ABRAHAM LINCOLN

THE PRAIRIE YEARS AND THE WAR YEARS
ONE-VOLUME EDITION

BY CARL SANDBURG

Abraham Lincoln: The Prairie Years *(Two Volumes)*, 1926
Abraham Lincoln: The War Years *(Four Volumes)*, 1939
Abraham Lincoln: The Prairie Years and The War Years *(One-Volume Edition)*, 1954
The Chicago Race Riots, 1919
The American Songbag, 1927
Steichen the Photographer, 1929
Potato Face, 1930
Mary Lincoln: Wife and Widow *(documented by Paul M. Angle)*, 1932
Storm over the Land, 1942
Home Front Memo, 1943
The Photographs of Abraham Lincoln *(with Frederick H. Meserve)*, 1944
Lincoln Collector: The Story of the Oliver R. Barrett Lincoln Collection, 1949
Always the Young Strangers, 1953
The Sandburg Range, 1957

NOVEL

Remembrance Rock, 1948

POETRY

Chicago Poems, 1916
Cornhuskers, 1918
Smoke and Steel, 1920
Slabs of the Sunburnt West, 1922
Selected Poems *(edited by Rebecca West)*, 1926
Good Morning, America, 1928
The People, Yes, 1936
Complete Poems, 1950
Harvest Poems: 1910-1960, 1960
Honey and Salt, 1963

FOR YOUNG FOLKS

Rootabaga Stories, 1922
Rootabaga Pigeons, 1923
Abe Lincoln Grows Up, 1928
Early Moon, 1930
Prairie-Town Boy, 1955
Wind Song, 1960

CARL SANDBURG

Abraham Lincoln

THE PRAIRIE YEARS AND THE WAR YEARS
ONE-VOLUME EDITION

☆ ☆ ☆

HARCOURT, BRACE & WORLD, INC.

New York

DEDICATION

To Harry and Marion Dolores Pratt, a handsome team of Lincoln scholars, who gave time and care to the new manuscript of the Prairie Years, wherefore the author is responsible for possible inaccuracies or errors—

To Paul M. Angle, a hardened veteran in the Lincoln field, a man of good will who can be relentlessly logical while hoping he is not "magisterial" in tone—

To Benjamin P. Thomas, a ballplayer and farmer who is a man of learning and integrity, possessed by Lincoln's dream of "man's vast future," a citizen with a deep and keen anxiety about the American Dream—

To Allan Nevins, whose four-volume *Ordeal of the Union* and *Emergence of Lincoln* are a massive and vivid presentation of the fourteen-year national scenes in which Lincoln moved in silence or speech till his first inaugural—

To the departed friends Lloyd Lewis, Oliver Barrett, Alf Harcourt, Stevie Benét, Jim Randall, Douglas Freeman, Henry Horner, Jake Buchbinder, whose shadows linger and whose fellowship endures—

To Edward Steichen, whose projected photographic exhibition "The Family of Man" will register his faith joined to Lincoln's in the unity of mankind and the hope of "freedom for all men everywhere"—

To my wife, Paula, whose counsel was ever of help and whose many ready and cheerful attentions are a part of this book—

To Catherine McCarthy, whose exacting toils in the compression of a six-volume work into one volume, whose skills, perspicacity and devotion are beyond praise, who merits an armful of roses in token of affectionate regard.

ACKNOWLEDGMENTS

To the faithful toilers on an incessantly changing manuscript: Helga Sandburg Golby, Marjorie Arnette Braye, Mari Jinishian, Mrs. Carl Sandburg.

PREFACE

As a growing boy in an Illinois prairie town I saw marching men who had fought under Grant and Sherman; I listened to stories of old-timers who had known Abraham Lincoln. At twenty in 1898 I served in the 6th Illinois Volunteers, our expedition to Porto Rico being commanded by General Nelson A. Miles, a brigadier general in some of the bloodiest battles of the Army of the Potomac in 1864. Our uniforms were the same light blue trousers and dark blue jackets with brass buttons as worn by the troops of the Army of the Potomac. We took swims in the Potomac River and had our first salt water swim in Charleston Harbor in sight of Fort Sumter.

The Lincoln lore of that time and place was of the man in his Illinois backgrounds and settings. When for thirty years and more I planned to make a certain portrait of Abraham Lincoln, it was as the country lawyer and prairie politician. But when I finished my *Prairie Years* portrait, Lincoln the Man had grown on me so that I went on to write *The War Years*. Now twenty-eight years after publication of the two-volume *Prairie Years* and nearly fifteen years after publication of the four-volume *War Years*, I have tried to compress the essential story of Lincoln the Man and President into one volume.

I have in this work, of course, consulted and made use of such new materials and researches as throw added light on the life and personality of Lincoln. Since the writing of *The Prairie Years* in the early 1920's there have been some thirty years of fiercely intensive research on the life of Lincoln before he became president. In no thirty-year period since the death of Lincoln has so rigorous and thorough an examination been given the facts and myths of the life of Lincoln. Listed separately at the back of the book are my "Sources and Acknowledgments." One may with no harm quote from Paul M. Angle: "I am convinced that annotation irritates almost everyone except professional historians . . . Still, if he is to play fair with his readers, the historical writer can hardly omit all mention of the materials he has used." Or from James G. Randall the cryptic: "Perhaps in general footnotes should be held guilty unless proved innocent." In all but four instances the texts as written by Lincoln, or as published, are followed literally without the use of [*sic*]. In three of these instances Lincoln stuttered in writing, but it is certain he did not stutter in speaking.

Walt Whitman saw Lincoln as "the grandest figure on the crowded canvas of the drama of the nineteenth century." In the story of a great pivotal figure at the vortex of a vast dark human struggle, we meet gaps and discrepancies. The teller of the story reports, within rigorous space limits, what is to him

vii

plain, moving, revealing. Every biographer of Lincoln is under compulsion to omit all or parts of Lincoln letters and speeches that he would like to include; this in part explains why any Lincoln biography is different from any or all other Lincoln biographies; each must choose and decide what sentences or paragraphs shed the light needed for the Lincoln portrait and story. Supposing all could be told, it would take a far longer time to tell it than was taken to enact it in life.

Here and there exist Lincoln letters not yet published but there are no expectations that they will throw important fresh light. As recently as February 1954 came the first publication of letters of Lincoln to Judge David Davis, which I have used herein as throwing slightly deeper gleams on Lincoln as a master politician. A national event was the opening at midnight on July 26, 1947, the "unveiling" as some termed it, of the long secret Robert T. Lincoln Collection in the Library of Congress. The next five days I did my best at reporting in seven newspaper columns for a syndicate what was revealed in the 18,300 letters, telegrams, manuscripts, miscellaneous data. The fourteen Lincoln scholars and authors present agreed that while no new light of importance was shed on Lincoln, the documents deepened and sharpened the outlines of the massive and subtle Lincoln as previously known. When I mentioned to Paul Angle a cynical editorial writer referring to us as "hagiographers" (saint worshippers), Paul said, "We could use a few real saints in this country now. And it's nice to live in a country where you can pick the saints you prefer to worship so long as you don't interfere with other saint worshippers."

Having read the million-word record of Lincoln's speeches and writings several times, Roy P. Basler sets forth, "The more fully Lincoln's varied career is traced . . . the more his genius grows and passes beyond each interpretation." Yankee Gamaliel Bradford put it briefly: "He still smiles and remains impenetrable."

To Joseph Fifer, Civil War soldier and later governor of Illinois, his favorite tribute to Lincoln was anonymous till after a six-year search he found that Homer Hoch of Kansas spoke it in the House of Representatives February 12, 1923:

"There is no new thing to be said about Lincoln. There is no new thing to be said of the mountains, or of the sea, or of the stars. The years go their way, but the same old mountains lift their granite shoulders above the drifting clouds; the same mysterious sea beats upon the shore; the same silent stars keep holy vigil above a tired world. But to the mountains and sea and stars men turn forever in unwearied homage. And thus with Lincoln. For he was a mountain in grandeur of soul, he was a sea in deep undervoice of mystic loneliness, he was a star in steadfast purity of purpose and service. And he abides."

On the 100th birthday anniversary of Lincoln, Brazilian Ambassador Joaquin Nabuco said: "With the increased velocity of modern changes, we do not know what the world will be a hundred years hence. For sure, the ideals of the generation of the year 2000 will not be the same of the generation of the year 1900. Nations will then be governed by currents of political thought which we can no more anticipate than the seventeenth century

could anticipate the political currents of the eighteenth, which still in part
sway us. But whether the spirit of authority, or that of freedom, increases,
Lincoln's legend will ever appear more luminous in the amalgamation of
centuries, because he supremely incarnated both those spirits."

CARL SANDBURG

Connemara Farm
Flat Rock, North Carolina
May 5, 1954

NOTES

Endpapers designed by Edward Steichen

Front—Hand of Lincoln from cast by Leonard Volk in Springfield 1860.
Back—Life mask of Lincoln by Clark Mills about February 1865. Original
of mask owned by Dr. Clarence L. Hay, son of John Hay. Photograph
from American Museum of Natural History.

The maps from *The Emergence of Lincoln* by Allan Nevins are used by
permission of the author and Charles Scribner's Sons.

In photograph captions herein, (Meserve) indicates the collection of Frederick Hill Meserve; (CS) indicates the author; (McLean) indicates
McLean County (Ill.) Historical Society; (USASC) indicates United
States Army Signal Corps; (McClees) indicates not a photographer but
a volume of photographic portraits published in 1859, owned by the
author.

CONTENTS

ILLUSTRATIONS

ABRAHAM LINCOLN

THE PRAIRIE YEARS AND THE WAR YEARS

ONE-VOLUME EDITION

CHAPTER 1

Wilderness Beginnings

IN THE year 1776, when the 13 American colonies gave to the world
their famous Declaration of Independence, there was a captain of Virginia militia living in Rockingham County named Abraham Lincoln. He had
a 210-acre farm deeded to him by his father, John Lincoln, one of the many
English, Scotch, Irish, German, Dutch settlers who were taking the green
hills and slopes of the Shenandoah Valley and putting their plows to unbroken ground long held by the Indians. These Lincolns in Virginia came
from Berks County in Pennsylvania and traced back to Lincolns in New
England and Old England. There was a strain of Quaker blood in them; they
were a serene, peaceable, obstinate people.

Abraham Lincoln had taken for a wife Bathsheba Herring, who bore him
three sons, Mordecai, Josiah and Thomas, and two daughters, Mary and
Nancy. This family Abraham Lincoln moved to Kentucky in 1782. For
years his friend Daniel Boone, coming back from trips to Kentucky, had
been telling of valleys there rich with black land and blue grass, game and
fish, tall timber and clear running waters. It called to him, that country
Boone talked about, where land was 40 cents an acre. Abraham Lincoln sold
his farm; they packed their belongings and joined a party heading down the
Wilderness Road through Cumberland Gap and up north and west into Kentucky. Abraham Lincoln located on the Green River, where he filed claims
for more than 2,000 acres.

One day about two years later, he was working in a field with his three
sons, and they saw him in a spasm of pain fall to the ground, just after the
boys had heard a rifle shot and the whine of a bullet. The boys yelled to
each other, "Indians!" Mordecai ran to a cabin nearby, Josiah started across
fields and woods to a fort to bring help. Six-year-old Tom stooped over his
father's bleeding body and wondered what he could do. He looked up to
see an Indian standing over him, a shining bangle hanging down over the
Indian's shoulder close to the heart. Then Tom saw the Indian's hands clutch
upward, saw him double with a groan and crumple to the ground. Mordecai
with a rifle at a peephole in the cabin had aimed his shot at the shining
bangle. Little Tom was so near he heard the bullet plug its hole into the
red man.

Thomas Lincoln, while growing up, lived in different places in Kentucky
with kith and kin, sometimes hiring out to farmers, mostly in Washington
County. Betweenwhiles he learned the carpenter's trade and cabinetmaking.
In his full growth he was about five feet nine, weighed about 185 pounds,
his muscles and ribs close-knit. His dark hazel eyes looked out from a round

face, from under coarse black hair. He could be short-spoken or reel off sayings, yarns, jokes. He made a reputation as a storyteller. He had little or no time for books, could read some, and could sign his name.

Thomas Lincoln at 19 had served in the Kentucky state militia. At 24 he was appointed a constable in Cumberland County. The next year he moved to Hardin County and served on a jury. He was trusted by a sheriff and paid by the county to guard a prisoner for six days. In the county jail he could see men bolted behind bars for not paying their debts and at the public whipping post both white and black men lashed on their naked backs. He saw prisoners in the stocks kneeling with hands and head clamped between two grooved planks; if a prisoner was dead drunk he was laid on his back with his feet fastened in the stocks till he was sober.

In 1803 Thomas Lincoln for "the sum of 118 pounds in hand paid" bought a 238-acre tract near Mill Creek, seven miles north of Elizabethtown, the county seat of Hardin County. In March 1805 he was one of four "patrollers" appointed in Hardin County to seize suspicious white characters or Negro slaves roving without permits. In March 1806 he was hired by Bleakley & Montgomery, storekeepers in Elizabethtown, to take a flatboat of their merchandise down the Ohio and Mississippi Rivers to New Orleans, earning 16 pounds in gold and a credit of 13 pounds in gold. Account books of the store had him occasionally buying "two twists of tobacco," one pound for 38 cents, and one pint of whisky for 21 cents.

And the books show that in May 1806 he went on a buying spree, purchasing "four skeins of silk," "five yards of linen," "four yards of coating," "one-fourth yard of scarlet cloth," several yards of "Jane" and of "Brown Holland," "three and one-half yards of cassemere," "one and one-quarter yards of red flannel," dozens of buttons, and other sundries. Earlier that year he had bought an aristocratic beaver hat for one pound six shillings and a pair of silk suspenders for $1.50. He was courting a woman he meant to marry and was buying clothes and dress goods intended for his bride and himself.

Thomas Lincoln was in love and his wedding set for June 12, 1806, at Beechland in Washington County. Nancy Hanks, the bride-to-be, was a daughter of Lucy Hanks and was sometimes called Nancy Sparrow as though she was an adopted daughter of Thomas and Elizabeth Sparrow whose house was her home.

Lucy Hanks had welcomed her child Nancy into life in Virginia about 1784. The name of the child's father seems to have vanished from any documents or letters that may have existed. His name stayed unknown to baffle and mystify the seekers who for years searched for records and sought evidence that might bring to light the name of the father of the girl child Nancy Hanks.

Lucy traveled to Kentucky carrying what was to her a precious bundle. She was perhaps 19 when she made this trip. She could toss her bundle into the air against a far, hazy line of blue mountains, catch it in her two hands as it came down, let it snuggle to her breast and feed, while she asked, "Here we come—where from?" If Lucy was married when Nancy was born it seemed that her husband either died and she became a widow or he lived and stayed on in Virginia or elsewhere. In either case she and their child had to get along as best they could without him.

Of how and where she lived in the years she was raising Nancy not much was remembered or recorded. There were those who said later that it was another Lucy Hanks, not the mother of Nancy, who was indicted November 24, 1789, by a grand jury in Mercer County Court for loose and shameless conduct with men. Months passed and there was no record of a trial of the Lucy Hanks indicted. In those months there came deeply into the life of the mother of Nancy a man named Henry Sparrow, Virginia-born, about her own age, a Revolutionary War veteran who had seen Lord Cornwallis' army surrendered to George Washington. Since his father's death in 1789 he had been caring for his widowed mother, sister and younger brother.

On April 26, 1790, Henry Sparrow, with a brother-in-law, John Daniel, gave bond for a license of marriage between himself and Lucy Hanks. On this same day Lucy Hanks, one of the few women of the time and locality who could read and write, wrote a certificate:

> I do sertify that I am
> of age and give my appro-
> bation freely for henry
> Sparrow to git out Lisons
> this or enny other day
> Given under my hand
> this day
> April 26th 1790
> day
> Lucey
> Hanks

Undersigned as witnesses were Robert Mitchell and John Berry, perhaps the same John Berry who had served on the jury that had indicted one Lucy Hanks. In the following May the Mercer County Court in the case "against Lucy Hanks, deft [defendant]" made a presentment recorded, "for reasons appearing to the court the suit is ordered to be discontinued." Whatever they meant by their indictment was wiped out as though she had changed for the better or they had been wrong in naming her in an indictment.

Nearly a year passed and Lucy Hanks and her way of living pleased Henry Sparrow. He wanted her for a life companion and, having their license that was issued April 26, 1790, they were, on April 3, 1791, married by the Baptist preacher, the Reverend John Bailey. Lucy Hanks Sparrow proved herself a woman of strengths and vitality, of passion for life and brave living. Of her eight children that came she saw to it in those days of little schooling that all of them learned to read and write, and two became preachers of reputation.

June 12, 1806, came and the home of Richard Berry at Beechland in Washington County saw men and women on horseback arriving for the wedding of 28-year-old Thomas Lincoln and 22-year-old Nancy Hanks. The groom was wearing his fancy beaver hat, a new black suit, his new silk suspenders. The bride's outfit had in it linen and silk, perhaps a dash somewhere of the "one-fourth yard of scarlet cloth" Tom had bought at Bleakley & Montgomery's. They had many relatives and friends in Washington County and the time was right to go to a wedding, what with spring planting and corn plowing over and the hay harvest yet to come. Nancy Hanks was at home in the big double log cabin of the Berrys. She had done sewing there for Mrs. Berry and it was Richard Berry who had joined Thomas Lincoln in signing the marriage bond, below his name writing "garden," meaning guardian. The six Negro slaves owned by Richard Berry were busy getting ready the food and "fixins" to follow the wedding ceremony. The Reverend Jesse Head arrived on his gray mare. He was a man they rhymed about:

> His nose is long and his hair is red,
> And he goes by the name of Jesse Head.

A hater of sin, he liked decency and good order and could pause in a sermon to step from the pulpit and throw out a disorderly mocker who had had a few drinks. The bride and groom stood up before him. He pronounced them man and wife and wrote for the county clerk that on June 12, 1806, Thomas Lincoln and Nancy Hanks had been joined together in the holy estate of matrimony "agreeable to the rites and ceremonies of the Methodist Episcopal Church."

Then came "the infare." One who was there remembered, "We had bear meat, venison, wild turkey and ducks, eggs wild and tame, maple sugar lumps tied on a string to bite off for coffee or whisky, syrup in big gourds, peach and honey, a sheep barbecued whole over coals of wood burned in a pit, and covered with green boughs to keep the juices in; and a race for the whisky bottle." Quite likely Henry Sparrow and his wife, Lucy Hanks Sparrow, rode over from Mercer County to join the wedding company. For them, as for the bride and groom, the solemn event of the day had a peculiar loveliness and Lucy could have a glad heart.

The new husband put his bride on a horse and they rode away on the red clay road along the timber trails to Elizabethtown to make a home in a cabin close to the county courthouse. At Bleakley & Montgomery's, Tom bought a half set of knives and forks, a half-dozen spoons, thread and needles, three skeins of silk, three pounds of tobacco—the silk for Nancy, the tobacco for himself. Tom worked as a carpenter, made cabinets, door frames, window sash and an occasional coffin. A child's coffin cost three dollars, a woman's six and a man's seven.

Tall, slender, dark-complexioned Nancy Hanks had happiness that year of 1806. One summer day she had news for her husband—a baby on the way! They rode out more often perhaps to the Little Mount Baptist Church where they were members and spoke prayers more often of hope for the child to come. Perhaps an added dark zeal came in the brief grace Thomas spoke at meals.

On February 10, 1807, the child came wellborn and they named her Sarah. Nancy washed and nursed her baby, made her wishes and prayers for the little one. It could be she was sad with sorrows like dark stars in blue mist, with hopes burned deep in her that beyond the everyday struggles, the babble and gabble of today, there might be what her brightest dreams told her. She read their Bible. One who knew her well said she was "a ready reader." She was a believer and knew—so much of what she believed was yonder—always yonder. Every day came cooking, keeping the fire going, scrubbing, washing, patching, with little time to think or sing of the glory she believed in—always yonder.

She saw her husband in trouble in law courts. He took a contract to hew timbers and help put up a new sawmill for Denton Geoghegan, spent days of hard work on the job. When Geoghegan wouldn't pay him, Tom filed suit and won. Geoghegan then started two suits against Lincoln, claiming the sawmill timbers were not hewn square and true. Tom Lincoln won both suits.

When he bought his second farm, 348½ acres on the South Fork of Nolin Creek, 18 miles southeast of Elizabethtown, he paid Isaac Bush $200 in cash and took on a small obligation due a former titleholder. This in 1808 made Tom Lincoln owner of 586½ acres of land, along with two lots in Elizabethtown and some livestock.

In May and the blossom-time of 1808, Tom and Nancy with the baby moved from Elizabethtown to the farm of George Brownfield, where Tom did carpenter and farm work. Near their cabin wild crab-apple trees stood thick and flourishing with riots of bloom and odor. And the smell of wild crab-apple blossoms, and the low crying of all wild things, came keen that summer to Nancy Hanks. The summer stars that year shook out pain and warning, strange and bittersweet laughters, for Nancy Hanks.

The same year saw Tom Lincoln's family moved to his land on the South Fork of Nolin Creek, about two and a half miles from Hodgenville. He was trying to farm stubborn ground and make a home in a cabin of logs he cut from timber nearby. The floor was packed-down dirt. One door, swung on leather hinges, let them in and out. One small window gave a lookout on the weather, the rain or snow, sun and trees, and the play of the rolling prairie and low hills. A stick-clay chimney carried the fire smoke up and away.

One morning in February 1809, Tom Lincoln came out of his cabin to the road, stopped a neighbor and asked him to tell "the granny woman," Aunt Peggy Walters, that Nancy would need help soon. On the morning of February 12, a Sunday, the granny woman was at the cabin. And she and Tom Lincoln and the moaning Nancy Hanks welcomed into a world of battle and blood, of whispering dreams and wistful dust, a new child, a boy.

A little later that morning Tom Lincoln threw extra wood on the fire, an extra bearskin over the mother, and walked two miles up the road to where the Sparrows, Tom and Betsy, lived. Dennis Hanks, the nine-year-old boy adopted by the Sparrows, met Tom at the door. In his slow way of talking Tom Lincoln told them, "Nancy's got a boy baby." A half-sheepish look was in his eyes, as though maybe more babies were not wanted in Kentucky just then.

Dennis Hanks took to his feet down the road to the Lincoln cabin. There he saw Nancy Hanks on a bed of poles cleated to a corner of the cabin, under warm bearskins. She turned her dark head from looking at the baby to look at Dennis and threw him a tired, white smile from her mouth and gray eyes. He stood watching the even, quiet breaths of this fresh, soft red baby. "What you goin' to name him, Nancy?" the boy asked. "Abraham," was the answer, "after his grandfather."

Soon came Betsy Sparrow. She washed the baby, put a yellow petticoat and a linsey shirt on him, cooked dried berries with wild honey for Nancy, put the one-room cabin in better order, kissed Nancy and comforted her, and went home, saying she would come again in the morning.

Dennis rolled up in a bearskin and slept by the fireplace that night. He listened to the crying of the newborn child once in the night and the feet of the father moving on the dirt floor to help the mother and the little one. In the morning he took a long look at the baby and said to himself, "Its skin looks just like red cherry pulp squeezed dry, in wrinkles."

He asked if he could hold the baby. Nancy, as she passed the little one into Dennis' arms, said, "Be keerful, Dennis, fur you air the fust boy he's ever seen." Dennis swung the baby back and forth, keeping up a chatter about how tickled he was to have a new cousin to play with. The baby screwed up its face and began crying with no letup. Dennis turned to Betsy Sparrow, handed her the baby and said, "Aunt, take him! He'll never come to much."

Thus the birthday scene reported years later by Dennis Hanks whose nimble mind sometimes invented more than he saw or heard. Peggy Walters, too, years later, gave the scene as her memory served: "I was twenty years old, then, and helping to bring a baby into the world was more of an event to me than it became afterward. But I was married young, and had a baby of my own, and I had helped mother who was quite famous as a granny woman. It was Saturday afternoon when Tom Lincoln sent over and asked me to come. They sent for Nancy's two aunts, Mis' Betsy Sparrow and Mis' Polly Friend. I was there before them, and we all had quite a spell to wait, and we got everything ready. Nancy had a good feather-bed under her; it wasn't a goose-feather bed, hardly anyone had that kind then, but good hen feathers. And she had blankets enough. A little girl there, two years old, Sarah, went to sleep before much of anything happened.

"Nancy had about as hard a time as most women, I reckon, easier than some and maybe harder than a few. The baby was born just about sunup, on Sunday morning. Nancy's two aunts took the baby and washed him and dressed him, and I looked after Nancy. And I remember after the baby was born, Tom came and stood beside the bed and looked down at Nancy lying there, so pale and so tired, and he stood there with that sort of hang-dog look that a man has, sort of guilty like, but mighty proud, and he says to me, 'Are you sure she's all right, Mis' Walters?' And Nancy kind of stuck out her hand and reached for his, and said, 'Yes, Tom, I'm all right.' And then she said, 'You're glad it's a boy, Tom, aren't you? So am I.'"

Whatever the exact particulars, the definite event on that 12th of February, 1809, was the birth of a boy they named Abraham after his grandfather who had been killed by Indians—born in silence and pain from a wilderness mother on a bed of perhaps cornhusks and perhaps hen feathers—with perhaps a laughing child prophecy later that he would "never come to much."

In the spring of 1811 Tom Lincoln moved his family ten miles northeast to a 230-acre farm he had bought on Knob Creek, where the soil was a little richer and there were more neighbors. The famous Cumberland Trail, the main pike from Louisville to Nashville, ran nearby the new log cabin Tom built, and they could see covered wagons with settlers heading south, west, north, peddlers with tinware and notions, gangs of slaves or "kaffles" moving on foot ahead of an overseer or slave trader on horseback, and sometimes in dandy carriages congressmen or legislative members going to sessions at Louisville.

Here little Abe grew out of one shirt into another, learned to walk and talk and as he grew bigger how to be a chore boy, to run errands, carry water, fill the woodbox, clean ashes from the fireplace. He learned the feel of blisters on his hands from using a hoe handle on rows of beans, onions, corn, potatoes. He ducked out of the way of the heels of the stallion and two brood mares his father kept and paid taxes on. That Knob Creek farm in their valley set round by high hills and deep gorges was the first home Abe Lincoln remembered. He told later how one Saturday afternoon other boys planted the corn in what was called "the big field" of seven acres. "I dropped the pumpkin seed. I dropped two seeds every other hill and every other row. The next Sunday morning there came a big rain in the hills, it did not rain a drop in the valley but the water coming down through the gorges washed ground, corn, pumpkin seeds and all clear off the field."

Again there were quiet and anxious days in 1812 when another baby was on the way; again came neighbor helpers and Nancy gave birth to her third child. They named him Thomas but he died a few days after and Sarah and Abe saw, in a coffin their father made, the little cold still face and made their first acquaintance with the look of death in a personal grief in their own one-room cabin.

Four miles a day Sarah and Abe walked when school kept and they were not needed at home. In a log schoolhouse with a dirt floor and one door, seated on puncheon benches with no backs, they learned the alphabet A to Z and numbers one to ten. It was called a "blab school"; the pupils before reciting read their lessons out loud to themselves to show they were busy studying. Their first teacher was Zachariah Riney, a Catholic, and the second one, Cabel Hazel, a former tavernkeeper. Under them young Abe learned to write and to like forming letters and shaping words. He said later that "anywhere and everywhere that lines could be drawn, there he improved his capacity for writing." He scrawled words with charcoal, he shaped them in the dust, in sand, in snow. Writing had a fascination for him.

Tom Lincoln worked hard and had a reputation for paying his debts. One year he was appointed a "road surveyor" to keep a certain stretch of road in repair, another time was named appraiser for an estate, and an 1814 tax book listed him as 15th among the 98 property owners named. In 1816 he paid taxes on four horses. In 1814, however, because of a flaw in title he sold his Mill Creek farm for 18 pounds less than he had paid for it; the tract survey in one place read "west" where it should have read "east." Another suit involved his title to the Nolin Creek farm, still another aimed to dispossess him of the Knob Creek farm. Meantime slavery was on the rise and in 1816 there were 1,238 slaves on the tax lists of Hardin County, one taxpayer owning 58 Negro slaves, men, women and children, on the books valued along with horses, cows and other livestock. So when Tom Lincoln in 1816 decided to move to Indiana it was, as Abe later wrote, "partly on account of slavery; but chiefly on account of the difficulty in land titles."

In December 1816, Tom Lincoln with Nancy, Sarah, Abe, four horses and their most needed household goods, made their breakaway from Kentucky, moving north and crossing the Ohio River into land then Perry County, later Spencer County, Indiana. They traveled a wild raw country, rolling land with trees everywhere, tall oaks and elms, maples, birches, dogwood, underbrush tied down by ever-winding grapevines, thin mist and winter damp rising from the ground as Tom, with Abe perhaps helping, sometimes went ahead with an ax and hacked out a trail. "It was a wild region, with many bears and other wild animals still in the woods," Abe wrote later, where "the panther's scream, filled night with fear" and "bears preyed on the swine." A lonesome country, settlers few, "about one human being to each square mile," families two and three miles apart.

They had toiled and hacked their way through wilderness when about 16 miles from the Ohio River they came to a rise of ground somewhat open near Little Pigeon Creek. Here the whole family pitched in and threw together a pole shed or "half-faced camp," at the open side a log fire kept burning night and day. In the next weeks of that winter Tom Lincoln, with help from neighbors and young Abe, now nearly eight, erected a cabin 18 by 20 feet, with a loft. Abe later wrote that he "though very young, was large of his age, and had an axe put into his hands at once; and was almost constantly handling that most useful instrument." The chinking of wet clay and grass ("wattle and daub") between the logs in the new cabin had not been finished in early February when something happened that a boy remembers after he is a grown man. Years later Abe wrote, "At this place A.[braham] took an early start as a hunter, which was never much improved afterwards. A few days before the completion of his eigth year, in the absence of his father, a flock of wild turkeys approached the new log-cabin, and A.[braham] with a rifle gun, standing inside, shot through a crack and killed one of them." Then came another sentence, "He has never since pulled a trigger on any larger game," making it clear that when they had deer or bear meat or other food from "larger game," it was not from his shooting. He didn't like shooting to kill and didn't care for a reputation as a hunter.

When Tom Lincoln built this cabin he didn't own the land it stood on. He was a "squatter." Not until October 15, 1817, after a 90-mile overland trip to Vincennes did he enter his claim for a quarter section of land, paying a first installment of $16 then and in December $64. The Government was selling him the land at $2.00 an acre; the $80 he had paid was one-fourth of the purchase price and he would have a clear title when he paid the other three-fourths. It had been a hard year, "pretty pinching times," as Abe put it later. They had to chop down trees, clear away underbrush, on what few acres they planted after plowing the hard unbroken sod. Their food was mostly game shot in the woods nearby, deer, bear, wild turkeys, ducks, geese. Wild pigeons in flocks sometimes darkened the sky. Their cabin lighting at night was from fire logs, pine knots, or hog fat. Sarah and Abe went barefoot from late spring till autumn frosts, brought home nuts and wild fruits, watched sometimes in the excitement of their father smoking out a bee tree for the honey. One drawback was water supply. Abe or Sarah had to walk nearly a mile to fetch spring water. Tom dug several wells but they all went dry.

They were part of the American Frontier, many others like them breaking ground never before broken, settling a new midwest country. On wagons by thousands slipping through the passes of the eastern mountains, or on flatboats, scows and steamboats on the Ohio River, they were heading west for the $2.00-an-acre Government land. Along pikes, roads and trails heading west were broken wagon wheels with grass growing up over the spokes and hubs, and nearby perhaps a rusty skillet and the bones of horses and men. They had stuck it out and lost. A saying, "The cowards never started and the weak ones died by the way," was unfair to the strong ones who died by the way of sudden maladies or long rains, windstorms, howling blizzards.

Some of those who came were hungry, even lustful, for land. Some were hunters, adventurers, outlaws, fugitives. Most were hoping for a home of their own. In December 1816, when the Lincolns came to Pigeon Creek, enough settlers had arrived in Indiana for it to be "admitted to the Union." It could be about then little Abe asked the solemn question, "The Union? What is the Union?"

A wagon one day late in 1817 brought into the Lincoln clearing their good Kentucky neighbors Tom and Betsy Sparrow and the odd quizzical 17-year-old Dennis Friend Hanks. For some years Dennis would be a chum of Abe's and on occasion would make free to say, "I am base born," explaining that his mother bore him before she married one Levi Hall. The Sparrows were to live in the Lincoln pole shed till they could locate land and settle. Hardly a year had passed, however, when Tom and Betsy Sparrow were taken down with the "milk sick," beginning with a whitish coat on the tongue, resulting, it was supposed, from cows eating white snakeroot or other growths that poisoned their milk. Tom and Betsy Sparrow died and were buried in September on a little hill in a clearing in the timbers nearby.

Soon after, there came to Nancy Hanks Lincoln that white coating of the tongue; her vitals burned; the tongue turned brownish; her feet and hands grew cold and colder, her pulse slow and slower. She knew she was dying, called for her children, and spoke to them her last dim choking words. Death came October 5, 1818, the banners of autumn flaming their crimsons over tall oaks and quiet maples. On a bed of poles cleated to the corner of the cabin, the body of Nancy Hanks Lincoln lay in peace and silence, the eyelids closed down in unbroken rest. To the children who tiptoed in, stood still, cried their tears of want and longing, whispered and heard only their own whispers answering, she looked as though new secrets had come to her in place of the old secrets given up with the breath of life.

Tom Lincoln took a log left over from the building of the cabin, and he and Dennis Hanks whipsawed it into planks, planed the planks smooth, and made them of a measure for a box to bury the dead wife and mother in. Little Abe, with a jackknife, whittled pine-wood pegs. And while Dennis and Abe held the planks, Tom bored holes and stuck the whittled pegs through the holes. This was the coffin they carried next day to the little timber clearing nearby, where a few weeks before they had buried Tom and Betsy Sparrow.

So Nancy Hanks Lincoln died, 34 years old, a pioneer sacrifice, with memories of monotonous, endless everyday chores, of mystic Bible verses read over and over for their promises, of blue wistful hills and a summer when the crab-apple blossoms flamed white and she carried a boy child into the world.

A hard year followed with 12-year-old Sarah as housekeeper and cook, and Tom Lincoln with the help of Dennis and Abe trying to clear more land, plant it, and make the farm a go. It was the year Abe was driving a horse at the mill. While he was putting a whiplash to the nag and calling, "Git up, you old hussy; git up, you old hussy," the horse let fly a fast hind foot that knocked Abe down and out of his senses just as he yelled, "Git up." He lay bleeding, was taken home, washed, put to bed, and lay all night unconscious. He spoke of it afterward as a mystery of the human mind, and later wrote of himself, "In his tenth year he was kicked by a horse, and apparantly killed for a time." Instead of dying, as was half expected, he came to, saying, "You old hussy," thus finishing what he started to say before he was knocked down and out.

Lonesome days came for Abe and Sarah in November when their father went away, promising to come back. He headed for Elizabethtown, Kentucky, through woods and across the Ohio River, to the house of the widow Sarah Bush Johnston. They said he argued straight-out: "I have no wife and you no husband. I came a-purpose to marry you. I knowed you from a gal and you knowed me from a boy. I've no time to lose; and if you're willin' let it be done straight off." She answered, "I got a few little debts," gave him a list and he paid them; and they were married December 2, 1819.

He could write his name; she "made her mark." Why the two of them took up with each other so quickly Dennis Hanks later said, "Tom had a kind o' way with women, an' maybe it was somethin' she took comfort in to have a man that didn't drink an' cuss none."

Abe and Sarah had a nice surprise one morning when four horses and a wagon came into their clearing, and their father jumped off, then Sarah Bush Lincoln, the new wife and mother, then her three children by her first husband, Sarah Elizabeth (13), Matilda (10), and John D. Johnston (9 years old). Next off the wagon came a feather mattress and pillows, a black walnut bureau, a large clothes chest, a table, chairs, pots and skillets, knives, forks, spoons.

"Here's your new mammy," his father told Abe as the boy looked up at a strong, large-boned, rosy woman, with a kindly face and eyes, a steady voice, steady ways. From the first she was warm and friendly for Abe's hands to touch. And his hands roved with curiosity over a feather pillow and a feather mattress.

The one-room cabin now sheltered eight people to feed and clothe. At bedtime the men and boys undressed first, the women and girls following, and by the code of decent folk no one was abashed. Dennis and Abe climbed on pegs to the loft for their sleep and liked it when later the logs were chinked against the rain or snow coming in on them. Dennis said "Aunt Sairy," the new mother, "had faculty and didn't 'pear to be hurried or worried none," that she got Tom to put in a floor and make "some good beds and cheers." Abe, like Dennis, said "cheers"; if he said "chairs" he would be taken as "uppety" and "too fine-haired."

In the earlier years he wore buckskin breeches and moccasins, a tow linen shirt and coonskin cap, "the way we all dressed them days," said Dennis

Hanks. For winter snow and slush they had "birch bark, with hickory bark soles, stropped on over yarn socks." And later, "when it got so we could keep chickens, an' have salt pork an' corn dodgers, an' gyardin saas an' molasses, an' have jeans pants an' cowhide boots to wear, we felt as if we was gittin' along in the world."

Eleven-year-old Abe went to school again. Years later he wrote of where he grew up, "There were some schools, so called; but no qualification was ever required of a teacher, beyond *'readin', writin', and cipherin''* to the Rule of Three. If a straggler supposed to understand latin, happened to sojourn in the neighborhood, he was looked upon as a wizzard." School kept at Pigeon Creek when a schoolmaster happened to drift in, usually in winter, and school was out when he drifted away. Andrew Crawford taught Abe in 1820, James Swaney two years later, and after a year of no school Abe learned from Azel Dorsey. The schoolmasters were paid by the parents in venison, hams, corn, animal skins and other produce. Four miles from home to school and four miles to home again Abe walked for his learning, saying later that "all his schooling did not amount to one year."

Abe kept his school sum book sheets as though they might be worth reading again with such rhymes as:

> Abraham Lincoln is my nam
> And with my pen I wrote the same
> I wrote in both hast and speed
> and left it here for fools to read

> Abraham Lincoln his hand and pen
> he will be good but god knows When

Dennis Hanks made an ink of blackberry briar root and copperas, an "ornery ink," he called it. And Abe with a turkey-buzzard quill would write his name and say, "Denny, look at that, will you? *Abraham Lincoln!* That stands fur me. Don't look a blamed bit like me!" And, said Dennis, "He'd stand and study it a spell. 'Peared to mean a heap to Abe."

Having learned to read Abe read all the books he could lay his hands on. Dennis, years later, tried to remember his cousin's reading habits. "I never seen Abe after he was twelve 'at he didn't have a book some'ers 'round. He'd put a book inside his shirt an' fill his pants pockets with corn dodgers, an' go off to plow or hoe. When noon come he'd set down under a tree, an' read an' eat. In the house at night, he'd tilt a cheer by the chimbly, an' set on his backbone an' read. I've seen a feller come in an' look at him, Abe not knowin' anybody was round, an' sneak out agin like a cat, an' say, 'Well, I'll be darned.' It didn't seem natural, nohow, to see a feller read like that. Aunt Sairy's never let the childern pester him. She always said Abe was goin' to be a great man some day. An' she wasn't goin' to have him hendered."

They heard Abe saying, "The things I want to know are in books; my best friend is the man who'll git me a book I ain't read." One fall afternoon he walked to see John Pitcher, a lawyer at Rockport, nearly 20 miles away, and borrowed a book he heard Pitcher had. A few days later, with his father and Dennis and John Hanks he shucked corn from early daylight till sundown. Then after supper he read the book till midnight, and next day at noon hardly knew the taste of his corn bread because of the book in front of him. So they told it.

He read many hours in the family Bible, the only book in their cabin. He borrowed and read *Aesop's Fables, Pilgrim's Progress, Robinson Crusoe,* Grimshaw's *History of the United States,* and Weems' *The Life of George Washington, with Curious Anecdotes, Equally Honorable to Himself and Exemplary to His Young Countrymen.* Books lighted lamps in the dark rooms of his gloomy hours.

When John Hanks, a cousin of Nancy Hanks, came to live with them about 1823, there were nine persons sleeping, eating, washing, mending, dressing and undressing in the one-room cabin, gathered close to the fireplace in zero weather. John Hanks and Dennis, with some neighbors, seemed to agree that while Abe wasn't "lazy" his mind was often on books to the neglect of work. A neighbor woman sized him up, "He could work when he wanted to, but he was no hand to pitch in like killing snakes." John Romine remarked, "Abe Lincoln worked for me . . . didn't love work half as much as his pay. He said to me one day that his father taught him to work, but he never taught him to love it."

When rain soaked Weems' *Life of Washington* that Josiah Crawford had loaned him, he confessed he had been careless and pulled fodder three days to pay for the book, made a clean sweep, till there wasn't an ear on a corn-stalk in the field of Josiah Crawford.

Farm boys in evenings at the store in Gentryville, a mile and a half from the Lincoln cabin, talked about how Abe Lincoln was always digging into books, picking a piece of charcoal to write on the fire shovel, shaving off what he wrote, and then writing more. Dennis Hanks said, "There's suthin' peculiarsome about Abe." It seemed that Abe made books tell him more than they told other people. The other farm boys had gone to school and read *The Kentucky Preceptor,* but Abe picked out such a question as "Who has the most right to complain, the Indian or the Negro?" and would talk about it, up and down in the cornfields. When he read in a book about a boat that came near a magnetic rock, and how the magnets in the rock pulled all the nails out of the boat so it went to pieces and the people in the boat found themselves floundering in water, Abe thought it was interesting and told it to others. When he sat with the girl, Kate Roby, with their bare feet in the creek, and she spoke of the moon rising, he explained to her it was the earth moving and not the moon—the moon only seemed to rise. Kate was surprised at such knowledge.

The years pass and Abe Lincoln grows up, at 17 standing six feet, nearly four inches, long-armed with rare strength in his muscles. At 18 he could take an ax at the end of the handle and hold it out from his shoulders in a straight horizontal line, easy and steady. He could make his ax flash and bite into a sugar maple or a sycamore, one neighbor saying, "He can sink an ax deeper into wood than any man I ever saw." He learned how suddenly life can spring a surprise. One day in the woods, as he was sharpening a wedge on a log, the ax glanced, nearly took his thumb off, and the cut after healing left a white scar for life. "You never cuss a good ax," was a saying then.

Sleep came deep to him after work outdoors, clearing timberland for crops, cutting brush and burning it, splitting rails, pulling crosscut saw and whip-saw, driving the shovel-plow, harrowing, spading, planting, hoeing, cradling grain, milking cows, helping neighbors at house-raisings, logrollings, corn-huskings, hog killings. He found he was fast and strong against other boys in sports. He earned board, clothes and lodgings, sometimes, working for a neighbor farmer.

Often Abe worked alone in the timbers, daylong with only the sound of his own ax, or his own voice speaking to himself, or the crackling and sway-ing of branches in the wind, or the cries and whirrs of animals, of brown and silver-gray squirrels, of partridges, hawks, crows, turkeys, grouse, sparrows and the occasional wildcat. In wilderness loneliness he companioned with trees, with the faces of open sky and weather in changing seasons, with that individual one-man instrument, the ax. Silence found him for her own. In the making of him, the element of silence was immense.

On a misunderstanding one time between Lincoln and William Grigsby, Grigsby flared so mad he challenged Abe to a fight. Abe looked at Grigsby, smiled and said the fight ought to be with John D. Johnston, Abe's step-brother. The day was set, each man with his seconds. The two fighters, stripped to the waist, mauled at each other with bare knuckles. A crowd formed a ring and stood cheering, yelling, hissing, and after a while saw Johnston getting the worst of it. The ring of the crowd was broken when Abe shouldered his way through, stepped out, took hold of Grigsby and threw him out of the center of the fight ring. Then, so they said, Abe Lin-coln called out, "I'm the big buck of this lick," and his eyes sweeping the circle of the crowd he challenged, "If any of you want to try it, come on and whet your horns." Wild fist-fighting came and for months around the store in Gentryville they argued about which gang whipped the other.

Asked by Farmer James Taylor if he could kill a hog, Abe answered, "If you will risk the hog I'll risk myself." He put barefoot boys to wading in a mud puddle near the horse trough, picked them up one by one, carried them to the house upside down, and walked their muddy feet across the ceiling. The stepmother came in, laughed at the foot tracks, told Abe he ought to be spanked—and he cleaned the ceiling so it looked new.

Education came to the youth Abe by many ways outside of schools and books. As he said later, he "picked up" education. He was the letter writer for the family and for neighbors. As he wrote he read the words out loud. He asked questions, "What do you want to say in the letter? How do you want to say it? Are you sure that's the best way to say it? Or do you think we can fix up a better way to say it?" This was a kind of training in grammar and English composition.

He walked 30 miles to a courthouse to hear lawyers speak and to see how they argued and acted. He heard roaring and ranting political speakers—and mimicked them. He listened to wandering evangelists who flung their arms and tore the air with their voices—and mimicked them. He told droll stories with his face screwed up in different ways. He tried to read people as keenly as he read books. He drank enough drams of whisky to learn he didn't like the taste and it wasn't good for his mind or body. He smoked enough to-bacco to learn he wouldn't care for it. He heard rollicking and bawdy verses

and songs and kept some of them for their earthy flavor and sometimes mean-
ingful intentions.

His stepmother was a rich silent force in his life. The family and the neighbors spoke of her sagacity and gumption, her sewing and mending, how
spick-and-span she kept her house, her pots, pans and kettles. Her faith in
God shone in works more than words, and hard as life was, she was thankful
to be alive. She understood Abe's gloomy spells better than anyone else and
he named her as a deep influence in him. "Abe never spoke a cross word
to me," she said and she found him truthful. Matilda in a wild prank hid and
leaped out onto Abe's back to give him a scare in a lonely timber. Pulling
her hands against his shoulders and pressing her knees against his back, she
brought him down to the ground. His ax blade cut her ankle and strips from
his shirt and her dress had to be torn to stop the bleeding. By then she was
sobbing over what to tell her mother; on Abe's advice she told her mother
the whole truth.

When Abe's sister Sarah, a year after marrying Aaron Grigsby, died in
childbirth in 1828, it was Sarah Bush Lincoln who spoke comfort to the
nearly 19-year-old son of Nancy Hanks at the burial of his sister. Yet somehow the stepmother couldn't lessen the bitterness Abe held toward Aaron
Grigsby, whether he blamed Grigsby for neglect of his sister or something
else. Two brothers of Aaron, Reuben and Charles Grigsby, on the same day
were marrying Betsy Ray and Matilda Hawkins and purposely forgot to invite Abe to the double wedding. It was then he put into circulation a piece
of writing titled "The Chronicles of Reuben," which had many in the neighborhood tittering if not laughing out loud at the Grigsbys. It told of what
a sumptuous affair it was, with music of harps, viols, rams' horns, and "accla-
mations" at the wedding feast. "Finally . . . the waiters took the two brides
upstairs, placing one in a bed at the right hand of the stairs and the other
on the left. The waiters came down, and Nancy the mother then gave directions to the waiters of the bridegrooms, and they took them upstairs but
placed them in the wrong beds. The waiters then all came downstairs. But
the mother, being fearful of a mistake, made inquiry of the waiters, and
learning the true facts took the light and sprang upstairs. It came to pass she
ran to one of the beds and exclaimed, 'O Lord, Reuben, you are in bed with
the wrong wife.' The young men, both alarmed at this, sprang out of bed
and ran with such violence against each other they came near knocking each
other down. The tumult gave evidence to those below that the mistake was
certain. At last they all came down and had a long conversation about who
made the mistake, but it could not be decided. So endeth the chapter."

A mile across the fields from the Lincoln home was the Pigeon Creek Baptist Church, a log meetinghouse put up in 1822. On June 7, 1823, William
Barker, who kept the minutes and records, wrote that the church "received
Brother Thomas Lincoln by letter." He was elected the next year with two
neighbors to serve as a committee of visitors to the Gilead church, and served
three years as church trustee. Strict watch was kept on the conduct of members and Tom served on committees to look into reported misconduct between husbands and wives, brothers and sisters, of neighbor against neighbor.

Most of the church people could read only the shortest words in the Bible,

Upper left: The older Sarah Bush Lincoln. Only known photograph of Lincoln's beloved stepmother [Meserve]. *Upper right:* Hannah Armstrong in later years. She sewed and cooked for the young Lincoln of New Salem days [CS]. *Lower:* Traditionally the one-room log cabin in which Lincoln was born. Now part of the Lincoln Memorial at Hodgenville, Kentucky [CS].

A page from Lincoln's sum book. Among the earliest known writings of Lincoln.
[Oliver R. Barrett Collection]

or none at all. They sat in the log meetinghouse on the split-log benches their own axes had shaped, listening to the preacher reading from the Bible.

To confess, to work hard, to be saving, to be decent, were the actions most praised and pleaded for in the sermons of the preachers. Next to denying Christ, the worst sins among the men were drinking, gambling, fighting, loafing, and among the women, gossiping, backbiting, sloth and slack habits. A place named Hell where men, women and children burned everlastingly in fires was the place where sinners would go.

In a timber grove one summer Sunday afternoon, a preacher yelled, shrieked, wrung his hands in sobs of hysterics, until a row of women were laid out to rest and recover in the shade of an oak tree, after they had moaned, shaken, danced up and down, worn themselves out with "the jerks" and fainted. And young Abe Lincoln, looking on, with sober face and quiet heart, was thoughtful about what he saw before his eyes.

Some families had prayers in the morning on arising, grace at breakfast, noon prayers and grace at dinner, grace at supper and evening prayers at bedtime. In those households, the manger at Bethlehem was a white miracle, the black Friday at Golgotha and the rocks rolled away for the resurrection were nearby realities of terror and comfort, dark power and sustenance. The Sabbath day, Christmas, Easter, were days for sober thoughts and sober faces, resignation, contemplation, rest, silence.

Beyond Indiana was something else; beyond the timber and underbrush, the malaria, milk sick, blood, sweat, tears, hands hard and crooked as the roots of walnut trees, there must be something else.

After a day of plowing corn, watching crop pests, whittling bean poles, capturing strayed cattle and fixing up a hole in a snake-rail fence, while the housewife made a kettle of soap, hoed the radishes and cabbages, milked the cows, and washed the baby, there was a consolation leading to easy slumber in the beatitudes: "Blessed are the meek: for they shall inherit the earth . . . Blessed are the peacemakers: for they shall be called the children of God." It was not their business to be sure of the arguments and the invincible logic that might underlie the Bible promises of Heaven and threats of Hell; it was for this the preacher was hired and paid by the corn, wheat, whisky, pork, linen, wool and other produce brought by the members of the church.

The Sabbath was not only a day for religious meetings. After the sermon, the members, who rode horses many miles to the meetinghouse, talked about crops, weather, births and deaths, the growing settlements, letters just come, politics, Indians and land titles.

Young Abraham Lincoln saw certain of these Christians with a clean burning fire, with inner reckonings that prompted them to silence or action or speech, and they could justify themselves with a simple and final explanation that all things should be done decently and in order. Their door strings were out to sinners deep in mire, to scorners seemingly past all redemption; the Jesus who lived with lawbreakers, thieves, lepers crying "Unclean!" was an instrument and a light vivifying into everyday use the abstractions behind the words "malice," "mercy," "charity."

They met understanding from the solemn young Lincoln who had refused to join his schoolmates in putting fire on a live mud turtle, and had written a paper arguing against cruelty to animals; who would bother to lug on his shoulders and save from freezing a man overloaded with whisky; who would get up before daylight and cross the fields to listen to the weird disconnected babbling of the young man, Matthew Gentry.

The footsteps of death, silent as the moving sundial of a tall sycamore, were a presence. Time and death, the partners who operate leaving no more track than mist, had to be reckoned in the scheme of life. A day is a shooting star. The young Lincoln had copied a rhyme:

> Time! what an empty vapor 'tis!
>   And days how swift they are:
> Swift as an Indian arrow—
>   Fly on like a shooting star,
> The present moment just is here,
>   Then slides away in haste,
> That we can never say they're ours,
>   But only say they're past.

His mother Nancy Hanks and her baby that didn't live, his sister Sarah and her baby that didn't live—time and the empty vapor had taken them; the rain and the snow beat on their graves. Matthew Gentry, son of the richest man in that part of Indiana, was in his right mind and then began babbling week in and week out the droolings of a disordered brain—time had done it without warning. On both man and the animals, time and death had their way. In a single week, the milk sick had taken four milk cows and 11 calves of Dennis Hanks, while Dennis too had nearly gone under.

At the Pigeon Creek settlement, while the structure of his bones, the build and hang of his torso and limbs, took shape, other elements, invisible yet permanent, traced their lines in the tissues of his head and heart.

Young Abraham had worked as a farm hand and ferry helper for James Taylor, who lived at the mouth of Anderson Creek and operated a ferry across the Ohio River. Here Abe saw steamboats, strings of flatboats loaded with farm produce, other boats with cargoes from manufacturing centers. Houseboats, arks, sleds, flatboats with small cabins in which families lived and kept house, floated toward their new homesteads; on some were women washing, children playing. Here was the life flow of a main artery of American civilization, at a vivid time of growth. Here at 18 Abe built a scow and was taking passengers from Bates Landing to steamboats in midstream. Two travelers anxious to get on a steamer came one day and he sculled them out and lifted their trunks on board. Each threw him a silver half-dollar. It gave him a new feeling; the most he had ever earned was 31 cents a day. And when one of the half-dollars slipped from him and sank in the river, that too gave him a new feeling.

One day, at a signal from the Kentucky shore, Lincoln rowed across. Two men jumped out of the brush and said they were going to "duck" him in the river. But looking him over more closely, they changed their minds. They were John and Lin Dill, brothers operating a ferry. All three went to Justice of the Peace Samuel Pate, near Lewisport, where John T. Dill swore out a warrant for the arrest of Abraham Lincoln, charged, on trial, with running a ferry without a license, in violation of Kentucky law.

Lincoln testified he had carried passengers from the Indiana shore only to the middle of the river, never to the Kentucky shore. Squire Pate dismissed the warrant against Lincoln; the Dills went away sore, and Lincoln had a long talk with Squire Pate and made a friend. Afterward on days when no passengers were in sight he sometimes sculled over and watched Squire Pate on "law day" handle cases.

James Gentry, with the largest farms in the Pigeon Creek clearings, and a landing on the Ohio River, had looked Lincoln over. He believed Abe could take a cargo of produce down the Mississippi to New Orleans. Abe built a flatboat, cut oaks for a double bottom of stout planks, and a deck shelter, two pairs of long oars at bow and stern, a check post, and a setting pole for steering. In charge of the boat Mr. Gentry had placed his son Allen, the 19-year-old Lincoln, "a hired hand," as he called himself. They loaded the boat and pushed off for a thousand-mile trip on the wide, winding water-way, where flatboats were tied up at night to the riverbank, and floated and poled by day amid changing currents, strings of other flatboats, and in the paths of the proud white steamboats. The river bends ahead must be watched with ready oars and sweeps or the flatboat heads in to shore. Strong winds crook the course of the boat, sometimes blowing it ashore; one man must hustle off in a rowboat, tie a hawser to a tree or stump, while another man on the boat has a rope at the check post; and they slow her down. Warning signals must be given to other craft at night, by waving lantern or firewood. So the flatboat, the "broadhorn," went down the Father of Waters, four to six miles an hour, the crew frying their own pork and cornmeal cakes, wash-ing their own shirts.

Below Baton Rouge, on the "Sugar Coast," they tied up at the plantation of Madame Duchesne one evening, put their boat in order, and dropped off to sleep. They woke to find seven Negroes on board trying to steal the cargo and kill the crew; the swift and long-armed Lincoln swung a crab-tree club, knocked some into the river, and with Allen Gentry chased others into the woods, both coming back to the boat bleeding. Lincoln laid a bandanna on a gash over his right eye that left a scar for life as it healed. Then they cut loose the boat and moved down the river.

At New Orleans they sold their cargo and flatboat and lingered a few days. For the first time young Lincoln saw a city of 40,000 people, a metropolis, a world port, with seagoing ships taking on cotton, sugar, tobacco and food-stuffs for Europe, a levee and wharves thick with planters, clerks, longshore-men and roustabouts loading and unloading cargoes. Sailors and deck hands from many nations and great world ports walked and straggled along, talking, shouting, roistering, their languages a fascinating jabber to the youths from Indiana. British, Yankee and French faces, Spanish, Mexican, Creole, the oc-casional free Negro and the frequent slave were on the streets. Gangs of chained slaves passed, headed for cotton plantations of a thousand and more acres. Women wearing bright slippers and flashy gowns; Creoles with dusks of eyes; quadroons and octoroons with soft elusive voices, streets lined with saloons and dens where men drank with men or chose from the women sipping their French wines or Jamaica rum at tables, sending signals with their eyes or fingers or openly slanging the sailors, rivermen, timber cruisers, and no lack of gamblers with dice or cards. An old city that had floated the flags of France and Britain and now of America. Here was a great and famous cathedral, here mansions of extravagant cost and upkeep, narrow streets with quaint iron grillwork fronting the second stories, live oaks drooping with Spanish moss, and many blocks of huts and hovels. The city had a feel of old times and customs, of mossy traditions, none of the raw and new as seen in Indiana.

Lincoln and Allen Gentry, heading for home after three months, rode an elegant steamboat up the Mississippi, the fare paid by James Gentry. Abe's wages at $8.00 a month, or what he hadn't spent out of $24, he paid over to his father, according to law and custom.

After a thousand miles of excitement and new sights every day, he worked a while in James Gentry's store in 1829. Then came a new excitement—Tom Lincoln was moving his family and kinfolk to Illinois where John Hanks had gone. A new outbreak of the milk sick had brought a neighborhood scare. Tom's farm wasn't paying well and John Hanks was writing letters about rich land and better crops. After paying for 80 acres at $2.00 an acre and improving it 14 years, Tom sold the land to Charles Grigsby for $125 cash. Moving came natural to Tom; he could tell about the family that had moved so often their chickens knew the signs of another moving; the chickens would walk up to the mover, stretch flat on the ground, and put their feet up to be tied for the next wagon trip.

Tom and Sarah Lincoln on December 12, 1829, had been granted by the Pigeon Creek Baptist Church a "letter of Dismission" showing they were regular members in good standing, this for use in Illinois. Sister Nancy Grigsby protested she was "not satisfied with Brother and Sister Lincoln." The trustees took back the "letter of Dismission" but after investigation turned it back to Brother and Sister Lincoln and appointed Brother Lincoln on a committee to straighten out a squabble between Sister Nancy Grigsby and Sister Betsy Crawford, details of which went into the church records.

They made wagons that winter, of wood all through, pegs, cleats, hickory withes, knots of bark holding some parts together, though the wheel rims were iron. They loaded bedclothes, skillets, ovens, furniture on three wagons, ready to go early morning of March 1, 1830. Abraham Lincoln had been for some days a citizen who "had reached his majority"; he could vote at elections, was lawfully free from paying his wages to his father; he could come and go now; he was footloose.

Two of the wagons had two yoke of oxen each and one wagon had four horses. On the wagons were Tom and Sarah Bush Lincoln, her three children, John D. Johnston; Sarah, with her husband Dennis Hanks and their daughters Sarah Jane, Nancy M. and Harriet, and son John Talbot; Matilda, with her husband Squire Hall and their son John; and Abraham Lincoln on and off an ox wagon with a goad coaxing or prodding the animals and bawling at them to get along. They stopped where night found them, cooked supper, slept, and started at daybreak. What with the ground freezing at night and thawing in the day, the oxen and horses slipped and tugged, the wagon axles groaned, the wooden pegs and cleats squeaked—a journey, Lincoln said later, "slow and tiresome." They forded rivers and creeks, often breaking their way through ice; at one river, Lincoln was reported telling it, "My little dog jumped out of the wagon and the ice being thin he broke through and was struggling for life. I could not bear to lose my dog, and I jumped out of the wagon and waded waist deep in the ice and water, got hold of him and helped him out and saved him."

At the first stretch of the Grand Prairie they saw long levels of land running, with no slopes or hollows, straight to the horizon. Grass stood up six and eight feet high with roots so tough and deep that trees couldn't get rootholds. They met settlers saying the tough sod had broken many plows, but after the first year of seed corn the yield would run 50 bushels to the acre, wheat averaging 25 to 30 bushels, oats 40 to 60 bushels.

After traveling over 200 miles to Macon County, Illinois, they found John Hanks, who showed them the location he had picked for them on the north bank of the Sangamon River, about ten miles southwest of Decatur, land joining timber and prairie. John Hanks had already cut the logs for their cabin which soon was finished. They built a smokehouse and barn, cleared some 15 acres, split rails to fence it, planted corn, after which Abraham with John Hanks split 3,000 rails for two neighbors, and as "sodbusters" broke 30 acres of virgin prairie for John Hanks' brother Charles.

It was a change from the monotony of hard farm work in that summer of 1830 for Abraham to make his first political speech in Illinois. He had been delivering speeches to trees, stumps, rows of corn and potatoes, just practicing, by himself. But when two legislative candidates spoke at a campaign meeting in front of Renshaw's store in Decatur, Abraham stepped up and advocated improvement of the Sangamon River for better navigation.

Fall came and most of the Lincoln family went down with chills, fever and ague, Tom and Sarah using many doses of a quinine and whisky tonic mixture from a Decatur store. Then in December a blizzard filled the sky and piled snow two and a half feet on the ground. Soon another drive of snow made a four-foot depth of it on the level, with high drifts here and there. Rain followed, froze, and more snow covered the icy crust. Wolves took their way with deer and cattle who broke through the crust and stood helpless. Fodder crops went to ruin; cows, hogs and horses died in the fields. Connections between houses, settlements, grain mills, broke down; for days in 12-below-zero weather, families were cut off, living on parched corn. Some died of cold, lacking wood to burn; some died of hunger, lacking corn. Those who came through alive, in after years called themselves "Snowbirds." Families like the Lincolns, with little of meat, corn and wood laid by, had it hard. Abraham in February made a try at reaching the William Warnick house, and crossing the Sangamon River broke through the ice and got his feet wet. Going on the two miles to the Warnick house, he nearly froze his feet. Mrs. Warnick put his feet in snow to take out the frostbite, then rubbed them with grease. For nine weeks that snow cover held the ground. Spring thaws came and sheets of water spread in wide miles on the prairies.

As the roads became passable, the Lincoln family and kin moved southeast a hundred miles to Coles County. Abraham had other plans and didn't go with them. He had "come of age."

CHAPTER 2

New Salem Days

IN FEBRUARY 1831, John Hanks had made an agreement with a man named Denton Offutt, a frontier hustler big with promises and a hard drinker, that he, Abe Lincoln and John D. Johnston would take a flatboat of cargo to New Orleans. Offutt was to have the flatboat and cargo ready and they were to meet him on the Sangamon River near the village of Spring-field as soon as the snow should go off. With traveling by land made difficult by floods, they bought a large canoe. And so, with his mother's cousin and his stepbrother, in the spring of 1831, Abraham Lincoln, 22 years old, floated down the Sangamon River, going to a new home, laughter and youth in his bones, in his heart a few pennies of dreams, in his head a rag bag of thoughts he could never expect to sell.

Leaving their canoe at Judy's Ferry and not finding Denton Offutt there, they walked to Springfield and at Andrew Elliott's Buckhorn Tavern found Offutt lush with liquor and promises and no flatboat. He hired them at $12 a month and sent them to Government timberland, where they cut down trees, got logs to Kirkpatrick's mill for planks and gunwales. Near their shanty and camp on the Sangamon River where the flatboat was shaping, the Sangamon County assessor, Erastus Wright, saw Lincoln in April with his "boots off, hat, coat and vest off. Pants rolled up to his knees and shirt wet with sweat and combing his fuzzie hair with his fingers as he pounded away on the boat."

In about four weeks they launched the boat, 80 feet long and 18 feet wide, loaded the cargo of barreled pork, corn and live hogs, and moved downstream from Sangamo Town, steering away from snags and low water, Lincoln on deck in blue homespun jeans, jacket, vest, rawhide boots with pantaloons stuffed in, and a felt hat once black but now, as the owner said, "sunburned till it was a combine of colors." On April 19, rounding the curve of the Sangamon at New Salem, the boat stuck on the Camron milldam, and hung with one-third of her slanted downward over the edge of the dam and filling slowly with water, while the cargo of pork barrels was sliding slowly so as to overweight one end. She hung there a day while all the people of New Salem came down to look. Then they saw Lincoln getting part of the cargo unloaded to the riverbank, boring a hole in the flatboat end as it hung over the dam to let the water out, plugging the hole, then dropping the boat over the dam and reloading cargo. As she headed toward the Mississippi water-course, New Salem talked about the cool head and ready wit of the long-shanked young man.

Lincoln, Hanks and John D. Johnston floated down the Mississippi River, meeting strings of flatboats and other river craft. Hanks, away from home longer than expected, left them at St. Louis. Stepping off the flatboat at New

Orleans, Lincoln walked nearly a mile, on flatboats, to reach shore. In New Orleans, Lincoln could read advertisements of traders, one giving notice: "I will at all times pay the highest cash prices for Negroes of every description, and will also attend to the sale of Negroes on commission, having a jail and yard fitted up expressly for boarding them." There were sellers advertising, "For sale—several likely girls from 10 to 18 years old, a woman 24, a very valuable woman 25, with three very likely children," while buyers indicated after the manner of one: "Wanted—I want to purchase twenty-five likely Negroes, between the ages of 18 and 25 years, male and female, for which I will pay the highest prices in cash."

Again Abraham could see the narrow cobblestoned streets and the women with rouged faces and teasing voices at the crib-house windows on side streets, Negroes shading from black to octoroon, ragged poor whites, sailors drunk and sober in a dozen different jargons, a dazzling parade of the humanly ugly and lovely in a mingling—what his eyes met again in the old strange city had him thoughtful and brooding. After a month or so, with Johnston, he took a steamboat north.

From New Orleans up the Mississippi on the steamboat and from St. Louis walking overland Lincoln must have wondered about New Salem village, the people there, his new job, the new life he was moving into. Offutt had rented the gristmill at the Sangamon River dam below the hilltop village and in St. Louis was buying a stock of goods for a new store. Lincoln was to be clerk in charge of store and mill at $15 a month and a back room to sleep in. Arriving in late July Lincoln walked the village street, looked over its dozen or more cabins, searched faces he expected to see many times for many months.

On August 1, 1831, he cast his first ballot. The polls were in the home of John Camron where Lincoln was boarding and getting acquainted with Camron's 11 daughters who teased him about his long legs and arms and heard him admit he "wasn't much to look at." Voting by word of mouth, each voter spoke to the election judges his candidates' names. A judge then called out the voter's name and his candidates, clerks recording the names "on poll sheets." Lincoln voted for a Henry Clay Whig for Congress—and against Joseph Duncan, then a Jackson man serving in Congress. He stayed around the polls most of the day talking cheerily, telling stories, making friends and getting acquainted with the names and faces of nearly all the men in the New Salem neighborhood.

The lizard story spun by the newcomer he said happened in Indiana. In a meetinghouse deep in the tall timbers, a preacher was delivering a sermon, wearing old-fashioned baggy pantaloons fastened with one button and no suspenders, his shirt held at the collar by one button. In a loud voice he announced his text, "I am the Christ, whom I shall represent today." About then a little blue lizard ran up under one pantaloon leg. The preacher went ahead with his sermon, slapping his leg. After a while the lizard came so high that the preacher was desperate, and, going on with his sermon, unbuttoned the one button that held his pantaloons; they dropped down and with a kick were off. By this time the lizard had changed his route and circled around under the shirt at the back, and the preacher, repeating his text, "I am the

Christ, whom I shall represent today," loosened his one collar button and with one sweeping movement off came the shirt. The congregation sat dazed, everything still for a minute; then a dignified elderly lady stood up slowly and, pointing a finger toward the pulpit, called out at the top of her voice, "I just want to say that if you represent Jesus Christ, sir, then I'm done with the Bible."

A little later men were telling of Lincoln, Offutt and a crew trying to load 30 large fat hogs onto a flatboat; the hogs were slippery and stubborn and the crew couldn't drive them on board. Offutt said, "Sew up their eyes," which was done, Lincoln helping, and writing it afterward, "In their blind condition they could not be driven out of the field they were in," so "they were tied and hauled on carts to the boat."

Boarding in the John Camron house Lincoln could hear at the eating table or in candlelight before bedtime how young was the village, how it was built on hope and promise. It was only in January 1829 that Camron and his partner James Rutledge had permission from the state legislature to build the dam that Lincoln had come to know so well. They had a survey made the following October, named the place New Salem, and in December that year they had sold their first lot for $12.50; on Christmas Day 1829 they had their post office in the new store of Samuel Hill and John McNeil. The growing village soon had three general stores, a cooper, two carpenters, a blacksmith and wagon-maker, a tanner, a hatter, a shoemaker, two doctors, a carding machine, two saloons, some 25 families and about 100 people, a squire and two constables living nearby. In easy driving distance were settlements of two to four or more houses along creek beds or in groves—Petersburg, Sand Ridge, Sugar Grove, Irish Grove, Clary's Grove, Indian Point, Athens, their trading center New Salem.

Far up in northern Illinois was a young village named Chicago, also built on hope and promise, like New Salem having about a dozen log cabins and a population of 100. The wide stretch of prairie between New Salem and Chicago was yet to have its tall grass and tough grass roots broken for crops from rich black soil. In southern Illinois the pioneers chose to farm where the sod was easier to break and near timber for firewood, fences, logs for cabins. These pioneers came mostly from Kentucky and Tennessee and had yet to see what crops could be raised on treeless prairies. A young and growing country and no one more sure and proud of New Salem's future than Denton Offutt, promoter, booster and boomer. He saw Lincoln as honest and able, picked him as a manager, told people, "He knows more than any man in the United States." Somehow at this particular time Offutt had an influence on Lincoln for good, perhaps made Lincoln feel more sure of himself. Lincoln never joined those who later blamed and belittled Offutt. There was something near tenderness in the way that, years later, Lincoln wrote, "Offutt, previously an entire stranger, conceived a liking for A.[braham] and believing he could turn him to account."

While waiting for Offutt in August 1831, Lincoln navigated a raft of household goods and a family, Texas bound, from New Salem to Beardstown and walked back to New Salem, jingling good pay.

On a lot Offutt bought for $10, he and Lincoln built a cabin of logs for the new store. Offutt's goods arrived and Lincoln stacked shelves and corners.

Soon stories got going about Lincoln's honesty, how he walked six miles to pay back a few cents a woman had overpaid for dry goods, and finding he had used a four-ounce weight instead of an eight, he walked miles to deliver to a woman the full order of tea she had paid for.

Offutt talked big about Lincoln as a wrestler and Bill Clary, who ran a saloon 30 steps north of the Offutt store, bet Offutt $10 that Lincoln couldn't throw Jack Armstrong, the Clary's Grove champion. Sports from miles around came to a level square next to Offutt's store to see the match; bets of money, knives, trinkets, tobacco, drinks, were put up. Armstrong, short and powerful, aimed from the first to get in close to his man and use his thick muscular strength. Lincoln held him off with long arms, wore down his strength, got him out of breath, surprised and "rattled." They pawed and clutched in many holds and twists till Lincoln threw Armstrong and had both shoulders to the grass. Armstrong's gang started toward Lincoln with cries and threats. Lincoln stepped to the Offutt store wall, braced himself, and told the gang he would fight, race or wrestle any who wanted to try him. Then Jack Armstrong broke through the gang, shook Lincoln's hand, told them Lincoln was "fair," and, "the best feller that ever broke into this settlement."

Some claimed it was a draw, and that after a long round of hard tussling and trying different holds, Lincoln said, "Jack, let's quit. I can't throw you— you can't throw me." One sure action everybody remembered was that Jack Armstrong gave Lincoln a warm handshake and they were close friends ever after. The Clary's Grove boys called on him sometimes to judge their horse races and cockfights, umpire their matches, and settle disputes. One story ran that Lincoln was on hand one day when an old man had agreed, for a gallon jug of whisky, to be rolled down a hill in a barrel. And Lincoln talked and laughed them out of doing it. He wasn't there on the day, as D. G. Burner told it, when the gang took an old man with a wooden leg, built a fire around the wooden leg, and held the man down till the wooden leg was burned off.

The Clary's Grove boys, it was told, had decided to see what stuff Abe had in him. First, he was to run a foot race with a man from Wolf. "Trot him out," said Abe. Second, he was to wrestle with a man from Little Grove. "All right," said Abe. Third, he must fight a man from Sand Ridge. "Nothing wrong about that," said Abe. The foot racer from Wolf couldn't pass Abe. The man from Little Grove, short and heavy, stripped for action, ran at Abe like a battering-ram. Abe stepped aside, caught his man by the nape of the neck, threw him heels over head, and gave him a fall that nearly broke the bones. A committee from the boys came up and told him, "You have sand in your craw and we will take you into our crowd." This, perhaps half true, was beginning to be told by Henry Onstot and others.

When a small gambler tricked Bill Greene, Lincoln's helper at the store, Lincoln told Bill to bet him the best fur hat in the store that he [Lincoln] could lift a barrel of whisky from the floor and hold it while he took a drink from the bunghole. Bill hunted up the gambler and made the bet. Lincoln sat squatting on the floor, lifted the barrel off the floor, rolled it on his knees till the bunghole reached his mouth, took a mouthful, let the barrel down— and stood up and spat out the whisky. Bill won his bet. It was Bill Greene who on the witness stand once, when a lawyer asked him who were the principal citizens of New Salem, answered, "There are no principal citizens; every man in New Salem neighborhood is a principal citizen."

In spare hours Lincoln had sessions with Mentor Graham, the local school-master, who told him of a grammar at John C. Vance's, six miles off; he walked the six miles, brought back the book, burned pine shavings at night in the Onstot cooper shop to light Samuel Kirkham's *English Grammar*. As he went further, he had Bill Greene hold the book and ask him questions. In the New Salem Debating Society, Lincoln in his first speech opened in a tone of apology, as though he wasn't sure of himself. He surprised both himself and those hearing him. James Rutledge, president of the society, was saying there was "more than wit and fun" in Abe's head.

In his work at the store, and in hours after work, he was meeting people, characters, faces, voices and motives, close up in a range and variety as never before in his life. James Rutledge, 50 years old, of medium height, warm-hearted, square in dealings, religious, born in South Carolina, had lived in Georgia, Tennessee, Kentucky, in White County, Illinois, on Concord Creek seven miles north of New Salem. The third of his nine children, Ann Mayes Rutledge, was 18, had auburn hair, blue eyes, a fair face, and Lincoln was to meet and know her. John M. Camron, Rutledge's partner and ten years younger, was a nephew of Mrs. Rutledge, had lived with or near them in White County and on Concord Creek. He was a massive, powerful man, had learned the millwright's trade, had become an ordained Cumberland Presby-terian minister, and sometimes preached in and around New Salem.

Dr. John Allen, a graduate of Dartmouth College Medical School, had left Vermont and come west for the climate, arriving in New Salem the same month as Lincoln. He was to prove himself a skilled physician and an earnest, obstinate man in his steady, quiet arguments against Negro slavery and alco-holic liquor. He went when called in all kinds of weather, sent bills for his services only to the well to do; all his fees from Sunday visits went into a fund for the church, the sick, the poor. Here was a Yankee for Lincoln to study; he had in his days met few Yankees.

There was Henry Sinco, a saloonkeeper, and Lincoln's vote August 1 had helped elect Sinco a village constable. There was James Pantier, who hunted big game, owned large tracts of land, wore a buckskin fringed shirt, some-times had cured snake bites by rubbings and mumblings. "Uncle Jimmy" would come in from Sand Ridge to a Cumberland Presbyterian Church meet-ing in a schoolhouse, repeat the sermon as the preacher spoke it, nod ap-proval or again shake a finger and in an undertone, "You are mistaken" or "Not so, brother."

Characters, men of personality and deed worth looking at and studying, these pioneers. The father of Lincoln's good friend, James Short, was pointed at as a veteran of the Revolutionary War; he had become a wild turkey hunter, and once in blazing away at 50, had killed 16 turkeys. Another vet-eran, Daddy Boger, of service under George Washington, lived in Wolf, wove bushel baskets of white oak splints, and would come to the village with a basket nest under each arm, trade his baskets, rest a while, and then start home. Lincoln definitely saw history in these men; he had read about them.

Then there was Granny Spears of Clary's Grove, often helping at houses where a new baby had come; stolen by Indians when a girl and living with them she had learned how to use herbs and make salves; a little dried-up woman whose chin and nose curved out and nearly touched. Farmer Sampson, with a big family, could tell of his beef hides tanned by Philemon Morris, then taken to the cobbler Alex Ferguson who had the foot measures of the family, and, with a two-bushel sack, he was taking home a dozen pairs of shoes. Tall, erect, an impressive figure was the Reverend John M. Berry, an 1812 veteran, whose sermons and prayers touched on the liquor evil with added depth because of his acquaintance with many a hard drinker. Samuel Hill and John McNeil were the keenest traders in the village, their store doing more business than any other. Hill was hot-tempered, crafty, thrifty, often called stingy. McNeil's face and talk could puzzle people; what was going on in his head and heart he didn't report.

Young Mr. Lincoln in late 1831 and early 1832 studied a book of legal forms, signed as a witness to four deeds, wrote in his own hand several legal documents, a bill of sale and a bond, each beginning "Know all men by these presents." With the help of his good friend, Bowling Green, the justice of the peace, he was edging into law and how to write the simpler documents.

On March 9, 1832, came the boldest and most important paper he had ever written, telling the public he was stepping into politics as a candidate for the legislature of the State of Illinois. The *Sangamo Journal* at Springfield printed it and it was issued as a handbill. There was in it the tone of a young man a little bashful about what he was doing—and yet unafraid of his ideas and his platform, ready to debate them with any comer. A railroad for the service of New Salem would cost too high; her one hope was steamboat traffic; therefore he favored all possible improvement of the Sangamon River; "if elected, any measure in the legislature having this for its object, which may appear judicious, will meet my approbation, and shall receive my support." He came out strong for education, books, religion, morality. "That every man may receive at least, a moderate education, and thereby be enabled to read the histories of his own and other countries, by which he may duly appreciate the value of our free institutions, appears to be an object of vital importance, even on this account alone, to say nothing of the advantages and satisfaction to be derived from all being able to read the scriptures and other works, both of a religious and moral nature, for themselves." Thus, for the benefit of any who might have heard otherwise, the young politician showed himself as favoring books, schools, churches, the Scriptures, religion, morality.

Touching on "the practice of loaning money at exorbitant rates of interest," it seemed to him as though "we are never to have an end to this baneful and corroding system." He mentioned "a direct tax of several thousand dollars annually laid on each county, for the benefit of a few individuals only," which might require "a law made setting a limit to the rates of usury." In his opinion such a law could be made "without materially injuring any class of people." He mentioned no specific cases of usury or of "cheating the law" but seemed to assume that his readers would know who and what he was talking about in three curious sentences: "In cases of extreme necessity, there could always be means found to cheat the law, while in all other cases it would have its intended effect. I would not favor . . . a law upon this subject, which might be very easily evaded. Let it be such that the labor and difficulty of evading it, could only be justified in cases of the greatest necessity."

He was young and would admit "it is probable I have already been more presuming than becomes me." What was his ambition? "I have no other so great as that of being truly esteemed of my fellow men, by rendering myself worthy of their esteem." He was throwing his case "exclusively upon the independent voters of this county," making clear, "I was born and have ever remained in the most humble walks of life. I have no wealthy or popular relations to recommend me." He closed in a manner having the gray glint of his eyes and the loose hang of his long arms: "If the good people in their wisdom shall see fit to keep me in the background, I have been too familiar with disappointments to be very much chagrined." That was all. He had made his first real start in politics.

In this same March of 1832, excitement ran high in the Sangamon country over the small, light-draft steamboat *Talisman* with merchandise cargo from Cincinnati arriving at Beardstown on the Illinois River, ready, when the ice jams cleared, to make the trip upstream to New Salem and Springfield. The shipmaster had asked for help; a boatload of men, Lincoln one of them, worked with long-handled poleaxes and crowbars clearing the channel of snags and overhanging branches. The *Talisman*, puffing her smoke and blowing her whistle, moved up the Sangamon; at New Salem and other points she got cheers, laughter and waving of hands from people seeing the first steamboat making headway up that river, their river. Tying up at Portland Landing, seven miles north of Springfield, the county seat with a population of 500, merchants there advertised the arrival of goods "direct from the East per steamer *Talisman*," and celebrated with a reception and dance in the county courthouse. It was a matter aside that the shipmaster had sent a dude captain, "a vainly dressed fellow," to command the boat and this deck officer had worried the ladies of Springfield by bringing along a flashily dressed woman not his wife, both of them drunk and loose-tongued at the festivities.

The trip of the *Talisman* downstream was "risky business." The high waters of the spring thaw had gone down making a more narrow river and shallow channel. At the wheel, as pilot, the boat officers put Rowan Herndon, New Salem grocer and a good boatsman, with Lincoln as assistant pilot. To get past New Salem they had to tear down part of the milldam. A slow four miles a day, sometimes nearly scraping river bottom, they made it to Beardstown. Walking back to New Salem, the two pilots could jingle a nice $40 apiece, their pay as navigators of the sometimes unnavigable Sangamon.

One morning in April 1832 a rider got off his mud-spattered, sweating horse in New Salem and gave notice of Governor John Reynolds calling for 400 thirty-day volunteers from the Sangamon County state militia to report at Beardstown April 24. The Illinois frontier, like nearly every other state to the east, was to have an Indian war. The 67-year-old Black Hawk, war leader of the Sauk and Fox tribes, on April 6 had crossed the Mississippi River into Illinois, saying his people would plant corn along the Rock River. He led 368 paint-faced and eagle-feathered warriors, nearly 1,000 women and children, and 450 horses. So came reports. For a hundred years his people had hunted, fished and planted in that prairie valley until treaties with the white men sent them west of the Mississippi. Now Black Hawk claimed that "land can not be sold," that "nothing can be sold but such things as can be carried away," and that wrong was done when red men drank too deep of the firewater of the white men and signed papers selling land. In days soon to come his whooping night riders on fast ponies left cabins in ashes and white men and women killed and scalped. Also red men tumbled off their horses from the rifle shots of white men. Any high cry in the night sent white settlers to their cabins and rifles. It was held against Black Hawk that in the War of 1812 he favored the British and fought as best he could for them.

Of this April, Lincoln said later, "Offutt's business was failing—had almost failed—when the Black-Hawk war of 1832 broke out." For months it seemed the store was run by Lincoln alone, while Offutt gave his time and funds to big and risky speculations in buying and shipping produce, leaving New Salem quietly in the spring of 1832 and not being heard of for years.

Lincoln borrowed a horse and rode nine miles to Richland Creek to join a company of friends and neighbors, mostly Clary's Grove boys. Voting for a captain, each man of the company stepped out and stood by either Lincoln or one William Kirkpatrick. Three-fourths of the men at once went to Lincoln—and then one by one those standing by Kirkpatrick left him till he was almost alone. Lincoln was to write, years later, that he was "surprized" at this election and had "not since had any success in life which gave him so much satisfaction." He at once appointed Jack Armstrong first sergeant, and nine days later promoted from the ranks his rival William Kirkpatrick. They marched to Beardstown and went into camp, part of an army of 1,600 mobilizing there.

To settle a dispute over which company should have a certain campground, Lincoln wrestled with Lorenzo D. Thompson. In their first feel-outs of each other, Lincoln called, "Boys, this is the most powerful man I ever had hold of." Lincoln was thrown twice and lost the match, saying later of Thompson, "He could have thrown a grizzly bear." After Lincoln went to the ground the second time, his men swarmed in and from over their heads came Lincoln's voice, "Boys, give up your bets. If this man hasn't thrown me fairly, he could."

No easy set of men to drill into obeying orders had Lincoln, and his first military order was answered, "Go to hell." He himself was a beginner in drill regulations, and once couldn't think of the order that would get two platoons endwise, two by two, for passing through a gate. So he commanded, "This company is dismissed for two minutes, when it will fall in again on the other side of the gate."

At the brigade quartermaster's office April 25 Lincoln drew corn, pork, salt, one barrel of flour and five and a half gallons of whisky for his company. After five days there was muttering and grumbling, discipline poor; it didn't seem the kind of a war they had expected and they wrote home about it. Lincoln's company was enrolled in the state service April 28 and Lincoln drew 30 muskets and bayonets, so it looked like there might be shooting. They began marching, 25 miles one day, 20 miles another, one night camping two miles from timber or water, men sleeping on cold, damp ground. They arrived at Yellow Banks (later Oquawka), noticed the citizens there serene and satisfied, some of the men wondering what the war was about. The food wasn't good so some soldiers shot hogs and enjoyed pork chops, and the farmers were heard from.

They marched to camp near the mouth of the Rock River where on May 9 Lincoln's company, with others, was sworn into the Federal service. The next day while the U.S. Regular Army troops moved on boats, the 1,500 militia marched 26 miles in swamp muck and wilderness brush along the left bank of the river, pushing and pulling when horses and wagons bogged. When night rains came the tents didn't shed water and Lincoln heard fagged men wail and curse, along with talk of deserting.

They marched to Prophetstown, to Dixon's Ferry where they heard two days later how, without orders, troops of Major Isaiah Stillman had at dusk rushed at Indian horsemen on a rise of ground about a mile from their camp, bringing on a fight that ended in a rout and left 12 white men dead. The next day General Samuel Whiteside's army, including Lincoln's company, marched to the battle scene, arriving near sunset to witness fallen white men who lay scalped and mangled. The next day, after burials, the army was drawn up in battle line for Black Hawk's spies to see they were ready for action, after which the hungry troops marched back to Dixon's Ferry and food and a speech by Governor Reynolds promising militiamen who were eager to go home that U.S. Regulars would arrive next day.

There were farmers anxious about their crops, there was gloom over the stragglers routed and sent flying by Black Hawk's horsemen, and a lessening confidence in officers. Once, against orders, someone shot off a pistol inside the camp; the authorities found it was Captain Lincoln; he was arrested, his sword taken away, and he was held in custody one day. Another time his men opened officers' supplies of whisky; some were dead drunk and others straggled on the march; a court-martial ordered Captain Lincoln to carry a wooden sword two days. "A hard set of men," said a Regular Army officer. Bill Greene remembered Lincoln saying to officers of the U.S. Regulars that his men "must be equal in all particulars" in rations and arms to the Regular Army and "resistance will hereafter be made to unjust orders," which threat of mutiny resulted in better treatment. Greene couldn't forget either how one day an old Indian, with a safe-conduct pass from a general, rambled into camp and men rushed to kill him. Lincoln jumped to the side of the Indian and said with a hard gleam, "Men, this must not be done." Some of the mob called him a coward and his answer came like a shot, "Choose your weapons!" Hot tempers cooled off as the Clary's Grove boys began backing Lincoln and they saw he was a captain who didn't presume on his authority.

They marched up Rock River, then to Stillman's battlefield, then back along the Rock River, some men believing they were being kept busy to lessen grumbling. On May 21 came news of an Indian party near Ottawa that killed, mangled and scalped three families, 15 persons, and took away alive two girls of 17 and 15. They marched up Sycamore Creek, arrived at Pottawatomie Village where spies the day before had found a number of scalps. At this point mutiny came, troops demanding discharge. Governor Reynolds called a conference of captains, including Lincoln, and had them vote on whether to follow the enemy or go home. A tie vote was announced and General Whiteside's temper blazed in saying he would no longer lead such men except to be discharged. Four days later, after marching to Ottawa, Lincoln's company and others were mustered out of the service. Lincoln certified his muster roll, marking three men as "absent without leave."

Lincoln re-enlisted for 20 days and May 29 was mustered as a private into a company of mounted Independent Rangers under Captain Elijah Iles, a pioneer trader, land dealer, and one of the founders of Springfield. His unit had former colonels, captains, lieutenants, and one general serving as privates. About this time Colonel Zachary Taylor of the U.S. Regulars had ordered a company of militia to march to Galena, and the men refusing to go, he had reported, "The more I see of the militia the less confidence I have of their effecting anything of importance." Nevertheless Captain Iles' company marched and camped alongside the small Apple River Fort near Galena where the night before Indians had stolen 12 horses and that afternoon had shot at and chased two men into the fort. The company slept with guns in their arms. Arriving the next day in Galena they found in the town of 400 so many people terrified that Captain Iles believed they would put up little or no resistance to Indians. Three days later the company again arrived at Dixon's Ferry, Iles reporting signs of Indians who seemed more anxious to get horses than scalps. A 45-mile march brought them to Fort Wilbourn on the Illinois River where Captain Iles' company was mustered out of service.

Lincoln on June 16 enlisted for the third time, becoming a 30-day private in the Independent Spy Corps of Captain Jacob M. Early, a Springfield physician and Methodist preacher who had been a private in the companies of Lincoln and Iles. On June 25 Early's Spy Corps was ordered out on an all-night march to Kellogg's Grove where the day before a main body of Sauks under Black Hawk, "secreted in a thicket," had surprised and routed the whites. Lincoln shortly after sunrise helped bury five men. As he told it afterward, each of the dead men "had a round, red spot on top of his head, about as big as a dollar where the redskins had taken his scalp." It was frightful, grotesque, "and the red sunlight seemed to paint everything all over." Captain Early wrote an extended report of the battle to General Henry Atkinson of the Regular Army.

The Spy Corps made several marches and on July 1 crossed into Michigan Territory (later Wisconsin), camping and throwing up breastworks near Turtle Village (later Beloit), sleeping on their muskets, Black Hawk being near. Next day Early's men marched in advance of the army to Lake Koshkonong and roundabout White Water and Burnt Village, and for four days performed spy and scout duty for General Atkinson's army of 450 Regulars, about 2,100 mounted volunteers, with 100 Indian allies. The general on July 9 wrote to General Winfield Scott that the country was so cut up with prairie, wood and swamp that it was "extremely difficult" to approach the enemy, many parts for miles being "entirely impassable even on foot." He had decided to dismiss the independent commands. On July 10 Captain Early's Spy Corps was mustered out at White Water on Rock River, honorably discharged "with the special thanks of Brigadier General H. Atkinson, Commander in Chief of the Army of the Illinois Frontier."

Black Hawk shaped and reshaped his army as a shadow, came and faded as a phantom, spread out false trails, set traps, lures and used the ambush. Yet the white men, though at cost, solved his style and used it to beat him.

The militia under General James D. Henry and other officers proved themselves equal and at times superior to the Regulars as they drove Black Hawk
north, marching in storm and night rains, performing an epic of endurance
and valor, outguessing the red men who had earlier tricked them. And the
end? Black Hawk, the prisoner, was taken to Washington, in the Executive
Mansion facing President Jackson, the red man saying to the white, "I—am—
a man—and you—are—another . . . I took up the hatchet to avenge injuries
which could no longer be borne . . . I say no more of it; all is known to
you."

On the night of his discharge Lincoln's horse was stolen; so was that of
his comrade George Harrison. In the 200 miles to Peoria they walked and
part way rode on the horses of comrades. Buying a canoe at Peoria, Lincoln
and Harrison steered by turns to Havana, sold the canoe, then walked to New
Salem. An army paymaster six months later in Springfield paid Lincoln some
$95 for his 80 days in the war. In those days Lincoln had seen deep into the
heart of the American volunteer soldier, why men go to war, march in mud,
sleep in rain on cold ground, eat pork raw when it can't be boiled, and kill
when the killing is good. On a later day an observer was to say he saw Lincoln's eyes misty in his mention of the American volunteer soldier.

Election Day was 18 days off, on August 6, and Lincoln traveled over
Sangamon County, gave the arguments in his long address issued in the spring.
At Pappsville, where a crowd had come to a sale, as he stepped on a box for
his speech he saw fellow citizens on the edge of the crowd in a fist fight.
He noticed his pilot friend Rowan Herndon getting the worst of it, stepped
off the box, shouldered his way to the fight, picked a man by the scruff of
the neck and the seat of the breeches, and threw him. Back on his box, he
swept the crowd with his eyes in a cool way as though what had happened
sort of happened every day, and then made a speech. Campaigning among
farmers, he pitched hay and cradled wheat in the fields and showed the farmers he was one of them; at crossroads he threw the crowbar and let the local
wrestlers try to get the "crotch hoist" on him. He closed his campaign with
a speech in the county courthouse at Springfield. On Election Day Lincoln
lost, running eighth in a field of 13 candidates. But in his own New Salem
precinct, he polled 277 of the 300 votes cast.

Later Lincoln wrote of himself after this August election, "He was now
without means and out of business, but was anxious to remain with his friends
who had treated him with so much generosity, especially as he had nothing
elsewhere to go to. He studied what he should do—thought of learning the
black-smith trade—thought of trying to study law—rather thought he could
not succeed at that without a better education."

He bought Rowan Herndon's interest in the partnership of Herndon and
William F. Berry, merchants, giving Herndon his promissory note. Then
Berry and Lincoln bought a stock of goods under peculiar conditions. Reuben
Radford at his store had spoken threats to Clary's Grove boys and one day
went away from his store telling his younger brother that if Clary's Grove
boys came in they should have two drinks apiece and no more. The boys
came, took their two drinks, stood the young clerk on his head, helped them-

selves at jugs and barrels, wrecked the store, broke the windows and rode away yelling on their ponies. Radford looked the wreck over and on the spot sold the stock to William G. Greene. The price was $400 which Greene made up by paying Radford $23 in cash and giving two notes for $188.50 each, secured by a mortgage on a New Salem lot. Lincoln drew and witnessed the mortgage, and on the same day he and Berry bought the stock from Greene, paying $265 cash, assuming Greene's notes to Radford, and throwing in a horse to boot. Thus Greene made a profit of $242 and one horse. Across later months there was more financing, several lawsuits and court judgments. They did nothing, as Lincoln said later, "but get deeper and deeper in debt" and "the store winked out."

During the fall and winter of 1832, business didn't pick up much. Berry wasn't interested, and Lincoln was reading and dreaming. Early harvest days came; the farmers bundled grain in russet fields. From the Salem hilltop the valley of the Sangamon River loitered off in a long stretch of lazy, dreamy haze and the harvest moon came in a wash of pumpkin colors. Lincoln could sit with uninterrupted thoughts, free day after day to turn and look into himself. He was having days that might nourish by letting him sit still and get at himself. He was growing as inevitably as summer corn in Illinois loam. Leaning against the doorpost of a store to which few customers came he was growing, in silence, as corn grows. He had bought at an auction in Springfield a copy of Blackstone, the first of the law books to read. One morning he sat barefoot on a woodpile, with a book. "What are you reading?" asked Squire Godbey. "I ain't reading; I'm studying." "Studying what?" "Law." "Good God Almighty!"

Lincoln later came across an account of "the peculiar manner" of his law studies: "His favorite place of study was a wooded knoll near New Salem, where he threw himself under a wide-spreading oak, and expansively made a reading desk of the hillside. Here he would pore over Blackstone day after day, shifting his position as the sun rose and sank, so as to keep in the shade, and utterly unconscious of everything but the principles of common law. People went by, and he took no account of them; the salutations of acquaintances were returned with silence, or a vacant stare; and altogether the manner of the absorbed student was not unlike that of one distraught." This picture of himself as a law student he accepted.

Business dropped off. Berry took out a license in March 1833 for Berry and Lincoln to keep a tavern and sell retail liquors. The required bond had both names, Lincoln and Berry, but neither signature was in Lincoln's well-known handwriting. The license specified they could sell whisky at 12½ cents a pint, brandies, gins, wine and rum, at various prices.

Selling pork, salt, powder, guns, trading calico prints and bonnets for eggs and furs had only a mild interest for Lincoln, but taking the cash of men and boys for hard liquor didn't come easy—and a few weeks after the firm got its license, Lincoln, in a deal of some kind, turned his interest in the store over to Berry. It could, however, have been about this time that, as he later told it, "Lincoln did work the latter part of one winter in a little still house, up at the head of a hollow." The stills ran in many odd corners, the supply endless, corn juice priced at $1.00 and less per gallon. At gatherings, barbecues, dances, sporting events, auction sales, weddings, funerals, camp meetings, the jug and the bottle were there. Dr. Allen, in his temperance appeals, found his fiercest opponents "among church members, most of whom had their barrels of whisky at home." Even the hardshell Baptist church was not then ready to take a stand against whisky. When Mentor Graham, the schoolmaster, joined the temperance movement, the church trustees suspended him. Then, to hold a balance, the trustees suspended another member who had gone blind drunk. This action puzzled one member who stood up in meeting and, shaking a half-full quart bottle so all could see, drawled, "Brethering, you have turned one member out beca'se he would not drink, and another beca'se he got drunk, and now I wants to ask a question. How much of this 'ere critter does a man have to drink to remain in full membership in this church?"

On May 7, 1833, as Lincoln told it, he "was appointed Postmaster at New-Salem—the office being too insignificant, to make his politics an objection." The pay would run about $50 a year, in commissions on receipts. He had to be in the office at Hill's store only long enough to receive and receipt for the mail which came twice a week by postrider at first and later by stage. Letters arrived written on sheets of paper folded and waxed, envelopes not yet in use. The sender of a letter paid no postage; that fell on whoever the letter was addressed to. Postage on a one-sheet letter was six cents for the first 30 miles, ten cents for 30 to 80 miles, and so on to 25 cents for more than 400 miles. Two sheets cost twice as much, three sheets three times as much, and with every letter Lincoln had to figure how many sheets, how far it had come, then mark the postage in the upper right corner of the outside sheet. If anyone didn't like his figuring as to the number of sheets the receiver could open the letter before the postmaster and settle the question.

Lincoln was free to read newspapers before delivering them, and he read "the public prints" as never before. The habit deepened in him of watching newspapers for political trends and issues. And he could find excitement at times in reading the speeches made in Congress at Washington as reported in full in the *Congressional Globe* subscribed for by John C. Vance. It was no pleasure for him to write later to the publishers, Blair & Rives, "Your subscriber at this place *John C. Vance*, is dead; and no person takes the paper from the office." It seemed he wasn't strict about regulations, and when George Spears sent a messenger with postage money for his newspapers and a note telling Lincoln he wanted a receipt, Lincoln replied he was "surprised" and, "the law requires News paper postage to be paid in advance and now that I have waited a full year you choose to wound my feelings by intimating that unless you get a receipt I will probably make you pay it again."

At times the post office was left unlocked for hours while citizens who called for mail helped themselves. The postmaster could send and receive letters free but franking a letter for someone else made him liable to a $10 fine. Not bothering about regulations, he wrote in the upper right corner of an outside sheet: "Free. A. Lincoln, P.M. New Salem Ills. Sept 22." The letter was from Matthew S. Marsh to a brother in Portsmouth, New Hampshire, and near its opening said: "The Post Master [Mr. Lincoln] is very careless about leaving his office open & unlocked during the day—half the time I go in & get my papers etc. without any one being there as was the case yesterday. The letter was only marked 25 & even if he had been there & known it was double he would not [have] charged me any more—luckily he is a very clever fellow & a particular friend of mine. If he is there when I carry this to the office—I will get him to 'Frank' it . . ." As between "particular" friends, could it have been that Marsh sometimes spoke to Lincoln as he did to his folks in his letter? Did he tell Lincoln that if no better chance offered he would teach a private school on Indian Creek, Morgan County, nearby a "sucker girl" of whom he wrote: "She posseses more qualities which assimilate with my peculiar disposition & comes nearer to the standard of what I consider essential in a wife than any girl I have ever seen. In stature middling height & slim—Light brown hair, black eyes, which suppress half their fire until she speaks, then through their soft disguise will flash an expression more of pride than ire . . . Her age 20. Such is all the discription I can give of the girl who at present stands highest in my estimation. How long she will continue to do so I cannot assure even myself as I have *naturally* a *fickle* disposition . . . I have one objection to marrying in this state & that is, the women have such an everlasting number of children—twelve is the least number that can be counted on." Did Marsh say the like to young Lincoln, of whom some were saying, "He can pump a man dry on any subject he is interested in"?

Marsh was good company, a man Lincoln could learn from. So was Jack Kelso, blacksmith, fisherman, trapper, a good rifle shot, a reader of Shakespeare and Burns. He recited from those authors, Lincoln listening while Kelso talked and fished, Lincoln joining in discussions but not in the bottle Kelso usually had handy. It was said that when other men were lush from drinking they wanted to fight but Kelso would recite Shakespeare and Burns.

Lincoln signed as witness to petitions and deeds, signed honorable discharges for members of his Black Hawk War company, accepted when after the war he was elected captain of militia in Clary's Grove, drew and attested mortgages, served as clerk with $1.00 of pay at September and November elections in New Salem, received $2.50 for taking poll books 18 miles to Springfield.

For earning a living, jobs at common labor were plenty; he worked as rail splitter, mill hand, farm hand, helped out at the Hill store. Meanwhile he read or dipped into Volney's *The Ruins of Empire,* Gibbon's *Decline and Fall of the Roman Empire,* Paine's *The Age of Reason.* And his debts haunted him. They added up to more when his former partner, William F. Berry, died on short notice in January 1835, his estate practically nothing, leaving Lincoln responsible for their joint obligations. Thus his debts ran to a total of $1,100—and they wouldn't laugh away. They were little rats, a rat for every dollar, and he could hear them in the night when he wanted to sleep.

Squire Bowling Green proved a friend and counselor, explained to Lincoln what he knew of the Illinois statutes, allowed Lincoln without fee to try small cases, examine witnesses and make arguments. The squire, not yet 50, weighed 250 pounds and was nicknamed "Pot" for his paunch. He held court wearing only a shirt and pants and once when two witnesses swore a hog didn't belong to Jack Kelso and Kelso swore it did, Squire Green decided,

"The two witnesses we have heard have sworn to a damned lie. I know this shoat, and I know he belongs to Jack Kelso."

In the fall of 1833 came Lincoln's entry into the most highly technical and responsible work he had known. Writing of it later, he said, "The Surveyor of Sangamon [County], offered to depute to A[braham] that portion of his work which was within his part of the county. He accepted, procured a compass and chain, studied Flint, and Gibson a little, and went at it. This procured bread, and kept soul and body together." There were farm sections, roads and towns needing their boundary lines marked clear and beyond doubt on maps—more than the county surveyor, John Calhoun, could handle. On the suggestion of Pollard Simmons, a farmer and Democratic politician living near New Salem, Calhoun, a Jackson Democrat, appointed Lincoln, who went 18 miles to Springfield to make sure he wasn't tied up politically and could speak as he pleased.

Then for six weeks, daytime and often all of nighttime, he had his head deep in Gibson's *Theory and Practice of Surveying* and Flint's *Treatise on Geometry, Trigonometry and Rectangular Surveying*. From decimal fractions one book ran on into logarithms, the use of mathematical instruments, operating the chain, circumferentor, surveying by intersections, changing the scale of maps, leveling, methods for mensuration of areas. Many nights, said Mentor Graham's daughter, she woke at midnight to see Lincoln and her father by the fire, figuring and explaining, her mother sometimes bringing fresh firewood for better lighting. On some nights he worked alone till daylight and it wore him down. He was fagged, and friends said he looked like a hard drinker after a two weeks' spree. Good people said, "You're killing yourself."

In six weeks, however, he had mastered his books, and Calhoun put him to work on the north end of Sangamon County. The open air and sun helped as he worked in field and timberland with compass and measurements. His pay was $2.50 for "establishing" a quarter section of land, $2.00 for a half-quarter, 25 cents to 37½ cents for small town lots. He surveyed the towns of Petersburg, Bath, New Boston, Albany, Huron, and others. He surveyed roads, school sections, pieces of farm land from four-acre plots to 160-acre farms. His surveys became known for care and accuracy and he was called on to settle boundary disputes. In Petersburg, however, he laid out one street crooked. Running it straight and regular, it would have put the house of Jemima Elmore and her family into the street. Lincoln knew her to be working a small farm with her children and she was the widow of Private Travice Elmore, honorable in service in Lincoln's company in the Black Hawk War.

For his surveying trips he had bought a horse, saddle and bridle from William Watkins for $57.86, and for nonpayment Watkins on April 26, 1834, got judgment in court and levied on Lincoln's personal possessions. It looked as though he would lose his surveying instruments. Then Bill Greene showed up and turned in a horse on the Watkins judgment—and James Short came from Sand Ridge to the auction Lincoln was too sad to attend and bid in the saddle, bridle, compass and other surveying instruments. When Short brought them to Lincoln it hit him as another surprise in his young life.

Short liked Lincoln as a serious student, a pleasant joker, and said that on a farm "he husks two loads of corn to my one."

In January 1834, after a survey for Russell Godbey, Lincoln bought two buckskins from Godbey and took them to Hannah Armstrong, the wife of Jack, who "foxed his pants," sewed leather between ankles and knees for protection against briars. The Armstrongs took him in two or three weeks at a time when he needed a place to stay, Hannah saying, "Abe would drink milk, eat mush, corn-bread and butter, rock the cradle while I got him something to eat. I foxed his pants, made his shirts. He would tell stories, joke people at parties. He would nurse babies—do anything to accomodate anybody." Jack one day had a hand in an affair that A. Y. Ellis said had Lincoln "out of temper and laughing at the same time." The boys had made a large fire of shavings and hemp stalks and bet a fellow Ellis called Ike that he couldn't run his bobtail pony through the fire. Ike got a hundred-yard start, came full tilt with his hat off, and just as he reached the blazing fire his pony "flew the track and pitched poor Ike into the flames." Lincoln ran to help, crying, "You have carried this thing far enough." He was mad though he couldn't help laughing, as Ellis saw him. Jack took Ike with scorched head and face to a doctor, who shaved the head and put salve on the burn. Jack was sorry and at his house next morning gave Ike a dram, his breakfast and a skin cap and sent him home.

Lincoln worked at occasional odd jobs when there was no surveying but he made it a point to find time to keep up his political connections. On March 1, 1834, he was secretary of a public meeting at New Salem which resolved on General James D. Henry, former sheriff of Sangamon County, as their choice for governor. General Henry had become a high name in the history of the Black Hawk War, a proven strategist and a soldier of courage who shared hardships with his men. He died of tuberculosis in New Orleans four days after the New Salem meeting that favored him and Lincoln couldn't stay away from a memorial service for Henry on April 20 in the courthouse at Springfield.

In those New Salem days were some saying Lincoln would be a great man, maybe governor or senator, anyhow a great lawyer, what with his studying of law. Others saw him as an awkward, gangly giant, a homely joker who could go gloomy and show it. It was noticed he had two shifting moods, one of the rollicking, droll story, one when he lapsed silent and solemn beyond any bystander to penetrate.

He moved amid odd happenings. He mourned with others when Rowan Herndon, while cleaning a rifle, accidentally pressed the trigger, the bullet striking his wife in the neck, bringing almost instant death. One winter morning he saw young Ab Trent, chopping away at the logs of an old pulled-down stable, Ab with rags instead of shoes on his feet. He told Lincoln he was earning a dollar to buy shoes. Lincoln told him to run to the store and warm his feet. And after a while Lincoln came to the store, handed Ab Trent his ax, and told him to collect the dollar and buy shoes; the wood was chopped. Later Ab, a Democrat, told friends he was going to vote for Lincoln for the legislature. And when the poll books showed that Ab Trent had voted against

Lincoln, Ab came to Lincoln with tears in his eyes and said his friends had got him drunk and had him vote against the way he intended.

In late summer or early fall of 1834 many people in New Salem, Lincoln included, wondered what had become of John McNeil. It was two years since he had left New Salem. Before leaving he had sold his interest in the Hill-McNeil store to Hill, but at 32 he was the owner of farms steadily rising in value and was rated one of the shrewdest and richest traders in New Salem. In money and looks he was considered by girls "a good catch." On December 9, 1831, Lincoln with Charles Maltby witnessed two deeds given by John Camron to John McNamar and it was then, if not earlier, that Lincoln learned John McNeil's real name was John McNamar. This also explained to Lincoln why as election clerk he didn't see McNeil's name on the poll books; the man was keeping his real name off election records. He said that he had left his family in New York State rather bad off and, setting out to make a fortune, he didn't want his family to trace and interfere with him, but he would in good time go back and help them when he had made his money.

The one person most anxious about him when he went away from New Salem in 1832 was, in all probability, the 19-year-old Ann Rutledge. They were engaged to marry and it was understood he would straighten out affairs of his family in New York State and in not too long a time would come back to her for the marriage. He rode away on a horse that had seen service in the Black Hawk War and it was said that he wrote to Ann from Ohio of a serious three weeks' sickness there and again had written her from New York, and she had answered his letters—and that was all.

A few months after he left in September 1832, James Rutledge and John M. Camron, the two founders of New Salem, having failed in business affairs, moved with their families into the double-log house of a farm near Sand Ridge that McNamar owned through payment to Camron of $400. It could have been that McNamar was showing goodness of heart to the family of his betrothed, at the same time acquiring trusted and responsible caretakers of his property while he was away. Possibly, too, he believed Ann's feeling about him would have added assurance out of her living on his land, the same land she might live on after their marriage. McNamar was a careful and exact man, insisted on clear understandings in all bargains—and a betrothal to him was a bargain between a man and a woman and their joint properties. What they wrote to each other about motives and intentions was in letters not kept and saved.

For nearly two years no one in New Salem had heard from the man who was afraid his folks would find him and had therefore changed his name. There was guessing and byplay of the kind in a later frontier song:

> Oh, what was your name in the States?
> Was it Thompson or Johnson or Bates?
>   Did you murder your wife and fly for your life?
>   Say, what was your name in the States?

Sharp gossips asked, "If he hid his real name what else might he be hiding? Did he run away from a wife or from a girl he got into trouble?" This was mostly idle chatter. For McNamar had a good name for straight dealing in business, for keeping sober, for no loose ways with girls and women. He was known for close bargains, had an eye for where values would rise; he required cash or land in payments, taking no promissory notes, one woman saying he was "cold as the multiplication table." He seemed to be the first of the early investors of New Salem to see that lack of river navigation and other conditions were to doom the village. He held off from loans to Camron and Rutledge when they began taking heavy losses on their sawmill and gristmill. He did accommodate them by paying $50 for half of Rutledge's 80 acres at Sand Ridge, seven miles from New Salem, and paying Camron $400 for one tract of 40 acres and another of 80 acres, also at Sand Ridge. He rode away from New Salem with no anxiety about promissory notes, the land he owned sure to rise in value.

And Lincoln, who called McNamar "Mack," who had surveyed the land McNamar owned, and who had lived under the same roof with Ann during the months "Mack" was a boarder at the Rutledge tavern, could hardly have been unaware of what she was going through. Her well-known betrothed had gone away saying he would be back soon; two years had gone by and except for a few weeks at the beginning no word had come from him. Did she talk over with Lincoln the questions, bitter and haunting, that harassed her? Had death taken her betrothed? Or was he alive and any day would see him riding into New Salem to claim her? And again, possibly, she kept a silence and so did Lincoln, and there was some kind of understanding beneath their joined silence.

Lincoln was to go away and stay away for months on important duties, writing her no letters that she kept and saved, she writing him no letters that he laid by as keepsakes. During the six weeks he mastered the surveying books, he could have seen her for only brief moments, if at all. And his surveying, as he said, "procured bread, and kept body and soul together." So definitely he was no man of property who like McNamar could offer her land and money, the creature comforts of life. He had arrived in New Salem "a piece of floating driftwood," as he later wrote, and was haunted by debts that had crept high on him. He was aware of large families, nine Rutledge children, 11 Camron daughters, Matthew Marsh writing "twelve is the least number," and a comment that central Illinois was "a hard country for women and cattle." His stepmother, Sarah Bush Lincoln, said he liked people in general, children and animals, but "he was not very fond of girls."

He was to tell T. W. S. Kidd in Springfield of his first dream of love. When he was "a little codger" in Indiana a wagon broke down near their place and a man, his wife and their two girls came to the Lincoln cabin, cooking their meals and staying till the wagon was fixed. "The woman had books and read us stories," Kidd reported Lincoln. "I took a great fancy to one of the girls. And when they were gone I thought of her a great deal, and one day sitting out in the sun by the house I wrote out a story in my mind." On his father's horse he rode after the wagon and surprised them. "I talked with the girl and persuaded her to elope with me, and that night I put her on my horse, and we started off across the prairie. After several hours we came to a camp; and when we rode up we found it was the one we had left a few hours before and we went in. The next night we tried again, and the same thing happened—the horse came back to the same place. And then we concluded not to elope. I stayed until I had persuaded her father to give her to me. I always meant to write that story out and publish it. I began once, but I concluded it was not much of a story. But I think that was the beginning of love with me."

A. Y. Ellis, who kept a store where Lincoln had helped out on busy days, recalled: "He always disliked to wait on the ladies. He preferred trading with the men and boys, as he used to say. He was a very shy man of ladies. On one occasion, when we boarded at the same log tavern, there came an old lady and her son and three stylish daughters, from the state of Virginia, and stopped there for two or three weeks; and during their stay, I do not remember of Mr. Lincoln ever eating at the same table when they did. I thought it was on account of his awkward appearance and his wearing apparel."

Did he tell Ann of any dream, daydream or reverie that came to him about love in general or a particular love for her? Or did he shrink from such talk because she might be clinging to some last desperate hope that her betrothed would return? Or did she lean to a belief that McNamar was gone for all time, then shifting to another awful possibility that he would surely come back to his land and properties, perhaps bringing a wife with him? Two years of silence could be heavy and wearing. She was 21 and Lincoln 25 and in the few visits he had time for in this year when surveying and politics pressed him hard, he may have gone no further than to be a comforter. He may have touched and stroked her auburn hair once or more as he looked deep into her blue eyes and said no slightest word as to what hopes lay deep in his heart. Her mother could remember her singing a hymn he liked, with a line, "Vain man, thy fond pursuits forbear." Both were figures of fate—he caught with debts, with surveying "to keep body and soul together" while flinging himself into intense political activities, she the victim of a betrothal that had become a mysterious scandal. They were both young, with hope endless, and it could have been he had moments when the sky was to him a sheaf of blue dreams and the rise of the blood-gold red of a full moon in the evening was almost too much to live, see and remember.

CHAPTER 3

The Young Legislator

ON APRIL 19, 1834, Lincoln's name ran again in the *Sangamo Journal* as a candidate for the state legislature. Before that and after, he attended all sorts of political powwows, large and small, and those for whom he surveyed, and those he delivered letters to, did not fail to hear he was in the running. He had become a regular wheel horse of the Whig party backed by John T. Stuart, a Springfield lawyer and county Whig leader. This time Lincoln gave out no long address on issues as two years before. With no presidential ticket in the field, voters were freer in personal choice. Bowling Green, a local Democratic leader, out of his liking for and belief in Lincoln, offered him the support of fellow Democrats. Lincoln hesitated, talked it over with Stuart, then accepted.

Strong Jackson men, believing Stuart wanted to run for Congress, were trying to cut Stuart down. At a shooting match for a beef at Clear Lake, Lincoln told Stuart of Jackson men proposing to him "that they would drop two of their men and take him up and vote for him," for the purpose of beating Stuart. "Lincoln acted fairly and honorably about it by coming to me," said Stuart. "I had great confidence in my strength—perhaps too much. But I told Lincoln to go and tell them that he would take their votes—that I would risk it—and I believe he did so."

So Lincoln played along with the Jackson Democrats who were after Stuart's scalp and with the Bowling Green Democrats who loved him for his own sake—speaking little on issues, and showing up, when there was time, any place he could meet voters face to face, shake hands, and let them know what he was like as a man, at Mechanicsburg taking a hand where fists were flying and ending the fight.

In the election for members of the Ninth General Assembly August 4, 1834, Lincoln ran second among 13 Sangamon County candidates, John Dawson having 1,390 votes, Lincoln, 1,376. Stuart ran fourth, with 1,164 votes, nosing out the one Democrat Stuart had "concentrated" against. Now at 25, Lincoln had won his first important political office, with better pay than ever before in his life, where he would train in the tangled and, to him, fascinating games of lawmaking and parliamentary management amid political labyrinths. After election he ran the post office, made surveys and appraisals, clerked in an October election, made court appearances in connection with his debts, and November 22 was elected a delegate to the State Education Convention to be held in Vandalia December 5. He had drawn closer to Stuart, who in the Black Hawk War had been major of the battalion in which Lincoln was a company captain, later serving as a private with Lincoln in Captain Iles' and Captain Early's companies. He had served two years in the legislature, and was an able lawyer, a handsome man, six feet tall, of Kentucky ancestry, a shut-mouthed manipulator whose nickname was "Jerry Sly." He deepened Lincoln's feeling about law study and loaned him law books.

A man of faith was Coleman Smoot, a well-to-do farmer, who lent Lincoln $200, Lincoln saying it was Smoot's penalty for voting for him. Lincoln paid a small pressing debt or two, bought cloth for a suit to be made at $60, and other apparel. With other members of the legislature, in the last week of November, he made the two-day 75-mile trip to Vandalia, the state capital, by stage. When later he saw a printed statement that he had walked to Vandalia, he wrote on the same page, "No harm, if true; but, in fact, not true."

Vandalia gave some the impression it had been there a long time and was a little tired though it was only 15 years old and had been the capital only 14 years. A town of some 800 people, it overlooked the Kaskaskia River and heavy timber, and to the north and west rolling prairie. Its streets, 80 feet wide, were lined mostly with log cabins, its sidewalks worn paths in grass. Five or six large frame buildings were taverns and boardinghouses, now filling their many empty rooms with legislators and lobbyists. Two weekly newspapers, one Democratic and the other Whig, advertised bedrooms, choice liquors and rewards for fugitive slaves. Main highways crossed the town, stages rolling in regularly, their wheels dusty or mud-coated, with passengers from all directions. The new jail had a "dungeon room" for stubborn birds and a "debtors' room." Into the latter Lincoln could stray for a look at men behind bars because they couldn't pay their debts.

He roomed with Stuart whose leadership made their room a Whig center. Here and in the legislature Lincoln was to meet men, most of them young, who would become governors, Congressmen, U.S. Senators, men of influence and portent. Here he would meet a short and almost dwarfish man, a little giant, thick of body with a massive head, 21 years old and absolutely confident of himself—Stephen A. Douglas lobbying for his selection as state's attorney of the First Circuit. Many members had their wives and daughters along and there was a social life new to Lincoln—parties, cotillions, music and flowers, elegant food and liquor, a brilliance of silk gowns and talk that ranged from idle gabble to profound conversation about the state and nation. Around the public square in candlelighted taverns, coffee rooms and hangouts, could be heard the talk and laughter of men eating, smoking, drinking, greeting, getting acquainted, and no lack of office seekers on the hunt.

On December 1, in a two-story ramshackle brick building facing the public square, meeting on the lower floor, the House was called to order, the members sitting in movable chairs, three to a table—cork inkstands, quill pens and writing paper on each table—and on the floor a sandbox as spittoon. A fireplace and stove heated the room. Three tin dippers hung over a pail of drinking water. Evening sessions were lighted by candles in tall holders. Ceiling plaster crashed down occasionally during speeches and roll calls; members got used to it.

Among the 54 representatives Lincoln could feel that if he was a greenhorn, so were the other 35 first-term members; there were 17 second-termers, and only one veteran of three previous terms. Three-fourths of them were born in Southern states, only one member a native of Illinois. Seven members had, like Lincoln, been captains in the Black Hawk War; many had been privates. More than half were farmers, one-fourth lawyers, with a sprinkling of merchants and mechanics. A "whole-hog" Jackson man was elected speaker, Lincoln with other Whigs voting for a less than "whole-hog" Jackson Democrat. Not till the seventh ballot did the House elect a doorkeeper, several candidates being hungry to be doorkeeper. In the next few days the House heard routine reports and joined in inaugurating Governor Joseph Duncan of Jacksonville, an 1812 war veteran who at 17 enlisted in the U.S. Infantry and performed heroic service, a Democrat who had known President Jackson personally when serving in Congress and was slowly moving toward joining the Whigs. Of the 11 standing committees Lincoln was appointed to the Committee on Public Accounts and Expenditures and he was to serve on several special committees.

On December 5 Lincoln stood up, unfolded to his full height, and gave notice of a bill he would introduce. And according to the rules, three days later he laid before them a bill to limit the jurisdiction of justices of the peace. The members were interested because they had that week rejected a proposal to give the justices wider powers. Days passed into weeks and Lincoln's bill was rewritten in select committee, reported to the House where a proposed amendment was debated, and the bill referred to a special committee, Lincoln being named to the committee. When finally reported with an amendment it passed the House 39 to 7 and was sent to the Senate where it died of indefinite postponement.

On his tenth day as a member he moved that it should not be in order "to offer amendments to any bill after its third reading," and his motion was tabled as too fresh and uninformed. Better luck came with passage of his bill to authorize his friend Samuel Musick to build a toll bridge across Salt Creek in Sangamon County, and another bill for three Sangamon friends "to view, mark and permanently locate" a road from Springfield to Miller's Ferry. He offered a resolution that "our Senators be instructed, and our Representatives requested" to procure a law through which Illinois would receive not less than 20 per cent of amounts paid into the Treasury of the United States for public lands lying within Illinois. The resolution was laid on the table, without a roll call, and Lincoln let it lay.

He worked and voted for incorporation of a new state bank in Springfield, the start of an alliance that would go further. He voted for a canal to connect the Illinois River with Lake Michigan, looking toward waterway hauls from mid-Illinois to the Atlantic. His votes generally ran with those of Stuart and the Whig minority. Several times members put in bills that were in Lincoln's handwriting and it seemed his hand was in more affairs than he openly showed.

The House shook nearer storm on the National Bank issue than on any other. President Jackson had gone into open battle with the Bank, refusing to favor it with a recharter, charging it was a "money power" that bought newspapers, politicians and Congressmen. Henry Clay, Daniel Webster and other leading Whigs clashed with Jackson, who made it an issue in 1832 when farmer and labor ballots gave Jackson 219 votes in the electoral college as against 49 for Clay. When the U.S. Senate denounced Jackson's course as lawless and unconstitutional, Jackson replied with a fierce protest which the Senate refused to print in its journal. Lincoln heard many hours of hot partisan debate on pro-Jackson and anti-National Bank resolutions. He voted with the Whigs on all such resolutions except once when he indicated he believed the U.S. Senate ought to have allowed Jackson's answer to the Senate to be printed in its journal.

Questions came up of salary raises, public roads, school funds, the public printer, the state militia, regulation of gamblers, leasing of convict labor. Lincoln worked on a committee which revived an earlier law to penalize the changing of brands on livestock with intent to steal. He served on another committee on an act "to simplify proceedings at law for the collection of debts."

Once he had the House laughing. It had nominated Samuel McHatton to be surveyor of Schuyler County and the Senate had appointed him, information then coming that there was no vacancy; the former surveyor still lived. On a motion that McHatton's nomination "be vacated" Lincoln remarked that the new surveyor could not legally oust the old one so long as the incumbent persisted in not dying. Let the matter be, he suggested, "so that if the old surveyor should hereafter conclude to die, there would be a new one ready without troubling the legislature." In the end the matter was laid on the table as Lincoln had suggested. Often there had been laughter when some member moved to lay a measure on the table "until next Fourth of July." One lobbyist noted Lincoln in this legislature as "raw-boned, angular, features deeply furrowed, ungraceful, almost uncouth . . . and yet there was a magnetism and dash about the man that made him a universal favorite."

Before midnight of February 13 the last batch of hacked and amended bills was passed and Lincoln in two days of below-zero weather rode the stage to New Salem.

After the fixed programs and schedules of Vandalia, the smoke-filled rooms and hullabaloo, Lincoln now rode lonely country roads and walked in open winter air over fields he was surveying. He had seen lawmaking and politics at a vortex and vague resolves deepened in him. And as he wrote later, he "still mixed in the surveying to pay board and clothing bills"; his law books, "dropped" when a legislature met, "were taken up again at the end of the session." The *Sangamo Journal* had announced he was its New Salem agent and would take "Meal, Buckwheat, flour, pork on newspaper accounts."

Before March was over he had completed several surveys, writing of posts, mounds, white oaks, Burr oaks, Spanish oaks, as land markers, writing scores of such meticulous sentences as: "Begining at the North East corner of the same at a White Oak 14 inches S 16 W. 78 Links White Oak 10 inches N 1 E. 66 Links." After March he seemed to have little surveying work over the rest of 1835. During that year, of whatever letters he wrote only three were kept and saved and they were scant and perfunctory, shedding no light on his personal life or love or growth. It was certain that Ann Rutledge and Lincoln knew each other and he took an interest in her; probably they formed some mutual attachment not made clear to the community; possibly they loved each other and her hand went into his long fingers whose bones told her of refuge and security. They were the only two persons who could tell what secret they shared, if any. It seemed definite that she had had letters from McNamar and probable that after a time she had once written him that she expected release from her pledge. Summer of 1835 came and in September it would be three years since McNamar had gone, more than two years since any letter had come from him.

Lincoln was reading law, hoping and expecting the next year to be admitted for practice. Later he advised a young student, "Get the books, and read and study them till you understand them in their principal features; and that is the main thing . . . Your own resolution to succeed, is more important than any other one thing." His resolution to study law drove him hard; friends worried about his health; he couldn't call on Ann often or for long. It was a seven-mile ride or walk when he called on her and her folks or at the nearby farm of "Uncle Jimmy" Short where Ann worked for a time. That she was earning wages meant the family was less well off than it had been and what money she saved could go for her expenses at the Jacksonville Female Academy 25 miles away which she "had a notion" to enter in the fall term. Her brother David was a student at Illinois College in Jacksonville and by a fellow student sent a three-in-one letter dated July 27, 1835, one to his father, another to a friend James Kittridge, and to his sister the following:

To Anna Rutledge:
Valued Sister. So far as I can understand Miss Graves will teach another school in the Diamond Grove. I am glad to hear that you have a notion of comeing to school, and I earnestly recommend to you that you would spare no time from improving your education and mind. Remember that Time is worth more than all gold therefore throw away none of your golden moments. I add nomore, but &c.
D. H. RUTLEDGE.

There seemed to have been an understanding between Ann and Lincoln, with no pledges, that they would take what luck might hand them in whatever was to happen, while they advanced their education. Lincoln had his debts, his law studies, his driving political ambitions, while she had her quandaries related to John McNamar. They would see what time might bring. August came and corn and grass stood stunted for lack of rain. Settlers came down with chills, fever, malaria, Lincoln for his aches taking spoonfuls of Peruvian bark, boneset tea, jalap and calomel.

Soon New Salem heard that Ann Rutledge lay fever-burned, her malady baffling the doctors. Many went out to the Rutledge place. Days passed. Her cousin, McGrady Rutledge, a year younger than Ann, rode to New Salem and told Lincoln of her sickness growing worse. Lincoln rode out and they let him in for what might be his last hour with her. He saw her pale face and wasted body, the blue eyes and auburn hair perhaps the same as always. Few words were spoken, probably, and he might have gone only so far as to let his bony right hand and gnarled fingers lie softly on a small white hand while he tried for a few monosyllables of bright hope.

A few days later, on August 25, 1835, death came to Ann Rutledge and burial was in nearby Concord cemetery. Whether Lincoln went to her funeral, whether he wept in grief with others at the sight of her face in the burial box, no one later seemed to know. Her cousin, McGrady Rutledge, wrote far later, "Lincoln took her death verry hard." A letter of Matthew Marsh September 17 had a tone as though the postmaster Lincoln was in good health and cheer. But this tells us nothing of Lincoln's inner feelings. Later when Lincoln was the center of incalculable death and agony and a friend rebuked him for telling funny stories, he cried back, "Don't you see that if I didn't laugh I would have to weep?" He did no doubt take Ann's death "verry hard" yet he was ambulant and doing his work as shown by a timberland survey he completed and dated September 24, 1835.

It was to come to pass that 30 years later New Salem villagers soberly spoke and wrote that Lincoln went out of his mind, wandered in the woods mumbling and crazy, and had to be locked up, all of which was exaggeration and reckless expansion of his taking Ann's death "verry hard." Woven with the recollections of his "insanity" were also the testimonies of what a deep flaming of lyric love there had been between him and Ann. A legend of a shining, deathless, holy and pure passion arose, spread, grew by some inherent vital sheen of its own or the need of those who wanted it, of Ann

Rutledge, as a poet wrote, "beloved in life of Abraham Lincoln / wedded to him, / not through union, / but through separation."

To this young raw country John McNamar returned three weeks after Ann died, bringing with him his aged mother, and reported that his father had died and he had straightened out what there was of the estate. What he said of Ann's passing and whether he visited the grave of his once-betrothed, of this there is no record. He may have gone the following December to attend at his farm the funeral services of her father who died at 54. Shortly after, he notified the Rutledge and Camron families they must move out from his place. Ann's younger sister, Sarah, lived to be 87 and at 86 an inquirer asked her where Ann had died and she answered, "I was only a little girl of six. It was not our house. The owner came back, and after father's death, we could not pay the rent. He turned mother out; and we had to move to Iowa and begin all over again. I remember how sad and how brave she was." To the question who was the owner of the house, she said, after thinking a while, "It was John McNamar! He was the man who turned mother out!"

In 1838 McNamar married and after the death of his first wife married again. Each ceremony was performed by a justice of the peace, one preacher taking note that the fees of ministers ran higher. McNamar built a commodious brick house on his farm and across the road a big barn for his fat livestock. Thirty years later when asked if he could locate the grave of Ann, he could give no help, though in one letter he wrote, "I cut the initials of Miss Ann Rutledge on a b[o]ard at the head of her grave thirty years ago." In another letter 30 years after Ann's death he wrote that there had been no rivalry between him and Lincoln and that Ann at the time she met Lincoln "attended a literary institution at Jacksonville, in company with her brother." He once intimated that Ann had died brokenhearted waiting for him and in a letter described her quaintly and with charm: "Miss Ann was a gentle Amiable Maiden without any of the airs of your city Belles but winsome and comly withal a blond in complection with golden hair, 'cherry red lips & a bonny Blue Eye.' " A Springfield lawyer in his brick farmhouse asked him where Ann had died and he pointed a trembling finger toward the west. "There, by that," he began, seeming choked with emotion, "there, by *that* currant bush, she died," giving the lawyer a first impression that he had bought the land because Ann had died on it, even though at the moment he had buried one wife and married a second. He became county assessor and proved honest and fair. He lived to be 78 unaware that in chronicles to come he would figure as an enigmatic lover.

Was there a blood strain in Lincoln that had its way in his affair with Ann Rutledge and in his entanglement with two women later? That could have been and was more than a possibility. Northwest in Hancock County were cousins and kinsmen of his, one of them, Mordecai Lincoln, a son of Lincoln's Uncle Mordecai. When living in Leitchfield, Grayson County, Kentucky, he was a tailor, a carpenter, a fiddler, but mostly a shoemaker, and at times a hard drinker. People called him a woman-hater, sworn never to marry. Yet letters showed him drawn deeply toward a girl named Patsy; they kept steady company till the evening when, under her mother's advice, it was said, she offered herself to Mordecai. And that night Mordecai had rushed from Patsy's house, didn't take time to stop in his home for his belongings, and headed for Fountain Green in Hancock County, Illinois. Patsy's father wrote a letter to Mordecai's cousin, James Lincoln, in Hancock County, of Patsy taking it hard, of the "painful circumstances of Mordecai's departure," and that Mordecai could have "stuck to the noble resolution [not to drink] he took six or seven months previous."

In Fountain Green Mordecai made wagons, cabinets, coffins, visited neighbors without telling them he was coming, talked politics, religion, gossip, played the violin, though no one could tell when he would go moody and sit brooding. His cousins, James and Abraham, a justice of the peace, and still other Lincolns, were talked about as changeable from infectious bright laughing moods to spells of gloom and silence. Though "Old Mord," as he was called before he was 40, had a name as a woman-hater, he had a secret heart. A letter he wrote to "My Favorite Girl, Elizabeth," said, "The first time I ever saw you in my life, my mind was filled with the site of your person, but such was the circumstances in my life that I thought it better for me never to see you nor any other girl that there was any likelihood of my becoming so greatly attached too. But by that means I have added fuel to the flame that is burning in my bosom . . . Elizabeth, I naturally hone for your company here with me, but when I look around you are not here. All that I could do is to nourish and cherish my strongest wishes . . ." He bought paper of robin's-egg blue for this letter and having written it he kept and saved it and never sent it to Elizabeth!

Still keeping a reputation as a woman-hater, when he was 50 he wrote "Dear Catherine," a schoolteacher who had been slandered, that he defended her good name, wanted her "the worst of anything," and if she could not accept him, let her think now and then of him as he always thought of her. This he mailed to Catherine, making a copy for himself, while he went on living alone with his dog, cat, books, lathe and tools. He lived on, often saying hard words of priests he didn't like, and dying in the Catholic faith in which his mother had reared him and his brothers and sisters.

In the Lincolns of Hancock County could there be any clues or derivations related to a wavering, hesitant love that Lincoln might have held for Ann Rutledge, a love so deep and strangely dazzling that it shook him with fear and gloom? Lincoln knew of his first cousin Mordecai living in Fountain Green and later was to go out of his way for a visit and talk with Mordecai.

Only Mordecai of the Lincolns at Fountain Green had the name of a woman-hater, but of the others it was said, "It seemed as if it was because they cared so much for women they were overwhelmed with the thought of marriage." They were known as men who could love women but were shy of marriage. They seemed to ask whether they loved enough and whether they had a right to marry. Among these Hancock County Lincolns there was never a divorce after marriage and for all their spells of gloom never a case of insanity.

Usher F. Linder wrote of Abe Lincoln and his uncle Mordecai being a good deal alike as storytellers. "No one took offense at Uncle Mord's stories. I heard him tell a bevy of fashionable girls that he knew a very large woman who had a husband so small that in the night she often mistook him for the

baby, and that one night she picked him up and was singing to him a soothing lullaby when he awoke and told her that the baby was on the other side
of the bed." Lincoln remarked, "Linder, I have often said that Uncle Mord
ran off with all the talents of the family."

In a snowfall over hills and rolling prairie Lincoln rode a stage, arriving
to see Vandalia blanketed white. A special session of the legislature opened
December 7, 1835. The senators on the upper floor were not feeling good
about fresh large cracks down the walls, the north wall bulging out and snow
sifting down on the floor which at its center had sunk half a foot. Over the
next six weeks 139 bills came up in the House; 17 railroads chartered for
Illinois towns that wanted to see the cars and hear the whistles. Half the bills
introduced were passed, the most important the one for the Illinois and
Michigan Canal, whereby wheat selling in Illinois at 50 cents the bushel, after
the Great Lakes haul, would bring $1.25 in Buffalo. Lincoln again put in a
bill "supplemental" to his of the previous session "for the relief of insolvent
debtors," which passed the House and failed in the Senate. He gave special
attention, writing one amendment, to a bill that passed to incorporate the
Beardstown and Sangamon Canal ending at the projected town of Huron at
Miller's Ferry northwest of New Salem. Friends of Lincoln had invested in
prospective Huron. Lincoln the next year was to own several lots there
which came to him for surveying services, besides buying a nearby tract of
47 acres. In a speech at Petersburg, he advised people to buy stock in the
canal and probably bought some of the stock himself, one of his few mild
adventures in speculation and management toward paying his debts. The
canal never got dug, but for a time it was a high hope of its promoters.
    At all times national politics boiled and seethed. Under orders from Presi-
dent Jackson a Democratic national convention had nominated Martin Van
Buren for President, Illinois Whigs favoring a former Jackson man, Hugh
White of Tennessee. The Whigs fought against resolutions praising Jackson
and Van Buren, and most of all against approval of nominating conventions,
a new way of naming candidates. Before this a man announcing he would
run for an office was then a candidate; under the new nominating conventions he would need the good will and the say-so of politicians, the *Sangamo
Journal*, speaking for most of the Whigs, saying the voter now must give up
private judgment and "be led up to the polls by a twine through the gristle
of the proboscis." The "whole-hog" Jackson men were aiming to get better
party loyalty from the "milk-and-cider" Jackson men, setting forth that they
would expel from the party any man not loyal to candidates nominated by
a party convention.
    Lincoln and Stuart were pleased that John Dawson, Sangamon County
Democrat, was switching to the Whigs. On an "act to improve the breed of
cattle," nicknamed "the little bull bill," providing for inspectors in each
township to keep bulls over one year of age from running at large, Lincoln
voted Nay, perhaps knowing the very names of farmers backing him who
had roving bulls. The reapportionment act, increasing the House from 55
to 91 members, went too far, Lincoln advised, but it satisfied him that Sangamon County was to have seven representatives instead of four. He collected $262 as his pay for the session and after adjournment January 18 rode

the stage homeward in that occasional fair and warmer Illinois winter weather that whispers of spring on the way.

Again Lincoln worked away as surveyor, law student, politician. He wrote, signed and got other signers to a petition to a county court for an increased allowance for support of Benjamin Elmore, the insane son of widow Jemima Elmore. He wrote wills, located roads, settled boundary disputes, and on March 26 advertised a reward for return of his horse, "a large bay horse, star in his forehead, eight years old, shod all round, and trots and paces." On March 24 the Sangamon Circuit Court recorded him as a person of good moral character, his first step toward admission to the bar and law practice. He advertised that 64 persons had uncalled-for letters which unless called for would be sent to the dead-letter office. On May 30 he handed out mail as postmaster for the last time and told his New Salem public that their post office was moved to Petersburg.

The convention system not yet operating, he put himself in the running in June as a candidate for the legislature, writing in the *Sangamo Journal,* "I go for all sharing the privileges of the government, who assist in bearing its burthens . . . admitting all whites to the right of suffrage, who pay taxes or bear arms, (by no means excluding females.)" And next November, "if alive," he would vote for Hugh L. White, the Whig candidate for President. He stumped the county, often speaking as one of a string of Whig candidates.

In Springfield he clashed with George Forquer, a lawyer who had switched from Whig to Democrat, then being appointed by the Jackson administration as register of the land office at $3,000 a year. On his elegant new frame house Forquer had put up the first lightning rod in that part of Illinois, a sight people went out of their way to see. After a speech in the courthouse by Lincoln, Forquer took the platform saying the young man who had just spoken was sailing too high and would have to be "taken down" and he was sorry the task devolved on him, then made what was termed a "slasher-gaff speech." Lincoln stood by with folded arms, stepped to the platform, made a quiet argument in reply and then, as others recalled it, a stormy finish: "I desire to live, and I desire place and distinction; but I would rather die now than, like the gentleman, live to see the day that I would change my politics for an office worth three thousand dollars a year, and then feel compelled to erect a lightning rod to protect a guilty conscience from an offended God." Some who were there said that friends carried Lincoln from the courthouse on their shoulders.

Of one of his speeches the *Sangamo Journal* said, "A girl might be born and become a mother before the Van Buren men will forget Mr. Lincoln." In the election August 1 the county gave Lincoln the highest vote of 17 candidates for the legislature. Sangamon County was taken by the Whigs, having now seven representatives and two senators.

Soon after this sweeping victory Lincoln in stride took his bar examination before two justices of the Supreme Court, passed, gave a dinner to his examiners, and on September 9, 1836, held in his hands a license to practice law in all the courts of Illinois. On October 5 he was in a Springfield court, appearing in a case for John T. Stuart, the beginning of their partnership as a law firm. In three related suits brought by James P. Hawthorn Lincoln was defending David Wooldridge. Hawthorn claimed Wooldridge was to furnish him two yoke of oxen to break up 20 acres of prairie sod ground and was to allow him to raise a crop of corn or wheat on a certain piece of ground; and Wooldridge had failed him in both cases. Furthermore, Hawthorn claimed damages because Wooldridge struck, beat, bruised, and knocked him down; plucked, pulled, and tore large quantities of hair from his head; with a stick and his fists struck Hawthorn many violent blows on or about the face, head, breast, back, shoulders, hips, legs and divers other parts of the body, and had with violence forced, pushed, thrust and gouged his fingers into Hawthorn's eyes.

Such were the allegations, including replevin action demanding return of a black and white yoke of steers, one black cow and calf, and one prairie plow. Lincoln's first move was to bring up a board bill for eight months which Hawthorn owed Wooldridge, amounting at $1.50 a week to $45.75. Also, besides a cash loan of $100, he had used for the same eight months a wagon and team for which he should pay $90. In proceedings out of court Lincoln lost on one count, with settlement on the other two, plaintiff and defendant dividing court costs.

In October and November he made three more known surveys and said good-by to surveying.

The tall Whigs from Sangamon County averaged six feet in height, Lincoln the longest, and were nicknamed the "Long Nine." Riding the stage to Vandalia two days, they talked about schemes and strategy that would carry through the legislature the one law more important to them than any other, an act to make Springfield the capital of Illinois. Arriving, they saw that Vandalia citizens, scared by the talk of moving the capital, had torn down the old building and were just finishing a new capitol in the center of the public square. Lincoln looked it over, stepping around workmen still on the job, tool sheds and piles of scaffolding lumber, piles of unused sand, brick and stone, perhaps laughing at the building hardly large enough to hold the new legislature, with no look toward future needs.

The legislature opened December 5, 1836, old members and 66 new ones smelling a pungent odor of fresh damp plaster. Governor Duncan's message advised state financial support for "all canals and railroads." On the 17 railroads and two canals chartered at the last session not a track had been laid nor a spade of dirt dug. The new dynamic member, Stephen A. Douglas, brought in a huge omnibus bill from the Committee on Internal Improvements. Nearly every town in the state wanted a railroad or canal and this bill would give it to them at a cost of $10,000,000, the state to sell bonds of that amount. On the same day the session began, this $10,000,000 program had been approved by an Internal Improvement State Convention, its delegates businessmen of wealth and power, including Thomas Mather, president of the State Bank in Springfield, of which bank Lincoln was continuously an active friend. As chairman of the Finance Committee Lincoln reported that the state had balanced its budget and had a surplus of $2,743.18, being strictly solvent.

The trading and logrolling began over the huge omnibus bill—"You scratch my back and I'll scratch yours." Lincoln had become Whig floor leader and with the Long Nine worked all the time at as many bargains and favors as possible for other members with an eye on the votes that would be needed to change the capital to Springfield. Across weeks the omnibus bill was changed, mangled, put together again, till every town and county had something from the "grab bag"—the railroad, track spur, canal, turnpike or other improvement it wanted. Lincoln, though not a member, spent so much time discussing amendments with the Internal Improvements Committee that one member later seemed to remember Lincoln was part of the committee. The West was young, immigrants by millions were to come, the future was all rosy, said the pioneer stock that believed in "boom or bust." Springfield was not alone in adding a thousand of population in seven years. The reckless, overloaded $10,000,000 Internal Improvements Bill passed by 61 to 25. There was a Council of Revision veto over which the bill was repassed by 53 to 20. Lincoln joined with a majority which voted to refuse to put the bill to a vote of the people.

On a bill to shape a new county out of Sangamon and other counties, making changes endangering the Long Nine politically, Lincoln maneuvered with amendments that defeated the bill. When Usher F. Linder put in resolutions for a sweeping investigation of the management of the State Bank of Illinois in Springfield, Lincoln made a long speech of cogent argument and pointed humor, saying Linder had "the faculty of entangling a subject, so that neither himself, or any other man, can find head or tail to it."

Back of an investigation that would cost ten or twelve thousand dollars, Lincoln saw rival interests. "These capitalists generally act harmoniously, and in concert, to fleece the people, and now, that they have got into a quarrel with themselves, we are called upon to appropriate the people's money to settle the quarrel." Lincoln denied being a special advocate of the Bank but he would stand against any politicians trying to harm the credit of the Bank. And the House heard him: "Mr. Chairman, this movement is exclusively the work of politicians; a set of men who have interests aside from the interests of the people, and who, to say the most of them, are, taken as a mass, at least one long step removed from honest men. I say this with the greater freedom because, being a politician myself, none can regard it as personal." Linder's resolution was trimmed to a limited investigation which ended in a report favorable to the bank. On a later bill to increase by $2,000,000 the capital stock of the bank, Lincoln voted Yea with the majority.

In three ballots for U.S. Senator, Lincoln voted for Archibald Williams of Quincy, a lawyer from Kentucky who had switched from Democrat to Whig. Election went to Richard M. Young, a circuit judge and a "milk-and-cider" Jackson man who ran ahead of a "whole-hog" Jackson man, Williams running third. In celebration fine wines and liquors flowed at a supper where dishes and goblets went flying and Stephen A. Douglas and James Shields danced on a table to the length of it amid cigar smoke, ribald songs and the laughter and follies of drinking men. Judge Young was pleased next day to pay $600 for the supper, cigars, drinks and damages.

Of Archibald Williams, Lincoln was to see more. They were tall and angular, alike in homely looks and humor. Williams' clothes were so careless that once a hotel clerk, seeing him loaf in a chair, begged pardon and asked, "Are you a guest of this hotel?" and Williams in a cool snarl, "Hell, no! I

am one of its victims, paying five dollars a day!" Williams was the kind of
man Lincoln could talk with about Andrew McCorkle, near Springfield, who
was afraid the railroads would scare his cows so they wouldn't give milk. Or
the mob that went to the house of a man and took him away and hanged
him to a tree; the night was dark and in the morning they saw they had
hanged the wrong man; and they went and told the widow, "The laugh is
on us!" Or the revolt of the small farmers against fines to be laid on them
when their "little bulls" strayed; they had roared so loud that the House on
December 19 had repealed its act of the previous session by 81 to 4. And it
bordered on humor of some generous kind when an omnibus bill granting
divorces to a number of persons was amended to read, "and all other persons
who are desirous of being divorced." Or a bill to provide a 50-cent bounty
for "wolf scalps with the ears thereon."

In the House were 64 Democrats to 27 Whigs but in the Senate the roll
was 22 Democrats to 18 Whigs. Through Lincoln's strategy the Senate first
took up a bill to "permanently locate the seat of government of the State of
Illinois." The bill passed and went to the House where maneuver and debate
began to rage. A Coles County man who had "been seen" by Lincoln, moved
an amendment which passed, that no less than $50,000 and two acres of land
must be donated by the new capital when chosen; this would be a mean
obstacle to rivals of Springfield. Other amendments, aimed at butchering the
bill, came up and failed in the late afternoon as candles were lighted and
members could see out of the windows a driving snow. Some members had
left the hall as though there would be only more monotonous amendments.
Then suddenly a motion was made to table the bill "until next Fourth of
July." And the motion passed by 39 to 38! Lincoln and the seven of the
Long Nine in the House voted Nay. It looked like the end for their hope
of making Springfield the new capital.

That night Lincoln called his Sangamon County colleagues into conference
and gave each an assignment. They went out into the driving snow and
knocked on doors. They found five members who had voted to table and
brought them to change their vote in the morning. They located absentees
of the afternoon who favored the bill and got their word to be surely on
hand in the morning. Of five members whom they had favored with votes
for railroads or canals they asked for a little gratitude. To others they threatened that in the Internal Improvements Bill, not yet passed by the Senate,
their two Sangamon senators and others might rub out some of the railroads
and canals. To Benjamin Enloe of Johnson County they pointed out that the
longest railroad in the state was to run along the west line of his county. Also
it seemed they promised to make Enloe warden of the state penitentiary,
which promise they kept that very month. From door to door and room to
room went Lincoln's colleagues using persuasions and threats.

Next morning, February 18, Enloe moved the bill "be re-considered." A
roll call demanded by Douglas showed 42 Yea and 40 Nay. One member
shifting from Yea to Nay would have killed the bill. A motion to table
"until the 4th of July next" lost by 37 to 46. It was hazardous and delicately
shaded politics Lincoln was playing.

Over the next week came more amendments and harassing tactics, including a motion to postpone selection of a new capital till December 1839. On the third reading of the bill February 24, 1837, the House passed it by 46 to 37. The House and Senate then held a joint session on location and the fourth ballot gave Springfield 73, Vandalia 16, Jacksonville 11, Peoria 8, Alton 6, Illiopolis 3—Henry Mills of Edwards voting for Purgatory on the third ballot. The losers charged "bargain and corruption." But it was all over and Springfield put on a jubilee; citizens howled and danced around a big bonfire blazing at the old whipping post on the public square till that relic was ashes.

In the Southern States it was against the law to speak against slavery; agitators of slave revolts would be hanged and had been. The 3,000,000 Negro workers in the Southern States on the tax books were livestock valued at more than a billion dollars. In political parties and churches, in business partnerships and families, the slavery question was beginning to split the country in two. The secret "Underground Railway" ran from Slave States across Free States and over the line into Canada. An antislavery man would keep a runaway slave in his house, cellar or barn, and at night or in a load of hay in the daytime, pass him along to the next "station." Officers and slaveowners came north with warrants hunting their runaway property; Illinois was seeing them often. Also bogus slave hunters in southern Illinois kidnaped free Negroes, took them to slave soil and sold them. The governor had sent a brief note with memorials from six states notifying the House that the slavery question was becoming a burning issue.

Amid this welter, Lincoln could understand his fellow members in resolutions declaring: "We highly disapprove of the formation of abolition societies; . . . the right of property in slaves is sacred to the slave-holding States by the Federal Constitution, and . . . they cannot be deprived of that right without their consent . . ."

Lincoln voted against these resolutions, joined by only five other members, one of them Dan Stone, a Yankee graduate of Middlebury College, a lawyer and a member of the Ohio Legislature before coming to Springfield in 1833. Stone and Lincoln, three days before the legislature adjourned March 6, recorded this protest in language completely courteous but quietly unmistakable in meaning:

Resolutions upon the subject of domestic slavery having passed both branches of the General Assembly at its present session, the undersigned hereby protest against the passage of the same.

They believe that the institution of slavery is founded on both injustice and bad policy; but that the promulgation of abolition doctrines tends rather to increase than abate its evils.

They believe that the Congress of the United States has no power under the constitution, to interfere with the institution of slavery in the different States.

They believe that the Congress of the United States has the power, under the constitution, to abolish slavery in the District of Columbia; but that that power ought not to be exercised unless at the request of the people of said District.

The difference between these opinions and those contained in the said resolutions, is their reason for entering this protest.

In December of this winter, Lincoln had written a drawling, hesitant, half-bashful letter to the daughter of a rich farmer in Green County, Kentucky, Miss Mary Owens, four months older than Lincoln, plump-faced, with a head of dark curly hair, large blue eyes, five feet five inches high. On her first visit to New Salem three years before, she had interested Lincoln; her sister, Mrs. Bennett Abell, at whose house Lincoln had stayed, played match-maker and wanted the two to get married. When starting for a visit with her sister in Kentucky, Mrs. Abell, perhaps only joking, said she would bring her sister back if Lincoln would marry her. And Lincoln said, perhaps only joking, that he accepted the proposal to become Mrs. Abell's brother-in-law.

When Miss Owens came back to New Salem with her sister in November 1836, Lincoln saw three years had worked changes, Miss Owens having lost bloom, lost teeth, and become stout. He made love to her, it seemed, in a rather easy careless way. And she held him off as one trained in Kentucky schools for refined young ladies, dressed in what one of the Greens called "the finest trimmings I ever saw." She noted Lincoln as "deficient in those little links which make up a woman's happiness." A party riding to Uncle Billy Greene's came to a creek branch with a treacherous crossing. Miss Owens noticed the other men helping their partners, Lincoln riding ahead of her without looking back. "You are a nice fellow!" heard Lincoln when she caught up with him. "I suppose you did not care whether my neck was broken or not." And he had laughed back a defense compliment; he knew she was smart enough to take care of herself. She climbed a steep hill with Lincoln and Mrs. Bowling Green, Lincoln joking and talking to her, not once offering to help carry the fat baby in Mrs. Green's arms. It seemed to Miss Owens to be "neglect" on Lincoln's part.

He puzzled her; in some things he was so softhearted. He told her he saw "a hog mired down" one day crossing a prairie and being "fixed up" in his best clothes, he said to himself he would pass on. But after he had passed on, the hog haunted him and seemed to be saying, "There, now my last hope is gone," and he had gone back and got the hog loose from the mire. Miss Owens had ideas about chivalry and wondered how a man could be so thoughtful about a mired hog and another time be so lost in his own feelings that he couldn't stay alongside his woman partner when riding across a dangerous creek. They had some vague understanding that they might marry. Lincoln had written her one letter she hadn't answered, and one cold, lonesome winter night, he wrote her a second letter:

VANDALIA, Decr. 13 1836

MARY

I have been sick ever since my arrival here, or I should have written sooner. It is but little difference, however, as I have verry little even yet to write. And more, the longer I can avoid the mortification of looking in the Post Office for your letter and not finding it, the better. You see I am mad about that *old letter* yet I dont like verry well to risk you again. I'll try you once more any how.

The new State House is not yet finished, and consequently the legislature is doing little or nothing. The Governor delivered an inflamtory political Message, and it is expected there will be some sparring between the parties about [it as] soon as the two Houses get to business. Taylor [deliv]ered up his petitions for the *New County* to one of [our me]mbers this morning. I am told that he dispairs [of its] success on account of all the members from Morg[an C]ounty opposing it. There are names enough on the petition[,] I think, to justify the members from our county in going for it; but if the members from Morgan oppose it, which they [say] they will, the chance will be bad.

Our chance to [take th]e seat of Government to Springfield is better than I ex[pected]. An Internal-Improvement Convention was held here since we met, which recommended a loan of several mill[ions] of dollars on the faith of the State to construct Rail Roads. Some of the legislature are for it[,] and some against it; which has the majority I can not tell. There is great strife and struggling for the office of U.S. Senator here at this time. It is probable we shall ease their pains in a few days. The opposition men have no candidate of their own, and consequently they smile as complacently at the angry snarls of the contending Van Buren candidates and their respective friends, as the christian does at Satan's rage. You recollect I mentioned in the outset of this letter that I had been unwell. That is the fact, though I believe I am about well now; but that, with other things I can not account for, have conspired and have gotten my spirits so low, that I feel that I would rather be any place in the world than here. I really can not endure the thought of staying here ten weeks. Write back as soon as you get this, and if possible say something that will please me, for really I have not [been] pleased since I left you. This letter is so dry and [stupid] that I am ashamed to send it, but with my pres[ent] feelings I can not do any better.

Give my respects to M[r. and] Mrs. Abell and family.

Your friend
LINCOLN

He was as cryptic in writing to her as she was in not writing to him. It was a letter of loneliness and of hunger for love and hope running low of any answering love.

Robert L. Wilson of the village of Athens and one of the Long Nine wrote of Lincoln as having "a quaint and peculiar way" and "he frequently startled us." He seemed a "born" politician. "We followed his lead; but he followed nobody's lead. It may almost be said that he did our thinking for us. He inspired respect, although he was careless and negligent . . . He was poverty itself, but independent." They had seen much of each other in the legislature and campaigning together, Wilson writing, "He sought company, and indulged in fun without stint . . . still when by himself, he told me that he was so overcome by mental depression, that he never dared carry a knife in his pocket; and as long as I was intimately acquainted with him, he never carried a pocketknife." At a banquet in Athens, Wilson gave the toast: "Abraham Lincoln; one of Nature's Noblemen."

In Springfield, Lincoln read lavish compliments to himself in the press and sat with the Long Nine and 60 guests at a game supper where one toast ran: "Abraham Lincoln: he has fulfilled the expectations of his friends, and disappointed the hopes of his enemies."

In April he packed his saddlebags to leave New Salem where six years before he had arrived, as he said, "a piece of floating driftwood," being now a licensed lawyer, a member of the state legislature and floor leader of the Whig party. The hilltop village, now fading to become a ghost town, had been to him a nourishing mother, a neighborhood of many names and faces that would always be dear and cherished with him, a friendly place with a peculiar equality between man and man, where Bill Greene was nearly correct in saying, "In New Salem every man is a principal citizen." Bitter hours but more sweet than bitter he had had. Here he had groped in darkness and grown toward light. Here newspapers, books, mathematics, law, the ways of people and life, had taken on new and subtle meanings for him.

CHAPTER 4

Lawyer in Springfield

SPRINGFIELD with 1,400 inhabitants in 1837 was selling to 18,000 people of the county a large part of their supplies, tools, groceries, and buying grain, pork and farm produce. There were 19 dry-goods besides other general stores, six churches, 11 lawyers and 18 doctors. Farm women coming to town wore shoes where they used to be barefoot; men had changed from moccasins to rawhide boots and shoes. Carriages held men in top boots and ruffled silk shirts, women in silks and laces. It was no wilderness that Abraham Lincoln, 28 years old, saw as he rode into Springfield April 15, 1837. Many of its people had come from Kentucky by horse, wagon and boat, across country not yet cleared of wolves, wildcats and horse thieves. A Yankee antislavery element in the Presbyterian Church had seceded to form a Second Presbyterian Church. And there were in Sangamon County 78 free Negroes, 20 registered indentured servants and six slaves.

Lincoln pulled in his horse at the general store of Joshua Speed. He asked the price of bedclothes for a single bedstead, which Speed figured at $17. "Cheap as it is, I have not the money to pay," he told Speed. "But if you will credit me until Christmas, and my experiment here as a lawyer is a success, I will pay you then. If I fail in that I will probably never pay you at all." Speed said afterward: "The tone of his voice was so melancholy that I felt for him . . . I thought I never saw so gloomy and melancholy a face in my life." Speed offered to share his own big double bed upstairs over the store. Lincoln took his saddlebags upstairs, came down with his face lit up and said, "Well, Speed, I'm moved." A friendship, to last long, began, as with William Butler, clerk of the Sangamon Circuit Court, who told Lincoln he could take his meals at the Butler home and there would be no mention of board bills.

The circuit courtroom was in a two-story building in Hoffman's Row, and upstairs over the courtroom was the law office of the new firm of Stuart & Lincoln: a little room with a few loose boards for bookshelves, an old wood stove, a table, a chair, a bench, a buffalo robe and a small bed. Stuart was running for Congress, so Lincoln most of the time handled all of their law practice in range of his ability. Between law cases he kept up his political fences, writing many letters.

In the street could be seen farmers hauling corn, wheat, potatoes and turnips in wagons; the axles creaked; husky voices bawled at the yokes of steers while the whip thongs lashed and cracked. Droves of hogs came past, in muddy weather wallowing over their knees, the hair of their flanks spattered, their curls of tails flipping as they grunted onward to sale and slaughter. And there were horses, men riding and driving who loved roans, grays, whites, black horses with white stockings, sorrels with a sorrel forelock down a white face, bays with a white star in the forehead. To Levi Davis, Esq., of Vandalia, Lincoln wrote on April 19, "We have, generally in this country, peace, health, and plenty, and no news." Yet his own peace of mind was clouded 18 days later when again he wrote Mary Owens. She would have to be poor and show her poverty, if she married him. He was willing to marry, if she so wished. His advice would be not to marry. The letter read:

SPRINGFIELD, May 7, 1837

FRIEND MARY

I have commenced two letters to send you before this, both of which displeased me before I got half done, and so I tore them up. The first I thought was'nt serious enough, and the second was on the other extreme. I shall send this, turn out as it may.

This thing of living in Springfield is rather a dull business after all, at least it is so to me. I am quite as lonesome here as [I] ever was anywhere in my life. I have been spoken to by but one woman since I've been here, and should not have been by her, if she could have avoided it. I've never been to church yet, nor probably shall not be soon. I stay away because I am conscious I should not know how to behave myself.

I am often thinking of what we said of your coming to live at Springfield. I am afraid you would not be satisfied. There is a great deal of flourishing about in carriages here, which it would be your doom to see without shareing in it. You would have to be poor without the means of hiding your poverty. Do you believe you could bear that patiently? Whatever woman may cast her lot with mine, should any ever do so, it is my intention to do all in my power to make her happy and contented; and there is nothing I can immagine, that would make me more unhappy than to fail in the effort. I know I should be much happier with you than the way I am, provided I saw no signs of discontent in you. What you have said to me may have been in jest, or I may have misunderstood it. If so, then let it be forgotten; if otherwise, I much wish you would think seriously before you decide. For my part I have already decided. What I have said I will most positively abide by, provided you wish it. My opinion is that you had better not do it. You have not been accustomed to hardship, and it may be more severe than you now immagine. I know you are capable of thinking correctly on any subject; and if you deliberate maturely upon this, before you decide, then I am willing to abide your decision.

You must write me a good long letter after you get this. You have nothing else to do, and though it might not seem interesting to you, after you had written it, it would be a good deal of company to me in this "busy wilderness." Tell your sister I dont want to hear any more about selling out and moving. That gives me the hypo whenever I think of it.

Yours, &c.

LINCOLN.

That summer Mary Owens and Lincoln saw each other and came to no understanding. On the day they parted, Lincoln wrote her another letter:

SPRINGFIELD, Aug. 16th 1837

FRIEND MARY.

You will, no doubt, think it rather strange, that I should write you a letter on the same day on which we parted; and I can only account for it by supposing, that seeing you lately makes me think of you more than usual, while at our late meeting we had but few expressions of thoughts. You must know that I can not see you, or think of you, with entire indifference; and yet it may be, that you, are mistaken in regard to what my real feelings towards you are. If I knew you were not, I should not trouble you with this letter. Perhaps any other man would know enough without further information; but I consider it *my* peculiar right to plead ignorance, and your bounden duty to allow the plea. I want in all cases to do right, and most particularly so, in all cases with women. I want, at this particular time, more than any thing else, to do right with you, and if I *knew* it would be doing right, as I rather suspect it would, to let you alone, I would do it. And for the purpose of making the matter as plain as possible, I now say, that you can now drop the subject, dismiss your thoughts (if you ever had any) from me forever, and leave this letter unanswered, without calling forth one accusing murmur from me. And I will even go further, and say, that if it will add any thing to your comfort, or peace of mind, to do so, it is my sincere wish that you should. Do not understand by this, that I wish to cut your acquaintance. I mean no such thing. What I do wish is, that our further acquaintance shall depend upon yourself. If such further acquaintance would contribute nothing to your happiness, I am sure it would not to mine. If you feel yourself in any degree bound to me, I am now willing to release you, provided you wish it; while, on the other hand, I am willing, and even anxious to bind you faster, if I can be convinced that it will, in any considerable degree, add to your happiness. This, indeed, is the whole question with me. Nothing would make me more miserable than to believe you miserable— nothing more happy, than to know you were so.

In what I have now said, I think I can not be misunderstood, and to make myself understood, is the only object of this letter.

If it suits you best to not answer this—farewell—a long life and a merry one attend you. But if you conclude to write back, speak as plainly as I do. There can be neither harm nor danger, in saying, to me, any thing you think, just in the manner you think it.

My respects to your sister.

Your friend

LINCOLN.

He mentioned no memory of a kiss. He was her "friend" rather than lover. What they had was an "acquaintance," so definitely no affair of passion. Months passed till the first day of April 1838. And comedy and glee lighted him as he wrote to Mrs. Orville H. Browning, who lived in Quincy. The wife of a colleague in the legislature, he had found her exceptionally gracious and understanding in conversation; she had a sense of humor lacking in her husband. On this April Fool's Day he confessed he had vanity, stupidity, and had made a fool of himself:

SPRINGFIELD, April 1. 1838.

DEAR MADAM:

Without appologising for being egotistical, I shall make the history of so much of my own life, as has elapsed since I saw you, the subject of this letter. And by the way I now discover, that, in order to give a full and inteligible account of the things I have done and suffered *since* I saw you, I shall necessarily have to relate some that happened *before*.

It was, then, in the autumn of 1836, that a married lady of my acquaintance, and who was a great friend of mine, being about to pay a visit to her father and other relatives residing in Kentucky, proposed to me, that on her return she would bring a sister of hers with her, upon condition that I would engage to become her brother-in-law with all convenient dispach. I, of course, accepted the proposal; for you know I could not have done otherwise, had I really been averse to it; but privately between you and me, I was most confoundedly well pleased with the project. I had seen the said sister some three years before, thought her inteligent and agreeable, and saw no good objection to plodding life through hand in hand with her. Time passed on, the lady took her journey, and in due time returned, sister in company sure enough. This stomached me a little; for it appeared to me, that her coming so readily showed that she was a trifle too willing; but on reflection it occured to me, that she might have been prevailed on by her married sister to come, without any thing concerning me ever having been mentioned to her; and so I concluded that if no other objection presented itself, I would consent to wave this. All this occured upon my *hearing* of her arrival in the neighbourhood; for, be it remembered, I had not yet *seen* her, except about three years previous, as before mentioned.

In a few days we had an interview, and although I had seen her before, she did not look as my immagination had pictured her. I knew she was over-size, but she now appeared a fair match for Falstaff; I knew she was called an "old maid", and I felt no *doubt* of the truth of at least half of the appelation; but now, when I beheld her, I could not for my life avoid thinking of my mother; and this, not from withered features, for her skin was too full of fat, to permit its contracting in to wrinkles; but from her want of teeth, weather-beaten appearance in general, and from a kind of notion that ran in my head, that *nothing* could have commenced at the size of infancy, and reached her present bulk in less than thirtyfive or forty years; and, in short, I was not all pleased with her. But what could I do? I had told her sister that I would take her for better or for worse; and I made a point of honor and conscience in all things, to stick to my word, especially if others had been induced to act on it, which in this case, I doubted not they had, for I was now fairly convinced, that no other man on earth would have her, and hence the conclusion that they were bent on holding me to my bargain. Well, thought I, I have said it, and, be consequences what they may, it shall not be my fault if I fail to do it. At once I determined to consider her my wife; and this done, all my powers of discovery were put to the rack, in search of perfections in her, which might be fairly set-off against her defects. I tried to immagine she was handsome, which, but for her unfortunate corpulency, was actually true. Exclusive of this, no woman that I have ever seen, has a finer face. I also tried to convince myself, that the mind was much more to be valued than the person; and in this, she was not inferior, as I could discover, to any with whom I had been acquainted.

Shortly after this, without attempting to come to any positive understanding with her, I set out for Vandalia, where and when you first saw me. During my stay there, I had letters from her, which did not change my opinion of either her intelect or intention; but on the contrary, confirmed it in both.

All this while, although I was fixed "firm as the surge repelling rock" in my resolution, I found I was continually repenting the rashness, which had led me to make it. Through life I have been in no bondage, either real or immaginary, from the thraldom of which I so much desired to be free.

After my return home, I saw nothing to change my opinion of her in any particular. She was the same and so was I. I now spent my time between planing how I might get along through life after my contemplated change of circumstances should have taken place; and how I might procrastinate the evil day for a time, which I really dreaded as much—perhaps more, than an irishman does the halter.

After all my suffering upon this deeply interesting subject, here I am, wholly unexpectedly, completely out of the "scrape"; and I now want to know, if you can guess how I got out of it. Out clear in every sense of the term; no violation of word, honor or conscience. I dont believe you can guess, and so I may as well tell you at once. As the lawyers say, it was done in the manner following, towit. After I had delayed the matter as long as I thought I could in honor do, which by the way had brought me round into the last fall, I concluded I might as well bring it to a consumation without further delay; and so I mustered my resolution, and made the proposal to her direct; but, shocking to relate, she answered, No. At first I supposed she did it through an affectation of modesty, which I thought but ill-become her, under the peculiar circumstances of her case; but on my renewal of the charge, I found she repeled it with greater firmness than before. I tried it again and again, but with the same success, or rather with the same want of success. I finally was forced to give it up, at which I verry unexpectedly found myself mortified almost beyond endurance. I was mortified, it seemed to me, in a hundred different ways. My vanity was deeply wounded by the reflection, that I had so long been too stupid to discover her intentions, and at the same time never doubting that I understood them perfectly; and also, that she whom I had taught myself to believe no body else would have, had actually rejected me with all my fancied greatness; and to cap the whole, I then, for the first time, began to suspect that I was really a little in love with her. But let it all go. I'll try and out live it. Others have been made fools of by the girls; but this can never be with truth said of me. I most emphatically, in this instance, made a fool of myself. I have now come to the conclusion never again to think of marrying; and for this reason; I can never be satisfied with any one who would be block-head enough to have me.

When you receive this, write me a long yarn about something to amuse me. Give my respects to Mr. Browning.

Your sincere friend

A. LINCOLN

The letter, like those to Miss Owens, was a self-portrait. He named no names but his own. Mr. and Mrs. Browning took it as the queer prank of a mind of fantasy and humor. The Rabelaisian streak in it was one well known to those who had heard Lincoln's storytelling. Had he named the woman he could have had credit as a vicious gossip. He rollicked on in the fun of having gotten out of a scrape. And yet in this period of his life he let himself go in sarcasm and satire that was to bring him shame and humiliation. He would change. He was to learn, at cost, how to use the qualities of pity and compassion that lay deeply and naturally in his heart, toward wiser reading and keener understanding of all men and women he met.

Later when Mrs. Abell visited her sister in Kentucky, Miss Owens told neighbors that Abe Lincoln said to Mrs. Abell, in Springfield, "Tell your sister that I think she was a great fool because she did not stay here and marry me." If true, he was as baffling to them as to himself in heart affairs.

The 1837 business panic had come, banks failing, depositors out of luck, loans called and money tight, the *Sangamo Journal* saying the "groan of hard times is echoed from one end of the country to the other." The State Bank in Springfield had "suspended specie payments"; you could have folding paper money but no coin, no hard money. Governor Duncan had called a special session of the legislature which met July 10 in Vandalia, voted against repeal of the $10,000,000 Internal Improvements scheme which the governor said was "fraught with evil." Approval of banks suspending specie payments was voted, Lincoln continuously defending the Springfield bank. On watch and swift, he was against repeated resolutions to repeal the bill making Springfield the state capital. After two weeks he was back in Springfield joining in the dirtiest mud-slinging campaign that Springfield politics had ever seen, "no holds barred," many old friendships to go on the rocks.

The Whigs were running for probate judge Dr. Anson G. Henry, egotist, orator, gadfly, peppery fighter who welcomed enemies. Against him was General James Adams, a lawyer, a veteran of the War of 1812 and a minor Indian war, 54 years old, and one of the old settlers of Springfield. The Adams men published insinuations that Henry, as a commissioner in the building of the new capitol, was a wild spender of the people's money. The Whigs called public meetings, appointed a bipartisan committee and white-washed Henry. The Whig sheriff Garret Elkin canceled his subscription to the new Democratic paper, the *Illinois Republican*, because of a mean article about Dr. Henry; that paper printed another mean article and Sheriff Elkin went to the office of the paper and horsewhipped the editor, George R. Weber. A brother of Weber got himself a knife, found Elkin and a friend Daniel Cutright and managed to sink the knife into both of them; the three involved were arrested.

Meantime, Mrs. Joseph Anderson, a widow, had come to Springfield to sell ten acres of land left her by her husband, only to find General Adams claimed that the ten acres had been signed over to him by her husband for a legal debt he owed Adams. Stuart and Lincoln took her case. Lincoln searched records and wrote six anonymous letters printed weekly in the *Sangamo Journal* which questioned "Gen. Adams's titles to certain tracts of land, and the manner in which he acquired them," and how Adams got a ten-year lease to two city lots for $10. Two days before the August 7 election a handbill, written but not signed by Lincoln, was given out over the town. It recited a series of alleged facts about the ten acres claimed by Mrs. Anderson and an assignment of judgment by Anderson to Adams being freshly handwritten in what appeared to be the handwriting of Adams. In effect, Lincoln was publicly accusing Adams of being a forger and swindler, this without a trial, with no evidence heard from the accused, and witnesses cited from only one side. It seemed Lincoln expected this handbill to blast Adams out of politics. He guessed wrong. In the August 7 election Adams won by 1,025 votes against 792 for Henry.

Adams now gave in the *Republican* a six-column reply to Lincoln and Lincoln in a one-column reply said affidavits offered by Adams were "all false as hell" and "I have a character to defend as well as Gen. Adams, but I disdain to *whine* about it as he does." Two weeks after election the *Sangamo Journal* reprinted the pre-election handbill. Instead of suing Lincoln and the *Journal* for libel Adams wrote another six columns for the *Republican*. Lincoln seemed to have played for a libel suit, hoping he could lay his evidence before a jury. As a final challenge to a libel suit, the *Sangamo*

Journal in November reprinted the pre-election handbill with its unmistakable implication that Adams was a forger and swindler, Adams making no answer. Nor did Adams take action when an editorial supposed to have been written by Lincoln was published in the *Sangamo Journal*, giving a copy of an indictment found against Adams in Oswego County, New York, in 1818, the crime charged being forgery of a deed. "A person of evil name and fame and of wicked disposition," was the *Journal*'s allusion to Adams.

In the course of replying to Lincoln, Adams had included Stephen T. Logan, an able and respected lawyer, as connected with Lincoln in forgery. Logan sued Adams for libel at $10,000 damages; the case was finally dismissed on Adams' payment of costs with a statement for the record that he "never intended" to charge Logan with forgery. In the courts the Stuart and Lincoln case of Mrs. Anderson for ten acres of land never came to trial, was dropped when Adams died; his widow and heirs got the ten acres. Through the entire affair Lincoln showed none of the management sagacity he had at Vandalia and little of the cool persuasive logic, mixed with good humor, of which he was capable at his best.

In law office routine Lincoln took depositions, drew deeds, filed declarations, bills of complaint, praecipes, perhaps taking an afternoon off when the famous Whig, Daniel Webster, made an hour and a half speech at a barbecue in a grove west of town. An official of the Post Office Department came one day to Springfield and asked about a certain amount of dollars and cents that had come into the hands of Lincoln as postmaster at New Salem. Lincoln brought out a sack and counted the money in it, the exact amount asked for by the inspector, who took the money, gave a receipt, and went away satisfied. People in trouble over land or money or love, witnesses, murderers, scandalmongers and slanderers, came to pour out their stories within the walls of the Stuart and Lincoln law office. In one of his first murder cases, Lincoln failed to save William Fraim, a 20-year-old, who in a drunken brawl killed a fellow laborer; he was convicted and hanged.

On a hot summer day Harvey Ross came to prove ownership of his farm at Macomb, needing the testimony of a witness near Springfield. Court had closed, Lincoln explained, but they would go out to Judge Thomas' farm. With a bundle of papers in one hand and in the other a red handkerchief for wiping sweat, Lincoln with Ross and the witness walked to the farm. The judge had gone to a tenant house on the north part of the farm, to help his men put up a corncrib and hog pen, said Mrs. Thomas; the main road would be a half-mile but cutting across the cornfield from the barn would be only a quarter-mile. They struck out Indian file, Lincoln still with papers in one hand and red handkerchief in the other. Arriving where the judge and his men were raising logs, Lincoln put the case to the judge, who looked over the papers, swore in the witness, and, with pen and ink from the tenant house, signed the documents. All were in shirt sleeves, and Lincoln remarked it was a kind of shirt-sleeve court they were holding. "Yes," laughed the judge, "a shirt-sleeve court in a cornfield." On Lincoln offering to roll up logs the judge guessed he could stand a little help, so they pitched in and when Ross asked the judge his fee the judge said he guessed their help was pay enough.

Lawyer Lincoln studied the face of Eliza Lloyd as she told of her husband, Peter, leaving her with a newborn baby, never furnishing support, becoming a habitual drunkard and, jailed for larceny, having broken jail. Lincoln wrote a bill of complaint "that the bonds of matrimony heretofore and now existing between the said Peter Lloyd and your oratrix be dissolved."

In a sensational murder case Stuart and Lincoln had their hands full in many weeks of 1838. Their last captain in the Black Hawk War, Jacob M. Early, a Democrat, had tangled with Henry B. Truett, another Democrat, over a political office. In the parlor of the Spottswood Hotel in Springfield they came to hot words and wild threats. On Truett drawing a pistol, Early picked up a chair to defend himself or to attack Truett. Truett shot Early dead. After indictment of Truett, Stephen A. Douglas was appointed prosecuting attorney, the regular prosecutor being a witness in the case. Assisting Stuart and Lincoln for the defense were attorneys, all Whig, Stephen T. Logan, Edward D. Baker and Cyrus Walker, who managed to get delays from March 14 till trial began October 9, when public feeling against Truett had simmered down. So many people had read or heard about the case, and formed opinions, that not till the third day was a twelfth juror agreed on.

Logan contended that Early, a larger man than Truett, with an uplifted chair in his hands, carried a deadly weapon, Truett believing the chair would come crashing on his head and kill him. Prosecutor Douglas insisted Truett came to the Spottswood Hotel with a gun, meaning to pick a fight with Early. Lincoln's plea to the jury was considered very effective and partly responsible for the verdict of acquittal for Truett. Before moving actively into the case in March, Stuart and Lincoln each accepted from Truett a note for $250 secured by a mortgage on two sections of land. That Truett was a man of violence who liked gunplay was a comment some years later when Truett, then in San Francisco, fought a duel and sank a bullet in his opponent.

In October 1837 the Reverend Jeremiah Porter was to speak against slavery in a church. A crowd gathered, some swearing they would mob him. Edward D. Baker cooled the crowd down, Porter made his address, but it took more wise handling of the crowd to get Porter out of town with no marks on him. At a citizens meeting in the courthouse a few days later, Judge Thomas C. Browne in the chair, resolutions were passed that "The doctrine of immediate emancipation . . . is at variance with christianity," and "abolitionists . . . are . . . dangerous members of society, and should be shunned by all good citizens." In nearby St. Louis a free mulatto named McIntosh resisting arrest had stabbed a deputy sheriff to death; a mob seized him in the street, took him to a suburb, chained him to a tree, burned him to death and the next morning boys threw stones at the skull as a target.

Into nearby Alton had moved a 35-year-old abolitionist Presbyterian minister, after editing a paper in St. Louis. His printing press arrived on a

Sunday and that night was dumped into the Mississippi River by unknown persons. Friendly citizens bought him another printing press which a mob took and threw into the river, as they did a third printing press after he had helped organize an Illinois antislavery society. Word came that Ohio abolitionists were sending him another printing press. It arrived and was moved into a warehouse where a guard was kept. A night mob stormed the warehouse November 7, 1837, and failing to get in, tried to set the warehouse on fire. Elijah Parish Lovejoy rushed out to stop the attempt at arson and fell dead from a mob bullet. His brother, Owen Lovejoy, a Congregational minister, knelt at the grave and vowed "never to forsake the cause that had been sprinkled with my brother's blood." Lincoln over at Springfield could not know that in years to come, amid inscrutable political labyrinths, he and Owen Lovejoy would understand and cling to each other, Lincoln to write, "To the day of his death, it would scarcely wrong any other to say, he was my most generous friend."

In a carefully written address, "The Perpetuation of Our Political Institutions," before the Young Men's Lyceum of Springfield in January 1838, Lincoln's theme was the spirit of violence in men overriding law and legal procedure. He pointed to the men of the Revolution who, at cost of death and mutilation, had won the liberties of men now being violated, saying, "whenever the vicious portion of population shall be permitted to gather . . . and burn churches, ravage and rob provision stores, throw printing presses into rivers, shoot editors, and hang and burn obnoxious persons at pleasure, and with impunity; depend on it, this Government cannot last." It was Lincoln's masterpiece of thought and speech up to this, his 29th year. No quotes from it could indicate the main closely woven fabric of the address. He dealt with momentous sacred ideas, basic in love of the American Dream, of personal liberty and individual responsibility. They were seeds in his mind foreshadowing growth. He spoke a toleration of free discussion; even abolitionists, keeping within the law, could have their say, a viewpoint not agreeable to the dominant southern element of Sangamon County who, if not in the listening audience, could read the printed text in the *Sangamo Journal*.

Again running for the legislature in the summer of 1838, Lincoln spent most of the campaign speaking for Stuart who was running for Congress against Douglas. Once when Stuart took sick, Lincoln went to Bloomington and debated with Douglas. Once in Archer G. Herndon's store, over a sloppy wet floor, Stuart and Douglas tussled and mauled each other, "fought like wildcats." And three days before election a Douglas speech in front of the Market House riled the tall, supple Stuart, who got a neck hold on the short, thick Douglas and dragged him around the Market House. Stuart came out of it with a scar for life where Douglas put a deep bite in his thumb. In the August 6 election Lincoln led in a field of 17 candidates. In a total of 36,495 votes, Stuart won over Douglas by the slim majority of 36 votes. Douglas cried for a recount but couldn't get it.

In Vandalia in December the Whigs nominated Lincoln for speaker of the House, and failing of election he worked as Whig floor leader. Again his maneuvers and votes favored the Internal Improvements spending, partly because he with others had so earnestly promised the funds for improvements to members who voted for Springfield as the new capital. Vandalia still had able members trying to keep her as the capital. Again Lincoln toiled on county reorganizations, on state reapportionment, and supported the Illinois and Michigan Canal. His main proposal, for the state to buy from the Federal Government public lands of about 20,000,000 acres at 25 cents an acre to be resold for $1.25 an acre, was approved, but came to no later results. Up till this time state tax money had come only from land owned by outsiders in Illinois and Lincoln voted for a new tax of 25 cents per $100 of assessed valuation on *all* real property in Illinois. To one member worried about property owners crying against the new law Lincoln said it took from the *"wealthy few"* rather than the *"many poor"* and definitely the wealthy few were "not sufficiently numerous to carry the elections."

He wrote William Butler and cleared up bad feeling between Butler and Ned Baker. "Your . . . letter to him was written while you were in a state of high excitement . . . it reached Baker while he was writhing under a severe tooth-ache." As to Butler writing of Lincoln's bad conduct in some piece of legislation, he wrote Butler, "I am willing to pledge myself in black and white to cut my own throat from ear to ear, if, when I meet you, you shall *seriously* say, that you believe me capable of betraying my friends for any price."

He wrote to Stuart as to some business or legislative matter, "Ewing wont do any thing. He is not worth a damn. Your friend A Lincoln." At his suggestion that the House membership should be limited to 99 or less, another member spoke of the Long Nine *"and old women"* seeming to favor the number 9. "Now," said Lincoln, "if any woman, old or young, ever thought there was any peculiar charm in this distinguished specimen of number 9, I have, as yet, been so unfortunate as not to have discovered it." After adjournment March 4 he rode out of Vandalia with perhaps a last backward look at the city he had helped rub off the map as the state capital.

Back in Springfield at law practice, Lincoln wrote his partner in Washington the news and for information wanted, as in one letter, "a d——d hawk billed yankee is here, besetting me at every turn I take, saying that Robt Kinzie never received the $80. to which he was entitled. Can you tell me any thing about the matter?" On payment of a fee, he would wrap "Stuart's half" in a piece of paper so marked.

He had seen the convention system working well for the Democrats and helped organize the first state Whig convention. It met in Springfield, named him one of five presidential electors for Illinois and a member of the State Central Committee. In December he made a speech of nearly two hours, an elaborate, intricate financial discussion of President Van Buren's scheme to replace the National Bank by a sub-treasury. He named high Democratic officials as making fortunes out of their stealings from the Government. "Look at Swartwout with his $1,200,000, Price with his $75,000, Harris with his $109,000." They and others had gone "scampering away with the public money to Texas, to Europe," and other spots of refuge. A *"running"* itch" was their malady, operating "very much like the cork-leg, in the comic song, did on its owner; which, when he had once got started on it, the more he tried to stop it, the more it would run away." In closing he registered an oath:

"Before High Heaven, and in the face of the world, I swear eternal fidelity to the just cause, as I deem it, of the land of my life, my liberty and my love." In a letter to Stuart he wrote, "Well, I made a big speech, which is in progress of printing in pamphlet form. I shall send you a copy."

In this December, the new capitol unfinished, the Senate met in the Methodist Church, the House in the Second Presbyterian Church. The Whigs had a majority of one in the House, each party 18 members in the Senate. Lincoln served on a committee to investigate the State Bank and signed a report which found, in the main, little mismanagement, though it was rated not good banking for the directors to allow Samuel Wiggins of Cincinnati to borrow $108,000 to pay installments on his $200,000 of bank stock, nor for the directors to make large loans to themselves and to favored individuals. Lincoln voted against forfeiture of the bank's charter, which passed, and then for a new law to revive the charter, which passed. He guided through passage a bill to incorporate the town of Springfield into a city. His amendment to the bill would make more than 12 per cent interest on loans illegal; it passed the House and died in the Senate, which pleased all loan sharks.

He voted against repeal of the big Internal Improvements Bill. This jungle of finance had by now brought the state into debt $17,000,000 and in less than two years the state was to stop payment of interest. Little was saved out of the vast wreck except the Illinois and Michigan Canal which Lincoln helped to save, and in time by able refinancing it was made a paying project. Lincoln and others kept the main colossal but crumbling scheme alive and Lincoln wrote to Stuart, to no avail, asking him to try to get action on Lincoln's plan of a previous session for the state to buy and sell public lands at a profit.

In that session the *Sangamo Journal* reported that Wickliff Kitchell in effect accused Lincoln of being drunkenly extravagant in favoring a bond issue of $1,500,000 to complete the Illinois and Michigan Canal. "Already prostrated by debt," said Kitchell, "that gentleman thinks it would be for the interest of the State to go still deeper." Kitchell told of a drunkard in Arkansas who "lost his reason" and lay in a dumb stupor from liquor. His wife couldn't bring him to. A neighbor came in and said "brandy toddy" might help. The drunk sat up at the word "toddy," saying, "That is the stuff!" Kitchell remarked, "It is so with the gentleman from Sangamon— more debt would be for the better."

Mr. Lincoln replied, "I beg leave to tell an anecdote. The gentleman's course the past winter reminds me of an eccentric old bachelor who lived in the Hoosier State. Like the gentleman from Montgomery [County], he was very famous for seeing *big bugaboos* in everything. He lived with an older brother, and one day he went out hunting. His brother heard him firing back of the field, and went out to see what was the matter. He found him loading and firing into the top of a tree. Not being able to discover anything in the tree, he asked him what he was firing at. He replied a squirrel—and kept on firing. His brother believing there was some humbug about the matter, examined his person, and found on one of his eyelashes a *big louse* crawling about. It is so with the gentleman from Montgomery. He imagines he can see squirrels every day, when they are nothing but *lice.*" "The House," said the *Sangamo Journal*, "was convulsed with laughter."

The national Whig convention in December 1839 nominated for President William Henry Harrison of Ohio, former Congressman and U.S. Senator, an 1812 war veteran and above all the commander and victor in the Battle of Tippecanoe defeating Chief Tecumseh. Nor did the Whigs fail to tell the country, howsoever true it might be, that Harrison lived in a plain log cabin and his drink was cider. Little mention was made that Harrison had lost his seat in Congress by voting against Missouri's admission to the Union unless as a Free and not a Slave State, which had its appeal to Lincoln as an early boomer of Harrison. Lincoln joined in the debating tournament in Springfield that ran eight straight evenings in December, Springfield learning, in a way, where Whig and Democrat stood. Lincoln as a four-time candidate for the legislature stumped his own district, and down into southern Illinois and over into Kentucky for the national ticket, often making two-hour speeches, at times debating with Douglas.

To a Whig conclave in Springfield in June 1840, came 15,000 people in wagons, carriages, horseback and afoot, in log cabins hauled by oxen. Thirty yoke of oxen drew one log cabin on wheels with live coons climbing a hickory tree and hard cider on tap by the cabin door. Lincoln's speech from a wagon was homely, familiar and natural, one man who heard it saying, "One story he told well illustrated the argument he was making. It was not an impure story, yet it was not one it would be seemly to publish." The *Illinois Register* said that on the platform he had too much of "an assumed clownishness" and should improve his manners.

The campaign raged around the 1837 panic, Democratic administration failures, hard times, and the Whig cry that the Democrats had been in office too long and it was time for a change. Feeling ran high and hot. Lincoln in March wrote to Stuart: "Yesterday Douglas, having chosen to consider himself insulted by something in the 'Journal,' undertook to cane Francis [the editor] in the street. Francis caught him by the hair and jammed him back against a market-cart, where the matter ended by Francis being pulled away from him. The whole affair was so ludicrous that Francis and everybody else (Douglas excepted) have been laughing about it ever since." Lincoln and Francis were two of five editors of a Whig paper, *The Old Soldier*. A "confidential" circular in stilted language tried to warm up every Whig party worker into personal activity, especially to see that all Whigs went to the polls. The wild campaign ended with Harrison as winner, with 234 electoral votes against Van Buren's 60, Harrison the first northern and western man to be sent to the White House. It was a famous campaign proving that sometimes the American democracy goes on a rampage and shows it has swift and terrific power, even though it is not sure what to do with that power.

Among Illinois Whigs were regrets. They carried their national ticket, but lost the state to the Democrats. This put a new color on a case they were interested in. Months earlier they had charged the Democrats with fraud in voting; thousands of Irish workmen in the canal zone had started a test action before a circuit judge who ruled that foreign-born inhabitants must be naturalized before they could vote. The Democrats took the case to the Supreme Court, knowing that if they lost the case they would lose thousands of votes.

Then came the newly elected legislature into session, with a Democratic majority. Douglas wrote a bill which became law. It set up five new supreme court judgeships; these with the four old judges would be the supreme court of the state besides doing the work of the circuit court judges, who were thrown out. The bill passed the Senate by a vote of 22 to 17, and the House by a vote of 45 to 43. By this move the Democrats saved the canal zone vote for their party, appointed Democrats as clerks in half the counties of the state as provided in the bill. Stephen A. Douglas, no longer register of the land office under a Whig national administration, was appointed a Supreme Court judge. The reply of the Whig party was a calm address issued by a committee of which Lincoln was a member, declaring "that the independence of the Judiciary has been destroyed—that hereafter our courts will be independent of the people, and entirely dependent upon the Legislature—that our rights of property and liberty of conscience can no longer be regarded as safe from the encroachments of unconstitutional legislation."

During one session the voting was often close; when the Democrats wanted a quorum and the Whigs didn't one day, the Democrats locked the door of the House to keep the quorum in. Lincoln, Joe Gillespie and another Whig raised a window and jumped out and hid. They were laughed at loud and long because they forgot they had voted on a motion to adjourn and by so voting had made a quorum that counted before they had vamoosed.

Lincoln joined with Whigs and Democrats and by 70 to 11 votes killed a bill to give the Territory of Wisconsin the 14 northern counties of Illinois. Thus Illinois kept in its border the vital and growing Great Lakes port of Chicago. The bright little prairie town of Galesburg in Knox County won incorporation by 52 to 31, Lincoln voting Aye. The session ended. An eastern visitor wrote, "The Assembly appeared to be composed all of young men, some of them mere boys; it forcibly reminded me of a debating school of boy students. I was more amused than instructed." Plainly he had missed some of the wild howling hours, and some of the "mere boys" he saw were beginning their ride to high place and power in the nation. In his Whig circular and in certain long speeches Lincoln let go with overcolored passages of a style that he later referred to as "fizzlegigs and fireworks." He was learning.

Several days in January 1841 Lincoln was in his seat only part of the day's session, on January 12 answering only two of the four roll calls; then for five straight days he was absent from the legislature. A letter of January 22 to a Whig member who had gone home had the current gossip: "We have been very much distressed, on Mr. Lincoln's account; hearing he had two Cat fits, and a Duck fit since we left. Is it true?" On January 24 the lawyer James Conkling was writing to a woman, "Poor L! how are the mighty fallen! He was confined about a week, but though he now appears again he is reduced and emaciated in appearance and seems scarcely to possess strength enough to speak above a whisper . . . he has experienced 'That surely 'tis the worst of pain To love and not be loved again.' " On January 20 Lincoln had written to Stuart in Washington, "I have, within the last few days, been making a most discreditable exhibition of myself in the way of hypochondriaism and thereby got an impression that Dr. Henry [Lincoln's physician] is necessary to my existence. Unless he gets that place [as Springfield postmaster] he leaves Springfield." The letter closed, "Pardon me for not writing more; I have not sufficient composure to write a long letter." He had met a woman and found his heart and mind in storm after storm.

Ninian W. Edwards of the Long Nine, a polished aristocrat and son of a former governor of Illinois, was the same age as Lincoln, and they had campaigned together and joined in Whig conferences. The Edwards' house, built of brick, stood two stories high and could have held a dozen prairie-farmer cabins. To this house in 1839 came a young woman from Lexington, Kentucky. She had been there two years before on a short visit. Now she had come to stay, Miss Mary Todd, a younger sister of Elizabeth, the wife of Ninian W. Edwards. Granddaughters of Todds who had fought through the American Revolution, their father, Robert Smith Todd, had been a captain in the War of 1812, had been clerk of the House and a state Senator, and was president of the Bank of Kentucky in Lexington.

Miss Mary Todd was 21, plump, swift, beaming. With her somewhat short figure sheathed in a gown of white with black stripes, low at the neck and giving free play to her swift neck muscles, the skirt fluffed out in a balloonish hoop, shod in modish ballroom slippers, she was a center of likes and dislikes among those who came to the house of her sister. For Lincoln, as he came to know her, she was lighted with magnets, the first aggressively brilliant feminine creature who had crossed his path so that he lost his head. One woman remarked that he didn't go as much as other young men for "ladies company." He saw in Mary Todd, with her pink-rose smooth soft skin, light brown hair hinting of bronze, ample bosom, flying glimpses of slippers, a triumph of some kind; she had finished schools where "the accomplishments" were taught; she spoke and read French. She had left her home in Kentucky because of a dispute with her stepmother. She was impetuous, picked the ridiculous angle, the weak point of anyone she disliked and spoke it with thrust of phrase. Her temper colored her; she could shine with radiance at a gift, a word, an arrival, a surprise, an achievement of a little cherished design, at winning a withheld consent. A shaft of wanted happiness could strike deep in her. Mary Todd was read, informed and versed in apparel and appearance. She hummed gay little ditties putting on a flowered bonnet and tying a double bowknot under her chin. A satisfying rose or ostrich plume in her hair was a psalm.

Her laughter could dimple in wreaths running to the core of her; she was born to impulses that rode her before she could ride them. After excesses of temper had worn her to exhaustion, she could rise and stand up to battle again for a purpose definitely formed. In the Edwards' circle they believed there were clues to her character in a remark she passed at a fireside party one evening. A young woman married to a rich man along in years was asked, "Why did you marry such a withered-up old buck?" and answered, "He had lots of houses and gold." And the quick-tongued Mary Todd in surprise: "Is that true? I would rather marry a good man, a man of mind,

with a hope and bright prospects ahead for position, fame, and power than
to marry all the houses, gold, and bones in the world."

In 1840 Lincoln and Mary Todd were engaged to be married. Ninian W.
Edwards and his wife had argued she was throwing herself away; it wasn't
a match; she and Lincoln came from different classes in society. Her stubborn Covenanter blood rose; she knew her own mind and spoke it; Lincoln
had a future; he was her man more than any other she had met.

The months passed. Lincoln, the solitary, the melancholy, was busy, lost,
abstracted; he couldn't go to all the parties, dances, concerts Mary Todd was
going to. She flared with jealousy and went with other men; she accused
him; tears; misunderstandings. They made up, fell out, made up again. The
wedding was set for New Year's Day, 1841.

And then something happened. The bride or the groom, or both, broke
the engagement. It was a phantom wedding, mentioned in hushes. There
was gossip and dispute about whether the wedding had been set for that date
at all. Lincoln was a haunted man. Was he sure he didn't love her? He walked
the streets of Springfield; he brooded, went to Dr. Henry's office, took Dr.
Henry's advice and wrote a long statement of his case for a doctor in Louisville. And the doctor answered that in this kind of case he could do nothing
without first a personal interview. Lincoln wrote his partner Stuart: "I am
now the most miserable man living. If what I feel were equally distributed
to the whole human family, there would not be one cheerful face on the
earth."

He was seeing Dr. Henry often, and wrote Stuart, "Whether I shall ever
be better I can not tell; I awfully forbode I shall not. To remain as I am is
impossible; I must die or be better, it appears to me. The matter you speak
of on my account, you may attend to as you say, unless you shall hear of
my condition forbidding it. I say this, because I fear I shall be unable to
attend to any business here, and a change of scene might help me. If I could
be myself, I would rather remain at home with Judge Logan. I can write no
more." He begged Stuart to go the limit in Washington toward the appointment of Dr. Henry as postmaster in Springfield. "You know I desired Dr.
Henry to have that place when you left; I now desire it more than ever."
He added that nearly all the Whig members of the legislature besides other
Whigs favored the doctor for postmaster. On Lincoln asking it, Stuart requested the new Secretary of State at Washington, Daniel Webster, to appoint Lincoln chargé d'affaires at Bogotá, far from Springfield, but nothing
came of it.

The legislature adjourned. Josh Speed was selling his store and going back
to his folks in Kentucky. Lincoln in a struggle to come back traveled to
Louisville in August and staying with Speed some three weeks shared talk
and counsel with that rare friend. Speed recalled Lincoln saying he had done
nothing to make any human being remember that he had lived; he wished to
live to connect his name with events of his day and generation and to the
interest of his fellow men. Slowly, he came back. A sweet and serene old
woman, Joshua Speed's mother, talked with him, gave him a mother's care,
and made him a present of an Oxford Bible.

In mid-September he was in Illinois again, writing to Speed's sister Mary about his tooth that failed of extraction when he was in Kentucky, "Well, that same old tooth got to paining me so much, that about a week since I had it torn out, bringing with it a bit of the jawbone . . . my mouth is now so sore that I can neither talk, nor eat."

CHAPTER 5

"I Am Going To Be Married"

JOSHUA SPEED, deep-chested, broad between the ears, had spots soft as May violets. And he and Abraham Lincoln told each other their secrets about women. "I do not feel my own sorrows much more keenly than I do yours," Lincoln wrote Speed in one letter. And again: "You know my desire to befriend you is everlasting."

The wedding day of Speed and Fanny Henning had been set; and Speed was afraid he didn't love her; it was wearing him down; the date of the wedding loomed as the hour for a sickly affair. He wrote Lincoln he was sick. And Lincoln wrote what was wrong with Speed's physical and mental system, a letter tender as loving hands swathing a feverish forehead, yet direct in its facing of immediate facts. It was a letter showing that Lincoln in unlucky endings of love affairs must have known deep-rooted, tangled, and baffling misery.

"You are *naturally of a nervous temperament*," he wrote. "And this I say from what I have seen of you personally, and what you have told me concerning your mother at various times, and concerning your brother William at the time his wife died." Besides this general cause, he gave three special reasons for Speed's condition—first, exposure to bad weather on his journey; second, "*the absence of all business and conversation of friends*, which might divert your mind, give it occasional rest from *that intensity* of thought, which will some times wear the sweetest idea thread-bare, and turn it to the bitterness of death. The third is, *the rapid and near approach of that crisis on which all your thoughts and feelings concentrate*."

Lincoln's broodings over the mysteries of personality, man's behavior, the baffling currents of body and mind, his ideas about his own shattered physical system were indicated in his telling Speed: "If . . . as I expect you will at some time, be agonized and distressed, let me, who have some reason to speak with judgement on such a subject, beseech you, to ascribe it to the causes I have mentioned; and not to some false and ruinous suggestion of the Devil . . . The *general one*, nervous debility, which is the key and conductor of all the particular ones, and without which *they* would be utterly harmless, though it *does* pertain to you, *does not* pertain to one in a thousand. It is out of this, that the painful difference between you and the mass of the world springs." That is, Lincoln believed that he and his friend had exceptional and sensitive personalities.

Lincoln was writing in part a personal confession in telling Speed: "I know what the painful point with you is, at all times when you are unhappy. It is an apprehension that you do not love her as you should. What nonsense! —How came you to court her? Was it because you thought she deserved it; and that you had given her reason to expect it? If it was for that, why did not the same reason make you court . . . at least twenty others of whom you can think, & to whom it would apply with greater force than to *her?* Did you court her for her wealth? Why, you knew she had none. But you say you *reasoned* yourself *into* it. What do you mean by that? Was it not, that you found yourself unable to *reason* yourself *out* of it? Did you not think, and partly form the purpose, of courting her the first time you ever saw or heard of her? . . . There was nothing *at that time* for reason to work upon. Whether she was moral, amiable, sensible, or even of good character, you did not, nor could not then know; except perhaps you might infer the last from the company you found her in. All you then did or could know of her, was her *personal appearance and deportment;* and these, if they impress at all, impress the *heart* and not the head.

"Say candidly, were not those heavenly *black eyes,* the whole basis of all your early *reasoning* on the subject? . . . Did you not go and take me all the way to Lexington and back, for no other purpose but to get to see her again . . . What earthly consideration would you take to find her scouting and despising you, and giving herself up to another? But of this you have no apprehension; and therefore you can not bring it home to your feelings. I shall be so anxious about you, that I want you to write me every mail."

Thus ended a letter which had begun, "My Dear Speed: Feeling, as you know I do, the deepest solicitude for the success of the enterprize you are engaged in, I adopt this as the last method I can invent to aid you, in case (which God forbid) you shall need any aid."

A few days before Speed's wedding, Lincoln wrote to the bridegroom. "I assure you I was not much hurt by what you wrote me of your excessively bad feeling at the time you wrote. Not that I am less capable of sympathising with you now than ever; . . . but because I hope and believe, that your present anxiety and distress about *her* health and *her* life, must and will forever banish those horid doubts, which I know you sometimes felt, as to the truth of your affection for her. If they can be once and forever removed. (and I almost feel a presentiment that the Almighty has sent your present affliction expressly for that object) surely, nothing can come in their stead, to fill their immeasurable measure of misery. The death scenes of those we love, are surely painful enough; but these we are prepared to, and expect to see. They happen to all, and all know they must happen . . . Should she, as you fear, be destined to an early grave, it is indeed, a great consolation to know that she is so well prepared to meet it. Her religion, which you once disliked so much, I will venture you now prize most highly."

Lincoln hoped Speed's melancholy forebodings as to Fanny's early death were not well founded. "I even hope, that ere this reaches you, she will have returned with improved and still improving health; and that you will have met her, and forgotten the sorrows of the past, in the enjoyment of the present. I would say more if I could; but it seems I have said enough. It really appears to me that you yourself ought to rejoice, and not sorrow, at this indubitable evidence of your undying affection for her. Why Speed, if you did not love her, although you might not wish her death, you would most calmly be resigned to it. Perhaps this point is no longer a question with you, and my pertenacious dwelling upon it, is a rude intrusion upon your feelings . . . You know the Hell I have suffered on that point, and how tender I am upon it. You know I do not mean wrong. I have been quite clear of hypo [hypochondria] since you left,—even better than I was along in the fall. I have seen Sarah [Rickard] but once. She seemed verry cheerful, and so, I said nothing to her about what we spoke of." Speed had "kept company" with Sarah and hoped she wasn't taking it hard that he was going to marry.

Speed's wedding day came; the knot was tied. And soon he read lines from Lincoln at Springfield: "When this shall reach you, you will have been Fanny's husband several days . . . But you will always hereafter, be on ground that I have never ocupied, and consequently, if advice were needed, I might advise wrong. I do fondly hope, however, that you will never again need any comfort from abroad. But should I be mistaken in this—should excessive pleasure still be accompanied with a painful counterpart at times, still let me urge you, as I have ever done, to remember in the dep[t]h and even the agony of despondency, that verry shortly you are to feel well again. I am now fully convinced, that you love her as ardently as you are capable of loving. Your ever being happy in her presence, and your intense anxiety about her health . . . would place this beyond all dispute in my mind.

"I incline to think it probable, that your nerves will fail you occasionally for a while; but once you get them fairly graded now, that trouble is over forever. I think if I were you, in case my mind were not exactly right, I would avoid being *idle* . . . If you went through the ceremony *calmly* . . . or even with sufficient composure not to excite alarm in any present, you are safe, beyond question." A postscript to one letter read, "I have been quite a man ever since you left."

The single man received a letter from his just-married friend, and wrote: "Yours of the 16th Inst. announcing that Miss Fanny and you 'are no more twain, but one flesh,' reached me this morning. I have no way of telling how much happiness I wish you both; tho' I believe you both can conceive it. I feel somwhat jealous of both of you now; you will be so exclusively concerned for one another, that I shall be forgotten entirely . . . I regret to learn that you have resolved to not return to Illinois. I shall be verry lonesome without you. How miserably things seem to be arranged in this world! If we have no friends, we have no pleasure; and if we have them, we are sure to lose them, and be doubly pained by the loss . . ."

The Washingtonian Temperance Society was so named because General George Washington had been a mild drinking man who knew when to stop. Lincoln on February 22, 1842, at a large gathering of Washingtonians, after riding in a carriage as "the orator of the day," gave an address on "Charity in Temperance Reform." He pictured the reformed drunkard as the best of temperance crusaders. Men selling liquor, and men drinking it, were blamed too much. Denunciation of them was both *"impolitic"* and "unjust." And why? "Because, it is not much in the nature of man to be driven to any thing; still less to be driven about that which is exclusively his own business . . . If you would win a man to your cause, *first* convince him that you are his sincere friend . . . Assume to dictate to his judgment, or to command his action, or to mark him as one to be shunned and despised, and he will retreat within himself . . . you shall no more be able to pierce him, than to penetrate the hard shell of a tortoise with a rye straw."

He sketched history, the practice of drinking "old as the world itself." The sideboard of the parson and the ragged pocket of the houseless loafer both held whisky. "Physicians prescribed it in this, that, and the other disease. Government provided it for its soldiers and sailors; and to have a rolling or raising, a husking or hoe-down, any where without it, was *positively insufferable*." The making of it was regarded as honorable.

Were the benefits of temperance to be only for the next generation, for posterity? "There is something so ludicrous in *promises* of good, or *threats* of evil, a great way off . . . 'Better lay down that spade you're stealing, Paddy,—if you don't you'll pay for it at the day of judgment.' 'Be the powers, if ye'll credit me so long, I'll take another, jist.'" And proud would be the title of that land in which "there shall be neither a slave nor a drunkard."

In the audience were reformed drunkards. Lincoln was keyed to these men. He didn't drink, but he did wish to say, "In my judgment, such of us as have never fallen victims, have been spared more from the absence of appetite, than from any mental or moral superiority over those who have."

And one young lawyer who liked his whisky stood at the door of the Second Presbyterian Church, as the people walked out, and reported he heard persons not pleased with the address, catching one remark, "It's a shame that he should be permitted to abuse us so in the house of the Lord." The *Illinois State Register* inquired whether Lincoln and other politicians had "joined the Washingtonian Society from any other than political motives," and "Would they have joined it if it had been exceedingly unpopular?"

Bowling Green died in this February and Lincoln went to the funeral at New Salem. The widow, Nancy Green, who had nursed Lincoln in sickness and fed him hot biscuits smothered in honey, asked him to speak. He stood at the side of the burial box, looked down at the still, white face of his old friend, teacher and companion, turned toward the mourners, the New Salem faces he knew so well. He may have been composed and spoken words of comfort and light. But one version had it that only a few broken and choked words came from him, tears ran down his face and he couldn't go on.

A few days after Joshua Speed's wedding, the newly married man wrote to Lincoln that he was still haunted by "something indescribably horrible and alarming." Lincoln's reply February 25, 1842, gave light on his own experience and methods of overcoming melancholy, "hypo," torment of mind and nerves. He wrote that he opened Speed's letter "with intense anxiety and trepidation—so much, that although it turned out better than I expected, I have hardly yet, at the distance of ten hours, become calm," and then, "I tell you, Speed, our *forebodings*, for which you and I are rather peculiar, are all the worst sort of nonsense." Lincoln believed he could see that since Speed's last letter, Speed had grown "*less miserable*" and not worse, writing:

"You say that 'something indescribably horrible and alarming still haunts you.['] You will not say *that* three months from now, I will venture. When your nerves once get steady now, the whole trouble will be over forever. Nor should you become impatient at their being very slow, in becoming steady. Again; you say you much fear that that Elysium of which you have dreamed so much, is never to be realized. Well, if it shall not, I dare swear, it will not be the fault of her who is now your wife. I now have no doubt that it is the peculiar misfortune of both you and me, to dream dreams of Elysium far exceeding all that any thing earthly can realize. Far short of your dreams as you may be, no woman could do more to realize them, than that same black eyed Fanny. If you could but contemplate her through my imagination, it would appear ridiculous to you, that any one should for a moment think of being unhappy with her. My old Father used to have a saying that 'If you make a bad bargain, *hug* it the tighter.'"

This letter was confidential and for Speed only. "I write another letter enclosing this, which you can show her, if she desires it. I do this . . . because, she would think strangely perhaps should you tell her that you receive no letters from me; or, telling her you do, should refuse to let her see them." For Speed in an earlier year, Lincoln had recited:

Whatever spiteful fools may say,
Each jealous, ranting yelper,
No woman ever went astray
Without a man to help her.

A month passed and Lincoln had news from Speed that the marriage was a complete success and bells rang merrily, Speed far happier than he ever expected to be. To which Lincoln replied: "I know you too well to suppose your expectations were not, at least sometimes, extravagant; and if the reality exceeds them all, I say, enough, dear Lord. I am not going beyond the truth, when I tell you, that the short space it took me to read your last letter, gave me more pleasure, than the total sum of all I have enjoyed since that fatal first of Jany. '41."

He referred to Mary Todd for the first time in his letters to Speed. ". . . it seems to me, I should have been entirely happy, but for the never-absent idea, that there is *one* still unhappy whom I have contributed to make so. That still kills my soul. I can not but reproach myself, for even wishing to be happy while she is otherwise. She accompanied a large party on the Rail Road cars, to Jacksonville last monday; and on her return, spoke, so that I heard of it, of having enjoyed the trip exceedingly. God be praised for that."

Three months later there came to Lincoln thanks and thanks from Speed for what he had done to bring and to keep Speed and Fanny Henning together. He wrote to Speed: "I am not sure there was any merit, with me, in the part I took in your difficulty; I was drawn to it as by fate . . . I could not have done less than I did. I always was superstitious; and as part of my superstition, I believe God made me one of the instruments of bringing your Fanny and you together, which union, I have no doubt He had fore-ordained. Whatever he designs, he will do for *me* yet . . . If, as you say, you have told Fanny *all*, I should have no objection to her seeing this letter, but for it's reference to our friend here. Let her seeing it, depend upon whether she has ever known any thing of my affair; and if she has not, do not let her."

"Our friend here" meant Mary Todd. Lincoln was now sure he had made a mistake, first of all in not taking Speed's advice to break off his engagement with Mary Todd, and then in not going through and keeping his resolve to marry her. "As to my having been displeased with your advice, surely you know better than that. I know you do; and therefore I will not labour to convince you. True, that subject is painfull to me; but it is not your silence, or the silence of all the world that can make me forget it. I acknowledge the correctness of your advice too; but before I resolve to do the one thing or the other, I must regain my confidence in my own ability to keep my resolves when they are made.

"In that ability, you know, I once prided myself as the only, or at least the chief, gem of my character; that gem I lost—how, and when, you too well know. I have not yet regained it; and until I do, I can not trust myself in any matter of much importance. I believe now that, had you understood my case at the time, as well as I understood yours afterwards, by the aid you would have given me, I should have sailed through clear; but that does not now afford me sufficient confidence, to begin that, or the like of that, again."

Such was the frank and pitiless self-revelation he did not wish Fanny Henning Speed to see unless she knew everything else. He closed his letter, "My respect and esteem to all your friends there; and, by your permission, my love to your Fanny." In one sentence he had sketched himself, "I am so poor, and make so little headway in the world, that I drop back in a month of idleness, as much as I gain in a year's rowing."

Mrs. Simeon Francis, wife of the editor of the *Sangamo Journal,* invited Lincoln to a party in her parlor, brought Lincoln and Miss Todd together and said, "Be friends again." Whatever of fate or woman-wit was at work, and whatever hesitations and broodings went on in Lincoln's heart, they were friends again. But they didn't tell the world so.

Joining the quiet little parties in the Francis house was Julia Jayne, who with Mary Todd, concocted articles printed in the *Sangamo Journal,* Whig satires on the state auditor of accounts, James Shields, his ways, manners and clothes. Of four letters signed "Rebecca" Lincoln wrote one, and it was in part overly gabby and mean, edging on malice—and yet often comic, as in reference to a gathering: "They wouldn't let no democrats in, for fear they'd disgust the ladies, or scare the little galls, or dirty the floor. I looked in at the window, and there was this same fellow Shields floatin about on the air, without heft or earthly substance, just like a lock of cat-fur where cats had been fightin . . . and the sweet distress he seemed to be in,—his very features in the exstatic agony of his soul, spoke audibly and distinctly— 'Dear Girls, *it is distressing,* but I cannot marry you all . . . it is not my fault that I am *so* handsome and *so* interesting.'" This anonymous letter of Lincoln's, signed only "Rebecca," ended, "If some change for the better is not made, its not long that neither Peggy, or I, or any of us, will have a cow left to milk, or a calf's tail to wring."

One "Rebecca" article written by Miss Todd and Miss Jayne read in part: "Now I want you to tell Mr. S. that rather than fight I'll make any apology, and if he wants *personal* satisfaction, let him only come here and he may squeeze my hand . . . Jeff tells me the way these fireeaters do is to give the challenged party choice of weapons, &c. which bein the case I'll tell you in confidence that I never fights with any thing but broom-sticks or hot water, or a shovel full of coals, or some such thing . . ."

Shields, a bachelor of 32, had been a lawyer ten years and a member of the legislature with Lincoln. He was a fighting Irishman born in Dungannon, County Tyrone, Ireland. He asked the *Sangamo Journal* editor who wrote the articles and was told Lincoln took all responsibility for them. Then Shields challenged Lincoln to a duel. Lincoln's seconds notified Shields' seconds that Lincoln chose to fight with cavalry broadswords, across a plank ten feet long and nine to twelve inches broad. The two parties traveled by horse and buggy, and by an old horse-ferry, and September 22 met on a sand bar in the Mississippi River, within three miles of Alton but located in the State of Missouri beyond reach of the Illinois laws against dueling.

Lincoln, seated on a log, practiced swings and swishes in the air with his cavalry broadsword, while friends, lawyers, seconds on both sides, held a long conference. After the main long one came shorter conferences with Lincoln and with Shields. Then a statement was issued declaring that although Mr. Lincoln was the writer of the article signed "Rebecca" in the *Sangamo Journal* of September 2, he had no intention of injuring the personal or private character or standing of Mr. Shields as a gentleman or a man, that he did not think that said article could produce such an effect; and had he anticipated such an effect, he would have foreborne to write it; said article was written solely for political effect, and not to gratify any personal pique against Mr. Shields, for he had none and knew of no cause for any. The duel had become a joke but Lincoln never afterward mentioned it and his friends saw it was a sore point that shouldn't be spoken of to him. A story arose and lived on that when first, as the challenged party, he had his choice of weapons, he said, "How about cow dung at five paces?"

At the meetings of Lincoln and Mary Todd in the Francis home, Miss Todd made it clear to him that if another date should be fixed for a wedding, it should not be set so far in the future as it was the time before. Lincoln agreed and early in October wrote to Speed: "You have now been the husband of a lovely woman nearly eight months. That you are happier now than you were the day you married her I well know . . . and the returning elasticity of spirits which is manifested in your letters. But I want to ask a closer question—'Are you now, in *feeling* as well as *judgement*, glad you are married as you are?' From any body but me, this would be an impudent question not to be tolerated; but I know you will pardon it in me. Please answer it quickly as I am impatient to know." Speed answered yes and yes, his marriage had brought happiness. A few weeks later, Lincoln came to the room of James Matheny, before Matheny was out of bed, telling his friend, "I am going to be married today."

On the street Lincoln met Ninian W. Edwards and told Edwards that he and Mary were to be married that evening. Edwards gave notice, "Mary is my ward, and she must be married at my house." When Edwards asked

Mary Todd if what he had heard was true, she told him it was true and they made the big Edwards house ready.

Lincoln took all care of a plain gold ring, the inside engraved: "Love is eternal." At the Edwards house on the evening of November 4, 1842, the Reverend Charles Dresser in canonical robes performed the ring ceremony of the Episcopal church for the groom, 33, and the bride, soon to be 24.

Afterward in talk about the wedding, Jim Matheny said Lincoln had "looked as if he was going to slaughter." Gossip at the Butler house where Lincoln roomed had it that, as he was dressing, Bill Butler's boy came in and asked, "Where are you going?" Lincoln answering, "To hell, I suppose." However dubious such gossip, Lincoln, seven days after his wedding, wrote to Sam Marshall at Shawneetown, discussed two law cases, and ended the letter: "Nothing new here, except my marrying, which to me, is matter of profound wonder."

The Lincoln couple boarded and roomed at $4.00 per week in the plain Globe Tavern, where their first baby came August 1, 1843, and was named Robert Todd. Soon after, they moved into their own home, bought for $1,500, a story-and-a-half frame house a few blocks from the city center. The framework and floors were oak, the laths hand-split hickory, the doors, door frames and weatherboarding black walnut. The house was painted, wrote one visitor, "a Quaker tint of light brown." In the back lot were a cistern, well and pump, a barn 30 by 13 feet, a carriage house 18 by 20. Three blocks east the cornfields began and farms mile after mile.

In the nine, and later, 15 counties of the Eighth Judicial District or "Eighth Circuit," Lincoln traveled and tried cases in most of the counties, though his largest practice was in Logan, Menard, Tazewell and Woodford, which were part of the Seventh Congressional District. He rode a horse or drove in a buggy, at times riding on rough roads an hour or two without passing a farmhouse on the open prairie. Mean was the journey in the mud of spring thaws, in the blowing sleet or snow and icy winds of winter. Heavy clothing, blankets or buffalo robes over knees and body, with shawl over shoulders, couldn't help the face and eyes that had to watch the horse and the road ahead. When pelting showers or steady rain came, he might stop at a farmhouse but if court was meeting next day, there was nothing to do but plod on in wet clothes.

The tavern bedrooms had usually only a bed, a spittoon, two split-bottom chairs, a washstand with a bowl and a pitcher of water, the guest in colder weather breaking the ice to wash his face. Some taverns had big rooms where a dozen or more lawyers slept of a night. In most of the sleepy little towns "court day" whetted excitement over trials to decide who would have to pay damages or go to jail. Among the lawyers was fellowship with men of rare brains and ability who would be heard from nationally, some of them to be close associates of Lincoln for years. Over the Eighth Circuit area, 120 miles long and 160 miles wide at its limit, ranging from Springfield to the Indiana line, Lincoln met pioneer frontier humanity at its best and worst, from the good and wise to the silly and aimless.

With Stuart away months in Congress, and busy with politics when at home, the heavy routine work fell on Lincoln, who had learned about all he could of law from Stuart. They parted cordially and Lincoln went into partnership with Stephen T. Logan, acknowledged leader of the Springfield bar. Nine years older than Lincoln, he was a former circuit judge, Scotch-Irish and Kentucky-born—a short sliver of a man with tight lips and a thin voice that could rasp, his hair frowsy and red. He wore linsey-woolsey shirts, heavy shoes, and never a necktie, yet he was known as one of the most neat, careful, scrupulous, particular, exact and profoundly learned lawyers in Illinois in preparing cases and analyzing principles involved. From him Lincoln was to learn more than he had known of the word "thorough" in law practice. Perhaps slight yet definite was the influence of Logan in Lincoln's writing later:

The true rule, in determining to embrace, or reject any thing, is not whether it have *any* evil in it; but whether it have more of evil, than of good. There are few things *wholly* evil, or *wholly* good. Almost every thing . . . is an inseparable compound of the two; so that our best judgment of the preponderance between them is continually demanded.

Lincoln argued in the Supreme Court the famous case of Bailey *vs*. Cromwell. Cromwell had sold Bailey a Negro girl, saying the girl was a slave. Bailey had given a note promising to pay cash for the slave. Lincoln argued, in part, that the girl was a free person until proven to be a slave, and, if not proven a slave, then she could not be sold nor bought and no cash could be exchanged between two men buying and selling her. The Supreme Court decided that the "girl being free" therefore "could not be the subject of a sale" and Bailey's promissory note was "illegal."

For Miss Eliza Cabot, a Menard County schoolteacher suing for slander, Lincoln won a verdict for $1,600. In one damage suit the best Lincoln could get for his client was one cent. In June 1842 Logan and Lincoln had eight bankruptcy cases in the U.S. District Court. They defended one bankrupt client, Charles H. Chapman, charged with perjury, Chapman getting five years in the penitentiary, though pardoned five months later. In such a case, it was generally understood among fellow attorneys that if Lincoln believed a client guilty, he made a poor showing before judge and jury.

Since 1839 Lincoln had traveled the circuit a few months each year. In DeWitt County he and Douglas were joint counsel in the defense of Spencer Turner indicted "for not having the fear of God before his eyes but being moved and seduced by the instigation of the Devil." Turner had assaulted one Matthew K. Martin with "a wooden stick of the value of ten cents" inflicting on the right temple of the said Martin "one mortal wound." The plea was not guilty and the jury was convinced of Turner's innocence.

Since joining Logan, Lincoln had more cases in the higher courts in Springfield. In December 1841 he argued 14 cases in the Supreme Court, losing only four. Of 24 cases in that court during 1842 and 1843 he lost only seven. But Logan was taking a son into partnership, and he saw, too, that Lincoln was about ready to head his own law firm. And Logan, a Whig, elected a member of the legislature in 1842, had an eye on going to Congress, as did Lincoln. The firm had, on Lincoln's advice, taken in as a law student a young man, William H. Herndon, nine years younger than Lincoln, who had clerked in the Speed store and slept upstairs. Shortly after Herndon's admittance to law practice in December 1844, Lincoln and he formed a partnership and opened their office. The younger man had spoken amazement at Lincoln's offer to take him on, Lincoln saying only, "Billy, I can trust you and you can trust me." From then on for years he was "Billy" and called the other man "Mr. Lincoln."

Herndon was intense, sensitive, had hair-trigger emotions. His grandfather in Virginia had given slaves their freedom; his father, a former store and tavern keeper, in politics had fought to make Illinois a Slave State. The son knew tavern life, and was near vanity about how he could read men by their eyes. He was of medium height, rawboned, with high cheekbones, dark eyes set far back, his shock of hair blue-black. He knew rough country boy talk and stories, tavern lingo, names of drinks, the slang of men about cards, horse races, chicken fights, women. Yet he was full of book learning, of torches and bonfires, had a flamboyance about freedom, justice, humanity. He was close to an element in Sangamon County that Lincoln termed "the shrewd wild boys." He liked his liquor, the bars and the topers and tipplers of the town. He was a Whig, was plain himself and was loved by many plain people. Lincoln, in a political letter, had referred to his own arrival in Sangamon "twelve years ago" as "a strange[r], friendless, uneducated, penniless boy, working on a flat boat—at ten dollars per month" and was now astonished "to learn that I have been put down here as the candidate of pride, wealth, and arristocratic family distinction." There was a factor of politics as well as law in his choosing for a partner the money-honest, highfalutin, whimsical, corn-on-the-cob, temperamental, convivial Bill Herndon.

CHAPTER 6

Running for Congress

NOW IF you should hear any one say that Lincoln don't want to go to Congress, I wish you as a personal friend of mine, would tell him you have reason to believe he is mistaken." Thus Lincoln was writing in mid-February 1843 to an active Whig, Richard S. Thomas. As a state party leader, with other Whigs, he wrote in March a campaign circular, an "Address to the People of Illinois," analyzing national issues, favoring a tariff for revenue rather than direct taxation, the National Bank opposed by the Democrats, a state income by sale of public lands; he warned hesitant Whigs they must use the convention system for nominations or go on losing to "the common enemy"; he pleaded for party unity, writing that "he whose wisdom surpasses that of all philosophers, has declared 'a house divided against itself cannot stand.'"

He tried to get the Sangamon County delegates to a district convention to endorse him for Congress, but the convention had pledged them to Edward D. Baker. Born in London, England, a Black Hawk War private, a lawyer certified in Carrollton, Illinois, once a state senator, Baker was one of the inner circle of Springfield Whigs, a brilliant and dramatic speaker who could shift modulations from hard ringing steel to rose and rainbow, a stubborn fighter moving with dash and gallantry. When "Ned" Baker loved a man or a cause, he could pour it out in lavish speech. And Lincoln's heart went out in admiration and affection for Ned Baker as perhaps to no other man in Springfield. Named a delegate to the district convention, pledged to support Baker, Lincoln wrote to Speed, "I shall be 'fixed' a good deal like a fellow who is made groomsman to the man what has cut him out, and is marrying his own dear 'gal'."

At the district convention in Pekin, a third rival, John J. Hardin, had a majority at hand for the nomination. Lincoln, for the sake of party unity, moved the nomination be made unanimous. Tall, well-tailored, having an air of command, a Transylvania University graduate, Hardin had been Lincoln's rival for Whig floor leadership in the legislature. In speech he stammered but had an ease and grace about it so no one minded. The Kentucky son of a distinguished U.S. Senator, a Black Hawk War veteran, a brigadier general of state militia, he had a paying law practice in Jacksonville and an ever-keen eye for a seat in Congress.

Lincoln engineered passage of a resolution by 18 votes to 14, whereby the convention, as individuals, recommended E. D. Baker as the Whig party nominee for Congress in 1844, subject to the decision of the convention then. It seemed that Lincoln, with Baker and Hardin, had made an arrangement that Baker would follow Hardin in 1844 as the nominee and Lincoln would follow Baker in 1846. Lincoln was later to remind Hardin of "the proposition made by me to you and Baker, that we should take a turn a piece." Hardin would claim the purpose of the resolution was "to soothe Baker's mortified feelings," Lincoln being certain that was not "*the sole*" object. Some delegates came away understanding that three Whig leaders had agreed on a rotation, "a turn a piece" in Congress.

Lincoln pledged himself to party harmony and when Hardin won his seat in Congress at the August election, Sangamon County gave him three times the majority of his own Morgan County. Nevertheless, when Lincoln voted August 7 he spoke out the names of only two candidates, constable and justice of the peace. Why he didn't vote for Hardin for Congress, nor for, nor against, any Whig candidates for the county offices, had no explanation from him. It was the more odd because in Whig circulars he had strictly urged all Whigs to go to the polls and vote for all Whigs. Possibly the election clerks were slovenly incomplete in recording what they heard. If he failed to vote for Hardin, it went unnoticed by opponents or rivals who could have used it against him. Hardin went to Congress, followed the Whig party line, and in 1844 stepped aside and let Baker have nomination and election.

Early in the 1844 presidential campaign, after bloody riots in Philadelphia, and Democratic forces blaming Whigs as wishing hate and violence toward "foreigners and Catholics," Lincoln at a public meeting in Springfield moved passage of resolutions he had written, "That the guarantee of the rights of conscience, as found in our Constitution, is most sacred and inviolable, and one that belongs no less to the Catholic, than to the Protestant; and that all attempts to abridge or interfere with these rights, either of Catholic or Protestant, directly or indirectly . . . shall ever have our most effective opposition." In late October he spoke in Indiana for the national ticket and Henry Clay, the third-time Whig candidate for President. Election Day found him in Gentryville, Indiana. In this November, James K. Polk of Tennessee won by 170 electoral votes over 105 for Clay, his Illinois majority 12,000.

When Baker came back from Washington, he hesitated about telling Lincoln he wouldn't run again, because of the chance Hardin might run and they both might lose out. Soon after, however, he told Lincoln that he would decline nomination—and when the next year another baby boy arrived at the Lincoln home, he was named Edward Baker Lincoln.

As Lincoln had feared and foreseen, Hardin wanted to run again. On January 7, 1846, Lincoln wrote Dr. Robert Boal, a party worker in Marshall County, "Since I saw you last fall . . . All has happenned as I then told you I expected it would—Baker's declining, Hardin's taking the track, and so on. If Hardin and I stood precisely equal—that is, if *neither* of us had been to congress, or if we *both* had—it would only accord with what I have always done, for the sake of peace, to give way to him; and I expect I should do it . . . But to yield to Hardin under present circumstances, seems to me as nothing else than yielding to one who would gladly sacrifice me altogether. This, I would rather not submit to. That Hardin is talented, energetic, usually generous and magnanimous, I have, before this, affirmed to you, and do not now deny. You know that my only argument is that 'turn about is fair play.' This he, practically at least, denies." When Hardin later saw county delegations moving toward Lincoln, he proposed that instead of nominating by convention the Whigs should poll the counties of the district, with no candidate allowed to electioneer outside his own county. Lincoln wrote to Hardin, "I am entirely satisfied with the old system under which you and Baker were successively nominated and elected to congress; and because the whigs of the District are well acquainted with that system."

At his office desk Lincoln dipped his goose-quill pen into an inkstand and wrote to editors, politicians, voters, precinct workers, saying in one letter, "I have . . . written to three or four of the most active whigs in each precinct of the county." He reckoned, in one letter, the counties for or against his nomination. A movement against him on foot in a town, he wrote the editor of the paper there, "I want you to let nothing prevent your getting an article in your paper, of *this week*." He could appeal frankly, "If your feelings towards me are the same as when I saw you (which I have no reason to doubt) I wish you would let nothing appear in your paper which may opperate against me. You understand. Matters stand just as they did when I saw you."

The blunt little sentence crept in often, "You understand." Some letters ended, "Confidential of course," or "Dont speak of this, lest they hear of it," or "For your eye only." There were times to travel in soft shoes. "It is my intention to take a quiet trip through the towns and neighbourhoods of Logan county, Delevan, Tremont, and on to & through the upper counties. Dont speak of this, or let it relax any of your vigilance. When I shall reach Tremont, we will talk every thing over at large." A direct personal appeal was phrased, "I now wish to say to you that if it be consistent with your feelings, you would set a few stakes for me." No personal feelings against

Hardin must be permitted. "I do not certainly know, but I strongly suspect, that Genl. Hardin wishes to run again. I know of no argument to give me a preference over him, unless it be 'Turn about is fair play.' " And again, to another: "It is my intention to give him [Hardin] the trial, unless clouds should rise, which are not yet discernable. This determination you need not however, as yet, announce in your paper—at least not as coming from me . . . In doing this, let nothing be said against Hardin—nothing deserves to be said against him. Let the pith of the whole argument be *'Turn about is fair play.'* "

Hardin began to feel outguessed and outplayed and wrote to Lincoln complaining. Lincoln, on February 7, 1846, answered with the longest political letter he had ever written, a masterpiece of merciless logic. Point by point he cornered Hardin, writing at its close, "In my letter to you, I reminded you that you had first at Washington, and afterwards at Pekin, said to me that if Baker succeeded he would most likely hang on as long as possible, while with you it would be different." Hardin's letter to him imputed "management," "manoevering," "combination" and had the reproach, "It is mortifying to discover that those with whom I have long acted & from whom I expected a different course, have considered it all fair to prevent my nomination to congress." Under such imputations, wrote Lincoln, "It is somewhat difficult to be patient." He ended, "I believe you do not mean to be unjust, or ungenerous; and I, therefore am slow to believe that you will not yet think *better* and think *differently* of this matter." Nine days later Hardin drew out of the contest, and the district convention at Petersburg, May 1, by acclamation nominated Lincoln for Congress in the one district in Illinois more certain than any other of Whig victory.

Against Lincoln the Democrats put up Peter Cartwright, a famous and rugged old-fashioned circuit rider, a storming evangelist, exhorter and Jackson Democrat. He had carried his Bible and rifle over wilderness, had more than once personally thrown out of church a drunk interrupting his sermon. He was thick-set, round-faced, and liked to refer to his wickedness at horse racing, card playing and dancing before he was converted. He was 61 and Lincoln 37, both of them very human. He had lived near New Salem, held camp meetings near there, and Lincoln had seen him and heard of his ways. A deacon spoke a cold, precise, correct prayer and Cartwright had to say, "Brother, three prayers like that would freeze hell over." When a presiding elder at a church meeting in Tennessee whispered to Cartwright, pointing out a visitor, "That's Andrew Jackson," the reply was: "And who's Andrew Jackson? If he's a sinner God'll damn him the same as he would a Guinea nigger."

Cartwright's men kept reports going: Lincoln's wife was a high-toned Episcopalian; Lincoln held drunkards as good as Christians and church members; Lincoln was a "deist" who believed in God but did not accept Christ nor the doctrines of atonement and punishment; Lincoln said, "Christ was a bastard." Lincoln put out a handbill giving the most complete and specific statement he had ever made publicly regarding his religion. It read:

A charge having got into circulation in some of the neighborhoods of this District, in substance that I am an open scoffer at Christianity, I have by the advice of some friends concluded to notice the subject in this form. That I am not a member of any Christian Church, is true; but I have never denied the truth of the

Scriptures; and I have never spoken with intentional disrespect of religion in general, or of any denomination of Christians in particular. It is true that in early life I was inclined to believe in what I understand is called the "Doctrine of Necessity"—that is, that the human mind is impelled to action, or held in rest by some power, over which the mind itself has no control; and I have sometimes (with one, two or three, but never publicly) tried to maintain this opinion in argument. The habit of arguing thus however, I have, entirely left off for more than five years. And I add here, I have always understood this same opinion to be held by several of the Christian denominations. The foregoing, is the whole truth, briefly stated, in relation to myself, upon this subject.

I do not think I could myself, be brought to support a man for office, whom I knew to be an open enemy of, and scoffer at, religion. Leaving the higher matter of eternal consequences, between him and his Maker, I still do not think any man has the right thus to insult the feelings, and injure the morals, of the community in which he may live. If, then, I was guilty of such conduct, I should blame no man who should condemn me for it; but I do blame those, whoever they may be, who falsely put such a charge in circulation against me.

He went to a religious meeting where Cartwright in due time said, "All who desire to give their hearts to God, and go to heaven, will stand." A sprinkling of men, women and children stood up. The preacher exhorted, "All who do not wish to go to hell will stand." All stood up—except Lincoln. Then Cartwright in his gravest voice: "I observe that many responded to the first invitation to give their hearts to God and go to heaven. And I further observe that all of you save one indicated that you did not desire to go to hell. The sole exception is Mr. Lincoln, who did not respond to either invitation. May I inquire of you, Mr. Lincoln, where you are going?"

Lincoln slowly rose: "I came here as a respectful listener. I did not know that I was to be singled out by Brother Cartwright. I believe in treating religious matters with due solemnity. I admit that the questions propounded by Brother Cartwright are of great importance. I did not feel called upon to answer as the rest did. Brother Cartwright asks me directly where I am going. I desire to reply with equal directness: I am going to Congress." Thus it was told.

Whig friends raised $200 for his personal campaign expenses. After the election he handed them back $199.25, saying he had spent only 75 cents in the campaign. The count of ballots gave Lincoln 6,340 votes, Cartwright 4,829, Walcott (Abolitionist) 249. He wrote to Speed, "Being elected to Congress, though I am very grateful to our friends, for having done it, has not pleased me as much as I expected."

Eleven days after Lincoln's nomination in May, Congress had declared a state of war between the United States and Mexico, authorizing an army of 50,000 volunteers and a war fund of $10,000,000 to be raised. In speeches Lincoln seemed briefly to advise all citizens to stand by the flag of the nation, supply all needs of the brave men at the fighting fronts, till an honorable peace could be secured. Trained rifle companies of young men offered service; of 8,370 volunteers in Illinois only 3,720 could be taken; they went down the Mississippi, across the Gulf to Texas, and on into baking hot deserts of Mexico.

Hardin enlisted and was appointed a colonel; he was to die a soldier of valor leading his men in the Battle of Buena Vista. James Shields was ap-

Upper left: Photograph of a daguerreotype. Earliest known portrait, possibly made in Washington about 1848 of Congressman Lincoln [Meserve]. *Upper right:* Joshua Speed, bosom friend with whom Lincoln shared confidences about women and marriage [Meserve]. *Center:* Peter Cartwright, circuit-rider evangelist who opposed Lincoln for Congress [McLean]. *Lower left:* Orville H. Browning, diarist and lawyer who tried cases with and against Lincoln [Meserve]. *Lower center:* Owen Lovejoy, Illinois antislavery Congressman from Princeton, Illinois, a cherished friend of Lincoln [USASC]. *Lower right:* Edward Dickinson Baker, Congressman, close political associate and friend of Lincoln [Meserve].

Upper left: Photograph of an ambrotype made in Macomb, Illinois, August 26, 1858, five days after debate with Douglas [Meserve]. *Upper right:* 1860 life mask of Lincoln. Original in bronze by Leonard Volk, owned by Frederick Meserve, photographed by Steichen. *Center left:* Joseph Medill, probably 1858, from a photograph loaned by Alicia Patterson. *Center right:* Ward Hill Lamon, lawyer and at times boon companion of Lincoln [Meserve]. *Lower left:* Isaac N. Arnold, Chicago lawyer and devoted political associate of Lincoln [USASC]. *Lower right:* William H. Herndon, 16 years the law partner of Lincoln [Huntington Library].

pointed brigadier general to command the Illinois troops and was to fall with a bullet through his lungs, leading a charge in the Battle of Cerro Gordo. Many of the young men wild to enlist had heard since 1836 of the Alamo, of San Jacinto, of almost incredibly heroic Texans against heavy odds overwhelming Mexican armies and winning independence for the Republic of Texas. The war now declared was, in part, for the boundary claimed by Texas, the Rio Grande.

Lincoln "never was much interested in the Texas question," as he wrote in October 1845, seemed only dimly aware of a variety of irresistible American forces acting by fact and dream. The fact was that Texas, New Mexico and California were passionately wanted in the domain of the United States because of the immense land and wealth foreseen in them. The dream was of "an ocean-bound republic," an America "from sea to sea." A Democratic editor saw this surge as Manifest Destiny; nothing could stop it. When Congress in March 1845 had passed resolutions to annex Texas, and a Texas convention in June was unanimous for joining the Union of States, the Mexican government warned that Texas was still a Mexican province. The Mexican Congress had voted $4,000,000 for war against Texas. President Polk ordered American troops in "protective occupation" on a strip of land in dispute at the Rio Grande. The inevitable clashes came—and the all-out war was on. Though the Americans were outnumbered four to one in nearly all actions, they had better cannon, riflemen and strategy. The battles ended September 14, 1847, when Mexico City was taken. The two outstanding generals, Winfield S. Scott and Zachary Taylor, were both Whigs. Texas, New Mexico and California came into the U.S. domain. The long and bitter dispute with Great Britain over the Oregon boundary, bringing war threats on both sides, was settled by Polk backing down from the cry of "54° 40' or fight" to 49°. So there was Manifest Destiny, "America from sea to sea"—the cost high in money and lives.

Lincoln saw more shame than glory in the political steps and procedures involved. In June 1846 he had seen Ned Baker return from Washington to raise an Illinois regiment, and start for Mexico, where he led Shields' brigade when Shields fell wounded. He had heard of Baker going to Washington the following December and ending a speech to Congress two days before he resigned his seat: "There are in the American Army many who strongly doubt the propriety of the war, and especially the manner of its commencement; who yet are ready to pour out their hearts' best blood, and their lives with it, on a foreign shore, in defense of the American flag and American glory." This, for Lincoln, was the Whig party policy and the music of the hour. He studied the passionate words of Senator Thomas Corwin, "If I were a Mexican, I would tell you, 'Have you not room in your own country to bury your dead men? If you come into mine, we will greet you with bloody hands and welcome you to hospitable graves.'"

Chicago was a four-day stage trip and Lincoln arrived in that city of 16,000 in July 1847, one of hundreds of delegates to the River and Harbor Convention, run by Whigs, and aimed to promote internal improvements and to rebuke laxity of the Polk administration. Thousands of out-of-town spectators, finding hotels and rooming houses overcrowded, slept on lake ships or camped in the streets, to be on hand in the morning in the big tent to see and hear famous men from all over the country. Here Lincoln met Tom Corwin of Ohio, Edward Bates and Thomas Hart Benton of Missouri, and Thurlow Weed, a Whig party boss in New York State. The notable New York lawyer David Dudley Field, spoke against certain internal improvements as unconstitutional; Horace Greeley wrote to his New York *Tribune* that "Hon. Abraham Lincoln, a tall specimen of an Illinoisan . . . was called out, and spoke briefly and happily." Some delegates remembered Lincoln answered Field's objection to federal improvement of the Illinois River because it ran through only one state, by asking through how many states the federally improved Hudson River ran.

Lincoln had his first look at mighty Lake Michigan, blue water moving on to meet the sky, a path for ship transport of wheat to New York and Europe. Farmers and wheat-buyers were hauling wheat to Chicago from 250 miles away; lines of 10 to 20 wagons headed for Chicago were common. Lincoln had no regrets over his long efforts for the canal to connect the Illinois River and Lake Michigan.

Lincoln's term in Congress was to start in December 1847; he went on riding the Eighth Circuit, driving a rattletrap buggy or on horseback, sometimes perhaps as he tied his horse to a hitching post, hearing a voice across the street, "That's the new Congressman Lincoln." It was a horsey country of horsey men. They spoke of one-horse towns, lawyers, doctors. They tied their horses to hitching posts half-chewed away by horse teeth. They brushed horse hair from their clothes after a drive. They carried feed bags of oats and spliced broken tugs with rope to last till they reached a harness shop.

His yearly income ranged from $1,200 to $1,500, comparing nicely with the governor's yearly $1,200 and a circuit judge's $750. By now he had probably paid the last of his personal "National Debt." An incomplete fee book of Lincoln and Herndon for 1845-47 showed fees from $3.00 to $100, most entries $10. Sometimes groceries and farm produce were accepted for fees. Lincoln was known to say he had no money sense, and never had money enough to fret him.

At Petersburg, he and Herndon, defending James Dorman, charged with manslaughter, won the case. Another client, Ammai Merill, charged with payments in counterfeit coin, got three years at hard labor in the penitentiary. Lincoln's friend, Samuel D. Marshall of Shawneetown, had taken the damage suit of Thomas Margrave against William G. Grable for the seduction of Margrave's daughter. Lincoln argued the case in Supreme Court, which affirmed the damages awarded by the lower court, and wrote Marshall his fee would be $5.00 and two years subscription to Marshall's paper, the *Illinois Republican*. In a divorce suit Lincoln penned his comment, "A pitiful story of marital discord."

"Feeling a little poetic this evening," Lincoln wrote in early 1846 to Andrew Johnston at Quincy, and he would send on "a piece of poetry of my own making," though "I find a deal of trouble to finish it." On a speaking trip that took him to Gentryville, old memories flooded in on him and he wrote "My Childhood Home I See Again," including verses about the insane son of James Gentry:

Poor Matthew! I have ne'er forgot
  When first with maddened will,
Yourself you maimed, your father fought,
  And mother strove to kill;

And terror spread, and neighbours ran,
  Your dang'rous strength to bind;
And soon a howling crazy man,
  Your limbs were fast confined.

How then you writhed and shrieked aloud,
  Your bones and sinews bared;
And fiendish on the gaping crowd,
  With burning eye-balls glared.

And begged, and swore, and wept, and prayed,
  With maniac laughter joined—
How fearful are the signs displayed,
  By pangs that kill the mind!

And when at length, tho' drear and long,
  Time soothed your fiercer woes—
How plaintively your mournful song,
  Upon the still night rose.

I've heard it oft, as if I dreamed,
  Far-distant, sweet, and lone;
The funeral dirge it ever seemed
  Of reason dead and gone.

To drink it's strains, I've stole away,
  All silently and still,
Ere yet the rising god of day
  Had streaked the Eastern hill.

But this is past and nought remains
  That raised you o'er the brute.
Your mad'ning shrieks and soothing strains
  Are like forever mute.

Now fare thee well: more thou the cause
  Than subject now of woe.
All mental pangs, but time's kind laws,
  Hast lost the power to know.

On his visit to Gentryville, Lincoln had seen Matthew Gentry, still alive, drooling, gentle, harmless, reminding Lincoln of

The very spot where grew the bread
  That formed my bones, I see.
How strange, old field, on thee to tread,
  And feel I'm part of thee!

This was not imagination: it was autobiographical confession. Later that year he sent Andrew Johnston another version of the poem, along with doggerel titled "The Bear Hunt." Published in the Quincy *Whig*, his verses did not carry Lincoln's name.

The mind of Lincoln enjoyed roving and questioning. He wrote at different times his independent thinking about the protective tariff which the Whigs favored. "In the early days of the world, the Almighty said to the first of our race 'In the sweat of thy face shalt thou eat bread'; and since then, if we except the *light* and the *air* of heaven, no good thing has been, or can be enjoyed by us, without having first cost labour. And, inasmuch [as] most good things are produced by labour, it follows that [all] such things of right belong to those whose labour has produced them. But it has so happened in all ages of the world, that *some* have laboured, and *others* have, without labour, enjoyed a large proportion of the fruits. This is wrong, and should not continue. To [secure] to each labourer the whole product of his labour, or as nearly as possible, is a most worthy object of any good government." How could a government effect this? One remedy would be to, "as far as possible, drive *useless* labour and *idleness* out of existence." For example, "Iron & every thing made of iron, can be produced, in sufficient abundance, [and] with as little labour, in the United States, as any where else in the world; therefore, all labour done in bringing iron & it's fabrics from a foreign country to the United States, is useless labour." As to cotton, "Why should it not be spun, wove &c. in the very neighbourhood where it both grows and is consumed, and the carrying thereby dispensed with?" He speculated on naked first principles: "If at any time all *labour* should cease, and all existing provisions be equally divided among the people, at the end of a single year there could scarcely be one human being left alive—all would have perished by want of subsistence . . . Universal *idleness* would speedily result in universal *ruin;* and . . . *useless labour* is, in this respect, the same as *idleness*." Therefore, reasoned Lincoln, to abandon the protective tariff "must result in the increase of both useless labour, and idleness."

In a long unsigned article in the Quincy *Whig*, April 15, 1846, Lincoln wrote of a case that had haunted him for five years. In June 1841 the three Trailor brothers, Archibald, William and Henry, had been seen with Archibald Fisher, who was known to carry considerable money on him. And Fisher had disappeared. Henry Trailor in a two-day examination denied and denied, finally confessing that his brothers had killed Fisher in woods northwest of Springfield and had brought the body back to where they had left Henry to stand watch at a buggy in a dense brush thicket. The two brothers then drove toward Hickox's millpond and returned in a half-hour saying they had put "him" in a safe place. The news spread like a prairie fire; wild talk ran of lynching. Hundreds of people seeking Fisher's body raked, fished, drained the millpond and tore down the dam to lower the water; cellars, wells, pits, were searched, fresh graves pried into, dead horses and dogs dug up, to no result.

A letter was published from the postmaster nearest William Trailor's home in Warren County, stating that William had returned home and was saying boastfully that Fisher was dead and had willed him $1,500. William and Archibald were arrested and put on trial, with Lincoln, Logan and Ned Baker in defense. Besides Henry Trailor's testimony, which cross-examination couldn't shake, a respectable lady testified to seeing William and Archibald with Fisher enter the timber northwest of town and return without Fisher. It was proved that since Fisher vanished, William and Archibald had passed an unusual number of gold pieces. Many witnesses testified to signs of a struggle in a thicket and a trail to buggy tracks that led in the direction of the millpond.

It looked as though the noose waited for the two defendants till a star witness arrived, Dr. Robert Gilmore from Warren County, who swore that Fisher was not only alive, but living in Gilmore's home, and only because of Fisher's low physical condition the doctor had not brought Fisher with him. "Gilmore also stated," wrote Lincoln, "that he had known Fisher for several years, and that he had understood he was subject to temporary derangement of mind, owing to an injury about his head received in early life. There was about Dr. Gilmore so much of the air and manner of truth, that his statement prevailed in the minds of the audience and of the court, and the Trailors were discharged; although they attempted no explanation of the circumstances proven by the other witnesses. On the next Monday, Myers [an officer] arrived in Springfield, bringing with him the now famed Fisher, in full life and proper person . . . it may well be doubted, whether a stranger affair ever really occurred. Much of the matter remains in mystery to this day. The going into the woods with Fisher, and returning without him, by the Trailors; their going into the woods at the same place the next day, after they professed to have given up the search, the signs of a struggle in the thicket, the buggy tracks at the edge of it; and the location of the thicket and the signs about it, corresponding precisely with Henry's story, are circumstances that have never been explained. William and Archibald have both died since—William in less than a year, and Archibald in about two years after the supposed murder. Henry is still living but never speaks of the subject."

Thus wrote Lincoln five years after the trial. In the week of the trial he wrote Speed an exciting, quizzical, 2,000-word account, ending, "Hart, the little drayman that hauled Molly [Mary Todd] home once, said it was too *damned* bad, to have so much trouble, and no hanging after all." Archibald Trailor, a 30-year-old carpenter, had always borne so good a name in Springfield that a few days after the trial a big public meeting passed resolutions of regret that he should ever have been accused of a crime. Also five years after the trial, a court awarded Logan and Lincoln $100 defense fees but the sheriff of Warren County reported he could find no property in the hands of James Smith, executor of the estate of William Trailor.

A few weeks before Lincoln's start to Washington he took the case of Robert Matson at Charleston. Matson, a young bachelor of a respectable Kentucky family, worked his large farm with slaves brought from Kentucky for the spring planting and sent back to Kentucky after the fall harvest, thus keeping within the Illinois law that no Negro or mulatto could stay in the state year after year "without a lawful certificate of freedom." But one slave

Matson had kept year after year as foreman and overseer, Anthony Bryant, who could read his Bible and preach Methodist sermons. Among slaves brought to the farm in the summer of 1845 was Bryant's wife, Jane, a shining mulatto said to be the daughter of a brother of Matson. Of her six children, three were plainly of mingled Negro and white blood, one girl having blue eyes and long red hair.

Matson's housekeeper, Mary Corbin, in jealous anger one day shrieked to Jane Bryant, "You're going back to Kentucky and you're going to be sold way down South in the cotton field." The terrorized Anthony Bryant rode at midnight two miles on horseback with his wife and one child, his other children afoot, to the inn of the antislavery Gideon M. Ashmore. A young doctor from Pennsylvania, Hiram Rutherford, sent word to other antislavery men to be ready for any chase and search by Matson. By a justice of peace action Matson got Jane Bryant and her children locked up in the county jail for 58 days. Next Matson was arrested and convicted of living unlawfully with Mary Corbin, a woman not his wife.

The main action came when Matson went into circuit court, calling for damages from Rutherford of $2,500 at slave property valuations. Rutherford found Lincoln tilted in a chair on the tavern veranda, having finished one story and about to start another, and they went to one side for a talk.

As Rutherford told his troubles, he noticed Lincoln growing sober, sad, looking far off, shaking his head in a sorry way. "At length, and with apparent reluctance, Lincoln answered that he could not defend me, because he had already been counselled with in Matson's interest," said Rutherford later. "This irritated me into expressions more or less bitter. He seemed to feel this, and endeavored in his plausible way to reconcile me to the proposition that, as a lawyer, he must represent and be faithful to those who counsel with and employ him. Although thoroughly in earnest I presume I was a little hasty. The interview and my quick temper made a deep impression on Mr. Lincoln, I am sure, because he dispatched a messenger to me followed by another message, that he could now easily and consistently free himself from Matson and was, therefore, in a position if I employed him to conduct my defense. But it was too late; my pride was up. Instead, I employed Charles H. Constable."

Before Judges Wilson and Treat, of the Supreme Court of the state, Lincoln and Usher F. Linder, as Matson's lawyers, seemed to expect to win by showing that Matson had no plans for permanently locating slaves in Illinois. And yet, Lincoln's statements sounded like a searching inquiry into the facts and elemental justice of the case, rather than an argument for a plaintiff. A Coles County lawyer, D. F. McIntyre, saw Lincoln as clumsy at favoring his client. He made no attempt to batter down the points of the opposition, and practically gave his case away by outright admission that if the Kentucky slaveowner had brought his slaves to Illinois for the purpose of working them and using them as slaves on the Coles County farm, the Negroes were thereby entitled to freedom. McIntyre noted that Lincoln said the whole case turned on one point. "Were these negroes passing over and crossing the State, and thus, as the law contemplates, *in transitu*, or were they actually located by consent of their master? If only crossing the State, that act did not free them, but if located, even indefinitely, by the consent of their owner and master, their emancipation logically followed." McIntyre noted further: "When Mr. Lincoln arose to make the closing argument, all eyes were fixed upon him to hear what reasons he could or would assign, in behalf of this slave holder, to induce the court to send this mother and her children back into lives of slavery. But strange to say Lincoln did not once touch upon the question of the right of Matson to take the negroes back to Kentucky. His main contention was that the question of the right of the negroes to their freedom could only be determined by a regular habeas corpus proceeding."

Judge Wilson leaned forward and asked: "Mr. Lincoln, your objection is simply to the form of the action by which, or in which this question should be tried, is it not?" "Yes, sir." Then came the high point of the day for Lincoln. Judge Wilson asked: "Now, if this case was being tried on issue joined in a habeas corpus, and it appeared there, as it does here, that this slave owner had brought this mother and her children, voluntarily, from the State of Kentucky, and had settled them down on his farm in this State, do you think, as a matter of law, that they did not thereby become free?" And Lincoln answered, "No, sir, I am not prepared to deny that they did."

Linder then argued, for Matson, that the Federal Constitution protected slaves as chattel property which could not lawfully be taken from Matson. But the court decree October 16, 1847, declared Jane Bryant and her children "are discharged from the custody as well of the Sheriff as of Robert Matson and all persons claiming them as slaves, and they shall be and remain free from all servitude whatever to any person or persons from henceforward and forever."

Matson that night slipped away, quit the county, and paid Lincoln no fee, Lincoln rather sure he had earned no fee. Rutherford saw Lincoln on leaving for Springfield and, "He gave no sign of regret because, as a lawyer, he had upheld the cause of the strong against the weak," Rutherford forgetting his own proud words when Lincoln twice went the limit trying to break into the case on the side he preferred.

Lincoln had begun wearing broadcloth, white shirts with white collar and black silk cravat, sideburns down three-fourths the length of his ears. Yet he was still known as carelessly groomed, his trousers mentioned as creeping to the ankles and higher, his hair rumpled, vest wrinkled, and at the end of a story putting his arms around his knees, raising his knees to his chin and rocking to and fro. Standing he loomed six feet four inches; seated he looked no taller than average, except for his knees rising above the chair's seat level.

When at home in Springfield, he cut wood, tended to the house stoves, curried his horse, milked the cow. Lincoln's words might have a wilderness air and log-cabin smack, the word "idea" more like "idee," and "really" a drawled Kentucky "ra-a-ly." He sang hardly at all but his voice had clear and appealing modulations in his speeches; in rare moments it rose to a startling and unforgettable high treble giving every syllable unmistakable meaning. In stoop of shoulders and a forward bend of his head there was a grace and familiarity making it easy for shorter people to look up into his face and talk with him.

In a criminal case Lincoln agreed with Usher F. Linder that each should make the longest speech he could, talking till he was used up. And, as Linder told it, Lincoln "ran out of wind" at the end of an hour, while he, Linder, rambled on three hours to the jury.

When Martin Van Buren stopped overnight in Rochester, friends took along Lincoln to entertain the former President. Van Buren said of the evening that his sides were sore from laughing. Lincoln might have told of the man selling a horse he guaranteed "sound of skin and skeleton and free from faults and faculties." Or the judge who, trying to be kindly, asked a convicted murderer, politically allied to him, "When would you like to be hung?" Or the lawyer jabbing at a hostile witness who had one large ear: "If he bit off the other ear he would look more like a man than a jackass." Or of the old man with whiskers so long it was said of him when he traveled, "His whiskers arrive a day in advance." Or of Abram Bale, the tall and powerful-voiced preacher from Kentucky, who, baptizing new converts in the Sangamon River, was leading a sister into the water, when her husband, watching from the bank, cried out: "Hold on, Bale! Hold on, Bale! Don't you drown her. I wouldn't take the best cow and calf in Menard County for her."

Once in a courthouse, Lincoln rattled off a lingo changing letters of words so that "cotton patch" became "potten catch" and "jackass" became "jassack," giving tricky twists to barnyard and tavern words. The court clerk asked Lincoln to write it out and took special care for years of the paper on which Lincoln scribbled verbal nonsense. The *Illinois State Register* termed him a "long-legged varmint" and "our jester and mountebank." A client seeing Lincoln with one leg on the office desk, said, "That's the longest leg I've ever seen in this country." Lincoln lifted the other leg to the desk, and, "Here's another one just like it." Or so it was told.

In the small clique of Springfield Whigs who had come to wield party controls, the opposition dubbed Lincoln the "Goliath of the Junto." On streets, in crowds or gatherings, Lincoln's tall frame stood out. He was noticed, pointed out, questions asked about him. He couldn't slide into any group of standing people without all eyes finding he was there. His head surmounting a group was gaunt and strange, onlookers remembering the high cheekbones, deep eye sockets, the coarse black hair bushy and tangled, the nose large and well shaped, the wide full-lipped mouth of many subtle changes from straight face to wide beaming smile. He was loose-jointed and comic with appeals in street-corner slang and dialect from the public square hitching posts; yet at moments he was as strange and far-off as the last dark sands of a red sunset, solemn as naked facts of death and hunger. He was a seeker. Among others and deep in his own inner self, he was a seeker.

Leasing his Springfield house for a yearly rental of $90, "the North-upstairs room" reserved for furniture storage, Lincoln on October 25, 1847, with wife, four-year-old Robert and 19-month-old Eddie, took stage for St. Louis, and after a week of steamboat and rail travel, arrived in Lexington, Kentucky. There relatives and friends could see Mary Todd Lincoln and her Congressman husband she took pride in showing. They stayed three weeks. Lincoln saw the cotton mills of Oldham, Todd & Company, worked by slave labor, driving out with his brother-in-law, Levi Todd, assistant manager.

He got the feel of a steadily growing antislavery movement in Kentucky. He saw slaves auctioned, saw them chained in gangs heading south to cotton fields, heard ominous news like that of "Cassily," a slave girl, under indictment for "mixing an ounce of pounded glass with gravy" and giving it to her master, John Hamilton, and his wife Martha. He had heard of the auction sale in Lexington of Eliza, a beautiful girl with dark lustrous eyes, straight black hair, rich olive complexion, only one sixty-fourth African, white yet a slave. A young Methodist minister, Calvin Fairbank, bid higher and higher against a thick-necked Frenchman from New Orleans. Reaching $1,200, the Frenchman asked, "How high are you going?" and Fairbank, "Higher than you, Monsieur." The bids rose to where Fairbank said slowly, "One thousand, four hundred and fifty dollars." Seeing the Frenchman hesitating, the sweating auctioneer pulled Eliza's dress back from her shoulders, showing her neck and breasts, and cried, "Who is going to lose a chance like this?" To the Frenchman's bid of $1,465, the minister bid $1,475. Hearing no more bids, the auctioneer shocked the crowd by "lifting her skirts" to "bare her body from feet to waist," and slapping her thigh as he called, "Who is going to be the winner of this prize?" Over the mutter and tumult of the crowd came the Frenchman's slow bid of "One thousand, five hundred and eighty dollars." The auctioneer lifted his gavel, called "one-two-three." Eliza turned a pained and piteous face toward Fairbank, who now bid "One thousand, five hundred and eighty-five." The auctioneer: "I'm going to sell this girl. Are you going to bid?" The Frenchman shook his head. Eliza fell in a faint. The auctioneer to Fairbank: "You've got her damned cheap, sir. What are you going to do with her?" And Fairbank cried, "Free her!" Most of the crowd shouted and yelled in glee. Fairbank was there by arrangement with Salmon P. Chase and Nicholas Longworth of Cincinnati, who had authorized him to bid as high as $25,000. Fairbank had since gone to the penitentiary for other antislavery activity and in his life was to serve 17 years behind bars.

Lincoln saw in the Todd and other homes the Negro house servants, their need to be clean, their handling of food and linen, the chasm between them and Negro field hands who lived in "quarters." He read books in the big library of Robert Todd, went to many parties and in the capital city of Kentucky met leading figures of the state and nation. He heard Henry Clay on November 13 before an immense audience: "Autumn has come, and the season of flowers has passed away . . . I too am in the autumn of life, and feel the frost of age," terming the Mexican War one of "unnecessary and offensive aggression," holding, "It is Mexico that is defending her firesides, her castles and her altars, not we." For the United States to take over Mexico and govern it, as some were urging, Clay saw as impossible, and there would be danger in acquiring a new area into which slavery could move.

CHAPTER 7

Congressman Lincoln

BY STAGE and rail the Lincoln family traveled seven days to arrive in Washington December 2, staying at Brown's Hotel, then moving to Mrs. Sprigg's boardinghouse on ground where later the Library of Congress was built. They saw a planned city with wide intersecting streets, squares, parks, a few noble buildings on spacious lawns, yet nearly everywhere a look of the unfinished, particularly the Capitol with its dark wooden dome, its two wings yet to be built. Cobblestoned Pennsylvania Avenue ran wide from the Capitol to the White House yet a heavy rain on Polk's inauguration day brought mudholes where parading soldiers slipped and sprawled.

Here lived 40,000 people, among them 8,000 free Negroes and 2,000 slaves. Here were mansions and slums; cowsheds, hog pens and privies in back yards; hogs, geese and chickens roving streets and alleys. Sidewalks were mostly of gravel or ashes. Thirty-seven churches of varied faiths competed with outnumbering saloons, card and dice joints, houses where women and girls aimed to please male customers. Ragged slaves drove produce wagons; gangs of slaves sold or to be sold at times moved in chains along streets. Lincoln saw a jail near the Capitol which he was to term "a sort of negro livery-stable," where Negroes were kept to be taken south "precisely like a drove of horses." Yet here too were libraries, museums, fountains, gardens, halls and offices where historic and momentous decisions were made, ceremonials, receptions, balls, occasions of state and grandeur, and all the dialects of America from Louisiana to Maine, the Southern drawl, the Yankee nasal twang, the differing western slang.

Lincoln liked Mrs. Sprigg's place, the lodgings and meals, the Whig antislavery members of Congress who ate there, especially the abolitionist war horse from Ohio, Joshua R. Giddings. When Lincoln couldn't referee a table dispute, he could usually break it up with an odd story that had point. But Mrs. Lincoln couldn't find company, attractions, women, social events of interest to her, and with her husband one of the busiest men in Congress, missing only seven roll calls in the long session that was opening, after three months of it she traveled with the two boys to her father's home in Lexington.

In the Hall of Representatives, after the oath of office, Lincoln drew a seat in the back row of the Whig side. Many faces and names in the House and over in the Senate became part of him, part of his life then and in years after. George Ashmun, John G. Palfrey and Robert Winthrop of Massachusetts, John Minor Botts of Virginia, Howell Cobb and Alexander Stephens of Georgia, Andrew Johnson of Tennessee, Robert C. Schenck of Ohio, Caleb B. Smith of Indiana, Jacob Thompson of Mississippi, David Wilmot of Pennsylvania—Lincoln could have no dim forevision of the events and tumults where those men would be joined or tangled with him.

He could see at one desk a little man with delicate sideburns, a mouth both sweet and severe. Eighty years old, this man had been professor of rhetoric at Harvard, U.S. Senator from Massachusetts, President of the United States from 1825 to 1829, after which he was in Congress for 17 years. In the foreign service in Paris he had seen Napoleon return from Elba. This was John Quincy Adams, one of the foremost and fiery Whigs to cry that the war with Mexico was instigated by slaveholders for the extension of slave territory. Over in the Senate Lincoln could see the Illinois wonder boy who had had two terms in the House, had been elected to a third, but resigned before taking his seat to start his first term in the upper chamber. Stephen A. Douglas quoted Frederick the Great, "Take possession first and negotiate afterward," and declared, "That is precisely what President Polk has done."

American armies in Mexico were clinching their hold on that country, which had cost the Government $27,000,000 and the people the lives of 27,000 soldiers. With Mexico beaten, questions rose: "What shall we force Mexico to pay us? Since she has no money, how much of her land shall we take? Or shall we take over all of Mexico?"

Lincoln on December 22 introduced resolutions respectfully requesting the President to inform the House as to the exact "spot of soil" where first "the blood of our *citizens* was so shed." He directly implied that the President had ordered American troops into land not established as American soil. The President, Lincoln said later, was attempting "to prove, by telling the *truth*, what he could not prove by telling the *whole truth*."

In the House January 12, 1848, Lincoln defended the vote of his party a few days before in declaring "that the war with Mexico was unnecessarily and unconstitutionally commenced by the President." He spoke of the course he and others followed. "When the war began, it was my opinion that all those who, because of knowing too *little*, or because of knowing too *much*, could not conscientiously approve the conduct of the President, in the beginning of it, should, nevertheless, as good citizens and patriots, remain silent on that point, at least till the war should be ended."

Since Mexico by revolution had overthrown the government of Spain, and Texas by revolution had thrown off the government of Mexico, Lincoln discussed the rights of peoples to revolutionize. "Any people anywhere, being inclined and having the power, have the *right* to rise up, and shake off the existing government, and form a new one that suits them better . . . Any portion of such people that *can*, *may* revolutionize, and make their *own*, of so much of the territory as they inhabit. More than this, a *majority* of any portion of such people may revolutionize, putting down a *minority*, intermingled with, or near about them, who may oppose their movement. Such minority, was precisely the case, of the tories of our own revolution. It is a quality of revolutions not to go by *old* lines, or *old* laws; but to break up both, and make new ones."

The President's justifications of himself reminded Lincoln that "I have sometimes seen a good lawyer, struggling for his client's neck, in a desparate case, employing every artifice to work round, befog, and cover up, with many words, some point arising in the case, which he *dared* not admit, and yet *could* not deny." He rehearsed the intricate Whig arguments that American troops invaded Mexican soil, and, "I more than suspect," as to the President, "that he is deeply conscious of being in the wrong,—that he feels the blood of this war, like the blood of Abel, is crying to Heaven against him . . . His mind, tasked beyond it's power, is running hither and thither, like some tortured creature, on a burning surface, finding no position, on which it can settle down, and be at peace . . . He knows not where he is. He is a bewildered, confounded, and miserably perplexed man. God grant he may be able to show, there is not something about his conscience, more painful than all his mental perplexity!"

It was a fiercely partisan speech, in a style Lincoln would in time abandon. He knew little or nothing of the pressure on Polk and misread Polk. For months the President hesitated; he *was* a miserably perplexed man. Of Robert Walker, his Secretary of the Treasury, the President noted in his diary, "He was for taking all of Mexico"; of Buchanan, his Secretary of State, the notation was similar. Finally, he wrote in his diary, after endless advice to seize the whole territory of the Mexican nation: "I replied that I was not prepared to go to that extent, and furthermore, that I did not desire that anything I said should be so obscure as to give rise to doubt or discussion as to what my true meaning was; that I had in my last message declared that I did not contemplate the conquest of Mexico."

Lincoln voted for all supplies and aid to soldiers in the field, and for every measure laying blame on Polk and the administration. He hoped the folks back home would understand his conduct. But many of the folks back home couldn't see it, not even Bill Herndon. The Belleville *Advocate* of March 2 reported a meeting in Clark County of "patriotic Whigs and Democrats" which resolved "That Abe Lincoln, the author of the 'Spotty' resolutions in Congress against his own country, may they be long remembered by his constituents, but may they cease to remember him, except to rebuke him." The *Illinois State Register* told of newspapers and public meetings that declared Lincoln to be "a second Benedict Arnold." The *Register* favored taking over all of Mexico and making it part of the United States.

In an emotion-drenched speech February 2, Alexander Stephens voiced the depths of Whig scorn of the President, in somewhat the vein of parts of Lincoln's speech some three weeks earlier. "The principle of waging war against a neighboring people to compel them to sell their country, is not only dishonorable, but disgraceful and infamous. What! shall it be said that American honor aims at nothing higher than land? . . . Never did I expect to see the day when the Executive of this country should announce that our honor was such a loathsome, beastly thing, that it could not be satisfied with any achievements in arms, however brilliant and glorious, but must feed on earth—gross, vile dirt!—and require even a prostrate foe to be robbed of mountain rocks and desert plains!"

Lincoln wrote to Herndon: "I just take up my pen to say, that Mr. Stephens of Georgia, a little slim, pale-faced, consumptive man, with a voice like Logan's, has just concluded the very best speech, of an hour's length, I ever heard. My old, withered, dry eyes, are full of tears yet. If he writes it out any thing like he delivered it, our people shall see a good many copies of it."

A new Senator from Mississippi, who at Buena Vista had stayed in his saddle with a bleeding foot till the battle was won, a cotton planter, Jefferson Davis, was saying Mexico was held by "title of conquest," that Yucatan should be annexed or England would take it, and if the American advance to the Isthmus was resisted, he favored war with Britain. His bill for ten regiments to garrison Mexico passed the Senate by 29 to 19 but was pigeonholed in the House, where Whigs controlled. The need of the South for new areas into which slavery could spread, and by which the South would have political representation to match that of the growing North, had brought splits and factions in both parties north and south.

Senator John C. Calhoun of South Carolina believed, "People do not understand liberty or majorities. The will of the majority is the will of a rabble. Progressive democracy is incompatible with liberty." His mantle of leadership seemed to be falling on Jefferson Davis who in this year of 1848 told the Senate that if folly, fanaticism, hate and corruption were to destroy the peace and prosperity of the Union, then "let the sections part . . . and let peace and good will subsist." With this readiness to break up the Union, the Southern Whigs, Toombs, Stephens, and above all Henry Clay, could not agree. In the North the Democrats were losing unity in several states on the issue of whether slavery should be extended into the new vast territories acquired and being settled. Among New York Democrats had come the "Hunkers," who were said to hanker after office on any principle, and the "Barnburners," so named after the Dutchman who burned down his barn to get rid of the rats. Also in New York were the elder Silver-Gray Whigs and the Radicals.

Over the country those having ears had heard of the Wilmot Proviso cutting across party lines, setting Southern Whigs against Northern, Southern Democrats angry with the Northern. Thirty-four-year-old David Wilmot of Pennsylvania, a Jacksonian Democrat who had fought for the rights of labor and against imprisonment for debt, had in 1846 offered a rider to the appropriations bill, a proviso that slavery would be shut out from all lands acquired by the Mexican War. Since then, over and over, this proviso had been moved as an amendment to this and that bill before Congress. Lincoln voted for the proviso, so he wrote, "at least" 40 times, he was sure. This hammering away at no further spread of slavery brought movements, outcries of injustice and interference, and threats of secession from Southern leaders.

Incidents constantly arose as one in February 1848 at Mrs. Sprigg's boardinghouse. The Negro servant in the house had been buying his freedom at a price of $300; he had paid all but $60 when, one day, two white men came to the house, knocked him down, tied and gagged him, took him to a slave jail, and had him sent to New Orleans for sale. Joshua Giddings asked for a hearing by the House and was voted down by 98 to 88.

One February morning John Quincy Adams stood up to speak, suddenly clutched his desk with groping fingers, then slumped to his chair, was carried out to linger and die, saying, "This is the last of earth, but I am content." In a final hour Henry Clay in tears had held the old man's hand. Lincoln served with a committee on arrangements; there was a funeral of state, many saying Mr. Adams could have no fear of the Recording Angel.

In the House post office was a storyteller's corner and fellowship. Stephens of Georgia could say, "I was as intimate with Mr. Lincoln as with any other man except perhaps Mr. Toombs." Lincoln could tell of Stuart and Douglas campaigning; arriving late one night at a tavern, the landlord showed them two beds, each with a man sleeping in it. Douglas asked their politics and the landlord pointed to one a Whig and the other a Democrat, Douglas saying, "Stuart, you sleep with the Whig and I'll sleep with the Democrat." Or the Kentucky justice of the peace, tired of two lawyers wrangling after his decision, speaking out: "If the court is right—and she think she air—why, then you air wrong, and she knows you is—shet up!"

Lincoln wrote to Herndon that "by way of getting the hang of the House," he had spoken on a post office question, and, "I was about as badly scared, and no worse, as I am when I speak in court." His House record showed him working hard and faithfully on petitions, appointments, pensions, documents for constituents, routine measures such as internal improvements, public roads, canals, rivers and harbors. He found the wrangling and quibbling much the same as in the Illinois Legislature. Once he counseled that to pay for canals with canal tolls and tonnage duties, before the canals were dug, was like the Irishman and his new boots: "I shall niver git 'em on till I wear 'em a day or two, and stretch 'em a little."

One evening at the library of the Supreme Court, after digging in many books and documents, Lincoln drew out volumes to read in his room at Mrs. Sprigg's. The library was going to close for the night, so he tied a large bandanna around the books, ran a stick through the knots, slung the stick over his shoulder, and walked out of the library. Wearing a short circular blue cloak he had bought since coming to Washington, he walked to his Capitol Hill lodging, where he read in his books, then took a brass key from his vest pocket and wound his watch, put his boot heels into a bootjack and pulled off his boots, blew out the candlelights and crept into a warm yellow flannel nightshirt that came down halfway between his knees and ankles.

In April he had written his wife, "Dear Mary: In this troublesome world, we are never quite satisfied. When you were here, I thought you hindered me some in attending to business; but now, having nothing but business—no variety—it has grown exceedingly tasteless to me. I hate to sit down and direct documents, and I hate to stay in this old room by myself." He wrote of shopping, as she wished, for "the little plaid stockings" to fit "Eddy's dear little feet," and "I wish you to enjoy yourself in every possible way . . . Very soon after you went away, I got what I think a very pretty set of shirt-bosom studs—modest little ones, jet, set in gold, only costing 50 cents a piece, or 1.50 for the whole. Suppose you do not prefix the 'Hon' to the address on your letters to me any more . . . and you are entirely free from head-ache? That is good—good—considering it is the first spring you have been free from it since we were acquainted. I am afraid you will get so well, and fat, and young, as to be wanting to marry again . . . I did not get rid of the impression of that foolish dream about dear Bobby till I got your letter written the same day. What did he and Eddy think of the little letters father sent them? Dont let the blessed fellows forget father." Their children were a common and warm bond.

In June he wrote to her at Lexington, "The leading matter in your letter, is your wish to return to this side of the Mountains. Will you be a *good girl* in all things, if I consent? Then come along, and that as *soon* as possible. Having got the idea in my head, I shall be impatient till I see you . . . Come on just as soon as you can. I want to see you, and our dear—*dear* boys very much. Every body here wants to see our dear Bobby." Her letter to him had said, "How much, I wish instead of writing, we were together this evening. I feel very sad away from you." But campaign duties pressed him and her visit to Washington couldn't be managed.

He wrote to her July 2 a long newsy letter ending, "By the way, you do not intend to do without a girl, because the one you had has left you? Get another as soon as you can to take charge of the dear codgers. Father expected to see you all sooner; but let it pass; stay as long as you please, and come when you please. Kiss and love the dear rascals." He signed his letters to her "Affectionately A. Lincoln," and hers to him were signed "Truly yours M.L."

It seemed byplay and banter in his ending a July letter to Herndon, "As to kissing a pretty girl, [I] know one very pretty one, but I guess she wont let me kiss her."

In a dignified speech June 20 Lincoln questioned intentions to amend the Constitution indicated in the Democratic platform. He advised, "No slight occasion should tempt us to touch it. Better not take the first step, which may lead to a habit of altering it . . . New provisions, would introduce new difficulties, and thus create, and increase appetite for still further change. No sir, let it stand as it is." On July 27 he told the House that "on the prominent questions . . . Gen: Taylor's course is at least as well defined as is Gen: Cass'" (the Democratic nominee), adding later, "I hope and *believe*, Gen: Taylor, if elected, would not veto the [Wilmot] Proviso. *But* I do not *know* it. Yet, if I knew he would, I still would vote for him. I should do so, because, in my judgment, his election alone, can defeat Gen: Cass; and because, *should* slavery thereby go to the territory we now have, just so much will certainly happen by the election of Cass."

After this candid presentation he swung into the comic vein of a stump speech before a rough-and-tumble crowd. He pointed to General Cass during nine years drawing ten rations a day from the Government at $730 a year. "At eating too, his capacities are shown to be quite as wonderful. From October 1821 to May 1822 he ate ten rations a day in Michigan, ten rations a day here in Washington, and near five dollars worth a day on the road between the two places! And then there is an important discovery in his example—the art of being paid for what one eats, instead of having to pay for it . . . Mr. Speaker, we have all heard of the animal standing in doubt between two stacks of hay, and starving to death. The like of that would never happen to Gen: Cass; place the stacks a thousand miles apart, he would stand stock still midway between them, and eat them both at once, and the green grass along the line would be apt to suffer some too at the same time . . . I have heard some things from New-York; and if they are true, one might well say of your party there, as a drunken fellow once said when he heard the reading of an indictment for hog-stealing. The clerk read on till he got to, and through the words 'did steal, take, and carry away, ten boars, ten sows, ten shoats, and ten pigs' at which he exclaimed 'Well, by golly, that is the most equally divided gang of hogs, I ever did hear of.' If there is any *other* gang of hogs more equally divided than the democrats of New-York are about this time, I have not heard of it." The Baltimore *American* said the speaker kept the House roaring.

Distinct, irrevocable events of 1848 were throwing shadows pointing to events lurking in farther shadows dark beyond reading. In February the Mexican War ended with a treaty; New Mexico and Upper California were ceded to the United States; the lower Rio Grande from its mouth to El Paso became the boundary of Texas; for territory acquired the United States was to pay Mexico $15,000,000. Calhoun, Davis, Rhett and others of the South were openly trying to organize secession of the Southern States from the Union. In the North was explosive force in the Free-Soil party which nominated the former Democratic President Martin Van Buren for President and Charles Francis Adams, son of John Quincy Adams, for Vice-President. Their platform called for "the rights of free labor against the aggressions of the slave power," cheap postage, "free grants" of land to actual settlers, with the slogan "Free Soil, Free Speech, Free Labor, and Free Men." Names that counted were in the new party, Salmon P. Chase of Ohio, Charles Sumner of Massachusetts, William Cullen Bryant, Longfellow, Lowell, Whittier, David Wilmot and others. Antislavery Whigs and Democrats were pouring into the new party in some states saying here was a cause to fight for, whereas the Whig and Democratic party platforms straddled, weasled and stood for nothing on any issue of the hour.

The great Whig hero, Daniel Webster, had a certain majesty but "lacked popular appeal." The other idolized veteran Whig hero, Henry Clay, had run three times and lost. And Lincoln, with Stephens and others, in a clique calling themselves "The Young Indians," served in the forefront of those who saw Zachary Taylor as the one candidate to win in the coming campaign. True enough, Taylor was owner on his Louisiana plantation of more than a hundred slaves, was naïve and somewhat ignorant of politics; he had never voted for President but said that had he voted for President in 1844 it would have been for Clay; he saw the Wilmot Proviso as "a mere bugbare" of agitators and it would disappear; he cautioned, "I am not an ultra Whig." But the name of "Old Zach" at 64 carried magic; he was honest, rugged, plain; against terrific odds his armies, by his keen strategy and dogged courage, had won for him the beloved nickname of "Old Rough and Ready." He had spoken of the war as uncalled-for and had moved his troops into action only under direct orders which he obeyed as a trained and loyal soldier.

In the Philadelphia convention in June the first ballot gave Taylor 111, Henry Clay 97, General Winfield Scott 43, Daniel Webster 22. As a delegate, Lincoln voted for Taylor on all ballots, cheered the nomination of Taylor on the fourth, and wrote to Illinois that Taylor's nomination took the Democrats "on the blind side" and "It turns the war thunder against them. The war is now to them, the gallows of Haman, which they built for us, and on which they are doomed to be hanged themselves." He could see a variety of factions, "all the odds and ends are with us"; all was high hope and confidence.

A letter of Herndon June 15 was "heart-sickening," "discouraging," Lincoln wrote, advising his young partner, "You must not wait to be brought forward by the older men. For instance do you suppose that I should ever have got into notice if I had waited to be hunted up and pushed forward by older men. You young men get together and form a Rough & Ready club . . . as you go along, gather up all the shrewd wild boys about town, whether just of age, or a little under age." Herndon had asked him to send along all speeches made about Taylor and Lincoln wrote that he had sent on the *Congressional Globe* containing "every speech made by every man" in both Houses, and, "Can I send any more? Can I send speeches that nobody has made?" Another Herndon letter questioned the motives of "the old men," and Lincoln wrote, "I suppose I am now one of the old men . . . I was young once, and I am sure I was never ungenerously thrust back . . . Allow me to assure you, that suspicion and jealousy never did help any man in any situation . . . You have been a laborious, studious young man" and he shouldn't allow his mind "to be improperly directed."

Because of the Whig party's "turn about is fair play" policy, Lincoln was not running for re-election to Congress. When news came to him of the August 7 election in Illinois, Stephen T. Logan, running for Lincoln's seat, had lost by 106 votes to a Mexican War veteran. Lincoln at headquarters of the national Whig committee was busy franking documents, helping edit a Whig paper *The Battery*, getting out campaign literature, writing political letters. He was assigned to speak in New England where the Free-Soilers had a threatening strength. By "steam cars" to New York and probably boat to Norwich he made the three-day trip that had him September 12 in Worcester, Massachusetts, where he declared that Taylor was "just the man to whom the interests, principles and prosperity of the country might be safely intrusted." The Free-Soil platform in general was like the pantaloons the Yankee peddler offered for sale, "large enough for any man, small enough for any boy." He spoke in New Bedford, Boston, Chelsea, Cambridge, and in a day speech at Dedham, a young Whig took note, "He wore a black alpaca sack coat, turned up the sleeves of this, and then the cuffs of his shirt. Next he loosened his necktie and soon after took it off altogether. He soon had his audience as by a spell. I never saw men more delighted. His style was the most familiar and offhand possible."

At Taunton a reporter wrote, "His awkward gesticulations, the ludicrous management of his voice and the comical expression of his countenance, all conspired to make his hearers laugh at the mere anticipation of the joke before it appeared." He quoted a sarcastic Free-Soiler, "General Taylor is a slaveholder, therefore we go for him to prevent the extension of slavery," and said the correct form of the syllogism should be: "General Taylor is a slaveholder, but he will do more to prevent the extension of slavery than any other man whom it is possible to elect, therefore we go for Taylor." At Tremont Temple in Boston he spoke after Governor William H. Seward of New York who was soon to be elected U.S. Senator. At their hotel Lincoln told Seward he had been thinking about Seward's speech, and, "I reckon you are right. We have got to deal with this slavery question, and got to give much more attention to it hereafter."

Traveling west Lincoln at Albany talked with Thurlow Weed and together they visited Millard Fillmore, Whig candidate for Vice-President. Next Lincoln saw Niagara Falls. He left Buffalo September 26 on the steamer *Globe* for a 1,047-mile cruise that had him in Chicago October 5. He wrote deep meditations on Niagara Falls, its "wonder" and "great charm," and how, "When Columbus first sought this continent—when Christ suffered on the cross—when Moses led Israel through the Red-Sea—nay, even, when Adam first came from the hand of his Maker—then as now, Niagara was roaring here . . . The Mammoth and Mastodon—now so long dead, that fragments of their monstrous bones, alone testify, that they ever lived, have gazed on Niagara." Lincoln's sense of history and the past, for all his incessant newspaper reading, came from books that became part of his mind.

In Chicago he spoke for the Whig ticket two hours to a crowd so large it had to adjourn from the courthouse to the public square. With Mrs. Lincoln and the children he traveled to Springfield. Of his two-hour speech in a Peoria stopover, the *Democratic Press* said, "Mr. Lincoln blew his nose, bobbed his head, threw up his coat tail, and delivered an immense amount of sound and fury." Before Election Day he spoke in eight or ten Illinois towns for the Whig ticket, always advising that a vote for the Free-Soil ticket might turn out to be a vote for Cass. As to the United States reaching out for more territory, he quoted the farmer about land, "I ain't greedy; I only want what jines mine."

Election returns (exclusive of South Carolina, where the legislature chose electors) gave a popular vote for Taylor 1,360,752; Cass 1,219,962; Van Buren 291,342. Ohio elected six Free-Soilers to Congress, other states six more, which forebode the slavery issue would blaze on. Cass had carried Illinois but there was comfort that Ned Baker, who had moved to Galena, was elected to Congress. Lincoln had written of him, "He is a good hand to raise a breeze." It counted a little, too, that his congressional district had given a whopping majority of more than 1,500 for Taylor. And the new legislature elected a new U.S. Senator, James Shields, a Democrat, with whom Lincoln had more than a slight acquaintance.

In a corner of his Springfield office Lincoln whittled and shaped a wooden model of a steamboat with "adjustable buoyant air chambers," "sliding spars," ropes and pulleys. On the Detroit River he had seen a steamboat stuck on a sand bar; barrels, boxes and empty casks forced under the vessel lifted it off. Lincoln finished a model, wrote a description of its workings, and the next year had it patented.

In late November 1848 Lincoln left Springfield for St. Louis and by steamboat up the Ohio River and then by rail reached Washington and took his seat in the House December 7, three days after the Thirtieth Congress had convened. While traveling, he wrote that he took "very extra care" of a letter containing money. "To make it more secure than it would be in my hat, where I carry most all my packages, I put it in my trunk."

He spoke briefly and moderately for river and harbor improvements by Federal aid and a more liberal policy in public lands for settlers, voting regularly for measures aimed at free governments in California and New Mexico, voting again for the Wilmot Proviso whenever it came up. He voted often against sweeping, straight-out abolitionist measures to prohibit slavery immediately and without reservations in the District of Columbia.

He loved his fellow boarder Joshua Giddings, a big, hearty, earnest, honest, rugged Buckeye of a man, but he couldn't vote for Giddings' bill to make a clean sweep-out of slavery in the District. Those who later saw Lincoln's growth beginning with his humiliations of this period gave him too little credit for the early sagacity of his resolution before the House January 10, 1849; on seeing no chance for its adoption he didn't introduce it as a bill. What he offered was the keenest solution then possible of the slavery problem in the District. In it was the foretokening that he could umpire between the North and the South, that he understood both sections without prejudice, that he could relate the tangled past to the uncertain future by offering only what might be workable in the immediate present.

He proposed that no new slaves could be brought into the District to live there, except temporarily the slaves, "necessary servants," of Government officers from slaveholding states. After January 1, 1850, all children born of slave mothers should be free, should be "reasonably supported and educated" by the owners of their mothers though owing "reasonable service" to such owners until arriving at an age to be determined. By these two provisions—no new slaves to be brought in and all children born of slaves to be free—and all living slaves in the District certain to die sometime, there would be a definite, calculable day when slavery would have vanished from the District. The President, Secretary of State and Secretary of the Treasury should be a board to determine the value of such slaves as owners "may desire to emancipate." Yet Congress must not impose its will on the District; therefore let it provide an election where all "free white male" voters could say whether they wanted such emancipation.

One proviso was to make trouble for Lincoln then and for years after. Washington authorities would be "empowered and required" to arrest and deliver to owners "all fugitive slaves escaping into said District." Lincoln said that he had shown his proposals to 15 leading citizens of the District and "he had authority to say that every one of them desired that some proposition like this should pass." The cry came from several members, "Who are they? Give us their names," to which Lincoln made no answer. In the many debates of various angles of the slavery question, he kept silence. Angry Free-Soilers, anxious antislavery and proslavery Whigs and Democrats clashed in wild disputes, and Lincoln sat still. He had begun waiting for unforeseen events sure to come.

He saw "Old Zach" inaugurated March 4, did his best at reaching the new Whig President and having him appoint Ned Baker to the Cabinet, but it didn't come off. He began writing letters and for months was to go on with letters asking the President or department heads to appoint this or that good Whig to this or that office. For several old friends he landed places, but he made some enemies; there were always the disgruntled and suspicious. He was to write to the Secretary of State that Taylor's habit of throwing appointments over to department heads was fixing in the public mind "the unjust and ruinous character of [the President] being a mere man of straw," and it could "damn us all inevitably."

Admitted March 7 to practice before the U.S. Supreme Court he argued a case appealed from an Illinois court, and lost it.

Back in Springfield, for months he carried on a furious and snarled campaign of letter writing, conferences, wirepulling, aimed at getting for himself or for some other Illinois Whig, the appointment of Commissioner of the General Land Office at Washington, salary $3,000 a year. The politics of the affair seemed to narrow down to where Lincoln would have to go after the office for himself or it would be lost to southern Illinois Whigs. Early in June he wrote to many: "Would you as soon I should have the General Land Office as any other Illinoian? If you would, write me to that effect at Washington, where I shall be soon. No time to lose." In June in Washington wearing a linen duster, he offered reasons why he, an original Taylor man, should be named over the Clay man who landed it. Justin Butterfield won through northern Illinois and Chicago influence, besides that of Daniel Webster and Henry Clay. When Secretary of State John M. Clayton notified Lincoln August 10, 1849, of his appointment as Secretary of the Territory of Oregon, he replied, "I respectfully decline the office" but he would be "greatly obliged" if the place be offered to Simeon Francis, editor of the oldest and leading Whig paper of the state.

CHAPTER 8

Back Home in Springfield

BACK in Springfield picking up law practice again he still had his sense of humor and the advice he had long ago given Speed that when feeling sad work is a cure. He liked the law. He was a born lawyer. He went to it, later writing, "From 1849 to 1854, both inclusive, I practiced law more assiduously than ever before." He traveled the Eighth Circuit, staying two days to two weeks in each county seat, in some years from September till Thanksgiving and from March till June away from his Springfield home. He kept in close touch with the people, their homes, kitchens, barns, fields, their churches, schools, hotels, saloons, their ways of working, worshiping, loafing.

In February 1850 the four-year-old boy Edward Baker Lincoln died. He could call to Eddie and the boy had no living ears to hear. The mother took it hard and it was his place to comfort and restore, if he could, a broken woman.

From the funeral sermon by the Reverend James Smith of the First Presbyterian Church, a friendship grew between the Lincoln family and Mr. Smith. He had been a wild boy in Scotland, a scoffer at religion, then a preacher in Kentucky; he could tell a story—he and Lincoln were good company. The Lincolns rented a pew; Mrs. Lincoln took the sacrament, and joined in membership. Mr. Smith presented Lincoln with his book, *The Christian's Defense*, a reply to infidels and atheists. Lincoln read the book, attended revival meetings, was interested, but when asked to join the church he said he "couldn't quite see it."

Close friends, such as Herndon and Matheny, saw Lincoln as a sort of infidel, saying he told them he couldn't see the Bible as the revelation of God, or Jesus as the Son of God. Lincoln, however, read the Bible closely, knew it from cover to cover, its famous texts, stories and psalms; he quoted it in talks to juries, in speeches, in letters. There were evangelical Christian church members who saw him as solemn, reverent, truly religious. Jesse W. Fell of Bloomington felt that Lincoln's views had likeness to those of the noted preachers, Theodore Parker and William Ellery Channing. Fell gave Lincoln a complete collection of Channing's sermons.

Over the year 1850 Lincoln could read in newspapers and the *Congressional Globe* of the tumults and hazards of political drama in Washington. Only by slender circumstance and hair-trigger chances was the Union saved. In Senate and House men of both sides of the Great Compromise shook their fists and cried threats. A Mississippi Senator, Foote, called a Missouri Senator, Benton, a "calumniator," a liar. Benton walked straight toward Foote, who pulled a revolver and cocked it. Benton tore open his coat and shirt, shouting, "I disdain to carry arms. Let him fire! Stand out of the way and let the assassin fire!" Other Senators rushed in, took the revolver from Foote, and the debate went on.

In January Henry Clay, whom Lincoln was to term "my beau ideal of a statesman," had introduced the omnibus bills and argued that only by compromise, by give and take, by each side north and south making concessions, could the Union be saved. As his bills came out of a special committee they would let California into the Union as a Free State; New Mexico and Utah would become territories, without reference to slavery; Texas would be paid for giving up boundary claims in New Mexico and having her other boundaries fixed; the slave trade in the District of Columbia would be abolished but slavery would continue so long as it was insisted on by Maryland, which had ceded the District land to the Federal Government. Last and most fiercely disputed was the proposed new Fugitive Slave Law, "with teeth in it"; the Negro claimed as a slave could not have a jury trial and could not testify; a Federal official would be empowered to decide ownership and if he decided for the Negro his fee was $5.00 but if his decision was for the owner his fee was $10; also anyone helping a runaway Negro was made liable to fine and imprisonment.

Daniel Webster on March 7 made a three-hour speech to crowded galleries. The eyes of the audience left him a few moments when the foremost interpreter of the doctrine of states' rights and secession, the aged John C. Calhoun, who was to die 24 days later, had his gaunt and bent form in a black cloak helped to the seat he had held so many years. Webster spoke for the Great Compromise, bill by bill, as the only agreement by which the Union could be held together. Mr. Lincoln out in Illinois must have dwelt with keen eyes on Mr. Webster's passionate exclamations toward his close:

"Secession! Peaceable secession! Sir, your eyes and mine are never destined to see that miracle. The dismemberment of this vast country without convulsion! The breaking up of the great deep without ruffling the surface! Who is so foolish . . . as to expect to see any such thing? . . . There can be no such thing as a peaceable secession." Webster had tried, in private conferences, to provide jury trial for the fugitive slave, but that was one of many matters to which in that hour he could not refer. Webster, wrote one of his intimate friends, was "a compound of strength and weakness, dust and divinity."

Henry Clay spoke, again and again, at times to storms of applause from crowded galleries. He rebuked personal ambitions. An individual man is "an atom, almost invisible without a magnifying glass . . . a drop of water in the great deep, which evaporates and is borne off by the winds; a grain of sand, which is soon gathered to the dust from which it sprung. Shall a being so small, so petty, so fleeting, so evanescent, oppose itself to onward march of a great nation, to subsist for ages and ages to come? . . . Forbid it God!"

President Taylor, it was known, had made up his mind that if Texans, as they were threatening, moved their troops to interfere with the New Mexico boundary, "I will take command of the army myself to enforce the laws." To the Southern Whigs, Toombs and Stephens, who called on him and said his action would bring civil war and dissolve the Union, he said, "If you men are taken in rebellion against the Union, I will hang you with less reluctance than I hanged spies and deserters in Mexico." Taylor was 65 and scandals, quarrels and insoluble problems had worn him. He sat three hours in the hot sun near the Washington Monument ceremonial on the Fourth of July, listening to orations calling for conciliation and national harmony. He drank ice water, went home to the White House and ate from a basket of cherries, disobeyed his doctor and drank goblets of iced milk and ate more cherries. He died July 9, saying, "I have endeavored to do my duty." With his death hope ran higher of passing the Great Compromise.

Serving as floor captain for the worn men, Clay and Webster, was Senator Douglas; he traded and rounded up votes; he framed provisions of the three most important bills; he maneuvered against the outspoken threats of immediate secession, made speeches for an ocean-to-ocean republic. He replied in anger and scorn to the Massachusetts Free-Soiler, Senator Charles Sumner, who called Douglas "a Northern man with Southern principles." Douglas heard and would never forget and would come back to it again and again that the Whig Senator from New York, William H. Seward, declared, ". . . there is a higher law than the Constitution, which regulates our authority . . ." He kept a wary eye on new Free-Soil Senators who held the Fugitive Slave Law to be infamous and said so. Douglas kept close to the new Whig President, Millard Fillmore, chubby-faced, moderate, suave, doing his best for the Great Compromise. By majorities of about one-third or more, the omnibus bills, some of them slightly modified, passed and became law. From January on through part of August the great debate had raged in Washington and spread over the country. Now cannon boomed over Washington, bonfires blazed, processions roared through the streets, stopping for speeches at the homes of Webster, Douglas and others. Drinking men said the occasion called for nothing less than every patriot to get stone blind drunk, which many of them did. And over the country there settled a curious, quiet, bland, enigmatic peace. In many a house men breathed easier and slept better because secession and possibly war had been stood off. The quiet was broken only by the abolitionists, Free-Soilers, antislavery men in both of the old parties, delivering their shrill or guttural curses on the new Fugitive Slave Law. Lincoln, two years later, in eulogizing Clay, would say of this new peace, "The nation has passed its perils, and is free, prosperous, and powerful."

In late May 1849 Dennis Hanks wrote Lincoln of the illness of his father Thomas Lincoln and, "He Craves to See you all the time & he wonts you to Come if you ar able to git hure, for you are his only Child that is of his own flush & blood . . . he wonts you to prepare to meet him in the un-known world, or in heven, for he think that ower Savour has a Crown of glory, prepared for *him* I wright this with a bursting hart . . ." A few days later came a letter from Augustus H. Chapman, who married a granddaughter of Sarah Bush Lincoln; the father was out of danger and would be well in a short time.

When later word came of his father on the Coles County farm dying in January 1851 Lincoln wrote to his stepbrother John D. Johnston:

I feel sure you have not failed to use my name, if necessary, to procure a doctor, or any thing else for Father in his present sickness. My business is such that I could hardly leave home now, if it were not, as it is, that my own wife is sick-abed. (It is a case of baby-sickness, and I suppose is not dangerous.) I sincerely hope Father may yet recover his health; but at all events, tell him to remember to call upon, and confide in, our great, and good, and merciful Maker; who will not turn away from him in any extremity. He notes the fall of a sparrow, and numbers the hairs of our heads; and He will not forget the dying man, who puts his trust in Him. Say to him that if we could meet now, it is doubtful whether it would not be more painful than pleasant; but that if it be his lot to go now, he will soon have a joyous meeting with many loved ones gone before; and where the rest of us, through the help of God, hope ere-long to join them.

When death came close, with a murmur from deep rivers and a cavern of dark stars, Lincoln could use Bible speech. The father died January 17, 1851, and the only son, with a crowded court calendar, including three Supreme Court cases, did not go to the funeral. Lincoln's final somber words to his father could be construed several ways. To be at the deathbed of one for whom you have even a small crumb of affection is definitely "more painful than pleasant." Thomas Lincoln to the last was a churchgoing, religious man, his invariable grace at meals, as reported by a local paper: "Fit and prepare us for humble service, we beg for Christ's sake. Amen."

When in Congress, Lincoln had written to his father, "I very cheerfully send you the twenty dollars, which sum you say is necessary to save your land from sale . . . Give my love to Mother, and all the connections. Affec-tionately your Son." Could there have been no slight pride or tone of warmth in his often quoting wise proverbs or quaint humor as coming from his father? "If you make a bad bargain, *hug* it the tighter." "Every man must skin his own skunk."

A local paper reported, "One day when alone with her husband, Mrs. Lincoln said, 'Thomas, we have lived together a long time and you have never yet told me whom you like best, your first wife or me.' Thomas replied, 'Oh, now, Sarah, that reminds me of old John Hardin down in Kentucky who had a fine-looking pair of horses, and a neighbor coming in one day and looking at them said, "John, which horse do you like best?" John said, "I can't tell; one of them kicks and the other bites and I don't know which is wust." ' It is plain to see where Abraham Lincoln got his talent for wit and apt illustration." When a third boy baby come to the Lincoln family in 1850 he was named William Wallace: the fourth one in 1853 was named Thomas after his grandfather, so Mrs. Lincoln wrote in a letter to Sarah Bush.

The next summer Lincoln as sole heir deeded the west 80 acres of his father's 120-acre farm to John D. Johnston, subject to Sarah Bush Lincoln's dower right. This stepbrother bothered him; Lincoln gave Johnston more free, sharp, peremptory advice than he did anyone else. While in Congress he refused to loan Johnston $80, well aware that Johnston was somewhat of a dude, handy with the girls, at times selling liquor by the jug. "You are not *lazy*, and still you *are* an *idler*. I doubt whether since I saw you, you have done a good whole day's work, in any one day . . . This habit of uselessly wasting time, is the whole difficulty." Lincoln promised that for every dollar Johnston would earn he would pay him another dollar. "You say you would almost give your place in Heaven for $70 or $80. Then you value your place in Heaven very cheaply . . . You have always been [kind] to me, and I do not now mean to be unkind to you . . . Affectionately Your brother."

On hearing that Johnston was going to sell his land and move to Missouri, he wrote, "What can you do in Missouri, better than here? Is the land any richer? Can you there, any more than here, raise corn, & wheat & oats, without work? Will any body there, any more than here, do your work for you? . . . Squirming & crawling about from place to place can do no good . . . part with the land you have, and my life upon it, you will never after, own a spot big enough to bury you in. Half you will get for the land, you spend in moving to Missouri, and the other half you will eat and drink, and wear out, & no foot of land will be bought . . . The Eastern forty acres I intend to keep for Mother while she lives—if you *will not cultivate it;* it will rent for enough to support her . . . Her Dower in the other two forties, she can let you have, and no thanks to [me] . . . Your thousand pretences . . . deceive no body but yourself. *Go to work* is the only cure for your case."

To this was added a postscript which might be termed the only known letter Lincoln wrote to his beloved stepmother, who was to say, "Abe was the best boy I ever saw. His mind and mine, what little I had, seemed to run together, more in the same channel." The postscript read:

A word for Mother:
Chapman tells me he wants you to go and live with him. If I were you I would try it awhile. If you get tired of it (as I think you will not) you can return to your own home. Chapman feels very kindly to you; and I have no doubt he will make your situation very pleasant. Sincerely your Son A. Lincoln

Later Lincoln had to warn Johnston not to sell land belonging to his mother. Johnston married a nice 16-year-old girl, got her parents to sell their land, and with the money moved to Arkansas, bought land, failed as a farmer and small-scale whisky distiller. Years later Lincoln saw a young son of Johnston in jail at Urbana for stealing a watch; Lincoln spent hours with the boy and then in kindly talk persuaded the owners of the watch to drop action against the boy.

After 11 years of marriage Lincoln and Mary Todd had stood together at the cradles of four babies, at the grave of one. For these little ones Lincoln was thankful. To handle them, play with them and watch them grow, pleased his sense of the solemn and the ridiculous.

The father and mother had come to understand that each was strong and each was weak. Habits held him that it was useless for her to try to break. If he chose to lie on the front room carpet, on the small of his back, reading, that was his way. If he came to the table in his shirt sleeves and ate his victuals absently, his eyes and thoughts far off, that too was his way. She tried to stop him from answering the front doorbell and leave it to the servant. But he would go to the front door in carpet slippers and shirt sleeves to ask what was wanted. Once two fine ladies came to see Mrs. Lincoln; he looked for her and asked the callers in, drawling, "She'll be down soon as she gets her trotting harness on."

When his wife wrangled with the iceman claiming an overcharge or when she screamed at John Mendonsa that she would pay only ten cents a quart for berries, that they were not worth 15 cents, he spoke quietly to her as "Mary," and did his best to straighten things. Mary had sewed her own clothes, had sewed clothes for the children; he let her manage the house In Springfield she was quoted as once saying, "Money! He never gives me any money; he leaves his pocketbook where I can take what I want."

In many matters Lincoln trusted her judgment. Herndon wrote much against her yet he noted: "She was an excellent judge of human nature, a better reader of men's motives than her husband and quick to detect those who had designs upon and sought to use him. She was, in a good sense, a stimulant. She kept him from lagging, was constantly prodding him to keep up the struggle. She wanted to be a leader in society. Realizing that Lincoln's rise in the world would elevate and strengthen her, she strove in every way to promote his fortunes, to keep him moving, and thereby win the world's applause." When Lincoln ordered bricks for a front fence to be "about two feet above ground" and when later they rebuilt the upper half-story, making a two-story house, Lincoln naturally consulted her every wish.

Talk about her over Springfield ran that she economized in the kitchen to have fine clothes; she had a terrible temper and tongue. That her husband had married her a thousand dollars in debt, that he charged low fees and had careless habits, that he trusted her and let her have her own way in the household economy, didn't fit well into the gossip. That she was at times a victim of mental disorder, that she was often sorry and full of regrets after a wild burst of temper, didn't make for exciting gossip.

She knew he liked cats and kittens as he did no other animals. She had written to him gaily from Kentucky of fun and trouble with kittens. Staying with one of the Grigsbys in Indiana a cat's yowling in the night broke all sleep and Lincoln got out of bed, held and quieted the cat and enjoyed it.

In July 1850 and in Chicago on a law case, Whigs pressed Lincoln to memorialize Zachary Taylor. He spoke as a Whig to Whigs, by inference defending the Whig policy toward the Mexican War. How Lincoln himself might wish to behave in crises when other men were losing their heads, he intimated in saying of Taylor: "He could not be *flurried,* and he could not be *scared* . . . He was alike averse to *sudden,* and to *startling* quarrels; and he pursued no man with *revenge.*"

When Henry Clay died in June 1852, Springfield stores closed, and after services in the Episcopal Church, a procession moved to the Hall of Representatives where Lincoln sketched Clay's long life, how Clay on occasions by his moderation and wisdom had held the Union together when it seemed ready to break. He quoted Clay on the American Colonization Society: "There is a moral fitness in the idea of returning to Africa her children, whose ancestors have been torn from her by the ruthless hand of fraud and violence. Transplanted in a foreign land, they will carry back to their native soil the rich fruits of religion, civilization, law and liberty." How desperate this hope, Lincoln was to learn at cost. Over the South were 3,204,000 slaves valued on tax books at more than one and one-half billion dollars. How to pay for them as property, if that were conceivable, and then "transplant" them to Africa, was the problem. With Henry Clay, Lincoln leaned on the hope of buying slave property and colonizing it in Africa, both laying blame on radical abolitionists who were saying they would welcome a breakup of the Union, and laying equal blame on proud Southern hotheads who saw slavery as a sanctioned institution for which they were ready to secede from the Union.

Lincoln in 1852 had for 20 years been a loyal Whig party leader who had shaken hands with nearly all active local Whig leaders over Illinois. He seemed to be merely a party wheel horse in his seven speeches in the 1852 campaign, discussing candidates and personalities rather than any great issues. Of Franklin Pierce, the Democratic candidate for President, he noted, "The first thing ever urged in his favor as a candidate was his having given a strange boy a cent to buy candy with." The inflation of Pierce as a heroic brigadier general in the Mexican War reminded him of oldtime militia rules. "No man is to wear more than five pounds of cod-fish for epaulets, or more than thirty yards of bologna sausages for a sash; and no two men are to dress alike, and if any two should dress alike the one that dresses most alike is to be fined."

He belittled statements of Douglas with a relentless logic that became comic and had an audience splitting its sides. He had never read Seward's "supposed proclamation of a 'higher law' " but if it was intended to "foment a disobedience to the constitution, or to the constitutional laws of the country, it has my unqualified condemnation." He praised General Winfield Scott, a hero of two wars, the third military candidate of the Whigs for

President. He had seen Southern Whigs favoring the Whig President Fillmore for the nomination but Seward and the extreme antislavery Whigs had swung the nomination to Scott. When Scott in the November election carried only four states, the question was asked by good Whigs, "Is the party falling to pieces?"

Herndon wrote that Lincoln was "the most secretive man" he ever knew. A Danville man said, "Lincoln doesn't show at first all that is in him." A lawyer who had tried cases with him, said, "You can never tell what Lincoln is going to do till he does it." Once during a criminal trial, Lincoln had been giving away one point after another, and as Lincoln was speaking to the jury, a colleague, Amzi McWilliams, whispered to other attorneys, "Lincoln will pitch in heavy now, for he has hid." Of two friendly lawyers, one said Lincoln "was harmless as a dove and wise as a serpent," and the other, "He respectfully listened to all advice, and rarely, if ever, followed it." Still another saw him as elusive: "While guilty of no duplicity, he could hide his thoughts and intentions more efficiently than any man with a historical record."

About the year 1850, wrote Herndon, he and Lincoln were driving in Lincoln's one-horse buggy to the Menard County Court. The case they were to try would touch on hereditary traits. "During the ride he spoke, for the first time in my hearing, of his mother, dwelling on . . . qualities he inherited from her. He said, among other things, that she was the illegitimate daughter of Lucy Hanks and a well-bred Virginia farmer or planter; and he argued that from this last source came his power of analysis, his logic, his mental activity, his ambition . . . His theory . . . had been, that, for certain reasons, illegitimate children are oftentimes sturdier and brighter than those born in lawful wedlock . . . The revelation—painful as it was—called up the recollection of his mother, and, as the buggy jolted over the road, he added ruefully, 'God bless my mother; all that I am or ever hope to be I owe to her,' and immediately lapsed into silence . . . We rode on for some time without exchanging a word."

Of this statement, a keen and thorough analyst of Herndon was to write that when Herndon related a fact as of his own observation, it might generally be accepted without question, while his derivations and guesses regarding the recollections of others might be full of errors. "As a matter of fact, the weight of independent evidence supports the truth of the statement, although proof beyond the possibility of a doubt has never been assembled. Even if it should be established that Nancy Hanks was born in lawful wedlock—a development which does not seem likely—Herndon's reliability would not necessarily be impaired. *The question is so difficult of solution that it would not be strange if Lincoln himself had been mistaken.*"

Herndon in 1840 had married Mary Maxcy, the daughter of Virginia-born James Maxcy, the first town constable of Springfield. Her quiet beauty was likened to a summer daisy in a meadow corner. She bore him six children, read books for him, gave him ease after his restless hours. Their home held rare happiness, and in a sense, they had a lifelong romance. This home Herndon would leave for the office which he opened at eight o'clock in the morning. Lincoln, when in town, would arrive at nine, and, wrote Herndon, "The first thing he did was to pick up a newspaper, spread himself out on an old sofa, one leg on a chair, and read aloud, much to my discomfort." Lincoln once explained to him, "When I read aloud two senses catch the idea: first, I see what I read; second, I hear it, and therefore I can remember it better."

Each of them had climbed narrow stairs, crossed a dark hallway, entered by a glass-paned door, to see worn familiar things of use—the sofa, the stove, two tables (one of them somewhat jack-knifed), a secretary with pigeonholes and drawers stuffed with papers, an earthenware inkpot with quill pens in reach, dingy windows looking out on a lonesome alley. Here they prepared cases, Lincoln writing most of the papers introduced in court, Herndon often doing the heavy research work on authorities and precedents.

Lincoln's silk stovepipe hat was part of his office, Herndon writing that it was his desk and memorandum book, holding bank book, letters and scribbled ideas placed in the hatband. To a fellow lawyer Lincoln once wrote of a lost letter, "I put it in my old hat, and buying a new one the next day, the old one was set aside, and so, the letter lost sight of for a time." Yet amid this seeming disorder the firm of Lincoln & Herndon in 1850 had 18 per cent of all cases in Sangamon County Circuit Court, in 1853 34 per cent, in 1854 30 per cent, and they rated as a leading law firm in a city of 6,000 having an exceptionally able set of attorneys. Herndon had moods of disgust with the law, once writing, "If you love the stories of murder—rape—fraud &c. a law office is a good place." The partners bothered little with bookkeeping, dividing fees equally, Lincoln sometimes putting money in an envelope he marked with the name of the case and "Herndon's half." Herndon only occasionally went on the circuit. Each appeared in many cases alone or with other lawyers, the rule being that they were never to be opposing counsel.

Herndon was bothered at times by Lincoln telling the same funny story on the same day to one client or politician after another. He saw, too, in other hours, Lincoln with a "woestruck face," gazing at the office floor or out the window, in a dark silence Herndon didn't dare interrupt. He tried to solve Lincoln's melancholy, whether it went back to heredity, environment, glands, slow blood circulation, or constipation, or thwarted love. Yet Herndon knew that his partner was, in degree, a steadying force in his own life, a sort of elder brother or affectionate uncle. When Herndon spoke as a red-hot abolitionist, Lincoln would tell him, "Billy, you're too rampant and spontaneous." He noted Lincoln's walk. "He put the whole foot flat down on the ground at once, not landing on the heel; he likewise lifted his foot all at once, not rising from the toe . . . The whole man, body and mind, worked slowly, as if it needed oiling." Then came Herndon as a brain specialist: "The convolutions of his brain are long; they do not snap quickly like a short, thick man's brain," which was pretentious guesswork, not commanding the respect that might be accorded his writing: "The enduring power of Mr. Lincoln's brain is wonderful. He can sit and think without food or rest longer than any man I ever met."

It came hard for Herndon when the boys, Willie and Tad, came to the office with their father on a Sunday morning while the mother was at church;

the boys pulled books off shelves, upset ink bottles, threw pencils into the spittoon, their father at his desk working as though the office were empty. It lingered with Herndon that Lincoln said to him more than once, "I shall meet with some terrible end." Out of what shadowed meditations could such a premonition come to be spoken? He took Shakespeare in his carpetbag on the circuit, it was known, but that wouldn't explain why one of his original bent would speak lines like Hamlet. When Joshua Speed said he had a quick mind, he denied it. "I am slow to learn, and slow to forget . . . My mind is like a piece of steel—very hard to scratch anything on it, and almost impossible after you get it there to rub it out."

An angry family trying to break a will, a man who with a knife had cut another man in the eye, a client of Lincoln's found guilty of manslaughter and sentenced to eight years at hard labor, the first three months in solitary confinement, another Lincoln client, a one-legged Mexican War veteran found guilty of robbing the mails of $15,000 in bank notes and sentenced to ten years—the likes of these came before Lincoln's eyes, their faces and voices beyond forgetting.

"She charges," he wrote in behalf of Eliza Jane Helmick, "that said complainant, while he yet lived with her, for the purpose of contriving evidence to procure a divorce from her, at various times, and in different ways, attempted to induce different men to make attempts upon the chastity of your Respondent." He wrote another lawyer of how he hadn't "pressed to the utmost" his case against a man: "I am really sorry for him—*poor* and a *cripple* as he is." In several cases he defended whisky sellers—and again at a trial in DeWitt County attended by more than a hundred women he defended nine women charged with riot; they had warned a saloonkeeper to close his place and when he didn't they smashed barrels and bottles and left him no whisky to sell; the jury found them guilty but the judge let them off with a fine of $2.00 each. More often came the humdrum cases involving properties and payments, estates, promissory notes, defaults, claims, mortgages, foreclosures, ejectments.

Little Harriet Beecher Stowe in 1852 had published a novel, *Uncle Tom's Cabin*, and by the device of dramatizing a black Christ lashed by a Yankee-born Satan, had led millions of people to believe that in the Slave States south of the Ohio River was a monstrous wrong. She ended her book with a prophecy: "This is an age of the world when nations are trembling and convulsed. A mighty influence is abroad, surging and heaving the world, as with an earthquake. And is America safe? Every nation that carries in its bosom great and unredressed injustice has in it the elements of this last convulsion."

Lincoln at a Springfield, Illinois, meeting wrote the resolutions of sympathy for Louis Kossuth and Hungarians in revolution against an arrogant and cruel monarchy. In notes for possible use, he wrote of "a society of equals" where every man had a chance. He had heard Southern men declare slaves better off in the South than hired laborers in the North. He would observe, "There is no permanent class of hired laborers amongst us. Twentyfive years ago, I was a hired laborer. The hired laborer of yesterday, labors on his own account to-day; and will hire others to labor for him to-morrow . . .

Although volume upon volume is written to prove slavery a very good thing, we never hear of the man who wishes to take the good of it, *by being a slave himself* . . . As Labor is the common *burthen* of our race, so the effort of *some* to shift their share of the burthen on to the shoulders of *others,* is the great, durable, curse of the race."

Emerson, the Concord preacher, saw war, revolution, violence, breeding in the antagonisms of bold, powerful men. "Vast property, gigantic interests, family connection, webs of party, cover the land with a network that immensely multiplies the dangers of war."

Lincoln caught the feel of change in the national air. He had seen the frontier move far west. He had seen St. Louis, with its 5,000 people, grow to 74,000 in 20 years, and Springfield from 700 to 6,000. Senator Douglas was telling of "a power in this nation greater than either the North or the South —a growing, increasing, swelling power, that will be able to speak the law to this nation, and to execute the law as spoken. That power is the country known as the great West—the Valley of the Mississippi." The human inflow from Europe kept coming into Illinois—Germans, Irish and English by tens of thousands. Fourteen steamboats, ice-locked in the Mississippi River near Cairo in the winter of 1854, were loaded with 2,000 German and Irish immigrants. Of new and old societies, unions, lodges, churches, it seemed that Lincoln belonged only to the Whig party and the American Colonization Society.

Between 1850 and 1860, the country's 23,000,000 people become 31,000,000, this being 2,000,000 more than Great Britain. In ten years 2,600,000 people arrive from overseas, in a single year 400,000. The East grows 21 per cent, the South 28 per cent, the Northwest 77 per cent, in population. Little towns peep up on the prairies where before were only gophers and jack rabbits.

Washington wrangles about the public lands, millions of acres northwest and southwest. Land speculators, interests, powerful in Washington, for reasons of their own do not want free land for actual settlers. A few Senators try to get a free homestead law and fail. Free land bills keep coming up in Congress.

The transcontinental railroad, the iron-built, ocean-going steamship, the power-driven factory—the owners and managers of these are to be a new breed of rulers of the earth. Between seaboard and the Mississippi comes the "iron horse" hauling pork and grain of the West to factory towns of the East, to vessels sailing to Europe; the cars return with sewing machines, churns, scissors, saws, steel tools. New reaping and threshing machinery comes. Singlehanded, a farmer gathers the crop on a quarter section. Grain drills, corn planters, wagons and buggies with springs under the boxes and seats are bought by the farmers. New churns and sewing machines help the farmer's wife. Steam fire engines, gas lighting systems, the use of anesthesia, the Hoe revolving cylinder press, vulcanized rubber, photography, arrive.

A territory of Kansas is organized, and from slave-soil Missouri, men with rifles ride over into Kansas and battle with abolitionists from New England for political control of Kansas. Emerson peers into years ahead and cries, "The hour is coming when the strongest will not be strong enough." On a late afternoon of any autumn day in those years, Abraham Lincoln in his rattletrap buggy over the prairie might have been lost deep in the swirl of his thoughts and his hope to read events to come.

Lincoln bought a book on logic, studied how to untangle fallacies and derive inexorable conclusions from established facts. On the circuit when with other lawyers, two in a bed, eight or ten in one hotel room, he read Euclid by the light of a candle after others had dropped off to sleep. Herndon and Lincoln had the same bed one night, and Herndon noticed his partner's legs pushing their feet out beyond the footboard of the bed, as he held Euclid close to the candlelight.

John T. Stuart saw Lincoln as a hopeless victim of melancholy. "Look at him now," said Stuart, in the McLean County Courthouse. "I turned a little," wrote Henry C. Whitney, Lincoln's fellow lawyer at Urbana, "and there beheld Lincoln sitting alone in the corner . . . wrapped in gloom." He seemed to be "pursuing in his mind some specific, sad subject, . . . through various sinuosities, and his sad face would assume, at times, deeper phases of grief . . . He was roused by the breaking up of court, when he emerged . . . like one awakened from sleep."

Herndon once found Lincoln covering sheets of paper with figures, signs, symbols. He told Herndon he was trying to square the circle. After a two days' struggle, worn down, he gave up trying to square the circle.

He penned notes trying to be as absolute as mathematics: "If A. can prove, however conclusively, that he may, of right, enslave B., why may not B. snatch the same argument, and prove equally, that he may enslave A?— You say A. is white, and B. is black. It is *color*, then; the lighter, having the right to enslave the darker? Take care. By this rule, you are to be slave to the first man you meet, with a fairer skin than your own. You do not mean *color* exactly?—You mean the whites are *intellectually* the superiors of the blacks, and, therefore have the right to enslave them? Take care again. By this rule, you are to be slave to the first man you meet, with an intellect superior to your own. But, say you, it is a question of *interest;* and, if you can make it your *interest*, you have the right to enslave another. Very well. And if he can make it his interest, he has the right to enslave you." Thus his private memorandum.

He wrote of the legitimate object of government being "to do for the people what needs to be done, but which they can not, by individual effort, do at all, or do so well, for themselves," such as "Making and maintaining roads, bridges, and the like; providing for the helpless young and afflicted; common schools; and disposing of deceased men's property." Military and civil departments were necessary. "If some men will kill, or beat, or constrain others, or despoil them of property, by force, fraud, or noncompliance with contracts, it is a common object with peaceful and just men to prevent it."

Out of the silent working of his inner life came forces no one outside of himself could know; they were his secret, his personality and purpose. He was in the toils of more than personal ambition. Politely, gently but firmly, he had told those who wanted him to run for the legislature or for Congress, that he wasn't in the running.

CHAPTER 9

Restless Growing America

THE CALIFORNIA "gold rush" of 1849 and what followed had the eyes of the world. San Francisco had become a world port. Sacramento, four lone houses in April 1849, became in six months a roaring crazy city of 10,000. Ten men in one week had shaken from the gravel in their hand-screens a million dollars in gold nuggets. More than once a single spade had sold for $1,000. Courts and law broke down in San Francisco and a Committee of Vigilantes took over the government.

Over the Great Plains moved wagon trains, a traveler counting 459 wagons in ten miles along the Platte River. A Peoria newspaper in 1854 counted 1,473 wagons in one month, movers going to Iowa. In a single week 12,000 immigrants arrived on railroad trains in Chicago. Cyrus McCormick's Chicago factory in 1854 sold 1,558 farming machines, mostly for both reaping and sowing, and was planning for 3,000 machines in 1855. The Department of State reported that Irish immigrants alone had in three years sent back to the old country nearly $15,000,000 for their kinfolk. A restless young growing America was moving toward a future beyond reading.

The peace of the Great Compromise had held up fairly well, broken by the endless crying of antislavery men against the new Fugitive Slave Law. The case of the slave, Anthony Burns, shook the country. He escaped from a Virginia plantation, stowed away on a ship for Boston, was arrested, and by a Federal commissioner ordered back to Virginia. A mob led by a minister broke into the courthouse to save Burns and in the fighting with Federal officers a deputy U.S. marshal was killed. Stores closed, doors and windows were draped in black, crowds lined the streets when the one lone Negro slave was marched to his Virginia-bound ship, escorted by dragoons, marines, loaded artillery, 12 companies of infantry, 120 personal friends of the U.S. marshal carrying drawn swords and loaded pistols. The affair cost the Government over $40,000. Like incidents, less dramatic, happened here and there over the country. In Chicago a fugitive slave was slipped out a courtroom window and when the Federal commissioner asked, "Where is the prisoner at the bar?" the answer came, "He is at rest in the bosom of the community."

Amid these changing scenes and issues, Douglas had become the foremost dramatic leader of the Democratic party, speaking, as he said, for "Young America" as against "Old Fogies," meaning Cass, Buchanan and other figures of hesitation. A younger element of the party boomed him for President in 1852 and he was only 39 when in the Democratic national convention on the 30th and 31st ballots he had more votes than any other candidate. He made his home in Chicago, where he bought land for a few dollars and sold one tract for $80,000. To the young University of Chicago he donated ten acres. He was close to all interests that wanted a railway to the Pacific. His tenacity had brought a rail route from the Great Lakes to the Gulf; the Illinois Central was thankful to him and let him have private cars for travel.

After the death of his wife in early 1853, when he went back to Congress he was noticed as bitter, bad-tempered, a sloven in dress, chewing tobacco and careless where he spat. He went abroad several months, seeing Russia and the Near East, and came back the oldtime Douglas who could put his hands on the shoulders of an old colleague or a young precinct worker and say, as though they were chums, "You—I count on your help." He was three years later to marry Adèle Cutts, a great-niece of Dolly Madison, a beautiful, warmhearted woman who proved to be a perfect helpmeet for a combative and furiously active husband. He made many long speeches, wrote few letters and those having little of self-revelation, kept no diary, seemed seldom if ever to have time for meditations on himself in particular or the whence and whither of all mankind.

In early 1854 came a bold, challenging action of Douglas that set the slavery issue boiling in a wild turmoil, Douglas having predicted, "It will raise a hell of a storm." Now 41, a battler, magnetic, with flashing blue eyes, chin drawn in, pivoting, elusive, he made a daring, spectacular play for reasons better known to himself than any he gave to the public. His lionlike head, his black pompadour swept back in waves, his deep bass voice, were seen and heard. Toiling, sweating, crying, he had coaxed, guided and jammed through Congress the Nebraska Bill, as it came to be known. It created two territories, Kansas on the south, Nebraska on the north; in each the voters would decide whether it should be free or slave soil. Nebraska then stretched far and wide, its area including all or part of the later states of Nebraska, North and South Dakota, Wyoming and Montana. There, in the future, under "popular sovereignty," said Douglas, "they could vote slavery up or down." Southern members had insisted on, and got, a provision expressly repealing the hitherto sacred Missouri Compromise; the line it drew between slave and free soil was wiped out.

As the news went across the country, not in the memory of living men had there been such recoils and explosions of opinion and passion over a political act and idea. Lincoln was roused as "by the sound of a fire-bell at night." In New England, 3,050 clergymen signed a widely published memorial to the U.S. Senate: "IN THE NAME OF ALMIGHTY GOD, AND IN HIS PRESENCE," we "solemnly protest against the passage of . . . the Nebraska bill." In Chicago 25 clergymen signed a like protest, followed by 500 ministers in the Northwest. Several longtime Democratic party leaders in Illinois gave it out that they were anti-Nebraska men. Traveling to Illinois, Douglas could see from his car window the burning of dummies bearing his name; in Ohio some women managed to present him with 30 pieces of silver. In Chicago in front of North Market Hall, on the hot night of September 1, he defied and insulted those against him; a crowd of 8,000 interrupted with questions, hisses, groans, boos, catcalls. They howled and hooted him till he looked at his watch, jammed his silk hat on his head, and left.

Among those who led in hooting Douglas were the Know-Nothings, members of the secret "Order of the Star Spangled Banner." When asked what the order stood for, members answered, "I know nothing." Each member on joining swore he would never vote for a foreigner or a Catholic for any office. Their slogans were, "Americans must rule America" and "No papacy in the Republic." Of millions of Irish and German immigrants, a large part were Catholic and they had become a power in large cities, throwing their strength most often to the Democrats, such as Douglas, who were more friendly to them than the Whigs in general. Two Catholic churches in Massachusetts had been wrecked and gutted—and a convent burned. A Protestant procession of 2,000 people in Newark, New Jersey, met an Irish mob and the fighting left one man dead and many wounded. Hibernian parades had been broken up by rioting Know-Nothings. Being secret in their operations, it was hard to guess what the Know-Nothings would show in the year's elections. Being openly anti-Nebraska and antislavery, they had drawn toward them many Democrats and an element of Whigs.

Before the year closed the Know-Nothings would surprise the country by electing mayors of Philadelphia and Washington. In alliance with Free-Soilers and former Whigs, they were to sweep Massachusetts with 63 per cent of all ballots, electing a Know-Nothing governor and legislature. They would have swept New York State but for the longtime proven friendships of Seward and Weed with groups of foreigners and Catholics. Lincoln gave out no word publicly but when Know-Nothings called on him he was reported as saying the red man in breechclout and with tomahawk was the true native American. "We pushed them from their homes, and now turn on others not fortunate enough to come over so early as we or our forefathers." He told of an Irishman who was asked why he wasn't born in America, and the answer, "Faith, I wanted to, but me mither wouldn't let me."

On a State Fair day in Springfield thousands who hated or loved Douglas stood in the cool night air of October 2 to see him on the Chenery House porch, torches lighting his face. His eyes flashed and lips trembled. "I tell you the time has not yet come when a handful of traitors in our camp can turn the great State of Illinois, with all her glorious history and traditions, into a negro-worshiping, negro-equality community." The next afternoon Douglas spoke three hours in the Statehouse. Had not the Missouri Compromise been practically wiped out by the Omnibus Bill of 1850? Was not the real question whether the people should rule, whether the voters in a territory should control their own affairs? If the people of Kansas and Nebraska were able to govern themselves, they were able to govern a few miserable Negroes. The crowd enjoyed it; cries came, "That's so!" "Hit 'em again." Lincoln comforted a pretty young woman abolitionist: "Don't bother, young lady. We'll hang the judge's hide on the fence tomorrow."

The next afternoon Lincoln spoke to the same crowd. "Wherever slavery is, it has been first introduced without law." He gave reasons for hating it as a "monstrous injustice," and added: "When southern people tell us they are no more responsible for the origin of slavery, than we; I acknowledge the fact. When it is said that the institution exists; and that it is very difficult to get rid of it, in any satisfactory way, I can understand and appreciate the saying. I surely will not blame them for not doing what I should not know how to do myself . . . What next? Free them, and make them politically and socially, our equals? My own feelings will not admit of this, and if mine would, we well know that those of the great mass of white people will not. Whether this feeling accords with justice and sound judgment, is not the sole question, if indeed, it is any part of it. A universal feeling, whether well or ill-founded, can not be safely disregarded."

And yet, while he could not say what should be done about slavery where it was already established and operating, he was sure it would be wrong to let it spread north. "Inasmuch as you do not object to my taking my hog to Nebraska, therefore I must not object to you taking your slave. Now, I admit this is perfectly logical, if there is no difference between hogs and negroes." And what should be done first of all? "The Missouri Compromise ought to be restored. For the sake of the Union, it ought to be restored." In Peoria 12 days later, he gave much the same speech to a crowd of thousands, wrote it out for publication, and it became widely known as the "Peoria Speech."

In the October elections of 1854, anti-Nebraska voters of all shades—former Whigs and Democrats, Know-Nothings, Fusionists—won by startling majorities. A combination in Pennsylvania elected 21 anti-Nebraska Congressmen as against four Nebraska. A Know-Nothing legislature in Massachusetts elected a Know-Nothing U.S. Senator. Maine, for years Democratic, saw the Anti-Nebraska Fusion Party electing a governor and carrying every congressional district, the same break from the past occurring in Iowa, Vermont and other states. Anti-Nebraska men rolled up a majority of 70,000, elected a Congressman in every Ohio district; they carried all but two districts in Indiana. Lincoln mentioned in his Peoria speech these sweeping political smashups, with a changed public opinion. He rebuked the "desperate assumption" of Douglas: "If a man will stand up and assert, and repeat, and re-assert, that two and two do not make four, I know nothing in the power of argument that can stop him . . . In such a case I can only commend him to the seventy thousand answers just in from Pennsylvania, Ohio, and Indiana."

At meetings in Ripon, Wisconsin, and Jackson, Michigan, citizens opposed to slavery extension, and coming from all parties, resolved in favor of a new party with a new name gathering anti-Nebraska Whigs and Democrats, also Free-Soilers, under one banner, and, "we will cooperate and be known as 'Republicans.' " In Wisconsin and Vermont conventions the name Republican was adopted. The New York *Tribune*'s Whig Almanac designated the 21 Congressmen from Ohio as Republicans, and in October 1854 Greeley was writing, "We consider the Whig party a thing of the past." In several county and congressional districts over Illinois the name Republican had been adopted, an Ottawa Democratic paper saying the Republican convention there was made up of "Whigs, abolitionists, know nothings, sore heads, and fag ends."

A group of radical abolitionists met in Springfield October 5 to organize an Illinois Republican party. Herndon, then calling himself an abolitionist, sat in with the group, and suddenly went in a hurry to Lincoln, saying, "Go home at once . . . Drive somewhere into the country and stay till this thing is over." And Lincoln, sending word to the radicals that he had law business in Tazewell County, drove away in his one-horse buggy. Herndon wrote, "On grounds of policy it would not do for him to occupy at that time such advanced ground as we were taking. On the other hand, it was equally as dangerous to refuse a speech for the Abolitionists." Later when Lincoln was named a member of the new state central committee of the new Republican party, he declined the honor, as without his authority, and refused to attend their meetings.

In the November 7 election the Democrats elected only four of the nine Illinois Congressmen, and to the legislature only 41 regular Democrats against 59 anti-Nebraska members of differing shades. Lincoln wrote the names of all members in alphabetical order and studied his chances for election to the seat of U.S. Senator James Shields. Late in 1854 he sent out many letters in the tone of one: "I have really got it into my head to try to be United States Senator; and if I could have your support my chances would be reasonably good." In February 1855 he watched in the Statehouse the election for U.S. Senator. He got 45 votes. Six more would have elected him. The balloting went on, his vote slumped to 15. The minute came when Lincoln saw that if he held his 15 loyal votes Governor Joel A. Matteson, a Douglas and tricky Nebraska Democrat playing what Lincoln termed "a double game," would be elected. Lincoln begged his steadfast 15 votes to go to Lyman Trumbull, anti-Nebraska bolter from the Democratic party. On the tenth ballot Trumbull was elected. The affair was snarled and shadowed, filled with strategies keen and subtle, and with treacheries plain and slimy.

Lincoln wrote to a friend: "I regret my defeat moderately, but I am not nervous about it." By not being stubborn he had won friends. He gave a dinner for all anti-Nebraska members of the legislature. Mrs. Lincoln had watched the balloting from the gallery and was bitter about it. Julia Jayne, the wife of Trumbull, had been bridesmaid at her wedding; they had joined in writing verse and letters to the *Sangamo Journal*, but forever after the night of Trumbull's election Mrs. Lincoln refused to speak to Julia or to receive a call from her.

Lincoln wrote to Speed: "I think I am a whig; but others say there are no whigs, and that I am an abolitionist . . . I now do no more than oppose the *extension* of slavery. I am not a Know-Nothing. That is certain. How could I be? How can any one who abhors the oppression of negroes, be in favor of degrading classes of white people? Our progress in degeneracy appears to me to be pretty rapid. As a nation, we began by declaring '*all men are created equal*.' We now practically read it 'all men are created equal, *except negroes*.' When the Know-Nothings get control, it will read 'all men are created equal, except negroes, *and foreigners, and catholics*.' When it comes to this I should prefer emigrating to some country where they make no pretence of loving liberty—to Russia, for instance, where despotism can be taken pure, and without the base alloy of hypocracy."

Polly, a free Negro woman in Springfield, had a son who worked on a steamboat to New Orleans where, not having papers to show he was a free Negro, he was jailed. The steamboat left without him and after a time he was advertised for sale to pay jail expenses. Polly came to Lincoln and Herndon about it. They went to Governor Matteson who said he could do nothing. Lincoln with Herndon and others raised by subscription the money to pay jail charges, and brought the boy back to Polly.

In August 1855 Lincoln wrote to Owen Lovejoy, "Not even *you* are more anxious to prevent the extension of slavery than I; and yet the political atmosphere is such, just now, that I fear to do any thing, lest I do wrong." Know-Nothing elements would be needed to combat the pro-Nebraska Democrats. "About us here, they [the Know-Nothings] are mostly my old political and personal friends; and I have hoped their organization would die out without the painful necessity of my taking an open stand against them. Of their principles I think little better than I do of those of the slavery extensionists. Indeed I do not perceive how any one professing to be sensitive to the wrongs of the negroes, can join in a league to degrade a class of white men." Few they were to whom Lincoln could write a letter of such candor which if published in that hour could do him harm. A peculiar bond of trust and understanding ran between him and the rugged Congregational minister over at Princeton, Illinois, who was a radical antislavery man.

One night in Danville at the McCormick House, the ladies' parlor was turned into a bedroom for Judge David Davis, who had a bed to himself, and for Lincoln and Henry C. Whitney, who slept two in a bed. Whitney wrote of it: "I was awakened early—before daylight—by my companion sitting up in bed, his figure dimly visible by the ghostly firelight, and talking the wildest and most incoherent nonsense all to himself. A stranger to Lincoln would have supposed he had suddenly gone insane. Of course I knew Lincoln and his idiosyncrasies, and felt no alarm, so I listened and laughed. After he had gone on in this way for, say, five minutes, while I was awake, and I knew not how long *before* I was awake, he sprang out of bed, hurriedly washed, and jumped into his clothes, put some wood on the fire, and then sat in front of it, moodily, dejectedly, in a most sombre and gloomy spell, till the breakfast bell rang, when he started, as if from sleep, and went with us to breakfast."

In 1856, on the Missouri and Kansas border, 200 men, women and children were shot, stabbed or burned to death in the fighting between free- and slave-state settlers and guerrillas. The money loss, in crops burned, cattle and horses stolen or killed, ran about $2,000,000. Each side aimed to settle Kansas with voters for its cause. In May, as the first state convention to organize the Republican party of Illinois was meeting in Bloomington, the town of Lawrence, Kansas, had been entered by riding and shooting men who burned the Free State Hotel, wrecked two printing offices and looted homes.

Senator Charles Sumner of Massachusetts, speaking on "The Crime Against Kansas," had lashed verbally South Carolina Senator Andrew P. Butler, saying Butler "has chosen a mistress . . . who, though ugly to others, is always lovely to him—I mean the harlot, Slavery." Butler had "with incoherent phrases, discharged the loose expectoration of his speech" on the people of Kansas. "He cannot open his mouth, but out there flies a blunder." And Congressman Preston Brooks, a nephew of Butler, had walked into the Senate chamber, and over the head and backbone of the seated Sumner had rained blows that broke to pieces a gutta-percha cane, beating his victim near to death. Over the North raged a fury almost tongue-tied. In the South was open or secret exultation; the man they hated and loathed more than any other in Congress had met punishment and would leave the Senate and suffer years before his wounds healed.

These events were in the air when political elements of Illinois and other states were holding conventions to organize state parties and to get up a national Republican party. Of delegates at Bloomington about one-fourth were regularly elected; others had appointed themselves. All stripes of political belief outside of the pro-Nebraska Democratic party were there: Whigs, bolting anti-Nebraska Democrats, Free-Soilers, Know-Nothings, abolitionists. Some who came were afraid that wild-eyed radicals would control.

The convention met in Major's Hall, upstairs over Humphrey's Cheap Store, near the courthouse square. The platform denounced Democratic policies and declared Congress had power to stop the extension of slavery and should use that power. After several delegates spoke, there were calls for Lincoln. He stood up. There were cries, "Take the platform," which he did. He observed, according to a Whitney version written many years later, "We are in a trying time"; then suddenly came the thrust, "Unless popular opinion makes itself very strongly felt, and a change is made in our present course, *blood will flow on account of Nebraska, and brother's hand will be raised against brother!* . . . We must not promise what we ought not, lest we be called on to perform what we cannot . . . We must not be led by excitement and passion to do that which our sober judgments would not approve in our cooler moments." He noted that the delegates had been collected from many different elements. Yet they were agreed, "*Slavery must be kept out of Kansas.*" The Nebraska Act was usurpation; it would result in making slavery national. "We are in a fair way to see this land of boasted freedom converted into a land of slavery in fact."

A terribly alive man stood before them. Joseph Medill, of the Chicago *Tribune*, and other newspaper writers felt their pencils slip away. Herndon and Whitney had started to take notes, then forgot they had pencils. Listeners moved up closer to the speaker. "I read once in a law book, 'A slave is a human being who is legally not a *person* but a *thing*.' And if the safeguards to liberty are broken down, as is now attempted, when they have made *things* of all the free negroes, how long, think you, before they will begin to make *things* of poor white men?"

He summarized history to show that freedom and equality, sacred to the men of the American Revolution, had become words it was fashionable to sneer at. He rehearsed current violent events. Should force be met with force? He could not say. "The time has not yet come, and if we are true to ourselves, may never come. Do not mistake that the ballot is stronger than the bullet." Applause came regularly. He was saying what the convention wanted said. He was telling why the Republican party was being organized. As applause roared and lingered, the orator walked slowly toward the back of the platform, looked at notes in his hand, took a fresh start and worked toward the front. To Bill Herndon and others he seemed taller than ever before. "He's been baptized," said Herndon, hearing Lincoln declare that no matter what was to happen, "We will say to the Southern disunionists, *We* won't go out of the Union, and you *shan't.*" The delegates rose from their seats, applauded, stamped, cheered, waved handkerchiefs, threw hats in the air, ran riot. He was their tongue and voice. He had deepened the passions and unified the faith of adherents of a partisan cause.

After it was all over, Whitney did the best he could at making notes of the speech. If Lincoln had written out the speech the record of it would be accurate and responsible. But it was known that what he said, if written and printed, would be taken as wild-eyed and radical, that a published text of his passionate declarations would bring fierce denunciations and would alienate moderates from his party. Delegates wrung Lincoln's hand, and William Hopkins of Grundy burst out, "Lincoln, I never swear, but that was the damnedest best speech I ever heard."

Anti-Nebraska "Long John" Wentworth, two inches taller than Lincoln, wrote in the Chicago *Democrat*, "Abraham Lincoln for an hour and a half held the assemblage spellbound by the power of his argument, the intense irony of his invective, the brilliancy of his eloquence. I shall not mar any of its fine proportions by attempting even a synopsis of it." He suggested, "Mr. Lincoln must write it out and let it go before all the people." This advice Lincoln also heard from others and refused to follow it. The speech carried drama, irony, anger, storm, and could be twisted too many ways to please the opposition. He would let it be a memory.

An Alton editor's brief summary of the speech, at the time the only one published, caught no single syllable of passionate oratory, and closed: "The Black Democracy were endeavoring to cite Henry Clay to reconcile old Whigs to their doctrine, and repaid them with the very cheap compliment of National Whigs." Whitney's version, written many years later, from notes made after the speech, had Lincoln closing: "While, in all probability, no resort to force will be needed, our moderation and forbearance will stand us in good stead when, if ever, we must make an appeal to battle and to the God of Hosts!!" Such a daring and flaming utterance, in those exact words, may not have come from Lincoln, but words of equally high and challenging import came from him that day in Bloomington. He delivered cold logic that he would have been willing to see in print. And he broke loose with blazing outbursts in regard to human freedom and the Union of States, which for that particular political hour were better kept out of print.

In the McLean County Circuit Court, Lincoln represented the Illinois Central Railroad, his retainer $200. He lost his case; the decision was that the railroad must pay a tax in every county through which it passed. The cost in taxes would mount into millions and bankrupt the corporation. Lincoln appealed to the Supreme Court, argued the case twice, and in January 1856 won a decision reversing the lower court. He presented to an official at their Chicago office his bill for $2,000. The official looked at it: "Why, this is as much as a first-class lawyer would have charged!" adding it was "as much as Daniel Webster himself would have charged."

Back on the circuit when he told other lawyers of it, they didn't know whether to laugh or cry; the corporation had been saved millions of dollars through Lincoln's victory in court. Lincoln started a suit against the Illinois Central for a fee of $5,000. The case was called; the lawyer for the railroad didn't show up; Lincoln was awarded his $5,000 one morning. When the railroad lawyer arrived and begged for a retrial, Lincoln was willing. The case was called later, and Lincoln read a statement signed by six of the highest-priced lawyers in Illinois that the sum of $5,000 for the services rendered in the case "is not unreasonable." Before the jury went out he told them he had been paid $200 by the railroad and they should make the verdict for $4,800. Which they did.

Thirty-eight days went by and the railroad company failed to pay the $4,800 fee. An execution was issued directing the sheriff to seize property of the railroad. Then the fee was paid. And high officers of the railroad explained, "The payment of so large a fee to a western lawyer would embarrass the general counsel with the board of directors in New York."

Lincoln deposited the $4,800 in the Springfield Marine and Fire Insurance Company, and later, in handing Herndon half the fee, he pushed it toward his partner, then held it back an instant, and said with a smile, "Billy, it seems to me it will be bad taste on your part to keep saying severe things I have heard from you about railroads and other corporations. Instead of criticizing them, you and I ought to thank God for letting this one fall into our hands." And Herndon wrote, "We both thanked the Lord for letting the Illinois Central Railroad fall into our hands."

He was more and more trusted with important affairs of property. The McLean County Bank retained him to bring suit against the City of Bloomington. In Springfield, the gasworks asked him to make certain their title to the two city lots on which they were located, which Lincoln did, later sending the gasworks a bill for $500.

A caller in his office one day asked Lincoln to use his influence in a certain legal quarter, offering him $500. Herndon wrote, "I heard him refuse the $500 over and over again. I went out and left them together. I suppose Lincoln got tired of refusing, for he finally took the money; but he never offered any of it to me; and it was noticeable that whenever he took money in this way, he never seemed to consider it his own or mine. In this case, he gave the money to the Germans in the town, who wanted to buy themselves a press. A few days after, he said to me in the coolest way, 'Herndon, I gave the Germans $250 of yours the other day.' 'I am glad you did, Mr. Lincoln,' I answered. Of course I could not say I was glad he took it."

On May 6, 1856, the steamboat *Effie Afton* rammed into a pier of the Rock Island Railroad bridge, took fire, and burned to a total loss, while part of the bridge burned and tumbled into the river. The owners of the *Effie Afton* sued the bridge company for damages. Lincoln represented the company at the hearing in Chicago, with Judge McLean presiding. In his argument Lincoln pointed to the growing travel from east to west being as important as the Mississippi traffic. It was ever growing larger, this east-to-west traffic, building up new country with a rapidity never before seen in the history of the world. In his own memory he had seen Illinois grow from almost empty spaces to a population of 1,500,000. One man had as good a right to cross a river as another had to sail up or down it. He asked if the products of the boundless, fertile country lying west must for all time be forced to stop on a western bank, be unloaded from the cars and loaded on a boat, and after passage across the river be reloaded into cars on the other side. Civilization in the region to the west was at issue. The jury listened two weeks and were locked up; when they came out they had agreed to disagree; their action was generally taken as a victory for railroads, bridges and Chicago, as against steamboats, rivers and St. Louis.

During noon recess of a case tried in Rock Island, it was told, Lincoln walked out to the railroad bridge and came to a boy sitting on the end of a tie with a fishing pole out over the water. And Lincoln, fresh from the squabbles and challenges of the courtroom, said to the boy, "Well, I suppose you know all about this river." And the boy, "Sure, mister, it was here before I was born and it's been here ever since." Lincoln smiled, "Well, it's good to be out here where there is so much fact and so little opinion."

A check for $500 came into Lincoln's hands, thus far his largest retaining fee. Cyrus H. McCormick of Chicago was bringing suit against John H. Manny of Rockford, claiming that Manny's patents, not lawful and valid, infringed on the McCormick rights. If McCormick could win his case he would stop the Manny factory at Rockford and get $400,000 as damages. His lawyers were Edward M. Dickerson and Reverdy Johnson, while Manny had George Harding, Edwin M. Stanton, Peter H. Watson and Abraham Lincoln.

Lincoln went to Rockford, saw the Manny reaper in the making, and went on to Cincinnati to argue before Judge McLean. Lincoln's colleague, Edwin M. Stanton, was a serious owl-eyed man, strict in language, dress, duty. When his eyes lighted on Lincoln at the Burnet House in Cincinnati, wearing heavy boots, loose clothes, farmer-looking, he used language reported as: "Where did that long-armed baboon come from?"

Up and down the courtroom walked Lincoln, in his coat pocket a manuscript of his argument. The moment came when Stanton told the court that only two arguments would be made for the defense. Lincoln was out, his carefully planned speech not delivered. The defense won, though not by his services. Back in Springfield he divided a $2,000 fee, half and half, with Herndon, saying he had been "roughly handled by that man Stanton," and mentioned Judge McLean as "an old granny," and, "If you were to point your finger at him and a darning needle at the same time he never would know which was the sharpest."

A woman client had Lincoln survey and lay off into lots a piece of land she owned near the Springfield city limits. He found that by some mistake the woman had become owner of three more acres of land than she was entitled to, and Charles Matheny, the former owner, was the loser of the three acres. Lincoln notified her she ought to pay the heirs of Matheny the price per acre first agreed on. The woman couldn't see it. Lincoln wrote her again; the Matheny heirs were poor and needed the money. And again he wrote explaining what seemed to him plain justice. One day the woman sent him payment in full and he hunted up the heirs and paid them out their money.

Whitney told of a murder case in which Lincoln "hedged" after getting into it. Leonard Swett and Whitney had spoken for the defense, and believed they would get a verdict of acquittal. Then Lincoln spoke to the jury, took up the facts and the evidence, and was all of a sudden making arguments and admissions that spoiled the case for the prisoner at the bar. The jury came in with a verdict that sent the client to the penitentiary for three years. And the case got to working in Lincoln's mind. Somehow he hadn't done just right. Having helped get the man in the penitentiary, he worked to get him out, and in a year handed him a pardon from the governor.

All other law cases were out when Lincoln threw himself into the defense of William ("Duff") Armstrong, the son of Hannah Armstrong. Before a coroner's jury a house painter named Charles Allen from Petersburg swore that he saw the fight between Armstrong and a man named Metzker, that it was between ten and eleven o'clock at night, and, by the light of a moon shining nearly straight over them, he saw Armstrong hit Metzker with a slung shot and throw away the slung shot which he, Allen, picked up.

In the trial at Beardstown Lincoln aimed to have young men on the jury; young, hot blood would understand his case better; the average age of the jurymen as finally picked, was 23. With each witness Lincoln tried to find some ground of old acquaintance. "Your name?" he asked one. "William Killian." "Bill Killian? Tell me, are you a son of old Jake Killian?" "Yes, sir." "Well, you are a smart boy if you take after your dad."

Again Allen swore he saw Armstrong by the light of a moon nearly overhead, on a clear night, hit Metzker with a slung shot. Nelson Watkins testified that he had been to camp meeting the day after the fight, that he had with him a slung shot, and that he had thrown it away because it was too heavy and bothersome to carry. He had made the slung shot himself, he testified; he had put an eggshell into the ground, filled it with lead, poured melted zinc over the lead, but the two metals wouldn't stick; then he had cut a cover from a calfskin boot leg, sewed it together with a squirrel-skin string, using a crooked awl to make the holes; and he had then cut a strip from a groundhog skin that he had tanned, and fixed it so it would fasten to his wrist.

Lincoln took out his knife, cut the string with which the cover was sewed, showed it to be squirrel-skin, and then took out the inside metals and showed they were of two different sorts that did not stick together— the slung shot Allen testified he had picked up was identical with the one Watkins testified he had made and thrown away. Meantime he had sent out for an almanac, and when the moment came he set the courtroom into a buzz of excitement, laughter, whispering, by showing that, instead of the moon being in the sky at "about where the sun is at ten o'clock in the morning," as the leading witness testified, a popular, well-known family almanac showed that on the night of August 29, 1857, the moon had set and gone down out of sight at three minutes before midnight, or exactly 11:57 P.M. The almanac raised the question whether there was enough light by which a murder could be competently and materially witnessed.

Lincoln told the jury he knew the Armstrongs; the wild boy, Duff Armstrong, he had held in his arms when Duff was a baby at Clary's Grove; he could tell good citizens from bad and if there was anything he was certain of, it was that the Armstrong people were good people; they were plain people; they worked for a living; they made their mistakes; but they were kindly, loving people, the salt of the earth. He had told the mother of Duff, "Aunt Hannah, your son will be free before sundown." And it so happened. As the jury had filed out to vote, one of the jurymen winked an eye at Duff, so he afterwards told it.

Lincoln was easygoing sometimes about collecting money owed to him by clients. John W. Bunn, the Springfield banker, was asked by a Chicago firm to have a local attorney help them in an attachment suit involving several thousand dollars; Lincoln won the suit and charged $25. The Chicago firm wrote Bunn, "We asked you to get the best lawyer in Springfield, and it certainly looks as if you had secured one of the cheapest."

A lease on a valuable hotel property in Quincy was handled by Lincoln for George P. Floyd, who mailed a check for $25, Lincoln replying: "You must think I am a high-priced man. You are too liberal with your money. Fifteen dollars is enough for the job. I send you a receipt for fifteen dollars, and return to you a ten-dollar bill." In co-operation with a Chicago lawyer he saved a farm in Brown County for Isaac Hawley, a Springfield man, and Hawley had $50 ready to pay a fee; Lincoln smiled into Hawley's face and drawled, "Well, Isaac, I think I will charge you about ten dollars." To another client he said, "I will charge you $25, and if you think that is too much I will make it less." A woman gave him a check to push a real-estate claim in court; he found the claim no good and told the woman on her next visit to his office that there was no action; she thanked him, took her papers and was going, when Lincoln said, "Wait—here is the check you gave me."

In the case of Samuel Short, living near Taylorville, Lincoln cleared him of charges of maliciously and feloniously firing a shotgun at boys stealing watermelons on Short's farm; Short didn't pay his fee and Lincoln collected it through a suit in the court of a justice of the peace. Ending a letter that notified a client his case was won, he wrote, "As the dutch Justice said, when he married folks 'Now, vere ish my hundred tollars?'" There was a personal tang or smack in slight things he did. A man asked him for advice on a point of law and he told the man he'd have to look it up; meeting the man again, he gave him the advice wanted, but when the man wished to know the fee, Lincoln answered there would be no fee because it was a point he ought to have known without looking it up.

On Herndon asking him why he was so prompt in always paying Herndon half the fees, the answer was, "Well, Billy, there are three reasons: first, unless I did so I might forget I had collected the money; secondly, I explain to you how and from whom I received the money, so that you will not be required to dun the man who paid it; thirdly, if I were to die you would have no evidence that I had your money."

A client complained to Whitney about the way he and Lincoln had managed a case; Whitney tried to get Lincoln to smooth it over with the client, Lincoln's answer being, "Let him howl." Usually he was calm, bland, easygoing with other lawyers; but sometimes he wasn't; Amzi McWilliams, handling a witness on Lincoln's side of a case, called out, "Oh! No! No!! No!!!" which brought Lincoln undoubling out of a chair with a slow yelling of, "Oh! Yes! Yes!! Yes!!!" putting a stop to the bulldozing of the witness.

A horse thief in the Champaign County jail told his local lawyer, William D. Somers, that he wanted Lincoln to help in the defense. When Lincoln and Somers arrived at the jail they found their client talking with his wife, who was in a delicate condition of health, Lincoln noticed. When the client handed Lincoln $10 and said that was all the money he had, Lincoln looked at the woman and asked: "How about your wife? Won't she need this?"

The answer was, "She'll get along somehow," which didn't satisfy Lincoln. He handed the woman $5.00, and divided the other five with Somers.

He had to take losses; once all around the circuit his cases were for defendants, and he was beaten every time; so he told Bunn, the banker, in Springfield. And he told of himself that people had said, without disturbing his self-respect, "Well, he isn't lawyer enough to hurt him."

Lincoln defended a man who had 35 indictments against him for obstruction of the public highway. He took to the Supreme Court of the state a case involving a dispute over the payment of $3.00 in a hog sale. He became versed in the questions whether a saloon license can be transferred, whether damages can be collected from a farmer who starts a prairie fire that spreads to other farms, whether the divorced wife of a man can compel him to give her custody of her children and to supply her the means for their support. A merchant set fire to his stock of goods, collected the insurance, bought a new stock, and was sued by the insurance company for possession of the new stock. A man and his wife were threatened with being put off a railroad train because they refused to pay excess cash fare, claiming that the station agent had no tickets to their point of destination; they sued the railroad company. Lincoln's memory was cross-indexed with tangled human causes.

They had their fun and stories on the circuit. Once in Champaign County Court Judge Davis absent-mindedly sentenced a young fellow to seven years in the *legislature* of the State of Illinois. Prosecutor Lamon whispered to the judge, who then changed legislature to *penitentiary*. Lincoln, one morning in Bloomington, meeting a young lawyer whose case had gone to the jury late the night before, asked what had become of his case; the young lawyer bemoaned, "It's gone to hell," and Lincoln, "Oh well, then you'll see it again." Lincoln enjoyed quoting to other lawyers from a book he had read about a man who far from being a liar "had such great regard for the truth that he spent most of his time embellishing it."

To illustrate a point, he would tell a fable: "A man on foot, with his clothes in a bundle, coming to a stream which he must ford, made elaborate preparations by stripping off his garments, adding them to his bundle, and, tying all to the top of a stick, which enabled him to raise the bundle high over his head to keep them dry during the crossing. He then fearlessly waded in and carefully made his way across the rippling stream, and found it in no place up to his ankles." In a law case having to do with hogs breaking through a fence and damaging crops, he told about a fence so crooked that whenever a hog went through a hole in it, the hog always came out on the same side from which it started.

A rich newcomer to Springfield wanted Lincoln to bring suit against an unlucky, crackbrained lawyer who owed him $2.50; Lincoln advised him to hold off; he said he would go to some other lawyer who was more willing. So Lincoln took the case, collected a $10 fee in advance, entered suit, hunted up the defendant and handed him half of the $10 and told him to show up in court and pay the debt. Which was done. And all litigants and the lawyer were satisfied.

On a 36-mile drive one October night, Lincoln, Swett and his wife, and Whitney were in a two-seated carriage; dark had come on as they rode into a river-bottom road in heavy timber with deep ditches alongside; and the horses and hubs plugged through mud. The driver stopped the horses; someone would have to go ahead and pilot; he didn't want to tip over as one of Frink & Walker's stages had done. Whitney jumped out, Lincoln after him; they rolled up their trousers, and arm in arm went ahead, calling back every minute or so. Lincoln sang, "Mortal man with face of clay, Here tomorrow, gone today," and other verses he made up. They drove into Danville later, laughing at October night weather and autumn mud.

He made safe, moderate investments. Speculations beckoned to others, but not to him. At hotels he took what was offered him with no complaint. He told his fellow lawyer Joe Gillespie he never felt easy when a waiter or a flunky was around. At a meeting of Republican editors in Decatur, he said he was a sort of interloper, and told of a woman on horseback meeting a man on a horse on a narrow trail. The woman stopped her horse, looked the man over: "Well for the land's sake, you are the homeliest man I ever saw!" The man excused himself, "Yes, Ma'am, but I can't help that," and the woman: "No, I suppose not, but you might stay at home."

Before posing for an ambrotype he ran his fingers through his hair to rumple it; on the stump or in jury speeches his hands wandered over his head and put the hair in disorder. Always, it was noticed, the linen he wore was clean; his barbers didn't let the sign of a beard start; he blacked his own boots. As to haircuts, grammar and technicalities, he wasn't so particular. In jury arguments and before a big crowd in Springfield, he wiped sweat from his face with a red silk handkerchief.

He read Joe Miller and repeated some of the jokes though he had a thousand fresher ones of his own; they sprouted by the waysides of his travel. For lawyers he would mimic a country justice: "If the court understand *herself* and she think she do." And there was John Moore, driving a yoke of red steers to Bloomington one Saturday, starting home with a jug, and emptying the jug into himself. Driving through timber a wheel hit a stump and threw the pole out of the ring of the yoke. The steers ran away; Moore slept till morning in the cart, and when he awoke and looked around, he said, "If my name is John Moore, I've lost a pair of steers; if my name ain't John Moore, I've found a cart."

And Lincoln had heard a farmer brag about his hay crop one year: "We stacked all we could outdoors, and then we put the rest of it in the barn." On a paper written by a lawyer, with too many words and pages, he remarked, "It's like the lazy preacher that used to write long sermons, and the explanation was, he got to writin' and was too lazy to stop."

Lincoln and Henry Grove of Peoria were attorneys at Metamora for the defense of 70-year-old Melissa Goings, indicted for the murder of her husband, a well-to-do farmer of 77. Testimony indicated he was choking her and she broke loose, got a stick of stove wood, and fractured his skull. The dead man had a name for quarreling and hard drinking and his last words were, "I expect she has killed me. If I get over it I will have revenge." Melissa Goings was held in $1,000 bail. Public feeling ran overwhelmingly in her favor. Indications were that Lincoln held a conference with the prosecuting attorney, and that on the day set for trial Mrs. Goings was granted time for a short conference with her lawyer, Mr. Lincoln. Then she left the court-house, was never again seen in Metamora, and the next day the case against her bondsmen was stricken from the docket. A court bailiff, Robert T. Cassell, later said that when he couldn't produce the defendant for trial he accused Lincoln of "running her off." Lincoln replied, "Oh no, Bob. I did not run her off. She wanted to know where she could get a good drink of water, and I told her there was mighty good water in Tennessee."

Friendships with Swett, Whitney and others on the circuit grew and deepened for Lincoln, and particularly that with fair-haired and pink-faced Judge David Davis, six years younger, five inches shorter, a hundred pounds heavier. A graduate of Kenyon College, Davis had come west and grown up with Bloomington. He had a keen eye for land deals and owned thousand-acre tracts. On his large farm near Bloomington he had a frame mansion where Lincoln stayed occasionally. In many ways the destinies of Davis and Lincoln were to interweave.

CHAPTER 10

The Deepening Slavery Issue

THE DEMOCRATIC national convention opened June 2, 1856, in Cincinnati, gave unanimous endorsement to the Nebraska Act, voted 138 to 120 against a Pacific railway, and after the 15th ballot went into a deadlock with 168½ votes for James Buchanan for President, 118½ for Douglas, a two-thirds vote being required to nominate. Douglas sent a letter saying the "embittered state of feeling" was a danger to the party and as Buchanan had a majority he was entitled to the nomination. On the 17th ballot Buchanan was nominated by unanimous vote. Buchanan had been away as minister to England, had taken no hand in the Kansas-Nebraska mess, and was rated a "safe" candidate. He and the platform faced to the past. The most human touch in the platform struck at the Know-Nothings; "a political crusade . . . against Catholics and foreign-born" had no place in the American system.

A fresher air and new causes moved the first national Republican convention in Philadelphia in mid-June. The newly born party's platform faced to the future; no extension of slavery, admission of Kansas as a Free State, "a railroad to the Pacific Ocean, by the most central and practicable route." No delegates came from the Deep South, only a few from the Border States; the party was sectional.

The nomination for President went to John C. Frémont; he had served as U.S. Senator from the Free State of California; as an explorer and "pathfinder" in western wilds he had made a name for daring and enduring hardship. He was overly dignified, an egotist, a greenhorn in politics, yet somehow he had never said or done anything radical that could harm him or the party. He was nominated by 359 votes, 196 going to U.S. Supreme Court Justice John McLean. Lincoln had favored the veteran Whig McLean as the man to draw the votes of the conservative Old Line Whigs. For Vice-President William L. Dayton of New Jersey, an able lawyer and former U.S. Senator, was nominated, the first ballot giving him 259 votes and Abraham Lincoln 110. The news reaching Lincoln, he laughed that it must be "some other Lincoln."

A February convention of Know-Nothings in Philadelphia had declared that only "*native*-born citizens" should hold office, and the foreign-born should vote only after "continued residence of twenty-one years." This political convention of the American party took a proslavery stand in endorsing the Kansas-Nebraska Bill, an antislavery faction walking out. Millard Fillmore, while in Europe, was nominated for President, and coming home, accepted. Fillmore had been a Whig Vice-President, had become a Whig President on the death of President Taylor, had a strong Whig following that would vote for him. And Lincoln in letters and in more than 50 speeches hammered it home that a Whig vote for Fillmore was a vote against the Republicans and a vote for Buchanan, the Democrat. He mentioned Fremont often but never with any slight flowering of praise. Also he handled Fillmore respectfully and tenderly, with no belittlement, saying nothing of the Know-Nothings who created and sponsored Fillmore as a candidate. He kept quiet about a convention of Old Line Whigs, presided over by Judge Edward Bates of Missouri, which in September endorsed Fillmore, "without adopting the peculiar doctrines" of the American party.

Lincoln stressed the slavery question most often. "The slaves of the South, at a moderate estimate, are worth a thousand million of dollars. Let it be permanently settled that this property may extend to new territory, without restraint, and it greatly *enhances*, perhaps quite *doubles*, its value at once." In Belleville, where Germans were in high proportion, the *Weekly Advocate* said that Lincoln referred to "the noble position" taken by the Germans, and, "When he called down the blessings of the Almighty on their heads, a thrill of sympathy and pleasure ran through his whole audience." The *Advocate* mentioned Lincoln as "this associate" of Frederick K. F. Hecker and banners reading, "Lincoln and Hecker." A revolutionary favoring a constitutional government to replace the monarchy, Hecker had been exiled from Germany. Hecker's home in St. Clair County had been burned down while he was making a Frémont speech. Lincoln had raised a fund to rebuild and wrote Hecker, "I hope you will not decline to accept."

At Galena July 23, 1856, Lincoln went radical. He spoke there in what was probably the tone of his "Lost Speech." In no other published speech did he refer to the naked might and force that could in the future be called into play. Fillmore in an Albany speech had charged that if the Republicans elected a President the event would dissolve the Union. "Who are the disunionists, you or we?" Lincoln asked. "We, the majority, would not strive to dissolve the Union; and if any attempt is made it must be by you, who so loudly stigmatize us as disunionists. But the Union, in any event, won't be dissolved. We don't want to dissolve it, and if you attempt it, *we won't let you*. With the purse and sword, the army and navy and treasury in our hands, and at our command, you *couldn't do it*. This Government would be very weak, indeed, if a majority, with a disciplined army and navy, and a well-filled treasury, could not preserve itself, when attacked by an unarmed, undisciplined, unorganized minority. All this talk about the dissolution of the Union is humbug—nothing but folly. *We won't* dissolve the Union, and *you shan't.*" Thus it was published in Galena and Springfield newspapers.

Of his day at Dixon, the Amboy *Times* said Lincoln "is about six feet high, crooked-legged, stoop-shouldered, spare-built, and anything but handsome in the face," but "as a close observer and cogent reasoner, he has few equals and perhaps no superior in the world . . . He attacks no man's character or motives, but fights with arguments." He spoke at Princeton with Lovejoy who was running for Congress, and at several meetings was joined with Senator Trumbull and William "Deacon" Bross of the Chicago *Daily Democratic Press.* He spoke at Atlanta [Illinois] in early September and again in late October. At a Shelbyville rally of Democrats, he debated with a local leader, the *Register* at Springfield saying his three-hour speech "was prosy and dull . . . all about 'freedom,' 'liberty' and niggers. He . . . dodged every issue."

His law practice got little of his time as he rode on trains, in buggies and wagons, to speak at many points including Bloomington, Urbana, Sterling, Paris, Grand View, Charleston, Oregon, Vandalia, Decatur, Lacon, the State Fair at Alton, Ottawa, Joliet, Peoria, Clinton, Pittsfield, Jacksonville, four speeches in Springfield, occasionally two speeches in one day. A crowd of 10,000 heard him in Kalamazoo, Michigan, where an abolitionist wrote he was "far too conservative and Union-loving."

In his own home Lincoln's arguments failed. Mrs. Lincoln wrote to a sister: "My weak woman's heart was too Southern in feeling to sympathize with any but Fillmore . . . he made so good a President & is so just a man & feels the *necessity* of keeping foreigners within bounds."

When the October and November election returns were all in, Buchanan had 174 electoral votes, Frémont 114, Fillmore 8. The popular vote was 1,838,169 for Buchanan, 1,341,264 for Frémont, 874,534 for Fillmore. Buchanan carried all the Slave States except Maryland, which Fillmore carried. Lincoln's fears of the Fillmore vote were seen in Illinois where the vote was 105,000 for Buchanan, 96,000 for Frémont, and 37,000 for Fillmore. Yet there was comfort. The Republicans had elected a Mexican War veteran, Colonel William H. Bissell, governor, and the state ticket had swept in.

The New York *Times* and the *Evening Post* reported that $150,000 was sent into Pennsylvania from the slaveholding states; that August Belmont of New York had contributed $50,000 for the Democrats; and that other Wall Street bankers and brokers, fearing disorder and damage to business from disunion, raised still another $100,000. "Very nearly $500,000" was spent by the Democrats, the New York *Times* estimated, while the Republican expenses were somewhat less. Enough was known to show that behind the Pennsylvania contest were special interests paying big money toward winning that state.

At a Chicago banquet Lincoln spoke the toast: "*The Union*—the North will maintain it—the South will not depart therefrom." All who didn't vote for Buchanan made a majority of 400,000. "We were divided between Frémont and Fillmore. Can we not come together, for the future . . . Let bygones be bygones. Let past differences, as nothing be." The central idea should be not "all citizens as citizens are equal" but the broader and better "all *men* are created equal." He was sure, "The human heart *is* with us—God is with us."

On March 6, 1857, in the U.S. Supreme Court room on the ground floor of the north wing of the Capitol, a hushed crowd listened to get every word read for three hours from a document by a man out of the past, an 81-year-old man, thin of body and furrowed of face, frail and fading, his voice at times a whisper. He had been Attorney General and Secretary of the Treasury under President Jackson who appointed him Chief Justice. He was Roger Brooke Taney, Maryland-born, a devout Catholic, free from scandal, highly respected in his profession, one lawyer terming him "apostolic" in conduct. He came from the tobacco-planting, slaveholding tidewater strip of Maryland but he had freed the slaves he inherited, except two or three too old to work whom he supported. At this time he was not yet over the shock of his wife's death from yellow fever and the death the next day of their last child, a beloved and beautiful daughter. He read for three hours the Supreme Court decision in the case of Dred Scott, a slave suing for freedom because he had been taken into territory where slavery was illegal under the Missouri Compromise; the Supreme Court of Missouri had sent him back into slavery because he had voluntarily returned to a Slave State. Four of the nine judges of the U.S. Supreme Court dissented, five being from Slave States. The decision declared that Congress did not have power to prohibit slavery in the Territories; the Missouri Compromise was unconstitutional; a slave was property and if a slaveowner took his property into a territory where the U.S. Constitution was the high law, his property could not be taken from him; a Negro slave or a free Negro whose ancestors were slaves, could not become a U.S. citizen. Negroes "were not intended to be included under the word 'citizens' " in the Constitution. "They had for more than a century before been regarded as beings of an inferior order, and altogether unfit to associate with the white race, either in social or political relations; and so far inferior that they had no rights which the white man was bound to respect, and that the negro might justly and lawfully be reduced to slavery for his benefit. He was bought and sold, and treated as an ordinary article of merchandise and traffic, whenever a profit could be made by it." Quoting from the Declaration of Independence "that all men are created equal," Taney read: "The general words above quoted would seem to embrace the whole human family . . . But it is too clear for dispute that the enslaved African race were not intended to be included."

Taney had hoped good would come from this decision but it set the slavery question seething. The New York *Tribune* said 6,000,000 people in the South had more weight in the Supreme Court than 16,000,000 people in the Free States. Lincoln, from now on for years, was to stress more than ever what he believed the Declaration of Independence meant by the clause "that all men are created equal." The question would recur, "If those who wrote and adopted the Constitution believed slavery to be a good thing, why did they insert a provision prohibiting the slave trade after the year 1808?" Into Lincoln's speech was to come more often that phrase "the Family of Man" as though mankind has unity and dignity.

Douglas in Springfield in June spoke for the court's decision. "Whoever resists the final decision of the highest judicial tribunal aims a deadly blow at our whole republican system of government." Lincoln two weeks later replied, "We know the court that made it, has often over-ruled its own decisions, and we shall do what we can to have it to over-rule this. We offer no *resistance* to it." Lincoln then quoted from a message of President Jackson in open resistance to a Supreme Court decision against a national bank, re-marking, "Again and again have I heard Judge Douglas denounce that bank decision, and applaud Gen. Jackson for disregarding it."

He mentioned Taney's lengthy insistence "that negroes were no part of the people" who made the Declaration of Independence or the Constitution. Lincoln then quoted from a dissenting court opinion showing that in five of the 13 original states, free Negroes were voters. He read from Douglas' speech that the signers of the Declaration of Independence "referred to the white race alone, and not to the African, when they declared all men to have been created equal—they were speaking of British subjects on this continent being equal to British subjects born and residing in Great Britain." Thus, said Lincoln, not only Negroes but, the "French, Germans and other white people of the world are all gone to pot along with the Judge's inferior races."

Of course the Declaration signers did not intend to declare "all men equal in all respects" but they did consider all men equal in "certain inalienable rights, among which are life, liberty and the pursuit of happiness." He men-tioned Douglas being "horrified at the thought of mixing blood by the white and black races," and commented, "In 1850 there were in the United States, 405,523 mulattoes. Very few of these are the offspring of whites and *free* blacks; nearly all have sprung from black *slaves* and white masters . . . In 1850 there were in the free states, 56,649 mulattoes; but for the most part they were not born there—they came from the slave States, ready made up. In the same year the slave States had 348,874 mulattoes all of home produc-tion . . . Could we have had our way, the chances of these black girls, ever mixing their blood with that of white people, would have been diminished at least to the extent that it could not have been done without their consent. But Judge Douglas is delighted to have them decided to be slaves."

Taney assumed "that the public estimate of the black man is more favor-able *now* than it was in the days of the Revolution" yet in states where formerly the free Negro could vote, that right had been taken away. More and more state constitutions forbade the legislature to abolish slavery or slaveowners to free slaves. Of the chattel slave Lincoln spoke a fateful and strangely cadenced meditation:

All the powers of earth seem rapidly combining against him. Mammon is after him; ambition follows, and philosophy follows, and the Theology of the day is fast joining the cry. They have him in his prison house; they have searched his person, and left no prying instrument with him. One after another they have closed the heavy iron doors upon him, and now they have him, as it were, bolted in with a lock of a hundred keys, which can never be unlocked without the con-currence of every key; the keys in the hands of a hundred different men, and they scattered to a hundred different and distant places; and they stand musing as to what invention, in all the dominions of mind and matter, can be produced to make the impossibility of his escape more complete than it is.

Never ending for months had been the unrest and the high crying over "Bleeding Kansas." Between November 5, 1855, and December 1, 1856, about 200 persons had been killed and far more wounded from guns and knives. The Emigrant Aid Society, with large eastern funds, had sent out thousands of antislavery settlers and the legislature was strongly antislavery. But by registration trickery in test oaths, by thousands of ballots from counties having only a few score of settlers, by threats of violence, and by refusal of thousands of antislavery voters to vote in a special election where they said their votes wouldn't be counted, the proslavery party "elected" a constitutional convention which met in Lecompton under Federal troop guard. The Lecompton constitution which they wrote, proslavery in its mumbo-jumbo clauses, was sent to Washington for approval by Congress.

While the debate dragged on for months in Congress, President Pierce sent two governors to Kansas, Buchanan sent another and another, and each failed at bringing order and peace. John W. Geary and Robert J. Walker were, in the aftermath, estimated to have been shrewd, keen and fair umpires in meeting demands from the desperate proslavery men who saw themselves more and more with every month outnumbered by antislavery settlers and immigrants—and whenever a fair election was held the proslavery party lost. A congressional committee went to Kansas, heard hundreds of witnesses and its report ran 1,206 pages. Only a long story, reciting election frauds, disputes, bickerings, burnings of houses and barns, shooting and stabbing affairs could begin to picture the tragic and moaning chaos of Kansas. Poll books stolen, election judges driven from their seats, illegal ballots by hundreds, voters coming to the polls hearing men with guns and knives, "Cut his throat!" "Tear his heart out!"—the witnesses gave names, dates, places.

Guerrillas, bushwackers, roving outlaw gangs were more common after the "Pottawatomie Creek Massacre." Tall, bearded John Brown, 56 years old, haunted by five free-state men killed, made a decision. He would kill five slave-state men, saying to one of his men, Townley, who didn't like the idea, "I have no choice. It has been decreed by Almighty God, ordained from eternity, that I should make an example of these men." On the night of May 24, 1857, he took two men and his four obedient sons, Owen, Frederick, Salmon and Oliver, each with a rifle, pistol and cutlass, and they went to three different cabins. In the Doyle cabin, the wife and mother begged to be let alone, but out into the night they dragged her husband and two sons, found next morning on the grass 200 yards from the cabin, the father shot in the head and stabbed in the breast, one son with arms and fingers cut off and a hole in his throat, the other son with holes in side, head and jaw. At Wilkinson's cabin past midnight they forced him to open the door, heard his sick wife plead, but he was found next day dead, with gashes in head and side. At the third cabin they took William Sherman who was found next morning with his skull split open and left hand cut off. The butchery was done mainly with two-edged cutlasses Brown had brought from Ohio.

Over the country in press and pulpit, on the platform, on sidewalks and in cigar stores and saloons, each side made its claims on the basis of distorted and incomplete reports. The sad fact that didn't come out till complete evidence was in made it clear that the victims slaughtered so coldly were merely plain illiterate farmers making a scant living and definitely not proslavery agitators. One son of Brown who didn't go along asked his father, "Did you have anything to do with that bloody affair on the Pottawatomie?" And John Brown: "I approved of it." The son: "Whoever did it, the act was uncalled for and wicked." And John Brown: "God is my judge. The people of Kansas will yet justify my course."

What with governors appointed by Pierce and Buchanan and more than a thousand U.S. Regular troops in Kansas, disorder and violence there slowed down, but in Washington in December 1857 the Lecompton constitution split the Democratic party wide open. At a coming election in Kansas the voters were to ballot, not on the constitution a rump convention had adopted, but on the single question of whether they adopted the constitution "with slavery" or "without slavery." Buchanan favored this election.

Douglas, before crowded galleries, made one of his great dramatic speeches. He denied the President's assertion that the Nebraska Act had carried an obligation merely to submit the slavery question and not the whole constitution. The election now arranged for this December in Kansas, said Douglas, offered Louis Napoleon's choice: Vote *yes* and be protected, vote *no* and be shot. Those in favor of it could vote for it, those against it couldn't vote at all. He had asked men who framed the Lecompton constitution about it. "They say that if they allowed a negative vote, the constitution would have been voted down by an overwhelming majority, and hence the fellows shall not be allowed to vote at all. [laughter] . . . If this constitution is to be forced down our throats, under a mode of submission that is a mockery and insult, I will resist it to the last." This speech was in a political year when the Boston scholar, George Ticknor, wrote to an English friend that American politics is "completely inexplicable."

In the eyes of some Republican leaders in the east Douglas became a hero; they suggested that Illinois Republicans in 1858 should support Douglas for Senator. Lincoln wrote to Trumbull in late December 1857: "What does the *New-York Tribune* mean by it's constant eulogising, and admiring, and magnifying Douglas? . . . Have they concluded that the republican cause, generally, can be best promoted by sacraficing us here in Illinois? . . . I am not complaining. I only wish a fair understanding."

Three months later when Buchanan was throwing out of office men put in by Douglas, postmasters, marshals, land and mail agents, Herndon wrote to Trumbull, "Lincoln and I are glad to death that Douglas has been crushed." But Douglas was far from crushed. With his Democratic following in Congress, joined with Republicans, he defeated Buchanan's proslavery measures for Kansas. Over the nation and in a large segment of his party Douglas had never before had such a peculiarly high and honorable standing. Many, however, in Republican and other circles, held that he was no particular hero in having done what he had to do; when Buchanan wanted to make a mockery of "popular sovereignty," his only course was to oppose Buchanan, even if it should smash party unity. He kept on saying he didn't care "whether slavery was voted up or down," and in that posture he was the same old Douglas.

Meantime the country was still staggering under the financial panic of 1857 with its bank wrecks, tumbling stocks, property value shrinkages. Processions of thousands of men marched in the Northern large cities with banners reading: "Hunger Is a Sharp Thorn" and "We Want Work."

CHAPTER 11

The Great Debates

THE POLITICAL letters of Lincoln early in 1858 showed more and more a rare skill in the management of men. He wrote Lovejoy that he had been in Lovejoy's district and the danger had been that the Democrats "would wheedle some republican to run against you." The letter was strictly confidential, "not that there is anything wrong in it; but that I have some highly valued friends who would not like me any the better for writing it." He wrote in other letters that he was not "setting stake" against Seward, that Greeley was honest though "a drag upon us," that the enemy trick was "to try to excite all sorts of suspicions and jealosies amongst us," and that "we need nothing so much as to get rid of unjust suspicions of one another." He wrote to Norman B. Judd, the Chicago railroad and corporation lawyer who was chairman of the state central committee, that if Herndon had been talking of Judd being "treacherous," he could promise it wouldn't be repeated. He wrote to Congressman Elihu B. Washburne that he never did believe rumors afloat about Washburne going for Douglas and, "I am satisfied you have done no wrong, and nobody has intended any wrong to you."

To another he wrote June 1 that he supposed it wasn't "necessary" that county conventions should make known their choice for U.S. Senator, though Lincoln must have known that an amazing number of county conventions would name him. The Chicago *Tribune* said on June 14 that the unprecedented action of 95 county Republican conventions endorsing Lincoln was a "remonstrance against outside intermeddling" by Greeley and easterners favoring Douglas.

Many Republicans were saying when their state convention met in Springfield June 16, 1858, "We know Douglas, we have fought him for years, and now we're going to give him the run of his life." On a unanimous vote the resolution passed, saying, "Abraham Lincoln is the first and only choice of the Republicans of Illinois for the U.S. Senate as the successor of Stephen A. Douglas." In the evening in the hall of the House of Representatives, Lincoln came, bowed to applause and cheers, murmured, "Mr. President and Gentlemen of the convention." Then he read a speech from manuscript. He had worked harder on it, revised it with more care, than any other speech in his life; he had read it the evening before to a group of party leaders who advised him not to deliver it. Now he read:

"If we could first know *where* we are, and *whither* we are tending, we could better judge *what* to do, and *how* to do it. We are now far into the *fifth* year, since a policy was initiated, with the *avowed* object, and *confident* promise, of putting an end to slavery agitation. Under the operation of that policy, that agitation has not only, *not ceased*, but has *constantly augmented*. In *my* opinion, it *will* not cease, until a *crisis* shall have been reached, and passed. 'A house divided against itself cannot stand.' I believe this government cannot endure, permanently half *slave* and half *free*. I do not expect the Union to be *dissolved*—I do not expect the house to *fall*—but I *do* expect it will cease to be divided. It will become *all* one thing, or *all* the other."

This was so plain that two farmers fixing fences on a rainy morning could talk it over. The speaker read on: "Either the *opponents* of slavery, will arrest the further spread of it, and place it where the public mind shall rest in the belief that it is in the course of ultimate extinction; or its *advocates* will push it forward, till it shall become alike lawful in *all* the States, *old* as well as *new, North* as well as *South*." He put together this and that circumstance and argued that while on the face of them the people could not be sure there was a conspiracy on foot to nationalize slavery, yet explanations were required. "Put *that* and *that* together, and we have another nice little niche, which we may, ere long, see filled with another Supreme Court decision, declaring that the Constitution of the United States does not permit a *state* to exclude slavery from its limits . . . Such a decision is all that slavery now lacks of being alike lawful in all the States." What interested the country most, as many newspapers published the speech in full, was its opening paragraph. It became known as the "House Divided" speech. It went far.

A court official in Springfield once asked Lincoln what special ability was most valuable for a winning politician, and quoted Lincoln's answer: "To be able to raise a cause which will produce an effect, and then fight the effect."

Douglas in Washington told a group of Republicans, "You have nominated a very able and a very honest man." To John W. Forney he said: "I shall have my hands full. Lincoln is the strong man of his party, the best stump speaker in the West." And again, "Of all the damned Whig rascals about Springfield, Abe Lincoln is the ablest and the most honest."

Douglas started west in June, his daily movements watched by the country. The Chicago *Times* reprinted from the Philadelphia *Press:* "Senator Douglas, accompanied by his beautiful and accomplished wife, arrived at the Girard House, en route for Chicago." Sixty miles out from Chicago, a special Illinois Central train with a brass band, flags and pennants met the Douglas party July 9 and escorted the statesman to Chicago. As he stepped out on the Lake Street balcony of the Tremont House that night, rockets and red fire lit the street. The crowd in the street was getting over a fight with hack drivers who had tried to plow through the mass of people and deliver guests at the Tremont House. One man was knocked down with the butt end of a whip, one driver pulled off his seat three times. As horses, people, and hack drivers were untangled, Judge Douglas began an hour and a half speech.

Upper left: Photograph made in Chicago in 1854 at 12 North Wells Street. Original presented to Chicago Historical Society by George Schneider. *Upper right:* Early photograph of Mary Todd Lincoln [CS]. *Lower left:* Stephen Arnold Douglas, powerful, dramatic political opponent of Lincoln for many years [Meserve]. *Lower right:* Adèle Cutts Douglas, second wife and rare helpmeet of the "Little Giant" [Meserve].

Second joint debate.
August 27. 1858 at Freeport, Illinois.
Lincoln, as reported in the Press & Tribune.
Douglas, as reported in the Chicago Times.

A. I do not stand to-day pledged to the abolition of slavery in the District of Columbia.

Q. 5. "I desire him to answer whether he stands pledged to the prohibition of the slave trade between the different States?"

A. I do not stand pledged to the prohibition of the slave trade between the different States.

Q. 6. "I desire to know whether he stands pledged to prohibit slavery in all the Territories of the United States, North as well as South of the Missouri Compromise line."

A. I am impliedly, if not expressly, pledged to a belief in the *right* and *duty* of Congress to prohibit slavery in all the United States Territories.

Q. 7. "I desire him to answer whether he is opposed to the acquisition of any new territory unless slavery is first prohibited therein."

A. I am not generally opposed to honest question of territory; and, in any given case I would or would not oppose such acquisition accordingly as I might think such acquisition would or would not *aggravate* the slavery question among ourselves.

Now, my friends, it will be perceived upon an examination of these questions and answers, that so far I have only answered that I was not *pledged* to this, that or the other. The Judge has not framed his interrogatories to ask me anything more than this, and I have answered in strict accordance with the interrogatories, and have answered truly that I am not *pledged* at all upon any of the points to which I have answered. But I am not disposed to hang upon the exact form of his interrogatory. I am rather disposed to take up at least some of these questions, and state what I really think upon them.

As to the first one, in regard to the Fugitive Slave Law, I have never hesitated to say, and I do not now hesitate to say, that I think, under the Constitution of the United States, the people of the Southern States are entitled to a Congressional Fugitive Slave Law. Having said that, I have had nothing to say in regard to the existing Fugitive Slave Law farther than this I think it should have been framed so as to be free from

ence to the State of Illinois, and I believe I am saying that which, if it would be *offensive* to any persons and render them enemies to myself, would be offensive to persons in this audience.

I now proceed to propound to the Judge the interrogatories, so far as I have framed them. I will bring forward a new installment when I get them ready. I will bring them forward now, only reaching to number four.

The first one is—

Question 1. If the people of Kansas shall, by means entirely unobjectionable in all other respects, adopt a State Constitution, and ask admission into the Union under it, *before* they have the requisite number of inhabitants according to the English Bill—some ninety-three thousand—will you vote to admit them?

Question 2. Can the people of a United States Territory, in any lawful way, against the wish of any citizen of the United States, exclude slavery from its limits prior to the formation of a State Constitution?

Q. 3. If the Supreme Court of the United States shall *decide* that States can not exclude slavery from their limits, are you in favor of acquiescing in, adopting and following such decision as a rule of political action?

Q. 4. Are you in favor of acquiring additional territory, in disregard of how such acquisition may affect the nation on the slavery question?

As introductory to these interrogatories which Judge Douglas propounded to me at Ottawa, he read a set of resolutions which he said Judge Trumbell and myself had participated in adopting, in the first Republican State Convention held at Springfield, in October, 1854. He insisted that I and Judge Trumbell, and perhaps, the entire Republican party were responsible for the doctrines contained in the set of resolutions which he read, and I understand that it was from that set of resolutions that he deduced the interrogatories which he propounded to me, using these resolutions as a sort of authority for propounding those ques-

Page from annotated and corrected newspaper reports of debates with Douglas, the only manuscript Lincoln ever prepared for book publication. [Alfred Whital Stern Collection of Lincolniana, Library of Congress]

Lincoln heard Douglas refer to him as "a kind, amiable, and intelligent gentleman, a good citizen and an honorable opponent." He heard Douglas say to the swarming thousands on the street: "Mr. Lincoln advocates boldly and clearly a war of sections, a war of the North against the South, of the free States against the slave States—a war of extermination—to be continued relentlessly until the one or the other shall be subdued, and all the States shall either become free or become slave."

The next night Lincoln spoke from the same Tremont House balcony to a crowd somewhat smaller; rockets blazed; the brass band of the German Republican Club from the Seventh Ward rendered music. And amid much on issues of the day Lincoln said: "I do not pretend that I would not like to go to the United States Senate, I make no such hypocritical pretense, but I do say to you that in this mighty issue, it is nothing to you—nothing to the mass of the people of the nation—whether or not Judge Douglas or myself shall ever be heard of after this night."

It was in this same month that A. P. Chapman wrote Lincoln of "Grand Mother Lincoln" (Sarah Bush) doing well, and, "I often take my Republican papers and read Extracts from them that Eulogise you you can hardly form an idea how proud it makes her. She often says Abram was always her best child & that he always treated her like a son. I told her I was a going to write you to day & and she says tell you she sent a heap of love to you & wants to see you once more very much . . ."

Lincoln wrote a challenge to debate and Douglas accepted. The two men would meet on platforms and clash on issues in cities in seven different parts of the state, all Illinois watching, the whole country listening. By the shorthand writing newly invented, reporters would give the country "full phonographic verbatim reports," newspapers told their readers.

In the Ottawa public square 12,000 listeners sat or stood in a broiling summer sun August 21 for the first debate. For three hours they listened. A train of 17 cars had come from Chicago. By train, boat, wagon, buggy and afoot people had arrived, waved flags, paraded and escorted their heroes.

Acres of people listened and, the speaking ended, they surged around their heroes and formed escorts. A dozen grinning Republicans lifted Lincoln to their shoulders, and a Republican crowd headed by a brass band saw him carried to Mayor Glover's home. "With his long arms about his carriers' shoulders, his long legs dangling nearly to the ground, his long face was an incessant contortion to wear a winning smile that succeeded in being only ghastly," said a Democratic newspaper. The Philadelphia *Press* reporter noted of Lincoln: "Poor fellow! he was writhing in the powerful grasp of an intellectual giant. His speech amounted to nothing." The New York *Evening Post* reporter wrote: "In repose, I must confess that 'Long Abe's' appearance is *not* comely. But stir him up and the fire of genius plays on every feature. Listening to him, calmly and unprejudiced, I was convinced that he has no superior as a stump speaker."

Next came Freeport, far in the northwestern corner of Illinois. A torchlight procession met Douglas; the Chicago *Times* counted 1,000 torches, the Chicago *Press* and *Tribune* 74. Lincoln rode to the speaking stand in a covered wagon drawn by six big white horses. Fifteen thousand people sat and stood listening through three hours of cloudy, chilly weather; mist and a fine drizzle drifted across the air. Some had come on the new sleeping cars from Chicago the night before. One train on the Galena road had 16 cars and 1,000 passengers.

Then debaters and shorthand reporters dropped south 300 miles, to a point south of Richmond, Virginia. The Jonesboro crowd numbered about 1,400 —most of them rather cool about the great debate. The place was on land wedged between the Slave States of Kentucky and Missouri; several carloads of passengers had come from those states to listen. The Chicago *Times* noted: "The enthusiasm in behalf of Douglas is intense; there is but one purpose, to reelect him to the Senate where he has won for himself and the State such imperishable renown." As to Lincoln's remarks, the Louisville *Journal* noted: "Let no one omit to read them. They are searching, scathing, stunning. They belong to what some one has graphically styled the *tomahawking* species."

Three days later debaters and reporters were up at Charleston, and there, said the Missouri *Republican*, "The joint discussion between the Tall Sucker and the Little Giant came off according to programme." Twelve thousand people came to the county fairgrounds—and listened.

On October 7, in the itinerary, came Galesburg, in Knox County. Twenty thousand people and more sat and stood hearing Lincoln and Douglas speak while a raw northwest wind tore flags and banners to rags. The damp air chilled the bones of those who forgot their overcoats. For three hours the two debaters spoke to people who buttoned their coats tighter and listened. They had come from the banks of the Cedar Fork Creek, the Spoon River, the Illinois, Rock and Mississippi Rivers, many with hands toughened on the plow handles, legs with hard, bunched muscles from tramping the clods behind a plow team. With ruddy and wind-bitten faces they were of the earth; they could stand the raw winds when there was something worth hearing and remembering.

Six days later, in Quincy, on the Mississippi River, 12,000 people came from Illinois, Iowa, Missouri, and sat and stood three hours hearing the debaters. And two days later, farther down river, looking from free-soil Illinois across to slave-soil Missouri, the debaters had their final match, in Alton, before 6,000 listeners.

One young man, Francis Grierson, kept a sharp impression of Lincoln at Alton. He "rose from his seat, stretched his long, bony limbs upward as if to get them into working order, and stood like some solitary pine on a lonely summit."

Two men had spoken in Illinois to audiences surpassing any in past American history in size and in eagerness to hear. Yet they also spoke to the nation. The main points of the debates reached millions of readers. Newspapers in the larger cities printed the reports in full. A book of passion, an almanac of American visions, victories, defeats, a catechism of national thought and hope, were in the paragraphs of the debates. A powerful fragment of America breathed in Douglas' saying at Quincy: "Let each State mind its own business and let its neighbors alone! . . . If we will stand by that principle, then Mr. Lincoln will find that this republic can exist forever divided into free and slave States . . . Stand by that great principle and we can go on as we have done, increasing in wealth, in population, in power, and in all the elements of greatness, until we shall be the admiration and terror of the world, . . . until we make this continent one ocean-bound republic."

Those who wished quiet about the slavery question, and those who didn't, understood Lincoln's inquiry: "You say it [slavery] is wrong; but don't you constantly . . . argue that this is not the right place to oppose it? You say it must not be opposed in the free States, because slavery is not here; it must not be opposed in the slave States, because it is there; it must not be opposed in politics, because that will make a fuss; it must not be opposed in the pulpit, because it is not religion. Then where is the place to oppose it? There is no suitable place to oppose it."

So many could respond to the Lincoln view: "Judge Douglas will have it that I want a negro wife. He never can be brought to understand that there is any middle ground on this subject. I have lived until my fiftieth year, and have never had a negro woman either for a slave or a wife, and I think I can live fifty centuries, for that matter, without having had one for either." Pointing to the Supreme Court decision that slaves as property could not be voted out of new territories, Lincoln said, "His [Douglas'] Supreme Court cooperating with him, has *squatted* his Squatter Sovereignty out." The argument had got down as thin as "soup made by boiling the shadow of a pigeon that had starved to death."

Douglas said he would not be brutal. "Humanity requires, and Christianity commands that you shall extend to every inferior being, and every dependent being, all the privileges, immunities and advantages which can be granted to them consistent with the safety of society." America was a young and growing nation. "It swarms as often as a hive of bees . . . In less than fifteen years, if the same progress that has distinguished this country for the last fifteen years continues, every foot of vacant land between this and the Pacific ocean, owned by the United States, will be occupied . . . And just as fast as our interests and our destiny require additional territory in the north, in the south, or on the islands of the ocean, I am for it, and when we acquire it will leave the people, . . . free to do as they please on the subject of slavery and every other question."

Lincoln cited a Supreme Court decision as "one of the thousand things constantly done to prepare the public mind to make property, and nothing but property, of the negro in all the states of this Union." Why was slavery referred to in "covert language" and not mentioned plainly and openly in the U.S. Constitution? Why were the words "negro" and "slavery" left out? Was it not always the single issue of quarrels? "Does it not enter into the churches and rend them asunder? What divided the great Methodist Church into two parts, North and South? What has raised this constant disturbance in every Presbyterian General Assembly that meets?" It was not politicians; this fact and issue of slavery operated on the minds of men and divided them in every avenue of society, in politics, religion, literature, morals. "That is the issue that will continue in this country when these poor tongues of Judge Douglas and myself shall be silent. It is the eternal struggle between these two principles . . . The one is the common right of humanity and the other the divine right of kings. It is the same . . . spirit that says, 'You work and toil and earn bread, and I'll eat it.' No matter in what shape it comes, whether from the mouth of a king who seeks to bestride the people of his own nation and live by the fruit of their labor, or from one race of men as an apology for enslaving another race, it is the same tyrannical principle."

At Freeport Lincoln put a series of questions to Douglas, one of them, "Can the people of a United States Territory, in any lawful way, against the wish of any citizen of the United States, exclude slavery from its limits prior to the formation of a State Constitution?" The answer of Douglas amounted to saying, "Yes." It raised a storm of opposition to him in the South, and lost him blocks of northern Democratic friends who wanted to maintain connections in the South.

When Douglas twisted his antislavery position into one of race equality, Lincoln replied it was an arrangement of words by which a man can prove a horse chestnut to be a chestnut horse. At Charleston he shook a finger at a man's face: "I assert that you are here to-day, and you undertake to prove me a liar by showing that you were in Mattoon yesterday. I say that you took your hat off your head, and you prove me a liar by putting it on your head. That is the whole force of Douglas' argument."

Of Lincoln's face in a hotel room in Quincy, David R. Locke wrote: "I never saw a more thoughtful face. I never saw a more dignified face. I never saw so sad a face." Nor could Locke forget that Lincoln had his boots off and explained, "I like to give my feet a chance to breathe."

On October 30, several thousand farmers out around Springfield hitched up their teams and drove into town to a Republican rally; Lincoln was to make his last speech of the campaign. Nine cars had come from Jacksonville and way stations. The Chicago & Alton brought 32 cars from McLean and Logan Counties, seats and aisles full, tops of the cars and two engine pilots crowded with passengers. Ten thousand swarmed around the Statehouse square, waves of people facing toward the speakers' stand.

Lincoln began his speech about two o'clock: "I stand here surrounded by friends—some *political, all personal friends*, I trust. May I be indulged, in this closing scene, to say a few words of myself? I have borne a laborious, and, in some respects to myself, a painful part in the contest."

He knew Galesburg to the north would vote about two to one for him and Jonesboro to the south three to one against him. He faced toward Jonesboro and all the South rather than Galesburg and the North. "The legal right of the Southern people to reclaim their fugitives I have constantly admitted. The legal right of Congress to interfere with their institution in the states, I have constantly denied . . . To the best of my judgment I have labored *for*, and not *against* the Union."

The issues were so immense, the required decisions so delicate, it was an hour for considerations beyond the personal. "As I have not felt, so I have not expressed any harsh sentiment towards our Southern bretheren. I have constantly declared, as I really believed, the only difference between them and us, is the difference of circumstances. I have meant to assail the motives of no party, or individual; and if I have, in any instance (of which I am not conscious) departed from my purpose, I regret it."

Then came words strange with a curious bittersweet. "I have said that in some respects the contest has been painful to me. Myself, and those with whom I act have been constantly accused of a purpose to destroy the union;

and bespattered with every immaginable odious epithet; and some who were friends, as it were but yesterday have made themselves most active in this. I have cultivated patience, and made no attempt at a retort."

And in the same tone, he ended. "Ambition has been ascribed to me. God knows how sincerely I prayed from the first that this field of ambition might not be opened. I claim no insensibility to political honors; but today could the Missouri restriction be restored, and the whole slavery question replaced on the old ground of 'toleration' by *necessity* where it exists, with unyielding hostility to the spread of it, on principle, I would, in consideration, gladly agree, that Judge Douglas should never be *out*, and I never *in*, an office, so long as we both or either, live."

The speech may have been longer. What he wrote that survived took less than 15 minutes. Packed with momentous meanings for people south and north, it was a sober appeal in an hour of hair-trigger tension. The local reporters raved over "the outpouring," "the gaily decorated stores and public buildings," "banners and flags flying," the Springfield *Journal* printing six columns of labored description, stilted narrative in commonplace style. The speech that would have taken a half column had this unconsciously silly and blandly ignorant report in the *Journal:* "At two o'clock, the vast multitude being congregated around the stand, Mr. Lincoln began his speech. We have neither time nor room to give even a sketch of his remarks to-day. Suffice it to say, the speech was one of his very best efforts, distinguished for its clearness and force, and for the satisfactory manner in which he exposed the . . . misrepresentations of the enemy. The conclusion of this speech was one of the most eloquent appeals ever addressed to the American people. It was received with spontaneous bursts of enthusiasm unequalled by any thing ever before enacted in this city." And not a paragraph, not a line or phrase, of the brief and great speech itself!

Henry Villard of the New York *Staats-Zeitung* wrote that a thunderstorm had come up the night before Election Day. Lincoln with Villard, at a flag station 20 miles west of Springfield, crawled into a railroad boxcar. They sat on the floor, chins on knees, talking in the dark. Villard felt the laughs "peculiar" as Lincoln rambled on about himself for U.S. Senator. "I am convinced that I am good enough for it; but, in spite of it all, I am saying to myself every day: 'It is too big a thing for you; you will never get it.' Mary [Mrs. Lincoln] insists, however, that I am going to be Senator and President of the United States, too."

And there was light enough in the boxcar for Villard to see Lincoln, with arms hugging knees, roaring another long laugh, and shaking in legs and arms at his wife's ambition for him to be President. The fun of it swept him as he shook out the words, "Just think of such a sucker as me as President!"

November 2, Election Day, arrived, wet and raw in northern Illinois. And though Lincoln had a majority of 4,085 votes over Douglas, Douglas because of a gerrymander held a majority of the legislature. Lincoln wrote to loyal friends, "Another explosion will soon come." Douglas managed to be supported as the best instrument both to *break down* and to *uphold* the slave power. "No ingenuity can keep this deception . . . up a great while." He was glad he made the race. "Though I now sink out of view, and shall be forgotten, I believe I have made some marks which will tell for the cause of civil liberty long after I am gone." And he joked; he was like the boy who stubbed his toe, "It hurt too bad to laugh, and he was too big to cry."

On January 5 the legislature elected Douglas. After the news Lincoln sat alone in his law office with his thoughts a while, blew out the light, locked the door, stepped down to the street, and started home. The path, worn pig-backed, was slippery. One foot slipped and knocked the other foot from under him. He was falling. He made a quick twist, caught himself, and said with a ripple, "It's a slip and not a fall!" The streak of superstition in him was touched. He said it again, "A slip and not a fall!"

And far off in Washington, Stephen A. Douglas was reading a telegram, from the *State Register,* "Glory to God and the Sucker Democracy, Douglas 54, Lincoln 46."

In November 1858 the *Illinois Gazette* at Lacon, the Chicago *Democrat,* the Olney, Illinois, *Times,* nominated Lincoln for President. The Cincinnati *Gazette* printed a letter nominating him, and a mass meeting at Sandusky, Ohio, called for him to head the Republican ticket in 1860.

In Bloomington, in December, Jesse Fell saw Lincoln coming out of the courthouse door. Fell was a land trader in thousand-acre tracts, a railroad promoter, a contractor for large lots of railroad ties off his timberland holdings. He was of Quaker blood, antislavery, Republican, a little below medium height, smooth-faced, honest-spoken, trusted and liked in Bloomington. He stepped across the street and asked Lincoln to go with him to the law office of his brother, Kersey H. Fell. A calm twilight was deepening, as Fell said: "Lincoln, I have been East, . . . travelling in all the New England States, save Maine; in New York, New Jersey, Pennsylvania, Ohio, Michigan, and Indiana; and everywhere I hear you talked about. Very frequently I have been asked, 'who is this man Lincoln, of your state?' . . . Being, as you know, an ardent Republican, and your friend, I usually told them, we had in Illinois, two giants instead of one; that Douglas was the little one, as they all knew, but that you were the big one which they didn't all know. But, seriously, Lincoln, Judge Douglas being so widely known, you are getting a national reputation through him . . . your speeches in whole or in part . . . have been pretty extensively published in the East . . . I have a decided impression, that if your popular history and efforts on the slavery question can be sufficiently brought before the people, you can be made a formidable, if not a successful, candidate for the Presidency."

Lincoln heard and, as Fell told it, replied: "Oh, Fell, what's the use of talking of me for the Presidency, whilst we have such men as Seward, Chase, and others, who are . . . so intimately associated with the principles of the Republican party. Everybody knows them. Nobody, scarcely, outside of Illinois, knows me."

Then Fell analyzed. Yes, Seward and Chase stood out as having rendered larger service to the Republican cause than Lincoln. "The truth is," said Fell, "they have rendered too much service, . . . have both made long records . . . and have said some very radical things, which, however just and true . . . would seriously damage them . . . if nominated . . . What the Republican party wants, to insure success in 1860, is a man of popular origin, of acknowledged ability, committed against slavery aggressions, who has no record to defend, and no radicalism of an offensive character . . . You have sprung from the humble walks of life . . . and if we can only get these facts sufficiently before the people, depend upon it, there is some chance for you."

And Fell went on, "Now, Mr. Lincoln, I come to the business part of this interview. My native State, Pennsylvania, will have a large number of votes to cast for somebody . . . Pennsylvania don't like, overmuch, New York and her politicians; she has a candidate, Cameron, of her own, but he will not be acceptable to a larger number of her own people, much less abroad, and will be dropped. Through an eminent jurist and essayist of my native county in Pennsylvania, favorably known throughout the state, I want to get up a well-considered, well-written newspaper article, telling the people who you are, and what you have done, that it may be circulated not only in that state, but elsewhere, and thus help in manufacturing sentiment in your favor. I know your public life and can furnish items that your modesty would forbid, but I don't know much about your private history: when you were born, and where, the names and origin of your parents, what you did in early life, what were your opportunities for education, etc., and I want you to give me these. Won't you do it?"

Lincoln had been listening and said: "Fell, I admit the force of much that you say, and admit that I am ambitious, and would like to be President; I am not insensible to the compliment you pay me, and the interest you manifest in the matter, but there is no such good luck in store for me, as the Presidency of these United States; besides, there is nothing in my early history that would interest you or anybody else; and as Judge Davis says, 'It won't pay.' "

Rising, Lincoln wrapped a thick gray and brown wool shawl around his bony shoulders, spoke good night, and started down the stairway, with Fell calling out that Lincoln must listen and do as he asked. Newspapers in small towns in Midwest states had begun asking, "Why not Abraham Lincoln for President of the United States?" Calls for Lincoln to speak, as the foremost Republican figure of the West, were coming from Kansas, Buffalo, Des Moines, Pittsburgh. Thurlow Weed, the New York boss, wired to Illinois, "Send Abram Lincoln to Albany immediately." Long John Wentworth, editor of the Chicago *Democrat*, a Republican paper, saw Lincoln looming, and told him he "needed somebody to run him"; in New York Seward had Weed to run him. Lincoln laughed, "Only events can make a President."

CHAPTER 12

Strange Friend and Friendly Stranger

LINCOLN was 51 years old. With each year since he had become a grown man, his name and ways, and stories about him, had been spreading among plain people and their children. So tall and so bony, with so peculiar a slouch and so easy a saunter, so sad and so haunted-looking, so quizzical and comic, as if hiding a lantern that lighted and went out and that he lighted again—he was the Strange Friend and the Friendly Stranger. Like something out of a picture book for children—he was. His form of slumping arches and his face of gaunt sockets were a shape a Great Artist had scrawled from careless clay.

He looked like an original plan for an extra-long horse or a lean tawny buffalo, that a Changer had suddenly whisked into a man-shape. Or he met the eye as a clumsy, mystical giant that had walked out of a Chinese or Russian fairy story, or a bogy who had stumbled out of an ancient Saxon myth with a handkerchief full of presents he wanted to divide among all the children in the world.

He didn't wear clothes. Rather, clothes hung upon him as if on a rack to dry, or on a loose ladder up a windswept chimney. His clothes, to keep the chill or the sun off, seemed to whisper, "He put us on when he was thinking about something else."

He dressed any which way at times, in broadcloth, a silk hat, a silk choker, and a flaming red silk handkerchief, so that one court clerk said Lincoln was "fashionably dressed, as neatly attired as any lawyer at court, except Ward Lamon." Or again, people said Lincoln looked like a huge skeleton with skin over the bones, and clothes covering the skin.

The stovepipe hat he wore sort of whistled softly: "I am not a hat at all; I am the little garret roof where he tucks in little thoughts he writes on pieces of paper." The hat, size seven and one-eighth, had a brim one and three-quarters inches wide. The inside band in which the more important letters and notes were tucked, measured two and three-quarters inches. The cylinder of the stovepipe was 22 inches in circumference. The hat was lined with heavy silk and, measured inside, exactly six inches deep. And people tried to guess what was going on under that hat. Written in pencil on the imitation satin paper that formed part of the lining was the signature "A. Lincoln, Springfield, Ill.," so that any forgetful person who might take the hat by mistake would know where to bring it back. Also the hatmaker, "George Hall, Springfield, Ill.," had printed his name in the hat so that Lincoln would know where to get another one just like it.

The umbrella with the name "Abraham Lincoln" stitched in, faded and drab from many rains and regular travels, looked sleepy and murmuring.

"Sometime we shall have all the sleep we want; we shall turn the law office over to the spiders and the cobwebs; and we shall quit politics for keeps."

There could have been times when children and dreamers looked at Abraham Lincoln and lazily drew their eyelids half shut and let their hearts roam about him—and they half-believed him to be a tall horse chestnut tree or a rangy horse or a big wagon or a log barn full of new-mown hay—something else or more than a man, a lawyer, a Republican candidate with principles, a prominent citizen—something spreading, elusive, and mysterious—the Strange Friend and the Friendly Stranger.

In Springfield and other places, something out of the ordinary seemed to connect with Abraham Lincoln's past, his birth, a mystery of where he came from. The wedding certificate of his father and mother was not known to be on record. Whispers floated of his origin as "low-flung," of circumstances so misty and strange that political friends wished they could be cleared up and made respectable. The wedding license of Thomas Lincoln and Nancy Hanks had been moved to a new county courthouse—where no one had thought to search.

The year of the big debates a boy had called out, "There goes old Mr. Lincoln," and Lincoln hearing it, remarked to a friend, "They commenced it when I was scarcely thirty years old." Often when people called him "Old Abe" they meant he had the texture and quaint friendliness of old handmade Bibles, old calfskin law books, weather-beaten oak and walnut planks, or wagon axles always willing in storm or stars.

A neighbor boy, Fred Dubois, joined with a gang who tied a string to knock off Lincoln's hat. "Letters and papers fell out of the hat and scattered over the sidewalk," said Dubois. "He stooped to pick them up and us boys climbed all over him." As a young man he played marbles with boys; as an older man he spun tops with his own boys, Tad and Willie.

When William Plato of Kane County came to his office with the little girl, Ella, he stood Ella on a chair and told her, "And you're not as tall as I am, even now." A girl skipping along a sidewalk stumbled on a brick and fell backward, just as Lincoln came along. He caught her, lifted her up in his arms, put her gently down and asked, "What is your name?" "Mary Tuft." "Well, Mary, when you reach home tell your mother you have rested in Abraham's bosom."

Old Aesop could not have invented a better fable than the one about the snakes in the bed, to show the harm of letting slavery into the new territories. "If there was a bed newly made up, to which the children were to be taken, and it was proposed to take a batch of young snakes and put them there with them, I take it no man would say there was any question how I ought to decide."

When Tad was late bringing home the milk he hunted the boy and came home with Tad on his shoulders and carrying the milk pail himself. Once he chased Tad and brought the little one home, holding him at arm's length; the father chuckled at his son's struggle to kick him in the face. Once as he lugged the howling Willie and Tad, a neighbor asked, "Why, Mr. Lincoln, what's the matter?" The answer: "Just what's the matter with the whole world. I've got three walnuts and each wants two."

In Rushville and towns circling around, they remembered the day he was there. The whole town turned out, among them young women of Rushville society, as such. One of the belles dangled a little Negro doll baby in Lincoln's face. He looked into her face and asked quietly, "Madam, are you the mother of that?" At many a corn shucking and Saturday night shindig, this incident had been told.

Germans and Irishmen had greetings from him. "I know enough German to know that Kaufman means merchant, and Schneider means tailor—am I not a good German scholar?" Or, "That reminds me of what the Irishman said, 'In this country one man is as good as another; and for the matter of that, very often a great deal better.'"

He told of the long-legged boy "sparking" a farmer's daughter when the hostile father came in with a shotgun; the boy jumped through a window, and running across the cabbage patch scared up a rabbit; in about two leaps the boy caught up with the rabbit, kicked it high in the air, and grunted, "Git out of the road and let somebody run that knows how." He told of a Kentucky horse sale where a small boy was riding a fine horse to show off points. A man whispered, "Look here, boy, hain't that horse got the splints?" and the boy, "Mister, I don't know what the splints is, but if it's good for him, he has got it; if it ain't good for him, he ain't got it."

Riding to Lewistown, an old acquaintance, a weather-beaten farmer, spoke of going to law with his next neighbor. "Been a neighbor of yours for long?" "Nigh onto fifteen year." "Part of the time you get along all right, don't you?" "I reckon we do." "Well, see this horse of mine? I sometimes get out of patience with him. But I know his faults; he does fairly well as horses go; it might take me a long time to get used to some other horse's faults; for all horses have faults."

Lincoln told of a balloonist going up in New Orleans, sailing for hours, and dropping his parachute over a cotton field. The gang of Negroes picking cotton saw a man coming down from the sky in blue silk, in silver spangles, wearing golden slippers. They ran—all but one old-timer who had rheumatism and couldn't get away. He waited till the balloonist hit the ground and walked toward him. Then he mumbled: "Howdy, Massa Jesus. How's yo' Pa?"

He liked to tell of the strict judge of whom it was said: "He would hang a man for blowing his nose in the street, but he would quash the indictment if it failed to specify which hand he blew it with."

He could write an angry letter, with hard names and hot epithets—and then throw it in the stove. He advised it was a help sometimes to write a hot letter and then burn it. On being told of a certain man saying, "I can't understand those speeches of Lincoln," he laughed, "There are always some fleas a dog can't reach."

Though the years had passed, he still believed, "Improvement in condition—is the order of things in a society of equals." And he still struggled under the load of that conundrum of history he had written ten years back: "As Labor is the common *burthen* of our race, so the effort of *some* to shift their share of the burthen on to the shoulders of *others*, is the great, durable, curse of the race."

He defended Peachy Harrison who killed Greek Grafton, a law student in the office of Lincoln & Herndon. On the witness stand came old Peter Cartwright, the famous circuit rider, grandfather of the accused murderer. "How long have you known the prisoner?" "I have known him since a babe; he laughed and cried on my knee." And Lincoln led on with more questions, till old Peter Cartwright was telling the last words that slowly choked out from the murdered man, three days after the stabbing: "I am dying; I will soon part with all I love on earth and I want you to say to my slayer that I forgive him. I want to leave this earth with a forgiveness of all who have in any way injured me." Lincoln had then begged the jury to be as forgiving as the murdered man. The handling of the grandfather as a witness cleared Peachy Harrison and set him free.

Over a period of some 20 years Lincoln had signed 20 petitions for pardons for convicted men, the governors of Illinois granting pardons in 14 cases. He had served as attorney for 14 of the convicted men and in some cases wrote his opinions and beliefs why the men should be set free. He wrote as to one of his clients that he was of a young family, had lost one arm, and had served five-sixths of his sentence, of another that it was "a miscarriage of justice," of two brothers sentenced to one year for stealing five shoats valued at $10 that the public was "greatly stirred" in their favor.

The name of the man had come to stand for what he was, plus beliefs, conjectures and guesses. He was spoken of as a "politician" in the sense that politics is a trade of cunning, ambitious, devious men. He chose a few issues on which to explain his mind fully. Some of his reticences were not evasions but retirements to cloisters of silence. Questions of life and destiny shook him close to prayers and tears in his own hidden corners and byways; the depths of the issues were too dark, too pitiless, inexorable, for a man to open his mouth and try to tell what he knew.

In the cave of winds in which he saw history in the making he was far more a listener than a talker. The high adventure of great poets, inventors, explorers, facing the unknown and the unknowable, was in his face and breath, and had come to be known, to a few, for the danger and bronze of it.

There was a word: democracy. Tongues of politics played with it. Lincoln had his slant at it. "As I would not be a *slave*, so I would not be a *master*. This expresses my idea of democracy. Whatever differs from this, to the extent of the difference, is no democracy."

He had faced men who had yelled, "I'll fight any man that's goin' to vote for that miserable skunk, Abe Lincoln." And he knew homes where solemn men declared, "I've seen Abe Lincoln when he played mournin' tunes on their heartstrings till they mourned with the mourners." He was taken, in some log cabins, as a helper of men. "When I went over to hear him at Alton," said one, "things looked onsartin. 'Peared like I had more'n I could stand up under. But he hadn't spoken more'n ten minutes afore I felt like I never had no load. I begin to feel ashamed o' bein' weary en complainin'."

He loved trees, was kin somehow to trees, his favorite the hard maple. Pine, cedar, spruce, cypress, had each their pine family ways for him. He could pick crossbreeds of trees that plainly belonged to no special family. He had found trees and men alike; on the face of them, the outside, they didn't tell their character. Life, wind, rain, lightning, events, told the fiber, what was clean or rotten.

What he said to a crowd at Lewistown one August afternoon of 1858 had been widely printed and many a reader found it deeply worth reading again and again. His theme was the Declaration of Independence and its phrase, "that all men are created equal," and have unalienable rights to "life, liberty and the pursuit of happiness." That document was a "majestic" interpretation:

This was their lofty, and wise, and noble understanding of the justice of the Creator to His creatures. [Applause.] Yes, gentlemen, to *all* His creatures, to the whole great family of man . . . They grasped not only the whole race of man then living, but they reached forward and seized upon the farthest posterity . . . Wise statesmen as they were, they knew the tendency of prosperity to breed tyrants, and so they established these great self-evident truths, that when in the distant future some man, some faction, some interest, should set up the doctrine that none but rich men, or none but white men, were entitled to life, liberty and the pursuit of happiness, their posterity might look up again to the Declaration of Independence and take courage to renew the battle which their fathers began . . . I charge you to drop every paltry and insignificant thought for any man's success. It is nothing; I am nothing; Judge Douglas is nothing. *But do not destroy that immortal emblem of Humanity—the Declaration of American Independence.*

Once in 1858 Lincoln wrote a meditation he didn't use in any of the debates. It was a private affair between him and his conscience:

. . . Yet I have never failed—do not now fail—to remember that in the republican cause there is a higher aim than that of mere office. I have not allowed myself to forget that the abolition of the Slave-trade by Great Brittain was agitated a hundred years before it was a final success; that the measure had it's open fire-eating opponents; it's stealthy "dont-care" opponents; it's dollar and cent opponents; it's inferior race opponents; its negro equality opponents; and its religion and good order opponents; that all these opponents got offices, and their adversaries got none. But I have also remembered that though they blazed, like tallow-candles for a century, at last they flickered in the socket, died out, stank in the dark for a brief season, and were remembered no more, even by the smell . . . I am proud, in my passing speck of time, to contribute an humble mite to that glorious consummation, which my own poor eyes may not last to see.

And that year he read at Bloomington a lecture on "Discoveries and Inventions," repeating it later in Springfield. Scheduled a second time at Bloomington he met so small an audience that he didn't bother to read his paper; he soon dropped the idea of being a "popular lecturer." What he read revealed him as a droll and whimsical humorist, a scholar and thinker, a keen observer and a man of contemplation who, if fate ordained, could have a rich and quiet life entirely free from political ambitions. He touched on man's first discovery or invention of clothes, of speech, of wind power for sailing, of the alphabet, of printing. Rulers and laws in time past had made it a crime to read or to own books. "It is difficult for us, *now* and *here*, to conceive how strong this slavery of the mind was; and how long it did, of necessity, take, to break it's shackles, and to get a habit of freedom of thought, established." A new country, such as America, "is most favorable—almost necessary—to the immancipation of thought, and the consequent advancement of civilization and the arts." Briefly and ironically, in passing, he went political, mentioning "the invention of negroes, or, of the present mode of using them, in 1434." Dominant in the paper he read was love of books, of pure science, of knowledge for its own sake, of a humanity creeping out of dark mist toward clear light.

Somewhere in this period Milton Hay of Springfield heard Lincoln speak offhand a rule or maxim in politics. Hay later passed it on to Joseph Fifer of Bloomington who found it so simple and so nicely singsong that he couldn't forget it: "You can fool some of the people all of the time, and all of the people some of the time, but you can't fool all of the people all of the time."

At a remark in Mayor Sanderson's house in Galesburg that he was "afraid of women," Lincoln laughed, "A woman is the only thing I am afraid of that I know can't hurt me." He told Whitney he hated going through the act of telling a hayrack full of girls in white gowns, each girl one state of the Union, "I also thank you for this beautiful basket of flowers." After a tea party at the home of Mayor Boyden of Urbana, the mayor and Whitney excused themselves for an hour, and left Lincoln alone with Mrs. Boyden, Mrs. Whitney, and her mother. Whitney, on returning, found Lincoln "ill at ease as a bashful country boy," eyes shifting from floor to ceiling and back, arms behind and then in front, then tangled as though he tried to hide them, and his long legs tying and untying themselves. Whitney couldn't understand it unless it was because he was alone in a room with three women.

A woman wrote her admiration of his course in politics, and he thanked her in a letter. "I have never corresponded much with ladies; and hence I postpone writing letters to them, as a business which I do not understand." Men knew of his saying, after giving money or time or a favor in answer to a pathetic but probably bogus appeal, "I thank God I wasn't born a woman."

Herndon believed Lincoln cloaked his ways with women by a rare and fine code, writing, "Mr. Lincoln had a strong, if not terrible passion for women. He could hardly keep his hands off a woman, and yet, much to his credit, he lived a pure and virtuous life. His idea was that a woman had as much right to violate the marriage vow as the man—no more and no less. His sense of right—his sense of justice—his honor forbade his violating his marriage vow. Judge Davis said to me, 'Mr. Lincoln's honor saved many a woman.' This I know. I have seen Lincoln tempted and I have seen him reject the approach of woman!"

A woman charged with keeping a house of ill fame was a client of Lincoln & Herndon; they asked for a change of venue; and Lincoln drove across the prairies from one town to another with the madam of the house and her girls. After the trial the madam was asked about Lincoln's talk with her. Yes, he told stories, and they were nearly all funny. Yes, but were the stories proper or improper, so to speak? Well—the madam hesitated—they were funny; she and all the girls laughed—but coming to think it over she believed the stories could have been told "with safety in the presence of ladies anywhere." Then she added, as though it ought to be told, "But that is more than I can say for Bill Herndon."

A curious friend and chum of Lincoln was Ward Hill Lamon, his Danville law partner, a young Virginian, dauntless, bull-necked, melodious, tall, commanding, often racy and smutty in talk, aristocratic and, drinking men said, magnificent in the amount of whisky he could carry. The first time he and Lincoln met, Lamon wore a swallow-tailed coat, white neckcloth, and ruffled silk shirt, and Lincoln: "Going to try your hand at law, are you? I don't think you would succeed at splitting rails." As the years passed a strange bond of loyalty between the two men grew. "Sing me a little song," was Lincoln's word to Lamon, who brought out a banjo and struck up the lively "Cousin Sally Downard," or "O Susanna," or the sad "Twenty Years Ago."

Women, music, poetry, art, pure science, all required more time than Lincoln had to give them. He liked to tell of the Indiana boy blurting out, "Abe, I don't s'pose there's anybody on earth likes gingerbread better'n I do—and gets less'n I do."

Herndon told of his partner coming to the office sometimes at seven in the morning when his usual hour to arrive was nine. Or of Lincoln at noon, having brought to the office a package of crackers and cheese, sitting alone eating. Mrs. Lincoln and Herndon hated each other. While Herndon was careless as to where he spat, she was not merely scrupulously neat and immaculate as to linen and baths, she was among the most ambitious women in Springfield in the matter of style and fashion. She knew of such affairs as Herndon getting drunk with two other men and breaking a windowpane that her husband had to hustle the money for so that the sheriff wouldn't lock up his law partner. She didn't like it that her husband had a drinking partner reckless with money, occasionally touching Lincoln for loans. She carried suspicions and nursed misgivings as to this swaggering upstart, radical in politics, transcendentalist in philosophy, antichurch.

At parties, balls, social gatherings, she moved, vital, sparkling, often needlessly insinuating or directly and swiftly insolent. If the music was bad, what was the need of her making unkind remarks about the orchestra? Chills, headaches, creepers of fear came; misunderstandings rose in waves so often around her; she was alone, so all alone, so like a child thrust into the Wrong Room.

At parties, balls, social gatherings, she trod the mazy waltzes in crinoline gowns, the curves of the hoop skirts shading down the plump curves of her figure. Once when talk turned to Lincoln and Douglas, she had said, "Mr. Lincoln may not be as handsome a figure, but people are perhaps not aware that his heart is as large as his arms are long."

She wrote to a sister in September 1857 of a trip east with her husband when he had law business in New York. A moment of happy dreaminess ran through part of her letter. "The summer has so strangely and rapidly passed away. Some portion of it was spent most pleasantly in traveling East. We visited Niagara, Canada, New York and other points of interest."

How often good times shone for them, only they two could tell. They were intense individuals, he having come through hypochondria, and she moving by swirls toward a day when she would cry out that hammers were knocking nails into her head, that hot wires were being drawn through her eyes. Between flare-ups and regrets, his was most often the spirit of accommodation. He was ten years older than she, with a talent for conciliation and adjustment.

There were times when she made herself pretty for him. One picture of her after 15 years of marriage shows dark ringlets of hair down her temples and about her ears, a little necklace circling her bare neck, three roses at her bosom, and a lily in her shapely hands.

Lincoln in 1857 sent an editor, John E. Rosette, a letter marked "Private":

Your note about the little paragraph in the Republican was received yesterday, since which time I have been too unwell to notice it. I had not supposed you wrote or approved it. The whole originated in mistake. You know by the conversation with me that I thought the establishment of the paper unfortunate, but I always expected to throw no obstacle in its way, and to patronize it to the extent of taking it and paying for one copy. When the paper was brought to my house, my wife said to me, "Now are you going to take another worthless little paper?" I said to her *evasively*, "I have not directed the paper to be left." From this, in my absence, she sent the message to the carrier. This is the whole story.

A lawyer was talking business to Lincoln once at home and suddenly the door opened. Mrs. Lincoln put her head in and snapped the question whether he had done an errand she told him to do. He looked up quietly, said he had been busy, but would attend to it as soon as he could. The woman wailed; she was neglected, abused, insulted. The door slammed; she was gone. The visiting lawyer, open-eyed, muttered his surprise. Lincoln laughed, "Why, if you knew how much good that little eruption did, what a relief it was to her, and if you knew her as well as I do, you would be glad she had had an opportunity to explode."

She was often anxious about her boys, had mistaken fears about their safety or health, exaggerated evils that might befall them. She gave parties for them and wrote with her own pen, in a smooth and even script, gracious invitations.

Mary Todd had married a genius who made demands; when he wanted to work, it was no time for interruptions or errands. For this brooding and often somber man she was wife, housekeeper, and counselor in personal and political affairs in so far as he permitted. She watched his "browsing" in the pantry and tried to bring him to regular meals. She had kept house years ago, too poor for a hired girl; they burned wood then; now they had a coal cookstove with four lids and a reservoir to warm rain water. She had chosen the beautiful, strong black-walnut cradle, into which she had put, one after the other, four boy babies.

She knew of the money cost in 1858 when he dropped nearly all law cases for months and paid his way at hotels and in 4,200 miles of travel, writing in one letter after the campaign closed, "I am absolutely without money now for even household purposes." At times he did the shopping, Herndon saying that of a winter's morning he might be seen around the market house, a basket on his arm, "his old gray shawl wrapped around his neck."

With their rising income and his taking place as the outstanding leader of his party, Mary Lincoln in the late 1850's enjoyed giving parties occasionally for two or three hundred people. Isaac N. Arnold noted of these evenings "everything orderly and refined," and "every guest perfectly at ease," with a table "famed for the excellence of many rare Kentucky dishes, and in season, loaded with venison, wild turkeys, prairie chickens, quail and other game." She had moved with him from lean years to the comforts of the well-to-do middle class. With ownership of his house and lot, with farm lands, and collectible bills he had out, Lincoln in 1859 had property worth perhaps $15,000 or more.

Drawn by Otto J. Schneider from Lincoln's hat and umbrella
in Chicago Historical Society

CHAPTER 13

"Only Events Can Make a President"

JOSEPH W. FIFER, later a governor of Illinois, a man of unusually accurate and tenacious memory, heard Lincoln speak in 1858 to an immense crowd in Bloomington. He stood ten feet from where Lincoln was speaking, turned around for a look, "And the faces of those listening thousands were as if carved out of rock on a mountainside—so still, so set!" The voice they heard was "metallic, clear, ringing, very penetrating." Fifer heard the voice at one point regarding the Negro, "In the right to eat the bread his own hands have earned he is the equal of Judge Douglas, or of myself, or of any living man." Then Lincoln "raised high his long right arm with the clenched hand on the end of it—high above his head—and he shook it in the air and then brought it down. And when he did that it—it made the hair on a man's head stand up, and the breath stop in his throat."

Lincoln's name had spread far as a speaker and thinker. In 1859 he made speaking trips in Illinois, Indiana, Ohio, Wisconsin, Iowa, Kansas, and had to refuse many invitations to speak. On these trips he met leading men of the Republican party. They could judge whether he was presidential timber. He had said, "Only events can make a president," and there were friends saying events might dictate that each other candidate was either too old, too radical or too conservative and that Lincoln was on points the one most available. Also on these speaking trips Lincoln kept in touch with undercurrents of politics and public feeling; he met men who were to be delegates to the national Republican party convention the next year.

At no time in his many addresses of this year did he hint that he might be a candidate for President the next year and when good Republican party men said something about Lincoln for President he brushed it off with remarks that he wasn't fit or, as he had told Fell, there were greater men than he the party could choose. Yet his speeches in Ohio had a simple finality, a merciless logic, often a solemnity woven with Bible verses. He tore to ribbons the pretenses of Douglas, Buchanan, Chief Justice Taney; his lamentations over the possible outspreading of slavery had a dark music. There were listeners who couldn't help thinking and feeling he stood before them a consecrated man with a warm heart, a cool head, and he might make an able President.

He tried to guide party policy, writing in June 1859 to Governor Chase about the Ohio Republican party platform demand for the "repeal of the atrocious Fugitive Slave Law." The proposition was "already damaging us here" in Illinois. If brought up in the next Republican national convention it would "explode" the convention and the party.

In May 1859 banker Jacob Bunn handling the deal, Lincoln bought for $400 the weekly German-language newspaper of Springfield, the *Illinois Staats-Anzeiger*. By the contract, Lincoln owned the type, press and other equipment, and Theodore Canisius, the editor, was to continue publishing a Republican paper in German with occasional articles in English. Those handling the deal kept it a secret; Lincoln said nothing of it to Herndon; no news of it was published. Editor Canisius had written Lincoln asking where he stood on the Massachusetts Act of 1859 providing that no foreign-born naturalized citizen could hold office or vote until two years after his naturalization. Lincoln wrote, "I am against it's adoption in Illinois, or in any other place, where I have a right to oppose it." Having "notoriety" for his efforts in behalf of the Negro, he would be "strangely inconsistent" if he favored "any project for curtailing the existing rights of *white men*, even though born in different lands, and speaking different languages from myself." Canisius published this letter and it was widely copied in other papers.

The census of the next year would show 1,300,000 foreigners in the country, 700,000 of them Germans, chiefly in the Northern States. They held a balance of political power in many states. Their editors and political leaders were many of them German university graduates who had taken a hand in the revolutions of 1830 or 1848 in Germany; some had served prison terms or escaped; they had been hunted men, coming to America as refugees and fugitives; they had their bitterness over the Fugitive Slave Law. One of the hunted was Lincoln's friend at Belleville, Gustave Koerner, who to escape arrest, fled Germany to France, then to St. Louis, later to become a Supreme Court justice in Illinois and lieutenant governor. Lincoln was now openly allying himself with these men. He had helped Germans write a resolution passed by the Republican state convention in 1856 declaring that "our naturalization laws . . . being just in principle, we are opposed to any change being made in them intended to enlarge the time now required to secure the rights of citizenship." This resolution a German editor had taken to the Philadelphia national convention of the Republican party where it was, in substance, adopted.

In September at Columbus, Ohio, Lincoln held the spread of slavery to be the only thing that ever had threatened the Union. Amid his sober reasonings and solemn appeals there was laughter at his saying of Douglas, "His explanations explanatory of explanations explained are interminable" and again of

Douglas' logic, "It is as impudent and absurd as if a prosecuting attorney should stand up before a jury, and ask them to convict A as the murderer of B, while B was walking alive before them."

Next day in Cincinnati, he declared: "We must prevent the outspreading of the institution . . . We must prevent the revival of the African slave trade and the enacting by Congress of a territorial slave code." To Kentuckians particularly, he wished to say: "We mean to remember that you are as good as we; that there is no difference between us other than the difference of circumstances. We mean to recognise and bear in mind always that you have as good hearts in your bosoms as other people, or as we claim to have, and treat you accordingly. We mean to marry your girls when we have a chance—the white ones I mean—and I have the honor to inform you that I once did have a chance in that way."

On the morning of September 30, 1859, at the Wisconsin State Fair in Milwaukee, Lincoln spoke as philosopher and scientist, even as a sort of inventor. "I have thought a good deal, in an abstract way, about a Steam Plow." In the four years past the ground planted with corn in Illinois had produced about 20 bushels to the acre. "The soil has never been pushed up to one-half of its capacity." He recommended "deeper plowing, analysis of soils, experiments with manures, and varieties of seeds, observance of seasons."

He saw the country as new and young; the hired laborer could get a farm for himself. "There is no such thing as a freeman being fatally fixed for life, in the condition of a hired laborer." Some reasons held: "Labor is prior to, and independent of, capital; that, in fact, capital is the fruit of labor, and could never have existed if labor had not *first* existed,—that labor can exist without capital, but that capital could never have existed without labor. Hence . . . labor is the superior—greatly the superior—of capital."

Was the working class to be the mudsills on which the structure of the upper class rested? "According to that theory," Lincoln told his farmers, "a blind horse upon a tread-mill, is a perfect illustration of what a laborer should be—all the better for being blind, that he could not tread out of place, or kick understandingly." By that theory education for the workers was regarded as dangerous. "A Yankee who could invent a strong *handed* man without a head would receive the everlasting gratitude of the 'mudsill' advocates." He spoke in simple words: "As each man has one mouth to be fed, and one pair of hands to furnish food, it was probably intended that that particular pair of hands should feed that particular mouth—that each head is the natural guardian, director, and protector of the hands and mouth inseparably connected with it; and that being so, every head should be cultivated, and improved, by whatever will add to its capacity for performing its charge. In one word Free Labor insists on universal education."

He walked around seeing the prize bulls and stallions, the blue-ribbon hens and roosters, and, chaffing with a bunch of farmers, patted a boy on the head: "My little man, I hope you live to vote the Republican ticket." The boy's father broke in, "If he ever does, I'll break his neck." And where a short strong man was lifting heavy weights, Lincoln tried his muscles at lifting, looked down at the short strong man and said, "Why, I could lick salt off the top of your head." In the evening at the Newhall House he made an offhand political speech and the next afternoon spoke in Beloit and in the evening at Janesville.

The editor of the *Wisconsin Pinery* at Stevens Point wrote: "He looks as if he was made for wading in deep water. He looks like an open-hearted, honest man who has grown sharp in fighting knaves. His face is swarthy and filled with very deep long thought-wrinkles. His voice is not heavy, but has a clear trumpet tone that can be heard an immense distance."

Herndon brought from Boston a book that Lincoln read, *The Impending Crisis of the South*, by Hinton Rowan Helper, who came from a slaveholding family that had lived a hundred years in the Carolinas. Helper gave formidable statistics showing that under the free labor system the North was growing richer and the people of the South sinking deeper in debt and poverty. Of the 6,184,477 people in the Slave States in 1850, only 347,525 were slaveholders. "As a general rule, poor white persons are regarded with less esteem and attention than Negroes and though the condition of the latter is wretched beyond description, vast numbers of the former are infinitely worse off." The South was shocked and aghast at the book, forbade its sale, and its men in Congress lashed out at any and all who read it or quoted from it.

Edwin A. Pollard of Virginia in his book *Black Diamonds* called for the African slave trade to be made lawful; then Negroes fresh from the jungles could be sold in Southern seaports at $100 to $150 a head. "The poor man might then hope to own a negro." Senator James H. Hammond, son of a Connecticut Yankee who had emigrated to South Carolina, told the North: "Our slaves are hired for life and well compensated. Yours are hired by the day, not cared for, and scantily compensated . . . Why, you meet more beggars in one day in the city of New York than you would meet in a lifetime in the whole South . . . Your slaves are white, of your own race. Our slaves do not vote. Yours do vote . . . If they knew that the ballot box is stronger than an army of bayonets, and could combine, where would you be? Your society would be reconstructed, your government overthrown, your property divided."

Abolitionists had stood up and interrupted church services to cry out it was a crime that the U.S. Constitution sanctioned slavery. Garrison had publicly burned a copy of the Constitution of the United States, calling it "a covenant with hell"; Henry Ward Beecher had held mock auctions of Negro women in his Brooklyn church; *Uncle Tom's Cabin* had sold in many editions and as a stage play held audiences breathless. The next census was to show that the 3,204,000 slaves of 1850 had increased to 3,953,500.

Out of Kansas came a man who ran slaves to freedom, burned barns, stole horses, and murdered men and boys without trial or hearing. He had come to Kansas from Ohio and New York, a descendant of *Mayflower* Pilgrim Fathers; two of his grandfathers fought in the Revolutionary War; at his house his 19 children partook in prayer and Scripture reading morning and night. He told eastern abolitionists action was the need, bold deeds. He had a saying: "One man and God can overturn the universe." Funds for rifles, pikes, wagons and stores were raised by wealthy and respectable citizens who in secret code termed the affair a "speculation in wool."

On Monday, October 17, 1859, the telegraph carried strange news. At the junction of the Shenandoah and Potomac Rivers, where Virginia and Maryland touch borders, in the rocky little town of Harpers Ferry, a U.S. Government arsenal and arms factory had been captured, the gates broken and watchmen made prisoners, slaveholders taken prisoner and their slaves told to spread the word of freedom to slaves everywhere—all of this between Sunday night and Monday daybreak.

Would the next news tell of slaves in revolt repeating the Nat Turner insurrection, with men, women and children butchered, homes looted and burned? The country breathed easier on Tuesday's news that Colonel Robert E. Lee, commanding 80 marines, had rushed a little engine-house fort where 18 men inside had fought till all were dead or wounded except two.

In a corner of the engine house, an old man with a flowing long beard said his name was John Brown. "Who sent you here?" they asked. "No man sent me here. It was my own prompting and that of my Maker." "What was your object?" "I came to free the slaves. I think it right to interfere with you to free those you hold in bondage." "And you say you believe in the Bible?" "Certainly I do." "Don't you know you are a seditionist, a traitor?" "I was trying to free the slaves." "You are mad and fanatical." "And I think you people of the South are mad and fanatical. Is it sane to think such a system can last? Is it sane to talk of war rather than give it up?"

The State of Virginia gave him a fair trial on charges of murder, treason and inciting slaves to rebellion; Northern friends sent him able lawyers; he was found guilty and sentenced to be hanged. He spoke calmly to the court. "Had I taken up arms in behalf of the rich, the powerful, the intelligent . . . or any of their class, every man in this court would have deemed it an act worthy of reward rather than of punishment . . . I see a book kissed here which is the Bible, and which teaches me that all things that I would have men do unto me, so must I do unto them. I endeavored to act up to that instruction. I fought for the poor; and I say it was right, for they are as good as any of you . . . God is no respecter of persons . . . Now, if it be deemed necessary that I should forfeit my life for the furtherance of the ends of justice . . . I say, let it be done."

Friends planned to steal him away from the death watch. He sent them word he would be more useful to freedom when dead. He wished to be a memory among young men. He was 59, but the average age of those who fought and died for his cause was a little over 25. He wrote in the Charles Town jail a last message before going to the gallows: "I, John Brown, am now quite certain that the crimes of this guilty land will never be purged away but with blood. I had, as I now think, vainly flattered myself that without much bloodshed it might be done." Beyond the 3,000 guardsmen with rifles and bayonets, he could see blue haze and a shining sun over the Blue Ridge Mountains. "This *is* a beautiful country; I never had the pleasure of really seeing it before."

He had written to the young abolitionist, Frank B. Sanborn, that he had always been "delighted with the doctrine that all men are created equal" and "the Savior's command, 'Thou shalt love thy neighbor as thyself,'" then adding, "Rather than have the doctrine fail in the world or in these States, it would be better that a whole generation, men, women and children, should die a violent death." His mother and grandmother had died insane and a maternal aunt and three maternal uncles suffered from the same dread taint of blood. His mind, somewhat off balance, dwelt on wholesale killings and with no haunting regrets over murders by his hand and direction in Kansas. He believed in his own right to doom others, and the power of God to doom wrongdoers everlastingly. "All our actions, even all the follies that led to this disaster, were decreed to happen ages before the world was made." He was only walking as God had ages ago foreordained. The sheriff asked, "Shall I give you the signal when the trap is to be sprung?" "No, no," came the even voice from the white beard. "Just get it over quickly."

John Brown's ghost did walk. The governor of Virginia, the jailer, spoke of how he died, without a quaver, cool, serene. Emerson, Thoreau, Victor Hugo compared him to Christ, to Socrates, to the great martyrs. Wendell Phillips said, "The lesson of the hour is insurrection." Abolitionists acclaimed him and spoke for disunion. The antislavery men had regrets; they knew the South was lashed and would retaliate. Senator Douglas called for a law to punish conspiracies, quoting Lincoln's House Divided and Seward's Irrepressible Conflict speeches to indicate that Republican politicians and their "revolutionary doctrines" had incited John Brown.

John Brown became a mystical and haunting challenge. Five of his moral and financial supporters crossed the Canadian border to be safe from investigation. His chief backer, Gerrit Smith, a quaint and lovable character who had expected a different performance from Brown, broke down in fear of indictment and misunderstanding; under "a troop of hallucinations," he was taken to the Utica, New York, Asylum for the Insane, where in six weeks he was restored to calm.

The New York *Herald* published, in full, Seward's Senate speech foretelling "the irrepressible conflict." Seward now said he was opposed to conspiracy, ambush, invasion and force as shown by Brown; he favored reason, suffrage and the spirit of the Christian religion. Yet his explanations could not wash away the radical stripes. Political observers commented that Seward's prestige as a candidate for President had been hard hit. Jesse Fell and Judge David Davis worked steadily on their plans to nominate their dark horse the coming May.

Lincoln in Elwood, Kansas, referred to the hanging of Brown, and speaking in the dining room of the Great Western Hotel, the Elwood *Free Press* reported, "He believed the attack of Brown wrong for two reasons. It was a violation of law and it was, as all such attacks must be, futile as far as any effect it might have on the extinction of a great evil . . . John Brown has shown great courage, rare unselfishness, as even Gov. Wise testifies. But no man, North or South, can approve of violence or crime."

Of the fierce issue shaking the country he said, "The Slaves constitute one seventh of our entire population. Wherever there is an element of this magnitude in a government it will be talked about." Kansas now had a constitution, a legislature, and was soon to ballot on territorial officers and a delegate to Congress. Lincoln spoke for the Republican ticket in Troy, Doniphan, Atchison, and at Leavenworth the *Times* reported: "In Brown's hatred of slavery the speaker sympathized with him. But Brown's insurrectionary attempt he emphatically denounced. He believed the old man insane, and had yet to find the first Republican who endorsed the proposed insurrection." He warned the Southern element, according to the Leavenworth *Register*, "If constitutionally we elect a President, and therefore you undertake to destroy the Union, it will be our duty to deal with you as old John Brown has been dealt with."

He rode in an open one-horse buggy on 20- and 30-mile drives over frozen roads across treeless prairie, the scattered sod houses of pioneers looking lonesome. Once on open prairie he met Henry Villard, traveling eastward from Colorado. They chatted a few minutes and Villard noticed Lincoln shivering, a raw northwest wind cutting through where the short overcoat left the legs poorly covered. Lincoln was glad to accept Villard's offer of a buffalo robe.

Keeping company with Lincoln over his Kansas trip, and having Lincoln as house guest in Leavenworth, was Mark W. Delahay, who had known Lincoln in Illinois and whose wife was distantly related to Lincoln's stepmother, Sarah Bush Lincoln. Delahay, eight years younger than Lincoln, was born in Maryland, had gone to Illinois and become a lawyer, had helped nominate and elect Lincoln to Congress, in 1853 practicing law for a year in Mobile, Alabama, then moving to Kansas. In Leavenworth as a Democrat he started the *Territorial Register* and upheld Douglas' "popular sovereignty." But after six months of the violence and terror of proslavery mobs and wild shooting horsemen from Missouri, he changed policy and his paper became an outspoken and vehement antislavery organ. While he was attending a Free State convention in 1855 at Lawrence, the proslavery "Kickapoo Rangers" wrecked his newspaper office and threw the type and part of the press into the Missouri River. He had helped organize the Republican party of Kansas and against a strong Seward-for-President opposition was doing his best for Lincoln. He had asked Lincoln to endorse him for U.S. Senator and Lincoln had replied, "Any open attempt on my part would injure you."

Delahay had a well-modeled face, a head of thick curly hair, a full beard and mustache, and habits of overtalking and overdrinking. At a small dinner party in his home, he rose from his chair, waved a carving knife and called out, "Gentlemen, I tell you, Mr. Lincoln will be our next president." Lincoln put in, "Oh, Delahay, hush," but Delahay shouted, "I feel it. I mean it." As the dishes were passed they may have discussed John A. Martin, later a governor of Kansas. As a sour and bitter pro-Seward man and as editor of the Atchison *Champion*, Martin let no item of news be printed in his paper about Lincoln's arrival in Atchison, reporting no word of Lincoln's speech to an Atchison audience.

Back in Springfield after nine days away, Lincoln wrote political letters. He tried to smooth over the bitter feud in the Republican party between Long John Wentworth and Norman B. Judd. Wentworth had published that Judd was linked with corruption and Judd had sued for libel, the Chicago *Tribune* backing him to the hilt. Lincoln suggested that Wentworth print a retraction and Judd drop his suit, for the sake of party unity, but no such actions came and in county and state conventions the Wentworth-Judd feud went on.

On December 20 Lincoln sent Jesse Fell the requested autobiography. His father and mother came from "second families." Indiana, where he grew up, "was a wild region." And his schooling? "There was absolutely nothing to excite ambition for education. Of course when I came of age I did not know much. Still somehow, I could read, write, and cipher to the Rule of Three; but that was all. I have not been to school since. The little advance I now have upon this store of education, I have picked up from time to time under the pressure of necessity." His country drawl was there. "I was raised to farm work." He closed, saying he had a "dark complexion, with coarse black hair, and grey eyes—no other marks or brands recollected." He noted for Fell, "There is not much of it, for the reason, I suppose, that there is not much of me. Of course, it must not appear to have been written by myself." Fell's Pennsylvania friend elaborated on the facts sent him and published in the *Chester County Times* a sketch going "all out" for Lincoln for President, many other papers reprinting it.

Letters kept coming about the House Divided speech. Just what did it mean? He would quote its opening paragraph, and write: "It puzzles me to make my meaning plainer. Look over it carefully, and conclude I meant all I said and did not mean anything I did not say, and you will have my meaning." And to close, "If you . . . will state to me some meaning which you suppose I had, I can, and will instantly tell you whether that was my meaning."

To a letter about the tariff question, he replied, "I have not thought much upon the subject recently . . . just now, the revival of that question, will not advance the cause itself, or the man who revives it . . . I should prefer, to not now, write a public letter upon the subject. I therefore wish this to be considered confidential." His decisions and choices in politics were dictated by swift-moving events. To Trumbull and all Republicans he made it clear he would not try for the U.S. senatorship in 1860; he and Trumbull were not rivals. "And yet I would rather have a full term in the Senate than in the Presidency," he wrote to Judd.

In April he had written T. J. Pickett, a Rock Island editor, "I must, in candor, say I do not think myself fit for the Presidency." In July 1859 he had written Samuel Galloway, a Columbus, Ohio, lawyer, "I must say I do not think myself fit for the Presidency." In November he wrote to a Pennsylvania man, W. E. Frazer, an intimation that he might be in the running. "I shall labor faithfully in the ranks, unless, as I think not probable, the judgment of the party shall assign me a different position." He knew Frazer was "feeling him out" and made clear he could enter no "combination . . . to the prejudice of all others." Still later he seemed to have an understanding with Norman Judd that he was to run for U.S. Senator in 1864 and toward that goal it would help if the Illinois delegates in the coming national convention were an instructed unit to vote for him for the presidential nomination. He wrote Judd, "I am not in a position where it would hurt much for me to not be nominated on the national ticket; but I am where it would hurt some for me to not get the Illinois delegates."

For nearly a year Lincoln had on hand what he called his "Scrap-book," writing, "It cost me a good deal of labor to get it up." From duplicate newspaper files he had clipped column by column, with careful scissoring, his and Douglas' main speeches of 1858 along with the full text of the Lincoln-Douglas debates. His own speeches were clipped from the friendly Chicago *Press & Tribune* while Douglas' speeches were clipped from the Chicago *Times*. These clippings he pasted neatly, two columns to a page, in a scrapbook bound in black boards, nine inches wide by 14 long, 95 pages numbered. He wrote on margins a few corrections and in scores of places his pencil struck out "Applause" or "Laughter" or "Cheers" or remarks shouted from the audience. In one place Douglas had nodded to a man, saying he knew this man would not vote for Lincoln, which the man seconded with a fast and blunt, "I'll be d——d if I do," and this Lincoln edited out.

In December came a letter from high Republican leaders in Ohio asking "for publication in permanent form" of the great debates of 1858. Lincoln wrote December 19 he was grateful for "the very flattering terms" of their request and, "I wish the reprint to be precisely as the copies I send, without any comment whatever." In January the Chicago *Press & Tribune* carried news that Ohio Republicans were publishing the Lincoln-Douglas debates as a campaign document, the Springfield *Journal* clipping it and adding it was "a most delicate and expressive compliment . . . The name of 'Old Abe,' the leader of the great Republican army of the Northwest, has become a word of power and might." Other newspapers chimed in. That the book would come off the press and go to an immense audience of readers gave Lincoln a quiet pride in the first book for which he had furnished a manuscript.

There would be readers enjoying such sentences as, "The Judge has set about seriously trying to make the impression that when we meet at different places I am literally in his clutches—that I am a poor, helpless, decrepit mouse," or, "I don't want to have a fight with Judge Douglas, and I have no way of making an argument up into the consistency of a corn-cob and stopping his mouth with it." Or the grinding cadenced statement: "I believe the entire records of the world, from the date of the Declaration of Independence up to within three years ago, may be searched in vain for one single affirmation, from one single man, that the negro was not included in the Declaration of Independence. I think I may defy Judge Douglas to show that he ever said so, that Washington ever said so, that any President ever said so, that any member of Congress ever said so, or that any living man upon the whole earth ever said so, until the necessities of the present policy of the Democratic party, in regard to slavery, had to invent that affirmation."

The title page read: "Political Debates between Hon. Abraham Lincoln and Hon. Stephen A. Douglas, in the Celebrated Campaign of 1858, in Illinois," the publishers Follett, Foster & Company, Columbus, Ohio. The book held the awesome heave and surge of the slavery issue and its companion, the dark threat of the Union dissolved. It gave the passionate devotion of Douglas to an ocean-bound republic of free white men, with what he termed "the inferior races," the Negro, the Indian, the Chinese coolie, barred from citizenship—and Lincoln's thousand-faceted defense of the clause, "that all men are created equal," and his high cries against the spread of slavery. In a sense, the book was a master mural of the American people in a given year.

Lincoln one October morning in 1859 "came rushing into the office," wrote Herndon, in his hands a letter inviting him to lecture in Brooklyn, in Plymouth Church, on the platform of Henry Ward Beecher. He thought it over, consulted with Herndon and others, and wrote the committee chairman, "I believe, after all, I shall make a political speech of it." Then over the winter weeks of late 1859 and early 1860 he toiled on the speech, at the State Library sinking himself in the *Congressional Globe*, the *Annals of Congress*, fingering through old mellowed newspaper files, in his office worming his way through his own six-volume Elliot's *Debates on the Federal Constitution*. This was to be no stump speech to prairie farmers. He would face a sophisticated metropolitan audience. The Chicago *Press & Tribune* on February 16, 1860, had sweepingly endorsed Lincoln for president, his character "the peer of any man yet named . . . more certain to carry Illinois and Indiana than any one else . . . great breadth and acuteness of intellect" and Lincoln would "never be President by virtue of intrigue and bargain." On February 23, as Lincoln left Springfield for New York, the *Illinois State Register* took its fling as to the coming speech: "Subject, not known, Consideration, $200 and expenses. Object, presidential capital. Effect, disappointment."

Arriving in New York he learned that the Young Men's Republican Union of New York City had arranged for his speech to be given in Cooper Union. At the Astor House he saw visitors, refused invitations to speak in New Jersey, went on working at his speech, noticed the *Tribune* called him "a man of the people, a champion of free labor." A Springfield Democrat, M. Brayman, wrote a letter February 27 telling of being at dinner with Lincoln, and admirers came to their table. "He turned half round and talked 'hoss' to them—introduced me as a Democrat, but one so good tempered that he and I could 'eat out of the *same rack, without a pole between us.*'"

A snowstorm interfered with traffic, and on the night of February 27 the Cooper Union audience didn't fill all the seats. About 1,500 people came, most of them paying the 25 cents admission; the door receipts were $367. The *Tribune* said that "since the days of Clay and Webster" there hadn't been a larger assemblage of the "intellect and moral culture" of the city of New York.

The eminent attorney, David Dudley Field, escorted the speaker to the platform, where among distinguished guests sat the innocent-faced Horace Greeley. William Cullen Bryant, editor of the *Evening Post*, author of "Thanatopsis" and "To a Waterfowl," told the audience of Lincoln's majority for the senatorship in Illinois and the legislative apportionment that elected Douglas. Bryant closed, "I have only, my friends, to pronounce the name of Abraham Lincoln of Illinois [loud cheering], to secure your profoundest attention."

A tall, gaunt frame came forward, on it a long, new suit of broadcloth, hanging creased and rumpled as it came out of his satchel. Applause began; the orator smiled, put his left hand to the lapel of his coat, and so stood as the greeting slowed down. "Mr. *Cheer*man," he said with Kentucky tang in his opening. He was slow getting started. There were Republicans not sure whether to laugh or feel sorry. As he got into his speech there came a change. They saw he had thought his way deeply among the issues and angers of the hour. He quoted Douglas: "Our fathers, when they framed the Government under which we live, understood this question [of slavery] just as well, and even better, than we do now." And who might these "fathers" be? Included must be the 39 framers of the original Constitution and the 76 members of the Congress who framed the amendments. And he went into a crisscross of roll calls, quotations, documents in established history, to prove "the fathers" held the Republican party view of restricting slavery. Did any one of "the fathers" ever say that the Federal Government should *not* have the power to control slavery in the Federal Territories? "I defy any man to show that any one of them ever, in his whole life, declared that." He said "neither the word 'slave' nor 'slavery' is to be found in the Constitution, nor the word 'property' even." They called the slave a "person." His master's legal right to him was phrased as "service or labor which may be due." Their purpose was "to exclude from the Constitution the idea that there could be property in man."

If the Republican party was "sectional" it was because of the Southern sectional efforts to extend slavery. The Republicans were not radical nor revolutionary but conservative and in line with the "fathers" who framed the Constitution. Yet, "I do not mean to say we are bound to follow implicitly in whatever our fathers did. To do so, would be to discard all the lights of current experience—to reject all progress—all improvement." There were those saying they could "not abide the election of a Republican President," in which event they would destroy the Union. "And then, you say, the great crime of having destroyed it will be upon us! That is cool. A highwayman holds a pistol to my ear, and mutters through his teeth, 'Stand and deliver, or I shall kill you, and then you will be a murderer!' "

Slave insurrections couldn't be blamed on the young Republican party; 23 years before the slave Nat Turner led a revolt in Virginia where three times as many lives were lost as at Harpers Ferry. "In the present state of things in the United States, I do not think a general, or even a very extensive slave insurrection, is possible . . . The slaves have no means of rapid communication . . . The explosive materials are everywhere in parcels; but there neither are, nor can be supplied, the indispensable connecting trains. Much is said by Southern people about the affection of slaves for their masters and mistresses; and a part of it, at least, is true." In any uprising plot among 20 individual slaves, "some one of them, to save the life of a favorite master or mistress, would divulge it . . . John Brown's effort . . . was an attempt by white men to get up a revolt among slaves, in which the slaves refused to participate. In fact, it was so absurd that the slaves, with all their ignorance, saw plainly enough it could not succeed."

In the quiet of some moments the only sound competing with the speaker's voice was the steady sizzle of the burning gaslights. The audience spread before him in a wide quarter-circle. Thick pillars sprang from floor to ceiling, white trunks dumb, inhuman. But the wide wedges of faces between were listening. "And now, if they would listen—as I suppose they will not—

I would address a few words to the Southern people." Then he dealt in simple words with the terrible ropes of circumstance that snarled and meshed the two sections of the country:

"The question recurs, what will satisfy them? Simply this: We must not only let them alone, but we must, somehow, convince them that we do let them alone . . . Wrong as we think slavery is, we can yet afford to let it alone where it is, because that much is due to the necessity arising from its actual presence in the nation; but can we, while our votes will prevent it, allow it to spread into the National Territories, and to overrun us here in these Free States? If our sense of duty forbids this, then let us stand by our duty, fearlessly and effectively."

He reasoned: "All they ask, we could readily grant, if we thought slavery right; all we ask, they could as readily grant, if they thought it wrong. Their thinking it right, and our thinking it wrong, is the precise fact upon which depends the whole controversy. Thinking it right, as they do, they are not to blame for desiring its full recognition, as being right; but, thinking it wrong, as we do, can we yield to them? Can we cast our votes with their view, and against our own?" To search for middle ground between the right and the wrong would be "vain as the search for a man who should be neither a living man nor a dead man." He finished: "Let us have faith that right makes might, and in that faith, let us, to the end, dare to do our duty as we understand it."

Applause came, outcries and cheers; hats went in the air and handkerchiefs waved; they crowded to shake the speaker's hand; a reporter blurted, "He's the greatest man since St. Paul" and scurried away to write: "No man ever before made such an impression on his first appeal to a New York audience."

The committee member, Charles C. Nott, walked with Lincoln, saw him limping, and asked, "Are you lame, Mr. Lincoln?" No, he wasn't lame; his new boots hurt his feet. They boarded a horse-drawn streetcar, and rode to where Nott had to hop off for the nearest way home. He told Lincoln just to keep on riding and the car would take him to the Astor House. And Nott watching the car go bumping up the street wasn't sure he had done right to get off; Lincoln looked sad and lonesome like a figure blown in with the drifts of the snowstorm.

In the morning Lincoln saw that four papers printed his speech in full, and learned there would be a pamphlet reprint of it. Brady photographed him; as the picture came out he looked a little satisfied with himself; it wasn't his usual sad face. But people liked it.

This week Joseph Medill in Washington sent to the Chicago *Press & Tribune* an editorial arguing that Lincoln could be elected President that year and Seward couldn't. Seward read it, hunted up Medill, and as Medill told it: "Seward 'blew me up' tremendously for having disappointed him, and preferring that 'prairie statesman,' as he called Lincoln. He gave me to understand that he was the chief teacher of the principles of the Republican party before Lincoln was known other than as a country lawyer in Illinois." The background instigators of Lincoln's appearance at Cooper Union were a faction long opposed to Seward and Weed; they were pleased to see Seward's stature cut down a little; they may have crossed their fingers when Lincoln asked for "harmony, one with another" and said, "Even though much provoked, let us do nothing through passion and ill temper."

Lincoln spoke for his party in New England and visited his boy, Robert, in school at Exeter, New Hampshire. At Hartford, the report ran, he cited one-sixth of the population of the United States looked upon as property, as nothing but property. "The cash value of these slaves, at a moderate estimate, is $2,000,000,000. This amount of property value has a vast influence on the minds of its owners, very naturally. The same amount of property would have an equal influence upon us if owned in the North. Human nature is the same—people at the South are the same as those at the North, barring the difference in circumstances."

Shoe factory workers on strike said they couldn't live on their wages of $250 a year. Douglas laid the strike on "this unfortunate sectional warfare"; Lincoln replied, "Thank God that we have a system of labor where there *can* be a strike." Thus at Hartford. At New Haven, the *Daily Palladium* reported him: "I do not pretend to know all about the matter . . . *I am glad to see that a system of labor prevails in New England under which laborers* CAN *strike* when they want to [Cheers,] where they are not obliged to work under all circumstances, and are not tied down and obliged to labor whether you pay them or not! [Cheers.] I *like* the system which lets a man quit when he wants to, and wish it might prevail everywhere. [Tremendous applause.] . . . I don't believe in a law to prevent a man from getting rich; it would do more harm than good. So while we do not propose any war upon capital, we do wish to allow the humblest man an equal chance to get rich with everybody else. [Applause.]"

He made speeches in Providence, Concord, Manchester, Dover, New Haven, Meriden, Norwich, and finally in Bridgeport on March 10, usually to "capacity audiences," several times escorted by brass bands and torchlight processions of cheering Republicans. About midway he wrote his wife, "I have been unable to escape this toil. If I had foreseen it, I think I would not have come east at all." He was hard put to make nine speeches "before reading audiences who had already seen all my ideas in print." He turned down invitations to speak in Philadelphia, Reading and Pittsburgh, being "far worn down." He thanked James A. Briggs for a $200 check for the Cooper Union speech, begged off any more speaking dates, but on March 11 did go with Briggs to hear Beecher preach in Brooklyn and to attend the Universalist Church of Edwin H. Chapin in New York. The next day he took the Erie Railroad for Chicago and two days later was home in Springfield, arriving, said the *Journal*, "in excellent health and in his usual spirits."

CHAPTER 14

"Mary, We're Elected"

WILLIAM H. SEWARD, eight years older than Lincoln, leading all other candidates for the Republican presidential nomination, was a New Yorker of Welsh-Irish stock, a slim, middle-sized man, stooped, white-haired, with a pointed nose, a slouching walk, a plain conversational tone in public speaking, "eyes secret but penetrating, a subtle, quick man, rejoicing in power." His friend and manager, Thurlow Weed, publisher of the Albany *Evening Journal*, ran a Seward publicity bureau, was in touch with large special interests and made free use of money in promoting Seward.

When governor of New York, Seward had brought into effect laws requiring jury trial for fugitive slaves, with defense counsel fees paid by the state. In the U.S. Senate, replying to Webster, Seward had said, ". . . there is *a higher law* than the Constitution, which regulates our authority over the domain." In October 1858 he spoke of the slavery issue as not "the work of fanatical agitators," but rather, "It is an *irrepressible conflict* between opposing and enduring forces, and it means that the United States must and will, sooner or later, become either entirely a slaveholding nation, or entirely a free-labor nation."

Southern voices and papers called him "monstrous and diabolical," some of his own advisers telling him he had gone too radical. He had retreated into explanations that he wasn't as radical as he sounded, but a stigma hung on him. While Lincoln went on month after month quoting from his House Divided speech, Seward refused to refresh memories about his "higher law" and "irrepressible conflict." Lincoln's speech had a mystic songlike quality while Seward's was bare intellectual doctrine.

Handsome, portly, overdignified Salmon P. Chase of Ohio, antislavery, radical, had twice been governor and served a term as U.S. Senator; he would get delegates from Ohio and elsewhere but didn't seem formidable. Judge Edward Bates of Missouri would have that state's delegates and a scattered following from elsewhere. He was 67, had married a South Carolinian's daughter who bore him 17 children. He had been a Whig Congressman and his backers said that as a Free-Soil Whig from a Border Slave State he would avert secession. He was smallish, bearded, a moderate Old Line Whig who kept a diary that whispered to him he would be President. In 1856 he had been a leader in an Old Line Whig convention at Baltimore which endorsed the American [Know-Nothing] party and he didn't know the full force of German editors and political leaders who had axes out for him and would throw a fierce strength against him.

John McLean, an Ohio Democrat, appointed associate justice of the U.S. Supreme Court by President Jackson, was in the running, his dissenting opinion in the Dred Scott case being in his favor. He was 75, and Lincoln wrote to Trumbull, "I do not believe he would accept it [the nomination]; . . . If he were ten years younger he would be our best candidate." McLean's health was failing and he was to die within a year, but he was mentioned in reckonings that did not include Lincoln.

Before mid-May the Lincoln-Douglas debates book, at 50 cents in paper or $1.00 clothbound, was to go into four editions; the pamphlet reprints of the Cooper Union speech were selling at one cent the copy, and there was a growing legend spreading wider of the tall homely man who was log-cabin born and had been flatboatman and rail splitter, struggling on to where his speech and thought were read nationwide. All this had created an aura about Lincoln that in the few weeks now left before the national Republican convention in May was to be the more effective because it was no forced growth. It had a way of dawning on men, "Why, yes, come to think of it, why not Lincoln? The more you look at him the more he is the man."

He had in 1859 traveled 4,000 miles to make 23 Republican speeches. He had covered more ground over America than any others of his party mentioned for President; born in Kentucky, he had traversed the Mississippi River in a flatboat to New Orleans, had lived in the national capital, had met audiences over all the Midwest as far out as Kansas, in New York City, and across New England. He had purposely in public hidden his hopes and strengths as a candidate and coming weeks would tell the results. He had followed this course long before John Wentworth's advice of February 6: "Look out for *prominence*. When it is ascertained that none of the prominent candidates can be nominated then ought to be your time."

Lincoln wrote to an Ohio delegate, of the coming Chicago convention, that Seward "is the very best candidate we could have for the North of Illinois, and the very *worst* for the South of it." With Chase of Ohio it would be the same, while Bates of Missouri would be the best for the south of Illinois and the worst for the north. And Judge McLean, if 15 or even 10 years younger, would be stronger than either Seward or Bates. "I am not the fittest person to answer the questions you ask [about candidates]. When not a very great man begins to be mentioned for a very great position, his head is very likely to be a little turned."

With Trumbull he would be "entirely frank," writing, "The taste *is* in my mouth a little." He repeated for Trumbull his view of the Seward, Chase and Bates followings in Illinois. Three small-town newspapers in Illinois had nominated Trumbull for President; the taste was a little in his mouth too and while he regarded himself as one of the darker dark horses, he favored McLean as against Lincoln, who had secured his election as U.S. Senator.

To another Ohio delegate Lincoln wrote: "Our policy, then, is to give no offence to others—leave them in a mood to come to us, if they shall be compelled to give up their first love. This, too, is dealing justly with all, and leaving us in a mood to support heartily whoever shall be nominated." In a Bloomington speech in April, he thrust at the Douglas logic: "If I cannot rightfully murder a man, I may tie him to the tail of a kicking horse, and let him kick the man to death."

Mark Delahay, as the Lincoln leader in Kansas, asked for money, Lincoln replying: "Allow me to say I can not enter the ring on the money basis— first, because, in the main, it is wrong; and secondly, I have not, and can not get, the money. I say, in the main, the use of money is wrong; but for certain objects, in a political contest, the use of some, is both right, and indispensable." He could make a distinct offer: "If you shall be appointed a delegate to Chicago, I will furnish one hundred dollars to bear the expences of the trip." In a second letter after Kansas elected a pro-Seward delegation he wrote to Delahay, "Come along to the convention, & I will do as I said about expenses."

Into the state Republican convention at Decatur on May 9 came John Hanks carrying two fence rails tied with flags and streamers, with the inscription, "Abraham Lincoln, the Rail Candidate for President in 1860: Two rails from a lot of 3,000 made in 1830 by Thos. Hanks and Abe Lincoln—whose father was the first pioneer of Macon County." Shouts followed: "Lincoln! Lincoln! Speech!" He thanked them with a sober face. Cheers: "Three times three for Honest Abe, our next President." Shouts from the convention: "Identify your work!" "It may be that I split these rails," and scrutinizing further, "Well, boys, I can only say that I have split a great many better-looking ones."

Thus the Rail Candidate was brought forth, and the nickname of Rail Splitter. The idea came from Richard Oglesby, a Decatur lawyer, Kentucky-raised, a plain and witty man, who shared Lincoln's belief in the people. He had hunted out John Hanks and planned the dramatization of Lincoln as "the Rail Splitter." Far more important was it that the convention instructed its delegates to the Chicago convention to vote as a unit for Lincoln; 7 of the 22 delegates personally preferred Seward, and Orville H. Browning's choice was Bates.

Two weeks earlier, at the national Democratic convention in Charleston, South Carolina, where the Douglas delegates held a majority control, but lacking the necessary two-thirds to nominate their hero, slavery men had split the party, and two separate wings of it were to hold conventions in June. The answers of Douglas to Lincoln in the Freeport debate and his break with the Buchanan administration had lost nearly all former trust of the South in him. William Lowndes Yancey of Alabama, tall, slender, with long black hair, spoke in a soft, musical yet tense voice for the minority. "The proposition you make, will bankrupt us of the South. Ours is the property invaded—ours the interests at stake . . . You would make a great seething caldron of passion and crime if you were able to consummate your measures." Ten days of speeches, ballots, wrangles, brought adjournment to Baltimore in June. Now it was taken as certain that there would be two Democratic parties in the field, one Northern, the other Southern, and Republican victory in November almost sure.

On May 9 in Baltimore was organized the new Constitutional Union party with a short platform calling for the maintenance of the Constitution, the Union and law enforcement. For President they nominated John Bell of Tennessee, a former Whig Congressman and U.S. Senator, for Vice-President, Edward Everett, a former Secretary of State and president of Harvard University. Not much was expected from them; their platform was not merely simple but too simple.

Illinois delegates were outfitting with silk hats and broadcloth suits for the Chicago Republican convention May 16. Lincoln was saying, "I am a little too much a candidate to stay home and not quite enough a candidate to go." Judd and others had made a special point of getting the convention for Chicago. They told the national committee that holding the convention in an eastern city would "run a big chance of losing the West." Chicago had become a symbol for audacity, enterprise and onward stride. Its population of 29,000 in 1850 had become 80,000 in 1855, and 109,000 in 1860; it betokened the "great Northwest" that had wrought transformations in American national politics. Its trade in hogs, cattle, wheat, corn, farm machinery, and the associated finance and transportation, made it the depot and crossroads for thousand-mile prairies. Out of it ran 15 railway lines with 150 railroad trains a day; on May 16, 1860, they had brought an estimated 40,000 strangers and 500 delegates to the convention. At the corner of Lake and Market Streets the Sauganash Hotel had been torn down, and a huge rambling lumber structure, to hold 10,000 people, had been put up and named the Wigwam. Chicago girls and women, with the help of young men, had made the big barnlike interior gay and brilliant with flags, bunting and streamers of red, white and blue.

Judge David Davis had adjourned the Eighth Circuit courts, took over the entire third floor of Chicago's finest hotel, the Tremont House, paying a rental of $300 for spacious Lincoln headquarters and rooms for his staff of Lincoln hustlers, evangelists, salesmen, pleaders, exhorters, schemers. Jesse Fell, once a Pennsylvanian, could mix with and interpret the pivotal Keystone delegates. Judd, as a railroad lawyer of close association with a Pennsylvania delegate who was a railroad lawyer, could make honest promises to the powerful interests who wanted a Pacific railway and other benefits. Leonard Swett, as a young man from Maine, might break, as he did, the Seward unity of that state's delegates. Richard J. Oglesby, as a Whig Free-Soiler raised in Kentucky, would do his best with his rough hearty jargon among the Kentucky delegates and those from Missouri. John M. Palmer, a loyal Democrat until the Kansas-Nebraska Bill, would be effective among former Democrats, while Gustave Koerner, the German-born refugee, would be a demon at breaking down the chances of Bates who in 1856 had lent his name to the Know-Nothings.

Judge Stephen T. Logan, William H. Herndon, Ward Hill Lamon, who knew Lincoln from close association, could testify where needed in personal talk with doubtful delegates. Helping on many errands and interviews would be the lawyers William W. Orme of Bloomington and Nathan M. Knapp of Winchester. Illinois state treasurer, William Butler, at whose house Lincoln once boarded, and Ozias M. Hatch, Illinois secretary of state, were no greenhorns in politics, and Jesse K. Dubois, state auditor, was about the closest coadjutor of the shrewd chief manipulator, Judge Davis. A born trader and man of affairs, Davis owned 10,000 acres of land in Iowa, many farms and tracts in Illinois, and was often rated a millionaire.

In the parlor of the Lincoln headquarters were cigars and wine, porter, brandy, whisky, for any delegate or important guest; the total bill, $321.50, was paid by Hatch and Lamon. They called in delegates and held quiet private talks or made speeches to groups; Thurlow Weed at his Seward headquarters in the Richmond House was using the same methods. Medill and Charles H. Ray of the *Tribune* were on hand with ideas and their influence. Weaving from caucus to caucus were Andrew G. Curtin of Pennsylvania and

Henry S. Lane of Indiana; each was running for governor in his state and each solemnly positive that their states would be lost if Seward was nominated. The same gospel of gloom about Seward came from David Dudley Field, George Opdyke and other New Yorkers who had come on to stop Seward. Innocent-faced Horace Greeley went hither and yon saying he had only goodwill toward Seward but the man to carry the country was Bates. A long roll could be called of the delegates who day and night buttonholed others and told them Seward couldn't carry the doubtful states of Pennsylvania, New Jersey, Indiana and Illinois.

From the midwest states people had swarmed into Chicago, proud and curious about the first great national convention to be held so far west. New York had sent a thousand to shout and cheer for Seward; among them was Tom Hyer, the champion heavyweight prize fighter. Pennsylvania sent 1,500 marchers to see the big show and help Pennsylvania. A Wisconsin delegate had to register at a cheap hotel where, after inspecting the bed, as he told it, "I spent the rest of the night in a chair, as sure as my name is Carl Schurz." Processions with brass bands and bright nobby uniforms marched, cheering candidates. During the three days of the convention the crowd outside the Wigwam was two and three times the size of the one inside; relays of orators made speeches. A thousand saloons had customers making holiday and hullabaloo. Mark Delahay wrote two rambling, boozy letters to Lincoln, reporting in his way that the confusion was confounding.

Delegate Knapp wrote to Lincoln May 14: "We are laboring to make you the second choice of all the Delegations we can where we can not make you first choice. We are dealing tenderly with delegates, taking them in detail, and making no fuss . . . brace your nerves for any result."

The day before the convention opened, May 15, Davis and Dubois wired Lincoln: "We are quiet but moving heaven & Earth. Nothing will beat us but old fogy politicians." The next day Judd's message was: "Dont be frightened. Keep cool. Things is working." On the afternoon of May 17 the platform was adopted in a sweep of yells and cheers. The Seward men then wanted to ballot on candidates; a motion to that effect was made but the chair said "the tally-sheets had not been prepared" and on a quick motion to adjourn and by a light unrecorded vote, Chairman George Ashmun announced the motion prevailed and the convention was adjourned. The moment was fateful; Seward men believed they could have nominated their man that afternoon. That May 17 the main Lincoln backers worked all night and clinched important deals. Davis telegraphed Lincoln: "Am very hopeful. Dont be Excited. Nearly dead with fatigue. Telegraph or write here very little."

Dubois and other Lincoln men went into conference with the Pennsylvania and Indiana delegations. "We worked like nailers," said Oglesby. Ray of the *Tribune* came to his chief, Medill. "We are going to have Indiana for Old Abe, sure." "How did you get it?" asked Medill. "By the Lord, we promised them everything they asked." Caleb B. Smith was to be Secretary of the Interior and William P. Dole, Commissioner of Indian Affairs; Indiana would vote a solid block for Lincoln on the first ballot. Pennsylvania with its block of 54 delegates wearing white hats would vote for Simon Cameron, as a favorite son, on the first ballot, and then were willing to go elsewhere. Judge

Davis dickered with them; Dubois telegraphed Lincoln the Cameron dele-gates could be had if Cameron was promised the Treasury Department. Lin-coln wired back, "I authorize no bargains and will be bound by none."

A message from Lincoln was carried to Chicago by Edward L. Baker, edi-tor of the Springfield *Journal;* it was a copy of a newspaper with markings of Seward speeches, with Lincoln's marginal notes, "I agree with Seward's 'Irrepressible Conflict,' but I do not endorse his 'Higher Law' doctrine," and then Lincoln's underlined words, "Make no contracts that will bind me." Why Lincoln should send such cryptic messages to old companions who were losing sleep, spending money and toiling fearfully to make him President was anybody's guess. He may have believed that in the rush and heat of events some corrupt bargain might be made, and he would have these messages to show. Definitely, too, out of his many years of close association with him he knew Davis' mind, will and conscience, and such peremptory messages from him would not stop the judge from a resolved purpose to nominate Lincoln.

What happened next was told by Whitney: "The bluff Dubois said, 'Damn Lincoln!' The polished Swett said, 'I am very sure if Lincoln was aware of the necessities ——' The critical Logan expectorated, 'The main difficulty with Lincoln is ——' Herndon ventured, 'Now, friend, I'll answer that.' But Davis cut the Gordian knot by brushing all aside with, 'Lincoln ain't here, and don't know what we have to meet, so we will go ahead, as if we hadn't heard from him, and he must ratify it!' "

In that mood they went to the Pennsylvania managers. When they were through they came down to the lobby of the Tremont House, where Medill of the *Tribune* had been smoking and thinking about a remark of Lincoln's that Pennsylvania would be important in the convention. As Medill saw 300-pound Judge Davis come heaving and puffing down the stairs about midnight, he stepped up to the judge and, as he told it later, asked him what Pennsyl-vania was going to do. And Judge Davis: "Damned if we haven't got them." "How did you get them?" "By paying their price."

Then came Ray, who had sat in and heard. And Medill asked his editor how Pennsylvania had been nailed down. "Why," said Ray, "we promised to put Simon Cameron in the Cabinet. They wanted assurances that we rep-resented Lincoln, and he would do what we said." "What have you agreed to give Cameron?" asked Medill. "The Treasury Department." "Good heav-ens! Give Cameron the Treasury Department? What will be left?" "Oh, what is the difference?" said Ray. "We are after a bigger thing than that; we want the Presidency and the Treasury is not a great stake to pay for it."

And so, with three state delegations solid, and with odd votes from Ohio and other states, the Lincoln men waited for the balloting, seeing to it, how-ever, that the convention seating committee carefully sandwiched the Penn-sylvania delegation between Illinois and Indiana.

When the platform was adopted the day before, leaving out mention of the Declaration of Independence, old Joshua R. Giddings arose, and said it was time to walk out of the Republican party. Then young George William Curtis of *Harper's Weekly* stood up and shamed the convention; the prin-ciple of the equality of men was written in and Giddings stayed on.

Seward victory was in the air; champagne fizzed at the Richmond House. Straw votes on all incoming railroad trains had given Seward overwhelming majorities. Michigan, Wisconsin, Minnesota, were a unit for Seward, as were the New York, Massachusetts (except four who were for Lincoln) and California delegations. Horace Greeley wired his New York *Tribune* that Seward seemed sure to win. Lincoln workers were saying with clenched fists and blazing eyes that the Republicans were beaten at the start if Seward headed the ticket. They scared a definite element who wanted to win; and again there were antislavery men such as Bryant of the New York *Evening Post* who believed Seward to be the same type as Daniel Webster, much intellect, little faith, none of the "mystic simplicity" of Lincoln.

Lamon had been to the printers of seat tickets. Young men worked nearly a whole night signing names of convention officers to counterfeit seat tickets so that next day Lincoln men could jam the hall and leave no seats for the Seward shouters. Hour on hour the bulk of the 40,000 strangers in Chicago kept up noise and tumult for Abraham Lincoln, for Old Abe, for the Rail Candidate. Judd had fixed it with the railroads so that any shouter who wished could set foot in Chicago at a low excursion rate. Men illuminated with moral fire, and others red-eyed with whisky, yelled, pranced, cut capers and vociferated for Lincoln.

On the first two days of the convention's routine business the Seward men were allowed by the Chicago managers to have free run of the floor. But on May 18, when sunrise saw thousands milling about the Wigwam doors, the Lincoln shouters were shoved through the doors till they filled all seats and standing room; hundreds of New York hurrah boys couldn't squeeze in. Lamon and Fell got a thousand men recruited for their lung power; they had been given tickets and were on hand. They watched their leaders, two men located on opposite sides of the Wigwam. One of them, Dr. Ames of Chicago, it was said, could "on a calm day" be heard clear across Lake Michigan. The other one, brought by Delegate Burton Cook from Ottawa, could give out with a warm monster voice. These two Leather Lungs watched Cook on the platform; when he took out his handkerchief they cut loose with all they had and kept it up till Cook put his handkerchief back. They were joined by the thousand recruits picked for voice noise.

Nomination speeches were in single sentences. Judd said, "I desire, on behalf of the delegation from Illinois, to put in nomination, as a candidate for President of the United States, Abraham Lincoln, of Illinois." Here Cook took out his handkerchief. "The idea of us Hoosiers and Suckers being out-screamed would have been bad," said Swett. "Five thousand people leaped to their seats, women not wanting, and the wild yell made vesper breathings of all that had preceded. A thousand steam whistles, ten acres of hotel gongs, a tribe of Comanches might have mingled in the scene unnoticed."

Seward had 173½ votes, Lincoln 102, and favorite sons and others the remainder of the votes on the first ballot. On the second ballot, Lincoln jumped to 181 as against Seward's 184½. On the third ballot, of the 465 votes Lincoln swept 231½ while Seward dropped to 180. Medill of the *Tribune* whispered to Cartter of Ohio, "If you can throw the Ohio delegation for Lincoln, Chase can have anything he wants." "H-how d'-d'ye know?"

stuttered Cartter, Medill answering, "I know, and you know I wouldn't promise if I didn't know."

Cartter called for a change of four votes from his state to Lincoln. Other delegates announced changes of votes to Lincoln. As the tellers footed up the totals, and the chairman waited for the figures, the chatter of 10,000 people stopped, the fluttering of ladies' fans ended, the scratching of pencils and the clicking of the telegraph dot-dash dash-dot-dash could be heard. The 900 reporters from everywhere in America clutched their pencils.

The chairman spoke. Of 465 votes, 364 were cast for the candidate highest, and "Abraham Lincoln, of Illinois, is selected as your candidate for President of the United States."

Chairmen of state delegations arose and made the nomination unanimous. The terrific emotional spree was over. Strong men hugged each other, wept, laughed and shrieked in each other's faces through tears. Judge Logan stood on a table, brandished his arms and yelled, swung wild his new silk hat and on somebody's head smashed it flat. Inside and outside the Wigwam it was a wild noon hour; hats, handkerchiefs, umbrellas, in the air; brass bands blaring; cannon explosions on the roof getting answers from city bells, riverboat and railroad whistles.

Hannibal Hamlin, the Maine senator, a former Democrat, was nominated for Vice-President, and thanks voted to the convention chairman, George Ashmun of Massachusetts. Seward's manager, Thurlow Weed, pressed the temples of his forehead to hold back tears but the tears came. Greeley wrote it was a fearful week he hoped never to see repeated. "If you had seen the Pennsylvania delegation, and known how much money Weed had in hand, you would not have believed we could do so well as we did . . . We had to rain red-hot bolts on them, however, to keep the majority from going for Seward."

Knapp telegraphed Lincoln: "We did it. Glory to God," and Fell: "City wild with excitement. From my inmost heart I congratulate you." Swett warned, "Dont let any one persuade you to come here," Dubois and Butler saying: "Do not come without we telegraph you," Judd more brief: "Do not come to Chicago," and Koerner briefest of all: "Dont come here."

On May 18 Lincoln walked from home to his office and was talking with two law students when the office door burst open and the *Journal* editor, Baker, told him of the first ballot in Chicago. They walked to the telegraph office, found no later news, and at the *Journal* office met a crowd shouting good news would be coming. Lincoln slouched in a chair but straightened up at the next news of his big gains on the second ballot. And when the wires sang that his nomination had been made unanimous, he knew that a great somber moment had come to him and the firing of 100 jubilant guns made a shadowed music. He read a flurry of gay telegrams, shook hands all round, then went home to tell the news and see his wife's face beam and glow. In the afternoon he shook hands with many callers.

Bonfires of boxes, barrels and brushwood lighted up the Sangamon River country that Friday night. A brass band and a cheering crowd at the Lincoln house surged to the front porch and called for a speech. He saw the honor of the nomination not for him personally but as the representative of a

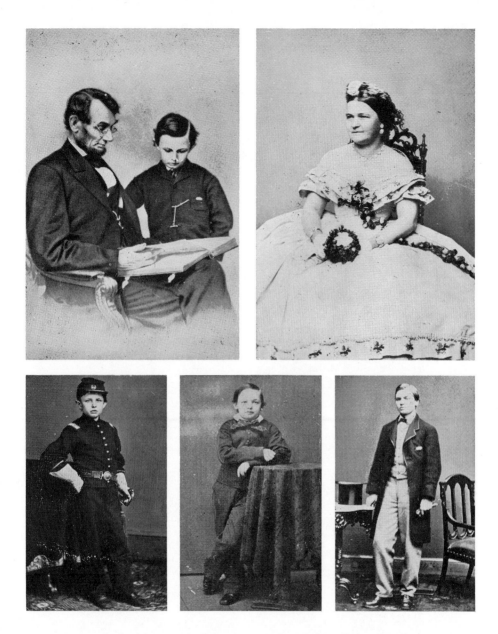

Upper left: Brady photograph of President Lincoln with his cherished youngest son and companion Thomas Todd ("Tad") [Meserve]. *Upper right:* Mrs. Abraham Lincoln in party gown, flowers, and jewels [Meserve]. *Lower left:* Tad in his uniform of "Colonel" in the U.S. Army [National Archives]. *Lower center:* William Wallace Lincoln, third son [CS]. *Lower right:* Robert Todd Lincoln, first-born of the four Lincoln sons [Meserve].

Upper: The Lincoln house in Springfield during 1860 campaign, Lincoln in white coat or linen duster at right of door [Meserve]. *Center left:* Photograph by Alexander Hesler in Springfield 1860. Original photograph loaned by Edward Steichen. *Center right:* David Davis, Eighth Circuit judge, landed millionaire, Lincoln's foremost political manager in 1860 [CS]. *Lower left:* William H. Seward, U.S. Senator from New York and titular leader of Republican party until Lincoln's nomination [CS]. *Lower right:* Thurlow Weed, editor of Albany *Evening Journal*, friend of Seward and his intensely active political manager [Meserve].

cause; he wished his house big enough so he could ask them all inside. Shouts and yells of hurrah parties broke on the night till the gray dawn of the morning after.

Judge Davis answered a question on what the wild week cost: "The entire expense of Lincoln's nomination, including headquarters, telegraphing, music, fare of delegations, and other incidentals, was less than $700."

Elements that Lincoln had described as "strange and discordant, gathered from the four winds," had formed a powerful party of youth, wild banners, pilgrims of faith and candlelight philosophers, besides hopeful politicians. Industrial, transportation and financial interests found this party promising. Pennsylvania, New York, New England, were satisfied as to both the tariff and the outlook for opening up the Great Plains to settlement and trade. "A Railroad to the Pacific Ocean is imperatively demanded by the interests of the whole country; the Federal Government ought to render immediate and efficient aid in its construction," read the Republican platform plank.

Hordes of politicians had hitched themselves to the Republican party seeing it as a winner; the Government was spending $80,000,000 a year; offices, contracts and favors lay that way; in their connections these politicians had manufacturing and mercantile interests, iron, steel, coal, oil, railroads and steamboats.

In its platform promises on tariff, on land and homestead laws, on farm and factory legislation to benefit workingmen, industry and business, the Republican party had a sincerity, was attending to issues in degree long neglected or evaded. Various practical interests saw to it that their political workers had front seats, committee places and influence in the new party. Before one issue all others shrank, that of union and the wage-labor system as against disunion and slave labor. Carl Schurz had yelled, to a storm of cheers, "We defy the whole slave power and the whole vassalage of hell." A cadence of exasperation, a strain of revolutionary rumble and mutter, rose, died down, and rose again.

The man in Springfield picked to carry the banner stood at moments as a shy and furtive figure. He wanted the place—and he didn't. His was precisely the clairvoyance that knew terrible days were ahead. He had his hesitations. And he was in the end the dark horse on whom the saddle was put. He could contemplate an old proverb: "The horse thinks one thing, he that saddles him another."

The notification committee at his house formally told Lincoln he was nominated for President. He formally replied, and later, after reading the platform, sent a letter of acceptance. He would co-operate, "imploring the assistance of Divine Providence."

In June the adjourned Democratic national convention met in Baltimore, and after bitter and furious debates, nominated Douglas of Illinois for President and Herschel Johnson, a Georgia unionist, for Vice-President. Delegates from 11 slave states walked out, bolted their old party, and nominated John C. Breckinridge of Kentucky for President and Joseph Lane of Oregon for Vice-President. They rejected with scorn and hate Douglas' "popular sovereignty" and his leadership; they believed with John Randolph who 40 years earlier had advised secession, saying, "Asking a state to surrender part of her sovereignty is like asking a lady to surrender part of her chastity." When Stephens of Georgia was asked what he was thinking, "Why, that men will be cutting one another's throats in a little while. In less than twelve months we shall be in a war, and that the bloodiest in history."

To Judge Davis came many letters asking how Lincoln, if elected, would deal with patronage and offices, with party factions, with coming issues and events. Davis requested Lincoln to guide him in answering such letters. Lincoln wrote May 26 for Davis "the body of such a letter as I think you should write . . . in your own handwriting," adding whatever assurances Davis might "think fit." The letter for Davis' use was vastly implicative, luminously shrewd yet wise, comprehensive yet brief, as an indication in that hour of the mingled peace and turmoil in Lincoln's mind and conscience. It read:

Since parting with you, I have had full, and frequent conversations with Mr. Lincoln. The substance of what he says is that he neither is nor will be, in advance of the election, committed to any man, clique, or faction; and that, in case the new administration shall devolve upon him, it will be his pleasure, and, in his view, the part of duty, and wisdom, to deal fairly with all. He thinks he will need the assistance of all; and that, even if he had friends to reward, or enemies to punish, as he has not, he could not afford to dispense with the best talents, nor to outrage the popular will in any locality.

From original letter written by Lincoln to David Davis

Judge Davis kept close track of the Midwest campaign, and August 24 wrote from Bloomington to Thurlow Weed that he had been in Indiana and found the Republican party in danger of losing that state. "They believe that with $10,000 the State can be carried . . . The election may run itself, as it is doing in a great many States, but, depend upon it, without pecuniary aid, there can be neither certainty nor efficiency." Among those keeping Lincoln in touch with the campaign machinery were Davis, Swett and Judd. Errands between Illinois, New York and Pennsylvania were indicated in a letter of Swett to Thurlow Weed: "We should be exceedingly glad to know your wishes and your views, and to serve you in any way in our power. I say this freely for myself because I feel it, and for Judge Davis, because, although now absent, I know his feelings. Of course, nobody is authorized to speak for Mr. Lincoln."

Wide-Awake clubs of young men in uniforms marched in torchlight processions. Seward spoke across the Northern States; Lincoln went to the railway station to pay him a cordial greeting when he passed through Springfield. Batteries and flotillas of orators spoke. They argued, threatened, promised, appealed to statistics, passions, history. But the high chosen spokesman of the party had little or nothing to say. He wrote a few letters, and shook hands with orators, politicians and reporters who came by the dozen and score to the house on Eighth Street. He spoke August 8 when railroads, buggies, horses and ox wagons brought 50,000 people to Springfield. He greeted them; the "fight for this cause" would go on "though I be dead and gone." He ended: "You will kindly let me be silent."

Follet, Foster & Company announced a biography of Lincoln, *authorized* by him, which brought his outburst, "I have scarcely been so much astounded by anything, as by their public announcement . . . I certainly knew they contemplated publishing a biography, and I certainly did not object to their doing so, *upon their own responsibility*." He had even helped them. But, "At the same time, I made myself tiresome, if not hoarse, with repeating to Mr. Howard, their only agent seen by me, my protest that I *authorized nothing*—would be *responsible for nothing*."

Five hack biographies sprouted in June. Later came more pretentious and competent biographies, bound in boards, one by William Dean Howells, the best by D. W. Bartlett, a 354-page volume with a steel engraving of Lincoln. Six editions were printed of the New York *Tribune*'s impressive *Political Text Book for 1860*, 248 pages of the most notable speeches and documents of all parties. In campaign literature the Republicans far surpassed the Democrats. Medals and coins were struck, one medal praising soap on one side and the candidate on the other. Requests for autographs flooded in. Wendell Phillips was asking, "Who is this huckster in politics?" Seward was saying, "No truer defender of the Republican faith could have been found."

Newspapers came, estimating Lincoln as "a third-rate country lawyer"; he lived "in low Hoosier style"; he "could not speak good grammar"; he delivered "coarse and clumsy jokes"; he was descended from "an African gorilla." Letters asked his view on this or that. And secretary John G. Nicolay sent all the same answer; his positions were well known when he was nominated; he must not now "embarrass the canvass."

Slimy, putrid and reeking, was an article in the Macomb, Illinois, *Eagle*, in August 1860, printing what it claimed to be "an extract of a speech made by Mr. Lincoln in 1844." It quoted Lincoln as saying:

Mr. Jefferson is a statesman whose praises are never out of the mouths of the Democratic party . . . The character of Jefferson was repulsive. Continually puling about liberty, equality, and the degrading curse of slavery, he brought his own children to the hammer, and made money of his debaucheries. Even at his death he did not manumit his numerous offspring, but left them soul and body to degradation and the cart whip. A daughter of this vaunted champion of democracy was sold some years ago at public auction in New Orleans.

A Republican broadside, campaign of 1860

To one who sent him a clipping of it, Lincoln wrote, "I do not recognize it as anything I have ever seen before, emanating from any source. I wish my name not to be used; but my friends will be entirely safe in denouncing the thing as a forgery." To a Boston group who invited him to a Jefferson birthday festival he had declined, writing:

Those claiming political descent from him have nearly ceased to breathe his name everywhere . . . soberly, it is now no child's play to save the principles of Jefferson from total overthrow in this nation . . . The principles of Jefferson are the definitions and axioms of free society . . . All honor to Jefferson—to the man, who, in the concrete pressure of a struggle for national independence by a single people, had the coolness, forecast, and capacity to introduce into a merely revolutionary document, an abstract truth, applicable to all men and all times, and so to embalm it there, that to-day, and in all coming days, it shall be a rebuke and a stumbling-block to the very harbingers of re-appearing tyranny and oppression.

John Locke Scripps, a Chicago *Tribune* editor, had a long interview with Lincoln, and on his request Lincoln wrote for his use a 2,500-word autobiography. From this Scripps wrote a 32-page close-print pamphlet titled "Life of Abraham Lincoln." Scripps wrote to a brother, "I have been getting out a campaign Life of Lincoln for the million which is published simultaneously by us [the Chicago *Tribune*] and by the *New York Tribune*." Though Scripps was rushed, and wrote against time, he produced a little book packed with a charming readable story having documents and dignity. A million copies at five cents apiece meant millions of readers now had a few answers to, "Who and what is Abraham Lincoln, his folks, his ways, his looks, his home, his beliefs and policies?" His education? "He was never in a college or an academy as a student, and was never, in fact, inside of a college or academy building until after he had commenced the practice of the law. He studied English grammar after he was twenty-three years of age; . . . he studied the six books of Euclid after he had served a term in Congress, and when he was forty years of age, amid the pressure of an extensive legal practice." He knew about hard work from "splitting rails, pulling the cross-cut and the whip-saw, driving the frower, plowing, harrowing, planting, hoeing, harvesting." He knew about sports. "In wrestling, jumping, running, throwing the maul and pitching the crow-bar, he always stood first among those of his own age."

Scripps in his book quoted Douglas as saying in one debate in 1858, "Lincoln is one of those peculiar men who perform with admirable skill everything they undertake." And Scripps wrote further: In many cases where "a poor client" had "justice and right on his side," Mr. Lincoln charged no fee and sometimes quietly slipped the client a five or ten dollar bill. His Mexican War record, his bill to abolish slavery in the District of Columbia, the debates with Douglas were elaborately documented. And personally, his six-feet-four-inch frame "is not muscular, but gaunt and wiry. In walking, his gait, though firm, is never brisk. He steps slowly and deliberately, almost always with his head inclined forward, and his hands clasped behind his back." At rest, his features were not handsome, "but when his fine, dark-grey eyes are lighted up by any emotion, and his features begin their play, he would be chosen from among a crowd as one who had in him not only the kindly sentiments which women love, but the heavier metal of which full-grown men and Presidents are made." As to religion, "He . . . is a pewholder and liberal supporter of the Presbyterian Church in Springfield, to which Mrs. Lincoln belongs." Scripps believed of Lincoln, "He has an exquisite sense of justice." On only this one point was Lincoln found "exquisite." Of the millions who read the pamphlet biography, many sat brooding, inquiring, thoughtful, about this fabulous human figure of their own time.

In this summer of 1860 Lincoln saw a powerful young political party shaping his figure into heroic stature, coloring his personality beyond reality. From hundreds of stump orators and newspapers came praise and outcry for "Abe," "Old Abe," "the Rail Candidate," "the Backwoodsman," "Honest Abe," "the Man of the People," the sagacious, eloquent Man of the Hour, one who starting from a dirt-floor cabin was to move on into the Executive Mansion in Washington.

What men there had been who had gone up against the test and gone down before it! What heartbreaking challenge there was in the act of heading a government where vast sensitive property interests and management problems called for practical executive ability, while millions of people hungered for some mystic bread of life, for land, roads, freedom. They were the titanic, breathing, groaning, snarling, singing, murmuring, irreckonable instrument through which, and on which, history, destiny, politicians worked —The People—the public that had to be reached for the making of public opinion.

Chicago politicians were saying Lincoln seemed to be in "rough everyday rig" in his pictures. Lincoln had written he would be "dressed up" if Hesler, the Chicago photographer, came to Springfield. And Hesler made four fine negatives of Lincoln in a stiff-bosomed, pleated shirt with pearl buttons. Volk, the sculptor, arrived, had a rose bouquet from Mrs. Lincoln, and presented her with a bust of her husband. A round stick was needed for Lincoln's hands while Volk made casts. Lincoln stepped out to the woodshed and returned to the dining room whittling a broom handle. The edges didn't need such careful whittling, Volk remarked. "Oh, well, I thought I would like to have it nice." Sitting for one portrait, as the likeness emerged Lincoln said, "There's the animal himself."

Douglas stumped the country in what seemed for him a losing fight; he went on tireless, men amazed at the way he wore out, went to bed, and came back fighting. At Norfolk, Virginia, in late August he told an audience of 7,000 that he wanted no votes except from men who desired the Union to be preserved. On a slip of paper handed him was the question whether, if the South seceded, he would advise resistance by force. To this he flashed, "I answer emphatically that it is the duty of the President of the United States and all others in authority under him to enforce the laws of the United States as passed by Congress and as the courts expound them . . . In other words, I think the President of the United States, whoever he may be, should treat all attempts to break up resistance to its laws as Old Hickory treated the Nullifiers in 1832." At Raleigh, North Carolina, he said he would "hang every man higher than Haman" who resisted Constitutional law. No Illinoisan would ever consent to pay duty on corn shipped down the Mississippi. "We furnish the water that makes the great river, and we will follow it throughout its whole course to the ocean, no matter who or what may stand before us."

At places in the North he favored "burying Southern disunionism and Northern abolitionism in the same grave," saying, too, that if Old Hickory were alive he would "hang Northern and Southern traitors on the same gallows." The Pacific railway and other dreams would never come true "unless you banish forever the slavery question from the halls of Congress and remand it to the people of each state and territory."

In Cedar Rapids, Iowa, on news in October of Republicans sweeping Pennsylvania, Douglas turned to his secretary, "Mr. Lincoln is the next President," adding, "We must try to save the Union. I will go South." In Tennessee, Georgia and Alabama, he spoke to large crowds, often amid threats and jeers of thugs and rotten fruit and eggs meant to reach his head. In Atlanta, Alexander Stephens, though Douglas was not his first choice for President, introduced Douglas with warm praise. Harassed and in sinking health, Douglas spoke in the Deep South with passion and storm in his voice of the love he held for the Union and his scorn of those who would break up the Union. Mr. Lincoln in Springfield must have been deeply moved when he read some of these Douglas speeches.

Letters kept coming to Lincoln—what would he do with slavery if elected? Would he interfere? Would it not be wise now to say plainly he wouldn't interfere? One he had answered, "Those who will not read, or heed, what I have already publicly said, would not read, or heed, a repetition of it." He wrote to a pro-Douglas Louisville editor, "I have *bad* men also to deal with, both North and South,—men who are eager for something new upon which to base new misrepresentations,—men who would like to frighten me, or, at least fix upon me the character of timidity and cowardice."

He wrote Swett about a matter concerning Weed and others, his main point in one sentence, "It can not have failed to strike you that these men ask for just, the same thing—*fairness*, and fairness only." But he ended the letter, "Burn this, not that there is any thing wrong in it; but because it is best not to be known that I write at all."

When the notification committee had called, he soberly brought them a pitcher of ice water. Mrs. Lincoln was all ready with bottles of champagne but Koerner warned that wouldn't do; it would be told against them. Lincoln loosened the stiff occasion by calling on a tall judge to stand up and measure height with him.

The campaign came to its last week. As the summer and fall drew on he was to those who met him the same friendly neighbor as always—but with more to think about. He shook hands with Whitney in a big crowd, and a half-hour later, seeing Whitney again, he shook hands and called him by name. "He didn't know me the first time," said Whitney.

Millions of people had by this time read his words of two years ago in the House Divided speech. They struck the soft, weird keynote of the hour. "If we could first know *where* we are, and *whither* we are tending, we could then better judge *what* to do, and *how* to do it."

Twice, since he had first so spoken, the corn had grown from seed to the full stalk and been harvested. In a book he had carried, it was told, "All rising to power is by a winding stair." As he went higher it was colder and lonelier. The last leaves were blowing off the trees and the final geese honking south. Winter would come and go before seed corn went into the ground again.

Early reports on election evening, November 6, gave Douglas 3,598 votes and Lincoln 3,556 in Sangamon County while in Springfield Lincoln had 1,395 against 1,326 for Douglas. From nine o'clock on he sat in the Springfield telegraph office. Lincoln with friends stepped across the street to where the Republican Ladies' Club had fixed a supper. The ladies rushed him. "How do you do, Mr. President?" Hardly were the men seated when a messenger rushed in waving a telegram. New York had gone Republican. Lincoln's election was clinched.

In the streets, and around the Statehouse, crowds surged, shouting themselves hoarse. The jubilee was still going as Lincoln walked home to say to a happy woman, "Mary, we're elected." The local *Journal* was saying, "Our city is as quiet as a young lady who has just found out that she is in love."

In Mobile, Alabama, Douglas had told a large audience that their rights would be far safer in the Union than outside. In the office of the *Register* he read dispatches. They told him only what he had expected. He tried

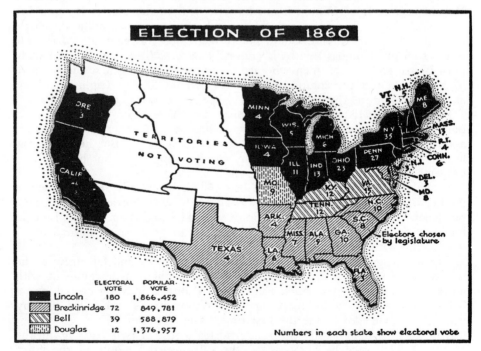

From Allan Nevins: *The Emergence of Lincoln*

to read the coming events in the light of his knowing from high sources that scores of powerful Southern leaders had their plans for secession on the election of Lincoln. He knew what his course would be. He had told the South what it would be. He was tired and sad but he had spent his life in storms and was ready for the next one.

The national count gave Lincoln 1,866,452 votes; Douglas, 1,376,957; Breckinridge, 849,781; Bell, 588,879. Lincoln had majorities in 17 Free States, Breckinridge carried 11 Slave States, Bell 3 Slave States. In the electoral college Douglas had only the 3 votes of New Jersey and the 9 of Missouri. The total electoral college votes looked a little silly, giving dim light on the popular balloting, with Lincoln, 180; Breckinridge, 72; Bell, 39; Douglas, 12. In a total of some 4,700,000 votes the other combined candidates had nearly a million more votes than Lincoln. Fifteen states gave him no electoral votes; in ten states of the South he didn't get a count of one popular vote. He was the most sectionally elected President the nation had ever had and the fact would be dinned into his ears.

Events marched and masked their meanings. Facts were gathering motion, whisking into new shapes and disguises every day. Dream shapes of future events danced into sight and out of sight, faded and came again, before a whirligig of triple mirrors.

CHAPTER 15

The House Dividing

LINCOLN'S election was a signal. The Atlanta newspaper, *Confederacy*, spoke for those who had visions of violence: "Let the consequences be what they may—whether the Potomac is crimsoned in human gore, and Pennsylvania Avenue is paved ten fathoms deep with mangled bodies, or whether the last vestige of liberty is swept from the face of the American continent, the South will never submit to such humiliation and degradation as the inauguration of Abraham Lincoln." This was in part bravado and blowoff and in part hope and determination.

Equally flaring and vivid in Boston was Wendell Phillips, speaking for an abolitionist faction: "Let the South march off, with flags and trumpets, and we will speed the parting guest . . . All hail, disunion! . . . Let the border states go. Then we part friends. The Union thus ended, the South no longer hates the North . . . The laws of trade will bind us together, as they do all other lands." Mildly the innocent-faced Greeley chimed in, "Let the erring sisters depart in peace."

In North Carolina, the Raleigh *Banner* spoke for a small segment of the South: "The big heart of the people is still in the Union. Less than a hundred politicians are endeavoring to destroy the liberties and usurp the rights of more than thirty millions of people. If the people permit it, they deserve the horrors of the civil war which will ensue."

South Carolina legislators voted to raise and equip 10,000 volunteer soldiers; Georgia voted $1,000,000 and Louisiana $500,000 for guns and men. Robert Toombs was saying: "It is admitted that you seek to outlaw $4,000,000,000 of property of our people . . . Is not that a cause of war?" But was secession the safest immediate way of managing this property? Jefferson Davis had hopes and doubts. And Alexander Stephens had written, "I consider slavery much more secure in the Union than out of it if our people were but wise."

In the day's mail for Lincoln came letters cursing him for an ape and a baboon who had brought the country evil. He was buffoon and monster; an abortion, an idiot; they prayed he would be flogged, burned, hanged, tortured. Pen sketches of gallows and daggers arrived from "oath-bound brotherhoods." Mrs. Lincoln saw unwrapped a painting on canvas, her husband with a rope around his neck, his feet chained, his body tarred and feathered.

A Tennessee woman wrote of her dream about how to keep out of war. Another suggested he should have all his food tasted. Still another letter told Lincoln to resign at the inaugural and appoint Douglas as the new President.

A chemist and metal-worker, A. W. Flanders of Burlington, Iowa, in letters to Nicolay, explained with intelligent detail that he could have made secretly a shirt of mail, of flexible chain armor, "plated with gold so that perspiration shall not affect it. It could be covered with silk and worn over an ordinary undershirt." Flanders would "be very happy to get this done for Mr. Lincoln," but his kindly and generous offer could not be accepted.

On the way to Chicago November 21 Lincoln made a two-minute speech at Bloomington, referred to the expressed will of the people, and, "I think very much of the people, as an old friend said he thought of woman. He said when he lost his first wife, who had been a great help to him in his business, he thought he was ruined—that he could never find another to fill her place. At length, however, he married another . . . and that his opinion now was that *any woman would do well who was well done by*."

In Chicago, as he had arranged by letters, he met Vice-President-elect Hamlin and Joshua Speed. He wasn't sure he had ever before met Hamlin but he had heard him speak in the Senate. Hamlin couldn't remember having met Lincoln but he had heard him in the House in a speech that had "auditors convulsed with laughter." People so crowded in on the two important men in the Tremont House that they went for their conference to a private home. Lincoln wished in appointments to hold a balance between Whigs who had turned Republican and Democrats who had turned Republican. He would trust Hamlin to name the New England member of his Cabinet for Secretary of the Navy, giving Hamlin three names he inclined to favor, Hamlin deciding on a former Jackson Democrat, Gideon Welles, a Hartford editor.

They both favored Seward for Secretary of State. Lincoln soon after wrote one short letter notifying Seward he would appoint him Secretary of State and a longer letter giving Seward Lincoln's belief "that your position in the public eye, your integrity, ability, learning," made the appointment "pre-eminently fit." These two letters Lincoln sent to Hamlin, writing, "Consult with Judge Trumbull; and if you and he see no reason to the contrary, de-

liver the letter to Governor Seward at once. If you see reason to the contrary, write me at once." Trumbull wasn't eager about Seward but he consented; so Hamlin delivered Lincoln's two letters to Seward, and Seward,
after pretending to think deeply about it, accepted.

With Joshua Speed, Lincoln discussed the outlook in Kentucky, possible
appointments there, and casually asked Speed how he was fixed for money,
income, wherewithal. Speed flashed back that he knew why Lincoln was
asking such a question and he didn't need any office Lincoln could offer him,
which pleased them both.

The trains into Springfield on a single day would unload hundreds of passengers, arriving to see the President-elect. Some carried shining faces; they
just wanted to look at him and tell him they hoped to God he'd live and have
good luck. Others, too, carried shining faces, singing, "Ain't we glad we
joined the Republicans?" They said they nominated and elected him President, and inquired about post offices, revenue collectorships, clerkships, sec-
retaryships. They wore him. Behind their smiles some had snouts like buz-
zards, pigs, rats. They were pap-seekers, sapsuckers, chair-warmers, hammock-
heroes, the office-sniffing mob that had killed Zach Taylor, that had killed
Tippecanoe Harrison. They wore Lincoln—worse than the signs of war.

The office seekers watched Lincoln's habits, waylaid him, wedged in, and
reminded him not to forget them. If personally refused, they sent appeals
again to Lincoln's ear through friends. One who kept coming, by one device
and another pressing claims on Lincoln, was Judge Davis. As Whitney told
it: "Lincoln inveighed to me in the bitterest terms against Judge Davis' greed
and importunity for office, and summarized his disgust in these words, 'I know
it is an awful thing for me to say, but I already wish some one else was here
in my place.' "

Smart alecks came, often committees of them, guffawing at their own lame
jokes, with thrusts of familiarity at Lincoln as though they might next be
tickling him in the ribs. Whitney saw Lincoln one afternoon, with smiling
humor, usher the last member of such a committee out of the door, and
Whitney remarked, "I wish I could take as rose-colored a view of the situation as you seem to." Lincoln's smiles had all crept back into the leathery
fissures of his face, as he told Whitney: "I hope you don't feel worse about
it than I do. I can't sleep nights."

Strong-hearted, black-eyed Hannah Armstrong came, the widow of Jack,
the mother of Duff. Lincoln took her two hands. They talked, homely and
heart-warming talk. He held the hands that had been good to him, so long
ago, when he was young and the sap ran wild in him. And as she was going:
"They'll kill ye, Abe." "Hannah, if they do kill me, I shall never die another
death."

The gray-bearded, quiet-mannered Judge Edward Bates on invitation visited Lincoln, and consented to be U.S. Attorney General, "a fine antique,"
ran one comment. Against Indiana and Illinois factions, Lincoln kept a convention pledge to appoint Caleb B. Smith of Indiana, a garden-variety spoils
politician, to be Secretary of the Interior. Norman B. Judd, the Republican

state chairman, wanted this or some other Cabinet place but couldn't swing it; Judge Davis worked against him and so did Mrs. Lincoln in writing Davis a letter of bitter dislike for Judd.

Thurlow Weed came from Albany, on Swett writing him that Lincoln wanted to see him about Cabinet matters. They talked politics and issues in general. Would Bates of Missouri do for Attorney General? Yes, Weed was sure; he paid tribute to Bates' personal reliability. Telegrams had come from prominent Republicans trying to head off appointments Weed might seek, Lincoln told the New York leader.

Lincoln had long trained himself to put men at their ease while pumping them with quiet questions, learning by asking, and asking with keen, soft persistence. He knew that Weed was in touch with such men of power as A. T. Stewart, leading New York merchant, and August Belmont, New York representative of the Rothschilds, international bankers, and one of the northern capitalists to whom the South was in debt $200,000,000. Also Lincoln learned in elaborate detail how Weed hated and feared radicals North and South and favored all possible conciliation and appeasement of the South.

Salmon P. Chase, newly elected U.S. Senator from Ohio, came by invitation. Lincoln said he "wasn't exactly prepared" to appoint Chase Secretary of the Treasury, but if he did, would Chase accept? Chase wouldn't promise. He'd think it over. And he went away to line up friends to put pressure on Lincoln to appoint him.

Simon Cameron came and after long talks left with a letter signed by Lincoln:

I think fit to notify you now, that by your permission, I shall, at the proper time, nominate you to the U.S. Senate, for confirmation as Secretary of the Treasury, or as Secretary of War—which of the two, I have not definitely decided. Please answer at your own earliest convenience.

Cameron's enemies brought evidence to Lincoln intended to show that Cameron was "the very incarnation of corruption" and his fortune "acquired by means forbidden to the man of honor." Lincoln wrote Cameron another letter; things had developed which made it impossible to take him into the Cabinet. Would he write a letter publicly declining any Cabinet place? And Cameron's answer was a bundle of recommendations outnumbering the opposition three to one; Lincoln later wrote Cameron that he wouldn't make a Cabinet appointment for Pennsylvania without consulting him.

Donn Piatt, an Ohio journalist, left Springfield to say, "Lincoln told us he felt like a surveyor in the wild woods of the West, who, while looking for a corner, kept an eye over his shoulder for an Indian."

Henry Villard earlier had written of Lincoln: "More than once I heard him 'with malice aforethought' get off purposely some repulsive fiction in order to rid himself of an uncomfortable caller. Again and again I felt disgust and humiliation that such a person should have been called upon to direct the destinies of a great nation." Villard later still, reporting for the New York *Herald*, judged the President-elect "a man of good heart and good intentions," but "not firm." Weeks passed and he definitely saw Lincoln as "a man of immense power and force of character and natural talent . . . a man to act and decide for himself . . . tremendously rough and tremendously honest and earnest." Thus judgments, in favor and against, shifted as the winds shift.

"Resistance to Lincoln is Obedience to God" flared a banner at an Alabama mass meeting; an orator swore that if need be their troops would march to the doors of the national Capitol over "fathoms of mangled bodies."

Against Southern advice that South Carolina wait till President Buchanan's term ended, Robert Barnwell Rhett and his forces had manipulated the precise dramatic event of secession. As a Congressman of six terms and a U.S. Senator of one term, as editor of the Charleston *Mercury*, as lawyer and churchman, as manager of the Charleston Bible Society, as vice-president of the Young Men's Temperance Society, as secretary of the Charleston Port Society for promoting the Christian gospel among seamen, as the father of 12 children, the driving motive of Rhett's life was to win secession and Southern independence, build a confederacy on the cornerstone of African slavery, and restore the African slave trade outlawed by the U.S. Constitution as of 1808. Rhett organized "minutemen" and vigilance committees, to make sure of delegates pledged to secession. He wrote the ordinance of disunion, and in secret session the convention's 169 delegates in St. Andrew's Hall at Charleston, December 16, 1860, passed it without debate in 45 minutes. A newly adopted flag brought a great shout, rocked the hall, and from lowlands to upcountry were bells, bonfires, torchlights, parades, shotgun salutes and cries of jubilee. One by one the six other Cotton States of the lower South joined South Carolina in leaving the Union.

Senators and Representatives from the South spoke sad and bitter farewells to Congress; U.S. postmasters, judges, district attorneys, customs collectors, by the hundreds sent their resignations to Washington. Of the 1,108 officers of the U.S. Regular Army, 387 were preparing resignations, many having already joined the Confederate armed forces. The U.S. mint at New Orleans and two smaller mints were taken over by the Confederate States, as were post offices and customhouses. Governors of seceded states marched in troops and took over U.S. forts that had cost $6,000,000.

Reports flew that Southern forces would seize Washington, Lincoln to be sworn in at some other place. Twenty-two carloads of troops were starting from Fort Leavenworth across Missouri for Baltimore. Cameron of Pennsylvania was saying, "Lincoln, if living, will take the oath of office on the Capitol steps." Dr. William Jayne of Springfield wrote to Trumbull, "Lincoln advised he would rather be hanged by the neck till he was dead on the steps of the Capitol than buy or beg a peaceful inauguration." Newly organized artillery companies were drilling in Chicago. A thousand Negro slaves were throwing up fortifications in Charleston, South Carolina. Governor Yates notified the legislature, "Illinois counts among her citizens 400,000 who can bear arms." Five million dollars and a hundred thousand troops would be offered by their state, Pennsylvania legislators were saying.

"The Revolution" was the top headline under which a New York daily paper assembled the news of the country. Nine columns were required on one day to report declarations of Southern conventions, and resignations from the Army, Navy and training academies. Stephens of Georgia had dug into history. "Revolutions are much easier started than controlled, and the men who begin them, even for the best purposes and object, seldom end them."

The New York *Herald*, circulating 77,000 copies daily, earning profits of $300,000 a year, advised in an editorial, "A grand opportunity now exists for Lincoln to avert impending ruin, and invest his name with an immortality far more enduring than would attach to it by his elevation to the Presidency. His withdrawal at this time from the scene of conflict, and the surrender of his claims to some national man who would be acceptable to both sections, would render him the peer of Washington in patriotism." And the *Herald* added: "If he persists in his present position . . . he will totter into a dishonoured grave, driven there perhaps by the hands of an assassin, leaving behind him a memory more excrable than that of Arnold—more despised than that of the traitor Catiline."

Senator Jefferson Davis, pale and just risen from a sickbed, in January spoke his words of parting: "I offer you my apology for any thing I may have done in the Senate, and I go remembering no injury I have received." His regrets coupled to a warning: "There will be no peace if you so will it." Swiftly, on Davis' walking out forever, Senator William M. Gwin of California would vote $100,000,000 for a Pacific railway. But Crittenden of Kentucky said that, with the Union "reeling about like a drunken man," he could not see a Pacific railway. "Build up the Union first; then talk about building up a railroad."

If Lincoln should try to retake the seized forts, he would have to kill in sickening numbers, said John Y. Brown of Kentucky. "From the blood of your victims, as from the fabled dragons' teeth, will spring up crops of armed men, whose religion it will be to hate and curse you." "Very well, sir," said Thaddeus Stevens. "Rather than show repentance for the election of Mr. Lincoln, with all its consequences, I would see this Government crumble into a thousand atoms."

Lincoln delivered remarks such as, "Please excuse me . . . from making a speech," and, "Let us at all times remember that all American citizens are brothers of a common country." He indicated in letters to Trumbull, Washburne and others at Washington they must stand for no further spread of slavery. "On that point hold firm, as with a chain of steel," he counseled, and warned, "The tug has to come, & better now, than any time hereafter." His close friend, Edward D. Baker, now U.S. Senator from Oregon, told the Senate that Lincoln would respect the Fugitive Slave Law. Also, Lincoln told friends privately that the forts seized by the seceded states would have to be retaken. But as to public declarations of policy on this and that, he was waiting.

Congressman William Kellogg of Canton, Illinois, one of the few most favored by Lincoln in patronage, held a long conference with Lincoln in Springfield January 21. Then Kellogg went to Washington, spoke for a mild compromise in his bill for extension of slavery into all new territories to be formed south of 36° 30′; he was howled down by the radicals of his party, and read out of the party by the Chicago *Tribune*—as both he and Lincoln had probably expected. One result of this Kellogg proposal was that the Unionist Democrats of southern Illinois, Indiana and Ohio, near the Slave State borders, could say to their people that when the Southern States left the Union, there was still a chance for slavery extension into the western territories. Then, too, the Slave States of Missouri and Kentucky had a fresh argument for staying in the Union. The action was mazy.

In the very air of the City of Washington was coming a sense of change, of an impending program to be wrought out on historic anvils in smoke and mist, of old bonds and moorings broken, of a formerly confident and dominant class giving way to an element a little raw and new to government and diplomacy, young and strange in its champing and chafing.

In the White House Buchanan suggested gently, "The election of any one of our citizens to the office of President does not of itself afford just cause for dissolving the Union." He could meditate on his serving as a private in the War of 1812 nearly 50 years before, of his horseback ride through blue-grass Kentucky, his temptation to settle in law practice there, and his going back to Lancaster, Pennsylvania. Elected a Congressman, he lived on, a bachelor, always reserved as to women. An estate of $300,000, out of 40 years of public officeholding, gave him little ease now, nor the comment "Buchanan has a winning way of making himself hateful."

He argued that seceded states had no right to secede, yet the Federal Government had no right to use force to stop them from seceding. He urged, however, the right of the Federal Government to use force against individuals, in spite of secession, to enforce Federal laws and hold Federal property. Yet his words lacked action to give them force. He wrote letters, negotiated, conferred, sent messengers, employed moral suasion against an organization making elaborate preparations to use guns. To Congressman Morrill of Vermont he was like an old man chuckling to his rowdy sons, *"Don't, but if I were you I would, and I can't help it if you do."*

One comfort to him was his niece, Harriet Lane, robust, with golden-brown hair, violet-blue eyes, a graduate of the Visitation Convent near Washington. A warship had been named for her, also a race horse, a flower, a fashionable gown and many a newborn girl child. "No American woman ever had more offers of marriage than Harriet Lane." Her uncle wrote the caution, "Never allow your affections to become interested, or engage yourself to any person, without my previous advice." They were chums; she shared as no others did his political secrets, with his warnings often not to tell others, for they "must tell it or burst."

While a hurricane was preparing, these two careful persons lived with their mild secrets in the White House. "Be quiet and discreet and say nothing"—the written advice of the old man to his niece was his own guiding motto. Once he termed himself "an old public functionary." "I at least meant well for my country," ran a line of his January message to Congress. To many he seemed half apparition, ready for the graveclothes that would swathe a past epoch.

Now they snarled in dog-fight tones in the halls of Congress. Now the radical abolitionist Ben Wade of Ohio kept a sawed-off shotgun in his desk. "Better for us that the fruitful earth be smitten and become dry dust," mourned Tom Corwin. "Better that the heavens for a time become brass and the ear of God deaf to our prayers; better that Famine with her cold and skinny fingers lay hold upon the throats of our wives and children . . . than that we should prove faithless to our trust . . . and all our bright hopes die out in that night which knows no coming dawn." This was a psalm for the people to hear. To Lincoln he sent an epistle for Lincoln's eye only:

. . . I cannot comprehend the madness of the times. Southern men are theoretically crazy. Extreme Northern men are practical fools. The latter are really quite as mad as the former. Treason is in the air around us everywhere. It goes by the name of patriotism. Men in Congress boldly avow it, and the public offices are full of acknowledged secessionists. God alone, I fear, can help us. Four or five States are gone, others are driving before the gale. I have looked on this horrid picture till I have been able to gaze on it with perfect calmness. I think, if you live, you may take the oath.

His dark words were addedly profound coming from the best wit and storyteller in Washington.

Only the hard of hearing had not heard of the Crittenden Compromise that winter. All territory north of the southern boundary line of Missouri to the Pacific Ocean would be free soil forever, and all territory south of that line would be slave soil forever, by Constitutional amendment, said the Crittenden Compromise; Congress would be forbidden ever to abolish slavery or interfere with it in Slave States or in the District of Columbia; the U.S. Government would pay slaveowners for slave property lost through action of mobs or law courts in the North. Thus Crittenden would bargain with the seceded states hoping they would stay in the Union. Who could blame Old Man Crittenden of Kentucky for this plan from his head, and heart? Of his two strong sons, Tom was for the Union and the Constitution and George was for secession and the Confederacy. And he wept over the House Divided.

Behind his compromise rallied Douglas, Edward D. Baker, Edward Everett, Thurlow Weed, August Belmont, Cyrus McCormick, many powerful newspapers, including the New York *Herald,* and such authentic and lovable advocates of peace as Tom Corwin. Petitions in its favor came to the Senate chamber in bales and stacks. The Crittenden Compromise marched up the hill, then down again; the forces against it had been long in growing and breeding. Behind each event operating for peace came another to cancel it.

General Winfield Scott, 75-year-old Virginian, military head of the U.S. Government, with headquarters in Winder's Building opposite the War Department, most often was to be found resting on an office sofa. At Chapultepec, Vera Cruz, Cerro Gordo, in the Mexican War he had held his saddle and ordered long marches and storming attacks and mapped the campaigns and run the armies. Six feet five inches tall, 300 pounds in weight, in shining gold braid and buttons, in broad epaulets and a long plumed hat, when he walked he seemed almost a parade by himself. Small boys waited of a morning to see him come out of his house and move like six regiments toward a waiting carriage. What with age, dropsy, vertigo and old bullets to carry, he could no longer mount a horse. To Scott's request for men and guns to garrison nine Southern forts against seizure, Buchanan wrote that to grant it would show on his part "a degree of inconsistency amounting almost to self-stultification." An Illinois Congressman presented his respects to General Scott with word from the President-elect, "Tell him, confidentially, I shall be obliged to him to be as well prepared as he can, to either hold or retake the forts, as the case may require, at and after the inauguration."

With inauguration day a few weeks off, letters warned Lincoln he would be killed before he reached Washington. He sent Thomas S. Mather, adjutant general of Illinois, to Washington to sound Winfield Scott on his loyalty. Mather came back to report he had found the Mexican War hero propped up with pillows, in bed, an old worn man with flesh in rolls over face and neck. His breathing heavy, he half choked and wheezed out the words: "Say to him that, when once here, I shall consider myself responsible for his safety. If necessary I'll plant cannon at both ends of Pennsylvania Avenue, and if any show their hands or even venture to raise a finger, I'll blow them to hell."

Delegates at Montgomery, Alabama, on February 4 organized a provisional government named the Confederate States of America, electing Jefferson Davis of Mississippi as President and Alexander Stephens of Georgia as Vice-President. Second to Robert Barnwell Rhett as a torch of revolution was William Lowndes Yancey of Alabama. And yet, in the seats of high power sat neither Yancey nor Rhett. Yancey and other extremists would have liked Rhett to be President. But a moderate element took the power, men who would rather have waited, who would have held a convention and presented demands to the North. In their newly adopted constitution they struck directly at Rhett, Yancey and the slave traders, and bid for international good will by expressly forbidding the African slave trade for all time.

Conventions in North Carolina and Arkansas deliberated, and joined the Confederacy. In Tennessee the voters balloted 105,000 to 47,000 in favor of secession, Union votes coming heavy from the mountaineers. In Virginia, three to one of 130,000 voters were in favor of "the Mother of Presidents" going into the Confederacy, the mountaineers chiefly being Unionist. In Texas, Governor Sam Houston refused to call the legislature and tried to stop secession, but was bowled over.

The California Senator, James A. McDougall, once an Eighth Circuit lawyer in Illinois, jingling his Mexican spurs like sleigh bells, his trousers thrust in his boots and his boots lifted on his senatorial desk, could see "as many minds as men and no end of wrangling," and was only sure, "I believe in women, wine, whiskey, and war." The less lush Henry Adams of Massachusetts was writing a brother, "No man is fit to take hold now who is not as cool as death."

It was sunset and dawn, moonrise and noon, dying time and birthing hour, dry leaves of the last of autumn and springtime blossom roots.

CHAPTER 16

"I Bid You an Affectionate Farewell"

WHEN a Brooklyn hatter one January day presented Lincoln with a black silk hat, he turned to say, "Well, wife, if nothing else comes out of this scrape, we are going to have some new clothes." Such attentions pleased Mrs. Lincoln. She had a sprightly manner of saying, "We are pleased with our advancement." In the hustle of deciding what to take along to the White House, when asked about many things to be done or not done, she would sometimes burst out, "God, no!" One winter morning she was burning papers in the alley when Jared P. Irwin, a neighbor, asked if he could have some of them. She said he was welcome and Irwin scraped from the fire several of the most interesting letters written by Mr. and Mrs. Lincoln to each other.

Pressure came on her to give her husband the names of men he should appoint to offices, with reasons why. Of one woman for whose husband she got a fat office, Mrs. Lincoln told another woman, "She little knows what a hard battle I had for it, and how near he came to getting nothing." She spoke of fears about her health, would mention "my racked frame" to other women, and say she hoped the chills she suffered from in earlier years would not return in Washington. She might find Washington a city of tears and shadows. She would go there with new clothes, fresh ribbons, and see. She made a trip in January to New York City, there meeting Robert, who came down from Harvard. She had as good a time as possible for her, choosing and buying gowns, hats, footwear and adornments becoming to one to be called "the First Lady of the Land."

Ordering things to wear, she could write instructions, "I am in need of two bonnets—I do not wish expensive ones, but I desire them of very fine quality and stylish." She wrote specifications to the milliner. "One bonnet, I wish fine, very fine, pretty shape. This I desire, to be trimmed with black love ribbons—with pearl edge. I cannot have it without the latter . . ." Villard wrote for the New York *Herald* January 26 of the President-elect "delighted" at the return of Mrs. Lincoln and Bob from the east. "Dutiful husband and father that he is, he had proceeded to the railroad depot for three successive nights in his anxiety to receive them, and that in spite of snow and cold. Mrs. Lincoln returned in good health and excellent spirits; whether she got a good scolding from Abraham for unexpectedly prolonging her absence, I am unable to say; but I know she found it rather difficult to part with the winter gayeties of New York." Villard noted, too, that Robert, fresh from Harvard, dressed in an elegance in "striking contrast to the loose, careless, awkward rigging of his Presidential father."

Lincoln rode to Mattoon, missed connections with a passenger train, and took the caboose of a freight train to Charleston. With a shawl over his shoulders, and his boots in slush, mud and ice, he picked his way in the late evening dusk alongside the tracks the length of the freight train to the station, where a buggy was ready. Friends took him to the house where he stayed overnight. Next day he drove eight miles out to an old farm. Sally Bush Lincoln and he put their arms around each other and listened to each other's heartbeats. They held hands and talked, they talked without holding hands. Each looked into eyes thrust back in deep sockets. She was all of a mother to him. He was her boy more than any born to her. He gave her a photograph of her boy, a hungry picture of him standing and wanting, wanting. He stroked her face a last time, kissed good-by and went away. She knew his heart would go roaming back often, that even when he rode in an open carriage in New York or Washington with soldiers, flags and cheering thousands along the streets, he might just as like be thinking of her in the old log farmhouse out in Coles County, Illinois.

The sunshine of the prairie summer and fall months would come sifting down with healing and strength; between harvest and corn-plowing there would be rains beating and blizzards howling; and there would be the silence after snowstorms with white drifts piled against the fences, barns and trees.

Lincoln cleaned out files, threw away useless odds and ends. Manuscripts he wished to preserve and didn't want to be encumbered with in Washington, he put into a carpetbag and gave to Elizabeth Todd Grimsley, whom he called "Cousin Lizzie." His "literary bureau," he termed it, and told Mrs. Grimsley to watch it with care but if he should not return to Springfield she might dispose of the manuscripts as she pleased. Among them were two drafts of his lecture "Discoveries and Inventions."

His regular secretary was a trusted, reliable, accurate, scrupulous young man, sober as a work horse, earnest as the multiplication table; he had freckles and reddish hair; a young Bavarian from the *Pike County Sucker*. This was John G. Nicolay, secretive, dependable, often carrying messages not to be written but whispered.

The other or second secretary, not strictly engaged as such, was going to Washington. Lincoln had said, "We can't take all Illinois with us down to Washington, but let Hay come." A keen and whimsical lad, John Hay. He had been class poet at Brown University, graduated, gone home to Warsaw, Illinois, then to Pike County, and later to Springfield to study law with his Uncle Milton, who had an office on the same floor as Lincoln & Herndon. He wrote notes in French to a sweetheart, and had a handsome, careless elegance all the girls in Springfield liked.

Between seven and twelve o'clock on the night of February 6, there came to the Lincoln home several hundred "ladies and gentlemen," wrote one correspondent, "the political elite of this State, and the beauty and fashion of this vicinity." It was the Lincolns' good-by house party. The President-elect stood near the front door shaking hands and nearby was Bob and Mrs. Lincoln and four of her sisters.

On one farewell day, as Lincoln was meeting people in Johnson's Block opposite the Chenery House, there came to him an old farmer, in butternut jeans, who had ridden horseback many miles since daybreak. And the old man was bent and worn with age, and nearly blind. He had known the Armstrongs and what Lincoln did for Duff Armstrong. And he came and put his old eyes close to Lincoln's face, peered and studied the lines of the face, burst into tears, and murmured, "It *is* him—it's the *same*." And after mentioning the Duff Armstrong case, he shook the hand of the President-elect and said solemnly two or three times, "God preserve you, Mr. Lincoln."

"Lincoln is letting his whiskers grow," men were saying in January, when his upper lip and cheeks were shaved but a stubble left on the chin. Then in February hair had grown over jaws, chin and throat, the upper lip shaven. This facial design was wrought by William Florville, a Haitian-born colored man, known as "Billy the Barber" whose shop in Springfield dated back to 1831. For more than 20 years he had shaved and done the haircuts of Lincoln while Lincoln handled several real-estate title cases for Billy who owned town lots and a farm. In his house was celebrated, it was said, the first Catholic mass in Springfield. He wrote for the Springfield *Journal* droll and charming praise of his razor skill, had keen humor, and Lincoln while being shaved undoubtedly picked up new funny stories.

Why Lincoln took to whiskers at this time nobody seemed to know. A girl in New York State had written begging him to raise a beard. An October letter from New York signed only "True Republicans" pleasantly but seriously asked him to "cultivate whiskers and wear standing collars." But something more than these random wishes guided him. Herndon, Whitney, Lamon, Nicolay, heard no explanation from him as to why after 52 years with a smooth face he should now change.

At sunset the evening before the day set for starting to Washington, Lincoln and Herndon sat in their office for a long talk about their 16 years as partners. Then Lincoln slumped on a sofa and looking up at the ceiling, mentioned that many a time after a Herndon drunk, people tried to get him to drop his partner and he told them that for all of his shortcomings he believed in Herndon. Thus Herndon wrote of it. Herndon said afterward: "I could have had any place for which I was fitted, but I thought too much of Lincoln to disgrace him. And I wanted to be free, drink whisky when I pleased." Herndon had one request, however, that Lincoln would speak to Governor Yates and have him reappointed state bank examiner, to which Lincoln agreed. As Lincoln gathered a bundle of papers and stood ready to leave, he told Herndon their partnership would go on, their "shingle" stay up. As they walked down the stairs Lincoln said he was "sick of office-holding already" and "I shudder when I think of the tasks that are still ahead."

In a dusty third-story locked room over the store of his brother-in-law, C. M. Smith, Lincoln, with a few books and documents he consulted, had hidden away from all callers while he worked on his inaugural address for March 4, in Washington, amid the cannon to be planted by General Scott. Two printers, sworn to secrecy, had in January set up and run off 20 copies of the address. Weeks had gone by. Nobody had told or been careless. The inaugural text was still a well-kept secret.

Lamon was called from Bloomington and told: "Hill, it looks as if we might have war. I want you with me, I must have you." And Lamon was going along, banjo, bulldog courage and all.

A queer dream or illusion had haunted Lincoln at times through the winter. On election evening he had thrown himself on a haircloth sofa at home, soon after the telegrams reported him President-elect. Looking into a bureau mirror across the room he saw himself full length, but with two faces. It bothered him; he got up; the illusion vanished; but when he lay down again there in the glass were two faces again, one more pale than the other. He got up again, mixed in the election excitement, forgot about it; but it haunted him. He told his wife and she too worried.

A few days later he tried it once more and the illusion of the two faces again registered to his eyes. But that was the last; the ghost since then wouldn't come back, he told his wife, who said it was a sign he would be elected to a second term, and the death pallor of one face meant he wouldn't live through his second term.

Lincoln took walks alone. Whitney ran across him in a section of Springfield where he had no business, unless to be walking alone. His arms were full of papers and bundles of mail. Where was he going? "Nowhere in particular," he told Whitney.

Clothes, furniture, books, the household goods were packed in boxes and trunks. The family took rooms a few days in the Chenery House; the old home was leased, horse, buggy and cow sold off, the German-language paper turned back to Canisius.

At the hotel Lincoln had roped his trunks himself, and had written, "A. Lincoln, The White House, Washington, D.C." on cards he fastened on the trunks.

A cold drizzle of rain was falling February 11 when Lincoln and his party of 15 were to leave Springfield on the eight o'clock at the Great Western Railway station. Chilly gray mist hung the circle of the prairie horizon. A short locomotive with a flat-topped smokestack stood puffing with a baggage car and special passenger car coupled on; a railroad president and superintendent were on board. A thousand people crowded in and around the brick station, inside of which Lincoln was standing, and one by one came hundreds of old friends, shaking hands, wishing him luck and Godspeed, all faces solemn. Even the huge Judge Davis, wearing a new white silk hat, was a somber figure.

A path was made for Lincoln from the station to his car; hands stretched out for one last handshake. He hadn't intended to make a speech; but on the platform of the car, as he turned and saw his home people, he took off his hat, stood perfectly still, and raised a hand for silence. They stood, with hats off.

Then he spoke slowly, amid the soft gray drizzle from the sky. Later, on the train he wrote with a pencil about half of his speech, dictating to Nicolay the remainder of his good-by words to Springfield: "My friends—No one, not in my situation, can appreciate my feeling of sadness at this parting. To this place, and the kindness of these people, I owe every thing. Here I have lived a quarter of a century, and have passed from a young to an old man. Here my children have been born, and one is buried. I now leave, not knowing when, or whether ever, I may return, with a task before me greater than that which rested upon Washington. Without the assistance of that Divine Being, who ever attended him, I cannot succeed. With that assistance I cannot fail. Trusting in Him, who can go with me, and remain with you and be every where for good, let us confidently hope that all will yet be well. To His care commending you, as I hope in your prayers you will commend me, I bid you an affectionate farewell."

Bells rang, there was a grinding of wheels, the train moved and carried Lincoln away from his home town and folks. The tears were not yet dry on some faces when the train had faded into the gray to the east.

At Tolono station, the last stop in Illinois, he said, "I am leaving you on an errand of national importance, attended, as you are aware, with considerable difficulties. Let us believe, as some poet has expressed it:—'Behind the cloud the sun is still shining.' I bid you an affectionate farewell."

And there were voices, "Good-by, Abe."

CHAPTER 17

America Whither?—Lincoln Journeys to Washington

"AMERICA whither?" was the question, with headache and heartache in several million homes, as Lincoln began his winding journey to Washington. There Congress had not yet, after canvass of electoral results, declared and certified him President-elect. There coming events were yet to unlock a box of secrets. In the hair-trigger suspense General Scott was saying to an aide, "A dog fight now might cause the gutters to run with blood." And he was putting guards at doorways and vantage points to make sure of order when the electoral vote for President would be canvassed February 13.

The high-priced lawyer, Rufus Choate, listening to foreign language opera in New York had told his daughter, "Interpret for me the libretto lest I dilate with the wrong emotion." In the changing chaos of the American scene, people were dilating with a thousand different interpretations. Lincoln was to be, if he could manage it, the supreme interpreter of the violent and contradictory motives swaying the country, the labor pains of the nation.

Only tall stacks of documents recording the steel of fact and the fog of dream could tell the intricate tale of the shaping of a national fate; of many newspapers North and South lying to their readers and pandering to party and special interests; of Southern planters and merchants $200,000,000 in debt to the North, chiefly to the money controllers of New York City; of the jealousy of Virginia and Kentucky slave breeders whose market was interfered with by the African slave traders; of the race question, one thing in the blizzard region of New England, where a Negro on the streets was a rare curiosity, and something else again in the deep drowsy tropical South, where in many areas Negroes outnumbered whites; of Southern slave traders who flouted the Constitutional law prohibiting the delivery of naked cargoes in the Gulf Coast canebrakes and everglades; of the law as to fugitive slaves mocked at by abolitionists stealing slave property and running it North to freedom; of abolitionists South and North hanged, shot, stabbed, mutilated; of the Northern manufacturer able to throw out men or machines no longer profitable while the Southern planter could not so easily scrap his production apparatus of living black men and women; of a new quantity production intricately organized in firearms and watch factories; of automatic machinery slightly guided by human hands producing shoes, fabrics, scissors, pins and imitation jewelry sold by a chain of Dollar Stores; of a wilderness of oil derricks sprung up in western Pennsylvania; of balloons soaring 23,000 feet and predictions of passenger balloons to Europe; of microscopically exact gauges to measure one ten-thousandth of an inch; of the far western State of Iowa having double the white population of South Carolina; of the persistent national vision of a railroad to the Pacific; of covered wagons heading west with signs "Ho for California," "Oregon or Death"; of 500 westbound wagons a day passing through Fort Kearney, Nebraska; of horse stages taking passengers across plains, deserts, mountains, in a regular 23-day run from St. Louis to San Francisco; of the pony express running mail from St. Joseph, Missouri, to San Francisco in 11 days, using 500 horses and 80 riders, each taking the sacks an average of 133⅓ miles; of farming machinery almost exclusively in the North that doubled and tripled crop land one man could handle; of woman's household work lightened by laborsaving sewing machines, churns, egg-beaters and the like; of Abraham Lincoln reading in his personal copy of *Blackwood's Magazine* that in 30 years the U.S. population would double and in 1940 reach 303,000,000; of immense stretches of the Great Plains where sod might yet be broken for unnumbered millions to come; of new empires of production and trade in the prospects of practical men who had in the past ten years spent $400,000,000 on railroads and canals between the Midwest and the Atlantic seaboard; of lands, homesteads and vast exploits waiting out yonder where the railroad whistle would shatter old solitudes; of backbreaking labor by Irish construction gangs on railroads and canals; of dog-eat-dog rivalries among merchants, manufacturers and other interests battling for customers and trade areas; of customers haggling over retail-store prices and the sensational announcement of A. T. Stewart's big store in New York that goods had one price only, as marked; of the clean and inexplicably mystic dream in many humble hearts of an indissoluble Federal Union of States; of the Mississippi River system draining 1,000,000 square miles of rich farm land, floating $60,000,000 worth of steamboats, hauling from 12 states North and South; of the certainty that the new Republican party power at Washington would aim to limit extension of slavery and put it in the course of "ultimate extinction"; of the 260,000 free Negroes of the South owning property valued at $25,000,000, one being the wealthiest landowner in Jefferson County, Virginia; of at least one in every hundred free Negroes owning one or two slaves, a few owning 50 or more; of the Southern poor white lacking slaves, land and the decent creature comforts of the Negro house servant, and often clutching as a dear personal possession the fact that he was not born black; of Northern factory hands and garment-trade workers paid a bare subsistence wage, out of which to guard against accident, sickness, old age, unemployment; of the vague hope across the South that Northwestern States might join their confederacy or form a confederacy of their own; of the one-crop Cotton States' heavy dependence on the Border Slave States and the North for food supplies, animal fodder, implements and clothing; of the Cotton States' delusion that New England and Europe were economic dependents of King Cotton; of the American system having densely intricate undergrowths, shot through from the growths of oncoming modern capitalism moderated and offset by an immense domain of cheap land absorbing otherwise disturbing and antagonistic elements.

Thus might run a jagged sketch of the Divided House over which Lincoln was to be Chief Magistrate.

The journey from Springfield to Washington brought Lincoln face to face with the governors and legislators of five states. He set foot in key cities; spoke with important men controlling politics, money, transportation, supplies; delivered more than 20 speeches; shook the hands of thousands of people; took his own look at immense crowds who wanted their look at the pivotal figure of the American scene.

Persons on board the Wabash Railroad train carrying the President-elect over the Indiana cornlands included press correspondents, old Eighth Circuit lawyers Ward Hill Lamon, Orville H. Browning, Jesse K. Dubois, Judge David Davis, Norman B. Judd of Chicago, four uniformed Regular Army officers, and 24-year-old Colonel Elmer Ephraim Ellsworth, whose Zouaves had swept the country, won championship colors, performed at West Point for Regular Army officers, and on the White House lawn. Crowds, one of 70,000, had seen their "lightning drill" with musket, bayonet, knapsack, in scarlet baggy trousers, red caps, blue jackets with orange and yellow trimmings. Later Ellsworth had gone to Springfield, had made the Lincoln & Herndon office his headquarters and delivered stump speeches for the Lincoln ticket.

The Wabash train drew into Indianapolis at five o'clock. To Governor Oliver P. Morton and "Fellow Citizens of the State of Indiana," Lincoln spoke of himself as "a mere instrument, an accidental instrument" of a great cause. Later in a speech from the balcony of the Bates House, he agreed with Solomon there is a time to keep silence and was quoted as saying: "*When men wrangle by the mouth with no certainty that they mean the same thing while using the same words, it perhaps would be as well if they would keep silence*."

On Lincoln's 52d birthday he set foot in Cincinnati, stepped into a carriage drawn by six white horses, and rode in a procession that included brass bands, fife-and-drum corps, La Fayette Guards, Rover Guards, German Yagers, Zouaves, Guthrie Greys, Washington Dragoons, citizens on horseback, in carriages, afoot.

The mayor introduced the President-elect. To Kentuckians just across the Ohio River he would say, "We mean to treat you, as near as we possibly can, as Washington, Jefferson, and Madison treated you," that "under the Providence of God, who has never deserted us . . . we shall again be brethren, forgetting all parties—ignoring all parties." As to Germans and other foreigners, "I esteem them no better than other people, nor any worse." This brought laughter. "It is not my nature, when I see a people borne down by the weight of their shackles—the oppression of tyranny—to make their life more bitter by heaping upon them greater burdens; but rather would I do all in my power to raise the yoke, than to add anything that would tend to crush them." This brought cheers and was too grave for laughter.

Not yet had Congress declared Lincoln President. Excitement ran high in Washington February 13. Crowds climbed up Capitol Hill for gallery seats, at every doorway finding armed guards. "No one could pass except Senators and Representatives, and those who had the written ticket of admission signed by the Speaker of the House or the presiding officer of the Senate," wrote L. E. Chittenden. "Even members of Congress could not pass in their friends." A Washington militia colonel in civilian clothes said his men and their rifles were within easy call. Pennsylvania Avenue, "choked with a howling angry mob," saw much street fighting and many arrests.

Tellers read the certificates state by state. John C. Breckinridge, the Vice-President, a Kentuckian whose heart lay deep with the secession cause, pronounced:

Abraham Lincoln, of Illinois, having received a majority of the whole number of electoral votes, is elected President of the United States for four years, commencing the 4th of March, 1861 . . .

Lincoln that day rode on his special train on the Little Miami Railroad to the capital of Ohio. To the state legislature at Columbus that night Lincoln made a speech peculiar from several angles: "I cannot but know what you all know, that, without a name, perhaps without a reason why I should have a name, there has fallen upon me a task such as did not rest even upon the Father of his Country . . . I turn, then, and look to the American people and to that God who has never forsaken them . . ." He spoke sentences that brought inquiry, derision, belittlement of him; he had his own purpose in the calm, deliberate words: "I have not maintained silence from any want of real anxiety. It is a good thing that there is no more than anxiety, for there is nothing going wrong. It is a consoling circumstance that when we look out there is nothing that really hurts anybody . . ."

The Lincoln special reached Pittsburgh February 14. He thanked Mayor Wilson and the citizens for a "flattering reception," again said he would speak on the country's "present distracted condition" when the time arrived, hoped that when he did finally speak he would say nothing to disappoint the people generally throughout the country, and once more threw out soothing words of a bright outlook, further baffling the better-informed philosophers.

At the town of Freedom, a coal-heaver yelled from the crowd, "Abe, they say you're the tallest man in the United States, but I don't believe you're any taller than I am." Lincoln replied, "Come up here and let's measure." The dusty shoveler in work clothes pushed through the crowd, stood back to back with the President-elect and they were exactly the same height. The crowd cheered. The two tall men grinned and shook hands. And here and there earnest people said it was no way for a public man to act with a coal-heaver, and what was the country coming to?

Into Ohio again and up to Cleveland chugged the special train. Artillery roared salutes. Through rain and mud two miles marched the procession of honor to the Weddell House. Again Lincoln spoke to his own purpose:

". . . Why all this excitement? Why all these complaints? As I said before, this crisis is all artificial. It has no foundation in facts. It was not argued up, as the saying is, and cannot, therefore, be argued down. Let it alone and it will go down of itself."

Thus from city to city, and no day of rest, and again six milk-white horses, or eight glossy blacks, with red plumes on their heads and flags in the harness, festoons and bunting of red, white and blue in the roaring streets, and packed human sidewalks.

Lincoln remembered a little girl who had written suggesting his face should have whiskers. He had answered it might look like a piece of "siily affec[ta]tion." Her town was Westfield, New York, and there he told the crowd, "I have a correspondent in this place, and if she is present I would like to see her." No one came forward. "Who is it? Give us her name," came from the crowd. "Her name is Grace Bedell." And Grace was led and carried to the platform, Lincoln saying, "She wrote me that she thought I would be better looking if I wore whiskers." He looked down at the little girl, "You see, I let these whiskers grow for you, Grace." Then he kissed her. Far and wide went the press item. The New York *Tribune* headlined "Old Abe Kissed by Pretty Girl." The St. Louis *Republican,* under the head of "Whiskers and Kisses," jibed: "If kissing pretty girls is a Presidential privilege, Mrs. Lincoln, who knows her rights and knowing dares maintain them, ought to insist on a veto power for herself."

Trying to stem the human surges around the President-elect in Buffalo, Major David Hunter of the Regular Army had his collarbone dislocated. A German Sängerbund offered songs. The crowd made merry over a man at a sawbuck sawing away to pay an election bet that Lincoln would lose. Again Lincoln said he knew the demonstration was not to him personally, and he would speak on national difficulties when he had all the light possible.

Eastward into the Erie Canal zone moved the Lincoln train in the morning. At Rochester he confessed to being overwhelmed "with this vast number of faces at this hour of the morning." The handsome platform rigged up for him at Syracuse was too much of a platform for such a speech as he would make, he said. At Utica he said he had no speech but appeared to see and be seen. So far as the ladies were concerned, he said, "I have the best of the bargain in the sight."

To governors and to key men, speaking in confidence, he counseled as he had written Governor Curtin: "I think you would do well to express, without passion, threat, or appearance of boasting, but nevertheless, with firmness, the purpose of yourself, and your state to maintain the Union at all hazzards. Also, if you can, procure the Legislature to pass resolutions to that effect."

While Lincoln crossed the Empire State from west to east February 18, news came over the wires that down in Montgomery, Alabama, amid thundering cannon and cheers from an immense crowd, Jefferson Davis took his oath as President of the Confederate States of America, six today and more tomorrow. For the first time since leaving home, Lincoln publicly admitted weariness, ending a short speech from the steps of the capitol at Albany, "I have neither the voice nor the strength to address you at any greater length."

The personal humility he had spoken in five states reached its lowest shrinking-point in the Hall of Assembly of the New York capitol: ". . . It is true that while I hold myself without mock modesty, the humblest of all individuals that have ever been elevated to the Presidency, I have a more difficult task to perform than any one of them. When the time comes I shall speak as well as I am able for the good of the present and future of this country—for the good both of the North and the South . . ."

Down the Hudson River, with greetings at Troy, Hudson, Peekskill. Then New York, the Front Door to America, where tall ships came in from the seven seas to one of the great world ports; where the 35,000 votes for Lincoln for President were a third of the total ballots; where had grown up the financial center of the country, with vast controls over trade, manufacture, transportation; where Mayor Fernando Wood had declared that New York should establish itself as a free city, separate from the Union, sovereign in itself like the seceded states of the South, thereby holding its trade and continuing "uninterrupted intercourse with every section" of the country; where bribe money had passed in franchise and city land deals; where the Mayor, as a party boss, had taken $5,000 apiece from two lawyers for nominations for Supreme Court judgeships; where the Mayor and his aldermen awarded a street-cleaning contract for $279,000 when another bid was $84,000 less; where the Mayor's personal fortune had risen to at least $250,000 out of politics; where only the corruption of the courts of justice had saved the Mayor from conviction of forgery, perjury and other crimes; where the Mayor and his brother Ben owned lotteries and were licensed as professional gamblers through charters from Southern States; where they owned the New York *Daily News* and openly advocated the rights of the Confederate States.

Lincoln rode in a procession of 30 carriages led by a platoon of mounted police. His open carriage, a barouche, had accommodated the Prince of Wales a few months before. At the Astor House 500 policemen held the crowds in line. For the first time on his journey Lincoln faced a crowd of peculiar curiosity, its silence having a touch of the sinister. The cheers and shouts were not like Buffalo, Columbus, Indianapolis.

In the City Hall next morning, surrounded by aldermen and writers for the press, Lincoln faced Mayor Wood, spoke thanks for the reception "given me . . . by a people who do not by a majority agree with me." And "in reference to the difficulties . . . of which your Honor thought fit to speak so becomingly, and so justly as I suppose, I can only say that I fully concur in the sentiments expressed." He was talking past Wood and to the country in saying: "This Union should never be abandoned unless it fails and the probability of its preservation shall cease to exist without throwing the passengers and cargo overboard."

White kid gloves were then in style for wear at opera but Lincoln, in a box at the new and sumptuous Academy of Music on Fourteenth Street and Irving Place, wore *black* kids on his large hands contrasting with the red-velvet box front. In a box opposite, a Southern man remarked to the ladies of his party, "I think we ought to send some flowers over the way to the Undertaker of the Union." The word spread, and the press commented on the one pair of black gloves in the packed house.

Mrs. Lincoln the same evening was holding a fairly successful reception in the parlors of the Astor House. Newspapers mentioned Mrs. August Belmont as among those present, which caused Mrs. Belmont to send a note to the newspapers saying she wished it known that she was not present. Tad and Willie went with a nursemaid and saw a play at Laura Keene's Theatre. With mother and father they saw Barnum's museum and its mammoth monstrosities and concatenated curiosities.

"Abe is becoming more grave," said the partly humorous weekly *Vanity Fair*. "He don't construct as many jokes as he did. He fears he will get things mixed up if he don't look out."

Greeley was saying in his morning *Tribune* that the questions were plopped at Lincoln: "What is to be the issue of this Southern effervescence? Are we really to have civil war?" And Greeley printed a version of a Lincoln fable:

"When I was a young lawyer, and Illinois was little settled, I, with other lawyers, used to ride the circuit. Once a long spell of pouring rain flooded the whole country. Ahead of us was Fox River, larger than all the rest, and we could not help saying to each other, 'If these small streams give us so much trouble, how shall we get over Fox River?' Darkness fell before we had reached that stream, and we all stopped at a log tavern, had our horses put up, and resolved to pass the night. Here we were right glad to fall in with the Methodist Presiding Elder of the circuit, who rode it in all weather, knew all its ways, and could tell us all about Fox River. So we all gathered around him, and asked him if he knew about the crossing of Fox River. 'O yes,' he replied, 'I know all about Fox River. I have crossed it often, and understand it well. But I have one fixed rule with regard to Fox River: *I never cross it till I reach it!*' " The earnest Greeley found this "characteristic of Lincoln and his way of regarding portents of trouble."

A second fable was offered New York political thinkers. "I once knew a good, sound churchman, whom we'll call Brown," Lincoln was quoted, "who was on a committee to erect a bridge over a dangerous and rapid river. Architect after architect failed, and at last Brown said he had a friend named Jones who had built several bridges and could build this. 'Let's have him in,' said the committee. In came Jones. 'Can you build this bridge, sir?' 'Yes,' replied Jones, 'I could build a bridge to the infernal regions, if necessary.' The sober committee were horrified, but when Jones retired Brown thought it fair to defend his friend. 'I know Jones so well,' said he, 'and he is so honest a man and so good an architect that, if he states soberly and positively that he can build a bridge to Hades—why, I believe it. But I have my doubts about the abutments on the infernal side.' " "So," Lincoln added, "when politicians said they could harmonize the Northern and Southern wings of the democracy, I believed them. But I had my doubts about the abutments on the Southern side."

The New York reception of the President-elect was the most elaborate, pretentious, detailed, expensive—and yet the coldest—of all on the Lincoln journey toward inauguration.

Before the New Jersey Assembly at Trenton he referred to himself again as of no personal importance and thanked them for receiving him as "the representative, for the time being, of the majesty of the people of the United

States . . . The man does not live who is more devoted to peace than I am. None who would do more to preserve it. But it may be necessary to put the foot down firmly. [Here the audience broke out in cheers so loud and long that for some moments it was impossible to hear Mr. Lincoln's voice.] And if I do my duty, and do right, you will sustain me, will you not?" Loud cheers, and cries of "Yes, yes, we will." He closed saying in effect that he might be the last President of the United States: "If it [the ship of state] should suffer attack now, there will be no pilot ever needed for another voyage."

He arrived in Philadelphia at four o'clock. In the hotel parlor Lincoln stood handshaking that night for an hour or two. Later in Norman B. Judd's room Lincoln met Allan Pinkerton, a railroad detective in the service of the Philadelphia, Wilmington & Baltimore Railroad, to guard trains and bridges and circumvent threatened explosions and fires. Pinkerton opened: "We have come to know, Mr. Lincoln, and beyond the shadow of a doubt, that there exists a plot to assassinate you. The attempt will be made on your way through Baltimore, day after tomorrow. I am here to help in outwitting the assassins." Lincoln sat with legs crossed, a good-natured curiosity on his face fading to a sober look. "I am listening, Mr. Pinkerton."

A barber named Fernandina was foremost among the conspirators, according to Pinkerton's spies, who, he said, had been at work for weeks and had become "bosom friends and inseparable companions" of the plotters. A melodramatic, maudlin speech by Fernandina at a secret meeting of the military company he captained was described by Pinkerton to Lincoln, the barber waving "a long glittering knife" over his head and crying: "This hireling Lincoln shall never, never be President. My life is of no consequence in a cause like this, and I am willing to give it for his. As Orsini gave his life for Italy, I am ready to die for the rights of the South and to crush out the abolitionist."

Pinkerton went personally to Baltimore, purporting to be a Georgia secessionist, and "Fernandina cordially grasped my hand, and we all retired to a private saloon." Fernandina was asked if there was no other way to save the South than by killing Lincoln. He replied, in the Pinkerton report: "No, as well might you attempt to move the Washington Monument yonder with your breath, as to change our purpose. He must die—and die he shall." With another drink by this time, he was asked about the police. He had fixed that, too: "They are all with us. I have seen the Chief Marshal of Police, and he is all right. In a week from today, Lincoln will be a corpse." Also it seemed that Pinkerton detected another conspirator named Hill, who also drank heavy and often, and also was ready, in his talk, to kill Lincoln. He said, in the Pinkerton report, "I shall immortalize myself by plunging a knife into Lincoln's heart."

Lincoln interrupted with many questions. Supporting Pinkerton's viewpoint were the practical Judd and the equally practical Samuel M. Felton, a railroad president who considered the evidence positive of a plot to burn railroad bridges, blow up trains, "and murder Mr. Lincoln on his way to Washington." Pinkerton gave details of a wild-eyed plot. The police chief at Baltimore was arranging to send only a small force to the railroad depot, where a gang of toughs would start a fight to draw off the policemen. Then the Fernandina assassins would close round the President-elect and deliver the fatal shot or knife thrust. "We propose," said Pinkerton, "to take you on to Washington this very night, Mr. President, and steal a march on your enemies."

Lincoln deliberated, then: "Gentlemen, I appreciate the suggestions, and while I can stand anything essential in the way of misrepresentation, I do not feel I can go to Washington tonight. Tomorrow morning I have promised to raise the flag over Independence Hall, and after that to visit the legislature at Harrisburg. Whatever the cost, these two promises I must fulfill. Thereafter I shall be ready to consider any plan you may adopt."

From Washington that night arrived Frederick W. Seward, son of Lincoln's announced Secretary of State. He found Chestnut Street and the Continental Hotel gay with a serenade to the President-elect, music, flowers, flags, buzzing conversations, and "brilliantly lighted parlours filled with ladies and gentlemen who had come to 'pay their respects.' " Lamon took Seward to Lincoln's bedroom. "Presently Colonel Lamon called me," wrote Seward of that night, "and we met Mr. Lincoln coming down the hall . . . After friendly greeting he sat down by the table under the gas light to peruse the letter I had brought." The communications his father had so secretly and hurriedly sent on, which Lincoln read deliberately twice, stressed a report of one Colonel Stone:

A New York detective officer on duty in Baltimore for three weeks past reports this morning that there is serious danger of violence to, and the assassination of, Mr. Lincoln in his passage through that city, should the time of that passage be known. He states that there are banded rowdies holding secret meetings, and that he has heard threats of mobbing and violence, and has himself heard men declare that if Mr. Lincoln was to be assassinated they would like to be the men . . . All risk might be easily avoided by a change in the traveling arrangements which would bring Mr. Lincoln and a portion of his party through Baltimore by a night train without previous notice.

"Did you hear any names mentioned?" Lincoln pressed. "Did you, for instance, ever hear anything said about such a name as Pinkerton?" No, Seward had heard no such name. Lincoln smiled. "If different persons, not knowing of each other's work, have been pursuing separate clues that led to the same result, why then it shows there may be something in it. But if this is only the same story, filtered through two channels, and reaching me in two ways, then that don't make it any stronger. Don't you see?" They discussed it further and Lincoln rose, "Well, we haven't got to decide it tonight, anyway."

In studying what to do Lincoln had to consider the silence of Baltimore and Maryland. Governor Thomas H. Hicks of that state favored the Union as against secession and was himself threatened with death by men proclaiming their volunteer militia would shoot down Northern soldiers en route to Washington, would burn supply depots and railroad bridges, would if war came march their corps to Washington and take that city. Governor Hicks had a seething and sensitive public to handle, a people ready to show what they could do with guns, clubs, stones, bricks, in street fighting. The marshal of police, George P. Kane, was an open secessionist.

At six o'clock that morning of February 22, Washington's Birthday, Lincoln amid cannon salutes and crowd applause pulled a rope and raised a flag over Independence Hall. Inside Independence Hall he spoke to an audience crowding all corners and overflowing. He had often pondered over the "dangers" incurred by the men who had assembled there and framed the Declaration. Not merely separation from a motherland, but liberty as a hope to all the world, for all future time, was the sentiment guiding them. "It was that which gave promise that in due time the weights should be lifted from the shoulders of all men, and that *all* should have an equal chance . . ." He asked if the country could be saved on that basis. If so he would consider himself one of the happiest men in the world. "But, if this country cannot be saved without giving up that principle—I was about to say I would rather be assassinated on this spot than surrender it." He could see no need of bloodshed and war. "And I may say in advance, there will be no blood shed unless it be forced upon the Government . . ."

Judd had been up nearly the whole night in a conference with Pinkerton and other men. They arranged for Lincoln to journey from Harrisburg on a two-car train that night under conditions they believed would deliver him safely in Washington the next morning. In Harrisburg, amid guns and platoons, Lincoln replied to Governor Curtin's welcome that under the weight of his great responsibility he brought an honest heart, but "I dare not tell you that I bring a head sufficient for it." He would lean on the people. "If my own strength should fail, I shall at least fall back upon these masses, who, I think, under any circumstances will not fail."

That evening Lincoln was at a table in the dining room of the Jones House in Harrisburg. He had made three speeches during the day, listened to other speeches longer than his own, talked with Governor Curtin and men of power in Pennsylvania, and held a conference with members of his party. For the first time others than Judd learned of the change in plans. Judd had told Lincoln these other old friends should know what was afoot, Lincoln approving. "I reckon they will laugh at us, Judd, but you had better get them together."

Lincoln told them, "Unless there are some other reasons besides fear of ridicule, I am disposed to carry out Judd's plan." A. K. McClure, legislative member and a founder of the Republican party, was sure he heard Lincoln say, "What would the nation think of its President stealing into its capital like a thief in the night?" while Governor Curtin declared the question not one for Lincoln to decide.

Close to six o'clock Lincoln was called from the dinner table, went upstairs to his room, changed his dinner dress for a traveling suit, and came down with a soft felt hat sticking in his pocket, and a folded shawl on his arm. A carriage was ready. Then, as Judd told it: "Mr. Lamon went first into the carriage; Col. Sumner of the regular army, was following close after Mr. Lincoln; I put my hand gently on his shoulder; he turned to see what was wanted, and before I could explain the carriage was off. The situation was a little awkward." Judd had tricked Colonel Sumner into a moment of delay, and to the Colonel's furious words Judd replied, "When we get to Washington, Mr. Lincoln shall determine what apology is due you."

Lincoln and Lamon, with a lone car to themselves, drawn by a lone locomotive of the Pennsylvania Railroad, rode out of Harrisburg, no lights on, Lamon carrying two ordinary pistols, two derringers and two large knives. Telegraph linemen had cut the wires; all telegrams into or out of Harrisburg were shut off till further orders.

In Philadelphia shortly after ten a carriage with Detective Pinkerton and Superintendent Kenney of the P. W. & B. Railroad met Lincoln and Lamon at the Pennsylvania Railroad station and took them to the P. W. & B. station, where they were put on the last car of the New York-Washington train. A woman detective working for Pinkerton had reserved rear berths of a sleeping-car, one for her "invalid brother" to be occupied by Lincoln, who was quickly in his berth with the curtains carefully drawn.

Unknown to Pinkerton or Lamon, on that last car a powerfully built man, armed with a revolver, slept in a berth engaged at New York. He was Superintendent John A. Kennedy of the New York police department, an officer of valor and integrity, who did not know that his detective, Bookstaver, had rushed on to Washington and reported his Baltimore findings to Seward. Kennedy was acting on reports received from his other two men in Baltimore, and his intention, as he slept in the same car with Lincoln that night, was to warn the authorities in Washington next morning that Lincoln would require safeguarding in his scheduled trip across Maryland the next day.

Baltimore was reached at 3:30 in the morning, and of the stop there Pinkerton wrote: "An officer of the road entered the car and whispered in my ear the welcome words 'All's well' . . ." An hour and more the train waited for a connecting train from the west. A drunken traveler on the train platform sang "Dixie," sang over and again how he would live and die in dear old Dixie. Lincoln murmured sleepily, said Pinkerton, "No doubt there will be a great time in Dixie by and by." Except for "a joke or two in an undertone," Lincoln was not heard from during the night, according to Lamon. At six in the morning the President-elect stepped off the train in Washington.

Thus ended the night ride of the vanishing and reappearing President-elect. The special train from Harrisburg drew into Baltimore in the afternoon like a clock with its hour hand gone, disappointing Mayor George Brown, city officials and an immense crowd. "At the Calvert station were not less than 10,000 people," wrote I. K. Bowen to Howell Cobb in Georgia, "and the moment the train arrived, supposing Lincoln was aboard, the most terrific cheers ever heard were sent up, three for the Southern Confederacy, three for 'gallant Jeff Davis,' and three groans for 'the Rail Splitter.' Had Lincoln been there, contrary to my preconceived opinions, he would have met with trouble . . ."

In many variations the tale went world-wide of the long-shanked Chief Magistrate in flight disguised in a Scotch plaid cap and a long military cloak. In thousands of journals it was repeated in news items, cartoons and editorial comment. Who started it? A lone press writer, Joseph Howard, a pathetic rascal who had a habit of getting newspapers into trouble with his frauds and hoaxes. Howard telegraphed his newspaper, the New York *Times*, a responsible journal friendly to Lincoln, of Lincoln's arrival in Washington: "He wore a Scotch plaid cap and a very long military cloak, so that he was entirely unrecognizable." The *Times* printed it. And the world took to it as a good story.

Lamon wrote that Lincoln "was convinced that he had committed a grave mistake in listening to the solicitations of a professional spy and of friends too easily alarmed." Nevertheless Lincoln's advisers may have saved his life, said Lamon, believing there was never a moment from then on during his days in Washington that he was not in danger of death by violence.

In the swirl of events to come there would be little time to thresh over the pros and cons of the night ride through Baltimore. Much other night riding lay ahead.

On February 4, 1861, the Peace Convention in Washington had begun its sessions behind closed doors. Though an air of secret and important deliberation was desired by many of the delegates, the main proceedings reached newspapers from day to day. Twenty-one Border and Northern States sent delegates; Michigan, Wisconsin and Minnesota let it be known they expected only useless or mischievous talk.

Mostly the delegates were old men. One day's session was given to eulogy over an aged and almost blind delegate who died before presenting his credentials. The presiding officer was a tottering, ashen ruin, John Tyler, once President of the United States. The record of the convention noted that nearly every speaker advised short speeches and then made a long one. The conflict of wills and opinion over the country was reproduced in the convention. On Lincoln's first evening in Washington the delegates called on him at nine o'clock in his Willard's Hotel suite, with no particular result.

Lincoln had breakfast with Seward the morning he arrived and at 11 called with Seward at the White House, chatted with President Buchanan, and shook hands with the Cabinet. In the afternoon he met the Illinois Congressmen and Senators, headed by Stephen A. Douglas. At seven he dined at Seward's home on F Street and at ten o'clock he received "reciprocal" calls from the Buchanan Cabinet members, also plenty of private citizens. Betweenwhiles he had held interviews with General Scott, Francis P. Blair, Sr., Montgomery Blair, many officials and would-be officials. Tomorrow was Sunday. Perhaps he would sleep.

Mrs. Lincoln and the three Lincoln boys took their first Washington breakfast with husband and father next morning. And Lincoln went with Seward to St. John's Church (Episcopal) that Sunday morning.

Two Republican party elements pressed Lincoln: the antislavery extremists Sumner, Chase, Wade, Stevens, and the conciliators Seward, Charles Francis Adams, Tom Corwin. "With which side would Lincoln be allied? That, north and south, was the question," wrote C. F. Adams, Jr., who saw Seward age ten years that winter. "These men had been brooding over the questions at issue and dwelling on them till their minds had lost their tone, and become morbid."

Sumner and Lincoln were getting acquainted. Up to Lincoln, Sumner would stride to tell him this or that *must* be done. The Senator from Massachusetts, the scholar in politics, the most elegantly tailored man in House or Senate, wearing maroon vests, fawn gaiters, blue-violet neckties, high silk hat, cape over shoulders, gold-headed cane, gold watch chain, was born in Boston to money and leisure. He had a handsomely modeled head, wavy locks of hair, sideburns; he was a beau, scholar, zealot, bachelor, 50 years old. His father, Charles Pinckney Sumner, had been named for a South Carolina statesman. His grandfather, Major Job Sumner, had marched through the Revolutionary War in hardship and danger alongside Major John Lucas of Georgia, and these two comrades from Massachusetts and Georgia were buried side by side in St. Paul's churchyard on Broadway, New York. He was the only man of whom Lincoln would remark, "Sumner thinks he runs me." Lincoln saw early what Henry Adams emphasized in letters of the hour, that Sumner had unaccountable dignity. "He stands six feet two in his stockings—a colossus holding his burning heart in his hand to light up the sea of life," wrote the poet Longfellow.

"I am in morals, not politics," said Sumner. He took it as his mission and role to tell the Senate and thereby the country North and South a series of tragic and horrible facts about slavery. He knew he was telling the truth. But he believed also that any such truth as he might omit was of no importance. The categories of fact always entering into the discussions of Lincoln and Seward as to slavery were out of Sumner's range and beyond his chosen role. Such points of understanding as might have come from association with Southerners were completely absent from his arguments. He mentioned the unmentionable, with a cold wrath and an evenly measured scorn, till at last there were Southern Senators and Representatives who wanted to see him suffer and die.

His own antislavery associates in the Senate had reservations about him, Grimes of Iowa writing to Mrs. Grimes that Sumner was "harsh, vindictive," and a friend of Ben Wade's noting: "For Wade there was a suspicion of arrogance, a flavor of sham, in the grand assumption of the splendid Sumner . . . Most men at each interview with him had to tell him who and what they were."

"The planter will one day take a slave for his harlot, and sell her the next as a being of some lower species, a beast of labor," Sumner quoted from Southey's *History of Brazil* in a Senate speech, Douglas replying, "We have had another dish of the classics served up, classic allusions, each one only distinguished for its lasciviousness and obscenity . . ." By degrees Sumner had come to stand for something the South wanted exterminated from the Union. He was perhaps the most perfect impersonation of what the South wanted to secede from. No other man in the Federal Government so thrust at the sin and guilt of the South while evading the issues of sin and guilt in the North.

In his Senate seat, after a session had closed and nearly all the members had left the chamber, Sumner had been struck on the head with a cane. The blows rained till the cane broke in pieces. Bruised and lacerated without warning or a chance to fight back, he struggled to rise and get at his unseen assailant, nearly wrenching loose his desk from the iron screws that held it to the floor, he was so powerful physically. Several of his enemies stood by with their unspoken wishes, "Let him suffer and die—it would be a blessing to the country," while Sumner lay senseless in an aisle, the blood flowing from his head. As the news of the assault went over the country, it set tongues raging in the North and deepened the sullen defiance of the South.

Then for Sumner had come pain, the sickbed, a wheel chair, years of grinding his teeth day by day as treatments, applications of fire, were given to heal a bruised spine and a partially disordered brain area. The assailant, Congressman Preston Brooks of South Carolina said he had only wanted to half-kill Sumner and watch him live and suffer. He had resigned his seat, had been re-elected by his constituents and presented with more canes and wishes that he would use them as he knew how. He died in bed of strangulation, clutching at his throat as if he would tear it open while he lay a victim of violent croup or acute inflammation of the throat.

In June 1860 Sumner stood up in the Senate for the speech marking his return to active politics. He had spent nearly four years in a wheel chair. What had been his meditations? What would the sick man now well again have to say? The old Sumner spoke: statistics, morals and a finality of doom. He pronounced an excommunication titled "The Barbarism of Slavery," put the slave masters of the South in a class with barbarous African tribal chiefs; he read the Southern people beyond the pale of civilization. He had collected "every instance of cruelty, violence, passion, coarseness, and vulgarity recorded as having happened within the Slave States," said the New York Times, which asked: "What general good can be hoped for from such envenomed attacks? Do they aid in the least the solution of what every sensible man acknowledges to be the most delicate and difficult problem of this age?" For reasons best known to himself he omitted completely his thought on the ways and means by which slave property valued at $3,000,000,000 could somehow be made nonproperty, could somehow be devalued to zero, and whether he favored forcible subjugation of Southern society toward that end.

In five campaign addresses Sumner had endorsed Abraham Lincoln, and later inquired as to the election, "What victory of the cartridge-box ever did so much?" and said of the crisis, "Happily, Abraham Lincoln [Prolonged cheers.] has those elements of character needed to carry us through . . . he is calm, prudent, wise, and also brave . . . the Union shall be preserved and made more precious by consecration to Human Rights."

Then came weeks that harassed Sumner, when old friends saw him as "morbid" and "crazy." The winds of doctrine roared in the caverns of his mind. Before he entered his career in politics he had been one of the foremost antiwar advocates in America, six printings having been circulated of his oration on "The True Grandeur of Nations," saying, "War crushes with bloody heel all justice, all happiness, all that is God-like in man," and, "In our age there can be no peace that is not honorable; there can be no war that is not dishonorable."

Old and tried friends were tenderly guiding the course of one possibly not fully recovered in a maimed head and spine. "Looks well in the face, but is feeble and walks with an uncertain step," Longfellow had written in his journal, writing later to Sumner in Europe, "It will not do to go limping through the remainder of your life with a tangled brain."

His occasional caution in politics was there in his telling Lincoln that Cameron was thief, corruptionist and hypocrite, and then in so consequential a matter refusing to give Lincoln one line of writing to that effect. In a scene where connivance and fraud were so prevalent, where men were so often controlled by personal material advancement, Sumner's charm and integrity were peculiar and extraordinary or he could not have held unwaveringly such friendships as he had with those other men of like integrity in varied walks, Longfellow the poet, John A. Andrew the politician, and Wendell Phillips the agitator. They took him as hero and crusader, Longfellow saying one could understand Sumner only through seeing what he *was* instead of emphasizing what he was *not.*

The gracious Julia Ward Howe asked him to meet some friends of hers at dinner. He said he wasn't interested and, "Really, Julia, I have lost all my interest in individuals." Her quick answer: "Why, Charles! God hasn't got as far as that yet." Few were aware that long before Lincoln's night ride into Washington, one of Sumner's wealthy Massachusetts friends, George Luther Stearns, a Medford ship chandler and abolitionist who had supplied John Brown with money and rifles, paid a bodyguard to watch and protect Sumner constantly.

"Sumner had never seen Lincoln before he came to Washington," wrote Carl Schurz. "When he met Lincoln he was greatly amazed and puzzled by what he saw and heard . . . Many thought that these two men, being so essentially different, could not possibly work together. But on the whole they did, and they were able to do so, because, however great the divergence of their views on some points, they believed in one another's sincerity."

On Sunday, March 3, Lincoln received in his room at Willard's the Virginia Congressman A. R. Boteler, who that afternoon had asked Congressman Benjamin Stanton of Ohio to withdraw his Force Bill, which would fix on the President complete authority over all regular and militia troops of the nation. Boteler said the bill if passed would force Virginia out of the Union. "The bill must pass the House this evening," Stanton had replied.

Boteler told Lincoln that the Force Bill was exciting painful anxiety in Virginia and frustrating patriotic efforts to prevent secession. He wrote of their chat: "It served to deepen the impression . . . that Mr. Lincoln was a kind-hearted man; that he was . . . by no means disposed to interfere, directly or indirectly, with the institutions of slavery in any of the States, or to yield to the clamorous demand of those bloody-minded extremists, who were then so very keen to cry 'havoc!' and 'let slip the dogs of war' . . ."

The House clock indicated nearly ten that night when Stanton called up his Force Bill for consideration. After two attempts to move adjournment, by Illinois Republican Washburne and Pennsylvania Republican Hickman, the floor was obtained by New York Republican John Cochrane, who before taking his seat renewed the motion to adjourn. By a vote of 77 to 60 the House adjourned and, wrote Boteler, "the Thirty-Sixth Congress expired on the following Monday of March 4, without having given to Mr. Lincoln the power to call out the militia and to accept the services of volunteers."

In those closing hours of Congress a bill was passed to forbid the Federal Government forever from interfering with slavery in any manner whatsoever in any Slave State—requiring three-fourths of the states of the Union to approve the measure as an amendment to the Constitution. This was as far as Congress could go within its powers to guarantee the South that whatever it intended to do as to slavery extension in the Territories, its policy was to let slavery alone in the Slave States. The act was in line with the Republican party platform and Lincoln's public and private declarations.

CHAPTER 18

Lincoln Takes the Oath as President

MARCH 4 dawned with pleasant weather that later turned bleak and chilly for the 25,000 strangers roving Washington. With hotels and rooming houses overcrowded, hundreds had slept on the porches of public buildings and on street sidewalks. Thousands filled the street around Willard's as the forenoon wore away. General Scott and Colonel Stone had arranged for riflemen in squads to be placed in hiding on the roofs of certain commanding houses along Pennsylvania Avenue. From windows of the Capitol wings riflemen were to watch the inauguration platform.

President Buchanan drove with Senator Baker of Oregon and Senator Pearce of Maryland from the White House to Willard's in an open carriage. Buchanan stepped out and soon returned arm in arm with Lincoln as police kept a path for them. Then the procession moved down Pennsylvania Avenue with representations from all branches of the Government. A new procession was formed to escort the President-elect to the east portico and the platform outdoors, where a crowd of at least 10,000 that had waited long gave its applause and scattering cheers.

Senator Douglas took a seat and looked over the crowd. One comment ran that rather than a sea of upturned faces it was a sea of silk hats and white shirt bosoms. Lincoln in a new tall hat, new black suit and black boots, expansive white shirt bosom, carrying an ebony cane with a gold head the size of a hen's egg, had the crowd matched.

Ned Baker's silver-bell voice rang out: "Fellow-citizens, I introduce to you Abraham Lincoln, the President-elect of the United States." The applause was a slight ripple. Then came the inaugural address; Lincoln drew the papers from an inside coat pocket, slowly pulled spectacles from another pocket, put them on, and read deliberately the fateful document.

Then stepped forward Chief Justice Taney, worn, shrunken, odd, with "the face of a galvanized corpse," said Mrs. Clay of Alabama. His hands shook with age, emotion, both, as he held out an open Bible toward the ninth President to be sworn in by him. Lincoln laid his left hand on the Bible, raised his right hand, and repeated after the Chief Justice the oath prescribed by the Constitution: "I do solemnly swear that I will faithfully execute the office of President of the United States, and will, to the best of my ability, preserve, protect, and defend the Constitution of the United States."

The artillery over on the slope boomed with all its guns a salute of thunder to the 16th President of the United States. That was all. The inauguration was over.

The inaugural address itself, as a state paper from the first administration of a new party, as a definition of policy and viewpoint, as a breaking of Lincoln's long silence, was the high point of the day. Beyond the immediate hearers was the vast unseen audience that would read the address in cold print. Never before in New York had such crowds waited at newspaper offices and jammed and scrambled for the first sheets wet from the press. In its week of delivery it was the most widely read and closely scrutinized utterance that had ever come from an American President. No previous manuscript from Lincoln's hand had been so carefully written by him, rearranged, modified. The draft made in Springfield underwent important changes, mainly deletions, under the suggestions of Seward and Browning, with Lincoln's added light as he traveled and events shifted.

The two closing sentences of Lincoln's original draft were too warlike, Seward believed. They read: "You can forbear the assault upon it [the Government]; I can not shrink from the defense of it. With you, and not with me, is the solemn question of 'Shall it be peace, or a sword?'" Lincoln dropped them. Seward believed "some words of affection, some of calm and cheerful confidence," should close the address and Lincoln revised a paragraph submitted by Seward.

The finished address Lincoln gave the world went to readers who searched and dug into every line and phrase. Reason and emotion wove through it —and hopes, fears, resolves. Parts of it read:

. . . Apprehension seems to exist among the people of the Southern States, that by the accession of a Republican Administration, their property, and their peace, and personal security, are to be endangered. There has never been any reasonable cause for such apprehension. Indeed, the most ample evidence to the contrary has all the while existed, and been open to their inspection. It is found in nearly all the published speeches of him who now addresses you. I do but quote from one of those speeches when I declare that "I have no purpose, directly or indirectly, to interfere with the institution of slavery in the States where it exists. I believe I have no lawful right to do so, and I have no inclination to do so." Those who nominated and elected me did so with full knowledge that I had made this, and many similar declarations, and had never recanted them . . .

There is much controversy about the delivering up of fugitives from service or labor. The clause I now read is as plainly written in the Constitution as any other of its provisions:

"No person held to service or labor in one State, under the laws thereof, escaping into another, shall, in consequence of any law or regulation therein, be discharged from such service or labor, but shall be delivered up on claim of the party to whom such service or labor may be due." . . .

There is some difference of opinion whether this clause should be enforced by national or by state authority; but surely that difference is not a very material one . . .

A disruption of the Federal Union heretofore only menaced, is now formidably attempted.

I hold, that in contemplation of universal law, and of the Constitution, the Union of these States is perpetual. Perpetuity is implied, if not expressed, in the fundamental law of all national governments. It is safe to assert that no government proper, ever had a provision in its organic law for its own termination . . .

The Union is much older than the Constitution. It was formed in fact, by the Articles of Association in 1774. It was matured and continued by the Declaration of Independence in 1776. It was further matured and the faith of all the then thirteen States expressly plighted and engaged that it should be perpetual, by the Articles of Confederation in 1778. And finally, in 1787, one of the declared objects for ordaining and establishing the Constitution, was *"to form a more perfect Union."* . . .

It follows from these views that no State, upon its own mere motion, can lawfully get out of the Union—that *resolves* and *ordinances* to that effect are legally void; and that acts of violence, within any State or States, against the authority of the United States, are insurrectionary or revolutionary, according to circumstances.

I therefore consider that, in view of the Constitution and the laws, the Union is unbroken; and, to the extent of my ability, I shall take care, as the Constitution itself expressly enjoins upon me, that the laws of the Union be faithfully executed in all the States. Doing this I deem to be only a simple duty on my part; and I shall perform it, so far as practicable, unless my rightful masters, the American people, shall withhold the requisite means, or, in some authoritative manner, direct the contrary. I trust this will not be regarded as a menace, but only as the declared purpose of the Union that it *will* constitutionally defend, and maintain itself.

In doing this there needs to be no bloodshed or violence; and there shall be none, unless it be forced upon the national authority. The power confided to me, will be used to hold, occupy, and possess the property, and places belonging to the government, and to collect the duties and imposts; but beyond what may be necessary for these objects, there will be no invasion—no using of force against, or among the people anywhere . . .

If a minority, in such case, will secede rather than acquiesce, they make a precedent which, in turn, will divide and ruin them; for a minority of their own will secede from them, whenever a majority refuses to be controlled by such minority. For instance, why may not any portion of a new confederacy, a year or two hence, arbitrarily secede again, precisely as portions of the present Union now claim to secede from it. All who cherish disunion sentiments are now being educated to the exact temper of doing this . . .

Plainly, the central idea of secession, is the essence of anarchy . . .

One section of our country believes slavery is *right,* and ought to be extended, while the other believes it is *wrong,* and ought not to be extended. This is the only substantial dispute . . .

Physically speaking, we cannot separate. We cannot remove our respective sections from each other, nor build an impassable wall between them. A husband and wife may be divorced, and go out of the presence, and beyond the reach of each other; but the different parts of our country cannot do this . . . Suppose you go to war, you cannot fight always; and when, after much loss on both sides, and no gain on either, you cease fighting, the identical old questions as to terms of intercourse, are again upon you.

This country, with its institutions, belongs to the people who inhabit it. Whenever they shall grow weary of the existing government, they can exercise their *constitutional* right of amending it, or their *revolutionary* right to dismember, or overthrow it. I cannot be ignorant of the fact that many worthy, and patriotic citizens are desirous of having the national constitution amended. While I make no recommendation of amendments, I fully recognize the rightful authority of the people over the whole subject, to be exercised in either of the modes prescribed in the instrument itself . . . I understand a proposed amendment to the Constitution—which amendment, however, I have not seen, has passed Congress, to the effect that the federal government, shall never interfere with the domestic institutions of the States, including that of persons held to service. To avoid misconstruction of what I have said, I depart from my purpose not to speak of particular amendments, so far as to say that, holding such a provision to now be implied constitutional law, I have no objection to its being made express, and irrevocable . . .

Why should there not be a patient confidence in the ultimate justice of the people? Is there any better, or equal hope, in the world? In our present differences, is either party without faith of being in the right? If the Almighty Ruler of nations, with his eternal truth and justice, be on your side of the North, or on yours of the South, that truth, and that justice, will surely prevail, by the judgment of this great tribunal, the American people . . .

While the people retain their virtue, and vigilence, no administration, by any extreme of wickedness or folly, can very seriously injure the government, in the short space of four years.

My countrymen, one and all, think calmly and *well*, upon this whole subject. Nothing valuable can be lost by taking time . . . Intelligence, patriotism, Christianity, and a firm reliance on Him, who has never yet forsaken this favored land, are still competent to adjust, in the best way, all our present difficulty.

In *your* hands, my dissatisfied fellow countrymen, and not in *mine*, is the momentous issue of civil war. The government will not assail *you*. You can have no conflict, without being yourselves the aggressors. *You* have no oath registered in Heaven to destroy the government, while *I* shall have the most solemn one to "preserve, protect and defend" it.

Thus flowed the reasonings, explanations, watchwords that ended Lincoln's long silence. He finished: "I am loth to close. We are not enemies, but friends. We must not be enemies. Though passion may have strained, it must not break our bonds of affection. The mystic chords of memory, stretching from every battle-field, and patriot grave, to every living heart and hearthstone, all over this broad land, will yet swell the chorus of the Union, when again touched, as surely they will be, by the better angels of our nature."

Far out in Iowa was a farmer who had written Lincoln not to yield: "Give the little finger and shortly the whole hand is required." Far down in Nolensville, Tennessee, W. N. Barnes had written him that the people there were "overwhelmingly loyal to the flag of their country." Barnes wanted a statement to circulate. Now he had it.

The Montgomery *Advertiser* in Alabama was sure the inaugural meant war, nothing less would satisfy "the abolition chief," and the artfully worded address was written by a pen more skillful than the Rail Splitter wielded.

"To twenty millions of people," said the New York *Tribune* of the address, "it will carry tidings, good or not, as the case may be, that the federal government of the United States is still in existence, with a Man at the head of it." Not one "fawning expression" could be found in it, observed the Boston *Transcript*. "The language is level to the popular mind, the plain, homespun language of a man accustomed to talk with the 'folks' and the 'neighbors,' whose words fit his facts and thoughts."

The New York *Herald* commented, "It would have been almost as instructive if President Lincoln had contented himself with telling his audience yesterday a funny story and letting them go"; however, the inaugural was

Upper left: Brady photograph made in Washington nine days before inauguration, 1861 [Meserve]. *Upper right:* Inauguration crowd before the unfinished Capitol March 4, 1861 [Meserve]. *Lower:* Pennsylvania Avenue, Washington, an 1861 sketch.

Upper left: Edwin McMasters Stanton of Ohio, second Secretary of War [CS]. *Upper right:* Simon Cameron of Pennsylvania, first Secretary of War [CS]. *Center left:* Gideon Welles of Connecticut, Secretary of the Navy, diarist extraordinary [USASC]. *Center right:* Salmon Portland Chase of Ohio, Secretary of the Treasury, constant Presidential aspirant [CS]. *Lower left:* Hannibal Hamlin of Maine, Vice-President [Meserve]. *Lower right:* General Winfield Scott, veteran of the Mexican War and the War of 1812, military head of the U.S. as Lincoln took office [CS].

"not a crude performance," for "it abounds with traits of craft and cunning." The Baltimore *Sun* read in the inaugural that "it assumes despotic authority, and intimates the design to exercise that authority to any extent of war and bloodshed. If it means what it says, it is the knell and requiem of the Union, and the death of hope." The Baltimore *Exchange* believed "the measures of Mr. Lincoln mean war"; while Douglas said publicly, "It is a peace offering rather than a war message."

The Richmond *Enquirer* saw in it "the cool, unimpassioned, deliberate language of the fanatic . . . Sectional war awaits only the signal gun . . . The question, 'Where shall Virginia go?' is answered by Mr. Lincoln. She must go *to war*." The Charleston *Mercury* announced, "It is our wisest policy to accept it as a declaration of war."

A group of Southern leaders meeting in Washington the night of the inauguration sent word to their Government: "We all agreed that it was Lincoln's purpose at once to attempt the collection of the revenue, to re-enforce and hold Fort Sumter and Pickens, and to retake the other places. He is a man of will and firmness. His cabinet will yield to him with alacrity."

Inauguration night saw an attempt at gaiety, the Union Ball, in a new building on Judiciary Square, the hall light-flooded by five large gas chandeliers. Lincoln shook hands from 8:15 till 10:30. The estimate was 25 hands a minute. His gloves were now *white* kids. He looked absent-minded, as young Henry Adams saw him, as though "no man living needed so much education as the new President but all the education he could get would not be enough."

The Marine Band played "Hail to the Chief" at 11. Lincoln entered leading the grand march, arm in arm with Mayor Berret, followed by Mrs. Lincoln arm in arm with Senator Stephen A. Douglas. Lincoln avoided waltz and square dance, but Mrs. Lincoln and Douglas were partners in a quadrille. Hundreds of women in crinoline trod the waltz, schottische, polka, mazurka. Mrs. Lincoln wore a new blue gown, a large blue feather in her hair. Many said it must be her happiest night of life, the realization of dreams long awaited. The ball over, Mr. and Mrs. Lincoln went for the first night in their new house of presences, shadows, ghosts.

As Lincoln slept that night, relays of ponies and men were rushing west from St. Joe, Missouri, with his inaugural address. They would be seven days and 17 hours reaching Sacramento, California, with his plea for the east and west coasts, the Great Lakes and the Gulf, the Rio Grande and the Penobscot, to belong to one common country.

"The President is determined he will have a compound Cabinet," Seward wrote to his wife. Seward objected to Chase in the Cabinet, and on Saturday, March 2, he had notified Lincoln he must "withdraw." Lincoln on Monday wrote to Seward: "I feel constrained to beg that you will countermand the withdrawal. The public interest, I think, demands that you should; and my personal feelings are deeply inlisted in the same direction." Handing the note to John Hay to copy, he said, "I can't afford to let Seward take the first trick." Next morning Seward with a polite note was back in the Cabinet. Thus the struggle between conservatives (Seward) and radicals (Chase) began. Lincoln wrote Seward for "an interview at once."

Thus far Lincoln's Cabinet slate, with two minor exceptions, stood as he had framed it late on election night in the Springfield telegraph office. When told, "They will eat you up," he replied, "They will be just as likely to eat each other up."

At noon on March 5 the Senate received and approved the new President's nominations: Secretary of State, William H. Seward; Secretary of the Treasury, Salmon P. Chase; Secretary of War, Simon Cameron; Secretary of the Navy, Gideon Welles; Secretary of the Interior, Caleb B. Smith; Attorney General, Edward Bates; Postmaster General, Montgomery Blair. The new Cabinet had four old-line Democrats (Chase, Cameron, Welles, Blair) and three old-line Whigs (Seward, Bates, Smith), a wrong balance, Lincoln heard many times, and made clear: "I'm something of an old-line Whig myself and I'll be there to make the parties even." These Cabinet men he would see and hear often; they would be stubborn with him and he with them.

Seward, eight years older than Lincoln, had been, until Lincoln's nomination and election, leader of the Republican party. As a New York man close to the controlling financial and commercial interests of the country, he sponsored protective tariffs, steamship subsidies, a bill for a railway to the Pacific. He analyzed canals, railroads, trade balances, tariffs, new factors in commerce, the stream of surplus capital and labor arriving from Europe, and foretold their economic role with a surer grasp than Lincoln. Although an Episcopalian, he had for years been close to Archbishop John Hughes of New York, the most influential Roman Catholic prelate in America. His start in politics was with the Anti-Masonic party, which elected him state senator in 1830. His recommendation as governor of New York that public-school funds be allotted to Catholics as well as to Protestants had brought the American or Know-Nothing faction clamoring against him within the Republican party.

He had quit snuff for cigars. His beautiful Arabian horses were pictured in *Harper's Weekly*. His five-course dinners at his Washington residence were a topic of smart society, and one of his loyal friends, Charles Francis Adams, Jr., noted: "When it came to drinking, Seward was, for a man of sixty, a free liver; at times his brandy-and-water would excite him, and set his tongue going with dangerous volubility; but I never saw him more affected than that—never anything approaching drunkenness. He simply liked the stimulus, and was very fond of champagne; and when he was loaded, his tongue wagged." Between this man and Lincoln was a friendship that would grow deeper.

Salmon Portland Chase had held off from taking the Treasury portfolio. Wrote Chase to J. T. Trowbridge, "Some rumor of my hesitation got abroad, and I was immediately pressed by the most urgent remonstrances not to decline. I finally yielded to this." He had been governor of Ohio and U.S. Senator, had received 49 ballots for the presidential nomination at Chicago, had expected that Seward's nomination would bring him second place on the ticket. An ambition to be President lay deep.

Tall and portly, Chase was spoken of as "handsome," as having "a stately figure," a "classic face." At 24 he married Katherine Jane Garniss, three years younger than himself, and within two years she died, leaving him a girl child who lived only four years. At 29 he married Eliza Ann Smith of Cincinnati, a girl of 18, who died six years later, having borne him three children, of whom only one had lived. A year later he married Sarah Bella Dunlop Ludlow of a well-known and propertied Cincinnati family; she died within six years, having borne him two children, of whom one lived. Thus he had across 17 years stood at the burial caskets of three wives and four children.

Out of these accumulated griefs he had two living daughters. One of them was a gleaming, vital creature, Katherine Jane Chase, known as Kate and born under strange stars. She had grown to be his chum and helper, playing chess with him, walking with him to the office, telling him what she got from a newly read book. Her glimpses into politics sometimes went further than his. She was as much a son as a daughter, men said.

Chase had lights for leading, though his gnawing ambition was a chronic personal ailment beyond remedy or easement. In early years in Cincinnati, he had taken without fee so many cases of black people claimed as fugitive slaves that Kentuckians called him "the attorney-general for runaway negroes." He had quit the Democratic party, led in organizing the Liberty party, then the Free-Soil party, ending with the Republicans. On a platform in Cincinnati he was hit with a brick, with rotten eggs. To abolitionists these were credentials. The way had been opened to commercial and corporation law practice; a fortune in money beckoned. He chose to throw his fate with runaway Negroes; also ambition dictated his politics.

When finally named by Lincoln, to refuse might isolate him, with risk to his moving higher. The story was easily half-true that he faced a mirror and bowed to himself, murmuring "President Chase."

Simon Cameron, the new Secretary of War, had proper claims to his portfolio. His white-hatted delegates to the Chicago convention had on the first presidential nomination ballot voted for him. Cameron's release of those delegates had started the stampede to Lincoln. Lincoln's managers had, without authority from Lincoln, pledged Cameron a Cabinet place.

Politics was a business, a sport, a passion with Cameron. At 62, for 20 years he had been the dominant political manager in Pennsylvania. His mother's father, a German, had fought in the Revolutionary War. His Scotch father was a country tailor, a poor provider, and nine-year-old Simon was adopted by a physician, at ten began typesetting, learned the printer's trade, and before he was 21 edited the Doylestown *Democrat*. On borrowed money Cameron became owner and editor of the Harrisburg *Intelligencer*. With a contract for state printing, his profits grew and more contracts came. He manipulated toward electing Andrew Jackson to a second term; the Federal patronage of Pennsylvania entire came into his hands.

Ten of Cameron's earlier years had been given to bank, railroad and canal building, getting a fortune. His nickname, "the Czar of Pennsylvania," rested on a reputation as the most skilled political manipulator in America. His decision had put Buchanan into the U.S. Senate twice. Then, suddenly seeing Buchanan's power rising to question his own in Pennsylvania, he organized the People's party, had himself elected U.S. Senator in 1856. In the same year he amalgamated Whigs, Know-Nothings, Republicans into the Union party of Pennsylvania, with a unique signed agreement by the national electors to give a solid vote for either Frémont, the national Republican candidate, or Fillmore, the national American or Know-Nothing candidate, if the electoral vote of the state would elect either to the presidency.

Loose gray clothes hung from his tall, slim frame. He was smooth of face, sharp-lipped, with a delicate straight nose, a finely chiseled mask touched with fox wariness. As he pronounced dry and pretendedly forthright decisions Cameron's face was more often mask than face. He wrought effects from behind the scenes. His setup of himself as a presidential possibility at the Chicago convention was one of his effects. He did not care to be President, but he came to Chicago with something to trade and got a pledge from Davis, Swett, Medill and others that with Lincoln elected he would be Secretary of the Treasury.

When it dawned on Lincoln that Cameron as Treasury head would look peculiar and call for dry wit, Lincoln named him for the War Department, took it back, named him again to stay. Cameron did not care deeply about any policies or principles involved in the affair, but when Chase, Sumner, Curtin, McClure and others started out to scalp and gut him politically, he stuck by his guns, brought as many witnesses as they to face Lincoln for him, his best ones Seward and Weed. When at last the opposition refused to prefer any charges against Cameron in writing, and all the accusations were exercises in oral denunciation, Lincoln said his name would stay on the original slate. The Keystone State with its iron and railroad domain was wanted by Lincoln for the national emergency, and Cameron was its leading link of business and politics. Lincoln appointed Cameron, though groaning, according to Whitney, as they talked about it, "How can I justify my title of Honest Old Abe with the appointment of a man like Cameron?"

Gideon Welles, the Connecticut Yankee named for Secretary of the Navy, was, like Cameron, an old Jackson Democrat. His newspaper, the Hartford *Times*, was among the earliest to cry Jackson for President. Lincoln saw Welles as a more than relatively honest Democrat who had quit his party on the slavery-extension issue, who as a Republican made a losing run for the governorship in 1855 and was chairman of his state's delegation to the Chicago convention. Fifty-eight years old, his short, thickset body had a massive head surmounted by a patriarchal wig, which with his white prophet's beard gave him a Neptune look. A smooth-shaven upper lip, and eyes kindly in repose, told those who met him not half what he could put into his diary. Lincoln put him at the head of all of Uncle Sam's seagoing vessels, and later made jokes about Uncle Gideon's not knowing bow from stern. His opinions and prejudices would run free, wide and faulty in the diary, but in recording fact as to what he saw and heard he would be a competent witness. Not all was going on that he believed or guessed, but what he put down as seeing and hearing was usually there.

Edward Bates, the new Attorney General, born in 1793, was a sergeant of volunteers in the War of 1812, going west and studying law in 1814 in St. Louis, then a settlement of 2,000 people. He had been attorney general of Missouri, a state senator, a Congressman. Events slowly piloted him to where he had no place to go but the Republican party. As a Free-Soil Whig from a Border State, it was argued that he was the man who as President could soften the shocks between the sections. His 48 votes on the first ballot at the Chicago convention sank to 22 on the third ballot and finally went to Lincoln. His course had been even and consistent. Most of his life Bates had been first a lawyer and secondly a politician. President Fillmore's offer to appoint him Secretary of War he had refused. He was quaint, old-fashioned, of a school that was passing. "An Old-Line Whig," said Bates, "is one who takes his whiskey regularly, and votes the Democratic ticket occasionally."

Caleb B. Smith of Indiana, Secretary of the Interior, was Boston-born, 1808, and taken to Ohio when six years old. Lawyer, editor, orator, at Connersville, Indiana, he became a Whig Congressman, held appointive Federal office, took up the practice of law in Cincinnati in 1850, and moved to Indianapolis in 1858. Of the new Cabinet members he was nearest the class of ordinary professional politician.

Montgomery Blair, Postmaster General, was viewed as a sign that among Lincoln's chosen advisers was the Blair family, headed by Old Man Blair, Francis Preston Blair, born in 1791 of a Scotch-Irish line, graduate of Transylvania University, a volunteer in the War of 1812, a fighting Jackson man through both of Jackson's stormy presidential terms, editing at Washington the *Globe,* which told Jackson's friends and enemies where to get on or off as to current issues.

His influence among Border State delegates joined to Montgomery's control of Maryland delegates, plus his son Frank's sway over Missouri delegates, were thrown to Lincoln on the third ballot at Chicago. His cordial relations with Lincoln, many feared, might grow into the same important intimacy he had held with Presidents Jackson and Van Buren. This fear was grounded partly on his tangible strength in having his first choice for President in 1860, Bates, as Attorney General, his old fellow Democrat, Welles, as Navy Department chief, his son-in-law, Gustavus Vasa Fox, slated to be Assistant Secretary of the Navy, another son-in-law, S. P. Lee, as a ranking admiral in the Navy, and finally his son Montgomery as Postmaster General. Subtle, cadaverous, bald, poised he was—persistent and silken in spinning his webs, delicately sensitive to political trends. Lincoln sought the views of this skilled professional politician. Often the views came unsought. The elder Blair was one of the few to whom Lincoln confidentially loaned a copy of the inaugural address for comment and suggestion.

Montgomery, born in 1813, had been district attorney for Missouri, mayor of St. Louis, judge of the court of common pleas. He had moved to Maryland to be near his large Federal Supreme Court practice. As counsel for Dred Scott, the fugitive slave, he won friends among antislavery men. He had helped get a lawyer to defend John Brown. He represented in Maryland the moderate wing of the Republican party as against the Henry Winter Davis radical faction. The Blair appointment resulted in protests to Lincoln nearly as furious as in the case of Cameron.

The man who would inherit this Cabinet and sit at the head of it in the event of Lincoln's death, Hannibal Hamlin, had been consulted about the Cabinet several times by Lincoln. At their meeting in Chicago, Lincoln said, "Mr. Hamlin, I desire to say to you that I shall accept, and shall always be willing to accept, in the very best spirit, any advice that you, the Vice-President, may give me." This was unusual. Hamlin said so. Except for Jackson and Van Buren, the relation between the Vice-Presidents and the Presidents had not as a rule been friendly. Hamlin pledged himself to be a friend and to render his humble advice as best he could.

Hamlin had been elected to Congress twice as a Democrat, had then been elected U.S. Senator as a Democrat, and on the slavery-extension issue had resigned as U.S. Senator, joined in organizing the Republican party in Maine, was elected governor of Maine, and resigned as governor to take a seat as one of the first Republicans in the U.S. Senate, later resigning as U.S. Senator to make the run for Vice-President on the Republican ticket. He was 52, tall and powerfully built, saying he did not need a revolver to guard against assassination, showing two fists that he said would take care of trouble. His face was swarthy, of a complexion so dark that many Southerners said and believed he was a mulatto and that his blood accounted for his radical anti-slavery sentiments. His recorded ancestors were of the pure English stock that settled the colony of Massachusetts. In college when he was 18 word came that his father was dead and he went back home to work the farm. Later he bought a country weekly paper, learned typesetting, studied law and oratory, and convinced the hardheaded, slow-going people of Maine that he should be their leading public servant.

Later in March Lincoln and his Cabinet gave a state dinner. William Howard Russell of the London *Times* wrote of being "surprised to find a diversity of accent almost as great as if a number of foreigners had been speaking English."

The new President had to give more hours daily to the Federal patronage, and applicants for places, than to all other items on the day's program. For 30 years, except eight Whig years, the thousands of Federal jobs had been the Democratic spoils of victory. The custom was for the new party to sweep out the old and put in new postmasters, port collectors, marshals, superintendents, paymasters, each having deputies, assistants, clerks. Thousands of the applicants had given time and money toward Republican victory, often with a clear promise of jobs.

At Willard's the main-floor corridors surged with office seekers, overflowing up the staircases into halls, reading room, barbershop, writing room, out on the porch and steps. From all over the North "the triumphant Republicans had winged their way to the prey." Many wore the new paper collars, some had linen. They crowded the Willard bar morning and night. Target cuspidors were circled with miss-shots. One excited pilgrim ordering breakfast for a crucial day called for black tea, toast, scrambled eggs, fresh spring shad, wild pigeon, pig's feet, two robins on toast, oysters, breads and cakes. One rushed out of the Willard barbershop, his face half-lathered, a towel under his chin, calling to a Senator about the place promised him. One stopped Lincoln in a hack at a street crossing and handed up his recommendation papers toward Lincoln, who frowned, burst out, "No! no! I won't open shop in the street," and rode on.

Of a visit of several days in Washington Herndon wrote that Lincoln could scarcely cease from referring to the persistence of office seekers. They slipped in, he said, through half-opened doors; they edged their way through crowds and thrust papers in his hands when he rode. Herndon quoted Lincoln in one outburst: "If our American society and the United States Government are demoralized and overthrown, it will come from the voracious desire for office, this wriggle to live without toil, work, and labor, from which I am not free myself."

The humorist Orpheus C. Kerr (Office Seeker) in April wrote: "Every soul of them knew old Abe when he was a child, and one old boy can even remember going for a doctor when his mother was born. I met one of them the other day (he is after the Moosehicmagunticook post-office), and his anecdotes of the President's boyhood brought tears to my eyes, and several tumblers to my lips."

Advice and philosophy crept into Lincoln notes to department heads. "This man wants to work—so uncommon a want that I think it ought to be gratified," began one note, and another: "The lady bearer of this says she has two sons who want to work. Set them at it if possible. Wanting to work is so rare a want that it should be encouraged." Not often was the tone so peremptory as in one note: "You must make a job for the bearer of this— make a job of it with the collector and have it done. You *can* do it for me and you *must*." A rebuke might go, as in a note to "Hon. Sec. of Interior": "How is this? I supposed I was appointing for register of wills a *citizen of this District*. Now the commission comes to me 'Moses Kelly, of *New Hampshire!*' I do not like this." One disgruntled place hunter snorted, "Why, I am one of those who made you President." And Lincoln started to dig into a pile of papers on his desk. "Yes, and it's a pretty mess you got me into!"

The President reached for friends he did not want to lose, writing to Senator Jacob Collamer of Vermont: "God help me! It is said I have offended you. Please tell me how."

In mid-March Senator John Sherman of Ohio introduced to Lincoln his brother William Tecumseh Sherman who, having just resigned as head of the Louisiana Military Academy, seeing war ahead, "may give you some information you want." Lincoln asked, "How are they getting along down there?" On Sherman fiercely replying, "They are preparing for war," the President said, "Oh, well, I guess we'll manage to keep house." And Sherman said no more to Lincoln, went away to take a job as street-railway superintendent in St. Louis at $40 a week, telling his brother what he had to tell politicians in general, Lincoln included: "You have got things in a hell of a fix, and you may get them out as best you can." Undoubtedly Sherman offered his services to the President in no ordinary office seeker's manner; he was asking no fat job, nor an easy life. Had Lincoln known of the steeled loyalty of this Ohio man, he would have met Sherman with a different greeting. However, the President was in a mood when he chose to show no anxiety, and this worried Sherman.

Seward heard from the President that John C. Frémont and William L. Dayton, Republican candidates for President and Vice-President in 1856, were to have respectively appointments as Ministers to France and England. This arrangement, proposed by Lincoln without consulting Seward, was "scarcely courteous" to his Secretary of State, and in the case of Frémont was "obnoxious" to Seward, who was no admirer of Frémont, according to C. F. Adams, Jr. "The President did not yield the point readily," and only persistent effort by Seward brought about the transfer of Dayton to Paris, and the naming of Charles Francis Adams, Sr., as Minister to the Court of St. James, London.

Carl Schurz was to be Minister to Spain and his case was argued up and down in the Cabinet. Seward declared that Schurz's record in insurrectionary, red-republican movements in Germany in 1848 would be frowned on by the Spanish monarchy. Lincoln replied that Schurz would be discreet; it ought not to be held against the man that he had made efforts for liberty; and it might be well for European governments to realize this. Chase and Blair agreed with Lincoln. Seward yielded, but didn't like it.

In the Cabinet, Chase, Cameron and Blair had their friends and allies to take care of in about the same proportion as Seward, a hundred asking an office that could go to only one. "Blair is nearly run to death with office seekers," wrote G. V. Fox to his wife. "They left him at 2 this morning and commenced at 8 this morning. The President is equally beset. I have seen Abe often." Among many wanting office was a belief that either money or influence could bring it, while Lincoln guessed he had "ten pegs where there was one hole to put them in." Often his salutation to a White House caller was, "Well, sir, I am glad to know that you have not come after an office."

In some quarters was a constant murmuring, such as that of Senator Sumner writing to an applicant for a foreign post: "Nobody who wishes to succeed should hail from Massachusetts or New York. Their claims are said to be exhausted." The New York complications got worse as Greeley and other anti-Seward Republicans worried in fear that Seward and Weed, getting control of Lincoln, would dictate all appointments. They called at the White House with a delegation, men who, as Lincoln well knew, had for years fought Seward and Weed for Republican party control in New York. They had gone to the Chicago convention hoping to stop the nomination of Seward. Lincoln said to the New Yorkers: "One side shall not gobble up everything. Make out a list of the places and men you want, and I will endeavor to apply the rule of give and take."

Seward on April 1 laid before Lincoln as odd a document as ever came from a department secretary to a chief magistrate, headed: "Some Thoughts for the President's Consideration." Seward numbered his thoughts. "First, we are at the end of a month's administration, and yet without a policy, either domestic or foreign." Second, "the need to meet applications for patronage" had prevented "attention to more grave matters." Third, "further delay . . . would not only bring scandal on the administration, but danger upon the country." Fourth, leave "foreign or general" appointments "for ulterior and occasional action." Fifth, "Change the question before the public from . . . slavery . . . to Union or disunion." (As though Lincoln had not for years lost sleep over how to do that very thing.) "I would terminate it [the occupation of Fort Sumter] as a safe means for changing the issue . . . This will raise distinctly the question of union or disunion." Yet the next sentence read, "I would maintain every fort and possession in the South."

Next Lincoln's eyes met weird proposals from his Secretary: "If satisfactory explanations are not received from Spain and France, [I] Would convene Congress and declare war against them. But whatever policy we adopt . . . it must be somebody's business to pursue and direct it incessantly. Either the President must do it himself, and be all the while active in it, or Devolve it on some member of his Cabinet . . . It is not in my especial province. But I neither seek to evade nor assume responsibility."

This was saying nearly straight out that Lincoln had fumbled and bumbled as a President and he, Seward, knew how to be one. And there in black ink on white paper was the strange and wild advice that by starting wars with Spain and France, the Union would be saved. The seceded Southern States would move back into the Union and fight under the Old Flag. Lincoln wrote in reply, "I have been considering your paper," pointed to his inaugural and quoted to show how definitely he had announced policies as to Sumter and union or disunion. "Upon your closing propositions," he wrote, ". . . I remark that if this must be done, *I* must do it." His closing words were soft, as though soothing a mind under strain. "When a general line of policy is adopted, I apprehend there is no danger of its being changed without good reason, or continuing to be a subject of unnecessary debate; still, upon points arising in its progress, I wish, and suppose I am entitled to have the advice of all the cabinet."

The Union was weaker than a month before because the administration had exhibited "a blindness and a stolidity without a parallel in the history of intelligent statesmanship," said the New York *Times*. Lincoln had "spent time and strength in feeding rapacious and selfish politicians, which should have been bestowed upon saving the Union," and "we tell him . . . that he must go up to a higher level than he has yet reached." This lent support to the *Herald*'s repeated jabs: "the Lincoln Administration is cowardly, mean, and vicious," the blame resting on "the incompetent, ignorant, and desperate 'Honest Abe.' "

William Cullen Bryant in a New York *Evening Post* editorial took the *Tribune* and *Times* outbursts as nervous and peevish. To frame in 30 days a clear policy for so complex a national situation was a hard matter, as Bryant saw it, and furthermore, how could the facile critics know that Lincoln had not fixed upon his policy, with a decision to make it known to the world by action instead of a windy proclamation?

Henry J. Raymond of the *Times* later went down to Washington, talked with Lincoln, and got his viewpoint: "I am like a man so busy in letting rooms in one end of his house, that he can't stop to put out the fire that is burning in the other."

CHAPTER 19

Sumter and War Challenge—Call for Troops

THE MORNING after inauguration Lincoln had studied dispatches from Major Robert Anderson, commander of Fort Sumter in Charleston Harbor, reporting that his food supplies would last four weeks or by careful saving perhaps 40 days. The Confederates stood ready to batter Fort Sumter and run down its flag whenever the word came from their Government at Montgomery.

When the Senate on March 25 requested from the President the Anderson dispatches to the War Department, the President replied, "I have, with the highest respect for the Senate, come to the conclusion that at the present moment the publication of it would be inexpedient." The Senators from Virginia, North Carolina, Tennessee, Arkansas, Texas, were in their seats answering roll call from day to day, their states not having officially and formally seceded.

Lincoln had called his Cabinet for its first meeting March 9 and put a written question, "Assuming it to be possible to now provision Fort Sumter, under all the circumstances, is it wise to attempt it?" The Cabinet members went away, returning March 16 with written answers. Seward advised No: it was not a time for the use of force. Chase advised Yes and No; Yes if it meant peace, No if the attempt was to bring on civil war, armies, million-dollar budgets. Cameron advised No, seeing that "no practical benefit will result to the country." Welles advised No: "I entertain doubts." Smith advised No: giving up Fort Sumter would cause "surprise and complaint" but it could be "explained and understood." Bates advised No: "I am willing to evacuate Fort Sumter." Blair was the only one with an unmodified Yes: Buchanan had hesitated and failed; Jackson had acted and won; provisioning the fort would "vindicate the hardy courage of the North, and the determination of the people and their President to maintain the authority of the Government." Thus the seven new counselors stood five against sending food to Anderson, one for it, and one neither for nor against it.

The President called in Assistant Secretary of the Navy Gustavus Vasa Fox, 39 years old. Born in Saugus, Massachusetts, a Naval Academy graduate of 18 years' service in coast survey, of Mexican War experience, commander of U.S. mail steamers, he resigned in 1856 to become agent of woolen mills in Lawrence, Massachusetts. On March 21, acting as Lincoln's messenger and observer, Fox had arrived in Fort Sumter under escort of a former friend, a Confederate captain formerly of the U.S. Navy, who stood within ear-shot while Major Anderson and Fox talked. Fox reported back to Lincoln that no time was to be lost; Anderson's final scraping of flour and last slab of bacon would be used up at noon April 15. On March 28 Lincoln instructed Fox to prepare a short order detailing the ships, men, supplies required for his plans to provision Fort Sumter. Lincoln kept a memorandum of this order for use in a day or two.

Lamon had arrived from a trip to Charleston. From the Governor of South Carolina he brought the message to Lincoln: "Nothing can prevent war except the acquiescence of the President of the United States in secession . . . Let your President attempt to reinforce Sumter, and the tocsin of war will be sounded from every hilltop and valley in the South."

The President on March 28 met his Cabinet in secret session. He read to them a memorandum from General Scott discouraging attempts to reinforce Sumter and advising, "The giving up of Forts Sumter and Pickens may be justified." This amazed several members. Blair was first to find his tongue and blurted out that the head of the Army was more than military, was "playing politician." Blair indicated that he blamed Seward's intrigue for this move. All agreed, however, that the advice of the head of the Army was not to be taken. The President asked the Cabinet to meet next day. And that night, said his secretaries, "Lincoln's eyes did not close in sleep." All night long his mind sought the realities behind multiple mirrors.

At noon next day the Cabinet met to discuss going to war. Bates wrote he would reinforce Fort Pickens, and "As to Fort Sumter, I think the time is come to either evacuate or relieve it." The President asked the others to write their views. Seward wrote: "I would at once, and at every cost, prepare for a war at Pensacola and Texas" and "I would instruct Major Anderson to retire from Fort Sumter forthwith." Chase would maintain Fort Pickens and provision Fort Sumter. Welles would make Fort Pickens impregnable, and as to Sumter, the Government was justified in "a peaceable attempt to send provisions to one of our own forts." Smith seemed to believe he would defend Fort Pickens and evacuate Fort Sumter, recognizing it as risky politically. Blair would hold Fort Pickens and fight "the head and front of this rebellion" at Fort Sumter. Cameron was absent. So the Cabinet stood three for and three against the evacuation of Sumter.

The Cabinet meeting over, the President brought out the memorandum of Captain Fox's order and at the bottom wrote an order on the Secretary of War: "Sir: I desire that an expedition, to move by sea, be got ready to sail as early as the 6th. of April next, the whole according to memorandum attached; and that you co-operate with the Secretary of the Navy for that object." This with a signed duplicate to the Secretary of the Navy was delivered, and Captain Fox started for New York to get ready the expedition.

A messenger went from Lincoln that week to Richmond, where a convention of delegates, debating over secession and voting against secession, had been sitting since February 13. The messenger gave to Judge George W. Summers Lincoln's request to come to Washington for a conference. Summers consulted other delegates and chose for the errand John B. Baldwin, who in a closed carriage arrived April 4 at the White House, and later wrote: "Mr. Lincoln received me very cordially . . . and said he desired to have some private conversation with me. He started through to a back room, opening into another room, but we found two gentlemen there engaged in writing; he seemed to think that would not do, and we passed across the hall into a small room opposite, and through that into a large front room . . . He locked the door, and . . . drew up two chairs and asked me to take a seat."

Precisely what Lincoln said in the interview was not clear in Baldwin's later recollections. Lincoln did vaguely say "something about a withdrawal of troops from Sumter on the ground of military necessity," and whatever the point was, Baldwin replied: "That will never do under heaven . . . Mr. President, I did not come here to argue with you . . . I tell you before God and man, that if there is a gun fired at Sumter, war is inevitable." Also Baldwin offered his surmise that if the Virginia convention did dissolve and its members did go home, another convention would be called in short order.

Efforts at peace were going on the rocks. Baldwin returned to Richmond declaring he had received from Lincoln "no pledge, no undertaking, no offer, no promise of any sort." Hay, Nicolay, Whitney, believed Lincoln gave Baldwin a message he failed to deliver. At a later time Lincoln, through a letter of Hay's, confirmed statements of Baldwin, as written, though having no corroboration then or since. Delegate Tarr of the Virginia convention later wrote Hay of hearing Baldwin say that he [Lincoln] "had sent for Mr. Baldwin, a member of the convention, and had him in the White House with him alone, and told him that if they would pass resolutions of adherence to the Union, then adjourn and go home, he, the President, would take the responsibility at the earliest proper time to withdraw the troops from Fort Sumter and do all within his line of duty to ward off collision." Hay replied that the President "directs me to state . . . that your first statement is substantially correct, but that for the present he still prefers that you withhold it from the public."

On April 1, 1861, Nicolay brought to Willard's a package of papers which he handed to Secretary Welles, who lived there. Welles read the papers; then, as Welles told it: "Without a moment's delay I went to the President with the package in my hand. He was alone in his office and, raising his head from the table at which he was writing, inquired, '*What have I done wrong?*'"

Then came the unraveling of a tangled affair. In Welles' hands were two papers signed by Lincoln, who after reading them said he was surprised he had sent such a document to the Secretary of the Navy. He had signed the papers without reading them, he told Welles; Seward with two or three young men had been at the White House through the day on a subject Seward had in hand. "It was Seward's specialty, to which he, the President, had yielded, but as it involved considerable details, he had left Mr. Seward to prepare the necessary papers."

Thus Welles heard Lincoln's explanation. "These papers he had signed, many of them without reading—for he had not time, and if he could not trust the Secretary of State he knew not whom he could trust. I asked who were associated with Mr. Seward. 'No one,' said the President, 'but these young men were here as clerks to write down his plans and orders.' I then asked if he knew the young men. He said one was Captain Meigs, another was a naval officer named Porter . . . He seemed disinclined to disclose or dwell on the project, but assured me he never would have signed that paper had he been aware of its contents, much of which had no connection with Mr. Seward's scheme . . . The President reiterated they were not his instructions, and wished me distinctly to understand they were not, though his name was appended to them—said the paper was an improper one—that he wished me to give it no more consideration than I thought proper— treat it as canceled—as if it had never been written."

Next day the tangle of orders and countermands became worse. Something of Navy Department feeling was reflected in Gustavus Vasa Fox's writing to his wife: "Mr. Seward got up this Pensacola expedition and the President signed the orders in ignorance and unknown to the Department. The President offers every apology possible and will do so in writing."

Among the papers Nicolay brought to Willard's for Welles to sign were instructions to the Secretary of the Navy, in the handwriting of Captain Meigs of the War Department, with a concluding sentence, "Captain Samuel Barron will relieve Captain Stringham in charge of the Bureau of detail," and the signature "Abraham Lincoln." Attached was a postscript in the handwriting of Lieutenant Porter, also signed "Abraham Lincoln," requesting of the Secretary of the Navy "that you will instruct Captain Barron to proceed and organize the Bureau of detail in the manner best adapted to meet the wants of the navy, taking cognizance of the discipline of the navy generally, detailing all officers for duty, taking charge of the recruiting of seamen, supervising charges made against officers, and all matters relating to duties which must be best understood by a sea officer."

The request proceeded: "You will please afford Captain Barron any facility for accomplishing this duty, transferring to his department the clerical force heretofore used for the purposes specified. It is to be understood that this officer will act by authority of the Secretary of the Navy, who will exercise such supervision as he may deem necessary."

Lincoln did not know when signing this appointment, nor Seward when advising Lincoln to sign it, that the man thereby appointed, Captain Samuel Barron, supposedly of the U.S. Navy, had five days before accepted a commission as a commodore in the Confederate States Navy! Nor could Lincoln or Seward under the circumstances have guessed that two weeks later Captain Barron would go to Richmond, take the oath of Confederate loyalty, and enter actively into building coast fortifications to defend Virginia and North Carolina against ships whose officers would have been detailed by him had he managed to get into the place to which Lincoln appointed him and from which Lincoln removed him the day Welles entered Lincoln's office in such anger that Lincoln's greeting was, "What have I done wrong?"

A naval lieutenant, Gwathmey, arrived in Secretary Welles' office and took from a belt strapped around his body under his shirt a letter from Captain Adams, senior naval officer in command of Fort Pickens. Welles learned that Adams was operating in obedience to an armistice negotiated by the Buchanan administration by which the U.S. Government was not to reinforce Fort Pickens provided the Confederate forces did not attack it.

Taking the letter to Lincoln, they decided to send word back to Adams to forget the armistice and to land troops. This message, however, could not be carried by Lieutenant Gwathmey. He was requesting that his resignation from the Navy be accepted; he was going to join the Confederates; he had been sufficiently loyal to his oath as an officer. So John Worden, a naval lieutenant whose loyalty to the Union was vouched for, received from the Secretary of the Navy a dispatch and was advised to memorize it, burn it, and on arriving in Florida make a certified copy as he remembered it. Worden did this, and Fort Pickens was reinforced the night of April 12.

The New York *Herald* spoke for a variety of powerful interests April 10: "Our only hope now against civil war of an indefinite duration seems to lie in the over-throw of the demoralizing, disorganizing, and destructive [Republican] sectional party, of which 'Honest Abe Lincoln' is the pliant instrument." "The new pilot was hurried to the helm in the midst of a tornado," wrote Emerson of Lincoln's first weeks in office. As yet, however, the tornado was merely beginning to get under way.

Fort Sumter, three miles out from Charleston, rising almost sheer with the rock walls of its island, was being ringed round with batteries, guns and 5,000 recruits under General P. G. T. Beauregard, constantly in touch with Governor F. W. Pickens of South Carolina and Secretary L. P. Walker of the Confederate War Department at Montgomery. Visitors to the U.S. Army officers or soldiers at Fort Sumter were challenged by Confederate pickets, had to show passes from Governor Pickens.

Three commissioners from the Confederate Government had arrived in Washington, instructed to "play with" Seward, which they did. And Seward had "played with" them. What to say to those commissioners, and how to say it without recognizing their Government, Seward took as his own prob- lem. He carried on furtive, indirect negotiations with them without consult- ing the President, whom he saw as lacking plan and decision, which was the view of the New York *Tribune*, the New York *Times*, the New York *Herald*.

The Confederate commissioners wrote and telegraphed their Government that the Lincoln administration would give up Sumter. Days passed. On March 30 the Governor of South Carolina was telegraphing the Confederate commissioners in Washington asking why Sumter was still flying the Stars and Stripes. April 2, the Confederate commissioners telegraphed their Gov- ernment: "The war wing presses on the President; he vibrates to that side . . . Their form of notice to us may be that of the coward, who gives it when he strikes."

Week by week the country had watched the emergence of Major Robert Anderson into a national figure. "Bob Anderson, my beau, Bob," ran a song line. He had kept a cool head and held on amid a thousand invitations to blunder. Even the Charleston *Mercury* complimented him as a gentleman whose word was good. He was a West Pointer, a sober churchman, born and raised in Kentucky. He had married a Georgia girl, had owned a plantation and slaves in Georgia and sold the slaves. He could see that his immediate duty was to obey orders from the U.S. Government but, according to one of his officers, if war came between the South and the North, and if his State of Kentucky seceded, he would go to Europe.

By now the Sumter garrison was stopped from getting fresh meat and vegetables at the Charleston market. By now there had arrived in Charleston a War Department clerk from Washington, Robert S. Chew, who on April 8 read to Governor Pickens a notification from President Lincoln:

Washington, April 6. 1861
Sir—You will proceed directly to Charleston, South Carolina; and if, on your ar- rival there, the flag of the United States shall be flying over Fort-Sumpter, and the Fort shall not have been attacked, you will procure an interview with Gov. Pickens, and read to him as follows:
"I am directed by the President of the United States to notify you to expect an attempt will be made to supply Fort-Sumpter with provisions only; and that, if such attempt be not resisted, no effort to throw in men, arms, or ammunition, will be made, without further notice, or in case of an attack upon the Fort"
After you shall have read this to Governor Pickens, deliver to him the copy of it herein inclosed, and retain this letter yourself.
But if, on your arrival at Charleston, you shall ascertain that Fort Sumpter shall have been already evacuated, or surrendered, by the United States force; or, shall have been attacked by an opposing force, you will seek no interview with Gov. Pickens, but return here forthwith.

The doubts of long months were at an end. Thus Lincoln framed an issue for his country and the world to look at and consider. Sumter was a symbol.

Jefferson Davis called his advisers into session at Montgomery to consider
Lincoln's message to Governor Pickens, which had been telegraphed on.
Robert Toombs, Secretary of State, read Lincoln's letter, and said, "The
firing on that fort will inaugurate a civil war greater than any the world has
yet seen; and I do not feel competent to advise you . . . You will wantonly
strike a hornet's nest which extends from mountains to ocean; legions, now
quiet, will swarm out and sting us to death . . ." President Davis, however,
decided in favor of attacking the fort, leaving to Beauregard the choice of
time and method.

On April 10 Governor Andrew Curtin of the great iron and coal State of
Pennsylvania read a note from Lincoln: "I think the necessity for being
ready increases. Look to it."

Beauregard on April 11 sent a little boat out to Sumter. A note to Anderson from Beauregard, his old-time affectionate pupil in artillery lessons at
West Point, read: "I am ordered by the Government of the Confederate
States to demand the evacuation of Fort Sumter . . . All proper facilities
will be afforded for the removal of yourself and command . . ." Major
Anderson wrote in answer: ". . . It is a demand with which I regret that my
sense of honor, and of my obligations to my Government, prevent my com-
pliance . . ." As Major Anderson handed this note to Beauregard's aides, he
made the remark, "Gentlemen, if you do not batter us to pieces, we shall be
starved out in a few days."

Now four men from Beauregard went in a boat out to Sumter. Past midnight they handed Major Anderson a note saying there would be no "useless
effusion of blood" if he would fix a stated time for his surrender. Anderson
called his officers; from one till three they consulted. And at 3:15 that morning Anderson gave his answer: "Cordially uniting with you in the desire to
avoid the useless effusion of blood, I will, if provided with the proper and
necessary means of transportation, evacuate Fort Sumter by noon on the
15th instant, and I will not in the meantime open my fire on your forces unless compelled to do so by some hostile act against this fort or the flag of my
Government . . . should I not receive prior to that time controlling instructions from my Government or additional supplies."

Within five minutes they gave Anderson a written answer:

Fort Sumter, S. C., April 12, 1861—3:20 A.M.
Sir:
By authority of Brigadier-General, commanding the Provisional Forces of the
Confederate States, we have the honor to notify you that he will open the fire
of his batteries on Fort Sumter in one hour from this time.
We have the honor to be, very respectfully, your obedient servant,
JAMES CHESNUT, JR.,
Aide-de-Camp.
STEPHEN D. LEE,
Captain, C. S. Army, Aide-de-Camp.

The four men got into their boat, with Chesnut musing over Major Anderson's parting words, "If we do not meet again on earth, I hope we may meet
in Heaven."

Old Edmund Ruffin—a farmer from Virginia, soil expert, farm paper editor, ally of Rhett, 67 years old, his face framed in venerable white ringlets

of hair—pulled the first gun of the war, and swore he would kill himself before he would ever live under the U.S. Government.

Mrs. James Chesnut, Jr., whose husband had helped get the guns going, wrote in her diary April 12 as the shooting began: "I do not pretend to go to sleep. How can I? If Anderson does not accept terms at four, the orders are he shall be fired upon. I count four, St. Michael's bells chime out and I begin to hope. At half-past four the heavy booming of a cannon. I sprang out of bed, and on my knees prostrate I prayed as I never prayed before."

Encircling batteries let loose all they had. The mortars and howitzers laughed. Wood fires on hulks at the inner harbor entrance and daybreak lighted one lonesome relief ship from Lincoln; it and two others arriving later could be of no help. Through daylight of the 12th and through the rain and darkness of the night of the 13th, the guns pounded Sumter with more than 3,000 shot and shell. Smoke, heat, vapor, stifled the garrison; the men hugged the ground with wet handkerchiefs over mouths and eyes till they could breathe again. The last biscuit was gone; they were down to pork only for food. The storm and dark of the early morning on the 13th ended with clear weather and a red sunrise.

Again offered the same terms of surrender as before, Anderson, after 33 hours of bombardment, gave up the fort. On Sunday, the 14th, he marched his garrison out with colors flying, drums beating, saluting his flag with 50 guns. They boarded one of the relief ships and headed north for New York Harbor. They had lost one man, killed in the accidental explosion of one of their own cannon. In their last glimpse of Fort Sumter they saw the new Confederate flag, Stars and Bars, flying. In his trunk Major Anderson had the flag he had defended; he wished to keep this burnt and shot flag and have it wrapped round him when laid in the grave.

On that Sunday of April 14, the White House had many visitors in and out all day. Senators and Congressmen came to say their people would stand by the Government, the President. The Cabinet met. A proclamation was framed. It named the States of South Carolina, Georgia, Alabama, Florida, Mississippi, Louisiana and Texas as having "combinations too powerful to be suppressed" by ordinary procedure of government.

"Now therefore, I, Abraham Lincoln, President of the United States, in virtue of the power in me vested by the Constitution and the laws, have thought fit to call forth, and hereby do call forth, the militia of the several States of the Union, to the aggregate number of seventy-five thousand, in order to suppress said combinations, and to cause the laws to be duly executed."

He called on "all loyal citizens" to defend the National Union and popular government, "to redress wrongs already long enough endured." The new army of volunteer soldiers was to retake forts and property "seized from the Union." Also, "in every event, the utmost care will be observed, consistently with the objects aforesaid, to avoid any devastation, any destruction of, or interference with, property, or any disturbance of peaceful citizens."

Also the proclamation called both Houses of Congress to meet at noon on the Fourth of July. The war of words was over and the naked test by steel weapons, so long foretold, was at last to begin.

From day to day since Lincoln was sworn in as President he had been moved toward war, saying casually to John Hay one day in April, "My policy is to have no policy." Day to day events dictated. How did he explain Sumter? "The assault upon and reduction of Fort Sumter was in no sense a matter of self-defense on the part of the assailants," he wrote later. "They well knew that the garrison in the fort could by no possibility commit aggression upon them. They knew—they were expressly notified—that the giving of bread to the few brave and hungry men of the garrison was all which would on that occasion be attempted."

The dilemma of a divided country Lincoln and Douglas discussed at the White House that Sunday of April 14, just after the flag came down at Sumter. Now Lincoln could be thankful that across the years of political strife between him and Douglas, the two had so spoken to and of each other that their personal relations had never reached a breaking point. The two foremost American political captains were closeted for a two-hour confidential talk, with only Congressman Ashmun in the room. Douglas read the proclamation to be published next morning, gave it his approval, though advising that he would call for 200,000 rather than 75,000 troops.

Douglas, at Willard's, wrote out a dispatch which next day went to the country through the Associated Press. He had called on the President and had "an interesting conversation on the present condition of the country," the substance of which was, on the part of Mr. Douglas, "that while he was unalterably opposed to the administration in all political issues, he was prepared to fully sustain the President in the exercise of all his constitutional functions, to preserve the Union, maintain the Government, and defend the capital. A firm policy and prompt action was necessary. The capital was in danger, and must be defended at all hazards, and at any expense of men and money." He added that he and the President "spoke of the present and future without any reference to the past." Douglas was a hoarse and worn man of dwindling vitality, but he struck with decisive words that sank deep in every one of his old loyal followers. He knew he had trumpets left, and he blew them to mass his cohorts behind Lincoln's maintenance of the Union.

Now came the day of April 15, 1861, for years afterward spoken of as "the day Lincoln made his first call for troops." What happened on that day was referred to as the Uprising of the People; they swarmed onto the streets, into public squares, into meeting halls and churches. The shooting of the Stars and Stripes off the Sumter flagstaff—and the Lincoln proclamation—acted as a vast magnet on a national multitude.

In a thousand cities, towns and villages the fever of hate, exaltation, speech, action, followed a similar course. Telegrams came notifying officers and militiamen to mobilize. Newspapers cried in high or low key the war song. Then came mass meetings, speeches by prominent citizens, lawyers, ministers, priests, military officers, veterans of the War of 1812 and the Mexican War, singing of "The Star-spangled Banner" and "America," fife-and-drum corps playing "Yankee Doodle." Funds were subscribed to raise and equip troops, resolutions passed, committees appointed to collect funds, to care for soldiers' families, to educate or trouble the unpatriotic. Women's societies were formed to knit and sew, prepare lint and bandages. Women and girls saw their husbands and sweethearts off to camp. Nearly every community had its men and boys marching away to the fifing of "The Girl I Left Behind Me." In churches and saloons, in city crowds and at country crossroads, the talk was of the War and "What will the President do next?"

In the large cities military units of the foreign-born were formed. Irishmen of New York made up four regiments: the 69th, Irish Zouaves, Irish Volunteers, St. Patrick Brigade. The Italian Legion made ready, also the Garibaldi Guards. Germans supplied the Steuben Volunteers, the German Rifles, the Turner Rifles, the De Kalb Regiment. The English and Irish Home Guards were proposed for men of former service in the British Army and Irish constabulary, while the British Volunteers were to recruit from British subjects in New York.

Bishop Matthew Simpson of the Methodist Episcopal church in a talk with the President gave his opinion that 75,000 men were but a beginning of the number needed; that the struggle would be long and severe. The New York *Herald,* shifting its outlook, voiced the new viewpoint of powerful business interests in declaring: "The business community demand that the war shall be *short;* and the more vigorously it is prosecuted the more speedily will it be closed. Business men can stand a temporary reverse. They can easily make arrangements for six months or a year. But they cannot endure a long, uncertain and tedious contest." Astor, Vanderbilt, Aspinwall, A. T. Stewart, Belmont of the House of Rothschild, the millionaires who had been at the breakfast to Lincoln when he came through New York, they and their cohorts and lawyers were now for war. Senator Douglas at Bellaire, Ohio, in Chicago at the Wigwam, in Springfield before the Illinois Legislature, was saying that the shortest way to peace would be stupendous and unanimous preparation for war.

None leaped so eagerly as the abolitionists at the ways now open for a war with slaveholders. "I was a Disunionist," said Wendell Phillips. "I did hate the Union, when Union meant lies in the pulpit and mobs in the streets, when Union meant making white men hypocrites and black men slaves . . . The only mistake I made was in supposing Massachusetts wholly choked with cotton dust and cankered with gold."

Gerrit Smith, abolitionist of means who had given 120,000 acres of land to 3,000 colored men, who had spent $16,000 on the Kansas civil war, told an audience at his home town of Peterboro, New York, that the last fugitive slave had been returned. "A few weeks ago I would have consented to let the slave states go without requiring the abolition of slavery . . . But now, since the Southern tiger has smeared himself with our blood, we will not, if we get him in our power, let him go without having drawn his teeth and claws." Gerrit Smith was offering to equip a regiment of colored troops, and was sending his only son, Greene Smith, into the army, insisting it be without soldier's pay.

Cheers and applause greeted the public reading of a letter of Archbishop John Hughes declaring for the Stars and Stripes: "This has been my flag and shall be till the end." At home and abroad, the Archbishop would have it wave "for a thousand years and afterward as long as Heaven permits, without limit of duration." On April 20, 50,000 people made their way to a Union mass meeting at Union Square in New York City. As William H. Appleton, publisher of books, stood at Broadway and Fourteenth Street watching the human swarm, he remarked to a friend, "We shall crush out this rebellion as an elephant would trample on a mouse."

Far from Union Square, in a cornfield near Iowa City, the farmer Governor Samuel J. Kirkwood saw an earnest man on a spent and foam-flecked horse. This corn-fed courier had been riding hours from Davenport on the Mississippi with a telegram he handed the Governor from the Secretary of War: "Call made on you tonight's mail for one regiment of militia for indefinite service." The Governor wrinkled his brow and gazed across a slope of cut cornstalks: "Why! The President wants a whole regiment of men! Do you suppose I can raise as many as that?" Yet a few days later, ten Iowa regiments were offered and Governor Kirkwood was telegraphing Washington: "For God's sake send us arms! We have the men."

At a Western religious conclave jubilant hosannas came from a bishop of the Methodist Episcopal church, the Reverend Edward R. Ames: "There has been held a grand Union convention amid the fortresses of the everlasting hills. The Rocky Mountains presided, the mighty Mississippi made the motion, the Allegheny Mountains seconded it and every mountain and hill, valley and plain, in this vast country, sent up a unanimous voice; Resolved, that we are one and inseparable and what God has joined together, let no man put asunder." It was a week of distinguished and inflammatory oratory.

Nathaniel Hawthorne wrote to his wife, "It was delightful to share in the heroic sentiment of the time, and to feel that I had a country . . . Though I approve the war as much as any man, I don't quite understand what we are fighting for." More distinct was Parson Brownlow, an editor in Knoxville, Tennessee, at the peril of his neck telling the world that though he was against abolition, he was for the Union and he would "fight the Secession leaders till Hell froze over and then fight on the ice."

Three delegates came to the White House as a special committee from the Virginia convention which in secret session had voted 60 to 53 against seceding from the Union. They politely inquired of Lincoln as to his intentions. He replied politely that his intentions were still the same as reported in his inaugural. He read over part of his inaugural, as though they had not read it carefully enough, and as though by patience they might find new clues in it: "The power confided to me will be used to hold, occupy, and possess the property and places belonging to the government . . ." They reported back to their convention—and Virginia, the Old Dominion, the Mother of Presidents, went out of the Union.

On April 17 when Virginia seceded, her troops were set in motion for a surprise march on the U.S. fort and arsenal at Harpers Ferry, the most dramatic point northward for raising her new flag. They arrived April 18 and took the fort and arsenal without fighting. The barrels and locks of 20,000 pistols and rifles were sent to Richmond to be remade. Two days later the U.S. navy yard at Norfolk, Virginia, was threatened, or the commander was afraid it was, and guns, munitions, ships and war property valued at $30,000,000 went up in smoke.

Robert E. Lee, Virginian, resigned from the U.S. Army, gave up his stately home on Arlington Heights overlooking Washington, to take command of the Army of Virginia. Long ago he had opposed slavery. He favored the Union but couldn't fight against his native state. Before resigning he was interviewed by Francis P. Blair, Sr., who said later: "I told him what President Lincoln wanted him to do; he wanted him to take command of the army . . . He said he could not, under any circumstances, consent to supersede his old commander [General Scott]. He asked me if I supposed the President would consider that proper. I said yes . . . The matter was talked over by President Lincoln and myself for some hours on two or three different occasions . . . The President and Secretary Cameron expressed themselves as anxious to give the command of our army to Robert E. Lee." Now Lee had gone to Richmond.

Lincoln had lost a commander that General Scott reckoned as worth 50,000 men. "Save in the defense of my native State I never again desire to draw my sword," Lee wrote to Scott. Two months before, in Texas, he had told army associates: "I fear the liberties of our country will be buried in the tomb of a great nation . . . If Virginia stands by the old Union, so will I. But if she secedes (though I do not believe in secession as a constitutional right, nor that there is sufficient cause for revolution) then I will still follow my native State with my sword, and, if need be, with my life." The break came hard for Lee.

The seething of propaganda began. Southern newspapers reported elaborate plans in the North to stir up insurrections of slaves, with robbery, arson, rape, murder. Northern newspapers reported a Northern woman teacher in a New Orleans grammar school as being stripped naked and tarred and feathered in Lafayette Square "for abolition sentiments expressed to her pupils." North and South, horrors were exaggerated or fabricated. The Petersburg, Virginia, *Express* told readers, "Old Abe has his legs in perfect readiness to run. He does not so much as take off his boots."

A volunteer White House Guard gathered under Cassius M. Clay, who would delay sailing as the new Minister to Russia, and Senator James H. Lane, the new Senator from the new State of Kansas. Both men had commanded troops in the Mexican War, had faced mobs in their antislavery careers. Both expected the war to begin in Washington and were ready for a last-ditch fight at the White House doors.

"The White House is turned into barracks," wrote Hay. Alarmists and cranks flitted into the halls and corridors, demanded to see the President or whispered they had information of plots, of attacks planned, of suspicious-looking steamers coming up the Potomac, of a mob that was to overwhelm the Executive Mansion, with picked men to seize and carry off the President. Washington was hemmed in.

From the governors of Border States came warlike answers to Lincoln's dispatch asking for quotas of troops: "Kentucky will furnish no troops for the wicked purpose of subduing her sister Southern States," replied Governor Beriah Magoffin. "Your requisition, in my judgment," replied Claiborne Jackson of Missouri, "is illegal, unconstitutional and revolutionary in its objects, inhuman and diabolical, and cannot be complied with."

President Davis at Montgomery announced that his Government would issue "letters of marque" giving authority to ships joining the Confederacy to seize U.S. vessels of commerce. Lincoln replied by proclaiming a blockade of ports of the seceded states.

Each day in bureaus and departments at Washington came new resignations, Southerners leaving to go south to fight. On all sides were spies inter-threading North and South. Lincoln later sketched the situation that week: "A disproportionate share of the Federal muskets and rifles had somehow found their way into these [seceded] States, and had been seized to be used against the government . . . Officers of the Federal army and navy had resigned in great numbers; and of those resigning a large number had taken up arms against the government."

On April 18 arrived 532 Pennsylvania boys from Pottsville, Lewistown, Reading, Allentown, whom Hay noted as "unlicked patriotism that has poured ragged and unarmed out of Pennsylvania." They had passed through Baltimore safely. Not so the 6th Massachusetts regiment the next day. As they marched from one station to another, changing trains, they met stones, bricks, pistols, from a crowd of Southern sympathizers. They answered with bullets. Four soldiers were killed, and 12 citizens. Two by two the 6th Massachusetts marched up Pennsylvania Avenue that evening to the Capitol, their 17 wounded on stretchers.

Now came word that the telegraph wires leading to the North were cut. The Baltimore telegraph office was in the hands of secessionists. The War Office said, "This stops all." With mails stopped, railroads crippled, bridges down, telegraph wires dead, it was not easy in Washington to laugh away the prediction of the New Orleans *Picayune* that Virginia's secession would result in "the removal of Lincoln and his Cabinet, and whatever he can carry away, to the safer neighborhood of Harrisburg or Cincinnati."

At what moment would some free-going body of Southern troops ride into the capital, seize the city, and kidnap the Government? These questions were asked in Washington. Then and later this was regarded as an easy possibility. There were Southerners eager for the undertaking.

More than idle wish or bluster lay back of the Richmond *Examiner*'s declaring: "There is one wild shout of fierce resolve to capture Washington City, at all and every human hazard. The filthy cage of unclean birds must and will be purified by fire . . . Our people can take it, and Scott the arch-traitor, and Lincoln the Beast, combined, cannot prevent it. The just indignation of an outraged and deeply injured people will teach the Illinois Ape to retrace his journey across the borders of the Free negro States still more rapidly than he came."

To Hay that week Lincoln talked about what seemed to him the key point of the hour: "For my own part, I consider the first necessity that is upon us, is of proving that popular government is not an absurdity. We must settle this question now,—whether in a free government the minority have the right to break it up whenever they choose. If we fail, it will go far to prove the incapability of the people to govern themselves."

Impatience was heard in the President's Cabinet. Chase wrote a belief that the President in lieu of any policy had "merely the general notion of drifting, the Micawber policy of waiting for something to turn up." Lincoln, however, was taking to himself one by one the powers of a dictator. He authorized a raid whereby at three o'clock the afternoon of April 20 U.S. marshals entered every major telegraph office in the Northern States and seized the originals of all telegrams sent and copies of all telegrams received during 12 months. Also the President dug into the Treasury of the United

States for millions of dollars—without due and required authority of Congress. At a meeting held Sunday, April 21, in the Navy Department, away from any spies and all observers in the White House, the Cabinet members joined with Lincoln in the placing of immense funds.

"It became necessary for me to choose," said Lincoln later, "whether I should let the government fall at once into ruin, or whether . . . availing myself of the broader powers conferred by the Constitution in cases of insurrection, I would make an effort to save it." Government money orders for million-dollar amounts Lincoln sent by private messengers, who went by way of Wheeling and Pittsburgh to New York.

In the Treasury building now were howitzers. At the Mint were howitzers. In the marble corridors of the Capitol were howitzers, muskets, provisions, munitions of war. In the Senate chamber slept the 6th Massachusetts boys. In the House of Representatives slept the Pennsylvania boys. At each Capitol doorway was a ten-foot barricade of sandbags, cement barrels, iron plate. The Georgetown flour mills' supply, 25,000 barrels, was seized as a war necessity.

Newspaper items in the North were creating impressions: "President Lincoln said to a Baltimore deputation that if the passage of U.S. troops was again obstructed he would lay their city in ashes. One of the deputation said that 75,000 Marylanders would contest the passage of troops over her soil. To this the President said that he supposed there was room enough in her soil to bury 75,000." One news writer reported Lincoln saying to a pair of the delegation, by way of illustration: "You have all heard of the Irishman who, when a fellow was cutting his throat with a blunt razor, complained that he *haggled* it. Now, if I can't have troops direct through Maryland, and must have them all the way round by water, or marched across out-of-the-way territory, I shall be *haggled*."

On April 23 a little mail arrived—and newspapers. Anderson and his garrison had arrived in New York and the town had gone wild over them! A Union Square mass meeting with 50,000 people shouting for the Union! Processions, speeches, enlistments of more men than the President called for! Million-dollar appropriations for the war! The famous crack regiment, the dandy 7th of New York, had marched down Broadway between vast walls of cheering crowds, heading south for Washington! The Governor of Rhode Island sailing with troops and guns for Washington!

So the news ran. And out of it all nothing had reached Washington except the few boys now sleeping on their guns in the Capitol building. "I saw the President repeatedly," wrote Henry Villard, "and he fairly groaned at the inexplicable delay of help." "I think I saw three vessels go up to the Navy Yard just now," the President scribbled to the Secretary of the Navy. "Will you please send down and learn what they are?"

The afternoon of April 23 Lincoln was alone in his office in the White House—or believed he was alone, though John Hay, quiet and unobtrusive, was there. And Hay saw Lincoln "after walking the floor alone in silent thought for nearly half an hour," stop at a window and gaze long and wistfully down the Potomac in the direction of the expected ships. And as he gazed he broke out with irrepressible anguish in the repeated exclamation "Why don't they come! Why don't they come!"

Schurz reported of a bad hour Lincoln had in that lonely time: "He told me of an incident which I wish I could repeat in his own language. One afternoon after he had issued his call for troops, he sat alone in this room, and a feeling came over him as if he were utterly deserted and helpless. He thought any moderately strong body of secessionist troops might come over the 'long bridge' across the Potomac, and just take him and the members of the Cabinet—the whole lot of them. Then he suddenly heard a sound like the boom of a cannon. 'There they are!' he said to himself. He expected every moment somebody would rush in with the report of an attack. The White House attendants, whom he interrogated, had heard nothing. But nobody came, and all remained still.

"Then he thought he would look after the thing himself. So he walked out, and walked, and walked, until he got to the Arsenal. There he found the doors all open, and not a soul to guard them. Anybody might have gone in and helped himself to the arms. There was perfect solitude and stillness all around. Then he walked back to the White House without noticing the slightest sign of disturbance. He met a few persons on the way, some of whom he asked whether they had not heard something like the boom of a cannon. Nobody had heard anything, and so he supposed it must have been a freak of his imagination."

On April 24, when as yet no troops had arrived, when Seward's messengers sent out by the dozen had not returned, soldiers and officers of the 6th Massachusetts, wounded in Baltimore street fighting, came to see the White House and the President. Lincoln spoke thanks to them for brave service, and wandered in his talk into the mystery of why the North allowed its Government to be isolated, imprisoned. It was a sad, ironic tone, noted Hay, in which he told them: "I don't believe there is any North! The Seventh Regiment is a myth! Rhode Island is not known in our geography any longer! You are the only Northern realities!"

A locomotive whistle shrieking hallelujah the next day, April 25, was followed by the marching—left, right, left, right—up Pennsylvania Avenue of the 7th New York. Then came 1,200 Rhode Islanders and a brigade of 1,200 from Massachusetts. A crippled locomotive at Annapolis had been repaired by Massachusetts mechanics; volunteer tracklayers put the road from Annapolis in running order again. A troop route to the North had been found. In a few days Washington had 10,000 defense troops. Now, for a time, Lincoln knew that the capital would still be at Washington.

CHAPTER 20

Jefferson Davis—His Government

THE CONFEDERATE Government, strengthened by the finally seceded States of Arkansas, Tennessee, North Carolina and Texas, moved the last week in May from Montgomery, Alabama, to Richmond, Virginia, to be nearer the Border States and the expected heavy fighting. Into Richmond streamed regiments from all parts of the South. The cry in the South, "On to Washington!" snarled straight into the cry from the North, "On to Richmond!"

From the Potomac River to the Gulf Coast and the Rio Grande ran the recruiting ground of this Confederate Army. Its line zigzagged 1,500 miles from Chesapeake Bay through Kentucky and out to the corners of Kansas. Its brain and will centered in the capitol, the executive mansion, the departments, at Richmond. Its chief weapon of defense was an army of 100,000 troops. The controls of this Government were out of the hands of those who had first given it breath and fire. Rhett of the True Perpetual Separationists was now only a member of the Confederate Congress with no executive authority; the efforts to appoint him Secretary of War had failed. Yancey was shelved as a commissioner to European nations, with no power to act and no special instructions.

Russell of the *Times* of London wrote in Charleston: "Both sexes and all ages are for the war. Secession is the fashion here. Young ladies sing for it; old ladies pray for it; young men are dying to fight for it; old men are ready to demonstrate it." Russell heard of a Mobile gentleman having a letter from his daughter: "She informs him she has been elected vivandière to a New Orleans regiment, with which she intends to push on to Washington and get a lock of Abe Lincoln's hair."

A new and a young Government it was at Richmond. "Where will I find the State Department?" an Englishman asked Robert Toombs, Secretary of State. "In my hat, sir," replied Toombs, "and the archives in my coat pocket." The impulsive Toombs was soon to resign and take to the camp and battlefield. He should have been Secretary of War, said many, but that place went to Leroy Pope Walker of Alabama, a lawyer and politician, harassed by technical matters of how a people with ports restricted or closed, and with no gun or arms factories or powder mills, should create those requisites. He was soon to step from office to field service, and this Confederate War Department at Richmond took on as Acting Assistant Secretary of War one Albert Taylor Bledsoe, a West Point graduate who had become a Protestant Episcopal clergyman, later a professor of mathematics, though part of his ten years as a practicing lawyer was spent in Springfield, Illinois, with an office adjoining that of Lincoln & Herndon.

The Secretary of the Treasury, Christopher Gustavus Memminger, an orphan-asylum boy, a German Lutheran born in Württemberg, a lawyer, businessman, and politician of exceptional integrity, founder of the public-school system in Charleston, was the one South Carolina name in the Cabinet. He arranged with Gazaway B. Lamar, the Southern secessionist president of the Bank of the Republic in New York, for a contract with the American Bank Note Company to engrave and print in New York the bonds and treasury notes of the Confederacy. "The work was handsomely executed on the best of bank note and bond paper," wrote Memminger, "but with all the precaution taken by Mr. Lamar, the entire issue fell into the hands of the Federal Government and was seized as contraband of war." Engravers rushed from Europe were therefore to direct the printing of Confederate money on paper brought from Baltimore by agents who ran the Federal picket lines.

The Navy head was Stephen R. Mallory of Florida, once chairman of the

Committee on Naval Affairs of the U.S. Senate, and having, as President Davis wrote, "for a landsman much knowledge of nautical affairs." Mallory was the one Roman Catholic of the Cabinet. The one Jew was Judah P. Benjamin of New Orleans, whose wife was a French Roman Catholic. Twice elected U.S. Senator from Louisiana, in his advocacy of the legal grounds for slavery, he once came close to a duel with Jefferson Davis. Once when defending slavery Benjamin was classified by Senator Wade of Ohio as "a Hebrew with Egyptian principles." He had a rare legal mind, and as Attorney General and later as Secretary of State was one of the few trusted helpers of President Davis; he toiled in his Richmond office from eight in the morning till past midnight, and was sometimes referred to as "the brains of the Confederacy." The one Texan in the Cabinet was the Postmaster General, J. H. Reagan, former Congressman, Indian fighter, and Southwestern pioneer.

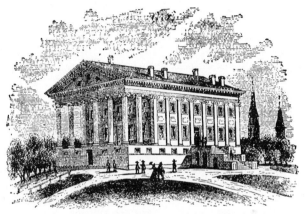

The State House at Richmond

Heading this Cabinet was a figure chosen as a military authority; he stood in the public eye as a moderate rather than a radical secessionist, having integrity and distinctively Southern qualities. This was the Mississippi cotton planter, West Point graduate, Black Hawk War lieutenant, Mexican War veteran wounded in service, U.S. Senator, Secretary of War under the Pierce administration, orator, horseman, man of fate—Jefferson Davis. He and Lincoln were both born in Kentucky, Davis a year earlier than Lincoln, one as a child carried north to free soil, the other as a suckling babe taken to the lower South.

Lincoln's army of 75,000 volunteers Davis termed a "posse comitatus" to round up 5,000,000 outlaws, and in the "singular document" calling for that army "the President was usurping a power granted exclusively to Congress." Davis would coldly and with studied politeness at intervals point to Lincoln as an ignorant usurper and a bloodthirsty despot, while Lincoln must speak and write as though Davis had no existence legal or personal, a nameless nobody, the invisible ghost of a glimmering hope.

When 17, Davis had replied to a sister's letter telling him of his father's death: "The intelligence contained in yours was more than sufficient to mar the satisfaction of hearing from anyone . . ." This formal manner, this icy perfection, was to stay with him. One of the rare times he dropped it was in his love letters to Sarah Knox Taylor, the 16-year-old daughter of Colonel Zachary Taylor at Fort Crawford, Wisconsin. "By dreams I have been lately almost crazy, for they were of you," he wrote to her, and again: "Kind, dear letter! I have kissed it often and often, and it has driven many mad notions from my brain." She was too young to marry, the father frowned. But Miss Taylor visited a Kentucky aunt, the young Lieutenant resigned from the Army, the couple were married in Kentucky and went to Mississippi near Vicksburg, to Brierfield, an 800-acre plantation given them by his brother, Joseph Davis, with 14 Negro slaves on credit. Malarial fever brought both of them down. In six weeks the bride of three months died in a delirium, singing an old hymn, "Fairy Bells," that she had from her mother.

An older brother brought to the plantation Miss Varina Howell, a 17-year-old girl from a well-to-do planter family at Natchez; she had soft liquid eyes, large curved eyebrows, with grace of speech and swift decisions. She was saved from mere prettiness by angular cheekbones and a full-lipped mournful mouth. She was 19 and he 37 when they married, and testimonies ran that she was the perfect helpmeet of a difficult man. When he was away she could write him that it was lonely for her "and I wish you had never loved me, and then I should not have encouraged myself to thinking of you . . . if you cannot come at least write more often . . . have more charity for me, dearest, and set me a better example." She was health to him physically and mentally, in loyalty a tigress.

His national reputation in politics began with his service in the U.S. Senate in 1847, his clashes with Douglas, his denials of secession purposes clouded by arguments that states had a Constitutional right to secede. Sam Houston of Texas briefly set forth that Davis was "ambitious as Lucifer and cold as a lizard." Another Southerner had it Davis "could not forget what ought not to be remembered." His wife wrote, "If anyone differs with Mr. Davis, he resents it and ascribes the difference to the perversity of his opponent." When for nothing much he challenged Senator Benjamin to a duel, it was called off, with Davis saying, "I have an infirmity of which I am heartily ashamed: when I am aroused in a matter, I lose control of my feelings and become personal." He lacked the skill to manage other men, but he was too positive a character to let others manage him, nor would he, as Lincoln did on occasion, let others believe they were managing him.

While Lincoln and Douglas were debating he said he wished they would tear each other to pieces like the Kilkenny cats. When on November 6 Lincoln, though lacking a majority vote, had carried the electors of every Northern State except New Jersey, Davis on November 10 had sent a letter to Rhett: "If South Carolina has determined to secede, I advise her to do so before the Government passes into hostile hands." On a sickbed racked by neuralgia, his left eye lost, Senator Davis talked with Seward, and the news came that Lincoln had declared he would concede almost every point at issue with the South except that no more Slave States could be made from Territories. Mississippi seceded January 9, and 11 days later Davis told the Senate he was officially notified of the secession of his state and must resign.

Tears were in many eyes at his saying they parted "not in hostility to

Upper left: Jefferson Davis, President of the Confederate States of America, former Senator from Mississippi and Mexican War veteran [McClees]. *Upper right:* Alexander Stephens of Georgia, Vice-President of the CSA, intimate with Lincoln when they were members of Congress [USASC]. *Center left:* Robert Barnwell Rhett of South Carolina, one of foremost instigators of secession [from *Battles and Leaders,* Century Co.]. *Center right:* William Lowndes Yancey, "fire-eater" orator who led Alabama into secession [Meserve]. *Lower left:* Christopher Gustavus Memminger of South Carolina, Württemburg born, Secretary of the Treasury of the CSA [Meserve]. *Lower right:* John C. Breckinridge, resigned U.S. Senator from Kentucky, Confederate general, later Secretary of War of the CSA [Meserve].

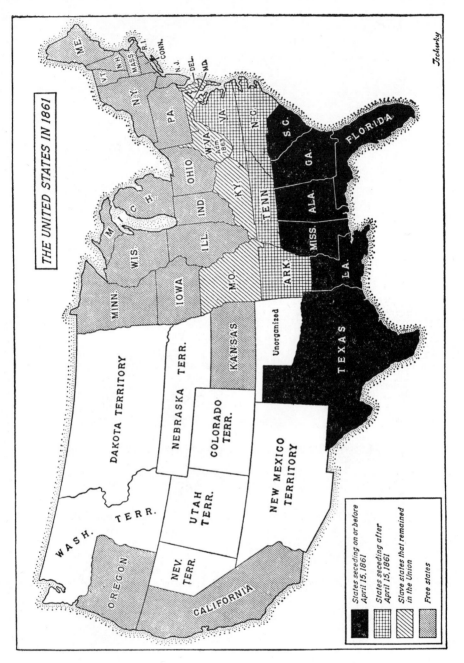

THE UNITED STATES IN 1861

ME
VT
N.H.
MASS.
R.I.
CONN.
N.Y.
N.J.
PA.
DEL.
MD.
W.VA
Adm
1863
VA
N.C.
S.C.
GA.
FLORIDA
OHIO
KY
TENN
ALA.
MISS.
MICH
WIS.
ILL.
IND
MO.
ARK.
LA.
MINN.
IOWA
DAKOTA TERRITORY
NEBRASKA TERR.
KANSAS
Unorganized
TEXAS
COLORADO TERR.
NEW MEXICO TERRITORY
WASH. TERR.
UTAH TERR.
NEV. TERR.
OREGON
CALIFORNIA

Ischrby

States seceding on or before
April 15, 1861

States seceding after
April 15, 1861

Slave states that remained
in the Union

Free states

From Allan Nevins: *The Emergence of Lincoln.*

others, not to injure any section of the country, not even for our own pecuniary benefit, but from the high and solemn motive of defending and protecting the rights we inherited, and which it is our duty to transmit unshorn to our children . . . It only remains for me to bid you a final adieu." At night, said his wife, in his restless tossing came often the prayer, "May God have us in his holy keeping, and grant that before it is too late peaceful counsels may prevail."

On February 10, with a warm spring sun pouring down on leaf and petal, he and Varina were in a rose garden trimming and cutting, as though bloodred roses carry ministrations. A messenger threaded his way through the bushes and handed Jefferson Davis a telegram. His wife tried to read his face while he read the telegram. His face took on grief and she was afraid evil news had arrived. "After a few minutes' painful silence he told me, as a man might speak of a sentence of death." The Montgomery delegates to the convention of the Confederate States of America had elected him provisional President, when so definitely he preferred campaign and battlefield to an administrative desk.

She wept a good-by and he rode to Montgomery, sleeping in his clothes, routed from the train by crowds roaring for their new President, calling for speeches, "bonfires at night, firing by day." After inauguration he wrote to her: "I thought it would have gratified you to have witnessed it, and have been a memory to our children."

Davis was a chosen spear of authority heading 11 states committed to him as against 23 states formally still in the Union with Lincoln, one side reckoned as having 9,000,000 people (including 3,900,000 slaves) as against 22,000,000 Northern people.

In the event of his death President Davis' place would be taken by a man who could himself have been President of the Confederate States by saying Yes to one condition. On the evening of February 8 delegates from six states came to Alexander Hamilton Stephens' room, their spokesman Robert Toombs, ever a warm personal friend of Stephens no matter how they disputed over politics.

"Aleck," said Toombs, "you are the choice of every man in Congress, and all of us are ready to pledge to help you form your Cabinet. There is only one point—those fellows from Virginia and the Border States want you to promise to strike the first blow. Those fellows say their States are hanging in the balance, ready to turn with the first blow. They know Buchanan will never dare to strike. They believe Lincoln will be as cowardly. Now they want the question settled in their States, and they want you, when the first opportunity offers—say, if the administration should attempt to re-enforce or provision Fort Sumter—to strike the first blow."

The massive and bulking Toombs had spoken his portentous message to the little frail Stephens. And there was silence. The shrunken and dwarfish figure sat composed, in his slow-burning hazel eyes a touch of clairvoyance and communion. Then slowly and distinctly, "No, I will never strike the first blow." Toombs roared, "Aleck!" and with a long look into the unflinching eyes of Stephens turned on his heel and with the other men strode from the room to where nightlong caucuses were picking another man for President.

"He had the look of being born out of season," said a woman of this

Aleck Stephens, who had fought the Know-Nothings and the anti-Catholic movements of Georgia with an unequivocal hostility, under warnings that he was wrecking the Whig party; who had thrice challenged tall heavy men to duels and had the reply in substance, "Pick some man your size."

Stephens wanted retirement, peace, poetry, philosophy, time for friendly talks, time at his home in Liberty Hall to bathe the sore eyes of his old blind dog Rio. Yet Toombs and the others made him Vice-President of the Confederacy. He understood the North and its Lincoln, once writing of old friendships in Congress, "I was as intimate with Mr. Lincoln as with any other man except perhaps Mr. Toombs."

CHAPTER 21

Turmoil—Fear—Hazards

THE LINCOLN administration hammered away at shaping a new and huge war establishment. On May 3 the President issued a proclamation calling into service 42,034 three-year volunteers, 22,714 enlisted men to add ten regiments to the regular U.S. Army, 18,000 seamen for blockade service—bringing the total of the Army to 156,861 and the Navy to 25,000. Day and night the President and other anxious officers worked on grand strategy and petty details.

From the windows of the White House Lincoln's spyglass caught the Confederate flag flying over the town of Alexandria eight miles down the Potomac River, where several heavy guns and 500 troops had been forwarded from Richmond.

After May '61, the U.S. mail service no longer ran into the seceded states. In this month too the Confederate Congress authorized all persons owing debts in the United States (except in Delaware, Maryland, Kentucky, Missouri and the District of Columbia) to pay the amount of those debts into the Confederate Treasury. According to R. G. Dun & Company, the South owed Northern merchants about $211,000,000, of which $169,000,000 was due in New York City.

By May 9 some 20,000 troops were in Washington. They included Colonel Elmer E. Ellsworth and the regiment of Fire Zouaves he had recruited in ten days from New York City fire-department men. New Yorkers had raised a fund of $60,000 for uniforms and arms. Ten different patterns of rifles were carried by Ellsworth's red-trousered ranks.

In bright moonlight on May 24 at two o'clock in the morning, squads of cavalry crossed the bridges leading from Washington across the Potomac into Virginia, and were followed by infantry and by engineers, who began crowning every hill for miles with defense trenches for the protection of the ten-mile-square District of Columbia surrounded by Slave States.

While a Michigan regiment marched toward the rear of Alexandria, Colonel Ellsworth's Fire Zouaves were to sail on transports down to that town of 10,000 and capture it. A Union sloop of war had preceded the transports and under a flag of truce had sent a message giving the Confederate troops one hour to leave town. Ellsworth was told the Confederate force of 500 had agreed to evacuate and, with a few straggling picket shots, they had done so.

Ellsworth started for the telegraph office to stop communication southward, taking a squad with him. They came to the Marshall House, a secondclass hotel, flying at the top of its flagpole the secession flag. Ellsworth threw open the front door and walked in to ask a barefoot man in shirt and trousers what sort of flag was over the roof. The man said he was only a boarder and knew nothing of it. Ellsworth sprang up the stairs, followed by his friends, to the third story, where with a ladder he mounted to the roof and cut down the secession flag.

Then, as the New York *Tribune* man told it: "We turned to descend, Corporal Brownell leading the way, and Ellsworth immediately following with the flag. As Brownell reached the first landing-place, after a descent of some dozen steps, a man jumped from a dark passage, and hardly noticing Brownell, leveled a double-barrelled gun square at the Colonel's breast. Brownell made a quick pass to turn the weapon aside, but the fellow's hand was firm, and he discharged one barrel straight to its aim, the slugs or buckshot entering the Colonel's heart, and killing him at the instant. I think my arm was resting on poor Ellsworth's shoulder at the moment; at any rate, he seemed to fall almost from my grasp. He was on the second or third step from the landing, and he dropped forward with that headlong weight which comes of sudden death." Brownell sent his own rifle slug into the face of Ellsworth's killer, "and before the man dropped, he thrust his saber-bayonet through and through the body."

Ellsworth's body was laid on a bed in a room nearby, the secession flag wrapped about his feet. The *Tribune* man left to make sure of the seizure of the telegraph office. "When I returned to the hotel, there was a terrible scene enacting. A woman had run from a lower room to the stairway where the body of the assassin lay, and cried aloud with an agony so heart-rending that no person could witness it without emotion. She flung her arms in the air, struck her brow madly, offered no reproaches, appeared almost regardless of our presence, and yielded only to her own frantic despair. It was her husband that had been shot—James W. Jackson, proprietor of the hotel"—the partly-dressed man who had told Ellsworth, "I am only a boarder here."

The body of Ellsworth arrived in Washington and was placed in a navy yard building. The tolling of bells went on, the flags of public buildings at half-mast. In the White House a New York *Herald* man, with Senator Wilson of Massachusetts, saw the President standing at a window looking out across the Potomac: "He did not move until we approached very closely, when he turned round abruptly, and advanced toward us, extending his hand: 'Excuse me, but I cannot talk.' . . . to our surprise the President burst into tears, and concealed his face in his handkerchief . . . 'I will make no apology, gentlemen,' said he, 'for my weakness; but I knew poor Ellsworth well and held him in high regard. Just as you entered the room, Captain Fox left me, after giving me the painful details of his unfortunate death.' "

Mrs. Lincoln visited the navy yard in the afternoon, left flowers, and talked with Corporal Brownell. An hour later, the embalming completed, she came again with the President, and they looked on the still face of Ellsworth, Lincoln moaning: "My boy! my boy! Was it necessary this sacrifice should be made?" Lincoln invited the Zouave guards to take the body to the White House for the funeral services.

They brought the body into the East Room, where Ellsworth lay in state and was viewed by thousands, had escorts with muffled drums and reversed arms. Then home at last to Mechanicsville, New York, for burial, arriving in a gale of wind and wild rain. Addressing a letter "To the Father and Mother of Col. Elmer E. Ellsworth," the President wrote: "In the untimely loss of your noble son, our affliction here, is scarcely less than your own . . . May God give you that consolation which is beyond all earthly power."

So Ellsworth became a legend identified with patriotic valor, the image of youth moving to drums and banners for the sake of emblems and a sacred, mystic cause.

In the Chicago Wigwam, Stephen A. Douglas had told an immense audience, "Before God it is the duty of every American citizen to rally around the flag of his country," and then gone home, to die. At his Oakenwald estate, overlooking Lake Michigan, in hearing of the Illinois Central locomotives, in a place that had always rested him, he argued stubbornly against the final adversary. Once in a delirium he called, "Telegraph to the President and let the column move on." The afternoon of June 3 his wife, holding his hand, asked if he had any last word for his boys and he answered, "Tell them to obey the laws and support the Constitution of the United States." These were telegraphed and generally recorded as his last words, though Chicago and New York newspaper accounts agreed in substance with that of the New York *Herald:* "When a few moments before his death, his wife leaned lovingly over him and sobbingly asked, 'Husband, do you know me? Will you kiss me?' he raised his eyes and smiled, and though too weak to speak, the movements of the muscles of his mouth evinced that he was making an almost dying struggle to comply with her request. His death was calm and peaceful; a few faint breaths after 9 o'clock; a slight rattling of his throat; a short, quick convulsive shudder, and Stephen A. Douglas passed into eternity."

His 48 years of life had taken his short, massive body through enough spectacular tumults, quarrels and dramas to fill a life of many more years. Northern Democrats mourned the lost giant of their party, while Republicans paid tribute to a leader who in a crisis had hushed mutiny among his followers.

Roll call of the Todd family of Lexington, Kentucky, found Mary Todd Lincoln's eldest brother Levi, and her half-sister Margaret Kellogg for the Union, while her youngest brother George and her three half-brothers Samuel, David and Alexander had joined the Confederate Army, and her half-sisters Emilie Helm, Martha White and Elodie Dawson were the wives of Confederate officers.

To the White House on Lincoln's invitation had come Ben Hardin Helm, West Pointer, son of a former governor of Kentucky, a Democrat, and the husband of Mary Todd Lincoln's "Little Sister" Emilie. During those few days the White House guest talked with old West Point comrades, some of them resigned and packing to go South. He was still undecided when as he left the White House Lincoln handed him an envelope holding a major's commission in the U.S. Army, saying: "Ben, here is something for you. Think it over for yourself and let me know what you will do." Mary Lincoln gave him a kiss to carry to Emilie and said, "Good-by, we hope to see you both very soon in Washington." After a long handclasp with Lincoln, Helm walked slowly down the stairs and out the door and was gone. Days passed and word came that he would wear the Confederate gray.

The fierce old Kentucky preacher and Union man, Robert Jefferson Breckinridge, could not get personal with his opposition. It included two of his own sons who were going into Confederate gray, one of them organizing a company for service under the Stars and Bars, and such kinsmen as his nephew John C. Breckinridge, and such illustrious Kentuckians as James B. Clay, the son of Henry Clay. Of his three sons only one was choosing the Stars and Stripes to fight under.

The Kentucky Legislature, after almost continuous session since January '61, adjourned sine die, proclaiming neutrality but still in the Union, and slowly drifting away from her sister Slave States to the south, who occasionally taunted Kentucky with "hesitation and cowardice." Joshua Speed and his brother James at Louisville had been allies of Dr. Breckinridge. Commissioned a brigadier general by Lincoln, Robert Anderson, who had said at Fort Sumter that if Kentucky seceded he would go to Europe, had set up headquarters in Cincinnati and given his best efforts to keep Kentucky in the Union. A naval lieutenant, William Nelson of Kentucky, had asked Lincoln to send him to his native state to stop secession. Nelson and others had distributed 10,000 rifles among Union men and Union military organizations. By stealth in the nighttime many a homeguard Unionist took to his arms his "Lincoln rifle" for use in emergency. Across the Ohio River on Ohio soil recruiting camps were set up, and some Ohio regiments had a fourth of their enrolled men from Kentucky. In the June balloting for members of the Congress Lincoln had called to meet July 4, Kentucky elected antisecessionists in nine out of the ten districts, the Union majority in the state being 54,700.

At the Baltimore election of April 24, 1861, only one ticket had been in the field, "States' Rights." Of 30,000 voters in the city, only 9,244 went to the polls and they all voted for secessionist members of the Maryland Legislature, which was to assemble two days later.

What with Union regiments increasing daily at Annapolis, Governor Hicks could have pleased the secessionist element by calling the legislature to Baltimore. Instead he convened it at the town of Frederick, a Unionist community but without Union troops. Such decisions favoring the Unionists came regularly from Governor Hicks. His message to the legislature reported his personal interviews with the President and the Cabinet, and the President's insistence that while he wished to avoid collisions through bringing troops across Maryland, military necessity required that such troops be brought to the defense of the national capital.

Slowly it became clear that the strength of secession in Maryland lay chiefly in a furiously active minority in Baltimore. William Rollinson Whittingham, Episcopal bishop of Maryland, was not of this minority. He rebuked clergymen who omitted the prayer for the President of the United States, and admonished them that the offense must not continue. A commission appointed by the Maryland Legislature reported May 6 that they had been courteously received by the President at Washington. They had differed as to fact, but on the general principle at issue, said the report, "The President concurred in the opinion that so long as Maryland had not taken, and was not taking, a hostile attitude toward the Federal Government, that the exclusive military occupation of her ways of communications, and the seizure of the property of her citizens, would be without justification."

Day by day the boiling point in Maryland receded as it became more evident that secession would result in devastating trade losses to Baltimore. Charleston at her distance could more easily be defiant. The days passed till 10, 20, 30 regiments had crossed Maryland to Washington. A military department under Brigadier General Benjamin F. Butler was set up at Annapolis.

In rain, darkness and thunder Butler moved 1,000 troops to Baltimore May 13, stacked arms on Federal Hill overlooking Baltimore, issued a proclamation that they were there to enforce respect and obedience to the laws of the United States. The North cheered Butler. He was continuing in the national scene his Massachusetts record for ingenuity and expedients, for sheer nerve and audacity, for the calculated exhibitions of a careerist, for the chameleon shifts of a wily criminal lawyer suspected by his own clients of a shaded and always partly defensible treachery. Heavy of body, with a well-rounded paunch, bald, sleepy-eyed with cunning, a cast in one eye, he was at every moment an actor with ready answers fitting his favorite combined role of the Man of the People and the Man Who Knows How. His militia troops in Massachusetts had elected him colonel, then brigadier general. To Carl Schurz passing through Annapolis, the chunky-shaped Butler was a little grotesque, was most evidently enjoying his power, and "keenly appreciating its theatrical possibilities."

As between two lawyers, Butler had told Lincoln that the order for him to leave with his brigade for Washington arrived when he was trying a case before a jury. He had quit his argument to the jury and got his case continued. It woke Lincoln to muse slowly, "I guess we both wish we were back trying cases."

Butler when removed from Maryland and put in charge of Fortress Monroe in Virginia protested personally to Lincoln; the treatment of him implied reproaches. The President, according to Butler's report, said very kindly and courteously, "The administration has done everything to remove every thought of reproach upon you."

They shook hands and Butler left to spread word that they were "the warmest personal friends." Not yet had Butler discredited himself. His performances in Maryland had heartened the North, and he was on form worth the high commission Lincoln handed him. Yet he was basically an actor, a political general, and a military politician, so that eventually when John Hay should say to Lincoln he believed Butler was the only man in the Army to whom power would be dangerous, Lincoln would reply: "Yes, he is like Jim Jett's brother. Jim used to say that his brother was the damndest scoundrel that ever lived, but in the infinite mercy of Providence he was also the damndest fool."

The Butler gift for expedients rang across the country again when in May fugitive slaves flocked by hundreds into his camp. The legal question Butler disposed of by his decision, "The negro must now be regarded as *contraband*" (like smuggled goods or anything forbidden to be supplied by neutrals to belligerents). The country picked up this word "contraband" as often untying knots of the Fugitive Slave Law. Many a runaway slave, after starving in timber and swamp, arrived in the Union lines to say with jubilation, "I'se contraband."

The next flare-up in Maryland ended with the Chief Justice of the U.S. Supreme Court tangled in dispute with the President. General George Cadwalader, in command of Fort McHenry near Baltimore, sent a squad of soldiers who at two o'clock the morning of May 25 roused one John Merryman from bed in his home at Hayfields and took him to Fort McHenry and locked him up "in close custody." Lawyers for Merryman appeared the same day before Roger B. Taney, who made his home in Baltimore. They denied that Merryman was guilty of reported charges of treason, prayed for a writ of habeas corpus. Chief Justice Taney issued the writ and commanded that General Cadwalader appear before him "and that you have with you the body of John Merryman."

General Cadwalader's response to Taney was brought by a staff member, Colonel Lee, who explained that the General was busy with pressing matters and then read a statement from the General that the aforesaid John Merryman was charged with treason, was publicly known to be holding a commission as lieutenant in a company having in their possession arms belonging to the United States, and avowing his purpose of armed hostility against the Government. "He has further to inform you that he is duly authorized by the President of the United States in such cases to suspend the writ of *habeas corpus* for public safety." After various proceedings neither Merryman nor Cadwalader appeared in court as ordered by Taney. The Chief Justice transmitted to the President a long written opinion on the ancient Anglo-Saxon custom of issuing writs of habeas corpus, with reminders and admonitions that the Executive himself should not violate law.

Police Marshal George P. Kane, whose methods clearly allied him with the Confederacy, was arrested at dawn June 27 and locked up at Fort McHenry. Four police commissioners, who were avowed secessionists, met and protested this action, and disbanded the city police force. So on July 1 the four police commissioners were also arrested and locked up in Fort McHenry. The secessionist trend in Maryland was definitely checked in June, when railroad schedules were re-established, Unionists were elected to Congress in the six districts of Maryland, and Governor Hicks was having no difficulty enlisting four regiments of men to serve within the limits of Maryland or for the defense of the national capital.

Lincoln's reply to Chief Justice Taney was given to the country in a message to Congress on July 4:

Soon after the first call for militia, it was considered a duty to authorize the Commanding General, in proper cases, according to his discretion, to suspend the privilege of the writ of habeas corpus; or, in other words, to arrest, and detain, without resort to the ordinary processes and forms of law, such individuals as he might deem dangerous to the public safety . . . Of course some consideration was given to the questions of power, and propriety, before this matter was acted upon . . . Are all the laws, *but one*, to go unexecuted, and the government itself go to pieces, lest that one be violated? Even in such a case, would not the official oath be broken, if the government should be overthrown . . . It was not believed that any law was violated . . . It was decided that we have a case of rebellion . . . Now it is insisted that Congress, and not the Executive, is vested with this power. But the Constitution itself, is silent as to which, or who, is to exercise the power . . .

Seward was still playing lingeringly with his old idea that a war with Great Britain might bring the Southern forces behind the old American flag in a solid Union. He believed nothing was to be lost by using a menacing tone to the British Government. His good friend in London, Minister Adams, took his reckless threats and turned them into well-measured reproaches and courteous arguments. Adams was English-blooded and had instincts that were at home in London, one saying his face could "outfreeze" that of any English gentleman with whom he had to dicker.

Queen Victoria's proclamation of May 13, 1861, took notice of hostilities "between the government of the United States of America and certain States styling themselves the Confederate States of America" and declared the "royal determination to maintain a strict and impartial neutrality in the contest between said contending parties." The Queen and her consort, Prince Albert, the political liberals and the masses of the English people leaned to the North in sympathy, while Prime Minister Palmerston and the officials and imperialistic cliques voiced by the London *Times* favored the South and in various technical rulings deviated far from strict neutrality. To the New York Rothschild agent, August Belmont, Palmerston said, "We do not like slavery, but we want cotton, and we dislike very much your Morrill tariff." A queer obstacle, not easily defined yet definitely operating, known as British Public Opinion, was about all that stopped Palmerston from giving complete recognition to the Southern Confederacy and lending it the British fleet.

To Carl Schurz departing for Spain Lincoln spoke about foreign affairs "with the same nonchalance with which he might have discussed an everyday law case at Springfield, Illinois." He told Schurz that if the administration had so far "stumbled along," as was said, it had, on the whole, "stumbled along in the right direction."

When the captain and crew of the privateer *Jefferson Davis* were convicted in Philadelphia of piracy, the decision was finally put up to Lincoln whether they should hang as pirates, in which event an equal number of Federal officers in Southern prisons, chosen by lot, would likewise be hanged, announced the Confederate Secretary of War. And Davis went so far as to name the 13 Union officers, selected by drawing of numbers, who would go to the gallows. Lincoln refused to begin a competition in hanging.

The President and the Cabinet through the new and often bungling personnels of their old departments were wrestling with crazy patterns of mili-

tary organization, red tape, confusions of counsels, inpouring brigades, telegrams exchanged daily or hourly with governors recruiting troops, the direction of four grades of troops: (1) regulars; (2) three-month volunteers; (3)
state militia; (4) three-year volunteers; besides independent troop units in
Border States still neutral.

In the furious, complex and driving labors of shaping effective armies for
grand strategic campaigns, General Scott was slow and fussy, his dropsy and
vertigo pathetic afflictions of an aged hero. In many cases Lincoln and Secretary Cameron went directly over Scott's head and ordered action on political grounds, if not military.

The new consul to Paris, John Bigelow, heard a conversation between
Lincoln and a Senator on army and field operations. "I observed no sign of
weakness in anything the President said," noted Bigelow. "What did impress
me, however, was what I can only describe as a *certain lack* of *sovereignty*.
He seemed to me, nor was it in the least strange that he did, like a man
utterly unconscious of the space which the President of the United States
occupied that day in the history of the human race . . . This impression was
strengthened by Mr. Lincoln's . . . frequent avowals of ignorance, which,
even where it exists, it is as well for a captain as far as possible to conceal
from the public."

In commissioning major generals of volunteers the President seemed to rest
chiefly on the judgment of Scott, who favored John E. Wool, John A. Dix,
Henry W. Halleck, Don Carlos Buell. The appointment of John C. Frémont
as a major general was mainly political, as were the appointments of Benjamin F. Butler and Nathaniel P. Banks. David Hunter, Edwin V. Sumner
and John Pope, who had accompanied Lincoln from Springfield to Harrisburg, were commissioned as brigadiers. Among the May and June appointees
as brigadiers nearly all had West Point training and Mexican War service
records.

William Tecumseh Sherman came again to the White House and left with
a colonel's commission. Sherman had amazed the President and given him a
healthy laugh by refusing a brigadier's commission and saying he would
rather work up from colonel. Sherman sent the St. Louis horsecar street rail-
ways a word of good-by as superintendent; he would do his best for the
war, though he was storm-tossed and haunted with impressions that men
North and South were blind and crazy, that greedy politicians had too large
a sway at Washington, and the war would end in a hundred years rather
than the hundred days many people were predicting. Another West Pointer,
Joseph E. Johnston of Virginia, of much the same feeling, in grief and tears
had just resigned as quartermaster general of the U.S. Army to go into Confederate gray.

Sherman had said to Lincoln, "Why don't you nominate Thomas?" meaning George H. Thomas, a Virginian and a West Pointer of long army experience. Lincoln replied that Thomas was born in Virginia and there were
doubts as to his loyalty. Sherman protested, "Mr. President, Old Tom is as
loyal as I am, and as a soldier he is superior to all on your list." Lincoln inquired, "Will you be responsible for him?" Sherman snapped, "With the
greatest pleasure." And Lincoln sent the nomination of Thomas as brigadier
general to the Senate that day.

Of a total of 1,108 U.S. Army officers, 387 had resigned to go South. These resigned Southerners, 288 of them West Point-trained, included promising officers, of actual field and battle service. Among West Pointers in Northern service were 162 born in Slave States. Among West Pointers gone South for service were 19 Northern-born men. Lincoln was writing in a message to Congress: "It is worthy of note, that while in this, the government's hour of trial, large numbers of those in the Army and Navy, who have been favored with the offices, have resigned, and proved false to the hand which had pampered them, not one common soldier, or common sailor is known to have deserted his flag. Great honor is due to those officers who remain true . . ."

In May and June '61 Lincoln was stressing popular government and maintenance of the Union above all issues. If the slavery issue was to come up front it would be through force of circumstances, through "yielding to partial and temporary departures, from necessity." This necessity had begun to work the moment the secession movement gained headway. It thrust the slavery issue forward for discussion and required that the millions of Negroes in the South be considered as a war factor, to be used by one side or both.

The South had a secret the North knew little of; the South had many doubts about slavery. Over the South not yet did they dare speak this secret. As to white-race superiority the South had no doubts. While it defended black-race slavery as a living institution, the South was not sure but that the institution was dying of some inherent malady.

Up in Maine the little woman who had written *Uncle Tom's Cabin* received in the mail one day a pair of Negro ears sent by someone who loathed her race-equality ideas.

In his message to Congress Lincoln was writing no line or word dealing with any phase of the Negro and slavery. The President kept an official loyalty to the Fugitive Slave Act. It seemed that fugitive slaves from Virginia, owned by secessionist Virginians, who fled into Butler's camp at Fortress Monroe were easily held as "contraband," having no intercessors for their owners at Washington. But Maryland slaves who drifted into District of Columbia and Virginia camps of the Union Army were immediately and hotly spoken for by Maryland Unionist members of Congress, sometimes for slaveowners who could not be shown as disloyal. So Lincoln began slowly evolving a policy of letting commanders and localities develop their own method of treating fugitive slaves, military necessity always to govern the method.

On July 6, 1861, Secretary of War Cameron notified Lincoln that 64 volunteer regiments of 900 men each, besides 1,200 Regulars, were in readiness around Washington, and the troops enrolled elsewhere over the North made a total of 225,000. Of this army, one of the largest the earth had ever seen, Lincoln was Commander in Chief. And he wrote his high pride of these volunteers in his message to Congress, for the world to know: "So large an army as the government has now on foot, was never before known, without a soldier in it, but who has taken his place there, of his own free choice. But more than this: there are many single Regiments whose members, one and another, possess full practical knowledge of all the arts, sciences, professions, and whatever else, whether useful or elegant, is known in the world . . ."

Pierre Gustave Toutant Beauregard, superintendent of the West Point

Military Academy before he resigned the previous winter, a Mexican War veteran, was now commanding an army of 20,000 Confederate troops near Washington at Manassas Junction. As the hero who had shot away the flag at Fort Sumter, he was called to Virginia to check Northern invasion. He began June 1 with a proclamation: "A reckless and unprincipled tyrant has invaded your soil. Abraham Lincoln, regardless of all moral, legal, and constitutional restraints, has thrown his Abolition hosts among you . . . All rules of civilized warfare are abandoned . . . Your honor and that of your wives and daughters, your fortunes, and your lives are involved in this momentous contest."

On July 4 when Congress assembled it was in the air that soon a battle would be fought near Washington. Greeley's *Tribune* clamored in headlines: "Forward to Richmond! Forward to Richmond! The Rebel Congress must not be allowed to meet there on the 20th of July! By that date the place must be held by the National Army!"

Business was worse, money scarce, loans slow. A short war was wanted. Everybody agreed on that. The time was already up for some three-month troops; the 4th Pennsylvania Volunteers and the 8th New York Artillery were calling for their discharges.

In his message to Congress the President gave a miniature history of the Fort Sumter affair, of how the fort was bombarded to its fall "without even awaiting the arrival of the provisioning expedition." It forced the questions: "Is there, in all republics, this inherent, and fatal weakness? . . . Must a government, of necessity, be too *strong* for the liberties of its own people, or too *weak* to maintain its own existence?" No choice was left but "to call out the war power of the Government." Applause swept the House at the recommendation "that you give the legal means for making this contest a short and decisive one" and for the work at least 400,000 men and $400,000,000.

The President then queried whether the Southern movement should be called "secession" or "rebellion," saying that the instigators of the movement understood the difference. "They knew they could make no advancement directly in the teeth of these strong and noble sentiments [of their people]. Accordingly they commenced by *an insidious debauching of the public mind*. [Italics added.] They invented an ingenious sophism . . . that any state of the Union may, *consistently* with the national Constitution, and therefore *lawfully*, and *peacefully*, withdraw from the Union, without the consent of the Union, or of any other state. The little disguise that the supposed right is to be exercised only for just cause, themselves to be the sole judges of its justice, is too thin to merit any notice. With rebellion thus *sugar-coated*, they have been *drugging the public mind* [italics added] of their section for more than thirty years; and, until at length, they have brought many good men to a willingness to take up arms against the government the day *after* some assemblage of men have enacted the farcical pretense of taking their State out of the Union, who could have been brought to no such thing the day *before* . . . To be consistent they must secede from one another, whenever they shall find it the easiest way of settling their debts, or effecting any other selfish, or unjust object."

The message was a brief for a client, a letter to the American people. The Northern press gave it greater approval than any utterance hitherto from

Lincoln. The editor of *Harper's Weekly*, George William Curtis, vented his enthusiasm in a letter: "I envy no other age. I believe with all my heart in the cause, and in Abe Lincoln. His message is the most truly American message ever delivered . . . Wonderfully acute, simple, sagacious, and of antique honesty! I can forgive the jokes and the big hands, and the inability to make bows. Some of us who doubted were wrong. This people is not rotten. What the young men dream, the old men shall see."

The Senate confirmed the President's appointments. A new army bill gave the President more than he asked, authorizing 500,000 three-year volunteers. A joint resolution to make legal and valid the extralegal, dictatorial and proscriptive acts of the President in the emergencies since his proclamation of war in April met little direct opposition, but was held up and laid away amid unfinished business from day to day. He had gone out of his way to do so many things without the required authority from Congress. Now Congress politely refused to sanction all he had done. Some of the murmuring took the form that he should have called Congress earlier and day by day asked its Yes or No.

Senator Baker of Oregon rang out: "I want sudden, bold, forward determined war; and I do not think anybody can conduct war of that kind as well as a Dictator."

CHAPTER 22

Bull Run—McClellan—Frémont—
The Trent Affair

T HE PRESIDENT on June 29 had called a Cabinet meeting before which General Irvin McDowell laid his plans. His army of 30,000 was to fight the 21,900 Confederates at Manassas under General Beauregard. Another Confederate army over in the Shenandoah Valley was to be held by a Union army under General Robert Patterson, also in the valley, and stopped from joining Beauregard. General Scott approved McDowell's battle plan but favored waiting till a larger army, better trained and prepared, could win victories that would be destructive.

Lincoln and his Cabinet, as political authorities yielding to the demand of the country for fighting, and considering that the time of the three-month troops was almost run out, overruled Scott. On McDowell's asking for more time to drill and discipline his troops, Lincoln remarked, "You are green, it is true, but they are green also."

The Battle of Bull Run, Sunday, July 21, 1861, was to a large and eager public a sort of sporting event, the day and place of combat announced beforehand, a crowd of spectators riding to the scene with lunch baskets as though for a picnic. On horseback, in buggies and gigs, Senators Trumbull,

Wade, Chandler, Grimes, Wilson, McDougall, besides Congressmen with emergency navy revolvers and pretty ladies in crinoline gowns, rode out to gaze on a modern battle. The word was that the Northern Shovelry would make Southern Chivalry bite the dust.

Lincoln went as usual that Sunday morning to the New York Avenue Presbyterian Church. During the afternoon he read telegrams from the battlefield, one every 10 or 15 minutes. A messenger from Scott arrived. All seemed favorable. The President went for a drive in his carriage, as usual of evenings. At six o'clock came Seward, pale, worn, hoarse, asking Nicolay and Hay, "Where is the President?" He had gone to drive, they told Seward, showing telegrams indicating victory. "Tell no one," came the words from Seward. "That is not true. The battle is lost." He had news that McDowell's army was retreating and calls were coming for General Scott to save Washington.

The President returned a half-hour later. Nicolay and Hay told him the news. "He listened in silence, without the slightest change of feature or expression, and walked away to army headquarters." There a dispatch from a captain of engineers read: "The day is lost. Save Washington and the remnants of this army. The routed troops will not re-form." General Scott refused to believe it. The Cabinet was called. Now came a telegram from McDowell. His army had gone to pieces, and was "a confused mob."

That night Lincoln lay on a lounge in the Cabinet room and heard eye-witnesses tell what they had seen from saddle, buggy or gig on the 20-mile ride from the battlefield. Strewn along roadways for miles were hats, coats, blankets, haversacks, canteens, rifles, broken harness, wagons upside down—the evidence of thousands of soldiers in panic and retreat to Washington.

At three that afternoon McDowell thought he had the battle won. An hour later his army was going to pieces. Yet back of the enemy lines there was panic; and as Jefferson Davis came from Richmond toward the battle lines, he saw many runaways and asked an old man how the battle had gone. "Our line was broken," was the answer. "All was confusion, the army routed and the battle lost."

McDowell's staff man, James B. Fry, recorded 16 officers and 444 men killed, 78 officers and 1,046 men wounded, 50 officers and 1,262 men missing, not including Congressman Alfred Ely of New York captured and sent to Libby Prison in Richmond. General Johnston officially reported Confederate losses at 378 killed, 1,489 wounded, and 30 missing.

After the hot, sweltering Sunday of the battle came a Monday of drizzling rain. Across Long Bridge over the Potomac, from daylight on, came lines of bedraggled men. Hour by hour these silhouettes of defeat trod the bridge to the capital. Thousands were taken into homes and fed.

Congress, the press, the pulpit, politicians, talkers, began fixing the blame. The regulars were to blame for driving their caissons at top speed through the regimental ranks when heading to the rear for ammunition. The three-month troops were to blame; two of their regiments, claiming their time of service was over, marched off the field as the cannons began to sing. The shoulder-straps, political brigadiers, colonels, majors, were only tin soldiers good for sham battles; at four o'clock, as the rout was developing, more than 12,000 volunteers had lost their regimental organization. The Senators, Congressmen, politicians, correspondents, civilians, hack drivers, ladies in crinoline, who had come to see the show, ran like sheep first of all and started the stampede. Thus ran talk, alibis, explanations.

But more than any other General Robert Patterson was blamed; if he had smashed at Johnston's army in the Shenandoah Valley, then Johnston's fresh regiments wouldn't have marched in and started the panic. To Lincoln he read orders, telegrams, letters, which he believed cleared him of failure. He must have a trial by his peers in order to stop the daily abuse laid on him. "The President replied that he would cheerfully accede to any practicable measure to do me justice, but that I need not expect to escape abuse as long as I was of any importance or value to the community, adding that he received infinitely more abuse than I did, but he had ceased to regard it, and I must learn to do the same."

"As for blame and causes," wrote George William Curtis in a private letter, "they are in our condition and character. We have undertaken to make war without in the least knowing how." And from this public calamity Curtis turned to the private grief of Henry Wadsworth Longfellow's wife burned to death in the tragic swift blazing of a crinoline gown.

In a letter to Lincoln from Greeley in New York, the foremost American editor was ready for an armistice, a national convention, peace, disbandment of forces. "The gloom in this city is funereal—for our dead at Bull Run were many, and they lie unburied yet. On every brow sits sullen, scorching, black despair." He would support any compromise Lincoln believed right. He closed, "Yours, in the depths of bitterness." Lincoln made no reply. To Hay later he spoke of the letter as "pusillanimous." Greeley, having helped bring on the tornado, was terrified at its first chaotic howlings.

Probing, analyzing, approving of Lincoln but more often scolding, were Horace Greeley and his newspaper. Among the 50,000 subscribers of the New York *Tribune* were nearly all the editors and news writers of America. Greeley had arrived in New York 20 years old, with $10 in his pocket, a greenhorn from Vermont farms who had picked up the trade of printer. He edited the *New Yorker*, the *Jeffersonian*, the *Log Cabin*, and in 1841 started his penny morning paper, the New York *Tribune*, which for 21 years was at the forefront reporting, if not advocating, every reform, radical idea and "ism" that came to view. "I have been branded aristocrat, communist, infidel, hypocrite, demagogue, disunionist, traitor, corruptionist, and so forth and so forth," he once declared in urging a friend not to class him also a poet. A half-myth the country talked about, he was fair, pink-skinned, baby-faced, blue-eyed with a stare of innocence. His cherubic face rose out of an under-chin beard, the voice a high squeal. He shuffled rather than walked, wore his cravat in disorder, one pant leg stuffed in one boot. He owned a farm at Chappaqua, 33 miles from New York, and liked to call himself a farmer. "Go West, young man" was his repeated advice, and in the westward flow of settlers a famous slogan.

Once, making a denial, he declared: "I never said all Democrats were saloon-keepers. What I said was that all saloon-keepers were Democrats." His office door was open, and when a man came in and bawled at the *Tribune*'s sins and errors, Greeley quietly scratched away at his two daily columns. Once a caller had used up his profanity and vituperation and was leaving; Greeley squeaked, "Come back, my friend, come back and relieve your mind."

Beggars and borrowers knew he was easy. He classified them as casual, chronic, or systematic, and usually let them know he knew they were lying about paying back the loan. To one borrower who paid back $20 he said, "You are the first one that has disappointed me."

At 25 he married Mary Y. Cheney, a Connecticut schoolteacher whom he met at a vegetarian boardinghouse in New York. She was slight, girlish-looking, a brunette with long curls falling below her shoulders. Their first child was fair, with notable complexion and hair that fell as "a shower of ruddy gold" to his shoulders; he died at five in an Asiatic cholera plague that infected New York in 1848. Another boy died at six from croup. One girl died at six months of age. Two infants died at childbirth. Of the seven Greeley children two daughters were alive.

"I didn't raise my children for this world but for the next," said the mother. Her freezing manners and sharp words kept many from making a second visit to the Chappaqua farm. They spoke of Mrs. Greeley snatching manuscripts from her husband's hand and throwing them in the fire so that he took to hotels occasionally to finish his editorials. And they spoke of him as being patient and not answering back.

Thousands of "self-made men" echoed his saying, "Of all horned cattle the most helpless in a printing office is a college graduate." Junius Henri Browne, of many years' service under Greeley, noted him wayward, moody, undisciplined. "His friends could not be certain of him, for he could not be certain of himself. He was not only unlike other men—he was unlike himself often."

Greeley recalled having seen Lincoln at the White House about two weeks after inauguration. And he had felt that Lincoln was too bland, too easygoing. His moaning letter to Lincoln just after Bull Run beginning "This is my seventh sleepless night" reflected his fear that Lincoln was not losing enough sleep over the war.

Lincoln gave his personal attention to the camps around Washington, kept close to men and officers, mixed with them. He rode in an open hack with Seward one day across the Potomac. Colonel William Tecumseh Sherman at a roadside asked if they were going to his camp. "Yes," said Lincoln. "We heard that you had got over the big scare, and we thought we would come over and see the boys." He asked Sherman into the hack. At the camp, noted Sherman, "Mr. Lincoln stood up and made one of the neatest, best, and most feeling addresses I ever listened to, referring to our disaster, the high duties that still devolved on us, and the brighter days to come."

When Lincoln had finished a speech to the 79th New York regiment, with his usual appeal that they should present grievances to him, one Highlander stepped forward, "Mr. President, we don't think Colonel Sherman has treated us very well," and rehearsed their being driven out of a barn to make room for the Colonel's horses. "Well, boys," said the President, "I have a great deal of respect for Colonel Sherman and if he turned you out of the barn I have no doubt it was for some good purpose. I presume he thought you would feel better if you went to work and tried to forget your troubles."

At the camp of the 69th New York (Irish), who had fought with impetuous valor and whose Colonel Michael Corcoran was taken prisoner in the thick of the fighting, "Mr. Lincoln made to them the same feeling address," wrote Sherman, "with more personal allusions, because of their special gallantry in the battle under Corcoran." Lincoln again made his offer to hear willingly the grievance of any man. An officer stepped forward who that morning had tried to quit the service and leave camp, saying, "Mr. President, this morning I went to speak to Colonel Sherman, and he threatened to shoot me." Lincoln: "Threatened to shoot you?" "Yes, sir, he threatened to shoot me." Lincoln looked at the officer, looked at Sherman, and then, stooping toward the officer as if to give a confidential message, and speaking in a stage whisper that could be heard for yards around, "Well, if I were you, and he threatened to shoot, I would not trust him, for I believe he would do it." The officer turned and vanished. The men whooped.

On the night of Bull Run, noted his secretaries, Lincoln did not go to bed, stayed on the lounge in the Cabinet room all night. The next night, having heard more accounts of the lost battle, he lay on a sofa in his office and penciled an outline of what must be done, a program for immediate action.

On Friday, July 26, the President had a call from Henry C. Whitney, fresh from Illinois. Whitney suggested, "Everything is drifting into the army, and I guess you will have to put me in." Lincoln said in a day or two he would make Whitney a quartermaster. The afternoon wore on. Congress was in session. War and revolution surged. Conversation between the two old friends ran from early afternoon till near sunset. The President needed a short holiday and took it. He "didn't care a cornhusk," according to Whitney, for those "who think that a statesman, like a blind horse in a treadmill, needs no rest, or that, like the conventional whitewashed statue of justice, he must always *pose* for dignified effect."

The Senate resolution to approve the President's unconstitutional acts done without approval of Congress during the emergency weeks, when Congress was not in session and could not then approve, was introduced the third day of the session. It would declare legal and valid the President's first call for state militia troops, his proclamation of blockade and action therein, his call for three-year volunteers and his increase of the Regular Army and the Navy, and not least of all his suspension of the ancient Anglo-Saxon writ of habeas corpus.

For weeks this resolution lay amid unfinished business. On August 5, the day before Congress adjourned, a bill to increase army pay came up for action and to this was added a rider declaring "that all the acts, proclamations, and orders of the President" relating to the militia and volunteers "are hereby approved and in all respects legalized and made valid, to the same intent and with the same effect as if they had been issued and done under the previous express authority and direction of the Congress of the United States." By a vote of 37 to 5 it passed the Senate, and by 74 to 19 the House, the Nays being Border State votes, with help from Ohio and Indiana. Thus the President failed of full approval, was not yet by Congress whitewashed of guilt as a usurper in what he did with the Regular Army, with closing ports by blockade, and with the hoary and precious right of the writ of habeas corpus.

Senator Preston King of New York made clear that he approved "the vigorous measures" of the Executive, "but I have a disinclination to pass upon a question the whole length and breadth and extent of which I do not entirely comprehend." John Sherman of Ohio presented his opinion: "I do not believe the President of the United States has the power to suspend the writ of *habeas corpus*, because that power is expressly given to Congress, and to Congress alone. I do not believe the President of the United States has the power to increase the regular army, because that power is expressly given by the Constitution to Congress alone. Still I approve of the action of the President. I believe the President did right. He did precisely what I would have done if I had been in his place—no more, no less; but I cannot here, in my place, as a Senator, under oath, declare that what he did do was legal."

When Congress adjourned August 6, it had given the President nearly all the practical measures he needed to proceed with the war. He was more of an executive than most of them had expected.

To his wife John Lothrop Motley was writing: "A grim winter is before us. Gather you rosebuds while you may. The war is to be a long one." In the blouse of a dead Confederate soldier at Fairfax Court House was a letter from a girl begging him to watch his own "precious life" while remembering "kill a Yankee for me."

The Army of the Potomac grew into 168,000 in November from 50,000 on July 22, when Washington had received its new commander, General George Brinton McClellan. McClellan was appointed by Lincoln by reason of an overwhelming weight of public and private opinion. He looked the part, with a well-modeled head, mustache and goatee, sat his saddle as a trained Man on Horseback, issued commands with authority, published proclamations modeled on Napoleon. Washington adopted him, the Army took to him, correspondents nicknamed him "Little Mac" and "the Young Napoleon."

Only the year before, he had married Ellen Mary Marcy, the daughter of a Regular Army officer, to whom he was now writing, "Who would have thought, when we were married, that I should so soon be called upon to save my country?" He had left her and a $10,000-a-year job as president of the Ohio & Mississippi Railroad at Cincinnati. He had been chief engineer and then vice-president of the Illinois Central Railroad, entertained Douglas in his Chicago home, and the only ballot he had ever cast was for Douglas. His *Manual on the Art of War*, his translation of a French book on bayonet exercises, were reputable. Commanding an army of 18,000 in West Virginia, he had overcome about two-thirds that number, giving the North the only actions thus far having semblance of military victories.

Not quite 35 now, he had entered West Point when only 15 years and seven months old; the regulation as to age was suspended in his case because of his superior health and physique and high standing in mental examinations; he had graduated second in a class of 59.

He was riding 12 hours a day and toiling till three in the morning organizing his army. On August 8, however, he wished his wife to know he had been "pestered to death with senators, etc." and had "a row with General Scott," and later, "I have scarcely slept one moment for the last three nights, knowing well that the enemy intend some movement."

One daily bulletin home read: "On Sunday, instead of going to church, was sent for by the President immediately after breakfast, and kept busy until midnight, when I returned from a long ride too tired to talk even. Yesterday in the saddle from ten to five, and then persecuted until after midnight. Today the President sent for me before I was up; have been at work ever since, and soon start out to receive a brigade and some batteries." When he had an army twice the size of the enemy camped near Manassas, he wrote his wife that he was sleeping with one eye open at night "looking out sharply for Beauregard, who, I think, has some notion of making a dash in this direction."

An illusion that the enemy outnumbered him kept growing. Day by day in personal interviews, in notes and letters, he called on the President, on Scott and others, for more and more men. "I am here in a terrible place; the enemy have from three to four times my force," he wrote his wife August 16, adding a few days later, "I do not *live* at all; merely exist, worked and worried half to death."

One day in late September when hazy gray folded the blue hills, and slashes of yellow and scarlet stood out on woodlands, McClellan rode with the President, the Secretary of War and Governor Curtin to a ceremonial of presenting flags to 15 Pennsylvania regiments. At a luncheon afterward McClellan invited the party to ride around his army and have a look at it. At one point they halted to view a Confederate flag on Munson's Hill, when McClellan "somewhat disturbed the equanimity of most of the party by saying we were just at that time outside of the Union lines." McClure noted Lincoln on a horse, "legs halfway between the under part of the girth and the ground, his long arms could have guided his horse by the ears," while the high silk hat somehow didn't belong. They drew rein before regiments that lifted genuine cheers for McClellan. Lincoln was impressed.

In November General Winfield Scott was retired on pay, with honors, and with tributes from the President and others. McClellan was now commissioned General in Chief, and at the White House Lincoln said to him, "I should be perfectly satisfied if I thought this vast increase of responsibility would not embarrass you." "It is a great relief, Sir!" said McClellan. "I feel as if several tons were taken from my shoulders today. I am now in contact with you, and the Secretary. I am not embarrassed by intervention." "Well," said Lincoln, as John Hay heard him, "draw on me for all the sense I have, and all the information. In addition to your present command, the supreme command of the army will entail a vast labor upon you." "I can do it all," McClellan said quietly.

When Lincoln had suggestions for McClellan which he did not care to put in writing, he took another course. He dated and signed a card September 30, 1861, reading, "Will Gen. McClellan please see Pay-Master Whitney a moment?" Whitney saw this as "an old habit Mr. Lincoln had of sending a verbal message on any subject he did not wish to put down in writing. He frequently sent verbal messages by those he could trust."

One night as they parted at McClellan's house the General said to Lincoln: "I intend to be careful and do as well as possible. Don't let them hurry me, is all I ask." "You shall have your own way in the matter, I assure you," replied Lincoln as he and John Hay started on their walk to the White House. Two nights later, on October 12, a telegram was handed Lincoln from Mc-

Clellan saying the enemy was before him in force and would probably attack in the morning. "If they attack," he added, "I shall beat them." This expected attack, like others expected, failed to arrive.

In November Lincoln, Seward and John Hay went to McClellan's house one evening. The General was at a wedding, said the servant, and would soon return. "We went in," wrote Hay in his diary, "and after we had waited about an hour, McC. came in and without paying any particular attention to the porter who told him the President was waiting to see him, went upstairs, passing the door of the room where the President and Secretary of State were seated. They waited about half-an-hour, and sent once more a servant to tell the General they were there; and the answer coolly came that the General had gone to bed."

Hay considered this deliberate snub the first sign of military authorities overriding the civil government. "Coming home I spoke to the President about the matter, but he seemed not to have noticed it, specially, saying it was better, at this time, not to be making points of etiquette & personal dignity." And the President said another day, "I will hold McClellan's horse if he will only bring us success."

Sometimes the President sent for McClellan to come to the White House. More often Lincoln called at McClellan's house. Once they met at Seward's house and McClellan's daily letter told his wife: "The President is honest and means well. As I parted from him on Seward's steps he said that it had been suggested to him that it was no more safe for me than for him to walk out at night without some attendant. I told him that I felt no fear; that no one would take the trouble to interfere with me. On which he deigned to remark that they would probably give more for my scalp at Richmond than for his."

A few days later, however, McClellan felt the President, pressing for action, was bothering him too much. At the home of Edwin M. Stanton he wrote, "I have not been at home for some three hours, but am concealed at Stanton's to dodge all enemies in shape of 'browsing' Presidents, etc."

McClellan's army now numbered more than 160,000; he had at least three times as many troops as the enemy at Manassas. Twice in that autumn of 1861 the spick-and-span platoons of the Army of the Potomac had passed in grand review before President Lincoln, the Cabinet, governors of states and ladies in silken crinoline. There had been autumn weather on which many commented—mild, pleasant days and cool nights, perfect weather for an army movement to redeem Bull Run, to end the war. Thus ran hope and talk.

On "a lovely, a rare October day" at Ball's Bluff, on high ground overlooking the Potomac, a few hundred Union soldiers were cornered, killed, captured. Their commander went down, a picked target of marksmen who sent several bullets into him as he came into the open calling to his troops to follow. Near sunset that day Lincoln, entering McClellan's headquarters, "spoke of the beauty of the afternoon" to a correspondent, who noted "the lines were deeper in the President's face than when I saw him in his own home, the cheeks more sunken." The telegraph was clicking off the minor battle of Ball's Bluff. The name of the killed commander, General Edward D. Baker, Lincoln's "Ned" Baker, came through. "Five minutes passed," wrote a correspondent, "and then Mr. Lincoln, unattended, with bowed head and tears rolling down his furrowed cheeks, his breast heaving, passed through the room. He almost fell as he stepped into the street. We sprang from our seats to render assistance, but he did not fall."

Gone now forever from Lincoln was a trumpet, a shield, an intimate companion and a bright light of loyalty, namesake of his second-born boy, his choice of all men to introduce him for a presidential inaugural address.

Driving snow came with the last week in November. Winter weather was on. Wool coats, heavy blankets, firewood, tents, huts, were the need. The war was costing more than $1,000,000 a day. A hazard was in the air. Would the Young Napoleon slog through in a winter campaign and take Richmond? If he should, said men of the South at Richmond, he would find it as Napoleon did Moscow, a city in ashes.

The war had not really set in as yet. Only that summer of '61 squads of Union recruits had marched down one side of a street in Louisville while recruits on the other side headed for the Confederate Army. On a railroad train in central Kentucky one car held a company of troops going to a Union camp while in another car was a company of Confederates.

The Kentucky Senator, John P. Breckinridge, once a Vice-President of the United States, had called at the White House to bid good-by to his kinswoman, Elizabeth Todd Grimsley. He was resigning as U.S. Senator and joining the Confederate Army as a brigadier general.

Secretary Cameron returned from a trip west in November to say that Sherman, now a brigadier general in Kentucky, insisted 200,000 troops would be required to hold his 300-mile line and move that line southward. Sherman was "insane," related a Cincinnati newspaper item widely reprinted in the North. He was ordered removed from command; the order was recalled. There was confusion and worse.

In a few cases Lincoln made colonels and brigadiers of politicians, "to keep them from fighting against the war with their mouths," said Whitney. Lincoln commissioned his old-time dueling challenger, James Shields, a brigadier general; he was one of several commissioned Democrats who were to make bright records. Illinois Republican editors complained that 40 out of 70 Illinois regiments had Democratic colonels.

In many cases Lincoln commissioned politicians and adventurers because they could raise troops; they had followings. One was Illinois Congressman John A. McClernand, a Douglas Democrat; another was John A. Logan, also a Douglas Democrat and a southern Illinois Congressman. In Logan's district a Pope County mass meeting declared for secession, and a mass meeting in Williamson County pledged itself to attach southern Illinois to the Confederacy. Lincoln had to gauge communities where uprisings die down and flare up again. The war thermometer varied.

One dark night Lincoln with four other men climbed up the tower of the Smithsonian Institution. Toward hills encircling Washington they flashed signals. Next day an army officer marched into Lincoln's office a prisoner, Professor Joseph Henry, secretary and director of the Smithsonian Institution, the most eminent man of learning in the employ of the U.S. Government. "Mr. President," said the officer, "I told you a month ago Professor Henry is a rebel. Last night at midnight he flashed red lights from the top of his building, signaling to the Secesh. I saw them myself."

Lincoln turned. "Now you're caught! What have you to say, Professor Henry, why sentence of death should not immediately be pronounced upon you?" Then, turning to the army officer, Lincoln explained that on the previous evening he and others had accompanied Henry to the Smithsonian tower and experimented with new army signals. The officer thereupon released from his custody a physicist of international repute.

In Missouri during the summer and fall of '61 the warfare had raw bones, pointed a sinister forefinger toward the future, and had its weight in moving Lincoln to write in a message to Congress: "In considering the policy to be adopted for suppressing the insurrection I have been anxious and careful that the inevitable conflict for this purpose shall not degenerate into a violent and remorseless revolutionary struggle."

Nathaniel Lyon, short, bearded, with dark-red hair and fiery temperament, drove himself hard, some of his raw volunteer troops saying he talked to them as if they were mules. The son of a Connecticut Yankee farmer, a West Pointer, Indian fighter in Florida, shot in the leg entering Mexico City with the American Army, Lyon handled regulars on the West Coast, at Forts Riley and Kearney, and came to St. Louis from Prairie Dog, Kansas. Congressman Frank Blair knew Lyon as a Union man and saw to it early that Lincoln appointed him commandant of the St. Louis arsenal. Lyon and Frank Blair had worked out their plans, which made it impossible for Missouri to secede from the Union. The Germans of St. Louis, who were mainly Union and antislavery, gave their help as valuable allies.

Lyon threw his army of 6,000 at more than twice that number of Confederates August 10, 1861, at Wilson's Creek. Bullets struck him near the ankle, on the thigh; one cut his scalp to the bone; his horse was shot. Mounting another horse, his face white from loss of blood, he ordered a bayonet charge and led it, tumbling off his horse into the arms of his orderly with a bullet hole close to the heart. His army retired, the enemy not following. The losses were about 1,200 killed and wounded on each side. Missouri boys of both armies lay dead in the cornfields alongside Kentucky, Iowa and Illinois boys. The Confederates gave over the body of Lyon. Crowds came to view the coffin as it journeyed to Connecticut, where the general assembly mourned its "beloved son."

An outcry arose when Congressman Frank Blair and others put the blame for Lyon's death, Wilson's Creek and other losses on General John Charles Frémont, commander of the Department of the West, with headquarters, troops and munitions at St. Louis. Frémont, in 1856 the first Republican party candidate for President, was born in Savannah, Georgia. Expelled from college in Charleston, South Carolina, for "continual disregard of discipline," he was an instructor of mathematics on a U.S. war sloop, a railroad surveyor in the Tennessee mountains, and became a lieutenant in the U.S. Topographical Corps. In Washington he fell in love with 15-year-old Jessie Benton, daughter of Senator Thomas H. Benton of Missouri. The Senator had him sent west of the Mississippi River on a surveying trip. He came back and ran away with Jessie; they were married, and thereafter the Benton home in St. Louis was his too, but he used it little. He led expeditions west, exploring the Rocky Mountains, South Pass, winning the first recorded climb up the highest point in the Wind River Mountains. Fremont Peak was named for him.

He clashed with the Spanish rulers of California, took a hand in overthrowing them and setting up the State of California, of which he was the first U.S. Senator. Then came land, gold mines, money pouring in at the rate of $75,000 a month, and Frémont's Mariposa estate of 46,000 acres, which had cost him $3,000, was estimated at $10,000,000. Then too came squatters, rival claims and the details of management and finance. He was in Paris trying to sell half of his estate when news came of Sumter. He offered his services and Lincoln with no waiting commissioned him a major general. At the White House he had talked with Lincoln of the plan for him to organize an army in the Northwest and go down the Mississippi and split the Confederacy in two.

Though he was head of the Western Department on July 3, Frémont lingered in Washington, delayed in New York, arrived in St. Louis on July 25; he directed entrenchments thrown around St. Louis, wore out relays of telegraphers with messages to governors and troop commanders. Many days he worked from five in the morning till midnight.

From the southwest corner of Missouri had come a messenger from Lyon begging Frémont to send him men. Frémont answered, "If he fights it will be on his own responsibility." Frémont had urged Lyon to retreat to Rolla, which would be falling back about halfway to St. Louis. And he started two regiments toward Lyon. But Lyon never saw them. For him war was fighting; he sought out the enemy. Lyon died in the drawn battle at Wilson's Creek. The memory rankled with men like Frank Blair.

"I will neither lose the state nor permit the enemy a foot of advantage," Frémont wrote Lincoln. "I have infused energy and activity into every department." Frémont addressed a telegram to "The President of the United States" inquiring, "Will the President read my urgent dispatch to the Secretary of War?" He received the reply on August 15: "Been answering your messages ever since day before yesterday. Do you receive the answers?"

Lincoln's anxiety about Frémont and Missouri grew as the mail brought stories of extravagance, blunders, favoritism, corruption. Frank Blair called on Frémont with General John M. Schofield, who wrote, "To my great surprise, no questions were asked, nor mention made, of the bloody field from which I had just come, where Lyon had been killed." Instead of wanting to learn any possible lessons from a tried soldier, Frémont led Schofield to a table and pointed out on maps the triumphant line of march his army would take. Blair and Schofield left Frémont's office. "We walked down the street for some time in silence. Then Blair turned to me and said, 'Well, what do you think of him?' I replied in words rather too strong to print. Blair said, 'I have been suspecting that for some time.'"

Frémont through the night of August 29 and far into the morning of August 30 worked on a proclamation. In pompous terms and with threats he didn't have power to enforce, he declared "martial law throughout the State of Missouri." Drawing the line of the Union Army across half the state, he promised that all persons north of this line caught "with arms in their hands" would be court-martialed and "if found guilty will be shot." Also "the property, real and personal, of all persons in the State of Missouri who shall take up arms against the United States, or who shall be directly proven to have taken an active part with their enemies in the field, is declared to be confiscated to the public use, and their slaves, if any they have, are hereby declared freemen."

Lincoln, along with the country, first heard of the proclamation through the newspapers. After getting an authentic text he wrote Frémont September 2: "Should you shoot a man, according to the proclamation, the Confederates would very certainly shoot our best man in their hands in retaliation; and so, man for man, indefinitely. It is therefore my order that you allow no man to be shot, under the proclamation, without first having my approbation or consent . . . The confiscation of property, and the liberating slaves of traiterous owners, will alarm our Southern Union friends, and turn them against us—perhaps ruin our rather fair prospect for Kentucky." He asked Frémont to modify the proclamation.

Frémont took six days to reply. And this letter to Lincoln was carried by a special messenger—Mrs. Frémont herself. She left St. Louis September 8 with her English maid, sitting two days and nights in a hot, overcrowded car, arriving in Washington the third day. She sent from Willard's a written request to know when she might deliver Frémont's letter to the President. A White House messenger brought back a card: "Now, at once. A. Lincoln."

Near nine in the evening she walked to the White House with Judge Edward Coles of New York, met the President in the Red Room and wrote of it: "I introduced Judge Coles, who then stepped into the deep doorway leading to the Blue Room—and there he remained walking to and fro, keeping in sight and hearing . . . He was struck at once, as I was, by the President's manner, which was hard . . . Nor did he offer me a seat. He talked standing, and both voice and manner made the impression that I was to be got rid of briefly . . . In answer to his question, 'Well?' I explained that the general wished so much to have his attention to the letter sent, that I had brought it to make sure it would reach him. He answered, not to that, but to the subject his own mind was upon, that 'It was a war for a great national idea, the Union, and that General Frémont should not have dragged the negro into it,—that he never would if he had consulted with Frank Blair. I sent Frank there to advise him.' He first mentioned the Blairs, in this astonishing connection. It was a *parti pris*, and as we walked back Judge Coles, who heard everything, said to me, 'This ends Frémont's part in the war. Seward and Montgomery Blair will see to that, and Lincoln does not seem to see the injustice, the wrong of receiving secret reports against him made by a man authorized to do so, and as everyone knows, with his mind often clouded by drink and always governed by personal motives' [meaning Frank Blair]."

When Mrs. Frémont began talking about the difficulty of conquering by arms alone, how England and the wide world would welcome a blow struck against slavery, she thought there was "a sneering tone" in the President's voice as he remarked, "You are quite a female politician." And Jessie Benton Frémont returned to St. Louis with contempt for Lincoln, hate for the Blairs and a sharper eye for conspirators against her husband. As Congressman J. B. Grinnell of Iowa reported Lincoln's version of the Jessie Frémont interview, she came "opening her case with mild expostulations, but left in anger flaunting her handkerchief before my face, and saying, 'Sir, the general will try titles with you! He is a man and I am his wife.' "

Lincoln's reply to Frémont September 11 pointed to the clause relating to confiscation of property and liberation of slaves, which "appeared to me to be objectionable, in it's non-conformity to the Act of Congress passed the 6th. of last August." He had therefore written his wish to Frémont that the clause be modified and now, "Your answer, just received, expresses the preference on your part, that I should make an open order for the modification, which I very cheerfully do."

From antislavery quarters rose a sure breeze of hostile criticism. Press, pulpit, men and women of antislavery fervor, spoke and wrote their scorn of Lincoln. Even Bill Herndon was writing to a friend: "Does the war go on to suit you? It does not suit me. Fremont's proclamation was right. Lincoln's modification of it was wrong."

Lincoln wrote in one letter: "Our adversaries have the power, and will certainly exercise it, to shoot as many of our men as we shoot of theirs. I did not say this in the public letter, because it is a subject I prefer not to discuss in the hearing of our enemies."

General Jeff Thompson, Confederate commander of the First Military District of Missouri, had issued a proclamation to meet Frémont's, announcing "most solemnly" that for every soldier of the state guard or of the Southern Army put to death as ordered by Frémont he would "hang, draw, and quarter a minion of said Abraham Lincoln."

It was a saying, "When the Blairs go in for a fight they go in for a funeral." Frémont, once their protégé, they had marked to be destroyed. Frémont fought back. Mrs. Frémont joined. Congressman Washburne headed a committee which investigated Frémont's department. Judges David Davis and Joseph Holt were appointed to direct an audit of accounts. War Secretary Cameron, with an adjutant general, went personally to St. Louis.

They all found extravagance, mismanagement, blunders, but no specific outstanding corruption. The total of contracts for food, guns, steamboats, uniforms, supplies, fortifications, ran to about $12,000,000. Nothing could be fastened on Frémont. He came through the search with a record for personal honesty. He let it be told that Frank Blair had asked him to give a contract for 40,000 uniforms to a friend of Blair and he had refused. He threw Blair into jail, let him go, arrested him a second time, and let him go. He suppressed the St. Louis *News*.

The Chicago Irish Brigade under Colonel James A. Mulligan defended Lexington eight days against 20,000 of the enemy and surrendered 1,600 men September 20. Blamed for this fresh loss of good troops, Frémont had notified General Scott at Washington: "I am taking the field myself . . . Please notify the President immediately." General Scott replied, "The President is glad you are hastening to the scene of action; his words are, 'he expects you to repair the disaster at Lexington without loss of time.' " Yet Frémont went on losing time.

And while Frémont sat with his dreams of war and glory, a man wearing clothes like a Southern planter got off a horse at the Frémont picket lines just beyond Springfield and told the pickets he was a messenger with information from the rebel lines. They let him in, the officer of the day taking him to the chief of staff. No, he couldn't see General Frémont, but they would pass in anything he wanted to tell Frémont. The man in the Southern-planter clothes refused this offer. Hours went by. And late in the evening the chief of staff took him to the office where General Frémont sat at the end of a long table.

The man ripped from his coat lining a paper and handed it to Frémont, who nervously unfolded it, read the name "A. Lincoln" signed to it, slammed the document down on the table, and frowned. "Sir, how did you get admission into my lines?" The man said he came in as a messenger bearing information from the "rebel" lines. Frémont waved him out. "That will do for the present."

Thus on November 2 Frémont was removed from command. Lincoln's removal order, dated October 24, had gone to General S. R. Curtis at St. Louis with instructions that the order was not to be handed Frémont if when reached by messenger "he shall then have, in personal command, fought and won a battle, or shall then be actually in a battle, or shall then be in the immediate presence of the enemy, in expectation of a battle." Curtis made copies of Lincoln's order and sent three messengers by separate routes with it. Curtis had heard of Frémont's arrangements for no removal order to be delivered. General Hunter temporarily took command. Other plans for reaching New Orleans were under way.

Frémont had lasted in Missouri just 100 days. In that time he made himself a hero in the eyes of nearly all the antislavery elements of the Northern States and of Europe. Sober citizens pulled the portraits of Lincoln from their walls and trampled under foot the face of the President, according to the Cincinnati *Gazette*. Wendell Phillips estimated Lincoln as "not a man like Frémont, to stamp the lava mass of the nation with an idea." Honoring Frémont in person, Henry Ward Beecher in his Brooklyn church said, "Your name will live and be remembered by a nation of freemen." James Russell Lowell, Greeley and Bryant spoke deep offense at Lincoln's treatment of Frémont. The Chicago *Tribune* denounced the President's action and pre-dicted grave humiliation unless the administration took a more vigorous policy.

The Springfield, Massachusetts, *Republican* editor, Samuel Bowles, wrote, "It is gratifying to know that we have a President who is loyal to law—when that is made to meet an emergency—as he is to meet an emergency for which no law is provided." The New York *Herald* said: "The President, who has always been known as an upright man, of late months, has justly earned the reputation of a wise and energetic statesman . . . The moderate and effective rebuke contained in his letter to Major-General Frémont is eminently worthy of admiration, both for the dignified and courteous lan-guage in which it is couched, and the death blow it strikes at all attempts of badly advised local commanders to overstep the legitimate sphere of their military duties."

Not for long could any man be the hero of the New York *Herald*. The foremost innovator in the journalism of his time, James Gordon Bennett, was studied by Lincoln as one of the powers to be kept on the Union side as far as possible. Brilliant and even bawdy in its endless chatterings, the

Herald was generally acknowledged to have circulation, resources and prestige surpassing any other American journal. Daily printing 84,000 copies, the *Herald* rated itself on April 9, 1861, as "the most largely circulated journal in the world." Two days before the bombardment of Fort Sumter the *Herald* said the only hope against civil war seemed to lie "in the overthrow of the demoralizing, disorganizing, and destructive sectional party, of which 'Honest Abe Lincoln' is the pliant instrument."

The *Herald* was concededly the only American newspaper of considerable circulation and influence in Europe. Its insolent anti-British tone, and its arrogant policy in general, misrepresented America, and Lincoln in his anxiety about foreign good will picked Thurlow Weed to approach Bennett. Weed pointed out that he and Bennett for 30 years had been political and personal enemies, but narrowed down to a choice from several proposed emissaries, Lincoln decided on Weed. At dinner and in a long conversation Bennett and Weed threshed over the issues. Bennett went on and on in bitter denunciation of Greeley, Garrison, Seward, Sumner, Wendell Phillips and Weed himself as having exasperated the South into the war. Weed returned to Washington, reported the interview, believed the President and the Cabinet were "gratified" over his diplomacy. The results were slender, if any. The *Herald* went on harpooning the British Empire.

Self-announced as "daily daguerreotype of American manners and thought" the *Herald*'s 66-year-old owner and editor, born of Roman Catholic parents in Keith, Scotland, had trained for priesthood at Aberdeen, had starved as a bookseller in Boston, had lived shabbily as a hack writer in New York. He issued his first four-page penny New York *Herald* in 1835, doing all the work except the printing himself, writing and shaping the whole paper on an editorial desk of one board slung over two dry-goods boxes, "one poor man in a cellar against the world," as he phrased it.

Then with years of toil from five in the morning till ten at night, scrambling, scandalizing, dramatizing, playing with a scale of shrieks and whispers delicately manipulated, Bennett built a world-famed newspaper. "The newspaper's function," he said, "is not to instruct but to startle."

He was first to print financial news on a large scale, regularly to expose stock-market frauds, to publish lists of bankrupts, to mock at "high society," and to give large spreads to bawdyhouse murders.

Four times in public places Bennett was beaten with canes, each time giving his readers a full report of the event as he saw and felt it. In the baffling human whirlpool of New York, Bennett was playing with paradoxical forces that were to be a heavy anxiety to the Lincoln administration. He kept close to the needs of business expansion and the widening streams of Northern capital that sought new fields and larger earnings.

After Bull Run the *Herald* counseled fresh determination and further preparations, almost in the tone of Lincoln's memoranda for immediate action; no panic, no bewilderment, as in the case of Greeley. Then on Lincoln's revoking Frémont's personal proclamation of Negro emancipation had come the *Herald*'s encomiums for Lincoln, praise in heaping measure, compliments that like fresh roses must soon wither and fade, petal by petal. With no cessation Bennett would continue putting the blame for the war on "nigger worshippers," sprinkling his editorial page with that phrase, and steadily maintaining that antislavery agitators were hypocrites rather than heroes.

To friends of Sumner who in September '61 urged Lincoln to issue a proclamation giving freedom to the slaves, he said, "It would do no good to go ahead any faster than the country would follow," Sumner's author friend, Charles Edwards Lester, writing that he heard the President add to this, "You know the old Latin motto, *festina lente*. How do the Italians, those bastard Romans, say the same thing now?" "They have improved on it, Mr. President. They say, *'Andante adagio, perchè ho premúra'*—'Go slow, because I am in a hurry.'" "That's it, exactly. I think Sumner and the rest of you would upset our applecart altogether, if you had your way. We'll fetch 'em; just give us a little time. We didn't go into the war to put down slavery, but to put the flag back."

In November '61 came a dramatic clash of English-speaking nations. The *Trent*, a British Royal Mail packet, one day out from Havana, was steaming serenely along the Bahama Channel. At noon November 8 she came to where the channel narrows to a width of 15 miles. There the *San Jacinto*, a screw sloop of the American Navy, was waiting.

The *Trent* hoisted the British colors. The *San Jacinto* ran up the Union flag. Also the *San Jacinto* fired a shot across the bow of the *Trent*. And as the British steamer showed no signs of slowing down, the American sloop sent a shell that burst in front of the bow of the *Trent*. This brought her to. Captain Moir of the *Trent* lifted a trumpet to his lips, and sang out, "What do you mean by heaving my vessel to in this way?" No answer came.

Three boats were leaving the *San Jacinto* with officers, sailors, marines. They rowed to the *Trent* in a few minutes, and Lieutenant D. MacNeill Fairfax, speaking for the commander of the *San Jacinto*, asked for the passenger list of the *Trent*. He had information that James M. Mason and John Slidell, newly appointed Confederate commissioners to Great Britain and France respectively, were on board.

Mr. Slidell standing near stepped up to Lieutenant Fairfax. "I am Mr. Slidell; do you want to see me?" Mr. Mason, also being near, stepped up, and as he and Lieutenant Fairfax had been introduced years before there was no need for him to say who he was. Next the Lieutenant asked for the secretaries to Messrs. Mason and Slidell and they were lined up. At this point the American Lieutenant informed the British Captain that he had been sent by his commander to arrest Messrs. Mason and Slidell and take them as prisoners on board the U.S. vessel nearby.

Among those with spyglasses on the *San Jacinto* was a heavy-jawed man with a dangerous eye and wavy locks of hair—Charles Wilkes, 63 years old, scientist, experimenter in astronomical observation, explorer of south-polar ice fields, authority on meteorology, author of 11 volumes and atlases.

Mrs. Slidell inquired who was the commander of the *San Jacinto*. "Your old acquaintance, Captain Wilkes," said Fairfax, which surprised Mrs. Slidell. She had sipped tea with him in Washington. "He is playing into our hands!" said Mrs. Slidell spunkily.

"Good-by, my dear, we shall meet in Paris in sixty days," said Mr. Slidell as he bade farewell to his wife. Lieutenant Fairfax went with him to his cabin for his luggage. There Slidell's daughter clung to him and begged to go with him. She wept as he was rowed with the three other prisoners to the *San Jacinto*. The two ships moved away toward different horizons and soon each was alone in the silence of the sea.

When the *Trent* passengers reached London November 27, they found themselves accepted heroes and heroines who had undergone severe tests. Commander Williams, the royal naval agent, told of "the marines rushing with the points of their bayonets at Miss Slidell," how she screamed, and it was then that he, Commander Williams, had just time "to put his body between her and the bayonets of the marines." England went into an uproar. The London *Times* fastened on Captain Wilkes: "He is an ideal Yankee. Swagger and ferocity, built on a foundation of vulgarity and cowardice, these are his characteristics, and these are the most prominent marks by which his countrymen, generally speaking, are known all over the world." The London *Morning Chronicle* tore its hair and gave the war party its cues: "Abraham Lincoln, whose accession to power was generally welcomed on this side of the Atlantic, has proved himself a feeble, confused and little-minded mediocrity. Mr. Seward, the firebrand at his elbow, is exerting himself to provoke a quarrel with all Europe."

On the intervention of Queen Victoria and Prince Albert, the severe instructions to Lord Lyons from Lord Palmerston, the Prime Minister, and Lord John Russell, Secretary for Foreign Affairs, were softened, and instead they framed a note for Seward and Lincoln to read. Mainly it asked whether Captain Wilkes had done what he did by his own wish and whim or at the command of his Government. If it was a Government order and in line with U.S. policy—then war! The ships of the best and biggest navy in the world were made ready. Eight thousand picked troops were put on transports and set sail for Canada.

By this time the United States had gone into an uproar. Yankee Doodle tore his shirt. The eagle was brought out to scream. "The Star-spangled Banner" blared its sonorous patriotism from multitudinous brass instruments. Captain Wilkes arrived at the port of New York with his prizes, marched down Broadway for a City Hall reception. Banquets were spread for him; in New York, Boston, he was dined, wined, toasted.

That the U.S. Government had in its clutches John Slidell was exciting to antislavery men, for Slidell had led in repealing the Missouri Compromise, was an author of the Fugitive Slave Law, had lengthily examined John Brown in jail, seeking information that might convict New England financial backers of Brown. Mason's record ran close to that of Slidell. The two of them personified the doctrines justifying slavery. America trembled with war fever. Famous lawyers such as Caleb Cushing and Edward Everett justified Wilkes as having the law with him, though other good lawyers like Charles Sumner and Charles Francis Adams were sure he was in the wrong.

Near midnight December 18 the Queen's messenger delivered to the British Minister in Washington the note from Her Majesty's Government. The London *Times* correspondent met Seward at a cotillon party "in very good humor and inclined to talk." Seward without a doubt was feeling extra good. "We will wrap the whole world in flames!" he told W. H. Russell, Prince de Joinville and others. "No power so remote that she will not feel the fire of our battle and be burned in our conflagration." Russell asked one of the guests if Seward was showing fight. "That's all bugaboo talk," was the explanation. "When Seward talks that way, he means to back down."

During the weeks of this fury Lincoln gave no inkling of what he would do. In his December message to Congress he made no reference to the matter. Galt, the Canadian financial Minister, in a White House visit asked the meaning of fortifications and depots of arms on the Great Lakes, Lincoln replying, "We must say something to satisfy the people." And what about the Mason and Slidell case? Galt inquired. "Oh, that'll be got along with," was the brief and equivocal response. Minister Lyons treasured the anecdote, and it was rehearsed in many legations that to a portentous diplomatic inquiry the American President had answered, "Oh, that'll be got along with."

So often the White House callers were asking, "Is it to be peace or war?" The President could ease the public mind by speaking just a few words, he was reminded. One politician kept pressing and received a Lincoln parable: "Your question reminds me of an incident which occurred out west. Two roughs were playing cards for high stakes, when one of them, suspecting his adversary of foul play, straightway drew his bowie-knife from his belt and pinned the hand of the other player upon the table, exclaiming: 'If you haven't got the ace of spades under your palm, I'll apologize.'"

Sumner showed Lincoln letters from Bright and Cobden of the British House of Commons, and wrote to Bright: "The President is much moved and astonished by the English intelligence. He is essentially honest and pacific in disposition, with a natural slowness. Yesterday he said to me, 'There will be no war unless England is bent on having one.'"

"One war at a time," was Lincoln's word to Seward. Blair was the only Cabinet member with Lincoln from the first. "The English didn't give us time to turn around," was a later comment of Lincoln's. "It was very humiliating, but we had one big war on hand and we didn't want two at the same time. England in the end will be the only one hurt."

Notes from the French, Austrian and Prussian governments were read to the Cabinet, advising the release of Mason and Slidell. Yet the tone of the press and of public opinion over the North was decidedly for war rather than a "backdown" to Britain.

Minister Adams put up a brave front and told the British government he was sure his Government was not responsible for Captain Wilkes' act. From week to week Adams was helpless till one day the mail brought Seward's note calling for arbitration and saying the captured Southern commissioners "will be cheerfully liberated." Discussion of this note had run two days in Lincoln's Cabinet, and Bates wrote: "There was great reluctance on the part of some of the members of the cabinet—and even the President himself"—to give up the Southern commissioners. However, it was so ordered. The British reply later took exception to minor points and acknowledged satisfaction as to "the reparation which Her Majesty and the British nation had a right to expect." Mason and Slidell were let out of their comfortable jail in Boston and placed on board a British war vessel to cross the Atlantic.

Lincoln had mixed feelings over the affair. To Horace Porter and others, on their request, he later gave what he regarded as the essentials. "It was a pretty bitter pill to swallow, but I contented myself with believing that

England's triumph in the matter would be short-lived, and that after ending our war successfully we would be so powerful that we could call her to account for all the embarrassments she had inflicted on us. I felt a good deal like the sick man in Illinois who was told he probably hadn't many days longer to live, and that he ought to make peace with any enemies he might have. He said the man he hated worst of all was a fellow named Brown in the next village and he guessed he had better begin on him. So Brown was sent for, and when he came the sick man began to say, in a voice 'as meek as Moses,' that he wanted to die at peace with all his fellow creatures, and he hoped he and Brown could now shake hands and bury all their enmity. The scene was becoming altogether too pathetic for Brown, who had to get out his handkerchief and wipe the gathering tears from his eyes. It wasn't long before he melted and gave his hand to his neighbor, and they had a regular love-feast. After a parting that would have softened the heart of a grindstone, Brown had about reached the room door, when the sick man rose up on his elbow and said, 'But, see here, Brown, if I *should* happen to get well, mind *that old grudge stands.*' "

CHAPTER 23

The Politics of War—Corruption

THE WAR cost was mounting toward $1,500,000 a day as the winter of '61 set in. Money was pouring in and out in larger aggregates, bigger numbers, than Federal bookkeeping ever before recorded. A long-drawn battle, with money as ammunition, had been fought between the North and the South in Great Britain and on the continent of Europe. The fighting—with gold, moneybags, credit—was over war supplies. The North outbid and outbought the South.

On the revolutionary advances in communication a magazine writer had noted, "Today newspapers multiplied by millions whiten the whole country every morning like the hoar frost." Lincoln's message to Congress in December '61 swept the national horizons. Westward from Omaha gangs of linemen had strung wires to the coast. "The President's message," said a dispatch, "read in Congress at 12 o'clock on Tuesday, was received by telegraph at San Francisco, and published early on Wednesday morning."

The message maintained in austere tone throughout that the Union was intact and its Government would ride the crisis and enforce its will. Lincoln opened with "great gratitude to God for unusual good health, and most abundant harvests." Kentucky "is now decidedly, and, I think, unchangeably," ranged on the side of the Union. Missouri had passed beyond seizure by the insurrectionists. The three states of Maryland, Kentucky and Missouri, "neither of which would promise a single soldier at first, have now an aggregate of not less than forty thousand in the field, for the Union."

In this message Lincoln changed from referring to himself as "he" or "the executive." After nine months as President he was "I." Where before he had written, "The executive deems it of importance," he now wrote, "I deem it of importance."

Three territories created by the last Congress, Colorado, Dakota, Nevada, had been organized, with civil administrations inaugurated. In this, and in other gestures, the President gave the impression of a young pioneer country striding into a vast and irreckonable future. He could see, with the Union maintained, promises for the future. "There are already among us those, who, if the Union be preserved, will live to see it contain 250 millions. The struggle of today, is not altogether for today—it is for a vast future also." One argument read:

Labor is prior to, and independent of, capital. Capital is only the fruit of labor, and could never have existed if labor had not first existed. Labor is the superior of capital, and deserves much the higher consideration. Capital has its rights, which are as worthy of protection as any other rights. Nor is it denied that there is, and probably always will be, a relation between labor and capital, producing mutual benefits. The error is in assuming that the whole labor of the community exists within that relation . . . Men with their families—wives, sons, and daughters—work for themselves, on their farms, in their houses, and in their shops, taking the whole product to themselves, and asking no favors of capital on the one hand, nor of hired laborers or slaves on the other. It is not forgotten that a considerable number of persons mingle their own labor with capital—that is, they labor with their own hands, and also buy or hire others to labor for them; but this is only a mixed, and not a distinct class . . .

Again: as has already been said, there is not, of necessity, any such thing as the free hired laborer being fixed to that condition for life. Many independent men everywhere in these States, a few years back in their lives, were hired laborers . . . This is the just, and generous, and prosperous system, which opens the way to all—gives hope to all, and consequent energy, and progress, and improvement of condition to all . . .

Declaring friendship for two Negro national governments the President could see no good reason for "withholding our recognition of the independence and sovereignty of Hayti and Liberia."

Five vessels being fitted out for the slave trade had been seized and condemned. Two mates of vessels engaged in the trade had been convicted. One captain "taken with a cargo of Africans on board his vessel" had been convicted of the highest grade of offense, punishable by death.

The Confiscation Act, by which Negroes belonging, as property, to disloyal slaveholders became freemen, was scrupulously recited in terms of law. "The legal claims of certain persons to the labor and service of certain other persons have become forfeited." In such numbers had these liberated Negroes come into the Union army lines and become Federal dependents, and so sure was it that more of them would arrive for disposal, that it now became necessary to have a permanent policy for their disposal.

The message drew more approval and perhaps less hostile comment in general than either the first inaugural or the July 4 message to Congress. Its most original feature concerned Negro freedom. Delicately, tentatively, and in the strictest of legal terms pertaining to the management of property, Lincoln projected his policy of gradual compensated emancipation. In substance his proposal was that the Border Slave States might enact laws for selling their slaves to the U.S. Government, which in turn should free the slaves and then take steps to colonize them.

Though the President had reported progress in suppression of the African slave trade, the New York *Times* estimated that 30,000 Africans were landed in Cuba the current year. Corruption, bribery, secret influence bought and paid for, marked each step of a slave ship's cruise from its first port clearance to the purchase of Negro tribesmen at the African Gold Coast on to permissions to sell in Cuba and later to smuggle the slaves into the Cotton States on the Gulf of Mexico.

The organized abolitionists expected little from the President. The executive committee of the American Anti-Slavery Society in its 28th annual report scored Lincoln as "under the delusion that soft words will salve the nation's sore." They analyzed him: "A sort of bland, respectable middle-man, between a very modest Right and the most arrogant and exacting Wrong . . . He thinks slavery wrong, but opposes the immediate abolition of it; believes it ought to be kept out of the Territories, but would admit it to the Union in new States . . . affirms the equality of white men and black in natural rights, but is 'not in favor of negro citizenship.' "

Wendell Phillips held that Lincoln was honest but "as a pint-pot may be full, and yet not be so full as a quart, so there is a vast difference between the honesty of a small man and the honesty of a statesman." Governor John Andrew with Mrs. Andrew, Julia Ward Howe and James Freeman Clarke talked with the President "mostly on indifferent topics." They took leave and "were out of hearing," as Julia Ward Howe wrote, when Clarke said of Lincoln, "We have seen it in his face; hopeless honesty—that is all!" This almost tallied with Attorney General Bates' writing in his diary, "The President is an excellent man, and in the main wise, but he lacks will and purpose, and I greatly fear he has not the power to command."

There came before Lincoln the case of Nathaniel Gordon of Maine, captain of a ship which had sailed to Africa and at the mouth of the Congo River had taken on board some 900 Negroes. Captured on the high seas and convicted as a slave trader, Gordon was sentenced to death by a judge declaring, "You are soon to pass into the presence of that God of the black man as well as the white man." Lincoln read the evidence, scrutinized many respectable names on a petition for pardon. Then he wrote a death sentence giving the doomed man an extra two weeks to live. It recited:

. . . Now, therefore, be it known, that I, Abraham Lincoln, President of the United States of America, have granted and do hereby grant unto him, the said Nathaniel Gordon, a respite of the above recited sentence, until Friday the 21st day of February, A.D. 1862, between the hours of twelve o'clock at noon and three o'clock in the afternoon of the said day, when the said sentence shall be executed.

In granting this respite it becomes my painful duty to admonish the prisoner that, relinquishing all expectation of pardon by Human Authority, he refer himself alone to the mercy of the common God and Father of all men.

Thus was sent to death the first and only slave trader in the history of the United States to be tried, convicted and hanged in accordance with the Constitution and Federal law. One of the prosecuting attorneys, Ethan Allen, told of extraordinary pressure on Lincoln to pardon Gordon.

From day to day as Congress met and in discussion, inquiry, report, touched every living and immediate question shaking the American people, the President had no special collaborator and spokesman in that body. Owen Lovejoy of Illinois and Albert Gallatin Riddle of Ohio were the only radical antislavery Congressmen—and Isaac N. Arnold of Chicago the only moderate—who spoke faith in the President.

When in December Congress appointed a Committee on the Conduct of the War, Lincoln saw it as one extreme intended to check another. Among its members were D. W. Gooch of Massachusetts, George W. Julian of Indiana, John Covode of Pennsylvania and Moses F. Odell of New York. Chiefly radical antislavery Republicans, they were headstrong men of brains, courage, ability, of long training in politics and the antislavery struggle; of the group the gadfly was Julian. Nothing less than genius shone and coruscated from some facets of this committee. They were to help Lincoln, and more often to interfere with him, for a long time. They sniffed out waste and corruption; they cleared away stenches; they muddled, accused men wrongly, roused fear and suspicion, and left ranklings; they wrangled and bombinated; they played with the glory and despair of democracy.

The chairman of the committee, Benjamin Franklin Wade, strode into the White House one day and stormily told Lincoln he must throw McClellan overboard. Lincoln asked who should then be put in McClellan's place. Snorted Wade, "Anybody!" Lincoln, coolly: "Wade, *anybody* will do for you but I must have *somebody*."

Short, deep-chested, defiant-looking Ben Wade was 61, of Puritan stock, his father a Revolutionary War soldier. Day laborer on the Erie Canal, farm hand, cattle-driver, schoolteacher, prosecuting attorney of Ashtabula County, he entered the Ohio Legislature and put through a bill forbidding that body to grant divorces. He fought against passage of the Fugitive Slave Law and then fought against its enforcement. He entered the U.S. Senate in 1851 as one of the small group of antislavery men who first dared, on broad policy grounds, to challenge the Southerners.

Senator Zachariah Chandler of Michigan, another member of the committee, had driven from the Bull Run battlefield to the White House, told of the battle, and urged the President to call for a half-million more troops to show the country that the Government was "just beginning to get mad." Detroit millionaire dry-goods merchant and landowner, "Zach" Chandler was of the breed of restless, rawboned New England Yankees who had pushed west, settled up the country, made money, and were restless to make history and more money.

Lyman Trumbull, another member, who had outplayed Lincoln for election to the U.S. Senate from Illinois in 1856, was cold, shrewd, scholarly, humanitarian though no friendly mixer, accurate in statement, no demagogue, a clean politician whose word was dependable. He often suspected Lincoln as cunning if not Machiavellian. An intangible factor in the relationship of Trumbull and Lincoln was the unrelenting hatred of Mrs. Lincoln for Julia Jayne Trumbull.

The Southern Union man on the committee was Senator Andrew Johnson, whose hammer-and-tongs oratory had rung across Tennessee in loyalty to the Lincoln administration. With never a day of regular school in his life, it was said, he had learned to read while sitting cross-legged at his trade of tailor in Greenville. Marrying the 16-year-old Eliza McCardle in 1827 turned out to be one of the blessings of his life. Supporting the Breckinridge ticket in 1860, he had fought secession tooth and nail and flaunted the Union banner in a Slave State nearly encircled by Slave States. More than once he had brought out his loaded revolver facing crowds ready to lynch him.

The Republican floor leader of the House of Representatives, chairman of the Committee on Ways and Means, a gnarled thorn tree of a man, "the master mind of the House," was not a member of the Committee on the Conduct of the War, but he had helped create it. And who could read Thaddeus Stevens' heart? He was as impenetrable as Abraham Lincoln, and as lonely and incessant in his broodings on the fate of man on the cold planet Earth. His mother was the high priceless memory of his life. He talked of her often. "She worked day and night to educate me." And when he became a lawyer with practice and money, he said, "I really think the greatest gratification of my life resulted from my ability to give my mother a farm of 250 acres, and a dairy of fourteen cows."

Though Stevens limped with a clubfoot, he was a horseman and a swimmer. His tongue was often sharp and, men said, malicious and arrogant. In the Pennsylvania Legislature he had put through bills that won him the name of father of the free-school system of the state. In law practice, investments, iron and furnace projects, Thaddeus Stevens had made one fortune of $200,000, lost it, made another, and had a reputation for paying his debts to the last dollar. His recreation was gambling. An old-timer said he lost and won and didn't seem to care. "He played with consummate coolness, never lost his temper, and never increased the amount of his bet." While his fellow players "were eating and drinking with the voracity of cormorants, he never indulged in anything more stimulating than a cracker and a sip of water."

His home people liked Stevens to the extent that his re-election to Congress in 1860 was by a vote of 12,065 to his opponent's 470. Meeting a Lancaster lawyer who had double-crossed him, he stood still, leaned on his cane and slowly clipped his words: "You must be a bastard, for I knew your mother's husband and he was a gentleman and an honest man!"

When in 1842 he had moved from Gettysburg to Lancaster, he had brought with him one who became the most talked-of woman in Lancaster. Lydia Smith was the widow of a Gettysburg Negro barber, by whom she had two children. She was a comely quadroon with Caucasian features and a skin of light-gold tint, a Roman Catholic communicant with Irish eyes, her maiden name Hamilton. For 20 years she was the clean, efficient, careful housekeeper of the bachelor attorney Thaddeus Stevens, herself quiet, discreet, retiring, reputed for poise and personal dignity. Some newspapers referred to her as "Mrs. Stevens," insisting that that title was used by some who had speaking acquaintance with her.

Stevens was a familiar of the hearts of murderers and at home in the chicanery of courts and the skulduggery of evidence. After Daniel Webster's famous speech on the Compromise of 1850, Stevens' quiet wrath found words:

"As I heard it, I could have cut his damned heart out." And after a neutral soothing speech of Seward in early '61, "I listened to every word and, by the living God, I haven't heard a thing."

He flashed with unexpected sarcasm; even Southern members laughed with him. Giving the floor to another member, he closed: "I now yield to Mr. B. who will make a few feeble remarks." Entering the House when a vote was being taken in a contested election case, and hearing from a party member that it was a case of "two damned rascals," he asked, "Which is *our* damned rascal?"

When Lincoln had declared a blockade of the seceded states, Stevens in a White House call made the point that a nation did not blockade its own ports and therefore the declaration of blockade was a tacit acknowledgment of Southern independence. According to Stevens, Lincoln said mildly: "Yes, that's a fact. I see the point now, but I don't know anything about the Law of Nations and I thought it was all right."

Born in 1793, Stevens had seen Jackson, Clay, Calhoun, Webster and Douglas rise and pass out. Nearly 70 now, he was bald and wore a heavy wig of black hair. An emphatic shake of the head sometimes jiggled the wig over one ear. When an abolitionist woman asked him for a lock of hair, he took off the wig and offered it to her. Scholar, wit, zealot of liberty, part fanatic, who could read the heart of limping, poker-faced old Thaddeus Stevens?

Early he had gone to warn Lincoln that Cameron had taking ways and might not be the man for War Department head. "You don't mean to say you think Cameron would steal?" Lincoln asked. "No," was the reply, "I don't think he would steal a red-hot stove." Lincoln repeated this to Cameron as good wit and perhaps a warning to be careful. Cameron insisted that Stevens must retract. So Stevens at the White House said, "Mr. Lincoln, why did you tell Cameron what I said to you?" "I thought it was a good joke and didn't think it would make him mad." "Well, he is very mad and made me promise to retract. I will now do so. I believe I told you he would *not* steal a red-hot stove. I now take that back."

In January '62 it was six months since McClellan had been put at the head of the Army of the Potomac. Money, men, bread, beef, gunpowder, arms, artillery, horses, had been given McClellan on a colossal scale. The army under him in the public prints and in common talk was rated the largest and finest known in modern history. And with this well-trained force of fresh troops he settled into winter quarters, the enemy army only two days' easy march away.

His army was made up mainly of boys in the early 20's, thousands of them 19 and under. They wrote home about their winter huts, pork and beans, coffee and soup from tin cups, epidemics of measles and mumps, digging trenches, putting up telegraph wires, clearing range for artillery with pick and shovel, throwing up earthworks, driving beef to camp, hauling military stores, dysentery, sore feet, roaches in hardtack, target practice, washing shirts and underwear in creeks and rivers.

In November McClellan wrote to his friend Barlow: "The President is perfectly honest and is really sound on the nigger question—I will answer for it now that things go right with him." Early in December Lincoln had handed

McClellan a carefully worked-out memorandum asking specific and technical questions about a forward movement. McClellan kept the memorandum ten days and sent it back with replies scribbled in pencil and a note dismissing all of Lincoln's suggestions: ". . . I have now my mind actively turned towards another plan of campaign." When officers of other armies called for more troops McClellan was surprised, sometimes shocked. General Sherman wired for 75,000 men to help the Western forces drive south; McClellan handed the dispatch to Lincoln, then at his headquarters, with the remark, "The man is crazy."

From week to week the contact grew worse between the political power, as embodied in Lincoln and Congress, and the military branch that asked for what it wanted. The political power tried to give it but the military branch did not seem to know this process was getting tiresome to the political end of the Government, which was closer to the people and the taxpayers.

Late in December McClellan fell sick with typhoid fever and took to his bed for three weeks. During those weeks he ran his armies, from the Atlantic to the Mississippi and beyond, from his bed. Lincoln wrote Chase a card January 2, 1862: "I have just been with General McClellan; and he is very much better." Days followed, however, when others came to McClellan's bedside and did business—but the President was kept outside, and failed to get polite entry.

What flitted through Lincoln's mind at this time was merely hinted at in an entry in the diary of Senator Browning: "Sunday Jany 12 A very warm day. Went to Dr. Gurleys Church in A.M. with dress coat & no overcoat . . . Had long talk with the President about the war—He told me he was thinking of taking the field himself, and suggested several plans of operation." Lincoln had been reading military treatises drawn from the Library of Congress, had held long conversations with officers widely versed in the theory of war, and considered himself as having grasped a few of the essentials.

In the Department of Missouri, General Halleck wrote Lincoln, mutinous "foreign" regiments calling for Frémont to command them had been disarmed; high officers were in the plot with the soldiers, Halleck believed; public property was robbed and plundered; discipline was going to pieces. Lincoln wrote on Halleck's letter: "It is exceedingly discouraging. As everywhere else, nothing can be done." Lincoln gave Gustave Koerner to Halleck, saying that Koerner could be made a brigadier general. "He is an educated and talented German gentleman, as true a man as lives. With his assistance you can set everything right with the Germans."

In memoranda kept by General McDowell were glimpses of Lincoln at the time McClellan lay sick and directing his armies. McDowell wrote of January 10, 1862: "Repaired to the President's house at eight o'clock, P.M. Found the President alone. Was taken into the small room in the north-east corner. Soon after we were joined by Brigadier-General Franklin, the Secretary of State, Governor Seward, the Secretary of the Treasury, and the Assistant-Secretary of War. The President was greatly disturbed at the state of affairs . . . said he was in great distress, and as he had been to General McClellan's house, and the General did not ask to see him; and as he must talk to somebody, he had sent for General Franklin and myself to obtain our opinion as to the possibility of soon commencing operations with the Army of the Potomac. To use his own expression, 'If something was not soon done, the bottom would be out of the whole affair; and if General McClellan did not want to use the army, he would like to borrow it provided he could see how it could be made to do something.'"

Two nights later somewhat the same group met—with McClellan present, up and out of bed. He refused to discuss proposed movements of the army. "Much conversation ensued, of rather a general character," ran McDowell's memorandum. "The Secretary of the Treasury then put a direct question to General McClellan to the effect as to what he intended doing with his army, and when he intended doing it?" After a long silence McClellan said a movement in Kentucky was to precede any from Washington. "After another pause he said he must say he was very unwilling to develop his plans, always believing that in military matters the fewer persons who were knowing them the better; that he would tell them if he was *ordered* to do so. The President then asked him if he counted upon any particular time; he did not ask what that time was, but had he in his own mind any particular time a movement could be commenced. He replied he had. Then, rejoined the President, I will adjourn this meeting."

Now that McClellan was up and they could get at him, the Committee on the Conduct of the War called him for a consultation. Senator Chandler spoke bluntly: "General McClellan, if I understand you correctly, before you strike at the rebels you want to be sure of plenty of room so that you can run in case they strike back." And this was seconded by Wade's sneer, "Or in case you get scared." McClellan then went into an explanation for the Senators of how wars are fought and how necessary it is for generals to have always available lines of retreat as well as lines of communication and supply.

Lincoln, while refusing to remove McClellan from command, as urged by radicals, was getting ready to let McClellan know who held authority. He issued on January 27 his General War Order No. 1, fixing February 22, 1862, as "the day for a general movement of the Land and Naval forces of the United States against the insurgent forces." He named the army "at & about, Fortress Monroe," the Army of the Potomac, the Army of Western Virginia, the army near Munfordville, Kentucky, the army and flotilla of gunboats at Cairo, Illinois, and a naval force in the Gulf of Mexico as ordered to be ready to move on that day. Department heads, commanders and subordinates "will severally be held to their strict and full responsibilities, for the prompt execution of this order." Four days later he followed this with "President's Special War Order No. 1" commanding that the Army of the Potomac, after providing for the defense of Washington, move on February 22 to seize and occupy Manassas Junction, "all details to be in the discretion of the general-in-chief." To this last he added a note to McClellan on February 3 urging his plan for a land attack on the Confederate army near Washington rather than an expedition by water for a peninsular attack on Richmond:

. . . If you will give me satisfactory answers to the following questions, I shall gladly yield my plan to yours. Does not your plan involve a greatly larger expenditure of *time*, and *money* than mine? Wherein is a victory *more certain* by your plan than mine? Wherein is a victory *more valuable* by your plan than mine? In fact, would it not be *less* valuable, in this, that it would break no great line of the enemie's communications, while mine would? In case of disaster, would not a retreat be more difficult by your plan than mine?

McClellan replied on the same day with a long letter showing his belief that by rapid enveloping movements on the peninsula near Richmond he could take the Confederate capital. A direct land attack on the Confederate army near Washington he could not approve. But he did have a mental picture of what he was going to do, for, wrote Secretary Chase, he came February 13 and said, "In ten days I shall be in Richmond . . . The ten days passed away; no movement, and no preparation for a movement, had been made."

McClellan gave consent to Lincoln's plucking Frémont from his retirement. There was created the Mountain Department in West Virginia, where Frémont took command of 25,000 men, later reinforced by 10,000. He was to follow a pet plan of Lincoln's, which he approved. The idea was to march over the mountains into East Tennessee, lend strength to the Unionist sentiment which dominated there, and seize the railroad at Knoxville. McClellan had no objections. And for the time being Lincoln had found a niche for the political and military figure about whom there clung such an aura of romance that thousands of boy babies in antislavery families were named Frémont.

A jobber from Vermont, Jim Fisk, twisted his swagger mustache and grinned with a cock of his eye, "You can sell anything to the government at almost any price you've got the guts to ask." His suite at Willard's welcomed Congressmen to a Havana cigar, a favorite drink and any kind of a dicker that would pay.

A report to Congress in December by the Committee on Government Contracts threw light on curious commissions and special favors, exorbitant prices charged the Government, and low-quality goods and articles delivered to the Army and Navy. Corruption so underlay the Government, wrote General Sherman in a private letter, that "even in this time of trial, cheating in clothes, blankets, flour, bread, everything, is universal."

To a resolution directing that the Secretary of War furnish the Senate with information as to contracts, amounts, names of contractors, dates, payments of money, Cameron made no reply. Months passed and Cameron sent neither information nor excuses nor regrets nor acknowledgments to the Senate.

Part of the clamor that arose was political and aimed at smearing the administration. Part of it traced to the jealousy of contractors and special interests not in favor with Cameron. Of this Lincoln was keenly aware. A delegation of New York and Boston bankers called on him and urged the removal of Cameron. "They talked very glibly," said Lincoln later to the portrait painter Frank B. Carpenter. Lincoln finally had to tell them: "Gentlemen, if you want General Cameron removed, you have only to bring me *one proved* case of dishonesty, and I promise you his 'head.' But I assure you I am not going to act on what seems to me the most unfounded gossip."

Firearms scandals were disposed of in a single sentence that, coming from Cameron with no facts or data, might be read in several ways: "Combinations among manufacturers, importers, and agents, for the sale of arms, have, in many cases, caused an undue increase in prices."

The catalogue of frauds and extortions was, said several journals, sickening. In the speeches of Holman, Trumbull, Dawes, Van Wyck, was no tone of persecution or of political maneuvering. They were Republican party men who wanted to get on with the war and win it, and they were sickened by the job of having first of all to combat men of their own party within the administration whom they termed "public enemies." They said they were well aware that disturbers, gossips, spies, informers, disgruntled competitors, jealous rivals in politics and business, not to mention newspaper sensationalists, were spreading exaggerated stories and rumors; it was no time for idle chatter but one for sticking strictly to the documentary record. Interruptions of their speeches were usually requests for further information. The methods and findings of the Committee on Government Contracts were almost universally accepted. The longer addresses of Representative Charles H. Van Wyck of New York had lamentation, depth of woe. He said, "The mania for stealing seems to have run through all the relations of Government—almost from the general to the drummer-boy; from those nearest the throne of power to the merest tide-waiter. Nearly every man who deals with the Government seems to feel or desire that it would not long survive, and each had a common right to plunder while it lived."

Van Wyck called the roll of rascals, gave cases and names, with the amounts stolen or the extortionate profits garnered, and alluded to them as the equivalents of incendiaries, horse thieves, dancing harlots. Was it a truth or a masked traitor's lie that every star of the sky stands as a sentinel over the graves where the patriot dead sleep? "The pirates who infest the ocean are not more deserving the execration of mankind than the gang who, on land, are suffered to feast upon the sweat of the poor and the blood of the brave."

To Nicolay, Lincoln said one day amid the furor: "It is a good thing for individuals that there is a Government to shove their acts upon. No man's shoulders are broad enough to bear what must be."

In the War Department Cameron personally was slovenly as to method, seemed to have no files or records in his office, and according to Representative Riddle, "in any official matter he would ask you to give its status and what he had last said about it." On being informed, "he would look about, find a scrap of paper, borrow your pencil, make a note, put the paper in one pocket of his trousers and your pencil in the other." Once a caller had to tell him, "The last thing you did in this case, Mr. Secretary, was to put my pencil in your pocket." After fussing with the often vague and indirect Cameron it was a relief, said Riddle, to go to Assistant Secretary Thomas A. Scott and meet an "electric brain and cool quiet manner."

Slowly the President had arrived at his appraisal, given to Nicolay, that Cameron was utterly ignorant and, regardless of the course of things, obnoxious to the country, selfish, incapable of organizing details, and—least of all—"openly discourteous to the President." To Sumner, A. B. Ely was writing: "Thaddeus Stevens said Cameron would add a million to his fortune. I guess he has done it."

The first open break between Lincoln and Cameron came in December '61 when the Secretary issued his annual report. Without having consulted the Executive, Cameron was thrusting himself forward as a spokesman of administration policy. The slave property of rebels should be confiscated, declared the paragraph that surprised and offended the President: "It is as clearly a right of the Government to arm slaves, when it may become necessary, as it is to use gunpowder taken from the enemy. Whether it is expedient to do so is purely a military question . . . If it shall be found that the men who have been held by the rebels are capable of bearing arms and performing efficient military service, it is the right, and may become the duty of the Government to arm and equip them, and employ their services against the rebels."

As Lincoln first glanced at the copy from the public printer placed in his hands, and his eye rested on the passage about arming the slaves, he was instantly aroused. And as the incident later came to the painter Carpenter, Lincoln spoke decisively: "This will never do! General Cameron must take no such responsibility. That is a question which belongs exclusively to me!" Telegrams went to the postmasters of the leading cities. The Cameron report was mailed back to Washington. A new edition was printed with the closing paragraph of the first edition omitted and a new paragraph substituted.

Newspapers had easily gotten copies of the Cameron report and published the suppressed paragraph alongside the final official one. The difference between the two was that the first sounded as though the administration was about ready to throw Negro troops into the war, while the later one suggested that the administration was still hesitating. Bursts of approval came from the antislavery ranks for Cameron, though it seemed on the part of Cameron too sudden a conversion to the cause of the Negro, in which he had hitherto been no radical. In the crusader's mantle he was a comic.

Both Lincoln and Cameron knew they had come to the parting of the ways. "Having corrected his minister's haste and imprudence," wrote Nicolay and Hay, "the President indulged in no further comment . . . They met in Cabinet consultations, or for the daily dispatch of routine business, with the same cordial ease as before." Cameron began to hint that his War Department duties wearied him and he would prefer a foreign mission. Lincoln said nothing for several weeks. Then a note of January 11, 1862, written by Lincoln to Cameron was made public: "As you have, more than once, expressed a desire for a change of position, I can now gratify you, consistently with my view of the public interest. I therefore propose nominating you to the Senate, next Monday, as minister to Russia."

In a private letter of the same date Lincoln wrote to Cameron that Cassius Marcellus Clay was returning from the post of Minister to Russia to fight for his country as a major general, and therefore the President could now offer that post to Mr. Cameron. "Should you accept it, you will bear with you the assurance of my undiminished confidence, of my affectionate esteem . . ." This letter, subscribed "Very sincerely Your friend, A. Lincoln," could be used by Cameron either at the court of the Czar or in Pennsylvania political circles for the information of any who wished to know how matters stood between him and the President. Cameron's reply of the same date "with profound respect" acknowledged the "kind and generous tone" of the President's letter.

Four days the Senate wrestled behind closed doors on the President's naming Cameron Minister to Russia. Cameron was confirmed January 17 by a vote of 28 to 14.

No other member of Lincoln's Cabinet seemed to have the complete approval accorded Edwin McMasters Stanton to replace Cameron. A Jackson Democrat replacing an ousted secessionist in President Buchanan's Cabinet as the Cotton States were seceding, he confidentially advised Seward and other Unionists of what went on in Cabinet meetings. Since then Stanton had been legal adviser to McClellan, to Cameron, John Dix and others. As the days passed he wrote letters to Buchanan, to Dix, to others, referring to "the painful imbecility of Lincoln," mentioning "distrust in the sincerity of Lincoln." He heard this and that and sped it onward in letters. "It is said that Lincoln takes the precaution of seeing no strangers alone." Bull Run was "another imbecility of the administration"; it was "the result of Lincoln's running the machine for five months." McClellan wrote as though amused and somewhat baffled by Stanton's frequently referring to Lincoln as the "original gorilla."

Often in handling people Stanton seemed to manage a fierce glare and a domineering, tempestuous manner. He was crazy or sick, more often just plainly difficult, according to various people. In fact, asthma was the lesser of his afflictions. Before Cameron sent to Lincoln his report favoring the arming of Negroes for Union service, he called in his legal adviser, Stanton. And Stanton gave approval to this clause and wrote an additional paragraph which Cameron adopted and inserted. By a tortuous path this nervous, asthmatic, strong man of many contradictions had come to be head of a War Department having authority over 600,000 soldiers. Moderates or conservatives like Seward, Cameron and McClellan endorsed him while in the same moment the radicals Chase, Wade and Sumner were saying, "He is one of us."

Stanton, the son of a widowed mother, at 13 years of age took care of her and a family of five. Working his way through Kenyon College, clerking in a bookstore in Columbus, Ohio, he met Mary Lamson, daughter of an Episcopal clergyman, carefully educated and, like himself, poor. They took their honeymoon in a 125-mile sleigh ride from Columbus to Cadiz, Ohio, where he began law practice, made money from the start, was known as stiff and proud rather than sociable, on occasion designated as "cheeky."

"He is accounted the first lawyer in America," said the Chicago *Tribune* of Stanton. That, however, took no account of the moody and hectic Stanton, of the weird undergrowths of behavior swarming behind his black whiskers and black bushy hair, his spectacled nearsighted eyes with a vehement stare, his stocky and deep-chested body. As a boy he trained snakes, and once horrified a quiet family of women and children by entering their home with two large wriggling snakes around his neck. When his child Lucy died, after her body had been buried a year he had it exhumed, cremated, and placed the ashes in a metal box which he kept in his own room.

The wife of his youth died in childbirth in 1844 and Stanton insisted she must wear her wedding clothes for burial. For years he went twice a week to decorate her grave, on Sundays always going alone, "to meet her," he said. Twelve years passed before he married the daughter of a wealthy merchant in Pittsburgh.

Stanton's favorite relaxation was to leave home of a morning with a market basket on his arm, walk slowly along to the grocer's and huckster's, and shop for the home pantry and icebox. He knew the Constitution and the price of eggs and was solemn about both. Born of a Quaker strain, he was raised a Methodist and became a devoted communicant of the Episcopal church. In odd intervals he was writing a book to be called *Poetry of God*, he told Donn Piatt. A vortex of action called. He sat in Buchanan's Cabinet across a table from John B. Floyd, secessionist and Secretary of War, as Floyd urged withdrawal of troops from Charleston Harbor. Stanton exploded with wrath, declaring that the surrender of Fort Sumter would be a crime equal to treason and all who took a hand in it should be hanged. Then months had passed with history in a whirligig, events seen in a mist, and he sat in Donn Piatt's room in Washington replying to a query from Mr. and Mrs. Piatt. "Yes, I am going to be Secretary of War to Old Abe." "What will you do?" was asked. "Do? . . . I will make Abe Lincoln President of the United States. I will force this man McClellan to fight or throw up."

At the War Department, at ten o'clock in the morning a room 15 by 20 feet began to fill up with claim agents, contractors, relatives of soldiers, Senators and Congressmen, all unable to get a private interview with the department head. At 11 there was a buzz and a stir and Stanton walked in, speaking to no one till he reached a high desk opposite the entrance. Then he picked out one by one those he would do business with. To a gushing office seeker he might say, "Sit down, sir, I'll attend to you by-and-by." He might roar at an officer, even a major general in brass buttons and gold stars: "Come, sir, what are you doing in Washington? You are not needed here. I'll see about mustering you out."

Some were troubled over the new titan who might go too far and try to run away with the whole concern, they told Lincoln. He drawled: "We may have to treat him as they are sometimes obliged to treat a Methodist minister I know of out West. He gets wrought up to so high a pitch of excitement in his prayers and exhortations, that they are obliged to put bricks in his pockets to keep him down. We may be obliged to serve Stanton in the same way, but I guess we'll let him jump awhile first."

Every day Stanton had his errands at the White House. At any hour he might be seen walking from the War Office taking telegrams, letters, official business, to the President. And Lincoln stepped over to the War Office nearly every day, sometimes during large troop movements or battles spending hours with his War Secretary over the latest wire news. The President gave wide and free play to Stanton's capacity for hard work and Stanton's enjoyment of personal power. In office less than two weeks, Stanton ordered the arrest of General Charles P. Stone in the Ball's Bluff disaster.

On Stanton's announcing to him the news of the arrest, the President said, "I suppose you have good reasons for it; and having good reasons, I am glad I knew nothing of it until it was done." Willie Lincoln lay sick with fever, and later in connection with the Stone affair the President wrote, "Owing to sickness in my family, the Secretary of War made the arrest without notifying me that he had it in contemplation." To a Senate request for information three months later the President answered: "In relation to Brigadier General Stone . . . he has not been tried because in the state of military operations, at the time of his arrest and since, the officers to constitute a court-martial, and for witnesses, could not be withdrawn from duty without serious injury to the service. He will be allowed a trial without any unnecessary delay; the charges and specifications will be furnished him in due season; and every facility for his defence will be afforded him by the War Department." And Stone was held in Fort Lafayette prison 189 days, released without trial and without charges having been preferred against him, then again restored to his brigadier shoulder straps.

Lincoln's response to a formal record of censure of Cameron was unexpected and took the form of a long message to Senate and House. The House had not struck at him; its language implied Lincoln had been betrayed by men he had trusted. Yet Lincoln defended those men. He reviewed the outbreak of the war, treason in all departments, and Washington beleaguered, and then gave Congress extended statements of what he had before told Congress in explanation of why he had assumed dictatorial powers.

He closed with a paragraph of explanatory comment which took all censure off Cameron and placed it on the entire administration, and which seemed to assume the situation had been so chaotic and the action so furious that it was a time to let some bygones be bygones: "Congress will see that I should be wanting equally in candor and in justice if I should leave the censure expressed in this resolution to rest exclusively or chiefly upon Mr. Cameron . . . It is due to Mr. Cameron to say that, although he fully approved the proceedings, they were not moved nor suggested by himself, and that not only the President but all the other heads of departments were at least equally responsible with him for whatever error, wrong, or fault was committed in the premises."

Nicolay and Hay noted: "Cameron gratefully remembered this voluntary and manly defense of his official integrity. He remained one of the most intimate and devoted of Lincoln's personal friends."

The great industrial State of Pennsylvania—with its iron and coal—nearest to Washington and most liable to invasion, was not to be torn by the political warfare and disruption that would have followed the particular sort of degradation Cameron's enemies would have put on him. The unblemished abolitionist Congressman Owen Lovejoy, with a curiously steady light of conscience for a lamp to his feet, might have dropped the word to Lincoln to try Cameron longer.

Yet the unremitting quest of individual profits and personal fortunes, behind war fronts where men were dying for proclaimed sacred causes, made a contrast heavy for the human mind to hold and endure.

CHAPTER 24

Donelson—Grant—Shiloh—*Monitor* and *Merrimac*—"Seven Days"—The Draft

LINCOLN called to Washington James B. Eads, a St. Louis man who had spent many days on the bottom sand and mud of the Mississippi River, salvaging ships with a diving bell he invented. Eads, back in St. Louis and under Government contract, got 4,000 men over the country working on his plans. In 100 days he had ready eight iron-plated, steam-propelled gunboats. These and more made up a flotilla commanded by Andrew H. Foote, a Connecticut Yankee Puritan sea dog, who in 1856 had lost 40 of his own men and killed 400 Chinese in the Canton River of China, who never swore nor drank nor allowed intoxicating liquor on shipboard; his prayer meetings and sermons among seamen were a topic in naval and other circles.

On February 6, 1862, Commodore Foote's gunboats escorted steamboats up the Tennessee River carrying 18 regiments under Brigadier General Ulysses S. Grant. They crowded the decks watching the scenery, 18,000 troops—cornhuskers, teamsters, rail splitters, shopmen, factory hands, college students, from Iowa, Nebraska, Illinois, Indiana, Ohio, Missouri, many of them not yet old enough to vote.

The gunboats stopped at Fort Henry, shelled it, and troops marched in and took its flag. The Confederate garrison had left for Fort Donelson on the Cumberland River. Grant marched his army 12 miles across country to Fort Donelson in fair weather, warm and balmy.

Foote took his gunboats down to the Ohio River, up the Cumberland, and exchanging shots with the Fort Donelson guns was disabled so that he had to steam downriver. This left Grant with 27,000 troops, counting new arrivals, to contest with 18,000 troops inside a fort. Before the fighting began a cold wind came, snow fell, the roads froze. In ten-above-zero weather men fired and loaded their muskets, and in the night huddled and shivered, seeking fences, brush, trees, logs, to keep off the wind. Neither side dared light a bivouac fire. Men and boys were found next morning frozen stiff.

On Sunday, February 16, telegrams began trickling into the War Department in Washington. General Simon B. Buckner, commanding Fort Donelson, had sent a messenger to Grant asking for "terms of capitulation" and Grant replied: "No terms except an unconditional and immediate surrender can be accepted. I propose to move immediately upon your works." And the Confederate commander was surrendering the fort and 13,828 prisoners. The battle losses were: Union, 500 killed, 2,108 wounded, 224 missing; Confederate, 231 killed, 1,534 wounded. The victory clinched Kentucky to the

Union, gave a foothold in Tennessee, sent Union armies 200 miles forward into enemy territory. It lighted up the gloom of the North and the hopes of Lincoln.

Ulysses S. Grant, an Ohio boy, graduated at West Point as number 21 in a class of 39. At West Point he rode a horse over a hurdle six feet six, a new record. At Monterey in the Mexican War he went for ammunition relief, riding under fire in Comanche style, clinging to the saddle with one leg while holding his head and body close to the side of the horse away from the enemy. He was five feet eight in height, wore a full beard, was nearly always a little disheveled, even sat for his picture with coat or hair in disorder. He had quiet manners, gravity, gray eyes, and a face with economy of expression.

At Fort Vancouver on the West Coast in 1854 no works or projects challenged him. He was homesick, carried in his inside coat pocket a worn pack of letters from his wife. Grant had married her without a regular proposal; they were buggy-driving across a flooded bridge when she cried, "I'm going to cling to you no matter what happens," and safely over, he asked, "How would you like to cling to me for the rest of your life?"

One day there came to Fort Vancouver a locket holding a long thin braid of a woman's hair interwoven with a little curl of a child's hair; this Grant wore around his neck. Why did he drink harder at this time? Was it loneliness for home? For he was warned that as a captain his drunkenness was bad for the regiment. He wrote out a blank resignation and gave it to the colonel; it was to be dated and sent to the War Department if whisky again got the best of him, which it did. He quit the Army.

Grant cleared land on 80 acres near St. Louis left to him by his wife's father. He became accustomed to two slaves given to his wife by her father, a slaveholder. He hauled wood ten miles into St. Louis at $10 a cord. He built himself a two-story house of logs, a masterpiece of simple design and craftsmanship, and named the place Hardscrabble. They traded Hardscrabble for a house and lot in St. Louis. As a real-estate salesman Grant failed. Friends said ague and rheumatism still held him; chills shook him on spring afternoons, weakened him so that he was dizzy and had to be helped to the omnibus he rode home in. He looked glum and felt useless. The family moved to Galena, Illinois, where he was selling hides to shoemakers and harness- and saddle-makers, his income $800 a year, when the war commenced. He went to Springfield, Illinois, was made colonel, and took a regiment to Missouri.

Chaplain James B. Crane, bringing him the *Missouri Democrat* one day in August, said, "I see that you are made brigadier-general." "Well, sir," said Grant, "that's some of Washburne's work. I knew Washburne in Galena. He was a strong Republican and I was a Democrat, and I thought from that he never liked me very much."

The country had now nicknamed him "Unconditional Surrender" Grant. Halleck wired McClellan, "His army seems to be as much demoralized by the victory of Fort Donelson as was that of the Potomac by the defeat of Bull Run." McClellan believed he understood the case, and wired back, "Do not hesitate to arrest Grant at once if the good of the service requires it."

Against intrigue, connivance and slander, Lincoln gave to Grant the stars of a major general. The President was more than interested in this plain fighter who had given the Union cause its first victories worth mentioning. Lincoln saw among the driving motives in the Fort Donelson victory the passion of the Northwest, his own region, for nationalism, for an unbreakable Union of States.

The laughter at McClellan now was wry, bitter. The Western forces had battled and won big points sooner than commanded in Lincoln's order setting February 22 as the day for a general movement of land and sea forces. Washington's Birthday came while McClellan's colossal Army of the Potomac kept to its tents and winter huts around Washington. Johnston nearby at Manassas had in his Confederate army less than one man for McClellan's three.

A clerk who handled much of the White House mail, William O. Stoddard, noted that Lincoln was "intensely, absorbingly interested" in the February 22 advance he had ordered. A staff officer from McClellan came and began explanations of why the advance could not be made February 22. "Why?" asked the President. The officer murmured, "The pontoon trains are not ready," and was interrupted, "Why in hell and damnation *ain't* they ready?" And as Stoddard saw it: "The officer could think of no satisfactory reply, but turned very hastily and left the room. Mr. Lincoln turned to the table and resumed the work before him."

Lincoln now stepped publicly into the handling of the Army of the Potomac, to the extent of publishing on March 7 and 8 his General War Orders No. 2 and No. 3. One directed McClellan to organize his army for active field operations into four corps, Lincoln naming the generals to command. The second ordered that whatever the field operations might take, enough troops should be left in and about Washington to leave the capital secure. This and other matters brought McClellan to the White House. On Sunday, March 9, while McClellan sat in conference with Lincoln and Stanton, a message came with news that Johnston's army at Manassas had moved out of its entrenchments, broken from winter quarters, and moved southward, leaving as mementoes many "Quaker guns"—logs on wheels, painted to look like cannon.

McClellan, shocked into action, that very Sunday ordered his army to march. At three the next morning he telegraphed Stanton, "The troops are in motion." He arrived at Bull Run Creek, at Manassas, and found it as reported—empty. Then he marched his army back again to Washington. To those asking why he did not push on, find the enemy and attack, he let it be known he was giving his troops a practice maneuver.

Among powerful financial, transportation and industrial interests gathered around such individuals as August Belmont, William H. Aspinwall, Cyrus McCormick, James Gordon Bennett, there was still faith in McClellan. Slowly too the impression grew in some circles that McClellan was interfered with too much by Stanton, by War Office bureaucrats, by the suspicious antislavery radicals.

Browning asked Lincoln if he still had confidence in McClellan and wrote: "He assured me he had . . . That he [McClellan] had now gone to Fortress Monroe with his Command, with orders to move on Richmond without delay, and that only on yesterday when McClelland came to take leave of him preparatory to marching, he shed tears when speaking of the cruel imputations upon his loyalty, and defending himself against them The President added that Genl Scott, and all the leading military men around him, had always assured him that McClelland possessed a very high order of military talent, and that he did not think they could all be mistaken . . . that he had studied McClelland . . . that he thought he had the capacity to make arrangements properly for a great conflict, but as the hour for action approached he became nervous and oppressed with the responsibility and hesitated to meet the crisis, but that he had given him peremptory orders to move now, and he must do it."

Eight days later Browning wrote of seeing the President and "He told me he was becoming impatient and dissatisfied with McClellan's sluggishness of action."

Lincoln had ordered McDowell with 40,000 troops to stay in and near Washington. The capture of the national capital would probably bring Britain and France to recognize the Confederate Government, the blockade would be broken, arms and supplies would pour into the South. Lincoln wrote McClellan: "My explicit order that Washington should, by the judgment of *all* the commanders of Army corps, be left entirely secure, had been neglected. It was precisely this that drove me to detain McDowell."

Then came bickering. McClellan was to claim he must have more troops. The War Office would ask why he did not have more than he claimed. "There is a curious mystery about the *number* of troops now with you," wrote Lincoln. "When I telegraphed you on the 6th. saying you had over 100,000 with you, I had just obtained from the Secretary of War, a statement, taken as he said, from your own returns, making 108,000 then with you, and *en route* to you. You now say you will have but 85,000 when all *en route* to you shall have reached you. How can the discrepancy of 23,000 be accounted for?" He tried gently to prod McClellan into moving forward and fighting. "Once more let me tell you, it is indispensable to *you* that you strike a blow. *I* am powerless to help this."

McClellan wrote his wife: "I have raised an awful row about McDowell's corps. The President very coolly telegraphed me . . . that he thought I had better break the enemy's lines at once! I was much tempted to reply that he had better come and do it himself." It also troubled McClellan that the President issued an order limiting his command to that of the Army of the Potomac. He wrote his wife of "rascality" and "traitors" in Washington.

In such a mood McClellan in April '62 headed the Army of the Potomac, on the peninsula before the Confederate entrenchments at Yorktown. Moving this army from Washington by water had required 113 steamers, 188 schooners, 88 barges, hauling for three weeks 121,500 men, 14,592 animals, 1,150 wagons, 44 batteries, 74 ambulances, besides pontoon bridges, telegraph materials, equipage, cattle, food, supplies.

McClellan kept his army at Yorktown for weeks while he threw up entrenchments, built batteries, installed big guns. "Do not misunderstand the apparent inaction here," he wrote to Lincoln. "Not a day, not an hour has been lost. Works have been constructed that may almost be called gigantic." And when at last McClellan's big guns were set to blow the enemy off the map, when finally Union troops moved out to capture the foe, they found nobody to fight. Again he had not heard Lincoln's warning: "the present hesitation to move upon an intrenched enemy, is but the story of Manassas repeated."

When at last after a month of siege the empty Confederate entrenchments were captured, McClellan telegraphed: "Yorktown is in our possession . . . No time shall be lost . . . I shall push the enemy to the wall." The total force under Johnston, who had evacuated, numbered 55,633 men, about one to two of McClellan's. They had waited till McClellan had finished building elaborate batteries, till McClellan was perfectly satisfied that he could shell and shatter all opposition. Then they drew off.

Other actions were staged elsewhere and with different results. Three days' fighting went on at Pea Ridge in the northwest corner of Arkansas between Missouri, Iowa, Illinois and Ohio regiments against Missouri, Arkansas and Texas regiments along with three Red Indian regiments. The Union forces lost 203 killed, 972 wounded, 174 missing, as against 800 to 1,000 killed, 200 to 300 missing, of the Confederates. The battle clinched Missouri deeper into the Union.

An action came as "a thrust into the vitals of the Confederacy." The sea dogs Commodore David Glasgow Farragut and Commodore David Dixon Porter, with battleships and mortar boats, along with Major General Ben Butler heading an army of land troops, ran and battered their way through the forts and batteries at New Orleans and captured the largest seaport and the most important metropolitan center of the South, a city of 168,000. An army of 10,000 Confederates left the city, their torches lighting 15,000 bales of cotton, a dozen large ships, several fine steamboats, unfinished gunboats and property worth millions of dollars.

In charge of the city as its military governor came Ben Butler, the former Breckinridge proslavery Democrat who had at one time striven to nominate Jefferson Davis for the Presidency of the United States. Butler tried to regulate newspapers, the food supply, money, flags permitted or prohibited. Regulating the women was no simple affair. They drew aside their skirts when they met Union officers and soldiers. They grimaced and taunted. They spat on the Union flag. They stepped off the sidewalk rather than pass a Yankee. Butler arrested the mayor, the chief of police and others, and put them in the guardhouse of a captured fort. In time the new governor was to be known among Southerners as "Beast Butler" or "Butler the Beast," or in token of stolen silverware, "Spoons Butler."

On the Tennessee River near the Mississippi State line at Shiloh Church and Pittsburg Landing, General Albert Sidney Johnston had hurled 40,000 Confederate troops in attack on 36,000 under Grant. The Union lines were steadily forced back. Would night find them driven to the bank of the wide Tennessee River and no bridge to cross? Sherman had three horses shot under him, got a bullet in the hand, another through his hat; a third grazed his shoulder. One tree about as thick as a lean man received 90 bullets, another tree 60. In a clearing between woodlands men lay so thick that careful walking was required not to step on the dead.

Toward evening Grant sat his horse, watching the Confederates try to take a hill guarded by a battery and Union gunboats. Someone asked him if things looked gloomy. He answered: "Delay counts for everything with us.

Tomorrow we shall attack them with fresh troops, and drive them, of course." Darkness fell on the Sabbath slaughter. Rain came in torrents on the tentless soldiers of the two armies. In the gray of dawn the Union troops moved in attack and that day, reinforced by 20,000 under Buell and 6,000 under Lew Wallace, drove the enemy to retreat. Albert Sidney Johnston, counted one of the most brilliant of Confederate commanders, was killed the day before, it was learned. The Union army lost 13,047 in killed, wounded and missing, the Confederates 10,694.

The President issued a proclamation: "It has pleased Almighty God to vouchsafe signal victories to the land and naval forces engaged in suppressing an internal rebellion, and at the same time to avert from our country the dangers of foreign intervention and invasion." He recommended to the people that "at their next weekly assemblages in their accustomed places of public worship" they should "especially acknowledge and render thanks to our Heavenly Father for these inestimable blessings." He spoke of hope for peace, harmony and unity in his own country, and beyond that "the establishment of fraternal relations among all the countries of the earth."

At first the joy over victory ran high in the North. Then this was modified by a widely spread story that Grant was drunk at Shiloh. Lincoln received at the White House one night at 11 o'clock his friend A. K. McClure, who as spokesman for a number of Republicans talked for nearly two hours on how "the tide of popular sentiment" was against Grant and Grant should be dismissed from the service so that the President could retain the confidence of the country. Lincoln let McClure talk with few interruptions. Then, as McClure reported it: "When I had said every thing that could be said from my standpoint, we lapsed into silence. Lincoln remained silent for what seemed a very long time. He then gathered himself up in his chair and said, in a tone of earnestness that I shall never forget, 'I can't spare this man—he fights!'"

In Richmond on February 22, 1862, Jefferson Davis had taken his inauguration oath for a six-year term of office. Heavy rain fell while President Davis under a canvas cover addressed a big crowd holding umbrellas: "After a series of successes and victories . . . we have recently met with serious disasters." He was referring to Fort Donelson. Pale, worn, resolved, and around him men also resolved, they would consecrate their toil, property, lives, to a nation of their own. Tears trickled down the faces of gray-headed men of the planter aristocracy. They joined in silence in the prayer of Davis spoken across the rain: "Acknowledging the Providence which has so visibly protected the Confederacy during its brief but eventful career, to Thee, O God! I trustingly commit myself, and prayerfully invoke Thy blessing on my country and its cause."

And in the White House the President was hit hard by a personal grief. The boys Tad and Willie, joined by two playmates from Cincinnati, Bud and Holly Taft, were often a comfort to him. Once they took rags and old clothes and made a doll they named Jack. In red baggy trousers, with a tight blue jacket and a red fez on his head, this Jack was a Zouave. And they sentenced Jack to be shot at sunrise for sleeping on picket duty. They were burying Jack when the head gardener asked, "Why don't you have Jack pardoned?" Into the White House chased the four boys, upstairs to a desk where a man dropped his work, heard them, and soberly wrote on a sheet of Executive Mansion stationery:

> The doll Jack is pardoned.
> By order of the President
> A. LINCOLN

To Julia Taft, sister of Bud and Holly, Tad gave this pardon paper, saying there would be no burying of Jack. In a week, however, Jack was hanging by the neck, dangling from the branch of a big bush in the garden, Tad saying, "Jack was a traitor and a spy."

Tad was dashing, valorous, often impudent; Willie more thoughtful and imaginative. All the main railroad stations from New York to Chicago were in Willie's memory and at his tongue's end. He could call them off, including Troy, Schenectady, Utica, Rome, including Ashtabula, Cleveland, Sandusky, Toledo. He spent hours drawing up timetables and would conduct an imaginary train from Chicago to New York with perfect precision. Also Willie spent hours curled up in a chair enjoying books, a grave, delicate boy. In his diary Attorney General Bates wrote that Willie was too much "idolized" by his parents. The boy had rare lights—and the father and mother made much of him.

Willie Lincoln went riding on his pony in a chilly rain and fell sick with a cold and fever in February '62, at a time when a White House ball was planned. The President spoke of the ball to Miss Dorothea Dix, wanted to stop it, had it announced officially there would be no dancing. "But the Marine band at the foot of the steps filled the house with music while the boy lay dying above," wrote one woman. "A sadder face than that of the President I have rarely seen. He was receiving at the large door of the East Room, speaking to the people as they came, but feeling so deeply that he spoke of what he felt and thought, instead of welcoming the guests. To General Frémont he at once said that his son was very ill and he feared for the result . . . The ball was becoming a ghastly failure."

During the next few days Willie called for Bud Taft, who came and held his hand. The President would come in, lean over and stroke Willie's hair. "Better go to bed, Bud," he said one night. Bud answered, "If I go he will call for me." Still another night Lincoln came in, found Bud asleep, picked him up and carried him off to another room.

A few days later Willie lay still and cold. Elizabeth Keckley, the mulatto seamstress and Mrs. Lincoln's trusted companion, wrote, "The light faded from his eyes, and the death-dew gathered on his brow." She had been on watch but did not see the end, telling of it: "I was worn out with watching, and was not in the room when Willie died, but was immediately sent for. I assisted in washing and dressing him, and then laid him on the bed, when Mr. Lincoln came in." He lifted the cover from the face of his child, gazed at it long, and murmured, "It is hard, hard, hard to have him die!" The mother wept long hours, moaned and shook with grief.

They closed down the lids over the blue eyes of the boy, parted his brown hair, put flowers from his mother in his pale, crossed hands, and soldiers, Senators, Cabinet officers, foreign Ministers, came to the funeral. The mother, too far spent, could not come. The body was later sent west to Illinois for burial. And the mother clutched at his memory and if his name was mentioned her voice shook and the tears came. "She could not bear to look upon his picture," said Mrs. Keckley. "And after his death she never crossed the threshold of the Guest's Room in which he died, or the Green Room in which he was embalmed."

The grief over Willie was hard to shake off; a month later in answering a letter which should have had an earlier reply the President wrote of "a domestic affliction" which "has delayed me so long." Among letters of condolence that had come was one, softhearted and sincere, from ex-President Pierce, mentioning that he too had once lost a boy he loved and could understand the grief.

On Sunday, March 9, 1862, news came that sent Secretary Welles hurrying to the President, who at once called the Cabinet. A U.S. 40-gun frigate, the *Merrimac*, had been fitted by the Confederates with a cast-iron ram, and covered with four-inch iron plates. On Saturday afternoon, she had met two Union war vessels, the *Congress* and the *Cumberland*, and shot and rammed their wooden hulls till they were helpless. Another Union war vessel, the *Minnesota*, also wooden, had been run aground. And the news was that the *Merrimac* would on Sunday morning be free to move on Washington or New York.

Welles told of one hope; the *Monitor*, a new type of sea-fighting craft, had arrived at Hampton Roads the night before. When Welles mentioned to Stanton that the *Monitor* carried only two guns, "his mingled look of incredulity and contempt cannot be described," wrote Welles. ". . . To me there was throughout the whole day something inexpressibly ludicrous in the wild, frantic talk, action, and rage of Stanton as he ran from room to room . . . swung his arms, scolded, and raved."

Stanton got Admiral Dahlgren to make ready 60 rock-laden canalboats to be sunk in the Potomac and obstruct the *Merrimac*. But Dahlgren refused to take further orders from the Secretary of War; he was in the Navy and that department had its own Secretary. According to Welles: "Stanton claimed that, instead of consulting and asking, the military could order naval assistance, and that it was the duty of the Secretary of the Navy and of naval officers to render it. President Lincoln would not, however, lend himself to this view of the subject."

Towed by a tug out of New York Harbor three days before, the little *Monitor* met rough weather; water broke over the engines, down the blower pipes and smokestacks; hand pumps were rigged and worked. Then the wind and high waves went down, or the *Monitor* would have gone to sea bottom. Once again fighting rough sea in shoals the captain and crew wondered if the hawser running to the tug would hold. It did and they rode out two storms.

They were a tired crew on the *Monitor*, twice nearly sunk, no food but hard sea biscuit on a storm-soaked vessel, and no sleep in 48 hours. Their commander, Lieutenant John Worden, said no captain ever had a better crew; the crew swore their captain was the best that ever walked a deck. As the Confederate *Merrimac* came on toward the *Minnesota* next morning, the little *Monitor* made straight for her, a David against a Goliath, ten guns on the *Merrimac* against two on the *Monitor*. "A cheesebox on a raft," "a tin can on a shingle," that was the *Monitor*, equipped with a revolving steel tower or turret, so that she could shoot from any position; and her raftlike deck was so low that it would be difficult for the big *Merrimac* to ram her.

The tiny *Monitor* moved around the giant *Merrimac* like a fast bantamweight circling a ponderous heavyweight. The big one crashed its ten guns against the little one. And the little one did not move except to answer with its two guns. A deep thrill went round the hearts of the men handling the guns in the *Monitor* turret when the first heavy slugs of the *Merrimac* thundered their impact on the outside of the turret. Sometimes it was hard to start

Battle between the *Monitor* and the *Merrimac*

the turret revolving. They hoped it would not snarl. "Once the *Merrimac* tried to ram us," wrote S. Dana Greene, lieutenant commander, "but Worden avoided the direct impact by skillful use of the helm, and she struck a glancing blow which did no damage."

The *Monitor* turret ran out of shells and she drew off for 15 minutes to bring up fresh ammunition. The *Merrimac*, drawing 22 feet, could not follow the *Monitor*, which could steam into water a little over 12 feet deep. The *Monitor* came back; again the two guns against ten trying to cripple or kill each other. "Again she came up on our quarter and fired twice," said a Confederate on the *Merrimac* after the fight. "The impact forced the side in bodily two or three inches. All the crews of the after guns were knocked over by the concussion, and bled from the nose or ears. Another shot in the same place would have penetrated."

The *Merrimac* ceased firing, and a gunnery officer was asked by his superior, "Why are you not firing, Mr. Eggleston?" "Why, our powder is very precious," called the lieutenant, "and after two hours' incessant firing I find that I can do her about as much damage by snapping my thumb at her every two minutes and a half."

At ten yards' distance a shell from the *Merrimac* hit the sighthole of the pilothouse, stunning Lieutenant Worden, filling his eyes with powder and blinding him, his face covered with blood. The *Monitor* drew off to care for its commander and to examine how badly the pilothouse was wrecked. The *Merrimac* drew off and steamed to Norfolk.

After six hours it was a drawn battle. Each side had made its mistakes. If the *Merrimac* had concentrated its entire fire on the *Monitor* pilothouse from the first, it would have destroyed the *Monitor*'s control. If the *Monitor* had shot at the *Merrimac*'s water line, where the armor was weak, it would have sunk the *Merrimac*. However, the two ships had taught the navies of the world a lesson. London and Paris declared that the era of wooden fighting craft was over. The Washington Government would now begin building a fleet of monitors. The blockade of Southern ports would go on.

In the crews of both ships were men writing home, as did S. Dana Greene, of being worn. "My men and myself were perfectly black with smoke and powder. All my underclothes were perfectly black, and my person was in the same condition . . . My nerves and muscles twitched . . . I lay down and tried to sleep—I might as well have tried to fly."

News of the battle came with pleasure to John Ericsson, the Swede who designed the *Monitor*. He grew up among mines and ironworks in Sweden, became a captain in the Army, resigned, invented an instrument for taking sea soundings, a hydrostatic weighing machine, artificial drafts that decreased smokestack size and economized fuel, a self-acting gunlock for naval cannon, a steam carriage in 1829 which ran 30 miles an hour. He came to the United States in 1839, and two years later furnished designs for a screw warship, "the first vessel having propelling machinery below water-line, out of reach of hostile shot." He improved gun carriages, optical instruments, won medals for innovations "in the management of heat."

His wife came from Sweden, joined him in New York, was as proud of his genius as he was of her beauty. And while she filled her time as best she could, Ericsson worked at the shop all day and stuck to his drawing table till midnight. After a time he found that she was, as he said, "jealous of a steam-engine." So she went to England. Ericsson sent her an allowance; they wrote letters to each other. He sent her passage money to cross the Atlantic and begin over their home life. It arrived to find her on a deathbed, a sister writing to Ericsson her last message for him: "I have always been a trouble to you. Forgive me." She could not quite gather his passion for tools, wheels, progress, man's quest in the material world.

This granitic man of quiet pride had written to the President in August '61 that "steel-clad vessels cannot be arrested in their course by land batteries." He was 58 when in '61 he laid his plans before a naval board of three commodores. They told him his plans had been considered when previously presented by a friend of Ericsson—and they were rejected. He asked why they had been rejected. Mainly, it turned out, they were afraid the *Monitor* as designed would upset; it lacked stability. So Ericsson talked about stability of vessels.

At one session of the naval board Lincoln and Cabinet members were present. All were surprised at the novelty of the plan. Some advised trying it; others ridiculed it. The session closed with Lincoln holding a pasteboard model of the *Monitor* and remarking: "All I have to say is what the girl said when she put her foot into the stocking. It strikes me there's something in it."

Finally they gave Ericsson a contract with a clause saying that if the

Monitor did not prove "invulnerable" he was to refund all Government money paid him. Croakings were in his ears as he went to New York, drew his final plans, and saw the ship built in exactly 100 days. When she went into action the final Government payment on her had not been made. Now he could read a letter from the chief engineer of the *Monitor* saying: "Thousands have this day blessed you. I have heard whole crews cheer you."

On the day after the *Merrimac-Monitor* battle Lincoln wrote advising Welles the *Monitor* could be easily boarded and captured, her turret wedged, her machinery drowned by pouring water. He passed on the advice from Lieutenant Worden that "she should not go sky-larking up to Norfolk."

A naval lieutenant arrived at a Cabinet meeting to tell the President the wounded Worden was at his house. The President dismissed the Cabinet. Ushering Lincoln into an upstairs room at his house, the naval lieutenant said, "Jack, here is the President come to see you." The President stood gazing down on Worden in bed, the scorched eyes closed, the torn face bandaged. "You do me great honor," murmured Worden. No answer came. The lieutenant turned to see Lincoln in tears with nothing to say for the moment. When he did find words he said: "It is not so. It is you who honor me and your country, and I will promote you." And he made Worden a captain that very day.

A few weeks later Lincoln, with Stanton and others, went down the Potomac in a steamer to Fortress Monroe, commanded by General John E. Wool. Near Kettle Bottom Shoals they saw a long line of boats. "Oh," said the President, as Welles noted it, "that is Stanton's navy. That is the fleet concerning which he and Mr. Welles became so excited in my room. Welles was incensed and opposed the scheme, and it has proved that Neptune was right. Stanton's navy is as useless as the paps of a man to a sucking child. They may be some show to amuse the child, but they are good for nothing for service."

After a long conference with Commodore Louis M. Goldsborough on his flagship the *Minnesota*, the fleet, by orders of the President, moved to attack Confederate batteries at Sewell's Point. The *Merrimac* came out, wavered, hesitated. Beyond and waiting stood the little *Monitor*. The *Merrimac* retreated and refused to give battle.

Ashore on horseback, the President with General Wool inspected troops, rode through the burned village of Hampton, destroyed by the Confederates when retiring before Union forces.

Commodore Goldsborough was summoned ashore by the President. Again an attack on the Sewell's Point batteries was ordered. The bombardment put one battery out of commission and revealed that a second battery was not as effective as supposed. The *Merrimac* steamed out slowly, paused, stood a while, again turned back, and looked as if she would fight only when she had to.

Lincoln had talked with a pilot, studied a chart, and found a landing place nearer to Norfolk than the one considered by General Wool. The President in a tug was scouting the shore line; Chase was aboard the *Miami*. "Several horsemen who seemed to be soldiers of the enemy, appeared on the beach," wrote Chase. "I sent to the President to ask if we should fire on them, and he replied negatively." Returning to General Wool and discussing plans for taking Norfolk from the Confederates, the President allowed Wool to use the landing the General preferred.

Six regiments were put on shore, marched to Norfolk, found it evacuated by the Confederates, with smoking ruins of large stores of military supplies. The mayor of Norfolk formally surrendered the city to General Wool. The President had been "greatly alarmed for our safety" by the report of General Mansfield, wrote Chase, "and you can imagine his delight when we told him Norfolk was ours. Mr. Stanton came into the President's room and was equally delighted. He fairly hugged General Wool."

The President, with Stanton and Chase, next day rode through the streets of captured Norfolk and gazed on the ruined hulk of the *Merrimac*, which the Confederates had blown up rather than risk another fight with the *Monitor*. Then the party sailed back to Washington on the steamer *Baltimore*, Chase writing to his daughter Janet: "So ended a brilliant week's campaign by the President; for I think it quite certain that if he had not gone down, Norfolk would still have been in the possession of the enemy . . . The whole coast is now virtually ours."

A curious week it was for Lincoln with his first experience at direct handling of sea and land forces, with fleet and field headquarters under his hat.

McClellan's army after nine months of organization, practice, drill, first went under fire in April '62, fought a rear-guard action at Williamsburg, and moved to White House Landing, 20 miles from Richmond. Meanwhile McClellan renewed his calls on the War Department and the President for more men and guns. Also he continued, with some of his generals, an undiminished political activity.

Long letters passed between McClellan and Lincoln on corps organization. Rain, mud, heavy roads, bogged his army, McClellan complained to Lincoln, who remarked to Hay that "he seemed to think, in defiance of Scripture, that Heaven sent its rain only on the just and not on the unjust."

One McClellan handicap was a fear that enemies among his own officers were leagued with enemies at Washington in plots against him. He wrote his wife May 1: "I shall be very glad when we are really ready to open fire, and then finish this confounded affair. I am tired of public life . . . the rebels on one side, and the abolitionists and other scoundrels on the other."

The wounded Confederate commander Joseph E. Johnston was replaced by Robert E. Lee. Lee sent Stonewall Jackson to the Shenandoah Valley. Jackson with 17,000 men swept the valley region and in 14 days marched his army 170 miles, routed 12,500 Union troops, captured $250,000 worth of supplies and property, took 3,000 prisoners and 9,000 rifles, a raid which threatened Washington so seriously that Lincoln called off McDowell from co-operation with McClellan. Strategy worked out by Lincoln, for bagging Jackson's army in the clutch of three Union armies, was logical enough. But Jackson was an illogical phantom, got away with his supplies and prisoners, and joined Lee at Richmond—as Lee had guessed he would. McClellan guessed that Lee must have at least 200,000 troops or he would not have dared to detach Jackson for the Shenandoah Valley operation. Lee had less than 83,000 when reinforced by Jackson.

Lincoln understood with McClellan that if the Army of the Potomac could smash the enemy army and take Richmond, it would set bells ringing over the North. On the other hand, the wreck of McClellan's army might mean the end of the Union cause. The hazards affected McClellan's mind. Over and again in letters to his wife he told her of his courage, his resolution, how firm he was. He mentioned his faith and his fearlessness often enough to show his own doubt of himself. These phases of McClellan haunted Lincoln, Stanton, Ben Wade, Zach Chandler. "He's got the slows," was one comment of Lincoln.

Lincoln wrote a letter for Seward to use among men of financial and political power who were insisting they must know precisely where the President stood. In this letter was a manner of oath: "I expect to maintain this contest until successful, or till I die, or am conquered, or my term expires, or Congress or the country forsakes me." The President was convincing. Seward and others got the governors of the North to sign a request that more troops be raised. Lincoln on July 1 made a call for 300,000 three-year men—wondering how the country would take it. He wrote to McClellan, who was calling for 50,000 more soldiers, to be patient.

The raising of new troops came addedly hard because of McClellan's handling of his army. The enemy struck at his White House Landing base of supplies, where food, guns, powder, wagons, mules, arrived from Washington, and what came to be known as the Seven Days' battles were on. McClellan ordered a change of base to Harrison's Landing on the James River. On McClellan's retreat Lee put in every last man and gun he had and tried to crumple up McClellan and capture his army. In the finish, and after bloody fighting, McClellan still held Harrison's Landing and had lost only 16,000 men as against 20,000 Confederate losses.

A complex and weary McClellan, after the first of the Seven Days' battles, telegraphed to Secretary Stanton: "I have seen too many dead and wounded comrades to feel otherwise than that the government has not sustained this army. If you do not do so now the game is lost." Then McClellan used accusing words: "If I save this army now, I tell you plainly that I owe no thanks to you or any person in Washington. You have done your best to sacrifice this army." Of these words, McClellan wrote his wife: "Of course they will never forgive me for that. I knew it when I wrote it."

But Lincoln and Stanton did not see the final accusing words of the telegram till much later. For Colonel E. S. Sanford, supervisor and censor of telegraphic messages, found these words to be outrageous, infamous, treasonable, designed by McClellan "to reach the public as a means of shifting the cause of defeat from his own to other shoulders." And Colonel Sanford took on himself the duty of cutting from the telegram what he regarded as treason. Lincoln replied to the mutilated telegram: "Save your Army at all events. Will send re-inforcements as fast as we can."

At one time, as McClellan came near Richmond, the gold and the archives of the Confederate Government were loaded on railroad cars ready to move in case McClellan reached the city.

On both sides were courage, tenacity. A correspondent saw a Federal soldier brought into a field hospital, "both legs torn off by a shell, both arms broken by bullets, the film of death glazing his eyes," but when spoken to he cried out, "I trust to God we are licking them!" At Malvern Hill a Confederate colonel had shouted: "Come on, come on, my men! Do you want to live forever?"

Gay humor lighted grim incidents. General O. O. Howard's right arm was shattered, and when he met General Phil Kearny, who had lost his left arm in Mexico, the two men shook hands on Howard's saying, "Hereafter we buy our gloves together."

For all his losses of men and material McClellan had won a victory. His cannon mounted tier on tier at Malvern Hill had mowed down the repeated lines of Confederates ordered up by Lee. Moving from Yorktown toward Richmond, McClellan had killed more of the enemy forces than they had of his. And now, having broken the fiercest blow the enemy could bring against him, he shrank under the protection of his gunboats at Harrison's Landing. The collapse of this campaign staggered Lincoln, who remarked of it later, "I was as nearly inconsolable as I could be and live." In a lighter vein he told Lamon: "It seems to me that McClellan has been wandering around and got lost. He's been hollering for help ever since he went south, wants somebody to . . . get him out of the place he's got into."

McClellan wrote the War Department, "To accomplish the great task of capturing Richmond and putting an end to this rebellion reinforcements should be sent to me rather much over than much less than 100,000 men." Lincoln said, "Sending men to that army is like shoveling fleas across a barnyard—not half of them get there." Still again, when another request came for more men, he said: "If I gave McClellan all the men he asks for they could not find room to lie down. They'd have to sleep standing up."

With Stanton, Lincoln started for Harrison's Landing, spent a day there, talked with McClellan, quizzed his generals, and found McClellan had 86,500 troops present for duty, 34,000 absent by authority, 3,700 absent without authority, his command including more than 120,000.

Lincoln and Stanton rode horseback alongside McClellan reviewing troops. Chaplain Joseph Twichell of a Connecticut regiment wrote his father July 9, 1862: "It did seem as though every moment the President's legs would become entangled with those of the horse he rode and both come down together . . . That arm with which he drew the rein, in its angles and position resembled the hind leg of a grasshopper—the hand before—the elbow away back over the horse's tail. The removal of his hat before each regiment was also a source of laughter in the style of its execution—the quick trot of the horse making it a feat of some difficulty, while from the same cause, his hold on it, while off, seemed very precarious. But, the boys liked him, in fact his popularity with the army is and has been universal. Most of our rulers and leaders fall into odium, but all have faith in Lincoln. 'When he finds it out,' they say, 'it will be stopped.'"

Lincoln returned to Washington carrying a long letter written by McClellan, giving freely his ideas on what policies should guide the Government. The war should be "conducted upon the highest principles known to Christian civilization." Private property should be respected; "radical views, especially upon slavery," would melt away the armies. McClellan was sincere in believing his advice would save the country. His sincerity was incomplete, however, else he would have informed Lincoln that Fernando Wood, the mayor of New York who in '61 tried to get his city to secede from the Union, had called on him in camp to talk politics. With Wood was another Democrat of national influence—and they told McClellan, as between Democrats, that he ought to be his party's candidate for President in the next campaign.

McClellan spoke of "saving" his army almost as though by some slight whim of mind or caprice of heart he might not choose to save it—and what then? His chief of staff and father-in-law, R. B. Marcy, deepened misgivings in Washington when in a talk with Stanton he remarked that he would not be surprised if McClellan's army should be forced to "capitulate." The lingo could mean anything. Browning noted: "This excited Stanton very much, and he went directly to the President and reported what had been said. It also excited the President, whereupon he sent for Marcy and said to him sternly, 'Genl I understand you have used the word "Capitulate"—that is a word not to be used in connection with our army &c.' Marcy blundered out some kind of explanation, excuse or apology."

The habit of blaming others for mistakes, accidents, fate, had grown on McClellan. He wrote to his wife, "I am tired of serving fools. God help my country!" He saw "incompetents" in Washington doing "injustice" to him. This, that, was "infamous."

Lincoln had called General Halleck from the West to serve as General in Chief of all land forces. Halleck was to puzzle Lincoln. Forty-seven years old, New York born, a West Pointer, an engineer with artillery in the Mexican War, he had written a book, *Elements of Military Art and Science*. When the war opened he was head of the leading law firm of San Francisco and major general of the state militia. After Shiloh he took the field, replacing Grant, moved slowly onward with pick and shovel, entrenching, making sure that his 100,000 would bag the enemy 50,000. After six weeks he had arrived at Corinth when the enemy had slipped out and was 50 miles away again. He reported this to Washington as a victory. But Lincoln was through with gathering more troops for McClellan, saying, reported Browning: "That if by magic he could reinforce McClelland with 100,000 men today he would be in an ecstasy over it, thank him for it, and tell him that he would go to Richmond tomorrow, but that when tomorrow came he would telegraph that he had certain information that the enemy had 400,000 men, and that he could not advance without reinforcements." Halleck was asking McClellan's generals whether they ought to stay before Richmond on the peninsula. Some said No, some Yes.

Slowly, at last, the whole story had to be told to the country of the Seven Days' battles. Out over the country, in homes where had been faith, doubts crept in. The national mood reached the White House, where the President sat in his library writing, "with directions to deny him to everybody." Senator Browning stepped in a moment and in the evening wrote, "He looked weary, care-worn and troubled. I shook hands with him, and asked him how he was. He said 'tolerably well' I remarked that I felt concerned about him—regretted that troubles crowded so heavily upon him, and feared his health was suffering. He held me by the hand, pressed it, and said in a very tender and touching tone—'Browning, I must die sometime,' I replied, 'your fortunes Mr. President are bound up with those of the Country, and disaster to one would be disaster to the other, and I hope you will do all you can to preserve your health and life.' He looked very sad, and there was a cadence of deep sadness in his voice. We parted I believe both of us with tears in our eyes."

The Army of the Potomac, its sick and wounded, its cannon and horses, its farm hands, shopmen, college boys, store clerks, was brought back from the peninsula to old places on the Potomac River within sight of the Capitol. And McClellan was relieved of command in the field and told to report for orders at Alexandria.

Hate, fear, jealousy, were rampant. To a man who came complaining against his superior officer, rather loose-mouthed, Lincoln merely said, "Go home and read Proverbs xxx, 10." And the man hunted up his Bible and read "Accuse not a servant unto his master, lest he curse thee, and thou be found guilty."

Lincoln had scolded McClellan, drollery ran, for not sending more complete and detailed reports of his army's progress. So McClellan sent a telegram to Lincoln one day: "Have captured two cows. What disposition should I make of them?" And Lincoln: "Milk 'em, George."

On August 4, 1862, Lincoln issued a second call for 300,000 troops. This meant conscription by the states, "the draft." Sheriffs and commissioners took lists of all men between 18 and 45 in counties and cities. Names written on folded ballots were shaken in a revolving wheel or drum-shaped box. A blindfolded man drew the names of those who were to go to war for nine months, or inside of five days pay a substitute to go.

Men who did not want to go to war, by thousands, filed exemption claims—they were physically unfit to go; they were citizens of other countries; they held to a religious belief that war was a sin. In ten days, 14,000 claims were filed in New York City. Thousands were crossing into Canada or buying steamship tickets for Europe. One steamer was overhauled at sea and all men passengers were taken back to New York.

Resistance and evasion of the attempts of the state governments to draft soldiers spread so far that the President issued a proclamation that "all persons discouraging volunteer enlistments, resisting militia drafts, or guilty of any disloyal practice, affording aid and comfort to Rebels against the authority of the United States" would come under martial law—and the writ of habeas corpus would be useless in any jail where they were held.

For Lincoln there were decisions—every day hundreds of decisions—Yes or No—take it or leave it—right or wrong.

Governor Andrew telegraphed he could not get "quick work" out of U.S. paymasters delaying transport of regiments. Lincoln wired: "Please say to these gentlemen that if they do not work quickly I will make quick work with them. In the name of all that is reasonable, how long does it take to pay a couple of Regts.?"

To Archbishop John Hughes the President wrote in late '61 with the salutation "Rt. Rev. Sir" and began: "I am sure you will pardon me if, in my ignorance, I do not address [you] with technical correctness." Though he could find no law authorizing his appointment of chaplains for hospitals, "yet the services of chaplains are more needed, perhaps, in the hospitals, than with the healthy soldiers in the field." Therefore he had given "a sort of quasi appointment" to three Protestant ministers and "If you perceive no objection, I will thank you to give me the name or names of one or more suitable persons of the Catholic Church, to whom I may with propriety, tender the same service." The President's personal touch with the Archbishop went into a closing sentence: "Many thanks for your kind, and judicious letters to Gov. Seward, and which he regularly allows me both the pleasure and the profit of perusing."

Some decisions came easy, such as signing the Pacific Railway Bill July 1, 1862. Rails were to be laid from the western Iowa line to San Francisco Bay. The Union Pacific and the Central Pacific corporations were to build the road, getting ten sections of land per mile alongside the right of way, with graduated Government loans on a per-mile basis—$16,000 for level work, $32,000 for desert work (the Great Basin), and $48,000 for mountain work. As the bill stood now, it was under "military necessity" an offer to railroad financiers to push through a job that would tie the two coasts closer.

He signed the Homestead Bill May 20, 1862, giving a farm free to any man who wanted to put a plow to unbroken sod. Immense tracts of land were thrown open in the Western Territories. Anyone a citizen of the United States or taking out first papers declaring intention of citizenship, paying a registration fee of $10 and staying on the same piece of ground five years, could have title papers making him the owner of 160 acres. Tens of thousands of Britons, Irish, Germans, Scandinavians came, many exclaiming, "What a good new country where they give away farms!" As a war measure touching enlarged food supply, and as an act fulfilling a Republican party pledge, Lincoln found it easy to sign the bill.

CHAPTER 25

Second Bull Run—Bloody Antietam— Chaos

THE POPULAR Orpheus C. Kerr [Robert H. Newell] and his nonsense helped relieve the gloom of some readers, including Lincoln. Kerr, August 9, 1862, set forth: "Notwithstanding the fact that President Lincoln is an honest man, my boy, the genius of Slumber has opened a large wholesale establishment here, and the tendency to repose is general." And three weeks later: "As every thing continues to indicate, my boy, that President Lincoln is an honest man, I am still of the opinion that the restoration of the Union is only a question of time, and will be accomplished some weeks previous to the commencement of the Millenium."

During that desperate, hammering summer of '62 Lincoln revolved often in his mind the curious failure of his 200,000 men in Virginia against half that number. Would he have to try one general, another and still another, and for how long?

Robert Edward Lee, 55 years old, had become the most portentous personality with whom Lincoln would have to contend in the months ahead. Lee had two rare gifts, patience with men and readiness with unforeseen circumstance. His training in handling and understanding men had been long, hard, varied and thorough. The smooth reciprocal functioning of Lee with Davis was almost startling in contrast to Lincoln and McClellan. Militarily Lee and Davis were one head of the Army of Northern Virginia. Where Davis would often fail to read the enemy mind Lee supplied the deficiency. Neither jealousy, envy, nor ambition, in any ordinary sense, gnawed at the heart of Lee.

Lee was a baby when taken in a family coach to Alexandria, Virginia. Growing up he became immersed in the legends of George Washington. Men who studied him closely said that one of his secrets was a grip on the character of Washington as a model, a hope and a light.

His mother, Ann Hill Carter Lee, was the daughter of Charles Carter, in his day reputed the richest man in Virginia except George Washington. Her inheritance had dwindled so far that West Point was the advisable place for her son's education. John C. Calhoun signed his appointment, and after graduation with high standing, he was married to Mary Custis, a frail blonde girl of whom it was said, "She loved wildflowers and old gardens and evening skies." She bore seven children in 14 years, and became a chronic invalid.

Lee had directed engineers and work gangs to cut ditches in Georgia mudbanks, to blast rock from the bed of the Mississippi for river channel improvement at St. Louis, to repair casemates in New York Harbor, to run pile drivers in Baltimore Harbor. His reputation for fair dealing spread far; when he assured an offending soldier, "You shall have justice," the answer was quick—"That is what I am afraid of."

Lee's only leave of absence during 30 years in the Army was an annoying year in which he acted as executor of the tangled estate of his wife's father, about that time writing, "I have no enjoyment in life now but what I derive from my children." Cold and austere he seemed on parade in his official uniform, panoplied for duty, though in the bosom of his family "he was very fond of having his hands tickled, and what was still more curious, it pleased and delighted him to take off his slippers and place his feet in our laps to have them tickled," said one of the sons. They would ask for more stories and he teased them. "No tickling, no story!" With a physical frame "solid as oak," trained to hardships and loneliness, Lee sipped wine occasionally, drank no hard liquor, cared nothing for tobacco.

In Alexandria he read of Virginia's secession. To a druggist in Alexandria he had remarked the day before, "I must say that I am one of those dull creatures that cannot see the good of secession." He sent Secretary Cameron his resignation and wrote to Scott: "I shall carry to the grave the most grateful recollections of your kind consideration, and your name and fame will always be dear to me . . . Save in defence of my native State, I never desire to again draw my sword." He had written a son, "While I wish to do what is right, I am unwilling to do what is wrong, either at the bidding of the South or the North." Of his hope for preservation of the Union he wrote, "I will cling to it to the last." He felt and resented "the aggressions of the

North," though "I am not pleased with the course of the 'Cotton States.' "
On the South Carolina proposals to legalize and reopen the African slave
trade he was decisive, writing a son: "One of their plans seems to be the
renewal of the slave trade. That I am opposed to on every ground." To his
wife in 1856 from western Texas he wrote his views: "In this enlightened
age, there are few I believe, but what will acknowledge, that slavery as an
institution, is a moral & political evil in any Country. It is useless to expatiate
on its disadvantages. I think it however a greater evil to the white than to
the black race, & while my feelings are strongly enlisted in behalf of the
latter, my sympathies are more strong for the former."

When offered high command of the Union armies, Lee had said, according
to Old Man Blair, "If I owned the four million slaves of the South I would
sacrifice them all to the Union," and then asked a question that Blair couldn't
answer: "But how can I draw my sword against Virginia?" The very asking
of the question included its answer.

"The war may last ten years," Lee had written his wife shortly after arriving in Richmond. He warned soldiers and politicians they were "on the
threshold of a long and bloody war," advising that they must plan with that
expectation, that he knew the Northern people well, and "they would never
yield except at the conclusion of a long and desperate struggle." Riding on
a field where one of his sons was fighting, he remarked, "That's right, my
son, drive those people back." Or again he would refer to the enemy as "our
friends across the river."

Suddenly, when General Joseph Johnston was wounded, Lee had been sent
forward to take in hand four different armies, weld them into a unit for action.
In a four months' campaign, at times outnumbered two to one, he had stopped
McClellan and earned a name as the savior of Richmond and the Confederacy.
To a doubting inquirer one of Lee's generals had said his first name was
"Audacity," that he would tower head and shoulders above all others in
audacity. In a conference with generals just before the Seven Days' battles,
one of them, busy with pencil and paper, was showing that McClellan with
superior forces could sweep on to Richmond. "Stop, stop!" said Lee. "If you
go to ciphering we are whipped beforehand."

Lee knew better than McClellan that war is a conflict of wills, and had
imposed his will on McClellan to the extent that McClellan believed he was
a loser when he was not, which was why he did not try to push through and
take Richmond after Malvern Hill. While Lee was leaving all Southern politics
to Jefferson Davis, McClellan concentrated his mind for many hours on the
political difficulties of the North and wrote the long letter instructing Lincoln
in the matter of Government policy. In one letter to Lincoln, McClellan estimated Lee as "personally brave and energetic to a fault" yet "too cautious
and weak under grave responsibility . . . likely to be timid and irresolute in
action. I am confident of success. Not only of success but of brilliant success."

Lee's right-hand man Thomas Jonathan Jackson also was born for war. His
valley campaign up and down the Shenandoah, in which he captured half of
one Union army, beat off three other armies with which Lincoln was trying
to trap him, and slipped through for a rapid march to join Lee, had become
a shining chronicle of the Confederacy. Lincoln from the White House undertook to direct continuously from day to day the field movements of sev-

eral armies. To Frémont, to Banks, to McDowell, with forces three times that of Jackson, Lincoln sent telegrams giving the reported movements of Jackson's "foot cavalry." During three weeks in a series of telegrams there glimmered Lincoln's hope that from his assorted varieties of armies in and about the Shenandoah, he might set up one little combination that would cross Jackson's path somewhere and damage or break that adventuring zealot. The opening telegrams on the same day advised Frémont: "Much—perhaps all—depends upon the celerity with which you can execute it. Put the utmost speed into it. Do not lose a minute"; and McDowell, "Every thing now depends upon the celerity and vigor of your movement."

But Jackson was putting on a campaign that for swift troop movement amazed the world. Thirty miles in 24 hours his infantry marched. With 17,000 men in this one month he won five battles, took many prisoners, sent to Richmond great wagon trains of captured muskets, munitions, medicines and supplies, threw Washington into a scare, made McDowell's army of 40,000 hug close to Washington. An order from Lincoln to McDowell that he should detach 20,000 men to reinforce Frémont for fighting Jackson, McDowell termed "a crushing blow" that he obeyed with "a heavy heart."

Why Lincoln at such a distance should have undertaken what he did was not clear, particularly when Frémont was the key and he knew from Missouri experience of Frémont's "celerity." His seriously telegraphing Frémont "Put the utmost speed into it. Do not lose a minute" was not in accord with his usual judgment of men.

Lincoln, advising with McDowell about starting to destroy Jackson, heard McDowell say he could begin marching the next Sunday but he had been excoriated all over the country for fighting Bull Run on a Sabbath. Lincoln hesitated and smiled. "Get a good ready and start on Monday," seemingly unaware that one day might be as decisive as death when hunting Jackson, even one Sabbath day.

Jackson's reverence for the Sabbath went so far that he would not mail his wife a letter to be carried in the mails on a Sunday nor would he open a letter received from her on a Sunday. But "with the blessing of an ever-kind Providence" he would fight, slay and deliver doom to the enemy if on a Sabbath the enemy looked ready for punishment. An orphan boy who managed to get into West Point, Jackson had graduated far below the class leader, George B. McClellan. His Mexican War record bright, he became professor of natural philosophy and artillery tactics in the Virginia Military Institute. Tall, rawboned, with big hands and a peculiar stride, he would walk alone, raise his right hand high over his head and let it down. He was either praying or easing himself physically—onlookers could not tell which. He had many books and two favorites, which he always carried in his mess kit—the Bible and a volume of Napoleon's maxims on war. His spiritual guide was Jesus of Nazareth, his professional and military inspiration the Little Corsican, whose 88 campaigns he had mastered from A to Z.

"His dyspepsia caused drowsiness," said General Daniel H. Hill, "and he often went to sleep in conversation with a friend . . ." His eyes went bad; he was ordered to do no reading by lamplight, and sat one hour, two hours, of an evening in silence with closed eyes or staring at the wall, concentrating on points arisen in his mind during the day. Alongside Negroes on his farm near Lexington he worked with his hands.

Gulping hard to get down whisky ordered by a physician, he said: "I like it; I always did, and that is the reason I never use it." Refusing a glass of brandy, he said to a fellow officer, "I am more afraid of it than of Yankee bullets."

He joined the Presbyterian church in Lexington, became a deacon, conducted a Sunday school for Negroes. He married Eleanor Junkin and a year later saw her and a newborn child to their double grave. Four years afterward he married Mary Anna Morrison, and their household ran like clockwork in its daily program. Letters of Jackson to his wife gushed with little excesses of romance. "When I gave my darling the last kiss" was a moment. He saluted her as "darling," "precious pet," "sunshine," "little jewel of mine," "esposita." He brandished swords about her head in play or leaped from hiding behind a door to take her in his arms.

Of all Southern commanders who had the ear of Lee and of Davis none was more fiercely in favor of defending by taking the offensive, of striking deep into Northern territory. Of his chief he said: "Lee is a phenomenon. He is the only man I would follow blindfold."

A new combination named the Army of Virginia, formed by the three commands of McDowell, Banks and Frémont, was headed by General John Pope. Frémont, however, decided to resign rather than serve under Pope. The new commander was a dashing horseman, his valor in battle impetuous and undisputed. He had been one of Lincoln's military escort en route to inauguration. Kentucky-born, a graduate of Transylvania University, his father a judge whom Lincoln had met in Illinois, a West Pointer, a Mexican War officer promoted for gallantry on the field, an engineer, surveyor, explorer, an 1860 Republican, John Pope had been continuously an army man, soldiering his lifework. His victories had brought in 1,300 prisoners at Blackwater, Missouri, and some 6,000 at Island No. 10 on the Mississippi. He wrote letters from "Headquarters in the Saddle," issued an address to his new command: "I have come to you from the West, where we have always seen the back of our enemies." His overconfidence ran into bombast. For Pope was facing two great proved fighters, two strange captains of men, Lee and Jackson.

In the last week of August '62, Lincoln sat up late every night, and one night through to a bitter dawn. Lee and Jackson were performing around Pope. Lincoln queried Burnside at Falmouth, "Any news from Gen. Pope?" He wired Banks at Manassas Junction, "Please tell me what news." He asked Haupt, "What news?" on August 30 and in a second telegram the same day, "Please send me the latest news." He telegraphed McClellan: "What news from direction of Manassas Junction? What generally?" McClellan replied he was clear that only two courses were open: first, to help Pope with all available forces; "second, to leave Pope to get out of his scrape, and at once use all our means to make the capital perfectly safe."

Lincoln puzzled over such words as "leave Pope to get out of his scrape." Did McClellan possibly mean that if Pope's army could win with men sent from the Army of the Potomac, then such men should *not* be sent? He answered McClellan: "I think your first alternative, towit, 'to concentrate all our available forces to open communication with Pope,' is the right one. But I wish not to control. That I now leave to Gen. Halleck, aided by your counsels."

McClellan was writing his wife: "I fancy that Pope is in retreat, though this is only a guess of mine . . . I don't see how I can remain in the service if placed under Pope, it would be too great a disgrace . . . I shall keep as clear as possible of the President and cabinet; endeavor to do what must be done with Halleck alone; so I shall get on better . . . I have just telegraphed very plainly to the President and Halleck what I think ought to be done . . . I am heart-sick with the folly and ignorance I see around me . . . I have seen neither the President nor the secretary since I arrived here . . ."

John Hay wrote in his diary of a horseback ride from Soldiers' Home to the White House with Lincoln, and of matters that made public would have further torn the country: "We talked about Bull Run and Pope's prospect. The President was very outspoken in regard to McClellan's present conduct. He said that it really seemed to him McC. wanted Pope defeated. The President seemed to think him a little crazy. Envy, jealousy and spite are probably a better explanation of his present conduct. He is constantly sending despatches to the President and Halleck asking what is his real position and command. He acts as chief alarmist and grand marplot of the Army . . ."

Stanton took Lincoln and Hay to his house. "A pleasant little dinner and a pretty wife as white and cold and motionless as marble, whose rare smiles seemed to pain her. Stanton was loud about the McC. business . . . He said that nothing but foul play could lose us this battle & that it rested with McC. and his friends. Stanton seemed to believe very strongly in Pope. So did the President for that matter."

Everything seemed to be going well on Saturday, August 30, as Lincoln and Hay saw it. "We went to bed expecting glad tidings at sunrise. But about eight o'clock the President came to my room as I was dressing and, calling me out, said 'Well, John, we are whipped again, I am afraid. The enemy reinforced on Pope and drove back his left wing and he has retired to Centreville where he says he will be able to hold his men. I don't like that expression. I don't like to hear him admit his men need holding.' "

On Sunday things began to look better. "The President was in a singularly defiant tone of mind. He often repeated, 'We must hurt this enemy before it gets away.' " On Monday when Hay spoke of the bad look of events, the President said: "No, Mr. Hay, we must whip these people now. Pope must fight them. If they are too strong for him, he can gradually retire to these fortifications. If this be not so, if we are really whipped we may as well stop fighting."

What with jealousy, spite, bickering, officialism, politics, pride, sloth, ignorance, large bodies of troops stayed quiet in scattered positions while Pope farther off was outguessed, flanked, surprised, hacked and harassed, and driven off from Bull Run Creek with slaughter. In combat and retreat he lost 14,000 out of 80,000; Lee lost 9,000 out of 54,000.

Stormy tides rocked Washington as the broken pieces of a defeated army straggled in. Outbound railroad trains were packed; thousands fled the national capital. The Federal Treasury building was barricaded with hundreds of barrels of cement. By order of the President clerks in the civil departments enrolled and began military drill. Stanton had important papers gathered into bundles to be carried away on horseback, if necessary.

This was the day that General M. C. Meigs saw Stanton issuing volleys of orders for the safety of the city. And Meigs wrote: "Lincoln, on the other hand, dropped into my room on his weary way to see Stanton, drew himself way down into a big chair, and, with a mingled groan and sigh exclaimed, 'Chase says we can't raise any more money; Pope is licked and McClellan has the diarrhoea. What shall I do? The bottom is out of the tub, the bottom is out of the tub!' I told the President to meet his generals with Stanton, fix the bottom back in the tub, rally the army, and order another advance at once. This seemed to brace him up a little and he went on to the War Department; but for the moment he was completely discouraged and downhearted. Stanton, on the other hand, was more full of power and vehement energy than ever."

The dying colonel of the 1st Michigan Cavalry wrote to his brother and sister: "I die midst the ring and clangor of battle, as I could wish . . . I am one of the victims of Pope's imbecility and McDowell's treason. Tell the President would he save the country he must not give our hallowed flag to such hands." The letter was published, discussed.

Three thousand convalescent soldiers were moved from Washington to Philadelphia to make room for serious cases from Bull Run. Floors in the Capitol, in the Patent Office building, were cleared for torn and mutilated men.

In this second panic at Bull Run one man satisfied Lincoln in everything, so Hay wrote. Haupt, the railroad man, took on duties outside his particular job, advancing supplies and munitions, rebuilding bridges, watching transport, telegraphing the President, working day and night with little food or sleep. "The President is particularly struck with the business-like character of his despatch, telling in the fewest words the information most sought for." It was some weeks earlier that Lincoln had told of seeing "the most remarkable structure that human eyes ever rested upon," and explained: "That man Haupt has built a bridge across Potomac Creek, about 400 feet long and nearly 100 feet high, over which loaded trains are running every hour, and upon my word, gentlemen, there is nothing in it but beanpoles and cornstalks." From a distance the green, new-cut timbers did look just so.

Pope was relieved of command and assigned to the Northwest to curb Indian tribes. Welles noted that the President "spoke favorably" of Pope and clearly believed he had not had a fair chance. "Pope," said the President, "did well, but there was an army prejudice against him, and it was necessary he should leave. He had gone off very angry, and not without cause, but circumstances controlled us." Lincoln probably told Pope and Halleck, as he did Welles, "We had the enemy in the hollow of our hands on Friday, if our generals, who are vexed with Pope, had done their duty; all of our present difficulties and reverses have been brought upon us by these quarrels of the generals."

Welles also recorded in this week that his convictions joined those of the President "that McClellan and his generals are this day stronger than the Administration with a considerable part of this Army of the Potomac." On a walk with the President, Welles noted the words: "I must have McClellan to reorganize the army and bring it out of chaos, but there has been a design —a purpose in breaking down Pope, without regard of consequences to the country. It is shocking to see and know this, but there is no remedy at present. McClellan has the army with him."

Stanton, Chase, Bates and Smith of the Cabinet had signed a paper in Stanton's handwriting, a remonstrance to be handed the President against McClellan's being once more entrusted with command of the army. Chase argued with Welles to sign. Welles held off, saying that while he wished to get rid of McClellan, it was not exactly fair to the President to be circulating such a paper behind his back. Then this paper disappeared, and Chase came to Welles with a second one, in the handwriting of Bates and with the same four signers as before. Welles said this second one was more reasonable in tone, but he told Chase he could not join with them.

The determination of Stanton and Chase was to remove, and if possible to disgrace, McClellan, as Welles saw it. "Chase frankly stated he desired it, that he deliberately believed McClellan ought to be shot, and should, were he President, be brought to summary punishment." Welles believed that McClellan hesitated in attack, had neither definite plans nor audacity, and was no fighting general. But he could not agree with Stanton and Chase that McClellan was "imbecile, a coward, a traitor." He wrote, "Chase was disappointed, and I think a little chagrined, because I would not unite in the written demand to the President."

Stanton came to see if he could not get Welles to sign. If Welles signed, that would make five out of seven in the Cabinet. "Stanton said, with some excitement, he knew of no particular obligations he was under to the President, who had called him to a difficult position and imposed upon him labors and responsibilities which no man could carry, and which were greatly increased by fastening upon him a commander who was constantly striving to embarrass him in his administration of the Department. He could not and would not submit to a continuance of this state of things." Welles admitted conditions were bad, severe on Stanton. Still he could not sign the paper.

Welles in his diary threw strange crosslights on the half-mutinous figures that sat around Lincoln's Cabinet table. Cabinet discussions went on without order or system, noted Welles, "but in the summing-up and conclusions the President, who was a patient listener and learner, concentrated results, and often determined questions adverse to the Secretary of State, regarding him and his opinions, as he did those of his other advisers, for what they were worth and generally no more."

At one Cabinet meeting Lincoln had all his counselors but one against him. He was reminded of a revival meeting in Illinois when a fellow with a few drinks too many in him had walked up the aisle to a front pew. All eyes were on him, but he didn't care; he joined in the singing, droned amen at the close of prayers, and as the meeting proceeded dozed off in sleep. Before the meeting ended the pastor asked the usual question: "Who are on the Lord's side?" and the congregation arose en masse. When the pastor asked, "Who are on the side of the Devil?" the dozing sleeper came to, heard part of the question, saw the parson standing, arose to his feet to say: "I don't exactly understand the question but I'll stand by you, parson, to the last. But it seems to me," he added reflectively, "that we're in a hopeless minority."

One advantage of Seward was resented. Like the President, he was a story-teller. While other Secretaries were toiling at their duties the Secretary of State "spent a considerable portion of every day with the President, patronizing and instructing him, hearing and telling anecdotes, relating interesting details of occurrences in the Senate, and inculcating his political party notions." And amid these Cabinet jealousies had come one deep cleavage. "Between Seward and Chase there was perpetual rivalry and mutual but courtly distrust . . ."

Before one Cabinet meeting Lincoln had gone with Halleck to McClellan and given him command of the Army again. But the actual words by which authority was once more handed over to him were not spoken by Lincoln. It was left to Halleck, Lincoln explaining to Welles, "I could not have done it, for I can never feel confident that he will do anything effectual." McClellan wrote his wife: "I was surprised this morning, when at breakfast, by a visit from the President and Halleck, in which the former expressed the opinion that the troubles now impending could be overcome better by me than anyone else. Pope is ordered to fall back on Washington, and, as he re-enters, everything is to come under my command again!"

Three days later, as Lincoln and Hay walked over to the telegraph office, Lincoln said: "McClellan is working like a beaver. He seems to be aroused to doing something, by the sort of snubbing he got last week. The Cabinet yesterday were unanimous against him. They were all ready to denounce me for it, except Blair. He [McClellan] has acted badly in this matter, but we must use what tools we have. There is no man in the Army who can man these fortifications and lick these troops into shape half as well as he." Hay spoke of the many letters coming in reflecting a feeling against McClellan. Lincoln commented: "Unquestionably he has acted badly toward Pope. He wanted him to fail. That is unpardonable. But he is too useful just now to sacrifice." And he added later, "If he can't fight himself, he excels in making others ready to fight." He admitted also that calling McClellan to power again was a good deal like "curing the bite with the hair of the dog."

Lincoln had, however, offered command in the field to Burnside, who would not take it, saying to the President, "I do not think that there is anyone who can do as much with that army as McClellan." Also, Lincoln had consented to the dismissal of three major generals, Porter, Franklin and Griffin, who were to have a court-martial on their conduct in the field. And with a heavy heart Lincoln agreed there should be a court of inquiry for McDowell.

"The President," said Chase, ". . . told me that the clamor against McDowell was so great that he [McDowell] could not lead his troops unless something was done to restore confidence; and proposed to me to suggest to him the asking for a Court of Inquiry." Both Chase and Stanton, along with Lincoln, had long ago become convinced that McDowell was a first-rate, loyal officer, never sulking nor talking loose nor taking a hand in military politics. McDowell went away "very sad," on a 15-day leave of absence, to return for the trial he asked.

A week after the Second Bull Run battle, Lincoln at the War Office referred to "the great number of stragglers he had seen coming into town this morning, and of the immense losses by desertion." Chase noted: "The President said he had felt badly all day." Next day, meeting a committee from New York who urged him to change his policy, "the President became vexed and said, in substance, 'It is plain enough what you want—you want to get Seward out of the Cabinet. There is not one of you who would not see the country ruined if you could turn out Seward.' "

On general policies Chase believed Lincoln had now drifted far out of line with his country and party. "The President," noted Chase, "with the most honest intentions in the world, and a naturally clear judgment and a true, unselfish patriotism, has yielded so much to Border State and negro-phobic counsels that he now finds it difficult to arrest his own descent towards the most fatal concessions."

At one Cabinet meeting, when Lincoln had brought up the matter of shifting and trying new generals, it came to A. K. McClure that the President said: "I think we'd better wait; perhaps a real fighting general will come along some of these days, and then we'll all be happy. If you go to mixing in a mix-up, you only make the muddle worse."

The yellow corn stood ripe in the fields of Maryland. Lee and Jackson knew that corn could help feed their armies. They marched gray and butternut regiments across the Potomac, ragged and footsore men who could fight, as the world knew.

McClellan with an army marched toward Lee. He was feeling better. His three dismissed major generals had been cleared without court-martial and restored to him by the President. McClellan wrote his wife, "The feeling of the government towards me, I am sure, is kind and trusting." Not in a year had he sent his wife any such pleasant words about the Government. His friend, Lincoln, against a majority of the Cabinet, had again put him at the head of a great army in the field.

Telegrams tumbled into the White House telling of Bragg's Confederate army in Kentucky slipping past Buell's army, which had been set to watch him. Bragg was marching north toward Cincinnati and Louisville, both cities anxious. Also Kirby Smith's men in gray had marched into Kentucky, chased the state legislature out of Frankfort, and captured Lexington, the home town of Mary Todd Lincoln.

"Where is General Bragg?" Lincoln queried in telegrams to several generals in the field. He wired Buell and others, "What degree of certainty have you, that Bragg, with his command, is not now in the valley of the Shenandoah, Virginia?" He wired McClellan, who was calling for reinforcements, that he could have 21,000 under Porter and "I am sending you all that can be spared."

Stonewall Jackson smashed at the Union garrison in Harpers Ferry, trapped them, and took 11,000 prisoners. Four days later, September 17, McClellan's 90,000 troops met Lee's army, about half that of McClellan in troop numbers, at Antietam Creek. Around a cornfield and a little white Dunker church, around a stone bridge, and in a pasture lane worn by cowpaths, surged a human tornado. General Joseph Hooker rode in the worst of the storm, and said of it, "Every stalk of corn in the northern and greater part of the field was cut as closely as could have been done with a knife, and the slain lay in rows precisely as they had stood in their ranks a few moments before." Hooker fell from his saddle with a bleeding foot. An old man with his white hair in the wind, Major General J. K. F. Mansfield, fell dead from his saddle. General Sedgwick was three times wounded, in shoulder, leg, wrist. Four other Union generals fell off their horses with wounds. On the Confederate side, Colonel B. B. Gayle of Alabama was surrounded, drew his revolver, called to his men, "We are flanked, boys, but let's die in our tracks," and fell riddled with bullets. "Don't let your horses tread on me," a wounded man called from a huddle of corpses where officers were picking their way through.

On a golden autumn Sabbath morning three-mile lines of men had faced each other with guns. And when the shooting was over the losses were put at 12,000 on each side. Lee crossed the Potomac, back into the South again. But McClellan did not follow though his chances of wiping out Lee's army were estimated by Longstreet: "We were so badly crushed that at the close of the day ten thousand fresh troops could have come in and taken Lee's army and everything it had. But McClellan did not know it." He had two soldiers to the enemy's one, completely superior cannon, rifles, supplies. He had 93,000 men answering roll call as Lee was fading down the Shenandoah Valley with less than 40,000.

Ten days after the Antietam battle McClellan wrote to his wife: "Not yet have I had a word from any one in Washington about the battle of the Antietam . . . except from the President in the following *beautiful* language, 'Your despatch received. God bless you and all with you! Cant you *bust* them some *even* before they get off?'!!!" Thus for his own purposes and satisfaction, in a highly responsible matter, McClellan could misquote and mangle the President's message, which read: "God bless you, and all with you. Destroy the rebel army, if possible."

Congressman William D. Kelley of Pittsburgh came to the White House and discussed with Lincoln the information that McClellan had held in reserve some 30,000 men, Fitz-John Porter's corps. They did not get into battle, had all their ammunition when the shooting was over. Kelley felt pity and sarcasm in the President's saying, "Whatever the troops and people may think and say of his failure to capture Lee's army and supplies, my censure should be tempered by the consciousness of the fact that I did not restore him to command for aggressive fighting, but as an organizer and a good hand at defending a position."

Lincoln, according to Kelley, was slow and deliberate as he said: "I am now stronger with the Army of the Potomac than McClellan. The supremacy of the civil power has been restored, and the Executive is again master of the situation. The troops know, that if I made a mistake in substituting Pope for McClellan, I was capable of rectifying it by again trusting him. They know, too, that neither Stanton nor I withheld anything from him at Antietam, and that it was not the administration, but their own former idol, who surrendered the just results of their terrible sacrifices and closed the great fight as a drawn battle, when, had he thrown Porter's corps of fresh men and other available troops upon Lee's army, he would inevitably have driven it in disorder to the river and captured most of it before sunset."

In a certain sense Lincoln felt at this time that the war had not really begun. The faults lay deep and were complex. He set forth his view to women at-

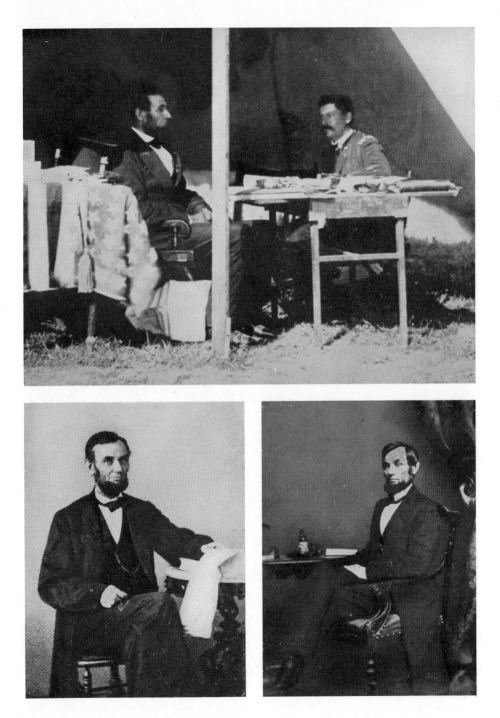

Upper: Lincoln, troubled about McClellan's "slows," pays a surprise visit to the Army of the Potomac commander in October 1862 [Meserve]. *Lower left:* One of a series of nine photographs by Alexander and James Gardner August 9, 1863 [Meserve]. *Lower right:* Photograph by Mathew B. Brady, probably 1862 [Meserve].

Lincoln facing McClellan in Antietam camp after the battle October 1862. The best photograph of Lincoln the tall man in the tall hat. Detail from photograph in Gardner Album No. 1 [Museum of Modern Art].

tending a national council to organize aid and relief for sick and wounded in the field. Among these devoted workers was Mary A. Livermore, wife of a Universalist clergyman and editor in Chicago. She had lent her strength to raising money and supplies, forming local groups that sent lint, bandages and comforts to the battlefields and hospitals. Before leaving for home they were calling on the President for some word of encouragement.

"I have no word of encouragement to give!" was the slow, blunt reply. The women were silent. They knew he was telling them what he could not well tell the country. The President went on: "The fact is the people have not yet made up their minds that we are at war with the South. They have not buckled down to the determination to fight this war through; for they have got the idea into their heads that we are going to get out of this fix somehow by strategy! That's the word—*strategy!* General McClellan thinks he is going to whip the Rebels by strategy; and the army has got the same notion . . ."

One of the women spoke of the uprisings of hundreds of thousands of volunteers, of valiant behavior at Donelson, Pea Ridge, Shiloh. The President admitted this, and then came back to his theme. "The people *have not* made up their minds that we are at war, I tell you! They think there is a royal road to peace, and that General McClellan is to find it. The army has not settled down into the conviction that we are in a terrible war that has got to be fought out—no; and the officers have not either . . . Whole regiments have two-thirds of their men absent—a great many by desertion, and a great many on leave granted by company officers, which is almost as bad . . . The deserters and furloughed men outnumber the recruits. To fill up the army is like undertaking to shovel fleas. You take up a shovelful but before you can dump them anywhere they are gone. It is like trying to ride a balky horse. You coax, and cheer, and spur, and lay on the whip, but you don't get ahead an inch—there you stick!"

Said one of the women, "Is not death the penalty for desertion? . . . Before many soldiers had suffered death for desertion, this wholesale depletion of the army would be ended." "Oh, no, no!" came the President's reply as he shook his sad head, ". . . if I should go to shooting men by scores for desertion, I should have such a hullabaloo about my ears as I have not heard yet, and I should deserve it. You cannot order men shot by dozens or twenties. People won't stand it and they ought not to stand it. No, we must change the condition of things some other way."

Mrs. Livermore saw his face having ghastly lines, his half-staggering gait like that of a man walking in his sleep.

CHAPTER 26

The Involved Slavery Issue—Preliminary Emancipation Proclamation

IN A ROCKING chair in a house on F Street in Washington a woman sat knitting. She made her home with her daughter, wife of Missouri Republican Congressman Frank P. Blair. She was old and blind and had a saying: "Of all things in the world I hate slavery the most—except abolitionism." Thus she carried a double hate, and she could tell which was heavier of the two. Over the country were single, triple and multiple hates. The sum of them made the war.

Lincoln heard the case of a Negro slave who ran away from his master, came to Washington, and was arrested. Chase and Montgomery Blair disputed before Lincoln. Chase would send the captured man into the Union Army; Blair would enforce the Fugitive Slave Law and return the Negro to his legal owner.

The harassed Lincoln said he was reminded of a man in Illinois terribly annoyed by a creditor who kept coming often and pressing him to pay the money he owed. Finally the poor debtor saw nothing to do but to "act crazy" whenever asked for the money. And Lincoln added: "I have on more than one occasion in this room, when beset by extremists on this question, been compelled to appear very mad. I think none of you will ever dispose of this subject without getting mad."

In the hysteria of a changing order, in the drive of forces uprooting a hoary and venerable past, many tongues were let loose and many snap judgments flung into the ears of men. Other extremists were saying the same as Wendell Phillips at a meeting near Boston August 1, 1862: the President "has no mind whatever. He has not uttered a word that gives even a twilight glimpse of any anti-slavery purpose. He may be honest—nobody cares whether the tortoise is honest or not; he has neither insight, nor prevision, nor decision." And, prophesied the agitator, "As long as you keep the present turtle at the head of the Government you make a pit with one hand and fill it with the other."

With a musical voice, with plain words and abrupt thought, Phillips held audiences rapt even when they hated his ideas. Parts of his speeches were splashes of gossip that other platform men could not manage. "The policy that prevails at Washington is to do nothing, and wait for events. I asked the lawyers of Illinois, who had practiced law with Mr. Lincoln for twenty years, 'Is he a man of decision, is he a man who can say no?' They all said, 'If you had gone to the Illinois bar, and selected the man least capable of saying no, it would have been Abraham Lincoln.'"

Some of the more visionary crusaders believed that with the slaveholders crushed, then would rise a nation of men and women all free, all Christian, "ultimately redeemed." First, however, must be the tragedy of sacrifice and vengeance.

Touched with sorrow yet awful with warning, was Julia Ward Howe's "Battle Hymn of the Republic":

Mine eyes have seen the glory of the coming of the Lord;
He is trampling out the vintage where the grapes of wrath are stored;
He hath loosed the fateful lightning of His terrible swift sword;
    His truth is marching on.

Published in February '62 her verses had now gone to singing millions. Of her trip to Washington and her visit with Lincoln, Mrs. Howe remembered sharply two things. Lincoln from where she sat was in line with the Gilbert Stuart painting of Washington and she tried to compare them. Also Lincoln remarked, "I once heered George Sumner tell a story." The way he pronounced "heered" fixed it in her memory.

Denunciation poured from abolitionists when the President dealt with a military order issued by his good friend Major General David Hunter, commanding at Port Royal, South Carolina. The General confiscated slaves and declared them free. Also, reasoning that martial law and slavery could not go together, the General declared all slaves in Georgia, Florida and South Carolina "forever free." Chase urged that these orders should stand, that nine-tenths of the country was for them.

Lincoln wrote to Chase, "No commanding general shall do such a thing, upon *my* responsibility, without consulting me." He again urged that the Federal Government co-operate with any Slave State in gradual compensated emancipation of the slaves. To the Border State people, "I do not argue— I beseech you to make arguments for yourselves." Afraid that they were not reading the drift of events, he warned them: "You cannot, if you would, be blind to the signs of the times. I beg of you a calm and enlarged consideration of them, ranging, if it may be, far above personal and partizan politics."

Border State Congressmen at the White House on Lincoln's invitation in July '62 heard him plead for graduated, compensated abolishment of slavery. "I intend no reproach or complaint," he said, "when I assure you that in my opinion, if you all had voted for the resolution . . . of last March, the war would now be substantially ended." He still believed the plan would be swift to end the war. With the slaves freed by purchase in the Border States, the other states farther south would see they could not long keep up the war. In time, as the war dragged on, slavery would be extinguished by mere friction, urged the President. The money spent for buying slaves and setting them free would shorten the war. "How much better to thus save the money which else we sink forever in the war. How much better to do it while we can, lest the war ere long render us pecuniarily unable to do it . . ."

And the Border State men went away, considered and discussed. But nothing came of Lincoln's hope to have the nation buy the slaves and set them free. The hatred of the administration head and his works ran deep among those in Kentucky committed to Jefferson Davis. One wrote for the

Kentucky Statesman: "This is the man who bids armies rise and fight and commands and dismisses generals at will. This is the man who proclaims (as such could only do) the equality of the races, black and white . . . Kneel down and kiss his royal feet, men of the South!"

Early in August '62 Sumner wrote of Lincoln to John Bright in England: "He is hard to move . . . I urged him on the 4th of July to put forth an edict of emancipation, telling him he could make the day more sacred and historic than ever. He replied, 'I would do it if I were not afraid that half the officers would fling down their arms and three more States would rise.'" Greeley in his *Tribune* of August 19, 1862, issued "The Prayer of Twenty Millions." As the first servant of the Republic, the President was required to execute the laws, declared Greeley, and, "We think you are strangely and disastrously remiss in the discharge of your official and imperative duty." Speaking for 20,000,000 people, as he assumed, Greeley wrote: "You are unduly influenced by the counsels, the representations, the menace of certain fossil politicians hailing from the border slave States." Also: "We complain that a large proportion of our regular army officers with many of the volunteers evince far more solicitude to uphold slavery than to put down the rebellion." Lincoln in a letter dated August 22, 1862, told the country in simple and skillfully wrought sentences what the war was for, as he saw it. Widely reprinted, probably reaching nearly all persons in the country who could read, the letter said:

. . . I would save the Union. I would save it the shortest way under the Constitution. The sooner the national authority can be restored; the nearer the Union will be "the Union as it was." If there be those who would not save the Union, unless they could at the same time *save* slavery, I do not agree with them. If there be those who would not save the Union unless they could at the same time *destroy* slavery, I do not agree with them. *My paramount object in this struggle is to save the Union, and is not either to save or to destroy slavery.* [Italics added.] If I could save the Union without freeing *any* slave, I would do it, and if I could save it by freeing *all* the slaves I would do it; and if I could save it by freeing some and leaving others alone I would also do that. What I do about slavery, and the colored race, I do because I believe it helps to save the Union; and what I forbear, I forbear because I do *not* believe it would help to save the Union. I shall do *less* whenever I shall believe what I am doing hurts the cause, and I shall do *more* whenever I shall believe doing more will help the cause. I shall try to correct errors when shown to be errors; and I shall adopt new views so fast as they shall appear to be true views.

I have here stated my purpose according to my view of *official* duty; and I intend no modification of my oft-expressed *personal* wish that all men every where could be free.

The Reverend Moncure Daniel Conway and the Reverend William Henry Channing, Unitarian antislavery clergymen, called by appointment at the Executive Mansion at eight o'clock one morning. As they waited in the anteroom, noted Conway: "A woman with a little child was waiting. She now and then wept but said nothing. The President saw her first, and she came out radiant. We conjectured some prisoner was that day released." They found the President "gracious." He agreed with Channing on plans for the nation to buy the slaves: compensated abolishment. He had for years favored this plan. He turned to Conway, who said the President could be the deliverer of the nation from its one great evil. What would not that man achieve for mankind who should free America from slavery? "Perhaps," said Lincoln, "we may be better able to do something in that direction after a while than we are now."

He half inquired from Conway whether it was not true that the anti-slavery people, being in a "movement," naturally met a good many who agreed with them. "You possibly may over-estimate the number in the country who hold such views. But the position in which I am placed brings me into some knowledge of opinions in all parts of the country and of many different kinds of people; and it appears to me that the great masses of this country care comparatively little about the negro, and are anxious only for military successes."

Thus stood the President, Conway reported far and wide. The two clergymen thanked him for his kindly reception. He remarked: "We shall need all the anti-slavery feeling in the country, and more; you can go home and try to bring the people to your views; and you may say anything you like about me, if that will help. Don't spare me!" This with a laugh. Then gravely: "When the hour comes for dealing with slavery, I trust I will be willing to do my duty though it cost my life. And, gentlemen, lives will be lost."

In that summer of '62 Lincoln had to consider such incidents as a Union officer, a Republican, drawing applause at a mass meeting for recruiting in Terre Haute, Indiana, when he shouted, "I hate a nigger worse than I hate the devil."

How the Border State men were shifting in degree was indicated in a Browning diary note: "Garrett Davis Senator from Kentucky, came in whilst I was with the President and in conversation upon the subject of slavery said that to save the Union he was willing, if necessary, to see slavery wiped out. Still he is very sensitive upon the subject."

And they were very sensitive, some of the Border State men, with armies passing to and fro through their cities, with guerrillas and bushwhackers playing havoc with their farms, barns, cattle, with informers shifting from one side to the other, with traders and merchants selling to whichever side would pay high prices. In a letter to a New Orleans man, Lincoln referred to the professed Union men who would neither help the Government nor permit the Government to do things without their help. They wished to stand by without taking sides. "They are to touch neither a sail nor a pump, but to be merely passengers,—dead-heads at that—to be carried snug and dry, throughout the storm, and safely landed right side up." There were true Union men whose sacrifices were beyond speech to praise. But there were others whose suggestions could only lead to a surrender of the Government. Lincoln was not in a boastful mood. "I shall not do *more* than I can, and I shall do *all* I can to save the government, which is my sworn duty as well as my personal inclination." And as if he might have struggled through tortuous windings to fix for himself one guiding point amid the intricacies, the President wrote. "I shall do nothing in malice. What I deal with is too vast for malicious dealing."

Cassius M. Clay, now a major general, had edited the antislavery *True American*, stumped Kentucky for Lincoln in 1860, and in a debate with a proslavery candidate received a deep stab wound in the left breast over the heart, yet managed to bury his own bowie knife to the hilt in the abdomen of his opponent. This muscular heavyweight, returned from the Russian Legation, came to tell Lincoln to free the slaves, that over Europe he found the governments ready to recognize the Confederacy, anxious to intervene, that an emancipation proclamation now would block these European autocracies. "Kentucky would go against us," said Lincoln, according to Clay. "And we have now as much as we can carry." Clay was decisive, telling the President: "You are mistaken . . ." Lincoln pondered, and at last said: "The Kentucky legislature is now in session. Go down and see how they stand and report to me." And Cash Clay had arrived to find the Kentucky Legislature in flight from approaching Confederate forces.

John Lothrop Motley, the Minister at Vienna, was writing home that having been in London, Paris, Berlin, he was sure that only one of three conditions would stave off European recognition of the Confederacy: (1) a great and conclusive battle crushing the Confederates; (2) the capture of cotton ports and release of large cotton supplies for European factories; (3) a clear-cut policy of emancipation for the slaves. Carl Schurz had reported likewise from Madrid. Lincoln, aware of these points, and at the suggestion of John Bright of the British House of Commons, wrote a resolution suitable for Bright to use:

Whereas, while heretofore States and nations have tolerated slavery, recently, for the first [time] in the world, an attempt has been made to construct a new nation, upon the basis of, and with the primary and fundamental object to maintain, enlarge and perpetuate human slavery; therefore,
Resolved, That no such embryo State should ever be recognized by, or admitted into, the family of Christian and civilized nations; and that all Christian and civilized men everywhere should, by all lawful means, resist to the utmost such recognition and admission.

On August 14, 1862, there came to the Executive Mansion the first committee of free Negroes to arrive by invitation of the President. Greetings and preliminaries over, the President explained that money had been put at his disposal by Congress for the purpose "of colonizing people of African descent," a cause he had long favored. One of those present wrote a memorandum of the words of the President.

"Why," Lincoln asked, "should the people of your race be colonized, and where? Why should they leave this country? . . . Your race suffers very greatly, many of them, by living among us, while ours suffers from your presence . . . Your race are suffering, in my judgment, the greatest wrong inflicted on any people. But even when you cease to be slaves, you are yet far removed from being placed on an equality with the white race . . ." The principal difficulty in the way of colonization, the President suggested to the committee of Negroes, was that "the free colored man cannot see that his comfort would be advanced by it." While slaves would gladly accept freedom on condition of leaving the United States for a colony, the free man would have "nothing to do with the idea . . ." Lincoln unfolded a plan for them to go to a country in Central America, rich in coal mines, farm land, harbors and other advantages. What they could do would depend on themselves. "Success does not as much depend on external help as on self-reliance . . . Could I get a hundred tolerably intelligent men, with their wives and children, and able to 'cut their own fodder,' so to speak? Can I have fifty? If I could find twenty-five able-bodied men, with a mixture of women and children,—good things in the family relation, I think,—I could make a successful commencement. I want you to let me know whether this can be done or not. This is the practical part of my wish to see you."

The President had in view for them to colonize a tract in the Republic of New Granada. But there were contending factions in the government of New Granada; necessary assurances could not be had of security, and the plan was soon abandoned. The enthusiasm of the free Negroes over such colonization was slight, almost negligible.

Lincoln signed an act ending Negro slavery in the District of Columbia, the Federal Government to buy the slaves at prices not exceeding $200 each. And, the President wishing it, there was provision for steamship tickets to Liberia or Haiti for any freed slaves who cared to go to those Negro republics. This act of Congress and the President was one of many laws, decisions, new precedents, that by percussion and abrasion, by erosion and attrition, were opening gaps in the legal status of slavery, wearing down its props and bulwarks.

Two plans the President struggled with incessantly, like an engineer wrestling to put bridges over a swollen river during a flood rush. One was to make practical the colonization of Negroes to be freed; the other was gradual compensated abolishment. He pointed to Kentucky as a state that recently through legal process had become the owner of slaves, and she sold none but liberated all.

The President asked, and Congress passed, an act recognizing the Negro republics of Haiti and Liberia, though the State Department modified this in announcing that a black man could not be received as a foreign Minister. This in turn was modified informally by the President in a talk with James Redpath, an agent of antislavery societies who had been to Haiti and reported to Lincoln that the Haitian President was profoundly grateful to the American President and so deeply appreciative that he was sending word by Redpath that, if it were the wish of Mr. Lincoln, he would not send to Washington a black man as Haitian Minister. As the Springfield *Republican* correspondent at Washington had it from Redpath, Lincoln hesitated a moment and then drawled, "You can tell the President of Hayti that I shan't tear my shirt if he sends a nigger here!"

When in a few months the Haitian Minister did arrive, C. Edwards Lester wrote of him as having "a finely formed, brilliant face, the complexion being rather dark, but his cheek glowing with the warm tint, and his eye with the liquid beauty of the Creole." Of Mr. Lincoln and the hearty reception accorded him at the White House, the Haitian Minister spoke with veneration, though no name was so dear to the Haitians as that of Charles Sumner. "Signor Carlo il Senatore! why, his picture is in every cottage in Hayti. He has done everything for us."

Congress revised the war regulations so as to forbid any officer of the Army or the Navy to use his forces to capture and return fugitive slaves. Another act provided that such officers could not hear evidence and try cases as to whether a runaway slave should be returned on the claim of an owner. A treaty was negotiated with Great Britain for suppression of the African slave trade. By another act of Congress all slaves in Territories of the United States were declared free. Further legislation provided for the education of Negro children, and Negroes were made admissible as mail-carriers.

These acts of Congress were capped by the Confiscation Act, which the President signed in July '62. Slaves owned by persons convicted of treason or rebellion should be made free, this act declared, and furthermore, slaves of rebels who escaped into Union army lines, or slaves whose masters had run away, or slaves found by the Union Army in places formerly occupied by rebel forces, should all be designated as prisoners of war and set free. Other bills provided that slaves entering Union Army lines could be put to work and earn their freedom; the President could enroll and employ Negroes for camp labor and military service, while the wives, mothers and children of such Negro slaves, if they were the property of armed "rebels," should be set free; the President was authorized "to employ as many persons of African descent as he may deem necessary and proper for the suppression of this rebellion, and for this purpose he may organize and use them in such manner as he may judge best for the public welfare."

Lincoln at first intended to veto the Confiscation Act and have it reframed. Instead he signed it, and returned it with his intended veto message attached, for future record. "It is startling to say that congress can free a slave within a state," ran part of this veto message, "and yet if it were said the ownership of the slave had first been transferred to the nation, and that congress had then liberated him, the difficulty would at once vanish." The slaves of a traitor were forfeited to the Government, which raised the question: "Shall they be made free, or sold to new masters?" He could see no objection to Congress' deciding in advance that they should be free.

Thus far all laws passed by Congress fully protected the ownership of slaves held by men loyal to the Union, or men not partaking in the rebellion. Not many were there of such Unionist slaveowners. All other owners of slaves were under the threat of confiscation of their property if and when the Union armies reached their plantations.

In the midst of these zigzags of public policy, *Harper's Weekly* saw the President as following a midway path, giving in to neither of the extremists. An editorial in May set forth: "In the President of the United States Providence has vouchsafed a leader whose moral perceptions are blinded neither by sophistry nor enthusiasm—who knows that permanent results must grow, and can not be prematurely seized." In a labyrinth of viewpoints Lincoln found himself encircled by groups trying to infiltrate him with their special ideas.

John W. Crisfield, once a fellow member of Congress with Lincoln, and now a member of a House committee to report on gradual compensated emancipation, came to Lincoln's office in July '62 and, according to Lamon, they exchanged remarks. "Well, Crisfield, how are you getting along with your report? Have you written it yet?" "No." "You had better come to an agreement. Niggers will never be cheaper."

On July 22, 1862, as the McClellan campaign for Richmond was fading in mist, mud and disaster, Lincoln called his Cabinet. And as he told it himself at a later time: "I felt that we . . . must change our tactics, or lose the game. I now determined upon the adoption of the emancipation policy . . . I prepared the original draft of the proclamation, and . . . I said to the Cabinet that I . . . had not called them together to ask their advice, but to lay the subject matter of a proclamation before them, suggestions as to which would be in order, after they had heard it read . . . Secretary Seward . . . said in substance, 'Mr. President, I approve of the proclamation, but I question the expediency of its issue at this juncture . . . It may be viewed as the last measure of an exhausted government, a cry for help . . .' His idea was that it would be considered our last *shriek*, on the retreat. 'Now,' continued Mr. Seward, 'while I approve the measure, I suggest, sir, that you postpone its issue, until you can give it to the country supported by military success . . .'

"I put the draft of the proclamation aside . . . Well, the next news we had was of Pope's disaster, at Bull Run. Things looked darker than ever. Finally, came the week of the battle of Antietam . . . The news came, I think, on Wednesday, that the advantage was on our side . . . I finished writing the second draft of the preliminary proclamation . . . called the Cabinet together to hear it, and it was published the following Monday."

At that Cabinet meeting September 22, 1862, the President opened by mentioning that Artemus Ward had sent him a book with a chapter in it titled "High-Handed Outrage at Utica." The President said he would read this chapter, which he thought very funny. It read in part:

In the Faul of 1856, I showed my show in Utiky, a trooly grate sitty in the State of New York . . . 1 day. . . . what was my skorn & disgust to see a big burly feller walk up to the cage containin my wax figgers of the Lord's Last Supper, and cease Judas Iscarrot by the feet and drag him out on the ground. He then commenced for to pound him as hard as he cood.

"What under the son are you abowt?" cried I.

Sez he, "What did you bring this pussylanermus cuss here for?" . . .

Sez I, "You egrejus ass, that air's a wax figger . . ."

Sez he, "That's all very well fur you to say, but I tell you, old man, that Judas Iscarrot can't show hisself in Utiky with impunerty by a darn site!" with which observashun he kaved in Judassis hed. The young man belonged to 1 of the first famerlies in Utiky. I sood him, and the Joory brawt in a verdick of Arson in the 3rd degree.

Lincoln enjoyed this clownery. So did other members of the Cabinet, though Seward laughed for fun while Chase smiled rather conventionally. Stanton sat glum and glowering.

Then Lincoln took a grave tone, with a solemn deliberation read the proclamation, commenting as he went along. It began with saying the war would go on for the Union, that the efforts would go on for buying and setting free the slaves of the Border States, and the colonizing of them; that on January 1, 1863, all slaves in states or parts of states in rebellion against the United States "shall be then, thenceforward, and forever free," and the Federal Government would "recognize the freedom of such persons." It was a preliminary proclamation.

Seward suggested adding the words "and maintain" after the word "recognize." Chase joined Seward in this, and it was done. Blair said he was for the principle involved, but the result of the proclamation would be to send the Border States into the arms of the secessionists; also it would give a club to hostile political elements in the North. Seward made another minor suggestion, that colonization should be only with the consent of the colonists; Negroes were to be sent out of the country only as they were willing to go. Lincoln put that in quickly. Then he asked Seward why he had not proposed both of his important changes at once. Seward hedged. And Lincoln said Seward reminded him of a hired man out West who came to the farmer one afternoon with news that one of a yoke of oxen had dropped dead. And after hesitating and waiting a while, the hired man said the other ox in the team had dropped dead too. The farmer asked, "Why didn't you tell me at once that both oxen were dead?" "Because," said the hired man, "I didn't want to hurt you by telling you too much at one time."

Two days later, September 24, on a Monday morning, this preliminary Emancipation Proclamation was published, for the country and the world to read. Serenaders came with a brass band to have music over the proclamation. The President addressed them from a White House balcony: ". . . I can only trust in God I have made no mistake . . . It is now for the country and the world to pass judgment on it, and, may be, take action upon it." He was "environed with difficulties," he soberly wished the crowd to know. "Yet they are scarcely so great as the difficulties of those who, upon the battle field, are endeavoring to purchase with their blood and their lives the future happiness and prosperity of this country." He wanted those soldiers with him. He was privately wondering how many of them now were stronger for him.

On invitation of Curtin a gathering of governors of Northern States met that day in Altoona, Pennsylvania, "to take measures for the more active support of the Government." It was in the minds of Andrew and other antislavery governors that they might frame a decision which would bring pressure on the President to remove McClellan from command and to issue some positive declaration against slavery. The ground had been cut from under them by Antietam and the Emancipation Proclamation. Sixteen of them signed an address to the President, pledging loyalty to the Union, endorsing the new emancipation policy, and suggesting that he should call for 100,000 more troops to be organized into a reserve corps for emergencies. Five governors held off from signing. They were from the Slave States Kentucky, Missouri, Maryland and Delaware, and the odd Northern bailiwick of New Jersey. While also pledging loyalty to the Union and support of the President, these five governors could not endorse the Emancipation Proclamation.

To justify their private and rather secretive conference during such a crisis, the governors appointed Andrew and Curtin a committee to see the President in Washington. They went back home to their state capitals encouraged and refreshed in faith, according to a close friend of Andrew.

The Democratic party, already campaigning for the November elections, raised the issue that the war for the Union had been changed to a war for abolition. McClellan wrote his wife that the President's proclamation, and other troubles, "render it almost impossible for me to retain my commission and self-respect at the same time." Lincoln had now gone over to the radicals, the Louisville *Democrat* and other papers told readers. "The abolitionists have pressed him into their service." John Hay spoke of editorials in the leading newspapers. The President said he had studied the matter so long that "he knew more about it than they did."

Beyond the newspapers and politicians were the People and Lincoln's question was: What were they thinking? In many quarters the proclamation was called grand, historic, and its author an immortal. Lincoln wrote in a letter marked "Strictly private," ". . . while commendation in newspapers and by distinguished individuals is all that a vain man could wish, the stocks have declined, and troops come forward more slowly than ever."

The President's act had been like a chemist tossing a tiny pinch of a powerful ingredient into a seething and shaking caldron. Colors and currents shifted and deepened. New channels cut their way far under the surface. The turmoil and the trembling became unreadable by any man. But below the fresh confusion was heaving some deep and irrevocable change.

The proclamation was aimed at Europe as well as North and South America. London *Punch* cartooned Lincoln with horns and a long tail. London, Henry Adams wrote, ". . . created a nightmare of its own and gave it the shape of Abraham Lincoln." In England, because of the cotton famine, nearly 500,000 men were out of work. In a single textile district of France were 130,000 unemployed. Yet a definite mass opinion favored the North as against the South.

The press and Premier Palmerston and the voices of the ruling class of England could not hope to change the basic instinct of the masses, now deeper in response to the Lincoln Government as against that of Davis at Richmond. In the inner circles of the ruling class it was admitted that now there would be increased difficulty for any European government to recognize the South.

A wave of fury swept the South. Lincoln was breaking the laws of civilized warfare, outraging private-property rights, inviting Negroes to kill, burn and rape, said statesmen, orators, newspapers. The Richmond *Enquirer* fumed, "What shall we call him? Coward, assassin, savage, murderer of women and babies? Or shall we consider them all as embodied in the word fiend, and call him Lincoln, the Fiend?"

Lincoln had warned nearly a year back that the contest might develop into "remorseless, revolutionary warfare." The awful responsibility of carrying on and finishing a war of conquest lay ahead.

Something new was in the writing—but what? Something was dying, something being born—but what?

Toward the end of this sad September Lincoln wrote a riddle that beset his mind, haunted his heart. He left it on his desk. It was not for publication. John Hay made a copy of it: "The will of God prevails. In great contests each party claims to act in accordance with the will of God. Both may be, and one must be, wrong. God cannot be for and against the same thing at the same time. In the present civil war it is quite possible that God's purpose is something different from the purpose of either party; and yet the human instrumentalities, working just as they do, are the best adaptation to effect his purpose. I am almost ready to say that this is probably true; that God wills this contest, and wills that it shall not end yet. By his mere great power on the minds of the new contestants, he could have either saved or destroyed the Union without a human contest. Yet the contest began. And having begun, he could give the final victory to either side any day. Yet the contest proceeds."

CHAPTER 27

McClellan's "Slows"—Election Losses—
Fredericksburg—'62 Message

WRITING from the Paris consulate, John Bigelow asked Weed, "Why doesn't Lincoln shoot somebody?" From his pivotal point of observation, however, Lincoln could find no unanimous opinion as to whom to shoot. In early October '62 Governor Morton of Indiana wrote to the President, "Another three months like the last six and we are lost—lost."

From day to day political questions interwove with military. At several Cabinet meetings the last week in September '62 came the matter of deporting freed Negroes. Blair and Bates, the Missouri members, favored forcible deportation, the President holding that only those should go who wished to go. He laid before Welles the maps, reports, titles and evidence having to do with the Chiriqui land grant in Panama, for Welles to make a decision as to whether the Navy Department should contract to buy coal from there, the coal to be mined by colonized free Negroes from the United States. "The President was earnest in the matter," wrote Welles in his diary; "wished to send the negroes out of the country," was "importunate."

Outside of Cabinet meetings Chase was telling Welles that Stanton felt useless and deemed it his duty to resign from the Cabinet. Welles said he was not surprised to hear it, that sooner or later either Stanton or some of the generals would have to go. "Chase said if Stanton went, he would go," wrote Welles. "It was due to Stanton and to ourselves that we should stand by him, and if one goes out, all had better go, certainly he [Chase] would." Thus Chase was trying to lay the way for a Cabinet departure, for all of them to quit at once.

Towering over immediate issues stood the sphinx of McClellan's army—how to get it moving. While McClellan "rested" his troops a visitor casually asked Lincoln what number of men he supposed the "rebels" had in the field. And according to *Leslie's Weekly*, he said seriously, "1,200,000 according to the best authority." The visitor turned pale and cried, "My God!" "Yes, sir," went on the President, "1,200,000—no doubt of it. You see, all our generals, when they get whipped, say the enemy outnumbers them from three to five to one, and I must believe them. We have 400,000 men in the field, and three times four makes twelve. Don't you see it?"

On October 1 Lincoln, without notifying McClellan, started for the Army of the Potomac camps. McClellan got word of Lincoln's being on the way, rode to Harpers Ferry, and was pleased to find that no Cabinet members or politicians were with the President, "merely some western officers." "His ostensible purpose," McClellan wrote his wife, "is to see the troops and the battle-field; I incline to think that the real purpose of his visit is to push me into a premature advance into Virginia."

They rode horseback all of one afternoon around the camps. Mathew B. Brady photographed them together sitting in McClellan's tent, Lincoln's right arm resting against a flag draping a table where his tall silk hat stood upside down between two stubs of candles.

The dim gray twilight just before dawn came over the hills of Maryland as Lincoln rose in the tent assigned to him. A few rooster crows drifted on the air from nearby farms. It was a quiet hour. Lincoln stood at the cot of Ozias M. Hatch, once secretary of state in Illinois, saying, "Come, Hatch, I want you to take a walk with me." Hatch got up without a word, the two of them dressed, and left the tent together. Lincoln led Hatch through the streets of a great tented city, amid avenues of little white canvas huts where thousands of soldiers were sleeping. Very little was spoken. "Lincoln seemed to be peculiarly serious," Hatch noted, "and his quiet, abstract way affected me also. It did not seem a time to speak. Nothing was to be said, nothing needed to be said."

They reached a commanding point in the hills where the rising sun spread its moving sheen over the stirring, half-awake army of men at their morning routine. The President waved his hand in a gesture of half-despair, and leaning toward Hatch, said in a husky and almost whispering voice, "Hatch— Hatch, what is all this?" "Why, Mr. Lincoln," said Hatch, "this is the Army of the Potomac." Lincoln hesitated a moment, and then straightening up, in a louder and clearer tone of voice: "No, Hatch, no. This is General McClellan's bodyguard." Nothing more was said. The two men walked slowly back to their tent.

At Frederick, Maryland, the troops were drawn up. The President told them it was not proper for him in his present position to make speeches. He gave thanks to the soldiers for good services, energy shown, hardships endured and blood shed for the Union. He hoped their children, and their children's children for a thousand generations to come, would enjoy the benefits of a united country.

Passing a house in which lay Confederate wounded, Lincoln asked to go in. A correspondent quoted him as saying they were "enemies through uncontrollable circumstances." After a silence, Confederates came forward and without words shook the hand of the President. Some were too sore and broken to walk or to sit up. The President went among these, took some by the hand, wished them good cheer, said they should have the best of care. The correspondent wrote, "Beholders wept at the interview, most of the Confederates, even, were moved to tears."

Lamon and others rode with the President in an ambulance a few miles to Porter's corps. On the way Lincoln said, "Lamon, sing one of your little sad songs." And Lamon sang "Twenty Years Ago," a melancholy Thomas Hood poem of which Lamon said, "Many a time, in the old days on the Illinois circuit, and often at the White House when he and I were alone, have I seen him in tears while I was rendering, in my poor way, that homely melody."

The song deepened Lincoln's sadness, and, said Lamon: "I then did what I had done many times before; I startled him from his melancholy by striking up a comic air, singing also a snatch from 'Picayune Butler,'" a blackface minstrel comic. Neither Lincoln nor Lamon had any notion that the singing in the ambulance that morning would be interpreted and spread on tongues of hate and malice, to be colored and magnified into an allegation, published and spoken, that while the slain still lay on the battlefield of Antietam, and the wounded were still languishing nearby, the President had called on a boisterous boon companion for a ribald song and had rollicked in laughter over it. So far would the slander spread that the two men were to talk it over in bitterness and prepare a completely detailed statement of what had happened, and then in quiet dignity withhold it from publication.

Two days later Lincoln was in Washington, and a telegram went to Mc-Clellan from Halleck, saying: "The President directs that you cross the Potomac and give battle to the enemy, or drive him south. Your army must move now, while the roads are good." No particular results came from this. McClellan may have thought the positive tone of the telegram was due to War Department politics. He believed he had done so well that he was entitled to a rest and asked the President for time. For Lincoln himself were no days off. But he wired McClellan, "You wish to see your family and I wish to oblige you," letting McClellan go to Philadelphia for a visit with wife and daughter.

Three weeks had gone by since Antietam. Yet McClellan stayed north of the Potomac with 100,000 men while Lee not far off in Virginia was recruiting his army from conscripts called up by the Richmond Government.

Repeatedly across months Lincoln remarked of McClellan, "He's got the slows." Like fact was the gossip that a Government official, getting a pass to see McClellan, remarked, "I'll report when I come back if I find the army." "Oh, you will," said Lincoln. "It's there. That's just the difficulty."

By latter October, it seemed, McClellan's dealings at Washington were entirely with Lincoln. "All his official correspondence is with the President direct and no one else," wrote Welles. To Lincoln, McClellan sent his calls for more shoes, mules, horses. To one of these Lincoln replied: "I have just read your despatch about sore tongued and fatiegued horses. Will you pardon me for asking what the horses of your army have done since the battle of Antietam that fatigues anything?" McClellan wrote to his wife, "It was one of those little flings that I can't get used to when they are not merited."

McClellan now slowly moved his army across the Potomac and put it about where Pope's army had lain before Second Bull Run. It was November. Lincoln told John Hay he would make a final judgment of McClellan. If he should permit Lee to cross the Blue Ridge and place himself between Richmond and the Army of the Potomac, Lincoln would remove McClellan from command. When Lee's army reached Culpeper Court House the test of McClellan was over.

The November elections of '62 nearly doubled the number of Democratic Congressmen, raising it from 44 to 75. In five states where Lincoln two years before had won the electoral vote, his party now lost; and the Democrats elected Horatio Seymour as governor of New York. The proadministration New York *Times* said the balloting registered "want of confidence" in the President.

Leslie's Weekly itemized: "When Colonel Forney inquired of him [Lincoln] how he felt about New York, he replied: 'Somewhat like that boy in Kentucky, who stubbed his toe while running to see his sweetheart. The boy said he was too big to cry, and far too badly hurt to laugh.'"

Lincoln wrote to Carl Schurz: "We have lost the elections . . ." and gave three main causes: "1. The democrats were left in a majority by our friends going to the war. 2. The democrats observed this & determined to re-instate themselves in power, and 3. Our newspaper's, by vilifying and disparaging the administration, furnished them all the weapons to do it with. Certainly, the ill-success of the war had much to do with this."

Political confusion of that hour was told in interviews Congressmen had with Lincoln just after the elections. William D. Kelley of Philadelphia came to the White House. Lincoln congratulated him on re-election, saying, as Kelley noted, "Sit down and tell me how it is that you, for whose election nobody seemed to hope, are returned with a good majority at your back, while so many of our friends about whom there was no doubt, have been badly beaten." Kelley said that six months earlier he would have been beaten, but he had been saved by his independent demand for a fighting general to replace McClellan.

J. K. Moorhead, Representative from the Pittsburgh district, heaved through the door, joined with the others in saying the administration had compromised, delayed, held on to McClellan too long. He told of riding to Harrisburg the day before with some of the best and most influential people of his state, including men who had one time been earnest Lincoln supporters. "They charged me," said Moorhead, "to tell you that when one of them said he would be glad to hear some morning that you had been found hanging from the post of a lamp at the door of the White House, others approved the expression."

At this, Kelley noted, the manner of the President changed. He was perfectly calm, and, in a subdued voice: "You need not be surprised to find that that suggestion has been executed any morning. The violent preliminaries to such an event would not surprise me. I have done things lately that must be incomprehensible to the people, and which cannot now be explained."

They talked about who should be named to replace McClellan. Kelley urged trying one general and another till the right man was found, the first change to be made soon. Kelley felt the President thoughtful but evasive in responding to several suggestions, "We shall see what we shall see."

Of the authenticated stories Lincoln used for illustration, one seemed to be reported by callers and visitors more than any other. Often his duties required him to be furtive and secretive beyond what he liked in political affairs. He would tell of the Irishman in Maine where state law prohibits the sale of alcoholic liquor. Having ordered a glass of lemonade and the glass set before him, the Irishman whispered to the druggist, "And now can ye pour in jist a wee drop of the creether unbeknownst to me?" In a public discussion of the use or misuse of presidential powers Lincoln once said, "I am like the Irishman, I have to do some things unbeknownst to myself."

The anti-McClellan group was holding sway. Fitz-John Porter was court-martialed on charges of disobedience, accused of helping to ruin Pope at Second Bull Run. A brave man, a highly competent officer, he was to be cashiered, drummed out of the Army. Don Carlos Buell, in the West, was under investigation by a commission which was to let him out as a major general. Lincoln was keeping hands off, allowing the authorized function-aries to have their way with Porter and Buell.

Old Frank Blair argued with Lincoln against McClellan's removal. Monty Blair told of this interview: "Lincoln . . . at the end of the conference rose up and stretched his long arms almost to the ceiling above him, saying, 'I said I would remove him if he let Lee's army get away from him, and I must do so. He has got the slows, Mr. Blair.' "

Two men traveled in a driving snowstorm near midnight November 7 to find the tent of General McClellan near Rectortown. They stepped in and shook off the snow from their overcoats. They had interrupted him in the writing of a letter to his wife. One of the men was Adjutant General C. P. Buckingham of the War Department. The other was Major General Ambrose Everett Burnside. Buckingham handed McClellan a message relieving him of command of the Army of the Potomac and ordering him to turn it over to Burnside. A second message told McClellan to report to Trenton, New Jersey, for further orders. McClellan finished the letter to his wife: "Alas for my poor country! . . . Do not be at all worried—I am not."

A farewell letter from McClellan read to the army was cheered. Where McClellan showed himself among the soldiers he was cheered. He had a way with him, a magnetism, and a figure and manner. The man taking his place, Burnside, came near weeping as he told McClellan he had refused to accept command until ordered.

According to Governor Andrew, Lincoln was asked what he would reply to McClellan's earlier advice on how to carry on the affairs of the nation. And Lincoln answered: "Nothing—but it made me think of the man whose horse kicked up and stuck his foot through the stirrup. He said to the horse, 'If you are going to get on I will get off.' "

McClellan's enemies seized on such incidents as one told by Colonel Albert V. Colburn of McClellan's staff—that when the General saw the Emancipa-tion Proclamation in the Baltimore *Sun*, he hurled the paper into a corner, exclaiming: "There! Look at that outrage! I shall resign tomorrow!" McClel-lan wrote to his wife the last of October, ". . . the good of the country requires me to submit to . . . men whom I know to be vastly my inferiors, socially, intellectually and morally. There never was a truer epithet applied to a certain individual than that of 'Gorilla.' "

No case was ever made out that McClellan was not brave and able. Only politicians, personal enemies, loose talkers, called him coward or sloven. At Malvern Hill and Antietam he performed superbly—and then failed to clinch and use what he had won. If he had been the bold ambitious plotter that Stanton, Chase and others saw, he would have marched his army to Wash-ington and seized the Government there, as he said many urged him to do.

His defect was that while he could not have instigated such treason himself, he did allow approaches to such treason to be talked freely in his staff and army without rebuke or repression from him.

His friend Aspinwall, the New York financier, who came to his camp, gave him the keen advice to go along with Lincoln's Emancipation Proclamation, say nothing, and be a soldier. From the way he wrote his wife of what Aspinwall told him, it would almost seem as though this was the first time he seriously considered the gift of silence on politics for a general heading an army given to him by a government wrestling with delicately shaded political questions.

Burnside spent three days with McClellan going over the army organization and plans. He was 39, a log-cabin boy, born at Liberty, Indiana, one of nine sons. His father, a state senator, got him a cadetship at West Point, where he met McClellan, Stonewall Jackson and others who rose in the Army. Burnside's Rhode Island regiment was among the first troops to arrive in Washington, where Lincoln often visited his camp. His chief distinction was in leading a joint naval and military force that early in 1862 captured Roanoke Island with 2,600 prisoners and 32 guns. This won applause, an embellished sword from Rhode Island, and the thanks of the Massachusetts and Ohio Legislatures.

When Burnside called at the White House Lincoln embraced him, and on Burnside's request promoted three of Burnside's brigadiers to major generals. Commanding a corps, he had been with McClellan on the Peninsula and through Antietam. A gathering of generals met him just after his latest promotion and congratulated him. Carl Schurz, now back from Spain and given his commission as major general, for which he had long ago asked Lincoln, wrote that Burnside thanked them "and then, with that transparent sincerity of his nature which made everyone believe what he said, he added that he knew he was not fit for so big a command, but he would do his best." It was touching.

Lincoln took the man who had been a friend of McClellan and who might inherit the good will of the Army for McClellan. Also he had found Burnside free of the plot and intrigue of army politics, exceptional in loyalty and sincerity.

In choosing the Fredericksburg locality for action Burnside was having his own way. "Somewhat to Mr. Lincoln's chagrin," noted Nicolay and Hay, "the first act of the new general was to object to the plan of campaign furnished to McClellan from Washington." Halleck had gone down to see Burnside about it, returned to Washington, laid the matter before Lincoln, who said Yes to Burnside's plan provided he "moved rapidly." Lincoln went down himself to see the army and Burnside. The President and the General had a long conference.

Now came Fredericksburg, a trap. Lee with 72,000 men was ready and waiting for Burnside with 113,000. For a month Burnside had been waiting for pontoons to cross the river. While the pontoons were on the way Lee made arrangements. Burnside's columns crossed over. They found hills spitting flame and metal, a sunken road swarming with riflemen waiting human prey. "A chicken can not live on that field when we open on it," a Confederate engineer had told General Longstreet of the plain facing Marye's

Hill. Meagher led his Irish Brigade of 1,315 up the hill and left 545 in the frozen mud. Hancock's division lost 40 of each 100 of its men. Between the fog of morning and twilight of evening 7,000 killed and wounded Union soldiers fell. The wounded lay 48 hours in the freezing cold before they were cared for. Some burned to death in long, dry grass set afire by cannon. Total Confederate losses were 5,309; Union, 12,653.

"Oh! those men! those men over there!" cried Burnside at his head-quarters, pointing across the river. "I am thinking of them all the time." Out of his grief came an idea. He would take his old corps, the 9th, and lead it against the stone wall and 300 cannon of the enemy. But his men would not let him think of it. In a rainy windstorm Burnside drew off his troops from Fredericksburg, back across the Rappahannock.

The morale of the army was hard hit. The troops had shown all the cour-age asked for. But with such commanders above them, what could they do? They asked that. On review they were called to give a cheer for their general. They hooted. Some went above Burnside and blamed Lincoln. More officers resigned. More privates deserted.

Lieutenant William Thompson Lusk wrote to his mother: "Alas, my poor country! It has strong limbs to march, brave hearts to dare—but the brains, the brains—have we no brains to use the arms and limbs and eager hearts with cunning? Perhaps Old Abe has some funny story to tell appropriate to the occasion. Alas, let us await the wise words of Father Abraham! . . . I believe Burnside to be brave and honest. The President I doubt not is honest, but 'let the shoemaker stick to his last.' Let Lincoln turn his talents to splitting rails. I prefer George McClellan to Abraham Lincoln, as Com-mander-in-Chief of the Army."

Burnside gave out a letter to Halleck taking all blame on himself, praising officers and men for gallantry, courage, endurance. "For the failure in the attack I am responsible," he wrote.

The President issued an address to the Army of the Potomac: "Although you were not successful, the attempt was not an error, nor the failure other than an accident. The courage with which you, in an open field, maintained the contest against an entrenched foe, and the consummate skill and success with which you crossed and re-crossed the river in the face of the enemy, show that you possess all the qualities of a great army, which will yet give victory to the cause of the country and of popular government."

Was the President thinking one thing privately and saying something else publicly as to the issues of the battle? Not according to William O. Stoddard of the White House staff, who wrote: "We lost fifty per cent more men than did the enemy, and yet there is sense in the awful arithmetic propounded by Mr. Lincoln. He says that if the same battle were to be fought over again, every day, through a week of days, with the same relative results, the army under Lee would be wiped out to its last man, the Army of the Potomac would still be a mighty host, the war would be over, the Confederacy gone. No general yet found can face the arithmetic, but the end of the war will be at hand when he shall be discovered."

A Department of Interior clerk, T. J. Barnet, wrote in a diary of hearing Lincoln after the Fredericksburg collapse, "If there is a worse place than

Hell, then I am in it." And on a later occasion, "I always meant that this war should have a peace in its belly."

A week passed and Burnside made ready for another move, ordered three days' rations in the men's haversacks. He seemed to have another battle in mind. These were hard days for Burnside, for on the same day that Lincoln warned him to make no forward movement, Halleck telegraphed him "to press the enemy," and some of his advisers urged him to win a victory and break the national gloom.

Lincoln now wrote Halleck it was his wish that Halleck go to Burnside, examine Burnside's plan, talk with the officers, get their judgment, notice their temper. "Gather all the elements for forming a judgment of your own; and then tell Gen. Burnside that you *do* approve, or that you do *not* approve his plan. Your military skill is useless to me, if you will not do this."

Halleck took this letter as insinuating. He asked to be relieved of his duties as General in Chief. Lincoln did not want to see Halleck go, as yet, and he did not want to hurt Halleck's feelings. So he "withdrew" the letter, writing the notation on it that it was "considered harsh by General Halleck." This being so, Halleck "withdrew" his request to be relieved.

The President's message to Congress December 1, 1862, opened with reports and comments on miscellaneous affairs and flowed on into discussions of the Union, slavery, the Negro. The argument for the Union mixed logic and sentiment: "A nation may be said to consist of its territory, its people, and its laws. The territory is the only part which is of certain durability." Laws change; people die; the land remains.

He pointed to "that portion of the earth's surface which is owned and inhabited by the people of the United States" as adapted to be the home of "one national family" and not for two or more. With the arrival of "steam, telegraphs, and intelligence," the modern inventions, there was still more advantage in having "one united people."

He pointed to the great interior region bounded by the Alleghenies on the east, Canada on the north, the Rockies on the west, and on the south by the line along which the cultures of corn and cotton meet. Already this region had 10,000,000 people and within 50 more years would have 50,000,000. "And yet this region has no sea-coast, touches no ocean anywhere." With separation of states it would have no outlet and would be cut off by physical barriers and trade regulations.

In previous messages Lincoln had not given so heavy an emphasis to the argument against secession in behalf of the Middle West from which he came. As the war had gone on he had found that the instinct for national solidarity was a deep one with the Midwestern people. Only six weeks before his message was delivered it was announced that Iowa was the first state to fill her quota under the call for 600,000 men; she had put every man into the field by voluntary enlistment, and all for three years of the war. The President was voicing Iowa, Ohio, Kansas and other states in declaring that "outlets, east, west, and south, are indispensable."

He pleaded: "Our strife pertains to ourselves—to the passing generations of men; and it can, without convulsion, be hushed forever with the passing of one generation." From this almost mystic appeal for the saving of the

Union he passed to a concrete proposal, the Constitution of the United States to be amended to provide that every state which abolished slavery at any time before January 1, 1900, should be paid for its freed slaves in U.S. bonds at a rate of interest and in sums to be agreed upon for each slave. Congress would be given express power to set aside money and otherwise provide for colonizing free colored persons. "Without slavery the rebellion could never have existed; without slavery it could not continue."

Each state could work out its own plan, and no two states were obliged to proceed alike. Before the end of the 37 years in which the proposed emancipation could be accomplished, the country would have probably 100,000,000 people instead of 37,000,000 to pay the cost. "The proposed emancipation would shorten the war, perpetuate peace, insure this increase of population, and proportionately the wealth of the country."

As to sending freed Negroes out of the country, he made his view clear again. "I cannot make it better known than it already is, that I strongly favor colonization. And yet I wish to say there is an objection urged against free colored persons remaining in the country, which is largely imaginary, if not sometimes malicious." It was insisted Negroes would injure and displace white laborers. On this he gave warnings. "If there ever could be a proper time for mere catch arguments, that time surely is not now. *In times like the present, men should utter nothing for which they would not willingly be responsible through time and in eternity.*" [Italics added.]

Every device of the art of persuasion that Lincoln had ever learned was put into this appeal. "The plan would, I am confident, secure peace more speedily, and maintain it more permanently, than can be done by force alone." It was the only way to end the war without victory, with something like permanent justice to all concerned. "All it would cost, considering amounts, and manner of payment . . . would be easier paid than will be the additional cost of the war, if we rely solely upon force. It is much—very much—that it would cost no blood at all."

Permanent constitutional results would be achieved. First, two-thirds of Congress, and afterwards three-fourths of the states, would have to concur in the plan. This would assure emancipation, end the struggle and save the Union for all time.

Was he getting too personal with the Senators and Congressmen? Did it seem too simple that he should assure them of a straight and clear way to cut through the vast labyrinth of interests back of the war? Perhaps so. For he felt it necessary to meet them on personal ground, as man to man. A gesture of true respect was required: "I do not forget the gravity which should characterize a paper addressed to the Congress of the nation by the Chief Magistrate of the nation. Nor do I forget that some of you are my seniors, nor that many of you have more experience than I, in the conduct of public affairs. Yet I trust that in view of the great responsibility resting upon me, you will perceive no want of respect to yourselves, in any undue earnestness I may seem to display."

He pleaded further that whatever objection might be made, still the question would recur, "Can we do better?" An old chapter in national life was over and another begun. "The dogmas of the quiet past, are inadequate to the stormy present. The occasion is piled high with difficulty, and we must rise with the occasion. As our case is new, so we must think anew, and act anew. We must disenthrall ourselves."

Possibly never before had Lincoln used that word "disenthrall." It was not a familiar word with him. He seemed almost to imply that though men might give physical emancipation to others who were oppressed, each individual must achieve his own disenthrallment, rise out of his old into a new self. A subtlety of philosophic thought was in the added suggestion, "In *giving* freedom to the *slave*, we *assure* freedom to the *free*—honorable alike in what we give, and what we preserve."

In his last paragraph he struck for motives to move men. "Fellow-citizens, *we* cannot escape history. We of this Congress and this administration, will be remembered in spite of ourselves. No personal significance or insignificance can spare one or another of us. The fiery trial through which we pass, will light us down, in honor or dishonor, to the latest generation."

He flung out sentences edging on irony. "We *say* we are for the Union. The world will not forget that we say this. We know how to save the Union. The world knows we do know how to save it. We—even *we here* —hold the power, and bear the responsibility . . . Other means may succeed; this could not fail. The way is plain, peaceful, generous, just—a way which, if followed, the world will forever applaud, and God must forever bless."

Thus ended the lesson. What came of it? No action at all except a faint groping toward compensated abolishment in the Slave State of Missouri. The Border States were too divided in viewpoint to act decisively. They were not yet cemented back into the Union. Lexington, Kentucky, on December 18 again fell into Confederate hands when Bedford Forrest's raiders drove off Illinois cavalry commanded by Colonel Robert G. Ingersoll of Peoria, Illinois.

The President's message was a compromise affair, aimed to throw sops of satisfaction into camps too hostile to be brought together for action. So said some. Others said he was riding a hobby, that as a Border State man he could not see that slavery must be destroyed root and branch first of all. Yet even to many who differed from him, who could not agree that his plan was practical, he delivered an impression of sincerely struggling to lift before men's eyes a banner worth sacrifice.

This December message prepared the way for the Emancipation Proclamation to be issued January 1, 1863—*if* the President should decide to issue it. The question was in the air whether he would. Radical antislavery men were saying the President would not dare issue the proclamation. Certain Border State men were saying he would not dare confiscate and destroy $1,000,000,000 in property values. Army men were not lacking to pronounce the judgment that such a proclamation would bring wholesale desertions, that entire companies and regiments would throw down their arms.

Senator Browning wrote in his diary of ". . . the hallucination the President seems to be laboring under that Congress can suppress the rebellion by adopting his plan of compensated emancipation."

CHAPTER 28

Thunder over the Cabinet—Murfreesboro

WHEN Chase told Senator Fessenden there was "a back-stairs influence" controlling the President, he knew Fessenden understood no one else was meant but Seward. That Seward with his cigars, cynicism, wit and nonsense, was the most companionable human being in the Cabinet had no bearing.

The Republican Senators in secret caucus December 15, 1862, discussed a letter written by Seward to Minister Adams six months before. Senator Sumner had taken the letter to Lincoln and asked if he had approved it. Lincoln said he had never seen the letter before. The newspapers got hold of this and raked Seward. The radicals claimed one more proof that Seward was a backstairs influence paralyzing the President's best intentions. Seward's offending letter had these words: "It seems as if the extreme advocates of African slavery and its most vehement opponents were acting in concert together to precipitate a servile war—the former by making the most desperate attempts to overthrow the Federal Union, the latter by demanding an edict of universal emancipation as a lawful and necessary, if not, as they say, the only legitimate way of saving the Union."

Senator Fessenden's memorandum of the secret caucus noted: "Silence ensued for a few moments, when Mr. Wilkinson [of Minnesota] said that in his opinion the country was ruined and the cause lost . . . The Secretary of State, Mr. Seward, exercised a controlling influence upon the mind of the President. He, Mr. Seward, had never believed in the war, and so long as he remained in the Cabinet nothing but defeat and disaster could be expected." Ben Wade followed, "particularly censuring the Executive for placing our armies under the command of officers who did not believe in the policy of the government and had no sympathy with its purposes." Senator Collamer found the difficulty in the fact that the President had no Cabinet in the true sense of the word. Fessenden said a duty was upon the Senate in the crisis at hand. It should, however, proceed cautiously and with unanimity or its action would alarm the country and weaken the hands of the Executive.

Browning noted in his diary that "old Ben Wade made a long speech in which he declared that the Senate should go in a body and demand of the President the removal or dismissal of Mr. Seward . . . he would never be satisfied until there was a Republican at the head of our armies."

The next day's caucus appointed a committee of nine to wait upon the President "and urge upon him changes in conduct and in the Cabinet which shall give the administration unity and vigor." The secret caucus was not yet over when Senator Preston King hurried to Seward's house, found his old colleague sitting in the library, and remarked: "I did not stay for the last vote, but just slipped out to tell you, for I thought you ought to know.

They were pledging each other to keep the proceedings secret, but I told
them I was not going to be bound."

Seward chewed a cigar and said, "They may do as they please about me,
but they shall not put the President in a false position." He called for pen
and paper and wrote to the President: "Sir, I hereby resign the office of Secretary of State, and beg that my resignation be accepted immediately." Five
minutes later King put the note in the hands of Lincoln, who read it, looked
up with surprise, and said, "What does this mean?" King told of the day's
events. Later in the evening Lincoln stepped over to Seward's house, spoke his
regrets to Seward, who remarked that it would be a relief to be free from
official cares. "Ah, yes, Governor," said Lincoln, "that will do very well for
you, but I am like the starling in Sterne's story, 'I can't get out.'"

Congressman Charles B. Sedgwick, a Syracuse, New York, lawyer wrote
to his wife: "I went to the President's with Thad. Stevens & Conklin to urge
him to accept Seward's resignation. With his usual adroitness & cunning
Seward, soon as he had tendered his resignation, began to send in his friends
to the President to frighten him into refusing to accept it & I wanted to do
what I could to counteract it . . . I fear the President needs strengthening
. . . I think you had better not show this letter at present."

Browning wrote of the next evening. ". . . the President . . . asked me
if I was at the caucus yesterday. I told him I was and the day before also.
Said he 'What do these men want?' I answered 'I hardly know Mr. President, but they are exceedingly violent towards the administration . . .' Said
he 'They wish to get rid of me, and I am sometimes half disposed to gratify
them . . . We are now on the brink of destruction. It appears to me the
Almighty is against us, and I can hardly see a ray of hope.' I answered 'Be
firm and we will yet save the Country. Do not be driven from your post.
You ought to have crushed the ultra, impracticable men last summer . . .'
He then said 'Why will men believe a lie, an absurd lie, that could not impose upon a child, and cling to it and repeat it in defiance of all evidence to
the contrary.' I understood this to refer to the charges against Mr. Seward."

The committee of Senators was to call on him at seven that night, Lincoln
told Browning—and added, "Since I heard last night of the proceedings of
the caucus I have been more distressed than by any event of my life." The
committee came that December night of '62, Collamer, Wade, Grimes, Fessenden, Trumbull, Sumner, Harris, Pomeroy and Howard. "The President
received us with his usual urbanity," Fessenden noted, though Browning had
seen Lincoln only a few minutes earlier wearing a troubled face and saying
he was "more distressed" than by any event of his life.

Collamer rose and read his carefully prepared paper. Its main points were
that the war for the Union must go on; the President should employ the
combined wisdom and deliberation of his Cabinet members, who in turn
should be unwaveringly for the war; it was unwise and unsafe to commit
military operations to anyone not a cordial believer and supporter of the
war as patriotic and just, rendered necessary by "a causeless and atrocious
rebellion."

Ben Wade stood up to say the war had been left in the hands of men who
had no sympathy with it or with the cause. Grimes and Howard rose to say
confidence in Seward was gone. Fessenden began with saying the Senate be-

lieved in the patriotism and integrity of the President, disclaiming any wish to dictate to him as to his Cabinet. He dwelt on the public belief that the Secretary of State was not in accord with a majority of the Cabinet. Again, in the conduct of the war almost every officer known as an antislavery man had been disgraced. The Democrats were using General McClellan for party purposes.

Sumner rose to say that Seward in official correspondence had made statements offensively disrespectful to Congress, and had written dispatches the President could not have seen or assented to. The President replied that it was Seward's habit to read the dispatches to him before they were sent, but they were not usually submitted to a Cabinet meeting. He did not recollect the letter to which Sumner referred.

"Some three hours were spent in conversation with the President," Fessenden noted, "but no definite action was discussed. The President said he would carefully examine and consider the paper submitted, expressed his satisfaction with the tone and temper of the committee, and we left him in apparently cheerful spirits, and so far as we could judge, pleased with the interview."

The actions against Seward had now taken three days. Tuesday and Wednesday the Republican Senators had caucused. Thursday their committee had organized and had gone to Lincoln for their evening interview. Lincoln called a Cabinet meeting for half-past ten Friday morning, December 19. All the members came except Seward.

Welles wrote in his diary, "The President says the evening was spent in a pretty free and animated conversation. No opposition was manifested towards any other member of the Cabinet than Mr. Seward . . . Him they charged, if not with infidelity, with indifference, with want of earnestness in the War . . . with too great ascendency and control of the President."

One of Lincoln's secretaries noted his telling the Cabinet of the Senate committee members: "While they seemed to believe in my honesty, they also appeared to think that when I had in me any good purpose or intention Seward contrived to suck it out of me unperceived." The President wished the Cabinet to know that he had told the committee he was shocked and grieved at "this movement."

After various remarks from Cabinet members, the President requested that the Cabinet should, with him, meet the committee of Senators. "This," noted Welles, "did not receive the approval of Mr. Chase, who said he had no knowledge whatever of the movement, or the resignation, until since he had entered the room." The President named half-past seven that evening for the interview.

Rumors were spreading that Seward had resigned. "On Thursday morning," wrote Fessenden, "I received information from a sure quarter that this rumor was well founded, but the fact was not generally known. The President, my informant stated, was much troubled about it." Wrote Browning, ". . . in the course of the afternoon I met him [the President] between the White House and the War Department, and remarked to him that I had heard that Mr. Seward had resigned, and asked him if it was so. He replied that he did not want that talked about at present, as he was trying to keep things along. This was all that passed. He cant 'keep them along.' The cabinet will go to pieces." Visitors at his house saw Seward packing up books and papers preparing to go home to Auburn, New York.

When the committee of Senators came to the White House that Friday night they did not know that Lincoln had arranged for them to meet the Cabinet, to sit face to face in a three-cornered session. The President told them he had invited the Cabinet, with the exception of Seward, to meet the committee for a free and friendly conversation in which all, including the President, should be on equal terms. He wished to know if the committee had any objection to talking over matters with the Cabinet. "Having had no opportunity for consultation, the committee had no objection," noted Fessenden.

The President opened by admitting that Cabinet meetings had not been very regular, excusing that fact for want of time. He believed most questions of importance had received reasonable consideration, was not aware of any divisions or want of unity. Decisions, so far as he knew, had general support after they were made. Seward, he believed, had been earnest in prosecution of the war, had not improperly interfered, had generally read to him the official correspondence, had sometimes consulted with Mr. Chase. The President then called on members of the Cabinet to say whether there had been any want of unity or of sufficient consultation.

Secretary Chase now protested earnestly, a little hotly, that he certainly would not have come to the meeting if he had known he was going to be arraigned before a committee of the Senate. He went on to say that questions of importance had generally been considered by the Cabinet, though perhaps not as fully as might be desired, that there had been no want of unity in the Cabinet but a general acquiescence on public measures; no member opposed a measure once decided on.

Fessenden was listening; Chase was not now saying in the three-cornered conference what he had been saying in private chats with Senators nor what he had been writing in letters. So Fessenden rose to repeat what he had two nights before told the President, that the Senators came with a desire to offer friendly advice and not to dictate to the President. Collamer said united counsels were needed. Grimes said again he had lost confidence in Seward. Sumner dragged out Seward's foreign correspondence again. Trumbull pointed to the President's own admissions that important questions were decided without full consideration. Bates cited the Constitution to show that the President need not consult his Cabinet unless he pleased. More talk followed. The hours were passing. "The President made several speeches in the course of the evening," wrote Fessenden, "and related several anecdotes, most of which I had heard before."

After hours of threshing over the issues and getting better acquainted, the President asked the Senators to give him their opinions as to whether Seward ought to leave the Cabinet. Collamer said he did not know how his constituents felt and he would not go beyond the paper he had handed the President. Grimes, Trumbull, Sumner, said Seward should go. Harris said No, that Seward's removal would be a calamity to the Republican party of New York. Pomeroy said he had once studied law in Seward's office but his confidence in Seward was gone. Howard said he had not spoken during the evening and would not. Chase suggested, "The members of the Cabinet had better withdraw." They did so. It was midnight. Senators Collamer and Harris took their hats and also went away. Fessenden then noted this conversation:

FESSENDEN: You have asked my opinion about Seward's removal. There is a current rumor that Mr. Seward has already resigned. If so, our opinions are of no consequence on that point.

THE PRESIDENT: I thought I told you last evening that Mr. Seward had tendered his resignation. I have it in my pocket, but have not yet made it public or accepted it.

FESSENDEN: Then, sir, the question seems to be whether Mr. Seward shall be requested to withdraw his resignation.

THE PRESIDENT: Yes.

The Senators left the White House. One of them, Trumbull, turned before going out, walked rapidly back to the President, and told him rather hotly that the Secretary of the Treasury had talked in a different tone the last time they had spoken. Fessenden wrote in his memorandum as to this Friday evening conversation: "It struck me that Mr. Chase seemed to have very much modified his opinions, often previously expressed to me, as to Mr. Seward's influence on the mind of the President and the want of unity in the Cabinet."

Browning asked Senator Collamer how Secretary Chase could venture to tell the committee that the Cabinet got along fairly well when he had been saying the opposite to the Senators privately. "He lied," answered Collamer.

It was one o'clock Saturday morning. The session had lasted five and a half hours. "It was observed by the Senators," wrote Fessenden, "that the President did not appear to be in so good spirits as when we left him on the preceding evening, and the opinion was expressed that he would make no change in his Cabinet. He said he had reason to fear 'a general smash-up' if Mr. Seward was removed."

Lincoln and Welles agreed next morning that while Seward's resignation should not be accepted by the President, neither should Seward get up on his dignity and press for immediate acceptance. Welles said he would go over and see Seward. Lincoln "earnestly" desired him to do so. Lincoln had a messenger sent to notify Chase that the President wished to see him.

Seward was pleased at Welles' report of his interview with the President. He said that "if the President and country required of him any duty in this emergency he did not feel at liberty to refuse it . . ." Back at the White House, Welles met Chase and Stanton in the President's office. Welles told them he was decidedly against accepting Seward's resignation. Neither would give a direct answer. The President came in, asked Welles if he "had seen the man." Welles said Yes and the man was agreed. The President turned to Chase. "I sent for you, for this matter is giving me great trouble."

Chase said he had been painfully affected by the meeting last evening, which was a total surprise to him. Then after some vague remarks he told the President he had written his resignation as Secretary of the Treasury. "Where is it?" asked Lincoln, his eyes lighting up. "I brought it with me," said Chase, taking the paper from his pocket. "I wrote it this morning." "Let me have it," said the President, reaching his long arm and fingers toward Chase, who held on to the paper and seemed to have something further to say before giving up the document. But the President was eager, did not notice Chase, took the letter, broke the seal and read it.

"This," said Lincoln, holding up the letter toward Welles with a triumphal laugh, "cuts the Gordian knot." His face of worry had changed to satisfaction. "I can dispose of this subject now without difficulty," he added as he turned on his chair. "I see my way clear."

Stanton was sitting with Chase, facing the fireplace. Stanton rose to say: "Mr. President, I informed you day before yesterday that I was ready to tender you my resignation. I wish you, sir, to consider my resignation at this time in your possession." "You may go to your Department," said Lincoln. "I don't want yours. This," holding out Chase's letter, "is all I want; this relieves me; my way is clear; the trouble is ended. I will detain neither of you longer." All three left the room, and Lincoln was alone.

When Senator Harris called soon after, Lincoln was beaming and cheerful. "Yes, Judge, I can ride on now, I've got a pumpkin in each end of my bag." (When farmers rode horseback to market two pumpkins in the bag thrown over the horse made a balanced load.) As the anecdote reached Senator Fessenden, the President had said: "Now I have the biggest half of the hog. I shall accept neither resignation."

The President sent polite notes to Seward and Chase that he could not let them quit and must ask them to take up again their duties. Seward replied that he had "cheerfully resumed" his functions. Chase held off. "I will sleep on it." Something rankled in Chase's bosom. He was afraid Lincoln had a sinister cunning that had outguessed and outwitted him. His pride was hurt. He wrote to the President: "Will you allow me to say that something you said or looked, when I handed you my resignation this morning, made on my mind the impression that having received the resignations both of Governor Seward and myself, you felt that you could relieve yourself from trouble by declining to accept either, and that this feeling was one of gratification?" However, after a Sunday of deep thinking Chase decided he would go back to his old place.

The Republican Senators caucused Monday, December 22, and heard the report of their committee, whose duty was over. Browning, however, felt called on to go to the President that night and suggest a new Cabinet be formed. The President said he believed he would rather try to get along with the Cabinet he had than try a new one.

Lincoln said later: "If I had yielded to that storm and dismissed Seward the thing would all have slumped over one way, and we should have been left with a scanty handful of supporters. When Chase gave in his resignation I saw that the game was in my hands, and I put it through."

Fessenden ended a letter to his family: "Yet such is the anomalous character of the President that no one can tell what a day may bring forth." Uneven, irregular, rather baffling, so Fessenden found the President; he could not read what was coming next from Lincoln, and it troubled him. Fessenden had clean hands and a rare sense of justice in politics, owning himself with a decency, with a spotless record. Yet the evils of gossip, greed, jealousy and personal ambition, amid furious and rushing events, had created various unfavorable impressions of the President. Fessenden had his and wrote to John Murray Forbes, who wanted to see Fessenden in the Cabinet: "No friend of mine should ever wish to see me there," for in the Cabinet no man could honestly be himself because of the interference of the President, and "You cannot change the President's character or conduct, unfortunately; he remained long enough at Springfield, surrounded by toadies and office-seekers, to persuade himself that he was specially chosen by the Almighty for this crisis, and well chosen. This conceit has never yet been beaten out of him . . ."

Forbes began his letter: "I must differ from you about the President. He has been in the hands of a vacillating, undecided man like Seward!"

Seward and Chase had a daily grasp of special and shifting situations. In diplomatic matters the President often told callers, "You'll have to see Seward about that," or on a financial detail, "That is for Chase to say—you go over and see him." Chase sat daily in conference on money, cash available, credit balances, the war cost of $2,000,000 a day. Chase was reporting in December '62 that the Government would have to borrow $600,000,000 the next year. By a single act of Congress that year, wherein the views of Chase were met, the "greenbacks" came, paper money to the amount of $150,000,000. Gold was hoarded, sent into hiding by paper money. The same act of Congress authorized a $500,000,000 bond issue, the Government to sell to the people, investors, banks, that amount of its promises to pay. Lincoln did not pretend grasp of it; long ago he had said he had "no money sense."

Armies of men marching in mud and sleeping on frozen ground, fighting bloody pitched battles, waited for back pay. Joseph Medill wrote: "Money cannot be supplied much longer to a beaten, demoralized and homesick army. Sometimes I think that nothing is left now but to fight for a boundary." Enigmas of cash and credit, of how paper money chases coin into hiding places, of bond issues to coax money out of hiding places and strongboxes, of the wish for money worth the same next week as this week—under these both Lincoln and Chase writhed.

The future was in bigger debt figures. Spaulding in the House said that $1,000,000,000 at least must be borrowed in the next 18 months. Expenses of the Government reached $2,500,000 a day, Sundays included. Government income from customs tariff, taxes and elsewhere was not over $600,000 a day, which left $1,900,000 to be pried loose from the banks and from the people by manipulation of bonds, notes, appeals to patriotic duty.

Lincoln met more with Seward than with Chase. His advice to Chase on how to raise money for the war was not needed by Chase; it was a special field, with no history of money ever having been written and no unquestionable handbook of finance supplied for such amateurs as Lincoln. His advice to Seward on problems of state was more needed. They were affairs seething and warm in human relationships. Here, working with Seward, Lincoln more often knew precisely what he was doing.

Seward informed him of how the Spanish, British and French governments were joining hands to collect money due from Mexico; so they gave diplomatic explanations. They announced they were not seeking new territory; they asked the United States to join their scheme. Slowly Seward and Lincoln had seen it become reasonably clear that Emperor Napoleon III of France was planning to beat the armies of Mexico, overthrow their republican government, and set up a royal throne, whereon would sit the Archduke Maximilian of Austria.

Throughout many conversations Seward made clear the view of the President that he did not question the right of the three European powers to join hands and seek redress of their grievances, even to war in Mexico, also that the President felt satisfaction in the assurance given by the powers that they would not seek to impair the right of the Mexican people to choose and freely to constitute the form of their government.

Intervention in America was a leading topic of diplomatic conversations in Europe. Leaders in England and France who favored recognition of the Confederacy found Russia a hindrance. Late in '62 a personal letter from President Lincoln was transmitted to the Russian Foreign Minister, Gorchakov, at St. Petersburg, by Acting American Minister Bayard Taylor. Their conversation was published by order of Congress, though Lincoln's letter to Gorchakov was not made known.

"Russia alone has stood by you from the first, and will continue to stand by you," said Gorchakov. "Proposals will be made to Russia to join in some plan of interference. She will refuse any invitation of the kind. You may rely upon it, she will not change." From none of the Great Powers of Europe had the United States been able to win so positive a declaration. In this decision Russia was aligning herself against England and France, who had fought her so recently in the war in the Crimea. Also Russia had no such textile industries as England and France, suffering from cotton famine.

Across Europe ran two extremes of opinion, with many moderate views intermingled. The liberal John Bright of England favored a united country in America, sent a letter to the Chamber of Commerce of New York. Bright wished it known that "there is no other country in which men have been so free and so prosperous as in yours, and that there is no other political constitution now in existence, in the preservation of which the human race is so deeply interested." The conservative London *Dispatch* phrased its view: "The real motives of the civil war are the continuance of the power of the North to tax the industry of the South, and the consolidation of a huge confederation to sweep every other power from the American continent, to enter into the politics of Europe with a Republican propaganda, and to bully the world."

An international world opinion favoring the North was Seward's steady objective. Often he brought to Lincoln's desk designs and schemes for approval on matters of broad policy. The President and his State Minister spent more and more time together, grew in respect and affection. "The President is the best of us," Seward had written to his wife. Often on Sunday mornings they had long talks, came nearer being cronies than any other two of the Cabinet.

Congress passed an act making West Virginia a state, seceding her from Virginia. Blair, Bates and Welles were against the act. Seward, Chase, Stanton, favored it, recommended that the President sign the bill. He did so, urging in a written opinion that her brave and good men regarded her admission into the Union as a matter of life and death. They had been true to the Union through severe trials. "We have so acted as to justify their hopes; and we can not fully retain their confidence, and co-operation if we seem to break faith with them."

Then Lincoln presented the quixotic phase of the matter. "The division of a State is dreaded as a precedent," he wrote. "But a measure made expedient by a war, is no precedent for times of peace. It is said that the admission of West-Virginia is secession, and tolerated only because it is our secession. Well, if we call it by that name, there is still difference enough between secession against the constitution, and secession in favor of the constitution." He did not like to do it but with a wry face he signed the bill.

From month to month Lincoln had met with Seward, Welles, the Cabinet and eminent attorneys in international law on the subject of mails captured on blockade-runners and the question whether such mails should be opened and used as evidence or be forwarded without opening. Welles contended the mails should be held and opened by the prize court which disposed of the captured ships and cargoes. Seward, however, had issued a circular of instructions to the State Department that captured mails should be given up, that in effect the State Department yielded any rights to examine and break the seals of mailbags and parcels.

"By special direction of the President, unusual courtesy and concession were made to neutrals," wrote Welles in a long letter to Seward at a time when the British Minister set up the claim that naval officers in the seizure of mails on the ship *Peterhoff* had violated U.S. Government instructions. The final action in the *Peterhoff* case came when the mails were given up by a U.S. district attorney who had applied to the prize court under direction of the Secretary of State, approved by the President. Seward, wrote Welles, having in a weak moment conceded an incontestable national right, "sought to extricate himself, not by retracing his steps, but by involving the President . . ."

Welles noted of Sumner's meeting with the President: ". . . He [the President] was confident we should have war with England if we presumed to open their mail bags, or break their seals or locks. They would not submit to it, and we were in no condition to plunge into a foreign war on a subject of so little importance . . . Of this idea of a war with England, Sumner could not dispossess him by argument, or by showing its absurdity. Whether it was real or affected ignorance, Sumner was not satisfied."

The President kept pressing his Navy Secretary and was "extremely anxious" to get at any specific cases of captured mail that had been searched. "I told him," noted Welles, "I remembered no specific mention." Perhaps the Federal district attorneys might have information. "The President said he would frame a letter to the district attorneys, and in the afternoon he brought in a form to be sent to the attorneys in Philadelphia, New York, and Boston."

Then other affairs arose and in their stride swept away the Cabinet disputes over whether Lincoln and Seward were yielding a legal right to Great Britain and if so, who was the loser by it.

Up on the border line of the wilderness settlements of the pioneers in Minnesota, five white people were murdered by Sioux red men. Federal Government agents had predicted the clash for many years because of seizures of Indian lands by white men, because of slow payment of promised funds to Indian tribes, and the trickery of white traders against individual Indians. Little Crow led the Sioux along the Minnesota River valley; they burned houses, violated women, slaughtered 490 whites, including women and children.

General Pope led his horsemen in pursuit, defeated Little Crow in battle. A military court put the Indians on trial, and partly in obedience to demands for revenge that swept the whole Northwest, the court sentenced 303 to be hanged.

Lincoln studied the record of the trial, and delayed. One by one, in his own handwriting, Lincoln listed those he would hang, 38 of them. The others, he wrote, would be held till further orders, "taking care that they neither escape, nor are subjected to any unlawful violence." On December 26, at Mankato, Minnesota, the 38 were hanged.

The President had insisted the trial record should "indicate the more guilty and influential of the culprits." In a message to Congress he pointed out that it was not definitely known who had fomented the Minnesota outbreak. "Suspicions, which may be unjust, need not to be stated." The President had learned, however, that Federal handling of Indians was not what it should be. He suggested a remodeling of the system and policy of treating Indians.

Lincoln took time to write a long letter to Miss Fanny McCullough at Bloomington, Illinois, beginning: "It is with deep grief that I learn of the death of your kind and brave Father; and, especially, that it is affecting your young heart beyond what is common." He was an older man telling her that time would teach her, the years would help. "In this sad world of ours, sorrow comes to all; and, to the young, it comes with bitterest agony, because it takes them unawares. The older have learned to ever expect it." She could not realize it now, but sometime she would be happy again. "The memory of your dear Father, instead of an agony, will yet be a sad sweet feeling in your heart, of a purer, and holier sort than you have known before."

Many times Lincoln had met and talked with her father, a Black Hawk War veteran, a Republican party man, circuit clerk and then sheriff of McLean County—a man who with one eye of no use and his left arm gone had at 51 helped organize the 4th Illinois Cavalry, commanding it in battles under Grant till far down in Mississippi he fell bullet-riddled, having shouted his last command.

Fanny McCullough could remember when she was a little girl and Lincoln used to hold her and her sister Nanny on his knees, telling their father, "These girls are not too old to be kissed."

On New Year's Eve, 1862, telegrams to the War Department reported one of the bloodiest battles of the war opening at Murfreesboro, Tennessee, along Stone's River, the Union army of Rosecrans fighting the Confederates under Bragg. The Confederates drove the right wing of the Union army back two miles, and Bragg sent a telegram of victory to Richmond on New Year's Eve: "God has given us a happy New Year." Lincoln went to bed that night with news of men marching in rain, sleeping on wet ground, fighting through mud, the South having made the gains of the day. Two days more of maneuvering and grappling went on between 41,000 under Rosecrans and 34,000 under Bragg. They fought in the rain and fog of raw winter days of short twilights. On the second day willing horses and cursing drivers couldn't get cannon moved over the soaked and slippery ground. One out of four men on the field was shot down, killed, wounded or taken prisoner; the Union army lost 12,906, the Confederates 11,739. Bragg retreated south.

And this huggermugger of smoke and steel, flame and blood, in Tennessee meant to the President far off in the White House one episode. The Union men of Tennessee would have easier going. The manpower of the South was cut down by so many figures. The war would never be ended by any one event, any single battle; the war might go on 20 or 30 years, ran the warning of Lincoln, Sherman and others.

Lincoln telegraphed Rosecrans: "God bless you, and all with you! Please tender to all, and accept for yourself, the Nation's gratitude for yours, and their, skill, endurance, and dauntless courage."

CHAPTER 29

Final Emancipation Proclamation, '63

ON JANUARY 1, 1863, the day set for the second and final Emancipation Proclamation, many doubted the President would issue the edict. Rumors ran in Washington that Lincoln on January 1 would withdraw, not issue, the proclamation. His courage, they were saying and writing, required bolstering, "puffing," as Greeley put it. John Murray Forbes of Boston wrote to Sumner that perhaps "a mixed deputation of laymen and clergy" could "try and influence" Lincoln to issue the document.

Harriet Beecher Stowe did not join with friends, nor with her brother Henry Ward Beecher, in suspicions that Lincoln would put off or evade the proclamation. The pioneer abolitionist agitator, William Lloyd Garrison, at the yearly meeting of the Anti-Slavery Society of Massachusetts, had rebuked the slurs of Wendell Phillips on the President's motives, holding "it is not wise for us to be too microscopic" in finding fault with the President.

Browning on December 31 wrote: "Some days ago I said to Judge Thomas [B. F. Thomas of the Massachusetts Supreme Court, 1853-59] that I thought he ought to go to the President and have a full, frank conversation with him in regard to the threatened proclamation of emancipation—that in my opinion it was fraught with evil, and evil only." Browning lamented: "The President was fatally bent upon his course, saying that if he should refuse to issue his proclamation there would be a rebellion in the north, and that a dictator would be placed over his head within the week. There is no hope. The proclamation will come—God grant it may [not] be productive of the mischief I fear."

Uprisings of Negro slaves would surely follow the impending proclamation, with murder and worse visited on the Southern people, several English journals predicted.

Congressman John Covode the last week of December found the President in his office walking back and forth with a troubled face. As to whether he would issue the proclamation, he said: "I have studied that matter well; my mind is made up . . . *It must be done. I am driven to it.* There is no other way out of our troubles. But although my duty is plain, it is in some respects painful, and I trust the people will understand that I act not in anger but in expectation of a greater good."

Copies of the proclamation were handed Cabinet members December 30. Next morning at ten they went into session. Seward and Welles suggested minor changes. Chase argued that the slaves should be declared free in entire states, with no parts or fractions stipulated as not being included. Also Chase had brought along a complete draft of a proclamation he had written himself. He suggested to Lincoln a closing sentence to read: "And upon this act, sincerely believed to be an act of justice warranted by the Constitution, and an act of duty demanded by the circumstances of the country, I invoke the considerate judgment of mankind, and the gracious favor of Almighty God." Said Chase, "I thought this, or something like it, would be appropriate." Lincoln adopted this sentence; he left out one clause and added that "military necessity" dictated the action.

Thirteen parishes in Louisiana and counties in Virginia around Norfolk were specifically excepted by Lincoln in the proclamation. Tennessee and the nonseceded Border Slave States of Missouri, Kentucky, Maryland and Delaware were not mentioned in the proclamation. In all these areas the slaves were not to be declared free. Blair argued that people long after would read and wonder why the Louisiana parishes and Virginia counties were excepted; they were in the very heart and back of slavery, and unless there was some good reason, unknown to him, he hoped they would not be excepted. Seward remarked, "I think so, too; I think they should not be excepted."

John P. Usher, First Assistant Secretary of the Interior, who was a week later appointed to take the place of Caleb B. Smith, resigning to take a judgeship in Indiana, noted Lincoln's reply: "Well, upon first view your objections are clearly good, but after I issued the proclamation of September 22, Mr. Bouligny of Louisiana, then here, came to see me. [John Edward Bouligny, elected to Congress as a National American from a New Orleans district, served from December 5, 1859, to March 4, 1861, the only Representative from a seceding state who did not leave his seat in Congress.] He was a great invalid, and had scarcely the strength to walk upstairs. He wanted to know of me if these parishes in Louisiana and New Orleans should hold an election and elect members of Congress whether I would not except them from this proclamation. I told him I would.

"No, I did not do that in so many words," continued Lincoln. "If he was here now he could not repeat any words I said which would amount to an absolute promise. But I know he understood me that way, and that is just the same to me. They have elected members, and they are here now, Union men, ready to take their seats, and they have elected a Union man from the Norfolk district."

Blair said, "If you have a promise out, I will not ask you to break it." Seward added: "No, no. We would not have you do that." Chase interposed, "Very true, they have elected Hahn and Flanders, but they have not yet got their seats, and it is not certain that they will." Chase was voicing the fear of Northern antislavery men that Southern Union men, sympathetic to slavery, would win added strength in Congress; he believed Congress might refuse to seat Hahn and Flanders.

Michael Hahn was Bavarian-born, a New Orleans high-school graduate, a lawyer who in politics had fought the Slidell faction in Louisiana, had done his best for Douglas for President in 1860, and favored gradual compensated abolishment of slavery. Benjamin Franklin Flanders was New Hampshire-born, a Dartmouth graduate, a high-school principal, and an editor and publisher in New Orleans; being an outspoken Union man, he had to leave that city early in '62, returning when the Union Army and Navy captured it that year.

On Chase's saying it was not certain that Hahn and Flanders would be seated, Lincoln rose from his chair. He was not easy about the matter. Usher noted that he walked rapidly back and forth across the room; looking over his shoulder at Chase, he burst out: "There it is, sir! I am to be bullied by Congress, am I? If I do I'll be durned." This ended the discussion.

That afternoon and next morning, as Lincoln rewrote the entire draft of the proclamation, he took his time, went to pains to have the penmanship plain, clear, unmistakable, in a manner solemn and testamentary. He had told Sumner, "I know very well that the name connected with this document will never be forgotten." The text was dry, strict, brief. Its sentences stood alone and sent out red runners against deep purple.

On the morning of New Year's Day the high officers of the Government, the civil, military and naval departments, the diplomatic corps in gold braid and official hats, arrived at the White House for the annual presidential reception. The carriages drove in the half-oval roadway, the horses champed, the important guests were delivered at the door; the long porch of the White House, the sidewalk and part of the lawn filled up with bystanders and beholders. The President began handshaking and greeting and went on for three hours.

That afternoon Seward and his son Fred walked over to the White House carrying Lincoln's own draft of the Emancipation Proclamation. Lincoln had left it with them for the State Department duly to engross. To be a complete document, the President must sign it. They found Lincoln alone in his office. The broad sheet was spread out before him on a table. He dipped his pen in an inkstand, held the pen in the air over the paper, hesitated, looked around, and said: "I never, in my life, felt more certain that I was doing right, than I do in signing this paper. But I have been receiving calls and shaking hands since nine o'clock this morning, till my arm is stiff and numb. Now this signature is one that will be closely examined, and if they find my hand trembled they will say, 'he had some compunctions.' But anyway, it is going to be done."

And with that he slowly and carefully wrote the name of Abraham Lincoln at the bottom of the Emancipation Proclamation, a bold, clear signature, though "slightly tremulous," Lincoln remarked. The others laughed, for it was better than he or they expected from fingers squeezed and wrenched by thousands that day. Then Seward signed, the great seal was affixed, and the document went into the archives of the State Department. The document—the most exciting news matter telegraphed, mailed, published, heralded over the world that day and month, for all that it was dry and formal—read:

BY THE PRESIDENT OF THE UNITED STATES OF AMERICA:

A Proclamation.

Whereas, on the twentysecond day of September, in the year of our Lord one thousand eight hundred and sixty two, a proclamation was issued by the President of the United States, containing, among other things, the following, towit:

"That on the first day of January, in the year of our Lord one thousand eight hundred and sixty-three, all persons held as slaves within any State or designated part of a State, the people whereof shall then be in rebellion against the United States, shall be then, thenceforward, and forever free; and the Executive Government of the United States, including the military and naval authority thereof, will recognize and maintain the freedom of such persons, and will do no act or acts to repress such persons, or any of them, in any efforts they may make for their actual freedom.

"That the Executive will, on the first day of January aforesaid, by proclamation, designate the States and parts of States, if any, in which the people thereof, respectively, shall then be in rebellion against the United States; and the fact that any State, or the people thereof, shall on that day be, in good faith, represented in the Congress of the United States by members chosen thereto at elections wherein a majority of the qualified voters of such State shall have participated, shall, in the absence of strong countervailing testimony, be deemed conclusive evidence that such State, and the people thereof, are not then in rebellion against the United States."

Now, therefore I, Abraham Lincoln, President of the United States, by virtue of the power in me vested as Commander-in-Chief, of the Army and Navy of the United States in time of actual armed rebellion against authority and government of the United States, and as a fit and necessary war measure for suppressing said rebellion, do, on this first day of January, in the year of our Lord one thousand eight hundred and sixty three, and in accordance with my purpose so to do publicly proclaimed for the full period of one hundred days, from the day first above mentioned, order and designate as the States and parts of States wherein the people thereof respectively, are this day in rebellion against the United States, the following, towit:

Arkansas, Texas, Louisiana, (except the Parishes of St. Bernard, Plaquemines, Jefferson, St. Johns, St. Charles, St. James, Ascension, Assumption, Terrebonne, Lafourche, St. Mary, St. Martin, and Orleans, including the city of New-Orleans) Mississippi, Alabama, Florida, Georgia, South-Carolina, North-Carolina, and Virginia, (except the fortyeight counties designated as West Virginia, and also the counties of Berkley, Accomac, Northampton, Elizabeth-City, York, Princess Ann, and Norfolk, including the cities of Norfolk & Portsmouth); and which excepted parts are, for the present, left precisely as if this proclamation were not issued.

And by virtue of the power, and for the purpose aforesaid, I do order and declare that all persons held as slaves within said designated States, and parts of

States, are, and henceforward shall be free; and that the Executive government of the United States, including the military and naval authorities thereof, will recognize and maintain the freedom of said persons.

And I hereby enjoin upon the people so declared to be free to abstain from all violence, unless in necessary self-defence; and I recommend to them that, in all cases when allowed, they labor faithfully for reasonable wages.

And I further declare and make known, that such persons of suitable condition, will be received into the armed service of the United States to garrison forts, positions, stations, and other places, and to man vessels of all sorts in said service.

And upon this act, sincerely believed to be an act of justice, warranted by the Constitution, upon military necessity, I invoke the considerate judgment of mankind, and the gracious favor of Almighty God.

Abraham Lincoln.

Lincoln's signature to Emancipation Proclamation—rarely he wrote his full name

Salutes of a hundred guns were fired in Pittsburgh, Buffalo, Boston, after newspapers published the proclamation. At night in Tremont Temple, Boston, it was read before an abolitionist crowd including the Negro members of the Union Progressive Association. Antislavery crowds held jubilation meetings, though some of the extremists said the document should have gone further, was too moderate. Meetings in some Northern cities lasted all night, with song, laughter, prayer, Negroes greeting the dawn kneeling and crying.

Critics took much the same view as they did of the preliminary proclamation in September. The London *Times* and the antiadministration press in general agreed with the New York *Herald:* "While the Proclamation leaves slavery untouched where his decree can be enforced, he emancipates slaves where his decree cannot be enforced. Friends of human rights will be at a loss to understand this discrimination." The Richmond *Examiner* spoke for much of the South in declaring the proclamation to be "the most startling political crime, the most stupid political blunder, yet known in American history," aimed at "servile insurrection," with the result that "Southern people have now only to choose between victory and death."

The proclamation struck at property valued on tax books at nearly $3,000,000,000. If not retracted and if finally sustained by the Union armies in the field, the newly issued document would take from Southerners, by force and without compensation, livestock classified and assessed with horses, cattle and mules, more than 3,900,000 head.

To those who shrank in horror, Lincoln later made his argument: ". . . I think the Constitution invests its commander-in-chief with the law of war in time of war. The most that can be said—if so much—is that slaves are property. Is there—has there ever been—any question that by the law of war, property, both of enemies and friends, may be taken when needed? . . . Civilized belligerents do all in their power to help themselves or hurt the enemy, except a few things regarded as barbarous or cruel."

Henry Adams in London wrote: "The Emancipation Proclamation has done more for us here than all our former victories and all our diplomacy. It is creating an almost convulsive reaction in our favor all over this country. The London Times furious and scolds like a drunken drab. Certain it is, however, that public opinion is very deeply stirred here and finds expression in meetings, addresses to President Lincoln, deputations to us, standing committees to agitate the subject and to affect opinion, and all the other symptoms of a great popular movement peculiarly unpleasant to the upper classes here because it rests on the spontaneous action of the laboring classes."

Foreign Minister Earl Russell in London, in a note to British Minister Lyons in Washington, saw no precedents to guide either as to the proclamation or in the matter of two public letters of the President of the United States, one addressed "To the Workingmen of Manchester," the other "To the Workingmen of London." It was not a custom for the ruling heads of nations to address letters to "workingmen" in other countries. Lincoln, however, had received addresses from bodies of workingmen in those cities giving him the hand of fellowship, and he replied: "I know and deeply deplore the sufferings which the workingmen at Manchester and in all Europe are called to endure in this crisis . . . Under these circumstances, I cannot but regard your decisive utterance upon the question as an instance of sublime Christian heroism which has not been surpassed in any age or in any country."

Around the world and into the masses of people whose tongues and imaginings create folk tales out of fact, there ran this item of the Strong Man who arose in his might and delivered an edict, spoke a few words fitly chosen, and thereupon the shackles and chains fell from the arms and ankles of men, women and children born to be chattels for toil and bondage.

The living issues coiled and tangled about Lincoln's feet were not, however, to be set smooth and straight by any one gesture, or a series of them, in behalf of freedom. His authority, worn often as a garment of thongs, was tied and knotted with responsibilities. Nailed with facts of inevitable fate was his leadership. The gestures of stretching forth his hand and bestowing freedom on chattel slaves while attempting to enforce his will by the violence of armies subjugating the masters of slaves on their home soil, the act of trying to hold a just balance between the opposed currents of freedom and authority, raised a riddle that gnawed in his thought many nights.

"A great day," wrote Longfellow that New Year's Day of '63. "The President's Proclamation for Emancipation of Slaves in the rebel States, goes into effect. A beautiful day, full of sunshine, ending in a tranquil moonlight night. May it be symbolical."

The argument over the President's authority to set up military governments in conquered areas went on in Congress, in the press, on platform and stump, on sidewalks, in homes and saloons. Thaddeus Stevens declared in February '63 that the President had ordered men to be elected to take their seats in Congress, had also directed what kind of men should be elected, "which, perhaps, was right enough, or we might have been overrun by secessionists." The two Congressmen elected from Louisiana, however, were objectionable to Stevens. He had said so when they were seated; he said so again and pressed for rejection of their credentials. He did not wish to be discourteous, but would expel them; they were from a conquered province that had not extinguished slavery.

The hope of the President that he might find 10 per cent of people in the Southern States who would take the oath of loyalty to the Union, and form a basis for reconstruction, was named "Lincoln's ten-per-cent plan."

Foreign and domestic affairs of a wide and kaleidoscopic character came under Lincoln's eye during early '63, toward the close of two years of war. In letters and speeches of the time were many guesses that the war would not end during Lincoln's administration.

CHAPTER 30

"More Horses Than Oats"—Office Seekers

AS MONTHS wore on and the offices were filled, the White House was overrun by young men who wanted commissions in the Army, credentials for raising regiments; officers seeking promotions or new assignments; men seeking contracts for supplies to the Army and Navy, commendations for newly invented rifles, cannon, munitions.

"Those around him strove from beginning to end to erect barriers to defend him against constant interruption," wrote Hay, "but the President himself was always the first to break them down. He disliked anything that kept people from him who wanted to see him." Senator Henry Wilson said he counseled, "You will wear yourself out," at which Lincoln smiled sadly. "They do not want much; they get but little, and I must see them."

The Republicans, new to power, were breezy about their errors in procedure, quick to ask why this or that could not be done. Lincoln usually heard state delegations, Senators and Congressmen, party leaders, before making appointments of importance for their states. Always, too, the governors of the states must have respectful hearing.

George Luther Stearns, Frank Bird and other Boston radicals came away from a session in which they had failed to budge Lincoln, Stearns saying, "There we were, with some able talkers among us, and we had the best position too; but the President held his ground against us." "I think he is the shrewdest man I ever met," said Frank Bird. "But not at all a Kentuckian. He is an old-fashioned Yankee in a western dress."

Donn Piatt wrote of once hearing Seward say that in the ability to manage saying No to office seekers, the President "had a cunning that was genius." In a care-laden hour, according to Schurz, the President pointed out to a friend an eager throng of office seekers and Congressmen in an anteroom and spoke these words: "Do you observe this? The rebellion is hard enough to overcome, but there you see something which, in the course of time, will become a greater danger to the republic than the rebellion itself."

General Egbert L. Viele, while military governor of Norfolk, spent many hours with the President in relaxed moods. He said, as Viele noted, "If I have one vice, and I can call it nothing else, it is not to be able to say 'No.' Thank God for not making me a woman, but if He had, I suppose He would have made me just as ugly as He did, and no one would ever have tempted me."

A young Ohioan, appointed to a South American consulate, came dressed as a dandy, "fit to kill." But he was gloomy. "Mr. President, I can't say I'm so very glad of this appointment after all. Why, I hear they have bugs down there that are liable to eat me up inside of a week." "Well, young man, if they do, they'll leave behind them a mighty good suit of clothes." Cabinet members protesting an appointment of a Democrat once received the reply: "Oh, I can't afford to punish every person who has seen fit to oppose my election. We want a competent man in this office." Cameron called in behalf of a young man who had been a pest in applying for a consulate. "Where do you want to have him sent?" asked the President. The Pennsylvania leader stepped to a large globe of the earth, put an arm around it as far as he could reach, and said, "I do not know what my finger is on, but send him there." And, it was told, he was accommodated.

A New England woman on a hospital errand entered the President's office unnoticed. A man was handing Lincoln a paper. Lincoln read it carelessly and said, "Yes, that is a sufficient endorsement for anybody; what do you want?" The woman did not hear the man's reply but later heard his sarcastic remark, "I see there are no vacancies among the brigadiers, from the fact that so many colonels are commanding brigades." At this, the President threw himself forward in his chair in such a way that she saw his "curious, comical expression." He was looking the man squarely in the face; and, with one hand softly patting the other, and the funny look pervading every line of his face, he said: "My friend, let me tell you something about that. You are a farmer, I believe; if not, you will understand me. Suppose you had a large cattle yard, full of all sorts of cattle—cows, oxen, and bulls—and you kept killing and selling and disposing of your cows and oxen, in one way and another, taking good care of your bulls. By and by you would find out that you had nothing but a yard full of old bulls, good for nothing under heaven. Now it will be just so with the army, if I don't stop making brigadier-generals." The man tried to laugh, but the effort was feeble. The woman caller noticed, however, that Lincoln "laughed enough for both"; in fact, laughed the man out of the room.

From a line of people at an informal reception came a shout: "Hello, Abe, how are ye? I'm in line and hev come for an orfice too." Lincoln recognized an old Sangamon County friend and told him "to hang onto himself and not kick the traces." They shook hands and after the reception Lincoln had to explain that his old friend could not handle the transactions in the office he wanted. With lips trembling, the friend sketched a world of personal history for Lincoln's understanding in saying, "Martha's dead, the gal is married, and I've guv Jim the forty." He moved closer and half whispered, "I knowed I wasn't eddicated enough to get the place but I kinder want to stay where I ken see Abe Linkern." And for a time he worked on the White House grounds.

Lincoln had to refuse an office sought by an old friend who was not fit for it, remarking to Noah Brooks, "I had rather resign my place and go away from here, if I considered only my personal feelings, but refuse him I must." The almost forgotten Denton Offutt turned up in a letter: "I hope you will Give me the Patten office or the office of Agricultural Department or the Commissary for Purchais of Horses Mules Beef for the Army or Mail agent . . . I have to be looking out to live . . ."

He remembered good friends of New Salem days—the goodhearted "Uncle Jimmy" Short and the shrewd Bill Greene—with offices at nice salaries. He remembered his brother-in-law, Ninian W. Edwards, no longer well off, with an appointment to quartermaster at $1,800 a year, and John A. Bailhache, an editor of the *Illinois State Journal*, with an appointment as a commissary. Illinois party men brought the President reports of the two men being free with money beyond salaries and making scandalous appointments of administration enemies. Lincoln transferred Edwards to Chicago and Bailhache to New York.

When Lincoln gave his good friend Lamon an appointment, Senator James Grimes of Iowa arose in the Senate to remark, "The President of the United States saw fit, in the plenitude of his wisdom, to import to this District from the State of Illinois Mr. Ward H. Lamon, and to appoint him the marshal!" Grimes charged that "this foreign satrap, Mr. Lamon, made a peremptory order, that no person—not even members of Congress—should be admitted to the [District] jail without first supplicating and securing a written permission to do so from him." Then Grimes went to the White House: "When, for the first time in six months, I attempted to approach the footstool of the power enthroned at the other end of the avenue, I was told that the President was engaged." Thus there was sarcasm, and men of importance played peanut politics. Nevertheless there was the factor that Lamon was not particularly antislavery and there were complaints that jailed Negroes were not really fugitive slaves, but free Negroes kidnaped by white ruffians.

A Senator, on learning from Lincoln that Halleck had negatived proposed military changes, asked the President why he didn't get Halleck out of the way. "Well—the fact is—the man who has no friends—should be taken care of."

A private poured out his complaints one summer afternoon as Provost Marshal Fry came in and heard Lincoln's reply, "That may all be so, but you must go to your officers about it." The private told his story two or three times more as Lincoln sat and gazed out the south window on the Potomac. At last the President turned. "Now, my man, go away, *go away!* I can not meddle in your case. I could as easily bail out the Potomac River with a teaspoon as attend to all the details of the army."

One soldier letter to Lincoln pleaded, "I am near starved if I get much thinner it will take two of us to make one shadder."

One pest of a politician came often asking offices, suggesting removals and creation of new offices, and Lincoln, reviewing his day's routine to a friend, said that at night as the closing act of the day "I look under the bed to see if So-and-So is there, and if not, I thank Heaven and bounce in."

A dispute over a high-salaried Ohio postmastership brought several delegations to the White House, and papers piled high in behalf of two men about equally competent. One day, bored by still another delegation, more arguments, even more petitions, the President called to a clerk: "This matter has got to end somehow. Bring me a pair of scales." They were brought. "Now put in all the petitions and letters in favor of one man and see how much they weigh, and then weigh the other fellow's pile." One bundle weighed three-quarters of a pound more than the other. "Make out an appointment," said the President, "for the man who has the heavier papers."

Senators and Congressmen came with letters begging offices for relatives soon to be married, for friends who were sick and had dependents. "I need the position for a living," wrote one to Sumner. "I have been unfortunate and poor." To Chase and other department heads, as to the President, came letters crying personal poverty as a basis for public office, in the tone of one: "God knows no one needs the appointment more than I do." The President liked to tell of a seedy fellow asking Seward for a consulate in Berlin, then Paris, then Liverpool, coming down to a clerkship in the State Department. Hearing these places were all filled, he said, "Well, then, will you lend me 5 dollars?"

The President needed reminders to make sure he would do a thing he was inclined to do. Thus Carl Schurz in a letter to Sumner: "I think he is inclined to send in my nomination tomorrow if he is reminded of it . . . I want to press you to do this reminding. Will you? It will cost you only five minutes."

Lincoln telegraphed S. B. Moody at Springfield, Illinois: "Which do you prefer Commissary or Quarter master? If appointed it must be without conditions." The matter was personal; when a Congressman later wished to name a postmaster in Springfield, Lincoln said, "I think I have promised that to old Mrs. Moody for her husband." The Congressman demurred: "Now, Mr. President, why can't you be liberal?" "Mrs. Moody would get down on me."

Personal sentiments would govern. William Kellogg, Jr., quit West Point under demerit; if he had not resigned he would have been dismissed. His father, an Illinois Congressman, reappointed the boy. A report by General Joseph G. Totten disapproved. Lincoln wrote the Secretary of War that the father was a friend of 20 years' standing. "This matter touches him very deeply—the feelings of a father for a child—as he thinks, all the future of his child. I can not be the instrument to crush his heart. According to strict rule he has the right to make the re-nomination. Let the appointment be made. It needs not to become a precedent." Thereafter Lincoln would have the rule that no resignation should be handed in by a cadet without express stipulation in writing that the resigning cadet would not take a re-nomination.

Murat Halstead of the Cincinnati *Commercial* sought men close to the President and tried to land a postmastership for a friend. As a poor loser, Halstead wrote his friend: "I use the mildest phrase when I say Lincoln is a weak, a miserably weak man; the wife is a fool—the laughing stock of the town, her vulgarity only the more conspicuous in consequence of her fine carriage and horses and servants in livery and fine dresses and her damnable airs . . . Lincoln is very busy with trifles, and lets everybody do as they please. He is opposed to stealing, but can't see the stealing that is done." Halstead retailed further information: "The way Chase manages Lincoln is to make him believe that he [Lincoln] is doing all things. The poor silly President sucks flattery as a pig sucks milk."

Chase did not bring to Lincoln a letter of February 19, 1863, from Halstead advising: "Can't you take him [Lincoln] by the throat and knock his head against a wall until he is brought to his senses on the war business? I do not speak wantonly when I say there are persons who feel that it was doing God service to kill him, if it were not feared that Hamlin is a bigger fool than he is." To John Sherman, Halstead wrote February 8, 1863, "If Lincoln was not a damned fool, we could get along yet. He is an awful, woeful ass."

A woman kept at Lincoln with letter after letter begging her husband's appointment. An extra long letter brought his question, ". . . what is it but an evidence that you intend to importune me for one thing, and another, and another, until, in self-defence, I must drop all and devote myself to find a place, even though I remove somebody else to do it, and thereby turn him & his friends upon me for indefinite future importunity, and hindrance from the legitimate duties for which I am supposed to be placed here?"

David R. Locke, Ohio editor, under the pen name of Petroleum V. Nasby, was writing sketches that had a national audience laughing at issues of the day. He flattened pompous patriots with his comic pot shots:

> 1st. I want a offis.
> 2d. I need a offis.
> 3d. A offis wood suit me; there4
> 4th. I shood like to hev a offis.

Beneath Locke's mockery shone affection, and the President wrote to the satirist: "Why don't you come to Washington and see me? Is there no place you want? Come on and I will give you any place you ask for—that you are capable of filling—and fit to fill." Locke was interested. The President had read some of his writings and was so pleased that in a generous outburst he wrote that Locke could have "any place he asked for."

Then, as Locke analyzed it, the President saw he was offering too much to a man he knew only through newspaper sketches, so the saving clause was added, "that you are capable of filling," and, to guard himself entirely, "that you are fit to fill." Locke did go to see Lincoln, but not to ask for a place. "He gave me an hour of his time," said the humorist, "and a delightful hour it was."

A well-dressed man asked merely that the President allow the use of his name for advertising a project in view. "No!" flashed the President. "No! I'll have nothing to do with this. Do you take the President of the United States to be a commission broker? You have come to the wrong place. There is the door!" The caller slunk away.

A governor of a state entered Lincoln's office bristling with complaints as to his state quota and enforcement. He had seen Fry and then Stanton for a session of loud angry words with each. Now it was Lincoln's turn. Fry for hours expected orders from the White House or at least a special summons. He was surprised to see the governor come in with a pleasant smile. Fry soon was saying to Lincoln: "I suppose you found it necessary to make large concessions to him."

"Oh, no, I did not concede anything," Fry noted the President's explanation. "You know how that Illinois farmer managed the big log that lay in the middle of his field! To the inquiries of his neighbors one Sunday, he announced that he had got rid of the big log. 'Got rid of it!' said they, 'how did you do it? It was too big to haul out, too knotty to split, and too wet and soggy to burn; what did you do?' 'Well, now, boys,' replied the farmer, 'if you won't divulge the secret, I'll tell you how I got rid of it—I ploughed around it.' Now," said Lincoln to Fry, "don't tell anybody, but that's the way I got rid of the governor. I ploughed around him, but it took me three mortal hours to do it, and I was afraid every minute he'd see what I was at."

How Lincoln could coax, argue and persuade, was in the adroit Thurlow Weed writing him, "I do not, when with you, say half I intend. Partly because I don't like to be a crank and partly because you talk me out of my convictions and apprehensions, so bear with me please now till I free my mind."

A letter to Postmaster General Blair in the summer of '63 went far in newspaper publication and discussion of it. The Lincoln opposition howled about it from many places; thousands of soldiers read it, forward and backward, for assurance. In two cases of postmasterships sought for widows whose husbands had fallen in battle, the President had endorsed them and now wrote: "These cases occurring on the same day, brought me to reflect more attentively than I had before done, as to what is fairly due from us here, in the dispensing of patronage, towards the men who, by fighting our battles, bear the chief burthen of saving our country. My conclusion is that, other claims and qualifications being equal, they have the better right; and this is especially applicable to the disabled soldier, and the deceased soldier's family."

A man came wearing a colonel's uniform, though no longer a colonel, dismissed for drunkenness on duty. Lincoln knew him. The man had a record for valor in battle. Lincoln heard the story. The man wanted back his old rank and place. Lincoln stood up, too moved and uneasy to stay in his chair. He took the soldier's right hand in both his own. Then slowly, tears in his voice, he told the man: "Colonel, I know your story. But you carry your own condemnation in your face." They were hard words to say, Judgment Day words. Later in referring to the case Lincoln told James M. Scovel, "I dare not restore this man to his rank and give him charge of a thousand men when he 'puts an enemy into his mouth to steal away his brain.'"

A one-legged soldier on crutches asked for some kind of a job; he had lost his leg in battle. "Let me look at your papers," said Lincoln. The man had none; he supposed his word was good. "What! no papers, no credentials, nothing to show how you lost your leg! How am I to know that you lost it in battle, or did not lose it by a trap after getting into somebody's orchard?" The President's face was droll. The honest-looking German workingman, turned soldier, earnestly muttered excuses. Lincoln saw this was no regular place seeker. Most of them came with papers too elaborately prepared. The chances were entirely in favor of any one-legged man having lost his leg in battle. "Well, it is dangerous for an army man to be wandering around without papers to show where he belongs and what he is, but I will see what can be done." Then he wrote a card for the man to take to a quartermaster who would attend to his case.

Once a humble man came asking to be made doorkeeper to the House and Lincoln let him down and out without hurting his feelings. Their conversation, as reported, ran: "So you want to be Doorkeeper to the House, eh?" "Yes, Mr. President." "Well, have you ever been a doorkeeper? Have you ever had any experience in doorkeeping?" "Well, no—no actual experience, sir." "Any theoretical experience? Any instructions in the duties and ethics of doorkeeping?" "Um—no." "Have you ever attended lectures on doorkeeping?" "No, sir." "Have you read any textbooks on the subject?" "No." "Have you conversed with anyone who has read such a book?" "No, sir, I'm afraid not, sir." "Well, then, my friend, don't you see that you haven't a single qualification for this important post?" "Yes, I do." And he took his hat and left humbly, seeming rather grateful to the President.

When Judge Baldwin of California asked for a pass through army lines to visit a brother in Virginia, the President inquired, "Have you applied to General Halleck?" "Yes, and met with a flat refusal." "Then you must see Stanton." "I have, and with the same result." "Well, then," drawled Lincoln, "I can do nothing; for you must know I have very little influence with this administration." In this case it was a pleasantry with Lincoln. The same remark to a soldier's widow, who asked for a sutler's appointment, was a sorry fact.

One day, going over applications and recommendations, Lincoln said he concurred in about all that Stanton proposed. "The only point I make is, there has got to be something done that will be unquestionably in the interest of the Dutch, and to that end I want Schimmelfennig appointed." "Mr. President, perhaps this Schimmel-what's-his-name is not as highly recommended as some other German officers." "No matter about that. His name will make up for any difference there may be, and I'll take the risk of his coming out all right." Then with a laugh he spoke each syllable of the name distinctly, accenting the last: "Schim-mel-fen-*nig* must be appointed."

A speculator pressed for a pass through army lines and a Treasury license to buy cotton. He was steadily refused. "Few things are so troublesome to the government," Lincoln had remarked, "as the fierceness with which the profits in trading are sought." This particular trader brought influence to bear on Lincoln, who signed the permit requested and told the man, "You will have to take it over to Stanton for countersigning." Later the trader came back, in a heat, saying Stanton had torn to pieces and stamped his feet on the paper signed by the President. Lincoln put on a surprised look and asked the man to tell exactly how the Secretary had acted. Then, pausing a moment, he told the speculator, "You go back and tell Stanton that I will tear up a dozen of his papers before Saturday night."

A plan for mingling eastern and western troops was urged on Lincoln by a committee headed by Lovejoy. Lincoln wrote a note to Stanton suggesting a transfer of regiments. "Did Lincoln give you an order of that kind?" asked the Secretary. "He did, sir," replied Lovejoy. "Then he is a damned fool!" said Stanton. "Do you mean to say the President is a damned fool?" "Yes, sir, if he gave you such an order as that." At the White House Lovejoy told what happened. "Did Stanton say I was a damned fool?" asked Lincoln. "He did, sir, and repeated it." The President was thoughtful. "If Stanton said I was a damned fool then I must be one. For he is nearly always right, and generally says what he means. I will step over and see him."

Thurlow Weed told Leonard Swett that Lincoln kept "a regular account book" of his appointments in New York, "dividing favors so as to give each faction more than it could get from any other source, yet never enough to satisfy its appetite." In giving out offices or favors, the President had one guiding principle, as Swett saw it: "An adhesion of all forces was indispensable to his success and the success of the country; hence he husbanded his means with nicety of calculation . . . He never wasted anything, and would always give more to his enemies than he would to his friends; and the reason was, he never had anything to spare, and in the close calculation of attaching the factions to him, he counted upon the abstract affection of his friends as an element to be offset against some gift with which he must appease his enemies. Hence, there was always some truth in the charge of his friends that he failed to reciprocate their devotion with his favors. The reason was, that he had only just so much to give away. 'He always had *more horses than oats.*'"

Late at night after a long talk on the quarreling political factions in Missouri and Kentucky, Swett was saying good-by and at the door Lincoln said, "I may not have made as great a President as some other man, but I believe I have kept these discordant elements together as well as anyone could."

When Justice McLean of the Supreme Court died late in '61, friends of Davis moved to place him on the high bench. Old Eighth Circuit lawyers became active. Swett spoke for him personally to Lincoln. Months passed, a year, a year and a half—and Judge Davis saw no move of Lincoln to appoint him. On the last day of the October term of court in '62 Davis notified the members of the McLean County bar to meet him in the old courthouse at Bloomington. He spoke to them: "My official connection with the people and bar of this circuit is about to terminate. The President has tendered me an appointment as Associate Justice of the Supreme Court of the United States which I shall accept, although distrustful of my abilities to discharge the duties of the office."

Davis called the roll on the little group of lawyers who during so many years had been boon companions. Three had become judges, two U.S. Senators, one wounded and two killed in battle, one President of the United States. Davis went on to Washington, where he wrote in a letter, "Mr. Lincoln is very kind, but care worn."

CHAPTER 31

Hooker—Chancellorsville—Calamity

THE ARMY of the Potomac in early '63 had lost—on the peninsula, twice at Bull Run, and again in the slaughter at Fredericksburg. It had, however, kept enemy bayonets out of Washington and the Free States. And other Northern armies, with naval co-operation, had captured all the Confederate strongholds—except Forts Sumter and Morgan—on the seacoast from Fortress Monroe in Virginia to points in Texas. Rosecrans was marching close to the

Alabama line, Grant was in Mississippi, Curtis in Arkansas, Banks in New Orleans.

The Richmond *Examiner*, reviewing the scene January 20, 1863, said, "The pledge once deemed foolish by the South, that he would 'hold, occupy and possess' all the forts belonging to the United States Government, has been redeemed almost to the letter by Lincoln."

A renewed play of commentary, a sharpened political activity, rose from extremist Democrats wholly against the war. Sumner wrote Franz Lieber in January: "These are dark hours. There are senators full of despair,—not I. The President tells me that he now fears 'the fire in the rear'—meaning the Democracy—especially at the Northwest—more than our military chances." When Burnside wrote for publication a letter taking all blame on himself for the Fredericksburg disaster, Lincoln told him he was the first man found who was willing to relieve the President of a particle of responsibility.

Burnside planned a night attack on Lee's army. On the night of January 20 as the army started, rain began slowly, a wind came up, the rain turned to sleet. Horses and wagons sank in the mud and were stuck all night. Men and mules failed to make headway with the pontoons, also with the unhitched cavalry steeds and the early morning ration of whisky ordered by Burnside for every man.

After breakfast at staff headquarters next morning General Hooker talked with a newspaperman about how the commanding general was incompetent, the President and Government at Washington were imbecile and "played out," a dictator was needed and the sooner the better.

Burnside resigned, was persuaded to withdraw his resignation, was relieved of duty, and January 25, 1863, the President ordered Hooker to the command of the Army of the Potomac. Chase was pleased; so were members of the Committee on the Conduct of the War; so were many people attracted by his fighting quality and a touch of the dramatic and impetuous about Hooker. "Now there is Joe Hooker," Nicolay heard the President say. "He can fight. I think that is pretty well established—but whether he can 'keep tavern' for a large army is not so sure."

Lamon urged Lincoln to look well to the fact that there was a scheme on foot to depose him, and to appoint a military dictator in his place. Lincoln laughed and said, as Lamon quoted him: "I think, for a man of accredited courage, you are the most panicky person I ever knew; you can see more dangers to me than all the other friends I have . . . now you have discovered a new danger; now you think the people of this great government are likely to turn me out of office. I do not fear this from the people any more than I fear assassination from an individual. Now, to show you my appreciation of what my French friends would call a *coup d'état*, let me read you a letter I have written to General Hooker." He opened the drawer of a table and took out and read a letter he sent to Hooker, dated January 26, 1863, later published and widely discussed:

General. I have placed you at the head of the Army of the Potomac. Of course I have done this upon what appear to me to be sufficient reasons. And yet I think it best for you to know that there are some things in regard to which, I am not quite satisfied with you. I believe you to be a brave and skilful soldier, which, of course, I like. I also believe you do not mix politics with your profession, in which you are right. You have confidence in yourself, which is a valuable, if not an indispensable quality. You are ambitious, which, within reasonable bounds, does good rather than harm. But I think that during Gen. Burnside's command of the Army, you have taken counsel of your ambition, and thwarted him as much as you could, in which you did a great wrong to the country, and to a most meritorious and honorable brother officer. I have heard, in such a way as to believe it, of your recently saying that both the Army and the Government needed a Dictator. Of course it was not *for* this, but in spite of it, that I have given you the command. Only those generals who gain successes, can set up dictators. What I now ask of you is military success, and I will risk the dictatorship. The government will support you to the utmost of it's ability, which is neither more nor less than it has done and will do for all commanders. I much fear that the spirit which you have aided to infuse into the Army, of criticising their Commander, and withholding confidence from him, will now turn upon you. I shall assist you as far as I can, to put it down. Neither you, nor Napoleon, if he were alive again, could get any good out of an army, while such a spirit prevails in it.

And now, beware of rashness. Beware of rashness, but with energy, and sleepless vigilance, go forward, and give us victories.

Not long after receiving the letter, Hooker stood with his back to a cozy fireplace in his log-and-canvas army hut. And looking quizzically at his only companion, Noah Brooks, newspaper correspondent, he said, "The President tells me that you know all about the letter he wrote to me when he put me in command of this army." Mr. Lincoln had read the letter to him, admitted Brooks. "Wouldn't you like to hear it again?" asked Hooker, drawing it from a pocket.

Hooker read, pausing to demur at one point: "The President is mistaken. I never thwarted Burnside in any way, shape or manner." Resuming the reading, Hooker's tone softened, and he finished the reading almost with tears in his eyes as he folded the letter, put it back in the breast of his coat, saying: "That is just such a letter as a father might write to his son. It is a beautiful letter, and, although I think he was harder on me than I deserved, I will say that I love the man who wrote it." Then Hooker added, "After I have got to Richmond, I shall give that letter to you to have published."

A handsome soldier, Hooker looked warlike for those to whom war is color, dash, valor. Blond of hair, with wavy ringlets, with a flushed and rosy face, 49 years old, he was tall, blue-eyed, had a martial air. A West Point graduate, brevetted captain for bravery at Monterey in the Mexican War, he was a farmer and superintendent of military roads on the West Coast when the war began.

So often came a reservation in the judgments of Hooker. "He could play the best game of poker I ever saw until it came to the point when he should go a thousand better, and then he would flunk," said a cavalry officer. Yet time and again Hooker had led his division into slaughter where men fell by platoons and his lines held their ground. At Williamsburg on the peninsula under McClellan he had 2,228 killed and wounded. He was nicknamed "Fighting Joe" Hooker. Shot in the foot at Antietam, he stayed in the saddle on the field with his men till the fighting was over. Often the words came from him "When I get to Richmond" or "After we have taken Richmond." Lincoln was near groaning as he said in confidence to Brooks: "That is the most depressing thing about Hooker. It seems to me that he is over-confident."

After a conference in the White House, Lincoln said with his good-by to Hooker, "General, we shall expect to have some good news from you very soon." Then the President turned to a young New Jersey cavalryman, Sergeant J. L. Stradling. "What can I do for you, my young friend?" A permit was wanted to ride a steamer to Aquia Creek, and join up with the cavalry again, after furlough. John Hay had written across a card: "To any steamboat captain going to the front, please give bearer transportation," which Lincoln signed.

The young Sergeant was about to leave when Lincoln said to Senator Wade and two others: "Senator, we have had the head of the Army here a few minutes ago, and learned from him all he cared to tell. Now we have here the tail of the Army, so let us get from him how the rank and file feel about matters. I mean no reflection on you, Sergeant, when I say the tail of the Army." The President then spoke of many men deserting that winter. There must be some good cause.

Stradling, flustered at first, now felt the President wanted him to speak frankly. "Mr. President, so far as I know, the Army has the utmost confidence in your honesty and ability to manage this war. So far as I can learn, the army had no faith in the ability of General Burnside . . . He . . . fought his battles like some people play the fiddle, by main strength and awkwardness." Senator Wade asked if there was any excuse for such a blunder as Fredericksburg. Lincoln spoke up, "This is very interesting to me, so please go ahead." The Sergeant explained that the country was an open one, with no real mountains or rivers; both flanks of the Confederate army could have been turned. "Even we privates wondered why such an attack was made. General Burnside must have known of the sunken road, for we of the cavalry had been over this road with General Bayard in 1862, and he must have informed General Burnside all about it. If General Burnside had possessed any military genius, he would have flanked Lee out of that strong position, and fought him where he could have had at least an equal chance."

The President said, as Stradling wrote it: "What you have stated, Sergeant, seems very plausible to me. When General Hooker left us but a few minutes ago, he said, 'Mr. President, I have the finest army that was ever assembled together, and I hope to send you good news very soon.' That is just the language General Burnside used when he left me shortly before the battle of Fredericksburg. And such a disaster that followed still makes my heart sick." The frank Sergeant, opening his mind and heart, said: "Mr. President, even privates when on the ground cannot help seeing and wondering why certain movements are made. I refer to the charges of General Hooker on our right. [Hooker had demurred against making these assaults but Burnside had insisted.] Our duty, however, is not to criticise, but to obey even if we get our heads knocked off. I have found that soldiers are willing to obey without hesitation and take the chances when they feel that their show is equal to that of the enemy.

"Mr. President, I approach the Emancipation Proclamation with great reluctance, for I know how your heart was set on issuing that document. So far as I am personally concerned, I heartily approve of it. But many of my comrades said that if they had known the war would free the 'niggers' they would never have enlisted, so many of them deserted. Others said they would not desert, but would not fight any more, and sought positions in the wagon train; the Ambulance Corps; the Quartermaster's Department, and other places, to get out of fighting."

The President, Senator Wade and the other gentlemen must have wondered what they had before them in such a straightaway talker. So thought the Sergeant. But he went on: "I was born a Quaker, and was therefore an anti-slavery young man when I entered the army. The issuing of the proclamation caused many to desert, no doubt, and the presence of General Burnside at the head of the army caused many others to leave."

The President sat still a moment or two, then said: "The proclamation was, as you state, very near to my heart. I thought about it and studied it in all its phases long before I began to put it on paper. I expected many soldiers would desert when the proclamation was issued, and I expected many who care nothing for the colored man would seize upon the proclamation as an excuse for deserting. I did not believe the number of deserters would materially affect the army. On the other hand, the issuing of the proclamation would probably bring into the ranks many who otherwise would not volunteer."

The President, during all of the conversation, Stradling noted, was a "woe-begone" man. "He did not smile, and his face did not lighten up once." "I thank you very much," said Lincoln, with a handshake, "and I trust you will reach the front in the morning." And Sergeant Stradling left the White House, slept on sacks of oats aboard the same steamer that carried General Hooker in its cabin that night. He wrote home of his visit to the Executive Mansion: "I was awful glad to get out, and when I did get away I felt as though I had been to a funeral. Senator Wade did smile once or twice, and so did the other two gentlemen who were present, but Lincoln did not even show the shadow of a smile. His long, sad and gloomy face haunted me for days afterward."

Slowly across weeks of February, March, April, the gloom of the Army of the Potomac changed toward gaiety. Hooker had found at the close of January that in round numbers 3,000 officers and 82,000 men of the ranks were absent; they were on the rolls of the army, but not answering roll call. Some were sick, wounded, on furlough. Others had run away. Homesickness, gloom and a general feeling of uselessness had brought an average of 200 desertions a day during the winter; relatives and friends sent express bundles to their loved ones, citizens' clothing for escape. Under a new rule express trains were searched, all citizens' clothing burned.

A new regime operated. Steadily a sulky army became willing and eager to fight. It lay at Fredericksburg, a day's buggy ride from Washington, so that important public men came for personal inspections, accompanied by wives and daughters in crinoline.

Early in April Hooker said that under his command was "a living army, and one well worthy of the republic." He also rated it "the finest army on the planet." He had 130,000 troops against Lee across the river with 60,000. The President kept in constant touch with the forging and welding of this new weapon for smiting the Confederacy, sending Hooker such communications as "Would like to have a letter from you as soon as convenient" and "How does it look now?" On April 3 he notified Hooker he would arrive at the Fredericksburg camp on Sunday and stay till Tuesday morning.

In an April snowfall, Lincoln with Tad, Mrs. Lincoln, and a few friends arrived at Aquia Creek water front, lined with transports and Government steamers unloading supplies for 130,000 men and 60,000 horses and mules. A crowd of army people cheered the arrival of the President. Lincoln insisted on going to the nearest hospital tent, stopping to speak with nearly every one of the sick and wounded, shaking hands with many, asking a question or two here and there, and leaving a kind word as he moved from cot to cot.

"More than once," noted Brooks, "as I followed the President through the long lines of weary sufferers, I noticed tears of gladness stealing down their pale faces; for they were made happy by looking into Lincoln's sympathetic countenance, touching his hand, and hearing his gentle voice; and when we rode away from the camp tremendous cheers rent the air from the soldiers, who stood in groups, eager to see the President."

Brooks mentioned to Lincoln one evening at headquarters after a day of riding at army inspection that he was looking rested and in better health. "It is a great relief to get away from Washington and the politicians," was the President's answer. "But nothing touches the tired spot."

On another evening in Hooker's hut, according to Brooks, the President looked cautiously about, saw they were alone, and in a half-jocular way took out from a pocket a small piece of paper and handed it to Brooks. On it were written the figures "216,718—146,000—169,000." Brooks studied the numbers with puzzled wonder; the President explained the first figures represented the sum total of the men on the rolls of the Army of the Potomac; the second were those of the actual available force, and the last represented the numerical strength to which the force might be increased when the army should move.

In a chat with Hooker, Lincoln said, "If you get to Richmond, General—" and was interrupted by Hooker: "Excuse me, Mr. President, but there is no 'if' in this case. I am going straight to Richmond if I live." Later Lincoln remarked mournfully to Brooks, "It is about the worst thing I have seen since I have been down here." By letter and by word he had tried to impress on Hooker that the objective was Lee's army and not Richmond.

On an eight-mile ride to a corps review, six mules pulled the ambulance over a rough corduroy road that jolted the passengers. At his wild mules the driver let fly volleys of oaths. Lincoln leaned forward, touched the driver on the shoulder, and said: "Excuse me, my friend, are you an Episcopalian?" The surprised driver looked around. "No, Mr. President, I am a Methodist." "Well, I thought you must be an Episcopalian, because you swear just like Governor Seward, who is a church warden." The driver stopped swearing. The ambulance plunged through jack oak and scrub pine. Lincoln pointed to stumps where an axman had done clever work, "a good butt"; or again to poor chopping.

Tad said he must see "graybacks," Confederate soldiers. Two staff men took Tad and his father on a frosty morning down to the picket line opposite Fredericksburg. They saw hills and a city war-swept, mansions and plain homes in ruins, farms desolated. Smoke rose from enemy campfires just above a stone wall where Burnside's men by thousands had weltered in blood. From a house that stood whole out of the wreckage floated a flag and Lincoln glimpsed the Confederate Stars and Bars.

Tobacco, coffee, newspapers and jackknives were being traded across the river between Confederate and Union pickets. They spoke good morning and saluted each other as "butternut" and "bluebelly."

From a reviewing stand the President, Hooker and the staff watched 17,000 horsemen file past, the biggest army of men on horses ever seen in the world, said Hooker, bigger even than the famous cavalry body of Marshal Murat with Napoleon. Mud flew from the horses' feet on ground soft with melting snow. On the fringe of the cavalry cloud came Tad, in a mounted orderly's charge, his gray cloak flying in the wind like a plume. The infantry filed past the President—four corps, 60,000 men, a forest of moving rifles and bayonets. Then came the reserve artillery force, some 400 cannon. Zouave regiments in baggy red trousers, crack drill troops, marched and made a contrast. Lincoln asked Hooker if fancy uniforms were not undesirable because they made better targets, the General replying that these uniforms had the effect of inciting a spirit of pride and neatness among the men.

Hour on hour in platoons and in company front, the Army of the Potomac, a sad army that had seen rivers of blood and anguish to the depths, marched by for the Commander in Chief in the reviewing stand, surrounded by his generals. "It was noticeable," recorded Brooks, "that the President merely touched his hat in return salute to the officers, but uncovered to the men in the ranks."

In the moving platoons that day were regulars, volunteers, conscripts, bounty men. From Boston, New York, Philadelphia, were sons of Daughters of the Revolution whose ancestors had fought ragged and shivering under George Washington from Valley Forge to Yorktown, and they were mingled in divisions with German, English, Scotch, Irish, Scandinavian, Jewish, Polish immigrants or children of immigrants, whose forefathers had fought with or against Bonaparte, Frederick the Great, Marlborough, Gustavus Adolphus, in decisive battles that had hammered out historic texts of the destiny of man.

In the 2d division of the 11th corps, Brigadier General Adolph von Steinwehr had in his command Colonel Adolphus Buschbeck, Major Alex von Schluembach, Colonel Patrick H. Jones and Lieutenant Colonel Lorenz Cantador. At the head of the 3d division rode Major General Carl Schurz with Brigadier General Alexander Schimmelfennig, leading Illinois, Ohio, New York and Pennsylvania regiments. Colonel W. Krzyzanowski, whose nomination by Lincoln to brigadier had failed of approval in the Senate, headed a New York regiment. Youths who had left their classes at Harvard, Kenyon, Oberlin, Knox and many other colleges were in the ranks; wild Irish from the sidewalks of New York; Bavarians and Prussians from St. Louis and Milwaukee. Green Mountain plowboys were there; farm hands from the cornfields and orchards of Michigan.

These platoons of regulars, volunteers, conscripts, bounty men, were marching for adventure and glory; for the country and the flag; for a united nation from coast to coast; for the abolition of chattel slavery; or because they were drafted and there was no escape; or because they were paid a bounty of cash.

In a hundred soldiers picked at random might be a hundred different explanations of why they had gone to war and become individual, mobile units of the Army of the Potomac. They were young, most of them in their early twenties, some in their teens—soft-haired youths, yet many of them fierce cubs of war ready to earn with pride and abandon the badge of courage.

Mrs. Lincoln wore, wrote the New York *Herald* man, "a rich black dress with narrow flounces, a black cape with broad trimming of velvet around the border and a plain hat of the same hue composed her costume. A shade of weariness, doubtless the result of her labors in behalf of the sick and wounded in Washington, rested upon her countenance but the change seemed pleasant to her. The President wore a dark sack overcoat and a fur muffler."

Instead of a lean cob with a docked tail, the President should have sat "a fair-sized cavalry horse of which there were plenty," wrote William F. Goodhue of Company C, 3d Wisconsin Infantry, to his home folks. "Mr. Lincoln sat his cob perfectly straight, and dressed as he was in dark clothes, it appeared as if he was an exclamation point astride of the small letter *m*."

General Darius N. Couch wrote: "Mr. Lincoln, sitting there with his hat off, his head bent, and seemingly meditating, suddenly turned to me and said, 'General Couch, what do you suppose will become of all these men when the war is over?' And it struck me as very pleasant that somebody had an idea that the war would sometime end."

In the Confederate army across the river horses were gaunt from lack of forage. Scurvy had begun to appear among troops lacking balanced rations. Cattle had arrived so thin that Lee asked to have them kept to fatten in the spring and salt meat issued instead. Through an unusually bleak and frigid winter some of Lee's troops had no blankets. Many wore coats and shoes in tatters. An evangelistic revival through the winter, in which religious leaders from Southern cities joined with chaplains, had brought thousands of converts and given a religious impress to the Army of Northern Virginia.

True it was "the Yanks were licked" at Charleston, dispatches told Lincoln. A fleet of ironclad vessels, long and carefully prepared, had failed to batter down Fort Sumter, and under fire from heavy shore batteries had retired somewhat crippled with one vessel sunk and two disabled. Because Charleston was a symbol, a starting point of secession, many in the North hoped it could be taken; they had expected much; they would wait.

The failure at Charleston led to Admiral Dahlgren's relieving Admiral Du Pont in command of the South Atlantic blockading squadron. Welles recorded Lincoln as saying: "Du Pont, as well as McClellan, hesitates—has *the slows*. McClellan always wanted more regiments; Du Pont is everlastingly asking for more gunboats, more ironclads. He will do nothing with any . . . He is no Farragut, though unquestionably a good routine officer, who obeys orders and in a general way carries out his instructions." Thus Lincoln kept touch personally with fleets and squadrons at sea as well as armies and expeditions on land.

"Write me often. I am very anxious," wrote Lincoln to Hooker a week after his visit to the army. He thanked Hooker for maps, newspapers and a letter which arrived April 28. "While I am anxious, please do not think I am impatient, or waste a moment's thought on me, to your own hindrance, or discomfort." He sent two telegrams to Hooker in the first week of May

Confederate Generals

Upper left: Robert Edward Lee [Library of Congress]. *Upper right:* Early photograph of Thomas J. ("Stonewall") Jackson [CS]. *Center left:* Joseph E. Johnston [Meserve]. *Center right:* Nathan Bedford Forrest [Meserve]. *Lower left:* J.E.B. ("Jeb") Stuart [Meserve]. *Lower right:* James Longstreet [Meserve].

Six Distinctive Wartime Women

Upper left: Harriet Beecher Stowe of *Uncle Tom's Cabin* [CS]. *Upper right:* Julia Ward Howe of "The Battle Hymn of the Republic" [CS]. *Center left:* Varina Howell Davis, wife of the Confederate President [Meserve]. *Center right:* The heroic Cordelia A. P. Harvey [CS]. *Lower left:* Kate Chase Sprague, "society" leader and politician [Meserve]. *Lower right:* Anna Dickinson, tempestuous, volatile orator [Meserve].

querying, "What news?" Hooker was letting no one into his secrets. "I heard him say," wrote Meade, "that not a human being knew his plans either in the army or at Washington."

On May 1 Hooker had brought most of his army across the Rappahannock River, to a crossroads named Chancellorsville. Hooker attacked, Lee counterattacked, and Hooker ordered his men to fall back. "Just as we reached the enemy we were recalled," wrote Meade, while General Couch, second to Hooker in command, said: "Hooker expected Lee to fall back without risking battle. Finding himself mistaken he assumed the defensive."

Early next morning Lee sent half his army under Stonewall Jackson on a march that took them till late in the afternoon, when they delivered a surprise attack that smashed the Union flank and rear. Next day Lee outguessed and outfought Hooker. With an army half the size of Hooker's, he so mangled and baffled the Union forces that Hooker called a council of his generals, of whom four voted to stay where they were and fight, two voted to retreat across the river. Hooker then ordered the retreat.

The white moon by night and the red sun by day had looked down on over 20,000 men who lay killed or wounded on the open farms and in the wilderness of trees, thickets and undergrowth, the figures giving Union losses at 11,000, Confederate at 10,000, not including 6,000 prisoners captured by Lee and 2,000 by Hooker. Numbers, however, could not tell nor measure the vacancy nor the Southern heartache left by the death of Stonewall Jackson, shot by his own men, it was reported, as he was inspecting positions in the zone of fire. A cannon ball had broken a mansion pillar against which General Hooker leaned, knocked him down, left him senseless a half-hour, dazed for an hour or more, while the battle lines rocked and tore on the second day.

Hooker had gone into battle with a good plan and dropped it when the enemy refused to do what he expected. He was sick with himself as he told Meade he was ready to turn over the army; he had had enough and almost wished he had never been born.

News of what happened to Hooker was slow reaching the White House. "I this P.M. met the President at the War Department," wrote Welles May 4. "He said he had a feverish anxiety to get facts; was constantly up and down, for nothing reliable came from the front." Noah Brooks found the President "anxious and harassed beyond any power of description," that while without any positive information Lincoln was certain in his own mind that "Hooker had been licked." He asked Brooks to go into the room occupied by his friend Dr. Henry, a guest, and wait for later news.

"In an hour or so, while the doctor and I sat talking, about 3 o'clock in the afternoon," wrote Brooks, "the door opened and Lincoln came into the room. He held a telegram in his hand, and as he closed the door and came toward us I mechanically noticed that his face, usually sallow, was ashen in hue. The paper on the wall behind him was of the tint known as 'French gray,' and even in that moment of sorrow and dread expectation, I vaguely took in the thought that the complexion of the anguished President's visage was like that of the wall. He gave me the telegram, and in a voice trembling with emotion, said 'Read it—news from the army.'

"The despatch was from General Butterfield, Hooker's chief of staff, addressed to the War Department, and was to the effect that the army had been withdrawn from the south side of the Rappahannock and was then 'safely encamped' in its former position. The appearance of the President, as I read aloud these fateful words, was piteous . . . broken . . . and so ghostlike. Clasping his hands behind his back, he walked up and down the room, saying 'My God! my God! What will the country say! What will the country say!' He seemed incapable of uttering any other words than these, and after a little time he hurriedly left the room."

Rumors flew over Washington that the President and Halleck had gone to the front; Hooker would be put under arrest; Halleck would command; Stanton had quit; Lee had cut Hooker to pieces and was moving on Washington; McClellan was coming by special train from New York to command, while Generals Sigel, Butler, Frémont, on the shelf, would soon arrive. The bar at Willard's was crowded; men with their feet on the brass rail drank hard liquor and conducted a war that existed in their own minds.

The President wrote May 7 to Hooker as though a good fighter had been sent reeling, wasn't hurt, and might make a swift comeback. "An early movement would . . . help," he wrote, asking if Hooker had in mind a plan wholly or partially formed. "If you have, prossecute it without interference from me . . ."

Lincoln's visit at the front was partly told in General Meade's letter to his wife: "I was summoned to headquarters, where I found the President and General Halleck. The former said he had come down to enquire for himself as to the condition of affairs and desired to see corps commanders . . . The President remarked that the result was in his judgment most unfortunate; that he did not blame any one . . . Nevertheless he thought its effect, both at home and abroad, would be more serious and injurious than any previous act of the war . . . Since seeing the President, he [Hooker] seems in better spirits . . ." Meantime as many explanations of the repulse at Chancellorsville had been published as were offered earlier to solve the first Bull Run rout.

Lee was carefully screening a movement that seemed to be aimed northward, possibly another invasion of Maryland. On June 14 Lincoln queried Hooker: "If the head of Lee's army is at Martinsburg and the tail of it on the plank road between Fredericksburg and Chancellorsville, the animal must be very slim somewhere. Could you not break him?"

Welles wrote he was puzzled that no condemnation of Hooker came from Lincoln: "The President . . . has a personal liking for Hooker, and clings to him when others give way." As though he had it from Sumner, Welles wrote: "The President said if Hooker had been killed by the shot which knocked over the pillar that stunned him, we should have been successful." As late as June 26, nearly seven weeks since the Battle of Chancellorsville, Hooker had done nothing to fret or harass Lee, and Lincoln gave to Welles the first inkling that he might have to let Hooker go.

Hearing that Lincoln was going to give him command of the army, the able and valorous corps commander General John F. Reynolds hurried to the White House and told Lincoln he did not want command of the Army of the Potomac and would not take it.

Lee rested his army, received new divisions of freshly conscripted troops, slipped away into the Shenandoah Valley, and by June 29 had crossed the Potomac, marched over Maryland, and had an army of 75,000 on Pennsylvania soil. Hooker broke camp with his army and moved it northward in scattered formation.

At Frederick, Maryland, a man in civilian clothes, riding in a buggy, begging, buying and wheedling his way through straggling parties of soldiers and wagon trains, arrived at three o'clock the morning of June 28 and went to the tent of General George Gordon Meade, was let in after wrangling. He woke Meade from sleep, saying he had come to give him trouble. Meade said his conscience was clear; he was prepared for bad news.

A letter from General in Chief Halleck was put in Meade's hands: "You will receive with this the order of the President placing you in command of the Army of the Potomac . . . You will not be hampered by any minute instructions from headquarters. Your army is free to act as you may deem proper under the circumstances as they arise." Meade argued with General James A. Hardie, chief of staff of the Secretary of War, who had brought the order. He did not want the place. But every point he made had been anticipated. Meade was ordered as a soldier to accept, which he did, issuing notice that day: "By direction of the President of the United States, I hereby assume command of the Army of the Potomac."

Lincoln met his Cabinet the Sunday morning Meade took command. "The President . . . drew from his pocket a telegram from General Hooker asking to be relieved," noted Welles. "The President said he had, for several days as the conflict became imminent, observed in Hooker the same failings that were witnessed in McClellan after the Battle of Antietam—a want of alacrity to obey, and a greedy call for more troops . . ." Chase, in a long polite letter to the President that day, intimated that trickery had been on foot in the ousting of Hooker.

A. K. McClure urged Lincoln to put McClellan again in command, which was also the wish of many business and professional men of New York and Philadelphia. Lincoln replied with two questions: "Do we gain anything by opening one leak to stop another? Do we gain anything by quieting one clamor merely to open another, and probably a larger one?"

Hooker asked Noah Brooks what the President had said about him. "I hesitated," said Brooks, "but when he pressed for a reply, I said that Lincoln had told me that he regarded Hooker very much as a father might a son who was lame, or who had some other physical infirmity. His love for his son would be even intensified by the reflection that the lad could never be a strong and successful man. The tears stood in Hooker's eyes as he heard this curious characterization of himself."

The next great battle, it seemed to many, would be a duel between Meade and Lee, somewhere in Pennsylvania, at Philadelphia, Chambersburg, Harrisburg, perhaps Gettysburg.

A soldier with both legs shot off was being carried to the rear in the recent fighting. And seeing a woman selling leathery-looking pies, he called out, "Say, old lady, are those pies sewed or pegged?" Also there was a high private at Chancellorsville who had been through several campaigns with a crockery mug, from which he was drinking coffee as his regiment awaited action. A stray bullet, just missing the coffee drinker's head, shattered the mug and left only its handle on his fingers. Turning his head toward the enemy, he growled, "Johnny, you can't do that again." Lincoln told of these to Brooks. "It seems as if neither death nor danger can quench the grim humor of the American soldier."

Now the war already had a considerable past. In a little wilderness clearing at Chancellorsville, a living soldier had come upon a dead one sitting with his back to a tree, looking at first sight almost alive enough to hold a conversation. He had sat there for months, since the battle the year before that gave him his long rest. He seemed to have a story and a philosophy to tell if the correct approach were made and he could be led into a quiet discussion. The living soldier, however, stood frozen in his foot tracks a few moments, gazing at the ashen face and the sockets where the eyes had withered—then he picked up his feet, let out a cry and ran. He had interrupted a silence where the slants of silver moons and the music of varying rains kept company with the one against the tree who sat so speechless, though having much to say.

CHAPTER 32

Will Grant Take Vicksburg?

ONE QUESTION weighed heavily on the Richmond Government in the spring of '63. Would Grant take Vicksburg? If so the Mississippi River would pass wholly into Union possession. Lincoln had talked about such a result to Commander D. D. Porter, pointing at a map and saying, as quoted by Porter: "See what a lot of land these fellows hold, of which Vicksburg is the key . . . Let us get Vicksburg and all that country is ours. The war can never be brought to a close until that key is in our pocket. I am acquainted with that region and know what I am talking about . . ."

From the fall of '62 till July 1 of '63 Grant performed with armies roundabout Vicksburg, marching troops along the Yazoo River, the Yalobusha, the Tallahatchie, amid the miasma of swamps and the tangles of live oak and Spanish moss, digging ditches and canals, chopping wood, building bridges, throwing up breastworks, standing waist-deep in the mud of rifle pits, sleeping in soaked fields and slogging on through monotonous heavy rains, enduring plagues of malarial fever, measles, mumps and smallpox. They became familiars of Five Mile Creek, Deer Creek, Eagle Bend, Moon Lake, Rolling Fork, the Big Sunflower, Muddy Bayou, the inlets and curves of the Mississippi River with its great sudden twist at the bluffs of Vicksburg, a city of 5,000 people, 250 feet above the river.

Grant's home-town Congressman, E. B. Washburne, wrote to Lincoln of Grant: "On this whole march for five days he has had neither a horse nor an orderly or servant, a blanket or overcoat or clean shirt. His entire baggage consists of a tooth brush." For weeks the army lived on the country, took the cattle, hogs, grain, supplies, from the farming sections where they were fighting.

Grant slogged and plodded, trying a plan to find it fail, devising another plan, hanging to his one purpose of taking Vicksburg. At one time Lincoln and Stanton had no word from him in ten days. His men marched 180 miles; fought five battles; killed more than the enemy; took 6,000 prisoners, 90 cannon, in 20 days. Porter's ironclad gunboats ran the fire of the heavy shore batteries around the long U bend of the Mississippi, took terrific pounding, lost coal barges and one transport, but came through with the armored flotilla safe. Two other flotillas were put on the Vicksburg operation, cutting off that city from all lines of communication in three directions. Twice Grant had tried to storm his way into Vicksburg, and failing, had settled down to pick and shovel, advancing trenches, stopping food and supplies for the city.

The commander of Vicksburg, John C. Pemberton, was a favorite of President Davis. A West Pointer, Mexican War veteran, Indian fighter, Pennsylvania-born and raised, a descendant of three generations of Quakers, his Northern birth was held against him. After Grant's second storming attempt, Pemberton spoke to his troops: "You have heard that I was incompetent and a traitor; and that it was my intention to sell Vicksburg. Follow me and you will see the cost at which I will sell Vicksburg. When the last pound of beef, bacon and flour, the last grain of corn, the last cow and hog and horse and dog shall have been consumed, and the last man shall have perished in the trenches, then, and only then, will I sell Vicksburg."

For six months and more Grant, to many people in the North, seemed to be wandering around, stumbling and bungling on a job beyond him. So crazily intricate became the layout that in early June Sherman wrote home: "I don't believe I can give you an idea of matters here. You will read so much about Vicksburg and the people now gathered about it that you will get bewildered." In March he had written, "No place on earth is favored by nature with natural defense such as Vicksburg, and I do believe the whole thing will fail"; another plan would have to be worked on.

Thus often the very spectators on the spot felt desperate, and newspaper correspondents had good reason, at times, to send the North stories of gloom and despair. Sherman arrested Thomas W. Knox, New York *Herald* correspondent, tried him by court-martial on the charge of writing letters for publication without submitting them to the commanding general. Knox was sentenced to stay outside of army lines. In Washington a committee of newspapermen laid the papers in the Knox case before Lincoln, who told the committee he couldn't embarrass his generals in the field, though he would be glad to serve Mr. Knox or any other loyal journalist. He began writing, with pauses, a statement to whom it might concern, that Knox's offense was "technical, rather than wilfully wrong" and the sentence should be revoked. "Now therefore said sentence is hereby so far revoked as to allow Mr. Knox to return to Gen. Grant's Head-Quarters, and to remain, if Gen. Grant shall give his express assent; and to again leave the Department, if Gen. Grant shall refuse such assent." This satisfied the committee.

Sherman stuck on with the army, held by affection and admiration for Grant, writing to his Senator brother that Grant was honest, able, sensible and a hero, which sentiments reached Lincoln. He was redheaded, lean, scrawny, this Sherman, with a mind of far wider range than usual in the army. One of the 11 children of a lawyer who served as judge of the Supreme Court of Ohio, he was taken into the home of Thomas Ewing, lawyer and famous Whig, when his father died. An 1840 West Pointer, Sherman saw Indian fighting in Florida, studied law, was an adjutant general in California during the Mexican War, managed a bank in San Francisco, operated a New York office for a St. Louis firm, practiced law in Leavenworth, Kansas, and at the opening of the war was superintendent of the Louisiana State Military Academy at Alexandria. He had seen the United States and anxiety rode him about it; newspapers, politicians, the educated classes, were corrupt, blind, selfish, garrulous, to the point of tragedy.

Early in the war it had racked Sherman's mind that there was to be wholesale and organized slaughter by prolonged combat between his Northern people against others "as good as ourselves." He had paced to and fro in the hall of a hotel in Cincinnati mumbling to himself, and his high-pitched commentaries had earned him the nickname of "Crazy" Sherman among those who misunderstood. For what seemed to him a just cause he would invoke terror. "To secure the navigation of the Mississippi River I would slay millions; on that point I am not only insane, but mad." Lincoln was yet to get acquainted with this lean, restless, hawk-eyed rider of war and apostle of conquest.

Charles A. Dana, once of the New York *Tribune*, had revolted at Greeley's muddled, equivocal support of Lincoln, had resigned, later was given full credentials to travel with Grant's army, see everything, and report to the President and the Secretary of War. Dana reported three remarkable men heading the campaign, Grant, Sherman and James B. McPherson, all Ohio-born, and between them "utmost confidence," no jealousy or bickering. "In their unpretending simplicity they were as alike as three peas." John A. Logan, the Douglas Democrat from far south in Illinois, Dana reported, was proving a heroic, brilliant, sometimes unsteady brigadier general.

Grant's home-town lawyer friend, now Assistant Adjutant General John A. Rawlins, Dana noted, gave himself no indulgence over Grant, "watches him day and night, and whenever he commits the folly of tasting liquor hastens to remind him that at the beginning of the war he gave him [Rawlins] his word of honor not to touch a drop." On a steamer trip up the Yazoo, Grant drank wine till he was too fuddled to make a decision as to how far upriver the boat should go, Dana ordering the steamer to return. "The next morning," wrote Dana, "Grant came out to breakfast fresh as a rose, clean shirt and all, quite himself." So faithful was the watch kept by Rawlins over Grant that no distinct occasion ever arose that scandal-bearers could point to and say that drink had brought disaster.

A steady stream of letters in the mail, and persistent callers at the White House, brought Lincoln the advice that for the sake of the country he must get rid of Grant. The tone of many ran like that of a letter of Murat Halstead, editor of the Cincinnati *Commercial*, to Secretary Chase. "How is it that Grant, who was behind at Fort Henry, drunk at Donelson, surprised and whipped at Shiloh, and driven back from Oxford, Miss., is still in command? Governor Chase, these things are true. Our noble army of the Mississippi is being wasted by the foolish, drunken, stupid Grant. He cannot organize or control or fight an army. I have no personal feeling about it; but I know he is an ass. There is not among the whole list of retired major-generals a man who is not Grant's superior."

On this letter Chase wrote an endorsement for Lincoln to read: "Reports concerning General Grant similar to the statements made by Mr. Halstead are too common to be safely or even prudently disregarded." In another letter in much the same vein, Halstead referred to Grant as "a jackass in the original package . . . a poor drunken imbecile . . . a poor stick sober and he is most of the time more than half drunk, and much of the time idiotically drunk."

Among White House callers one day came John M. Thayer, a brigadier from Grant's army, who was for special reasons making a trip east. Fixing an earnest and somewhat quizzical look on Thayer, Lincoln asked, "Well, what kind of a fellow is Grant?" Thayer replied that Grant was a real commander, popular with the army, making plans and throwing all his energies into their execution. Thayer said he had had opportunities to observe Grant during two years of service. "It has been charged in northern newspapers that Grant was under the influence of liquor on the fields of Donelson and Shiloh. The charge is atrocious, wickedly false. I saw him repeatedly during the battles of Donelson and Shiloh on the field, and if there were any sober men on the field, Grant was one of them."

"It is a relief to me to hear this statement from you," said Lincoln, "for though I have not lost confidence in Grant, I have been a good deal annoyed by reports which have reached me of his intemperance . . . Delegation after delegation has called on me with the same request, 'Recall Grant from command' . . . One day a delegation headed by a distinguished doctor of divinity from New York, called on me and made the familiar . . . protest against Grant being retained in his command. After the clergyman had concluded his remarks, I asked if any others desired to add anything to what had already been said. They replied that they did not. Then looking as serious as I could, I said: 'Doctor, can you tell me where General Grant gets his liquor?' The doctor seemed quite nonplussed, but replied that he could not. I then said to him: 'I am very sorry, for if you could tell me I would direct the Chief Quartermaster of the army to lay in a large stock of the same kind of liquor, and would also direct him to furnish a supply to some of my other generals who have never yet won a victory.'" Lincoln handed Thayer a friendly slap on the leg, lay back in his chair, had a laugh.

Nicolay and Hay noted that when overzealous people had accused Grant of intemperance, Lincoln's reply was, "If I knew what brand of whiskey he drinks I would send a barrel or so to some other generals." At one time, Nicolay noted, Grant's standing had sunk so low with newspapers, politicians and a large public that Lincoln remarked, "I think Grant has hardly a friend left, except myself."

During June, Grant's army, earlier numbering only about 40,000, was reinforced to 70,000 and more. The plantations of Jefferson Davis and his brother Joseph had been captured and supplies from them lent aid to the Union cause. A world audience was looking on and wondering how many days or months the siege might last.

The marching of Lee with 80,000 Confederate troops up into Pennsylvania, with Meade and the Army of the Potomac trailing him for battle, hoping to stop him, was a bold movement, partly made on the chance that the danger to Northern cities would cause Lincoln and Halleck to draw off troops from Grant to fight Lee. In such event it was believed Pemberton might cut his way out of the seven miles of Union trenches encircling Vicksburg.

In hundreds of caves dug in the clay hillsides of the besieged city, women and children wondered how long till the end. One eyewitness told of seeing a woman faint as a shell burst a few feet from her. He saw three children knocked down by the dirt flung out from one explosion. "The little ones picked themselves up, and wiping the dust from their eyes, hastened on." Said another, "I saw one bright young bride whose arm shattered by a piece of shell had been amputated." Yet these were minor incidents to the thousands whose daily monotonous menu of mule and horse meat with parched corn had run out in latter June. Pemberton, as he had said he would, killed the last dog for food. Then he fed the men of his garrison on rats, cane shoots and bark. Some of the men standing in the firing trenches were wobbly on their legs. Pemberton was obeying instructions from President Davis to hold Vicksburg at all costs.

CHAPTER 33

Deep Shadows—Lincoln in Early '63

IN THE months between Fredericksburg and Chancellorsville, events swirled round the peculiar pivot where Lincoln moved, and put him into further personal isolation. So often daylight seemed to break—and it was a false dawn—and it was as yet night. When hope came singing a soft song, it was more than once shattered by the brass laughter of cannon and sudden bayonets preceding the rebel yell.

Said Howell Cobb of Georgia in early '63: "Only two things stand in the way of an amicable settlement of the whole difficulty: the Landing of the Pilgrims and Original Sin."

The first combat of Negro troops against white had taken place in the Vicksburg area when 1,000 enlisted Union black men defended Milliken's Bend from an attack of some 2,000 Confederates. The fighting was mainly hand-to-hand. General Elias S. Dennis said, "White and black men were lying side by side, pierced by bayonets. Two men, one white and the other black, were found side by side, each with the other's bayonet through his body." As such news spread North it intensified agitation for and against the use of more Negro regiments. In the deepening bitterness General John M. Thayer and others heard Lincoln say his main anxiety was in the North. "The enemy behind us is more dangerous to the country than the enemy before us."

The Richmond Government could not have planted a readier spokesman in Congress at Washington than it had in Clement L. Vallandigham saying that more than 1,000,000 had been called to arms: "Seventy-five thousand first . . . then eighty-three thousand more were demanded; and three hundred and ten thousand responded . . . The President next asked for four hundred thousand, and Congress . . . gave him five hundred thousand; and, not to be outdone, he took six hundred and thirty-seven thousand. Half of these melted away in their first campaign." Should the war go on? "I answer no—not a day, not an hour," shouted Vallandigham. He outlined a plan for the soldiers of both armies to fraternize and go home, while the governments at Washington and Richmond should not even negotiate a treaty of peace.

A peace man of shaded sincerity, Vallandigham of Dayton, Ohio, had the country's eye. His father, a Presbyterian minister, traced directly to a Huguenot driven out of France for religious convictions, settling in Virginia in 1690. His mother was Scotch-Irish. Teaching school at Snow Hill, Maryland, he studied at night; he practiced law in Columbus, Ohio, served in the state legislature and, known as an extreme proslavery man, lost several campaigns for judge, lieutenant governor, member of Congress. Tall, bearded, sonorous, his self-righteousness gave him a personal exaltation: "I had rather that my right arm were plucked from its socket, and cast into eternal burnings, than, with my convictions, to have . . . defiled my soul with the guilt of moral perjury . . . I would that my voice could penetrate the most impenetrable of all recesses, the precincts of the White House." He became specific. "Stop fighting. Make an armistice—no formal treaty . . . Buy and sell . . . Open up railroads . . . Visit the North and West . . . the South. Exchange newspapers. Migrate. Intermarry. Let slavery alone. Hold elections at the appointed times. Let us choose a new President in sixty-four."

More adroit was Wilbur Fisk Storey, publisher of the Chicago Times, a broken-down newspaper he had vitalized and made the voice of the extremist enemies of the Lincoln administration. A Vermont boy, he had been printer's devil, typesetter in New York, and drifting west had edited Democratic newspapers at La Porte and Mishawaka, Indiana. In Michigan he was postmaster at Jackson under President Polk, in two cities had run drugstores, had given eight years to building up the Detroit Free Press, earning $30,000 for himself, and in 1861 at 42 had begun to give Chicago and the Middle West a morning paper that was gossipy, sensational, fearless, devious.

A tight-lipped, short-spoken man, his face whiskered except for the upper lip, Storey cultivated suspicion as a habit. During March '63 the Chicago Times printed items about "the impeachment of the President at the opening of the next session of Congress . . . the crimes committed by the Executive . . . have furnished ample grounds for his impeachment; and every true patriot will rejoice to learn that he is to be brought to punishment . . ."

Without basis or explanation, the New York Day Book, the Chicago Times and like party organs printed the one sentence: "The President's son, 'Bob,' as he is called, a lad of some twenty summers, has made half a million dollars in government contracts." That was the item entire. How or where the President's son made his money, by what particular contracts, was not told or hinted at.

Old Sam Medary was a philosopher, a natural dissenter and fanatic protestant, whose weekly newspaper, the Crisis at Columbus, Ohio, presented the ancient Anglo-Saxon case for personal liberty. Born of a Quaker mother, he was in his editorials eloquently antiwar and consistently held Lincoln all wrong, on the premise that all wars are all wrong.

Bluff, gray-bearded, sincere Sam Medary, 62 years old, could sit at his desk and keep up a running conversation with any visitor as his pen chased along writing an editorial. "Abe Linkin reminds us of a little anecdote we once heard, very foolish and no nub to it," he wrote. Or "If Abe Lincoln is the Government, with his army of official thieves, would it not be an act of patriotism to notify such a Government to skedaddle as soon as possible?" The President's course was "serpentine," said the *Crisis*.

A mob one night wrecked the print shop, smashed the editorial desks, and Editor Medary issued a number blaming soldiers from Camp Chase, egged on by the *Ohio State Journal* editor, whom he characterized as "dirty pup," "hired pimp," "daily associate of burglars," "gloating hyena"; the Republicans concerned were "idiots and knavish asses."

One morsel of utterance from Lincoln was seized on. Editors and orators of the opposition hurled their strength at Lincoln's fragment in his inaugural address: "Suppose you go to war, you cannot fight always; and when, after much loss on both sides, and no gain on either, you cease fighting, the identical old questions, as to terms of intercourse, are again upon you." They demurred to Lincoln's progressions in styling the Negroes in 1859 "negroes"; in 1860, "colored men"; in 1861, "intelligent contrabands"; in 1862, "free Americans of African descent."

In New York City, Samuel F. B. Morse, inventor of the electric telegraph, headed the Society for the Diffusion of Political Knowledge, sending forth showers of Peace Democrat pamphlets. To a brother-in-law Morse wrote that Lincoln was "weak," "vacillating," "illiterate," "a President without brains."

Northern fleets and armies had shattered and desolated Southern cities with houses mute as dried skulls. This, while in the North many streams of life flowed on as if the war had never been heard of.

Lincoln was "the Baboon President," "a low-bred obscene clown," if you believed the Atlanta *Intelligencer* while Robert E. Lee had with his own hands flogged a slave girl and poured brine on her bleeding wounds, if you believed the Boston *Transcript*. Each side played for hate.

New York Peace Democrats took fresh vigor from their new governor, Horatio Seymour, 53, a man of inherited fortune who had served as mayor of Utica, speaker of the state assembly, lieutenant governor, delegate to national conventions. Seymour shaved his face, liked a muffler of whiskers under his jaws; ringlets of hair circled his bald pate. He called for an end to "the incompetents" at Washington who would never save the nation; he said compromise measures could have prevented the war. The Emancipation Proclamation, Seymour said on taking office, violated the Constitution; to free 4,000,000 Negro slaves, the North would require a military despotism.

Lincoln wrote to Seymour in March '63 a letter so openly friendly that Seymour was suspicious as he read: "You and I are substantially strangers; and I write this chiefly that we may become better acquainted. I, for the time being, am at the head of a nation which is in great peril; and you are at the head of the greatest State of that nation . . . In the performance of my duty, the co-operation of your State, as that of others, is needed—in fact, is indispensable. This alone is a sufficient reason why I should wish to be at a good understanding with you. Please write me at least as long a letter as this —of course, saying in it, just what you think fit." Seymour sent a brother to Washington to convey assurances of loyal support and to protest against arbitrary arrests.

A New York *Tribune* editorial March 25, 1863, noted that politically the war issue dwarfed all others: " 'Tell your brother,' said President Lincoln lately to the brother of a prominent Democratic aspirant to the Presidency, 'that he can not be the next President of the United States unless there shall *be* a United States to preside over.' "

On the last day before a new Congress with new Democratic members would take their seats, a Conscription Act was passed empowering the Government to divide the country into districts with provost marshals and enrollment boards authorized to raise troops by drafting all able-bodied citizens between 20 and 45.

Debate raged on what the Constitution meant in saying "The . . . writ of habeas corpus shall not be suspended, unless when in cases of rebellion or invasion the public safety may require it." Had the President alone the power to suspend the writ, or did he need Congress to tell him when? This issue would not down. English history and law seemed to favor Parliament as against the King, and Congress as against the President. Lincoln himself had seldom directly ordered arrests of the sort complained of. But Stanton and Seward had, and Lincoln had not interfered.

Seward telegrams would read, "Arrest Leonard Sturtevant and send him to Fort La Fayette," or, "Send William Pierce to Fort La Fayette." Stanton would notify a U.S. marshal that John Watson was in Boston at No. 2 Oliver Place. "Watch him, look out for the clothes and letters, and seize them and arrest him when it is the right time. Don't let him see or communicate with anyone, but bring him immediately to Washington." Men arrested were charged with treason, disloyalty, inciting or participating in riot, aiding and abetting rebels, defrauding the Government, stealing Government property, robbing the U.S. mail, blockade-running, smuggling, spying, enticing soldiers to desert, aiding and harboring deserters, defrauding recruits of bounty, horse-stealing. The charges went into the records or again they did not.

The terror of secret and arbitrary arrests was softened somewhat by the Habeas Corpus bill of March 3, 1863. The Secretaries of State and of War were directed to furnish courts with names of all persons held as prisoners by authority of the Secretaries or the President. Congress made it clear that control over the habeas corpus writ rested with Congress, yet it directly authorized the President to suspend the writ. This was carefully done so that no appearance was presented of any conflict of authority between the President and Congress.

From house to house enrollers in the spring of '63 took the names of men and boys fit for the Army. Cripples, the deaf and dumb, the blind and other defectives were exempt. So were the only son of a widowed mother, the only son of aged and infirm parents, others having dependents. In a family where two or more sons of aged and infirm parents were drafted, the father if living, or if dead the mother, must say which son would stay home and which go to war. Also anyone having $300 cash, and willing to pay it as "bounty" to a substitute, was exempt and could stay at home and laugh at the war.

Western governors reported the secret Knights of the Golden Circle as disguising itself under various names, with oaths, passwords, rituals and rifles, aiming to encourage desertion, defeat the draft, and protect its members by force. In a few weeks 2,600 deserters had been arrested. Seventeen deserters fortified a log cabin and, provisioned by neighbors, defied siege. Two draft-enrollers were murdered in Indiana; women threw eggs, men rioted with clubs, guns, bricks. In a Pennsylvania county one enroller was forced to quit taking names, another was shot, the sawmill of another was burned. The Molly Maguires, an Irish miners' secret society in Pennsylvania, made resistance; coal operators refused to give the names of leaders to the Government in fear their breakers might be burned; Stanton sent troops to quell the disturbers.

In St. Louis, the Reverend Dr. McPheeters refused to declare himself for the Union; he baptized a baby with the name of a Confederate general. A provost marshal arrested McPheeters and took control of the church. Lincoln studied the matter and wrote to General Curtis: "I tell you frankly, I believe he does sympathize with the rebels; but the question remains whether such a man, of unquestioned good moral character . . . can, with safety to the government be exiled, upon the suspicion of his secret sympathies . . . I must add that the U.S. government must not . . . undertake to run the churches . . . It will not do for the U.S. to appoint Trustees . . . or other agents for the churches."

Illinois had 2,001 deserters arrested in six months. In January the wholesale desertions and fraternizing with the enemy among troops of the 109th Illinois regiment began to look so much like a mutiny that the entire regiment was arrested, disarmed and put under guard at Holly Springs, Mississippi; these were recruits from southern Illinois, from a triangle of land wedged between the Slave States of Kentucky and Missouri. They were disgusted with Lincoln and the Emancipation Proclamation; they had enlisted to fight for the Union, "not to free the niggers." The Democratic majority in the Illinois Legislature prepared bills to restore the habeas corpus writ, to bar Negroes from entering Illinois, and otherwise to oppose the Federal Government. Then for the first time in the history of Illinois a governor prorogued the legislature, disbanded them, ordered them to go home.

Governor Morton telegraphed Lincoln he expected the Indiana Legislature in January '63 to acknowledge the Southern Confederacy. Though the legislature did not go that far, it did return the Governor's message with insults and a resolution saying the policies of Governor Seymour of New York were a better model. Also this Indiana Legislature tried to take military power from the Governor, with the result that the Republican members stayed away, there was no quorum, and the legislature adjourned without appropriations of money to run the state government. Needing $250,000, Governor Morton went to Washington and got it from a fund of $2,000,000 set aside for munitions of war, to be used where rebellion existed or was threatened.

The Knights of the Golden Circle claimed 1,000,000 members. At its height it probably had thousands on its rolls. The army secret service penetrated it, one private soldier joining and becoming Grand Secretary for the State of Kentucky. The Government kept informed, guarded against upheavals, arrested ringleaders, and convicted them whenever possible. Naturally, too, some of the spies and informers reported men they personally hated, paid off old grudges. Also some officials credentialed from Washington used their powers like fools and petty tyrants.

The Sons of Liberty, the Circle of Hosts, the Union Relief Society, the Order of American Knights and other oath-bound secret societies of like aims progressed in size. They sometimes bought a storekeeper's stock entire of Colt revolvers, rifles and ammunition. Union men horsewhipped by masked committees in lonesome woodlands at night, Union men shot down in their own homes by Southern sympathizers, had their friends and kin who banded and took oaths. Violence met violence.

Protests of innocence came often from men plainly guilty. They reminded Lincoln of a governor who visited a state prison. The convicts one by one had the same story of innocence and of wrongs done them. At last the governor came to one who frankly said he had committed a crime and the sentence given him was perfect justice. "I must pardon you," said the governor. "I can't have you here corrupting all these good men."

The seething of strife was not eased in the spring of '63 by Order No. 38 issued by General Burnside commanding the Department of the Ohio, with Cincinnati headquarters. Treason, of course, was forbidden, and giving aid and comfort to the enemy. Order No. 38 was positive: "The habit of declaring sympathy for the enemy will not be allowed in this department," thereby making Burnside and his officers the judges of what was "sympathy" and how many times "sympathy" had to be declared to become a habit. They would also decide whether treason hid and lurked in the words of any suspect, Order No. 38 admonishing, "It must be distinctly understood that treason, express or implied, will not be tolerated in this department."

Vallandigham, now out of Congress, went from city to city with his cry: "If it be really the design of the administration to force this issue, then come arrest, come exile, come death itself! I am ready here to-night to meet it." On May 1 at Mount Vernon, Ohio, he rode in a parade four miles long of wagons, buggies, carriages, horsemen and a six-horse float holding 34 pretty flower girls. The *Democratic Banner* of Mount Vernon reported it "a proud and glorious day." On the platform sat Congressmen Samuel S. Cox and George Hunt Pendleton. Vallandigham had practiced for his speech. He gave again his ideas that the Government at Washington was a despotism, had rejected peace offers, was waging war to liberate black slaves and enslave white men; no men deserving to be free would submit to its conscription. Order No. 38 was a base usurpation of arbitrary power; he despised it, spat upon it and trampled it under his feet. The President was "King Lincoln," and he would advise the people to come together at the ballot box and hurl the tyrant from his throne. Applause came often. Vallandigham faced acres of people, thousands beyond reach of his voice. They led him on. His defiance and scorn of the Government ran further than in any previous hour in his career.

Three army captains from Cincinnati, in plain clothes, up close to the platform, took notes and reported to Burnside. Three nights later soldiers arrived and went to Vallandigham's home at three in the morning. Fire bells tolled while soldiers with axes battered down doors, reached Vallandigham, gave him a few minutes to dress, then took him to the train for Cincinnati. A crowd of some 500 moved to the Dayton *Journal,* a Republican newspaper, broke the office windows with bricks and stones, smashed the doors, fired revolvers, put a torch to the building, gutted it.

Vallandigham from a jail cell in Cincinnati issued, without censorship, an address: "I am a Democrat—for the Constitution, for law, for the Union, for liberty—this is my only 'crime.' In obedience to the demand of Northern abolition disunionists and traitors, I am here in bonds today." A military commission tried Vallandigham and sentenced him to Fort Warren, Boston Harbor, till the war was over.

Anger, indignation and high crying rose from many newspapers and partisan Democrats. Burnside telegraphed the President he would resign if so desired. The President replied: "When I shall wish to supersede you I will let you know. All the cabinet regretted the necessity of arresting, for instance, Vallandigham, some perhaps, doubting, that there was a real necessity for it—but, being done, all were for seeing you through with it."

Lincoln's choice now seemed to lie between approval of the sentence or annulment of it. He chose still another course. The order was telegraphed to Burnside: "The President directs that without delay you send C. L. Vallandigham under secure guard to the headquarters of General Rosecrans, to be put by him beyond our military lines; and in case of his return within our lines, he be arrested and kept in close custody for the term specified in his sentence."

Vallandigham issued, without censorship, another address: "Because despotism and superior force so will it, I go within the Confederate lines . . . in vain the malice of enemies shall thus continue to give color to the calumnies and misrepresentations of the past two years." To his wife Vallandigham wrote: "I am as calm and unmoved as ever. Bear it all like a woman—a heroine. Take care of my dear, dear boy till I return. All goes well for the cause."

In Murfreesboro, Tennessee, General Rosecrans gave the prisoner a lecture ending, ". . . do you know that unless I protect you with a guard my soldiers will tear you to pieces in an instant?" Vallandigham replied: "Draw your soldiers up in a hollow square to-morrow morning . . . I will guarantee that when they have heard me through they will be more willing to tear Lincoln and yourself to pieces than they will Vallandigham."

At a house near the farthest outlying Confederate picket line, Vallandigham was left in the early morning by Union officers. At noon an ambulance took him to Bragg's headquarters; messages arrived inviting him to the hospitality of the South. He went to Wilmington, North Carolina, reporting on parole.

Meantime on June 1 General Burnside ordered the Chicago *Times* suppressed. Soldiers from Camp Douglas left the work of guarding Confederate prisoners, marched downtown and seized the newspaper plant. Copperheads made speeches that night to a Chicago crowd of 20,000 people on Court House Square. Mobs threatened to sack and burn the Chicago *Tribune* in retaliation. Senator Lyman Trumbull, Congressman Isaac N. Arnold and other Republicans held a conference with leading Democrats and telegraphed resolutions to the President asking him to revoke Burnside's order.

Lincoln wrote Stanton that many dispatches had been received June 4 "which, with former ones, induce me to believe we should revoke or suspend the order suspending the Chicago Times, and if you concur in opinion, please have it done." And the order which had brought Chicago close to mob war was revoked. The Chicago *Times* again appeared as usual with its customary columns of curses on Lincoln and all his works.

Meantime the state convention of the Democratic party of Ohio solemnly nominated the exiled Vallandigham for governor while tongues raged at Lincoln who had "banished" their leader. On June 12, 1863, Lincoln gave to the country a letter addressed to "Hon. Erastus Corning & others," the resolutions committee of the Albany Democratic convention which had blasted at the administration and demanded Vallandigham's return to freedom. Lincoln's letter covered the main points brought against him as to personal liberty, jails, gags, handcuffs.

As a Chief Magistrate he saw a distinction between peacetime arrests and the jailing of men during a gigantic rebellion. "The former is directed at the small per centage of ordinary and continuous perpetration of crime; while the latter is directed at sudden and extensive uprisings against the government, which, at most, will succeed or fail, in no great length of time. In the latter case, arrests are made, not so much for what has been done, as for what probably would be done . . . In such cases the purposes of men are much more easily understood, than in cases of ordinary crime."

Would a search of history reveal one civil war where the prevailing government had not used individuals with violence and injustice in cases where civil rights were involved? "Nothing is better known to history than that courts of justice are utterly incompetent to such cases. Civil courts are organized for trials of individuals . . . in quiet times . . . Even in times of peace, bands of horse-thieves and robbers frequently grow too numerous and powerful for the ordinary courts of justice. But what comparison, in numbers, have such bands ever borne to the insurgent sympathizers even in many of the loyal states? Again, a jury too frequently have at least one member, more ready to hang the panel than to hang the traitor. And yet again, he who dissuades one man from volunteering, or induces one soldier to desert, weakens the Union cause as much as he who kills a union soldier in battle. Yet this dissuasion, or inducement, may be so conducted as to be no defined crime of which any civil court would take cognizance."

Pointing to the death penalty as a requisite of military organization, he inquired: "Must I shoot a simple-minded soldier boy who deserts, while I must not touch a hair of a wiley agitator who induces him to desert? This is none the less injurious when effected by getting a father, or brother, or friend, into a public meeting, and there working upon his feelings, till he is persuaded to write the soldier boy, that he is fighting in a bad cause, for a wicked administration of a contemptible government, too weak to arrest and punish him if he shall desert. I think that in such a case, to silence the agitator, and save the boy, is not only constitutional, but, withal, a great mercy."

The authors of the Albany resolutions had referred to themselves as "democrats" rather than as "American citizens" in time of national peril. "I would have preferred to meet you upon a level one step higher than any party platform . . . But since you have denied me this, I will yet be thankful, for the country's sake, that not all democrats have done so." The general who arrested and tried Vallandigham, also the judge who denied the writ of habeas corpus to Vallandigham, were both Democrats. "And still more, of all those democrats who are nobly exposing their lives and shedding their blood on the battle-field, I have learned that many approve the course taken with Mr. V. while I have not heard of a single one condemning it."

The President believed that as the confusion of opinion and action of wartime fell into more regular channels "the necessity for arbitrary dealing" might decrease. He so desired. "Still, I must continue to do so much as may seem to be required by the public safety."

To the foregoing a reply was made by Ohio Vallandigham Democrats who called and read it to Lincoln. They asked, "not as a favor," that Vallandigham be given back his rights as a citizen. Their "earnestness" about the Constitution being violated the President in his reply saw as noteworthy and would add: "You claim that men may, if they choose, embarrass those whose duty it is, to combat a giant rebellion, and then be dealt with in turn, only as if there was no rebellion. The constitution itself rejects this view."

He wrote of how "armed combinations" had resisted arrests of deserters, had resisted draft enrollment, and "quite a number of assassinations" had occurred. "These had to be met by military force, and this again has led to bloodshed and death . . . this hindrance, of the military, including maiming and murder, is due to the course in which Mr. V. has been engaged, in a greater degree than to any other cause; and is due to him personally, in a greater degree than to any other one man . . . With all this before their eyes the convention you represent have nominated Mr. V. for Governor of Ohio; and both they and you, have declared the purpose to sustain the national Union by all constitutional means. But, of course, they and you, in common, reserve to yourselves to decide what are constitutional means . . . Your own attitude, therefore, encourages desertion, resistance to the draft and the like, because it teaches those who incline to desert, and to escape the draft, to believe it is your purpose to protect them." He closed in the tone of one at the head of a government: "Still, in regard to Mr. V. and all others, I must hereafter as heretofore, do so much as the public safety may seem to require."

Those who had relatives in the Army read the dispatch three or four times a week in the newspapers: "Two or more deserters were shot this morning." And *Harper's Weekly* inquired, "Instead of wanting Vallandigham back, ought we not rather to demand of the President, in justice and mercy, that a few more examples be made of Northern traitors?"

The President heard from the Peace Democrats in one key, the antislavery radicals in another. Said Wendell Phillips: "I believe that the President may do anything to save the Union. He may take a man's houses, his lands, his bank-stock, his horses, his slaves,—anything to save the Union . . . We need one step further,—an act of Congress abolishing slavery wherever our flag waves . . ." Whose will and wit could be trusted? "None of them—I am utterly impartial,—neither President nor Cabinet nor Senate . . ." It seemed "childish" for the President, "in bo-peep secrecy, to hide himself in the White House and launch a proclamation at us on a first day of January. The nation should have known it sixty days before."

On the slave question: "The President is an honest man; that is, he is Kentucky honest . . . the very prejudices and moral callousness which made him in 1860 an available candidate . . . necessarily makes him a poor leader,— rather no leader at all,—in a crisis like this."

An excited delegation of clergymen, troubled about the conduct of the war, came with protests. The President heard them through and, as the reading public had it from newspapers, he replied: "Gentlemen, suppose all the property you were worth was in gold, and you had put it in the hands of Blondin to carry across the Niagara River on a rope, would you shake the cable, or keep shouting out to him, 'Blondin, stand up a little straighter!— Blondin, stoop a little more—go a little faster—lean a little more to the north —lean a little more to the south'? No! you would hold your breath as well as your tongue, and keep your hands off until he was safe over. The Government is carrying an immense weight. Untold treasures are in their hands. They are doing the very best they can. Don't badger them. Keep silence, and we'll get you safe across."

The New York *Times* took as "one of the deepest sensations of the war" the order of General Grant excluding all Jews as a class from his military department. "The order, to be sure, was promptly set aside by the President but the affront to the Jews conveyed by its issue, was not so easily effaced."

Thousands of Negroes had been enlisted as soldiers in the first six months of 1863. Adjutant General Lorenzo Thomas of the War Department, in the lower Mississippi region in March, reported renewed faith in arming the blacks. He addressed 11,000 troops of two divisions, mentioning the rebels keeping at home all their slaves to raise subsistence for the armies in the field. "The administration has determined . . . to take their negroes and compel them to send back a portion of their whites to cultivate their deserted plantations. They must do this or their armies will starve."

Thomas had gone over his message thoroughly with Lincoln and Stanton. "I charge you all if any of this unfortunate race come within your lines . . . that you receive them kindly and cordially . . . They are to be received with open arms; they are to be fed and clothed; they are to be armed . . . I am here to say that I am authorized to raise as many regiments of blacks as I can. I am authorized to give commissions from the highest to the lowest."

Word had spread of the Confederate Government's order that white officers commanding Negro troops should never be taken prisoner, but put to death. Officers and men listening to the Adjutant General well knew this. "I desire only those whose hearts are in it, and to them alone will I give commissions . . . While I am authorized thus, in the name of the Secretary of War, I have the fullest authority to dismiss from the army any man, be his rank what it may, whom I find maltreating the freedmen . . . This, fellow soldiers, is the determined policy of the administration. You all know full well when the President of the United States, though said to be slow in coming to a determination, when he once puts his foot down, it is there, and he is not going to take it up." The War Department in May '63 announced a new bureau to handle Negro recruiting.

From Port Hudson on the Mississippi June 14 came word that colored troops under General Paine had led an assault, put their flag on a fort parapet amid fearful slaughter, leaving their commander wounded in front of the enemy's works as they retired. A half-mile away on a call for volunteers to go back and rescue the General, 16 stepped out from the colored regiments, moved forward in squads of four. And they brought back their general's body though only two of the 16 Negroes were alive.

A new status of the Negro was slowly taking form. In August '62 for the first time was sworn testimony taken from a Negro in a court of law in Virginia. Also Negro strikebreakers in New York were attacked by strikers, and in Chicago Negroes employed in meat-packing plants were assaulted by unemployed white men. The colored man was becoming an American citizen.

Stories arose that Confederate troops had a law to themselves: "Kill every nigger!" No distinctions would be made in battle as between free Negroes and fugitive slaves. Written petitions and spoken appeals came to Lincoln that he must retaliate: kill one Confederate white prisoner for every Negro Union soldier executed.

Negroes marching to war—with weapons—to kill—and to kill white men—it was at first a little unreal. Longfellow wrote in his diary May 28, 1863, of a visit to Boston: "Saw the first regiment of blacks march through Beacon Street. An imposing sight, with something wild and strange about it, like a dream. At last the North consents to let the Negro fight for freedom."

In an Indiana town, controlled by Copperheads, Sojourner Truth was introduced to speak at an antislavery meeting. A local physician and leading Copperhead rose and said word had spread over the community that the speaker of the evening was a man in woman's disguise; it was the wish of many present that the speaker of the evening should show her breasts to a committee of ladies. Sojourner Truth, tall, strong, unafraid, illiterate though having a natural grace of speech and body, stood silent a few moments. Then she loosed the clothing of her bosom, showed her breasts, and said in her own simple words and her deep contralto voice that these breasts she was showing had nursed black children, yes, but *more white children than black*. The audience sat spellbound. A few Copperheads slowly filed out. Toward one of them who had a look of hate and doubt on his face, Sojourner Truth shook her breasts with the melancholy query, "You want to suck?" And in this atmosphere, the gaunt black woman, the former slave, began her plea for the freedom of her race.

Strange was the play of men's thought and imagination around the Negro and his role. Antislavery journals reprinted from the Memphis *Bulletin:* "A Negro went into a menagerie, in which was a large baboon in a cage. He approached the cage closely while the baboon went through several gyrations, such as nodding and shaking his head, holding out his hands to shake, etc., to the evident delight of both Negro and baboon. Finally, the baboon seemed so intelligent and knowing, the Negro addressed him some remarks, which the baboon only answered by a nod of the head. At length the Negro was still more delighted, and broke forth with the remark, 'You're right; don't open your month, kase if you spokes a word the white man'l have a shovel in your hand in less dan a minit.' "

There came to Lincoln the foremost of fugitive slaves. By authority of the President to Governor Andrew of Massachusetts to raise two regiments of colored men, this ex-slave had led in recruiting the 54th and 55th Massachusetts regiments, two of his own sons in the 54th. Hundreds of black men of the 54th, and their white colonel, had been killed assaulting a fort in South

Carolina, the white colonel's body resting, as South Carolinians reported, "between layers of dead niggers." And Lincoln held his first conference on important business of state with a mulatto, Frederick Douglass. Born in Maryland of a black slave mother, his father a white man, Douglass had grown up as a plantation boy living through winters without shoes or stockings. He grew to a superb physical strength, worked in shipyards as a calker, and learned to read. In the red shirt and bandanna of a sailor, with papers loaned to him by a free Negro, he rode out of Baltimore on a railroad train. In New York he recognized on Broadway another escaped slave, who told him to stay away from all Negroes, as there were informers among them who would send him back where he came from for a few dollars' reward. Then Douglass met abolitionists who paid his way to New Bedford, where he worked at his trade of calker.

Antislavery men noticed he was a natural orator and sent him from city to city to tell of his life as a slave. He had sent word to a free black woman in Maryland, who came North, married him and they made a home in Rochester, New York, where in the cellar they once had 11 runaway Negroes.

Douglass read Lincoln as completely mistaken in his Negro colonization policy. "The colored race can never be respected anywhere till they are respected in America." According to Douglass, the President listened with patience and silence, was serious, even troubled. To the point that colored soldiers ought to receive the same wages as white soldiers, the President said that employment of colored soldiers at all was a great gain to the colored people; that the wisdom of making colored men soldiers was still doubted; that their enlistment was a serious offense to popular prejudice; that they had larger motives for being soldiers than white men; that they ought to be willing to enter the service upon any conditions; that the fact they were not to receive the same pay as white soldiers seemed a necessary concession to smooth the way to their employment as soldiers, but that ultimately they would receive the same pay as whites.

On the second point, that colored prisoners should receive the same protection and be exchanged as readily and on the same terms as white prisoners, and that there should be retaliation for the shooting or hanging of colored prisoners, the President said the case was more difficult. Retaliation was a terrible remedy—once begun, no telling where it would end; that if he could get hold of the Confederate soldiers who had been guilty of treating colored soldiers as felons, he could easily retaliate, but the thought of hanging men for a crime perpetrated by others was revolting to his feelings. "In all this," noted Douglass, "I saw the tender heart of the man rather than the stern warrior and Commander-in-Chief of the American army and navy, and while I could not agree with him, I could but respect his humane spirit."

On the third point, that colored soldiers who performed great and uncommon service on the battlefield should be rewarded by distinction and promotion precisely as were white soldiers, the President had less difficulty, though he did not absolutely commit himself, simply saying he would sign any commissions for colored soldiers which his Secretary of War should commend to him. "Though I was not entirely satisfied with his views," noted

Douglass, "I was so well satisfied with the man and with the educating tendency of the conflict, I determined to go on with the recruiting."

In an interlude of their talk Lincoln asked, "Who is this Phillips who has been pitching into me?" adding later: "Well, tell him to go on. Let him make the people willing to go in for emancipation; and I'll go with them."

From Memphis early in '63 Charles A. Dana reported to the War Department "a mania for sudden fortunes made in cotton, raging in a vast population of Jews and Yankees." Under Federal permits they bought cotton low from Southern planters and sold high to New England textile works. Dana himself had put in $10,000, gone into partnership with a cotton expert, and was in line to make a fortune, yet he wrote to Stanton, "I should be false to my duty did I . . . fail to implore you to put an end to an evil so enormous, so insidious."

Grant agreed with Stanton; the cotton trade was corrupting in and out of the Army; the profits of it should go to the Government. Dana arrived in Washington, had many conversations with Lincoln and Stanton. The President in March issued a proclamation outlawing all commercial intercourse with insurrectionary states except under Treasury Department regulations. One public sale by an army quartermaster of 500 bales of cotton confiscated by Grant at Oxford and Holly Springs, Mississippi, brought over $1,500,000 cash, nearly paying the cost of Grant's supplies and stores burned by the enemy at Oxford.

A war prosperity was on, gold rising in price, paper money getting cheaper. Amos A. Lawrence, humanitarian millionaire merchant of Boston, wrote to Sumner: "Cheap money makes speculation, rising prices and rapid fortunes, but it will not make patriots. Volunteers will not be found for the army when paper fortunes are so quickly made at home; and drafting will be resisted . . . We must have Sunday all over the land, instead of feasting and gambling."

A New York *World* editorial writer saw a new moneyed class attaining domination: ". . . This is the age of shoddy. The new brown-stone palaces on Fifth Avenue, the new equipages at the Park, the new diamonds which dazzle unaccustomed eyes, the new silks and satins which rustle overloudly, as if to demand attention, the new people who live in the palaces, and ride in the carriages, and wear the diamonds and silks—all are shoddy. From devil's dust they sprang, and unto devil's dust they shall return. They set or follow the shoddy fashions, and fondly imagine themselves à la mode de Paris, when they are only à la mode de shoddy . . . Six days in the week they are shoddy business men. On the seventh day they are shoddy Christians."

Food prices had slowly gone up; clothes, house rent, coal, gas, cost more. This pressure on workingmen brought an agitation in New York that resulted in new trade-unions. The *World* reported a mass meeting in Cooper Union with the building crammed to capacity and hundreds waiting outside. Nearly all trades were represented, and resolutions were adopted unanimously pointing to wage rates inadequate to the cost of living and urging all trades to organize and send delegates to a central body.

In spite of corruption and chicanery, an economic system of new factors was getting deep rootholds. Colt's firearms factory at Hartford, Connecticut, declared a 30 per cent dividend for 1862. Aspinwall, Vanderbilt, Drew, Gould and others foresaw, once the war ended, an era of money-making, speculations and developments, individual fortunes to surpass by far any reckonings of finance in the former generation. Immigration was bringing to American shores a supply of workers that would result in a labor market more than requisite to the needs of capitalist industry.

The National Bank Act of February '63 was presented as a device to get money to run the war, while gaining stability in currency through co-operation with the bankers, bondholders and business interests having cash and resources. Therefore it stipulated gold payment of interest on bonds. Five or more persons, under the National Bank Act, could associate and form a bank having capital of $50,000 or more. On depositing in the U.S. Treasury interest-bearing bonds to the amount of one-third of the paid-in capital of the bank, the Government would engrave money for them, National Bank certificates, to the amount of 90 per cent of the par value of the bonds deposited. The banks would use these new certificates for carrying on a regular banking business, receiving the full profit as though they were the bank's own notes. Also the banks would receive, from the Government, interest payment in gold on the bonds deposited in the Treasury.

Thus the double profit of banker's interest on Government guaranteed and supervised money issues, and the gold-paid interest on bonds, was the inducement by which Chase, with Lincoln's complete endorsement, proposed to rally cash resources to the war for the Union. Also the aim was to bring order out of chaos in currency. Across the country were in circulation more than 8,300 sorts of paper money of solvent banks, according to one financial writer, while the issues of fraudulent, broken and worthless banks brought the total up to more than 13,000.

"Shinplasters" was the nickname for much of this mongrel money; once a soldier had used them as plasters for a wounded shinbone. Bills of the banks of one state found no circulation in another. A traveler passing through several states might have to change his money several times, pay heavy discounts and sometimes commissions. Of Government greenbacks $175 would buy $100 of gold money, perhaps moving toward the time Chase had in mind when he said earlier, "The war must go on until the rebellion is put down, if we have to put out paper until it takes a thousand dollars to buy a breakfast." Chase had urged the National Bank Act as "a firm anchorage to the Union of States," which would "reconcile as far as practicable the interests of existing institutions with those of the whole people." Lincoln in his December '62 message to Congress advocated its passage.

A Republican element, holding the view of Thaddeus Stevens that it was a moneylender's measure, unjust to the debtor class, had little to say by way of criticism, waited to see if it would bring in the war funds promised while also, as Lincoln hoped, operating to "protect labor against the evils of a vicious currency." From opposition Democrats, few in number and influence, an outcry arose that the new national banking system would create a more insidious centralization of money power than the old Bank of the United States which Andrew Jackson had destroyed.

In these financial matters, Nicolay and Hay noted, "Mr. Chase had the constant support of the President," who sometimes made suggestions but did not insist on their being adopted. When the Secretary needed his help with Congress, the President gave it ungrudgingly to the one department of the Government where he was least expert.

A committee of New Yorkers asked the President for a gunboat to protect their city. Lincoln was puzzled. The committee were introduced as "gentlemen representing $100,000,000 in their own right." Lincoln heard them through, and in his speech, as Lawrence Weldon heard it, said: ". . . It is impossible for me, in the condition of things, to furnish you a gun-boat. The credit of the Government is at a very low ebb. Greenbacks are not worth more than 40 or 50 cents on the dollar, and in this condition of things, if I was worth half as much as you gentlemen are represented to be, and as badly frightened as you seem to be, I would build a gun-boat and give it to the Government." Weldon quoted one who listened as saying he "never saw one hundred millions sink to such insignificant proportions as it did when that committee recrossed the threshold of the White House, sadder but wiser men."

The spring and early summer of '63 saw Lincoln's rating among large groups of respectable people of influence sink lower than at any time since he had become President. Richard H. Dana, author of *Two Years Before the Mast*, also an able attorney who had managed Government cases in prize courts, wrote in March to Charles Francis Adams in London: "As to the politics of Washington, the most striking thing is the absence of personal loyalty to the President. It does not exist. He has no admirers, no enthusiastic supporters, none to bet on his head . . . He has a kind of shrewdness and common sense, mother-wit, and slipshod, low-levelled honesty, that made him a good Western jury lawyer. But he is an unutterable calamity to us where he is."

One of the three Republican Congressmen—three and no more—who defended Lincoln on the floor of the House was Albert G. Riddle of Ohio. For weeks the denunciations of the President by his own party men had flowed on, mixed with clamor and sniping criticism, Riddle interposing that "the just limit of manly debate" had been "brutally outraged." The press had "caught up and reëchoed" the clamor. If the masses of people should believe what they were hearing, "no power on earth can save us from destruction, for they would shiver the only arm that must bring us safety." Riddle would have them remember: "The war is greater than the President; greater than the two Houses of Congress . . . greater than all together; and it controls them all, and dictates its own policy; and woe to the men or party that will not heed its dictation."

Amid the snarling chaos of the winter of 1862-63 there were indications of a secret movement to impeach Lincoln. Stubbornly had he followed his own middle course, earning in both parties enemies who for different reasons wanted him out of the way. There were radical Republicans who wanted a man obedient to their wishes. There were reactionaries in both parties who hoped the confusion of an impeachment would slow down the war, bring back habeas corpus and other civil rights. Long after this embryo conspiracy had failed of its aim, Cameron said to an interviewer, Howard Carroll, in guarded statements that would implicate neither dead nor living Republicans:

"Late in 1862 or early in 1863 there can be no doubt that a secret effort was made to bring about the ejectment of President Lincoln from the White House . . . I received from a number of the most prominent gentlemen an invitation to visit Washington and attend a meeting . . . to be held in regard to national affairs . . . I went to the capital, and . . . soon discovered that their real object was to find means by which the President could be impeached and turned out of office . . . I was asked for my advice. I gave it, stating . . . that it would be little short of madness to interfere with the Administration."

The talk of a Southern woman spy in the White House arrived at the point where Senate members of the Committee on the Conduct of the War set a secret morning session for attention to reports that Mrs. Lincoln was a disloyalist. One member of the committee told of what happened. "We had just been called to order by the Chairman, when the officer stationed at the committee room door came in with a half-frightened expression on his face. Before he had opportunity to make explanation, we understood the reason for his excitement, and were ourselves almost overwhelmed with astonishment. For at the foot of the Committee table, standing solitary, his hat in his hand, his form towering, Abraham Lincoln stood. Had he come by some incantation, thus of a sudden appearing before us unannounced, we could not have been more astounded." There was an "almost unhuman sadness" in the eyes, and "above all an indescribable sense of his complete isolation" which the committee member felt had to do with fundamental senses of the apparition. "No one spoke, for no one knew what to say. The President had not been asked to come before the Committee, nor was it suspected that he had information that we were to investigate reports, which, if true, fastened treason upon his family in the White House."

At last the caller spoke slowly, with control, though with a depth of sorrow in the tone of voice: "I, Abraham Lincoln, President of the United States, appear of my own volition before this Committee of the Senate to say that I, of my own knowledge, know that it is untrue that any of my family hold treasonable communication with the enemy." Having attested this, he went away as silent and solitary as he had come. "We sat for some moments speechless. Then by tacit agreement, no word being spoken, the Committee dropped all consideration of the rumors that the wife of the President was betraying the Union. We were so greatly affected that the Committee adjourned for the day."

The author of *Uncle Tom's Cabin* came to the White House, and Lincoln, as she related it, strode toward her with two outreached hands and greeted her, "So you're the little woman who wrote the book that made this great war," and as they seated themselves at the fireplace, "I do love an open fire; I always had one to home." They talked of the years of plowshares beaten into swords. Mrs. Stowe felt about him "a dry, weary, patient pain, that many mistook for insensibility." He said of the war, "Whichever way it ends, I have the impression I shan't last long after it's over."

"Rest," he said to Noah Brooks after a horseback ride. "I don't know about 'the rest' as you call it. I suppose it is good for the body. But the tired part of me is *inside* and out of reach."

Lincoln had been daily riding the three miles between the White House and Soldiers' Home, where the family lived through the hot-weather months. Lamon had been urging that the President have a military escort, the President each time laughing it off. One morning he met Lamon. While still on the horse Lincoln said, "I have something to tell you"; they went to the President's office, locked the doors. As Lamon later wrote down the talk of Lincoln, he said he would not be sure of the exact words but was giving them to the best of his recollection: "Understand me, I do not want to oppose my pride of opinion against light and reason, but I am in such a state of 'betweenity' in my conclusions that I can't say that the judgment of *this court* is prepared to proclaim a reliable 'decision upon the facts presented.'" He paused. Lamon: "Go on, go on."

"Last night, about 11 o'clock, I went out to the Soldiers' Home alone, riding *Old Abe*, as you call him (a horse he delighted in riding), and when I arrived at the foot of the hill on the road leading to the entrance of the Home grounds, I was jogging along at a slow gait . . . when suddenly I was aroused—I may say the arousement lifted me out of my saddle as well as out of my wits—by the report of a rifle, and seemingly the gunner was not fifty yards from where my contemplations ended and my accelerated transit began. My erratic namesake, with little warning . . . and with one reckless bound . . . unceremoniously separated me from my eight-dollar plug-hat, with which I parted company without any assent, expressed or implied, upon my part. At a break-neck speed we soon arrived in a haven of safety. Meanwhile I was left in doubt whether death was more desirable from being thrown from a runaway federal horse, or as the tragic result of a rifle-ball fired by a disloyal bushwhacker in the middle of the night."

This was all told in what Lamon termed "a spirit of levity," as though the little affair might be exaggerated in importance. Lincoln seemed to want to believe it a joke. "Now," he went on, "in the face of this testimony in favor of your theory of danger to me, personally, I can't bring myself to believe that anyone has shot or will deliberately shoot at me with the purpose of killing me; although I must acknowledge that I heard this fellow's bullet whistle at an uncomfortably short distance from these headquarters of mine. I have about concluded that the shot was the result of accident. It may be that someone on his return from a day's hunt, regardless of the course of his discharge, fired off his gun as a precautionary measure of safety to his family after reaching his house." This was said with much seriousness.

He then playfully proceeded: "I tell you there is no time on record equal to that made by the two Old Abes on that occasion. The historic ride of John Gilpin, and Henry Wilson's memorable display of bareback equestrianship on the stray army mule from the scenes of the battle of Bull Run, a year ago, are nothing in comparison to mine, either in point of time made or in ludicrous pageantry . . . This whole thing seems farcical. No good can result at this time from giving it publicity . . . I do not want it understood that I share your apprehensions. I never have."

Lamon sat studying a companion who to him had always seemed prepared for the inevitable, for fate, always careless about his personal safety, and at this time not yet recovered from sorrow over the death of his son Willie.

Lamon protested: "The time . . . may not be far distant when this republic will be minus a pretty respectable President."

Death was in the air. So was birth. What was dying men did not know. What was being born none could say.

CHAPTER 34

The Man in the White House

THE WHITE HOUSE or Executive Mansion gave a feeling of Time. The statue of Thomas Jefferson in front of the main portico stood with green mold and verdigris. The grounds during Lincoln's first year had a smooth outward serenity. Yet hidden in shrubbery were armed men and in a basement room troops with muskets and bayonets. Two riflemen in bushes stood ready to cover the movements of any person walking from the main gate to the building entry.

The Charleston *Mercury* reprinted, October 14, 1862, a New York *Herald* item: "The President's life is considered unsafe by many persons here . . . the personal safety of the commander-in-chief ought to be looked after with the utmost diligence." The President held that the only effective way to avoid all risk was to shut himself up in an iron box, where he could not possibly perform the duties of President. "Why put up the bars when the fence is down all around? If they kill me, the next man will be just as bad for them; and in a country like this, where our habits are simple, and must be, assassination is always possible, and will come if they are determined upon it."

Company K of the 150th Pennsylvania Volunteers went on guard duty the first week in September and in a way became part of the White House family, taking care of Tad's goats and doing other chores. "He always called me Joe," said one private. The President asked about their sick, sometimes personally looked after passes and furloughs.

Of many callers and hangers-on, only one was named by Lincoln as a possible assassin, wrote Lamon. Nearing 60, side-whiskered, gray and bald as a buzzard, large of head, paunched of belly, wearing a red flannel vest, a broad-brimmed hat, a flowing blue cape from the shoulders, Adam Gurowski would come into the President's office and give advice in a sharp peremptory tone, his voice tense. Behind large green goggles one good eye glared and blazed, while a sightless one stayed mute and pitiful, as he would snort to people that Lincoln was "the great shifter, the great political shuffler," lacked energy and executive ability, was even "a beast," or "Chase is a thousand times more fit for a President than Lincoln or Seward."

Gurowski was a studied croaker. "The country is marching to its tomb, but the grave-diggers will not confess their crime . . . O God! O God! to witness how by the hands of Lincoln-Seward-McClellan, this noblest human structure is crumbled . . ." He had held a job under Greeley and been let out. His slanderous talk and published slurs on Seward had resulted in his dismissal as a translator from the State Department. As a European republican revolutionary and as a scholar and author of political volumes, Gurowski assumed that the American Republic needed his counsel and experience. At the White House Lincoln kept an eye on him. Lamon wrote he heard Lincoln more than once remark: "Gurowski is the only man who has given me a serious thought of a personal nature. From the known disposition of the man, he is dangerous wherever he may be. I have sometimes thought that he might try to take my life. It would be just like him to do such a thing."

At one of many White House functions the British Minister Lord Lyons had, as required by custom, read a long paper one morning, formally notifying the U.S. Government that a prince of the royal family in England had taken unto himself a wife. Lincoln listened gravely throughout, and the ceremony over, took the bachelor Minister by the hand, then quietly, "And now, Lord Lyons, go thou and do likewise."

The main executive office and workroom on the second floor, 25 by 40 feet, had a large white marble fireplace, with brass andirons and a high brass fender, a few chairs, two hair-covered sofas, and a large oak table for Cabinet meetings. Lighting was by gas jets in glass globes, or when needed, by kerosene lamps. Tall windows opened on a sweep of lawn to the south, on the unfinished Washington Monument, the Smithsonian Institution, the Potomac River, Alexandria, and slopes alive with white tents, beef cattle, wagons, men of the army. Between the windows was a large armchair in which the President usually sat at a table for his writing. A pull at a bell cord would bring Nicolay or Hay from the next room. A tall desk with many pigeonholes stood nearby at the south wall. Among books were the *United States Statutes*, the Bible and Shakespeare's plays. At times the table had been littered with treatises on the art and science of war. Two or three frames held maps on which blue and red pins told where the armies were moving, fighting, camping.

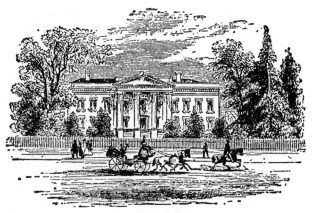

The White House

Once when visitors called to pay respects, a secretary placed papers on a table for signature. The President excused himself: "Just wait now until I sign some papers, that this government may go on." At the finish of an afternoon's work with the secretaries he would say: "Boys, I reckon that'll do. We'll shut up shop for the rest of the day."

The President more than once heard a crying child in the arms of a woman belowstairs and sent word asking what the woman wanted. Or again he might hear a bawling voice, "I want to see Old Abe," or a seeker of a contract orating: "The President must be made to understand, sir, that the eyes of the people are on him, sir! They are watching him, sir!"

A woman demanded a colonel's commission for her son, not as a favor but as a right. "Sir, my grandfather fought at Lexington, my father fought at New Orleans, and my husband was killed at Monterey." She left the office and went down the stairs with a dismissal in her ears: "I guess, Madam, your family has done enough for the country. It is time to give someone else a chance."

The President was at his desk often before seven in the morning, after "sleep light and capricious," noted Hay. His White House bed, nine feet long, nearly nine feet high at the headboard, had bunches of grapes and flying birds carved in its black walnut. Nearby was a marble-topped table with four stork-shaped legs; under its center was a bird's nest of black walnut filled with little wooden bird eggs.

In the earlier days of the administration a digest of the day's news was ready for the President before breakfast at nine o'clock. Then he would usually go over to the War Office, read telegrams, discuss "the situation" with Halleck or Stanton; back at the White House, he would take up the morning mail with his secretaries. Tuesday and Friday were usually for Cabinet meetings. On other days a stack of cards from callers would be sifted for old acquaintances and persons on urgent business.

"On other days [than Tuesday and Friday]," wrote Hay, "it was the President's custom at about that hour [noon], to order the doors to be opened and all who were waiting to be admitted. The crowd would rush in, thronging the narrow room, and one by one would make their wants known." Some came merely to shake hands, to wish Godspeed, others for help or mercy, wailing their woe. Still others lingered, stood at the walls, hanging back in hope of having a private interview.

"Late in the day," wrote Hay, "he usually drove out for an hour's airing; at six o'clock he dined. His breakfast was an egg and a cup of coffee; at luncheon he rarely took more than a biscuit and a glass of milk, a plate of fruit in its season; at dinner he ate sparingly of one or two courses. He drank little or no wine . . . and never used tobacco. He pretended to begin business at ten o'clock in the morning, but in reality the ante-rooms and halls were full long before that hour—people anxious to get the first axe ground. He was extremely unmethodical; it was a struggle on Nicolay's part and mine to get him to adopt some systematic rules. He would break through every regulation as fast as it was made. Anything that kept the people away from him he disapproved. He wrote very few letters and did not read one in fifty that he received . . . He signed, without reading them, the letters I wrote in his name. He wrote, perhaps half a dozen a week himself—not more . . .

The house remained full of people nearly all day. Sometimes, though rarely, he would shut himself up and see no one. He scarcely ever looked into a newspaper unless I called his attention to an article on some special subject. He frequently said, 'I know more about it than any of them.'"

Early in the administration Seward wrote his wife, "The President proposes to do all his work." That did not last long. He learned to detail routine and to assign work to others. "At first," wrote Fred Seward, "when I would take up to the President a paper for his signature, he would spread it out and carefully read the whole of it. But this usage was speedily abandoned, and he would hastily say, 'Your father says this is all right, does he? Well, I guess he knows. Where do I put my name?'" The procedure got him into several tangled affairs. More and more, however, as the months passed the letters and documents were sifted for his attention and signature.

T. B. Bancroft stood for an hour within three feet of Lincoln's desk, waiting to ask for a pass through Army of Potomac lines to visit the son of a friend in the 3d Pennsylvania Cavalry. Bancroft had waited half an hour with about 50 others in the Blue Room belowstairs until the announcement from a colored attendant that the President was ready to receive them, when the crowd rushed pell-mell upstairs into the office. Wrote Bancroft: "Mr. Lincoln sat at the back end of the enclosure . . . a pair of short-shanked gold spectacles sat low down upon his nose, and he could easily look over them." A boy in army blue took the chair, handing his papers to the President, who read them and said, "And you want to be a captain?" "Yes, sir." "And what do you want to be captain of? Have you got a company?" "No, sir, but my officers told me that I could get a captain's commission if I were to present my case to you." "My boy—excuse my calling you a boy—how old are you?" "Sixteen." "Yes, you are a boy, and from what your officers say of you, a worthy boy and a good soldier, but commissions as captains are generally given by the governors of the States." "My officers said *you* could give me a commission." "And so I could, but to be a captain you should have a company or something to be captain of. You know a man is not a husband until he gets a wife—neither is a woman a wife until she gets a husband. I might give you a commission as captain and send you back to the Army of the Potomac, where you would have nothing to be captain of, and you would be like a loose horse down there with nothing to do and no one having any use for you."

The boy began breaking, tears in his eyes. The President put a hand on the boy's shoulder, patting while he spoke: "My son, go back to the army, continue to do your duty as you find it to do, and with the zeal you have hitherto shown, you will not have to ask for promotion, it will seek *you*. I may say that had we more like you in the army, my hopes of the successful outcome of this war would be far stronger than they are at present. Shake hands with me, and go back the little man and brave soldier that you came." The boy stepped away as if he had been home to see a wise and kindly father.

A Washington resident complained that a man with a hand organ disturbed him day and night by grinding out music in front of his house. Lincoln: "I'll tell you what to do. Speak to Stanton about it, and tell him to send Baker [secret-service head] after the man. Baker will steal the organ

and throw its owner into the Old Capitol [Prison], and you'll never be troubled with his noise again."

A farmer from a border county in Virginia claimed that Union soldiers
had taken a horse and a lot of hay from his farm and he would now like the
President to send him to the proper department to have his claims paid. The
President referred him to a claim department, and was reminded of a steamboat running at full speed on a Western river one day when a boy tugged
at the captain's coat sleeve and cried for the boat to stop: "I've lost my
apple overboard."

A young chiropodist, Isachar Zacharie, an English Jew, was introduced,
with the result later that Lincoln wrote a testimonial: "Dr. Zacharie has
operated on my feet with great success, and considerable addition to my
comfort." The satirists had their day, the New York *Herald* saying: "Dr.
Zacharie has made his début on the national stage to cut the Presidential
corns."

Came a full-bosomed woman of rare face and gleam. "I have three sons in
the army, Mr. Lincoln." "You may well be proud of that, madam." "There
were four, but my eldest boy—" and that was all she could say as she passed
on with his low-spoken "God bless you, madam" in her ear.

A fleshy and dignified man, stern and homely of face, entered one day in
swallow-tail coat, ruffled shirt, white cravat, orange gloves. His watch chain
had a topaz seal, his cane a gold head. He looked "ominous," said Lamon,
and gave the President the impression, "I'm in for it now." The conversation
ran on in a chilly way. The visitor, keeping a frozen face, shocked the President with his closing remarks as he was about to leave: "Mr. President, I
have no business with you, none whatever. I was at the Chicago convention
as a friend of Mr. Seward. I have watched you narrowly ever since your
inauguration, and I called merely to pay my respects. What I want to say
is this: I think you are doing everything for the good of the country that
is in the power of man to do. You are on the right track. As one of your
constituents I now say to you, do in the future as you damn please, and I
will support you!" Lincoln almost collapsed with glee. He took the visitor's
hand: "I thought you came here to tell me how to take Richmond." They
looked into each other's faces. "Sit down, my friend," said the President.
"Sit down, I am delighted to see you. Lunch with us today. I have not seen
enough of you yet."

In an interlude of business he got acquainted with a new orderly, asking
name, age, what place he called home, and "Is your mother living? Do you
send her money regularly?"—then meditative talk that it means much for a
mother to have a good son and the mother lives a hard life with a son not
trustworthy and loving. That orderly only a few days before had been
offered $100 for dispatches he carried from the President. He held off till
$200 was paid him, then whipped out a revolver and took the briber pris-
oner, later finding out the briber was a secret-service operative and he as an
orderly was being tested.

Congressman A. W. Clark of Watertown, New York, pleaded for a constituent who had one boy killed in battle, another dying in prison and a
third son sick at Harpers Ferry—the mother at home having gone insane.
The father sat by and wept while the Congressman begged for him to take

the sick boy home, as it might help bring back the wandering reason of the mother. Lincoln listened, asked no questions, and wrote "Discharge this man."

Thus ran a few specimens of the stream of thousands who wore the thresholds of the White House, nicked its banisters, smoothed the door-knobs, and spoke their wants and errands. When told this procedure was wearing on him, Lincoln said these were his "public opinion baths."

In a day's clamor and confusion, Nicolay noted the President saying: "I'll do the very best I can, the very best I know how. And I mean to keep doing so till the end. If the end brings me out all right what is said against me won't amount to anything. If the end brings me out wrong, ten angels swearing I was right would make no difference."

An old Springfield friend after an evening in the White House drawled: "How does it feel to be President of the United States?" "You have heard about the man tarred and feathered and ridden out of town on a rail? A man in the crowd asked him how he liked it, and his reply was that if it wasn't for the honor of the thing, he would much rather walk."

"Who has been abusing me in the Senate today?" he asked Senator Morrill in his office one day. The Senator hoped none of them were abusing him knowingly and willfully. "Oh, well," said Lincoln, "I don't mean that. Personally you are all very kind—but I know we do not all agree as to what this administration should do and how it ought to be done . . . I do not know but that God has created some one man great enough to comprehend the whole of this stupendous crisis from beginning to end, and endowed him with sufficient wisdom to manage and direct it. I confess I do not fully understand and foresee it all. But I am placed where I am obliged to the best of my poor ability to deal with it. And that being the case, I can only go just as fast as I can see how to go."

Seward mentioned to his son that he had known people to arrive early and sleep for hours in the hall of the White House waiting to interview the President. Writhing under the grind once, the President told General Schenck, "If to be the head of Hell is as hard as what I have to undergo here, I could find it in my heart to pity Satan himself."

The military telegraph office at the War Department was for Lincoln both a refuge and a news source. The bonds were close between Lincoln and David Homer Bates, manager of the office, and the chief of staff, Thomas T. Eckert. The President was more at ease among the telegraph operators than amid the general run of politicians and office seekers. Bates noted that Lincoln carried in his pocket at one time a well-worn copy in small compass of *Macbeth* and *The Merry Wives of Windsor*, from which he read aloud. "On one occasion," said Bates, "I was his only auditor and he recited several passages to me with as much interest apparently as if there had been a full house." Occasionally he questioned the omission of certain passages of a Shakespeare play as acted.

At a large flat-topped desk Lincoln went through flimsies of telegrams received. When he got to the bottom of the new telegrams, and began again reading important ones he had sifted out for second and more careful reading, he often said, "Well, I guess I have got down to the raisins." Operator

A. B. Chandler asked what this meant, which brought the story of a little girl who often overate of raisins, and one day followed the raisins with many other goodies. It made her sick; she began vomiting, and after a time the raisins began to come up. She gasped and looked at her mother. "Well, I will be better now, I guess, for I have got down to the raisins."

In this telegraph room Lincoln had first heard of the killing of Ellsworth, of the first and second Bull Run routs, of the Seven Days' battles and McClellan's cry for help at Harrison's Landing, of the *Monitor* crippling the *Merrimac*, of the Antietam shaded victory, of Burnside and Hooker failing at Fredericksburg and Chancellorsville, of blood "up to the bridles of horses," of Lee moving his army far up in Pennsylvania toward Gettysburg. Here Lincoln received a telegram about a skirmish in Virginia where "opposing troops fought the enemy to a standstill," which reminded him of two dogs barking through a fence, continuing their barking until they came to a gate, when both ran off in opposite directions. Here he quoted from Petroleum V. Nasby: "Oil's well that ends well"; and after one of McClellan's peninsular defeats, from Orpheus C. Kerr: "Victory has once again perched upon the banners of the conquerors."

An official letter on one desk had the signature of John Wintrup, operator at Wilmington, written with extraordinary and sweeping flourishes; Lincoln's eye caught it. "That reminds me of a short-legged man in a big overcoat, the tail of which was so long that it wiped out his footprints in the snow."

A dispatch from General Schenck reported a skirmish in Virginia and 30 prisoners taken, all armed with Colt's revolvers. Lincoln read it and with a twinkle of eye said to the operator that with customary newspaper exaggeration of army news they might be sure in the next day's prints that "all the little Colt's revolvers would have grown into horse-pistols."

A message from a part of McClellan's command once reported that Union pickets still held Ball's Cross Roads and "no firing had been heard *since* sunset." The President asked if any firing had been heard *before* sunset, and the answer being that none was reported, he laughed about the man who spoke of a supposed freak of nature, "The child was *black* from his hips *down*," and on being asked the color from the hips *up*, replied, "Why, *black*, of course."

Mrs. Lincoln had, inevitably, become a topic. "I went to the reception at Mrs. Eames'," wrote Charles Francis Adams, Jr. "If the President caught it at dinner, his wife caught it at the reception. All manner of stories about her were flying around; she wanted to do the right thing, but not knowing how, was too weak and proud to ask; she was going to put the White House on an economical basis, and, to that end, was about to dismiss 'the help' as she called the servants; some of whom, it was asserted, had already left because 'they must live with gentlefolks'; she had got hold of newspaper reporters and railroad conductors, as the best persons to go to for advice and direction. Numberless stories of this sort were current."

Her hand was in squabbles over who should have post offices and West Point cadetships. While the President was steering a delicate course trying to hold his Cabinet together, she wrote October 4, 1862, to James Gordon

Bennett, whose editorials were clamoring for a Cabinet shake-up: "From all parties the cry for a 'change of cabinet' comes. I hold a letter, just received from Governor Sprague [of Rhodᵣ Island], in my hand, who is quite as earnest as you have been on the subject."

She had been pleased rather than troubled that the New York *Herald* printed two and three columns a day about her arrival at the Long Branch beach resort, her baggage, accommodations, companions, visits, amusements, toilets, gowns, seclusions. "Mrs. Lincoln, looking like a queen in her long train and magnificent coronet of flowers, stood near the centre of the room, surrounded by a brilliant suite, bowing as the ladies were presented to her . . . Before her, forming a sort of semi-circle, were a number of gentlemen, dressed *en règle,* in all the glory of fine black suits and heavy white neckties."

Bonnet gossip by a correspondent who signed merely "Burleigh" ran in several newspapers. "A number of cities are contending for the honor of furnishing a hat for the head that reclines on Abraham's bosom . . . In New York from Canal to Fourteenth, from Philadelphia to Bangor, can be seen on exhibition a 'Bonnet for Mrs. President Lincoln.' These establishments send on and notify Mrs. Lincoln that they have a love of a bonnet, which they are desirous to present to her as a testimonial of their loyalty and great regard for her personally. The amiable and kind-hearted lady of the White House (for such she is) condescends to accept the gift, and at once 'Mrs. Lincoln's Hat' is on exhibition and crowds flock to see it. And such a hat! a condensed milliner's stock in trade, arched high enough to admit a canal boat under it, scalloped, fluted and plaited."

"Her manner was too animated, her laugh too frequent," wrote a woman. Congressman Washburne, entirely friendly to Lincoln, wrote to his wife, "Mrs. Lincoln came last night; I shall not express my opinion of her until I see you." John Lothrop Motley wrote to Mrs. Motley that he found her "youngish, with very round white arms, well dressed, chatty enough, and if she would not, like all the South and West, say 'Sir' to you every instant, as if you were a royal personage, she would be quite agreeable." Welles wrote in his diary: "Mrs. Lincoln has the credit of excluding Judd of Chicago from the Cabinet."

On New Year's Day, 1863, Browning rode in her carriage. "Mrs. Lincoln told me she had been, the night before, with Old Isaac Newton, out to Georgetown, to see a Mrs. Laury, a spiritualist and she had made wonderful revelations to her about her little son Willy who died last winter, and also about things on the earth. Among other things she revealed that the cabinet were all enemies of the President, working for themselves, and that they would have to be dismissed."

Her conversation and letters had much to do with executive details, as in writing, "Nicolay told me, that Caleb Smith said to him, a few days since that he had just received a letter from Kellogg, of Cincinnati that he did not know why he had received his appointment as consul. Is not the idea preposterous?" To Murat Halstead, the Cincinnati editor who in private letters referred to her as silly and vain, she sent information: "I write you in great haste to say that after all the excitement General Banks is to be returned to his command at New Orleans, and the great Nation will be comforted with the idea that he *is* not to be in the Cabinet."

When she took her boys to Niagara Falls and returned, when she stopped at the Metropolitan Hotel in New York and shopped at the big stores, it was chronicled from day to day. *Leslie's Weekly* gave brief items: "Mrs. Lincoln held a brilliant levee at the White House on Saturday evening. She was superbly dressed." Once *Leslie's* had the one-sentence item: "The reports that Mrs. Lincoln was in an interesting condition are untrue."

The run of press items about Southern relatives was steady. One day: "New Orleans papers state that D. H. Todd, brother-in-law of Mr. Lincoln, has been appointed a lieutenant in the Confederate army." Another day: "The Rebel officer who called the roll of our prisoners at Houston is Lieutenant Todd, a brother of the wife of President Lincoln. He is tall, fat, and savage against the 'Yankees.'" Or again: "Eleven second cousins of Mrs. Lincoln are members of the Carolina Light Dragoons of the Confederate forces."

One summer day in '63 Mrs. Lincoln's carriage horses ran away. "She threw herself out of her carriage," reported a newspaper. "Fortunately no bones were broken, and after some restoratives she was taken to her residence." The husband and father telegraphed Robert at Harvard: "Don't be uneasy. Your mother very slightly hurt by fall."

Mrs. Lincoln visited hospitals, gave time and care to sick and wounded. She interceded with General McClellan, won pardon for a soldier ordered shot. McClellan in letters referred to her as "Mrs. President." From several dressmakers who applied she had chosen the comely mulatto woman, Mrs. Elizabeth Keckley, who once had been dressmaker to the wife of Jefferson Davis. The first spring and summer 15 new dresses were made, and as time passed Mrs. Lincoln felt a rare loyalty and spirit of service in Elizabeth Keckley, giving her trust and confidence not offered to others.

Away on frequent shopping trips to New York or Philadelphia, she had telegrams from her husband: "Do not come on the night train. It is too cold. Come in the morning." Or: "Your three despatches received. I am very well, and am glad to hear that you and Tad are so." Or the domestic news that he was "tolerably well" and "have not rode out much yet, but have at last got new tires on the carriage wheels, and perhaps shall ride out soon now." Gossip once had it that when they first entered a White House carriage he had grinned. "Well, mother, this is just about the slickest glass hack in town, isn't it?"

In diary and letters John Hay used the nicknames "Tycoon" and "The Ancient" for Lincoln. Mrs. Lincoln was "Madame," and occasionally the "Hellcat" who could become more "Hell-cattical day by day." The secretaries could not always agree with her opinion that wages specified for an unfilled position in the White House might be handed to her directly. She questioned whether the Government or the secretaries should pay for the grain of the secretaries' horses in the White House stables. The two secretaries eventually were to find it more comfortable to move from the White House and lodge at Willard's.

The boy Tad meant more to Lincoln than anyone else. They were chums. "Often I sat by Tad's father reporting to him about some important matter that I had been ordered to inquire into," wrote Charles A. Dana, "and he would have this boy on his knee; and, while he would perfectly understand the report, the striking thing about him was his affection for the child." Tad usually slept with him, wrote John Hay. Often late at night the boy came to the President's office: "He would lie around until he fell asleep, and Lincoln would shoulder him and take him off to bed."

"Tad" was short for Tadpole, a wriggler, nervous, active. With a defective palate, his occasional "papa dear" sounded more like "pappy day." He could burst into the President's office and call out what he wanted. Or again Tad would give three sharp raps and two slow thumps on the door, three dots and two dashes he had learned in the war telegraph office. "I've got to let him in," Lincoln would say, "because I promised never to go back on the code."

A party of Boston ladies one day admired the velvet carpet, plush upholstery, mahogany furniture and pompous chandeliers of the East Room. The air was quiet, dignified. Then a slam-bang racket, a shrill voice, "Look out there!"—and young Tad came through flourishing a long whip, driving two goats hitched tandem to a kitchen chair. These goats figured in telegrams to Mrs. Lincoln, away with Tad on a visit: "Tell Tad the goats and father are very well, especially the goats." To "My dear Wife" in August '63 Lincoln wrote of weather and politics and to "tell dear Tad" of his "Nanny Goat" lost. "The gardener kept complaining that she destroyed the flowers, till it was concluded to bring her down to the White House. This was done, and the second day she had disappeared, and has not been heard of since. This is the last we know of poor 'Nanny.'"

The boy did things with a rush. "I was once sitting with the President in the library," wrote Brooks, "when Tad tore into the room in search of something, and having found it, he threw himself on his father like a small thunderbolt, gave him one wild, fierce hug, and without a word, fled from the room before his father could put out a hand to detain him." Tutors came and went, Brooks noted. "None stayed long enough to learn much about the boy; but he knew them before they had been one day in the house." Of this the father would say: "Let him run. There's time enough yet for him to learn his letters and get poky."

A Kentucky delegation was held off, couldn't get in. For political reasons Lincoln did not want to meet them. They were half-cursing among themselves when Tad laughed to them, "Do you want to see Old Abe?" They laughed "Yes," and the boy scooted in to his father. "Papa, may I introduce some friends to you?" "Yes, son." And Tad brought in the men whom the President had carefully avoided for a week, introduced them with formality —and the President reached for the boy, took him on his lap, kissed him and told him it was all right and that he had gone through the introductions like a little gentleman.

Tad enjoyed strutting along with Captain Bennett inspecting the cavalry on White House guard duty. The Captain one morning saw the men getting lax and bawled them out. "The condition of the quarters is disgraceful," his voice rasped. "Instead of being kept as they should be kept, they look like—" and while he hesitated Tad shrilled "hell!" For the rest of that day discipline was not so good. Nor again one cold night when the corporal of the guard every half-hour blew a police whistle signaling sentinels to walk their horses fast and change places. This lessened monotony and helped warm men and horses. Tad that night went to the corporal of the guard, asked to see the whistle, took it and ran for the White House. From a second-story window he leaned out and blew it. The men and horses shifted places. Again the whistle and again the shod horses sounding on the cobblestones. For a half-hour Tad kept this up till he had had his fun and then came out and handed back the whistle to the corporal of the guard, along with a bowl of Roman punch from the reception room, where the diplomatic corps was having a party. Thus Robert W. McBride of the guard detail, and others, told of it.

Julia Taft was small and slight for her 16 years, wore long curls, flew from one room to another in a ruffled white frock and blue sash. Lincoln called her "Jew-ly," told her she was a "flibbertigibbet." Once he held a handful of small photographs over her head. "Do you want my picture, Jewly?" She danced on her tiptoes, saying, "Please," and heard, "Give me a kiss and you can have it." The shy girl reached up, he leaned over, and she gave him a peck on the cheek. Into his arms he swept her with, "Now we will pick out a good one."

Another girl playing with Lincoln's big heavy watch asked him if it could be broken. "Of course it can't. Why, little girl, you hit it as hard as you can with a bunch of wool and even that won't break it." He asked a little boy some questions the lad enjoyed answering, patted the fellow on the shoulder, and sent him away with the pleasant but puzzling remark in his ears, "Well, you'll be a man before your mother yet."

Charles A. Dana spoke to Lincoln of his little girl, who wanted to shake hands. Lincoln walked over, took up the girl, kissed her and talked to her. Dana considered it worth mentioning. Important men of high office usually lacked a natural and easy grace in handling a child. With Lincoln, Dana noticed, the child felt easy, as if in the arms of Santa Claus or at home as with some friendly, shaggy big animal dependable in danger.

No child shrank from his presence, it was noted, and the little ones enjoyed him as they might a trusted horse. His face lighted when a little girl walked away after he had bent and kissed her, calling out, "Why, he is only a man after all!" And he knew what was in the heart of another he took on his lap in his office; as he chatted with her she called to her father, "Oh, Pa! he isn't ugly at all; he's just beautiful!"

Robert T. Lincoln, his press nickname "the Prince of Rails," away at Harvard, never saw his father, even during vacations, for more than ten minutes of talk at a time, so he said. Stepping up to his father at one reception and bowing with severe formality, "Good evening, Mr. Lincoln," his father handed Robert a gentle open-handed slap across the face. The two of them in a carriage one day were halted at a street corner by marching troops. "Father was always eager to know which state they came from. And in his eagerness to know from where they hailed, father opened the door and stepping half way out, shouted to a group of workmen standing close by, 'What is that, boys?' meaning where did they come from. One short, little red-haired man fixed him with a withering glance and retorted, 'It's a regiment, you damned old fool.' In a fit of laughter father closed the door, and when his mirth had somewhat subsided, turned to me and said, 'Bob, it does a man good sometimes to hear the truth.' A bit later, somewhat sadly he added, 'And sometimes I think that's just what I am, a damned old fool.'"

Mrs. Lincoln's afternoon receptions and the President's public levees were held regularly during the winters. Usually twice a week, on Tuesday evenings at so-called dress receptions and on Saturday evenings at a less formal function, the President met all who came. "A majority of the visitors went in full dress," wrote Noah Brooks, "the ladies in laces, feathers, silks, and satins, without bonnets; and the gentlemen in evening dress . . . Here and there a day-laborer, looking as though he had just left his work-bench, or a hard-working clerk with ink-stained linen, added to the popular character of the assembly . . . So vast were the crowds, and so affectionate their greetings, that Mr. Lincoln's right hand was often so swollen that he would be unable to use it readily for hours afterward. The white kid glove of his right hand, when the operation of handshaking was over, always looked as if it had been dragged through a dust-bin." Much of the time the President went through the handshaking sort of absent-minded. "His thoughts were apt to be far from the crowds of strangers that passed before him."

The query came, Why not take a vacation and rest? "I sincerely wish war was a pleasanter and easier business than it is, but it does not admit of holidays." At his desk one day his casual word on the hour was, "I wish George Washington or some of the old patriots were here in my place so that I could have a little rest."

Noah Brooks, somewhat scholar and dreamer, a failure as merchant in Illinois and farmer in Kansas, correspondent of the Sacramento *Union*, writing under the pen name of "Castine" news letters widely reprinted on the West Coast, often had close touch with Lincoln, and wrote of one phase: "I have known impressionable women, touched by his sad face and his gentle bearing, to go away in tears. Once I found him sitting in his chair so collapsed and weary that he did not look up or speak when I addressed him. He put out his hand, mechanically, as if to shake hands, when I told him I had come at his bidding. It was several minutes before he was roused enough to say that he 'had had a hard day.' "

In one news letter the third year of the war Noah Brooks wrote, "The President is affable and kind, but his immediate subordinates are snobby and unpopular." What Nicolay and Hay had done to Brooks, and why he disliked them, Brooks didn't say beyond writing, "These secretaries are young men, and the least said of them the better, perhaps."

The friendship of the President and Noah Brooks steadily deepened. Brooks wrote in one news letter: "It does appear to me that it is impossible to designate any man in public life whose character and antecedents would warrant us in the belief that we have anyone now living whose talents and abilities would fit him to administer this Government better than it has been conducted through the past stormy years by the honesty, patriotism, and far-sighted sagacity of Abraham Lincoln . . ." Brooks was tired of the mud-slinging. Scandalous stories, slanders innumerable, he had heard of Mrs. Lincoln and the President's family, from "loyal people, more shame to them, not knowing the truth of what they repeat . . . Shame upon these he-gossips and envious retailers of small slanders. Mrs. Lincoln, I am glad to be able to say from personal knowledge, is a true American woman."

Out at Soldiers' Home were trees and cool shade, long sweeps of grassy land. In its 500 acres were drives that overlooked the city, the Potomac and wide landscapes. In the birds and the flowers Lincoln had only a passing interest. But there were trees—oak, chestnut, beech—maple and cypress and cedar—and they gave rest and companionship. He was still a kinsman of these growths that struggled out of the ground and sprawled and spread against the sky and kept their rootholds till storm, disaster, or time and age brought them down.

On the way to Soldiers' Home the Lincoln carriage passed through a city where one traveler had commented that everything worth looking at seemed unfinished. In March '63 the public grounds around the unfinished Washington Monument held droves of cattle, 10,000 beeves on the hoof. Shed hospitals covered acres in the outlying suburbs; one of the better they named the Lincoln Hospital.

Into churches, museums, art galleries, public offices and private mansions had arrived from battlefields the wounded and dying. The passing months saw more and more of wooden-legged men, men with empty sleeves, on crutches, wearing slings and bandages.

From a population of 60,000 the city had gone above 200,000. Among the newcomers were contractors, freed Negroes, blockade-runners, traders, sutlers, office seekers, elocutionists, gamblers, keepers of concert saloons with waiter girls, liquor dealers, candy-criers, umbrella-menders, embalmers, undertakers, manufacturers of artificial limbs, patent-medicine peddlers, receivers of stolen goods, pickpockets, burglars, sneak thieves.

Of the new arrivals of footloose women it was noted they ranged "from dashing courtesans who entertained in brownstone fronts to drunken creatures summarily ejected from army camps." One observer wrote: "Houses of ill fame are scattered all through the city. With rare exceptions, however, they have not yet ventured to intrude into respectable neighborhoods. A few of these houses are superbly furnished, and are conducted in the most magnificent style. The women are either young, or in the prime of life, and are frequently beautiful and accomplished. They come from all parts of the country, and they rarely return more than two seasons in succession, for their life soon breaks down their beauty. The majority of the 'patrons' of the better class houses are men of nominal respectability, men high in public life, officers of the army and navy, Governors of States, lawyers, doctors, and the very best class of the city population. Some come under the influence of liquor, others in cool blood."

Beer, whisky, performances of nude or scantily dressed women, brought many a soldier boy into saloon concert halls to awake later on the streets with empty pockets. Into his drinks someone had slipped "knockout drops." At intervals the lower grade of houses were raided by police or provost marshals.

The Washington correspondent of the New York *Independent* wrote in '63: "In broad daylight a few days ago, in front of the Presidential mansion . . . a woman clad in . . . fashionable garments with diamonds flashing from her slender fingers, sat upon the stone balustrade, unable to proceed . . . At last she rose . . . swaying to and fro . . . The carriage of a foreign minister . . . stopped, took in the lady, and carried her to her luxurious home. For the lady is wealthy, occupies a high social position, but she was drunk in the streets of Washington."

The high-class gambling houses, located mostly on Pennsylvania Avenue, were carpeted, gilded, frescoed, garnished with paintings and statuary for the players of faro and poker. At the four leading establishments, where introductions were necessary, could be found governors, members of Congress, department officials, clerks, contractors, paymasters. In one place there was the tradition of a Congressman who broke the bank in a single night's play, winning over $100,000. The gambling places shaded off into all styles, ending at the bottom, where smooth-spoken women plied the young infantrymen with drink and played them out of their last payday greenbacks. Colonel La Fayette C. Baker reported to Stanton in the summer of '63 that 163 gaming houses in full blast required attention.

Of the gaudy and bawdy features of Washington, John Hay wrote, "This miserable sprawling village imagines itself a city because it is wicked, as a boy thinks he is a man when he smokes and swears." One diary entry of Hay in the summer of '63 gave a picture: "I rode out to Soldiers' Home with the Tycoon tonight . . . Had a talk on philology for which the T. has a little indulged inclination. Rode home in the dark amid a party of drunken gamblers & harlots returning in the twilight from [erased]."

Walt Whitman, author of *Leaves of Grass*, prophet of the Average Man, crier of America as the greatest country in the world—in the making—wrote to the New York *Times* in the summer of '63: "I see the President almost every day, as I happen to live where he passes to or from his lodgings out of town . . . He always has a company of twenty-five or thirty cavalry, with sabres drawn, and held upright over their shoulders . . . Mr. Lincoln generally rides a good-sized easy-going gray horse, is dress'd in plain black, somewhat rusty and dusty; wears a black stiff hat, and looks about as ordinary in attire, &c., as the commonest man . . . I saw very plainly the President's dark brown face, with the deep cut lines, the eyes, &c., always to me with a deep latent sadness in the expression. Sometimes the President comes and goes in an open barouche. The cavalry always accompany him, with drawn sabres . . . None of the artists have caught the deep, though subtle and indirect expression of this man's face. They have only caught the surface. There is something else there. One of the great portrait painters of two or three centuries ago is needed."

This poet at Fredericksburg saw the mutilated and languishing on blankets laid on the bare frozen ground, lucky if layers of pine or dry leaves were between the blanket and the hard clay. "No cots; seldom a mattress," he wrote. "I go around from one case to another. I do not see that I do much good to these wounded and dying; but I can not leave them. Once in a while some youngster holds on to me convulsively, and I do what I can for him . . . sit near him for hours if he wishes it."

Hearing the screams of men lifted into ambulances, among the cases of diarrhea, pneumonia, fever, typhoid, amid the mangled, among "the agonized and damned," he said they had met terrible human tests, and noted: "Here I see, not at intervals, but quite always, how certain man, our American man—how he holds himself cool and unquestioned master above all pains and bloody mutilations."

In soft weather one moonlit February night Whitman sauntered over Washington: "Tonight took a long look at the President's house. The white portico

—the palace-like, tall, round, columns, spotless as snow—the tender and soft moonlight, flooding the pale marble—everywhere a hazy, thin, blue moonlace, hanging in the air—the White House of future poems, and of dreams and dramas . . . sentries at the gates, by the portico, silent, pacing there in blue overcoats." Another evening he went to the foot of Sixth Street and saw two boatloads of wounded from Chancellorsville put off during a heavy downpour, to lie in torchlight with the rain on their faces and blankets till ambulances should arrive in an hour or two at the wharves. "The men make little or no ado, whatever their sufferings."

A letter for two boys in New York went from him in March '63. "I think well of the President. He has a face like a Hoosier Michael Angelo, so awful ugly it becomes beautiful, with its strange mouth, its deep cut, criss-cross lines, and its doughnut complexion . . . I do not dwell on the supposed failures of his government; he has shown I sometimes think an almost supernatural tact in keeping the ship afloat at all."

A New York lawyer, George Templeton Strong, wrote in his diary of hearing Lincoln say "thar" for "there," "git" for "get," "ye" for "you," "heered" for "heard," "one of 'em," for "one of them," "wa-al" for "well," once hearing the sentence, "I haint been caught lyin' yet, and I don't mean to be." Strong wrote of hearing the President read to a group of men a victory telegram from Pea Ridge, Missouri, and with an undignified elation, the preface: "Here's the dispatch. Now, as the showman says, 'Ladies and gentlemen, this remarkable specimen is the celebrated he-goat of the mountings, and he makes the following noise, to wit.'" Strong wrote, too: "He is a barbarian, Scythian, yahoo, a gorilla, in respect of outward polish, but a most sensible, straightforward old codger. The best president we have had since old Jackson's time." Strong asked mercy for a seaman he believed wrongfully convicted of manslaughter and heard the President: "It must be referred to the Attorney General, but I guess it will be all right, for me and the Attorney General's very chicken hearted!"

One Englishman wrote of his meeting in Lincoln "two bright dreamy eyes that seem to gaze through you without looking at you." Hay said of Lincoln's gaze at one suspicious character, "He looked through him to the buttons on the back of his coat."

An English author, Edward Dicey, recorded an anecdote. "At the first council of war, after the President assumed the supreme command-in-chief of the army, in place of McClellan, the General did not attend, and excused himself next day by saying he had forgotten the appointment. 'Ah, now,' remarked Mr. Lincoln, 'I recollect once being engaged in a case for rape, and the counsel for the defence asked the woman why, if, as she said, the rape was committed on a Sunday, she did not tell her husband till the following Wednesday? and when the woman answered, she did not happen to recollect it—the case was dismissed at once.'" Stories like these, added Dicey, "read dull enough in print, unless you could give also the dry chuckle with which they are accompanied, and the gleam in the speaker's eye, as, with the action habitual to him, he rubs his hand down the side of his long leg."

Nicolay held there were many pictures of Lincoln; no portrait: "Graphic art was powerless before a face that moved through a thousand delicate gradations of line and contour, light and shade, sparkle of the eye and curve of the lip, in the long gamut of expression from grave to gay, and back again from the rollicking jollity of laughter to that far-away look."

Gustave Koerner wrote, "Something about the man, the face, is unfathomable." Congressman Henry Laurens Dawes of Massachusetts said early in the administration: "There is something in his face which I cannot understand. He is great. We can safely trust the Union to him." And later he would remember Lincoln's face as "a title-page of anxiety and distress." His counselors found him "calmer and clearer-sighted" than they. "The political sagacity of no other man was ever equal to that which enabled him to gather around him in earnest support of his administration, rivalries, opposing purposes, conflicting theories, and implacable enmities, which would have rent asunder any other administration. He grew wiser and broader and stronger as difficulties thickened and perils multiplied, till the end found him the wonder in our history. I could never quite fathom his thoughts. But as I saw how he overcame obstacles and escaped entanglements, it grew upon me that he was wiser than the men around him, that the nation had no other man for the place to which he was assigned by the Great Disposer."

A beaming and officious visitor slid into the office one day as Lincoln sat writing and chirruped, "Oh, why should the spirit of mortal be proud?" The President turned a noncommittal face. "My dear sir, I see no reason whatever," and went on writing.

The wearing of gloves for ceremony he regarded as "cruelty to animals," said Lamon, who witnessed Lincoln at a levee trying to give an extra hearty handshake to an old Illinois friend—when his white kids burst with a rip and a snort. The procession of guests heard: "Well, my old friend, this is a general bustification. You and I were never intended to wear these things. They are a failure to shake hands with between old friends like us." And he went on handshaking without gloves. With Mrs. Lincoln he drove to a hotel to get a man and wife, old friends from the West, to take them for a drive. As the man got into the carriage seat alongside Lincoln he was fixed out with brand-new gloves, his wife's doing. So Lincoln began pulling on his gloves —just as the other fellow shed his with the cry, "No! no! no! put up your gloves, Mr. Lincoln," and they rode along and had a good old-time visit. "He disliked gloves," said Brooks, "and once I saw him extract seven or eight pairs of gloves from an overcoat pocket where they had accumulated after having been furnished to him by Mrs. Lincoln."

Meeting a soldier six feet seven, Lincoln surveyed him and asked, "Say, friend, does your head know when your feet get cold?" A strapping cornhusker easily three inches taller than the President had the greeting, "Really, I must look up to you; if you ever get into a deep place you ought to be able to wade out."

The honeymooning midgets, General Tom Thumb and wife, under P. T. Barnum's management, entered the Executive Mansion one evening and stood in a reception room filled with Cabinet members, Senators, generals, Congressmen, others including families unto the smallest children. The couple advanced in what Grace Greenwood saw as "pigeon-like stateliness," almost to the feet of the President: "With profound respect they looked up, up, to his kindly face. It was pleasant to see their tall host bend, and bend, to take their little hands in his great palm, holding Madame's with special chariness, as though it were a robin's egg, and he were afraid of breaking it. He made them feel from the first as though he regarded them as real folks, presented them very courteously and soberly to Mrs. Lincoln."

In the Patent Office Hospital the President, Mrs. Lincoln, Mrs. Abner Doubleday and Noah Brooks visited the patients. Lincoln and Brooks lingered at the cot of a wounded soldier who held with a weak white hand a tract just given him by a well-dressed lady performing good works. The soldier read the title of the tract and began laughing. Lincoln noticed that the lady of good works was still nearby, told the soldier undoubtedly the lady meant well. "It is hardly fair for you to laugh at her gift." The soldier: "Mr. President, how can I help laughing a little? She has given me a tract on the 'Sin of Dancing' and both of my legs are shot off."

In Halleck's office one evening in the summer of '63 Lincoln discussed plans for a joint naval and land attack on Charleston, illustrating gradual approaches of artillery and infantry with three or four lead pencils and pen handles which he arranged in parallels and shifted according to his notions of the strategy. Gustavus Vasa Fox came in, agreed with Lincoln, but Halleck could not see it, and as Lincoln walked home that evening he spoke to Brooks of his discouragement with what he termed "General Halleck's habitual attitude of demur."

Inquiries as to the physical law or mechanical principle that underlay a phenomenon or operation came frequently from Lincoln. "Unless very much preoccupied," wrote Brooks, "he never heard any reference to anything that he did not understand without asking for further information." He would ask, "What do you suppose makes that tree grow that way?" and was not satisfied until he had found out. Or he would take one of his boy's toys to pieces, find out how it was made, and put it together again. Tad had occasion more than once, said Brooks, to bewail his father's curiosity.

The politician, the Executive, the quixotic human being, were inextricable. On board the steamer *Daylight,* which had performed bravely down the Potomac, Lincoln stood where a half-dozen members of the crew brought a tarpaulin to protect him from rain while he insisted on shaking hands with the crew. A fireman in shirt sleeves was the last up, his face and hands sooty and smoked, saying, "My hand isn't fit to give you, sir, but there's not a man aboard loves you more than I do." "Put that hand in mine," cried the President. "It has been blackened by making fires for the Union." Or again on the B. & O. Railroad when a conductor asked him, "Why do you always bother shaking hands with the engineer and fireman, whose hands are always covered with soot and grease?" the answer came, "That will all wash off, but I always want to see and know the men I am riding behind."

When he could not grant a favor, he would generally make an appearance of so doing. A committee requested him to take action in certain claim cases—and he did not want to act. However, it looked like action, and partially satisfied the committee, when he wrote a formal order on Secretary Welles to send him the evidence in the cases. He told Welles later there was no other way to get rid of the callers. An old acquaintance in Illinois, having organized a bank under the new National Bank Act, wrote offering some of the stock to Lincoln, who replied with thanks, saying he recognized that stock in a good national bank would be a good thing to hold, but he did not feel that he, as President, ought to profit from a law which had been passed under his administration. "He seemed to wish to avoid even the appearance of evil," said the banker.

John Eaton was 35, had been superintendent of schools in Toledo, Ohio, had become a Presbyterian minister and as chaplain of the 27th Ohio Volunteers had seen active service in Missouri, twice being taken prisoner and more than once preaching to Confederate soldiers on request of their commanders. "The freedom with which he discussed public affairs with me often filled me with amazement," wrote Eaton. The President spoke one day "quite fully" of the opposition, expressing surprise that there should be so much antagonism to his policy in the ranks of the great abolitionists. The criticism of such men as Greeley and Wendell Phillips was "a great grief and trial" to Lincoln, Eaton believed. "Of a well-known abolitionist and orator," wrote Eaton, "the President once exclaimed in one of his rare moments of impatience, 'He's a thistle! I don't see why God lets him live!'"

Dispatches lay before the President one morning from a Northern governor who in one telegram after another was sending threats and warnings. Lincoln made a few guesses that worked out as he foretold: "Those despatches don't mean anything. The Governor is like a boy I saw once at a launching. When everything was ready they picked out a boy and sent him under the ship to knock away the trigger and let her go. At the critical moment everything depended on the boy. He had to do the job well by a direct, vigourous blow, and then lie flat and keep still while the ship slid over him. The boy did everything right, but he yelled as if he were being murdered from the time he got under the keel until he got out. I thought the hide was all scraped off his back; but he wasn't hurt at all. The master of the yard told me that this boy was always chosen for that job, that he did his work well, that he never had been hurt, but that he always squealed in that way. That's just the way with Governor Blank. Make up your minds that he is not hurt, and that he is doing his work right, and pay no attention to his squealing. He only wants to make you understand how hard his task is, and that he is on hand performing it."

A report having much useless language lay on his desk, the work of a Congressional committee regarding a newly devised gun. "I should want a new lease of life to read this through," groaned the President. "Why can't an investigating committee show a grain of common sense? If I send a man to buy a horse for me, I expect him to tell me that horse's points—not how many hairs he has in his tail."

A big cavalry raid had filled the newspapers and raised noisy enthusiasm, but failed to cut the enemy's communications. Lincoln remarked to Whitney, "That was good circus riding; it will do to fill a column in the newspapers, but I don't see that it has brought anything else to pass."

A young brigadier with a small cavalry troop strayed into Confederate lines in Virginia and was captured. Receiving the report, Lincoln said he was sorry to lose the horses. "I can make a better brigadier any day, but those horses cost the government $125 a head."

To Thomas L. James of Utica, New York, the President said, "I do not lead; I only follow." When the Prince de Joinville asked what was his policy, he replied: "I have none. I pass my life preventing the storm from blowing down the tent, and I drive in the pegs as fast as they are pulled up."

In company with Judge Jesse L. Williams of Indiana, the Reverend Mr. Livingston discussed Lincoln's letter to General Curtis about the Reverend Dr. McPheeters in St. Louis, charged with disloyalty. Said the Judge, "On the trial of Dr. McPheeters by the general assembly of the Presbyterian Church, your letter to General Curtis was read. But the curious part of the affair was this: One party read a portion of your letter and claimed the President was on their side, and the other party read another portion of the same letter and claimed the President was on their side. So it seems, Mr. President, that it is not so easy to tell where you stand."

Lincoln joined in the laughter and was reminded of an Illinois farmer and his son out in the woods hunting a sow. After a long search they came to a creek branch, where they found hog tracks, and signs of a snout rooting, for some distance on both sides of the branch. The old man said to his boy, "Now, John, you take up on this side of the branch and I'll go up t'other, for I believe the old critter is on both sides."

A sense of speech values in Lincoln registered in such degree that he could say of another, "He can compress the most words into the smallest ideas of any man I ever met." Nicolay heard him tell of a Southwestern orator who "mounted the rostrum, threw back his head, shined his eyes, and left the consequences to God."

Robert B. Nay, released from prison on Lincoln's order, came with a letter of introduction co-signed by Senator Reverdy Johnson, on which Lincoln wrote, "I will not say thee 'Nay.'" On an envelope from Salmon P. Chase he wrote, "Nix." On a note from Seward, "What do you say to sending Bradford R. Wood to the Sandwich Islands?" the President wrote, "It won't do. Must have a tip-top man there next time." On a large envelope holding the documents related to a dispute between an admiral and a general as to their crossed-up authorities, the President wrote neatly, "Submitted to Mars & Neptune." After Shiloh a colonel wrote belittling Grant and Sherman, and Lincoln wrote, "Today I verbally told Col. Worthington that I did not think him fit for a colonel; & now upon his *urgent* request I put it in writing."

When Mrs. Gideon Welles mentioned certain malignant reports in newspapers and someone present said, "The papers are not always reliable," Lincoln interjected, "That is to say, Mrs. Welles, they lie and then they *re-lie*." A woman who had asked the President to use his authority in her behalf at the War Department quoted him: "It's of no use, madam, for me to go. They do things in their own way over there, and I don't amount to pig tracks in the War Department."

He was afraid of long speeches and had a fear of sentiment when fact and reasoning had not laid the way for it. His effort at a flag-raising speech before the south front of the Treasury building was one sentence only: "The part assigned to me is to raise the flag, which, if there be no fault in the machinery, I will do, and when up, it will be for the people to keep it up." Suppose the war ran on three years, four, and seemed at no end, what then?

An anxious White House visitor asked that. "Oh, there is no alternative but to keep pegging away."

He could refer to men loyal with "buts" and "ifs" and "ands." The Mississippi Valley was "this Egypt of the West." What was past was past; "broken eggs cannot be mended." To Illinois sponsors of a proposed major general he wrote that "major-generalships are not as plenty as blackberries." The Republican party should not become "a mere sucked egg, all shell and no meat, the principle all sucked out."

A foreign diplomat demurred at Lincoln's condemning a certain Greek history as tedious. "The author of that history, Mr. President, is one of the profoundest scholars of the age. Indeed, it may be doubted whether any man of our generation has plunged more deeply in the sacred fount of learning." "Yes," said Lincoln, "or come up dryer."

In an office cabinet divided into pigeonholes were compartments for correspondence and memoranda. Greeley had a pigeonhole. So did each of several letter-writing generals. And one labeled "W. & W." Brooks was curious about, Lincoln laughing: "That's Weed and Wood—Thurlow and Fernandy—that's a pair of 'em."

Because of the unwanted publicity and the interruptions of politicians and office seekers, Lincoln arranged with managers of two theaters that he could go in privately by the stage door and slip into a stage box without being seen from the audience. "Concealed by the friendly screen of the drapery, he saw many plays without public observation," said Brooks. He saw the notable Edwin Forrest in *King Lear,* and when John McCullough played Edgar, Lincoln asked Brooks, "Do you suppose he would come to the box if we sent for him?" Brooks said the actor would undoubtedly be gratified. And McCullough came, in stage rags and straw, and received discriminating praise and thanks for an evening of pleasure given the President.

Into the White House one day a Congressman brought Jean Louis Rodolphe Agassiz, the world's foremost ichthyologist, authority on fishes, fossils, animal life, glaciers, professor of geology and zoology at Harvard—sometimes referred to as the greatest man of learning in the United States. "Agassiz!" blurted Lincoln to Brooks. "I never met him yet." Brooks started to leave. "Don't go, don't go. Sit down and let us see what we can pick up that's new from this great man."

As Agassiz and Lincoln talked, the conversation did not seem very learned to Brooks: "Each man was simplicity itself. Lincoln asked for the correct pronunciation and derivation of Agassiz's name, and both men prattled on about curious proper names in various languages." Agassiz asked Lincoln if he had ever lectured any, Lincoln having offered some of his speculations on man's discoveries and inventions: "I think I can show, at least in a fanciful way, that all the modern inventions were known centuries ago." Agassiz urged him to finish the lecture. Perhaps sometime he would, Lincoln guessed. The two men shook hands warmly, Agassiz left, and Lincoln smiled quizzically at Brooks: "Well, I wasn't so badly scared after all, were you?" Brooks said it seemed as though Lincoln had expected to be weighed down by the great man's learning. Lincoln admitted to Brooks that he had cross-examined Agassiz on "things not in the books."

Did the President vacillate? Was he managed by others? Men and journals shifted in view. The New York *Herald* in May '63 approved Lincoln's reversal of a court-martial order for the hanging as traitors of citizens of loyal states captured wearing uniforms of Confederate officers. Lincoln had declared them to be merely prisoners of war.

In the President's discussions of peace, said the London *Spectator*, "He expresses ideas, which, however quaint, have nevertheless a kind of dreamy vastness not without its attraction. The thoughts of the man are too big for his mouth." He was saying that a nation can be divided but "the earth abideth forever," that a generation could be crushed but geography dictated the Union could not be sundered. As to the rivers and mountains, "all are better than one or either, and all of right belong to this people and their successors forever." No possible severing of the land but would multiply and not mitigate the evils among the American states. "It is an oddly worded argument," said the *Spectator*, "the earth being treated as if it were a living creature, an Estate of the Republic with an equal vote on its destiny."

At home and abroad judgments came oftener that America had at last a President who was All-American. He embodied his country in that he had no precedents to guide his footsteps; he was not one more individual of a continuing tradition, with the dominant lines of the mold already cast for him by Chief Magistrates who had gone before.

The inventive Yankee, the Western frontiersman and pioneer, the Kentuckian of laughter and dreams, had found blend in one man who was the national head. In the "dreamy vastness" noted by the *Spectator*, in the pith of the folk words "the thoughts of the man are too big for his mouth," was the feel of something vague that ran deep in many American hearts, that hovered close to a vision for which men would fight, struggle and die, a grand though blurred chance that Lincoln might be leading them toward something greater than they could have believed might come true.

Also around Lincoln gathered some of the hope that a democracy can choose a man, set him up high with power and honor, and the very act does something to the man himself, raises up new gifts, modulations, controls, outlooks, wisdoms, inside the man, so that he is something else again than he was before they sifted him out and anointed him to take an oath and solemnly sign himself for the hard and terrible, eye-filling and center-staged role of Head of the Nation.

To be alive for the work, he must carry in his breast Cape Cod, the Shenandoah, the Mississippi, the Gulf, the Rocky Mountains, the Sacramento, the Great Plains, the Great Lakes, their dialects and shibboleths. He must be instinct with the regions of corn, textile mills, cotton, tobacco, gold, coal, zinc, iron. He would be written as a Father of his People if his record ran well, one whose heart beat with understanding of the many who came to the Executive Mansion.

In no one of the 31 rooms of the White House was Lincoln at home. Back and forth in this house strode phantoms—red platoons of boys vanished into the war—thin white-spoken ghosts of women who would never again hold those boys in their arms—they made a soft moaning the imagination could hear in the dark night and the gray dawn.

To think incessantly of blood and steel, steel and blood, the argument without end by the mouths of brass cannon, of a mystic cause carried aloft and sung on dripping and crimson bayonet points—to think so and thus across nights and months folding up into years, was a wearing and a grinding that brought questions. What is this teaching and who learns from it and where does it lead? "If we could first know where we are and whither we are tending, we could better judge what to do and how to do it."

The dew came on the White House lawn and the moonlight spread lace of white films in the night and the syringa and the bridal wreath blossomed and the birds fluttered in the bushes and nested in the sycamore and the veery thrush fluted with never a weariness. The war drums rolled and the telegraph clicked off mortality lists, now a thousand, now ten thousand in a day. Yet there were moments when the processes of men seemed to be only an evil dream and justice lay in deeper transitions than those wrought by men dedicated to kill or be killed.

Beyond the black smoke lay what salvations and jubilees? Death was in the air. So was birth. What was dying no man was knowing. What was being born no man could say.

CHAPTER 35

Gettysburg—Vicksburg Siege— Deep Tides, '63

THE Cincinnati *Gazette* correspondent with the Army of the Potomac chanced to hear Lincoln say, "I tell you I think a great deal of that fine fellow Meade." Meade's father was a merchant, shipowner, U.S. naval agent in Cadiz, Spain. Born in Cadiz in 1815, graduated from West Point, the son took a hand in fighting Seminole Indians, resigned from the Army, worked on War Department surveys, was brevetted first lieutenant for gallantry in the Mexican War, and for five years was a lighthouse-builder among Florida reefs. He married Margaretta, daughter of John Sergeant, noted Philadelphia lawyer, in 1840, and often when away on duty wrote her a letter every day; in these were many references to "Our Saviour," to "the will of God and the uncertainty of human plans and projects," and his own "innumerable sins," which he prayed would be forgiven.

After Meade's appointment as brigadier general of volunteers August 31, 1861, he had seen active and often front-line service in every battle of the Army of the Potomac—except for a short interval of recovery from a gunshot wound at New Market Road on the Peninsula. In camp at Fredericksburg he had told Lincoln he believed the army was gratified with the President's revocation of General Hunter's emancipation proclamation, writing to his wife that the President said, "I am trying to do my duty, but no one can imagine what influences are brought to bear upon me." From camp at

Falmouth he wrote her of "a very handsome and pleasant dinner" with the President and Mrs. Lincoln.

Meade quietly confessed to his wife, by letter: "I have been making myself (or at least trying to do so) very agreeable to Mrs. Lincoln, who seems an amiable sort of personage. In view also of the vacant brigadier-ship in the regular army, I have ventured to tell the President one or two stories, and I think I have made decided progress in his affections." Ten weeks later, however, there crashed on Meade, against his wish, an order he could not disobey, the President's appointment of him to the command of the Army of the Potomac.

Where McClellan most often wrote to his wife that any lack of success on his part must be laid on others, Meade more often was moderate and apologetic, writing to his wife, "Sometimes I have a little sinking at the heart, when reflecting that perhaps I may fail at the grand scratch; but I try to console myself with the belief that I shall probably do as well as most of my neighbors, and that your firm faith must be founded on some reasonable groundwork."

The President on June 15, 1863, issued a call for 100,000 troops—from Pennsylvania 50,000, Maryland 10,000, West Virginia 10,000, Ohio 30,000—to serve for six months unless sooner discharged. The Secretary of War called for help from the governors of 13 states. Thirty regiments of Pennsylvania militia, besides artillery and cavalry, and 19 regiments from New York were mobilized at Harrisburg under General Couch from the Army of the Potomac.

From day to day through latter June the news overshadowing all else in the public prints was that of Lee's army. Far behind Lee now was Richmond and its small defensive force. When he had requisitioned for rations, it was said the Confederate Commissary General replied, "If General Lee wishes rations let him seek them in Pennsylvania." When Lee had been asked about a Union army taking Richmond while he was away, he smiled, it was said. "In that case we shall swap queens." He and his chief, Davis, had decided that "valuable results" might follow the taking of Harrisburg, Philadelphia, Baltimore, Washington; besides immense amounts of supplies, provisions, munitions, there would be European recognition. Men well informed believed that Lee had nearly 100,000 men and 250 cannon, so Simon Cameron at Harrisburg sent word to Lincoln.

Lee's men were in a high and handsome stride. Twice within seven months, though far outnumbered, they had routed, sent reeling, the Army of the Potomac. "There were never such men in an army before," said Lee. "They will go anywhere and do anything if properly led." The English Lieutenant Colonel Fremantle, traveling with the invading army, noted that the universal feeling in the army was "one of profound contempt for an enemy whom they have beaten so constantly."

Fremantle wrote of Hood's ragged Jacks from Texas, Alabama, Arkansas, marching through Chambersburg with cheers and laughter at the taunts of scowling, well-dressed women: "One female had seen fit to adorn her ample bosom with a huge Yankee flag, and she stood at the door of her house, her countenance expressing the greatest contempt for the barefooted Rebs; several companies passed her without taking any notice; but at length a Texan gravely remarked, 'Take care, madam, for Hood's boys are great at storming breastworks when the Yankee colors is on them.' . . . The patriotic lady beat a precipitate retreat." No repartee was flung at a gaunt woman with a face of doom who cried from a window at the passing troops: "Look at Pharaoh's army going to the Red Sea." To a woman who sang "The Star-spangled Banner" at him, General Lee lifted his hat and rode on. From another window a woman gazed at the cool and impressive Lee riding by and murmured, "Oh, I wish he was ours!"

Like a foretokening a girl in Greencastle, "sweet sixteen and never yet kissed," came running out of a house at Pickett's Virginians, her face flushed and her eyes blazing. For an apron she wore the Union flag. And she hurled a *défi:* "Come and take it, the man that dares!" Pickett bowed, sweeping his hat. His soldiers gave the girl a long cheer and a gale of bright laughter.

The Springfield *Republican* urged Lincoln himself to take the field; he was as good a strategist as the Northern generals had proved, and his personal presence would arouse enthusiasm. Lincoln's instructions to Meade ran that not Richmond but Lee's army must be the objective. Meade followed Lee with orders from Lincoln "to find and fight" the enemy. From day to day neither Meade nor Lee had been certain where the other was. Lee would rather have taken Harrisburg, its stores and supplies, and then battled Meade on the way to Philadelphia.

Lee rode his horse along roads winding through bright summer land-scapes to find himself suddenly looking at the smoke of a battle he had not ordered or planned. Some of his own marching divisions had become en-tangled with enemy columns, traded shots, and a battle had begun that was to swirl around the little town of Gettysburg. Lee could draw away or carry on; he decided to carry on.

The stakes were immense, the chances fair. The new Union commander had never planned a battle nor handled a big army in the wild upsets of frontal combat on a wide line. Also 58 regiments of Northern veterans who had fought at Antietam, Fredericksburg, Chancellorsville, had gone home, their time up, their places filled by militia and raw recruits.

One factor was against Lee: he would have to tell his cannoneers to go slow and count their shells, while Meade's artillery could fire on and on from an endless supply. Also Lee was away from his Virginia, where he knew the ground and the people, while Meade's men were fighting for their homes, women, barns, cattle and fields against invaders and strangers, as Meade saw and felt it.

Lee hammered at the Union left wing the first day, the right wing the second day, Meade on that day sending word to Lincoln that the enemy was "repulsed at all points." On the third day, July 3, 1863, Lee smashed at Meade's center. Under Longstreet's command, General George Edward Pickett, a tall arrow of a man, with mustache and goatee, with long ringlets of auburn hair flying as he galloped his horse, headed 15,000 men who had nearly a mile to go up a slow slope of land to reach the Union center. Before starting his men on their charge to the Union center, Pickett handed Long-street a letter to a girl in Richmond he was to marry if he lived. Longstreet had ordered Pickett to go forward and Pickett had penciled on the back of the envelope, "If Old Peter's [Longstreet's] nod means death, good-bye, and

God bless you, little one!" An officer held out a flask of whisky: "Take a drink with me; in an hour you'll be in hell or glory." And Pickett said No; he had promised "the little girl" he wouldn't.

Across the long rise of open ground, with the blue flag of Virginia floating ahead, over field and meadow Pickett's 15,000 marched steadily and smoothly, almost as if on a drill ground. Solid shot, grape and canister, from the Union artillery plowed through them, and later a wild rain of rifle bullets. Seven-eighths of a mile they marched in the open sunlight, every man a target for the Union marksmen behind stone fences and breastworks. They obeyed orders; Uncle Robert had said they would go anywhere and do anything. As men fell their places were filled, the ranks closed up. As officers tumbled off horses it was taken as expected in battle. Perhaps half who started reached the Union lines surmounting Cemetery Ridge. Then came cold steel, the bayonet, the clubbed musket. The strongest and last line of the enemy was reached. "The Confederate battle flag waved over his defences," said a Confederate major, "and the fighting over the wall became hand to hand, but more than half having already fallen, our line was too weak to rout the enemy."

Meade rode up white-faced to hear it was a repulse and cried, "Thank God!" Lee commented: "They deserved success as far as it can be deserved by human valor and fortitude. More may have been required of them than they were able to perform." To one of his colonels Lee said, "This has been a sad day for us, a sad day, but we cannot expect always to gain victories." As a heavy rainfall came on the night of July 4 Lee ordered a retreat toward the Potomac.

Meade was seen that day sitting in the open on a stone, his head in his hand, willing it should rain, thankful that his army had, as he phrased it, driven "the invaders from our soil." For three days and nights Meade wasn't out of his clothes, took only snatches of sleep, while he had spoken the controlling decisions to his corps commanders in the bloodiest battle of modern warfare up till that time. Tabulations ran that the Union army lost 23,000 killed, wounded and missing, the Confederate army 28,000. Pickett came out of it alive to write his Virginia girl, "Your soldier lives and mourns and but for you, he would rather, a million times rather, be back there with his dead to sleep for all time in an unknown grave."

One tree in line of fire had 250 bullets in it, another tree 110. Farmer Rummel's cow lane was piled with 30 dead horses. Farmer Rummel found two cavalrymen who had fought afoot, killed each other and fallen with their feet touching, each with a bloody saber in his hand. A Virginian and a 3d Pennsylvania man had fought on horseback, hacking each other's head and shoulders with sabers; they clinched and their horses ran out from under them; they were found with stiff and bloody fingers fastened in each other. The peg-leg Confederate General Ewell, struck by a bullet, had chirped merrily to General John B. Gordon, "It don't hurt a bit to be shot in a wooden leg."

The brave and able General John F. Reynolds, who had once peremptorily refused Lincoln's offer of command of the Army of the Potomac, felt a bullet sink into his neck, called to his men, "Forward! for God's sake, forward!" and fell into the arms of a captain with the words, "Good God, Wilcox, I am killed."

Confederate bayonets had taken Union cannon and Union bayonets had retaken the cannon. Round Top, Little Round Top, Culp's Hill, rang with the yells of men shooting and men shot. Meadows of white daisies were pock-marked by horse hoofs. Dead and wounded lay scattered in rows, in little sudden piles. The first battle of the war fought outside a Slave State was over. Lee could have managed it better. So could Meade. The arguments began.

Meade issued an order thanking the Army of the Potomac for glorious results: "An enemy superior in numbers and flushed with the pride of a successful invasion, attempted to overcome and destroy this Army. Utterly baffled and defeated, he has now withdrawn from the contest . . . The Commanding General looks to the Army for greater efforts to drive from our soil every vestige of the presence of the invader."

On the wall map in his office, Lincoln had watched the colored pins as they changed to indicate military positions. Zach Chandler came in, spoke of painful anxiety because the fate of the nation seemed to hang in the balance, noted "the restless solicitude of Mr. Lincoln, as he paced up and down the room, reading despatches, soliloquizing, and often stopping to trace positions on the map."

The President announced to the country July 4 that news had arrived up to 10 P.M. July 3 such as to cover with honor the Army of the Potomac, to promise great success to the cause of the Union, and to claim condolence for the many gallant fallen. "For this he especially desires that on this day He whose will, not ours, should ever be done be everywhere remembered and reverenced with profoundest gratitude."

Fry of the Adjutant General's office had noticed Lincoln clinging to the War Office and devouring every scrap of news as it came over the wires. "I saw him read General Meade's congratulatory order to the Army of the Potomac. When he came to the sentence about 'driving the invaders from our soil,' an expression of disappointment settled upon his face, his hands dropped upon his knees, and in tones of anguish he exclaimed, ' "Drive the *invaders* from our soil." My God! Is that all?' "

Lincoln sent from Soldiers' Home a telegram to Halleck saying he had left the telegraph office "a good deal dissatisfied." He quoted from Meade's address about driving "the invaders from our soil," saying, "You know I did not like the phrase." Since then had come word that the enemy was crossing its wounded over the Potomac.

While the Battle of Gettysburg was being fought the President had wondered what was happening to Grant. For months he had been haunted by the colossal Vicksburg affair. Grant was trying to starve out one Confederate army in Vicksburg while he held off other Confederate armies from reaching Vicksburg. Against many representations and pleadings Lincoln had kept Grant in command and was hoping for great results. But the months passed.

When Lee's van was a day's march from Harrisburg, Lincoln had issued a long letter to an Ohio Democratic committee regarding habeas corpus and the Constitution; sent General R. H. Milroy a sharp letter for losing a division of troops and blaming it on the West Pointers who were his superiors; written a note of comfort to General David Hunter that he must not grumble so much, for he was still held in respect and esteem. On the third day's fighting he took time to pardon a deserter sentenced to be shot.

Welles July 7 was just saying good afternoon to a distinguished delegation when a dispatch was handed to him with news from Admiral Porter at Vicksburg; that city, its defenses and Pemberton's army of some 30,000 troops had surrendered to Grant and the Union army. Welles excused himself and headed for the Executive Mansion; he found the President with Chase and others, pointing on a map to details of Grant's movements.

Welles gave the news of the Porter telegram. The President rose at once, said they would not discuss Vicksburg and the map any more, and, "I myself will telegraph this news to General Meade." He took his hat as if to go, suddenly stopped and looked down with a shining face at Welles, took him by the hand, put an arm around him and broke forth: "What can we do for the Secretary of the Navy for this glorious intelligence? He is always giving us good news. I cannot, in words, tell you my joy over this result. It is great, Mr. Welles, it is great!"

The two of them walked out across the White House lawn. "This," said the President, "will relieve Banks. It will inspire me." Welles thought the opportunity good to request the President to insist upon his own views, to enforce them, not only on Meade but on Halleck. Lincoln directed Halleck to send word at once to Meade that Vicksburg had surrendered to Grant July 4, and furthermore: "Now, if General Meade can complete his work, so gloriously prosecuted thus far, by the literal or substantial destruction of Lee's army, the rebellion will be over."

Over the North as the news spread were mass meetings and speeches, rejoicing, firing of guns, ringing of bells. In hundreds of cities large and small were celebrations with torchlight processions, songs, jubilation, refreshments. "The price of gold . . . fell ten or fifteen cents and the whole country is joyous," wrote Welles. A brass band and a big crowd serenaded the President at the White House. He spoke to the crowd: ". . . in a succession of battles in Pennsylvania, near to us, through three days, so rapidly fought that they might be called one great battle on the 1st, 2d and 3d of the month of July; and on the 4th the cohorts of those who opposed the declaration that all men are created equal, 'turned tail' and run. Gentlemen, this is a glorious theme, and the occasion for a speech, but I am not prepared to make one worthy of the occasion." He would praise those who had fought so bravely. "I dislike to mention the name of one single officer, lest I might do wrong to those I might forget."

The colloquial phrase "turned tail" was as old to him as his boyhood and had the graphic edge he wished to convey. But it wasn't correct English, and he would hear about such language. He closed with a breezy and careless sentence that would do him no good among the purists of diction. "Having said this much, I will now take the music."

An odd number was Grant, a long way from home, bagging an entire army, winning the greatest Union victory of the war thus far, clearing the Mississippi River of its last Confederate hold, yet failing to send word to

Washington—unless he let it go at telling Admiral Porter the Navy should be first to wire the big news to Washington. This was more of Grant's careless ways. Welles wrote, "The Secretary of War and General Halleck are much dissatisfied that Admiral Porter should have sent me information of the capture of Vicksburg in advance of any word from General Grant, and also with me for spreading it at once over the country without verification from the War Office."

The detailed facts arrived at Washington of Grant receiving 31,600 prisoners, 172 cannon, 60,000 muskets. Port Hudson, a little farther south on the Mississippi, had fallen to General Banks with 6,000 prisoners, 51 cannon, 5,000 muskets. The starved Confederates filed out of Vicksburg in silence, the Union soldiers obeying Grant's instructions "to be orderly and quiet as these prisoners pass, and to make no offensive remarks." They were paroled, Grant explaining they were largely from the Southwest. "I knew many of them were tired of the war and would get home just as soon as they could." The prisoners included Lieutenant General John C. Pemberton, a favorite of President Davis, 4 major generals, 15 brigadiers, 80 staff officers.

Lincoln's eager anxiety about a military drama enacted along river bends where he had navigated flatboats, was told in a tender handshake letter of July 13, 1863, to Grant: ". . . I write this now as a grateful acknowledgment for the almost inestimable service you have done the country . . . I never had any faith, except a general hope that you knew better than I, that the Yazoo Pass expedition, and the like, could succeed. When you got below, and took Port-Gibson, Grand Gulf, and vicinity, I thought you should go down the river and join Gen. Banks; and when you turned Northward East of the Big Black, I feared it was a mistake. I now wish to make the personal acknowledgment that you were right, and I was wrong."

Meade was writing to Halleck July 8, "I think the decisive battle of the war will be fought in a few days," receiving from Halleck two days later the advice, "I think it will be best for you to postpone a general battle till you can concentrate all your forces and get up your reserves and reinforcements." On July 12 Meade reported to Halleck that he would attack next day "unless something intervenes to prevent it," recognizing that delay would strengthen the enemy and would not increase his own force. The war telegraph office operator Albert B. Chandler said that when this dispatch arrived from Meade, Lincoln paced the room wringing his hands and saying, "They will be ready to fight a magnificent battle when there is no enemy there to fight."

Next day Halleck wired Meade in words surely Lincoln rather than Halleck: "You are strong enough to attack and defeat the enemy before he can effect a crossing. Act upon your own judgment and make your generals execute your orders. Call no council of war. It is proverbial that councils of war never fight. Reinforcements are being pushed on as rapidly as possible. Do not let the enemy escape."

The night before, however, Meade had already called a council of war, finding that only two of his corps commanders wanted to fight. Meade himself was for immediate combat, but when the discussion was over decided to wait. The Monday following Meade's council of war, July 13, Hay's diary noted "the President begins to grow anxious and impatient about Meade's silence." The morning of the 14th "the President seemed depressed by Meade's despatches of last night. They were so cautiously & almost timidly worded—talking about reconnoitering to find the enemy's weak place, and other such." The President said he feared Meade would do nothing. About noon came a dispatch. The enemy had got away unhurt. The President was deeply grieved. "We had them within our grasp," he said to Hay. "We had only to stretch forth our hands & they were ours. And nothing I could say or do could make the Army move." It seemed to Hay that one of the President's dispatches to Meade of a few days before "must have cut like a scourge," but Meade returned so reasonable and earnest a reply that the President concluded Meade knew best what he was doing.

Welles recorded of July 14 that as Cabinet members were gathering, "Stanton said abruptly and curtly he knew nothing of Lee's crossing. 'I do,' said the President emphatically, with a look of painful rebuke to Stanton. 'If he has not got all of his men across, he soon will.' " Lincoln said he did not believe they could take up anything in the Cabinet for that day. Welles walked out slowly. The President hurried and overtook Welles. They walked across the White House lawn to the departments and stopped to talk a few moments at the gate. Welles believed he could never forget the voice and face of the President as he spoke. "And that, my God, is the last of this Army of the Potomac! There is bad faith somewhere. Meade has been pressed and urged, but only one of his generals was for an immediate attack, was ready to pounce on Lee; the rest held back. What does it mean, Mr. Welles? Great God! what does it mean?"

On July 14 Lincoln wrote a long bitter letter to Meade: "I do not believe you appreciate the magnitude of the misfortune involved in Lee's escape. He was within your easy grasp, and to have closed upon him would, in connection with our other late successes, have ended the war . . . Your golden opportunity is gone, and I am distressed immeasurably because of it. I beg you will not consider this a prossecution, or persecution of yourself. As you had learned that I was dissatisfied, I have thought it best to kindly tell you why." This letter never reached Meade, Lincoln later scribbling on the envelope "never sent or signed." It lacked the tone of Lincoln's remark to Simon Cameron in a later reference to Meade: "Why should we censure a man who has done so much for his country because he did not do a little more?"

Robert Lincoln said he went into his father's room to find him "in tears, with head bowed upon his arms resting on the table at which he sat." To the question, "Why, what is the matter, father?" the answer came slowly, "My boy, I have just learned that at a council of war, of Meade and his Generals, it had been determined not to pursue Lee, and now the opportune chance of ending this bitter struggle is lost."

A few days having passed, he could see it was well he had not sent Meade the letter he meant to be kindly but which was not kindly. Having met in Meade a rare humility and sincerity throughout their many difficult interchanges, Lincoln sent through Howard the salutation that Meade was more than a brave and skillful officer, was "a true man."

As the days passed Welles continued to blame chiefly General in Chief Halleck: "In this whole summer's campaign I have been unable to see, hear, or obtain evidence of power, or will, or talent, or originality on the part of

General Halleck. He has suggested nothing, decided nothing, done nothing but scold and smoke and scratch his elbows."

On the last day of the Battle of Gettysburg Alexander H. Stephens, Vice-President of the Confederate States, had with one companion started down the James River from Richmond in a small steamer, aiming to reach Washington as commissioners of the Confederate Government and hold a conference with the President of the United States. Their dispatch of July 4 requested permission to pass through the blockade. The final decision after much consultation was in a telegram sent by Lincoln to the blockading admiral: "The request of A. H. Stephens is inadmissible. The customary agents and channels are adequate for all needful communication and conference between the United States forces and the insurgents." Thus did Lincoln dismiss his old-time colleague.

There was issued a "Proclamation of Thanksgiving," July 15, 1863, by the President. In diapasons of Old Testament prose, in the attitude of piety in which the name of Almighty God was invoked, Lincoln emerged as a man of faith. "It has pleased Almighty God to hearken to the supplications and prayers of an afflicted people," ran the opening chords, "and to vouchsafe to the army and the navy of the United States victories on land and on the sea so signal and so effective as to furnish reasonable grounds for augmented confidence that the Union of these States will be maintained, their constitution preserved, and their peace and prosperity permanently restored . . . It is meet and right to recognize and confess the presence of the Almighty Father and the power of His Hand equally in these triumphs and in these sorrows:

"Now, therefore, be it known that I do set apart Thursday the 6th. day of August next, to be observed as a day for National Thanksgiving, Praise and Prayer, and I invite the People of the United States to assemble on that occasion in their customary places of worship, and in the forms approved by their own consciences, render the homage due to the Divine Majesty, for the wonderful things he has done in the Nation's behalf . . ."

On the date this proclamation was issued the dignity and majesty of the U.S. Government was being challenged, upset, smeared with insult and threatened with the disorders and violence of revolution, in the largest city in the United States.

During the three days of July 13, 14, 15, mobs or crowds in New York City met by prearrangement, with a specific design as to what points they would attack and carry, drove out the U.S. provost marshal from his office at 43d Street and Third Avenue, wrecked the wheel or revolving drum from which the names of drafted men were drawn, tore to pieces the books and papers, poured turpentine on the floor, set the building on fire, fought off police and firemen, and the draft office and six adjoining buildings burned. They wrecked and burned the U.S. draft office on Broadway two doors from 29th Street, looted stores nearby, and burned 12 buildings; they smashed windows and doors and sacked the home of Republican Mayor Opdyke and burned at midnight the home of U.S. Postmaster Abram Wakeman, first stripping the premises of furniture and clothing; they burned a ferry house, hotels, drugstores, clothing stores, factories, saloons where they were refused free liquor, police stations, a Methodist church, a Protestant mission, the

Colored Orphan Asylum at 43d Street and Lexington Avenue. They drove out 40 policemen and 15 armed workmen from the state arsenal at 21st Street and Second Avenue, trampling over five of their dead, seizing muskets and cartridges, setting the building on fire; they hanged a Negro from a tree on Clarkson Street and burned the body with loud howling; they hanged three a day of Negroes; they hanged to a lamppost a captain of the 11th regiment of the state guard; they hanged, shot or beat and trampled to death at least 30 Negroes and so terrorized the colored population that it disappeared up-state and across to New Jersey. They erected for protection and refuge barricades on First Avenue from 11th to 14th Streets, on Ninth Avenue from 32d to 43d Streets, with smaller barricades across intersecting thoroughfares. They sang "We'll hang old Greeley to a sour apple tree, and send him straight to hell!"; they yelled "To hell with the draft and the war!" and "Tell Old Abe to come to New York!"

The mobs were not driven in their work by mere blind wrath. Somebody had done some thinking, somebody had chosen a time when all the state guards the governor could scrape together had gone to Gettysburg. The only organized force ready against the first riots was a police department of 1,500 members. With club and revolver they had fought night and day, and their dead lay in scores, their wounded by the hundreds.

The mobs of the first day's riots aimed straight at a thing they hated: the Draft. It was a Monday, and on the previous Saturday 1,200 names had been picked by a blindfolded man out of the wheel. These 1,200 names had been published, and unless something happened to make the Government change its mind most of the men answering to these 1,200 names would be put into uniforms and sent to fight.

If they believed such newspapers as the *World*, the *Journal of Commerce*, the *Express*, the *Daily News*, the *Day Book*, the *Mercury*, they were to be the willing cannon fodder of a tyrannical and oppressive Government daily violating the Constitution and the fundamental law of the land. Said the *Daily News*: "The people are notified that one out of about two and a half of our citizens are to be brought off into Messrs. Lincoln & Company's charnel-house. God forbid!"

The newspapers had printed the Fourth of July speech of Franklin Pierce, former President of the United States, at a great Democratic mass meeting at Concord, New Hampshire. Said Pierce, "It is made criminal for that noble martyr of free speech, Mr. Vallandigham, to discuss public affairs in Ohio—ay, even here, in time of war the mere arbitrary will of the President takes the place of the Constitution." Governor Seymour of New York told a Fourth of July audience that the country was on "the very verge of destruction" because of Government coercion, "seizing our persons, infringing upon our rights, insulting our homes . . . men deprived of the right of trial by jury, men torn from their homes by midnight intruders."

By the time the subtle arguments of the newspapers and of Pierce and Seymour had been simplified into plain words for the 400,000 foreign-born citizens of New York, of whom 203,740 were Irish, they had lost their fine philosophic distinctions. And far beyond any discussion was the terribly simple and outstanding fact that any man having $300 could buy his freedom from the draft. It was "a rich man's war and a poor man's fight," ran the talk in 5,000 saloons and 20 times as many homes.

Drafted men, their relatives and friends, reinforced by thousands of sympathizers who favored some kind of direct action, gathered early the morning of July 13 in vacant lots with clubs, staves, cart rungs, pieces of iron, and moved as if by agreement to a lot near Central Park where they organized, began patrolling the city, and put the first sign of their wrath and vengeance on the draft offices wrecked and burned. The first acts of the three days' tornado had some semblance of an uprising of the people against a Government discriminating in its conscription between the rich and the poor. The second and third days, however, saw the events come under the sway of the city's criminal and gang elements, then numbering between 50,000 and 70,000, who swarmed out for loot and the work of getting the police defied and overrun.

Governor Seymour probably set forth a sincere viewpoint in a proclamation calling for enforcement of law and order. He meant to say he might have favored a few small riots which would show a healthy Democratic opposition to the draft, but when the mobs ran wild and made war against the rich, it was time to place the emphasis on property, safety, strict law enforcement, rather than on personal liberty and the class discrimination of the Conscription Act.

Besides the many mobs carrying banners inscribed "No Draft" and "No $300 Arrangements with Us," there had been many other mobs with varied and mixed motives. Class war was the cry behind the big placards of one division: "The Poor Man's Blood for the Rich Man's Money." Eagerness for loot lay back of the stripping of houses of jewelry, plate, furniture, rugs, clothes. Primitive race antagonism, set aflame by political malevolence, underlay the hanging and beating of black men by white men. In thousands of boys the savage was unleashed; they robbed houses and set them on fire; they beat to death with fists and clubs the young Negro cripple Abraham Franklin; they tore off the clothes of Jeremiah Robinson, who was trying to escape to a ferryboat wearing his wife's dress and hood, threw him to the pavement, kicked him in the face and ribs, killed him and threw the body into the river.

Robert Nugent, assistant provost marshal in charge of conscription, received the second day of the riots a telegram from his Washington chief, James B. Fry, directing him to suspend the draft. Governor Seymour and Mayor Opdyke clamored that he should publish this order. Nugent said he had no authority, but he finally consented to sign his name to a notice: "The draft has been suspended in New York City and Brooklyn," which was published in newspapers. This had a marked quieting effect.

The storm in the streets began to slow down as though winds had changed. There was added quieting effect as infantry, cavalry, artillery, from the Army of the Potomac commenced arriving.

On July 14, the second of the three-day riots, a telegram dated at the War Department, Washington, and signed "A. Lincoln" went addressed to Robert T. Lincoln, Fifth Avenue Hotel, New York, with the query, "Why do I hear no more of you?"

After 150 Regular Army soldiers with ball cartridges had faced a crowd of 2,000, fired in the air, and received a volley of stones in reply, and had then shot into the swarming and defiant mass, killing 12 and wounding more, the hullabaloo began to die down.

Soon afterward James R. Gilmore, who had sent Lincoln reports on the riots from the New York *Tribune* office, called on Lincoln at the White House and asked why the President could not say Yes or No to the recommendation for a special commissioner to expose the instigators of the riots. Lincoln hesitated and in a peculiar half-bantering manner, according to Gilmore, replied: "Well, you see if I had said no, I should have admitted that I dare not enforce the laws, and consequently have no business to be President of the United States. If I had said yes, and had appointed the judge, I should—as he would have done his duty—have simply touched a match to a barrel of gunpowder. You have heard of sitting on a volcano. We are sitting upon two; one is blazing away already, and the other will blaze away the moment we scrape a little loose dirt from the top of the crater. Better let the dirt alone,—at least for the present. One rebellion at a time is about as much as we can conveniently handle."

Governor Seymour wrote to the President asking for suspension of the draft, the President replying that he could not consent. "*Time* is too important." Due credit in the quota would be made for volunteers, Lincoln stipulated; he also said he would be willing to facilitate a decision from the U.S. Supreme Court on whether the draft law was constitutional. "But I can not consent to lose the *time* while it is being obtained . . ." His purpose was to be "just and constitutional; and yet practical." He was yielding nothing to the astute and persistent Governor who had so often given words of hope to New York City that the draft would be got rid of.

Lincoln did during those hectic summer weeks prepare an address to the country giving the facts and logic which dictated his actions in the draft. Having written this argument, Lincoln filed it away in a pigeonhole of personal papers and it was not heard of till long afterward. One relentlessly logical passage read: "There can be no army without men. Men can be had only voluntarily, or involuntarily. We have ceased to obtain them voluntarily; and to obtain them involuntarily, is the draft—the conscription. If you dispute the fact, and declare that men can still be had voluntarily in sufficient numbers prove the assertion by yourselves volunteering in such numbers, and I shall gladly give up the draft. Or if not a sufficient number, but any one of you will volunteer, he for his single self, will escape all the horrors of the draft; and will thereby do only what each one of at least a million of his manly brethren have already done. Their toil and blood have been given as much for you as themselves. Shall it all be lost rather than that you too, will bear your part?"

His mind had dwelt, evidently, on a law to enforce universal selective service, the Government taking all men physically fit, no man escaping by purchase or substitution. Such conscription was operating in several European monarchies and republics, but as Lincoln looked out across the American scene in 1863, he seemed to believe it could not then be put to work in the United States, even if he could find Congressmen to advocate it. Perhaps the opposition had more than a demagogue's idle phrase in the cry "The rich man's money against the poor man's blood."

His elaborately prepared address, said Nicolay and Hay, was intended more especially for the honest and patriotic Democrats of the North, "but after he had finished it, doubts arose in his mind as to the propriety or the expediency of addressing the public directly in that manner," and "with reserve and abnegation, after writing it, he resolved to suppress so admirable a paper." He laid his paper aside as a meditation that had exercised his mind and sharpened his humility and perhaps deepened his patience.

New York City saw on August 19, 1863, no less than 10,000 troops from the Army of the Potomac assisted by the 1st Division New York State Guards. Governor Seymour proclaimed that citizens should obey the law of Congress as to conscription. New draft offices went into operation. Cavalry patrols rode up and down the streets.

The draft proceeded, meeting covert instead of open resistance. Tammany, Tweed, A. Oakey Hall, Fernando Wood and his brother Ben, the *World*, the *Express*, the *Day Book*, the *Mercury*, many scurrying politicians, examining physicians, and fixers, lawyers, did their work. Upward of $5,000,000 was appropriated by the municipality of New York for draft-evasion purposes. According to the "infallible" record which Lincoln had mentioned to Seymour, of 292,441 men whose names were drawn from the wheels 39,877 failed to report for examination. Of the remaining 252,564, for good or bad reasons 164,394 were exempted. This left 88,170 available for duty, of whom 52,288 bought exemptions at $300 apiece, which yielded the Government $15,686,400. The original 292,441 names were thus cut down to 35,882 men, of whom 26,002 hired substitutes to go to war for them. This left 9,880 who lacked political pull or seemed to want to join the army and fight.

There now arose at Niagara Falls, Canada, Clement L. Vallandigham, crying that on British soil he was a freeman but if he crossed over into the U.S.A. he was a felon and would be clapped into jail. Discussion of habeas corpus and the right of free speech flared higher. The New York *World* declared that the crime of arresting Vallandigham was a Lincoln blunder and inquired why the President had not arrested Fernando Wood for remarks at New York mass meetings as treasonable as those of Vallandigham in Ohio.

Mrs. Vallandigham left her home in Dayton, Ohio, to join her husband at Windsor, Canada, opposite Detroit, to help him campaign from there. It was reported she told her friends that she never expected to return from Canada until she did so as the wife of the governor of Ohio. This reminded Lincoln of a man out in Illinois running for supervisor on the county board. On leaving home election morning he said, "Wife, tonight you shall sleep with the supervisor from this township." News came in the evening that her husband was beaten in the election, and she was all dressed up for going out when she met her defeated man at the door. "Wife, where are you going all dressed up this time of night?" he exclaimed. "Going?" she countered. "Why, you told me this morning that I should sleep tonight with the supervisor of this town and as the other man was elected instead of you, I was going to his house." Whereupon the husband, as newspapers quoted Lincoln, "acknowledged the corn, she didn't go out, and he bought a new Brussels carpet for the parlor."

During those six weeks of Vallandigham's banishment Lee had been re-pulsed at Gettysburg; Grant had taken Vicksburg and Confederate power on the Mississippi River was gone; a violent three-day uprising in the largest city in the North, and minor revolts at other points, had been brought under con-trol. Lincoln, pleased at the outlook, wrote a letter that James C. Conkling read at an immense mass meeting in Springfield, Illinois: "There are those who are dissatisfied with me. To such I would say: You desire peace; and you blame me that we do not have it." One way to peace was to suppress the rebellion by force of arms. "This, I am trying to do. Are you for it? If you are, so far we are agreed. If you are not for it, a second way is, to give up the Union. I am against this. Are you for it? If you are, you should say so plainly. If you are not for *force*, nor yet for *dissolution*, there only remains some imaginable *compromise*."

He promised that if any peace proposition came from those who controlled the Confederate Army, "It shall not be rejected, and kept a secret from you." There was another issue. "You are dissatisfied with me about the negro . . . I suggested compensated emancipation; to which you replied you wished not to be taxed to buy negroes. But I had not asked you to be taxed to buy ne-groes, except in such way, as to save you from greater taxation to save the Union exclusively by other means."

He launched into the finish of what was really a paper aimed at the masses of people in America and Europe: "The signs look better. The Father of Waters again goes unvexed to the sea . . . And while those who have cleared the great river may well be proud, even that is not all. It is hard to say that anything has been more bravely, and well done, than at Antietam, Murfrees-boro, Gettysburg, and on many fields of lesser note. Nor must Uncle Sam's Web-feet be forgotten. At all the watery margins they have been present. Not only on the deep sea, the broad bay, and the rapid river, but also up the narrow muddy bayou, and wherever the ground was a little damp, they have been, and made their tracks. Thanks to all. For the great republic—for the principle it lives by, and keeps alive—for man's vast future,—thanks to all.

"Peace does not appear so distant as it did. I hope it will come soon, and come to stay; and so come as to be worth the keeping in all future time. It will then have been proved that, among free men, there can be no successful appeal from the ballot to the bullet; and that they who take such appeal are sure to lose their case, and pay the cost. And then, there will be some black men who can remember that, with silent tongue, and clenched teeth, and steady eye, and well-poised bayonet, they have helped mankind on to this great consummation; while, I fear, there will be some white ones, unable to forget that, with malignant heart, and deceitful speech, they strove to hinder it. Still, let us not be over-sanguine of a speedy final triumph. Let us be quite sober. Let us diligently apply the means, never doubting that a just God, in his own good time, will give us the rightful result."

No previous letter, address or state paper of Lincoln's received such warm-hearted comment. Many newspapers joined with the New York *Times* seeing it as having hard sense, a temper defying malice. "Even the Copperhead gnaws upon it as vainly as a viper upon a file. The most consummate rhetorician never used language more pat to the purpose and still there is not a word not familiar to the plainest plowman . . . Abraham Lincoln is today the most popular man in the Republic . . ."

The New York *World* was saying, "Nature has not endowed Mr. Lincoln with a single great or commanding quality. He has indeed a certain homely untutored shrewdness and vulgar honesty . . . but no . . . higher degree of consideration than belongs to a village lawyer . . ." The London *Times* was annoyed at Lincoln's latest letter: "The persons, if there be any such, to whom such jargon can appear impressive or even intelligible, must have faculties and tastes of which we can form no idea."

Living in the same house, seeing the chief in many moods, Hay was writing, "The Tycoon is in fine whack. I have rarely seen him more serene & busy. He is managing this war, the draft, foreign relations, and planning a reconstruction of the Union, all at once. I never knew with what tyrannous authority he rules the Cabinet, till now. The most important things he decides & there is no cavil . . . There is no man in the country, so wise, so gentle and so firm. I believe the hand of God placed him where he is."

In September '63 the Boston publisher Benjamin B. Russell issued a collection of *The Letters of President Lincoln on Questions of National Policy*, with a preface, as though the letters were literature and unique reading matter. The sheaf filled 22 pages, and sold at eight cents a copy, two copies 15 cents.

By the carefully wrought appeal in simple words aimed to reach millions of readers and by the face-to-face contact with thousands who came to the White House, Lincoln was holding to the single purpose of adding momentum to what there was of popular will for war. The late summer and early fall of '63 seemed to mark a deepening of loyalties to Lincoln and his vision of where to go and how.

The President needed anchors, needed hope. A million volunteers had answered his call and given toil and blood for the cause of which he was the mouthpiece. Soon he was to order a draft for 300,000 more conscripts. He had told Mary Livermore there was little realization of the agony and cost that yet lay ahead. The reports of Grant and Sherman far down in the intestinal center of the Confederacy told him their belief that the war had only truly begun, as it could only be ended by complete and bloody conquest. So furiously had it raged thus far that both sides had often been left no time to bury their dead.

CHAPTER 36

Lincoln at Storm Center

FROM the Big Black River in Mississippi, Sherman was writing to Lincoln: "The South must be ruled by us, or she will rule us. We must conquer them, or ourselves be conquered. They ask, and will have, nothing else, and talk of compromise is bosh; for we know they would even scorn the offer . . . I would not coax them, or even meet them half-way, but make them so sick of war that generations would pass away before they would again appeal to it . . . The people of this country in after-years will be better citizens from the dear-bought experience of the present crisis. Let them learn it now, and learn it well, that good citizens must obey as well as command."

A fierce insolence would Vallandigham, Seymour, the organization Democrats, have found in this treatise if Sherman had let it be published as Lincoln proposed. "I know what I say when I repeat that the insurgents of the South sneer at all overtures looking to their interests . . . They tell me to my face that they respect Grant, McPherson, and our brave associates who fight manfully and well for a principle, but despise the Copperheads and sneaks at the North, who profess friendship for the South and opposition to the war, as mere covers for their knavery and poltroonery."

Sherman invoked his doctrine of terror: "Our officers, marshals, and courts, must penetrate into the innermost recesses of their land, . . . that it makes no difference whether it be in one year, or two, or ten, or twenty; that we will remove and destroy every obstacle, if need be, take every life, every acre of land, every particle of property, every thing that to us seems proper; that we will not cease till the end is attained . . ."

When the vaguely furtive and definitely garrulous James R. Gilmore of the New York *Tribune* came again with a scheme, Lincoln listened. It was doubtful whether Lincoln gave Gilmore a glad hand and took him to his bosom in the easy and familiar way Gilmore wrote about it. Yet it seemed definite that Gilmore and others in the summer of '63 interested Lincoln, at least mildly and tentatively, in plans to sound out Zebulon B. Vance, the 33-year-old governor of North Carolina, on how far Vance might be willing to go toward bringing his state back into the Union.

The break between Vance and the Davis Government ran deep, the feeling bitter. The planter aristocracy, the slaveholders, the original secessionists, had no such hold in North Carolina as in the Cotton States. Her mountaineers, farmers, seacoast population, were "different." Vance spoke for his people when he served notice on the Richmond Government that his state troops would go into action against Confederate authorities who should try to override the right of any citizen to the writ of habeas corpus. Vance protested to Richmond against Confederate War Department officers "engaging in speculations of private account" in North Carolina. Vance telegraphed and wrote Davis that a Georgia regiment, its men and officers, started a riot the night of September 9, burned and destroyed the Raleigh *Standard*, and in retaliation a mob of citizens the next morning burned and destroyed the Raleigh *State Journal*. "I feel very sad in the contemplation of these outrages," Vance told Davis. "The distance is quite short to either anarchy or despotism, when armed soldiers, led by their officers, can with impunity outrage the laws of a State."

The Georgia regiment that had wrecked and burned the Raleigh *Standard* newspaper plant hated its peace tone, hated a four-column address published July 31, 1863. Governor Vance had helped, it was said, to write the address with its cry, "The great demand of the people of this part of the State is *peace;* peace upon any terms that will not enslave and degrade us."

Vance would welcome reunion of the states and "any peace compatible with honor," according to the information Gilmore brought Lincoln. He had it, he said, from Edward Kidder, a merchant of Wilmington, North Carolina. Born in New Hampshire, Kidder had gone to Wilmington in 1826 when he was 21, had lived there ever since, "accumulating a vast fortune, and having larger business transactions than any other man in the State." Lincoln read Kidder's confidential report of a talk with Governor Vance. Slavery was dead, the report ran, the Confederacy hopeless, and Vance favored a return to the Union on terms of honor and equity. Therefore Kidder hoped Gilmore would run the blockade into Wilmington, interview Governor Vance at Kidder's home, bringing to Vance Lincoln's peace terms.

In the months that followed, with further errands and with the plans changing, nothing much directly came of the scheme. Whether Lincoln reached across the state lines and convinced Governor Vance that peace efforts would be worth while was not clear. It was clear as daylight, however, that a few months after Gilmore and Kidder had laid their plans before Lincoln, Governor Vance was going nearly as far as Lincoln could wish in blunt suggestions and arguments sent to Jefferson Davis. A letter of Vance to Davis in December '63 was a straight and open plea for "some effort at negotiation with the enemy."

There was a Union sentiment in North Carolina, as in several areas of the South—as in one county in Alabama having no slaves and sending no troops to the Confederate armies. Lincoln was responsive to all such Union areas. What he did in some cases might never be known. In many affairs he was careful to keep no record.

The French government advised the American Minister in Paris that the sooner the American government showed a willingness to recognize the government of Archduke Maximilian, set up in Mexico by French armies, the sooner would those armies be ready to leave Mexico. Seward replied that the determination of the President was to err on the side of neutrality, if he erred at all, as between France and Mexico.

In plainer words than the covert phrasings of diplomacy, Lincoln had answered General John M. Thayer's query, "Mr. President, how about the French army in Mexico?" He shrugged his shoulders and wrinkled his eyebrows. "I'm not exactly 'skeered,' but I don't like the looks of the thing. Napoleon has taken advantage of our weakness in our time of trouble, and has attempted to found a monarchy on the soil of Mexico in utter disregard of the Monroe doctrine. My policy is, attend to only one trouble at a time. If we get well out of our present difficulties and restore the Union, I propose to notify Louis Napoleon that it is about time to take his army out of Mexico. When that army is gone, the Mexicans will take care of Maximilian."

Heading the Military Department of Missouri was General John M. Schofield, 32 years old, cool, sober, a West Pointer, professor of physics, chief of staff for General Lyon in the fighting at Wilson's Creek. Now he was Lincoln's main buffer in a Slave State seething with civil war. To the President, he reported the return of thousands of soldiers from defeated Confederate armies at Vicksburg and elsewhere. At first organized secretly as gangs, they joined up into regiments and small armies; they had raided, foraged supplies from Unionists, stolen money and horses, burned houses and railroad bridges, looted villages and towns, shot and hanged Union men. Toward keeping order Schofield organized ten regiments of Federal troops. Once he estimated there were 5,000 armed and banded guerrillas in Missouri.

Schofield's authority often tangled with that of Missouri's provisional governor, 65-year-old Hamilton Rowan Gamble. Virginia-born of Irish immigrants, his wife from South Carolina, Gamble had been member of the legislature, secretary of state, presiding judge of the state supreme court. He had pronounced Lincoln's call for troops in April '61 unconstitutional and had leaned toward those who wished to make Missouri independent of both North and South, repelling invaders whether in blue or in gray. As chairman of the committee on Federal relations in the state constitutional convention of '61, Gamble hoped for "amicable adjustment" without civil war. That same convention appointed him provisional governor of the state, replacing the regularly elected Claiborne F. Jackson, whom Unionist forces had run out of the state capital.

Gamble wrote that the radicals were "openly and loudly" threatening to overthrow the state provisional government by violence. Lincoln replied that Schofield would take care of the violence, that it was not a party but individual radicals making the threats. "I have seen no occasion to make a distinction against the provisional government because of its not having been chosen and inaugurated in the usual way. Nor have I seen any cause to suspect it of unfaithfulness to the Union."

Yet Lincoln knew that the face of Gamble was toward the past, that the emancipation ordinance passed by the conservative convention in the summer of '63 was evasive, odorous of politics, setting the year 1870 for slavery to "cease" in Missouri, but to "cease" under the peculiar conditions that all slaves over 40 would still be slaves till they died, while all slaves under 12 would be slaves until they were 23, and those of all other ages until the Fourth of July, 1876. In the atmosphere of the convention that passed this ordinance Governor Gamble felt called on to offer his resignation, but it was refused by a vote of 51 to 29.

A delegation of German radicals from Missouri called at the White House and later published their report that the President had refused their demands for dismissal of Seward, Blair and Halleck, had declined their requests that he restore Frémont, Sigel and Butler to important commands.

In Missouri excitement flared high as the radical Union Emancipation convention met, with delegates from four-fifths of the counties of the state. The high cry in Jefferson City September 1 was that Governor Gamble's "pro-slavery" provisional government was paralyzing Federal power. A Committee of Seventy, one from each county in the state, was appointed to call on the President and lay their cause before him. At train stops on the way to Washington this committee was hailed by brass bands, antislavery delegations and orators. At Washington they were joined by a Committee of Eighteen from Kansas on the same errand.

Lincoln told Hay that if they could show that Schofield had done anything wrong, their case was made, that he believed they were against Schofield because Schofield would not take sides with them. "I think I understand this matter perfectly and I cannot do anything contrary to my convictions, to please these men, earnest and powerful as they may be." Meanwhile the Missouri-Kansas committees dominated the Washington scene, took in a big reception to themselves at the Union League Hall, where Gamble was denounced and immediate emancipation demanded.

The delegation took two days to prepare an address to the President. The wrongs their people had borne were heavy. Crimes and outrages they alleged and enumerated for Lincoln's eye. They were exasperated men whose voices rose out of mixed motives of war and politics; public service and private revenge; the hangover of greed and corruption among Frémont's associates, of connivance and trickery by the Blairs in their animosities toward Frémont and others, of anger that Schofield had lent detachments of Enrolled Militia to Grant for the Vicksburg operation, of wrath that Lincoln and members of Congress were trying to emancipate the slaves of Missouri by gradual purchase instead of direct bestowal of freedom by proclamation, of indignation at Schofield's Order No. 92 prohibiting Kansans from pursuing guerrillas over the state line, of disgruntlement on the part of some with the apportionment of Federal offices and favors, of suspicion on the part of others that Lincoln's policy was Kentuckian and his leanings pro-slavery.

Their prepared address to the President voiced three demands. First, General Schofield must be relieved, and General Butler appointed in his stead. Second, the system of Enrolled Militia in Missouri must be broken up and national forces substituted. Third, at elections persons must not be allowed to vote who were not entitled by law to do so.

At nine o'clock the morning of September 30, the 88 delegates walked through the great front doors into the White House. Then the great front doors were locked and stayed locked till the conference was over. At the committees' own request, all reporters and spectators were barred.

Lincoln looked along panels of faces. His eyes roved over stubborn men, in the main sincere, some with a genius of courage and sacrifice. He told John Hay later: "They are nearer to me than the other side, in thought and sentiment, though bitterly hostile personally. They are utterly lawless—the onhandiest devils in the world to deal with—but after all, their faces are set Zionwards."

The address was read to the President by the chairman, Charles Daniel Drake, a St. Louis lawyer, 52 years old, educated as a midshipman in the U.S. Navy, author of notable law treatises, member of the Missouri Legislature, an early leader against secession. His voice carried what Enos Clarke, another St. Louis delegate, described as "a deep, impressive, stentorian tone." And Enos Clarke took note that while Chairman Drake read, the President listened with patient attention, and when the reading was over rose slowly, and with a deliberation born of what they knew not, began a lengthy reply. Said Clarke: "I shall never forget the intense chagrin and disappointment we all felt at the treatment of the matter in the beginning of his reply . . . He gave us the impression of a pettifogger speaking before a justice of the peace jury. But as he talked on and made searching inquiries of members of the delegation and invited debate, it became manifest that his manner at the beginning was really the foil of a master . . ."

Enos Clarke recalled Lincoln saying: "You gentlemen must bear in mind that in performing the duties of the office I hold I must represent no one section, but I must act for all sections of the Union in trying to maintain the supremacy of the Government." This from Lincoln had been heard over and again privately, publicly, in letters and speeches. Clarke, however, caught another expression that could not have been anticipated. "I desire to so conduct the affairs of this administration that if, at the end, when I come to lay down the reins of power, I have lost every other friend on earth, I shall at least have one friend left, and that friend shall be down inside of me."

Two hours ran on, some of it in speechmaking, some in random talk. Hay noted the President saying he could not give a hasty answer. "I will take your address, carefully consider it, and respond at my earliest convenience . . ." As President, he had uniformly refused to give the governor exclusive control of the Missouri State Militia, while on the other hand the Enrolled Militia existed solely under state laws with which he had no right to interfere. As to Schofield, Lincoln was sorry they had not made specific complaints. "I cannot act on vague impressions." He went into details as to Schofield's record. "I know nothing to his disadvantage. I am not personally acquainted with him. I have with him no personal relations. If you will allege a definite wrong-doing, and, having clearly made your point, prove it, I shall remove him." The suspension of habeas corpus by Schofield in Missouri was in obedience to the President's official decree. "You object to its being used in Missouri. In other words, that which is right when employed against opponents is wrong when employed against yourselves. Still, I will consider that."

They objected to Schofield's muzzling the press. "As to that," continued Lincoln, "I think when an officer in any department finds that a newspaper is pursuing a course calculated to embarrass his operations and stir up sedition and tumult, he has the right to lay hands upon it and suppress it, but in no other case. I approved the order in question after the 'Missouri Democrat' had also approved it." A delegate interrupted: "We thought it was to be used against the other side." And Lincoln agreed, "Certainly you did. Your ideas of justice seem to depend on the application of it."

Hay noted that as an inquisition the morning did not work out, Lincoln meeting each point, issue, grievance, "with a quick counter-statement so brief and clinching that the several volunteer spokesmen who came forward to support the main address retired, one by one, disconcerted and overwhelmed." The formal session drew to a close with Lincoln saying: "Still you appear to come before me as my friends, if I agree with you, and not otherwise. I do not here speak of mere personal friendship. When I speak of my friends I mean those who are friendly to my measures, to the policy of the Government." They knew the President was referring to loyal Union men who might even be proslavery in viewpoint when he said: "If a man votes for supplies of men and money, encourages enlistments, discourages desertions, does all in his power to carry the war on to a successful issue, I have no right to question him for his abstract political opinions. I must make a dividing line somewhere between those who are opponents of the Government, and those who only approve peculiar features of my Administration while they sustain the Government."

One of the men from Missouri felt Lincoln was not so quick in his answers, not so much at ease as Hay believed. "The President in the course of his reply hesitated a great deal," said this man, "and was manifestly, as he said, very much troubled over affairs in Missouri. He said they were a source of more anxiety to him than we could imagine. He regretted that some of the men who had founded the Republican party should now be arrayed apparently against his administration." Twice before, the Missourian had met Lincoln, and had not seen such a perplexed look on Lincoln's face. "When he said he was *bothered* about this thing he showed it. He spoke kindly, yet now and then there was a little rasping tone in his voice that seemed to say, 'You men ought to fix this thing up without *tormenting* me.' But he never lost his temper."

When all points had been covered, and there seemed nothing more to say, Chairman Drake stepped forward. "Mr. President, the time has now come when we can no longer trespass upon your attention but must take leave of you." Then came the most impressive moment of the two hours, Drake saying the men who stood before the President now would return, many of them to homes surrounded by "rebel" sentiment. "Many of them, sir, in returning there do so at the risk of their lives, and if any of those lives are sacrificed by reason of the military administration of this government, let me tell you, sir, that their blood will be upon your garments and not upon ours." This was terribly, though only partly, true and near to ghastly prophecy. Enos Clarke noted that during this address of Drake "the President stood before the delegation with tears streaming down his cheeks, seeming deeply agitated."

One by one the delegates shook hands with the President and took leave. To Clarke it was memorable; he shook hands, walked off with others, and at the door turned for a final look. "Mr. Lincoln had met some personal acquaintances with whom he was exchanging pleasantries, and instead of the tears of a few moments before, he was indulging in hearty laughter. This rapid and wonderful transition from one extreme to the other impressed me greatly."

The next night Secretary Chase opened his home and gave the delegation a reception, told them he was heartily in sympathy with their mission. On to New York went the delegates to a rousing public meeting in Cooper Union, where William Cullen Bryant spoke for them, where the President was threatened with revolutionary action if he did not yield to their demands.

As in other cases, Lincoln now stood by his men. In a long letter October 5 to the Missouri-Kansas Committee he said that in their address of September 30, besides four supplementary ones on October 3, enough of "suffering and wrong" was stated.

Yet the whole case, as presented, fails to convince me, that Gen. Schofield, or the Enrolled Militia, is responsible for that suffering and wrong . . . We are in civil war. In such cases there always is a main question; but in this case that question is a perplexing compound—Union and Slavery. It thus becomes a question not of two sides merely, but of at least four sides, even among those who are for the Union, saying nothing of those who are against it. Thus, those who are for the Union *with,* but not *without* slavery—those for it *without,* but not *with*—those for it *with* or *without,* but prefer it *with*—and those for it *with* or *without,* but prefer it *without.* Among these again, is a subdivision of those who are for *gradual* but not for *immediate*, and those who are for *immediate*, but not for *gradual* extinction of slavery. It is easy to conceive that all these shades of opinion, and even more, may be sincerely entertained by honest and truthful men. Yet, all being for the Union, by reason of these differences, each will prefer a different way of sustaining the Union. At once sincerity is questioned, and motives are assailed. Actual war coming, blood grows hot, and blood is spilled. Thought is forced from old channels into confusion. Deception breeds and thrives. Confidence dies, and universal suspicion reigns. Each man feels an impulse to kill his neighbor, lest he be first killed by him. Revenge and retaliation follow. And all this, as before said, may be among honest men only. But this is not all. Every foul bird comes abroad, and every dirty reptile rises up. These add crime to confusion. Strong measures, deemed indispensable but harsh at best, such men make worse by mal-administration. Murders for old grudges, and murders for pelf, proceed under any cloak that will best cover for the occasion.

Finally, he had directed General Schofield that the request of the committee regarding elections was proper. The third demand of the Committee of Seventy was granted.

In his own serious advice to Schofield, Lincoln made it plain he had no immediate hope of peace for that region. In the young, blond, whiskered Schofield had been found an administrator who understood Lincoln once writing to him: "If both factions, or neither, shall abuse you, you will probably be about right. Beware of being assailed by one, and praised by the other."

What to do about the Negro and slavery in this Slave State was covered in three sentences to Schofield: "Allow no part of the Military under your command, to be engaged in either returning fugitive slaves, or in forcing, or enticing slaves from their homes; and, so far as practicable, enforce the same forbearance upon the people . . . Allow no one to enlist colored troops, except upon orders from you, or from here through you. Allow no one to assume the functions of confiscating property, under the law of congress, or other wise, except upon orders from here."

A deepening trend was seen in the Cincinnati *Telegraph and Advocate*, under auspices of the Roman Catholic Archbishop of Cincinnati, in July advising its readers that Negro slavery was virtually abolished; it would oppose on moral and religious grounds all efforts to restore or re-establish it.

The new governor of Kentucky, Thomas E. Bramlette, in his September inaugural spoke against the arming of Negroes; he asked what could be done with such soldiers at the end of the war. He was speaking for those of his Slave State who knew that such soldiers would bring grave problems.

A vision was coming to many that somehow amid the confusions of emancipation proclamations, enforced conscription, habeas corpus, there belonged in the picture many regiments of black men fighting for whatever the war was about. "I want to see 200,000 black soldiers in the field," Charles Francis Adams, Jr.—no radical—wrote to his father, "and then I shall think it time to have peace." From the South now, since Gettysburg and Vicksburg, came less emphasis on the right of secession and the cry more often that the South was in a defensive war.

Habits of stealing and lying changed for the better when freed Negroes came into the contraband camps. So alleged the American Freedmen's Inquiry

Commission, headed by Robert Dale Owen, in their report published in June '63, saying, ". . . one of the first acts of the Negroes, when they found themselves free, was to establish schools at their own expense." The former crime of learning to read being no longer a crime, made some of them glad. They were starting churches. Also now that they could be married and have a family life if they chose, some were taking that course. "The Negro is found quite ready to copy whatever he believes are the rights and obligations of what he looks up to as the superior race."

The pathos of mixed bloods, and the fact of a mulatto woman being in more peril from a Northern white soldier than from a black freedman, was recited by the commission. "Many colored women think it more disgraceful to be black than to be illegitimate; for it is especially in regard to white men that their ideas and habits as to this matter are perverted. A case came to the knowledge of the commission, in which a mulatto girl deemed it beneath her to associate with her half sister, a black, the daughter of her mother's husband, her own father being a white man." The commission inserted in its report sentences over which Lincoln, possibly, both laughed and cried as he read: ". . . Our Chief Magistrate would probably be surprised to learn with what reverence, bordering on superstition, he is regarded by these poor people. Recently, at Beaufort, a gang of colored men . . . at work on the wharf, were discussing the qualifications of the President—how he had dispersed their masters, and what he would undoubtedly do hereafter for the colored race—when an aged, white-headed Negro —a 'praise-man' (as the phrase is) amongst them—with all the solemnity of an old prophet, broke forth: *'What do you know 'bout Massa Linkum? Massa Linkum be ebrywhere. He walk de earth like de Lord.'*"

CHAPTER 37

Chickamauga—Elections Won, '63

AFTER the drawn battle at Murfreesboro in January '63, General Rosecrans kept the Army of the Cumberland at that same place in Tennessee for six months, fortifying, drilling, setting no troops into motion. Late in June '63 Rosecrans marched his forces through rough and broken country, and by September 9 had, without a battle, maneuvered the Confederate army under Bragg out of Chattanooga and put his own troops into that strategic center. While on this operation, Rosecrans wrote to Lincoln early in August reciting conditions: bad roads, bad weather, cavalry weakness, long hauls for bridge material.

"I think," Lincoln replied, "you must have inferred more than Gen Halleck has intended, as to any dissatisfaction of mine with you . . ." He wrote of anxiety while Rosecrans stayed inactive as Grant was threatened at Vicksburg by Johnston's army, which might any day have been joined by Bragg's army.

In the matter of supplies, road and weather conditions, campaign requisites, what he thought he had to have before he could start fighting, Rosecrans seemed as muddled and querulous as McClellan the year before. The complaints of Rosecrans, however, did not insinuate that jealous plotters and malicious geese at Washington were trying to snare and frustrate him. Lincoln met this personal quality, and never in his letters and telegrams to Rosecrans took on the peremptory manner, the ironic tone, he had latterly used with McClellan. On one slight affair the President telegraphed Rosecrans: "In no case have I intended to censure you, or to question your ability . . . I frequently make mistakes myself, in the many things I am compelled to do hastily." It may have come to Lincoln that into Rosecrans' ear had been poured an offer, by James R. Gilmore, that Horace Greeley and others wanted to run him for President. And Rosecrans had said No, "My place is in the army."

Rosecrans, 44 years old, was born in Kingston, Ohio. Graduating fifth in the class of 1842 at West Point, he served four years as professor of natural philosophy and of engineering at the national academy. He had organized a kerosene manufacturing company just before the war began, quit coal oil and money-making, and served with credit under McClellan in West Virginia; he came through hard fighting at Corinth and Murfreesboro, rated as an able commanding officer, not lacking piety. To his brother, Bishop Rosecrans, the General wrote a letter published in the *Catholic Telegraph* at Cincinnati excoriating Northern "rebel leaders" who foment guerrilla warfare.

The Richmond War Department had arranged for Longstreet with 20,000 troops from the Army of Northern Virginia to be sent by railroad down across the Carolinas and up into far northern Georgia to the help of Bragg. This gave Bragg 70,000 troops as against Rosecrans' 57,000. The two armies grappled at Chickamauga Creek near Crawfish Spring September 19, 1863.

Hay noted: "Sunday morning, the 20th of September, the President showed me Rosecrans' despatches of the day before, detailing the first day's fighting, and promising a complete victory the next day. The President was a little uneasy over the promise."

Late that Sunday afternoon Dana at Chattanooga wired: "My report to-day is of deplorable importance. Chickamauga is as fatal a name in our history as Bull Run." The right and center were shattered. The left wing, under the Union Virginian General George H. Thomas, held. Till sunset, till darkness and night, his 25,000 men held solid on a horseshoe of a rocky hillock against twice their number. One brigade ran out of ammunition and met Longstreet's veterans with the bayonet. Next day Thomas began moving in good order to Chattanooga, Bragg failing to make another attack.

A heavy day's work had been done that Sunday, with Union killed, wounded and missing reckoned at 16,000, Confederate at 18,000, a larger affair in blood loss than Antietam.

Enough news of the battle reached Lincoln that Sunday night so he could not sleep. Welles noted on Monday: "The President came to me this afternoon with the latest news. He was feeling badly. Tells me a dispatch was sent to him at the Soldiers' Home shortly after he got asleep, and so disturbed him that he had no more rest, but arose and came to the city and passed the remainder of the night awake and watchful."

Hay's diary read: "The next morning [September 21] he [the President] came into my bedroom before I was up, & sitting down on my bed said, 'Well, Rosecrans has been whipped, as I feared. I have feared it for several days. I believe I feel trouble in the air before it comes.' " To Rosecrans that day Lincoln sent a telegram: "Be of good cheer. We have unabated confidence in you, and in your soldiers and officers. In the main you must be the judge as to what is to be done . . ."

On the evening of September 23 John Hay rode out by moonlight to Soldiers' Home to bring the President to Washington for a night council of war; Stanton with dark news from Chattanooga was shaken by one of his frenzies of excitement. Hay found the President abed. "I delivered my message to him as he robed himself & he was considerably disturbed. I assured him as far as I could that it meant nothing serious, but he thought otherwise, as it was the first time Stanton had ever sent for him." According to Chase's memorandum of the meeting, much conversation followed, the President and Halleck disinclined to weaken Meade, Seward and Chase decisive for reinforcing Rosecrans.

At 2:30 A.M. September 24, Meade was ordered by telegraph to prepare two army corps, under General Hooker, ready for transport, with five days' cooked provisions, with baggage, artillery, ammunition, horses, to follow. Further appeals came from Rosecrans and Dana; soon the enemy might cut off their communications and supplies. Stanton told Eckert to work out a rail schedule to Chattanooga. At 8 A.M. Eckert reported the troop transport could be done in 15 days. Stanton jumped for joy. "The plan was so well laid and withal so sensible," wrote Bates, "that Lincoln and Stanton both indorsed it." Superintendent Thomas A. Scott of the Pennsylvania Railroad and officers of the Baltimore & Ohio and other railroads were called to Washington, and arrangements completed. Scott went to Louisville, a midway point, kept the wires hot with brief messages; from Bealeton, Virginia, to Chattanooga, Tennessee, 1,233 miles, 23,000 men were transported in 11½ days.

To Mrs. Lincoln at the Fifth Avenue Hotel in New York, the President September 24 telegraphed as to Chickamauga that the Union army was worsted mainly in yielding ground. "According to rebel accounts . . . they lost six killed, and eight wounded. Of the killed, one Major Genl. and five Brigadiers, including your brother-in-law, Helm." Now Lincoln wrote for his wife's stepmother at Lexington, Kentucky: "Allow Mrs. Robert S. Todd, widow, to go south and bring her daughter, Mrs. General B. Hardin Helm, with her children, north to Kentucky."

Every day while Rosecrans had operated around Chattanooga that month the President had been keeping an anxious watch on East Tennessee, a region of mountaineers and hill people who owned no slaves and whose hearts, many of them, Lincoln knew were with the Union cause. In that region kinfolk of his had lived and died.

While Rosecrans marched toward Chattanooga, and Lincoln was urging Burnside with the Army of the Ohio to take Knoxville and occupy East Tennessee, once more a delegation from that region called at the White House to lay their wrongs before the President. And the President did not have the heart to face them and talk with them. He wrote them a groaning and bitter letter, saying he knew well what they had been waiting for when on successive days they sent cards and notes asking an interview which he refused. "I knew it was the same true, and painful story, which Gov. Johnson, Mr. Maynard, Dr. Clements and others have been telling me for more than two years. I also knew that meeting you could do no good; because I have all the while done, and shall continue to do the best for you I could, and can. I do as much for East Tennessee as I would, or could, if my own home, and family were in Knoxville." He mentioned the difficulties of getting an army into the region and keeping it there. No one could fail to see those difficulties "unless it may be those who are driven mad and blind by their sufferings."

Then in three weeks, early in September, Burnside and the Army of the Ohio had crossed the Tennessee line, entered Kingston, and marched into Knoxville to be met by cheering crowds. Flags long hidden were flashed out into sunlight, officers and soldiers welcomed into homes.

Though repeatedly ordered to join Rosecrans, Burnside delayed, and September 25 Lincoln wrote him: ". . . On the 19th. you telegraph once from Knoxville, and twice from Greenville, acknowledging receipt of order, and saying you will hurry support to Rosecrans. On the 20th. you telegraph again from Knoxville, saying you will do all you can, and are hurrying troops to Rosecrans. On the 21st. you telegraph from Morristown, saying you will hurry support to Rosecrans; and now your despatch of the 23rd. comes in from Carter's Station, still farther away from Rosecrans."

The letter was a patient and weary framing of the query to Burnside "How can you be so stupid?" Having written it, Lincoln delayed sending it. Then he decided not to send it at all. Instead he sent Burnside two telegrams suggesting that troops be rushed to Rosecrans at Chattanooga.

Meantime came charges that three major generals, McCook, Crittenden, Negley, had, during the Chickamauga battle, sought personal safety or had mismanaged their forces. The President issued orders for a court of inquiry. The court met, heard evidence and cleared the generals of conduct unbecoming to officers.

Rosecrans under strain was cracking, putting into telegrams to Lincoln many complaints of poor communications and subsistence, and such generalties as "Our future is not bright." In a telegram October 12 Lincoln tried heartening Rosecrans: "You and Burnside now have him [the enemy] by the throat, and he must break your hold, or perish . . . Sherman *is* coming to you."

The Confederates had a hold on the Tennessee River by which they blocked water transport of food and supplies for Rosecrans' army; and the long rough wagon route that met rail connections with Nashville was threatened. The Dana reports ran gloomier that second week in October; Rosecrans was "dawdling" while catastrophe hung close, starvation or disorderly retreat. And on October 16: "The incapacity of the commander is astonishing, and it often seems difficult to believe him of sound mind. His imbecility appears to be contagious."

The same day Halleck wrote to Grant at Cairo, Illinois: "You will receive herewith the orders of the President of the United States placing you in command of the Departments of the Ohio, Cumberland and Tennessee."

Thus Lincoln put Grant at the head of all military operations west of the Alleghenies. "It is left optional with you to supersede General G. H. Thomas or not."

After a personal conference at Indianapolis with Stanton, Grant, by a rail route and a final horseback trip of 55 miles, arrived at Chattanooga October 23. Rosecrans had left October 20 to report at Cincinnati for further orders. To Hay October 24 the President said that ever since Chickamauga Rosecrans had been "confused and stunned like a duck hit on the head."

George Henry Thomas, "the Rock of Chickamauga," was a peculiar instance, a Virginia-born West Pointer who stayed with the Union. Appointed a colonel in April '61, and with others required to renew his oath of allegiance to the U.S. Government, Thomas replied, "I don't care; I would just as soon take the oath before each meal during my life if the department saw fit to order it." Thomas, now 47, saw service in Indian wars and in the Mexican War, was an artillery instructor at West Point, a cavalry major. At Mill Springs Thomas had shown a flash, at Murfreesboro fire and flint, at Chickamauga granite steadiness and volcanic resistance. Slowly in the trampling and grinding of events George Henry Thomas was arriving at his own.

A laconic streak underlay the sluggish outside of him. In a council of generals at Murfreesboro, when asked by Rosecrans to protect a proposed retreat, he woke from a nap to say, "This army can't retreat." In a like council at Chickamauga he dozed, and only came out of the doze to mutter repeatedly, "Strengthen the left," almost as though he read in a crystal ball the terrible necessity of the next day, when everything crumbled except himself and the left wing. This brevity functioned again when after a battle he was asked whether the dead should be buried in the order of the states they came from. "No, no," said Old Pap Thomas. "Mix them up. I am tired of State rights."

Now Thomas was joined with Sherman and other tried commanders, with Grant as chief of the West, with forces massed at Chattanooga near the Alabama and Georgia state lines, wedging toward the Deep South as if hoping to cut it in two.

Meade September 24 was writing his wife: "I was summoned to Washington and informed that the President considered my army too large for a merely defensive one . . . The President is the best judge of where the armies can be best employed, and if he chooses to place this army strictly on the defensive, I have no right to object or murmur . . . There still existed a feverish anxiety that I should try and do something."

One staff man wrote that though the newspapers were mentioning "the fine autumn weather" for fighting, Meade was not going to risk another Fredericksburg. Lincoln, however, was willing to take that risk, and October 16 wrote to Halleck his guess that Lee, overestimating the number of soldiers stripped from Meade for Western duty, might fight in the open. The President made a proposal for Meade to consider, an offer at no time previously made to a general in the field: "If Gen. Meade can now attack him [Lee] on a field no worse than equal for us, and will do so with all the skill and courage, which he, his officers and men possess, the honor will be his if he succeeds, and the blame may be mine if he fails."

The offer of Lincoln to Meade reached the press and was published. Lincoln evidently wished it made known that, as the newspapers said, he had ordered Meade "to pursue after Lee's army, to find the enemy, and to fight him wherever found; and that he [the President] would be responsible for Meade's defeat, if he should be defeated." It seemed as though Lincoln took this step so there could be no possible mistake in the public mind that he wanted fighting, had ordered fighting, and would blame no commander if there was fighting that brought more useless slaughter. A hostile and defeatist press poured its scorn on "this silly and most unmilitary order," as the Chicago *Times* termed it in an article headed "Exposure of Lincoln's Folly."

But Lee had again outguessed Meade, as Meade humbly and frankly confessed to his wife in a note from Warrenton, Virginia, four days later: "Lee has retired across the Rappahannock, after completely destroying the railroad on which I depend for my supplies. His object is to prevent my advance, and in the meantime send more troops to Bragg. This was a deep game, and I am free to admit that in the playing of it he has got the advantage of me."

When Lincoln groaned to Hay or Welles, or to himself alone, over the inaction of the Army of the Potomac, it was not because of any trickery, evasion or politics of that army's commander. For Meade had not asked command. It had been thrust on him. And always with the gravest courtesy he made it plain to Lincoln, Halleck and Stanton that if they believed he was "too slow or prudent," as he phrased it, he would willingly fight under some-one else. On October 23 he wrote to Mrs. Meade: "Yesterday I received an order to repair to Washington, to see the President. I . . . was detained so late that I remained there all night . . . The President was, as he always is, very considerate and kind. He found no fault with my operations, although it was very evident he was disappointed that I had not got a battle out of Lee. He coincided with me that there was not much to be gained by any farther advance; but General Halleck was very urgent that something should be done, but what that something was he did not define."

From the Southern press and home strategists, Lee was receiving the same sort of criticism as that heaped on Meade in the North. Like Meade, he was too slow and too prudent, ran many an editorial. They were both Christian gentlemen, Meade and Lee, clean, reverent and pious, each strict in the observance of Episcopal forms, praying regularly to the same God while they led their hosts seeking to mangle and eviscerate each other.

In promoting Admiral Dahlgren, Lincoln gave his approval to aggressive tactics at Charleston, whatever the increased cost. During six days in August a fleet of monitors and gunboats bombarded Charleston; an army of 18,000 troops waited while 12 batteries of heavy rifled cannon opened fire at a two-mile distance; in one 40-minute period they dropped 120,000 pounds of projectiles into the defending forts. A storming column of Negro soldiers led by the white Colonel Robert Gould Shaw, of an old and distinguished Boston family, captured Fort Wagner. Shaw, "the blue-eyed child of fortune," crying, "Onward, boys!" fell dead from bullets, and became an enshrined memory and a symbol to the antislavery forces of the North.

Lincoln read the news telegraphed by the commanding general, August 24: "Fort Sumter is today a shapeless and harmless mass of ruins." As later news trickled in it turned out that the much-hated city still serenely held her own. And though Fort Sumter seemed to be a ruin, it kept a garrison. For many months Charleston was let alone.

From cities and towns of the North a steady stream of men and boys in blue moved south, always south, month by month filling gaps in the ranks. The machinery of the draft was working. Among generals it was commented that the substitutes, bounty men, human material pressed into service by the enrolling officers, were not as good soldier stuff as the earlier recruits of the war.

To the President came many instances of Federal judges releasing drafted men through habeas corpus proceedings. The Cabinet September 14 saw Lincoln in a warlike mood, going so far as to say he might have to arrest a few Federal judges. "The President was very determined," noted Welles, "and intimated that he would not only enforce the law, but if Judge Lowry [Lowrie] and others continued to interfere and interrupt the draft he would send them after Vallandigham."

Of another Cabinet session next morning Chase recorded it came out that two U.S. court judges in Pennsylvania—Cadwalader at Philadelphia and McCandless at Pittsburgh—had released more drafted men by far than all the state courts put together. Stanton's view was that these two Federal judges had taken a hand in "some very gross proceedings, under color of judicial authority, manifestly intended to interfere with the recruiting and maintenance of the army."

On September 15 was issued a proclamation as finally drafted by Seward. Solemnly it was made known by the President that "the privilege of the writ of *habeas corpus* is suspended throughout the United States" and this suspension would continue till modified or revoked by a later proclamation. A sonorous pronouncement it would be when read by a provost marshal, in support of the marshal's saying in effect to the judge, "I'm going to take this drafted man away with me and put him in the army and your court can't stop me because I have the United States Army and Navy backing me."

Hay wrote to Nicolay August 7 of Washington being "dismal now as a defaced tombstone." Part of the dismal air came from the conscription. On Executive Mansion stationery Hay wrote: "The draft fell pretty heavily in our end of town. William Johnston (cullud) was taken while polishing the Executive boots . . . A clerk in the War Department named Ramsey committed suicide on hearing he was drafted."

While the President in early October was dealing with habeas corpus, with the committee of radicals from Missouri and Kansas, with Burnside in Tennessee, Rosecrans at Chattanooga and Meade in Virginia, besides many routine matters, Seward took on the work of writing a Thanksgiving proclamation, which the President signed. Over the signature of A. Lincoln came the pronouncement, "I do therefore invite my fellow citizens in every part of the United States, and also those who are at sea and those who are sojourning in foreign lands, to set apart and observe the last Thursday of November next, as a day of Thanksgiving and Praise to our beneficent Father who dwelleth in the Heavens."

The changed air of expectation that the Union cause would yet win, the shift from the gloom of the first half of '63, made the basis for thanksgiving.

With the Gettysburg and Vicksburg victories, one of them ending Confederate hopes of winning by invasion of the North, the other sending the Mississippi "unvexed to the sea," many considered the war at an end or nearly so. Intangible psychic factors played on both sides. The North wondered why the South didn't quit.

The South dug deeper into itself for new motives and began fighting with despair for honor, for a mystic pennant, for a lost cause that could eventually be looked back on as having had a clean death. "The drums that beat for the advance into Pennsylvania seemed to many of us to be beating the funeral march of the dead Confederacy," later wrote General Daniel H. Hill, one of Lee's ablest lieutenants, now in the West with Bragg. "Duty, however, was to be done faithfully and unflinchingly to the last . . . The waning fortunes of the Confederacy were developing a vast amount of 'latent unionism' in the breasts of the original secessionists, those fiery zealots who in '61 proclaimed that 'one Southern could whip three Yankees.' The negroes and the fire-eaters with 'changed hearts' were now most excellent spies."

Both Lee and Davis, after the July defeats, issued appeals to soldiers to come back to the army. Davis offered pardon to officers and men absent without leave who would return in 20 days. Wives, mothers, sisters, daughters of the Confederacy were beseeched by the Richmond head of their Government, "If all now absent return to the ranks you will equal in numbers the invaders."

Thousands of Confederate deserters in the mountains of Alabama fought off cavalry sent to arrest them. The Confederate Bureau of Ordnance asked for the church bells of Georgia to be melted and remolded for war. One gold dollar bought ten paper Confederate dollars. A Louisiana father, beginning to doubt the Southern orators, was writing his son in the Confederate Army, "This war was got up drunk but they will have to settle it sober."

In a call for 300,000 more troops October 16, 1863, Lincoln said the new men were wanted to follow up and clinch the winning streak of Union armies that summer. The document stipulated that quotas would be *required* from the various states. In reality it was another executive order for a draft. Between provost marshals and various state officials, particularly Governor Seymour of New York, there began discussions and quarrels as to methods of drafting. The war, the draft, habeas corpus suspension, had been denounced at five overflow meetings in and around Cooper Union in New York City June 3, 1863, at a Peace Convention. "God did not intend that we should succeed in this war," said the convention's address to the public. "Had He intended it He would not have placed in command a Lincoln with such coadjutors as Butler or Burnside." As the address was read to the convention, "the groans and hisses for the President, and the cheers for Vallandigham and peace were specially vigorous," said the New York *Times*. Bartenders in saloons roundabout served patrons with "Jeff Davis cocktails," "Stonewall punches," "Sumter bumpers."

Under the heading "Lincoln to Be Declared Perpetual President," the *Crisis* October 7 said, "It is now stated that a bill has been prepared and will be placed before the next Congress declaring Lincoln President while the war lasts."

The fast and furious fall campaign in the Buckeye State revolved around

Lincoln. Ohio mass meetings at which orators excoriated the President, and with metaphors nailed his hide to the barn door, drew thousands of people. Crowds did not number 30,000 and 40,000 as often as the Democratic press claimed, yet the Copperhead clans did gather in tens of thousands. And the Union party meetings drew tens of thousands. Not since the Lincoln-Douglas debates had the prairie electorate gathered in such numbers and with so high an excitement. George E. Pugh, candidate for lieutenant governor, shouted from the campaign platform that if his running mate, Vallandigham, were elected governor there would be "fifty thousand fully armed and equipped freemen of Ohio to receive their Governor-elect at the Canadian line and escort him to the State House to see that he takes the oath of office."

On October 13, Election Day in Ohio and Pennsylvania, Welles called at the White House, and noted, "The President says he feels nervous." The wires that night clicked off news that the Ohio Copperhead ticket had the votes of 185,000 citizens and 2,200 soldiers of Ohio. However, John Brough of the Union party was elected governor by a majority of 61,920 in the citizen vote and 39,179 in the soldier ballots, a total of over 101,000. Pennsylvania returns gave Governor Curtin re-election by a 41,000 majority. A letter from General McClellan endorsing Curtin's opponent had had little effect.

Welles on October 14 found Lincoln relieved of the gloom of the day before. "He told me he had more anxiety in regard to the election results of yesterday than he had in 1860 when he was chosen. He could not, he said, have believed four years ago that one genuine American voter would, or could be induced to, vote for such a man as Vallandigham."

At the Maryland election the Governor's party, Conservative Union, was sunk with a vote of 15,984 as against 36,360 for the candidates of the Unconditional Union or Emancipation party. Four on the latter ticket were among the five new Congressmen elected, and the Emancipationists won a majority in both houses of the legislature.

In the Border Slave States of Delaware and Kentucky the Union party also won, while in Missouri the Union Emancipationist radicals swept into so many legislative seats that the two U.S. Senatorships were divided between Union party factions, one to B. Gratz Brown, a leading radical, the other to John B. Henderson, a conservative. Lincoln was pleased. The event fitted the turmoil. He wired friends at Jefferson City, Missouri: "Yours saying Brown and Henderson are elected Senators, is received. I understand, this is one and one. If so, it is knocking heads together to some purpose."

In all the Northern States except New Jersey, the Union party ticket swept the field. A Chicago newspaper exulted: "Everywhere it has been a slaughter of Copperheads. Springfield, Ill., went Union by 138, a gain of 440 since 1862." In the State House at Springfield sat Governor Dick Yates, who when lit up was a blunt and familiar talker. In the campaign he had made a speech to a Methodist conference at Springfield and was quoted: "I have visited Old Abe and urged him to use more radical measures and he has said to me, 'Never mind, Dick, it will be all right yet. Hold still and see the salvation of the Lord!' (Loud and prolonged cheering, stamping of feet, etc.)" The speech had something, and was argued about in the tall-grass weeklies, even the New York *Herald* saying that immense applause from the people had greeted "the above Cromwellian phrase."

CHAPTER 38

Lincoln Speaks at Gettysburg

A PRINTED invitation notified Lincoln that on Thursday, November 19, 1863, exercises would be held for the dedication of a National Soldiers' Cemetery at Gettysburg.

The duties of orator of the day had fallen on Edward Everett. Born in 1794, he had been U.S. Senator, governor of Massachusetts, member of Congress, Secretary of State under Fillmore, Minister to Great Britain, Phi Beta Kappa poet at Harvard, professor of Greek at Harvard, president of Harvard. His wife was Charlotte Gray Brooks, daughter of Peter Chardon Brooks, first of American marine and life-insurance millionaires. Serene stars had watched over their home life and children until Everett's wife was sent to a private retreat, incurably insane. A lifelong friendship took root between him and her father; they shared a sorrow.

The Union of States was a holy concept to Everett, and the slavery issue secondary, though when president of Harvard from 1846 to 1849 he refused to draw the color line, saying in the case of a Negro applicant, Beverly Williams, that "If this boy passes the examinations, he will be admitted." Not often was he so provocative. Suave, handsomely venerable in his 69th year, Everett was a natural choice of the Pennsylvania commissioners. He notified them that he would appear for the Gettysburg dedication November 19.

Lincoln meanwhile, in reply to the printed invitation, sent word to the commissioners that he would be present at the ceremonies. The commissioners then considered whether the President should be asked to deliver an address. Clark E. Carr of Galesburg, Illinois, representing his state on the Board of Commissioners, noted that the decision of the board to invite Lincoln to speak was "an afterthought."

David Wills of Gettysburg, as the special agent of Governor Curtin and also acting for the several states, by letter informed Lincoln, ". . . I am authorized by the Governors of the various States to invite you to be present and participate in these ceremonies . . . It is the desire that after the oration, you, as Chief Executive of the nation, formally set apart these grounds to their sacred use by a few appropriate remarks." "The invitation," wrote Carr, "was not settled upon and sent to Mr. Lincoln until the second of November, more than six weeks after Mr. Everett had been invited to speak, and but little more than two weeks before the exercises were held."

Lamon noted that Lincoln wrote part of his intended Gettysburg address in Washington, covered a sheet of foolscap paper with a memorandum of it, and before taking it out of his hat and reading it to Lamon he said it was not at all satisfactory to him. He had been too busy to give it the time he would like to.

The armies of Meade and Grant required attention. And there were such unforeseen affairs as the marriage of Kate Chase, daughter of the Secretary of the Treasury, at the most brilliant wedding the new Northern regime had as yet put on in Washington. The bridegroom was Governor William Sprague of Rhode Island, handsome of figure, an heir of wealth, iron and textile manufacturer, railroad and bank president, artillery officer with a record of a horse shot from under him at Bull Run, U.S. Senator by election in the spring of '63. He was 33 years old, had paid $11,000 for one of his string of horses, and his bride of 28 had beauty plus wit and a gift for politics. Lincoln, attending alone, and bringing a dainty fan as a present for the bride, probably went because that was better than to let talk run as to why he did not go. He dropped in and left early.

Two men, in the weeks just before the Gettysburg ceremonies, had done their best to make him see himself as a world spokesman of democracy, popular government, the mass of people as opposed to aristocrats, classes and special interests. John Murray Forbes, having read Lincoln's lively stump-speech letter to the Springfield, Illinois, mass meeting, wrote to Sumner September 3, "I delight in the President's plain letter to plain people!" Forbes followed this five days later with a letter which Sumner carried to the White House and handed to Lincoln.

An aristocracy ruled the South and controlled it for war, believed Forbes, pointing to "the aristocratic class who own twenty negroes and upwards" as numbering "about 28,000 persons, which is about the 1/8th part of 5,000,000" whites. So Forbes urged, "Let the people North and South see this line clearly defined between the people and the aristocrats, and the war will be over! Bonaparte, when under the republic, fighting despots of Europe, did as much by his bulletins as he did by his bayonets. You," Forbes urged the President, "have the same opportunity . . . My suggestion, then, is that you should seize an early opportunity and any subsequent chance, to teach your great audience of plain people that the war is not the North against the South, but the people against the aristocrats."

This same idea Forbes wrote to William Evans, an English liberal, who was to call on the President. "I wish you could make him see and feel," said Forbes, "that you and Bright and others represent the democratic element in Great Britain, and that you look upon him as fighting the battle of democracy for all the world! I wish our people understood this as well as yours do!" And William Evans after seeing Lincoln wrote Forbes November 3: "Your suggestions were duly attended to."

Thus while Lincoln shaped his speech to be made at Gettysburg he did not lack specific advice to stand up and be a world spokesman. Some newspapers now had it that the President was going to make a stump speech over the graves of the Gettysburg dead as a political play. Talk ran in Washington that by attending Governor Curtin's "show" the President would strengthen himself with the Curtin faction without alienating the opposing Cameron clique.

Though the Gettysburg dedication was to be under interstate auspices, it had tremendous national significance for Lincoln; on the platform would be the state governors whose co-operation with him was of vast importance. Also widely mouthed and printed had been the slander and libel that on his visit to the battlefield of Antietam nearly a year before he had laughed obscenely at his own funny stories and called on Lamon to sing a cheap comic song. Perhaps he might go to Gettysburg and let it be seen how he demeaned himself on a somber landscape of sacrifice.

His personal touch with Gettysburg, by telegraph, mail, courier and by a throng of associations, made it a place of great realities to him. Just after the battle there, a woman had come to his office, the doorman saying she had been "crying and taking on" for several days trying to see the President. Her husband and three sons were in the army. On part of her husband's pay she had lived for a time, till money from him stopped coming. She was hard put to scrape a living and needed one of her boys to help.

The President listened to her, standing at a fireplace, hands behind him, head bowed, motionless. The woman finished her plea. Slowly and almost as if talking to himself alone the words came and only those words: "I have two, and you have none." He crossed the room, wrote an order for the military discharge of one of her sons. On a special sheet of paper he wrote full and detailed instructions where to go and what to say in order to get her boy back.

In a few days the doorman told the President the same woman was again on hand crying and taking on. "Let her in," was the word. She had found doors opening to her and officials ready to help on seeing the President's written words she carried. She had located her boy's camp, regiment, company. She had found him, yes, wounded at Gettysburg, dying in a hospital, and had followed him to the grave. And, she begged, would the President now give her the next one of her boys?

As before he stood at the fireplace, hands behind him, head bent low, motionless. Slowly and almost as if talking to himself alone the words came and as before only those words: "I have two, and you have none." He crossed the room to his desk and began writing. As though nothing else was to do she followed, stood by his chair as he wrote, put her hand on the President's head, smoothed his thick and disorderly hair with motherly fingers. He signed an order giving her the next of her boys, stood up, put the priceless paper in her hand as he choked out the one word, "There!" and with long quick steps was gone from the room with her sobs and cries of thanks in his ears.

Thus the Kentuckian, James Speed, gathered the incident and told it. By many strange ways Gettysburg was to Lincoln a fact in crimson mist.

Thaddeus Stevens said in November '63 that Lincoln was a "dead card" in the political deck. He favored Chase as a more thoroughgoing antislavery man for the next President, and hearing that Lincoln and Seward were going to Gettysburg, but not Chase, he clipped his words, "The dead going to eulogize the dead."

On November 17 the President issued a little proclamation fixing a township line "within the City of Omaha" as the starting point for the Union Pacific Railway. Congress had made it his duty to do this.

The Gettysburg speech was shaping at the same time that Lincoln was preparing his annual message to Congress, assembling it in less than three weeks. In that message he would point to "actual commencement of work upon the Pacific railroad," his own act of fixing an initial point being the most tangible part of the commencement.

When Lincoln boarded the train for Gettysburg November 18, his best chum in the world, Tad, lay sick abed and the doctors not sure what ailed him. The mother still mourned for Willie and was hysterical about Tad. But the President felt imperative duty called him to Gettysburg.

Provost Marshal General Fry as a War Department escort came to the White House, but the President was late in getting into the carriage for the drive to the station. They had no time to lose, Fry remarked. Lincoln said he felt like an Illinois man who was going to be hanged and as the man passed along the road on the way to the gallows the crowds kept pushing into the way and blocking passage. The condemned man at last called out, "Boys, you needn't be in such a hurry to get ahead, there won't be any fun till I get there."

Flags and red, white and blue bunting decorated the four-car special train. Aboard were three Cabinet members, Seward, Usher and Blair, Nicolay and Hay, Army and Navy representatives, newspapermen, the French and Italian Ministers and attachés. The rear third of the last coach had a drawing room, where from time to time the President talked with nearly everyone aboard as they came and went. Approaching Hanover Junction, he arose and said, "Gentlemen, this is all very pleasant, but the people will expect me to say something to them tomorrow, and I must give the matter some thought." He then returned to the rear room of the car.

An elderly gentleman got on the train and, shaking hands, told the President he had lost a son at Little Round Top at Gettysburg. The President answered he feared a visit to that spot would open fresh wounds, and yet if the end of sacrifice had been reached "we could give thanks even amidst our tears." They quoted from his unburdening to this old man: "When I think of the sacrifices of life yet to be offered, and the hearts and homes yet to be made desolate before this dreadful war is over, my heart is like lead within me, and I feel at times like hiding in deep darkness." At one stop a little girl lifted to an open window thrust a bunch of rosebuds into the car. "Flowerth for the President." Lincoln stepped over, bent down, kissed her face. "You are a little rosebud yourself."

At sundown the train pulled into Gettysburg and Lincoln was driven to the Wills residence. A sleepy little country town of 3,500 was overflowing with human pulses again. Private homes were filled with notables and non-descripts. Hundreds slept on the floors of hotels. Military bands blared till late in the night serenading whomsoever. The weather was mild and the moon up for those who chose to go a-roaming. Serenaders called on the President and heard him: "In my position it is sometimes important that I should not say foolish things. [A voice: "If you can help it."] It very often happens that the only way to help it is to say nothing at all. Believing that is my present condition this evening, I must beg of you to excuse me from addressing you further."

At dinner in the Wills home that evening Lincoln met Edward Everett, Governor Curtin and others. About 11 o'clock, he gathered his sheets of paper and went next door for a half-hour with his Secretary of State. Whether Seward made slight or material alterations in the text was known only to Lincoln and Seward. It was midnight or later that Lincoln went to sleep. He slept better for having a telegram from Stanton reporting there was no real war news and "On inquiry Mrs. Lincoln informs me that your son is better this evening."

Fifteen thousand, some said 30,000 or 50,000, people were on Cemetery Hill for the exercises next day when the procession from Gettysburg arrived afoot and horseback—members of the U.S. Government, the Army and Navy, governors of states, mayors of cities, a regiment of troops, hospital corps, telegraph company representatives, Knights Templar, Masonic Fraternity, Odd Fellows and other benevolent associations, the press, fire departments, citizens of Pennsylvania and other states. At ten o'clock Lincoln in a black suit, high silk hat and white gloves came out of the Wills residence, mounted a horse, and held a reception on horseback. At 11 the parade began to move. Clark E. Carr, just behind the President, believed he noticed that the President sat erect and looked majestic to begin with and then got to thinking so that his body leaned forward, his arms hung limp, his head bent far down.

A long telegram from Stanton at ten o'clock had been handed him. Burnside seemed safe though threatened at Knoxville, Grant was starting a big battle at Chattanooga, and "Mrs. Lincoln reports your son's health as a great deal better and he will be out today."

The march began. "Mr. Lincoln was mounted upon a young and beautiful chestnut horse, the largest in the Cumberland Valley," wrote Lieutenant Cochrane. This seemed the first occasion that anyone had looked at the President mounted with a feeling that just the right horse had been picked to match his physical length.

The march was over in 15 minutes. But Mr. Everett, the orator of the day, had not arrived. Bands played till noon. Mr. Everett arrived. On the platform sat Governors Curtin of Pennsylvania, Bradford of Maryland, Morton of Indiana, Seymour of New York, Parker of New Jersey, Dennison of Ohio, with ex-Governor Tod and Governor-elect Brough of Ohio, Edward Everett and his daughter, Major Generals Schenck, Stahel, Doubleday and Couch, Brigadier General Gibbon and Provost Marshal General Fry, foreign Ministers, members of Congress, Colonel Ward Hill Lamon, Secretary Usher, and the President of the United States with Secretary Seward and Postmaster General Blair immediately at his left.

The U.S. House chaplain, the Reverend Thomas H. Stockton, offered a prayer while the thousands stood with uncovered heads. Benjamin B. French, officer in charge of buildings in Washington, introduced the Honorable Edward Everett, who rose, bowed low to Lincoln, saying, "Mr. President." Lincoln responded, "Mr. Everett."

The orator of the day then stood in silence before a crowd that stretched to limits that would test his voice. Beyond and around were the wheat fields, the meadows, the peach orchards, long slopes of land, and five and seven miles further the contemplative blue ridge of a low mountain range. His eyes could sweep all this as he faced the audience. He had taken note of it in his prepared address. "Overlooking these broad fields now reposing from the labors of the waning year, the mighty Alleghanies dimly towering before us, the graves of our brethren beneath our feet, it is with hesitation that I raise my poor voice to break the eloquent silence of God and Nature . . .

As my eye ranges over the fields whose sods were so lately moistened by the blood of gallant and loyal men, I feel, as never before, how truly it was said of old that it is sweet and becoming to die for one's country."

He gave an outline of how the war began, traversed decisive features of the three days' battles at Gettysburg, discussed the doctrine of state sovereignty and denounced it, drew parallels from European history, and came to his peroration quoting Pericles on dead patriots: "The whole earth is the sepulchre of illustrious men." He had spoken for one hour and 57 minutes, some said a trifle over two hours, repeating almost word for word an address that occupied nearly two newspaper pages.

Everett came to his closing sentence without a faltering voice: "Down to the latest period of recorded time, in the glorious annals of our common country there will be no brighter page than that which relates THE BATTLES OF GETTYSBURG." It was the effort of his life and embodied the perfections of the school of oratory in which he had spent his career. His poise, and chiefly some quality of inside goodheartedness, held most of his audience to him.

The Baltimore Glee Club sang an ode written for the occasion by Benjamin B. French. Having read Everett's address, Lincoln knew when the moment drew near for him to speak. He took out his own manuscript from a coat pocket, put on his steel-bowed glasses, stirred in his chair, looked over the manuscript, and put it back in his pocket. The Baltimore Glee Club finished. Ward Hill Lamon rose and spoke the words "The President of the United States," who rose, and holding in one hand the two sheets of paper at which he occasionally glanced, delivered the address in his high-pitched and clear-carrying voice. The Cincinnati *Commercial* reporter wrote, "The President rises slowly, draws from his pocket a paper, and, when commotion subsides, in a sharp, unmusical treble voice, reads the brief and pithy remarks." Hay wrote in his diary, "The President, in a firm, free way, with more grace than is his wont, said his half dozen words of consecration." Charles Hale of the Boston *Advertiser*, also officially representing Governor Andrew of Massachusetts, had notebook and pencil in hand, took down the slow-spoken words of the President:

Fourscore and seven years ago, our fathers brought forth upon this continent a new nation, conceived in liberty and dedicated to the proposition that all men are created equal.

Now we are engaged in a great civil war, testing whether that nation—or any nation, so conceived and so dedicated—can long endure.

We are met on a great battle-field of that war. We are met to dedicate a portion of it as the final resting place of those who have given their lives that that nation might live.

It is altogether fitting and proper that we should do this.

But, in a larger sense, we cannot dedicate, we cannot consecrate, we cannot hallow, this ground. The brave men, living and dead, who struggled here, have consecrated it, far above our power to add or to detract.

The world will very little note nor long remember what we say here; but it can never forget what they did here.

It is for us, the living, rather, to be dedicated, here, to the unfinished work that they have thus far so nobly carried on. It is rather for us to be here dedicated to the great task remaining before us; that from these honored dead we take increased devotion to that cause for which they here gave the last full measure of devotion;

that we here highly resolve that these dead shall not have died in vain; that the nation shall, under God, have a new birth of freedom, and that government of the people, by the people, for the people, shall not perish from the earth.

In the written copy of his speech from which he read Lincoln used the phrase "our poor power." In other copies of the speech which he wrote out later he again used the phrase "our poor power." So it was evident that he meant to use the word "poor" when speaking to his audience, but he omitted it. Also in the copy held in his hands while facing the audience he had not written the words "under God," though he did speak those words and include them in later copies which he wrote. Therefore the words "under God" were decided upon after he wrote the text the night before at the Wills residence.

The New York *Tribune* and many other newspapers indicated "(Applause.)" at five places in the address and "(Long continued applause.)" at the end. The applause, however, according to most of the responsible witnesses, was formal, a tribute to the occasion. Ten sentences had been spoken in less than three minutes. A photographer had made ready to record a great historic moment, had bustled about with his dry plates, his black box on a tripod, and before he had his head under the hood for an exposure, the President had said "by the people, for the people" and the nick of time was past for a photograph.

The New York *Tribune* man and other like observers merely reported the words of the address with the one preceding sentence: "The dedicatory remarks were then delivered by the President." Strictly, no address as such was on the program from him. He was down for a few "dedicatory remarks." Lamon wrote that Lincoln told him just after delivering the speech that he had regret over not having prepared it with greater care. "Lamon, that speech won't *scour*. It is a flat failure and the people are disappointed." On the farms where Lincoln grew up, when wet soil stuck to the mold board of a plow they said it didn't "scour."

The nearby *Patriot and Union* of Harrisburg took its fling: "The President succeeded on this occasion because he acted without sense and without constraint in a panorama that was gotten up more for the benefit of his party than for the glory of the nation and the honor of the dead . . . We pass over the silly remarks of the President; for the credit of the nation we are willing that the veil of oblivion shall be dropped over them and that they shall no more be repeated or thought of."

The Chicago *Times* held that "Mr. Lincoln did most foully traduce the motives of the men who were slain at Gettysburg" in his reference to "a new birth of freedom," adding, "They gave their lives to maintain the old government, and the only Constitution and Union . . . The cheek of every American must tingle with shame as he reads the silly, flat, and dish-watery utterances of the man who has to be pointed out to intelligent foreigners as the President of the United States."

The Chicago *Tribune* had a reporter who telegraphed (unless some editor who read the address added his own independent opinion) a sentence: "The dedicatory remarks of President Lincoln will live among the annals of man." The Cincinnati *Gazette* reporter added after the text of the address, "That this was the right thing in the right place, and a perfect thing in every respect, was the universal encomium."

The American correspondent of the London *Times* wrote that "the ceremony was rendered ludicrous by some of the sallies of that poor President Lincoln . . . Anything more dull and commonplace it would not be easy to produce." Count Gurowski wrote in his diary, "Lincoln spoke, with one eye to a future platform and to re-election."

The Philadelphia *Evening Bulletin* said thousands who would not read the elaborate oration of Mr. Everett would read the President's few words "and not many will do it without a moistening of the eye and a swelling of the heart." The Providence *Journal* reminded readers of the saying that the hardest thing in the world is to make a good five-minute speech: "We know not where to look for a more admirable speech than the brief one which the President made at the close of Mr. Everett's oration."

Lincoln had spoken of an idea, a proposition, a concept, worth dying for, which brought from a Richmond newspaper a countering question and answer, "For what are we fighting? An abstraction."

The Springfield *Republican* comment ran: "Surpassingly fine as Mr. Everett's oration was in the Gettysburg consecration, the rhetorical honors of the occasion were won by President Lincoln. His little speech is a perfect gem; deep in feeling, compact in thought and expression, and tasteful and elegant in every word and comma. Then it has the merit of unexpectedness in its verbal perfection and beauty. We had grown so accustomed to homely and imperfect phrase in his productions that we had come to think it was the law of his utterance. But this shows he can talk handsomely as well as act sensibly. Turn back and read it over, it will repay study as a model speech."

"The Lounger" in *Harper's Weekly* inquired why the ceremony at Gettysburg was one of the most striking events of the war. "The President and the Cabinet were there, with famous soldiers and civilians. The oration by Mr. Everett was smooth and cold . . . The few words of the President were from the heart to the heart. They can not be read, even, without kindling emotion. 'The world will little note nor long remember what we say here, but it can never forget what they did here.' It was as simple and felicitous and earnest a word as was ever spoken."

Everett's opinion was written to Lincoln the next day: "I should be glad if I could flatter myself that I came as near to the central idea of the occasion in two hours as you did in two minutes." Lincoln's immediate reply was: "In our respective parts yesterday, you could not have been excused to make a short address, nor I a long one. I am pleased to know that, in your judgment, the little I did say was not entirely a failure."

At Everett's request Lincoln wrote with pen and ink a copy of his Gettysburg Address, and the manuscript was auctioned at a Sanitary Fair in New York for the benefit of soldiers. On request of George Bancroft, the historian, he wrote another copy for a Soldiers' and Sailors' Fair at Baltimore. He wrote still another to be lithographed as a facsimile in a publication, *Autographed Leaves of Our Country's Authors*. For Mr. Wills, his host at Gettysburg, he wrote another. The first draft, written in Washington, and the second one,

Upper left: Photograph by Alexander Gardner November 15, 1863, four days before the Gettysburg speech. Stern, austere, one of the most popular portraits of Lincoln [Meserve]. *Upper right:* Henry J. Raymond, editor and publisher of the New York *Times* and 1864 campaign biographer of Lincoln [Meserve]. *Lower left:* Andrew G. Curtin, Governor of Pennsylvania [CS]. *Lower center:* John A. Andrew, Governor of Massachusetts [CS]. *Lower right:* Horace Greeley, editor of the New York *Tribune* [CS].

Upper left: Union infantry rank and file [USASC]. *Upper right:* Commander in Chief of the armed forces of the U.S., Brady photograph February 9, 1864 [Meserve]. *Center:* Union officers and privates [CS]. *Lower left:* Confederate rank and file troopers captured at Gettysburg [CS]. *Lower right:* Escaped slaves, "contrabands," outfitted for labor inside Union lines [CS].

held while delivering it, went into Hay's hands to be eventually presented to the Library of Congress.

The ride to Washington took until midnight. Lincoln was weary, talked little, stretched out on one of the side seats in the drawing room and had a wet towel laid across his eyes and forehead.

He had stood that day, the world's foremost spokesman of popular government, saying that democracy was yet worth fighting for. What he meant by "a new birth of freedom" for the nation could have a thousand interpretations. The taller riddles of democracy stood up out of the address. It had the dream touch of vast and furious events epitomized for any foreteller to read what was to come. His cadences sang the ancient song that where there is freedom men have fought and sacrificed for it, and that freedom is worth men's dying for. For the first time since he became President he had on a dramatic occasion declaimed, howsoever it might be read, Jefferson's proposition which had been a slogan of the Revolutionary War—"All men are created equal"—leaving no other inference than that he regarded the Negro slave as a man. His outwardly smooth sentences were inside of them gnarled and tough with the enigmas of the American experiment.

Back at Gettysburg the blue haze of the Cumberland Mountains had dimmed till they were a blur in a nocturne. The moon was up and fell with a bland golden benevolence on the new-made graves of soldiers, on the sepulchers of old settlers, on the horse carcasses of which the onrush of war had not yet permitted removal. The New York *Herald* man walked amid them and ended the story he sent his paper: "The air, the trees, the graves are silent. Even the relic hunters are gone now. And the soldiers here never wake to the sound of reveille."

In many a country cottage over the land, a tall old clock in a quiet corner told time in a tick-tock deliberation. Whether the orchard branches hung with pink-spray blossoms or icicles of sleet, whether the outside news was seedtime or harvest, rain or drouth, births or deaths, the swing of the pendulum was right and left and right and left in a tick-tock deliberation.

The face and dial of the clock had known the eyes of a boy who listened to its tick-tock and learned to read its minute and hour hands. And the boy had seen years measured off by the swinging pendulum, had grown to man size, had gone away. And the people in the cottage knew that the clock would stand there and the boy would never again come into the room and look at the clock with the query, "What is the time?"

In a row of graves of the Unidentified the boy would sleep long in the dedicated final resting place at Gettysburg. Why he had gone away and why he would never come back had roots in some mystery of flags and drums, of national fate in which individuals sink as in a deep sea, of men swallowed and vanished in a man-made storm of smoke and steel.

The mystery deepened and moved with ancient music and inviolable consolation because a solemn Man of Authority had stood at the graves of the Unidentified and spoken the words "We can not consecrate—we can not hallow—this ground. The brave men, living and dead, who struggled here, have consecrated it far above our poor power to add or detract . . . from these honored dead we take increased devotion to that cause for which they gave the last full measure of devotion."

To the backward and forward pendulum swing of a tall old clock in a quiet corner they might read those cadenced words while outside the windows the first flurry of snow blew across the orchard and down over the meadow, the beginnings of winter in a gun-metal gloaming to be later arched with a star-flung sky.

CHAPTER 39

Epic '63 Draws to a Close

A WEEK after Lincoln's return from Gettysburg, Hay wrote to Nicolay: "The President is sick in bed. Bilious." Still later came definite information. The President had varioloid, a mild form of smallpox. Owen Lovejoy sent in his name, waited in the reception room, saw a door open just enough to frame Lincoln in a dressing gown saying, "Lovejoy, are you afraid?" "No, I have had the small-pox." And walking in, he heard Lincoln: "Lovejoy, there is one good thing about this. I now have something I can give everybody." Press items told of office seekers suddenly fleeing the White House on hearing what ailed the President.

An epic of action around Chattanooga came to its high point and Lincoln on a sickbed could read a Grant telegram: "Lookout Mountain top, all the rifle-pits in Chattanooga Valley, and Missionary Ridge entire, have been carried and now held by us," and a dispatch from Thomas: "Missionary Ridge was carried simultaneously at six different points . . . Among the prisoners are many who were paroled at Vicksburg." And again from Grant on November 27: "I am just in from the front. The rout of the enemy is most complete . . . The pursuit will continue to Red Clay in the morning, for which place I shall start in a few hours."

For the first time in a large-scale combat, Confederate soldiers had been routed, had run away. They had valor, as they had shown at Chickamauga. What explained their panic? The usual answer was Bragg, upright, moral, irascible, disputatious, censorious, dyspeptic, nervous, so harsh with his corrections and criticisms that the discipline of his army had gone to pieces. Grant had studied Bragg, knew him as Lee knew McClellan, and gauged his plans accordingly. Bragg had cornered Grant, put his army within gunshot range overlooking the Union army, making retreat for Grant "almost certain annihilation," said Grant. Then the rank and file of Grant's army had thrown orders to the wind and taken mountains away from an army holding the top ridges with cannon and rifle pits.

Anger at Jeff Davis, and mistrust of him, arose among some of his best aides because of his not knowing Bragg was second-rate. And Jeff Davis answered by appointing his friend Bragg Chief of Staff of the Confederate armies, with headquarters in Richmond. Newspapers of the North spread the story before their readers the last Thursday of November, the Day of Thanksgiving proclaimed by the President weeks earlier.

Now Sherman could be released with an army to march on Knoxville and relieve Longstreet's siege of Burnside there—which Sherman did in a clean, fast operation. Now Grant and Sherman could lay their plans to move farther south—on Atlanta—perhaps drive a wedge and split the Confederacy that lay east of the Mississippi.

The President's annual message to Congress began with "renewed, and profoundest gratitude to God" for another year "of health, and of sufficiently abundant harvests." Efforts to stir up foreign wars had failed. The treaty between the United States and Great Britain for suppression of the slave trade was working. The national banking law passed by Congress had proved a valuable support to public credit. The troops were being paid punctually. And the people? The President saluted them. "By no people were the burdens incident to a great war ever more cheerfully borne."

The report of the Secretary of War, "a document of great interest," was too valuable to summarize. The Union Navy was tightening its blockade of the enemy. More than 1,000 vessels had been captured; prizes amounted to $13,000,000. New navy yards were wanted. Enlisted seamen in 1861 numbered 7,500, now 34,000. The post office had taken in nearly as much money as it had spent and might soon become self-sustaining. Though a great war was on, 1,456,514 acres of land had been taken up under the new Homestead Law. The President agreed that the law should be modified to favor soldiers and sailors of Federal service.

The breath of a new and roaring age, intricate with man's new-found devices, rose at intervals throughout the message. A continuous line of telegraph from Russia to the Pacific Coast was being wrought under arrangements effected with the Russian Emperor. The proposed international telegraph across the Atlantic Ocean, and a telegraph line from Washington to the seaboard forts and the Gulf of Mexico, deserved reasonable outlay from Congress.

The Executive invited a backward look at the war. The "rebel" borders were pressed still farther back, the Mississippi opened, Tennessee and Arkansas cleared of insurgent control, slaveowners "now declare openly for emancipation," Maryland and Missouri disputing only as to the best mode of removing slavery within their own limits. Of former slaves 100,000 were in the U.S. military service, half of them bearing arms. "So far as tested, it is difficult to say they are not as good soldiers as any."

Looking to the present and future, the President had thought fit to issue a Proclamation of Amnesty and Reconstruction, a copy of it being transmitted to Congress. To those who wanted it the Union Government would give amnesty, forget what had been. Reconstruction, the bringing together again of the departed brothers into the Union, would begin with amnesty. This was the theory and the hope, not explicitly formulated, that underlay the proclamation and the oath Lincoln discussed for Congress in his message. He cited his constitutional pardoning power: through the rebellion many persons were guilty of treason; the President was authorized to extend pardon and amnesty on conditions he deemed expedient. Full pardon would be granted with restoration of property, except as to slaves and where rights of third parties intervened, and on condition that every such person took an oath:

. . . in presence of Almighty God, that I will henceforth faithfully support, protect and defend the Constitution of the United States, and the union of the States thereunder; and that I will, in like manner, abide by and faithfully support all acts of Congress . . . and . . . abide by and faithfully support all proclamations of the President made during the existing rebellion having reference to slaves . . . So help me God.

The proclamation had no reference to states that had kept loyal governments, never seceded—meaning Missouri, Kentucky, Maryland, Delaware. The intention of the proclamation was to give a mode by which national authority and loyal state governments might be re-established. The President's message reasoned for the amnesty proclamation. "The form of an oath is given, but no man is coerced to take it. The man is only promised a pardon in case he voluntarily takes the oath . . ."

The Executive set at rest all talk that the Emancipation Proclamation would be revoked. "While I remain in my present position I shall not attempt to retract or modify the emancipation proclamation; nor shall I return to slavery any person who is free by the terms of that proclamation, or by any of the acts of Congress." Before this sentence the silence in the hall was "profound," noted Noah Brooks, but with its reading "an irresistible burst of applause" swept the main floor and galleries.

Movements for emancipation in states not included in the Emancipation Proclamation were "matters of profound gratulation." He still favored gradual emancipation by Federal purchase of slaves. "While I do not repeat in detail what I have heretofore so earnestly urged upon this subject, my general views and feelings remain unchanged."

Noah Brooks in his news letter two days later found Senator Sumner "irate because his doctrine of State suicide finds no responsive echo" in the President's message. As a "vent to this half-concealed anger," wrote Brooks, "during the delivery of the Message the distinguished Senator from Massachusetts exhibited his petulance to the galleries by eccentric motions in his chair, pitching his documents and books upon the floor in ill-tempered disgust." Sumner still held that the seceded states had by secession committed suicide and should be governed as territories, conquered provinces on trial and under compulsion.

Lincoln spoke of the newborn fury of some of the Missouri radicals. Hay wrote December 13 of the President "very much displeased" at fresh reports from Missouri. Congressman Washburne had been in Missouri and saw, or thought he saw, that Schofield was overplaying his hand in factional politics; when Washburne spoke of electing Gratz Brown and J. B. Henderson as U.S. Senators, one from each faction, Schofield had replied he would not consent to the election of Brown. Also Brown had told the President that Schofield had refused to consent to a state constitutional convention, even though Brown had promised in that event he would as U.S. Senator vote to confirm Schofield as a major general. "These things," wrote Hay, "the President says, are obviously transcendent of his instructions to Schofield and must not be permitted. He has sent for Schofield to come to Washington and explain these grave matters."

Schofield in the White House heard Lincoln and replied the facts were that the desired union of conservatives and radicals in Missouri was impossible; they were more bitterly opposed to each other than either was to the Democrats. According to Schofield, Lincoln promptly dismissed the subject, "I believe you, Schofield; those fellows have been lying to me again." Later, from Congressman James S. Rollins, Schofield heard that one group of Missouri politicians had called on the President and given a version of Missouri affairs. The President had opened a little right-hand drawer of his desk, taken out a letter from Schofield, read it to them and said, "*That* is the truth about the matter; you fellows are lying to me."

To the Secretary of War, Lincoln wrote: "I believe Gen. Schofield must be relieved from command of the Department of Missouri; otherwise a question of veracity, in relation to his declarations as to his interfering, or not, with the Missouri Legislature, will be made with him, which will create an additional amount of trouble, not to be overcome by even a correct decision of the question." Lincoln sent to the Senate a nomination of Schofield for major general. There a majority favored it. But by a small minority, controlling the Military Committee, it was hung up against the President's wishes for weeks.

Then came word from Grant that General Foster, heading the Department and Army of the Ohio, was leaving on account of ill-health. On being asked whom to appoint in Foster's place, Grant wired, "Either McPherson or Schofield." Halleck handed Grant's dispatch to Schofield, who carried it to Lincoln saying he would take all chances on the new job. Lincoln: "Why, Schofield, that cuts the knot, don't it? Tell Halleck to come over here, and we will fix it right away." Then Schofield was appointed and transferred, with Rosecrans taking his place in Missouri.

The New York *Times* was saying that Lincoln's refusal to identify himself with either side in Missouri exhibited broad-souled patriotism, singleness of purpose. "Mr. Lincoln never forgets he is President of the nation and his prime duty is to save the nation from the rebellion which has threatened to destroy it. He . . . consequently can not be drawn into any petty strife."

This month of December '63 seemed to mark the beginning of a period in which, North and South, extremists more often referred to Confederate leaders ending on the gallows. Hanging with rigor, system, ceremonial, lay in the imaginings of the more fiery Republican radicals.

The Richmond *Examiner* editorial writer, Edward A. Pollard, in December quoted from Lincoln's Amnesty Proclamation and set down his judgment as a historian: "In proposing these utterly infamous terms, this Yankee monster of inhumanity and falsehood, had the audacity to declare that in some of the Confederate States the elements of reconstruction were ready for action . . . This insulting and brutal proposition of the Yankee Government was the apt response to those few cowardly factions which in North Carolina, and in some parts of Georgia and Alabama, hinted at 'reconstruction.' "

The New York *Metropolitan Record* queried: "Ye war Democrats, what do you think of being told that the black soldier is just as good as the white, for this is the amount of the President's message? What next? Shall we look among the black race for the President's successor?" The *Record* had no patience "with the great criminal who now occupies the Presidential chair."

In the week of the President's message, and while he yet lay sick, a New

York *World* editorial reprinted in the Detroit *Free Press* joined in a remarkably human commentary. From those extremist opposition organs came generous wishes:

We believe we but echo the feelings of the whole country, without distinction
of party, in sincerely hoping that the President will soon be restored to health
and strength . . . His death at this time would tend to prolong the war . . .
Mr. Lincoln has oftentimes acted wrongly, unwisely, arbitrarily; but still he
hesitates before he takes an extreme position, and is willing to obey, although not
always quick to perceive, the drift of public opinion. Without elevation of character, he has a self-poise, a reticence, an indisposition to commit himself, which
in many a trying crisis has saved him from being the utter tool of the madmen
whose folly brought on the war . . .
So heaven help Abraham Lincoln, and restore him to his wonted health and
strength.

A history rather than a biography would be required for recording the
life of Lincoln, wrote James Russell Lowell, of the *North American Review*,
in an article on Lincoln in January '64. An eminent Bostonian, author of
Yankee dialect verse, poet, essayist, critic, Harvard professor in the chair
of modern languages and belles-lettres—Lowell sketched Lincoln as ". . . so
gently guiding public sentiment that he seems to follow it, by so yielding
doubtful points that he can be firm without seeming obstinate in essential
ones." People come in time to see that such a political leader has shaken
himself loose and is free from temper and prejudice. ". . . perhaps none
of our Presidents since Washington has stood so firm in the confidence of
the people as he does after three years of stormy administration . . . At first
he was so slow that he tired out all those who see no evidence of progress
but in blowing up the engine; then he was so fast, that he took the breath
away from those who think there is no getting on safely while there is a spark
of fire under the boilers . . . Mr. Lincoln . . . has always waited . . . till
the right moment brought up all his reserves."
Lowell months before had written in a private letter: "Lincoln may be
right, for aught I know, but I guess an ounce of Frémont is worth a pound
of long Abraham. Mr. Lincoln seems to have the theory of carrying on the
war without hurting the enemy. He is incapable, of understanding that they
ought to be hurt." Lowell now enfigured Lincoln as a logger in a crazy river
snatching his way on a shaky raft and trying to hold to the main current
through rapids. "He is still in wild water, but we have faith that his skill and
sureness of eye will bring him out right at last." The very homeliness of Lincoln's genius was its distinction, thought Lowell. "His kingship was conspicuous by its workday homespun. Never was ruler so absolute as he, nor
so little conscious of it; for he was the incarnate common-sense of the people."

The new Congress in December '63, by the New York *Tribune Almanac*,
had in the House 102 Republicans and unconditional Unionists, 75 Democrats,
9 Border State men; in the Senate 36 Republicans and unconditional Unionists, 9 Democrats and 5 conditional Unionists.
One set of reports about himself that year the President did not bother to
answer. Over and again the opposition newspapers large and small said that

his salary was to be raised from $25,000 to $100,000 a year, as he wished, that he was drawing his salary in gold while the soldiers were paid in greenbacks, that his length of time in office was to be fixed by Congress for a life term, as he wished.

Day after day the question of the Negro and his destiny crossed the events of each hour. He was "the inevitable Sambo," "the everlasting nigger," the living interrogation point. To one side he incarnated the slavery issue, to the other the race-equality problem. The trend of feeling against slavery went on deepening. Francis George Shaw of Boston wrote to the President, "My only son, Colonel Robert Gould Shaw of the 54th Regiment Massachusetts Volunteers (colored troops) was killed on the parapet of Fort Wagner in South Carolina, and now lies buried in its ditch among his brave and devoted followers." To the request of Colonel Shaw's friends for his corpse came a reply it was "buried under a layer of niggers." The father urged the President to take immediate measures for protection to colored troops. "If our son's services and death shall contribute in any degree towards securing to our colored troops that equal justice which is a holy right of every loyal defender of our beloved country, we shall esteem our great loss a blessing."

Antislavery Roman Catholics declared their convictions in a more positive tone. The Christmas issue of the *Catholic Telegraph*, December 24, 1863, published: "It seems that there is a Priest in Kentucky who is still holding forth in favor of slavery. He ought to hide in the Mammoth Cave and associate with the fossils . . . A Catholic Priest, in the holy times of Christmas, advocating slavery! Handing over women and children into infamous bondage with one hand and offering incense with the other to the infant Saviour— THE REDEEMER OF ALL! What a subject for meditation before the altar on Christmas morning! If slavery must have its advocates let them be found amongst the laity, and not amongst the Priests." The sermon on the war given by Archbishop John Hughes August 17, 1862, was resented by Southern Catholics, by Northern antiwar groups; he replied to criticisms of his course printed in the Baltimore *Catholic Mirror*. He broke his connection with the fiercely antiwar and anti-Lincoln *Metropolitan Record*.

That the year of '63 was coming to an end with not one Negro slave revolt, not one scene of killing and plunder, as a result of the Emancipation Proclamation, made the going easier for Lincoln.

But for the New Year's season the *Crisis* reprinted a lamentation from the Zanesville, Ohio, *Aurora:* "The people of the North owe Mr. Lincoln but eternal hatred and scorn. There are 500,000 new made graves; there are 500,000 orphans; there are 200,000 widows . . . thieves in the Treasury, provost marshals in the seats of justice, butchers in the pulpit—and these are the things which we owe Mr. Lincoln. As the Lord liveth, we shall pay him all we owe him some day—him, and all the bloody band of traitors, plunderers and knaves."

That Christmas Lincoln wrote a letter of thanks for a solid gold watch to James H. Hoes, Esq., a Chicago jeweler. Hoes had donated the watch to the first Sanitary Commission Fair held in Chicago, as a token to be awarded the one person making the largest contribution of funds to the fair. Lincoln donated his original hand-written draft of the Emancipation Proclamation; it sold at auction for $3,000. A Chicago publisher was assigning territory to canvassers selling lithographed copies of "The Emancipation Proclamation, Genuine Facsimile in President Lincoln's Handwriting."

To Usher F. Linder, Douglas Democrat and storytelling lawyer of the old "orgmathorial" Eighth Circuit, Lincoln sent a Christmas gift. Linder's boy had joined the Confederate Army, had been taken prisoner, and his father sent letters to Lincoln asking a pardon. Weeks passed and Linder received a note dated December 26, 1863: "Your son Dan. has just left me, with my order to the Sec. of War, to administer to him the oath of allegiance, discharge him & send him to you."

The year of 1863 saw glimmering of the last hopes of the Richmond Government for European recognition. The despair of Jefferson Davis as to overseas help, as to ships or money from England was set forth in his December message to the Confederate Congress. Davis dwelt at such length and so bitterly on the point that he was rebuked by some of the Southern newspapers for overemphasis of it. Rhett and Yancey among civilians, and the former slave trader General Bedford Forrest, a military leader perhaps as great in his own field as Stonewall Jackson, had said, "If we are not fighting for slavery, then what are we fighting for?" They were told that the outlawing of the African slave trade by the Confederacy in '61 was a gesture for European good will with a hope of recognition as a World Power among nations. Yet that recognition had not come. All maneuvers and prayers for it had failed.

As early as '61, Archbishop John Hughes had come to Washington, met Lincoln and the Cabinet, indicated that he could not take official appointment. At the President's request, however, joined to that of his old friend Seward, the Archbishop became one of the President's personal agents with full powers to set forth the Union cause in Europe. The Archbishop had interviewed the French Emperor, attended a canonization of martyrs in Rome, laid the cornerstone of a new Catholic university in Dublin built partly from moneys collected in America. In this tour of eight months over Europe the Archbishop spoke the pro-Northern views which he gave in a published letter to the pro-Southern Archbishop of New Orleans.

Meanwhile the war, the Emancipation Proclamation, the messages of Lincoln, the antislavery propaganda, had sharpened the instinct against slavery among masses of people in all countries. In homes and at work millions in Europe had asked, "What is this slavery in America?" the simplest answer being, "It is where a white man owns a black man like he owns a horse, a cow or a dog," the talk going farther, "What about the black women and children?" "The white man owns them too." "He can breed them, beat them, sell them?" "Yes." "Oh! oh!"

Uncle Tom and Simon Legree, Little Eva, and Eliza crossing the ice pursued by bloodhounds, had been presented on stages of world capitals and in hundreds of smaller cities. A thousand folk tales had gone traveling of the mixed bloods of white and Negro races, of fathers selling their children, of lusts and sins and concubines, of fantastic tricks of fate involving those legally proved to have one drop of Negro blood.

A long letter to the Loyal National League of New York came from "friends of America" in France. Among signers were the Count de Gasparin, Protestant, former Minister of Public Instruction; Augustin Cochin, Catholic, author of *The Abolition of Slavery;* Henri Martin, Catholic, Republican, author of a history of France; Edouard Laboulaye, professor in the Collège de France, "moderate Catholic, moderate Republican." They gave Lincoln and his administration complete approval in a propaganda document of 17 pages dated October 31, 1863, and reprinted some weeks later in America.

Italian republican liberals sent to Lincoln a cadenced address lavish with Latin gestures, its first signer the famous fighting patriot Giuseppe Garibaldi. Señor Don Matias Romero, envoy of the Republic of Mexico, presented his credentials at the White House. An army of some 25,000 French soldiers and a fleet were holding a large part of Mexico. But the fugitive President Juarez had in the field perhaps 27,000 troops. Lincoln read a response to Señor Romero: ". . . Thanking you for the liberal sentiments you have expressed for the United States, and congratulating you upon the renewed confidence which your government has reposed in you, it is with unaffected pleasure that I bid you welcome to Washington."

In Great Britain, with the "mother-tongue," were crosscurrents as complex and varied as in the United States, as muddled as Missouri. The Emancipation Proclamation, mass meetings of workingmen formulating resolutions and addresses to Lincoln, had roused the active friends of the South, who organized Southern Clubs, gathered in men of influence, and carried on propaganda favoring the Confederacy. In April, three days' subscriptions in London to a Confederate loan amounted to 9,000,000 pounds sterling; later it ran to a total of 16,000,000 pounds, subscribers paying 15 per cent down. The last week in June '63 a motion in the House of Commons for recognition of the Southern Confederacy as a sovereign state was shelved by adjournment and by the speeches and tactics of John Bright and a handful of liberals. When, a little later, news arrived of the victories of Gettysburg and Vicksburg, the motion had lost what chance it ever had.

A *North British Review* writer came to the nub of the matter for many of the British. He quoted from pamphlets and personal letters of Americans showing their almost barbaric faith that "the hand of God" was shaping America. "Citizens of the United States are born with a giant ambition in their brains; and almost the first syllables they lisp have a sort of trumpet twang, as thus, 'Here I come, ready to grasp a sceptre and to rule the world.' "

For all the quaffing of toasts to the British Queen and her people, Lincoln and Seward saw that their only dependable well-wisher in Europe, except republican Switzerland, was the land of absolutist monarchy, Russia, the farthest of European extremes from "government of the people, by the people, for the people." Seward arranged secret understandings with Russia so momentous that he must have consulted with Lincoln about them. In America perhaps only Seward and Lincoln knew what conditional assurances were given the Russian government as to the purchase of the peninsula of Alaska. Not to Nicolay nor Hay nor Noah Brooks, nor to others to whom the President sometimes revealed secrets of state, did he give any inklings. And not even to his bosom friend Thurlow Weed did Seward give clues. Estimates ran that it was worth from $1,400,000 to $10,000,000. The United States was to buy it as soon as convenient, the purchase price to include certain naval expenses of the Russian government—some such understanding was worked out between the Washington and St. Petersburg governments.

Early in October '63 one Russian fleet lay in San Francisco harbor, another at New York with five first-class war vessels. Stalwart Muscovites in gay uniforms, outlandish whiskers, in excellent Russian, indifferent French and worse English, added merriment wherever they went. They sat for Brady photographs. They visited Meade's headquarters in Virginia, fell from the upper decks of cavalry horses, ate heartily, carried their liquor well.

Special writers filled many newspaper columns with tales of the Russian naval visitors, giving an extra spread to one shipboard reception where U.S. military officers and Mrs. Lincoln drank to the health of the Czar. The Richmond *Examiner* drew a parallel: "The Czar emancipates the serfs from their bondage of centuries, and puts forth the whole strength of his empire to enslave the Poles. Lincoln proclaims freedom to the African, and strives at the same time to subjugate free born Americans."

The essential viewpoint of Seward and Lincoln was probably hit off by *Harper's Weekly:* "England and France have recognized the belligerent rights of the rebels . . . Russia has not."

To Bayard Taylor, author of travel books, who had served as secretary of the American Legation at St. Petersburg under Minister Cameron, Lincoln wrote in December '63: "I think a good lecture or two on 'Serfs, Serfdom, and Emancipation in Russia' would be both interesting and valuable. Could not you get up such a thing?" Not long after, Taylor was addressing lyceum audiences on "Russia and the Russians." And Hay mentioned in his diary that the President went one evening to hear Taylor's lecture.

A Southern Union man, James Louis Petigru of Charleston, South Carolina, 74 years old, had gone as worn and infirm oaks fall; even Rhett said he could not find words to tell what a man this had been. At the first gun of the war Petigru had said, "I never believed that slavery would last a hundred years, now I know it won't last five." His name for appointment to the U.S. Supreme Court to replace Justice McLean or Justice Campbell was seriously laid before Lincoln and by him gravely considered.

Of Lincoln, Petigru had no high opinion, writing in March '62, "The *Mercury* has thrown off all reserve and proclaims J. D. [Jefferson Davis] is unfit for his place. I am myself afraid that he is but little better qualified for it than Lincoln is for his." Now Petigru was beyond the war and his daughter was to write in his epitaph, "In the great Civil War he withstood his People for his Country, but his People did homage to the Man who held his conscience higher than their praise."

Both sides had laid under earth brigadiers and major generals, the South mourning Stonewall Jackson, Van Dorn, Helm, Paxton, Tracy, Tilghman, Pender, both Garnetts, Barksdale, Preston Smith; the North its Reynolds, Berry, Sill, Lytle, Bayard, Sanders, Buford, Corcoran. The Union commissions had come to Lincoln's desk and he had signed them; the War Department reports had come to his desk that they were through with commissions. Colleges, societies, lodges, clubs, were treasuring in creped rosters the names of their dead who had not availed themselves of the $300 clause.

When General Michael Corcoran, who had proved his valor often under fire, died from the fall of a horse on him, a comrade of the Fenian Brotherhood in New York intoned a requiem: "Deep in the green sod let him rest under the starry arch of the Republic he so nobly served and within sight of that city where his name will never sound strange."

Major General John A. Logan, on furlough from Grant's army, had spoken to the people of Du Quoin, Illinois: "How do they know we are all abolitionists, regular straight-outs? Did we tell them so? Did we say so? Why is it? Well, I will tell you. It is because we are in the army and Abraham Lincoln is President. That is the reason. These men don't know enough or don't want to know that Abraham Lincoln, because he is President don't own the Government. This is our Government. This war ain't fighting for Mr. Lincoln. It is fighting for the Union, for the Government . . . I have seen Democrats shot down and buried in the same grave with the Republican and the Abolitionist. They are all fighting for the same country, the same ground . . . You will again see the great railroads running from the North to the South, from the East to the West."

The human causes operating in America were many and varied and moving, requiring the brush of chaos to do a mural of the crossed interests of climate and geography, of native and foreign blood streams, of bread-and-butter necessity, of cultural environment, of mystic hopes. As they passed before Lincoln in their many guises and dialects, he considered, decided, waited, looked often abstracted, seemed more often to have his mind elsewhere than in Washington.

Lincoln was at the vortex of the revolution to break the power of the Southern planter aristocracy and usher in the dominance of the financial and industrial interests centered in New York City. He may have seen Paris correspondence of the New York *Times* at the year's end: "The popularity of Mr. Lincoln has much advanced abroad by his late acts . . . I heard a leading French politician say lately: 'You Americans don't appreciate Mr. Lincoln at his proper value. No monarch in Europe could carry on such a colossal war in front while harassed by so many factions and fault-finders behind . . . On every side I hear people begin to say that Mr. Lincoln will merit more than a biography—he will merit a history.' "

Newspapers were printing a strangely worded psalm of praise for Lincoln the man, spoken in the 1863 Thanksgiving sermon at the Second Presbyterian Church of Auburn, New York, by its pastor, the Reverend Henry Fowler. The progress of the President kept pace with the progress of the people, Fowler believed, comparing it with the time in Jewish history when the prophet Samuel was the mediator between a passing and a coming epoch. "Such an epoch of perplexity, transition, change, is not often witnessed. In every such passage of a nation there ought to be a character like that of Samuel. Misunderstood and misrepresented at the time; attacked from both sides; charged with not going far enough and with going too far; charged with saying too much and saying too little, he slowly, conscientiously and honestly works out the mighty problem. He was not a founder of a new state of things like Moses; he was not a champion of the existing order of things like Elijah. He stood between the two; between the living and the dead; between the past and the present; between the old and the new; with that sympathy for each which at such a period is the best hope for any permanent solution of the questions which torment it. He has but little praise from partisans, but is the careful healer binding up the wounds of the age . . .

"His awkward speech and yet more awkward silence, his uncouth manners, his grammar self-taught and partly forgotten . . . doing nothing when he knows not what to do; hesitating at nothing when he sees the right; lacking the recognized qualification of a party leader, and yet leading his party as no other man can; sustaining his political enemies in Missouri to their defeat, sustaining his political friends in Maryland to their victory; conservative in his sympathies and radical in his acts . . . his religion consisting in truthfulness, temperance, asking good people to pray for him and publicly acknowledging in events the hand of God, he stands before you as the type of 'Brother Jonathan,' a not perfect man and yet more precious than fine gold." The President took such outpourings to heart. As prose it had a touch of his own flavor.

New Year's Day of 1864 came, and Benjamin Perley Poore noted at the morning reception in the White House: "Mr. Lincoln was in excellent spirits, giving each passer-by a cordial greeting and a warm shake of the hand, while for some there was a quiet joke." Mrs. Lincoln stood at his right hand, wearing purple silk trimmed with black velvet and lace, a lace necktie fastened with a pearl pin, a white plume topping her headdress. At noon the doors were thrown open for the people to pour through in a continuous stream for two hours. "A living tide which swept in, eddied around the President and his wife, and then surged into the East Room which was a maelstrom of humanity, uniforms, black coats, gay female attire, and citizens generally." Noah Brooks' eye took in Mrs. Lincoln lacking mourning garb for the first time in the more than twenty months since Willie Lincoln died.

While the President had lain abed with varioloid, an immense crowd had streamed down Pennsylvania Avenue to the Capitol grounds looking skyward toward the Capitol dome. The bronze legs and torso of the massive heroic figure of a helmeted woman representing Armed Freedom, after years of lying helpless and forlorn on the ground below, had been lifted to the top of the dome. And on this day, precisely at noon, the last section of this 19½-foot high bronze statue, consisting of the head and shoulders of the incomplete goddess, left the mass of material at the foot of the dome and moved serenely upward, drawn by a slender wire cable.

From a chaos of timbered scaffolding the head and shoulders emerged and swung lightly and calmly into place joined to her torso. A workman drove a ringing sledge hammer three times. The Union banner ran up a flagstaff. Artillery roared a salute.

To one onlooker, Noah Brooks, the prolonged and loud shout of the crowd seemed to say to the azure that day: "Take her, oh, heavens blue and gay, take her to thy protecting arms, with all her bronze and all her charms."

John Eaton of Toledo, Ohio, had talked with Lincoln one day about the statue of Armed Freedom to be hoisted over the Capitol dome, new marble pillars to be installed on the Senate wing, a massive and richly embellished bronze door being made for the main central portal. People were saying it was an extravagance during wartime, Eaton remarked. Lincoln answered, "If people see the Capitol going on, it is a sign we intend the Union shall go on."

CHAPTER 40

Grant Given High Command, '64

AS A FORMER Douglas Democrat now for the war and the Union, Grant was accepted and endorsed by an element that could never see Lincoln as their leader. The powerful New York *Herald* spoke for a miscellany of interests when through the winter of '63 and '64 it kept up a cry for Grant for President, "Grant, the People's Candidate." Many other newspapers joined in.

Lincoln had never seen Grant. He knew Grant only from what he read and what he heard in talk about his best fighter. To Congressman Washburne, Lincoln said: "About all I know of Grant I have got from you. I have never seen him. Who else besides you knows anything about Grant?" Washburne: "I know very little about him. He is my townsman but I never saw very much of him. The only man who really knows Grant is Jones. He has summered and wintered with him." Washburne referred to a Galena man, J. Russell Jones, a U.S. marshal at Chicago who had visited with Grant in Mississippi.

Lincoln wired Jones to come on to Washington. Jones picked up his mail on the way to the depot and opened it on the train. In it was a letter from Grant answering one Jones had written urging the General to pay no attention to the newspapers trying to run him for President. Grant was saying that he had as big a job as one man could ask, that he was out to suppress the "rebellion," and everything that reached him trying to push him into politics went into the wastebasket. Arriving in Washington, Jones sent word he would be glad to call when convenient and the President set eight o'clock that evening. Then as Jones told it: "The President gave directions to say to all that he was engaged for the evening . . . opened the conversation by saying that he was anxious to see somebody from the West with whom he could talk upon the general situation . . . Mr. Lincoln made no allusion whatever to Grant. I had been there but a few minutes, however, when I fancied he would like to talk about Grant. 'Mr. President, if you will excuse me for interrupting you, I want to ask you kindly to read a letter that I got from my box as I was on my way to the train.' Whereupon I gave him Grant's letter. He read it with evident interest. When he came to the part where Grant said that it would be impossible for him to think of the presidency as long as there was a possibility of retaining Mr. Lincoln in the office, he read no further, but arose and, approaching me, put his hand on my shoulder and said: 'My son, you will never know how gratifying that is to me.

No man knows, when that presidential grub gets to gnawing at him, just how deep it will get until he has tried it; and I didn't know but what there was one gnawing at Grant.' The fact was that this was just what Mr. Lincoln wanted to know."

Among the first acts of Congress that winter was the voting of a medal of thanks to Grant for his victories. The country had its first word from Grant, as to running for President, in January '64: "I aspire only to one political office. When this war is over, I mean to run for Mayor of Galena [his Illinois home town], and if elected, I intend to have the sidewalk fixed up between my house and the depot." Some comment ran like that of *Leslie's Weekly:* "If General Grant should go on joking in this dry style, he will soon joke Lincoln out of the next nomination."

To his father February 20 Grant wrote cautioning the old man not to believe all he read in the public prints. "I am not a candidate for any office. All I want is to be left alone to fight this war out." America had its chuckle over Mrs. Grant's saying to a New York *Herald* interviewer, "I have no doubt Mr. Grant will succeed, for he is a very obstinate man." Lincoln thereafter occasionally spoke of "Mr. Grant, as Mrs. Grant calls him."

Bills in House and Senate to revive the rank of lieutenant general of the armies of the United States on February 26 passed both houses. On February 29 the President signed the bill, named Grant for the newly created office and the Senate confirmed it.

And now Halleck at last was to go. Lincoln had told Hay and others on various occasions, "I am Halleck's friend because he has no others." Also to Hay, Lincoln had said that Halleck was "little more . . . than a first-rate clerk."

Grant at Nashville wrote to Sherman that his personal success in the war was due to the energy and skill of his subordinates, above all to Sherman and McPherson. "I feel all the gratitude this letter can express, giving it the most flattering construction." Sherman groaned over the prospect of Grant's leaving. "For God's sake and your country's sake, come out of Washington . . . Come West; take to yourself the whole Mississippi Valley." Sherman knew that for Grant, as for himself, the war was for a river and whether that river should belong to one or several nations. Also both knew that political forces in Washington could hamstring the best of commanders.

Grant traveled toward Washington with his 14-year-old boy Fred, and his chief of staff John Rawlins. Crowds and cheers met Grant as the train moved on to Washington. There on the evening of March 8 he walked into Willard's and asked for a room. The clerk said he had only a top-floor room. Grant said that would do—and signed the register. The clerk took a look at the name and then jumped fast to assign Grant the best in the house. Grant walked into the dining room and was ordering food when word passed among the guests, "It's Grant," and questions: "Where is he?" "Which is he?" Someone stood on a chair and called for three cheers for Grant. Three cheers rang out. The diners pounded on tables, waved napkins, threatened the glassware, yelled the name of Grant, Grant, Grant!

After a few minutes, as Noah Brooks noted it, "General Grant, looking very much astonished and perhaps annoyed, rose to his feet, awkwardly rubbed his mustache with his napkin, bowed, resumed his seat and attempted to finish his dinner." The diners then seemed slowly to get the idea that Grant had come to the dining room for a meal. And they let him eat in peace.

Soon Grant was on his way with Senator Cameron to report to the President at the White House, in a tarnished uniform with a major general's stars on the shoulder straps. "He had no gait, no station, no manner, rough, light-brown whiskers, rather a scrubby look," wrote Richard Henry Dana. "He had a cigar in his mouth, and rather the look of a man who did, or once did, take a little too much to drink . . . a slightly seedy look, as if he was out of office and on half pay, nothing to do but hang around, a clear blue eye and a look of resolution, as if he could not be trifled with, and an entire indifference to the crowd about him . . . He does not march, nor quite walk, but pitches along as if the next step would bring him on his nose."

It was the night of the President's weekly reception. A buzz and a murmur ran round the big East Room, reaching the President with news that Grant would soon step into the room. As the General entered, a hush fell on the crowd. They moved back and made a pathway. Lincoln saw him coming, put out his long bony hand for the shorter and smaller one of Grant's. "I'm glad to see you, General." The two men stood a moment with struck hands.

Lincoln introduced the General to Seward, who escorted him toward Mrs. Lincoln in the East Room. The buzz of talk became a hullabaloo. The crowd swirled around the short bullet-shaped man who embodied Donelson, Shiloh, Vicksburg, Chattanooga, in his rough frame. They cheered and yelled, jammed toward him, men and women wanting to touch his hands. He "blushed like a schoolgirl," shook hands till sweat poured down his face. Veins on his forehead bulged red. He dropped a remark later that it was a hotter spot than he had ever known in battle.

"Stand up so we can all have a look at you!" came cries. And the shrinking war hero stepped up on a sofa and stood where they could look at him. Then he made a tour of the room with Mrs. Lincoln's arm in his. Lincoln, with a lady on his arm, followed, his fissured face lighted, taking in all the contrasts that appealed to his sense of humor. Ladies caught in the crush had their laces torn and crinolines mashed; many got up on chairs, tables, sofas, to be out of harm's way or to get a better view.

"It was the only real mob I ever saw in the White House," wrote Noah Brooks. "For once at least the President of the United States was not the chief figure in the picture. The little scared-looking man who stood on a crimson-covered sofa was the idol of the hour. He remained on view for a short time, then he was quietly smuggled out by friendly hands."

Grant returned when the crowd was gone and met Lincoln with Stanton and Nicolay in a small drawing room. And Lincoln did nearly all the talking —all of it on the point that the next day, when he was to hand formally to Grant the new commission, each of them should say little, but what they did say should be pat to the occasion. Grant put in his inside coat pocket a copy of the President's speech and, saying good night, left the room with Stanton. Next day at one o'clock the Cabinet, Halleck, Grant's son Fred, Rawlins, Owen Lovejoy and Nicolay assembled to hear two little speeches that were telegraphed to the wide world.

Lincoln, facing Grant, read four sentences: "General Grant, The nation's appreciation of what you have done, and it's reliance upon you for what remains to do, in the existing great struggle, are now presented with this commission, constituting you Lieutenant General in the Army of the United States. With this high honor devolves upon you also, a corresponding responsibility. As the country herein trusts you, so, under God, it will sustain you. I scarcely need to add that with what I here speak for the nation goes my own hearty personal concurrence."

Grant held a half-sheet of note paper, on it a hurried lead-pencil scrawl. "His embarrassment was evident and extreme," noted Nicolay. "He found his own writing very difficult to read." The speech, however, fitted Grant as he read, facing Lincoln, his three-sentence response: "Mr. President: I accept this commission with gratitude for the high honor confered. With the aid of the noble armies that have fought in so many fields for our common country, it will be my earnest endeavor not to disappoint your expectations. I feel the full weight of the responsibilities now devolving on me and know that if they are met it will be due to those armies, and above all to the favor of that Providence which leads both Nations and men."

The news of Lincoln and Grant meeting, their two simple little speeches, was at once a universal press and sidewalk topic. The North brightened a little. The South saw Northern morale changed, at least slightly, for the better.

Grant rode by rail to the Army of the Potomac headquarters at Brandy Station, talked with Meade, felt out the spirit of the officers and men, said nothing much. Of intrigue and wirepulling in Washington he had heard and seen not a little in this week. Senators Wade and Chandler had been to the President and called for removal of Meade from command of the Army of the Potomac. Grant found Meade sincere, generous, open-minded, and told Meade he had no thought of a substitute for him.

No other man of high command in Washington had been so completely noncommittal regarding future plans as Grant. He was a good listener, and of his first interview with Lincoln alone, Grant wrote: "He stated to me that he had never professed to be a military man or to know how campaigns should be conducted, and never wanted to interfere in them: but that procrastination on the part of commanders, and the pressure from the people at the North and Congress, *which was always with him,* forced him into issuing his series of 'Military Orders'—one, two, three, etc. He did not know but they were all wrong, and did know that some of them were. All he wanted or had ever wanted was someone who would take the responsibility and act . . . I did not communicate my plans to the President, nor did I to the Secretary of War or to General Halleck."

After four days in Washington Grant told Lincoln he would go west, be gone about nine days, then return and direct operations from eastern headquarters. Of his four-day stay in Washington he said to Lincoln, "This has been rather the warmest campaign I have witnessed during the war."

Before starting west, Grant ordered Sherman in command of all Western armies, McPherson to take Sherman's department, John A. Logan being given McPherson's corps. He rode to Nashville, talked with Sherman on a campaign plan, huge but simple. As Sherman put it: Grant "was to go for Lee and I was to go for Joe Johnston." That was all. The two of them believed they would start a never-ending hammering, a pressure of irresistible pincers—and close out the war.

Returning to Washington, Grant found himself hailed as the most popular man in the United States. "He hardly slept on his long journey east," said the New York *Tribune*, "yet he went to work at once." Grant ordered so many troops away from Washington for service with the Army of the Potomac that Stanton showed anxiety, even nervousness, about the small garrisons that would be left to man the forts around the capital. "I have already sent the men to the front," Grant replied to Stanton's questions. Stanton held this contrary to his plans; he would order the men back, saying, "We will see the President about that. I will have to take you to the President." Grant: "That is right. The President ranks us both." Then Stanton, in Lincoln's office facing the seated President, "Now, General, state your case." Grant: "I have no case to state. I am satisfied as it is." And Lincoln, after hearing Stanton's argument that Grant was exceeding his authority and putting Washington in danger by stripping the garrison, spoke: "Now, Mr. Secretary, you know we have been trying to manage this army for nearly three years and you know we haven't done much with it. We sent over the mountains and brought Mr. Grant, as Mrs. Grant calls him, to manage it for us; and now I guess we'd better let Mr. Grant have his own way." And there the matter rested. The incident was told and published, many believing it had a quality of the three men partaking.

Lincoln's own way of telling Grant to call on the administration for troops, but not too many, took the form of an ancient fable. "He said he thought he could illustrate what he wanted to say by a story," wrote Grant. "At one time there was a great war among the animals, and one side had great difficulty in getting a commander who had sufficient confidence in himself. Finally, they found a monkey, by the name of Jocko, who said that he thought he could command their army if his tail could be made a little longer. So they got more tail and spliced it on to his caudal appendage. He looked at it admiringly, and then thought he ought to have a little more still. This was added, and again he called for more. The splicing process was repeated many times, until they had coiled Jocko's tail around the room, filling all the space. Still he called for more tail and, there being no other place to coil it, they began wrapping it around his shoulders. He continued his call for more, and they kept on winding the additional tail about him until its weight broke him down."

Phil Sheridan arrived in Washington early in April. Grant had appointed him to head the combined cavalry of the Army of the Potomac. Five feet five inches high, less than 130 pounds in weight—a total stranger to Washington and service in the east—young-looking, 33 years old, cool and guarded he was, refusing to tell anybody how to win the war. Halleck took him to Stanton and it was a meeting with no compliments. Halleck took him to the White House. Lincoln offered Sheridan both his hands, said he hoped Sheridan would fulfill Grant's expectations, and added that the cavalry of the Army of the Potomac had not gone so far as it might have.

At Culpeper Court House with Grant next day Sheridan again felt at home. A black-haired Irish Catholic boy who went from Perry County, Ohio, to West Point, Sheridan had followed soldiering ever since. As a fighter leading men against odds he had proved his wild and stubborn ways at Murfreesboro, Chickamauga and Chattanooga. Grant heard doubts spoken in Washington about Sheridan. They would soon find out whether Sheridan could fight, answered Grant. Lincoln about this time was asked for an opinion of Sheridan and limited himself to saying: "I will tell you just what kind of a chap he is. He is one of those long-armed fellows with short legs that can scratch his shins without having to stoop over."

In snow and rain of the last week in March, Grant and Rawlins set up headquarters at Culpeper Court House with the Army of the Potomac. Into their hands came daily reports and dispatches from troops on a line that ran 1,200 miles from the Atlantic to the Rio Grande, 21 army corps, 18 departments, with 800,000 men enrolled, 533,000 present and fit for duty. On a day soon to come the armies were to move, Butler up the James River, Grant and Meade across the Rapidan, Sigel up the Shenandoah, Averell in West Virginia, Sherman and Thomas from Chattanooga, and Banks up the Red River toward Texas.

Hitherto armies had acted independently, "like a balky team, no two ever pulling together," said Grant, as he explained to Lincoln that each army was to hammer away at enemy armies, railroads and supplies, "until by mere attrition, if in no other way, there should be nothing left to him." Grant and Meade in the east, and Sherman and Thomas in the west, were to be a giant nutcracker having the South crushed when they should finally meet. Thus Grant outlined the grand strategy to Lincoln.

"The President has been powerfully reminded," wrote Hay in his diary, "by General Grant's present movements and plans, of his [the President's] old suggestion so constantly made and as constantly neglected, to Buell & Hooker, et al., to move at once upon the enemy's whole line so as to bring into action . . . our great superiority of numbers . . . This idea of his own, the Pres^t recognized with especial pleasure when Grant said it was his intention to make all the line useful—those not fighting could help the fighting. 'Those not skinning can hold a leg,' added Lincoln."

Grant was to hit Lee so hard in Virginia that Lee could send no help to Johnston in Georgia. Sherman was to hit Johnston so heavily in Georgia that Johnston would never shift troops to Lee in Virginia. So they hoped and planned. Grant's orders to his scattered subcommanders were relayed through Halleck at Washington. Burnside was taking his orders from Grant.

The Burnside corps had mobilized at Annapolis, its veterans of Roanoke, the Peninsula, Antietam, Fredericksburg, Chancellorsville and Knoxville being joined by new recruits that included several Negro regiments. They passed in review before the President standing on the balcony of Willard's. The black troops cheered, laughed, threw their caps in the air, marching past the signer of the Emancipation Proclamation. A rain blew up and soaked the marchers. Bystanders urged Lincoln to go in out of the rain. "If *they* can stand it, I guess I can," he answered as burnt and shot-riddled flags swept by on Pennsylvania Avenue.

Grant took a six-mile ride to see Meade, talking as he rode with Colonel Horace Porter of his favorable impression of Lincoln, of how frankly Lincoln had said he did not want to know Grant's plans. A delegation of "crossroads wiseacres," as Lincoln told it to Grant, criticized Grant for paroling Pemberton's army at Vicksburg and Lincoln gave the delegation a story with a moral:

Sykes had a yellow dog he set great store by, but there were a lot of small boys around the village, and that's always a bad thing for dogs, you know. These boys didn't share Sykes's views, and they were not disposed to let the dog have a fair show. Even Sykes had to admit that the dog was getting unpopular; in fact, it was soon seen that a prejudice was growing up against that dog that threatened to wreck all his future prospects in life. The boys, after meditating how they could get the best of him, finally fixed up a cartridge with a long fuse, put the cartridge in a piece of meat, dropped the meat in the road in front of Sykes's door, and then perched themselves on a fence a good distance off, holding the end of the fuse in their hands. Then they whistled for the dog. When he came out he scented the bait, and bolted the meat, cartridge and all. The boys touched off the fuse with a cigar, and in about a second a report came from that dog that sounded like a clap of thunder. Sykes came bouncing out of the house, and yelled, "What's up? Anything busted?" There was no reply, except a snicker from the small boys roosting on the fence; but as Sykes looked up he saw the whole air filled with pieces of yellow dog. He picked up the biggest piece he could find, a portion of the back with a part of the tail still hanging to it, and after turning it round and looking it all over, he said, "Well, I guess he'll never be much account again—as a dog." And I guess Pemberton's forces will never be much account again—as an army. The delegation began looking around for their hats before I had quite got to the end of the story, and I was never bothered any more after that about superseding the commander of the Army of the Tennessee.

Lincoln adopted a set form to meet one question and, according to the Chicago *Journal*, the dialogue ran:

VISITOR: When will the army move?
LINCOLN: Ask General Grant.
VISITOR: General Grant will not tell me.
LINCOLN: Neither will he tell me.

CHAPTER 41

Will His Party Renominate Lincoln?

AS THE ruthless Republican floor leader, Thad Stevens, kept pushing his program of no mercy to the South, press editorials and street talk of citizens over the North mentioned more often the day when Jefferson Davis and secession leaders would be hanged or shot. Wholesale executions of "rebels" were forecast.

The tone of Congress had an assurance as though the United States would stand for a long time, and there would be in the North a growing World Power, gigantic in commerce and industry from coast to coast. In the South was a deepening courage of despair over the terrorizing possibility that the

Confederacy might die, the old South vanish, with its ruling class sunk. One hope still held that the peace party at the North might so weaken the Lincoln administration that in time it would give up the war as hopeless.

To combat those Southern hopes and wear them down was Lincoln's set task. As part of that task he could never afford to lose contact with Congress nor let serious cleavage arise. A worse deliberative body might have been wished on him. He sought the brains and ability there. Reasonable advice, discussion and inquiry, and no tone of faultfinding, stood forth in his papers in the *Congressional Globe* pages so often sprinkled with the item, "A message in writing was received from the President of the United States, by Mr. Nicolay, his Private Secretary." He would communicate a report "in obedience to the resolution of the Senate." He would "earnestly recommend" that a law be modified. He would "invite the early attention of Congress" to a subject. Or he would lay before Congress a letter from an important committee representing four large Northern cities not clear on what should be done for their increasing population of free Negroes. "Not having the time to form a mature judgment of my own as to whether the plan they suggest is the best, I submit the whole subject to Congress, deeming that their attention thereto is almost imperatively demanded."

Early in '64 several newspapers agreed with the Detroit *Free Press* man at Washington: "Not a single Senator can be named as favorable to Lincoln's renomination for President." Any Senator who might want Lincoln for a second term was not making himself heard. On this the Republican party organs were mainly silent.

In the House only one Congressman was definitely committed to Lincoln. A Pennsylvania editor visiting Washington said to Thaddeus Stevens, "Introduce me to some member of Congress friendly to Mr. Lincoln's renomination." "Come with me," said Stevens. He took the editor to Isaac N. Arnold and said: "Here is a man who wants to find a Lincoln member of Congress. You are the only one I know, and I have come over to introduce my friend to you." "Thank you," said Arnold. "I know a good many such and I will present your friend to them, and I wish you, Mr. Stevens, were with us." Thus the scrupulous Arnold recorded the incident.

Mixed motives of Stevens and some of his associates could be gathered from part of a letter of Stevens that year to an intimate, J. B. McPherson: "How little of the rights of war and the law of nations our Pres't knows! But what are we to do? Condemn privately and applaud publicly!"

The only remarks then favoring Lincoln's renomination for President delivered in either Senate or House came from Arnold in the first week of the year and in March. ". . . I ask the ardent and impatient friends of freedom to put implicit faith in Abraham Lincoln. If you deem him slow, or if you think he has made mistakes, remember how often time has vindicated his wisdom. The masses of the people everywhere trust and love him . . . You have a Chief Magistrate . . . sagacious, firm, upright, and true. Somewhat rude and rough, it may be, but under this rough exterior you have the real and true hero . . . Taking the last five years, and Mr. Lincoln has exerted a greater influence upon the popular heart and in forming public opinion than any other man."

Thus Isaac N. Arnold, 49 years old, once a country schoolteacher in New York State, city clerk of Chicago in 1837, practicing attorney of Cook County, put into the *Congressional Globe* an estimate of Lincoln as a hero. Not then nor in many months after did any member of the House or Senate stand up and deliver any similar estimate.

Washburne in November '63 wrote to Lincoln for two executive favors and asking whether the party could count on the President to run for a second term. Lincoln replied that he was enclosing a leave of absence for one of Washburne's brothers from army duty, that to another brother he was tendering the customs collectorship of Portland, Maine, giving Washburne all that was asked for. To this Lincoln added thanks for kind words and intentions, and "A second term would be a great honor and a great labor, which, together, perhaps I would not decline if tendered."

Of Owen Lovejoy in early '64 it should be noted that he was a sick man for months. Lincoln had one note from him saying: "I am gaining very slowly. It is hard work drawing the sled uphill." And Lincoln had repeatedly visited Lovejoy's bedside, once telling the veteran abolitionist: "This war is eating my life out. I have a strong impression that I shall not live to see the end."

"The opposition to Mr. Lincoln," wrote the Indiana Republican Congressman George W. Julian, "was secretly cherished by many of the ablest and most patriotic men of the day . . . Of the more earnest and thorough-going Republicans in both Houses of Congress, probably not one in ten really favored it [his renomination]." No writer of the day laid open clearly the springs and motives of this opposition, or the exact extent of it. Of course, Lincoln had gone too far—or not far enough—in his acts and policies; he was the Man Between. Yet this would not explain why Congress was sore, suspicious, jealous, almost completely silent about his hold on the people. For nearly all political forecasters in early '64 saw the deep popular current over the North with the President. The New York *Herald*, the New York *World*, the Detroit *Free Press*, proclaimed it as an unpleasant fact, while the New York *Times* and other newspapers agreed with the Chicago *Tribune:* "So far as can be gathered, the public generally mean to elect Mr. Lincoln, when the time comes for an election . . . God meant him for President, or the nation is deceived."

A friend of Governor John Andrew of Massachusetts noted that Lincoln's offhand behavior at times had so lowered opinion of him that it was a factor in the secrecy that enveloped the choice of a President in '64. This secrecy, also noted Governor Andrew's friend, "is something marvelous; there were so many concerned in it; when it *all* comes out, it will make a curious page in the history of the time." He wrote:

. . . reports from Washington in 1863 did impute a frivolity of language and demeanor in the President, which could not but offend many earnest men . . . There was a characteristic anecdote related . . . The legislature has been famous for passing resolutions against slavery . . . a committee brought in a resolve in the fewest words possible.

A friend of the Governor, who also held an official position, desired to present it personally to the President. It was accordingly written on parchment, with the great seal annexed, and plenty of red tape. Arrived in Washington, the messenger by appointment met the President at eleven o'clock the next day, to present this resolve of the Commonwealth of Massachusetts.

The Chief Magistrate of the nation sat in an armchair, with one leg over the elbow, while the emissary of Massachusetts presented the parchment with a little speech.

The President took the document, slowly unrolled it, and remarked in a quaint way, "Well, it isn't long enough to scare a fellow!" It is not remarkable that the Massachusetts official said as he left the room, "That is certainly an extraordinary person to be President of the United States!"

Thus one incident drawing Andrew toward the anti-Lincoln movement. It was ominous. For Andrew rated as no mere ordinary politician riding the antislavery bandwagon. He had raised troops and funds with a loyalty hardly equaled by any other state governor. He was spoken of by friends as a hope for the Presidency because of clean, rugged manhood he carried. Located in the antislavery crusade's most active center, surrounded by good men impatient with the President's slowness on that issue, Governor Andrew was looking elsewhere than to Lincoln for a Chief Magistrate. He wrote just after the President issued the Emancipation Proclamation, "It is a poor document, but a mighty act, slow, somewhat halting, wrong in its delay until January, but grand and sublime after all." Andrew sat on Beacon Hill now, a square-built, deep-chested man, curly hair topping his round head, a face smooth with kindliness, almost boyishly cherubic, his eyes peering from behind spectacles, wanting results out of his loyal toiling, decisions quicker than Lincoln could give them.

In early February Lyman Trumbull wrote to H. G. McPike of Alton, Illinois: "The feeling for Mr. Lincoln's re-election *seems* to be very general, but much of it I discover is only on the surface. You would be surprised, in talking with public men we meet here, to find how few, when you come to get at their real sentiment, are for Mr. Lincoln's reëlection. There is a distrust and fear that he is too undecided and inefficient to put down the rebellion. You need not be surprised if a reaction sets in before the nomination, in favor of some man supposed to possess more energy and less inclination to trust our brave boys in the hands and under the leadership of generals who have no heart in the war. The opposition to Mr. L. may not show itself at all, but if it ever breaks out there will be more of it than now appears."

The warm kindliness of the New York *Evening Post* had veered into a slight chill: "We deprecate the agitation of a Presidential nomination as premature . . . a great and important work is yet to be done before we can distinguish the man likely to be approved by the people or who is most worthy to be intrusted with the administration of the government during the next four years."

In a one-column editorial in mid-February '64 Greeley sounded a Joshua ram's horn blast that he hoped would send Lincoln's Jericho walls toppling. Did Mr. Lincoln so overtop all other candidates that no others should be considered? "We answer in the negative," wrote Greeley. "Heartily agreeing that Mr. Lincoln has done well, we do not regard it as at all demonstrated that Gov. Chase, Gen. Frémont, Gen. Butler, or Gen. Grant, cannot do *as* well." In reprinting this one-column blast of Greeley, the Chicago *Tribune* credited "its preliminary remarks" as of no account, "being merely the flour-ish of Greeley's knife before he stabs," editorially estimating Lincoln's ability "at least equal, if not superior to that of any man likely to be elected."

The Republicans had five candidates for President whom the New York *World* set down "in the order of their availability and probable chances": Abraham Lincoln, Salmon P. Chase, John C. Frémont, Nathaniel P. Banks, Benjamin F. Butler. To defeat Lincoln would be simply to nominate Chase, deduced the *World*. "Only the adherents of Chase have any interest in thwarting Lincoln."

Ben Butler hovered available. Chase men offered him second place with their guiding star, Butler smiling that he might yet take Richmond and come thundering home in first place on the Union ticket. Sumner's availability was hinted at slightly. And Sumner's secretary, the studious and scrupulous Edward L. Pierce, recorded Sumner's "distrust of Mr. Lincoln's fitness for his place."

Senators and Congressmen joining in this anti-Lincoln movement had nearly all been handed their share of patronage by the President. He had met them more than halfway in policies of emancipation and arming the Negro. This worried Thurlow Weed in New York, who once wrote to Judge David Davis, "They will all be against him in 1864, why does he persist in giving them weapons to defeat his renomination?"

With a touch of dawn maroon and a faint odor of forget-me-nots, Miss Anna Elizabeth Dickinson flitted into the Washington scene pro-Lincoln and faded out anti-Lincoln. She had won name as a Girl Orator, had developed gifts of swift and withering sarcasm, had nursed and brought along an eloquence that made her a torch of promise to thousands who had heard her on the platform. Her chestnut curls cut close to her clean-shapen head, her virginal beauty, her symmetrical figure, her complete self-possession, her contralto fullness of voice, her discussions of momentous issues beginning gravely and flowing into sudden passionate appeals for the redemption of mankind and the holiness of human freedom—these had brought comparisons of her with the Maid of Orleans who saved France when all others despaired.

She was just past 21 when on January 16, 1864, she spoke in the hall of the House of Representatives, Speaker Colfax sitting on her right hand, Vice-President Hamlin on her left, the President on a bench farther in the foreground, the affair bringing $1,031 for the Freedmen's Relief Association. "How, to such youthful lips, flowed so easily such stately language!" wrote N. P. Willis. Others called it just another stump speech. She referred to the President as though he should be renominated and re-elected. Said the Detroit *Free Press* one day, "The strong-minded Anna Dickinson has renominated the weak-minded Abraham Lincoln."

Two months later Miss Dickinson, in Metropolitan Hall in Chicago, ran on to say that the President's Amnesty Proclamation was a piece of Northern meanness and a usurpation of the functions of Congress: "The President is a lawyer, and a Western one at that; it is a wonder he does not know that the oaths of such men [reconstructed rebels] are but as idle wind . . . These men must be punished. South Carolina should be cut up into twenty acre lots, and as many negroes settled on them as can be got there."

A month later Miss Dickinson called at the White House, interviewed the President, then went to Boston and in a public lecture satirized the administration and caricatured Lincoln, his twang and his clothes, as she reported her interview. He had said to her: "They tell me you are on my side. I want to know how it is." She told him his emancipation policy was not moving fast enough and pleaded for justice to the Negro.

The President answered, "That reminds me of a story." She had to reply: "I did not come here to hear stories. I can read better ones in the papers any day than you can tell me." He showed her his correspondence with officials in Louisiana and asked her what she thought of his plan of reconstruction there. She replied, "Sir, I think it all wrong; as radically bad as can be." The President then "sugar-plummed" her, as Miss Dickinson phrased it. He told her she could talk better than he, and so forth. Ending their conversation, he remarked, "All I can say is, if the radicals want me to lead, let them get out of the way and let me lead." And, said Miss Dickinson to her Boston audience, "When he said that, I came out and remarked to a friend, 'I have spoken my last word to President Lincoln.'"

From speech to speech Wendell Phillips went on, graphic and simple, and however mistaken and however heady, with a peculiar joy in being temperamentally stubborn. He debonairly justified himself: "Mr. Lincoln is a growing man. And why does he grow? Because we water him."

The bland, bald, large-mouthed William Lloyd Garrison stood up. He had helped nurse the abolition movement, had gone to jail for it, had in one hour stood with a rope around his neck while a mob howled around him—all before young Phillips had enlisted in the cause. "Has not the President," asked the old war horse, "gone as fast and as far as the people would sustain him? ('No, no.') Mr. Lincoln has travelled as fast toward the negro as popular sentiment would warrant him. Butler and Grant have sustained the President's policy. ('No, no, no.') And what about Frémont? Events have occurred within a year greatly to diminish my faith in Frémont. Not a word from him in reference to the President's proclamation of amnesty. What a glorious opportunity was there lost! Then we have had the arming of one hundred thousand blacks, and still not one word of encouragement from Frémont."

Plainly, to the upper circles of Plymouth Church, Brooklyn, the answer was Frémont and nobody else. And it was nothing to talk about in Plymouth Church circles that a son of Henry Ward Beecher, not yet of age, had been commissioned an officer in the Army of the Potomac and, caught in conduct unbecoming to an officer, had been forced to resign. In anxiety and shame Beecher had gone to his handsome young friend, Theodore Tilton, who in turn went straight to the then Secretary of War Cameron and begged for a commission in the Regular Army for young Beecher. From Cameron, Tilton went to the White House and Lincoln signed the appointment of young Harry Beecher, lieutenant of artillery, Regulars.

Wrote Beecher to Chase of the President: "His mind works in the right *directions*, but seldom works clearly and cleanly. His bread is of unbolted flour, & much straw, too, mixes in the bran, & sometimes gravel stones." Beecher had written in the *Independent:* "The President seems to be a man without any sense of the value of time . . . Our armies have been managed as if they were a body of nurses in a foundling hospital."

Early in '64 the New York *World* presented General McClellan as the one man of worth, dignity and patriotism for nomination by the Democratic party to overwhelm Lincoln. In this effort the *World* served financial, industrial and transportation interests represented in politics by Erastus Corning and Dean Richmond of the New York Central Railroad; by William Henry Aspinwall of the New-York-to-San Francisco steamship lines and the Panama Isthmus 49-mile railway which up to 1859 had netted him a fortune of $6,000,000; and more directly and dominantly by August Belmont, politically and financially the most eminent Jew in America.

Born in a rich landholding family in Rhenish Prussia in 1816, Belmont at 14 had worked without pay as office boy, swept and dusted the rooms of the powerful banking firm of Rothschild Brothers in Frankfort while learning finance. In the panic year 1837 he set up in New York his own banking house of August Belmont & Company, his great asset being the agency for the Rothschilds in America. Becoming a U.S. citizen, Belmont served on foreign missions, was U.S. Minister to Holland, championed Stephen A. Douglas at the 1860 Baltimore convention, saw himself chosen chairman of the national Democratic committee. He wore side whiskers, owned ponies and enjoyed horse races, collected rare porcelains and masterpieces of painting. And Belmont had anger and courage, for in 1841 he had fought, because of a woman, a duel at Elkton, Indiana, with William Hayward of South Carolina, took a bullet wound and thereafter walked through life with a limp. After an interview with Lincoln and Seward, Belmont had gone to Europe and quietly warned financial circles that the Southern Confederacy was not a good business risk, wreaking practical damage to the South under cover. From England he transmitted to Lincoln a short message he had from an interview with Palmerston: "We do not like slavery, but we need cotton, and hate your Morrill protective tariff."

Belmont had helped raise and equip the first regiment of German troops enlisted in New York City. As a Union man through the war he had run somewhat the course of Governor Seymour. He had sent on to Washington an extract from a letter written at New Orleans, expecting it would be shown to Lincoln. "The time has arrived when Mr. Lincoln must take a decisive course," it read. "Trying to please everybody, he will satisfy nobody." And Lincoln in a long letter to Belmont had urged that his reconstruction policy was clear for those who would read and understand rather than write complaining letters northward. "Broken eggs cannot be mended; but Louisiana has nothing to do now but to take her place in the Union as it was, barring the already broken eggs. The sooner she does so, the smaller will be the amount . . . past mending."

Belmont joined with Aspinwall in belief that McClellan was a "genius" and, as President, would manage to save the Union without entanglement on the slavery issue. With Seymour he stood for a party policy of unmistakable opposition to the Republicans in power; otherwise the Democratic party would be swallowed and cease to exist in a proposed new National Union party foreshadowed by Lincoln and Weed.

Manton Marble, publisher of the New York *World*, was ably meeting the wishes of Belmont, who was credited with financially backing the newspaper. No other newspaper, not even the New York *Herald*, so incessantly cried down Chase and Federal money affairs on its financial page. They directly insinuated that by advance knowledge of money measures Chase and others were piling up fortunes for themselves. That Chase was in debt, and had to manage carefully to pay small loans from time to time, could never be known to those who believed half they read in the *World*'s financial page.

The President had ended free speech and a free press in America, the *World* said in April, being itself free to say: "In the knots of two or three which sometimes gather, Mr. Lincoln's stories quite as often occupy the time as the momentous interests of a great nation, divided by traitors, ridden by fanatics and cursed with an imbecility in administration only less criminal than treason."

The *World* made public, now nearly two years after its writing, McClellan's letter handed to Lincoln at Harrison's Landing, Virginia, in 1862, in which McClellan unfolded for Lincoln his ideas on how the country ought to be run. On the slavery issue he was not merely reserved but noncommittal: he would not interfere with the institution, it seemed, but he threw no light on what form of compromise could be made with it. Still he held to his declaration: "The Constitution and the Union must be preserved, whatever may be the cost in time, treasure and blood."

Lincoln's darkly solemn letter of April 4 to A. G. Hodges of Kentucky staggered many readers. Hodges with other Border State men had interviewed Lincoln. Lincoln at Hodges' request put into writing, for the country to read, what he had told them face to face in the White House: "I am naturally anti-slavery. If slavery is not wrong, nothing is wrong. I can not remember when I did not so think, and feel." He went on: "I claim not to have controlled events, but confess plainly that events have controlled me." This had the opposition hard put for pertinent comment. Something in it was as basic and strange as the House Divided speech. "Now, at the end of three years struggle the nation's condition is not what either party, or any man devised, or expected. God alone can claim it. Whither it is tending seems plain. If God now wills the removal of a great wrong, and wills also that we of the North as well as you of the South, shall pay fairly for our complicity in that wrong, impartial history will find therein new cause to attest and revere the justice and goodness of God."

An old question bothered Senators and Congressmen and found its way into editorials. The *World* on February 11, 1864, headed one: "Ought a President to Re-elect Himself?" In a sentence in Lincoln's '61 inaugural address, said the one-term advocates who were becoming vocal, it could be seen that the President had pledged himself to one term and no more. That sentence ran, "I now enter upon the same task [as fifteen previous Executives] for the brief constitutional term of four years, under great and peculiar difficulty." Entirely aside from this point, Chase held it had now become an American tradition that the President should not serve a second term; for 30 years no President had served two terms, and the custom was established. Chase wrote this in many letters.

Those favoring the one-term tradition from week to week could glean no satisfaction from Lincoln personally. He had nothing, not even an anecdote, about a second term. Until he should say he was a candidate they were up a row of stumps. He was waiting. What he was waiting for he did not say. Swett noted, "Lincoln kept an eye out for the spot where the lightning was going to strike and tried to be on that spot." Lincoln's belief in lightning was allied to his belief in luck, to his sleep-visioned nature, to the superstitious element, the will of Providence, the dreaming bones that swayed him in vaster matters.

The grinding drama of drums and blood and agony went on. Three years of these rocking lines of destroyers seeking each other and unable to destroy to an end. Three years of it and no foreteller had foretold it as it happened. "God alone can claim it." Inexorable laws and deep-running forces of human society and national life had operated. Any one man in their midst had better count himself of small moment in the blood and slime of the hour. Could it be an hour to step out and form combinations and huckster a candidacy with an eye on November next? Before November would come terrific decisions of men with snarling guns and plunging bayonets. Beyond and out there where men lay rolled in their gray blankets by the bivouac fire under frost or falling rain or white moon—out there lay the dictates of the November election, the action that would sway the November voters.

When Lincoln was actually in a political campaign, as Swett saw him, he never believed in going out to line up factions and interests in his favor. He kept hands off. "I believe he earnestly desired that nomination. He was much more eager for it than he was for the first, and yet from the beginning he discouraged all efforts on the part of his friends to obtain it."

Swett, who had performed confidential errands too delicate to record in telegrams or letters, in Washington in the early months of '64 noted that for a year and more the adversaries of Lincoln had been at work for themselves. "Chase had three or four secret societies and an immense patronage extending all over the country. Frémont was constantly at work, yet Lincoln would never do anything either to hinder them or to help himself." Swett threw his light on how Lincoln managed campaigns by ignoring men and by ignoring all small causes, but by closely calculating the tendencies of events and the great forces which were producing logical results.

The hard-drinking Governor Dick Yates of Illinois early in '64 saw that he belonged politically in the deeper-running Lincoln current, saying in Bryan Hall, Chicago: "It is no use, as I heard a friend of mine say today; the politicians may try to fix it up, but the people will have Old Abe and nobody else. (Applause.) I must confess I am for him first, last and all the time. (Applause.) It is no time to change fronts when you are in the presence of the enemy . . . I stand up here to say that from long acquaintance with him, he is not only one of the honestest men that God ever made, but in clear, cool, statesmanlike judgment, he is without a peer in the history of the world."

Lincoln held no mood fixed and frozen. His eye caught light and shadow, color and mass, in the flow and heave of a reality he termed Public Opinion. His moods ranged with those of the People in a democracy that in spite of war kept a wide measure of freedom in personal expression.

Conscience and expediency told him, rightly or wrongly, for weal or woe, that he himself in justice should continue to be the instrument of the American people to finish the war, and if it might be, to bind up the wounds and heal the scars without malice. Anxiety weighed him down in these moods. Deep gongs rang. He referred to himself as well as Chase, Frémont and

Butler in the remark that J. Russell Jones, Provost Marshal General James Fry and Congressman John Kasson said they heard from him as to the desire to be President: "No man knows what that gnawing is till he has had it."

Without a doubt, too, Lincoln felt a loyalty due from him to people who trusted him, who saw logic and sense in what he was doing, who were afraid to try some other man as President. It was to them Lincoln's Government and Lincoln's Army that held the boys and men from so many homes. Father Abraham was not merely a nickname. He cared. They trusted him as he trusted them. There was this kinship between him and a certain legion of loyalists. He seemed to reason that if they wanted him to go on as President they would have their way—and if they didn't want him, he could stand that if they could.

He heard from his legion often, once in March '64 when the Chicago *Tribune* carried an editorial paragraph: "A sturdy farmer from Oskaloosa, Iowa, one of the bone and sinew class, called upon us yesterday in relation to business matters. Before leaving, we asked him how Mr. Lincoln stood in Iowa. 'Stands?' said the old farmer, with glistening eyes and raising his brawny fist, 'Old Abe stands seventeen feet higher in Iowa than any other man in the United States!' "

A like enthusiasm was found by a Cincinnati *Gazette* writer who in February interviewed John Bright. He quoted this leading English liberal as saying that the re-election of Lincoln would be the hardest blow the North could inflict on the South that year. Bright refused to worry over what he heard of Lincoln as too slow, though he believed a change of Cabinet should be demanded, adding, "Mr. Lincoln is like a waiter in a large eating house where all the bells are ringing at once; he cannot serve them all at once, and so some grumblers are to be expected."

In February '64 the New York *Herald*'s satirically excessive compliments meant to carry barbs: "As a joker Mr. Lincoln is unique. With the caustic wit of Diogenes he combines the best qualities of all the other celebrated jokers of the world. He is more poetical than Horace, more spicy than Juvenal, more anecdotal than Aesop, more juicy than Boccaccio, more mellow than rollicking Rabelais, and more often quoted than the veteran Joe Miller." The idea was that a clown ran the Government. To seven sarcastic reasons why Lincoln should be a candidate again the New York *World* added, "He writes worse English than any President we ever had," and he surpassed in stories "from the broad smutty to the diluted Joe Miller."

The New York *Evening Post* served Lincoln in April by printing on page one a column and more of Lincoln stories and anecdotes. They rendered none of Lincoln's ease in dialect and of course could not carry his personal mimicry and facial mobility.

Not yet was there a photograph of a smiling Lincoln. A face "woebegone" the Quaker boy, Sergeant Spradling, saw at the White House and saw again in waking moments between sleeps at night for days afterward.

While the army had its quota always of deserters, stragglers and malingerers, the mass of sentiment there plainly favored "Old Abe." Thousands of soldier letters written home told this. Letters of protest and murmuring were few in comparison. A veteran on furlough spoke in Chicago on whether the soldiers wanted Lincoln re-elected. He cocked his eyes with a reckless glint: "Why, of course they do. We all re-enlisted to see this thing through, and Old Abe must re-enlist too. He mustered us in and we'll be damned if he shan't stay where he is until he has mustered us out. We'll never give up till every rebel acknowledges he is the Constitutional President . . . I don't give a cuss for this country if the beaten side has a right to bolt after an election; it would not be fit to live in."

Harriet Beecher Stowe having words for what moved her, wrote for the January number of the *Watchman and Reflector* of Boston, with flow and stride:

The world has seen and wondered at the greatest sign and marvel of our day, to-wit, a plain working man of the people, with no more culture, instruction or education than any such workingman may obtain for himself, called on to conduct the passage of a great people through a crisis involving the destinies of the whole world . . .

Lincoln's strength is of a peculiar kind; it is not aggressive so much as passive, and among passive things it is like the strength not so much of a stone buttress, as of a wire cable. It is strength swaying to every influence, yielding on this side and on that to popular needs, yet tenaciously and inflexibly bound to carry its great end; and probably by no other kind of strength could our national ship have been drawn safely thus far during the tossings and tempests which beset her way.

Surrounded by all sorts of conflicting claims, by traitors, by half-hearted, timid men, by Border State men and free State men, by radical Abolitionists and Conservatives, he has listened to all, weighed the words of all, waited, observed, yielded now here and now there, but in the main kept one inflexible, honest purpose, and drawn the national ship through.

Justice David Davis, his ear to the winds of gossip and change, wrote to a brother-in-law: "The politicians in and out of Congress, it is the current belief, would put Mr. Lincoln aside if they dared. They know their constituents don't back them, and hence they gamble rather than make open war." Seeing itself in a losing contest to nominate General Grant, the New York *Herald* crawfished. "Mr. Lincoln will be the regular nominee of his party. He is in the field and has the reins of the party in his hand. He will enter the canvass as the embodiment of all the blunders, follies, and corruptions of his administration."

Henry C. Work of Chicago added another song to his "Kingdom Coming" and "Wake, Nicodemus"—titled "Washington and Lincoln." One gave the country independence, the other saved the Union and set a people free, said the song. The lines were flamboyant. The cohorts of August Belmont and the New York *World* frowned at it. To them it was flapdoodle. Yet the song strode. As poetry it was so-so. As the offering of Henry C. Work, among greatest of popular song writers, it had import.

Francis Bicknell Carpenter, portrait painter, wished to give his public a momentous historic setting for Lincoln. A rich lawyer friend assured Carpenter six months' income for work on his vision, and Speaker Colfax and Congressman Lovejoy recommended him to the President. Carpenter at a White House reception heard Lincoln with a twinkle of the eye, playfully, "Do you think, Mr. Carpenter, that you can make a handsome picture of *me?*" In his office he said, "Well, Mr. Carpenter, we will turn you loose in here, and try to give you a good chance to work out your idea." In the painting the Cabinet members were to be seated and standing around the President seated at a table, in their midst at the exact center of the design that world-famous parchment, the Emancipation Proclamation. This was the idea Carpenter outlined.

The 37-year-old painter was given the run of the White House, assigned the state dining room with its big chandeliers for lighting his night work, which sometimes lasted till daylight. Carpenter sat with his sketchbook in the President's office, worried visitors hearing from the President, "He is but a painter." At Cabinet meetings Carpenter sketched, the President having explained, "He has an idea of painting a picture of us all together."

More than once Carpenter walked the streets of Washington late at night with Lincoln, no escort or guard. In the temporary studio of sculptor Swayne in the Treasury Building, Lincoln sat for a bust, replying to a query from Swayne that he did not write the verses "Why Should the Spirit of Mortal Be Proud?" though they were often signed with his name. When Carpenter asked for it Lincoln recited the poem.

Carpenter told the President of a New York *Tribune* account, from a correspondent within the Confederate lines, of an elaborate conspiracy worked out in Richmond to kidnap the President, or if kidnaping failed to assassinate him. Lincoln asked for the details, which Carpenter gave him. He smiled as though he could not believe it, "Well, even if true, I do not see what the Rebels would gain by killing or getting possession of me. I am but a single individual, and it would not help their cause or make the least difference in the progress of the war. Everything would go right on just the same." Ever since his nomination at Chicago the regular installment of threats came in the week's mail, and they no longer bothered him, he informed Carpenter. This surprised him, said the young painter. "Oh," said Lincoln, "there is nothing like getting *used* to things!"

On the evening of the day Lincoln reviewed Burnside's corps, Governor Curtin came with a friend to the President's office. And in their talk Curtin referred to the volunteer citizen soldier as "worthy of profound respect." Lincoln gave quiet assent, Carpenter noting a "peculiar dreaminess" creep over his face, as if he could not find words should he try to speak his heart about volunteers his heart knew.

Carpenter made himself at home in the White House, kept busy on his big painting, saw the President and Cabinet on and off parade. He told Lincoln of odd happenings and Lincoln replied with stories, none of which offended him, said the conventional Carpenter. Carpenter repeated Lincoln stories, correcting vocabulary at times, making the words nicer. Where Lincoln said "skunks" or "polecats" in a story, Carpenter, in retelling it, said "those little black and white spotted animals which it is not necessary to name."

While Carpenter wrestled with his work of art the New York *Herald* and other newspapers printed a story that Mrs. Lincoln came in one day to watch him with his paints and brushes and saluted him, "Well, Mr. Carpenter, how are you getting along with your happy family?"

Carpenter in February called on Lovejoy, saw him sit up and take nourishment, saying he was better, not knowing he had only three months to live.

On his death Lincoln said to Carpenter, "Lovejoy was the best friend I had in Congress."

Several Copperhead editors made peculiar comment when Lovejoy died. They saluted him as a true man holding mistaken ideas. Underlying these salutations it could be seen that these Copperhead editors divided anti-slavery men into genuine heroes and counterfeit, true crusaders and bogus.

And to the end Lovejoy, his once magnificent physical frame nearly used up, burned with a loyalty to the President. According to Carpenter, his words ran: "I tell you, Mr. Lincoln is at heart as strong an antislavery man as any of them, but he is compelled to *feel* his way . . . His mind acts slowly, but when he moves, it is *forward*. You will never find him receding from a position once taken. It is of no use talking, or getting up conventions against him. He is going to be the candidate and is sure to be reëlected. 'It was foreordained from the foundation of the world.' "

The dying Lovejoy was writing in a letter to Garrison February 22, 1864, "I write you, although ill-health compels me to do it by the hand of another, to express to you my gratification at the position you have taken in reference to Mr. Lincoln. I am satisfied, as the old theologians used to say in reference to the world, that if he is not the best conceivable President he is the best possible."

CHAPTER 42

Jay Cooke—Cash for War—Hard Times and Flush

THE UNION Government was spending easily more than $2,000,000 a day for the war. Chase had reason to say that while the other departments stood at the spigots he had to worry about the barrel. Lincoln met the wishes of Chase in many delicate particulars of appointments, arrangements, measures, that would bring in the cash to keep the war going.

In offices across the street from the Treasury Building Jay Cooke & Company hung up their sign. In January '64 this company finished the selling of $513,000,000 worth of U.S. bonds, the issue being oversubscribed, so that Congress had to act in order to legalize the millions over the half-billion. The commission of Jay Cooke on these immense sales was $\frac{1}{4}$ of 1 per cent, out of which he paid the costs of a large sales force and advertising space in hundreds of newspapers. He had persistently refused offers of Chase to appoint him an Assistant Secretary of the Treasury, his title being merely U.S. Subscription Agent.

The bond-selling campaigns of Cooke under Chase's authority satisfied Lincoln to the extent that he kept his hands off, seeing Cooke only two or three times during many months. Once Cooke had finished breakfast with Chase when a servant announced the President at the door in a carriage with

Attorney General Bates. The Secretary went out to the carriage and learned that Cabinet members and their ladies were going that day to a drill review of 10,000 men seven miles beyond Georgetown. Chase begged to be excused. Lincoln insisted on Chase's going and told him to bring Cooke along. As they rode across the country Cooke noticed the President enjoying the holiday. Cooke got to looking at Bates' head of black hair with white whiskers and mustache and said to Bates that his own father had been just like that, not a gray hair in his head but when he grew a beard it always came out white. Cooke said he wondered what was the philosophical and scientific explanation. And according to Cooke, Lincoln gave a quizzical look at Bates and said, "Oh, Mr. Cooke, that is easily accounted for." "I shall be glad to know the reason." "Well, it could hardly be otherwise. The cause is that he uses his jaws more than he does his brain."

Also, Cooke noted, "We all laughed heartily at this impromptu and original joke at Mr. Bates' expense and, as I gave the substance of it to some newspaper men the next day it was published far and wide as one of Lincoln's original sayings."

Jay Cooke's father, Eleutheros Cooke, had built the first stone house in the new town of Sandusky, Ohio, and practicing law, launching a railroad with horse-drawn cars, sitting in Congress at Washington, never lacked fluency of speech. Young Jay read his father's speeches in the *Congressional Globe*, built a 16-inch-long steamboat propelled by power from an old clock spring, took a hand in defending a Negro bootblack from the attacks of other debating-society members who said they could not allow a Negro to listen to their discussions. Jay had clerked in a store, studied bookkeeping, traveled to St. Louis where he again clerked in a store, practiced penmanship in a night school. In Philadelphia, again a clerk, he rose to be at 21 a partner and active manager of E. W. Clark & Company, the largest private banking house in the United States. He married Dorothea Elizabeth Allen, the daughter of a Maryland planter and slaveowner, and she bore him two sons and two daughters.

When the house of E. W. Clark & Company crashed in the 1857 panic, Jay Cooke went in for railroad reorganization, joined the best canals of Pennsylvania into one system. In 1861 he had his own banking house in Philadelphia and introduced himself to the U.S. Treasury officials by sending on Federal loan subscriptions without compensation. Early that year he won national reputation and the gratitude of Governor Curtin by selling at par $3,000,000 in bonds issued by Pennsylvania, which was almost bankrupt.

Both Lincoln and Chase were responsive to the advice of Jay Cooke transmitted through his brother Henry: "I would advise Gov. Chase . . . to keep on the right side of those capitalists who are disposed to dabble in the loans, etc., of the government, and if they do make sometimes a handsome margin it is no more than they are entitled to in such times as these. They can be very useful to the government. I repeat that the Governor should keep on the right side of the capitalists till he gets into smoother water."

The New York *Herald* soon was saying that a delegation of the bankers had appeared in Washington making no secret of their errand of notifying the President that his management of the war had incurred their displeasure, and as they were paying the costs of it, they had come to recommend to him changes in his policy.

Congressman Kellogg stood up to say: "We have summoned the youth; they have come. I would summon the capital; and if it does not come voluntarily, before this republic shall go down or one star be lost I would take every cent from the treasury of the states, from the treasury of capitalists, from the treasury of individuals and press it into the use of the government."

Jay Cooke's plan was to go over the heads of the bankers and reach the small investors, the masses of people who could buy a $100 bond or more, the very ranks from which the bankers got their depositors. His drive got under way in the spring of '63 to sell $500,000,000 of five-twenties, bonds paying 6 per cent interest for 20 years or redeemable in government gold within five years. The newspaper campaign of direct advertising, informative news accounts and editorial comment on the five-twenty bonds that Jay Cooke set going was the most far-reaching, deliberately organized affair of the sort that America had ever seen. At one time 1,800 daily and weekly journals were printing paid advertising. Disloyal sheets that hated the Lincoln administration and all its works could not bring themselves to hate Jay Cooke's cash to the extent of not printing live news, which he sent them fresh from the hands of his large staff of skilled writers.

The telegraph bill ran over $40 a day. From the first weeks, when subscriptions varied from less to more than $1,000,000 a day, on into later weeks when the daily totals were from $2,000,000 to $6,000,000, the drive of Jay Cooke's vision and bustling energy spread out and animated the philosophy of the North. Foreign-language newspapers were brought in. They too published in German, Italian, Yiddish, Polish, advertisements explaining the five-twenty bonds.

Thus Jay Cooke—with Chase backing him and Lincoln backing Chase—put the impress of his personality on the country, outranking Greeley, Beecher and Barnum in his ability to get action from masses of people. His news writers were quick to relay the information to editors that in the week after the Army of the Potomac took its heavy slaughter at Chancellorsville no less than $8,000,000 in bonds were bought.

The tumbling river of cash flowing in to Jay Cooke, and from him to the Lincoln Government, for men, guns, horses, mules, hardtack and beans to carry on the war, was possible partly because of the breezy, valiant, inextinguishable optimism of Jay Cooke as to his country. Behind a thousand phrasings that came from him lay his theory that the war was an incident, a minor circumstance, in a deep stream of economic events crowding the United States forward into a future of dizzy figures in railroad, steamship, mill, mine and oil financing. Steamers from Europe in 1863 had brought to America 182,808 new laborers and homesteaders, the port of New York doubling its arrivals over the previous year, with 92,000 from Ireland, 35,000 from Germany, 18,000 from England, 11,000 from other countries.

Lincoln's friends Swett and Lamon gambled in oil and quicksilver stocks and went flat broke. The New York merchant A. T. Stewart paid a tax on $4,000,000 of income; William B. Astor's income was $1,300,000; Cornelius Vanderbilt's $576,000; J. P. Morgan's $53,000. Joshua Bates of Boston, American partner of the Barings of London, died leaving an estate of $8,000,000.

California had dug out $70,000,000 in gold and silver the previous year, and other states $30,000,000. Four out of five white men in California were bachelors, and every steamship from the port of New York for the West Coast held scores of marriageable women sailing to where they would try their luck. In the rush for copper and iron lands in the Lake Superior region entries for 26,000 acres were made in the one month of February '64. The *Tribune* of St. Joseph, Missouri, noted on March 10, 1864, that since February 1, 400 teams and wagons had crossed the Missouri River headed for Western mining regions. East and west were fortune seekers who with Jay Cooke could see a future worth gambling on.

Small, comfortable fortunes had sprung up by thousands across the Northern and Border States, not to mention the Gulf State of Louisiana. Snug accumulations of wartime profits came out of selling wooden and metal legs and arms to men mutilated in battle, and out of providing substitutes to go forth to battle. Hundreds of neat bank deposits traced back to blockade-running and to forbidden traffic in liquor, medical supplies and scarce ingredients of war munitions.

Good to look at and all too rare was the instance cited by a son of George Luther Stearns, the Boston merchant and Negro recruiting officer: "A Boston firm for whom Mr. Stearns had obtained a lucrative government contract, from which they probably had derived a larger profit than they deserved, sent him a cheque for two thousand dollars, which he returned with a note saying as politely as possible that to partake in such transactions was as culpable as theft."

General Sherman cursed the merchants of Cincinnati for readiness to trade the enemy anything for a profit. Grant cursed Lincoln's friend Swett for trying to trade in hay at exceptional profits, and when Swett told Lincoln that Grant had threatened to shoot him if he went into hay deals, Lincoln told Swett to beware, for Grant generally kept his word. Yet the ordinarily scrupulous though occasionally obtuse Grant did not see anything wrong in his giving a kinsman by marriage an inside track on cotton-trading profits, until Rawlins exploded and shamed him about it. To a request of Ohio's first war governor, William Dennison, that Lincoln give a letter of recommendation to military and naval authorities in behalf of a cotton trader, Nicolay wired, "The President thinks he cannot safely write that class of letters."

Personal success in business, a stake that would assure a man comfort for life, was a motive so tangibly in the air that Lincoln, according to Whitney, advised his old law associate that Western land deals could bring him $50,000 in not so long a time. Letters of David Davis, Swett, Lamon, Orme and the Eighth Circuit "orgmathorial" lawyers were touched with hopes and groans related to whether this one or that among them would come through with a stake to give financial security for life. Secretary Welles made the mistake of letting a kinsman by marriage have a rather large-sized fortune as a commission on the negotiation of vessel sales to the Navy; he was fiercely satirized in *Leslie's Weekly*, the New York *World* and the New York *Herald*. But because huge amounts were involved it was generally accepted that Welles took a proper course in letting it be handled at a rather low percentage by a man he considered responsible. Repeatedly in his diary Welles bemoaned the palpable rascals who came trying to sell him worn-out ships at fancy prices.

From Dana and Grant to Stanton and then Lincoln went the cases of several cotton speculators trying to snake out profit-yielding bales of fiber for textile mills. Stanton organized a secret-service force that uncovered corrupt practices and frauds. Dana as Stanton's assistant carried this further and broke down the game of many a thieving quartermaster and contractor.

General James Grant Wilson noted one difficulty was that some of the most competent and most energetic contractors were the most dishonest, could not be content with a fair profit. "In tents, a lighter cloth or a few inches off the size; in harness, split leather; in saddles, inferior materials and workmanship; in shoes, paper soles; in clothes, shoddy; in mixed horse feed, chaff and a larger proportion of the cheaper grain . . . Every contractor had to be watched." As if this merely was a repetition of European experience, *Blackwood's Magazine* in England commented, "A great war always creates more scoundrels than it kills."

The higher up the hypocrite and thief uncovered by Stanton's secret service, the louder the howling from some newspapers and the heavier the pressure from politicians to let him go. Wilson noted that governors, Congressmen, Senators and even the President himself were pressed into the service of the "best citizens" who had been caught cheating the Government. In the winter of 1863-64 Dana helped supervise the buying of 3,000,000 pairs of trousers, 5,000,000 flannel shirts and drawers, 7,000,000 pairs of socks, 325,000 mess pans, 207,000 camp kettles, 13,000 drums, 14,830 fifes. The War Department paid out from June '63 to June '64 more than $250,000,000.

A procession of mouthpieces and fixers twined in and out of Lincoln's office from week to week, and he had to sit not merely as judge and jury passing on their guilt or innocence and the punishment due; beyond that he had to ask whether the Union cause at the military front, and at the political and economic rear, would be served by his judgment. When a large share of a swindler's stealings had been returned and a Senator of considerable influence interceded for a thief of highly respectable position, Lincoln leaned to what Dana called "moderation," though privately exclaiming to John Eaton that the Senator was "too crooked to lie still." In dealing with various stripes of fox, wolf and hog caught with a smear of guilt on their snouts, Lincoln was more often blamed for "sympathy and clemency" than for vindictiveness. Heavy files of evidence and many intricate considerations stood in the backgrounds of an item in *Leslie's* in June: "The *New York Tribune* says that Capt. Sam Black, U.S. Quartermaster, who was recently convicted at Louisville of perpetrating enormous frauds on the Government, has been pardoned; and that Hall & Smith, Western horse contractors, who had likewise been found guilty of the same offence, have had their sentence suspended."

A tangled affair moved from May 8, 1863, when Lincoln signed the writ his old friend Swett wanted, to August 19, 1863, when the New Almaden gold mine in California at a ridiculously low price passed into the hands of a corporation in which Swett was a stockholder and for which he was a paid attorney. For Swett, Lincoln had no reproaches. In a way he knew Swett better than Swett knew himself. Swett was not so bad, only too anxious about getting a stake for life—too easily played on by sharpers, who paid Swett not as a lawyer but as one who had access to the President.

Lincoln would probably not have disagreed with Bates' diary entry of March 9: "The demoralising effect of this civil war is plainly visible in

every department of life. The abuse of official powers and the thirst for dishonest gain are now so common that they cease to shock."

Oliver Wendell Holmes wrote: "Multitudes have grown rich and for what?
To put gilt bands on coachmen's hats? To sweep the sidewalks with the
heaviest silks the toiling French can send us? To float through life the passive
shuttlecocks of fashion, from the avenue to the beaches and back again from
the beaches to the avenue?"

New York hotels, theaters, jewelers' retail stores and women's wear establishments were surpassing all former sales records. The shopping crowds and
what they were doing was an endless topic in the newspapers. A class of reckless war-profit spenders were named the "Shoddy," a word from the textile
trade where a compound of refuse and sweepings pounded, rolled, glued and
smoothed into the external form and gloss of cloth was known as shoddy.
Harper's Monthly of July '64 in a scornful commentary told of soldiers on
the first day's march or in their first storm finding their jackets and trousers,
overcoats and blankets, scattering to the winds in rags or breaking into scraps
and dust under a driving rain. "Shoddy has ever since become a word to
represent the fraudulent contractor who makes a display of his ill-gotten
gains."

Leslie's Weekly believed it significant that $2,000,000 in diamonds had been
imported the previous year. "No wonder Shoddy glitters in the sunlight of
Central Park or the gaslight of its own palatial residence; no wonder the
jeweler's hands are full, setting gems, while the soldier's feet blister in his
paper-soled shoes, and his bare elbows emerge from his worn jacket sleeves."
The same editor complained of New York given up to the leg drama, "legs,
physical and of unpadded proportions, female pedals as necessary to dramatic
success as is a prima donna in an opera." The man who buttoned his vest
with diamonds, accompanied by the woman whose hair shook with the glitter
of gold dust, went shopping, saying, "We don't feel this war."

When in a slum hut of Columbus, Ohio, the widow of a soldier killed at
Chickamauga died lacking food and the decencies of life, the Mahoning
Sentinel threw a diatribe: "Wealth revels in luxury and worth starves in
poverty—shoddy swells in bogus jewelry and like a rotten mackerel emits a
dazzling glow from its vulgar splendor—in this paradise of parasites and
patriots." This was not a Copperhead political outpouring. It was a cry of
the same human pitch as the lamentations of the pro-Lincoln *Harper's
Monthly*.

While winter snow blew along the city streets, it troubled Oliver Wendell
Holmes that fresh peaches at $24 a basket should be offered in show windows
to buyers who had money to throw at the birds. The customers of luxury-
dealers made merry over the war. It was a pretty little war and had been good
to them, in their slang a "High Daddy."

Prices of food and clothing soared upward while wages stood still or rose
slowly. The very process that brought fortunes to speculators and sure-thing
gamblers cut the wages and buying power of the workman. As if by instinct
and with no traditions or practice for guidance, the working class began using
the weapon termed the strike. The very word "strike" was so novel that
some newspapers put it in quotes as though it were slang or colloquial, not yet
fully accepted in good language. The year 1864 saw more strikes than all

previous years in American history. In March the engineers on all railroads entering Chicago were on strike. On the Galena & Chicago Union Railroad the cry was that the company was not meeting an alleged January agreement to pay wages of $3 a day; the strike was broken in two days by engineers who went back to work reinforced by engineers brought on from New York and other eastern cities. The Brotherhood of the Foot-Board, born in Detroit in '63, grew into the reorganized Grand International Brotherhood of Locomotive Engineers in '64.

Payday dollars would buy so little in May '64 that the Chicago newspapers told their readers one day that in desperation the common laborers on every railroad running out of Chicago, except one, were on strike for a wage raise from $1.50 a day to $1.75. The printers in New York, Chicago and other cities formed their Typographical Union, the bakers, the tailors, the iron-workers, the coopers, the journeymen cordwainers, the seamen, each in their own craft, organized a union or "protective association" or "benevolent society," usually meeting behind closed doors. In some cases the labor union was recognized and took permanent form. More often there was a confused development out of which came somewhat better conditions for the workers.

The only strike where Lincoln seemed to have stepped in with his influence as President was but partly told of in his letter of December 21, 1863, to the Secretary of War: "Sending a note to the Secretary of the Navy as I promised, he called over and said that the strikes in the Ship-yards had thrown the completion of vessels back so much, that he thought Gen. Gilmores proposition entirely proper. He only wishes (and in which I concur) that Gen. Gilmore will courteously confer with and explain to Admiral Dahlgren." General Gillmore had a proposition for meeting the demands of the strikers. Admiral Dahlgren did not agree with Gillmore. Lincoln in effect ordered the two of them to get together and settle the strike, Lincoln concurring with Gillmore.

In St. Louis when newspaper printers went on strike General Rosecrans detailed soldiers to take the places of strikers. The union printers sent in a report to Lincoln on their side of the case. And it became a tradition of the labor movement that the President sent word that servants of the Federal Government should not interfere with legitimate demands of labor—and the strikebreaking soldiers were withdrawn.

In the textile trades, in the factories and the homework system, the hours were inhumanly long and the wages so low that respectable newspapers frequently published the figures as though for the amazement of readers that human beings could subsist on so few dollars a week. A strike of factory girls in Paterson, New Jersey, was for higher wages through cutting down the workday from 12 and 16 to 10 hours a day.

The necessities of poor and pretty women were made the means of their debauchery by high Government officials, so believed the sober Springfield *Republican*. An editorial summarized Washington scandals which flashed working-girl melodramas of fact through many newspaper columns, all soberly and sadly confirmed as to fact in House reports of May and June. "A bureau of the Treasury Department made a house of seduction and prostitution. Members of Congress putting their mistresses into clerkships. An honorable Senator knocked down in the street by a woman he had outraged. Whisky drinking ad libitum. The government cheated in contracts and openly robbed by its employés. Writes our most careful correspondent, a long resident at the capital, 'Washington was never quite so villainously corrupt as at the present time . . .'"

In the brighter view $5,000,000 of privately raised funds was given to the Sanitary Commission for its many-sided help to soldiers in camp, on battle-field and in hospital. Bedding, clothing, vegetables, supplies, upwards of $15,000,000 worth, went from the people back home to the boys at the front. Endowment funds to colleges ran into millions of dollars.

Of all classes the war was falling most heavily on the soldier, Lincoln re-marked in closing a Sanitary Fair in Washington. To the soldier, staking his life and often giving it, went the highest merit. Next perhaps would come the women of America, who had been the chief agents in these fairs for the relief of suffering soldiers and their families. Said the President, "I have never stud-ied the art of paying compliments to women; but I must say that if all that has been said by orators and poets since the creation of the world in praise of women were applied to the women of America, it would not do them justice for their conduct during this war. I will close by saying God bless the women of America!"

So ran intersecting human streaks across America while Jay Cooke carried on his drive that brought a Niagara of money into the U.S. Treasury, raising in less than 11 months over $500,000,000, a financial feat that to cold Euro-pean observers indicated some peculiar unity of purpose in the North, and resources that might yet surpass Great Britain's.

Through the advertising and circular literature of the campaign had run a quiet promotion of the idea that Secretary Chase was the most prominent executive at Washington and would make an able President of the United States. Lincoln's estimates of Chase always included high appraisal of heavy labor in a difficult field.

George William Curtis, lavish and loyal friend of Lincoln in his *Harper's Weekly* editorials, wrote to a friend the first week in April, "I have seen Lincoln tête-à-tête since I saw you, and my personal impression of him con-firmed my previous feeling." Curtis was 15 years younger than Lincoln, remembered that Lincoln shook hands with him in the manner of a father as they parted, and said: "Don't be troubled. I guess we shall come through."

Two sentences from Lincoln in early '64 had been picked up and in private conversations and public prints threshed out as significant texts or as silly excuses. One was spoken at the Philadelphia Sanitary Fair: "It is difficult to say a sensible thing nowadays." The other was from the Hodges letter: "I claim not to have controlled events, but confess plainly that events have controlled me." Though spacious and simple as sky and air, these two sen-tences were like the kaleidoscopic American scene. They could be read as having any shade or tint chosen to suit the views of any interpreter.

What was dying might be a little better known than two or three years before. What was being born was more of an enigma than ever.

CHAPTER 43

Chase Thirsts to Run for President

THREE California Congressmen on request called on Secretary Chase in his private office. He had resolved to remove all of the leading Federal appointees of his department at San Francisco. He read to the seated and interested Congressmen a list of the new appointees. The Congressmen had nothing to say, Chase having told them his decision in the matter was irrevocable. They took their hats and walked over to the White House and paid their respects to the President without saying anything about what had just happened. Then they went to New York to take steamships for San Francisco. While they lingered in New York, Noah Brooks was summoned to the White House. There Brooks learned that the President had just heard of the wholesale removals and appointments determined by Secretary Chase.

The President tramped up and down the long room swinging his arms. "Tell me," he demanded of Brooks, "are those California Congressmen angry because the San Francisco mint and custom-house appointments were agreed on without their consent?" It seemed so, replied Brooks. "But the appointments are not agreed on," continued Lincoln. "Nothing is agreed on. I got the impression the California Congressmen were consulted and were satisfied . . . Were they very mad?" Not very, said Brooks. Still they were sore. "The President then angrily asked why I had not told him this before," ran Brooks' account. "I replied that it was not my affair . . . The President expressed his astonishment that he had been kept in the dark about so grave a matter as the emptying and filling of the most important federal offices on the Pacific coast. Then he anxiously asked if there was any way by which the California Congressmen could be reached and brought back."

One had sailed and was now on the high seas, Brooks answered, but two of them were still in New York. Lincoln handed a telegraph blank to Brooks and told him to wire the two Congressmen asking them to return to Washington to see the President, Brooks to sign the telegram.

The two Congressmen came and Lincoln slowly and carefully broke down the list of appointments fixed by Secretary Chase. He told Brooks that Chase was "exceedingly hurt" by the interference with his plans. In the shift of affairs Chase offered to appoint one of the two California Congressmen who had returned to Washington as collector of the port at San Francisco. The President suggested that all three California Congressmen should get together in San Francisco, agree on a list of appointments, and send it to him for approval. This was not agreed on. However, when the two California Congressmen finally took steamer from New York for the West Coast, one of them, Frederick Low, carried with him his commission as collector of the port at San Francisco.

About the same time the Senate threw out an appointment made by Chase to the office of internal revenue collector at Hartford, Connecticut. Chase sent Lincoln a long letter insisting that the President again send the name of Mark Howard, Chase's man, to the Senate, and if the Senate again threw out the Howard appointment, to let Chase then give the President another name to offer the balky Senate. Equally insistent but much shorter was Lincoln's reply to Chase saying that Senator Dixon of Connecticut and Congressman Loomis, both of Hartford, joined in recommending Edward Goodman for the appointment. "I will thank you therefore to send me a nomination, at once, for Mr. Goodman."

Next day Chase again wrote those words which became familiar to Lincoln: "I respectfully resign"—whatever the "respectfully" might mean. But this resignation Chase did not send to Lincoln, partly because, as Chase explained in a note to Lincoln, Senator Dixon sent him a note "of great personal respect and kindness" and he, Chase, had replied to Senator Dixon also with great personal respect and kindness, upon which Senator Dixon had called on Chase, and the entire matter was to go over for further consideration of the President. However, Chase made it clear that his purpose was "to secure fit men for responsible places" without control of appointments by Senators or Representatives. Otherwise "I feel that I can not be useful to you or the country in my present position." From month to month these summary notices were served on the President that any moment his Treasury head was ready to quit.

Letters of protest came to Lincoln from Puget Sound citizens who wanted Victor Smith thrown out of the collector's office in that district. Smith had been an Ohio man, a personal and political friend of Chase, an abolitionist, a spiritualist who believed in rappings, spouted his pet "isms," and was an "eccentric functionary." While collector of customs at Port Townsend, Washington Territory, Smith managed to induce the Government to move the customhouse to another place named Port Angelos, which, combined with Smith's arrogant personal manners, raised an outcry from businessmen, politicians and ordinary citizens that he was a nuisance and an evil to the West Coast.

Joining in the demands on Lincoln for Smith's removal and the return of the customhouse to its first point were, according to Brooks, every other Federal officer and nearly every prominent citizen in the Puget Sound district. Among the prominent citizens seeking Smith's official scalp was Anson G. Henry, formerly of Springfield, Illinois, and personal physician years back to a sufferer from hypochondria named Abraham Lincoln, who as President had appointed Henry surveyor general of the Territory of Washington. Henry was among those who gave their word to the President that Smith was a worthless vagabond and an audit might show him a defaulter.

A delegation that seemed to include everybody then in Washington, official and unofficial, from the Pacific Coast, came and filed with the President formal charges against Victor Smith and called for his removal. Lincoln sent Chase a note to "please send me, at once, an appointment of Henry Clay Wilson" to replace Victor Smith. He explained to Chase that his mind was made up to remove Smith, yet in so doing he had not decided that the charges against Smith were true but had only decided that the dissatisfaction with Smith was too great. "But I believe he is your personal acquaintance & friend; and if you shall desire it, I will try to find some other place for him."

Chase on a Monday wrote to Lincoln, "This information surprised and greatly pained me; for I had not thought it possible that you would remove an officer of my department without awaiting the result." Also on this Monday Chase read a note from Lincoln saying he had learned that the man, Henry Clay Wilson, he had appointed Friday to replace Victor Smith was dead, and therefore Lincoln would appoint one Frederick A. Wilson.

Two days later Lincoln sent Chase a letter giving his approval to several matters and closing, "*Please send me over the commission for Lewis C. Gunn, as you recommend, for collector of customs at Puget Sound.*" Smith besought Chase to have himself reappointed and Chase replied that Smith was mistaken as to the influence of words from Chase to the administration. "If any word of mine would make you collector again you would be reappointed."

In one phase the Victor Smith affair was a duel of political strength as between Smith and Dr. Henry. Though both were followers of the spiritualist cult and believed they could talk with the dead and departed of another realm, the two men loathed each other and never spoke as they passed by. On the steamer *Brother Jonathan,* bound from San Francisco to Portland, Mr. Smith and Dr. Henry were both drowned when that vessel struck a reef and sank.

In Chase's department were more than 10,000 job-holders high and low, and according to Nicolay and Hay, the President let Chase have his way as to all of these except in rare cases, seldom interfering. The two secretaries saw Chase trying to undermine Lincoln. "He regarded himself as the friend of Mr. Lincoln; to him and to others he made strong protestations of friendly feeling, which he undoubtedly thought were sincere; but he held so poor an opinion of the President's intellect and character in comparison with his own, that he could not believe the people so blind as deliberately to prefer the President to himself."

Still later the secretaries agreed as to Chase, "There never was a man who found it so easy to delude himself." This may have been the key to the wormings and gyrations of Chase. Under the portentous exterior of the handsomest man in the Cabinet was an oversized marionette borne down by delusions of grandeur. Two sorry points Nicolay and Hay recorded of Chase. He had what they called, for want of a better word, "self-love." And he had no sense of humor to tell him when others might be hiding laughter at him.

"Chase looks and acts as if he meant to be the next President," Richard Henry Dana had written from Washington to Charles Francis Adams at London in March '63. A few days after a visit with Lincoln in December, Thurlow Weed wrote from Albany to John Bigelow in Paris: "Mr. Chase's report is very able, and his huge banking machine will make him strong. But how pitiable it is to know that his eye is single—not to the welfare of his country but to the presidency! Mr. Lincoln says he is 'trying to keep that maggot out of his head,' but he cannot."

In scores of letters written to politicians, editors, ministers, Chase over a two-year period sought to spread the impression that in the midst of incompetents he was the one man who would know how if given the power. "Had there been here an administration in the true sense of the word," he wrote to the Reverend Dr. J. Leavitt, January 24, 1864, "—a President conferring with his Cabinet and taking their united judgments . . . we could have spoken boldly and defied the world." To Wayne MacVeagh, Republican state committee chairman of Pennsylvania, two days later: "Oh, for a vigorous, earnest, thorough prosecution of this war!" To Judge Thomas F. Key of Cincinnati the same day: "Some friends are sanguine that my name will receive favorable consideration from the people in connection with the Presidency. I tell them that I can take no part in anything they may propose to do, except by trying to merit confidence where I am." To Thomas Heaton, a Treasury Department agent at Cincinnati: "So far as the Presidency is concerned, I must leave that wholly to the people . . . Whatever disposition they make of it I shall be content."

Perhaps no one else wrote more shifting and contradictory opinions than did Chase of Lincoln. To the wealthiest man in the Senate, his son-in-law, Chase wrote November 26, 1863, that he could never be driven into any hostile or unfriendly position as to Mr. Lincoln. "His course toward me has always been so fair and kind." He dwelt at length on his "respect and affection" for Mr. Lincoln. Yet in the same letter he made the point that no President should have a second term, and "I think a man of different qualities from those of the President will be needed for the next four years."

From his desk Chase sent out dozens of curiously stilted self-portraits of the noble and worthy citizen, the man of grasp, dignity and patience, who against his deeper inclinations would serve his country as Chief Magistrate if called on. He evolved forty ways of saying what he wrote a Wisconsin man in December '63, "There is certainly a purpose to use my name, and I do not feel bound to object to it." Over and again Welles' diary entries had one tone: Chase "lamented the President's want of energy and force, which he said paralyzed everything. His weakness was crushing us. I did not respond to this distinct feeler, and the conversation changed."

From the number of long letters Chase wrote in fixing his political fences, and from the number of interviews and conferences he held toward the same end, it could be estimated that he was giving perhaps half of his time to nursing along his high political hope.

While Carpenter from day to day painted, Lincoln often brought visitors down to see the work of art and, said Carpenter, he came by himself sometimes three and four times in a single day. In his many remarks, seldom did Lincoln indulge in any personal comments on his Cabinet members. However, one day, Carpenter noted, "with a sly twinkle of the eye, he turned to a senatorial friend and said: 'Mrs. Lincoln calls Mr. Carpenter's group *The Happy Family*.'"

A short, thickset man wearing side whiskers and the latest cut of clothes, carrying a monocle in the English manner and sporting a gold-headed walking stick, came to see Lincoln while the Chase movement was under way. And Lincoln gave this man plenty of time and talked much with him. He was Henry Jarvis Raymond, editor and owner of the most distinctly pro-Lincoln daily organ in New York City, the *Times*, the one morning newspaper that tried to hurl back the daily javelins of Greeley, Bennett, Brooks, Fernando Wood. A Congressman-elect from New York State had pressed Lincoln for official action in an important matter, according to Carpenter, and the answer from Lincoln was: "You must see Raymond about this. He is my *Lieutenant-General* in politics. Whatever he says is right in the premises, shall be done."

Raymond was 44 years old. Born in Lima, New York, a University of Vermont graduate, teacher in a young ladies' seminary, he was once editor of a literary weekly. He founded the New York *Times* in 1851 and edited it for a public that wanted more trustworthy reporting of the day's news than was to be had in the brilliant and slimy *Herald* or in the quirks and shifts of the *Tribune*.

A delegate to the Whig national convention of 1850, later lieutenant governor of New York, Raymond had helped organize the Republican party in 1856, stumped for Frémont, in 1858 independently swung away to support of Stephen A. Douglas for President, but in 1860 swung back to Lincoln. He was close to Weed and Seward; the triumvirate of Seward-Weed-Raymond was often satirized and excoriated. And now Raymond worked on the most comprehensive and formidable biography of Lincoln that had ever been attempted, to be published late in the spring. That Raymond in '61 was so hopeless of the Lincoln administration that he urged in his newspaper a provisional government and a dictator [George Law] to replace Lincoln would not be told in the biography. That a movement to nominate Chase for President was supported by scores of Republican leaders in Washington early in '64 would not be told. Except for political family secrets not worth telling in a campaign year, it would be a first-rate campaign biography.

"The most violent opposition to Mr. Lincoln," wrote Raymond, "came from those most persistent and most clamorous in their exactions." In so terrible a crisis, it was unavoidable that "vast multitudes of active and ambitious men should be disappointed in their expectations of position and personal gain," this resulting in powerful and organized efforts against the renomination of Lincoln. "The President has achieved a wonderful success" in maintaining through terrible trials "a reputation with the great body of the people, for unsullied integrity, of purpose and of conduct, which even Washington did not surpass, and which no other President since Washington has equalled." Raymond elaborated this "unspotted character" as a key point in the national situation, as also Lincoln's remarkable faculty of "putting things" in simple language that carried precise ideas. "It gives to his public papers a weight and influence with the mass of the people, which no public man of this country has ever attained. And this is heightened by the atmosphere of humor which seems to pervade his mind, and which is just as natural to it and as attractive and softening a portion of it, as the smoky hues of Indian summer are of the charming season to which they belong."

As to the candidacy of Chase, Lincoln gave an anecdote that Raymond passed on to Carpenter: " 'R[aymond], you were brought up on a farm, were you not? Then you know what a *chin fly* is. My brother and I . . . were once ploughing corn on a Kentucky farm, I driving the horse, and he holding the plough. The horse was lazy; but on one occasion rushed across the field so that I, with my long legs, could scarcely keep pace with him. On reaching the end of the furrow, I found an enormous *chin fly* fastened upon him, and knocked him off. My brother asked me what I did that for. I told him I didn't want the old horse bitten in that way. "Why," said my brother, "that's all that made him go!" Now,' added Lincoln, 'if Mr. C[hase] has a presidential *chin fly* biting him, I'm not going to knock him off, if it will only make his department go.' "

Lincoln possibly told the story much as they gave it. Others heard the story and it was widely published as from Lincoln.

A story was printed about Chase one day giving Lincoln a gloomy recital of the financial situation, gold going higher and greenbacks sinking, and "What can be done about it?" Lincoln: "Well, Mr. Secretary, I don't know unless you give your paper mill another turn." At which Chase almost swore as he flustered out.

Republican and Democratic papers enjoyed reprinting facetious charges of the New York *Herald* that Mr. Chase was "putting his own portrait upon the greenbacks of *small* denominations, which everybody sees, while he sticks Mr. Lincoln's comical phiz upon the *large* bills, in order that he may make himself generally known to the public."

John Hay wrote one day: "I do not know whether the nation is worthy of the President for another term, I know the people want him . . . But politicians are strong yet and he is not 'their kind of a cat.' "

In the fall of '63 Hay had spoken to Lincoln of Chase's "trying to cut under" the administration, the President saying, "Whenever he sees that an important matter is troubling me, if I am compelled to decide it in a way to give offense to some man of influence he always ranges himself in opposition to me and persuades the victim that he would have arranged it differently. It was so with Gen. Frémont—Genl Hunter when I annulled his hasty proclamation—with Gen. Butler when he was recalled from New Orleans— with these Missouri people when they called . . . I am entirely indifferent as to his success or failure in these schemes, so long as he does his duty as the head of the Treasury Department."

On Rosecrans' removal from command after Chickamauga and before his appointment to the Department of Missouri, Hay told the President that Chase would try to make capital out of it. The President laughed. "I suppose he will, like the bluebottle fly, lay his eggs in every rotten spot he can find." In measuring men and reading their hearts Lincoln had the advantage that Chase seldom if ever laughed at himself. To Chase a fool was a dunce and every day in the week a dunce. For Lincoln any dunce might have off days and even the wicked were not wicked all the time.

Chase could only be mystified by a story the New York *Evening Post* laid to Lincoln about a general who hinted to Lincoln that many people took it as settled that he would accept a renomination for President. Lincoln was reminded of an Illinois State official when an itinerant preacher asked for a permit to lecture in the State House. "On what subject?" was asked, and the reply, "On the second coming of our Saviour." "Oh, bosh," said the official, "if our Saviour had ever been to Springfield and got away with his life, he'd be too smart to think of coming back again." This, related the New York *Evening Post*, Mr. Lincoln said was very much his case about the renomination.

That Chase—like Lincoln—wanted to keep clear of anything about which bothersome questions could be asked was seen in his returning to Jay Cooke a $4,200 profit that Cooke had earned for him in a railway stock deal, explaining to Cooke that he must "avoid every act which could give occasion to any suspicion," and "In order to be able to render the most efficient service to our country, it is essential for me to *be* right as well as to *seem* right, and to *seem* right as well as to *be* right."

Theodore Tilton in the *Independent* stressed the fact that Lincoln in writing the Emancipation Proclamation forgot to mention God and it was Chase who suggested the closing phrase which invoked "the gracious favor of Almighty God." A friend said to Lincoln he felt it was improper of Tilton to publish such matters at such a time and Chase had probably seen Tilton and was responsible. Lincoln: "Oh, Mr. Chase had nothing to do with it; I think *I* mentioned the circumstance to Mr. Tilton myself." Thus the man who had it from Lincoln told it to Carpenter.

The Union League Club of Philadelphia came out strong for Lincoln's renomination, the National Union Club of Philadelphia chiming in. In New York City the National Conference Committee of the Union Lincoln Association issued an address "To the Loyal Citizens of the United States" declaring that in electing an "occupant for the presidential chair" the people should choose "a true leader," one "tried and not found wanting," naming Abraham Lincoln. When some postmasters over the country who favored Lincoln's renomination posted this imposing New York declaration where any and all purchasers of postage stamps could see it, the New York *World* howled that the administration had issued an order coercing the postal service into peanut politics.

Horace Greeley a month earlier at an antislavery meeting came forward to say he thought about the largest man in this Government was Governor Chase, a statesman who had been fighting on the hardest ground of all to manage and whose battles had all been victorious. As usual, Greeley wrote and printed a long cool editorial to buttress his short impetuous speech. Hay noted of this: "The Pres^t was greatly amused at Greeley's hasty Chase explosion and its elaborate explanation in the *Tribune*."

While Greeley grumbled and sputtered, some of the most cunning and ruthless political manipulators in the country began working on an upshoot of expression that would cry the mass sentiment favoring Lincoln. Simon Cameron and John W. Forney, practiced professional politicians of the Keystone State, at one extreme, and swaggering gun-fighting Jim Lane of Kansas at another end, saw work ahead they could do. So did the Blair boys and Old Man Blair, besides many political workers who knew left hand from right.

Among Union members of the Pennsylvania Legislature early in January a paper was passed around. An address to the President, it was, saying that the voters of Pennsylvania had endorsed his policies generously at the recent election and "We are only responding to their demand when we thus publicly announce our unshaken preference for your reëlection to the Presidency in 1864." Signed by every Union member of senate and assembly, this paper was sent to Lincoln January 14 by Simon Cameron with the message, "You are now fairly launched on our second voyage . . . Providence has decreed your reëlection, and no combination of the wicked can prevent it."

A New Hampshire State convention of the Union party had already met January 6 to nominate a state ticket, and before the chairman knew exactly what he was doing with so many Treasury Department employees present, the delegates had sent up rockets and declared for Lincoln's renomination. The Union Central Committee of New York unanimously took like action, and in sending the news to Lincoln, Senator Morgan said, "It is going to be difficult to restrain the boys, and there is not much use in trying to do so." With only one dissenting voice both houses of the Kansas Legislature endorsed renomination of the President. The Union members of the legislature of New Jersey joined in saying, without disparagement of other true men, "You are the choice of the people."

California legislators, almost unanimously, declared, "While we revere and honor other noble patriots who have performed their parts, the people will look to Abraham Lincoln as the instrument selected by Providence to lead their country in safety through its perils." In much the same tone the legislatures of Maryland, Michigan, Wisconsin, Rhode Island, declared themselves, as also state conventions in Minnesota, Iowa, Indiana, New Hampshire, Connecticut. When February '64 ended, 14 states had by official action gone on record speaking their preference for Lincoln for a second term.

During the first two months of '64 money was spent, political workers hired, and literature, open and secret, was spread by the quietly working Chase organization. The Washington branch of Jay Cooke & Company, through Henry D. Cooke, was involved in expenditures estimated at $20,000, while Senator Sprague's payments were put at $10,000. The Cooke firm made an outright gift of $5,000 to the Chase committee, of which Senator Samuel C. Pomeroy of Kansas was chairman, and gave a check for $2,000 for the writing and placing of an article about Chase in the *Atlantic Monthly*. And working modestly, quiet as a church mouse, yet fertile of resource and quick of wit, was Kate Chase Sprague, swept and driven by ambition.

While the Chase band wagon was trying at once to make a noise and be quiet, the mass sentiment favoring Lincoln was exploded and reverberated through the state legislatures. Pomeroy and his committee decided in February on a bold play. A circular was prepared—for private and confidential distribution. It was said to be a joint product of Sumner, Stevens, Henry Winter Davis and Wade, though signed by Pomeroy only. Printed copies were mailed over the country and marked "private and confidential." From men inside the President's own party went this appeal to Union men that they must counteract the President's attempt to re-elect himself through using the official machinery of the Government: (1) His re-election was impossible because of the combinations that would be against him; (2) on the face of the President's record his second term would be worse than his first; (3) a second term would give the President more power than was safe for republican institutions; (4) Chase on the other hand would guarantee economy and purity in the Government; (5) the unorganized Chase strength needed only systematic effort to win. Each of these points was made in elaborate and unmistakable language running nearly 600 words.

The *National Intelligencer* at Washington spread this document in full over its pages, for newspapers everywhere to reprint. And the Chase workers, who had counted on secrecy till they had a strength worth bringing into the open, were all surprised, some shocked, Chase himself aghast. Clear and plain to all who read the text of the circular was the shame that the "Committee of

Prominent Senators, Representatives and Citizens" who issued the document were so afraid of being caught doing it that they did not sign. In so bold and raw a piece of work it was best to be anonymous. But their work was dragged into the daylight. And they scurried from newspapermen asking, "Who wrote it?" The Democratic press jibed at the Republicans in the words of the New York *World*, "Go on, gentlemen! wash your dirty linen in public." The document which became notorious as "The Pomeroy Secret Circular" had odd declarations:

. . . even were the reëlection of Mr. Lincoln desirable, it is practically impossible against the union of influences which will oppose him.

. . . we find united in Hon. Salmon P. Chase more of the qualities needed in a President during the next four years than are combined in any other available candidate . . .

. . . the discussion of the Presidential question . . . has developed a popularity and strength in Mr. Chase unexpected even to his warmest admirers . . .

A central organization has been effected, which already has its connections in all the States, and the object of which is to enable his friends everywhere most effectually to promote his elevation to the Presidency . . .

While the circular was still being mailed out, and read as strictly private and confidential, many copies fell into the hands of Lincoln workers and soon began coming to the White House. The President, according to Nicolay, was absolutely without curiosity in regard to attacks on himself, refused to look at the circulars; they piled up "unread" on Nicolay's desk.

On the day the *National Intelligencer* burst into print with the circular, Chase wrote a sick-at-heart letter to Lincoln saying it was probable he had already seen a letter printed in the *Intelligencer*. Until he saw it in print, "I had no knowledge of the existence of this letter." Several gentlemen had called on him some weeks before and urged him to allow his name to be used toward election as Chief Magistrate. They said their views were shared by many earnest friends. He had replied that his usefulness as head of the Treasury Department might be impaired. They had come again. "We had several interviews." They gave their judgment that he could still be useful while his name was used. "I accepted their judgment as decisive." Chase then wrote more warmly toned feelings than had ever before shown in his letters to Lincoln. "For yourself I cherish sincere respect and esteem; and, permit me to add, affection. Differences of opinion as to administrative action have not changed these sentiments; nor have they been changed by assaults upon me by persons who profess themselves the special representatives of your views and policy . . ."

Lincoln studied this letter with its careful excuses, its blurred justifications, its embarrassed self-portraiture. Next day, February 23, he wrote a one-sentence note to Chase: "Yours of yesterday in relation to the paper issued by Senator Pomeroy was duly received; and I write this note merely to say I will answer a little more fully when I can find the leisure to do so." Lincoln waited six more days. Robert Lincoln on this sixth day was home from Harvard on vacation, strolled into his father's room; his father showed him a long reply to Chase. The son was surprised that his father had not read the Pomeroy Circular and said so. The father stopped the son sternly, saying that a good many others had tried to tell him something it did not suit him to hear, and he asked Robert to call a messenger to take the letter to Chase.

Chase could study the letter, a self-portrait in exchange for the one received from Chase: "I would have taken time to answer yours of the 22nd. sooner, only that I did not suppose any evil could result from the delay . . . on consideration, I find there is really very little to say. My knowledge of Mr. Pomeroy's letter having been made *public* came to me only the day you wrote; but I had, in spite of myself, known of it's *existence* several days before. I have not yet read it, and I think I shall not. I was not shocked, or surprised by the appearance of the letter, because I had had knowledge of Mr. Pomeroy's Committee, and of secret issues which I supposed came from it, and of secret agents who I supposed were sent out by it, for several weeks. I have known just as little of these things as my own friends have allowed me to know. They bring the documents to me, but I do not read them—they tell me what they think fit to tell me, but I do not inquire for more . . . Whether you shall remain at the head of the Treasury Department is a question which I will not allow myself to consider from any stand-point other than my judgment of the public service; and, in that view, I do not perceive occasion for a change."

Three days later Chase was worried lest Lincoln might give out for publication the interesting letters that had passed between them. He wrote a note for Henry Villard, now of the New York *Tribune*, to carry to the President, who wrote to Chase: "In consequence of a call Mr. Villard makes on me, having a note from you to him, I am induced to say I have no wish for the publication of the correspondence between yourself and me in relation to the Pomeroy Circular—in fact, rather prefer to avoid an unnecessary exhibition—yet you are at liberty, without in the least offending me, to allow the publication, if you choose."

As Chase reread the letters between him and Lincoln he knew he would be the worse damaged by publication. When one of Chase's most loyal friends, Robert B. Warden, read the letters later he wrote that he, Warden, nearly lost his head and was tempted to agree with Tom Corwin's having told Lincoln that Chase was "embodied perfidy."

Thaddeus Stevens as a Chase worker in Pennsylvania had been powerless against Cameron and Forney. Jim Lane in Kansas had overridden the Pomeroy forces. The son-in-law Sprague in Rhode Island had not been able to swing that tiny bailiwick. The Blair family, old Frank and young Frank and Postmaster General Montgomery, had put their influence and advice where it counted.

Still Chase hoped on. Ohio might come his way. His home state might say Yes. Surely the Buckeyes would want their old governor for a White House figure. But the Ohio legislative members plopped one and all for Lincoln. And Chase wrote to the former Ohio Congressman A. G. Riddle, early in March: "I am trying to keep all Presidential aspirations out of my head. I fancy that as President I could take care of the Treasury better with the help of a Secretary than I can as Secretary without the help of a President. But our Ohio folks don't want me enough." He wrote James C. Hall of Toledo that under circumstances that might arise, or that could be arranged, he would lead the Democratic party for the sake of Union, Freedom and Justice. Compared with the cause for which he stood, he wrote, "persons and even parties are nothing."

In such peculiar twilights had Chase run his candidacy that when he requested by letter "no further considerations be given" to his name, it was not taken that he strictly meant what he said. As the Chase boom wavered and sank early in March, Henry Ward Beecher in a Philadelphia speech came forward with flowers of approval for Lincoln as always a man of honest principles rather than tricky expedients, the homely President of a homely people, faithful to the great political truths of the American system. "He has shown the world that successful government is not the mystery that only a privileged few can enact."

As weeks passed Chase continued writing the same sort of letters as before about the waste and bungling of the administration, the President's lacking a firm mind and a strong hand to guide the nation. "It seems as if there were no limit to expense . . . The spigot in Uncle Abe's barrel is made twice as big as the bung-hole."

The National Union party convention which would renominate Lincoln—or not—was to meet in Baltimore June 7, according to a call of its national committee in February. This would be too soon, said Greeley, Bryant and others. Raymond, *Harper's Weekly* and others asked, "Why not?" The ground swell of mass sentiment was for Lincoln, and an early convention would be good strategy. One or two inexplicable disasters might send the mass sentiment dwindling.

A restless but uncrystallized labor movement over the country would cast its ballots in the coming campaign. Lincoln met a small section of it when a committee from the New York Workingmen's Democratic Republican Association called to inform him their association had elected him an honorary member. They had organized the year before and favored trade-unions and bargaining of employees with employers. "The honorary membership in your Association," said the President, ". . . is gratefully accepted. You comprehend, as your address shows, that the existing rebellion, means more, and tends to more, than the perpetuation of African Slavery—that it is, in fact, a war upon the rights of all working people."

He touched on the New York draft riots of the year before: "The most notable feature of a disturbance in your city last summer, was the hanging of some working people by other working people. It should never be so. The strongest bond of human sympathy, outside of the family relation, should be one uniting all working people, of all nations, and tongues, and kindreds. Nor should this lead to a war upon property, or the owners of property. Property is the fruit of labor—property is desirable——is a positive good in the world. That some should be rich, shows that others may become rich, and hence is just encouragement to industry and enterprise. Let not him who is houseless pull down the house of another; but let him labor diligently and build one for himself, thus by example assuring that his own shall be safe from violence when built."

In an autograph album for a Sanitary Fair next day Lincoln wrote: "I never knew a man who wished to be himself a slave. Consider if you know any *good* thing, that no man desires for himself."

In the autograph, in the address to the workingmen's committee, he knew he was helping create opinion, and the mass of his personal contacts and their impression were a part of the political campaign of the year.

A pleasant and idle tale spread in talk and print. Lincoln had gone to a black prophetess in Georgetown. Like King Saul in the Bible, he asked about his future. The voodoo woman went into a dark room to raise up mystic spirits and speak with them, returning to the consultation parlor to tell Lincoln, "General Grant will capture Richmond, you will be the next President—but beware of Chase."

CHAPTER 44

Spring of '64—Blood and Anger

NEVADA'S miners, prospectors, gamblers, gold- and silver-hunters, with 26,000 voters, wanted to have a state and be in the Union. She liked the idea of her little desert population sending a Congressman and two Senators to Washington. Two out of three voters were Republican.

The President called on Assistant Secretary of War Charles A. Dana, who wrote of what followed. Lincoln told Dana the administration had decided the Constitution should be amended to prohibit slavery; this was not only a change in national policy but a most important military measure equivalent to new armies in the field, worth at least a million men, tending to paralyze and break the continuity of enemy ideas. To pass such an amendment would require approval by three-fourths of the states. Nevada might be of critical importance as a state. Dana quoted Lincoln, "It is easier to admit Nevada than to raise another million soldiers."

The Senate bill of February 24, 1864, authorized a Nevada convention the first Monday in July, to declare on behalf of the people that they adopt the Constitution of the United States and to frame a state government. In the House through March this bill was held up by lack of votes. Stevens, the floor leader, simply couldn't line up a majority for it.

Lincoln walked over to Dana's office, said: "Dana, I am very anxious about this vote. It has got to be taken next week. The time is very short. It is going to be a great deal closer than I wish it was . . . There are three [members of Congress] that you can deal with better than anybody else, perhaps, as you know them all. I wish you would send for them." Lincoln told Dana who they were. Dana considered it unnecessary to tell their names to anyone not immediately concerned. One was from New Jersey and two from New York. "What will they be likely to want?" asked Dana. The President said, ". . . It makes no difference what they want. Here is the alternative: that we carry this vote, or be compelled to raise another million, and I don't know how many more, men, and fight no one knows how long. It is a question of three votes or new armies." "Well, sir, what shall I say to these gentlemen?" "I don't know, but whatever promise you make to them I will perform."

Dana sent for the men and saw them one by one. Two wanted each an internal-revenue collector's appointment. "You shall have it," said Dana. The third wanted a customhouse appointment in New York at about $20,000 a year. The Congressman, a Democrat, wanted a Republican appointed. When the Congressman had stated his case, Dana asked, "Do you want that?" "Yes." "Well, you shall have it." "I understand, of course, that you are not saying this on your own authority?" "No. I am saying it on the authority of the President." So the extra votes needed to pass the Nevada bill through the House were gotten. And the Yeas and Nays on the vote in Senate and House were not indexed or recorded in the *Congressional Globe*, whether through clerical inattention or by official arrangement.

Dana believed he and Lincoln knew precisely the fine, thin lines of right, wrong and expediency that wove through this piece of politics. Lincoln had chosen for an intermediary in an intricate operation, a man of delicate methods who had been a terror to fraudulent contractors and get-rich-quick cotton traders, and whose faith in Lincoln had depths. "Lincoln was a supreme politician," wrote Dana. "He understood politics because he understood human nature."

Hay had talked with the President in December about reconstruction in Florida, the possibility of getting one-tenth of the voters in the state to swear Union allegiance and be recorded as U.S. citizens in an oath book. To General Q. A. Gillmore, in whose department Florida lay, Lincoln wrote January 13 that he had commissioned Hay a major in the army and Hay with oath books and blank certificates would arrive and explain to General Gillmore the President's general views on the subject of reconstructing a loyal state government in Florida. "It is desirable for all to cooperate; but if irreconcileable differences of opinion shall arise, you are master. I wish the thing done in the most speedy way possible, so that, when done, it lie within the range of the late proclamation on the subject . . ."

Hay sailed to Gillmore's headquarters on the South Carolina coast, assured the General it was not the President's intention to do anything to embarrass his military operations. At Jacksonville, Florida, Hay read the President's proclamation of amnesty to a line-up of prisoners, explained that if they signed the oath book, certificates to that effect would be issued to them and they would be allowed to go home. Otherwise they would be sent North as prisoners of war for exchange. "There is to be neither force nor persuasion used in the matter. You decide for y^rselves." They signed, nearly half making their mark. They were tired of the war.

Then came shocking news. General Truman Seymour, a Regular Army officer in charge of some 5,500 men, sought out a Confederate force of about the same size at Olustee River in a picked position, welcoming battle. The Union loss was 1,800, the Confederate half that. Seymour's orders from Gillmore had been to wait. But he had plunged and his army was routed.

With Union bayonets in disgrace for the moment, Hay had a harder time enrolling loyal Unionists. He went to Fernandina, where he got a few more names, noted: "Some refused to sign, on the ground that they were not repentant rebels." On March 3 he wrote, "I am sure that we cannot now get the President's 10th." His hopes vanished that the required 10 per cent of voters to form a state government could be enrolled.

Sailing back to Washington, Hay could read in the New York *Herald* or *World* that the President would not hesitate at murder to win political ends, that Hay had joined with the President in a reckless conspiracy to overawe Florida with military power, to elect himself as a Congressman, to deliver a set of Florida delegates for the President at the nominating convention in June. "Price of Three Votes for the Presidency! One Thousand Lives!" trumpeted the New York *Herald*, while the *World* day after day rehearsed the allegations in new phrases.

The written instructions of Lincoln to Hay and to Gillmore, along with Gillmore's explicit orders to General Seymour, were made public, and it was seen that a brave general in Florida had taken a chance, risked a battle and lost. This amid the hullabaloo of passing weeks came to be regarded as the central fact.

In many forms ran accusations that the President had an eye on Southern delegates to help renominate him. The accusers hoped he would wait until after the November elections before taking a hand in reconstruction, out of fear that anything he did might look as though he were hunting delegates. Sardonic and miserable contradictions were beginning to whirl around the very word "reconstruction." Out of so much death, ashes and devastation, what could in the end be reconstructed? In its beginning it was to rest on a 10 per cent of oath-bound voters regarded as betrayers and outcasts by those whose bayonets and taxes were still keeping the Confederacy alive. The oath itself had lost sanctity in the story of the soldiers who caught a rattlesnake, took it to camp, administered the oath, and let it go.

That wholesale and regimented oath-taking might easily become ridiculous was in Lincoln's mind when he issued the Amnesty Proclamation in December; he had warned that it was only a method, a mode, for re-establishing national authority. He heard in January '64 from General Banks, commanding the Department of the Gulf, that there were loyal Union people in Louisiana who wished to avoid taking the oath prescribed. The President replied: ". . . it is not even a modification of anything I have heretofore said when I tell you that you are at liberty to adopt any rule which shall admit to vote any unquestionably loyal free-state men and none others. And yet I do wish they would all take the oath."

Far down in that changing patchwork of military and civil governments, Louisiana, Lincoln tried to guide General Nathaniel Prentiss Banks, a Democrat, three times governor of Massachusetts. Amid clashing authorities Lincoln wrote him assurance. "I deeply regret to have said or done anything which could give you pain, or uneasiness. I have all the while intended you to be *master* . . ." While fortunes large and small were being harvested in a thousand shady Gulf Coast traffickings, Banks kept an instinct for what Nicolay and Hay named "honorable poverty" rather than such cash winnings as Ben Butler's brother took out of the Crescent City.

Lincoln tried to steer Banks in the governing of some 17 of the 48 parishes of Louisiana controlled by Union armies, an area holding a fourth of the slaves of Louisiana. He would like to see the state recognize the Emancipation

Proclamation. "And while she is at it, I think it would not be objectionable for her to adopt some practical system by which the two races could gradually live themselves out of their old relation to each other, and both come out better prepared for the new. Education for young blacks should be included in the plan."

Banks on January 11 proclaimed an election to be held February 22. Free white male voters who had taken the oath of allegiance cast over 11,000 ballots, of which the Banks candidate Michael Hahn received 6,183, J. Q. A. Fellows, a proslavery conservative, 2,996, and B. F. Flanders, 2,232.

In his Louisiana domain Governor Michael Hahn estimated that in three-fourths of the state allegiance lay mainly with the Confederate governor and the legislature in session at the capitol in Shreveport. Hahn was 34 years old. Born in Bavaria, he was as a baby carried by his parents to a ship for New York; he moved with them to New Orleans, where he graduated from the law department of the University of Louisiana, became president of the school board in New Orleans, clung fast to Douglas in politics, though an outspoken antislavery man.

To Hahn, Lincoln wrote a letter marked "Private": "I congratulate you on having fixed your name in history as the first-free-state Governor of Louisiana. Now you are about to have a Convention which, among other things, will probably define the elective franchise. I barely suggest for your private consideration, whether some of the colored people may not be let in—as, for instance, the very intelligent, and especially those who have fought gallantly in our ranks. They would probably help, in some trying time to come, to keep the jewel of liberty within the family of freedom."

With this the President included a one-sentence letter, perhaps equally important, notifying Hahn that until further orders he would be military governor of Louisiana. Thus if his civil authority given him by election was questioned, he could call out the troops and riot squads.

Banks headed in March the Red River expedition of some 40,000 men. And the forces mishandled by Banks were beaten and sent reeling so that Banks was glad to get his army safe in Alexandria, 80 miles back eastward from the town where 20 days earlier he had written John Hay he was anxious lest the enemy might not give him battle.

Lincoln, Seward, Halleck, Grant, Sherman, newspaper correspondents and the cotton traders had, affirmatively or negatively, shared in getting the expedition started and in direction of it after it got going. Banks was pleased to get back with it to the Mississippi and disperse it into various commands. Charges arose that the collapsed Red River expedition had as its main objective capture of immense supplies of cotton to be sold by the Union Government to relieve the textile-mill famine and to put millions of dollars into the U.S. Treasury.

Two men had turned up at Alexandria on the Red River with cotton trading permits in the President's handwriting, William Butler and Thomas L. Casey of Springfield, Illinois, old personal friends of Lincoln. What little cotton they collected was taken away from them by the army and put to military use. But their appearance at the Red River camp with presidential permits set many tongues going. "Much odium was excited by the circumstance," wrote Greeley.

"Reflections more or less severe were cast upon the President," wrote Nicolay and Hay. The secretaries pointed to a pressure "almost incredible" on the President to grant such permits, "and he sometimes, though very seldom, gave way." The letter of the President to Congressman Kellogg audibly groaning his refusal to give a trading permit, was quoted. "I think you do not know how embarrassing your request is," he wrote. Few things were so troublesome to the Government as the fierceness with which the profits in cotton trading were sought. "The temptation is so great that nearly everybody wishes to be in it; and, when in, the question of profit controls all, regardless of whether the cotton-seller is loyal or rebel, or whether he is paid in cornmeal or gunpowder . . . The officers of the army, in numerous instances, are believed to connive and share the profits, and thus the army itself is diverted from fighting the rebels to speculating in cotton . . ."

Kellogg had urged that the President could let him have one or two trading permits and the public need know nothing of it. That had been done. The President noted: "One case cannot be kept a secret. The authority given would be utterly ineffectual until it is shown, and when shown, everybody knows of it."

In May, Banks was relieved of his command and resigned his army commission. "The President gave me too much to do—more than any other major-general in the army," he wrote, as fact and not complaint. Sherman had written Lincoln and Halleck that he deemed it "very unwise at this time or for years to come, to revive the State governments of Louisiana, etc., or to institute in this quarter any civil government in which the local people have much to say." This, however, was precisely what Banks under Lincoln's guidance was trying to do with one hand while with the other he was to slay Confederate armies.

Lincoln and Banks agreed that, if only for its effect on politics and war morale in the North, the ballot should be given to at least a part of the free Negro population. Governor Hahn hoped to work out Lincoln's suggestion that Negroes who had fought for the Union, and possibly those who could read and write, should be the first Negro voters.

Grant suggested General E. R. S. Canby to supersede Banks and it was so ordered. But Lincoln and Banks remained friends and Banks was staying on in New Orleans advising with the Louisiana constitutional convention and reporting to Lincoln.

After General Frederick Steele's column of 13,000 Union troops had marched into Little Rock, the capital of Arkansas, September 13, 1863, a large part of the state came under Union control. Eight regiments of Arkansas citizens had been enlisted under the Union flag. And early in January the President sent oath books and blank certificates to General Steele, for use in reorganizing a state government. Word came to Lincoln of a series of Union meetings with speeches and resolutions and election of delegates to a convention of 44 members who claimed to represent 22 of the 54 counties of the State of Arkansas.

This convention on January 22, 1864, declared secession null and void, slavery abolished immediately and unconditionally, and the Confederate debt repudiated. An address to the voters of Arkansas adopted January 23 frankly acknowledged "that while we could not properly claim to be the people of Arkansas in convention assembled," yet as representatives of a considerable portion of the state, and understanding the sentiment of citizens desiring a government under U.S. authority, they had determined to present a state constitution for the voters to ballot on. They appointed and inaugurated for provisional governor one Isaac Murphy, 62 years old, born near Pittsburgh, Pennsylvania, schoolteacher, lawyer, California gold-hunter, civil engineer and public-land surveyor. As a member in May '61 of the state convention which decided that Arkansas would secede, Murphy was the one delegate voting against secession. He became a staff officer of General Steele and his son Frank a major in the 1st Arkansas U.S. Infantry.

General Steele proclaimed an election for March 14 as scheduled by the convention, the polls to be kept open three days. The returns gave 12,179 votes for the new constitution and 226 against it; for Isaac Murphy, with no opposition candidate for governor, 12,430 ballots were cast by oath-of-allegiance voters in 40 counties. With brass bands, flags and formalities the new state government was sworn in and took office April 11. Its two U.S. Senators-elect and its three Congressmen-elect went to Washington, presented their credentials, heard the wrangling and the squabbling in Senate and House over how the occupied Southern States should be reconstructed, and came back home to tell their people that not yet, though maybe after a while, they might be admitted to seats.

Bushwhackers had sprung up around Little Rock in such force that it was not safe to go a mile out of the capital. Brigadier General C. C. Andrews wrote to Lincoln: "A large majority of planters have taken the oath, pretend to acquiesce in the proclamation setting their slaves free, and still cling to their slaves and to the hope that they will sometime again hold them as slaves." To Lincoln as well as to Rosecrans came Missouri reports of vagabonds, thieves, marauders, bushwhackers, guerrillas, incendiaries, by tens, twenties, hundreds, often wearing the Federal uniform.

A dramatic history-making figure rose out of Missouri affairs, ready to embroil Lincoln in a fiery episode. Born in Lexington, Kentucky, a Princeton graduate who studied law in Washington, Frank Blair, Jr., now 43 years old, was admitted to the bar in Kentucky, practiced in St. Louis, trapped bear and wolf in the Rocky Mountains, fought in the Mexican War, again practiced law in St. Louis, edited the *Missouri Democrat*, went to the legislature, helped found the Republican party in 1856. One of the first Republicans in Congress, in 1857 he advocated compensated emancipation and colonization of the Negroes five years before Lincoln brought those issues to Congress.

Blair had been commissioned general of a brigade he raised himself, and ordered to join Grant at Milliken's Bend in Mississippi. "I dreaded his coming," said Grant, who had known Blair in St. Louis and voted against him for Congress in 1858. To Grant, Blair seemed one more political general, one more politician with unearned stars on the shoulder straps. Then at Chickasaw Bluffs, Arkansas Post, at Hard Times Landing and Champion's Hill, on the Big Black and the Yazoo, Blair had fought in muddy bayous and across cornfields, sending lines of skirmishers or storming columns against the enemy. Grant said he was disappointed, agreeably so, in Frank Blair, "no man braver than he, nor . . . any who obeyed all orders . . . with more unquestioning alacrity." Therefore Grant deduced that Blair was "one man as a soldier, another as a politician." The Senate approved Lincoln's commissioning him major general.

Then Stanton out of suspicion and dislike of the Blair tribe issued an order relieving General Blair of command, having, the Blairs and their friends said, "the effrontery to declare that he did so by order of the President." Sherman still wanted Blair in the saddle with the 15th corps. So did Grant. And Lincoln called on Stanton to revoke the order relieving Blair.

Blair asked his brother Montgomery in the Cabinet to find out the wishes of the President. He would be guided by those wishes. Lincoln wrote to Montgomery Blair:

Some days ago I understood you to say that your brother, Gen. Frank Blair, desires to be guided by my wishes as to whether he will occupy his seat in congress or remain in the field. My wish, then, is compounded of what I believe will be best for the country, and best for him. And it is, that he will come here, put his military commission in my hands, take his seat, go into caucus with our friends, abide the nominations, help elect the nominees, and thus aid to organize a House of Representatives which will really support the government in the war. If the result shall be the election of himself as Speaker, let him serve in that position; if not, let him re-take his commission, and return to the Army. For the country this will heal a dangerous schism . . . He is rising in military skill and usefulness. His recent appointment to the command of a corps, by one so competent to judge as Gen. Sherman, proves this. In that line he can serve both the country and himself more profitably than he could as a member of congress on the floor. The foregoing is what I would say, if Frank Blair were my brother instead of yours.

Frank Blair was still in rain and sleet among Union fighters in Tennessee while Congress organized and elected Colfax Speaker of the House. On January 12, 1864, however, Frank Blair took his seat in Congress. Those who had hated the sight of him the last time they saw him now hated him all the more. Stanton's relieving him from command was considered personal animus. They were uneasy; Blair outclassed them in the point that he could sit a horse and keep a cool head while handling a corps of 30,000 troops in a style up to the requirements of the terrible Sherman.

Blair defended the President's Amnesty Proclamation as wise statesmanship. He challenged a provision for the lands, estates and properties of the South to be seized and partitioned among freed slaves and Union soldiers. Blair would recall Senator Benton's aphorism, "Our troubles come from the uneasy politicians and our safety from the tranquil masses."

With praise for the President, Blair mingled his plea for slaveholders loyal to the Union to be paid for their slaves made free. In this speech of February 5, 1864, Blair put himself on record with the few Lincoln men in Congress. In doing so he set himself up as an interpreter of the President's mind and took on the tone of a spokesman and a defender, so that those who heard or read his speech might believe that the Blair family and the President were in perfect accord. It was a habit and a method that both Montgomery and Frank Blair had. And Lincoln knew its political folly when he wrote to Montgomery that Frank was "in danger of being permanently separated from those with whom only he can ever have a real sympathy—the sincere op-

SPRING OF '64—BLOOD AND ANGER

ponents of slavery." Lincoln saw Blair tearing wider the split between radicals and moderates in Congress, and therefore was making arrangements with Grant and Sherman for Blair to take again his corps command.

Blair struck at Chase in a resolution calling for a committee of five from Congress to investigate acts of the Treasury Department, "to report whether any frauds have been practiced on the Government," whether any favoritism had been shown, and whether the enemy had been helped. The Chase men struck back.

Blair had bought brandy to the amount of 225 gallons and a scandalously large amount of whisky, claret, Catawba wine, besides 25 half-barrels of ale and 225 boxes of canned fruit, while he was at Vicksburg in June '63, according to photographic copies of an order signed by Major General Blair and eight staff officers. This order was published in newspapers and photographic copies of it were circulated among members of Congress. The permit of the customs collector at St. Louis invoiced the purchase at $8,651. The inference of the Chase men and the Missouri radicals seeking Blair's scalp was that Blair and his staff men on duty at Vicksburg could not possibly drink 225 gallons of brandy and a larger amount of other liquors during the war, and the goods had been ordered for speculation and profits. Blair had told the House that the liquor order was a forgery and B. R. Bonner, assistant special treasury agent in St. Louis, would substantiate the fact.

Blair took the floor and requested the House to appoint a committee of three to investigate. A coast-to-coast committee of William Higby of California, Brutus J. Clay of Kentucky and John V. S. L. Pruyn of New York was appointed and reported a month later, April 23, that it appeared satisfactorily in evidence before them that "one Michael Powers, representing himself to be an agent of the Treasury Department . . . had offered his services" to procure a moderate amount of liquor, tobacco and cigars for General Blair and his staff, to cost not more than $175. Since Blair and his officers had signed the order, it had been altered. An order for goods to cost less than $175 had been item by item changed to cost $8,651.

"I am . . . loth . . . to consume the time," began Blair in a speech that ran ten columns in the *Congressional Globe*. When the atrocious slander against him had first been published he was commanding the 15th army corps on its march from Memphis to Chattanooga to drive Bragg from Lookout Mountain and Missionary Ridge. Following publication of the slander, he had been superseded in command. Not satisfied with having thus humiliated him, the originators of the calumny had reiterated it on his return to the House. He spoke regrets at having employed the language ("liar, falsifier, scoundrel") which he did in the House, though making it clear he was still using that same language outside the House. He would not go extensively into the matter of the "forgery perpetrated by a person in the employ of the Treasury Department, uttered and put into circulation by a special agent of the Treasury Department, and printed in a newspaper pensioned by the Secretary of the Treasury." These guilty men he would not follow longer. "These dogs have been set on me by their master, and since I have whipped them back into their kennel I mean to hold their master responsible for this outrage and not the curs who have been set upon me." The liquor order had been made public by a Treasury agent who knew it was a forgery, after the goods it called for had been seized as contraband, after he, Blair, had been assailed in newspapers as a whisky speculator, and "because I had attacked Mr. Chase in a speech in St. Louis and assailed his trade regulations."

Everything true or false that Blair could think of that might possibly blacken or smear Chase was hurled out before a gaping, amazed Congress and press gallery. The same Chase who had opposed the President on the reinforcement of Fort Sumter and would have abandoned the war at the start now favored a war to annihilate the loyal state governments of the South. One letter from the head of a large financial institution in New York City mentioned rumors afloat there: the Secretary of the Treasury had "given to his son-in-law, Governor Sprague, a permit to buy cotton at the South, by which he will probably make . . . $2,000,000." When a congressional committee should make the inquiry that he, Blair, had called for, they would find plenty. "And Mr. Chase cannot escape . . . However deeply the committee may lay the whitewash on, it cannot conceal the dark background."

And though Mr. Chase had written a letter saying he had retired from the canvass for the presidential nomination, that letter was written because the "strictly private" Pomeroy Circular, being made public, had cut the ground from under him. "He wanted to get down under the ground and work there in the dark as he is now doing, running the Pomeroy machine on the public money as vigorously as ever."

When Blair had finished, he had only come short of openly saying he believed Chase to be a respectable masquerading scoundrel, a whited sepulcher, coward, liar, hypocrite, thief and snake in the grass. The leader of one factional clan in politics had been hit below the belt and had hit back—below the belt. It was a double foul, and not easy for Lincoln to referee.

The House two days later asked the President to tell them whether Blair was a Congressman or a general. The President three days later sent the House an explanation:

. . . when Gen. Grant was made Lieut. General, producing some change of commanders, Gen. Blair sought to be assigned to the command of a corps. This was made known to Generals Grant and Sherman and assented to by them, and the particular corps for him designated. This was all arranged and understood, as now remembered, so much as a month ago; but the formal withdrawal of Gen. Blair's resignation, and making the order assigning him to the command of the corps, were not consummated at the War Department until last week—perhaps on the 23rd. of April, Inst. As a summary of the whole it may be stated that Gen. Blair holds no military commission or appointment, other than as herein stated; and that it is believed he is now acting as a Major General upon the assumed validity of the commission herein stated . . .

The House next day by a vote of 84 to 28 requested the President to send over copies of all documents concerned in the matter. He did so, and Senate and House threshed over the question of whether the President had authority thus to hold resignations. Again the President was overstepping the Constitution and taking powers that belonged to Congress, said several earnest, worthy statesmen, besides several windy blatherskites. The matter finally was referred to a committee, where it lingered and was not brought up.

Late in the day of Blair's speech burning up Chase, Albert Gallatin Riddle, an Ohio friend of Chase, was shown into the railroad car on which Chase was soon starting for Baltimore. "He [Chase] was alone, and in a frightful rage, and controlled himself with difficulty while he explained the cause," noted Riddle. "The recital in a hoarse, constrained voice, seemed to rekindle his anger . . . Mr. Chase thought of remaining in the city, and at once tendering his resignation to the President."

Riddle called on the President with another Ohio Congressman, Rufus Paine Spalding. "The jealous and exacting abolitionists," said the standing Riddle to the seated Lincoln, "forgetting how impossible it is that you can be guilty of an attack upon your Secretary . . . believe that Blair must have had at least your countenance in this wretched business." The President rose from his chair, came around the table, took each man by the hand, then went to the table, took up some papers, and, standing, addressed the two Congressmen for half an hour.

Long before Frank's speech denouncing Chase, he had sent, on Frank's request, an order to the War Department to have him restored as a major general. He heard no more of it till about noon of the day of Frank's last speech, when Frank had called and said the all-important order had not been made. The President then sent a messenger to the Adjutant General, who replied that Mr. Blair was not known in the department as an officer, whereupon the President ordered his resignation as major general to be canceled, which was done. "Within three hours," said Lincoln, as Riddle noted it, "I heard that this speech had been made, when I knew *that another beehive was kicked over*. My first thought was to have cancelled the orders restoring him to the army. Perhaps this would have been best. On such reflection as I was able to give to the matter, however, I concluded to let them stand. If I was wrong in this, the injury to the service can be set right. And thus you see how far I am responsible for Frank Blair's assaults on Mr. Chase."

The visit of Riddle and Spalding with the President lasted two hours, and they were pleased to go away with their message for Chase and the abolitionists. As matters stood, Chase did not insist on the President's making the public disavowal which at first he had said must be conceded.

Meanwhile in this April of 1864, came news of an affair, the central figure of which was Confederate Major General Nathan Bedford Forrest, born for war. Fifteen horses had been killed under him. At Murfreesboro, Shiloh, Chickamauga, he was in the vortex. No other commanding officer North or South, it was believed, had sat his horse and personally sabered to death so many of the enemy. A log-cabin boy from middle Tennessee, Forrest had never seen West Point nor read a book on military tactics. In Memphis as a real-estate dealer and slave trader he had made a fortune, bought cotton plantations, and when the war started had an income of $30,000 a year. He had raised several regiments, sometimes outfitting them with horses, equipment and rations by raids on Union supply centers. His record for swift movement and fast fighting was compared to that of Stonewall Jackson. His answer to a woman who asked him the secret of his success was, "Ma'am, I got thar fust with the most men." One of his written orders read, "Tell Bell to move up and fetch all he's got." He took whisky only when wounded, spoke prayers in his tent every night, and before wading into the enemy, if there were time, he had a chaplain ask God's blessing on ranks of men with hats off. He had sent pistol balls into more than one runaway trooper of his command.

As a slave trader he had the faint enigmatic odor that traditionally excluded slave traders from exclusive social circles of the South. When it was urged that the war was for Southern independence and not slavery, Forrest replied, "If we aint fightin' fer slavery then I'd like to know what we are fightin' fer." With some 4,000 men Forrest moved up from Mississippi into Tennessee, struck at Sherman's supply connections, enlarged and strengthened his army.

At Fort Pillow, on the Mississippi 40 miles north of Memphis, Forrest with 6,000 troops drove the 600 defenders from outworks into the fort. While his white flags of truce were in the air he served notice that he would storm the fort. The Union commanders claimed that while thus negotiating under flags of truce Forrest moved his troops into better positions, violating the laws of civilized warfare. Forrest's regiments rushed the fort, took it, and put to death over half the garrison, Forrest claiming the fort flag had not been hauled down in token of surrender and in accord with civilized military law. Of the 262 Negro soldiers in the garrison nearly all were killed, wounded in escape, or buried alive.

The news shocked the North. Press, pulpit and politicians of antislavery trend cried the affair as a fiendish atrocity demanding retaliation. Ben Wade for the Senate and Daniel W. Gooch of Massachusetts for the House were appointed a committee to find the facts. They reported "at least 300 were murdered in cold blood after the post was in possession of the rebels and our men had thrown down their arms and ceased to offer resistance . . . Men, women, even children, were shot down, beaten, hacked with sabres; children not more than ten years old were forced to stand up and face their murderers while being shot; sick and wounded were butchered without mercy . . ."

Whether one side tricked the other under a flag of truce was left in doubt; perhaps neither side could have cleared up the point. But a historian would have to record that a certain moment arrived when Forrest's men were no longer fighting a battle in a war between civilized nations; they were sharing in a race riot, a mass lynching, and the event became an orgy of unleashed primitive human animals riding a storm of anger and vengeance. "Kill the God damned nigger!" ran the recurring line of the published testimony. "Kill all the niggers!" shouted one Confederate officer. General Forrest, riding among scattered wounded Negroes, called out that he knew some of them. "They've been in my nigger-yard in Memphis."

Perhaps half or more of Forrest's men were horrified at what was happening. What they saw was not war but mass murder out of race hatred. They tried to stop it. But it was a cyclone. According to a Negro private of the 6th U.S. Artillery one Confederate officer shouted to his men, "Boys, I will have you arrested if you don't stop killing them boys," another Confederate officer yelling the answer, "Damn it, let them go on; it isn't our law to take any negro prisoners; kill every one of them." Repeatedly the witnesses told of Southern officers ordering men not to shoot, or of Confederate men in the ranks pleading mercy for enemy Negroes and whites. But discipline was gone. What began as a battle ended as a race riot with wholesale murder.

A telegram of Forrest to Richmond reported driving the enemy into Fort Pillow and demanding surrender, "which was declined." Then: "I stormed the fort, and after a contest of thirty minutes captured the entire garrison, killing 500 and taking 100 prisoners . . . I sustained a loss of 20 killed and 60 wounded." Forrest at Paducah and at Columbus in weeks immediately preceding had indicated that if he must storm the works "no quarter" would be shown the Negro troops. His view was made clearer a few weeks later when he wrote to a Union general, "I regard captured negroes as I do other captured property, and not as captured soldiers."

Six days after the Fort Pillow massacre Lincoln spoke at a Sanitary Fair, reminded his Baltimore audience that in looking out on so many people assembled to serve the Union soldiers, the fact was that three years earlier the same soldiers could not so much as pass through Baltimore. "We all declare for liberty; but in using the same *word* we do not all mean the same *thing*. With some the word liberty may mean for each man to do as he pleases with himself, and the product of his labor; while with others the same word may mean for some men to do as they please with other men, and the product of other men's labor . . . The shepherd drives the wolf from the sheep's throat, for which the sheep thanks the shepherd as a *liberator*, while the wolf denounces him for the same act as the destroyer of liberty, especially as the sheep was a black one. Plainly the sheep and the wolf are not agreed upon a definition of the word liberty; and precisely the same difference prevails to-day among us human creatures, even in the North, and all professing to love liberty . . ."

On another subject he felt he ought to say a word: "A painful rumor, true, I fear, has reached us of the massacre, by the rebel forces, at Fort Pillow . . . of some three hundred colored soldiers and white officers . . . There seems to be some anxiety in the public mind whether the government is doing it's duty to the colored soldier, and to the service, at this point . . . We are having the Fort-Pillow affair thoroughly investigated; and such investigation will probably show conclusively how the truth is. If, after all that has been said, it shall turn out that there has been no massacre . . . it will be almost safe to say there has been none, and will be none elsewhere. If there has been the massacre of three hundred there, or even the tenth part of three hundred, it will be conclusively proved; and being so proved, the retribution shall as surely come. It will be matter of grave consideration in what exact course to apply the retribution; but in the supposed case, it must come."

In the storm of guns and blood and death soon to be let loose by Grant and Sherman against Lee and Johnston, in the reddening streams and the shouting and the crying with black silence after, and then the renewal of crimson explosions and the gray monotonous weariness—in this terrific grapple of guns and living wills and dying testaments the Fort Pillow affair was to sink to a lesser significance.

CHAPTER 45

Grant's Offensive, '64—Free Press— Lincoln Visits the Army

ACROSS the Rapidan River and into the Wilderness of Spotsylvania, Grant with some 120,000 men had vanished at midnight May 4. On a piece of ground ranging 10 to 12 miles across in any direction Grant was to meet Lee's army. Grant had two men to Lee's one. Lee, as Grant came on, could choose where he wanted to fight Grant. For Grant's men, crossing a river, seeking their opponent and going to him, it would be at times a groping in the dark.

Lincoln sat scanning flimsies in the telegraph room, and during Thursday, May 5, and past midnight of Friday, May 6, had no news of Grant. A locomotive ordered by Lincoln brought a cub reporter, Henry E. Wing, from 30 miles away for a two-o'clock-in-the-morning interview. As Wing told it to Lincoln, Grant had given orders for a daybreak offensive against the enemy and had said to him on leaving, "If you do see the President, see him alone and tell him that General Grant says there will be no turning back." Until four that Saturday morning the man and the youth talked, Lincoln squeezing from Wing every last point as to what he had seen and heard.

While Lincoln tried to sleep, Grant sat by a campfire, his hat slouched low, the collar of his blue overcoat hiding most of his face. He smoked a cigar, slowly chewed it, sat motionless except for an occasional shift of one leg over the other. Grant had lost 14,000 men, killed, wounded or missing, in 48 hours of fighting. Ambulances streaming north choked the roadways. Lee had lost more than he could spare as Grant hour on hour ordered up assaulting columns. After such desperate fighting it was customary to rest an army. Grant could decide to hold back—or go on.

As hours passed after midnight, slouched and grizzled, outwardly calm as bronze and steel but underneath shaken in turmoil, Grant did his thinking and made his decision. He would move on. His reasoning included his proposition, "Accident often decides the fate of battle." He could name the simple accidents that had operated against him and against Lee that day. He reasoned too that there would be an advantage in doing what the other fellow did not want him to do. He would move on, toward Richmond, by the left, toward Spotsylvania Court House. And Lee was at Spotsylvania, again in Grant's path. Till dawn of May 13 the combat went on at Spotsylvania. For ten days the Army of the Potomac had marched and fought continuously, losing 26,815 killed and wounded, 4,183 missing. The Confederates gave out no records of losses, though on the basis of prisoners taken by Grant, it was plain that Lee's army was being mercilessly slashed of irreplaceable manpower.

In the evening Lincoln spoke to serenaders of "our commanders . . . following up their victories resolutely and successfully," and "Gen. Grant has not been jostled in his purposes . . . he has made all his points, and to-day he is on his line as he purposed before he moved his armies . . . I commend you to keep yourselves in the same tranquil mood that is characteristic of that brave and loyal man."

During this week Carpenter in the White House studied every shade of expression in the exterior Lincoln. "Absorbed in his papers, he would become unconscious of my presence . . . In repose, it was the saddest face I ever knew. There were days when I could scarcely look into it without crying. The first week of the battles of the Wilderness he scarcely slept at all . . . One of these days, I met him, clad in a long morning wrapper, pacing back and forth a narrow passage leading to one of the windows, his hands behind him, great black rings under his eyes, his head bent forward upon his breast." Of this same day John W. Forney wrote that he heard Lincoln cry "My God! my God!" over 20,000 men killed and wounded in a few days' fighting.

Good news from the battle front had to be shared. Lincoln could not lie abed with it. "The President came in last night in his shirt & told us of the retirement of the enemy from his works at Spotsylvania & our pursuit," wrote Hay May 14. Considering the wear and tear of events, Hay estimated that Lincoln was holding his weight well.

Leslie's Weekly recorded a gentleman remarking to Lincoln that nothing could cheat him of election as President again except Grant's capture of Richmond when the Democrats would nominate Grant for President. "Well," said the President, "I feel very much like the man who said he didn't want to die particularly, but if he had got to die that was precisely the disease he would like to die of." Worrying friends suggested more than once that he should beware of General Grant. His usual reply, according to his secretaries: "If he takes Richmond, let him have it."

Now emerged Phil Sheridan. His cavalry swept round the flank of Lee's army, tore up ten miles of railway, released 400 Union prisoners, struck the reserve stores of Lee's supplies, destroyed 504,000 rations of bread and 904,000 of meat, and in combat six miles from Richmond killed the dauntless and priceless cavalry officer, J. E. B. Stuart, 31 years old, Lee's most irreplaceable general officer, "the eyes of the army."

Grant's pride and joy among major generals, the dauntless and priceless John Sedgwick, took a sharpshooter's bullet in his brain one May day as he smiled in jest to his soldiers his last words, "Don't duck; they couldn't hit an elephant at that distance." Once Lincoln had offered him command of the Army of the Potomac and in modesty Sedgwick declined it. He was afraid of nothing except immeasurable personal responsibility.

By the left again Grant moved, to Cold Harbor, almost in sight of the steeples of Richmond. There he ordered a frontal assault that in 22 minutes lost 3,000 men. The night of June 3 saw 7,000 Union soldiers dead or ready for hospitals, as against Confederate losses of 1,200 to 1,500. "I have always regretted that the last assault at Cold Harbor was ever made," wrote Grant later. It was 30 days since he had crossed the Rapidan and forced Lee into a succession of battles. Never before had the Army of Northern Virginia been pressed from point to point and day to day of fighting by an Army of the

Potomac that never rested or quit. A new mental and psychic factor was entering the war.

What was this new triple combination of Grant in Virginia, Sherman in Georgia and Lincoln at Washington? Would Lincoln, the recruiting agent and supply man at Washington, and Grant and Sherman with men and bayonets, carry on till they established the authority of the Federal Government at Washington over all the states of the old Union?

No longer could Lee go out in the open and send assaulting columns at the Army of the Potomac. The Richmond Government was near its last line of conscripts. Among Lee's men the question was: Will this battle never end? Why kill and kill only to see that army come further south? Among Grant's men the question was: Why should we over and again lose two and three to one fighting an entrenched enemy who forces us to come to him?

Suddenly Grant made a complete shift in his style of fighting. While Lee waited for direct combat and bloody frontal assaults, Grant moved—by night—in so shrouded a secrecy that only a few high officers knew where the army was going. Lee's skirmishers next day brought him word that the long trenches in front of Cold Harbor were empty. Grant was gone. A long march, and the wide James River crossed, brought Grant's army to the Petersburg defenses of Richmond. In four days of assaults 10,000 Union troops were now lost as against half that number of the enemy. On June 19 Grant sent word to Washington that he would order no more assaults. For a time he would rest his army. From the Wilderness through Cold Harbor he had lost 54,000 men, nearly as many as the entire force under Lee, but reinforcements had brought his army to about the same number he had when he crossed the Rapidan in early May.

While the bloody assaults at Petersburg were under way Grant had a telegram from Lincoln June 15, 1864: "Have just read your despatch of 1 P.M. yesterday. I begin to see it. You will succeed. God bless you all." This implied salutations on the grand strategy. For Grant was directing several armies. Sigel in the Shenandoah had failed him. Butler on the James River had dallied and lost big chances. But Sheridan had performed, while Sherman was steadily approaching Atlanta. Long toils were ahead. Could Sherman and Grant press through and join their armies? If so, the war would be over. "I begin to see it," Lincoln wired Grant.

Lincoln continued service as Grant's head recruiting officer. "War, at the best, is terrible, and this war of ours, in its magnitude and in its duration, is one of the most terrible," said the President at a Sanitary Fair in Philadelphia. "If I shall discover that General Grant . . . can be greatly facilitated in [his] work by a sudden pouring forward of men and assistance, will you give them to me? [Cries of "yes."] Then, I say, stand ready, for I am watching for the chance."

On May 18 at 4 A.M., the press deadline near, there had come to all New York newspapers a proclamation in which the President fixed May 26 as a day of fasting, humiliation and prayer for the nation, called for 400,000 men to be conscripted, and took on a tone of mourning as though the war was lost. Dated at the Executive Mansion, Washington, it opened: "In all seasons of exigency it becomes a nation carefully to scrutinize its line of conduct, humbly to approach the Throne of Grace, and meekly to implore forgive-

Union Generals

Upper left: William Tecumseh Sherman [Meserve]. *Upper right:* Ulysses Simpson Grant [Meserve]. *Lower, left to right:* George Gordon Meade [CS], Joseph Hooker [CS], Ambrose E. Burnside [Meserve], Henry W. Halleck [Meserve].

Upper: Lincoln photographed by Brady February 9, 1864, with his private secretaries, John Hay (left) and John G. Nicolay (right), who accompanied the President-elect to Washington and were White House residents [Meserve]. *Lower:* National Union party campaign *carte de visite* [CS] and the three humorists who were close friends of Lincoln, *left to right:* Robert H. Newell (Orpheus C. Kerr, or "Office Seeker"), David R. Locke (Petroleum Vesuvius Nasby), Charles Farrar Browne (Artemus Ward) [Meserve].

ness, wisdom, and guidance . . . With a heavy heart, but an undiminished confidence in our cause, I approach the performance of a duty . . . by my sense of weakness before [the] almighty . . ."

The *Herald*, *Tribune* and *Times* editors had received in their offices the same Associated Press manifold sheets as the *World* and the *Journal of Commerce*. The fishy tone of its opening: "Fellow-Citizens of the United States" made it suspect. The *Herald* printed it, but did not send out the one early edition containing it. The two newspapers foremost in violent opposition to the President, however, printed it as a news follow-up on their repeated items about the President's shattered physical health.

Stanton the next morning, according to Nicolay and Hay, wrote a dispatch, with Lincoln's signature, to Major General John A. Dix, commanding in New York: "Whereas there has been wickedly and traitorously printed and published this morning in the New York 'World' and New York 'Journal of Commerce' . . . a false and spurious proclamation . . . purporting to be signed by the President . . . you are therefore hereby commanded forthwith to arrest and imprison . . . the editors, proprietors, and publishers of the aforesaid newspapers." To Governor Yates at Springfield, Illinois, Lincoln wired: "If any such proclamation has appeared, it is a forgery." Seward issued a statement: "The paper is an absolute forgery." Dix arrested the editors of the *World* and the *Journal of Commerce*, under later orders let them go, but for two days would not let them print and sell their papers.

Dix telegraphed Stanton he was sending to Fort Lafayette one Joseph Howard, found to be the author of the forged proclamation. "He is a newspaper man . . . has been very frank in his confession, says it was a stock-jobbing operation." The President directed that, while the editors had no right to plead ignorance or want of criminal intent, he was not disposed "to visit them with vindictive punishment" and authorized Dix to restore to them their establishments. The editor of the *World*, Manton Marble, signed columns of editorials terming the Chief Magistrate tyrant, usurper and despot who had destroyed "freedom of the press." Marble invited and defied the President to again close down the *World*, which didn't happen.

Stanton had rushed the decision to suppress the two papers without asking the President about it, according to Nicolay and Hay. The case was similar to the arrest of Vallandigham and the suppression of the Chicago *Times;* in both the President indicated afterward that he would have preferred another course of action.

Joe Howard meditated in a cell at Fort Lafayette on the easy money he had expected from the rise of gold resulting from his hoax, on the brokers in cahoots with him who had also lost out, on his former days as secretary to the Reverend Henry Ward Beecher, on newspapers over the country saying: "Howard . . . wrote the hoax story in relation to Mr. Lincoln's escape 'in a Scotch cap and long military cloak.'" After a few weeks in jail, Howard was released by order of the President, on request of Henry Ward Beecher.

Governor Seymour called on District Attorney A. Oakey Hall of New York City to punish those who in the suppression of newspapers had offended the law. General John A. Dix and four other army officers were arrested, though not jailed, the proceedings polite and legal. In the finish, Seymour was baffled by Lincoln's order to Major General Dix that until further orders he must stay in command in New York and, in effect, use the U.S. Army and Navy before he let the likes of Seymour and the New York *World* put him in jail.

Elsewhere over the land mobs of Union men had gone far in the suppression of newspapers. In the three preceding months the *Constitution and Union* at Fairfield, Iowa, was destroyed, as was the *Northumberland Democrat* and the Sunbury *Democrat* in Pennsylvania; the Youngstown *Mahoning Sentinel*, the Dayton *Empire*, the Greenville *Democrat*, the Lancaster *Eagle* and the Wauseon *Democrat* in Ohio; the Laporte *Democrat* in Indiana; the Chester *Picket Guard* and the *Gallatin County Democrat* in Illinois; the Belleville *Volksblatt* and the Louisiana *Union* in Missouri. In these cases the mobs demolished office and plant so they could not get out a paper. In Columbus, Ohio, the editor of the *Crisis* was seized and imprisoned; the editor of the *Mahoning Sentinel* narrowly escaped death. Editors at several points were "seized" and sometimes roughly handled. The two-day suppression of two New York newspapers was in accord with a mass trend of the first half of '64.

On the morning of the bogus proclamation the price of gold made fast upswings and the New York Stock Exchange was feverish. To gold speculators who took it as genuine the proclamation meant that Grant was losing and gold would go higher. The antics and greed of these gamblers had recently been attacked by Congress in a bill empowering the Secretary of the Treasury to sell surplus gold. Carpenter heard Governor Curtin remark to Lincoln one day, "I see by the quotations that Chase's movement has already knocked gold down several per cent." Lincoln's face knotted. "Curtin, what do you think of those fellows in Wall Street, who are gambling in gold at such a time as this?" "They are a set of sharks." "For my part," bringing a clenched fist down on a table, "I wish every one of them had his *devilish* head shot off."

In his own mind the President believed the war would last a longer time than he dared to tell the public, according to Noah Brooks. He wrote that on June 14 the President was impatient with the people who expected Grant would take Richmond before the autumn leaves began to fall.

Down the Potomac and around to the James River Lincoln and Tad rode on a white river steamer and June 21 Lincoln stepped from upper deck to gangway, wrung the hand of his General in Chief, spoke appreciation. Lincoln chatted at Grant's headquarters and rode to the Butler and Meade commands. Astride a horse he wore a tall black silk hat, black trousers and frock coat. Wrote Horace Porter, "By the time he had reached the troops he was completely covered with dust, and the black color of his clothes had changed to Confederate gray . . . his trousers gradually worked up above his ankles, and gave him the appearance of a country farmer riding into town wearing his Sunday clothes. However, the troops were so lost in admiration of the man that the humorous aspect did not seem to strike them. The soldiers rapidly passed the word along the line that 'Uncle Abe' had joined them, and cheers broke forth from all the commands, and enthusiastic shouts and even words of familiar greeting met him on all sides."

After a while Grant suggested they should ride on and see the colored troops. Lincoln said, "Oh, yes. I want to take a look at those boys. I read with the greatest delight the account in Mr. Dana's despatch of how gallantly they behaved. He said they took six out of the sixteen guns captured that day. I was opposed on nearly every side when I first favored the raising of colored regiments; but they have proved their efficiency, and I am glad they have kept pace with the white troops in the recent assaults . . ."

At the 18th corps camp Lincoln met a torrent of black men who circled roundabout him. Tears ran down some faces. Cheers, laughter, songs, mixed and rang in the air. "God bress Massa Linkum!" "De Lawd save Fader Abraham!" They waved their hands, brandished their arms, kissed the hands of their mystic hero, crowded around fondling his horse, bridle and saddle. "The President," noted Porter, "rode with bared head; the tears had started to his eyes and his voice was broken."

Lincoln next morning cruised upriver, amid the gunboats, met Admiral Lee and General Butler, saw breastworks and parapets and heard army men explain them. Some particularly strong positions recently seized and fortified were pointed out and brought Lincoln's remark to Butler, "When Grant once gets possession of a place, he holds on to it as if he had inherited it." He sailed back to Washington with new-made friends in the army, not the least of them the General in Chief. Their bonds drawing closer would need yet to be stronger.

The Chicago *Times* quoted a Missouri Frémonter as saying Lincoln's head was "too light for the weight of his foot," and the war was conducted in the manner of the man found climbing trees to catch woodpeckers. On being told he could never catch woodpeckers that way, he hollered back, "Well, if I don't catch any I'll worry them like hell."

Unionist newspapers dwelt on Libby Prison in Richmond limiting letters to six lines and one prisoner writing: "My dear Wife—Yours received—no hope of exchange—send corn starch—want socks—no money—rheumatism in left shoulder—pickles very good—send sausages—God bless you—kiss the baby —Hail Columbia! Your devoted Husband."

In an album that held autographs of all the Presidents of the United States Lincoln wrote his signature. The actress Fanny Kemble donated it to the New York Sanitary Fair.

Over the land stood houses where the war losses came close home. "My oldest boy, not yet twenty," wrote the poet Longfellow to a friend, "in the last battle on the Rapidan shot through both shoulders with a rifle-ball, is now at home. He comes down into my study every day, and is propped up in a great chair. How brave these boys are! Not a single murmur or complaint, though he has a wound through him a foot long. He pretends it does not hurt him."

Homeward went a musician from the Virginia fighting When he had arrived in hospital, according to the New York *Tribune*, the surgeon said he must be lashed down while a leg was amputated. "No," said the soldier. "Never! Is there a violin in camp?" They brought one. He put it under his chin, tuned it, laughed. "Now, doctor, begin." And he went on playing the violin "without missing a note or moving a muscle" during 40 minutes while they sawed his leg off.

The Buffalo *Express* hung up a slogan: "God—Grant—Victory."

CHAPTER 46

The Lincoln-Johnson Ticket of the National Union Party

JUSTICE DAVID DAVIS and Thurlow Weed as between two practical party managers wanted more action from Lincoln toward clinching the nomination for President. To General Orme, Davis confided in a letter: "Mr. Lincoln seems disposed to let the thing run itself and if the people elect him he will be thankful, but won't use means to secure the thing. Mr. Lincoln annoys me more than I can express, by his persistence in letting things take their course—without effort or organization."

Swett wrote to Orme, "Lincoln out of 150 delegates elected previous to May 25, figures them all up for him." The National Union convention was ten days away. And so far no delegates had been picked for anyone but Lincoln.

John Charles Frémont and followers in Cleveland, Ohio, May 31, 1864, organized a party. They met eight days before the National Union convention at Baltimore in order to notify that convention it must not nominate Lincoln. Their platform: the constitutional prohibition of slavery, free speech and a free press, a one-term Presidency, reconstruction of states to be left entirely with Congress. They nominated for President Major General John C. Frémont and for Vice-President Brigadier General John Cochrane. They named their new party Radical Democracy. Frémont accepted the nomination and announced he had resigned as major general in the U.S. Army. He approved of the platform, except the plank calling for seizure of conquered slave soil and its division among soldiers and sailors of the United States. Mildly he spoke. "Had Mr. Lincoln remained faithful to the principles he was elected to defend, no schism could have been created and no contest would have been possible," declared the man who had been the Republican party candidate for President in 1856.

The morning after the convention, according to Nicolay and Hay, a friend gave Lincoln an account of it, and said that instead of the many thousands expected there were present at no time more than 400. The President reached for the Bible on his desk, searched a moment, then read: "And everyone that was in distress, and everyone that was in debt, and everyone that was discontented, gathered themselves unto him; and he became a captain over them; and there were with him about four hundred men."

On June 4, three days before the Baltimore convention, a mass meeting of 20,000 people in Union Square heard ex-Mayor George Opdyke, Senator Pomeroy, Magnus Gross, Hiram Walbridge, James T. Brady, General T. F. Meagher and other orators pay tribute to General Grant. The announced and express purpose of the meeting was "to honor General Grant." The inference was that Grant should be nominated at Baltimore instead of Lincoln. Grant's name in the air as the man of the hour, the doer of straight-away deeds, might suddenly be plucked for service by the emotional delegates of the Baltimore convention.

As the convention date drew near it was plain to many a radical politician that it would be easier sledding in their home territory if they were for Lincoln. Senator Jim Lane of Kansas, who had once led in taking a committee of Missouri-Kansas radicals to the White House for protest of the President's policy, was now on the band wagon, bringing to Baltimore a set of delegates he said were "all vindictive friends of the President."

Of the many who interviewed the President, his secretaries noted: "They were all welcomed with genial and cordial courtesy, but received not the slightest intimation of what would be agreeable to him. The most powerful politicians from New York and Pennsylvania were listened to with no more confidential consideration than the shy and awkward representatives of the rebellious States, who had elected themselves in sutlers' tents and in the shadow of department headquarters."

Hay wrote June 5 that delegations genuine, bogus and irregular saw the President. C. Bullitt "with Louisiana in his trousers' pocket," somewhat stampeded by political rumors in New York, was feeling "uneasy in his seat." "Florida was sending two delegations," Hay noted. "Neither will get in. Each attacks the other as unprincipled tricksters." Then came an odd paragraph: "The South Carolina delegation came in yesterday. The Pres^t says, 'Let them in.' 'They are a swindle,' I said. 'They won't swindle me,' quoth the Tycoon. They filed in: a few sutlers, cotton-dealers, and negroes, presented a petition & retired."

June 7 the Baltimore convention of the National Union party met. The name National Union was adopted as a gesture of respect or even reverence for Democrats fighting in the Union armies and those who had continuously supported the Lincoln administration. June 7 Grant was still burying his dead four days after the bloody repulse at Cold Harbor. June 7 the gold speculators in New York were crazy and wild-eyed over the betting that gold, now higher than ever, would go higher yet. June 7 and potatoes were quoted at $160 a bushel in Richmond, cabbage at $10 a head.

The executive committee chairman, Senator Morgan, called the convention to order at noon in sweltering weather. Morgan then turned the convention over to the Reverend Dr. Robert J. Breckinridge of Kentucky, chosen by the national committee for temporary chairman, though it became a Breckinridge family tradition that Lincoln had asked the national committee to choose Breckinridge. The white-haired, bearded and grizzled preacher took the platform amid cheers for the "Old War Horse of Kentucky." Delegates knew they were gazing on an old man who had a nephew and two sons serving as officers in the Confederate Army.

A whirlwind of applause shook rafters and beams at a sentence from Breckinridge: "Does any man doubt . . . that Abraham Lincoln shall be the
nominee?" But other solemn duties lay ahead. They would have to tell the
country why they were fighting the war. They would have to beware of
party politics and sink all for the Union. "As a Union party, I will follow
you to the ends of the earth, and to the gates of death. (Applause.) But as an
Abolition party—as a Republican party—as a Whig party—as a Democratic
party—as an American party, I will not follow you one foot." As to slavery
the venerable Kentuckian was crystalline. "I join myself with those who say,
away with it forever; and I fervently pray God that the day may come when
throughout the whole land every man may be as free as you are, and as
capable of enjoying regulated liberty."

After a prayer, Thad Stevens took the floor and objected to the admission of delegates from states "in secession." He had no doubt "excellent men
. . . from such States" were present, but protested against any "recognition
of the right of States which now belong to the Southern Confederacy to be
represented here."

Then arose Horace Maynard of Tennessee, tall and spare, his long black
hair, high brow and strong straight nose having brought him the nickname
of the "Narragansett Indian." Maynard's high-pitched voice measured out
sentences, punctuated by gestures with a forearm and a quivering index
finger; he carried to every seat in the theater. His eyes grew wet with tears
and many in the audience sobbed aloud as he pictured the conditions of his
people and faltered at voicing their desolation. "For you that drink in the
cool breezes of the Northern air, it is easy to rally to the flag . . . But we
represent those who have stood in the very furnace of the rebellion, those
who have met treason eye to eye, and face to face, and fought from the
beginning for the support of the flag and the honor of our country. (Great
applause.)" Outnumbered and often outlawed, they had seen their sons conscripted in the Confederate Army, their property confiscated, homes burned,
brutal guerrilla raids, imprisonment and execution of leaders, and all the woe
of a land where contending armies sweep back and forth. A storm of applause swept the main floor and galleries when Maynard finished.

At the evening session the permanent chairman of the convention, ex-
Governor William Dennison of Ohio, alluded to the forthcoming unanimous
nomination for the Presidency, of "the wise and good man whose unselfish
devotion to the country, in the administration of the Government has secured to him not only the admiration, but the warmest affection of every
friend of constitutional liberty. (Applause.)"

Next morning the convention voted 440 to 4 in favor of seating the Missouri radicals who had obstructed and harassed Lincoln and by a series of
roll calls sifted what it wanted. Only the delegates from South Carolina were
thrown out entirely. The Virginia and Florida delegations were admitted to
seats with no right to vote. Arkansas and Louisiana were given seats and the
right to vote. By 310 to 151 the convention gave Tennessee delegates seats
with the right to vote.

The report of the platform committee, offered by its chairman, Henry J.
Raymond, resolved in favor of the war, the Union, the Constitution; pledged
itself to everything possible to quell the then raging rebellion; no compro-

mise with rebels; a deathblow at the gigantic evil of slavery through a con-stitutional prohibition of it; thanks and everlasting gratitude to the soldiers and sailors of the Union cause and promise of "ample and permanent provi-sion for those of their survivors who have received disabling and honorable wounds in the service of the country"; approval and applause of "the practical wisdom, the . . . unswerving fidelity to the Constitution . . . with which Abraham Lincoln has discharged, under circumstances of unparalleled diffi-culty, the great duties and responsibilities of the Presidential office"; justice and protection to all men employed in the Union armies "without regard to distinction of color"; liberal and just encouragement of foreign immigration to "this nation, the asylum of the oppressed of all nations"; speedy construc-tion of the railroad to the Pacific Coast; inviolate redemption of the public debt, economy and responsibility in public expenditures, vigorous and just taxation.

The radical mood was seen in a pledge of the first plank for "bringing to the punishment due to their crimes the Rebels and traitors arrayed against" the Government. The tone indicated criminal trials and hanging of Con-federate leaders if and when the North won the war. This part of the plat-form Lincoln would have revised or deleted.

Nominations were in order. Cameron had sent to the clerk's desk a written resolution with a demand that it be read. The convention heard a call for the unanimous renomination of Abraham Lincoln of Illinois and Hannibal Ham-lin of Maine.

"A frightful clamor shook the hall," wrote Brooks. "Almost every delegate was on his feet objecting or hurrahing . . . For a few minutes pandemonium reigned, and in the midst of it Cameron stood with his arms folded, grimly smiling, regarding with composure the storm that he had raised. After the turmoil had spent itself . . . Raymond of New York, in an incisive, clear-cut speech, advocated nomination by a call of States . . ." Raymond's reso-lution passed.

The roll call began. Maine announced 16 votes for Lincoln. New Hamp-shire, coming next, tried a little speechmaking but was choked off with cries of "No speeches!" From then on each state announced its vote without oratory. One by one the undivided delegations threw in their ballots for Lincoln. Only one snag broke the smooth and orderly unanimity. The Mis-souri delegation announced it was under positive instructions to cast its 22 votes for Ulysses S. Grant. "This caused a sensation," wrote Brooks, "and growls of disapproval arose from all parts of the convention." Before the result of the balloting was announced Hume of Missouri moved that the nomination of Lincoln be declared unanimous. This under the rules could not be done until the secretary read the results: 484 votes for Lincoln, 22 for Grant. Missouri then changed its vote, and the secretary gave the grand total of 506 for Lincoln.

A storm of cheers was let loose, lasting many minutes, dying down and then flaring up again. "Men hurrahed, embraced one another," noted Brooks, "threw up their hats, danced in the aisles or on the platform, jumped on the benches, waved flags, yelled, and committed every possible extravagance . . . One of the most comical sights I beheld was that of Horace Maynard and Henry J. Raymond alternately hugging each other and shaking hands."

The hilarity over, they settled down to nominations for Vice-President. Cameron presented, under instructions of his state, he said, the name of Hannibal Hamlin. A New York delegate "in behalf of a portion" of his delegation proposed Daniel S. Dickinson of New York. Indiana, under instructions of its state convention, offered Governor Andrew Johnson of Tennessee. Horace Maynard seconded, saying Johnson "in the furnace of treason" would stand by the convention's declarations "as long as his reason remains unimpaired, and as long as breath is given him by his God."

On roll call Maine was solid for Hamlin. The number of votes Johnson had picked up in other New England States was surprising. Connecticut plopped solid its 12 for Johnson. Massachusetts split with 17 for Dickinson, 3 for Hamlin, 2 for Butler. The chairman was solemn, the convention too, as the New York tally was read: Johnson 32, Dickinson 28, Hamlin 6. Delegates pondered. Louisiana split evenly between Dickinson and Johnson. Arkansas threw its 10 votes to Johnson and Tennessee its 15. The Missouri radicals gladly pinned a rose on Ben Butler with 20 votes, though 2 put in for Johnson. The final total was shocking and almost unbelievable to the Hamlin men: Johnson 200, Dickinson 108, Hamlin 150.

Kentucky now announced that its complimentary vote of 21 for its General Rousseau and 1 for Tod would be thrown to Johnson. Oregon and Kansas followed for Johnson. A wave of applause came with Cameron handing Pennsylvania's 52 to Johnson. As New Jersey swung into line Senator Morrill of Maine, Hamlin's manager, who the night before had been publicly and privately confident of Hamlin's chances, changed the vote of Maine in favor of the Tennessee tailor. The convention secretary announced: Johnson 494, Dickinson 17, Hamlin 9.

A. K. McClure's judgment ran with Lamon's that "Lincoln was guided in what he did, or what he did not, in planning the great campaign of his life that involved the destiny of the country itself, by the single purpose of making success as nearly certain as possible." McClure saw "not a trace of prejudice or even unfriendliness toward Hamlin" in all that Lincoln said in their second interview.

Two reasons Lincoln gave McClure for Johnson's candidacy. First, he was the ablest of all War Democrats and in a position to draw that element toward the Government; Johnson was then dramatically before the people in his work of restoring his state to the Union. The second reason was with Lincoln stronger and more imperative, according to McClure. "Lincoln was firmly convinced that by no other method could the Union sentiment abroad be so greatly inspired and strengthened as by the nomination and election of a representative Southern man to the Vice-Presidency from one of the rebellious States in the very heart of the Confederacy."

Nicolay was to say that McClure misstated the facts, that Lincoln had kept his hand out of the nomination of Johnson, that McClure imputed double-dealing to an honest Chief Magistrate. McClure was to reply that he did not at all accuse Lincoln of deceit or insincerity. "It was quite as much a necessity for Lincoln to conceal his movements for the nomination of Johnson as it was, in his judgment, a necessity for him to nominate a Southern man and a War Democrat. He simply acted with rare sagacity and discretion in his movements, and with fidelity to the country."

The ancient factor of effective oratory had swayed the convention toward Johnson, several observers noted. The most memorable voices were those of the Border State men, Breckinridge, Brownlow and Maynard. In two speeches Maynard with fierce and moving phrases named Johnson as someone to think about. There was design wrought from some quarter in the staging of these scarred orators for their early roles at the convention.

"Of Andrew Johnson it is enough to say that there is no man in the country, unless it be Mr. Lincoln himself, whom the rebels more cordially hate," said *Harper's Weekly* in June. "He fought them in the Senate, when they counted upon his aid, and he has fought them steadily ever since." Greeley in the *Tribune* saw as "happy" the nomination of Johnson, who had "never wavered or faltered" in the Union cause, a man who would be hanged at noon on the day the Confederates captured him. From various points now was voiced one thought or instinct that had lain behind the framing of the Lincoln-Johnson ticket: it would nationalize the Republican party; no longer would Lincoln stand as the head of a sectional party.

The plan so odious and stenchladen to the radicals, known as "Lincoln's ten-per-cent plan," had only to be announced for Johnson to leap to embrace it. In a speech six months earlier Johnson had said: "Abraham Lincoln is a honest man and is going to put down this infernal rebellion. He is for a free government and I stand by him . . ."

Of medium height, a little swarthy of skin, with fine shoulders and a deep chest, Johnson carried a massive head. His deep-set and darkly piercing eyes looked at men without fear. Weapons and threats had no effect on him. If an idea or an impulse of depth moved him, he acted on it and stood by it. Physically he trusted the revolver in his right hip pocket and spiritually he had an ego that rested on a bulwark he called his conscience. He wore clean linen, was almost dainty about his collar and his shirt front, had small hands and feet; but the blandishments of the social set couldn't sway him.

From his beginnings in politics Johnson had voiced the poor whites as against the exclusive and propertied aristocracy which for 30 years had ruled the South and unduly controlled at Washington. Sometimes he was brave unto stubborn folly. He could wear his hate of the aristocrats and his passion for democracy till it was a pose and an overdone attitude. He could be so overly zealous to stand square and clear on a human issue that important half-lights of it were lost to him. Perhaps only such a man could have been the first to so manage a seceded state that it could give some color of promise to "Lincoln's ten-per-cent plan."

Many messages of congratulation rolled in to Lincoln on his renomination but none from Johnson. Many telegrams and letters came to Johnson but none from Lincoln. Each said publicly that the ticket was a good one. But neither sent word to the other that it was pleasant they were running mates.

Horace White, from a wire in the convention hall had sent Lincoln the first message of congratulation on renomination. This with the news from Nicolay arrived at the War Department telegraph office. When Major Eckert congratulated him, his face lighted elusively. "What! Am I renominated?" Operator Tinker showed him Nicolay's telegram. "Send it right over to the Madam. She will be more interested than I am."

To a committee the next day notifying him of his nomination, the President answered: "I will neither conceal my gratification, nor restrain the expression of my gratitude . . ." The same day he said to a National Union League delegation: "I have not permitted myself, gentlemen, to conclude that I am the best man in the country; but I am reminded, in this connection, of a story of an old Dutch farmer, who remarked to a companion once that 'it was not best to swap horses when crossing streams.' "

The convention platform and the President's public addresses had projected above all other immediate issues the need of a Constitutional amendment to prohibit slavery. But one week after the convention adjourned, when the House of Representatives took up a joint resolution to that effect, 64 members voted Nay, and it failed for lack of a two-thirds majority. The Nay votes were all Democratic and forecast a campaign issue.

In Middletown, Connecticut, a clergyman lighted his front door with a transparency quoting from Genesis 22:15: "The angel of the Lord called unto Abraham out of heaven a second time." The Troy *Times* was naïve and sweet. "If Mr. Lincoln has fallen into errors and made mistakes—if he has done some things that he ought not to have done, and left undone some things that he ought to have done, who that was ever called upon to do so much has erred so little?"

Hannibal Hamlin in Bangor, Maine, three days after the convention spoke of the President as "a man of eminent abilities," as one who would "lead the nation out of its present difficulty and plant it on the eternal principle of liberty," as one "whom the people loved."

The New York *World* on June 9 spoke for August Belmont and many wealthy and respectable Democrats. "In a crisis of the most appalling magnitude, requiring statesmanship of the highest order, the country is asked to consider the claims of two ignorant, boorish, third-rate backwoods lawyers, for the highest stations in the government."

"I, A. Lincoln, hereby nominate myself as a candidate for reëlection," said the Chicago *Times* June 11. Various anti-Lincoln journals reprinted a long editorial from the Richmond *Dispatch,* not entirely courteous: "We say of Old Abe it would be impossible to find such another ass in the United States, and therefore, we say let him stay."

A one-column letter of Wendell Phillips in the *Independent* was reprinted in the New York *Tribune,* the New York *World* and across the country. "The Baltimore Convention was largely a mob of speculators and contractors willing to leave to their friend, Mr. Lincoln, his usurped power of reconstruction." Its "meaningless and hypocritical platform" was "a mixture of claptrap compliments and brave demands forced by the Cleveland movement . . . As long as you keep the present turtle at the head of the Government you make a pit with one hand and fill it with the other." Of the gyrations of Phillips *Harper's* remarked: "Mr. Phillips has no right whatever to call them hypocrites . . . his vast vituperation and bitter assaults . . . are things which make many an admiring friend sad and sorry for him, and will they not one day make him profoundly sorry for himself?"

Party lines were shaken. Two men, one a Republican and the other a Democrat, were heading a National Union ticket. The great American game of politics was in chaos. In Maine and California, in Ohio and Connecticut, the state governors were War Democrats. In the patronage portioned out by the President, the War Democrats got more than a fair share, said organization Republicans.

The supreme American botanist, president of the American Academy of Arts and Sciences, Asa Gray, saw Lincoln at this time as having deep roots in good loam. To his English friend Charles Darwin, Gray wrote, "Homely, honest, ungainly Lincoln is the representative man of the country."

Twice in the week of the Baltimore convention William Lloyd Garrison had interviews with Lincoln. At one interview Theodore Tilton of the *Independent* accompanied Garrison, and it seemed that both hardened abolitionists would swing in for the Lincoln and Johnson ticket. Garrison and Tilton had taken a walk around Baltimore and tried to find the old jail that once held abolitionist Garrison many years back for voicing subversive doctrines. They said they couldn't find the jail and Lincoln laughed. "Well, Mr. Garrison, when you first went to Baltimore you couldn't get *out;* but the second time you couldn't get *in!*"

From a photograph by Gardner of Lincoln seated, with Nicolay and Hay standing, *Harper's Weekly* made a drawing which it presented to its readers the week after the Baltimore convention. "In this earnest care-worn face," it commented, "saddened by a solemn sense of the great responsibility which in God's providence has devolved upon him, we see the man who said to his neighbors, as he left his home three years ago, that he was called to a graver task than any chief magistrate since Washington. Through an infinite perplexity of events the faith of the President has never faltered . . . Look thoughtfully at this rugged face. In its candor, its sagacity, its calmness, its steadiness and strength, there is especially conspicuous the distinctive American. Turn then to the portrait of General Grant . . . and there you see another purely American face, the same homely honesty, capacity and tenacity. Children of the people both of them . . . these two men illustrate at once the character of American civilization. There is but one prayer in the great multitude of American hearts today, God bless President Lincoln and General Grant!"

In a thin mist of evening air with willows nearby trembling to a low breeze, amid a cool dew flung out by old oaks above them, Lincoln on the Soldiers' Home grounds stood with others silent over a thoughtful twilight. By and by, as a California woman remembered it and soon wrote home to San Francisco, Lincoln said softly:

> " 'How sleep the brave, who sink to rest
> By all their country's wishes blest—' "

She was too "easily melted," wrote the California woman. "It made us cry." And she heard him further in the purpling shadows:

> " 'And women o'er the graves shall weep,
> Where nameless heroes calmly sleep.' "

CHAPTER 47

Washington on the Defensive—Peace Babblings

THE NIGHT of June 14, 1864, a man in his room in Hiron's House, Windsor, Canada, stands before a mirror and in an amateur way arranges himself a disguise. On his unshaven upper lip he smooths a large false mustache, over the close-trimmed beard of his chin and jaws a long flowing set of whiskers. He blackens his reddish eyebrows. Under trousers and vest he buttons a bed pillow.

Nobody bothers him as he rides the ferry to Detroit. A customs officer punches him lightly in the stomach and lets it go at that. A policeman in Detroit is suspicious, takes him to a street gaslight, looks him over and lets him go. On a train out of Detroit a passenger bends down to whisper, "I know your voice but you are safe from me." Snuggled in the berth of a sleeping car he rides safely overnight to Hamilton, Ohio.

This is the return of the Honorable Clement L. Vallandigham from alien land to native soil. He spoke to a convention that day: "I return of my own act . . . I was abducted from my home and forced into banishment. The assertion or insinuation of the President, that I was arrested because laboring with some effect to prevent the raising of troops . . . is absolutely false . . ."

Noah Brooks in Lincoln's office referred to Vallandigham in Ohio. The President, with a quizzical look: "What! has Vallandigham got back?" Brooks had to say everybody knew it, and heard from the President: "Dear me! I supposed he was in a foreign land. Anyhow, I hope I do not know that he is in the United States; and I shall not, unless he says or does something to draw attention to him."

June 27, 1864, Chase sent the President the nomination of Maunsell B. Field for Assistant Treasurer at New York. Lincoln next day wrote Chase: "I cannot, without much embarrassment, make this appointment, principally because of Senator Morgan's very firm opposition to it," and naming three men Morgan had mentioned to Chase. "It will really oblige me if you will make choice among these three . . ."

Chase wrote asking an interview and the President the same day replied reciting inexorable political considerations, and, "When I received your note this forenoon suggesting a verbal conversation . . . I hesitated, because the difficulty does not, in the main part, lie within the range of a conversation between you and me. As the proverb goes, no man knows so well where the shoe pinches as he who wears it . . ."

The tone of this was a little new to Chase. Once more he resigned. This made four times. And now Lincoln wrote to Chase that his resignation was accepted. "Of all I have said in commendation of your ability and fidelity, I have nothing to unsay; and yet you and I have reached a point of mutual embarrassment in our official relations which it seems cannot be overcome, or longer sustained, consistently with the public service." In his diary Chase wrote: "So my official life closes. I have laid broad foundations . . . I am too earnest, too anti-slavery, and, say, too radical, to make the President willing to have me connected with the Administration, just as my opinion is that he is not earnest enough, not anti-slavery enough, not radical enough."

The summer had brought stench of scandal. The New York *World* and other hostile newspapers day on day aired the matter of women from the Printing Bureau of the Treasury Department dressing in men's attire and attending at the Canterbury Inn in Washington lewd performances to which men only were supposed to have admission. Two newspaper columns of affidavits recited details giving the impression that the Treasury Department offices held a fast and loose set of public servants. This to one as spotless as Chase in relation to women was not to be laughed off. The New York *Tribune* presented Chase's view that the affair was a conspiracy and dirty politics.

Hay read mixed motives. The resignation came when gold reached a new high point, when despair over government finance was deepest. The political motive, however, outweighed all others, the yearnings of Chase in his remark to the editor of the Indianapolis *Independent*, "After all, I believe that I would rather that the people should wonder why I wasn't President than why I was."

Lincoln named former Governor David Tod of Ohio, an old Douglas Democrat, to replace Chase. The Senate Finance Committee called in a body on Lincoln to protest that Tod hadn't the ability. A telegram from Tod to the President said his health would not permit him to head the Treasury. So Tod was out of the way.

Early next morning the President wrote out a nomination for William Pitt Fessenden, Senator from Maine, to fill the vacancy. The Senate took about one minute to confirm the nomination unanimously.

As chairman of the Senate Finance Committee Fessenden knew the money market was feverish, public confidence wavering; yet his friends were saying a financial crash would follow his refusal. He wrote: "Foreseeing nothing but entire prostration of my physical powers, and feeling that to take the Treasury in its exhausted condition would probably result in destroying what little reputation I had, it was still my duty to hazard both life and reputation if by so doing I could avert a crisis so imminent. I consented, therefore, to make the sacrifice."

Telegrams and letters of approval beyond precedent had poured in on Fessenden. The New York and Boston clearinghouses, bankers and merchants in all quarters, it seemed, urged his acceptance of the President's nomination when it was reported he would refuse. At the first report that Fessenden was to be Secretary of the Treasury, Government bonds advanced, pork declined $10 a barrel, and all provisions went to lower prices.

Fessenden was sworn in. The press held forth in compliments such as never before, except in the case of Grant, over a major Lincoln appointment. Hay quoted the President: "It is very singular, considering that this appointment of F.'s is so popular when made, that no one ever mentioned his name to me for that place . . ."

Fessenden had attacked the administration on the $300 clause of the draft law. He would credit the Government with the best intentions and would sustain it thoroughly, but he was opposed to "the system of high bounties which made people forget that their first duty was to the country."

Three of Fessenden's four sons had gone into the Army. Sam had been killed in battle at Centerville in '62; the others had won advancement by valor and ability to brigadier general and colonel. In '64 Frank was on the Red River in Arkansas, Jim with one leg gone was on Hooker's staff with Sherman trying to take Atlanta.

Starting as a young lawyer in Portland, Maine, Fessenden had become a Whig Congressman, later a Senator, helped found the Republican party, watched the tariff, fisheries and shipping interests of his state, clashed with Welles over Maine's share of favors and patronage, and was now to undergo the trials of an executive. The national debt was $1,700,000,000, the Treasury almost empty, the war costing $2,000,000 a day.

For several weeks it would seem Fessenden held off from making arrangements with Cooke, saying in effect that newspapers and politicians had made out too strong a case against Cooke's garnering a large comfortable fortune for himself in the selling of Government bonds. Out of interviews with Fessenden and Lincoln it followed that Jay Cooke & Company were once more harnessed into Government service.

Seventeen days before Chase resigned Congress had passed the Gold Bill and the President signed it. To buy or sell gold for delivery later than the day of signing the contract was made a crime. To contract to buy or sell gold not in the hands of the seller when selling was made a crime. The purpose was to stop speculation and gambling in gold. In the past six months gold had steadily climbed from 150 to 250. The Gold Bill made the course of gold crazier than before. It cavorted and somersaulted so fast in such a price range that it was the gambler's perfect delight. And actual gold was sent into deeper hiding and became scarcer for its functions of paying interest on Government bonds and foreign exchange.

After the 17 days of gold-price acrobatics Congress repealed the Gold Bill and the President signed the repeal. From then on the gold gamblers were accepted by the Government as an evil beyond control. Nothing came of a Union League meeting in June '64 urging that "Congress at once order the erection of scaffolds for hanging" the gold speculators.

In the deep gloom months of July and August '64, the barometric indicator, gold, was to say that Lincoln and the Union Government were failing. Thirty-nine dollars of gold would buy $100 of greenbacks. This was the bottom gold price of the Union Government's paper promises to pay. One interpretation was that the holders of gold in those months had less hope than ever of the Union Government winning its war.

On July 4 of this gloomy summer Congress adjourned. Among the bills piled on the President's desk for signature was one that would slash the slender supports on which the "Lincoln ten-per-cent plan" rested. Since December '63, when the President had launched his plan, much had happened to it. Then Hay wrote in his diary that all factions in Congress seemed to agree, and on the reading of the President's message, "Men acted as if the millennium had come. Chandler was delighted, Sumner was beaming." Border State men said they were satisfied.

Then slowly had come deepening suspicions of the President's motives, more open claims that the states in secession had committed suicide and that the President was impossible in his plan for a loyal 10 per cent to be authorized to reorganize the governments of those states. Henry Winter Davis led this opposition in the House, and Ben Wade in the Senate. Davis was tall, slender, with wavy hair and a curly mustache, a musical voice, mental caliber, oratorical and theatrical style. Born in a Maryland slaveholding family, he had come to hate slavery as fiercely as any New Englander. In politics first a Whig, then an American or Know-Nothing, he became a Republican. That Monty Blair of Maryland should be named Postmaster General was a stench in his nostrils. He led in Maryland a faction that hated Blair.

Davis brought in a bill intended to block the restoration efforts already started by the President in Louisiana and Tennessee; the measure aimed to stop the spread of the President's policy in other Southern States. In the House Davis was the one radical most often reminded by Thaddeus Stevens that he was going too far and ought to take what he could get now. The one speaker who could draw in more members from the cloakrooms than any other was Davis. He spoke his guess and vision for the Negro with cadence: "The folly of our ancestors and the wisdom of the Almighty, in its inscrutable purpose, having allowed them to come here and planted them here, they have a right to remain here to the latest syllable of recorded time."

The quixotic political artist, Davis, with his ally Ben Wade, saw a wide chasm between them and the President. They nursed suspicions into what they believed were facts. The President was too slow, too hesitant, too loose with expedient, they believed, and Congress would be more firm. New state governments could be referred "to no authority except the judgment and will of the majority of Congress," said Davis in behalf of his bill of February 15, 1864. Under the bill the President with Senate consent would appoint for each state in rebellion a provisional governor to serve until Congress recognized a regular civil government as existing therein, the loyal people of the state entitled to elect delegates to re-establish a state government. "Until therefore," said Davis, "Congress recognize a State government, organized under its auspices, there is no government in the rebel States except the authority of Congress." Davis rejected the President's Amnesty Proclamation and its "ten-per-cent plan" as lacking guarantees.

The debate ran long, a festival of constitutional lawyers. How and when does a state become a state, and under what conditions can it lose its face as a state and again later have its face put back? This question was argued up, down and across. The unconstitutional and despotic acts of the President would be legalized and perpetuated by the proposed bill, declared Representative Charles Denison of Pennsylvania. Perry of New Jersey was positive the Machiavellian hand of the President was behind the bill. Nor was Thaddeus Stevens satisfied with the Davis bill. "It does not, in my judgment, meet the evil." Its acknowledgment that the "rebel States have rights under the

Constitution" he would deny. His chief objection was that the bill removed the opportunity of confiscating the property of the disloyal.

By 73 to 59 the Davis bill passed the House May 4, 1864. In the Senate its course had been guided by Wade, who said: "The Executive ought not to be permitted to handle this great question to his own liking." That a state should have self-government originated by one-tenth of the population seemed to Wade absurd, anti-republican, anomalous and entirely subversive.

In what the President had thus far done he was "equally a usurper with Caesar, Cromwell and Bonaparte," said Garrett Davis of Kentucky. In exploiting the Peace Democrat viewpoint Garrett Davis spread over the pages of the *Congressional Globe* a diatribe of several thousand words on Lincoln's ambition, desire for re-election, love of power and money. "He is no statesman, but a mere political charlatan. He has inordinate vanity and conceit. He is a consummate dissembler, and an adroit and sagacious demagogue." The tentative and hazardous state governments set up by the President in Louisiana, Tennessee and Arkansas were denounced by Garrett Davis as "lawless and daring political enterprises" intended to garner electoral votes in the coming November.

The main bill of Wade, which had been on the Senators' desks for five months, passed July 2, 1864, by 26 Yeas to 3 Nays, with no less than 20 Senators absent. The bill went into conference. Wade moved that the Senate agree to the House [Davis] bill. The Senate agreed by 18 Yeas and 14 Nays, no less than 17 Senators being absent.

In the months the bill had been before Congress, "The President declined to exercise any influence on the debate," said his secretaries, meaning that no Senators or Representatives were privately called in by the President to hear a request that they should do the best they could against it.

Into this confusion and perplexity four days after Congress adjourned the President stepped with an amazing document. He issued a proclamation reciting that Congress had passed a bill to guarantee republican form of government to certain states, and "the said bill was presented to the President of the United States for his approval less than one hour before the *sine die* adjournment of said session, and was not signed by him." Never before had an Executive assumed to reject those provisions in a legislative measure he disliked and to adopt those acceptable to him. And he went straight to the people proclaiming what he did. He had neither signed the bill nor vetoed it. "He put it in his pocket." Madison and others had used this pocket veto. He was "fully satisfied" with part of the bill but as to other parts he was "unprepared." The key of the matter was in his saying he could not be "inflexibly committed to any single plan of restoration." Over the heads of Congress and its embittered and warring factions, he put his case to the country and the people.

Ben Wade and Henry Winter Davis raged privately and stormed publicly. In the New York *Tribune* of August 5 they published their joint answer to Lincoln, picked up and reprinted over the country, "The Wade-Davis Manifesto." The language was fierce and polite at once. They hoped to blast the pinions from under the President and blister his name and give him a lesson. Addressing themselves "To the Supporters of the Government," they said they had "read without surprise, but not without indignation" the President's proclamation of July 8. They would maintain it was a right and a duty "to check the encroachments of the Executive on the authority of Congress, and to require it to confine itself to its proper sphere." The President did not sign the bill in question. "The bill did not therefore become a law; and it is therefore nothing. The proclamation is neither an approval nor a veto of the bill; it is therefore a document unknown to the laws and Constitution of the United States . . . The committee sent to ascertain if the President had any further communication for the House of Representatives reported that he had none; and the friends of the bill, who had anxiously waited on him to ascertain its fate, had already been informed that the President had resolved not to sign it. The time of presentation, therefore, had nothing to do with his failure to approve it.

"The President persists in recognizing those shadows of governments in Arkansas and Louisiana, which Congress formally declared should not be recognized—whose representatives and senators were repelled by formal votes of both Houses of Congress . . . They are the mere creatures of his will." The President held "the electoral votes of the rebel states at the dictation of his personal ambition." He had "greatly presumed" and they would give warning. "He must understand . . . that the whole body of the Union men of Congress will not submit to be impeached by him of rash and unconstitutional legislation; and if he wishes our support he must confine himself to his executive duties—to obey and to execute, not make the law."

On hearing the rasp and snarl of this family quarrel in the Republican party the opposition rejoiced. One who was hot under the collar came to Lincoln about it. And according to Carpenter, the President philosophized: "It is not worth fretting about; it reminds me of an old acquaintance, who, having a son of a scientific turn, bought him a microscope. The boy went around experimenting with his glass on everything that came in his way. One day, at the dinner-table, his father took up a piece of cheese. 'Don't eat that, father,' said the boy; 'it is full of *wrigglers*.' 'My son,' replied the old gentleman, taking, at the same time, a huge bite, 'let 'em *wriggle*; I can stand it if they can.' "

Welles wrote: "The President, in a conversation with Blair and myself on the Wade and Davis protest, remarked that he had not, and probably should not read it." And Welles strayed into dejection over the President's having advised only with Seward on his pocket-veto proclamation, having called no Cabinet meeting on it.

The main landscape of the country was too somber for people to care that Wade and Davis had lost their heads or that Davis by his false stride was to fail of nomination and lose his seat in Congress to a Unionist colonel who had come near death from wounds in the Wilderness. One viewpoint was given by *Harper's Weekly*. "We have read with pain the manifesto of Messrs. Wade and Winter Davis, not because of its envenomed hostility to the President, but because of its ill-tempered spirit, which proves conclusively the unfitness of either of the gentlemen for grave counselors in a time of national peril . . . It was the President's constitutional right to let the bill drop and say nothing more about it."

In the three days immediately preceding his proclamation concerning the Wade-Davis bill the President issued, with detailed reasons, a proclamation suspending the writ of habeas corpus in Kentucky, and another proclamation, by direction of Congress, appointing the first Thursday of August as a day of national humiliation and prayer.

Once more General Robert E. Lee played a bold defensive game and struck fear into the heart of the Union cause. He gave Jubal A. Early and John C. Breckinridge an army of 20,000 men. Sheltered by the Blue Ridge Mountains, they marched up the Shenandoah Valley, slipped through a pass, headed for Washington.

Early's men collected $20,000 cash at Hagerstown, tore up 24 miles of Baltimore & Ohio Railroad tracks, wrecked and burned mills, workshops, factories, at Baltimore burned the home of Governor Bradford, reached Silver Spring and in sight of the Capitol dome seized private papers, valuables, whisky, in the home of Postmaster General Blair, and then set the house afire. "Baltimore is in great peril," telegraphed a mayor's committee to Lincoln, asking for troops. Lincoln wired: "I have not a single soldier but whom is being disposed by the Military for the best protection of all. By latest accounts the enemy is moving on Washington. They can not fly to either place. Let us be vigilant but keep cool. I hope neither Baltimore or Washington will be sacked."

Lew Wallace, department commander at Baltimore, had marched troops out to Monocacy, fought a battle and, heavily outnumbered, was routed. His defeat delayed Early's army one day. That one day, it was generally admitted, saved Washington from the shame of capture. Gustavus Vasa Fox, without the President's knowing it, had a steamer ready for him in case the city was taken. In the Gold Room in New York June 11 the wild-eyed gamblers saw gold go to its peak price of 285.

Raw troops and soldiers just out of hospital made up the 20,000 men scraped together for manning the forts around Washington against Early, who had cut all wires north and July 11 marched his men on the Seventh Street Road that would lead him straight to the offices, arsenals, gold and silver, of the U.S. Government. Early halted his men just a little over two miles from Soldiers' Home, where Lincoln the night before had gone to bed when a squad from the War Department arrived with word from Stanton that he must get back to the city in a hurry. The President dressed and rode to the Executive Mansion.

Next day Lincoln saw through a spyglass transport steamers at Alexandria coming to unload two magnificent divisions of veteran troops fresh from Grant at City Point. The President met them at the wharf, touched his hat to them; they cheered and he waved his hand and smiled and they sent up more and more cheers. No mail, no telegrams, arrived from the outer world that day of July 12 in Washington.

From where Lincoln stood on a Fort Stevens rampart that afternoon he could see the swaying skirmish lines and later the marching brigade of General Daniel D. Bidwell, a police justice from Buffalo, New York, who had enlisted in '61 as a private, advanced in rank, and with his men had heard the bullets sing from Antietam through Gettysburg and the Wilderness. Out across parched fields, dust and a haze of summer heat marched Bidwell's men in perfect order, to drive the enemy from a house and orchard near the Silver Spring Road. Up a rise of ground in the face of a withering fire they moved, took their point and pushed the enemy pickets back for a mile—the cost 280 men killed and wounded.

While Lincoln stood watching this bloody drama a bullet whizzed five feet from him and struck Surgeon Crawford of the 102d Pennsylvania in the ankle. Within three feet of the President an officer fell with a death wound. Those who were there said he was cool and thoughtful, seemed unconscious of danger, and looked like a Commander in Chief. "Amid the whizzing bullets," wrote Nicolay and Hay, the President held to his place "with . . . grave and passive countenance," till finally "General Wright peremptorily represented to him the needless risk he was running." Official records gave the Union losses at 380 killed and 319 wounded.

Next morning Early's army was gone. Again on July 14 Washington had mail and telegrams. Somewhere toward the Shenandoah Valley marched Early's army with its plunder-laden wagons, audacity on its banners, money in its strongboxes, shoes on feet that had started north barefoot. Early got away for the same reason, it was said, that he arrived. "Nobody stopped him."

And why? The answer would require a diagram of the overlapping authorities and departments; of many physical and psychic factors, of slackness, fears, jealousies, rivalries. Nicolay and Hay recorded: "Everybody was eager for the pursuit [of Early] to begin; but Grant was too far away to give the necessary orders; the President, true to the position he had taken when Grant was made general-in-chief, would not interfere, though he observed with anguish the undisturbed retreat of Early." Halleck assumed that he was in fact, as he ranked, a chief of staff and not a commander from whom strategy was required. "Put Halleck in command of 20,000 men," said Ben Wade, "and he would not scare three sitting geese from their nests." "Today," wrote Bates in his diary, "I spoke my mind very plainly, to the Prest. (in presence of Seward, Welles and Usher) about the ignorant imbecility of the late military operations, and my contempt for Genl. Halleck."

On July 25 Grant sent a dynamic constructive proposal to Lincoln on "the necessity of having the four departments of the Susquehanna, the Middle, West Virginia, and Washington, under one head." He had made this proposal before and the War Department had rejected it. Now he was urging it again. And again he was naming General William B. Franklin, one of the abler major generals of distinguished field service, "as a suitable person to command the whole." Two days later the Secretary of War notified not General Franklin, but Halleck, that "the President directs me to instruct you that all the military operations" of the four departments and all the forces in those departments, "are placed under your general command."

It seemed that Grant wanted Franklin, or some other proven field general, at the head of the defense of Washington, while Stanton wanted the desk strategist, Halleck, elevated from staff chief to commander. And as between Stanton and Grant the President was saying Yes to Stanton and No to Grant. On the face of the matter Lincoln was going back on Grant and taking a stand with the established political bureaucrats who muddled instead of performing. Stanton's order accommodating Grant by joining four departments into one, and then giving Grant the last man Grant would have picked to head the new four-in-one department, was dated July 27.

And on that day Grant took to drink. Had Rawlins been there, Rawlins would have cursed him and put up arguments and returned to cursing and Grant would have stayed sober. As it was, Rawlins on July 28 got back from Washington to write his wife: "I find the General in my absence digressed from his true path. The God of Heaven only knows how long I am to serve my country as the guardian of the habits of him whom it has honored."

Whether the death of Major General James B. McPherson could have had anything to do with Grant's drinking on July 27, Rawlins did not write his wife. Five days before, McPherson, bronzed, tall, tireless, in boots and gauntlets on a beautiful black horse, had ridden away from a talk with Sherman to examine the cause of a new roaring note in the firing on the left of their army near Atlanta. McPherson was only 35, with a future of hope ahead of him and a sweetheart dated to marry him when Atlanta should be taken. And McPherson's black horse had come racing back with saddle empty. Later they found him with a bullet near his heart—a soldier so rare that Grant had him in mind to take Sherman's place if anything happened to Sherman, a friend and comrade so rare that Sherman at the news paced back and forth in a headquarters room barking orders, barking his grief, tears running down his cheeks into the red beard. Grant too at the news had wet eyes, and his voice broke in saying, "The country has lost one of its best soldiers, and I have lost my best friend."

What was the balancing circumstance that made Lincoln say Yes when Stanton brought him the suggestion that Halleck and not Franklin must head the new four-in-one department? Could Stanton have boldly said to Lincoln that he must have this point or he would resign? Would that have been past Stanton? And could Lincoln at this hour have taken on himself the burden of finding a new Secretary of War to replace Stanton? If so, who would make a better one than Stanton? In telegrams they exchanged July 28 and 29 it was evident that Grant and Lincoln each understood delicate and involved matters of administration and personnel they could neither write nor telegraph. Both men were working at a furious pace in the fevered air of decisive events. On July 19 Grant had telegraphed the President a suggestion to call for another draft of 300,000 men and Lincoln had replied: "I suppose you had not seen the call for 500,000 made the day before, and which I suppose covers the case. Always glad to have your suggestions."

In grief over losing his library and many valuable papers when Early's men ransacked, looted and burned his Silver Spring house, Monty Blair said nothing better could be expected while "poltroons and cowards" manned the War Department. Ready tongues carried this to Halleck. At once Halleck had to write about it to Stanton. "I desire to know whether such wholesale denouncement and accusation by a member of the Cabinet receives the sanction and support of the President of the United States." Stanton chose to pass the letter without comment to the President, who remarked, "Men will speak their minds freely in this country," and wrote to the Secretary of War:

". . . Gen. Halleck's letter . . . in substance demands of me that if I approve the remarks, I shall strike the names of those officers from the rolls; and that if I do not approve them, the Post-Master-General shall be dismissed from the Cabinet. Whether the remarks were really made I do not know; nor do I suppose such knowledge is necessary to a correct response.

If they were made, I do *not* approve them; and yet, under the circumstances, I would not dismiss a member of the Cabinet therefor. I do not consider what may have been hastily said in a moment of vexation at so severe a loss, is sufficient ground for so grave a step. Besides this, *truth* is generally the best vindication against slander. I propose continuing to be myself the judge as to when a member of the Cabinet shall be dismissed." Thus Lincoln was peremptory, decisive, perfectly understanding and sweetly courteous, in a single letter.

In the cross play of hates, guesses were made as to whether some of the Federal Government servants hated each other any less than they hated the enemy. A peculiar mental attitude or a hoodoo spell pervaded much of Washington. Lincoln and Grant were aware of it. Grant on August 1 acted to evade it; he notified Halleck that he was sending Sheridan to "expel the enemy from the border." Sheridan's record and status, his complete aloofness from the desk strategists of Washington, were such that there was nothing they could do about it. Lincoln approved the action and August 3 sent Grant a telegram momentous in its confession of a spirit that held powerful sway: "I have seen your despatch in which you say 'I want Sheridan put in command of all the troops in the field, with instructions to put himself South of the enemy, and follow him to the death. Wherever the enemy goes, let our troops go also.' This, I think, is exactly right, as to how our forces should move. But please look over the despatches you may have receved from here, even since you made that order, and discover, if you can, that there is any idea in the head of anyone here, of 'putting our army *South* of the enemy' or of following him to the *death*' in any direction. I repeat to you it will neither be done nor attempted unless you watch it every day, and hour, and force it."

Grant journeyed from south of Richmond to Monocacy north of Washington, August 6, 1864, for personal communication with Sheridan; his telegrams through the War Department were too often translated into something else. Or as he put it later: "I knew it was impossible for me to get orders through Washington to Sheridan to make a move, because they would be stopped there and such orders as Halleck's caution (and that of the Secretary of War) would suggest would be given instead, and would, no doubt, be contradictory to mine." The four times' use of "would" had to be read more than once—and then there was no mistaking what Grant meant to say.

Weeks were to pass with Sheridan on trial, with Sherman on trial, one in the Shenandoah, the other in Georgia, two commanders not yet proved as Grant had been proved, both of them held by Grant as unbeatable. And the delays and failure of immediate victory were blamed, by those in black moods for blaming that summer, chiefly on the President, who upheld all three and never let up in his efforts to meet their requirements.

Later in a political matter Sherman refused to correct a policy of Grant when so requested, saying, "Grant stood by me when I was crazy, and I stood by him when he was drunk, and now we stand by each other."

Halleck had written to Sherman that the President wished to give him appointment as a major general in the Regular Army. "I wish you to say to the President," wrote Sherman, "that I would prefer he should not nominate me or anyone." He had all the rank he needed.

With the Armies of the Cumberland, Tennessee and Ohio joined into a force of 99,000, Sherman began his campaign from Chattanooga aimed at the capture of Atlanta. Between him and Atlanta was a Confederate army of 41,000, soon reinforced to 62,000, commanded by the master strategist General Joseph E. Johnston. Carrying scars of wounds from Florida Indian wars, from Cerro Gordo and Chapultepec in the Mexican War, from Seven Pines in the Peninsular campaign near Richmond, now 57 years old, a West Pointer, a Virginian who had never owned slaves, a clean sportsman of a fighter, a silent, cautious Fabian—little Joe Johnston, familiar with the red hills of Georgia, seemed the one marshal in gray best able to stop or delay Sherman. He led Sherman on. He fought and faded and waited. At Dalton, past Buzzard's Roost, through Snake Creek Gap, back to Resaca and Cassville, across the Etowah, through Allatoona Pass, and after clashes at New Hope Church, not until Kenesaw Mountain did Johnston in his slowly maneuvered retreat lure Sherman into a frontal attack.

Sherman piled in his men on the fortified lines of Johnston hoping to break through and win victory and Atlanta. Sherman lost 3,000 as against the Confederate's 800. "One or two more such assaults would use up this army," said Old Pap Thomas. Not least of Johnston's hopes was the one that he could hold off any Sherman victory until the November elections in the North. He would like to make Sherman's efforts look useless in order to persuade Northern citizens that the Lincoln administration was useless.

Davis and Bragg at Richmond wanted more decisive action. Davis on July 17 replaced Johnston with General John B. Hood, who, they knew, would not wait and fade and hope. In 11 days Hood fought and lost three battles at a cost of 10,841 men to Sherman's 9,719. Sherman had at last reached the Atlanta area. But would he take Atlanta? The North hoped. And the North despaired. Why did it take so long? Why had the whole war gone on so long? From Lincoln the last week of July Sherman had a long telegram which closed: "My profoundest thanks to you and your whole Army for the present campaign so far."

Many were tired of the war, its cost, its betrayals and corruptions. Peace movements gained headway from this feeling in the North and the South. Fernando Wood in seeking to have Congress empower the President to appoint commissioners to discuss peace terms with Southern representatives was playing with this sentiment. To Davis in Richmond and to others Governor Zebulon B. Vance of North Carolina wrote of "discontent" in his state. "I have concluded it will be impossible to remove it except by some effort at negotiation with the enemy." Davis gave Vance three instances wherein he had made "distinct efforts" to communicate with Lincoln, never once connecting, and to send peace proposals was "to invite insult and contumely, and to subject ourselves to indignity without the slightest chance of being listened to."

The New York *World* and its country newspaper following would not let their readers forget that Lincoln's inaugural address carried the portentous words: "Suppose you go to war, you cannot fight always; and when, after much loss on both sides, and no gain on either, you cease fighting, the identical old questions, as to terms of intercourse, are again upon you."

Horace Greeley in July '64 received a letter from a fellow signing himself "William Cornell Jewett of Colorado." Jewett wrote many letters—to Lincoln, to Jeff Davis, to the New York *Herald*. Jewett needed listeners. Now he picked on Greeley, writing, "I am authorized to state to you, for your use only, not the public, that two ambassadors of Davis & Co. are now in Canada, with full and complete powers for a peace." If the President would accord protection for these "ambassadors" they would meet in Niagara Falls whomsoever Lincoln might choose to send for a private interview.

The quavering Greeley again wrote to Lincoln one of his long letters, both pleading and cudgeling. Lincoln discounted Jewett's story but within two days wrote to Greeley: "If you can find, any person anywhere professing to have any proposition of Jefferson Davis in writing, for peace, embracing the restoration of the Union and abandonment of slavery, what ever else it embraces, say to him he may come to me with you, and that if he really brings such proposition, he shall, at the least, have safe conduct, with the paper (and without publicity, if he choose) to the point where you shall have met him. The same, if there be two or more persons."

On July 13 Greeley again wrote Lincoln; now he had confidential information that the two Confederate ambassadors waiting and ready to cross over from Canada and talk peace terms at Niagara Falls were the Honorable Clement C. Clay of Alabama and the Honorable Jacob Thompson of Mississippi, each an ex-U.S. Senator from his state. Lincoln telegraphed two days later: "I was not expecting you to *send* me a letter, but to *bring* me a man, or men. Mr. Hay goes to you with my answer."

In New York Hay handed Greeley Lincoln's letter which stated his disappointment over Greeley's not having produced the commissioners and "if they would consent to come, on being shown my letter to you of the 9th. Inst. . . . bring them. I not only intend a sincere effort for peace, but I intend that you shall be a personal witness that it is made." Greeley didn't like the letter, noted Hay, said he was the worst man the President could have picked for such a mission. Lincoln, it was evident to Hay, was pressing the matter. Whatever reality or illusion might be hovering on the Canadian border, he was going to smoke it out.

At the town of Niagara Falls Greeley met Jewett and sent by him a letter to Clay, Thompson and a University of Virginia professor, James P. Holcombe, saying he was informed they were accredited from Richmond as bearing propositions looking toward peace, that they desired to visit Washington in their mission, George N. Sanders accompanying them, and "if my information be thus far substantially correct, I am authorized by the President of the United States to tender you his safe conduct on the journey proposed." Greeley heard in reply that Jacob Thompson was not one of them, that none of them had authority to act for the Richmond Government, but they were acquainted with the views of their Government and could easily get credentials, or other agents could be accredited in their place, if they could be sent to Richmond armed with "the circumstances disclosed in this correspondence."

Greeley telegraphed Lincoln the substance of this letter. Lincoln consulted with Seward and gave Hay a paper in his own handwriting to take to Niagara. There on July 20 Hay saw Greeley nettled and perplexed at reading:

> Executive Mansion,
> Washington, July 18, 1864.
>
> To Whom it may concern:
> Any proposition which embraces the restoration of peace, the integrity of the whole Union, and the abandonment of slavery, and which comes by and with an authority that can control the armies now at war against the United States will be received and considered by the Executive government of the United States, and will be met by liberal terms on other substantial and collateral points; and the bearer, or bearers thereof shall have safe-conduct both ways.
>
> ABRAHAM LINCOLN

Greeley proposed bringing Jewett into conference. Hay declined. Greeley then refused to cross the suspension bridge into Canada unless Hay would go with him and deliver the Lincoln paper into Confederate hands. The two then crossed the bridge, met Holcombe in a hotel room in Clifton, Canada, and handed him the President's letter. Greeley took a train for New York, but before doing so had an interview with Jewett, unknown to Hay. Hay stayed on a day and then wrote Holcombe asking when he might be favored with a reply to the communication addressed "To Whom it may concern." "Mr. Holcombe greatly regrets," was the reply, "if his [Hay's] return to Washington has been delayed by any expectation of an answer." Jewett then wrote the Confederate emissaries that Greeley was gone and he regretted "the sad termination of the initiatory steps taken for peace," placing the blame on "the change made by the President in his instructions"; they could communicate with Greeley through him, Jewett.

The Confederates replied with compliments and a long letter to Greeley, holding the President responsible for the collapse of peace hopes. Without notifying Hay, Jewett gave this letter to the press, letting Hay know afterward that this was a mild form of revenge. The letter made interesting reading for a gloom-struck nation. Those who saw the President as "indecisive" had a new item to contemplate. Others saw the President as more astute, if not wiser, than they had expected.

There was drama bordering on farce in the Confederate diplomats, at the end of the suspension bridge connecting the United States and Canada, accusing Lincoln of high crimes. They assumed people would believe the President's duty was to invite unauthorized Confederate agents to Washington to receive peace terms to carry to Richmond. They had hoped to use Bennett of the New York *Herald* for their game, Sanders remarking to Hay once, "I wanted old Bennett to come up, but he was afraid to come." They had used Jewett to lure Greeley, Jewett having followed his first letter to Greeley with a telegram: "Will you come here? Parties have full power." Greeley had believed the parties had full power; Lincoln hadn't and by a little memorandum addressed to nobody or anybody had thwarted them. Greeley's course in the end brought ridicule on him; Lincoln at a climactic point turned the incident into a dramatic presentation of his Government's viewpoint as to peace proposals.

Another peace mission was undertaken by Colonel James Frazier Jaquess, a Methodist clergyman from Illinois commissioned to raise and lead the 73d Illinois Volunteers, and James R. Gilmore, a newspaperman. Without Government authority from Lincoln, it was permitted by him under pressure. Under flags of truce the two men arrived in Richmond, and in an evening interview with Jefferson Davis, they had from him the declaration: "I worked night and day for twelve years to prevent it [war], but I could not. The North was mad and blind, would not let us govern ourselves, and so the war came; now it must go on until the last man of this generation falls in his tracks and his children seize his musket and fight our battles, *unless you acknowledge our right to self-government*. We are not fighting for slavery. We are fighting for independence, and that, or extermination, we *will* have."

Gilmore published the interview in the *Atlantic Monthly*, and the article, widely reprinted, went to millions of readers. At Niagara, through Greeley, Lincoln had given the world his peace terms; at Richmond, Davis had made himself clear.

Intricate in vast detail, droll, fantastic, comic in various phases, the Greeley and Jaquess-Gilmore peace missions had been affairs of risk. Any slight circumstance could have put Lincoln in a false light. Only a certain procedure of guns, men, blood and iron, could bring peace, it seemed. "Peace," said *Leslie's Weekly* August 6, 1864, "must come through the powerful negotiations of Gens. Grant and Sherman."

CHAPTER 48

"The Darkest Month of the War"— August '64

SPEAKING in February '64, Senator Henry S. Lane of Indiana said the operation of the $300 clause in the conscription act had not been in favor of the poor man. "The poor man had to go at all events; he could not raise the $300; but it has operated, perhaps, beneficially upon the middle classes, and has exempted the rich entirely, for they could all pay the $300 exemption." What did it matter that $12,000,000 had been paid into the Government Treasury for draft exemptions? The measure was not intended to raise revenue. "We need men more than money. If we could print soldiers as fast as we print greenbacks, there would be something in this argument; but it cannot be done."

Congress had kept to itself certain strict powers. The President could be a dictator in enforcement of the draft law, but he was limited to *advising* Congress what the draft law should say. And so, June 8, 1864, Executive Document No. 97 went to Congress with the signature of Abraham Lincoln: "I have the honor to submit, for the consideration of Congress, a letter and

inclosure from the Secretary of War, with my concurrence in the recommendation therein made." The letter enclosed, signed by Stanton and addressed "To the President," recommended "a repeal of the clause in the enrollment act commonly known as the $300 clause."

Attached to Stanton's recommendation was a report signed by Provost
Marshal General Fry on the operation of the enrollment act as amended by
Congress February 24, 1864. "I invite your attention," noted Fry, "to the
small proportion of soldiers being obtained under the existing law. I see no
reason to believe that the Army can be materially strengthened by draft so
long as the $300 clause is in force."

Congressman Schenck brought before the House a bill to repeal previous
draft laws. It declared "hereafter no payment of money shall be accepted or
received by the Government to release any enrolled or drafted man from
obligation to perform military duty." One exception was made. Any man
could send a substitute for himself if it be his father, brother or son. Schenck
mentioned the President as seeing "the necessity for having men and not
money only to carry on this war against the rebels, and finding the present
existing enrolling act does not produce men by a draft, because of . . . circumstances, such as commutation and substitution, and other things which
intervene to prevent the procuring of men." Schenck raised a class issue in
his argument, saying the committee proposed such limits in conscription that
"no man, whether a man of means or not, whether rich or poor, shall in any
case get rid of furnishing a substitute unless he be one of his own blood."

Representative John W. Chandler of New York said that though the bill
masked itself as "a poor man's friend" it was nevertheless drawn from "the
horrid example of the European system. The President is given unlimited
control over the lives of every family in the land."

James G. Blaine of Maine moved to strike out the first section of the bill,
saying it was made to appear "that the *people* need to be goaded and driven";
that a "*compulsory* draft" would require troops to shoot down rioters and
demonstrators; that the people were "patriotically willing" and there was no
necessity for a conscription "absolutely merciless and sweeping"; that the
draft as it was being enforced would bring "a very large amount of money
with which to pay bounties to volunteers." His own state was raising its
quota, said Blaine; other parts of the Union might be disorderly, but not
Maine.

If Blaine's motion should pass, it would kill the bill and defeat Lincoln,
Stanton, Schenck and the Military Affairs Committee in their attempt to get
universal selective military service, making money payments unlawful. "Do
not, I pray you," cried Blaine, "by any action here proclaim to the world that
you have no faith in the loyal people of the United States." The debate was
brief; the Yeas and Nays were called for. And the President, the War Department and Schenck were beaten by a vote of Yeas 100, Nays 50, not
voting 32.

The 50 Congressmen who with Lincoln gambled their political futures (by
risking the ill will of all potential drafted men having $300 with which they
wished to buy exemption) were Republicans. The 100 who voted to keep
the $300 exemption clause were Republicans joined by a minority of Demo-
crats, including George H. Pendleton of Ohio, close political ally of Val-

landigham. Congressmen plainly were afraid that the drastic action proposed by Stanton, concurred in by Lincoln, and advocated by Schenck, Frank P. Blair and others on the floor, would offend men of influence and property in their home districts, resulting possibly in upheavals and violence. Mostly these fears were kept under, were left plainly implied.

In the Senate political instinct ran the same as in the House. The Senators were decisively for bounties and substitutes. Also they were as hazy and groping as House members on the ways and means of getting soldiers. The ballots ran close, as in the House, and about a proportional number stayed away and didn't get into the record. Wade, Wilson, Reverdy Johnson and other Senators spoke fears of giving the President power to draft men for three years. The result might be a country ruled by a military despotism working through a horde of professional soldiers.

Schenck in the House and Sprague in the Senate had pointed out how clear it was that the President, the Cabinet and the War Department wanted the $300 commutation clause absolutely repealed. This was done by such a device that in the campaign of that year it could be said in speech and pamphlet and editorial that the commutation clause *was* absolutely repealed. Yet what was substituted for it was nearly an equivalent. The President had authority to call for *volunteers* for one, two or three years, the one-year men to be paid $100 bounty, the two-year men $200, the three-year men $300, each receiving the final one-third installment of his bounty on completion of service.

On a clear-cut issue between Lincoln and Congress he was refused by overwhelming votes what he asked for in an essential point for carrying on the war. The refusal of Congress extended to Grant and Sherman, who favored a policy of no money payments and no substitutes entangling and retarding the draft. Grant and Sherman stressed the point that money payments brought a poorer brand of soldiers. Lincoln was speaking both as an executive in office and as a political candidate with re-election at stake in four months. He was willing to take his chances on whatever disorder might result from a new principle in the draft. And in face of political unrest and a vast gloom savage with suspicion and recrimination, Lincoln two weeks after the draft act was passed by Congress July 4, 1864, proclaimed a call for a half-million volunteers.

With the $300 clause done away with, any man drafted must either go into the Army himself or pay someone else to go for him. Such a substitute had to be either an alien, a veteran of two years' service, or a boy under 20. Hustlers, in the business of finding substitutes and selling them to those who wished to buy, came forward. "Wanted. Irishmen, Englishmen, Scotchmen, Germans, Frenchmen, to enlist as volunteers." Thus one amid columns of similar ads, paid for at regular rates, in the New York *Herald*. Only four days after the President's proclamation one New York *Herald* ad made the appeal: "It is clearly to the interest of every man liable to military duty to procure an alien substitute at once and save dollars, cents and worry. The price of substitutes will soon reach $1,200, because of the great bounties that will be offered by cities, towns and States."

"Six hundred dollars cash paid for substitutes," ran one ad in newspapers of Cincinnati, where on August 20 prices went to $1,200 and $1,500 for substitutes, for men to replace the fallen or the vanished in the ranks of Grant and Sherman. "A nice farm of eighty acres worth $600" was offered by one lacking cash and seeking a substitute.

Under way in northern New York State was a stampede of men seeking draft evasion, wrote the provost marshal of Albany requesting authority to stop the men at the Canadian border. Thousands of "miserable, cowardly Copperhead scoundrels" were fleeing across Minnesota for the Canadian border, ran a report from Milwaukee. An Ohio writer put the case with more care, observing for *Appleton's Annual Cyclopaedia:* "The voluntary absentee-ism from the State of persons liable to military service, on the approach or during the pendency of the draft, was estimated to exceed twenty thousand. A large number left during the ten days allowed by law between draft and notification . . . in some cases, there were not men enough left in the town-ships to fill the quota. Many men drafted in one section of the State went into other sections."

Amid chaos, gloom, forebodings over the country, amid howlings that they were inhuman monsters and God would bring them retribution, Lincoln and Stanton carried through, with every employable resource at their hands, the procurement of troops to maintain the strength of Grant's and Sherman's armies, to impress the Southern people anew with the man power of the North. "All who will not help should be put in petticoats and deprived of the right to vote in the affairs of the nation," Sherman wrote home. "This army is much reduced in strength by deaths, sickness, and expiration of service. It looks hard to see regiments march away when their time is up."

What Congress did, after many conferences between Senate and House, was to provide that pay equal to that of the white soldiers should be given to all regularly enlisted "persons of color who were free" April 19, 1861. This resulted in an ingenious oath being used in many of the Negro regiments. Drawn up by Colonel E. N. Hallowell of the Massachusetts 54th, it required men to swear that they "owed no man unrequited labor on or before the 19th day of April, 1861." Thus they might be swearing to the truth and the fact, though they would be evading the category in which the U.S. Consti-tution still held them as chattels and property. Here and there, said Massa-chusetts colonels, were black men whose pride put them above a trick oath for evading a Constitution which still held them as chattels and property.

The necessity of men killing men, since there was a war on, stood forth in Lincoln's writing to Vice-President Hamlin that on the issuance of the Emancipation Proclamation troops came forward more slowly than ever: "The North responds to the proclamation sufficiently in breath; but breath alone kills no rebels." Killings were wanted. Enough killings would end the war. "I have seen your despatch," he wired Grant one hot August day of '64, "expressing your unwillingness to break your hold where you are. Neither am I willing. Hold on with a bull-dog grip, and chew & choke as much as possible."

From Chicago came a committee of three appointed at a mass meeting to ask the Secretary of War for a new enrollment figure. Their quota had been put too high, they believed. Stanton refused any concession. So they went to Lincoln, who said, "I will go with you to Stanton and hear both sides." Head-ing the committee was Joseph Medill, editor of the Chicago *Tribune,* who argued before Lincoln, Stanton and Fry that the Chicago quota should be lowered. Chicago had already sent 22,000 men and was drained. Lincoln heard the argument sitting quietly, and in time lifted his head and spoke.

"Gentlemen," he said, as Medill's memory served, "after Boston, Chicago has been the chief instrument in bringing this war on the country. The Northwest has opposed the South as the Northeast has opposed the South. You called for war until we had it. You called for emancipation and I have given it to you. Whatever you have asked for you have had. Now you come here begging to be let off from the call for men which I have made to carry out the war which you have demanded. You ought to be ashamed of yourselves. I have a right to expect better things of you. Go home and raise your 6,000 extra men. And you, Medill, are acting like a coward. You and your *Tribune* have had more influence than any paper in the Northwest in making this war. You can influence great masses, and yet you cry to be spared at a moment when your cause is suffering. Go home and send us those men."

Some sort of writhing, intense speech like that came from Lincoln, and as Medill confessed: "I couldn't say anything. It was the first time I ever was whipped, and I didn't have an answer. We all got up and went out, and when the door closed, one of my colleagues said, 'Well, gentlemen, the old man is right. We ought to be ashamed of ourselves. Let us never say anything about this, but go home and raise the men.' And we did, 6,000 men, making 28,000 in the war from a city of 156,000."

"I hev lost, sence Stanton's order to draft, the use of wun eye entirely, and hev kronic inflammashen in the other," wrote Petroleum V. Nasby, gloom-chaser for the President. "My teeth is all unsound, my palit ain't eggsactly rite, and I hev hed bronkeetis 31 yeres last Joon. At present I hev a koff, the paroxisms uv wich is friteful 2 behold. I am afflictid with kronic diarrear and kostivness. I am rupcherd in 9 places, and am entirely enveloped with trusses. I hev korns and bunions on both feet, wich wood prevent me from marchin."

Walt Whitman wrote from Washington to his mother that the feeling was "savage & hot" against draft evaders. "I do not feel it in my heart to abuse the poor people, or call for a rope or bullets for them, but that is all the talk here, even in the hospitals." The author of "Blow, Bugles, Blow!" who had welcomed war, like many others who brooded over the balances of justice in it now felt himself blown to and fro in its windy passions. "The deeper they go in with the draft, the more trouble it is likely to make. I have changed my opinions and feelings on the subject. We are in the midst of strange and terrible times. One is pulled a dozen different ways in his mind, & hardly knows what to think or do." And of the President and General Burnside reviewing the 9th corps parade up Pennsylvania Avenue Whitman wrote to "dearest mother": "Five regiments of new black troops looked and marched very well. It looked funny to see the President standing with his hat off to them just the same as the rest as they passed by."

When a man enlisted as a substitute, pocketed the cash bounty, jumped elsewhere to enlist again and pocket another cash bounty, he was known as a "bounty-jumper." Newspapers carried a stream of items about fugitive and captured bounty-jumpers. One sentenced to four years in the Albany penitentiary confessed to having jumped the bounty 32 times.

Those who took flight to evade the draft, known as "skedaddlers," changed their names and sought localities where voters and officials were hostile to the Lincoln administration. They moved to lonely mining camps or settlements unfriendly to provost marshals and reached by hard travel.

A Vermont woman, according to *Leslie's*, having an errand in Canada, was shocked at meeting her husband in Montreal. Had she not received official word from the Government that her husband had died on the field of battle as a hero? Had she not mourned and put on widow's garb, and later married another man? Now she learned from him that he had nursed no wish to fall with honor on the field of glory, and therefore had stuffed her letters to him, her photographs, her locks of shining bronze hair, into the pockets and bosom of a dead soldier, removing from the corpse any contradictory evidence. Then he had deserted and made his way to Canada. He promised her, "I'll never trouble you again," and she warned him not to.

In the war chronicle of the summer of '64, with its plodding in blood and muck, were two bright spots for the Union cause. On a Sunday morning in June, outside the international line off the coast of France at Cherbourg, two ships met and battled. The one flying the Confederate flag had cruised thousands of miles in the South Atlantic and Indian Oceans since August '63, had captured 62 merchantmen, and burned most of them at sea. She was the hated and feared *Alabama*, British-built, her seamen and gunners mainly British.

The *Kearsarge* had long trailed the *Alabama* and at last penned her in Cherbourg Harbor. Three hundred and seventy shells from the *Alabama* left the *Kearsarge* practically undamaged, with only the loss of a smokestack, while nearly every one of the 173 projectiles from the *Kearsarge* found its target and tore open the sides of the *Alabama* till she began sinking. Forty were killed on the *Alabama* under the Confederate flag; on the *Kearsarge* the losses were three men wounded, of whom one died.

In August, the Confederacy lost its most essential port on the Gulf of Mexico. Lashed to a flagship mast and leading his fleet into Mobile Bay, Admiral Farragut prayed, "O God, who created man and gave him reason, direct me what to do. Shall I go on?" His order, "Damn the torpedoes! Full speed ahead!" became a Unionist slogan. His fleet captured the ram *Tennessee*, rated one of the most powerful vessels of war afloat in any waters, and with land forces reduced the three forts guarding Mobile. Lincoln termed it a "brilliant achievement."

Lincoln with Grant believed a strangle hold was being put on the South. But a large number of people, some of them highly vocal in this August of '64, did not so believe or were not particularly interested in believing in anything connected with continuance of the war.

Near the town of Mount Vernon, Ohio, lived a farmer and his wife who believed that Vallandigham was telling the truth about the war, that Lincoln was a deceiver, a monster and a fiend perpetuating a needless war, the woman saying to her children, "Lincoln! how I loathe that name between my lips!" To her Vallandigham was a hero and brave truthteller. Nothing Lincoln said reached her. She and her husband worked their farm without help, kept a sober and orderly household, read their Bible and went to a Congregational church on the Sabbath, had no traffic with ill-gotten gains of the war. They were for peace. They saw Lincoln as against peace. And her children, not yet of age to be drafted, heard her with immemorial woe and hate in her voice, "Lincoln! how I loathe that name between my lips!"

Here and there despair over the war became despair over the President and his seeming failures. "The war and its constant expectations and anxieties oppress me," wrote James Russell Lowell. "I cannot think. I hear bad things about Mr. Lincoln and try not to believe them." William Cullen Bryant wrote to John M. Forbes of "the Seward and Weed faction filling all the offices with its creatures," saying further, "I am so disgusted with Lincoln's behavior that I cannot muster respectful terms in which to write him." From Bloomington August 4 David Davis wrote to a brother that while in Chicago he had talked with many people from different parts of the country and found growing uneasiness and distrust. "People are getting tired of the war. Some of them can't see a ray of light. I am speaking of good men. Two years ago I succeeded in raising 1,300 men in this county. It took about ten days. There is no note now of any volunteering . . . There is faith in the administration, and yet you will hear *whispering* inquiries as to whether the plan they are pursuing is the best . . . Keep these views to yourself, and burn this letter."

Former President Millard Fillmore August 10, 1864, was writing to John T. Stuart, urging that "all men who value their own liberty should unite to change the administration . . . for without this all is lost." One other living ex-President, Franklin Pierce, was saying the same where he thought it might help to crush Lincoln.

Across weeks of August '64, a movement, necessarily secret, among Republican party leaders operated with the aim of replacing Lincoln with another nominee for President. The Jonah of the Ship of State was Lincoln. He should be flung overboard. Among Republican conferences in New York City was one at the home of David Dudley Field August 14, with Greeley, Mayor George Opdyke, Parke Godwin of the *Evening Post*, William Curtis Noyes, Henry Winter Davis, Theodore Tilton, Franz Lieber and 20 or more others. It was agreed that a committee should request Lincoln to withdraw as a presidential candidate. The name of Grant was most favored to replace that of Lincoln. A call was prepared for a convention to be held in Cincinnati September 28.

"Mr. Lincoln is already beaten," wrote Greeley to Mayor Opdyke. "We must have another ticket to save us from utter overthrow. If we had such a ticket as could be had by naming Grant, Butler, or Sherman for President, and Farragut as Vice, we could make a fight yet."

The antislavery wheel horse, John Jay, believed a letter might be prepared which would "compel Mr. Lincoln's acquiescence" to another nominating convention. Senator Charles Sumner indicated his wish that Lincoln should withdraw, but in case Lincoln should refuse it would not be so good. "It may be," wrote Sumner, "that Mr. Lincoln will see that we shall all be stronger and more united under another candidate."

Whitelaw Reid of the Cincinnati *Gazette* wrote to the committee's secretary: "That which I could do in the direction you indicate has been done in inducing the *Gazette* to come out for Mr. Lincoln's withdrawal. The article has been telegraphed east, and I hope has done some good." Rugged John Andrew spoke for himself and others of unquestionably clean motives when he wrote to Greeley: "Mr. Lincoln *ought* to lead the country. But he is essentially lacking in the quality of leadership, which is a gift of God and not a device of man."

Carl Schurz rode with Lincoln in a carriage from the White House to Soldiers' Home. Lincoln said he would not complain of the burden of care put on his shoulders. "They urge me with almost violent language to withdraw from the contest, although I have been unanimously nominated . . . God knows, I have at least tried very hard to do my duty, to do right to everybody and wrong to nobody. And now to have it said by men who have been my friends and who ought to know me better, that I have been seduced by what they call the lust of power, and that I have been doing this and that unscrupulous thing hurtful to the common cause, only to keep myself in office! Have they thought of that common cause when trying to break me down? I hope they have." So he went on, as if speaking to himself, noted Schurz, sometimes as if Schurz were not there at all.

"Ten days since, I told Mr. Lincoln that his re-election was an impossibility," wrote Thurlow Weed to Seward August 22. "Mr. Raymond, who has just left me, says that unless some prompt and bold step be now taken all is lost. The people are wild for peace. They are told that the President will only listen to terms of peace on condition slavery be abandoned." Therefore Weed was urging that the President should offer the Richmond Government the conditions of the Crittenden Compromise of the winter of '60-'61, with the Union to be restored and the South writing its own constitutional sanction of slave property.

Events had brought new and definite viewpoints to the President. To Judge Joseph T. Mills and ex-Governor A. W. Randall of Wisconsin at Soldiers' Home Lincoln unburdened himself. "There are now between 1 & 200 thousand black men in the service of the Union . . . There have been men who have proposed to me to return to slavery the black warriors of Port Hudson and Olustee to their masters to conciliate the South. I should be damned in time and eternity for so doing. The world shall know that I will keep my faith to friends and enemies, come what will. My enemies say I am now carrying on this war for the sole purpose of abolition. It is & will be carried on so long as I am President for the sole purpose of restoring the Union. But no human power can subdue this rebellion without using the Emancipation lever as I have done . . . My enemies condemn my emancipation policy. Let them prove by the history of this war, that we can restore the Union without it.

"Freedom has given us the control of 200,000 able bodied men, born & raised on southern soil. It will give us more yet. Just so much it has sub[t]racted from the strength of our enemies, & instead of alienating the south from us, there are evidences of a fraternal feeling growing up between our own & rebel soldiers." This gave him a glow. He seemed to welcome news of fraternal feeling rather than hate, as though should the Union be saved, that fraternal feeling could be built on.

The Badger State visitors saw Lincoln enter the room with shoulders inclined forward, gait rapid "and shuffling, ample understandings with large slippers, and Briarian arms, a face radiant with intelligence and humor." A version of this peculiarly significant interview *Harper's Weekly* of New York reprinted from the *Grant County Herald* of Wisconsin, whereupon scores of newspapers in America and the London *Spectator* and other journals in England gave it to their readers.

Raymond was hearing but one report. "The tide is setting strongly against us." Washburne in Illinois, Cameron in Pennsylvania, were saying their states at the moment were against the administration. Only strenuous efforts could carry Indiana, Governor Morton had written. Two special causes were assigned for this feeling against the administration: want of military success, and "the impression in some minds, the fear and suspicion in others, that we are not to have peace in any event under this Administration until slavery is abandoned." The suspicion seemed widespread that peace with Union was to be had. "It is idle to reason with this belief—still more idle to denounce it." Therefore Raymond would suggest the President appoint a commission to proffer peace to Davis "on the sole condition of acknowledging the supremacy of the Constitution—all other questions to be settled in a convention of the people of all the States."

Raymond waited in New York. From the President came no reply. In Washington the President was viewing the national situation. He was a candidate for re-election with as yet no opponent. It would be a week or more before the Democrats at Chicago would name a man to run against him; yet the signs were that he was already beaten by whoever might be named. In his own later words, "At this period we had no adversary and seemed to have no friends." When his Cabinet met August 23, he handed around a sheet of paper so folded and pasted that what was inside could not be read. He requested each member to sign his name across the back of the sheet. Each one wrote not knowing what he was signing. It was a memorandum for possible future use:

Executive Mansion,
Washington, Aug. 23, 1864.

This morning, as for some days past, it seems exceedingly probable that this Administration will not be re-elected. Then it will be my duty to so co-operate with the President elect, as to save the Union between the election and the inauguration; as he will have secured his election on such ground that he can not possibly save it afterwards.

A. LINCOLN

Two days later Raymond and the national executive committee of the Republican party, not having heard from the President that he would publicly proffer peace to the Richmond Government, arrived at the White House. They were, according to Nicolay and Hay, "in obvious depression and panic." Raymond was in a final and confidential session with the President and three Cabinet members when Welles entered. "I went in as usual unannounced," wrote Welles in his diary. "I found Messrs. Seward, Fessenden, and Stanton with Raymond . . . in consultation with the President. The President was making some statement as to a document of his, and said he supposed his style was peculiar and had its earmarks, so that it could not be mistaken. He kept on talking as if there had been no addition to the company, and as if I had been expected and belonged there. But the topic was not pursued by the others when the President ceased. Some inquiry was put to me in regard to intelligence from the fleet at Mobile . . . Mr. Fessenden rose and, putting his mouth to the ear of the President, began to whisper, and as soon as I could answer the brief inquiries, I left the room. It was easy to perceive that Seward, Stanton, and Raymond were disconcerted by my appearance. Except the whispering by Fessenden I saw nothing particular on his part."

Nicolay wrote to Hay in Illinois as between two cronies: "Hell is to pay. The New York politicians have got a stampede on that is about to swamp everything. Raymond and the National Committee are here to-day. R. thinks a commission to Richmond is about the only salt to save us; while the Tycoon sees and says it would be utter ruination. The matter is now undergoing consultation. Weak-kneed damned fools . . . are in the movement for a new candidate to supplant the Tycoon. Everything is darkness and doubt and discouragement."

And what of the document Welles heard the President say was in his own "peculiar" style, having his personal "earmarks"? Lincoln had written it to meet squarely the proposals of Raymond for a peace proffer to Richmond. Dated August 24, 1864, it was concrete, exact, decisive as a slide rule measuring in fractions:

Sir:
You will proceed forthwith and obtain, if possible, a conference for peace with Hon. Jefferson Davis, or any person by him authorized for that purpose.

You will address him in entirely respectful terms, at all events, and in any that may be indispensable to secure the conference.

At said conference you will propose, on behalf this government, that upon the restoration of the Union and the national authority, the war shall cease at once, all remaining questions to be left for adjustment by peaceful modes. If this be accepted hostilities to cease at once.

If it be not accepted, you will then request to be informed what terms, if any embracing the restoration of the Union, would be accepted. If any such be presented you in answer, you will forthwith report the same to this government, and await further instructions.

If the presentation of any terms embracing the restoration of the Union be declined, you will then request to be informed what terms of peace would be accepted; and on receiving any answer, report the same to this government, and await further instructions.

As Nicolay wrote in his private notebook, the President "and the stronger half of the Cabinet, Seward, Stanton, and Fessenden," showed Raymond that they had thoroughly considered and discussed his proposals of a peace proffer. "He very readily concurred with them in the opinion that to follow his plan of sending a commission to Richmond would be worse than losing the Presidential contest—it would be ignominiously surrendering it in advance. Nevertheless the visit of himself and committee here did great good. They found the President and cabinet much better informed than themselves, and went home encouraged and cheered." And into files to which Greeley and Bennet. had no access went the unused, unsent peace proffer.

Returning to New York, Raymond threw amazement into the Republican anti-Lincoln ranks with his positive statements in the *Times* that peace negotiation stories had no bottom; "the President stands firm against every solicitation to postpone the draft"; and as to rumors of this and that about the Government, "You may rest assured . . . its sole and undivided purpose is to prosecute the war until the rebellion is quelled."

And perhaps it was the mercurial Bennett himself who in the *Herald*, the day after Raymond's return, mocked and gabbed and jibed: "The Republican leaders may have their personal quarrels, or their shoddy quarrels, or their nigger quarrels with Old Abe; but he has the whiphand of them, and they will soon be bobbing back into the Republican fold, like sheep who have gone astray . . .

"Whatever they say now, we venture to predict that Wade and his tail; and Bryant and his tail; and Wendell Phillips and his tail; and Weed, Barney, Chase and their tails; and Winter Davis, Raymond, Opdyke and Forney who have no tails; will all make tracks for Old Abe's plantation, and soon will be found crowing and blowing, and vowing and writing, and swearing and stumping the state on his side, declaring that he and he alone, is the hope of the nation, the bugaboo of Jeff Davis, the first of Conservatives, the best of Abolitionists, the purest of patriots, the most gullible of mankind, the easiest President to manage, and the person especially predestined and foreordained by Providence to carry on the war, free the niggers, and give all the faithful a fair share of the spoils. The spectacle will be ridiculous; but it is inevitable."

John Eaton, with a pass signed by the President was authorized to "visit Gen. Grant at City Point, Va." Grant held strictly to army matters in the talk of the two men that ran past midnight. Eaton was interested, but was trying to find some entering wedge on political affairs. Finally he mentioned to Grant a conversation on a railroad train with army men who had asked Eaton if he thought Grant could be induced to run as a citizen's candidate for President. "The question is," said Eaton to Grant, "not whether you wish to run, but whether you could be compelled to run in answer to the demand of the people for a candidate who should save the Union."

Grant's instant reply amazed Eaton. The General brought his clenched fists down hard on the strap arms of his camp chair, "They can't do it! They can't compel me to do it." "Have you said this to the President?" "No, I have not thought it worth while to assure the President of my opinion. I consider it as important to the cause that he should be elected as that the army should be successful in the field."

Eaton, back at Washington, entering Lincoln's office heard the eager question, "Well, what did you find?" "You were right." And the President "fairly glowed with satisfaction," noted Eaton, as he heard Lincoln say, "I told you that they could not get him to run until he had closed out the rebellion."

Grant resumed his noncommittal attitude toward Lincoln as a candidate for the Presidency. To the country Grant gave no sign that he was for or against Lincoln. Lincoln may have guessed that Grant had a fear of the Washington hotbed of intrigues and the political guile that had been a curse on the Army of the Potomac. Lincoln may have instigated the mission of Congressman Washburne to Grant asking him to publish a letter in favor of Lincoln's election. If Washburne carried back to Lincoln what Grant had to say,

Lincoln might have taken a healthy laugh for himself. Grant told Washburne that "for the President to answer all the charges the opposition would bring against him would be like setting a maiden to work to prove her chastity."

Grant's letter for publication dated at City Point, August 16, 1864, took no sides with any Republican or Democratic party faction, was neither pro- nor anti-Lincoln. And in its closing paragraph it endorsed by inference the President's emancipation policy. The old Steve Douglas Democrat, Grant, was saying by implication that the slavery issue had progressed to where the complications were inexorable: there was nothing else to do but free the slaves and make a peace that kept the slaves free. Regarding the war and the draft he wished to give the impression that the Confederacy was becoming a hollow shell sucked of its vitality.

"I state to all citizens who visit me that all we want now to insure an early restoration of the Union is determined unity of sentiment in the North. The Rebels have now in their ranks their last man . . . They have robbed the cradle and the grave equally to get their present force. Besides what they lose in frequent skirmishes and battles, they are now losing from desertions and other causes at least one regiment per day . . . Their only hope now is a divided North, and this might give them reinforcements from Kentucky, Tennessee, Maryland and Missouri, while it would weaken us . . . they are exceedingly anxious to hold out until after the Presidential election; for they have many hopes upon its result." This letter Stanton withheld for later pub- lication, probably after conference with Lincoln, as though written appeals could be of little use in that dark August.

Editor Sam Bowles of the Springfield *Republican* had to write in a letter: "Do you notice that the Anti-Slavery Standard and the Liberator, representa- tives of the old Abolitionists, are both earnest for Lincoln? Yet a new crop of radicals have sprung up, who are resisting the President and making mischief. Chase is going around, peddling his griefs in private ears, and sowing dissatis- faction about Lincoln." Chase amid his other doings had opened a corre- spondence with August Belmont, chairman of the Democratic national com- mittee, letting Belmont know that if the Democratic party at its Chicago convention would insert a platform plank declaring for the abolition of slav- ery, he, Chase, would then be willing to run as the Democratic candidate for the Presidency.

Lincoln knew that no words, explanations, persuasions, letters, speeches, could save his cause. Only bayonets triumphant and red-dripping with Con- federate defeat could bring anything like magic or potency to anything he might have to say. While decisive events waited he would manage a course as best he could, saying: "The pilots on our western rivers steer from point to point, as they call it—setting the course of the boat no farther than they can see. And that is all I propose to do in the great problems that are set before us."

A summer for sure it had been of steering from point to point, from Sher- man's drive toward Atlanta and Grant's lunges at Richmond to the arrival of Early at the gates of Washington and the sinking of the *Alabama* and the capture of Mobile; from the smooth unanimous nomination of Lincoln at Baltimore to the clawing scorn of the Wade-Davis Manifesto; from the peace missions of Greeley at Niagara and Jaquess-Gilmore at Richmond to the secret Republican party manipulations hoping to replace Lincoln at the head of the ticket; from draft legislation authorizing conscripts to buy substitutes to the attempt to detach 50,000 men from Grant's army to enforce the draft in Northern cities, oath-bound secret societies threatening to take over the Government at Washington and one committee of Republican party leaders begging the President not to make his call for a draft of a half-million men until after the November election. He had given reply: "What is the Presidency worth to me if I have no country?"

Midsummer, Lincoln had told a Boston *Journal* man: "I have faith in the people. They will not consent to disunion. The danger is, in their being misled. Let them know the truth and the country is safe." He looked haggard and careworn to the correspondent, who said, "You are wearing yourself out with work." "I can't work less. But it isn't that. Work never troubled me. Things look badly, and I can't avoid anxiety . . . I feel a presentiment that I shall not outlast the rebellion. When it is over, my work will be done."

William Bross one August day found Lincoln "cordial but rather melancholy." A brother of Bross had fallen at the head of his regiment in fighting before Petersburg and Bross was on his way to recover the body. Deepchested, heavily full-bearded with bristling hairs, flashing-eyed, one of the owners and editors of the Chicago *Tribune*, Bross was the Union party candidate for lieutenant governor of Illinois. Lincoln asked Bross anxiously for news from the West. Gloom hung over the West and the entire country, Bross believed. Lincoln agreed that neither of them could shut their eyes to the condition, Bross saying that the people expected a more vigorous prosecution of the war; more troops and appliances would be forthcoming from the people, if called for. And Bross felt assured that Lincoln spoke his "inmost sentiments" in a brief and graphic commentary which Lincoln plainly wished Bross to carry back to the Union men of Illinois: "I will tell you what the people want. They want and must have, *success*. But whether that come or not, I shall stay *right here* and do my duty. Here I shall be. And they may come and hang me on that tree [pointing out of the window], but, God helping me, I shall never desert my post."

In the progress of the war Lincoln had constantly drawn closer to the churches. He replied to one delegation in May '64: "It is no fault in others that the Methodist Church sends more soldiers to the field, more nurses to the hospital, and more prayers to heaven than any. God bless the Methodist Church. Bless all the churches." And replying to a Baptist delegation later in the same day: "I have had great cause of gratitude for the support so unanimously given by all Christian denominations of the country."

Late in the summer of '64 came a committee of colored people from Baltimore, their spokesman in an elaborate address presenting Lincoln with a richly wrought Bible. He could only now say as so often before, "It has always been a sentiment with me that all mankind should be free . . . To you I return my most sincere thanks for the very elegant copy of the great Book of God which you present."

Writing to the Quaker woman Eliza P. Gurney, Lincoln dwelt on the searchings of conscience that might divide a man in time of war: "I am much

indebted to the good christian people of the country for their constant prayers and consolations; and to no one of them, more than to yourself. The
purposes of the Almighty are perfect, and must prevail, though we erring
mortals may fail to accurately perceive them in advance. We hoped for a
happy termination of this terrible war long before this; but God knows best,
and has ruled otherwise. We shall yet acknowledge His wisdom and our
own error therein. Meanwhile we must work earnestly in the best lights He
gives us, trusting that so working still conduces to the great ends He ordains.
Surely He intends some great good to follow this mighty convulsion, which
no mortal could make, and no mortal could stay."

CHAPTER 49

The Fierce Fall Campaign of '64

BEFORE leaving for Chicago to report the Democratic national convention, Noah Brooks heard Lincoln: "They must nominate a Peace Democrat on a war platform, or a War Democrat on a peace platform; and I
personally can't say that I care much which they do."

In the same Wigwam in Chicago where Lincoln had been nominated in
1860, the convention met August 29, a boiling kettle of partisans that included Peace Democrats, War Democrats, Whigs, Know-Nothings, Conservatives, states' rights extremists who endorsed secession, millionaires in broadcloth, run-down politicians in paper collars, men who had braved mobs and
suffered for the rights of free speech and a free press, and a remnant of
Confederate loyalists who could not be open about their efforts. The delegates were called to order by August Belmont.

On taking the gavel as permanent chairman, Governor Seymour said the
present administration could not now save the Union if it would, but "If the
administration cannot save this Union, we can. (Loud applause.) Mr. Lincoln
values many things above the Union; we put it first of all." The platform then
adopted declared for the Union, the Constitution, civil liberty, and "care,
protection, and regard" for the soldiers of the country.

Against persistent opposition Vallandigham in the resolutions committee
carried through a straight-out peace plank declaring "that immediate efforts
be made for a cessation of hostilities, with a view to an ultimate convention
of the States."

The measures of immediate action on taking power, directly pledged in
the platform, were: (1) the armies would be ordered to cease hostilities and
go home; (2) the Southern States would then be asked to join a convention
to restore the Union; (3) free speech and a free press would be allowed and
no matter what the opposition to the Government there would be no arbitrary arrests, while habeas corpus and trial by jury would return.

Delegate Stambaugh of Ohio believed "they might search hell over and
they could not find a worse candidate than Abraham Lincoln." Delegate

Alexander, a circuit court judge from Kentucky, made public, according to the Chicago *Times*, his favorite anecdote "of a Kentucky gentleman who thought that as Mr. Lincoln was so fond of the negro, he should have one of the slain ones skinned and made into a pair of moccasins for his daily wear." The Honorable W. W. O'Brien, a Peoria delegate, was certain that the convention's candidate for President would on the next fourth of March "apply his boot to 'Old Abe's posterior' and kick him out of the Presidential chair."

Vallandigham on the streets was cheered. As a delegate he was a presence. John J. Van Alen of New York early intimated that he and others would not accept the nomination of McClellan for President, nor any candidate "with the smell of war on his garments." These anti-McClellan peace men were given a free hand in writing a peace plank.

On the final showdown George B. McClellan had 202½ votes as against little more than one-tenth of that number for one T. H. Seymour of Connecticut. Vallandigham amid cheers moved that the nomination of McClellan for President be made unanimous, which was done with further cheers. Senator George H. Pendleton of Ohio, on his record entirely satisfactory to the peace men, was named for Vice-President. The politicians went home fairly well satisfied. Was not victory in the air? In that week did not everyone know that the leading prophets and weather vanes of the Republican party were conceding defeat?

Then fate stepped in. Like a moving hour hand on a clock of doom came news flung world wide, news setting crowds of Northern loyalists to dancing with mirth and howling with glee, news centering about one little dispatch from Sherman September 3. Lincoln read a flimsy saying: "So Atlanta is ours and fairly won . . . Since May 5th we have been in one constant battle or skirmish, and need rest."

The dull ache of defeat and failure in many hearts took a change. In all news sheets the first item, the one story overwhelming all others, was around Sherman's words: "Atlanta is ours and fairly won." A strategic crossroads, supply depot and transportation center of a pivotal Cotton State in the Deep South was gone. Vicksburg, New Orleans and the Mississippi River gone, Kentucky, Tennessee and Nashville gone, Mobile gone. Lee and his army penned between Grant and Richmond for how long? Bells rang again, guns boomed.

The President requested thanksgiving to be offered in all places of worship the following Sunday and announced: "The national thanks are herewith tendered by the President to Major General William T. Sherman, and the gallant officers and soldiers of his command before Atlanta . . . The marches, battles, sieges . . . must render it famous in the annals of war . . ."

A few days later the country read McClellan's acceptance of the nomination for President in a letter throwing no light on what he would do about slavery except let it alone. "The Union is the one condition of peace—we ask no more."

As gently as McClellan could put it to those favoring immediate peace on any terms—and they were an influential fraction of his party—he seemed to be saying with a finality, hesitant yet final, that if the states out of the Union refused to come back on his invitation if he were President, then he would fight them. He hoped for peace "without the effusion of another drop of blood" but possibly there might have to be more fighting if the Union were to be saved. The General wrote: "Let me add, what I doubt not was, although unexpressed, the sentiment of the Convention, as it is of the people they represent, that when any one State is willing to return to the Union, it should be received at once, with a full guarantee of all its constitutional rights . . . the Union must be preserved at all hazards. I could not look in the face my gallant comrades of the army and navy who have survived so many bloody battles, and tell them . . . we had abandoned that Union for which we have so often periled our lives. A vast majority of our people, whether in the army and navy or at home, would, as I would, hail with unbounded joy the permanent restoration of peace, on the basis of the Union under the Constitution, without the effusion of another drop of blood. But no peace can be permanent without Union." Having thus deftly and gently thrown out the most labored point of the Chicago platform, McClellan closed in a belief "that the views here expressed are those of the Convention and the people you represent."

Vallandigham for the Peace Democrats scoffed at McClellan's repudiation. "The Chicago platform enunciated its policy and principles by authority and was binding upon every Democrat, and by them the Democratic Administration must and should be governed."

Now in this September of '64 Phil Sheridan was heard from. For the first time in the war the Shenandoah Valley saw a destroyer with a system. Whatever would nourish man or provide fodder for beast was to be taken or burned or spoiled. When Grant's order should be met, then a crow would have to carry its own rations flying over the valley. At Harrisonburg from Gibbs Hill, residents counted 20 barns in the same hour lighting the dark night of the valley as the flames roared upward.

Four days' fighting at Winchester and Fisher's Hill followed Grant's order "Go in!" and Sheridan's telegram to Grant the night of September 19 had first place in all news sheets of the country: "I attacked the forces of General Early . . . completely defeated him, and driving him through Winchester, captured about 2,500 prisoners, 5 pieces of artillery, 9 army flags, and most of their wounded." To his army next day Sheridan read a telegram signed "A. Lincoln": "Have just heard of your great victory. God bless you all, officers and men. Strongly inclined to come up and see you."

A *Harper's Weekly* writer had noticed a man at a news bulletin board reading one of Sheridan's dispatches to Grant and commenting, "A few more such victories and Abe Lincoln will be elected in November." They were what Lincoln had wanted. No campaign speeches could equal them. The least he could do was appoint Sheridan a brigadier general in the Regular Army and place him in permanent command of the Middle Division, which he did.

A committee appointed by the Rockingham County Court later estimated $25,000,000 worth of property had been destroyed by Sheridan's troops, itemizing 50,000 bushels of corn, 100,000 bushels of wheat, 450 barns, one furnace, three factories, 30 dwelling houses, 31 mills, besides livestock. Grant's order had said: "If the war is to last another year we want the Shenandoah Valley to remain a barren waste."

In a Washington dispatch Whitelaw Reid voiced those who had sought to replace Lincoln with another candidate. "The general apathy and discontent and the apparent certainty of Mr. Lincoln's defeat" had all changed. Greeley announced that the *Tribune* would "henceforth fly the banner of Abraham Lincoln for President." Chase spoke likewise and prepared to go on the stump with speeches alongside Ben Wade and Henry Winter Davis. Gloomy August became a September edged with a few splinters of dawn.

On September 22 a letter was published of Frémont dropping his third party and coming out for Lincoln. And next day Lincoln asked Blair to leave the Cabinet and Blair did. Whether Lincoln made a deal for Frémont's return to the fold on condition of Blair's being ushered out of the Cabinet was anybody's guess. It came as a necessary piece of work for Lincoln to write in his letter to Blair: "You very well know that this proceeds from no dissatisfaction of mine with you personally or officially. Your uniform kindness has been unsurpassed by that of any friend . . ."

Welles asked Blair what had led up to it. Blair said he had no doubt he was "a peace-offering to Frémont and his friends." The secretaries Nicolay and Hay would not stress any one factor as bringing the President to oust his Postmaster General. Blair "wearied the President by insisting upon it that all the leading Republicans were Lincoln's enemies." Lincoln lost the fine edge of his patience, once saying to Blair in the hearing of John Hay, "It is much better not to be led from the region of reason into that of hot blood by imputing to public men motives which they do not avow."

"The union of the Republican party has become a paramount necessity," ran Frémont's letter withdrawing his candidacy in favor of "the Republican candidate pledged to the reëstablishment of the Union without slavery . . . however hesitating his policy may be." Frémont could have said too that fate was playing hard with him in his 44,000-acre Mariposa estate in California, once valued at $10,000,000, that debts on it had reached a total of $1,250,000 with interest charges of $13,000 monthly, that one fee of $200,000 had been charged him by David Dudley Field for attorney's services, that by frauds not strictly illegal and by mismanagement and bad turns of luck he was slowly being eased out of an almost fabulous fortune in land and gold. His brownstone mansion in New York and his summer home north of Tarrytown, the big gray-stone house that commanded a beautiful view of Tappan Zee, were to go in pawn and then fail to meet the demands.

Some newspapers made much of a remark dropped by Simon Cameron that in the event of re-election the President would call around him fresh and earnest men. Hay referred to this. Lincoln said: "They need not be especially savage about a change. There are now only 3 left of the original Cabinet."

William Dennison, lawyer, president of the Exchange Bank of Columbus, governor of Ohio the first two years of the war, a cordial friend of the Blair family, was in Lincoln's mind to fill the vacant Cabinet office. On September 24 the President telegraphed Dennison: "Mr. Blair has resigned and I appoint you Postmaster-General. Come on immediately."

For campaign purposes both parties now made use of the long letter McClellan had handed to Lincoln at Harrison's Landing more than two years before. The Democrats offered it as a modest self-portrayal of a Christian gentleman, a soldier and a statesman. The Republicans picked at it in editorials and squibs, the more radical editors saying its ego and covert insolence should have brought instant removal of a general stepping so completely out of the military field into politics.

On one point the Republicans and Democrats seemed to agree: that on July 7, 1862, when he dated that letter, and for some time before, McClellan had the definite notion in his head that he might make a good President and had carefully studied what he would announce as his policies if he were a candidate. Whether or not Fernando Wood had seduced McClellan into politics, as some believed, it was now in McClellan's favor that Wood announced in view of McClellan's repudiation of the Chicago platform he, Wood, could not support McClellan for President.

When this September swing into party unity had been accomplished Lincoln was in "a more gleeful humor," according to Lamon, who found him alone one evening and met the greeting, "I am glad you have come in. Lamon, do you know that 'we have met the enemy, and they are *ourn*'? I think the cabal of obstructionists 'am busted'! . . . I now am inspired with the hope that our disturbed country further requires the valuable services of your humble servant. 'Jordan has been a hard road to travel,' but I feel now that, notwithstanding the enemies I have made and the faults I have committed, I'll be *dumped* on the right side of that stream."

Of the few "obstructionists" still unyielding was Wendell Phillips, writing as late as September 27 to Elizabeth Cady Stanton: "I would cut off both hands before doing anything to aid Abraham Lincoln's election . . . Justice is still more to me than Union." This was September. October was to see Phillips on the stump for Lincoln, and Thad Stevens commending "the firm grasp of the pilot at the helm," who had risen above "Border State seductions and Republican cowardice."

Collections for the campaign went on, among government employees and elsewhere. Leonard Swett wrote to his wife that he and Congressman Washburne had managed to get a campaign fund of $100,000, assuring her: "Don't think it is for improper purposes. It is not . . . Innumerable expenses have to be incurred."

John Hay noted September 23: "Senator Harlan thinks that Bennett's support [with the New York *Herald*] is so important, especially considered as to its bearing on the soldier vote, that it would pay to offer him a foreign mission for it." Lincoln, it seemed, definitely promised to appoint James Gordon Bennett U.S. Envoy Extraordinary and Minister Plenipotentiary to France. An associate, confidant and go-between of Bennett's, W. O. Bartlett, wrote to Bennett November 4, 1864:

I am from Washington, fresh from the bosom of Father Abraham. I had a full conversation with him, alone, on Tuesday evening, at the White House, in regard to yourself, among other things.

I said to him: "There are but few days now before the election. If Mr. Bennett is not *certainly* to have the offer of the French Mission, I want to know it *now*. It is important to me."

We discussed the course which the *Herald* had pursued, at length, and I will tell you, verbally, at your convenience, what he said; but he concluded with the remark that in regard to the understanding between him and me, about Mr. Bennett, he had been a *"shut pan,* to every body"; and that he *expected to do that thing* (appoint you to France) *as much as he expected to live.* He repeated: *"I expect to do it as certainly as I do to be re-elected myself."*

It carried Lincoln's lingo. Bennett and his *Herald* were of moment for the election a week away. And far more in the labors to follow a re-election would it count for Lincoln to have good will and co-operation from that most humanly interesting newspaper in the Western Hemisphere.

Marshaled solidly behind McClellan were powerful forces, the banking and transportation interests linked with August Belmont, Dean Richmond, Aspinwall, the industrialist churchman seen pre-eminently in Cyrus H. McCormick of Chicago, an array of respectably wealthy, intellectual or aristocratic types embodied in Horatio Seymour of New York and Robert C. Winthrop of Boston. Marching along were two-fisted and riotous elements, joined by those to whom the race issue was uppermost, fearful the Emancipation Proclamation might bring political and social equality. The recoil over McClellan's repudiation of the peace platform came in some of the most vocal sections of the party. The *Metropolitan Record* and the *Daily News* in New York announced they could not go along with McClellan. The *Crisis* at Columbus, Ohio, held that "fraudulent sale is not binding in law" and the "sell-out" in Chicago was treachery. With Vallandigham these organs continued their attacks on Lincoln, pouted disapproval of McClellan, and seemed to be saying they hoped McClellan could be elected, after which they could force him into respect for the Chicago demand for peace through "cessation of hostilities." This too seemed to be the position of McClellan's running mate, Senator George H. Pendleton.

A letter of the Reverend Dr. Moncure Conway in the Boston *Commonwealth* reported Conway, with antislavery associates, interviewing the President. And the careful and scrupulous Conway recorded the President as saying: "Gentlemen, it is generally the case that a man who begins a work is not the best man to carry it on to a successful termination. I believe it was so in the case of Moses, wasn't it? He got the children of Israel out of Egypt, but the Lord selected somebody else to bring them to their journey's end. A pioneer has hard work to do, and generally gets so battered and spattered that people prefer another, even though they may accept the principle." Conway commented: "Under him [Lincoln] the war was begun; he had to deal with the disaffected; is it not possible that he has become so *battered and spattered* as to make it well for him to give up the leadership to some Joshua?"

The printing press worked overtime. The electorate saw literature hauled by the ton. Pamphlets, leaflets, brochures, cards, tracts, envelopes colored with party emblems, in quantity lots came to voters. The Republicans seemed to outdo the Democrats in the amount of educational material, but no voter went hungry who wanted reading matter that lambasted Lincoln and sang the praises of McClellan. A list of horrors, including the debauchery of young women and the jailing of boys in foul and dismal cells for two years, filled a fearsome Democratic brochure titled *Mr. Lincoln's Arbitrary Arrests.*

In one leaflet was an anecdote from General Schenck in an Ohio speech. The Chicago peace platform with a war candidate reminded Schenck of an old lady selling apples at the courthouse door in Cincinnati. On a customer asking, "Are they sweet or sour?" she would lead on into finding out what might be wanted by the assurance, "Why, sir, they are rather acid; a sort of low tart, inclined to be very sweet."

A speech of Carl Schurz at Philadelphia, September 16, was an extraordinary effort in persuasion. The Union Congressional Committee circulated it among all groups, with emphasis on the Germans. Schurz had grown restless in command of a corps of instruction at Nashville and had taken to the stump after a conference with Lincoln. Undoubtedly they had one of their long talks again. And probably Lincoln wrote parts of Schurz's speech or Schurz, with his remarkably acute literal memory, incorporated something of the flair and wording of Lincoln's conversation into a speech. "The mouth of the Mississippi in the hands of a foreign power? Let it be so and half our independence is gone . . . The people of the United States have bought the mouth of the Mississippi, once with their money, and twice with their blood. To give it away would be merely to produce the necessity of buying it a fourth time. Can the South yield it? No. Can the North do without it? No. And then?"

The vote for the platform at Chicago was far more unanimous than the vote for the candidate, in which connection Schurz would speak from experience: "There is no American who does not know that a President's policy is not made by him alone, but by those who have made him." In closing Schurz let the American Eagle scream. In 50 years the country would have 100,-000,000 people, in another century 500,000,000, and the purpose of the North was a free republic *"so strong that its pleasure will be consulted before any power on earth will undertake to disturb the peace of the world."*

In a Union party pamphlet Professor Edouard Laboulaye spoke for French liberals. "The world is a solidarity, and the cause of America is the cause of liberty." So long as a society of 30,000,000 people across the Atlantic lived "under a government of their choice, with laws made by themselves," Europe could hope. "But should liberty become eclipsed in the New World, it would become night in Europe," and power would go to "the whole school which believes only in violence and in success." Therefore Laboulaye and his associates were "praying God that the name which shall stand on the ballot [of November] shall be that of honest and upright Abraham Lincoln." From the English liberal leader John Bright in a letter to Greeley came the wish that Lincoln be re-elected because it would over Europe "and indeed throughout the world" deepen men's faith in republican institutions.

Three speeches of Lincoln to Ohio regiments, "three months' men" going home, gave his attempt to tell in a few simple words what the shooting and crying, the war, was about. "A free government where every man has a right to be equal with every other man" was endangered. "Nowhere in the world is presented a government of so much liberty and equality. To the humblest and poorest amongst us are held out the highest privileges and positions. The present moment finds me at the White House, yet there is as good a chance for your children as there was for my father's. I happen, temporarily, to occupy this White House. I am a living witness that any one of your children may look to come here as my father's child has."

A committee of McClellan Democrats carrying an elaborate document of protest arrived at the White House and John Lellyet of Nashville read the recital of their wrongs to Lincoln. Lincoln was brusque. "May I inquire how long it took you and the New York politicians to concoct that paper?" Lellyet replied that none but Tennesseans had had a hand in it. Lincoln: "I expect to let the friends of George B. McClellan manage their side of this contest in their own way, and I will manage my side of it in my way." Adding that he might make some further answer in writing, Lincoln closed. They saw he was abrupt and filed out.

Mingled flamboyance and romance of democracy as it moved in Andrew Johnson came to the fore one October night as he rose to address the torch-lighted faces of a crowd that included practically the entire Negro population of Nashville. He had a proclamation to make: "Standing here upon the steps of the Capitol, with the past history of the State to witness, the present condition to guide, and its future to encourage me, I, Andrew Johnson, do hereby proclaim freedom, full, broad and unconditional, to every man in Tennessee." A roar of rejoicing and a wild clamor of gladness broke from Negro throats, drums and trumpets added jubilation, and banners waved over circling torches. Johnson's voice rang again. "This damnable aristocracy should be pulled down. No longer should the wives and daughters of the colored men of Tennessee be dragged into a concubinage compared to which polygamy was a virtue." Radicals who had found Lincoln a poor instrument for their measures began saying, "Johnson is our man, one of us."

Singing "Blow ye the trumpet, blow," 144 Negro delegates met in Syracuse, New York, four October days. They spoke for the free Negroes of 18 states, including seven Slave States, and organized the National Equal Rights League, petitioning Congress to remove "invidious distinctions, based upon color, as to pay, labor, and promotion" among Negro troops. Thanks were accorded the President and Congress for opening the way to colored mail carriers, for abolishing slavery in the District of Columbia, for recognition of the Negro republics Liberia and Haiti, for a retaliatory military order invoked because of "barbarous treatment of the colored soldiers of the Union army by the rebels." Further and special thanks were accorded Senator Sumner and General Butler.

On October 11 the stump speakers and the tub thumpers paused slightly, the torchlights and the transparencies halted a moment, and there was less fury in the pamphlets blown loose as wild geese across the autumn sky. The electorate went to the polls that day in Pennsylvania, Ohio and Indiana. At eight o'clock in the evening the President with Hay walked over to the War Department.

The telegraph keys clicked. Governor Morton and the entire Republican ticket in Indiana were elected by 20,000 majority, with a gain of four Congressmen. Pennsylvania's Congressmen, equally divided between two parties, changed to 15 Republicans against 9 Democrats. The Union ticket carried Ohio by 54,000 and the 14 Democrats and 5 Republicans of '62 shifted now to 17 Republicans and 2 Democrats in Congress. The defamatory Peace

Democrat "Sunset" Cox lost his seat to Samuel Shellabarger. Not least was the news from Maryland and her adoption of a new state constitution abolishing slavery; the majority was slim, the soldier vote giving emancipation its day.

On October 12 Roger Brooke Taney died and the President must name a new Chief Justice. Spheres of influence formed and sought to have Lincoln name Montgomery Blair, Bates, Fessenden, Salmon P. Chase or some other one. And Lincoln was to hear them and to wait and to consider carefully and hold his patience.

Browning sounded Fessenden on whether he would permit his friends to mention Browning to the President for Chief Justice and heard Fessenden's refusal. To the War, Treasury and State Departments in the morning, to his room in the afternoon, went Mr. Browning, ex-U.S. Senator Browning, holder of the seat vacated by Steve Douglas until Illinois had gone Democratic again. He was the one old-time Illinois lawyer associated with Lincoln who most often was seen at the White House. "At the Departments in the forenoon, and at work at my room in the afternoon" ran the most frequent item of his diary, though the next most frequent seemed to be "At night went to the President's." And unless the President was over at the War Department Browning was let in. The President liked his company, though it seemed that along in the fall of '64 the President came to look at Browning as one of the most peculiarly befuddled individuals that had come out of the war, and he became less free in outpourings of mind and spirit to Browning.

When Smith had retired as Secretary of the Interior, Browning had hoped the President would agree with Mrs. Lincoln that he should have the place. When Browning brought to the President the matter of the vacant Chief Justiceship, he was not without faint hope he might be the man. Known as a familiar of the President, for him doors swung open when he sent his card in at the departments. He rode with the President and navy heads to the navy yards to witness the throwing of rockets and signals from 6- and 12-pound guns. He worked in his office till night "then went and saw the President about fees in the Phillips cases, about Adml Wilke's case, and about appointment of Eben Moore to Montano."

Browning refused the request of Seward and the President that he take the appointment of commissioner for claim adjustments of the Hudson Bay and Puget Sound agricultural companies. "I find the duties will be very arduous, and the compensation $5000 inadequate." When the hay contractors Covert & Farlin had been arrested and put on trial before a court-martial charged with fraud, the hay contractors hired the two lawyers in Washington nearest to the President in confidence and longest in acquaintance, Orville H. Browning and Leonard Swett. To the War Department, to the Quartermaster General, to the Judge Advocate went Browning, sometimes in company with Swett, with the result that the hay contractors got "an extension of 30 days to enable them to fill their contracts— They discharged from arrest and proceedings in Court Martial suspended," according to Browning's diary.

Wearing a serenity bland and colorless, almost empty of humor, precise in the forms and manners, overly vain about his scruples, Browning went here and there, saw everybody who was anybody, made the entries in his diary, two lines, ten lines, without elation or melancholy, earnest and careful. When a band of serenaders came to his Quincy home the night of McClellan's nomination for President, Browning was earnest and scrupulous enough to tell them he was not a Democrat, yet sufficiently careful to repeat that McClellan was "a great general" and would have his support if elected President. In like manner he would support Frémont or any other administration. The name of Browning's intimate personal friend and political benefactor, then a candidate for re-election, escaped his mention. He may have wished that Lincoln might be President another four years, but the wish did not reach his tongue. It was likewise when Browning spoke before a crowd jubilating over the capture of Atlanta. Then too, as he wrote in his diary, "I carefully avoided subjects of a merely partizan character, and made no allusion to the Presidential candidates." On September 16, 1864, his entire diary entry read: "Honorable C. B. Lawrence dined with me today. Has urged me earnestly to declare myself in favor of the re election of Mr. Lincoln."

The days ran on through the campaign and Browning was to hold back from any word that he would vote for Lincoln. His calls on the President seemed to increase and nearly always the favor he asked was granted. "At night went to the Presidents and got order for release of Capt Saml Black." "At Presidents and got order for Judge Advocate Burnett to examine & report on cases . . . and of Captain Black." Nothing less than "an interview of three hours" with the President was accorded him one evening "in regard to Capt Blacks case." Or again one Sunday: "At night went to the Presidents, and got an order for the release of Ludwell Y. Browning, a rebel prisoner at Camp Douglas."

Only once in his diary did Browning record an open rebuff from the President. Browning possibly omitted some points of circumstance in the entry:

At night went to see the President on behalf of Mrs Fitz, a loyal widow of Mississippi owning a cotton plantation there, and from whom the U S Army had taken all her slaves amounting to 47, and 10,000 bushels of corn—She is now a refugee in St Louis, reduced to indigence She asks no compensation for her slaves, but wishes the government to give her a sufficient number of negroes out of those accumulated upon its hands to work her farm the ensuing season, and enable her to raise a crop of cotton, she to pay them out of the proceeds the same wages which the government pays those it employs. I made the proposition to the President thinking it reasonable and just, and worthy at least of being considered.

He became very much excited, and did not discuss the proposition at all, but said with great vehemence he had rather take a rope and hang himself than to do it. That there were a great many poor women who had never had any property at all who were suffering as much as Mrs Fitz—that her condition was a necessary consequence of the rebellion, and that the government could not make good the losses occasioned by rebels. I reminded him that she was loyal, and that her property had been taken from her by her own government, and was now being used by it, and I thought it a case eminently proper for some sort of remuneration, and her demand reasonable, and certainly entitled to respectful consideration. He replied that she had lost no property—that her slaves were free when they were taken, and that she was entitled to no compensation.

I called his attention to the fact that a portion of her slaves, at least, had been taken in 1862, before his proclamation, and put upon our gun boats, when he replied in a very excited manner that he had rather throw up, than to do what was asked, and would not do anything about it. I left him in no very good humor.

All the numerous past incidents of trust, affection and benefits bestowed on him did not bring out Browning in favor of Lincoln for President. He said nothing for or against a second term for Lincoln. To that extent Browning helped the McClellan ticket and cause.

Unionist serenaders from Baltimore arrived at the White House in late October, and facing them, Lincoln made reference to Democratic newspaper clamor that the Lincoln administration aimed to keep its power whatever the verdict at the polls in November. Lincoln told the serenaders that in contrast "others regard the fact that the Chicago Convention adjourned, not *sine die*, but to meet again, if called to do so by a particular individual, as the intimation of a purpose that if their nominee shall be elected, he will at once seize control of the government." He hoped the people would suffer no uneasiness on either point, delivering himself of momentous words:

"I am struggling to maintain government, not to overthrow it. I am struggling especially to prevent others from overthrowing it. I therefore say, that if I shall live, I shall remain President until the fourth of next March; and that whoever shall be constitutionally elected therefor in November, shall be duly installed as President on the fourth of March; and that in the interval I shall do my utmost that whoever is to hold the helm for the next voyage, shall start with the best possible chance to save the ship. This is due to the people both on principle, and under the constitution . . .

"I may add that in this purpose to save the country and it's liberties, no classes of people seem so nearly unanamous as the soldiers in the field and the seamen afloat. Do they not have the hardest of it? Who should quail while they do not? God bless the soldiers and seamen, with all their brave commanders."

A call signed by eminent and influential Democrats of the past endorsed the Lincoln-Johnson ticket. The call asked what kind of a Democratic party it was that excluded John A. Dix, Alexander T. Stewart, Theodore Roosevelt, Sr., R. B. Roosevelt, Peter Cooper, John A. Logan, John M. Palmer and many others who till now had had no political home except the Democratic party. "If these men are not Democrats, who are?"

"Should the soldier in the field have the right to vote in elections?" Two Union party pamphlets called the roll on the various states. *Harper's Weekly* summarized the points. In New York the Union men passed a soldier-vote bill by 65 Yeas to 59 Copperhead Nays; Governor Seymour vetoed the bill, but the Unionists went over his head and against prolonged Copperhead opposition procured a soldier-vote amendment to the state constitution. In New Hampshire the law passed the legislature by 175 to 105. In Rhode Island, Connecticut, Maine, Michigan, Ohio and other states the only opposition was from McClellan-for-President men. In New Jersey 31 Copperhead Nays against 19 Union Yeas defeated the soldier vote, and likewise in Delaware. In Michigan the soldiers in the field were accorded the ballot over the opposition of the "Detroit *Free Press* and the entire Copperhead press." In California, Iowa, Minnesota and Missouri it was Union men against Copperheads that won the soldier's right to vote. In Indiana a Copperhead legislature naturally refused it. In Ohio in the October election, out of 55,000 soldier votes a majority of 48,000 were for the Union party candidates.

In more than one case officious army politicians refused a pass, previously promised, to a soldier wearing a McClellan campaign badge. Friends of one such soldier brought his case before Lincoln, who investigated, sent for the soldier, and then handed him a pass in the President's own handwriting along with a handshake and "God bless you, my boy. Show them that. It'll take you home."

The draft meanwhile proceeded. The relentless dragnet moved. Grant and Sherman wanted men. "Leading Republicans all over the country," noted Nicolay and Hay, "fearing the effect of the draft upon the elections, begged the President to withdraw the call or suspend operations under it." Cameron advised against it in Pennsylvania. Chase telegraphed from Ohio urging a three weeks' suspension. To an Ohio committee earnestly requesting suspension until after the November elections, Lincoln quietly answered, "What is the Presidency worth to me if I have no country?"

Twice came Governor Morton of Indiana, whose soldiers could not vote in the field, applying for the return of all Indiana soldiers possible on Election Day. And at Lincoln's refusal to go over the heads of his generals and order the soldiers home to vote, it was suggested that if Indiana went Democratic she could give no more help to the Government. Lincoln met this point: "It is better that we should both be beaten than that the forces in front of the enemy should be weakened and perhaps defeated on account of the absence of these men." Morton suggested that no Indiana troops be kept in hospitals outside his state and that all troops unfit for service be sent home. On these points Lincoln got action. And Stanton had Lincoln's approval in ordering home from Sherman's army for campaigning in Indiana six prominent Hoosier officers, along with Major Generals Logan and Frank Blair to stump Indiana and nearby states. In fact, Logan later wrote to Sherman that "when I left on leave after the Atlanta campaign, to canvass for Mr. Lincoln, I did it at the special and private request of the President. This I kept to myself and never made it public."

"There was a constant succession of telegrams from all parts of the country," wrote Dana of the War Office, "requesting that leave of absence be extended to this or that officer, in order that his district at home might have the benefit of his vote and political influence. Furloughs were asked for private soldiers whose presence in close districts was deemed of especial importance, and there was a widespread demand that men on detached service and convalescents in hospitals be sent home. All the power and influence of the War Department, then something enormous from the vast expenditure and extensive relations of the war, was employed to secure the re-election of Mr. Lincoln. The political struggle was most intense, and the interest taken in it, both in the White House and in the War Department, was almost painful."

Along the Canadian border and the shore lines of the Great Lakes there were in the summer and fall of '64 plots, adventures, explosions, robberies, espionage, propaganda. From the dwindling hoard of Confederate gold, Jacob Thompson of Mississippi, formerly Secretary of the Interior under Buchanan, passed money to Sons of Liberty for armed revolts to be started in various states. "Lincoln had the power and would certainly use it to reëlect himself," wrote Thompson later in a report to Judah P. Benjamin at Richmond, "and there was no hope but in force. The belief was entertained and freely expressed, that by a bold, vigorous and concerted movement . . . Illinois, Indiana, and Ohio could be seized and held." Plans were laid in detail for a general uprising on an appointed day, seizure of arsenals at Indianapolis, Springfield, Chicago and Columbus, release of Confederate prisoners at four camps, arming of prisoners, overthrow of the state governments in Ohio, Indiana, Illinois, Missouri, formation of a Northwestern Confederacy. Then they would dictate peace.

The uprising collapsed. The Confederate operations from Canada annoyed the North but they were more noisy than effective. Thompson, who was Jeff Davis' personal choice for the work of embroiling the Northwestern States in an uprising, lacked the required touch; he moved at cost and found the result was a rubber dagger limp on the hide of a rhinoceros.

Again Sheridan, his men and horses, were heard from. When the hour cried for it Sheridan had the genius of a daredevil who could make other men in the mass want to be daredevils. At ten o'clock the night of October 19 Sheridan telegraphed Grant: "My army at Cedar Creek was attacked this morning before daylight, and . . . in fact, most of the line . . . driven in confusion with the loss of twenty pieces of artillery. I hastened from Winchester, where I was on my return from Washington, and found the armies between Middletown and Newtown, having been driven back about four miles. I here took the affair in hand . . . formed a compact line of battle, just in time to repulse an attack of the enemy, which was handsomely done at about 1 P.M. At 3 P.M., after some changes of the cavalry from the left to the right flank, I attacked, with great vigor, driving and routing the enemy, capturing, according to the last report, forty-three pieces of artillery, and very many prisoners . . . Affairs at times looked badly, but by the gallantry of our brave officers and men disaster has been converted into a splendid victory."

Lincoln telegraphed Sheridan October 22: "With great pleasure I tender to you and your brave army, the thanks of the Nation, and my own personal admiration and gratitude, for the month's operations in the Shenandoah Valley; and especially for the splendid work of October 19, 1864."

Twenty days before the November elections Sheridan gave the North one of the most dramatic victories of the war, following a methodical devastation of the Shenandoah Valley, with the result soon to come that his own army and the shattered forces of Early would be transferred to operations before Richmond. From innumerable platforms of the North were recited the verses of "Sheridan's Ride" by Thomas Buchanan Read. As a campaign tract it was fetching. As he heard this piece many and many a time Sheridan said he believed that what people liked best in the poem was the horse.

Soon now, on November 8, the American electorate would choose between Lincoln and the Baltimore platform and McClellan and the Chicago platform as revised by McClellan. That day of ballots would fix a momentous decision in the life of the American people.

CHAPTER 50

Lincoln's Laughter—and His Religion

LINCOLN was the first true humorist to occupy the White House. No other President of the United States had come to be identified, for good or bad, with a relish for the comic. This had brought him to folk masses as a living man they could feel and picture. The *Saturday Review* of London said: "One advantage which the Americans now have in national joking is the possession of a President who is not only the First Magistrate, but the Chief Joker, of the land. Collections of American jests are advertised as containing 'Mr. Lincoln's latest jokes,' and some of his stories are certainly good . . . The Puritan familiarity without intention of irreverence we have in the camp story of the Colonel (reprinted in all American papers), who, hearing from his Baptist chaplain that there had been ten conversions in a rival regiment, exclaimed, 'Do you say so? Sergeant Jones! detail fifteen men of my regiment for immediate baptism.' "

Before Lincoln's renomination at Baltimore the New York *Herald* did its best to attach infamy to Lincoln as a jester, "a joke incarnated, his election a very sorry joke, and the idea that such a man as he should be the President of such a country as this a very ridiculous joke."

In one little mock biography, originally intended to wrap up Lincoln as entirely ridiculous, a genius of nonsense let himself go: "Mr. Lincoln stands six feet twelve in his socks, which he changes once every ten days. His anatomy is composed mostly of bones, and when walking he resembles the offspring of a happy marriage between a derrick and a windmill. When speaking he reminds one of the old signal-telegraph that used to stand on Staten Island. His head is shaped something like a rutabago, and his complexion is that of a Saratoga trunk. His hands and feet are plenty large enough, and in society he has the air of having too many of them. The glove-makers have not yet had time to construct gloves that will fit him. In his habits he is by no means foppish, though he brushes his hair sometimes, and is said to wash. He swears fluently. A strict temperance man himself, he does not object to another man's being pretty drunk, especially when he is about to make a bargain with him. He is fond of fried liver and onions, and is a member of the church. He can hardly be called handsome, though he is certainly much better looking since he had the small-pox."

An Illinois cavalry colonel, John F. Farnsworth, quoted Lincoln on his storytelling: "Some of the stories are not so nice as they might be, but I tell you the truth when I say that a funny story, if it has the element of genuine wit, has the same effect on me that I suppose a good square drink of whiskey has on an old toper; it puts new life into me." Lamon said the President used stories as a laugh cure for a drooping friend or for his own

Lincoln telling little stories in camp

Lincoln writing his letter of acceptance

Lincoln assuming command of
the Army and Navy

Lincoln splitting rails in Sangamon

Drawings from a campaign comic life of Lincoln

melancholy, yet also to clinch an argument, to lay bare a fallacy, to disarm an antagonist, but most often the stories were "labor-saving contrivances."

"I am glad to take the hand of the man, who, with the help of Almighty God will put down this rebellion," said an earnest citizen in line at a reception. The answer flashed, "You are more than half right, sir." To one asking whether the town of Lincoln, Illinois, was named after him, Lincoln said: "Well, it was named after I was."

Perhaps one-sixth of the stories credited to him were old acquaintances, Lincoln told Noah Brooks. The other five-sixths came from other and better storytellers than himself. "I remember a good story when I hear it, but I never invented anything original. I am only a retail dealer."

Many yarns, anecdotes and puns credited to Lincoln were definitely inventions of others who took Lincoln as a handy peg on which to hang them. His own admitted stories might number a hundred, noted Nicolay. On the flyleaf of a replete book of *Anecdotes of Abraham Lincoln*, Isaac N. Arnold wrote that in his judgment about half were probably stories Lincoln had actually told.

Sometimes, noted Sumner, Lincoln insisted that he had "no invention, only a good memory" for anecdotes. And Sumner, it seemed, cultivated a manner of keeping some actual sense of humor hidden, or he could not have managed one of the best metaphors coined about the way Lincoln used stories to support argument. "His ideas moved," noted Sumner, "as the beasts entered Noah's ark, in pairs."

And of Lincoln's humor operating with iron and without anecdote, Sumner had an instance of the President saying to him of a political antagonist indifferent to slavery: "I suppose the institution of slavery really looks small to him. He is so put up by nature, that a lash upon his back would hurt him, but a lash upon anybody else's back does not hurt him." Fearful lashes on the back had been taken by Sumner, and any study of the relations of Lincoln and Sumner could not leave out Lincoln's awareness of the long-drawnout suffering Sumner had borne. Lincoln possibly even suspected what Sumner's best friend Longfellow had written in a diary, that the spinal lacerations from the cane of Preston Brooks had not left the brain unaffected.

In the telegraph office one evening Lincoln confessed to David Homer Bates that his storytelling was a habit formed in his younger days and his case was like that of an old colored man on a plantation, who let his work slide to preach to the other slaves. His master rebuked him, but the old man had the spirit of the gospel in him, kept on preaching, even when he knew the lash might be waiting for him. At last one day he was ordered to report at the Big House. There the master scolded, told him he would get hard punishment next time he was caught preaching. Tears came to his eyes:

"But, marsa, I jest cain't help it; I allus has to draw infrunces from de Bible textes when dey comes into my haid. Doesn't you, marsa?" "Well, uncle, I suspect I do something of that kind myself at times, but there is one text I never could understand, and if you can draw the right inference from it, I will cancel my order and let you preach to your heart's content." "What is de tex, marsa?" " 'The ass snuffeth up the east wind.' Now, uncle, what inference do you draw from such a text?" "Well, marsa, I's neber heerd dat tex' befo', but I 'spect de infrunce is she gotter snuff a long time befo' she git fat!"

Carpenter after his six months in the White House could not recollect a Lincoln story "which would have been out of place uttered in a ladies' drawing-room." Isaac N. Arnold endorsed this as his own observation of Lincoln over a 20-year period. These friends, however, were neither the crony familiars nor the bores and nuisances to whom Lincoln told his stories questioned as "not in good taste."

Lincoln's transition from mood to mood impressed Andrew D. White, educator and a member of the New York State senate. White saw Lincoln in the White House "dressed in a rather dusty suit of black," resembling "some rural tourist who had blundered into the place." Lincoln entered the room and approached White's group. He seemed, to White, "less at home there than any other person present" as he "looked about for an instant as if in doubt where he should go." Others had seen and written of the same thing. And White's impression recorded itself: "As he came toward us in a sort of awkward, perfunctory way his face seemed to me one of the saddest I had ever seen, and when he had reached us he held out his hand to the first stranger, then to the second and so on all with the air of a melancholy automaton. But suddenly someone in the company said something which amused him and instantly there came in his face a most marvelous transformation. I have never seen anything like it in any other human being. His features were lighted, his eyes radiant, he responded to sundry remarks humorously, then dryly, and thenceforward was cordial and hearty."

By mid-1863 several large editions of Lincoln joke books had been printed and sold. *Old Abe's Jokes—Fresh from Abraham's Bosom* ran the title of one and *Old Abe's Joker, or Wit at the White House* another. One page had a bad-tempered old fellow calling to a noisy boy, "What are you hollering for when I'm going by?" The boy: "What are you going by for when I'm hollering?" This had its parallels when one day Lincoln came into the telegraph office, found Major Eckert counting greenbacks, and Lincoln said it seemed the Major never came to the office any more except when he had money to count. Eckert said it was just a coincidence, but it reminded him of Mansfield, Ohio, where a certain tailor was very stylish in dress and airy in manner. A groceryman, seeing the tailor passing one day, puffed himself up and gave a long blow. The tailor snorted, "I'll learn you not to blow when I'm passing," the groceryman answering, "And I'll learn you not to pass when I'm blowing."

Lincoln found this very good—like the man in an open buggy caught at night on a country road in a heavy downpour of rain. He was hurrying to shelter, passing a farmhouse where a man somewhat drunk put his head out of a window and yelled, "Hullo! hullo!" The traveler stopped his buggy in the rain and asked what was wanted. "Nothing of you," came the voice at the window. "Well, what in the damnation do you yell hullo for when people are passing?" "Well, what in the damnation are you passing for when people are yelling hullo?"

Lincoln heard from Alexander Stephens when they were in Congress, and may have retailed, the incident of an undersized lawyer in an acrimonious stump debate with the massive Robert Toombs. Toombs called out, "Why, I could button your ears back and swallow you whole." The little fellow retorted, "And if you did, you would have more brains in your stomach than you ever had in your head."

A current quip was adapted as personal to the President. "I feel patriotic," said an old rowdy. "What do you mean by feeling patriotic?" inquired the President, standing by. "Why, I feel as if I wanted to kill somebody or steal something." Under the heading "Old Abe's Story of New Jersey"—politically more anti-Unionist than any other of the Northern States—was the tale of a shipwrecked sailor drifting toward land, where friendly hands flung him a rope. He took hold of the rope, asking, "What country is this?" and hearing "New Jersey" let go the rope and moaned, "I guess I'll float a little farther!" A man visiting a hospital in Washington noticed a soldier in one bed "laughing and talking about the President." The visitor was educated, drew fine distinctions, and said to the soldier, "You must be very slightly wounded." "Yes," said the soldier. "Very slightly—I have lost only one leg."

The joke books, with like published material, were giving a large mass of people an impression of a plain, neighborly, somewhat droll man, nobody's fool, at home to common folks. He could refer to a soprano voice so high that it had to be climbed over by a ladder or a German worried because "somebody tied my dog loose." A Boston man wished information. "You never swear, Mr. President, do you?" And Lincoln laughed, not loud but deep, the Bostonian noted. "Oh, I don't have to. You know I have Stanton in my Cabinet."

Grown-up men and women, even nations, at times were like the little girl Lincoln told Gustave Koerner about. She asked her mother if she could run out and play. The mother refused, and the girl begged harder, kept teasing till the mother gave her a whipping. When that was over the girl said, "Now, ma, I can surely run out and play."

A newly elected Congressman came in, Lincoln knowing him to have a sense of humor, for the gay greeting was: "Come in here and tell me what you know. It won't take long."

To illustrate a shifting political policy, Lincoln told of a farm boy whose father instructed him in plowing a new furrow. "Steer for that yoke of oxen standing at the further end of the field." The father went away. The boy followed instructions. But the oxen began moving. The boy followed them around the field, furrowed a circle instead of a line!

An ex-governor brought up the case of a woman named Betsy Ann Dougherty. "She did my washing for a long time. Her husband went off and joined the rebel army, and I wish you would give her a protection paper." Lamon was looking on, noted the President masked his humor and with inimitable gravity inquired, "Is Betsy Ann a good washer-woman?" She was indeed, said the ex-governor. "Is your Betsy Ann an obliging woman?" She was certainly very kind, the ex-governor responded soberly. "Could she do other things than wash?" the President asked without batting an eyelash. Oh, yes, she was very kind—very. "Where is Betsy Ann?" It came out she was in New York, wanted to come back to Missouri, but was afraid of banishment. "Is anybody meddling with her?" "No; but she is afraid to come back unless you give her a protection paper." Thereupon, noted Lamon, Lincoln turned to his desk and wrote on a card, which he signed: "Let Betsy Ann Dougherty alone as long as she behaves herself." Handing over the card, he said it should be given to Betsy Ann. "But, Mr. President, couldn't you write a few words to the officers that would insure her protection?" "No, officers have no time now to read letters. Tell Betsy Ann to put a string to this card and hang it around her neck. When the officers see this, they will keep their hands off your Betsy Ann."

Lamon gave this as an instance of Lincoln using "mirth-provoking trifles" out of the day's routine for relaxation. When the ex-governor, accompanied by a committee from Missouri, had left with his card for Betsy Ann, Lincoln had a laugh about it, and then, said Lamon, "relapsed into his accustomed melancholy, contemplative mood, as if looking for something else—looking for the end." He sat in thought for a time at the desk and turned to Lamon. "This case of our old friend, the governor, and his Betsy Ann, is a fair sample of the trifles I am constantly asked to give my attention to. I wish I had no more serious questions to deal with. If there were more Betsy Anns and fewer fellows like her husband, we should be better off. She seems to have laundered the governor to his full satisfaction, but I am sorry she didn't keep her husband washed cleaner."

During the Trent Affair Lincoln urged, "The less risk we run the better," and mentioned a recent battle where amid furious fire of shot and shell an officer drew his revolver and ordered a running soldier: "Go to the front with your regiment or I'll shoot you." The private yelled, "Shoot and be damned—what's one bullet to a whole hatful?!" Once when the interference of foreign nations with American affairs was under discussion, the President was quoted in a reminiscence of early Indiana days when he had called at a farmhouse overrun with children managed by a redheaded mother who kept a whip and made everyone come to time at her orders. "There's trouble here, and lots of it," she blurted, "but I kin manage my own affairs without the help of outsiders. This is jest a family row, but I'll teach these brats their places ef I have to lick the hide off every one of them. I don't do much talkin', but I run this house, an' I don't want no one sneakin' round tryin' to find out how I do it, either." Lincoln ended: "That's the case with us. We must let the other nations know that we propose to settle our family row in our own way."

At a mention of some persons' not capitalizing the name of the Deity, the President was reminded of a Confederate soldier's letter saying the Yankees would be licked in the next battle "if goddlemity spares our lives."

Brigadier General John Gross Barnard, chief engineer to the Army of the Potomac in the Peninsula campaign, told of the President asking General McClellan why such heavy embankments and gun emplacements had been located to the north of Washington. McClellan replied: "Why, Mr. President, if under any circumstances, however fortuitous, the enemy, by any chance or freak, should in a last resort get in behind Washington in his efforts to capture the city, why, there is the fort to defend it." The precaution, said the President, reminded him of a lyceum in Springfield. "The question was, 'Why does man have breasts?' and after long debate was submitted to the presiding judge who wisely decided 'that if under any circumstances, however fortuitous, or by any chance or freak, no matter what the nature or by what cause, a man should have a baby, there would be the breasts to nurse it.'"

One anecdote Nicolay heard in use by Lincoln was of a backwoods housewife in her messed-up log cabin, many ragtag children running around. A wandering Methodist preacher tried to sell her a Bible and she didn't like the way he pushed some questions. Shouldn't every home have a Bible? Did they have a Bible in this home? Her sharp answer came that of course they owned a Bible. If so, where was it? the man asked. She began a hunt, finding no Bible. She called the children and they joined in the hunt. At last one of them dug up from some corner and held up in triumph a few torn and ragged pages of Holy Writ. The man tried to argue this was no Bible, and how could they pretend it was? The woman stuck to her claims. Of course they had a Bible in the house. "But I had no idea we were so nearly out!"

The seizure early in the war of all copies of dispatches in the major telegraph offices of the country uncovered names, individuals, disloyalties, to an extent shocking. Lincoln told of an Illinois farmer who for years had prized and loved a soaring elm tree that spread its branches near his house. One day, the farmer saw a squirrel scurry up the giant elm's trunk and suddenly disappear in a hole. Looking farther, he found the great tree hollow, the whole inside rotten and ready to fall. The farmer moaned to his wife, "My God! I wish I had never seen that squirrel!" Lincoln pointed to the piles of telltale dispatches: "And I wish we had never seen what we have seen today."

Hay heard Lincoln tell of a conscript recruit unable to name his father, explaining, "Captain, sir, I guess I'm just a camp-meetin' baby." More long-spun was one Lincoln told Lamon, in connection with current turmoil between North and South. A man chased around a tree by a bull gained on the bull and got it by the tail. The bull pawed, snorted, broke into a run, the man after it still holding to the tail and bawling, "Darn you, who commenced this fuss?"

Governor Yates gave to the 10th Illinois Cavalry, according to the Chicago *Tribune* of February 4, 1864, a message brought by "my friend Bill Green of Menard County." Green before leaving Washington had asked, "Mr. Lincoln, what shall I say to the people of Illinois?" "Say to them," replied the President, "that I have Jeff Davis by the throat." And from the 10th Illinois Cavalry applause and cheers roared.

A California Republican, Cornelius Cole, called on business so tangled that it reminded Lincoln of a young Universalist preacher who came to Springfield. Three ministers of orthodox churches agreed "to take turns and preach this young fellow down." A Methodist preached the first sermon. "He commenced by telling his large congregation how happily they were all situated in Springfield. Launching into his sermon the Methodist shouted, 'And now comes a preacher preaching a doctrine that all men shall be saved. But, my brethren, let us hope for better things.' " This one Seward too had heard, repeating it as a sample of Lincoln humor.

Another caller told about a friend, early in the war, ordered out of New Orleans as a Unionist. He asked to see the writ by which he was expelled, and the Confederate committee told him their government was issuing no illegal writs, and he would have to get out of his own free will. Lincoln then told of a St. Louis hotelkeeper who claimed a record no one had ever died in his hotel. "Whenever a guest was dying in his house, he carried him out to die in the street."

A general was being outmaneuvered in West Virginia. At the high danger point Lincoln said the general was like a man out west who put his boy inside a barrel to hold up the head while the father pounded down the hoops. When the job was done the father saw he hadn't figured on how to get the boy out again. "Some people can succeed better in getting themselves and others corked up than in getting uncorked."

Of a Union and a Confederate army maneuvering as if they might soon be fighting, though not reaching the combat stage, Welles noted the President's remark they were like "two dogs that get less eager to fight the nearer they come to each other." Fears were telegraphed by Burnside's command, lost down in Tennessee and not heard of for some time. Lincoln told of Sally Ward on an Illinois farm with 14 children. Sometimes one of them got hurt and let out a loud cry somewhere in the cornfield or the timber. Then Sally Ward would sing out, "Thank Heaven there's one of my children that ain't dead yet."

Signing a brigadier general's commission for Napoleon Jackson Tecumseh Dana, Lincoln pronounced the name; it would "certainly frighten the enemy." Wishing to check a newspaper Biblical reference, Lincoln asked for a copy of the Bible. A polite offer to get a Bible came from Albert Johnson, Stanton's secretary, described by David Homer Bates as "a very obsequious, dapper little man." Johnson soon brought in and laid before the President a Bible. Lincoln looked up the reference he wanted. Johnson meantime had left the room. Then, according to Bates, Lincoln arose with a smile. "I am always interested in the movements of Johnson. Now let me show you how he did that." Then in mimicry, Lincoln took the Bible in his hands, presented it in a very obsequious style to Major Eckert and said, "That is the way Johnson did that." This, noted Bates, created a laugh among those looking on. An odd little functionary, a curious and incessant yes-man to Stanton, Lincoln impersonated in a funny little errand with a Bible.

Lincoln's tough hide, or lack of fine sensibilities, in Donn Piatt's view, was traced tersely by the Wendell Phillips expression that Lincoln was "the white trash of the South spawned on Illinois." Educated men troubled themselves with attempts to reduce to simple points the shifting lights and glooms of the Lincoln personality.

Galusha Grow told of his taking a Pennsylvania infantry company to see the President, who stepped out of the White House, looked around, put his hand behind him. "When I get this handkerchief out of this coat-tail pocket I intend to shake hands with you boys!"

To illustrate the petty jealousies and bickerings among Congressmen and army generals, James M. Scovel said Lincoln told the story of two Illinois men, one Farmer Jones, a churchman gifted in prayer, the other Fiddler Simpkins, welcome at every country merry-making. At one prayer meeting Brother Jones made a wonderful prayer which touched the hearts of all. And Brother Simpkins felt called on to rise and say, "Brethring and sistring, I know that I can't make half as good a prayer as Brother Jones, but by the grace of God I *can* fiddle the shirt off of him."

"Can this man Lincoln *ever* be serious?" wrote Richard Henry Dana in a letter. For the President would tell, in the midst of tremendous efforts to draft a new army, of the boy under fire whose commanding officer called, "You are crying like a baby," getting the answer, "I knows it, Ginral. I wish I was a baby, and a gal-baby, too, and then I wouldn't have been conscripted."

The telegrapher Bates heard of Lincoln telling about a man going into an asylum and meeting a little old fellow who demanded a salute. "I am Julius Caesar." The salute was given, the man went on his errand, returned soon, and again the little fellow demanded a salute. "I am Napoleon Bonaparte." "Yes, Napoleon, but a while ago you told me you were Julius Caesar." "Yes, but that was by another mother!" And there was the man who asked a friend to lend him a clean boiled shirt, getting the answer, "I have only two shirts, the one I have just taken off, and the one I have just put on—which will you have?"

Lincoln heard the telegrapher Bates tell of a man who enters a theater just as the curtain goes up. So interested is the man in looking at what is happening on the stage that he puts his tall silk hat, open side up, on the seat next to him, without noticing a very stout woman who is nearsighted. She sits down. There is a crunching noise. The owner of the flattened hat reaches out for it as the stout woman rises. He looks at his hat, looks at her: "Madam, I could have told you my hat wouldn't fit you before you tried it on." Dozens of such stories in the repetitions came to be told as though these things had happened to Lincoln.

On the day after Fredericksburg the staunch old friend, Isaac N. Arnold, entered Lincoln's office, was asked to sit down. Lincoln then read from Artemus Ward. One spring he got "swampt in the exterior of New York State, one dark and stormy night, when the winds Blue pityusly, and I was forced to tie up with the Shakers." He knocked at a door. "A solum female, looking sumwhat like a last year's beanpole stuck into a long meal bag, axed me was I athurst and did I hunger? to which I urbanely ansered 'a few.'" That Lincoln should wish to read this nonsense while the ambulances were yet hauling thousands of wounded from the frozen mud flats of the Rappahannock River was amazing to Congressman Arnold. As he said afterward he was "shocked." He inquired, "Mr. President, is it possible that with the whole land bowed in sorrow and covered with a pall in the presence of yesterday's fearful reverse, you can indulge in such levity?" Then, Arnold said, the President threw down the Artemus Ward book, tears streamed down his cheeks, his physical frame quivered as he burst forth, "Mr. Arnold, if I could not get momentary respite from the crushing burden I am constantly carrying, my heart would break!" And with that pent-up cry let out, it came over Arnold that the laughter of Lincoln at times was a mask.

Possibly only a crony from the old Eighth Circuit could have called out the peculiar humor Leonard Swett met one gloomy day of the summer of '64. Grant was pounding toward Richmond, the ambulances groaned with their loads, hospitals filled beyond capacity. Men should be rushed to the front. This and much else Swett poured out to Lincoln, with a flood of suggestions on what should be done and immediately. "The President was sitting by an open window," noted Swett. "And as I paused, a bird lit upon a branch just outside and was twittering and singing joyously. Mr. Lincoln, imitating the bird, said: '*tweet, tweet, tweet;* isn't he singing sweetly?' I felt as if my legs had been cut from under me. I rose, took my hat, and said, 'I see the country is safer than I thought.' As I moved toward the door, Mr. Lincoln called out in his hearty, familiar way, 'Here, Swett, come back and sit down.' Then he went on: 'It is impossible for a man in my position not to have thought of all those things. Weeks ago every man capable of bearing arms was ordered to the front, and everything you suggested has been done.'"

Far and wide through newspaper reprints went an eyewitness account of Lincoln's pertinence, bordering on horseplay, during a spiritualist séance in the White House arranged by Mrs. Lincoln. Curiously enough there was little or no hostile comment on this procedure. It was one of a series of odd incidents that built up a portrait of an American in the White House who could be keen, possibly wise, amid the ludicrous, the shallow, the bottomless.

Though paper was costly in '64 and its newspaper size diminished, the

Charleston *Mercury* went on reprinting occasional Lincoln wit from Northern newspapers, one incident going far. A minister in a delegation meeting the President "hoped the Lord is on our side." The President: "I don't agree with you." There was amazement. The President continued: "I am not at all concerned about that, for we know that the Lord is always on the side of the right. But it is my constant anxiety and prayer that I and this nation should be on the Lord's side."

"Lincoln is called the American Aesop," said the New York *Herald*, November 21, 1863, a week later taking the liberty of inventing a comic insidious anecdote as from the President's mouth.

To run down all the suspicions, insinuations, inveracities, innuendoes, uttered against a man in his place, said Lincoln, "would be a perpetual flea hunt."

The foremost funnymen of the age, the leading American comics, understood Lincoln. They shaded their foolery and colored their jests as if in the White House was one of their own. Artemus Ward, Petroleum Vesuvius Nasby, Orpheus C. Kerr, Miles O'Reilly, the young burblers of the satirical weekly *Vanity Fair*, all wrote with a gay though covert affection for the President. And it came to them that the President was one of their faithful readers, seemed to believe they were important voices of democracy in a living republic.

Forty thousand copies had been sold of *Artemus Ward: His Book* published in May '62. The author, Charles Farrar Browne, was only 28 years old. Born in Waterford, Maine, his father was a justice of the peace, his mother of Puritan stock, the son writing, "I think we came from Jerusalem, for my mother's name was Levi, and we had a Moses and a Nathan in the family, but my poor brother's name was Cyrus so, perhaps, that makes us Persians." He learned typesetting on the Skowhegan *Clarion*. Drifting west as a tramp printer, Browne finally took a $12-a-week job as reporter on the Cleveland *Plain-Dealer*, going then to the staff of *Vanity Fair* in New York.

One Ward sketch "In Washington" had a mock interview with Lincoln:

I called on Abe. He received me kindly. I handed him my umbreller, and told him I'd have a check for it if he pleased. "That," sed he, "puts me in mind of a little story. There was a man out in our parts who was so mean that he took his wife's coffin out of the back winder for fear he would rub the paint off the doorway. Wall, about this time there was a man in a adjacent town who had a green cotton umbreller."

"Did it fit him well? Was it custom made? Was he measured for it?"

"Measured for what?" said Abe.

"The umbreller?"

"Wall, as I was sayin'," continnerd the President, treatin the interruption with apparent contempt, "this man sed he'd known that there umbreller ever since it was a parasol. Ha, ha, ha!"

"Yes," sed I, larfin in a respectful manner, "but what has this man with the umbreller to do with the man who took his wife's coffin out of the back winder?"

"To be sure," said Abe—"what was it? I must have got two stories mixed together, which puts me in mind of another lit——"

"Never mind, Your Excellency. I called to congratulate you on your career, which has been a honest and a good one—unscared and unmoved by Secesh in front of you and Abbolish at the back of you—each one of which is a little wuss than the other if possible!

"Tell E. Stanton that his boldness, honesty, and vigger merits all prase, but to keep his under-garmints on. E. Stanton has appeerently only one weakness, which it is, he can't allus keep his under-garmints from flyin up over his hed. I mean that he occasionally dances in a peck-measure, and he don't look graceful at it."

I took my departer. "Good bye, old sweetness!" sed Abe, shakin me cordgully by the hand.

"Adoo, my Prahayrie flower!" I replied, and made my exit. "Twenty-five thousand dollars a year and found," I soliloquised, as I walked down the street, "is putty good wages for a man with a modist appytite, but I reckon that it is wurth it to run the White House."

David R. Locke's letters dated at "Confederate X Roads which is in the State of Kentucky," had their signer, the Reverend Petroleum Vesuvius Nasby, set up as pastor of a church and a seeker of office. Lincoln kept a pamphlet of these Nasby letters in a desk drawer. Locke was a year older than Ward, and like Ward had been a tramp printer, learning to set type on the Cortland, New York, *Democrat*, serving on the Pittsburgh *Chronicle*, having a hand in running newspapers in Plymouth, Mansfield, Bucyrus and Bellefontaine, Ohio. In April '62, in a Findlay, Ohio, newspaper he ran the first of the Nasby letters, dating it at Wingert's Corners, a village in Crawford County where the citizens almost to a man were secessionists.

Fifteen Negroes had arrived at the place, "yesterday another arrove," and P. V. Nasby, alarmed, prepared resolutions: "Wareas, we vew with alarm the ackshun uv the President uv the U. S., in recommendin the immejit emansipashun uv the slaves uv our misgided Suthern brethrin, and his evident intenshun uv kolonizin on em in the North, and the heft on em in Wingert's Corners; and Wareas, Eny man hevin the intellect uv a brass-mounted jackass kin easily see that the 2 races want never intendid to live together; and Wareas, Bein in the magority, we kin do as we please and ez the nigger haint no vote he kant help hisself; therefore be it Resolved, That the crude, undeodorized Afrikin is a disgustin obgik. Resolved, That this Convenshun, when it hez its feet washed, smells sweeter nor the Afrikin in his normal condishun, and is there4 his sooperior."

One Nasby piece Lincoln carried a clipping of in his vest pocket and memorized. And Noah Brooks told of an evening at Soldiers' Home when visitors came and talk fell on freed slaves in the Border States. Lincoln stood before the fireplace and recited from the Wingert's Corners piece: "Arouse to wunst! Rally agin Conway! Rally agin Sweet! Rally agin Hegler's family! Rally agin the porter at the Reed House! Rally agin the cook at the Crook House! Rally agin the nigger widder in Vance's Addishun! Rally agin Missis Umstid! Rally agin Missis Umstid's children by her first husband! Rally agin Missis Umstid's children by her sekkund husband! Rally agin all the rest uv Missis Umstid's children! Rally agin the nigger that cum yisterday! Rally agin the saddle-culurd girl that yoost 2 be hear! Ameriky for white men!" Lincoln at intervals used to quote these mock rallying cries, said Brooks, long after other men had read and forgotten them.

Sometimes before reading aloud from the pamphlet of Nasby papers taken from his desk drawer, Lincoln made such remarks as one to Sumner, "For the genius to write these things, I would gladly give up my office," or as he told several officials and private citizens one evening, "I am going to write Petroleum to come down here, and I intend to tell him if he will communicate his talent to me, I will swap places with him." These javelins of horselaugh journalism Lincoln welcomed. They fought for his cause. It was not strange he got out of bed and paraded around the White House past midnight to find someone else awake to share his reading of Nasby.

Robert H. Newell, creator of Orpheus C. Kerr (Office Seeker), was under 30, of Scotch-Welsh stock, a New York City boy; his father was the inventor of a sewing machine that had won gold medals at the London and Vienna world expositions. While young Newell served as assistant editor of the New York *Sunday Mercury*, he wrote letters dated at Washington or in the field with the Army of the Potomac. He opened one with "not wishing to expire prematurely of inanity." On the face of them his sketches were an escape from inanity. Of the national capital he alleged: "The most interesting natural curiosity here, next to Secretary Welles' beard, is the office of the Secretary of the Interior. Covered with spider-webs, and clothed in the dust of ages, sit the Secretary and his clerks, like so many respectable mummies in a neglected pyramid."

While this humorist steadily upheld Lincoln and the Union cause, and directed ridicule at the South and the Copperheads, he also kept on with sarcasm and irony aimed at the pretenses and pomps of war, at showy military heroes, at loud-mouthed statesmen. Kerr burlesqued McClellan's careful instructions for the return of slaves to their owners, with the order: "If any nigger comes within the lines of the United States Army to give information, whatsomever, of the movements of the enemy, the aforesaid shall have his head knocked off, and be returned to his lawful owner, according to the groceries and provisions of the Fugitive Slave Ack."

In the month that Lincoln finally removed McClellan, Kerr argued that as the army had marched 15 miles in six weeks, they were going up steep hills and Lincoln had a choice of removing either the Blue Ridge or McClellan. To have removed the Blue Ridge would have been "construed into proof that the Honest Abe had yielded to the fiendish clamor of the crazy Abolitionists." Also it would occasion heartburnings among the Democrats. "Hence our Honest Abe has concluded to leave the Blue Ridge where it is, and remove the idolized General."

A letter of Kerr published in early '63 led off with a deep-toned psalm of praise to Lincoln: "Standing a head and shoulders above the other men in power, he is the object at which the capricious lightnings of the storm first strike; and were he a man of wax, instead of the grand old rock he is, there would be nothing left of him but a shapeless and inert mass of pliable material by this time. There are deep traces of the storm upon his countenance, but they are the sculpture of the tempest on a natural block of granite . . . Abused and misrepresented by his political foes, alternately cajoled and reproached by his other foes,—his political friends,—he still pursues the honest tenor of the obvious Right, and smiles at calumny. His good-nature is a lamp that never goes out, but burns, with a steady light, in the temple of his mortality . . ."

Hours of easy reading for two years prepared Lincoln's reply to General Meigs' query who this person Orpheus C. Kerr might be. "Why, have you not read those papers? They are in two volumes; any one who has not read them is a heathen." The Kerr papers were uneven and sporadic in production as compared with those of Nasby and Ward, this possibly resulting from his adventures in search of a wife. He married in September '61 the actress-poet Adah Isaacs Menken, who had divorced Alexander Isaacs Menken, a wealthy Cincinnati dry-goods merchant, her first husband, and John C. Heenan, a famous prize fighter, her second husband. Dazzling stage success in Baltimore after her marriage to Kerr brought her a gift of diamonds worth $1,500; she announced herself a secessionist, was arrested and released on parole, while her husband went merrily along writing for the Union. He sailed with her in July '63 to San Francisco, where she won the plaudits of a group including Mark Twain, Bret Harte, Artemus Ward, Joaquin Miller and others. Kerr in April '64 sailed with her from San Francisco down to the Isthmus. There she embarked for London, where her poetry and acting met higher praise than ever before—and her husband in New York never saw her again. While his beautiful and insatiably ambitious wife pursued her career, Kerr followed his bent toward nothing in particular. He would have been heartbroken except for the balance wheel that once enabled him to write, "Our President, my boy, has a tail for every emergency, as a rat-trap has an emergency for every tail."

Thus the three most eminent American comic writers favored Lincoln and generated good will and affection for him and his cause.

Two Quakeresses in a railway coach were overheard in a conversation: "I think Jefferson will succeed." "Why does thee think so?" "Because Jefferson is a praying man." "And so is Abraham a praying man." "Yes, but the Lord will think Abraham is joking."

This in newspapers added the information that Lincoln said it was the best story about himself he had "ever read in the papers." Lincoln let this story spread. Nevertheless his most deliberate public appearances and utterances encouraged no one to take him for a trifler. The series of photographs by Brady, Gardner and others without exception portrayed a man sober, solemn, grim.

Continuously Lincoln gave no definite impression that he belonged to any particular church or endorsed any special faith or doctrine. That he was a man of piety and of deep religious belief was conveyed to large numbers of people by unmistakable expressions in his speeches and messages. The President and his wife usually drove to the New York Avenue Presbyterian Church but sometimes walked, accompanied by a guard, arriving punctually and never delaying Dr. Gurley's opening of the services, wrote the guard Crook. The President and his wife would walk down the center aisle, and on the right take the eighth pew from the pulpit. During this proceeding, wrote Crook, "out of respect for the great office he occupied, those in the church when the President arrived would rise from their seats and remain standing."

The good, upright, usually well-tempered Fessenden, it was told over Washington, in a rage over some unjust distribution of patronage turned loose a flow of "intemperate language" on Lincoln one morning. Lincoln kept cool. The fury of his Maine friend spent itself. Lincoln inquired gently, "You are an Episcopalian, aren't you, Senator?" "Yes, sir. I belong to that church." "I thought so. You Episcopalians all swear alike. Seward is an Episcopalian. But Stanton is a Presbyterian. You ought to hear him swear." Then Lincoln went on telling about several varieties of profanity, and he and Fessenden settled down to an even-toned conversation.

The press in October '63 reported a call paid Lincoln by members of the Baltimore (Old School) Presbyterian Synod. The Moderator, the Reverend Dr. Septimus Tustin, said the synod wished as a body to pay their respects, and that each member "belonged to the Kingdom of God, and each was loyal to the Government." The President's reply, in the Associated Press report, read in part: "I have often wished that I was a more devout man than I am. Nevertheless, amid the greatest difficulties of my Administration, when I could not see any other resort, I would place my whole reliance in God, knowing that all would go well, and that He would decide for the right. I thank you, gentlemen, in the name of the religious bodies which you represent, and in the name of the Common Father, for this expression of your respect. I cannot say more."

To Methodist and Baptist delegations of ministers the President had spoken with rich praise. His speech one May day in '62 began: "I welcome here the representatives of the Evangelical Lutherans of the United States. I accept with gratitude their assurances of . . . sympathy and support . . . in an important crisis which involves, in my judgment, not only the civil and religious liberties of our own dear land, but in a large degree the civil and religious liberties of mankind in many countries and through many ages." That he had a creed of some religious faith, which he might be able to amplify in extenso if required, he would have them know by his closing statement to them: "I now humbly and reverently, in your presence, reiterate the acknowledgment of that dependence, not doubting that, if it shall please the Divine Being who determines the destinies of nations that this shall remain a united people, they will, humbly seeking the Divine guidance, make their prolonged national existence a source of new benefits to themselves and their successors, and to all classes and conditions of mankind."

Bishop Ames as chairman headed a large Methodist delegation that came to the White House in May '64 to present an address. The President read to them his reply:

In response to your address, allow me to attest the accuracy of it's historical statements; indorse the sentiments it expresses; and thank you, in the nation's name, for the sure promise it gives.

Nobly sustained as the government has been by all the churches, I would utter nothing which might, in the least, appear invidious against any. Yet, without this, it may fairly be said that the Methodist Episcopal Church, not less devoted than the best, is, by it's greater numbers, the most important of all. It is no fault in others that the Methodist Church sends more soldiers to the field, more nurses to the hospital, and more prayers to Heaven than any. God bless the Methodist Church—bless all the churches—and blessed be God, Who, in this our great trial, giveth us the churches.

After handshaking, the delegates took leave amid a general smile over one saying, "Mr. President, we all hope the country will rest in Abraham's bosom for the next four years."

In proclamations, in recommendations of thanksgiving or of fasting and prayer, in numerous references to God, Providence, the Almighty, the Common Father, sometimes having their meaning colored by special events or conditions, Lincoln had given the impression to a multitude that he might have a creed. At a later time a clergyman sought to formulate such a creed from Lincoln's own words, changing the text merely to the extent of transposing pronouns from plural to singular, making other slight modifications, and prefixing the words "I believe." These were parts of such a creed:

I believe in national humiliation, fasting, and prayer, in keeping a day holy to the Lord, devoted to the humble discharge of the religious duties proper to such a solemn occasion.

. . . I believe in Him whose will, not ours, should be done.

I believe the people of the United States, in the forms approved by their own consciences, should render the homage due to the Divine Majesty for the wonderful things He has done in the nation's behalf, and invoke the influence of His Holy Spirit to subdue anger.

. . . I believe in His eternal truth and justice.

I believe the will of God prevails; without Him all human reliance is vain; without the assistance of that Divine Being I cannot succeed; with that assistance I cannot fail.

I believe I am a humble instrument in the hands of our Heavenly Father; I desire that all my works and acts may be according to His will; and that it may be so, I give thanks to the Almighty and seek his Aid.

I believe in praise to Almighty God, the beneficent Creator and Ruler of the Universe.

Among steadfast loyal friends of Lincoln, keenly attuned to the Lincoln personality, was Jesse Fell who wrote it was a "well-known fact" that on religion "Mr. Lincoln seldom communicated to anyone his views." After free and familiar talks on religion, Fell had presented to Lincoln Channing's sermons, printed entire, and Fell wrote that Lincoln's beliefs were "derived from conversations with him at different times during a considerable period." Of those beliefs the scrupulous recorder, Jesse Fell, wrote:

On the innate depravity of man, the character and office of the great head of the Church, the Atonement, the infallibility of the written revelation, the performance of miracles, the nature and design of present and future rewards and punishments (as they are popularly called) and many other subjects, he held opinions utterly at variance with what are usually taught in the Church. I should say that his expressed views on these and kindred subjects were such as, in the estimation of most believers, would place him entirely outside the Christian pale. Yet to my mind, such was not the true position, since his principles and practices and the spirit of his whole life were of the very kind we universally agree to call Christian; and I think this conclusion is in no wise affected by the circumstance that he never attached himself to any religious society whatever.

His religious views were eminently practical and are summed up, as I think, in these two propositions: "the fatherhood of God, and the brotherhood of man." He fully believed in a superintending and overruling Providence that guides and controls the operations of the world, but maintained that law and order, not their violation or suspension, are the appointed means by which this Providence is exercised.

Noah Brooks, out of his close and continuous friendship with the President, wrote of "something touching in his childlike and simple reliance upon Divine aid," especially in extremities of fateful events. Then, "though prayer and reading of the Scriptures was his constant habit, he more earnestly than ever sought that strength which is promised when mortal help faileth." Brooks said Lincoln could quote whole chapters of Isaiah, and the New Testament and the Psalms were fixed in his memory. He would sometimes correct a misquotation of Scripture and give chapter and verse where it could be found. Once in regard to his own age and strength he quoted, "His eye was not dim, nor his natural force abated." He found meaning in the Scriptural phrase, "the stars in their courses fought against Sisera."

To Joshua Speed's mother the President sent a photograph of himself inscribed: "For Mrs. Lucy G. Speed, from whose pious hand I accepted the present of an Oxford Bible twenty years ago."

Months after the Battle of Fredericksburg came word of the Massachusetts soldier who had carried over his heart a pocket Bible that stopped and held a rifle ball. The President sent the boy another Bible, with a personal inscription.

Out of the Cold Harbor slaughter emerged Carter E. Prince of the 4th Maine Volunteers. A bullet hit his suspender buckle and carried it through the New Testament in the pocket of his blouse. Pushed by the bullet, the buckle went through all the chapters between Revelation and St. Mark and came to rest at Mark 12:36, where is recorded the saying of the Lord: "Sit thou on my right hand, till I make thine enemies thy footstool."

With such incidents, and with men who could speak at firsthand of them, Lincoln became familiar.

A distinct trend toward a deeper religious note, a piety more assured of itself because more definitely derived from inner and private growths of Lincoln himself, this could be seen as the President from year to year fitted himself more deeply and awarely into the mantle and authorities of Chief Magistrate.

To others besides Alexander H. Stephens, Lincoln had a "mystic" zeal for the Union cause. In one sense Lincoln saw himself as a crusader and a holiness preacher for an indissoluble unity of one common country. To the sacred devotions of his own cause he would join any others of capacity for sacred devotions.

He could not be impervious to the Reformed Presbyterian Church ("Scotch Covenanters"), through a committee in dark months of 1863, "by every consideration drawn from the Word of God" enjoining him "not to be moved from the path of duty on which you have so auspiciously entered, either by the threats or blandishments of the enemies of human progress." Nor could he have been unmoved by the New School Presbyterians in 1862 through their General Assembly sending word: "Since the day of your inauguration, the thousands of our membership have followed you with unceasing prayer, besieging the throne of Heaven in your behalf."

The German Reformed Synod, the Lutheran General Synod, the Moravian Synod, had passed resolutions of varied texts declaring themselves in favor of the war. In the autumn of '64 the Congregational churches of New York, New Jersey and Pennsylvania placed themselves squarely in favor of Lincoln's re-election through the declarations of their General Association: "Make the decision of the people on the 8th of November final and fatal to the hopes of traitors in arms and conspirators in political councils."

The Roman Catholic church was less demonstrative and vocal than the Protestants. But it was a Roman Catholic, General William S. Rosecrans, who had resisted the pressure of Greeley to place him at the head of the Union ticket instead of Lincoln. And General Rosecrans' brother, a Catholic bishop in Cincinnati, had continuously approved of Lincoln's progressive antislavery policy. Archbishop John Hughes, despite his tardiness of action during his illness while the New York antidraft riots raged, had kept in close touch with Secretary Seward and rendered important loyalist service. In the ranks and among the shoulder straps of the Union armies Catholics of several nationalities, and particularly the Irish, had records for gallant and distinguished service.

As a Chief Magistrate having a common bond with all of these faiths and churches that moved toward a national unity beyond any future breaking, Lincoln's piety was manifest. A blood fellowship of death and suffering moved him.

Answering a kindly letter from Rhode Island Quakers, Lincoln acknowledged that he expected no reputation as a peace man while up to his armpits in war blood. "Engaged as I am, in a great war, I fear it will be difficult for the world to understand how fully I appreciate the principles of peace inculcated in this letter and everywhere by the Society of Friends." That such true and perfect lovers of peace as the Quakers could send him from their Iowa organization, through Senator Harlan, an address voicing accord with him, was deeply moving.

According to an interview reported by the Iowa Congressman, James F. Wilson, in June '62, when Jeb Stuart had taken his gray horsemen in a circle around McClellan's army and cut the communications, Lincoln had remarked there was no news: "Not one word . . . I don't know that we have an army." One member of the delegation with which Wilson called urged a more resolute policy on slavery. "Slavery must be stricken down wherever it exists," this radical emphasized. "If we do not do right I believe God will let us go our own way to our ruin. But if we do right, I believe He will lead us safely out of this wilderness, crown our arms with victory, and restore our now disservered Union."

Wilson saw that this trend of speech affected the President deeply, and expected "from the play of his features and the sparkle of his eyes" there would be a response. The listless Lincoln slowly arose to full height, "his right arm outstretched towards the gentleman who had just ceased speaking, his face aglow like the face of a prophet," saying to his admonisher, "My faith is greater than yours," agreeing fully with what had been said of the role of God and Providence. Then he proceeded: "But I also believe He will compel us to do right in order that He may do these things, not so much because we desire them as that they accord with His plans of dealing with this nation, in the midst of which He means to establish justice. I think He means that we shall do more than we have yet done in furtherance of His plans, and He will open the way for our doing it. I have felt His hand upon me in great trials and submitted to His guidance, and I trust that as He shall further open the way I will be ready to walk therein, relying on His help and trusting in His goodness and wisdom."

Wilson added that Lincoln, with his dejection gone, resumed his seat and in a reassured tone continued. "Sometimes it seems necessary that we should be confronted with perils which threaten us with disaster in order that we may not get puffed up and forget Him who has much work for us yet to do."

John W. Widney of Piqua, Ohio, a sergeant wounded at the Wilderness, starting a furlough home for complete recovery before return to duty, saw Lincoln on the White House walk from the War Office, "dressed in black, with frock coat, stove-pipe hat, walking slowly, shoulders bent forward, hands folded behind his back." Lincoln asked the Sergeant, "What State and regiment?" Widney answered, and Lincoln, with a "God bless you and I hope you will get home safe," passed into the White House while Widney stood gazing and feeling a "burden of sorrow" on the shoulders under the stovepipe hat. Widney was a churchman who favored his Bible and said that no other words fitted the moment for him like those of (to use his words) an old prophet: "O Jerusalem, Jerusalem, how often would I have gathered thee beneath my wings, as a hen gathers her chicks, but ye would not."

CHAPTER 51

The Pardoner

IN, THROUGH and around the city of Washington moved the signs of human storm. Out of the storm and into the White House over its heavy carpets and past the tall mirrors came the spick-and-span, the dustily ragged and worn. Before Lincoln's eyes the drama surged in lines and waves, and his mood varied from telling a man, "The only thing to do is to keep pegging away," and once murmuring half-dreamily to a Michigan woman: "I'm a tired man. Sometimes I'm the tiredest man on earth."

The city and suburbs, all the main streets, in latter '64 swarmed with soldiers, "more than ever before," wrote Walt Whitman in his journal. Blue pants and coats were everywhere. "The clump of crutches is heard up the stairs of the paymasters' offices, groups often waiting long and wearily in the cold. Furloughed men, singly, in small squads, make their way to the Baltimore depot. Patrol detachments move around, examining passes, arresting all soldiers without them. They do not question the one-legged, or men badly disabled or maimed, but all others are stopt." Of a large brick mansion on the banks of the Rappahannock, used as a hospital during a battle, Whitman had noted, "Out doors, at the foot of a tree, within ten yards of the front of the house, I notice a heap of amputated feet, legs, arms, hands, &tc., a full load for a one-horse cart."

The city of Washington seemed to be one immense hospital. The inadequate and cruder equipment of the earlier war years had grown into a vast establishment, much of it still temporary and improvised. Churches, private homes and government buildings were commandeered. Board barracks and white army tents met the eyes of the President on almost any walk or ride around the city.

Late in October '64 Whitman wrote of seeing squads of Union Army deserters, over 300 of them, marching between armed guards along Pennsylvania Avenue, "all sorts of rigs, all sorts of hats and caps, many fine-looking young fellows, some shame-faced, some sickly, most of them dirty, shirts very dirty and long worn, &c . . . (I hear that desertions from the army now in the field have often averaged 10,000 a month)."

The timebeat of the war went on, bluecoat streams pouring south, miles of men and boots, leather, hardtack, tents, steel, lead, powder, guns. As miles of wagon supplies, mountains of hardtack, were used up, more and more poured south. And moving north, flung back out of the muddy and bloody recoils, came stragglers, deserters, bounty-jumpers, the furloughed, the sick and wounded—while beyond the battle fronts toward the south, living skeletons in prison offered prayers that the timebeat of the war would end, that the sad music of rifle volleys and cannonading guns would close over in some sweet silence.

At one crowded White House reception, when so many people pressed into the room that handshaking had to be dispensed with, Lincoln stood bowing acknowledgments. Then his eyes fell on a soldier, pale, crippled, moving through with a plainly dressed mother. Before they could get to the door Lincoln made his way to them, took each by the hand, told them he was interested they had come, and he could not let them go without his welcome. He said to young Henry E. Wing, the New York *Tribune* cub who scouted among many regiments and reported to the President on the rank-and-file feeling in the armies, "I would rather be defeated with the soldier vote behind me than to be elected without it."

The number of soldiers who felt they had met Lincoln personally, now in latter '64, ran into many thousands. At reviews he had dismounted from his horse, walked along the company lines, shaken hands with soldiers in the front rank and reaching through to the rear file, and spoken such words as, "Glad to see you looking so well, boys, glad to meet you."

The flimsy excuses some brought him, hoping for a furlough, the good and valid reasons others had—these too he knew. Out of the hospitals from fevers and amputations they came to the White House, some shaken, palsied, dumb, blind.

Widows and mothers who had lost husbands and sons in the war numbered more than 150,000 in February '64, according to claims filed in the Pension Office. Not often was the President troubled by claimants in connection with the dead. But those with petitions in behalf of the living came every hour of the day. And many of the living were young. The war was being fought by the young. Not yet voters, all of them under 21, were some 30 per cent of the troops in the U.S. armies. Another 30 per cent were 21 to 24. Still another 30 per cent were from 25 to 30, leaving only 10 per cent over 30.

A cadaverous young man, white of face, his clothes hanging loose, was given a chair. He talked for half an hour about himself and army conditions, under Lincoln's questioning. The 40 pieces of bone that had oozed out from his shoulder wound, were laid out on a desk and examined. On his original commission as lieutenant the President wrote an endorsement. When this was presented next morning to the officer having power to act, the officer looked disturbed, finally said, "This seems peremptory in its terms," and issued an order for back pay due and too long refused. After a furlough the young lieutenant returned to service and within a year stepped in to say thanks for a commission as captain, and to show Lincoln he was now plump, erect and hoping he looked every inch a soldier, even though 40 pieces of bone were lacking from one shoulder.

Major C. J. Stohlbrand walked in one day and handed Lincoln "important dispatches" from General Sherman. A Swedish-blooded citizen from the West, he had volunteered at Lincoln's first call in '61 and served continuously, at times in field emergencies acting as colonel or brigadier general. No promotions coming, he was leaving the service. Sherman didn't want to lose his Major Stohlbrand, asked him to go home by way of Washington and hand some "important dispatches" to the President. Lincoln opened the sealed papers, read them and put out his hand. "How do you do, General?" Stohlbrand corrected, "I am no general; I am only a major." Laughed Lincoln: "You are mistaken. You are a general." And in a few hours, with his commission signed by Lincoln, Stohlbrand was on his way back to Sherman's army.

Old Jim Conner of Miami County, Indiana, arrived home from a long trip to tell what had happened to him. His four sons and some neighbor boys were with the Army of the Potomac and he had gone with his Congressman to ask Stanton for a pass to see the boys. Stanton said No, and soon Old Jim and the Congressman were seeing Lincoln, Conner crying, "My God! I'll never go back home to face those women." The President thought it over, and then: "Conner, I can't overrule Stanton, but I need a special commissioner to go among the rank and file of the army to find out what the soldiers of this country think of the government in its greatest crisis. Conner, will you be a special commissioner?"

In a voice of high rage a crippled private near the War Office was cursing out the Government from the President down, just as Lincoln happened along and asked what was the matter. "I want my money. I've been discharged here and can't get my pay." Lincoln told the private he used to practice law and maybe could help. Lincoln sat down at the foot of the tree, ran over the papers handed him, wrote a notation on the back of one and told the private to take them to Chief Clerk Potts of the War Department. Lincoln walked on, and A. W. Swann of Albuquerque, New Mexico, who had been looking on, asked the private if he knew who he had been talking with. "Some ugly old fellow who pretends to be a lawyer," was the guess. Then Swann went with the private, saw him get the money due him, saw him stand sort of puzzled as to whether he ought to be glad or sorry he had cursed the President to his face.

An earnest Republican of proved deeds asked that his son be appointed an army paymaster. How old was the son? "He is twenty—well, nearly twenty-one." "Nearly twenty-one! I wouldn't appoint the angel Gabriel a paymaster if he wasn't twenty-one!"

A 14-year-old who had run away from his Kansas home and enlisted began crying as he read a note Lincoln wrote for him to carry to Stanton. The boy had expected he would be shot at sunrise. But instead he read words to this effect: "Hadn't we better spank this drummer boy and send him back home to Leavenworth?" Lincoln sent the lad to a hotel and arranged for his ticket home.

"The boy is not going to be *shot*," Congressman Kellogg cried at a refusal from Stanton, near midnight, the execution set for sunrise. Kellogg went to the White House, broke down the refusals of the guards, reached the room where the President lay in bed, and cried: "This man must not be shot. I can't help what he may have done. Why, he is an old neighbor of mine; I can't allow him to be shot!" Lincoln stayed in bed, listened quietly to the pleas of a man he had known many years, then slowly: "Well, I don't believe *shooting* will do him any good. Give me that pen."

To his desk, to the tents of his generals in the field, came the appeals of valorous fighters found guilty of drunkenness, looting, of being absent without leave, of many varieties of insolence or disobedience. Lincoln's view joined that of Sherman regarding some of his 8th Missouri lawbreakers. "Their conduct for courage under my own eye was such that I would have pardoned them for anything short of high treason."

Press accounts told of an army surgeon court-martialed and his attorney bringing the papers to Lincoln, who read the indictment of "drunkenness," commenting, "That's bad, very bad," and further along as to "insulting a lady": "That's bad, too. An officer shouldn't insult a lady, by any means."

Lincoln read further the specifications regarding an attempt to kiss a lady, scratched his head, looked up to the attorney. "Really, I don't know about this. There are exceptions to every rule but as a general thing it's very hard to insult a lady by kissing her. But it seems the doctor only *attempted* to kiss her—perhaps the insult consisted in his not fully succeeding. I don't know as I ought to interfere in behalf of a man who attempts to kiss a lady and doesn't do it."

The attorney urged that a third party had made the complaint, with no evidence that the lady herself felt insulted. "That's a fact," said the President. "We can easily dispose of the kissing part. But I must look into the drunkenness a little. I can't overlook that. I'll have to get good evidence that it was strictly a New Year's offence, and is not a common occurrence with the doctor." He took the case under advisement.

Lincoln took a deep interest in James Madison Cutts, a brother of the second wife of Senator Douglas and secretary to Douglas through all the hard campaigning of 1860. After graduation at 24 from Harvard Law School, Cutts had gone west, stood at the bedside of the dying Douglas, then enlisted as a private in the Union Army. In May '61, Cutts had presented to Lincoln a letter of recommendation from Douglas and Lincoln had appointed him a captain in the Regular Army. While a staff officer under Burnside, Cutts wrote two letters to the President pouring out hate of Burnside's highhanded methods. For this and another offense a court-martial had found Cutts guilty of conduct unbecoming to an officer and gentleman. He had been caught in a hotel hallway standing on a valise looking through a transom at a woman undressing. The President had approved the findings of the court-martial but changed the sentence of dismissal from the Army to a reprimand. Lincoln wrote that he would not "add a pang to what you have already suffered," and then as father to son:

You were convicted of two offences. One of them, not of great enormity, and yet greatly to be avoided [the hotel hallway affair], I feel sure you are in no danger of repeating. The other [insubordination] you are not so well assured against . . . No man resolved to make the most of himself, can spare time for personal contention. Still less can he afford to take all the consequences, including the vitiating of his temper, and the loss of self-control. Yield larger things to which you can show no more than equal right; and yield lesser ones, though clearly your own. Better give your path to a dog, than be bitten by him in contesting for the right. Even killing the dog would not cure the bite.

In the mood indicated deal henceforth with your fellow men, and especially with your brother officers; and even the unpleasant events you are passing from will not have been profitless to you.

In a sense the reprimand was a quiet portrait of Lincoln himself. Captain Cutts took it and in the forefront as a field officer under Grant earned an award, the "Medal of Honor of the United States." For three distinct acts of extraordinary bravery, his triple medal read: "For gallantry at Wilderness, Spotsylvania, and Petersburg, 1864." Among those proud of it was the widowed sister, Adèle Cutts Douglas.

In April '64 came a letter from a Quaker girl in Washington County, Pennsylvania, giving "a brief history connected with myself and would be husband." They had been engaged for some years. In August '62 he enlisted for three years. In October '63 he was furloughed to go home and vote. "It was our design to marry while he was at home and under those determinations we very foolishly indulged too freely in matrimonial affairs . . ." She named the father of her unborn child, a private in the 140th Pennsylvania Volunteers with the Army of the Potomac. Word had come from him that army orders forbade soldiers writing furlough-begging letters to those higher up. Therefore she wrote to the President. On the back of her letter Lincoln wrote April 14, 1864, to the Secretary of War: "Send him to her by all means."

David R. Locke, on the second of the only two calls he paid Lincoln in Washington, asked a pardon for an Ohio deserter who had enlisted and kissed good-by to a girl he was engaged to marry. She would be true to her hero who had marched away to war. So he believed. Then rumors came to him. A rival she had rejected, a rival he hated, was keeping company with her. She was pretty. She liked company. What was happening? While he was at the battle fronts perhaps the hated rival would win her. He applied for a furlough. It was refused him. Reckless and half-crazy, he deserted, went home, found the rumors partly true, but he had come in time. He married the girl. Then came his arrest, trial and sentence to be shot. "I stated the circumstances, giving the young fellow a good character," wrote the creator of Petroleum V. Nasby, "and the President at once signed a pardon."

With the pardon went Lincoln's comment to Locke: "I want to punish the young man—probably in less than a year he will wish I had withheld the pardon. We can't tell, though. I suppose when I was a young man I should have done the same fool thing."

The same Duff or William Armstrong that Lincoln had helped clear of a murder charge, the son of Hannah and Jack Armstrong, himself explained his case: "The four brothers of us enlisted. Jim was wounded at Belmont. Pleasant died. I served on. Mother took a notion she wanted me. People laughed at her when she said she would write to the President, but she said, 'Please goodness, I am a-going to try it.' She got Squire Garber of Petersburg to write to 'Uncle Abe,' and in a few days mother got a telegram signed 'A. Lincoln,' telling her I had been honorably discharged. I was at Elmira, New York, helping pick up deserters, and a discharge was the last thing I dreamed of."

In the chronicle of Confederate spies saved from death by Lincoln was Lieutenant Samuel B. Davis of Delaware, son of a Presbyterian minister, 24 years old, tall, slender, handsome, dauntless, distant kin to Jefferson Davis, who sent him on a secret mission to Ohio. His hair dyed, traveling on a British passport with a false name, he was recognized by two Union soldiers who got on at Newark, Ohio, as an officer on duty when they were Confederate prisoners. In the main room of the Newark jail young Davis was seen to remove his coat, rip open the lining, take out dispatches and drawings penciled on white silk. These he burned at a stove around which other prisoners were gathered.

On trial, Davis pleaded "not guilty of being a spy" but "guilty of being a bearer of dispatches." The judge advocate argued that he had been found within the Union lines in disguise and under a false name at places where he could have obtained valuable information, whether he did or not. Lieutenant Davis proposed to show by testimony of President Davis and Secretary of State Judah P. Benjamin that he was sent as a bearer of dispatches. The court-martial refused a continuance of the trial for the purpose of getting such testimony. Young Davis made a speech. He faced, as he spoke, several haggard and battered Union veterans, some with empty sleeves. They were cold as he began. When he finished his short speech they were not so cold.

The day was set for his hanging on Johnson's Island near Sandusky, Ohio. Among those who asked Lincoln for suspension of sentence were William T. McClintick, president of the Cincinnati & Marietta Railroad, and Senator Saulsbury of Delaware, one of the most violent of Senate critics of Lincoln. Saulsbury wrote to Lincoln: "You know I am neither your personal nor political friend, but Senator Douglas once told me you were a kind-hearted man. Read the inclosed speech of this young officer condemned as a spy. There is nothing like it in history save Robert Emmet's. I ask you to act in this matter as the President of the United States should act."

How could Saulsbury, reputed the hardest drinker in the Senate, sometimes attending public sessions drunk, have guessed that such a note would hit where Lincoln was weak? Lincoln undoubtedly read more than once the little gem of a note from Saulsbury with its wonderfully sober dignity. Then he must have read more than once the little speech of Lieutenant Samuel B. Davis facing haggard and battered Union veterans: "I fear nothing on this earth. I do not fear to die. I am young and I would like to live, but I deem him unworthy who should ask pity of his foemen. Some of you have wounds and scars. I can show them, too. You are serving your country as best you may. I have done the same. I can look to God with a clear conscience, and whenever the Chief Magistrate of this nation shall say 'Go,' whether upon the scaffold or by the bullets of your soldiery, I will show you how to die."

The day set for the hanging drew near. Lieutenant Davis wrote to Major Lewis H. Bond: "The court of which you are the judge-advocate having sentenced me to be hung, at least grant the request of one whose days are numbered. I desire that, if possible, one or more members of the court will come and witness my execution. Take this as the request of one who is about to be launched into eternity. Come and see it done, and you shall at least have the satisfaction of knowing that you hung a brave man. Be kind enough to answer this hasty note. It is not written through disrespect, but for the reason I have already assigned." Judge Advocate Bond wrote that he would be there with regret and sadness, that "by your manly conduct and heroic bearing under the most trying circumstances, you have won the respect and excited the admiration of your foemen."

The evening before the hanging date the scaffold lumber, the rope, had been tested, and the headquarters commandant at Johnson's Island had gone to bed expecting first thing in the morning to witness the neck of young Davis broken in due process of law. A pounding at the door woke the commandant from his sleep. A messenger handed him an order from the President directing that the execution be suspended and the prisoner sent to Fort Warren. The grounds in international law for a death sentence were clear. But Lincoln held international law not always applicable to a civil war where hope was nursed of reconciliations to come.

Dr. David M. Wright, a reputable citizen of Norfolk, Virginia, tried by a military commission, was sentenced to be hanged for murder. Judge Advocate General Holt, on Lincoln's request, sent a transcript of the trial to the President, with an opinion that the deed was "undefended assassination." Petitioners surpassing in number those of any other pardon appeal during the war, it seemed, protested to Lincoln from the North, the South and Canada, with letters, telegrams, personal calls. "Do not let execution be done until my further order," Lincoln telegraphed Fortress Monroe.

A crying issue stood out. Up one of the main streets of Norfolk July 11, 1863, had marched a company of Negro troops. At their head was Anson L. Sanborn, a second lieutenant of the 1st U.S. Colored Troops. From the sidewalks came taunts and hoots. Among onlookers was Dr. Wright, a man of exceptional works and good character, widely known. He was suddenly in a clash with Lieutenant Sanborn, drew a revolver, shot the 20-year-old officer dead.

War Secretary Seddon at Richmond endorsed one petition with sympathy over the "natural indignation of Dr. Wright at the shameful spectacle [of Negro troops], and his prompt vindication of his honor." The daughter of Dr. Wright was permitted an extended visit alone with him in his prison cell. He walked out of the prison—in her clothes—beginning his escape. A Union officer in the street noticed his walk as "a masculine stride" and took Dr. Wright back to his cell.

On October 7 Lincoln had delayed execution nearly three months and wrote that no proper question remained open except as to the alleged insanity of the accused. On that point, including all evidence from counsel of the accused, a noted alienist wrote findings that Wright was not insane prior to the killing, "that he has not been insane since, and is not insane now." Therefore the President was directing that the sentence of death be carried into execution October 16. On pleas of one of Wright's attorneys Lincoln postponed execution to October 23, adding, "This is intended for his preparation and is final."

On October 17 the Fortress Monroe commandant telegraphed Lincoln that Dr. Wright's wife desired to visit Washington to intercede with the President for her husband's life. He replied: "It would be useless for Mrs. Dr. Wright to come here. The subject is a very painful one, but the case is settled."

The day before October 23, according to David Homer Bates, his office associate Richard O'Brien, "was approached by a man who said that if he would anticipate a telegram which was hourly expected from President Lincoln granting a reprieve, he would be paid $20,000 in gold, and would be given free passage to England on a blockade runner. O'Brien indignantly refused the bribe."

October 23 dawned. Hope had not died in some quarters that in the last hour a telegram from Lincoln might arrive. Hours passed. No Executive Mansion telegram came. At 11:20 in the morning word was put on the wires: "Dr. Wright was executed this morning." On the scaffold his last words came from tremulous lips: "Gentlemen, the act which I committed was done without the slightest malice."

A young Virginia woman whose family had long been familiars of the Blairs was brought to Lincoln by Old Man Blair. He had warned her beforehand; she was impulsive and must be careful not by any word to betray her Confederate sympathies. She wished a pass to visit her brother, a Confederate soldier and a prisoner in the Union lines. Her eyes flashed. She was a vivid presence. The President bent toward her, searched her face, and, "You are, of course, loyal?"

She hesitated a moment, met his gaze frankly, then, "Yes, loyal to the heart's core—to Virginia!" He kept his eyes on her face a moment longer, went to a desk, wrote a line or two and handed her a folded paper. She bowed herself out with Mr. Blair, who was saying: "Didn't I warn you to be very careful? You have only yourself to blame." She unfolded the paper and read words to this effect signed by the President: "Pass Miss —— ——; she is an honest girl and can be trusted."

Mrs. Thomas Theophilus Brown, her baby in her arms, came to the President September 7, 1863; she had been to the War Department and elsewhere, in fear and anxiety over her husband and his brother, taken prisoners at Gettysburg. Their home was in Alexandria, Virginia. Though they had fought with the Confederate Army, they were not spies. Yet they had been held for weeks in Old Capitol Prison and it was whispered would be shot as spies. Lincoln heard her through. She was crying when she finished. Her baby, however, was smiling and making eyes at Lincoln. Lincoln added to the confusion. He lifted the baby up in his arms and held her to his cheeks. The baby burbled, "Papa." Lincoln laughed, put the baby back in the mother's arms, walked to and fro a few times, then wrote a paper for Mrs. Brown to take to Stanton. At the door he said, "Mrs. Brown, you are a brave little woman." The paper she carried read in part: "This lady says . . . they were conscripted into the rebel army, and were never for the rebel cause, and are now willing to do anything reasonable to be at liberty. This may be true, and if true they should be liberated. Please take hold of the case, and do what may seem proper in it."

Official action for this woman was rapid. Having taken the oath of Union allegiance, three days later at the prison gates the two brothers walked out free men. And Mrs. Thomas Theophilus Brown kissed her ragged, shaggy husband, trembling with fever and nerves, his feet torn and scarred. She took him home to Alexandria and nursed him back to health, waiting till he was strong again before she dared to tell him of the man farther up the river, in the White House, who understood her language and heard their baby call him "Papa."

With the North squeezing the South toward its last loaf of bread and final bullet, Lincoln looked to the day when it would be an advantage to have a political record free from vengeance, with no avowals of punishment and retribution to come.

A pitiless logic at times led men from bad to worse, with no going back. In more than one case Stanton and other Cabinet members strictly were on the side of right and abstract justice with Lincoln ordering a course for the sake of political considerations not to be laughed off lightly in a republic at war with itself.

The President once dropped a few kind words about the enemy. They were human beings—were they not? One could not be completely remorseless, even in war. The line must be drawn somewhere. An elderly woman in the reception room flashed a question; how could he speak kindly of his enemies when he should rather destroy them. "What, madam?" slowly as he gazed into her face, "do I not destroy them when I make them my friends?" This type of anecdote gained circulation, in both England and America.

Once Thad Stevens asked a pardon for a young constituent who had gone to sleep on picket duty. Lincoln handed Stevens a telegraph blank, Stevens wrote a reprieve, signed "A. Lincoln" to the dispatch, and sent a messenger on the run to a telegraph office. This happened soon after an informal agreement between Lincoln and Stanton that the President would consult the War Secretary on reprieves in capital cases.

"I see, Mr. President," huffed Stanton on his early entry into Lincoln's office, "you have signed another reprieve contrary to your agreement not to do so without first consulting the War Department." "No. I have signed no reprieve. I have kept my word." "But I just saw one going over the wires. And your name is signed to it." "But I did not write it." "Did not write it! Who did write it?" "Your friend, Thad Stevens." Stanton took his hat and left.

A sobbing old man told the President his son with Butler's army had been convicted of a crime and sentenced by court-martial to be shot. The President read a telegram from General Butler protesting against executive interference with army courts-martial. The dazed old man shook with a desperate grief, Lincoln watching a minute, and "By jings, Butler or no Butler, here goes," wrote a few words. He showed them to the old man, a presidential signed order that the son was "not to be shot until further orders from me."

The old man was still in grief. "I thought it was to be a pardon. But you say 'not to be shot till further orders,' and you may order him shot next week." Lincoln smiled. "Well, my old friend, I see you are not very well acquainted with me. If your son never looks on death till further orders come from me to shoot him, he will live to be a great deal older than Methuselah."

A young woman in neat and plain dress was heard with respect and frank speech. "My poor girl, you have come with no governor, or senator, or member of Congress, to plead your cause. You seem honest and truthful, and *you don't wear hoops;* and I'll be whipped but I'll pardon your brother!"

An ancient rule of law held that pirates should be hanged. Nevertheless Lincoln pardoned a pirate, Alfred Rubery, captured in San Francisco in March '63 and held in jail for months till released on order of the President. Two reasons were given the public. The pirate was a British subject. And John Bright had written to the President asking the pardon as a favor. "In consideration of Mr. Bright's eminent services, the President at once acceded to his request," said *Leslie's Weekly*, January 2, 1864. "Mr. Bright has some strange friends." The comment was too easy. Lincoln saw little to be gained in that hour by hanging a British subject. And he believed John Bright was entitled to one pardon and no questions asked.

In the case of Louis A. Welton, sentenced to prison, Senator Morgan, Thurlow Weed and Raymond of the *Times*, were asking Lincoln to pardon him. Lincoln plainly believed the man to be a liar and a scoundrel taking profits out of trading with the enemy. Yet Lincoln pardoned Welton. It was the last week in August '64. The three men asking Welton's pardon were not to be thrust away with abrupt refusals. Lincoln wrote a statement giving his belief that Welton was a falsifier and a species of traitor intent on money-making from treason, and his further belief that Welton ought not to be pardoned. However if Messrs. Morgan, Weed and Raymond would on the same sheet with his statement of the case write their requests for Welton's pardon it would be done in deference to their wishes. Two of the three petitioners did so. Welton was saved from prison. Lincoln held in his possession a paper which the opposition would have seized on as luridly scandalous had it been made public:

Mr. Louis A. Welton came from the rebel lines into ours with a written contract to furnish large supplies to the rebels, was arrested with the contract in his possession, and has been sentenced to imprisonment for it. He, and his friends complain of this, on no substantial evidence whatever, but simply because his word, only given after his arrest, that he only took the contract as a means of escaping from the rebel lines, was not accepted as a full defence. He perceives that if this had been true he would have destroyed the contract so soon as it had served his purpose in getting him across the lines; but not having done this, and being caught with the paper on him, he tells this other absurd story that he kept the paper in the belief that our government would join him in taking the profit of fulfiling the contract.

This is my understanding of the case; and I can not conceive of a case of a man found in possession of a contract to furnish rebel supplies, who can not escape, if this be held a sufficient ground of escape. It is simply for the accused to escape by telling a very absurd and improbable story. Now, if Senator Morgan, and Mr. Weed, and Mr. Raymond, will not argue with me that I *ought* to discharge this man, but will, in writing on this sheet, simply request me to do it, I will do it solely in deference to their wishes.

A. LINCOLN

Then appearing on the same sheet of paper were the endorsements:

We respectfully request the President to pardon the within named Louis A. Welton, now at Fort Delaware.

THURLOW WEED.

I have read Mr. Welton's statement and if it is true, (and I know no reason for distrusting it,) his pardon would be an act of *justice*. I concur in Mr. Weed's request.

H. J. RAYMOND.

Lincoln's hands-off attitude in some cases may have meant he had heard enough of the case to believe the court-martial findings were probably true and correct. Or it may have been that, much as he would have liked to take a day or two for the study of the extended evidence in a case, he had no such day or two to spare.

Congressman Kellogg brought in the affair of a helter-skelter lad who before the war served six months in the Regular Army, deserted, came home, told his father nothing about it, sobered up and settled down. Later the boy volunteered at the beginning of the war, helped raise a regiment, was elected one of its officers, and in a charge across a bridge during one battle saw his colonel at his side killed and took wounds himself. Then an old-timer of the Regular Army recognized him, and let him know he would be exposed as a deserter. He managed to get furloughed home, told his father he would "die first" rather than be arrested as a deserter. Lincoln wasn't interested until the charge across the bridge. "Do you say the young man was wounded?" "Yes, badly." "Then," musingly, "then he has shed his blood for his country." And with a brightening, "Kellogg, isn't there something in Scripture about the 'shedding of blood' being the 'remission of sins'?" "Guess you're about right there." "It is a good point, and there is no going behind it." The President took a pen, wrote a pardon without condition or reservation.

An anxious old woman came with Congressman Charles Denison of Pennsylvania. Her son, John Russell, a private soldier, was under sentence to be shot in 48 hours. Lincoln heard them and sent for the papers in the case. It seemed that in a recent bloody battle Russell's captain had run away and after the battle found half of his command lost. Russell, meeting his captain, walked toward him, rifle in hand, and burst out, "Captain, you're a damned coward and ought to be shot for cowardice." The captain pulled his revolver; others came between them. The captain then charged insubordination, got a court-martial to give the lad a death sentence. Lincoln revoked the court-martial findings and ordered Private Russell restored to his command in good standing.

Joseph Holt, Judge Advocate General, laid before the President a flagrant case of a soldier in the heat of battle, affecting others by his cowardice, throwing down his gun and hiding behind a tree stump. The court-martial found he had neither father nor mother living, nor wife nor child; he was a thief, stealing from comrades on duty, by all standards unfit to wear the uniform. "Here is a case," said Judge Holt to the President, "exactly within your requirements; he does not deny his guilt; he will serve his country better dead than living . . . no relations to mourn for him . . . not fit to be in the ranks of patriots."

The President ran his long fingers through his hair: "Well, after all, Judge, I think I must put this with my leg cases." Judge Holt frowned. Was this a humorous matter? "What do you mean by leg cases, sir?" "Why, why, do you see those papers crowded into those pigeonholes? They are the cases that you call by that long title 'cowardice in the face of the enemy,' but I call them, for short, my 'leg cases.' But I put it to you, and I leave it for you to decide for yourself: if Almighty God gives a man a cowardly pair of legs how can he help their running away with him?"

On several bounty-jumpers Lincoln let the firing squads do their work. He refused mercy to bounty-jumpers—or again he intervened. The eccentric versatility of Robert Lane appealed to him. Lane enlisted first in Loomis' battery, left the service on a physical-disability discharge, stayed in Detroit, bobbed up in Nashville with a sutler, clowned with a circus, performed as a sword-swallower, rode a horse in a Kentucky cavalry regiment, was next heard of as a sergeant in one Indiana infantry company, leaving that for another. While held in an Indiana penitentiary Robert Lane was by court-martial ordered to be shot. Lincoln for reasons known to himself commuted the sentence of this flagrant bounty-jumper and scalawag to one year's hard labor with chain and ball. Possibly he saw genius and wit allied to madness in the case of Robert Lane.

A newspaperman and an Ohio colonel, after an interview on Great Lakes commerce, requested Lincoln to hear an old man waiting outside whose boy was to be shot. They waited. Nicolay came in with the old man's card, leaned over Lincoln's chair and whispered. Lincoln spoke, harassed yet decisive: "Tell him I will not see him. I cannot. Don't ask me again. Tell him I have read the papers in the case, all of them, fully, word for word. The boy deserted three times, the last time when on guard at Washington, and he cannot be pardoned. I will not interfere. He must be shot."

One guerrilla failing of mercy at Lincoln's hands was a Missouri leader named Nichols. Judge Holt gave Carpenter details about Nichols. "He was in the habit of filling the ears of Unionists who fell into his hands with gunpowder, setting fire to it, and blowing their heads to pieces. When captured, a number of human *ears* were found on his person."

The guard Crook took note of a woman intercepting Tad in a corridor, telling Tad her boys and girls were cold and starving because their father was shut up in prison and couldn't work for them. Tad ran to his father with the story. The father sat at a desk with papers, an absent look on his face, said he would look into the case as soon as he had time. Tad clung to his father's knees and begged till his father listened. And Tad ran back and told the woman her husband would be set free. The woman blessed him and cried, and Tad cried, and Crook said he had to cry too.

A rough rider of the Confederate Mosby's raiders awaited the firing squad while his wife came to Lincoln with her story. The President, knowing how fierce Mosby's men were in the field, asked her what kind of a husband her man was. Did he get drunk? Did he beat her and the children? "No, no," said the wife. "He is a good man, a good husband. He loves me. He loves the children. And we can't live without him. The only trouble is that he is a fool about politics. I live in the North, born there, and if I can get him home he will do no more fighting for the South." "Well," said Lincoln as he thumbed through the papers, "I will pardon your husband and turn him over to you for safe keeping." Here the woman broke into tears, into a sobbing beyond control. "My dear woman, if I had known how badly it was going to make you feel, I never would have pardoned him." "You don't understand me," she cried between sobs, in a fresh flow of tears. "Yes, yes, I do. And if you don't go away at once I shall be crying with you."

A woman knelt to give thanks for the release of her husband. "Don't kneel to me but thank God and go" was the President's dismissal of her.

There were tender scenes with no overplaying of them. A woman with tears filling her eyes tried to speak gratitude for a "suspension of execution" granted her husband. "Good-by, Mr. Lincoln. I shall probably never see you again till we meet in heaven." She had taken one of his hands. He took her right hand in both of his. They walked to the door as he spoke softly: "I am afraid with all my troubles I shall never get to the resting-place you speak of. But if I do, I am sure I shall find you. That you wish me to get there is, I believe, the best wish you could make for me. Good-by."

"If he has no friend I'll be his friend," was Lincoln's remark as he penned a reprieve for one unbespoken. Once he sat up in his nightshirt, just awakened from sleep, heard the story of a 19-year-old boy having fallen asleep on picket duty, wrote a reprieve in bed, then worried that the order might go wrong, dressed himself and went over to the War Department to make sure the order was understood. This was one story and a likely one. Another ran that in fear a similar pardon order might go astray he sent telegrams to four different authorities. Of one of these pardons saving the life of a sleeping picket, he remarked to a Congressman as he read an order he had written: "I could not think of going into eternity with the blood of that poor young man on my skirts. It is not to be wondered at that a boy, raised on the farm, probably in the habit of going to bed at dark, should, when required to watch, fall asleep; and I cannot consent to shooting him for such an act."

On Monday morning, September 9, 1861, the 3rd Vermont Volunteers regiment was drawn up to hear the reading of General Order No. 8, issued by General McClellan. It began with reciting William Scott's trial and sentence, the appeals of brigade, regiment and company officers, together with privates, that Scott's life be spared. "And," it continued, "the President of the United States had expressed a wish that, as this is the first condemnation to death in the army for this crime, mercy may be extended to the criminal. This fact, viewed in connection with the inexperience of the condemned as a soldier, his previous good conduct and general good character, and the urgent entreaties made in his behalf, have determined the Major General to grant the pardon so earnestly prayed for." Then came a warning that pardons might not always be given to boys who slept on sentinel duty, as it was an offense to which "all nations affix the penalty of death." Then came the order releasing Scott for duty with his regiment.

This same William Scott seven months later among the fresh growths and blooms of Virginia springtime at Lee's Mill took the burning messages of six bullets into his body. All he could give Lincoln or his country or his God was now given.

Pardon appeals where an executive Yes or No must decide whether a soldier face the firing squad—these troubled from several approaches. From a cold practical viewpoint it was good politics to have a reputation as a pardoner, softhearted rather than hardhearted, even though it affected army behavior. Mothers and sisters wept as the President one day signed a reprieve. "Well, I have made one family happy, but I don't know about the discipline of the army!"

In the seven days between December 26, 1863, and January 3, 1864, six soldiers received pardons or stays of death sentences from the President. "Do not execute him till further order" or "Suspend execution of sentence and forward record of trial for examination" was the repeated essential of the telegrams. The most sweeping order of this class ever sent by the President was on December 10, 1863, to Major General Butler at Fortress Monroe: "Please suspend execution in any and all sentences of death in your Department until further orders." To the army of no other general than Butler did it seem that Lincoln issued so inclusive an order regarding stays of execution. Butler seemed to be the one major general who openly and directly blamed his military losses on the President's lack of severity. Butler gave his answer why the war was lasting so long: "Pusillanimity and want of executive force of the government."

Donn Piatt wrote of how he heard Brigadier General Daniel Tyler of Connecticut in an antechamber of the War Department tell the President that reverses in Kentucky and Tennessee were due to the one condition that Bragg, the Confederate commander, had shot his deserters, but "if we attempt to shoot a deserter, you pardon him and our army is without discipline." Tyler went on: "Why do you interfere? Congress has taken from you all responsibility." The President, swiftly and impatiently: "Yes, Congress has taken the responsibility and left the women to howl about me." And he strode away.

Many opponents and critics of Lincoln believed that realistic political and military purposes moved him entirely in his pardons. The popular belief in Lincoln's mercy was "erroneous," Donn Piatt would say. "His good-natured manner misled the common mind." Piatt doubted whether Lincoln "had at all a kind, forgiving nature," pointing to history and successful leaders of men as "round, oily, elastic" on the outside, giving way in trifles, while "angular, hard," on the inner purposes. In his guess at this phase of Lincoln, Piatt was half-correct at least. Lincoln had disciplined himself to hide his deeper purposes under the spoken immediate ones. He could be smooth toward rough ends when he considered it necessary. "I heard Secretary Seward say," wrote

Piatt, "that President Lincoln 'had a cunning that was genius.'" Coming from
Seward that was some manner of tribute.

The sound of musketry fire blew from Virginia camps into the White
House one afternoon as Lincoln sat with John Eaton. He stepped to an open
window and looked to the Virginia shore. "When he turned again, the tears
were running down his cheeks," wrote the responsible Eaton, who heard him
say, "This is the day when they shoot deserters." Nevertheless it was not so
easy as that. By his pardons he had lowered army morale. "Some of our officers feel that," he said to Eaton. "Our" officers had that feeling. After all it
was "our" army and he too was part of "they" who were shooting deserters.

To what extent did the President's frequent pardons interfere with army
discipline? Chauncey M. Depew was to answer by quoting General Sherman.
"How did you carry out the sentences of your court-martials and escape
Lincoln's pardons?" Depew asked. Sherman answered, "I shot them first!"
Whatever the irregular or illegal device used by Sherman in this respect, it
was probably also used by Grant, Thomas, Sheridan and every other commander who won campaigns and battles.

Well enough was it known in the army that being saved from a firing
squad by a President's pardon often meant iron bars, prison fare, close confinement, hard labor, the ball and chain. Far and wide went the press item in
1864: "President Lincoln directed that the sentences of all deserters who had
been condemned to death by court-martial, and that had not been otherwise
acted upon by him, be mitigated to imprisonment during the war at the Dry
Tortugas, Florida, where they would be sent under guard." In a tropical
climate, cut off by the sea, with war-torn states and the Atlantic Ocean between them and the Northern home states, some of the deserters, thieves,
cowards, "leg cases," mutineers, malingerers, bounty-jumpers, doing the lock
step in the Dry Tortugas Islands wrote home that it was a hard life.

In a single year the army courts-martial were handling 30,000 cases of
offenders against military law. Many capital cases eventually drifted to Lincoln's desk. Of one hot summer afternoon John Hay wrote in his diary that
the President spent six hours on court-martial transcripts, catching at any
fact that would justify saving a life. In one case he doubted "it would make
any man better to shoot him," urging that if the Government kept him alive
it could at least get some work out of him. One endorsement read, "Let him
fight instead of shooting him."

The young Indiana Democratic Congressman Daniel W. Voorhees heard
from Lincoln the confession: "No one need ever expect me to sanction the
shooting of a man for running away in battle. I won't do it. A man can't help
being a coward any more than he could help being a humpback." It was on
another White House call, according to Voorhees, that Lincoln, with a pathetic look of anxious pain, made the little inquiry, "Voorhees, don't it seem
strange to you that I who could never so much as cut off the head of a
chicken, should be elected, or selected, into the midst of all this blood?"

CHAPTER 52

The Man Who Had Become the Issue

THE MAN Lincoln, his person and mind, had come to be the pivotal issue of the 1864 campaign. Some would vote for him with no particular faith, others in a loyalty that had seldom or never swerved. In the chaos of the times he was to these folk a beacon light that in moments almost flickered out into a black despair, yet returned to shine without wavering. His life in the White House, his decisions, speeches and messages issued from there, went out over the country for interpretations, for thanks, curses, doubts. Those interpretations would be told of in the November 8 ballot boxes.

"The great West is with you," Ralph Emerson of Rockford, Illinois, assured him. "Yes—but I am sometimes reminded of Old Mother Partington on the sea beach. A big storm came up and the waves began to rise till the water came in under her cabin door. She got a broom and went to sweeping it out. But the water rose higher and higher, to her knees, to her waist, at last to her chin. But she kept on sweeping and exclaiming, 'I'll keep on sweeping as long as the broom lasts, and we will see whether the storm or the broom will last the longest.' " At the final words, according to Emerson, Lincoln's jaws came together, his face grim rather than funny.

In Illinois, Dick Oglesby, recovered from bullet wounds, was running for governor on the Union ticket and saying that in 1858 at Urbana in a walk with Lincoln—he distinctly recalled it—Lincoln told him, "Remember, Dick, to keep close to the people—they are always right and will mislead no one."

Nathaniel Hawthorne nursed his complex grief over the awful war game and died in '64, mostly of heartbreak, from looking too close and too long at the riddle Lincoln had formulated in the Gettysburg speech. Mrs. Hawthorne had once written her husband of "a paragraph in the paper about your being at Washington, and that the President received you with especial graciousness . . . I suspect the President is a jewel. I like him very well." She loved her husband and wrote as a lover. "If it were not such a bore, I could wish thou mightest be President through this crisis . . . I should not wonder if thy great presence in Washington might affect the moral air and work good. If you like the President, then give him my love and blessing."

Of Lincoln's plea for gradual compensated emancipation, she wrote, "The President's immortal special message fills me with unbounded satisfaction. It is so almost superhumanly wise, moderate, fitting that I am ready to believe an angel came straight from heaven to him with it. He must be honest and true, or an angel would not come to him. Mary Mann says she thinks the message feeble, and not to the point. But I think a man shows strength when he can be moderate at such a moment as this. Thou hadst better give my regards to the President."

The lights of such spirits as hers did reach Lincoln. Precious affection came his way. Motives beyond price were unbosomed to him. They lighted, changed and deepened him, perhaps saddened him. He had hours when, like Hawthorne, he hardly knew what took his strength away. Of one vicious personal criticism of him, he said mildly that it wasn't well timed; and of one bitter political enemy, "I've been told that insanity is hereditary in his family, and I think we will admit the plea in his case."

Events moved him to change his policies. Some were baffled by his transitions. Congressman John B. Alley suddenly found the President differed with him on a matter where they had been agreed. "Mr. President, you have changed your mind entirely within a short time." "Yes, I have. And I don't think much of a man who is not wiser today than he was yesterday."

Every phase of the war lived and rang in the rooms of the White House, where, according to Crook, "As he went upstairs and entered his own room, Lincoln's last act was to turn to the guard on duty in the corridor and wish him good-night. Then he would enter his room, and close the door, and I— if it were my turn to stand guard—would settle down for eight hours of duty." In the silence of the night was despair—and hope. Though torn with intestinal violence, the Government of the United States was still a vast going concern, having immense transactions in land, money, shipbuilding, the first tentative projections of the Union Pacific Railway under way, an around-the-earth international telegraph system being wrought toward reality, mails being carried, pensions paid to widows and orphans, river and harbor works in process, emigrants thronging U.S. consulates in Europe with anxiety to go to "the free country" overseas. And the question running over the world: Would the Union Government be able to hammer out an indissoluble unity of its states? Alongside this world of red war and this other world of constructive realities in which Lincoln had to immerse himself daily, there was the formal realm of conventions, of "society," of ordained contacts necessary to the role of being President. The night of the weekly reception—more often termed a levee—"was always a trying one to the President," wrote Carpenter.

Seven biographies published in '64 presented Lincoln favorably for various audiences of readers. Several small paper-covered books issued by the opposition were chiefly humorous and satirical. Immense editions were sold of an issue of the monthly *Beadle Dime Library* by O. J. Victor and another "popular life" by the Reverend William M. Thayer of Boston. Each emphasized the opportunity before any American poor boy who wished "to climb the heights."

Leslie's Weekly enumerated "sweet scented compliments" paid by the opposition press to the President of the United States, namely: ape, gorilla, fool, filthy storyteller, despot, liar, thief, braggart, buffoon, usurper, monster, tortoise, ignoramus, old scoundrel, perjurer, robber, swindler, tyrant, fiend, butcher, land pirate.

The effect of this savage verbal warfare? In October '64 *Harper's Weekly* appraised it: "The personal character of the President is the rock upon which the Opposition is wrecked. It dashes against him and his administration, hissing and venomous, but falls back again baffled . . . the popular confidence in the unswerving fidelity and purity of purpose of the President has smiled the storm to scorn." *Harper's Weekly, Harper's Monthly*, the *Atlantic Monthly, Leslie's Weekly, Godey's Lady's Book*, the larger part of the more formidable and solid periodicals, either in quiet and reserved tones or with direct and sonorous declarations, favored Lincoln and the National Union ticket during the campaign.

Lamon and Piatt accepted with full credence an account by the economist and financier Amasa Walker of an interview he and Chase had with Lincoln about a proposed greenback issue Chase feared was unconstitutional. Piatt wrote:

Mr. Chase made a long and elaborate constitutional argument against the proposed measure . . . said Mr. Lincoln . . . "This thing reminds me of a story I read in a newspaper the other day. It was of an Italian captain, who ran his vessel on a rock and knocked a hole in her bottom. He set his men to pumping and he went to prayers before a figure of the Virgin in the bow of the ship. The leak gained on them. It looked at last as if the vessel would go down with all on board. The captain, at length, in a fit of rage at not having his prayers answered, seized the figure of the Virgin and threw it overboard. Suddenly the leak stopped, the water was pumped out, and the vessel got safely into port. When docked for repairs, the statue of the Virgin Mary was found stuck headforemost in the hole."
"I don't see, Mr. President, the precise application of your story," said Mr. Chase.
"Why . . . I don't intend precisely to throw the Virgin Mary overboard, and by that I mean the Constitution, but I will stick it in the hole if I can. These rebels are violating the Constitution to destroy the Union. I will violate the Constitution, if necessary, to save the Union, and I suspect . . . that our Constitution is going to have a rough time of it before we get done with this row. Now, what I want to know is whether, Constitution aside, this project of issuing interest-bearing notes is a good one."
"I must say," responded Mr. Chase, "that with the exception you make, it is not only a good one, but the only way open to us to raise money. If you say so, I will do my best to put it into immediate and practical operation, and you will never hear from me any opposition on this subject."

One October evening in '64 a torchlight procession of hundreds of Negroes marched to the White House lawn, carrying banners and transparencies, a brass band blaring, loud and repeated cheers bringing the President. He looked out from the portico on jubilant black faces, heard in the half-lighted darkness their moving hoarse voices, and began, "I have to guess, my friends, the object of this call which has taken me quite by surprise this evening." Then according to Noah Brooks' news report, a spokesman shouted, "The emancipator of Maryland, sah!" The newly adopted constitution of that state was in their favor. The President proceeded: "It is no secret that I have wished, and still do wish, mankind everywhere to be free." (Great cheering and cries of "God bless Abraham Lincoln.")

The tall, gaunt, slave-born black woman Sojourner Truth arrived at the Executive Mansion from Battle Creek, Michigan, "a long and halting journey," she said. The President gave Sojourner his hand, bowed. "I am pleased to see you." Then Sojourner released her speech poem: "Mr. President, when you first took your seat I feared you would be torn to pieces, for I likened you unto Daniel, who was thrown into the lions' den; and if the lions did not tear you to pieces, I knew that it would be God that had saved you; and I said if He spared me I would see you before the four years expired, and He has done so, and now I am here to see you for myself." He took the little book she brought out, and as Sojourner phrased it, "The same hand that signed the death-warrant of slavery wrote as follows":

For Aunty Sojourner Truth,
Oct. 29, 1864.   A. Lincoln

Lincoln wrote checks payable to "Mr. Johns, a sick man," "Lucy (colored woman)," and a wanderer on the White House lawn, "Colored Man, with one Leg." And how and why he endorsed notes for other Negroes was not a matter of publicity and news. To the ears of Nicolay it came, however, that a cashier of one of the Washington banks, meeting an old friend of Lincoln on the street one morning, had to say: "That President of yours is the oddest man alive. Why, he endorses notes for niggers!"

In the Executive Mansion for the first two years no colored persons were employed. "But," wrote Brooks, "the President has succeeded in getting about him a corps of attachés of Hibernian descent." Brooks wrote that the Irish coachman "did not consider it his business to run errands. This coming to the President's ears he ordered up the carriage next morning at six o'clock and sent a member of his household in the equipage to the Avenue where he bought a paper and rode back, with the mortified coachee on the box."

To the White House often had come the master photographer Mathew B. Brady. Since February '60, at the time of the Cooper Union speech, Brady had by autumn of '64 photographed Lincoln more than 30 times. From his profitable portrait gallery on Broadway and Tenth, New York, Brady had come to the war with his camera. Out in the camps, on the march and on battlefields Brady and his assistants made both single and stereoscopic wet-plate exposures and were achieving a camera record comprising thousands of convincing likenesses of scenes and people. Lincoln wrote and signed a heavy card with the large scrawl "Pass Brady," which took Brady nearly everywhere he cared to go.

Collections of *cartes de visite*, photographs of fine clarity and definition of line, mounted on small cards usually 2¼ by 3½ inches, were in many thousands of homes. Brady and Gardner photographs of Lincoln were often on show there. Frequently the illustrated weeklies, *Harper's* and *Leslie's*, and occasionally the daily newspapers, published large drawings from photographs, so that Lincoln's face and figure had become familiar to those who read, and of course to some who enjoyed pictures though they couldn't read.

A Connecticut painter's portrait of Lincoln, done for Secretary Welles, hung for a time in Lincoln's office. Welles, turning toward it one afternoon, said it was a successful likeness. From Lincoln came a hesitant "Yes," noted Carpenter, and then a story of a Western man who had himself painted secretly, giving his wife the picture for a birthday present. "Horridly like," she pronounced it. "And that," said Lincoln, "seems to me a just criticism of *this!*"

Carpenter's painting, "The First Reading of the Emancipation Proclamation by President Lincoln to His Cabinet" was nearly finished. In his six months' stay he and Lincoln had passed many pleasant hours. Thirty-four years old, slender and delicate, with bushy black hair, devout in religion and strict in manners, Carpenter had a loyalty to the President and a belief that his painting would be a help. "I must go in and take one more look at the picture before you leave us," said Lincoln one July day. Carpenter spoke of the unvarying kindness the President had always shown him. Lincoln listened, kept gazing on the picture, and turned to say, "Carpenter, I believe I am about as glad over the success of this work as you are." By permission of the President the painting, when finished, was placed in the East Room, open to the public for two days, and was viewed by several thousand visitors.

At 11 o'clock one night Carpenter found Lincoln alone signing military commissions. He went on signing, presently remarking, "I do not, as you see, pretend to read over these documents. I see that Stanton has signed them, so I conclude they are all right." He chatted and wrote, finished the lot, rose, stretched, "Well, I have got that job *husked out*, now I guess I will go over to the War Department before I go to bed, and see if there is any news."

Readers saw with interest press items of Mrs. Lincoln paying a complimentary visit to General Scott at West Point and receiving a salute of 15 guns; of her going to Harvard in June to attend the graduation of Robert; of her buying a set of earrings and a pin for $3,000 and a shawl for $5,000 on successive shopping trips to New York City; of her sister Martha Todd White of Selma, Alabama, receiving a pass signed by the President giving her passage, with baggage, through the Union Army lines, resulting in rumors and accusations that she had been accorded special privileges and had smuggled contraband goods, including, *Leslie's Weekly* alleged mistakenly, "a rebel uniform, the buttons of which were gold, worth $40,000."

Cases of assorted wines and liquors piled high in the White House cellar. Arrivals of whisky, brandy, rum were acknowledged with thanks and word that they were to be distributed among hospitals.

Blue Room, East Room, Red Room, Green Room, long and stately with lofty ceilings, with gas chandeliers spreading like huge jungle flowers of glass further decked with glittering balloons of whitened glass—these on the downstairs floor of the White House overlooked much small talk and idle chatter. Seven o'clock strictly was the hour for state dinners, according to the Department of State. On request it furnished the White House with elaborate details on tradition and accepted form. At times the stairways leading up to the offices were blocked with callers and curiosity seekers.

Somehow the tale went forth and became published as fact that Senator Sumner strolled in to find the President polishing his own boots. "Why, Mr. President, do you black your own boots?" "Whose boots did you think I blacked?"

Congressman Alley's version ran that Chase found Lincoln rubbing his leather footwear with a brush. Remarks were exchanged. "Mr. Lincoln, gentlemen don't black their own boots." "Whose boots do they black?"

A dusty and worn dispatch-bearer with secret papers of importance handed them to the President seated alone in his office. And young Major Gerrard Whitehead of the Philadelphia City Troop took a seat where the President motioned him and watched the President fall into a deep study, lost entirely in the revelations of the dispatches.

"The one window of the room was open," Whitehead wrote. "Across the sultry sky came up heavy thunder clouds. The storm broke and rain began to pour into the room. The officer did not think of moving while the Commander in Chief of the Army was so engrossed. So he sat and watched the rain form a pool on the floor and slowly trickle across it, almost to the feet of the President, absorbed and unconscious. At last Mr. Lincoln made his decision, seemed to rouse from his deep reflections and becoming conscious of the young despatch bearer, told him to return in an hour, when the answering despatch would be ready for him."

On occasion Lincoln kept a weather eye on his caller, as when in April '64 press items told of "the lunatic who harangued the President, claiming to have been elected President in 1856." And again when an incoherent individual styling himself "Major General of the Anti-Renters," babbled that he had been imprisoned in "Castle Thunder" in Richmond, raved over vast schemes to end the war, was led away and adjudged insane.

That the President's earlier suspicions of Count Adam Gurowski were partly justified was seen in August '64 when that neurotic growler was locked up in a police station and after a hearing before a magistrate was fined $5. Witnesses testified that Gurowski had "attempted to discipline" the Washington Fire Department. Yelling that they were moving too slow toward the conflagration, "he drew a pistol on the firemen to make them run faster."

One evening Robert W. McBride, serving as corporal of the guard, picketed his horse in the rear of the White House and was standing in the driveway of the front portico. As he stood there he saw the President come out alone and walk to the edge of the portico where the steps began. There under a lighted gas jet the President stood, alone. His hands behind him, he stood there in a reverie. A few feet away, across the driveway, Corporal McBride had drawn his saber and stood at attention. As a corporal it was his duty to stand at attention and salute any officer, and particularly the Commander in Chief of the armies of the United States.

"Just how long he stood there I do not know," said McBride. "I know he stood there so long I became very tired." It was to McBride as though, were some marksman hidden anywhere, the President wished to make himself a perfect target by standing alone in the full light of the gas jet. But after a time, possibly several minutes, he came down the steps, and hardly seeming to notice the corporal, nevertheless gravely lifted his hat as a return salute and walked toward the War Department, alone. In about a half-hour he came back, alone.

Stanton's anxiety over the President's safety continued. He gave one standing order. Although the President might come to the War Office at midnight alone, as happened often, he should never be permitted to return alone, but must be escorted by a file of four soldiers and a noncommissioned officer.

During the autumn of '64 the cavalry guard at Soldiers' Home was cautioned repeatedly to be "extremely vigilant," and according to its lieutenant, George C. Ashmun, "the whole company was kept under arms with horses saddled," ready for any night disturbance. The President was leaving the house late at night, taking solitary walks. Of one Lincoln ramble alone under the stars Ashmun noted: "One beautiful Indian Summer night, about 12 o'clock, as I was returning across the grounds from a visit to one of our pickets who had fired at something, I saw a man walking leisurely and alone across the path I was taking. As I came nearer I saw it was Mr. Lincoln. At an earlier hour I would have kept from speaking, but, prompted by anxiety, I said, 'Mr. President, isn't it rather risky to be out here at this hour?' He answered, 'Oh, I guess not—I couldn't rest and thought I'd take a walk.' He was quite a distance outside the line of infantry guards about the house where the family was staying. He turned back after I spoke to him, and I passed on to where the escort was camped."

Four police officers in November '64 were detailed by the chief of police of the District of Columbia, to serve as special guards for the President. They were John F. Parker, Alfonso Dunn, Alexander Smith and Thomas Pendel. On Pendel's later being appointed doorkeeper, that vacancy was filled by William H. Crook. Noted Crook, "The night guards were expected to protect the President on his expeditions to and from the War Department, or while he was at any place of amusement, and to patrol the corridor outside his room while he slept."

In March and April of '64 the New York *Tribune* gave the country several news letters from a Washington correspondent who named one Colonel Margrave as having submitted to the Confederate War Department plans to kidnap Lincoln and carry him to Richmond, "or if it should be found impossible to escape with him to the rebel lines, to assassinate him." The story did not quite stand up, yet was taken in some circles friendly to Lincoln as perhaps having a slight basis—"Where there is so much smoke there must be some fire." The New York *World* said: "This ridiculous canard was telegraphed all over the country, and has found its way into nearly every journal in the land. It is absurd on its face. Mr. Lincoln is of much more service to the rebels where he is than if they had him in Richmond."

Of an odd affair about mid-August '64, nothing should be said, ran Lincoln's advice to John W. Nichols, a guard since the summer of '62. Nichols, on duty at the large gate entrance to the Soldiers' Home grounds, one night about eleven heard a rifle shot in the direction of the city and soon after heard the hoofbeats of a horse coming nearer and nearer. In two or three minutes a horse came dashing up. On it Nichols saw the President, bareheaded, and Nichols helped to quiet a favorite saddle horse. The President was now saying: "He came pretty near getting away with me, didn't he? He got the bit in his teeth before I could draw rein." To Nichols' query about his hat the President answered that somebody had fired a gun off down at the foot of the hill, and that his horse had become scared and had jerked his hat off.

Nichols led the horse to the executive cottage, held it while the President dismounted and went into the house, then saw the horse to the stables. Nichols with a corporal began a search for the hat. At a point where the sound of the shot had come from, a driveway intersection with the main road, they found the President's hat, the familiar plain silk stovepipe. "Upon examination," proceeded Nichols' story, "we discovered a *bullet-hole* through the crown. We searched the locality thoroughly, but without avail. Next day I gave Mr. Lincoln his hat, and called his attention to the bullet-hole. He made some humorous remark, to the effect that it was made by some foolish marksman and was not intended for him; but added that he wished nothing said about the matter. We all felt confident it was an attempt to kill the President, and after that he never rode alone."

This made twice that Lincoln lost his hat while riding at night, the first time telling Lamon about it as a comic affair worth a laugh.

To the theater Lincoln continued to go, though warned that he was an easy target. He heard of clergymen murmuring about his moral support of the playhouse. One Hay diary entry read: "Spent the evening at the theatre with President, Mrs. L., Mrs. Hunter, Cameron and Nicolay. J. Wilkes Booth in the 'Marble Heart.' Rather tame than otherwise."

Alone often, yet again with varied companions, Tad or Mrs. Lincoln, or Hay, Brooks, Sumner and others, the President went to the drama, visiting Grover's Theatre perhaps a hundred times since coming to Washington. When there was opera at Grover's, Mrs. Lincoln invariably attended with the President. "Mr. Grover, I really enjoy a minstrel show," Lincoln suggested once. And when Grover later announced Hooley's Minstrels soon to come Lincoln laughed. "Well, that was thoughtful of you."

Once in '64 Tad quietly slipped away from a box at Grover's. And soon the father saw his boy on stage with a chorus singing "The Battle Cry of Freedom," Tad half lost in a Union Army blue uniform blouse.

To Grover's one night came Mr. and Mrs. Lincoln with Speaker Colfax, and no guard or other company. Grover met them at the curb, conducted them from their carriage, through a private passage to their box. After the play he took them by the same passage to the street, where they found a crowd of more than a hundred jeering and laughing around the President's carriage. Grover opened the carriage door, handed his guests in and watched a scene grotesque and sad.

On the carriage box holding the reins of two lively horses sat a boy who had been a drummer, had lost an arm in battle, had then been given a place at the White House. The regular coachman, a young man clumsy from drink, jabbering in Irish brogue, was trying to climb onto the box. Three hours earlier, invited for a few drinks, he had left his horses in charge of the one-armed boy. The crowd saw him slump to the street cobblestones and slowly get to his feet. "He staggered slightly," wrote Grover, "and then with a supreme effort, clambered over the wheel, landed on the box, seized the reins from the hand of the drummer-boy, and turning to take his seat—fell sprawling his full length on the sidewalk. The jeering shout which followed had a threatening tone. Any overt act, the throwing of a stone, might have resulted in catastrophe."

Grover took the reins, sprang to the box, started the span of horses, asked the President where to drive, took Speaker Colfax home first, then delivered the White House folks to their home where Lincoln spoke grateful words. Leonard Grover wrote with a modest accuracy: "Some people went so far as to say that I had saved Mr. Lincoln's life. I knew that I had extricated him from a very annoying situation." The drunken coachman and the one-armed drummer-boy were lost in a confusion of chronicles.

Lincoln had seen for the first time a performance of *Hamlet*, with Edwin Booth in the leading role. It had "at all times a peculiar charm for Mr.

Lincoln's mind," noted Carpenter, who quoted Lincoln: "There is one passage very apt to be slurred over by the actor . . . It is the soliloquy of the king, after the murder . . ." He took up the words:

"O! my offence is rank, it smells to heaven;
It hath the primal eldest curse upon 't . . ."

The entire passage of 37 lines moved from him smoothly, with feeling and shadings; Carpenter rated it "unsurpassed by anything I ever witnessed upon the stage." With a natural ease Lincoln then stepped into the character of Richard and gave the famous soliloquy with a power that to Carpenter "made it seem like a new creation." Carpenter laid down palette and brushes, gave a burst of handclapping applause.

To Carpenter he once read aloud his letter to the Owen Lovejoy Monument Association, as though the lines were worth his intoning: "Let him have the marble monument along with the well-assured and more enduring one in the hearts of those who love liberty unselfishly for all men."

In April '61 Lincoln had appointed Mark Delahay to be surveyor general for Kansas and Nebraska. In October '63 Delahay resigned and Lincoln named him U.S. District Judge for Kansas. Letters and speeches against Delahay had to do mainly with his being "so ignorant as a lawyer that no one would employ him," and with his itch for unearned money and his heavy drinking. Yet Lincoln over a powerful opposition drove through the nomination. And the friend to whom Lincoln had shown so unfailing a loyalty began a course of conduct on the Federal bench that resulted eventually in his being impeached on charges of incompetency, corruption, drunkenness on and off the bench, Delahay resigning while the impeachment committee was taking testimony.

Thus ran in brief essentials the course of the only man it was ever known to whom Lincoln promised and paid money for personal political promotion. Whatever the underlying facts, they were probably more essential than any that came to light. One consideration operated. As far back as 1846 Delahay as a Whig party man had worked loyally and actively to nominate and elect Lincoln to Congress. He had come from Kansas to be part of the White House guard in the spring of '61 when mail, telegraph and railroad communication with the outside world were cut off. This loyal activity Lincoln couldn't forget—and there was the vague factor that Delahay's wife was distant kin of Lincoln's beloved stepmother.

Often in subdued corners was talk of Colonel La Fayette C. Baker, chief of the Detective Bureau, a czar of various underworlds. He had 1,000 to 2,000 men operating under his orders, their webs and tentacles flung out among the just and the unjust, his bureau under Stanton. Baker's grandfather, named Remember Baker, was a Revolutionary War captain under Ethan Allen, and his father, named Green Mountain Boy Baker, was a Michigan farmer whose boy went east, then west, to become one of the most active members of the Vigilante Committee that overrode the openly lawless of San Francisco.

Early in the war La Fayette Baker had gone afoot, so he said, to Richmond, and returned with a detailed story of being arrested, jailed and having several interviews with Jefferson Davis during his three-week trip. It became definitely known that he could tell a story to his own advantage, that he could be careless with facts. He was often clever—or again merely glib and loose Stanton believed him useful in tracing conspiracies and thwarting Confederate spies. His work was naturally such that he made enemies and roused ill will. Welles wrote that from what he had heard and seen Colonel Baker was "wholly unreliable, regardless of character and the rights of persons, incapable of discrimination, and zealous to do something sensational."

Register of the Treasury Lucius E. Chittenden pictured Baker as "cruel and rapacious"; his detectives were put on the rolls "without recommendation, investigation, or any inquiry." Usually the suspect arrested was handcuffed, and brought to Baker's office, then in the basement of the Treasury building. There the suspect was "subjected to a brow-beating examination, in which Baker was said to rival in impudence some heads of the criminal bar," this examination being repeated as often as he, Baker, chose. "Men were kept in his rooms for weeks, without warrant, affidavit, or other semblance of authority. If the accused took any measures for his own protection, he was hurried to the Old Capitol Prison, where he was beyond the reach of the civil authorities.

"Corruption spread like a contagious disease, wherever the operations of these detectives extended . . . Honest manufacturers and dealers, who paid their taxes, were pursued without mercy for the most technical breaches of the law, and were quickly driven out of business. The dishonest rapidly accumulated wealth, which they could well afford to share with their protectors." Turning to a concrete instance, Chittenden wrote of catching Colonel Baker in the act of forgery and "Perfectly unabashed, without a blush, the fellow smiled as he looked me in the face and said, 'That game didn't work, did it?' " This secret-service head once said he had 2,000 men inside and outside Washington, reporting to him their findings, and he at the central controls. Others than Chittenden felt Baker was an ever-lurking evil shadow over the administration.

Baker had a way of talking and writing as though he were a confidant and a trusted operative of the President. "I was sent for by Mr. Lincoln," or "I was summoned to report in person to Mr. Lincoln." Yet there seemed to be no record of the President writing any communication to Baker or to anyone else about Baker, and none of Lincoln's closer associates recorded that he had any intimacy with Baker.

Senator Wilkinson of Minnesota heard presentations to Lincoln by Senators Sumner, Wade and others, hotly urging removal of a prominent official. "The President listened with his head down," noted Wilkinson. "At the conclusion he looked up with a sorrowful face and said, 'Well, gentlemen, it does seem to me that whenever I have a particular friend in office, everybody is down on him.' This ended the matter, and the official was not removed."

Among odd political fish with whom Lincoln dealt was one he named in a note to Stanton in November '63: "I personally wish Jacob R. Freese, of New-Jersey, to be appointed a Colonel for a colored regiment—and this regardless of whether he can tell the exact shade of Julius Caesar's hair."

Nothing seemed to come of this. Freese the next year while editing a newspaper in New Jersey wrote to Secretary Chase proposing that he be made collector of revenue in that state. This could be done through Chase removing the man holding the office, who was "a warm Lincoln supporter." Once in office as collector, Freese explained, he could make certain that all Treasury officials would be Chase-for-President workers at the proper time. Furthermore, the office would furnish an excuse for Freese visiting all parts of the state and building a Chase-for-President movement. This didn't seem to interest Chase, possibly because Freese's newspaper never had any real Chase-for-President editorials or news items. In September '64 Lincoln wrote the New Jersey Senator John C. Ten Eyck: "Dr. J. R. Freese, now editor of a leading Union Journal in New-Jersey, resided, for a time, in Illinois, where & when I made his acquaintance, and since when I have enjoyed much of his friendship. He is somewhat wounded with me now, that I do not recognize him as he thinks I ought. I wish to appoint him a Provost-Marshal in your State. May I have your approval?" In the moving stream of politics Lincoln accommodated himself to changing events regardless of the exact shade of Julius Caesar's hair.

Well enough Lincoln knew that two men he had just appointed to nice offices had talked mean about him. On Lamon asking why he should put them in office, he answered that Lamon couldn't *think* one of them to be half as mean as he *knew* him to be. "But I can't run this thing on the theory that every officeholder must think I am the greatest man in the nation."

Several delegations had presented claims, each for his own man to get a forthcoming appointment. And Lincoln one day refused to receive as a caller an old and dear personal friend, because the friend was one of the candidates for the appointment. Carpenter heard his regrets: "If I was less *thin-skinned* about such things, I should get along much better." Another time he had to refuse a sutlership to a soldier who had served three years with an honorable record, because of Stanton saying the place should go to a soldier who had lost an arm or a leg. "I have thousands of applications like this every day," the President was quoted, "but we cannot satisfy all for this reason, that these positions are like office-seekers—there are too many pigs for the tits."

Whitney noted his repeated refusals to a man who wanted appointment as an inspector of army horses, and the final outburst, "I hain't got anything to give you!" In one state two party factions were each pushing for their own man to fill a high position. The President passed by both factions, made an appointment neither faction could criticize, an able army officer who in valiant service had lost a leg.

The phrase "lame duck" entered political lingo. A Western Senator on introducing his successor to Lincoln put in his request for himself to be Commissioner of Indian Affairs. Lincoln cut him short, it was said, and later explained: "I hate to have old friends like the Senator go away. And another thing I usually find out is that a Senator or Representative out of business is a sort of *lame duck*. He has to be provided for."

A Methodist minister, claiming relation to the inventor of ironclad gunboats, wished to be a hospital chaplain. The President could do nothing and said so curtly. The place seeker had heard that such appointments were made by the President. The President made clear: "When there are vacancies I appoint, not without."

Into the hands of Josiah Gilbert Holland, special writer for and one-fourth owner of the Springfield *Republican*, came a letter written by an extraordinary woman who had several interviews with President Lincoln on successive days. Her account of these days achieved a vivid word portrait of a man writhing, elusive, tormented, lighted with awkward humors, using words sometimes to mask his thought. Her account was put in print by Holland.

She was Mrs. Louis Powell Harvey, wife of the Governor of Wisconsin elected in 1861. Her husband was drowned while moving supplies for soldiers wounded in the Battle of Shiloh. She asked Governor Edward Salomon of Wisconsin for permission to visit hospitals in the Western military depot as an agent of the state. Southward along the Mississippi River she visited many general hospitals. She saw Northern boys wasting away in the heat of semitropical summers, noxious and contagious diseases bringing the mortality too high, taking many who might under different climatic and sanitary conditions have lived. She met surgeons appalled at conditions.

She entered alone to find the President alone "in a folded-up sort of way, in his arm-chair." He held her letter, made a feint at rising, looked from under his eyebrows. "Mrs. Harvey?" He took her hand, "hoped she was well," gave no smile of welcome. She read his face, deep-lined, almost stern. He motioned her to a chair. He finished her letter, looked up, ran his fingers through his slightly silvered dark-brown hair. "Madam, this matter of northern hospitals has been talked of a great deal, and I thought it was settled; but it seems this is not the case. What have you got to say about it?"

"Simply this," she replied, "that many soldiers, sick in our western army on the Mississippi, must have northern air, or die. There are thousands of graves along the Mississippi and Yazoo, for which the government is responsible—ignorantly, undoubtedly; but this ignorance must not continue. If you will permit these men to come North, you will have ten men in one year where you have got one now."

Shrugging his shoulders, smiling: "If your reasoning were correct, your argument would be a good one. I don't see how sending one sick man North is going to give us ten well ones." The lady: "You understand me, I think." "Yes, yes," said he, "I understand you; but if they go North they will desert, and where is the difference?" Her reply: "Dead men cannot fight, and they may not desert." "A fine way to decimate the army!" exclaimed the President. "We should never get a man back—not one—not one." "Pardon me," responded the lady, "but I believe you are mistaken. You do not understand our people. They are as true and as loyal to the government as yourself. The loyalty is among the common soldiers, and they are the chief sufferers." Almost with contempt Lincoln replied, "This is your opinion!"

In this exhibition of petulance, were there signs the President saw he was being undermined? "Mrs. Harvey," said he earnestly, "how many men of the Army of the Potomac do you suppose the government was paying at the battle of Antietam? . . ." He threw himself awkwardly around in his chair, with one leg over the arm, and spoke slowly: "This war might have been finished at that time, if every man had been in his place who was able to be there . . . The consequences, you know, proved nearly disastrous." The President paused.

Her response came: "It was very sad; but the delinquents were certainly not in northern hospitals . . ." The President: "Well, well; you go and call on the Secretary of War and see what he says." He then took her letter, and wrote on the back: "Admit Mrs. Harvey at once . . . She is a lady of intelligence, and talks sense. A. Lincoln." "May I return to you, Mr. Lincoln?" she inquired. "Certainly," said he, gently. Then Mrs. Harvey in Mr. Stanton's office was treated with great kindness, but he had to be guided by the medical authorities.

She returned to the President. No one was waiting. She passed directly into the President's room. Mr. Lincoln motioned her to a chair, inquired what the Secretary of War had said to her. She gave him a full account, and added, "I have nowhere to go but to you." He replied: "I will see the Secretary of War myself, to-night; and you may come again in the morning." He then dismissed her, she noted, "in the kindest manner and with the kindest words."

Had he from this moment determined to grant the woman her request? In these interviews he seemed to be arguing against and opposing his own decisions.

In the morning, she returned. The President said good morning, pointed to a chair, seemed annoyed at something, and waited for her to speak. She waited for him. "Well?" said he, after a minute of delay. "Well?" replied his visitor.

He looked up under his eyebrows, a little startled, and inquired, "Have you nothing to say?" "Nothing," she replied, "until I hear your decision. Have you decided? You know you bade me come this morning." "No, I have not decided; and I believe this idea of northern hospitals is a great humbug, and I am tired of hearing about it."

The woman pitied him in his weak and irritable mood. "I regret to add a feather's weight to your already overwhelming care and responsibility. I would rather have stayed at home." With a feeble smile, he responded, "I wish you had."

She was earnest, and replied: "Nothing would have given me greater pleasure, sir; but a keen sense of duty to this government, justice and mercy to its most loyal supporters, and regard for your honor and position, made me come . . . Mr. Lincoln, I do believe you will yet be grateful for my coming . . . I plead for the lives of those who were the first to hasten to the support of this government, who helped to place you where you are—for men who have done all they could; and now, when flesh and nerve and muscle are gone, who still pray for your life, and the life of the republic. They scarcely ask for that for which I plead. They expect to sacrifice their lives for their country. I know that, if they could come North, they could live, and be well, strong men again—at least many of them. I say I know, because I was sick among them last spring, surrounded by every comfort, with the best of care, and determined to get well. I grew weaker and weaker, day by day, until, not being under military law, my friends brought me North. I recovered entirely by breathing northern air."

Mr. Lincoln's expression of face changed often, but he did not take his eyes from her. He seemed distressed at being convinced she was speaking the truth. His face contracted almost painfully. "You assume to know more than I do." The tears almost came in the woman's eyes. "Pardon me, Mr. Lincoln, I intend no disrespect; but it is because of this knowledge, and because I do know what you do not know, that I come to you. If you had known what I know, and had not already ordered what I ask, I should know that an appeal to you would be in vain; but I believe in you. I believe the people have not trusted you in vain. The question only is—do you believe me, or not? If you believe in me, you will give us hospitals; if not—well."

"You assume to know more than surgeons do," said Lincoln, sharply. "Oh no," she replied: "I could not perform an amputation nearly so well as some of them do! But this is true: I do not come here for your favor. I am no aspirant for military favor or promotion . . . For eight long months—from early morning until late at night, sometimes—I have visited the regimental and general hospitals on the Mississippi, from Quincy to Vicksburg; and I come to you from the cots of men who have died, and who might have lived if you had permitted it. This is hard to say, but it is true."

While she was speaking the last sentences, Lincoln's brow set with hard furrows; a look of pain gathered on his whole face. Then he sharply asked her how many men her state had sent to the field. She replied, "About fifty thousand." "That means," he responded, "that she has about twenty thousand now." With an unpleasant voice and manner he continued. "You need not look so sober; they are not all dead." The veins filled in his face painfully; one across his forehead was fearfully large and blue. Then, with an impatient movement of his whole frame: "I have a good mind to dismiss them all from the service, and have no more trouble with them."

Mrs. Harvey was astonished. She knew he was not in earnest. They sat looking at one another in silence. He had become very pale. At last she broke the silence. "They have been faithful to the government; they have been faithful to you; they will still be loyal to the government, do what you will with them. But, if you will grant my petition, you will be glad as long as you live. The prayers of grateful hearts will give you strength in the hour of trial, and strong and willing arms will return to fight your battles."

The President bowed his head and, with a look of sadness she thought impossible for language to describe, said, "*I shall never be glad any more.*" All severity had passed away from his face, and he seemed looking inward and backward, unconscious that he was not alone. Great burdens he had borne, terrible anxieties that had poisoned his life at the fountain, peaceful scenes he had forever left behind—did these sweep across his memory? And then the added thought that perhaps his mistaken judgment had done injustice to the men who had fought the nation's battles.

The woman said, "Oh! do not say so, Mr. Lincoln, for who will have so much reason to rejoice as yourself, when the government shall be restored—as it will be?" "I know—I know," he said, pressing a hand on either side, "but the springs of life are wearing away, and I shall not last." She asked him if he felt that his great cares were injuring his health. "No," he replied; "not directly, perhaps." She asked him if he slept well. He never was "a good sleeper," he replied, and of course slept now less than ever before.

The woman, feeling that she had occupied too much of his time, rose to take her leave. "Have you decided upon your answer to me?" "No," he replied, "come to-morrow morning:—stop, it is cabinet-meeting to-morrow. Yes, come at twelve o'clock; there is not much for the cabinet to do to-morrow."

The next morning Mrs. Harvey found that her interview had prostrated her, but at twelve o'clock she was at the White House. The President sent her word that the Cabinet would adjourn soon, and that she must wait. For three long hours she waited, receiving occasional messages to the effect that the Cabinet would soon adjourn, and he would then see her.

She was in distress, expecting defeat. She walked the room, and gazed at the maps, and at last she heard the sound of feet. The Cabinet had adjourned. The President did not send for her, but came shuffling into the room, rubbing his hands, and saying, "My dear madam, I am sorry I have kept you waiting so long, but we have this moment adjourned." "My waiting is no matter," she replied, "but you must be very tired, and we will not talk to-night."

Bidding her to a seat, she having risen as he entered, he sat down at her side, and quietly remarked, "I only wish to say to you that an order which is equivalent to the granting of a hospital in your state, has been issued from the War Department, nearly twenty-four hours."

The woman could make no reply, except through the tears that sprang at once. Lincoln looked on, and enjoyed it. When at last she could command her voice, she said: "God bless you!" Then, as doubts came as to the order, she said earnestly, "Do you mean, really and truly, that we are going to have a hospital now?" With a look full of benevolence and tenderness—such a look, the woman wrote, "as rarely illuminates any face"—he said, "I do most certainly hope so." Then he told her to come on the following morning, and he would give her a copy of the order.

But she was too much affected to talk; and noticing this, he changed the subject, asking her to look at a map which hung in the room, representing the great battlegrounds of Europe. ". . . a great work, whoever executed it. Who was it, Mr. President?" "McClellan," he answered, and added: "He certainly did do this well. He did it while he was at West Point."

Next morning, sick with the excitement through which she had passed, Mrs. Harvey was at the White House again. She found more than 50 persons waiting for an audience; so she sent in her name, and said she would call again. The messenger said he thought the President would see her, and she had better be seated. Soon afterward he informed her that the President would see her. As she passed in, she heard the words from one of the waiting throng: "She has been here six days; and, what is more, she is going to win."

As she entered, the President smiled pleasantly, drew a chair to his side, and said, "Come here, and sit down." As she did so, he handed her a copy of the coveted order. She thanked him, and apologized for not being more promptly at the house; she had been sick all night. "Did joy make you sick?" he inquired. "I suppose," he added, "you would have been mad if I had said 'no.'" She replied, "No, Mr. Lincoln, I should have been neither angry nor sick." "What would you have done?" "I should have been here at nine o'clock this morning." "Well," said he, laughing, "I think I have acted wisely then."

Then he turned suddenly and looked into her face as he said, "Don't you ever get angry?" She replied that she never did when she had an important object to attain. There was more conversation on the naming of the hospital. The woman rose, and said, "You will not wish to see me again." "I did not say that, and I shall not say it," said the President. "You have been very kind to me, and I am very grateful for it."

He looked up at her from under his eyebrows, in his peculiar way, and said, "You almost think I am handsome, don't you?" His face was full of benevolence, and his countenance lighted by a cordial smile; and it was not strange that Mrs. Harvey exclaimed, "You are perfectly lovely to me *now*, Mr. Lincoln." The President colored a little, and laughed a good deal at the impulsive response, and reached out his hand to bid her farewell. She took it reverently, bowed her head upon it, and, bowing, prayed: "God bless you, Abraham Lincoln." Then she turned, heard his good-by and was gone.

Thus ran one transcript, more scrupulously complete and accurate, without a doubt, than perhaps half the accounts of what Lincoln said and did within eyesight and earshot of those who gave the accounts. Her return from the Secretary of War to say "I have nowhere to go but to you" struck him with its simplicity. Her waiting for him to speak was proper. Her "Well?" to his "Well?" could not have been better. To his startled "Have you nothing to say?" came her "Nothing until I hear your decision," the perfect essence of truth. To her abrupt point that she would "rather have stayed at home" than add "a feather's weight" to his overwhelming care, his "I wish you had" was probably with design, as again his later "You assume to know more than I do."

During this third interview in which he told her that he believed her project "a great humbug," everything she asked for had already been granted, an order issued, as he told her the next day, "issued from the War Department, nearly twenty-four hours." Then in the last one of their interviews he had been luminous with humor, shining with a benevolent wit, sharing with her the gladness that came through her tears, refuting his own cry that he would never be glad again—naïve and bubbling his query "You almost think I am handsome, don't you?"

Mrs. Harvey went away to be a witness of the building of the Harvey Hospital at Madison, Wisconsin, named for her husband, another general hospital at Prairie du Chien, and still another in Milwaukee—three hospitals resulting from her interviews with her President.

Had the people and events of those tornado years shaped Lincoln more and more into a man paradoxically harder than ever, yet also more delicate and tenuous in human judgments and affairs? Was there more often a phantom touch in what he did? Did certain men and women who studied him either close up or from far away feel that a strange shade and a ghost, having often a healing power, moving toward wider and surer human solidarity, lived and spoke in the White House? For such as there were of these, who knew an intimacy with Lincoln even when he was at his loneliest, who were ready to uphold him when they had no inkling of where his next decision might bring the country—for these one writer tried in *Harper's Weekly* of September 24, 1864, to voice a faith and offer a parable bearing on the election to come in November. This was George William Curtis, signing his paragraphs with his initials.

He could see a ship torn and worn with a long voyage, met by head winds and baffling currents. "A feeling of disappointment and despondency takes possession of the passengers and the crew, and each one attributes to the officer of the ship the inevitable and necessary delays and discouragements . . ." Then the long-wished-for land heaves into view. "Certainty takes the place of disappointed hopes, and they feel with mortification and regret how unjust they have been to the officer whose every hour and thought has been devoted to their welfare, and who has at length brought them with safety, and with a prosperous voyage, to the end of their journey."

Beyond parties or partisan success were other motives to which G.W.C. would appeal in this popular pictorial weekly magazine going to nearly all towns of the North and camps of the Union Army. Though no loyal heart could envision Mr. Lincoln replaced "by some other, any other, man," his influence could not end with his discontinuance of power. "There is a fame which no station or absence of station can add to or diminish. His work, like that of the most obscure soldier who lies buried under the sod of Gettysburg or Antietam, has been done . . . Faithful and consecrated to the service of his country, his memory, though it were nameless as that of any private in our armies or any nurse in our hospitals, will, like theirs, be sweet in the heart of every true American . . ."

A San Francisco woman wrote for a home newspaper of how she quoted for Lincoln a line from Starr King's burial speech for Ned Baker—"Hither in future ages they shall bring . . . the sacred ashes of the advocate and soldier of liberty"—and of how in evening mist among the Soldiers' Home trees Lincoln kindled to the picture of a grand procession in solemn hush winding its way through street crowds of San Francisco on up the heights to the open grave on Lone Mountain. "It seemed to rise before them out of the quiet sea, a vast mausoleum from the hand of God, wherein to lay the dead."

There amid grasses where sea wind and land wind met they had laid for his long sleep the old and treasured friend whose death at Ball's Bluff had meant tears and grief to Lincoln. Now, thought the woman, this weary though lighted and strange man, Lincoln, seemed almost to be dreaming of rest for himself sometime, perhaps in envy of the rest that had come to the bright and daring Ned Baker. He gave a eulogy of his old friend "in a few deep-toned words."

CHAPTER 53

Election Day, November 8, 1864

OF NOVEMBER 8, 1864, the day of the national election, John Hay wrote that the White House was "still and almost deserted." The sky hung gray. Rain fell. About noon Brooks called on the President "and to my surprise found him entirely alone, as if by common consent everybody had avoided the White House." Lincoln had no ease, saying to Brooks: "I am just enough of a politician to know that there was not much doubt about the result of the Baltimore convention; but about this thing I am very far from being certain. I wish I were certain."

At seven o'clock that evening Lincoln with Hay stepped out of the White House into a night of wild rain and storm. They splashed across the grounds to the War Department telegraph office. At a side door a wet and steaming sentinel huddled in a rubber coat. As Lincoln entered the second-floor telegraph office a dispatch was put in his hands from Forney at Philadelphia claiming 10,000 majority there. "Forney," said Lincoln, "is a little excitable." To Mrs. Lincoln he sent over early reports, saying, "She is more anxious than I."

In Stanton's office later Lincoln saw Gustavus Vasa Fox in glee over two hated opponents beaten. "You have more of that feeling of personal resentment than I," said Lincoln, Hay noted. "Perhaps I may have too little of it, but I never thought it paid. A man has not time to spend half his life in quarrels. If any man ceases to attack me, I never remember the past against him."

The wires worked badly because of the rain-and-wind storm. In a long lull about ten, wrote Brooks, "The President amused the little company in the War Office with entertaining reminiscences and anecdotes." In and out moved Eckert, handing telegrams to Stanton, the President then studying them and commenting. "Presently there came a lull in the returns," wrote Charles A. Dana of the evening, "and Mr. Lincoln called me to a place by his side.

" 'Dana,' said he, 'have you ever read any of the writings of Petroleum V. Nasby?' 'No, sir,' I said: 'I have only looked at some of them, and they seemed to be quite funny.' 'Well,' said he, 'let me read you a specimen'; and, pulling out a thin yellow-covered pamphlet from his breast pocket, he began to read aloud. Mr. Stanton viewed these proceedings with great impatience, as I could see, but Mr. Lincoln paid no attention to that. He would read a page or a story, pause to consider a new election telegram, and then open the book again and go ahead with a new passage . . .

"Mr. Stanton went to the door and beckoned me into the next room. I shall never forget the fire of his indignation . . . that when the safety of the republic was thus at issue . . . the leader, the man most deeply concerned

. . . could turn aside to read such balderdash and to laugh at such frivolous jests was, to his mind, repugnant, even damnable. He could not understand, apparently, that . . . this was Mr. Lincoln's prevailing characteristic—that the safety and sanity of his intelligence were maintained and preserved."

As the evening wore on the wires worked badly from Illinois and from states west of the Mississippi. The returns in, however, were running close to the tabulation Lincoln had made weeks before of his own estimates. Toward midnight, noted Brooks, "It was certain that Lincoln had been reëlected, and the few gentlemen left in the office congratulated him very warmly on the result. Lincoln took the matter very calmly, showing not the least elation or excitement, but said that he would admit that he was glad to be relieved of all suspense, grateful that the verdict of the people was likely to be so full, clear, and unmistakable that there could be no dispute." At a midnight supper, Hay noted, "The President went awkwardly and hospitably to work shovelling out the fried oysters." It was two in the morning when he started to leave the War Office, at the door meeting serenaders with a brass band, with cheers calling for a speech. The rain, the storm, was over.

The President told them, "I earnestly believe that the consequences of this day's work, if it be as you assure me and as now seems probable, will be to the lasting advantage, if not to the very salvation, of the country . . . I do not impugn the motives of any one opposed to me. It is no pleasure to me to triumph over any one; but I give thanks to the Almighty for this evidence of the people's resolution to stand by free government and the rights of humanity."

A day of great fate was over. There was no going behind the returns. Complete tabulations yet to come were a mere formality. At thousands of polling places some 4,000,000 men had marked ballots. A nation had made a decision.

Chaos, hate, suspicion, mistrust, vengeance, dark doubts, were in the air. But the marking, handling, counting, of the ballots went on in quiet and good order, fraud or violence showing only in minor incidents. The miscounts and repeaters were only ordinary. Free speech and license to print were so operating that either side would have flared forth about any flagrant departure from the customary election methods.

The American electorate, "the People," spoke on whether a colossal, heavy, weary war should go on, under the same leadership as it had begun, on whether the same guiding mind and personality should keep the central control and power. On a day of rain and wind that wrecked telegraph systems, the people said Yes to Lincoln.

Brooks directly quoted Lincoln as saying the day after: "I should be the veriest shallow and self-conceited blockhead upon this footstool if, in my discharge of the duties which are put upon me in this place, I should hope to get along without the wisdom which comes from God and not from men."

The election returns when analyzed admonished humility. In the Electoral College vote, all the Northern States except Kentucky, Delaware and New Jersey went to Lincoln. But it was not so sweeping a triumph in the total of popular ballots. They gave Lincoln a majority of slightly more than 400,000. The votes for Lincoln from coast to coast, 2,203,831, represented 55.09 per cent of all that were cast, said *Appleton's Annual Cyclopaedia* for

1864. McClellan had 44.91 per cent of the total: between New York and San Francisco were 1,797,019 male voters opposed to Lincoln, his administration and his policies. In New York City McClellan carried by 78,746 against Lincoln's 36,673; in the Empire State Lincoln won with 50.47 per cent of the vote as against McClellan's 49.53 per cent. It was formidable that 212 of the Electoral College votes should go to Lincoln, with McClellan getting only 21. But a study of three states with the largest electoral votes, New York, Pennsylvania and Ohio, showed Lincoln receiving 930,269 to 843,862 for McClellan, a difference of only 86,407 votes, but giving Lincoln 80 in the Electoral College. Had these three key states by their narrow margin gone for McClellan and been joined by two or three other states, McClellan would have been elected.

Humility was counseled even in the one little news bulletin: "The official majority of votes cast for General McClellan in Mr. Lincoln's own county of Sangamon, Illinois, is 376." Also a study of Illinois returns showed that every county bounding Sangamon had gone for McClellan and against Lincoln. But in the one spot in the returns where Lincoln's heart would have been sore had not the ballots thundered and roared high for him—the soldier vote—he won home big, the forecast being fulfilled that they would vote as they shot.

Grant wired from City Point, "The victory is worth more to the country than a battle won." General Frank Blair wrote to Hay from Georgia, where he headed an army corps under Sherman, "The vote in this army today is almost unanimous for Lincoln. Give Uncle Abe my compliments."

And highlighted in the background of Lincoln's victory was the fact that hundreds of thousands of soldiers whose ballots would have been given to the President had no chance to vote, either because of required marching and fighting, or because their home-state legislatures had refused them the right of voting in the field. And in the foul rooms of Libby Prison at Richmond the votes were 276 for Lincoln, 95 for McClellan.

On the night of November 10 a procession with banners, lanterns, transparencies marched to the White House, surged around the main entrance and filled the front grounds. The newly elected President stepped out of a window opening on the north portico and the crowd uproar was many minutes going down. Lincoln made ready to read his script to the people. Hay stood alongside with a candle to light the written page. "Not very graceful," he smiled to Hay, "but I am growing old enough not to care much for the manner of doing things."

"It has long been a grave question," Lincoln began, under the night stars, "whether any government, not *too* strong for the liberties of its people, can be strong *enough* to maintain its own existence, in great emergencies. On this point the present rebellion brought our republic to a severe test . . . the election was a necessity. We can not have free government without elections; and if the rebellion could force us to forego, or postpone a national election, it might fairly claim to have already conquered and ruined us . . . Human-nature will not change. In any future great national trial, compared with the men of this, we shall have as weak, and as strong; as silly and as wise; as bad and good . . . Gold is good in its place; but living, brave, patriotic men, are better than gold."

Left: Brady photograph February 9, 1864. Robert Todd Lincoln considered this the best photograph of his father [Meserve]. *Upper center:* Walt Whitman, the great poet of the War and of Lincoln [Meserve]. *Upper right:* John Bright, member of the British House of Commons, constantly a spokesman of Lincoln and his policies [CS]. *Lower center:* Thomas Eckert, a War Telegraph Office crony of Lincoln [USASC]. *Lower right:* Carl Schurz of Wisconsin, youthful German revolutionary, Minister to Spain, later Major General, brilliant '64 campaign orator [CS].

Upper left: Brady photograph February 9, 1864 [Meserve]. *Upper right:* Andrew Johnson of Tennessee, elected Vice-President 1864 [USASC]. *Lower, left to right:* John C. Frémont, explorer, California millionaire rancher, Major General, politician constantly at odds with Lincoln [Meserve], Charles Sumner, Boston antislavery aristocrat, U.S. Senator from Massachusetts [CS], Benjamin F. Butler, Massachusetts lawyer who "could strut sitting down," Major General constantly playing politics [CS], Clement L. Vallandigham of Ohio, Congressman and violent opponent of Lincoln [McClees].

He voiced the human spirit he would prefer to have breathing across the future. "So long as I have been here I have not willingly planted a thorn in any man's bosom. While I am deeply sensible to the high compliment of a re-election; and duly grateful, as I trust, to Almighty God for having directed my countrymen to a right conclusion, as I think, for their own good, it adds nothing to my satisfaction that any other man may be disappointed or pained by the result . . . And now, let me close by asking three hearty cheers for our brave soldiers and seamen and their gallant and skilful commanders." The applause and cheers roared. Then slowly the faces, lights and voices dwindled. The White House lawn took on its accustomed night shadows of trees, fences, buildings, and silence.

The outlook Lincoln had voiced was toward conciliation—no retaliation, no reprisals, no thorns knowingly planted in the bosoms of others. On November 11 at the Cabinet meeting the President took from his desk the folded and pasted memorandum that Cabinet members had signed August 23 without knowing what it said. He read it with its now odd-sounding statement of probability "that this Administration will not be re-elected."

On Election Day McClellan resigned as a major general in the Regular Army. To fill this vacancy Lincoln signed a commission for General Philip H. Sheridan. McClellan began on his plans for a trip to Europe, which would keep him away from the American scene and its war for many months.

The Charleston *Mercury* on November 22 printed Lincoln's speech of November 10, in full. The news item preceding the speech read: "The Abolition Clubs of Washington went to Lincoln's White House on Thursday evening, and, after firing off a cannon, proceeded to hurrah, etc., until the Gorilla came out and made the following speech." Confederate newspapers in the main interpreted for their readers the election of Lincoln as an advantage to their cause. A Richmond *Sentinel* commentary held: "There are some names more odious among us even than that of Abraham Lincoln. We know Seward as a snake, a cunning plotter of mischief and contriver of frauds wherever his faith is pledged. We know Sumner as a mouthing thunderer of great words, but of weak spine and trembling knees. We know Butler as a beast. Compared with these detestable qualities Mr. Lincoln's joking propensities appear, if puerile, yet harmless. If they excite our contempt, they yet appeal to our good nature."

A cartoon in *Harper's Weekly*, titled "Long ABRAHAM LINCOLN a little Longer," stretched Lincoln's length of form till he soared to an impossible height.

Overseas that political fraction known as liberals had relief and joy over Lincoln's re-election. In France, said the *Journal des débats*, "It is the first time that a people in possession of universal suffrage has been called to pronounce directly and finally for or against the continuation of a painful war." Never in any other land, it seemed, had a people in the waste and anguish of war voted Yes or No, freely and without hindrance, whether a war should go on.

The *Spectator* of London, November 26, saw the North had pronounced by a majority that "though its land be covered with hospitals and its cities filled with bankrupts, though every family weep for its sons and the course

of material civilization be thrown back centuries, it is ready to fight manfully on rather than freedom should be proved a chimera . . . Had the
North shrunk, or even faltered, had she refused the necessary sacrifices or
accepted the evil compromise, the cause of liberty would have received a
heavy, perhaps a deadly wound." New England, the West, the great States
of New York and Pennsylvania, had declared that Mr. Lincoln, "this shrewd
peasant with his noble purpose and his deadly tenacity, expresses their resolve; that despite endless charges of oppression and occasional realities of
failure, despite uncouthness and occasional want of tact, he is the fitting
mouth-piece of the nation in its struggle for life or death." The *Spectator*
writer from his long-distance view listed the mighty factors of advantage
that lay with Lincoln. "He is securely President until March, 1869." Victory
now needed only persistence. "And persistence is the one quality Mr. Lincoln is certain not to lack."

Consul Bigelow in Paris wrote November 22 of Lincoln's election as
". . . more significant than is realized even in America . . . more worthy of
a National thanksgiving than any event, humanly speaking, which has occurred since the Revolution."

Grant's telegram to Lincoln held true. The November election counted
for more than a great battle won. It answered many questions. Would the
war go on? Yes, more brutally than before. Would conscription go on?
Yes, and with less outspoken opposition. Those claiming free speech and a
free press? They would be less noisy and foul, though not giving up old
habits. Some were a little stunned and helpless.

"Our people are excited," read a telegram November 25 from Governor
Curtin, "by a rumor that three States have offered to return to their allegiance. Is it true?" Lincoln's instant and positive reply: "I have no knowledge, information, or belief, that three States, or any state, offer to resume
allegiance."

The morning after Election Day Hay's diary recorded: "W. H. L.
[Ward Hill Lamon] came to my room to talk over the Chief Justiceship
. . . He took a glass of whiskey and then, refusing my offer of a bed, went
out &, rolling himself up in his cloak, lay down at the President's door;
passing the night in that attitude of touching and dumb fidelity, with a small
arsenal of pistols & bowie knives around him. In the morning he went away
leaving my blankets at my door, before I or the President were awake."

CHAPTER 54

Lincoln Names a Chief Justice

W HO WOULD be named as Chief Justice? In the press, in political
circles, across tea cups and over whisky toddies, there was guess and
gossip. Of the eminent New York attorney William M. Evarts, Justice
Swayne, Justice David Davis, there was public mention. Attorney General

Bates modestly and privately mentioned in his diary that his appointment would be a fitting close to his career. Fessenden said for himself he could not consent. Browning wrote: "Called on the President and urged on him the appointment of Mr. Stanton as chief Justice. He said nothing in reply to what I urged except to admit Mr. Stantons ability, and fine qualifications."

Formidable pressure arose for Montgomery Blair. James Gordon Bennett and Thurlow Weed, an odd team of editors, went to Washington and held a conference with Blair on how to stop Chase, whom everyone considered in the lead.

Across November the President heard a series of delegations and individual callers and gave them no committals. Union League Club men from Philadelphia spoke for Chase, and read a signed memorial. The President replied: "Will you do me the favor to leave that paper with me? I want it in order that, if I appoint Mr. Chase, I may show the friends of the other persons for whom the office is solicited by how powerful an influence and by what strong personal recommendations the claims of Mr. Chase were supported." The Union Leaguers, pleased and satisfied at this, then noticed the President had not finished. He had merely paused. Now he went on. "And I want the paper also in order that, if I should appoint any other person, I may show his friends how powerful an influence and what strong personal recommendations I was obliged to disregard in appointing him." The Philadelphians walked out knowing no more than when they came.

Richard Henry Dana and Judge E. R. Hoar called together and told Lincoln that if, as rumor had it, he had determined to appoint Chase they would not proceed to suggest other men. Lincoln replied, Judge Hoar wrote: "Mr. Chase is a very able man. He is a very ambitious man and I think on the subject of the presidency a little insane. He has not always behaved very well lately and people say to me, 'Now is the time to *crush him out.*' Well, I'm not in favor of crushing anybody out! If there is anything that a man can do and do it well, I say let him do it. Give him a chance."

Chase personally seemed to have high hopes at first. Later he was not so sure what the President would do. Days passed into weeks. The deliberation of the President seemed ominous to Chase. Behind the scenes it seemed that Lincoln had only one distinct doubt and this he spoke to one after another of those who came to the front for Chase. He considered sending for Chase to see whether he would dismiss at once and forever the Presidency from his mind. But when Lincoln broached this to Sumner, noted Nicolay and Hay, "he saw in a moment's conversation how liable to misapprehension such action would be . . . the construction which Mr. Chase would inevitably place upon such a proposition coming from his twice successful rival."

When one day Nicolay brought a letter from Chase, Lincoln asked, "What is it about?" "Simply a kind and friendly letter." Lincoln, without reading it and with a shrewd smile: "File it with his other recommendations."

From active enemies of Chase in Ohio came spoken and written protests against his appointment. From Treasury Department officials, from the

Blair and other groups, came many descriptions of Chase as too partisan, too ignorant of men, too much of a grumbler and a marplot. Nicolay and Hay noted the President heard with respect any points of merit they had against Chase but when they tried to remind him of how and when Chase had sought to undermine him, "he sternly checked them." The secretaries believed Lincoln intended from the first to appoint Chase. To Nicolay he said, using boyhood Kentucky lingo, "I shall be very 'shut pan' about this matter."

The young Illinois Congressman Shelby M. Cullom heard of Chase letters with mean insinuations about Lincoln being offered for the President's reading and of his comment, "If Mr. Chase has said some hard things about me, I in turn have said some hard things about him, which, I guess, squares the account." And on another occasion, "I know meaner things about Mr. Chase than any of these men can tell me."

Congress had assembled. On December 6, at whatever risk and not unaware there were risks, guided by joined motives of statecraft and political balances, the President named Chase for Chief Justice.

"He communicated his intention to no one," noted his secretaries, and wrote out the nomination with his own hand. Without reference to a committee and with no discussion the Senate at once unanimously confirmed the appointment. Chase wrote to the President: "Before I sleep I must thank you for this mark of your confidence, and especially for the manner in which the nomination was made."

Congressman John B. Alley, so he wrote, had entered the President's library to hear Lincoln: "Although I may have appeared to you and to Mr. Sumner to have been opposed to Chase's appointment, there never has been a moment since the breath left old Taney's body that I did not conceive it to be the best thing to do to appoint Mr. Chase . . ." Alley repeated that the action was magnanimous and patriotic. Lincoln: "As to his talk about me, I do not mind that. Chase is, on the whole, a pretty good fellow and a very able man. His only trouble is that he has 'the White House fever' a little too bad, but I hope this may cure him and that he will be satisfied."

Nicolay and Hay saw Chase take his place on the bench with a conscientious desire to do his whole duty in his great office, and yet, "He still considered himself called upon to counteract the mischievous tendencies of the President towards conciliation and hasty reconstruction. His slighting references to him [the President] in his [Chase's] letters and diaries continued from the hour he took his place on the bench." Chase had been especially pressed upon the President by the radical antislavery wing of their party. Lincoln for his own political reasons was giving them what they wanted. He was hoping for more harmony toward his own plans for reconstruction in the South.

As the author of the National Bank Act, as an acquaintance of August Belmont who proposed in the summer of '64 the conditions under which he [Chase] would join the Democratic party, as a man of "a certain solid weight of character," Chase was not offensive to a large section of conservatives. The appointment, once made, met with little opposition, and, noted

Nicolay and Hay, was "received with the greatest satisfaction throughout the Union."

Were the lines being more sharply drawn for a more continuous challenge by Congress of the executive power? It seemed so when in latter November Attorney General Bates resigned because of age and long service and the President sent to the Senate the appointment of James Speed of Kentucky. This brother of Joshua Speed, Lincoln's old bosom friend, had been an outspoken Union loyalist from the first, raised troops, and served to keep Kentucky in the Union. As an able attorney his record was unspotted.

The Senate Judiciary Committee held up the President's nomination several days, according to Noah Brooks, not because they hesitated at confirming Speed, but, as one of that committee said, "to convey a mild insinuation to the President that they did not know who James Speed of Kentucky was."

The somber and dignified old Supreme Court was filled to its limits December 15 with people who came to see Chase sworn in. The new Chief Justice read the oath of office in a clear but tremulous voice. Then, laying down the paper, he lifted his right hand, looked upward to the noble dome, and with deep feeling, "So help me God." Over the room was a breathless hush. The Chief Justice took his seat.

In the Buckeye State some who had long known Salmon P. Chase politically were unkind enough to recall a saying they had heard from him— "Be satisfied with skim milk when you can't get cream."

CHAPTER 55

The "Lost Army"—The South in Fire and Blood—War Prisons

IN LATE '64, observers in America and Europe hung breathless and wondering over the audacity and fate of a general and an army that had vanished. To his wife the head of this adventure wrote that he would come out of it reputed a great general or just plain crazy. Sherman had not seen the newborn baby who had arrived at his home in June. The baby would die while he was gone, while millions were wondering where he was, and he would accept this as war.

"If you can whip Lee," Sherman had written in September to Grant as between family men, "and I can march to the Atlantic, I think Uncle Abe will give us a twenty days' leave of absence to see the young folks." This he was writing in Georgia, where he had taken Atlanta. Nearby was Hood's army, which Jefferson Davis was saying had every advantage of being on home ground, so that it would yet cut Sherman's communications and destroy Sherman. To Grant, Sherman offered his plan. He would divide his army, give Thomas 60,000 with which to take care of Hood's 41,000, and then himself start on a thousand-mile march which was to end by joining Grant in Virginia, pausing at Savannah-by-the-Sea.

Thousands of people abroad and in the South would reason, wrote Sher-- man, "If the North can march an army right through the South it is proof positive that the North can prevail in this contest . . . Mr. Lincoln's elec- tion, which is assured, coupled with the conclusion thus reached, makes a logical whole."

Grant wired Lincoln: "Sherman's proposition is the best that can be adopted . . . Such an army as Sherman has, and with such a commander, is hard to corner or capture." This seemed to be a day of acid test for Lincoln on whether he would get behind his two best proven generals. Within three hours after Grant's telegram arrived, Stanton telegraphed Sherman com- plete approval.

It seemed as though Grant trusted Sherman completely, except for a day or two of wavering on the point of Sherman's faith that Thomas could take care of Hood. In the end Grant decided he would accept Sherman's judgment of what Thomas could do. And Lincoln, with his natural caution enforced by the bitter opposition of Grant's chief of staff, Rawlins, and by Halleck's placid routine disapproval, had nevertheless thrown himself into complete trust of Grant and Sherman. This trio of Lincoln, Grant and Sherman now worked in a co-operation as smooth as that which had long existed between Lee and Davis.

When Grant had heard of steps Lincoln was taking in Georgia in Septem- ber toward beginnings of reconstruction, he had wired Stanton, "Please ad- vise the President not to attempt to doctor up a State government for Georgia by the appointment of citizens in any capacity whatever. Leave Sherman to treat all questions in his own way, the President reserving his power to approve or disapprove of his actions." And Lincoln had accepted Grant's wish for him to go slow in any "doctoring" of state governments where Union armies were operating.

Sherman had not intended to burn as much of Atlanta as did burn. His chief engineer under orders wrecked all railroads in and about Atlanta, heated the rails red hot and twisted them around trees. Then smokestacks were pulled down, furnace arches broken, steam machinery smashed, holes punched in all boilers, all devices of industrial production wrecked against possible use. Before this work had begun, firebugs had set in flame a score of buildings, General Slocum offering a reward of $500 for the detection of any soldier involved. Atlanta buildings, 1,800, went up in smoke.

Sherman rode into the city with an aide near sunset November 15. Roses still bloomed in a few gardens of fine houses and Atlanta was a quiet city, not soothed but calm with a hint of heavy fate. The night held little quiet as an engineer corps fired more fallen buildings, as flames spread to a wrecked arsenal and shell explosions rattled the windows of hundreds of homes where no sleepers lay to be awakened. A fire department of soldiers struggled sev- eral hours of the night, managing to hold the fire mainly to the downtown and industrial districts, as intended. When Sherman rode out of the city at seven the next morning, a third, perhaps more, of Atlanta lay in ashes.

Toward the east and southward, toward Savannah and the Atlantic Ocean, toward a path that was to twist upward in the Carolinas, Sherman turned his horse. He knew this country. He had crossed many parts of it and lived in it several years of the 1840's. The ways of its people had been under his eye in part when he was superintendent of the Louisiana State Military Academy. The Macon *Telegraph* called him Judas Iscariot, a betrayer, a creature of depravity, a demon "of a thousand fiends."

Toward the east by the Decatur road Sherman paused on a hill and took a last look at smoking Atlanta. On the horizons around him a bright sun slanted down on the shining rifles of 55,000 picked men, veterans of proved capacity for action, for marching, for legwork, for many disease immunities, survivors of hard campaigns. Each man carried 40 rounds of cartridges, and in wagons were enough more to make 200 rounds per man. The sun slanted too on 65 cannon, each drawn by four teams of horses. Six-mule wagons, 2,500 of them, hauled supplies and forage. And 600 ambulances, two horses to each, were prepared for battle service. Between Sherman and his friend Grant at Richmond lay a thousand miles of cities and towns, lands, swamps and rivers, alive with a bitterly hostile people hating with a deepening despair.

To his wife Sherman had written less than a month before that in revolutions men fall and rise, are praised and then insulted. He was in a dark mood, writing: "Grant, Sheridan and I are now the popular favorites, but neither of us will survive this war. Some other must rise greater than either of us, and he has not yet manifested himself." Of the cheery soldiers singing in sun-bright weather on the start from Atlanta he was to write her: "I never saw a more confident army. The soldiers think I know everything and that they can do anything." In late October he had written her he was on a hazardous feat. "And you will not hear from me for months. The War Department will know my whereabouts, and the Rebels, and you will be able to guess."

This army had 218 regiments, all but 33 from Western States, 52 from Ohio, 50 from Illinois, 27 from Indiana, 13 from Wisconsin, 10 from Michigan, 15 from Iowa, 3 from Minnesota, 10 from Missouri, 4 from Kentucky. From New York were 16 regiments, from Pennsylvania 10, from New Jersey 3, from Massachusetts and Connecticut 2 each. They would be heard from—sometime. The word of Sherman to Grant, to the War Department and the President, was that communications were cut off from central Georgia and his next message he hoped to send from somewhere on the Atlantic Coast.

Starting November 15, marching in four columns sweeping a path 20 to 40 or more miles wide, this army began a systematic campaign of destruction. "The State of Georgia alone," Jefferson Davis had said in a recent speech in Augusta, "produces food enough not only for her own people and the army within but feeds too the Army of Virginia." On this storehouse and granary of the Confederacy worked the destroyers. What the army could not eat or carry away it burned, spoiled, ruined.

Now they had their war, was Sherman's thought, the war they had asked for. Until now the Border States had taken the punishment. Now it had come to the doorsills of the Deep South. Now sometimes you couldn't see the roses and the magnolia trees for the depot and warehouse smoke, for the dust of marching columns and rumbling wagons.

An argument began, to last long. Was Sherman a modern impersonation of Attila the Hun, a manner of sadist, a wanton and a monster who took pleasure in seeing an enemy people suffer? Or was he a soldier doing a necessary job, a kindhearted family man who wanted to end the war and saw no other way but the tactics he was using? Both sides made out a case. Wrote Sherman, ". . . the rebels . . . had forced us into the war, and . . . deserved all they got and *more*."

His conscience worried Sherman less than his sense of timing. He and Grant would join their armies some day, if their timing was right. Then the war would end. He traveled light. The saddlebags which his orderly carried held "a change of underclothing, my maps, a flask of whiskey, and a bunch of cigars." He could live as plainly as rank-and-file soldiers; they had seen him sleep in his blanket on cold ground. He watched over details till midnight and past, was out early in the morning, made up lost sleep sometimes with 10- and 15-minute naps on the ground during the day. When his troops had orders to do things that at first seemed impossible they said, "Well, *he* can't make a mistake."

A line of bridges on fire toward the rear one day, a private grunted comfortably, "Guess, Charley, Sherman has set the river on fire," Charley answering, "Well, if he has, I reckon it's all right." A stock anecdote had it that two Confederates on outpost duty were overheard trading rumors. "The Yanks can't get any more rations by railroad, for Wheeler has blown up the tunnel at Dalton." "Oh, hell, don't you know Sherman carries along a duplicate tunnel?"

Of the railroad-wrecking, wrote Sherman, "I gave it my personal attention." Bonfires were made of crossties, the iron rails laid on and when red hot carried to telegraph poles or trees and twisted around to make what were nicknamed "Sherman hairpins," though sometimes called "Lincoln gimlets." Or again they were "Jeff Davis neckties." A month of this and 265 miles of railway were *un*built.

Each brigade commander had authority to detail a forage company, usually about 50 men headed by one or two commissioned officers. Before daylight this party would leave, knowing where to rejoin their command on the march later in the day. On foot five or six miles from the brigade route, they visited every plantation and farm within range. On a farm wagon or a family carriage they loaded bacon, corn meal, turkeys, ducks, chickens, "everything that could be used as food or forage," to use Sherman's words. They regained the main road, usually in advance of their wagon train, and delivered to the brigade commissary the day's supplies gathered.

Candidly Sherman admitted, "No doubt, many acts of pillage, robbery and violence, were committed by these parties of foragers, usually called 'bummers.'" Stories came to him of jewelry taken from women, of family silverware dug up from hiding places, and of plunder of value that never reached the commissary. "But these acts were exceptional and incidental. I never heard of any cases of murder or rape." The unruly and the malicious would get out of hand, and in his official report to the War Department Sherman wrote of this hoodlum element, "A little loose in foraging they 'did some things they ought not to have done.'"

Yet no careful reading was required of the criticisms voiced by Governor Brown and General Beauregard the previous August to see they meant to say that the Confederate cavalry under General Wheeler had its own bummers. Robert Toombs then was writing to Stephens that Wheeler's band "consumes more than the whole army," was helping "accelerate the evil day," and as to their Confederate commander, Wheeler, "I hope to God he will never get back to Georgia." A letter to Secretary Seddon published in the Charleston *Mercury* went into many particulars of this Confederate unit having plunderers who took carpets, blankets, furniture in private houses, "by force in the presence of the owners."

Kilpatrick's cavalry did more than any other unit to earn a bad name for Sherman's army. They did lay hands on old men and choke them till the secret hiding places of coin, silver or jewelry were divulged. They did put their dirty boots on white bed linen, dance on polished floors to the piano music of howling comrades, smash the piano with gun butts. They did drag feather beds outdoors and scatter the feathers like a small snowstorm. They did scare women, though the incidence of rape was not conclusive in more than one or two cases. They did make free with Negro women and set special value on shapely mulattoes. But they were veteran troopers, hard fighters. Sherman tolerated them, partly because of his own belief that as tough soldiers for loyal active service they were among the best the earth had ever seen, partly because to set up a military police to watch and discipline his own men would delay when delay might be at heavy cost.

How many hundreds or thousands of stragglers, skulkers and deserters from the Confederate Army there were at this time in Georgia could not get into official records; in Georgia and all the Southern and Border States were roving bands of bushwhackers and guerrillas, lawless, desperate, living on the country. General Lee, seeing his losses by desertion on the increase in latter '64, suggested to President Davis it might be advisable to serve notice that deserters would have their rights to citizenship and property taken away. Governor Vance of North Carolina had the same year given out a long and fierce malediction on "the vile wretch who skulked in the woods, or the still viler coward who aided him, while his bleeding country was calling in vain for his help," telling them they must consider what their brave comrades would do to them when peace and independence were secured. "Ye that shelter, conceal, and feed these miserable depredators, think you that you will be spared? Nay! Never-failing eyes have marked you, every one." Misdeeds near to atrocities had been committed, according to Vance's proclamation.

In more than one case deserters said they had heard that if Lincoln was elected in November the war would be over, that it was common talk that with Lincoln President again the South would quit fighting. Many rumors of the Confederacy being on its last legs encouraged desertion. Union commanders circulated Lincoln's proclamation offering amnesty. Across picket posts, through printed circulars, by means open and secret, the report spread that deserters into the Union lines would meet good treatment. That the earlier Confederate unity was breaking, that cracks and seams had come in their governmental structure, was known to the Georgians, who saw their state legislature joined with those of Mississippi and North Carolina in refusals to take as constitutional the act of their Congress at Richmond in suspending the writ of habeas corpus. And timed with Sherman's march from Atlanta toward the sea ran the rumor that President Davis was to be impeached. It was not a harmonious Confederate Georgia over which Sherman was laying devastation. Daily as Sherman's troops swung along on the march came remarks from sidewalks, from roadsides. Most often there was silence. But General Hazen noted that the most typical expression from the Georgians was: "Why don't you go over to South Carolina and serve them this way? They started it."

One of Sherman's staff men wrote of seeing a black woman, holding a mulatto baby, point at Sherman with the cry, "Dar's de man dat rules de world!" At many a crossroads the Negroes came singing and cavorting in a faith that now their masters were overcome and the long-promised emancipation was at hand. Sherman however continued his former policy of telling them that in the right and proper hour to come they would have freedom to work for themselves instead of their masters, that they must not now harm their masters. "We don't want that." To Grant's advice that he should acquire Negroes and arm and organize them as best he could, Sherman paid no attention. In a plantation house at the crossing of the Ulcofauhatchee River he explained to an old, gray-haired Negro, "of as fine a head as I ever saw," that "we wanted the slaves to remain where they were, and not to load us down with useless mouths, which would eat up the food for our fighting men; that our success was their assured freedom; that we could receive a few of their young, hearty men as pioneers; but that if they followed us in swarms of old and young, feeble and helpless, it would simply cripple us in our great task." Sherman believed that this old man spread this message far, got it carried from mouth to mouth to an extent that saved the army from taking on a host of refugees that might have spelled famine. Some 25,000 Negroes in all, it was estimated, from time to time joined the army and were fed by it, three-fourths of them perhaps turning back homesick or unwilling or unable to stand the pace.

One raw, cold night Sherman found himself in a double-hewed log house, saw a box marked "Howell Cobb," learned from Negroes he was in the home of a Confederate brigadier general, onetime U.S. Senator from Georgia, Secretary of the U.S. Treasury under Buchanan. "Of course, we confiscated his property, and found it rich in corn, beans, peanuts, and sorghum-molasses." Sherman sent word to a staff general "to spare nothing," and that night on the Cobb plantation huge bonfires blazed.

Arriving next day at the state capital, Milledgeville, they found Governor Joseph Brown, the state officials, and the members of the legislature gone, the Governor's mansion stripped of carpets, curtains, furniture, food. Here Federal troops used stacks of Confederate paper money for a breakfast fire. Here Federal officers held a mock session in the state legislative chamber, repealed the Ordinance of Secession, voted the state back into the Union, made sarcastic speeches, and appointed a committee officially to kick the buttocks of Governor Brown and President Davis. Here were late newspapers from over the South, one having an appeal from General Beauregard to the people of Georgia to arise, obstruct, be confident, be resolute, and "Sherman's army will soon starve in your midst." Also a proclamation from Senator B. H. Hill, cosigned at Richmond by Secretary of War Seddon, that with firm and prompt action, "You have now the best opportunity ever presented to destroy the enemy." And while Sherman in Milledgeville read these and other items, thousands of bales of cotton got the torch, many cotton gins and presses were wrecked, and as Sherman reported, "I burned the railroad buildings and the arsenals; the statehouse and Governor's Mansion I left unharmed." That Governor Brown had transported the cabbages from his cellar and left the state archives for the invaders was taken by Sherman as a sign of a hurried departure, if nothing more.

The marching army moved on, no pauses, no days of rest, feeding on the fat of the land with a more savory bill of fare than any army during the war thus far. "It was gravy every day." Juicy steaks, pork chops, fried chicken, ham and eggs, yams rolled in Indian meal, sorghum syrup—at moments the war was a picnic and a frolic. Not so of course when the route shifted from east southward toward Savannah, when ground under the feet of one column heaved in explosion and several men were torn by shells and torpedoes, whereupon Sherman ordered Confederate prisoners to be marched ahead. They accommodated and dug up a line of buried torpedoes.

Sherman's army feinted toward the cities of Augusta and Macon, made no real move at them, slipped smoothly past them. No time now for the taking of cities. Confederate cavalry detached from Hood's army skirmished a little with Sherman's advance but undertook no real clash with the Union horse troops under Kilpatrick. The convicts, on Sherman's approach let loose from the state prison at Milledgeville for military service, were no help to further good order in Georgia that month. Some of them, joined up with deserters, drifters, bushwhackers, posed as Wheeler's cavalry and raided here and there for loot. "People show little spirit," wired a defending general from Augusta to Richmond. There and at Macon were the only signs of any organized resistance to Sherman, and at these spots Sherman refused to pause. At Macon "every man was in the trenches," said the Augusta *Constitutionalist*, adding that when members of the state legislature passed through the city they were arrested and an attempt made to put them in military service. "But they were exempt by law and refused to serve."

Sherman's men as seasoned soldiers more often gave misleading than correct information when they were asked what would be the route of the army. As less and less could be gleaned from Southern newspapers, the Union army marching in Georgia, the "lost army," became a world mystery, for speculation and surmise in the North and in Europe. "If Sherman has really left his army in the air and started off without a base to march from Georgia to South Carolina," said the experts of the *Army and Navy Gazette* in England, "he has done either one of the most brilliant or one of the most foolish things ever performed by a military leader." Sherman would either come out decorated for "the success of sublime audacity" or ridiculed for "the most tremendous disaster that ever befell an armed host," believed the London *Herald*, adding that he might become "the scoff of mankind and the humiliation of the United States." The London *Times* found itself fascinated by a piece of drama: "military history has recorded no stranger marvel than the mysterious expedition of General Sherman, on an unknown route against an undiscoverable enemy."

Henry Adams wrote in early December from London to his brother with the Army of the Potomac, "Popular opinion here declares louder than ever that Sherman is lost . . . The interest felt in his march is enormous, however, and if he arrives as successfully as I expect, at the sea, you may rely upon it that the moral effect of his demonstration on Europe will be greater than that of any other event of the war. It will finish the rebs on this side."

Grant said to a visiting committee: "Sherman is acting by order and I am waiting on him. Just as soon as I hear he is at some one of the points designated on the seacoast I will take Richmond. Were I to move now without advices from Sherman, Lee would evacuate Richmond, taking his army somewhere South and I would have to follow him to keep him from jumping on Sherman."

To a serenading party on the night of December 6 the President was brief and intimate: "I believe I shall never be old enough to speak without embarrassment when I have [nothing] to talk about. I have no good news to tell you, and yet I have no bad news to tell. We have talked of elections until there is nothing more to say about them. The most interesting news we now have is from Sherman. We all know where he went in at, but I can't tell where he will come out at. I will now close by proposing three cheers for Gen. Sherman and his army."

Sherman's brother, the Ohio Senator, came in anxiety over published Southern reports of his brother in retreat and disaster. Could anyone tell him the facts? Lincoln said: "Oh, no, I know the hole he went in at, but I can't tell you what hole he will come out of." Some two weeks after Sherman disappeared A. K. McClure in Lincoln's office was leaving when he heard, "McClure, wouldn't you like to hear something about Sherman?" McClure turned eagerly and Lincoln laughed. "Well, I'll be hanged if I wouldn't myself."

Carpenter noted Lincoln during a White House reception shaking hands with a continuous stream of people. And along came an old friend, whose name and face should be perfectly familiar to Lincoln. But Lincoln gave him only the same handshake and abstract greeting as any unknown. The old friend stood still and spoke again to Lincoln, who roused, shook himself out of a dark-brown study, again took his old friend's hand, and, "Excuse me for not noticing you. I was thinking of a man down South."

Richmond papers had no stories of attacks or effective actions against Sherman. Lincoln worried. "I assured him," wrote Grant to Sherman later, "with the army you had and you in command of it, there was no danger." Grant heard of Lincoln comforting inquirers: "Grant says they are safe with such a general, and that if they cannot get out where they want to, they can crawl back by the hole they went in at."

The same point in a less blunt style went into Lincoln's message to Congress December 6: "The most remarkable feature in the military operations of the year is General Sherman's attempted march of three hundred miles directly through the insurgent region. It tends to show a great increase of our relative strength that our General-in-Chief should feel able to confront and hold in check every active force of the enemy, and yet to detach a well-appointed large army to move on such an expedition. The result not yet being known, conjecture in regard to it is not here indulged."

That was all. Brooks puzzled; here was nothing about the direction of march or the point from which news of Sherman was expected. Laying the sheet of paper down and taking off his spectacles, Lincoln laughed at Brooks' disappointment, and added kindly, "Well, my dear fellow, that's all that Congress will know about it, anyhow."

A curious sentence which could serve several purposes was written into the first draft of the message to Congress. Then later Lincoln ran his pen through this sentence: "We must conclude that he [the General in Chief] feels our cause could, if need be, survive the loss of the whole detached force; while, by the risk, he takes a chance for the great advantages which would follow success." It could be taken to mean that Lincoln was not sharing the "risk" with Grant and Sherman.

In early December Colonel A. H. Markland of Grant's staff was leaving with mail for Sherman's army. He didn't know where he would deliver it, not knowing where he would find Sherman. Grant had told Markland to step in and see whether Lincoln had some message for Sherman. Lincoln was in a conference, but on seeing Markland's card had him shown in at once. He arose, crossed the room, meeting Markland halfway, and with a handshake: "Well, Colonel, I got word from General Grant that you were going to find Sherman, and that you would take him any message I might have. I know you will find him, because we always get good news from you. Say to General Sherman, for me, whenever and wherever you see him, 'God bless him and God bless his army.' That is as much as I can say, and more than I can write." He held Markland's hand and looked him in the eye all the time he was saying this. Tears gathered in his eyes, his lips trembled, and his voice shook, according to Markland, who noted: "He shook my hand, bade me good-by, and I proceeded toward the door, when he called to me. When I looked back he was standing like a statue where I had left him. 'Now, remember what I say,' and then he repeated the message."

An army for 32 days to the outside world "lost sight of," as Sherman phrased it, now had behind it 300 miles of naked smokestacks, burned culverts, shattered trestleworks, wailing humanity. Of the railroads every rail was twisted beyond use, every tie, bridge, tank, woodshed and depot building burned. Thirty miles ran the devastation on either side of the line from Atlanta, estimated Sherman. Kilpatrick's 5,000 horsemen had ravaged beyond the reach of foot troops. For the economy of powder they had sabered hogs, knocked horses between the ears with axes, killing more than a hundred horses on one plantation with a fine mansion, and shooting every bloodhound, mastiff or other dog that looked as though it could track runaway Negroes in swamps and forest. Over many square miles of this area now was left not a chicken, not a pig, not a horse nor cow nor sheep, not a smokehouse ham nor side of bacon, not a standing corncrib with a forgotten bushel, not a mule to plow land with, not a piece of railroad track, nor cars nor locomotives nor a bunker of coal.

On December 10 General Howard's right wing stood ten miles from Savannah. To Washington Howard sent a telegram notifying the Government that the march had won through. By scouts overland to Port Royal, South Carolina, and wire relays, this good-news message reached Washington the evening of December 14. Next day Halleck passed on to Lincoln Howard's dispatch: "We have met with perfect success thus far, troops in fine spirit and General Sherman near by."

Over the North flashed this news. Across streets in town, over roads and fields in the country, went the jubilant cry that Sherman had got to Savannah. From Boston to Council Bluffs and points west there were cheers and prayers of thanks.

On December 13 Sherman with staff officers climbed to the top of a rice mill, looked toward the sea for the fleet, looked toward a forest edge where the 15th corps was ready to move on Fort McAllister. The fort overlooked a river needed for supply transport between Sherman and the fleet—if the fleet had arrived as planned. For hours Sherman and his aides kept their lookout. It was near sundown when a smokestack took clearer form, at last could be seen, and later a flag wigwagged the words, "Who are you?" "General Sherman," said the rice-mill flag. "Is Fort McAlister taken yet?" asked the ship. "Not yet, but it will be in a minute."

As though this was a signal, Sherman's old Shiloh division under General William B. Hazen broke from cover, sharpshooters running out to fling themselves flat on the ground and pick off enemy gunners, the whole line soon charging through a hail of shot, shell and rifle bullets, rushing the defenses, soon dancing on the parapets of Fort McAllister.

By the light of a pale moon this December 13 Sherman rode a fast yawl downstream, boarded the Union ship, the *Dandelion,* and before midnight was writing dispatches to be read five days later by Stanton, Halleck and Lincoln—and parts of them passed on to a world starving for news and sure fact.

Back with his army again, Sherman saw Colonel A. H. Markland with sacks of mail. Men and officers whooped with glee over the first letters from home in many weeks. Sherman's eyes danced when Colonel Markland spoke the message from Lincoln.

Savannah fell, its garrison of 9,000 under General Hardee moving out and away toward the north the night of December 20. Sherman wrote Lincoln a message: "I beg to present you as a Christmas gift, the city of Savannah, with one hundred and fifty guns and plenty of ammunition, also about twenty-five thousand bales of cotton." The day after Christmas Lincoln wrote a letter to Sherman and sent it South: "When you were about leaving Atlanta for the Atlantic coast, I was *anxious,* if not fearful; but feeling that you were the better judge, and remembering that 'nothing risked, nothing gained' I did not interfere. Now, the undertaking being a success, the honor is all yours; for I believe none of us went farther than to acquiesce . . . Please make my grateful acknowledgments to your whole army, officers and men."

Lingering hesitations that Sherman had about Lincoln were wearing away, and the degree of trust that Lincoln held for him and Grant was deepening. The three were now closer than ever. Later Sherman was to write that the acclaim over the march to the sea pleased him, but "I experienced more satisfaction in giving to his [Lincoln's] overburdened and weary soul one gleam of satisfaction and happiness."

Stanton refused at this time to join the others in a Merry Christmas mood. To Grant he wrote: "It is a sore disappointment that Hardee was able to get off his 15,000 from Sherman's 60,000. It looks like protracting the war while their armies continue to escape."

The campaigning in Tennessee was strange and involved, with none of the dramatic simplicity of Sherman's march, General Schofield writing Sherman that they in Tennessee had the work while he in Georgia had the fun. Schofield on leaving Sherman and trying to connect his force of 29,000 with Thomas at Nashville had to fight a battle with Hood's 41,000 Confederate troops at Franklin, Hood in desperate frontal attacks thrown back with losses of 6,000 as against 2,300 on the Union side. Schofield drew off. Hood followed. Schofield joined Thomas at Nashville. There Hood camped with his army, now reduced to 26,000, intending as he said in a report of December 11 "to force the enemy to take the initiative."

Washington worried. Stanton December 2 had telegraphed Grant: "The President feels solicitous about the disposition of General Thomas to lay in fortifications for an indefinite period . . . This looks like the McClellan and Rosecrans strategy of do nothing and let the rebels raid the country. The President wishes you to consider the matter." The phrasing was Stanton's. On this same December 2 Grant had sent two dispatches to Thomas urging him to take the offensive, Thomas replying that in two or three days he would probably be ready.

Thomas, as Sherman saw him, had on occasion a granite-and-glacier certainty of movement. As West Point classmates, as young lieutenants in the same Regular Army regiment for ten years, they became "precious" to each other, Sherman feeling that "never since the world began did such absolute confidence exist between commander and commanded, and among the many mistakes I made I trace some of his earnest and vehement advice."

On December 8 Grant had wired Halleck: "If Thomas has not struck yet, he ought to be ordered to hand over his command to Schofield. There is no better man to repel an attack than Thomas but I fear he is too cautious to ever take the initiative."

To Grant from Halleck came a telegram, in all probability on so grave a matter having had scrutiny or perhaps revision by the President, reading: "If you wish General Thomas relieved, give the order. No one here will interfere. The responsibility, however, will be yours, as no one here, so far as I am informed, wishes General Thomas removed."

Grant on this December 8 tried a further telegram to Thomas: "Why not attack at once? By all means avoid the contingency of a foot-race to see which, you or Hood, can beat to the Ohio." Thomas still delayed. In cavalry Hood outnumbered him four to one; he was getting remounts and hoped to have a force of 6,000. He wired Grant that in troop concentration and transport "I have made every effort possible." Grant, receiving this December 9, wired Halleck that as Thomas had not yet attacked, "Please telegraph orders relieving him at once, and placing Schofield in command." The order was made out. Before telegraphing it to Nashville Halleck asked Grant if he still wished it to be forwarded. Grant replied, "You will suspend the order until it is seen whether he will do anything."

Thomas called his corps commanders, told them of the orders to attack Hood. The generals agreed that their commander should not fight on the slippery hills around Nashville till he was ready. No news of an attack reaching Grant, he wired December 11, "Let there be no further delay," Thomas replying, "I will obey the order as promptly as possible. The whole country is covered with a perfect sheet of ice and sleet." He would have attacked "yesterday had it not been for the storm."

Grant on December 13 ordered Logan to Nashville to replace Thomas in command. Logan started. Then Grant for the first time since he had become lieutenant general himself started on a trip back west, for Tennessee, to take personal charge there. Grant had reached Washington. Logan was at Louisville, Kentucky, less than a day's travel from Nashville. To both of them came news that Thomas had launched his troops at Hood's army.

Thomas telegraphed December 15: "I attacked the enemy's left this morning, and drove it from the river below the city very nearly to the Franklin pike, a distance of about eight miles . . . The troops behaved splendidly, all taking their share in assaulting and carrying the enemy's breast works." That night the whole army slept on its guns in line of battle and next day pushed a broken and retreating enemy at all points. "I beheld," later wrote Hood, "for the first and only time a Confederate army abandon the field in confusion." No rout of the war had been so complete. One factor was the cavalry for which Thomas had delayed action. Hood's army as a unit vanished. Parts of it, to the number of 15,000 men, held intact through the generalship of Forrest, who saved them for other Confederate commands. The Confederate losses in killed and wounded at least equaled the Union casualties of 3,000—and 4,462 Confederate prisoners were taken.

Sherman took pride in his friend "Old Tom" and was to write of this battle that it was the only one of the war "which annihilated an army." A famous metaphor was coined: the Rock of Chickamauga became the Sledge of Nashville. Congratulations came from many, including Grant, Sherman, Stanton, Sheridan, Lincoln's of December 16 reading: "Please accept for yourself, officers, and men, the nation's thanks for your good work of yesterday. You made a magnificent beginning. A grand consummation is within your easy reach. Do not let it slip." To a commission naming Thomas for the vacant major generalship in the Regular Army Grant and Lincoln joined their signatures.

For Grant the week had been, according to Colonel Horace Porter, "the most anxious period of his entire military career," and before the victory came "he suffered mental torture." To Grant, Thomas was one piece in a big game involving other pieces and Grant was trying to time and co-ordinate them toward destroying the three Confederate armies left. When Thomas won, there were only two. The extent of Lincoln's hand in the affair did not appear. He seemed to have watched every phase of it keenly, "solicitous" that by no one's mistake should there be more "McClellan and Rosecrans strategy," yet when Grant put it up to him to relieve Thomas he insisted that must be Grant's act. One of the three remaining Confederate armies having been destroyed, Grant went from Washington to Burlington, New Jersey, and spent a day of rejoicing with his wife and family.

Grant's anxiety to play no favorites, to keep clear of the politics always seething in the Army, showed one day in Washington when Sherman's army was "lost" in Georgia. He then gave the President and Secretary of War a list of eight major generals and 33 brigadiers whose services the Government "could dispense with to advantage." In the matter of letting out "these useless officers," noted Colonel Porter, Grant was entirely impartial, the list having some of his warm personal friends. The President said: "Why, I find that lots of officers on this list are very close friends of yours. Do you want them all dropped?" General Grant: "That's very true, Mr. President. But my personal friends are not always good generals, and I think it but just to adhere to my recommendations."

Lee's distressing need for men ran back in part to an order of Grant in April that not another Confederate prisoner of war should be paroled or exchanged until certain conditions were met that Grant probably knew would never be met. Cruel it was, he admitted, but necessary. "Every man we hold, when released on parole or otherwise, becomes an active soldier against us at once either directly or indirectly . . . If we hold those caught they amount to no more than dead men." At the particular time in late summer when the Confederate Government proposed to exchange prisoners man for man, said Grant, it "would insure Sherman's defeat" and "compromise safety" at Richmond.

Many were the influences brought to bear on Lincoln to reverse or modify this policy of Grant. Arguments based on political power and made in the name of reason, cries and prayers for the sake of humanity, rang in his ears. But Lincoln stood by his general. He let Grant have his way. And at this time there raged over the North a propaganda of horror with proposals of vengeance for the inhuman handling of Union soldiers in Southern prisons. They were starved. And they died of starvation. This was fact. They festered in rags and became living skeletons, chilled and shivering. This, for many, was fact. Atrocities monstrous and almost beyond belief were told of in Northern newspapers and pulpits and on political platforms. These too had some basis of fact. But the South had its answers. And these too held facts. Where in the South were any such parades of pleasure and riots of luxury as could be seen in the metropolitan centers of the North? A shelf of competent testimony would reduce to a verdict of both sides making war as war had always been made and meaning brought to the word "agony." The so-called laws of war were being violated, as in former wars, as an incident of humanity in the mass being violated—on both sides. Over this Lincoln troubled his mind and heart and was to refer to it in his second inaugural address.

A 27-acre piece of marshland in southwestern Georgia, fenced and stockaded for Union prisoners, bare of trees and hiding places, was Andersonville. A man going there died a dirty and lingering death; or killed himself by stepping over a line where guards at once put a bullet through him for attempted escape; or lost his mind; or by slim chance issued forth to freedom somehow with a woebegone look and a wild-animal stare in his eyes. When a few of these hunted ones had crept into Sherman's camp one night at Milledgeville, the sight of them brought mutterings of revenge.

The place named Andersonville won distinction as the one spot on the North American map where war was more hideous to look at than any other spot that could be named. In its close-packed and swarming population was less food and more scurvy and starvation; less soap and more filth, scabs and lice; less medicine and more gangrene, fever, diarrhea, ulcers, sores, hemorrhages, bleeding gums and swollen lips symptomatic of scurvy, than anywhere else in America.

The bloodiest battle of the war had not taken such a toll of death as Andersonville from June to September 1864, with its record of 8,589 dying. This reduced the peak population of 32,000 and enlarged the average space of six square feet per man. Vice-President Stephens suggested that Jefferson Davis visit Andersonville, that the Confederate President make a solemn speech to the prisoners and let them go home and tell the North the South was fighting only for independence.

Where lay the blame? On both sides. So wrote a Confederate prisoner, Henry M. Stanley, later an African explorer, of what he saw in a human "cattle-yard" named Camp Douglas at Chicago. On the way to the latrines Stanley saw "crowds of sick men who had fallen prostrate from weakness, and given themselves wholly to despair, and while they crawled or wallowed in their filth, they cursed or blasphemed as often as they groaned." Every morning came wagons whereon Stanley saw the corpses rolled in their blankets "piled one upon another, as the New Zealand frozen mutton carcasses are carted from the docks!"

Had Lincoln been looking toward a policy of vengeance on the South, had he joined with Thad Stevens and the now powerful group who planned to visit retribution on the ruling class of the South, he could not have wished for a better issue than Andersonville. He could have set in motion such whirlwinds of hate as the war had not yet seen. A grumbling and muttering had begun that the President took no action in this field, assertions, wrote Carpenter, that he showed "a criminal indifference to the sufferings of our prisoners at Libby, Andersonville, and other places." There was the record, said these critics: nowhere in any public address or message of the President could you find any allusion to the Union soldiers murdered by foul treatment in Southern prisons. Purposely Lincoln avoided discussion of it. The issue had not become sharp till this fourth year of the war. For maddening the Northern people into war effort the issue could have been useful earlier in the war. But now it could do no good toward the ends of reconciliation and rebuilding which Lincoln hoped for beyond the war's end. So he was saying nothing. Partly the animus in the matter was political.

"When the reports, in an authentic form, first reached Washington of the sufferings of the Union prisoners," wrote Carpenter, "I know he [the President] was greatly excited and overcome by them." He was told that justice demanded a stern retaliation, that like treatment should be given Confederate prisoners, and according to Carpenter, he said to Congressman M. F. Odell with deep feeling, "I can never, never starve men like that!" and again, "Whatever others may say or do, I never can, and I never will, be accessory to such treatment of human beings."

The Southern summer heat was bad for men from the North, and the

Northern zero winter weather not so good for those from the South. Official statistics ran that 12 of every 100 Confederate prisoners died in the North, and 15 of every 100 Union captives in the South. Medical men agreed that the Southern troops were undernourished because of their own armies' inferior food supply, and therefore less resistant to disease.

Want and hunger threatened the life arteries of the Confederacy less than its own internal strife. The November message of President Davis to the Confederate Congress spoke desperately of conspiracies, of traitors and spies inside their own house. What any state capital announced was more important and authoritative to the people of that state than any proclamations from the Richmond Government. This faith in states' rights as much as want or military defeat was a gnawing and devitalizing factor in the Confederacy.

The Richmond *Whig* had spoken for an element with deep-rooted instincts about states' rights when it suggested dropping the name of Confederate States and substituting The Allied Nations or The Allied Republics. "We are sorry to see the word 'national' sometimes used with reference to Confederate affairs. We think it should be henceforth a forbidden word. This Confederacy is not a nation, but a league of nations."

Mrs. Chesnut, now in Columbia, South Carolina, wrote when Sherman was two days out from Atlanta moving toward the seacoast, "Fire and the sword are for us here; that is the word." A letter came to her from Mrs. Jefferson Davis saying she was tired of hoping and being disappointed. Her news from Richmond was that some people expected another attack soon, "but I think the avalanche will not slide until the spring." For Mrs. Davis, wrote Mrs. Chesnut, "my heart aches."

Into Mrs. Chesnut's Columbia house came a Connecticut-born woman with Northern relatives who spoke of Sherman opening a way at last so that she could go to Europe or to the North and live in comfort and ease. "I dare say she takes me for a fool," ran the diary entry that day. "I sat there dumb, although she was in my own house. I have heard of a woman so enraged that she struck some one over the head with a shovel. To-day, for the first time in my life, I know how that mad woman felt. I could have given Mrs. S. the benefit of shovel and tongs both."

Now came news of Hood's army broken and scattered, and, wrote Mrs. Chesnut, "maybe I am benumbed." A Miss Rhett was visiting her, "a brilliant woman and very agreeable," who had a saying, "The world, you know, is composed of men, women, and Rhetts." Now, said the diary, "we feel that if we are to lose our negroes, we would as soon see Sherman free them as the Confederate Government; freeing negroes is the last Confederate Government craze. We are a little too slow about it; that is all." Mournful and Biblical was her mood of December 19: "The deep waters are closing over us and we are in this house, like the outsiders at the time of the flood."

CHAPTER 56

The Bitter Year of '64 Comes to a Close

IN NEW YORK CITY November 25, 1864, with phosphorus and turpentine as starters, 11 New York hotels began blazing at about the same time. The flames were caught in time and put out by quick-witted hotel workers. At Barnum's Museum, at Niblo's Garden where an audience of 3,000 was seeing a play, at the Winter Garden Theatre, the terrorizing cry of "Fire!" was raised. Cool heads slowed down the near-panics while fires were snuffed out. In this episode the same Federal secret-service operative who had carried dispatches between the Richmond Government and the Confederate commissioners in Canada brought Stanton, Dana and Lincoln information that enabled them to have the arson bugs arrested. One of the guilty was hanged, others sent to prison.

It may have been that Jacob Thompson, operating from Canada with a fund of $300,000 supplied from Richmond, expected a job at Chicago to be his masterpiece. The plot there was that at Camp Douglas, on election night, November 8, Sons of Liberty should throw in their forces, release and arm the 8,000 Confederate prisoners, "cut the telegraph wires, burn the railroad depots, seize the banks and stores containing arms and ammunition, take possession of the city and commence the release of other Confederate prisoners in Illinois and Indiana." The commandant at Camp Douglas, however, early got word of the plot, and two nights before the break was to come he arrested an English soldier, four Confederates, two Sons of Liberty. Later he arrested seven more Sons of Liberty. A military commission dealt out prison sentences to several and decreed death for one.

Was the South in heartbreak and despair now using tactics it would not have considered when the war opened? Suffering had come to Charleston, seared by a fire loss of $7,000,000, raked by shells, bombs, the awe of single incidents such as the killing of Miss Pickens, daughter of ex-Governor Pickens. One May morning she was married to Lieutenant de Rochelle, ran the *Mercury* account. "The wedding party had assembled at the house of General Bonham, when a shell from the Union forces penetrated the house and wounded the bride so that she died soon afterward. The marriage ceremony was completed as she lay dying on the floor."

At Camden Mrs. Chesnut was haunted by her memory of little Joe Davis, son of the Confederate President, killed by falling from a high porch to a brick pavement. And in the drawing room of the executive mansion at midnight she could hear the tramp of Mr. Davis' step as he walked back and forth in the room above, not another sound, the whole house silent as death. Next day thousands of children at little Joe's grave each had a green bough or a bunch of flowers to throw on a pile of crosses and evergreens.

The fighting men of South Carolina had all gone to the front, wrote Mrs.

Chesnut. "Only old men and little boys are at home now." She read a column list of South Carolina dead and wounded in clashes with Grant's men, shuddering at news of Grant receiving 25,000 fresh troops in one relay. "Old Lincoln says in his quaint backwoods way, 'Keep a-peggin.' Now we can only peg out." A harsh play on words. The peg legs were too many.

"It is impossible to sleep here," wrote Mrs. Chesnut, "because it is so solemn and still. The moonlight shines in my window sad and white." She was as grave and vivid now as when in April '61, the first guns booming to bring down the parapets of Fort Sumter, she had leaped from her bed and knelt in prayer over what was to come.

In her Richmond stay she had gone shopping, "and paid $30.00 for a pair of gloves; $50.00 for a pair of slippers; $24.00 for six spools of thread; $32.00 for five miserable, shabby little pocket handkerchiefs." Soon they would be saying in Richmond, "You take your money to market in a market basket and bring home what you buy in your pocketbook." Money—it was getting ridiculous. As Confederate money sank in value from month to month pathos and pity touched deeper the Confederate cause.

Now in the North and in Europe it was taken as full of portent that President Davis recommended to his Congress that slaves be drafted for the Confederate armies. This plan would throw 400,000 able-bodied and armed black men against the Northern armies. Slavery would not be abolished, but the enlisted Negroes would be given freedom. Factions in the Confederate Congress with polite contempt offered other plans to fill the thinning armies.

As with each year the South had dwindled in man power, in money and economic resources, in commerce and industry, in the comforts or necessities of life, the North had gained. In steel, oil, railroads, munitions, textiles and other industries, scores of large fortunes were already made, many others on their way. The fast and luxurious living in most of the large cities still contrasted with sacrifices on the march, in camp and on the battlefields. Travelers from Europe commented in surprise at seeing seaboard cities of a North at war with so few signs of war and such throngs of spenders and pleasure hunters as in no European cities. From Great Britain, especially Ireland, and from Germany and the Scandinavian countries, fresh populations poured in.

Westward across the plains and to the West Coast poured an endless migration, some of it to escape the draft. From March 1 to August 10, 1864, 9,300 teams and wagons passed Fort Kearney, Nebraska. One fast traveler on the road from St. Joseph, Missouri, to Fort Kearney passed 400 wagons in one day. At Council Bluffs in April and May a line of teams three miles long waited their turn to cross a ferry whose capacity was 200 in its operation day and night. By the middle of June it was estimated 75,000 men, 30,000 horses and mules, 75,000 cattle, had made the crossing. With each year farmers of the Midwest and Northwest bought more planters, reapers, threshers for putting in crops and harvesting; these labor-saving farm machines made more men available for Grant and Sherman.

America had these lights and contradictions in 1864. Any historian of them in their vast and moving variety needed a gift for showing chaos in the current scene and a weave of paradox leading to the future. A mystic dream of a majestic republic holding to human freedom and equal oppor-

tunity ran parallel to motives of hard cash and pay dirt. These were to shape
a future already begun, swaying indistinctly in many a speech or saying of
Lincoln.

In the fourth December of the war, Lincoln sent his message to Congress.
The tone continuously traveled with high assumption that the United States
was a going concern, that the Union of States was fated to become a great
World Power.

The President read the message to his Cabinet December 3. The briefs of
several Cabinet members were kept in the message "pretty much in their
own words," noted Welles. One unusual matter came up, indicating the favor
in which church leaders were held by Lincoln and an innovation to which,
it seemed, he would have consented had the Cabinet agreed. "One paragraph,"
wrote Welles, "proposing an Amendment to the Constitution recognizing
the Deity in that instrument met with no favorable response from any one
member of the Cabinet. The President, before reading it, expressed his own
doubts in regard to it, but it had been urged by certain religionists."

Foreign affairs were in a "reasonably satisfactory" condition. The Republic
of Liberia should be given a gunboat at moderate cost, paying the United
States for it in installments. Such a beginning of a navy would "stimulate a
generous ambition" in this young Negro nation. An international telegraph
system, the Atlantic cable, and co-operation toward "world-encircling communication" were approved. A rebellion "long flagrant" in China "has at last
been suppressed," with "the co-operating good offices of this government
and of the other western commercial States." Emphasis was laid on the "extension of our commerce" and a "more intimate intercourse" with China.
Japan in performing treaty stipulations "is inconstant and capricious," though
good progress had been effected by the Western Powers "moving with enlightened concert." Money claims of the United States had been allowed by
the Japanese or put in course of settlement. One Virginia port, Norfolk, and
two Florida ports, Fernandina and Pensacola, were now open, and foreign
merchants might consider whether it was not "safer and more profitable" to
use those ports than to risk blockade-running.

Thus far the message was chiefly Seward. Lincoln's hand became evident
in a paragraph on the slave trade and those who did a business of shipping
and selling black folk. "For myself, I have no doubt of the power and duty of
the Executive, under the law of nations, to exclude enemies of the human race
from an asylum in the United States."

The Treasury Department had taken in over $1,000,000,000 in cash and
disbursed nearly as much for the Army and Navy. "Taxation should be still
further increased." The paragraph completely endorsing the national banking
system probably represented the views of Secretary Fessenden, with Lincoln
in agreement.

The Navy now could show 671 vessels. Across the past year its actual increases over and above all losses by shipwreck and battle were 83 vessels, 167
guns and 42,427 tons. During the year 324 ships had been captured, making
a total of 1,379 since the war commenced. Sales of condemned prize property
had brought more than $14,000,000.

The Army and Navy could read of "liberal provisions" made by Congress for pensions. During the year ending June 30, 16,770 invalid soldiers and 271 invalid seamen had been added to the rolls. Of widows, orphans and dependent mothers, a total of 22,198 were on the army pension rolls and 248 on the navy rolls. Homesteaders had entered more than 4,000,000 acres of public land. Open to settlement were 133,000,000 acres of surveyed land. The Union Pacific railway had "assurance of success."

The President pointed to "the most important branch of national resources —that of living men." The North in spite of war losses had 145,551 more voters at the polls in November '64 than four years before. The fact stood out "that we have *more* men *now* than we had when the war *began;* that we are not exhausted, nor in process of exhaustion; that we are *gaining* strength, and may, if need be, maintain the contest indefinitely."

Of the word "reconstruction" Lincoln steered clear. Already it had become tinged with suspicion. Important movements had occurred during the year, wrote the President, "to the effect of moulding society for durability in the Union." Short of complete success, he admitted, but much in the right direction was it that 12,000 citizens in each of the States of Arkansas and Louisiana "have organized loyal State governments with free constitutions, and are earnestly struggling to maintain and administer them." Similar movements more extensive, though less definite, in Missouri, Kentucky and Tennessee "should not be overlooked."

The President now dealt with the crowded rumors and flying reports that peace was to be had through negotiation. "On careful consideration of all the evidence accessible it seems to me that no attempt at negotiation with the insurgent leader could result in any good. He would accept nothing short of severance of the Union—precisely what we will not and cannot give. His declarations to this effect are explicit and oft-repeated. He does not attempt to deceive us . . . What is true, however, of him who heads the insurgent cause, is not necessarily true of those who follow. Although he cannot re-accept the Union, they can. Some of them, we know, already desire peace and reunion. The number of such may increase . . ."

He seemed to leave a quite direct inference that for himself he would be found, if and when the war closed, using his authority for the help and sustenance of men in the South who might have to consider vindictive enemies in Washington. "Pardons and remissions of forfeitures, however, would still be within Executive control. In what spirit and temper his control would be exercised can be fairly judged of by the past." Pardon and amnesty had been offered a year ago "to all, except certain designated classes." These latter, it was made known then, were "still within contemplation of special clemency."

As to slavery, the President was brief but more decisive than in any other part of the message: "I repeat the declaration made a year ago that 'while I remain in my present position I shall not attempt to retract or modify the emancipation proclamation, nor shall I return to slavery any person who is free by the terms of that proclamation, or by any of the Acts of Congress.' If the people should, by whatever mode or means, make it an Executive duty to re-enslave such persons, another, and not I, must be their instrument to perform it."

Dry with a cool Lincolnian finality, touched with a faint preposterous irony, was the closing one-sentence paragraph: "In stating a single condition of peace, I mean simply to say that the war will cease on the part of the government, whenever it shall have ceased on the part of those who began it."

Far and wide went this document. By Union armies it was spread into Confederate areas where Confederate newspapers had not reprinted it from Northern journals. In Europe it was studied and discussed in state chambers and on the streets. Over the Northern States it was examined for every shading of fear and hope and promise.

Opposition journals in the North agreed in various ways with the London *Times,* which said: "For ourselves, we never read a public document less calculated to inspire hope," adding the gratuitous comment that it was "the most uncomfortable President's address ever read to the American House of Representatives."

Harper's Weekly judged it a "calm, simple, concise statement of public affairs," and could understand a Northern opposition, "in common with the rebels," finding the message very "unconciliatory." Its tranquil tone of faith in the people, its dignity toward other Powers, its lofty confidence in peace and union "make the Message, now familiar to the country, one of the . . . most truly American papers in our political history."

Lincoln's anonymous friend in the *Spectator* of London found his latest message "drier, shrewder, and more tenacious than ever." The peace terms offered by Mr. Lincoln were "precisely the terms every monarchy in Europe always offers to rebels." His war policy held to that of the Roman patrician who would "spare the submissive, but war out the proud." His amnesty was free to everybody. His proud roll call of national resources, "of which Americans never weary," none the less had great meaning. "Faith is the source of strength."

Dry, informative, again casual as a locomotive, came the President's proclamation of December 19 calling for 300,000 more troops.

Now into only one port of the South could blockade-runners bring supplies. This port of Wilmington, North Carolina, would be lost if its defending Fort Fisher should fall. General Butler worked out a scheme to run a powder-loaded steamer near the shore under the fort, have a clockwork blow up the boat, and in the ensuing havoc and confusion move in troops to take the fort.

Admiral Porter with a naval squadron, General Butler with troop transports, joined their efforts. After Butler sailed from Fortress Monroe "three days of fine weather were squandered," according to Grant. Then heavy storms delayed action. At last on the night of December 23 the powder steamer was towed in near the fort, the clockwork set and everybody left. "At two o'clock in the morning," wrote Grant, "the explosion took place— and produced no more effect on the fort, or anything else on land, than the bursting of a boiler anywhere on the Atlantic Ocean." Porter shelled the fort with no damaging results. Butler landed troops, won footings, then drew away, put his troops back on the transports and told Porter he was through.

Grant telegraphed the President December 28 that the Wilmington expedition had proved "a gross and culpable failure," that he hoped it would be known who was to blame. Grant, however, on hearing from Admiral Porter that the army had quit when they nearly had Fort Fisher, sent word to Porter to hold on, to stay near Wilmington, that they would soon close that last Confederate port through which came medicine, food, metals, clothing, salt, arms, blankets, from Europe.

The President would soon name another man to replace Stanton, had run persistent reports since the November election. "This subject was brought up by the President in his conversation with the general-in-chief," wrote Grant's aide, Colonel Porter, "and he was considerate enough to say that in case such a change should occur, he would not appoint another secretary without giving the general an opportunity to express his views as to the selection." Grant's reply to Lincoln, as Porter noted it: "I doubt very much whether you could select as efficient a Secretary of War as the present incumbent. He is not only a man of untiring energy and devotion to duty, but even his worst enemies never for a moment doubt his personal integrity and the purity of his motives . . ." Grant privately continued to believe Stanton "timid" as a warrior, too freely arrogant in the handling of Grant's telegrams when it suited him, but Grant had no one else in mind now who better fitted the needs of the hour.

And Stanton, though in breaking health, regarded himself as an image of war and a hurler of thunderbolts. At the doorway of the war telegraph office one evening he stood, without coming in. At a table sat Lincoln writing. In the doorway Stanton postured volcanic and warlike to look at. The operator Chandler wrote of the tableau: "Mr. Lincoln did not notice him at first. As he looked up from his writing and perceived Stanton standing there, he bowed low and said with much gravity, 'Good-evening, Mars.' "

A Cabinet shake-up coming, ran rumors—a house cleaning. But it was idle talk. In neither major nor minor offices did Lincoln intend to use a broom. "I have made up my mind to make very few changes in the offices in my gift for my second term," he told one caller. "I think, now, that I shall not move a single man, except for delinquency. To remove a man is very easy, but when I go to fill his place, there are twenty applicants, and of these I must make nineteen enemies."

To Seward the Paris Consul Bigelow more than once sent word, "Burn this Mss when you have read it." Seward once replied that a note was duly "received, read, and burned," as suggested, and "The contents are known only to the President here." This latter concerned the death December 1 of Minister William L. Dayton in Paris, in the hotel apartment of a woman not his wife, the body being immediately removed to Dayton's house. This was done, according to Bigelow, "before the police could interfere, for should they become aware of what had happened they would insist upon holding an inquest upon the premises, which would involve many inconveniences, all of which would be avoided by placing the body within the precincts of the legation." Bigelow recited the insistence of the unfortunate hostess upon riding up to the legation with the body to explain how it happened. They wished to discourage her, but she insisted. "What will Mrs. Dayton think?" she exclaimed. "My reputation is involved. I must go at once." And so she went. According to the doctor's report, wrote Bigelow in a later unofficial account, Dayton "after some pleasantry on entering the apartment, called upon his hostess to give three cheers for Abraham Lincoln, the news of whose re-election had just recently reached Paris. He soon complained of feeling unwell," and died from apoplexy before the doctor's arrival. Thus a matter kept secret by the Paris Legation in Europe, and by Seward and Lincoln in America, did not reach a press which would have reveled in the details.

Had the November election given a mandate to Congress or to the President? Was it the duty of Congress now to challenge the Executive and cut down his powers? A test vote came in mid-December. Henry Winter Davis demanded a vote on his resolution that Congress had "a constitutional right to an authoritative voice" in foreign affairs, and, "it is the constitutional duty of the President to respect that policy . . . in diplomatic negotiations." Without debate or inquiry the House voted on a motion of Representative Farnsworth to lay the Winter Davis resolution on the table. This passed with 69 Yeas, 63 Nays, not voting 50.

Thus in mid-December of '64 the respect and adherence of Congress to Lincoln seemed to hang in a balance of about 69 with him, 63 against him, and 50 undecided, wavering, sick or not interested. Those with him were nearly all his own party men. Those against him were the opposition party, allied with nearly as many of his own party. Those not voting were mostly of his own party.

In stature and sagacity the President now stood on a different footing with Congress. The campaign and the election had brought an impression that Lincoln was a politician of keener touch, an Executive of more designing statecraft, than they had given him credit for. Fair words and lavish estimates spoke Thad Stevens on the President's message. "It is brief (a great virtue in public documents), it treats of subjects of great importance, not only to the nation but to the whole family of man. I do not think I am extravagant when I say that it is the most important and best message that has been communicated to Congress for the last sixty years."

Stevens saw an opposition trying to save from destruction "the darling institution of the Democratic party, the institution of human bondage." Compromise on this was sought. They condemned the "President's determination to insist on the abandonment of slavery." When the President's own leading friends besought him to compromise, he refused to sue for peace. "There never was a day since Abraham Lincoln was elected President that he stood so high . . . in the estimation of the people as at this moment." The guiding fear of Stevens was that the war by compromise evasions might end without slavery uprooted.

John M. Palmer, the Union Democrat of Illinois, waited in a White House anteroom one morning till he was told to enter the President's room. As Palmer told it, he found Lincoln in the hands of the barber, and Lincoln called: "Come in, Palmer, come in. You're home folks. I can shave before you. I couldn't before those others, and I have to do it sometime." They chatted about this and that, Palmer finally speaking in a frank and jovial mood. "Mr. Lincoln, if anybody had told me that in a great crisis like this the people were going out to a little one-horse town and pick out a one-horse lawyer for President I wouldn't have believed it." Lincoln whirled in his chair, his face white with lather, a towel under his chin. Palmer at first thought the President was angry. Sweeping the barber away, Lincoln leaned forward, put a hand on Palmer's knee and said: "Neither would I. But it was a time when a man with a policy would have been fatal to the country. I have never had a policy. I have simply tried to do what seemed best as each day came."

The degree of Doctor of Laws, awarded by Knox College, at Galesburg, Illinois, an abolitionist and solidly Republican community, was less a surprise to Lincoln than a like degree conferred by the trustees of the College of New Jersey.

To Lincoln's desk in September had come a request from Governor Andrew in behalf of a widow living at 15 Dover Street, Boston. She had sent her five sons into the Union armies and all had been killed in action, according to Andrew's information from his state adjutant general, William Schouler.

On request of the War Department the adjutant general of Massachusetts made an investigation and officially certified the names, regiments and dates of death of Mrs. Bixby's five sons. This document came to Lincoln in mid-October. He could have then written a letter to Mrs. Bixby and made it public for campaign purposes. Instead, he waited. As on occasion with certain speeches or letters, he probably wrote a first draft of the letter and later changed the phrasing. On November 21 he dated the letter and sent it through the War Department to Adjutant General Schouler of Massachusetts. He addressed it to "Mrs. Bixby, Boston, Massachusetts." Her first name, Lydia, and her address in Boston, were not given. Adjutant General Schouler received the letter in an envelope addressed to himself and copied the letter. On Thanksgiving Day the General took a holiday dinner and a present of money raised among good people of Boston and delivered them at 15 Dover Street to Mrs. Bixby—along with Lincoln's letter to her. She read on that Thanksgiving Day:

I have been shown in the files of the War Department a statement of the Adjutant General of Massachusetts, that you are the mother of five sons who have died gloriously on the field of battle.

I feel how weak and fruitless must be any words of mine which should attempt to beguile you from the grief of a loss so overwhelming. But I cannot refrain from tendering to you the consolation that may be found in the thanks of the Republic they died to save.

I pray that our Heavenly Father may assuage the anguish of your bereavement, and leave you only the cherished memory of the loved and lost, and the solemn pride that must be yours, to have laid so costly a sacrifice upon the altar of Freedom. Yours, very sincerely and respectfully, A. LINCOLN.

This was the text as Schouler had copied it and as he gave it to the Boston newspapers.

Later research was to show that of the five Bixby boys Charles died in action at Fredericksburg and Oliver met death at Petersburg. Henry was reported killed at Gettysburg, was in reality taken prisoner, exchanged, returned to his mother in good health. George too was taken prisoner, secured his release by enlistment as a Confederate soldier, and was of record as having "deserted to the enemy." Edward Bixby, on the muster rolls as 18 years of age, became homesick, and his mother swore that he was only 16, had enlisted against her will, that he had periods of insanity. The order for his discharge was issued, but the worrying boy had deserted the Army and gone to sea as a sailor.

In substance, then, had the actual facts been known, what was the extent of Mrs. Bixby's sacrifice? Whether all five died on the field of battle, or only two, four of her sons had been poured away into the river of war—the two who had deserted were as lost to her as the two who had died. The one who had returned alive had fought at Gettysburg. If sacrifice could be transmuted into cold figures, she deserved the distinction and fame Lincoln gave her name. From her womb had gone blood to the altars of the Union cause. Lincoln was not deceived nor John Andrew fooled nor the War Department taken unaware.

The response to the Bixby letter, the love of its words and music that arose over the country, lay in the fact that in so many thousands of homes they did love the Union; they did hate slavery; mournfully but willingly they had sent their boys to take a chance with death on the field of battle. The war was not all waste and filth and corruption. More darkly than the Gettysburg speech the letter wove its awful implication that human freedom so often was paid for with agony.

As a living human target who daily walked with a lurking and elusive shadow of death, as a Chief Magistrate who had twice had his hat shot off by an unknown would-be assassin, Lincoln was completely entitled to be a spokesman for the boy phantoms who had fought his war and now no longer answered roll call. Side by side with Governor Andrew's communication to the President about Mrs. Bixby was presented the case of Otis Newhall of Lynn, Massachusetts, and his five vacant chairs at home. George F. Newhall had met the steel of death at Second Bull Run. Edward had begun marching and fighting in October '61 and had gone on with the Army of the Potomac to the battle of the Wilderness in May '64, when he was taken prisoner. Henry and Herman Newhall were two sharpshooters who enlisted in October '61, had stayed on through, and were now with Grant at Petersburg. This left James O. Newhall, who enlisted in January '62, fought through to Spotsylvania Court House in May '64, when he received wounds and went to hospital. Now James had recovered, and his father, not wanting all the chairs at home vacant, had proposed Governor Andrew's recommendation to Lincoln that James be discharged "as a graceful recognition of the claim of a patriotic family." To the Newhall family Lincoln gave the discharge asked for, and to Mrs. Bixby a letter the world read.

As the months passed after Lincoln's first inaugural address, his sense of the comic, his occasional role of comedian, stayed with him, while significantly on the other hand he came to know more keenly and fittingly what could be done with the authoritative mantle of President. He learned how better to wear it publicly, to adjust it as the garment of a solemn spokesman. He believed the majesty of the office backed him in telling Congress that "the fiery trial" through which they were all passing would be written as history and the players weighed and the balances cast up. At Gettysburg he stood in a ceremonial role. Across many months of '64 his authority hung by such threads that he knew his cue was silence; no statements could be wrung from him. Again in the Bixby letter he performed a rite, managing language as though he might be a ship captain at midnight by lantern light dropping black roses into the immemorial sea for mystic remembrance and consecration.

A speech of the President in December reached the public in an unusual way. He sent for Noah Brooks "to hear a story." He had the story partly written. With a sheet five or six inches wide on one knee, his legs crossed, sunk comfortably in his armchair, he asked Brooks to wait till he finished. Soon he gave it to Brooks, who saw at the top of the sheet an underscored heading, followed by a paragraph. It read:

THE PRESIDENT'S LAST, SHORTEST, AND BEST SPEECH.

On thursday of last week two ladies from Tennessee came before the President asking the release of their husbands held as prisoners of war at Johnson's Island. They were put off till friday, when they came again; and were again put off to saturday. At each of the interviews one of the ladies urged that her husband was a religious man. On saturday the President ordered the release of the prisoners, and then said to this lady "You say your husband is a religious man; tell him when you meet him, that I say I am not much of a judge of religion, but that, in my opinion, the religion that sets men to rebel and fight against their government, because, as they think, that government does not sufficiently help *some* men to eat their bread on the sweat of *other* men's faces, is not the sort of religion upon which people can get to heaven!"

He remarked to Brooks that he wanted it copied and printed in the Washington *Chronicle*, adding, "Don't wait to send it to California in your correspondence. I've a childish desire to see it in print right away." So Brooks took it to the *Chronicle* and it was widely reprinted. "Lincoln," noted Brooks, "showed a surprising amount of gratification over this trifle."

The day before Christmas of '64 after one favor, the commutation of a death sentence, Welles pressed for another from the President. Miss Laura Jones of Richmond was engaged to be married to a man in Richmond, three years back. In Washington, having nursed her mother back to health, she wanted to return to Richmond and see her betrothed. In a letter to an old friend, Mrs. Gideon Welles, she prayed for help in getting a pass through Union lines. Noted Welles, "The poor girl . . . says truly the years of her youth are passing away. I knew if the President read the letter, Laura would get the pass."

Without reading the letter the President at once said he would give Miss Laura Jones her pass. Welles made it plain that "her sympathies were with the Secessionists, and it would be better he should read her own statement." But Lincoln wouldn't read her letter to Mrs. Welles. "He . . . said he would let her go; the war had depopulated the country and prevented marriages enough."

New Year's Eve came, the fourth for Lincoln in the White House. On the first one McClellan, with a magnificently prepared army, had gone into winter quarters without fighting, the shame of Bull Run not redeemed and the North yet to try its faith in itself. The second New Year's Eve could look back on a year highlighted by the weary Peninsula campaign, the jubilant capture of Fort Donelson, New Orleans taken, bloody Shiloh, the Second Bull Run shame, McClellan and Lee at Antietam, the preliminary Emancipation Proclamation, the delays of McClellan and his dismissal, the needless butchery at Fredericksburg. The third New Year's Eve had brought the final Emancipation Proclamation, the rout of Chancellorsville, New York draft and race riots, the turning point of the war at Gettysburg and Vicksburg, the shouting at narrowly shaded Chickamauga fighting, the cries from men in blue at the top of Lookout Mountain, the speech at Gettysburg, the beginning of the sunset of the Confederacy.

Now here was the fourth New Year's Eve looking back on Grant named to head all the Union armies, plunging into the Wilderness and on through Spotsylvania, Cold Harbor, Petersburg, with overwhelming troops and resources battering Lee pitilessly while Early's gray horsemen reached the gates of Washington with their smoke to be seen from White House windows, while Sherman took Atlanta and marched to the sea and took Savannah, while Sheridan scattered Early's army from the Shenandoah and Thomas became the sledge that broke Hood's army into the first Confederate rout of the war, while the Navy sank the *Alabama*, took Mobile and tightened its throttling grip on all Southern ports—a fateful year that had seen the President of the United States win a party renomination against the almost unanimous disapproval of his party members in the House and Senate, winning a national election in November that looked dark and all lost in August, winning in a fairly conducted contest, amid good order, so that the longer one gazed at the November ballots, the more they seemed to say momentously that the Union would be held together and the underlying cause of the war, the propertied institution of slavery, outlawed forever. Not so bitter as the other three was the taste of this New Year's Eve. Across the horizons of the New Year of 1865, however, were signs of the storm to take new phases. Heavy labors lay ahead, and much mist of human confusion.

The diplomatic corps in sashes and epaulets promenaded over the reception rooms of the White House. Members of the Senate and House, the Cabinet, and in larger numbers than ever before the Public were there to shake hands with the President New Year's Day.

Had Miss Betsey Canedy of Fall River, Massachusetts, been in line that day and paused for conversation with Lincoln, she could have told him of what she heard while teaching a school of Negro pupils at Norfolk, Virginia. To Negro carpenters at work on the school building one day she showed a plaster bust of Abraham Lincoln. What they said impressed Miss Canedy and some of it she wrote down: "He's brought us safe through the Red Sea." "He looks as deep as the sea himself." "He's king of the United States." "He ought to be king of all the world." "We must all pray to the Lord to carry him safe through, for it 'pears like he's got everything hitched to him." "There has been a right smart praying for him, and it mustn't stop now."

Among onlookers outside the White House, seemingly innocent bystanders enjoying a show worth while, were groups of Negroes. Nearly two hours they hung around gazing at those coming and going. Nearly two hours they waited, some of them wearing fine clothes, others in pickings from various discards ready for the rag bag.

At last they agreed the time had come for them to go in. Why not? Who would throw them out? Surely not the one man in the house they wanted to see. And an observer for the New York *Independent* wrote: "For two long hours Mr. Lincoln had been shaking the hands of the 'sovereigns,' and had become excessively weary, and his grasp languid; but here his nerves rallied at the unwonted sight, and he welcomed this motley crowd with a heartiness that made them wild with exceeding joy. They laughed and wept, and wept and laughed—exclaiming, through their blinding tears: 'God bless you!' 'God bless Abraham Lincoln!' 'God bress Marse Linkum!' Those who witnessed this scene will not soon forget it. For a long distance down the Avenue, on my way home, I heard fast young men cursing the President for this act; but all the way the refrain rang in my ears,—'God bless Abraham Lincoln!' "

CHAPTER 57

"Forever Free"—The Thirteenth Amendment

MORE than 1,300,000 slaves had been freed "by the Lincoln Administration or by the events of the war," indicated a statistical table in the Philadelphia *North American* in November '64. Of slaves when the war began one out of three now was free—under the Emancipation Proclamation of "military necessity." The Federal Constitution, however, still held these slaves to be property, except in Missouri and Maryland, two states which had legalized emancipation.

In many published incidents figured a changed Negro. *Leslie's Weekly* reported a Negro who took a hand in a guerrilla fight: "We fit 'em, we whopt 'em, and we kotched ten uv 'em." *Harper's Monthly* told of Confederate prisoners at Rock Island, Illinois, under Negro guards—and one guard, suddenly seeing the man who once owned him, crying out, "Hullo, massa! *bottom rail top!*"

To make all Negroes free under the law and the Constitution, Lincoln in his December message pointed to the last session of Congress. Then "a proposed amendment of the Constitution abolishing slavery throughout the United States, passed the Senate, but failed for lack of the requisite two-thirds vote in the House of Representatives."

The Senate was safe; 13 Democrats there had joined the four who voted with the Republicans the year before. But the House looked doubtful. For more than a year Lincoln had foreseen a narrow margin. Toward this day he planned when he instigated the admission into the Union of Nevada with her added votes, when he called in Charles A. Dana and arranged for patronage gifts that would have raised a high and noisy scandal if known to the opposition. Again toward this crisis Lincoln had looked when one day only two votes were needed to make a two-thirds majority in the House. Representative John B. Alley wrote: "Two members of the House were sent for and Mr. Lincoln said that those two votes must be procured. When asked, 'How?' he remarked: 'I am President of the United States, clothed with great power. The abolition of slavery by constitutional provision settles the fate, for all coming time, not only of the millions now in bondage, but of unborn millions to come—a measure of such importance that *those two votes must be procured*. I leave it to you to determine how it shall be done; but remember that I am President of the United States, clothed with immense power, and I expect you to procure those votes.' These gentlemen understood the significance of the remark. The votes were procured."

Alley's reserve indicated he had further particulars of a sort he did not care to mention. A practical man was Alley, his hide and leather trade in Lynn, Massachusetts, and his other business interests not suffering through his political dealings.

One of the largest slaveholders in Missouri, James S. Rollins, several times consulted with the President about the proposed Constitutional amendment. Rollins heard Lincoln in early January: "This is my chief hope and main reliance to bring the war to a speedy close, and I have sent for you as an old Whig friend to come and see me, that I might make an appeal for you to vote for this amendment. It is going to be very close. A few votes one way or the other will decide it."

Rollins' response was quick. The President didn't need to send for him on this matter. "Although I . . . have the misfortune to be one of the largest slave-owners in the county where I reside, I had already determined to vote for the thirteenth amendment." Then, as Rollins told it, "He arose from his chair, and grasping me by the hand, gave it a hearty shake, and said, 'I am most delighted to hear that.' " The President then asked how various Missouri Representatives stood. Rollins named those he knew to be for or against the bill. And on Rollins saying he was "on easy terms" with the entire Missouri delegation, Lincoln asked if he wouldn't "talk with those who might be persuaded to vote for the amendment," and to report soon what was the prospect. Congressman Rollins agreed.

Sumner had introduced bills to curb what he termed a usurped power of taxation in New Jersey. Railroad interests affected were seeking to get Sumner to drop these bills, for the time, in exchange for Democratic Representatives of New Jersey voting for the Constitutional amendment to abolish slavery. Nicolay's memorandum indicated the desperate tactics being used to gather a few more needed votes.

This was January 18. On the 31st at noon the galleries of the House are filled to overflowing, in the air a subdued hum of excitement. After formal preliminaries, the joint resolution for a Constitutional amendment to outlaw "slavery or involuntary servitude," except for crimes, is up for final decision.

Ashley yields the floor to a Democrat, Archibald McAllister of Pennsylvania, who announces he will change his vote of Nay last June to Yea. "In voting for the present measure I cast my vote against the cornerstone of the southern confederacy." Applause from the Republican side. Ashley again yields the floor to a Democrat, Alexander H. Coffroth of Pennsylvania, who says the Constitution has been amended before and he favors amending it now by removing slavery as a cause of future strife. Applause from the Republican side. Ashley now yields the remainder of his time to Herrick of New York, whereupon Johnson of Pennsylvania protests the proceeding is getting arbitrary. "One gentleman occupies the floor and farms it out to whoever he pleases." Speaker Colfax upholds Ashley and reads the rules.

A Kentucky Democrat, Aaron Harding, rises to rebuke two Kentucky colleagues who have changed their minds since the vote of June '64, after which he proceeds to justify slavery by familiar and conventional arguments.

Martin Kalbfleisch, a Democrat from Brooklyn, stands up and reads 22 sheets of heavy words meaning nothing much except that he has the words. The clock says three. Speaker Colfax announces the hour for voting has arrived. Kalbfleisch says he has only six more pages to read. Speaker Colfax lets him drone on. The proposed amendment, "as if it were in truth an amendment," proceeds Kalbfleisch, "I regard as subversive of the spirit of that instrument [the Constitution]." Now as ever before he must vote against gentlemen "seeking to lay sacrilegious hands upon that venerated and almost sacred instrument, our glorious Constitution." Kalbfleisch finishes. The speeches are over. Not a Republican has made an argument. They are there to vote. The Democrats for and against have had their say on this day when only roll calls count.

On two roll calls the House refuses to table, refuses to reconsider. The hour of the final vote comes nearer. The galleries fill till standing room is gone. Crowded to the doors are the corridors and lobbies, faces beyond faces wondering if the two-thirds vote will be there. Into the reporters' gallery sweeps "a mob of well-dressed women," as Noah Brooks describes them. With "good grace" the press writers give up their seats to the crinoline girls. The Senate seems to have come over in a body. Grave spectators are four Associate Justices of the Supreme Court and the highly tensed Chief Justice Chase.

The Yeas and Nays are ordered. Alley, Allison, Ames, Anderson and so on. These are all Republicans, their Yeas expected. Comes the name of James E. English, a Connecticut Democrat. He shouts "Aye!" A long roll of applause bursts from the gallery and Republican House members. The Speaker hammers with his gavel. The tumult goes down. Again the voice of the clerk can be heard. For the Republican Ayes as the roll call goes on there is quiet. But with each Democrat shooting his vocal Aye at the calling of his name there is a tumult of handclapping, cheers, laughter, the noisemaking of pent-up emotion let loose. Eleven Democrats answer Aye.

The roll call reaches the W's and Y's; the Wood brothers, Ben and Fernando of New York City, vote for slavery and Yeamen of Kentucky for freedom.

Swift pencils add up the lists. The clerk whispers to the Speaker who announces that the question is decided in the affirmative—Yeas 119, Nays 56, not voting 8. And, said the *Congressional Globe:* ". . . the two thirds required by the Constitution of the United States having voted in favor thereof, the joint resolution was passed."

A mass of still faces break shining and lighting. Emotions explode into a storm of cheers. Men in tears throw their arms around each other. The crowds stand up, many mounting their seats, to shout their glee. Man after man goes handshaking and backslapping. A cloud of women's handkerchiefs wave and float. Ten minutes go by before this hurricane of feeling lets down.

Outside is thunder. The air is torn. Someone has ordered three batteries of regular artillery on Capitol Hill to cry joy with a salute of 100 guns.

Victory came by the margin of three men voting Yea. Eight Democrats stayed away from this House session. Something was due these eight Democrats, absent, noted Nicolay and Hay, "not altogether by accident."

News coming next day that Illinois had ratified the amendment, starting the line-up of three-fourths of the states necessary to amend the Constitution, Lincoln smiled. "This ends the job. I feel proud that Illinois is a little ahead." To the White House that night came a crowd with a brass band, serenaders shouting for the President. At a window they saw standing in half-lights and shadows the solemn central figure of the drama of emancipation. He remarked, "There is a task yet before us—to go forward and consummate by the votes of the States that which Congress so nobly began yesterday. (Applause and cries—'They will do it.')"

The solemn figure at the shadowy window could also have mentioned that this latest and formidable act of Congress was only an empty mouthing of phrases unless the bayonets of Grant and Sherman would give an awful meaning to the seizure without compensation of property sanctioned by the Constitution and once valued at $3,000,000,000. A popular cartoon portrayed a Negro laughing—"Now I'm nobody's nigger but my own."

William Lloyd Garrison made his acknowledgments in the *Liberator:* "To whom is the country more immediately indebted for this vital and saving amendment of the Constitution than, perhaps, to any other man? I believe I may confidently answer—to the humble railsplitter of Illinois—to the Presidential chainbreaker for millions of the oppressed—to Abraham Lincoln!"

CHAPTER 58

Heavy Smoke—Dark Smoke

A SOCIAL revolution moved toward its final collapses and shadows. The Southern planter class read a handwriting on the wall of fate. Not yet did the letters spell out the shape of their doom—but doom enough had already come to make it a dark story.

To Davis and Lee there seemed this winter a last hope of holding out against the North by giving freedom to blacks who would fight. The hour seemed at hand when the Confederacy had conscripted its last white man—and the efforts of Davis and Lee to put black men in fighting service were blocked by the extremist element.

Those blaming Jefferson Davis for Southern failure were in part hunting a scapegoat. He personified the Southern planter class in its pride, its aristocratic feudal outlook, its lack of touch with an almost world-wide abhorrence of slavery as distinguished from what was called "nigger-loving." The war years rolled on and Davis failed to become either an idol or a name and a figure of faith—like Robert E. Lee. Yet Lee had never been such a spokesman of the Confederate cause as Davis. On the death of his wife's mother in 1862 Lee emancipated the slaves to which his family fell heir. Privately Lee spoke of slavery as a sinister, insidious, menacing institution—the view of his high exemplar George Washington. As a voice of states' rights and secession Lee had no reputation at all. In his very silence about why the war was being fought, in the wide and deep love for him for keeping silence while he fought so magnificently, there was some clue to the human dignity of a certain remnant of the Confederacy ready for sacrifice rather than submission to those they termed invaders.

As the pressure became fiercer in early '65 Lee consented, in perfect accord with Davis, to take chief command of all the Confederate armies. As a first move he appointed General Joseph E. Johnston to head an army, made from various fragments, to block the path of Sherman from Savannah up across the Carolinas. This reflected Lee's judgment that Davis had been mistaken in his abrupt dismissal of Johnston.

The Charleston *Mercury* changed its mind about Lincoln and said in January '65: "When Abraham Lincoln took the chair of the Presidency of the United States, he promised in his flat-boat lingo, to 'run the machine as he found it' . . . he has run it with a stern, inflexible purpose, a bold, steady hand, a vigilant, active eye, a sleepless energy, a fanatic spirit, and an eye single to his end—conquest—emancipation . . . Blackguard and buffoon as he is, he has pursued his end with an energy as untiring as an Indian, and a singleness of purpose that might almost be called patriotic. If he were not an unscrupulous knave in his end, and a fanatic in his political views, he would undoubtedly command our respect as a ruler . . . Abroad and at home, he has exercised alike the same ceaseless energy and circumspection."

Late on the night of January 15, after three days' bombardment, Fort Fisher fell. Wilmington, the last open port of the Confederacy, was closed to incoming supplies and outgoing cotton. To no one was it more galling news than to Major General Benjamin F. Butler. Political and military circles were amazed at the news from Washington January 13; it was "now specifically stated that on January 6 Lieutenant General Grant indicated to President Lincoln his earnest wish that Major General Butler be forthwith relieved of his command," and next day the President directed the Adjutant General to issue the order deposing Butler and ordering him to report at Lowell, Massachusetts, his home.

Amid hue and cry and guess and gossip, Grant and Lincoln got rid of the one man in the Union armies who stood foremost as a potential dictator. He was the one commander who, under conceivable circumstances, which Hay had in mind, would not have hesitated at marching an army to Washington, taking over the Government, and issuing regulations to the country.

In the summer of '64 Grant and Lincoln could have told the country during those gloom months that Richmond stood untaken because Butler had miserably blundered. Such an explanation, however true, would have brought scorn and blame on Grant and Lincoln for letting Butler blunder, for keeping in command of the Army of the James a politician "who could strut sitting down." Pertinent was the question of why Grant did not let Butler out in the summer of '64. The reason was plain, tacitly understood between Grant and Lincoln. Butler had a national political following. Shifting, as the war rolled on, from his former loyalty to the proslavery wing of the Democratic party, he turned radical on the slavery issue, radical enough so that Wendell Phillips publicly and repeatedly wished Butler were President instead of Lincoln.

Disputes over how to run the war rose less often now. The war machine ran with fewer blowups. To Lincoln's desk came fewer tangled military matters for his final decision. During many sessions of House and Senate the war was scarcely mentioned. Discussions ran as though the call now was to build the Pacific railway, improve rivers and harbors, dig canals, make land grants to railroads and homesteaders, perfect coast surveys, ease commerce between the states, resettle Indian tribes. The Secretary of the Interior reported on some 4,250,000 acres of public land sold and granted, railroads and homesteaders moving toward a future of expected booms.

The draft had stiffer enforcement, less resistance and evasion. Deserters met less mercy. On Governor's Island a large crowd saw the hanging of a bounty-jumper who had three times pocketed his money and three times deserted. Near City Point with elaborate military ritual thousands of troops formed in a square and saw a firing squad shoot a soldier who had deserted, received pardon, returned to his regiment and deserted again. Over the country went the story of it, with crayon sketches by artists who caught its horror.

In late January the outcry about Northern men languishing in Southern prisons reached the point where Grant decided to relent. In October '64 he had asked Lee whether the Confederate Government would deliver in exchange colored troops "the same as white soldiers," Lee rejoining that "negroes belonging to our citizens are not considered subjects of exchange." On January 24, 1865, however, when the Confederate Government again offered to exchange man for man, Grant accepted the offer without mention of color.

The information service of Grant gave him the advantage of Lee. Deserters each month by thousands, tired of short rations and hard fare in the Confederate Army, crossed the picket lines, nightly expected and welcomed by the Union forces. Always some of them would talk.

Three days after Savannah fell Old Man Blair was on hand and Lincoln wrote one sentence on a card: "Allow the bearer, F. P. Blair, Senr. to pass our lines, go South and return." Blair took a naval boat from City Point to Richmond. At the Confederate White House Blair dined with Davis, fraternized with old cronies of days agone in the Democratic party, noticed with surprise how many able-bodied men were walking the streets, men he would have expected to be in Lee's army.

On January 12, closeted with the Confederate President for a secret interview, Blair spilled his various proposals, kept from the outside world till long afterward. Blair wrote for Lincoln a report of this interview, of how he told Davis of his relations with Lincoln, that Lincoln "shunned an interview with me, until I perceived that he did not wish to hear me, but desired I should go without any explanation of my object."

Out of their suave and guarded confabulations came one thin result; Davis suggested he was willing to send men to some conference and the men he would appoint could be relied on by Mr. Lincoln. A letter written by Davis for Blair to carry back to Lincoln read in closing: ". . . notwithstanding the rejection of our former offers, I would, if you could promise that a commissioner, minister, or other agent would be received, appoint one immediately, and renew the effort to enter into conference, with a view to secure peace to the two countries."

For Blair at the White House Lincoln wrote a one-sentence letter to Davis via Blair: "Your having shown me Mr. Davis' letter to you of the 12th. Inst., you may say to him that I have constantly been, am now, and shall continue, ready to receive any agent whom he, or any other influential person now resisting the national authority, may informally send to me, with the view of securing peace to the people of our one common country."

Thus the Davis letter ending with the words "the two countries" had Lincoln's letter in reply ending with the phrase "our one common country." And where Davis had referred to Lincoln as President of "etc." Lincoln now alluded to "Mr." Davis as though whatever Davis might be President of he was definitely a "Mr." The score was about even.

Now for the first time since the Confederate capital had been moved to Richmond, Davis asked his Vice-President to meet him in conference. Stephens suggested the names of three commissioners. Davis agreed with one of the names, John A. Campbell, Assistant Secretary of War and former U.S. Supreme Court Justice, added R. M. T. Hunter, Senator and ex-Secretary of State, and Stephens himself. These were all three "peace men" or "submissionists" rather than uncompromising last-ditchers. Their instruction by Davis read: "In conformity with the letter of Mr. Lincoln, of which the foregoing is a copy, you are requested to proceed to Washington City for informal conference with him upon the issues involved in the existing war, and for the purpose of securing peace to the two countries."

With his fellow commissioners Stephens came to the Union Army lines the evening of January 29, claiming an understanding with General Grant to pass them on their way to Washington. On this being telegraphed to Washington, Lincoln at once sent Major Eckert of the war telegraph office with written directions to let the commissioners in with safe-conduct if they would say in writing they were ready to talk peace on the basis of the President's note of January 18, peace for "our one common country." Before Eckert arrived with this message the commissioners applied by a written note to General Grant for permission "to proceed to Washington to hold a conference with President Lincoln upon the subject of the existing war, and with a view of ascertaining upon what terms it may be terminated."

On receiving their note Grant at once telegraphed it to Stanton and Lincoln. Lincoln sent Seward to meet the commissioners at Fortress Monroe with written instructions that he was to make known to them three things as indispensable to peace: "1. The restoration of the national authority throughout all the States. 2. No receding, by the Executive of the United States on the Slavery question, from the position assumed thereon, in the late Annual

Message to Congress, and in preceding documents. 3. No cessation of hostilities short of an end of the war, and the disbanding of all forces hostile to the government."

Seward started February 1, while Lincoln telegraphed Grant to let the war go on while peace was talked. "Let nothing which is transpiring, change, hinder, or delay your Military movements, or plans." Grant promised in reply there would be no armistice, that troops were "kept in readiness to move at the shortest notice."

General Meade wrote to his wife that when the Confederate commissioners came within the Union lines "our men cheered loudly, and the soldiers on both sides cried out lustily, 'Peace! Peace!' " This was meant as "a compliment" to the Confederate agents, and, believed Meade, "was so taken by them."

The three commissioners had been considering the very explicit instructions from the President of the United States, brought to them by Eckert, that they must agree in writing to no peace talk except on the basis of the President's note to Blair of January 18, peace for "our one common country." Their answer was a refusal. Their mission seemed at an end. Eckert telegraphed Lincoln their reply was "not satisfactory" and notified the commissioners they could not proceed.

About an hour after their refusal to meet Lincoln's terms, Grant sent a long telegram to the Secretary of War, stating "confidentially, but not officially—to become a matter of record" that he was convinced on conversation with Messrs. Hunter and Stephens "that their intentions are good and their desire sincere to restore peace and union." Grant admitted he was in "an awkward position," fearing a bad influence from the commissioners going away with no results. He saw the difficulties of receiving them and did not know what to recommend. Grant put the high point of his letter: "I am sorry, however, that Mr. Lincoln cannot have an interview with the two names in this despatch [Stephens and Hunter], if not all three now within our lines."

Lincoln next morning walked over to the War Office, read Major Eckert's report, was framing a telegram to call Seward back, when Grant's long telegram was put in his hands. "This despatch," wrote Lincoln later, "changed my purpose." He at once wired Grant: "Say to the gentlemen I will meet them personally at Fortress Monroe, as soon as I can get there."

The President went in a hurry and with secrecy. Even the trustworthy Nicolay was not told. The news leaked from several sources. Welles in his diary grumbled over it. "None of the Cabinet were advised of this move, and without exception, I think, it struck them unfavorably." Meantime down the Potomac on a naval vessel Lincoln journeyed.

"On the night of the 2nd. [of February]," ran Lincoln's account, "I reached Hampton Roads   . . On the morning of the 3rd., the three gentlemen, Messrs Stephens, Hunter and Campbell, came aboard of our Steamer and had an interview with the Secretary of State and myself of several hours duration. No question of preliminaries to the meeting was then and there made or mentioned. No other person was present; no papers were exchanged, or produced; and it was, in advance, agreed that the conversation was to be informal, and verbal merely." The instructions the President had written for Seward were insisted on. Five astute men of politics and law talked four hours in a steamboat saloon. What went on in the minds of the five men, the tangled cross-purposes underlying their words, no onlooker could have caught and reported.

As between drinking men Seward on his arrival had sent the commissioners three bottles of whisky, though aware that Stephens never took more than a teaspoon of it at a time. Hunter, who had spent most of his life in Washington, genially asked Seward: "Governor, how is the Capitol? Is it finished?" Whereupon Seward described the new dome and the great brass door.

There might be a "continental question" on which they could adjust the strife, Stephens once led off, Lincoln rejoining that Mr. Blair in Richmond on matters in Mexico had spoken with no authority from him. The people of the North were as responsible for slavery as the people of the South (as Stephens heard Lincoln say) and "He knew some [in the North] who were in favor of an appropriation as high as four hundred millions of dollars for this purpose [paying owners for the loss of slaves]. 'I could mention persons,' said he, 'whose names would astonish you, who are willing to do this if the war shall now cease.' "

On Hunter's saying it seemed that Lincoln's terms forced the Confederate people to choose nothing else than unconditional surrender and submission, Seward with quiet dignity insisted that "no words like unconditional submission had been used" nor any harsh phrases meaning degradation or humiliation. With peace, said Seward, the Southern people would again be under the Constitution "with all their rights secured thereby."

The opening query of the conference had come from Stephens to Lincoln: "Well, Mr. President, is there no way of putting an end to the present trouble . . . existing between the different States and sections of *the country?*" In this Stephens did not go so far as Lincoln's term "our one common country," but he did with intention and meaning, as his first stroke at the conference, abandon the Davis phrase "two countries."

It was news to the Confederate commissioners that the U.S. Congress on January 31 had passed the 13th Amendment to the Constitution and when this should also pass three-fourths of the state legislatures, it would outlaw and abolish slavery.

Lincoln stressed the point that even if the Confederate States should consider coming back into the Union, he could not make any bargains with armed forces making war on his Government. At this Hunter pointed to King Charles I of England and how that monarch bargained with people in arms against his Government. Hunter's argument was long and elaborate, insisting that peace could come through Lincoln's recognizing the right of Davis to make a treaty. "Mr. Lincoln's face," ran a later newspaper account by Stephens, "then wore that indescribable expression which generally preceded his hardest hits, and he remarked: 'Upon questions of history I must refer you to Mr. Seward, for he is posted in such things, and I don't pretend to be bright. My only distinct recollection of the matter is that Charles lost his head.' That settled Mr. Hunter for a while."

A hush fell over the conference when Lincoln felt required to contradict gravely and directly remarks made by the Confederate commissioners. His words were measured and sounded like doom: the conduct of certain rebel leaders had been such that they had plainly forfeited all right to immunity from punishment for the highest crime known to law. He had come to the brink of saying they should be strung up for treason, should hang high and lonesome as traitors.

After a quiet pause Hunter gave Lincoln a steady, searching look, and then very deliberately: "Mr. President, if we understand you correctly, you think that we of the Confederacy have committed treason; that we are traitors to your government; that we have forfeited our rights, and are proper subjects for the hangman. Is not that about what your words imply?" "Yes," rejoined Lincoln. "You have stated the proposition better than I did. That is about the size of it!" Another somewhat painful pause, then Hunter with a pleasant smile: "Well, Mr. Lincoln, we have about concluded that we shall not be hanged as long as you are President—if we behave ourselves."

An Augusta, Georgia, *Chronicle* interview with Stephens later related: "Hunter declared that he had never entertained any fears for his person or life from so mild a government as that of the United States. To which Mr. Lincoln retorted that he, also, had felt easy as to the Rebels, but not always so easy about the lampposts around Washington City,—a hint that he had already done more favors for the Rebels than was exactly popular with the radical men of his own party. Mr. Lincoln's manner had now grown more positive. He suggested that it would be better for the Rebel States to return at once than to risk the chances of continuing the war, and the increasing bitterness of feeling in Congress. The time might come, he said, when they would not be considered as an erring people invited back to citizenship, but would be looked upon as enemies to be exterminated or ruined."

A fellowship resting on thin fire, in a far cavern of gloom, seemed to have renewal between Lincoln and Stephens. Stephens came aboard the steamer wearing a coarse gray woolen overcoat that came down nearly to his feet. He looked almost like an average-sized man, though his weight was only 90 pounds. Lincoln had come into the steamer saloon and stood watching the dwarfish Georgian shake loose and step out of his huge overcoat, unwinding a long wool muffler and several shawls. Lincoln moved toward Little Aleck, whom he had not seen in 16 years, and with a smile and handshake: "Never have I seen so small a nubbin come out of so much husk." Thus Stephens remembered and told it.

Now came the friendly handshakings ending the Hampton Roads confer-ence, a world of nations and people watching, a horde of journalists and politicians puzzling. Stephens again asked Lincoln to reconsider Blair's stalk-ing horse, the plan of an armistice on the basis of a Mexican expedition com-manded by Jeff Davis. Lincoln: ". . . I will reconsider it; but I do not think my mind will change." And further: "Well, Stephens, there has been nothing we could do for our country. Is there anything I can do for you person-ally?" "Nothing." Then Little Aleck's pale face brightened. "Unless you can send me my nephew who has been for twenty months a prisoner on John-son's Island." Lincoln's face too brightened. "I shall be glad to do it. Let me have his name."

The Confederate commissioners were put in a rowboat and taken to their steamer. Then a rowboat with a Negro at the oars headed for their steamer; he reached their deck with a basket of champagne and a note with the com-pliments of Mr. Seward. The commissioners waved their handkerchiefs in acknowledgment. Then they saw Mr. Seward, and speaking through a boatswain's trumpet, his words came clear: *"Keep the champagne, but return the negro!"* Thus ran the final informal words of the Hampton Roads conference.

In Washington were curiosity and fury. In New York the stock market was nervous and wavering. The gold speculators were crazy to go but couldn't figure which way. Lincoln and Seward rode a steamer up Chesapeake Bay for Annapolis where a crowd was on hand to see the President; newspapermen failed to wring anything definite from Lincoln or Seward.

Next day, February 4, the Cabinet heard from Lincoln and Seward that the conference had no results. A peculiar array of counselors it was, all against him the following day when at an evening session the President laid before them one of the boldest constructive proposals he had ever made. All were Christian churchmen, though each one withheld himself from joining Lincoln in an act for which an argument could be made that it was laden and shining with the spirit of the Sermon on the Mount.

Lincoln this day of February 5 had spent most of his time on a message and proclamation to go to the Senate and House, asking those "honorable bodies" to resolve that the President of the United States be empowered, in his discretion, to pay $400,000,000 to various Southern States, which were named. Six per cent Government bonds would form the payment, "to be distributed among said States *pro rata* on their respective slave populations, as shown by the census of 1860; and no part of said sum to be paid unless all resistance to the national authority shall be abandoned and cease, on or before the first day of April next." The adoption of such a resolution was sought "with a view to embody it, with other propositions, in a proclamation looking to peace and re-union." The proclamation would say ". . . that war will cease, and armies be reduced to a basis of peace; that all political offences will be pardoned; that all property, except slaves, liable to confiscation or forfeiture, will be released therefrom, except in cases of intervening interests of third parties; and that liberality will be recommended to congress upon all points not lying within executive control."

This document Lincoln had confidentially laid before his Cabinet. Wrote Nicolay and Hay: "There was but little discussion of the proposition. The President's evident earnestness on the one side, and the unanimous dissent of the Cabinet on the other, probably created an awkward situation which could be best relieved by silence on each hand." Usher wrote of the President somewhat surprised at all the Cabinet being opposed, and asking, "How long will the war last?" No one answered, so the President took it on himself: "A hundred days. We are spending now in carrying on the war three millions a day, which will amount to all this money, besides all the lives." With a deep sigh, noted Usher, he added, "But you are all opposed to me, and I will not send the message."

On the back of the manuscript of this proposed message, under date of February 5, 1865, Lincoln wrote: "To-day these papers, which explain themselves, were drawn up and submitted to the Cabinet & unanamously disapproved by them." He signed his name as though it was history and should be of record.

Welles with his colleagues saw the President in this a schemer rather than a solid statesman. "The Rebels would misconstrue it if the offer were made. If attempted and defeated it would do harm." Welles, whose judgment probably reflected that of most of the Cabinet, believed his guess was better than that of Lincoln on how the South would take the proposal. Also Welles looked toward Congress and the Lincoln opposition there rather than toward the country and the people, the forces by which Lincoln the year before had overcome the almost unanimous array of politicians in Congress opposed to him.

So the war would go on. The majestic and incalculably dynamic gesture Lincoln asked for, was out. A policy of nonretaliation, of "molding society for durability in the Union," as he hoped in the December message, would have to come slowly. His confidential advisers were thinking of Washington and Congress and politics; he was thinking of the great everyday masses of people North and South. The Cabinet was correct in feeling that the present controlling Southern politicians would hoot his proposed proclamation. But beyond might be a mass of Southern people moving and acting when those politicians were discredited as prophets and bankrupt as statesmen.

When the Confederate commissioners came back with their report, Richmond was turned upside down humanly. Jefferson Davis spoke; death or humiliation he would prefer "sooner than we should ever be united again." With curled lips of scorn he referred to the archantagonist "His Majesty Abraham the First" and prophesied that the Confederacy would yet "compel the Yankees, in less than twelve months, to petition us for peace on our own terms."

Little Aleck Stephens heard it as oratory bold, lofty, undaunted, but he was reminded of the Light Brigade at Balaklava and the Frenchman who summarized its useless sacrifice: "It is brilliant; it is grand; but it is not war."

Stephens reached his home at Crawfordsville, Georgia, February 20, where, as he wrote later, "I remained in perfect retirement." Stephens was too far committed to the states' rights theory to go as far as Lincoln advised. On the other hand his conscience did allow him to go home, stay there, keep silence and watch the movement of a tragic drama where his voice lacked authority.

Lincoln in Washington sent a telegram to the Johnson's Island prison. Lieutenant Stephens was pleased to hear at headquarters that the President wanted to see him. They put him on a sleigh to ride 20 miles across the ice on Lake Erie to Sandusky. He rode the railroad cars to Washington, and at the White House found the President half sitting and half slouched on a table, talking with Seward. Lincoln rose, and with a smile: "I saw your uncle, the Honorable Alexander H. Stephens, recently at Hampton Roads. I told your uncle I would send you to him." The Lieutenant was deeply moved and just a little dizzy over the next words from the President: "You have the freedom of the city as long as you please to remain here. When you want to go home, let me know, and I will pass you through the lines." Two weeks the Lieutenant stayed in Washington, finding old friends of his own and his uncle's who entertained him. He put on weight, gained strength.

When ready to go to Richmond, Mr. Lincoln gave him a letter to carry to his uncle: "Your nephew, Lieut. Stephens, goes to you, bearing this note.

Please, in return, to select and send to me, that officer of the same rank, imprisoned at Richmond, whose physical condition most urgently requires his release." He signed a pass through the Union Army and then did a sentimental thing. He handed the Confederate lieutenant a photograph of himself: "You had better take that along. It is considered quite a curiosity down your way, I believe." Did Mr. Lincoln want to help Mr. Stephens remember what an old laughing friend looked like?

In the Senate Wilson of Massachusetts was saying that Grant would have won the war by now if three months ago he could have had a reinforcement of 50,000 or 75,000 men to which he was entitled. On the basis of "a report in circulation" Wilson would like to convict the President of failing to get Grant troops needed to end the war. Wilson was taking part in a concerted move to drag down the executive and raise up the legislative end of the Government.

In the same week Ben Wade tore into the President's "pretensions" in Louisiana, saying of Lincoln's ten-per-cent plan that it was "the most absurd and impracticable that ever haunted the imagination of a statesman." Wade could hit hard, if not always clean. Perfect courtesy got mixed with a smoothflowing insolence in short words. Doolittle of Wisconsin undertook a defense of the President and came off a bad second.

In the House session February 8, Stevens put through a resolution, much like one of Sumner's in the Senate, requesting the President to report on Hampton Roads. Many Senate and House members nursed a sullen mistrust of Lincoln's latest errand. With more than a few it was a baffled and inarticulate hate of the President. When Lincoln had followed Seward to Hampton Roads and the completely unexpected news of it went forth over Washington, undercurrents of excitement and frustration raged and whirled, wrote Noah Brooks. "The Peace Democrats went about the corridors of the hotels and the Capitol, saying that Lincoln had at last come to their way of thinking, and had gone to Hampton Roads to open peace negotiations. The radicals were in a fury of rage. They bitterly complained that the President was about to give up the political fruits which had been already gathered from the long and exhausting military struggle." The moderate Republicans of unshaken faith in Lincoln were in a minority; they failed to convince the radicals that Lincoln would not give ground on emancipation.

Thad Stevens among the bitterest, according to Brooks, was saying "that if the country were to vote over again for President of the United States, Benjamin F. Butler, and not Abraham Lincoln, would be their choice." And for the first time since Lincoln had been President a faction of his own political party, ruthless men of no hesitations about extreme methods, mentioned the final and desperate weapon they might use against him. "Others," wrote Brooks, "of the same uncompromising and unreasonable stripe [as Stevens] actually hinted at impeachment and trial."

Certainly the February 7 speech of radical Representative George W. Julian set the frame and laid the scene for a possible impeachment of Lincoln. In case the radicals should find that his report on Hampton Roads was considered by them a betrayal of their cause, Julian had opened the course with a first blast. In some 10,000 words Julian reviewed the war as a procession of mistakes, chiefly by the administration and its head. The negative, sickly and awkward policies of the administration, hoped Julian, would not be resumed.

On this day Welles found Lincoln waiting for the Cabinet to come in, "reading with much enjoyment certain portions of Petroleum V. Nasby": "Cussid be Sherman, for he took Atlanta. And he marcht thro the Confedrisy, and respected not the feelins of ennybody. And the people of the South lift up their voisis and weep, becoz their niggers are not. And he took Savanner, and cotton enuff 2 hev satisfide Bookannon's cabbynet. And he turns his eyes toward Charleston, and is serusly thinkin uv Richmond. The wind bloweth where it listeth—he listeth where he goeth."

One rumor now gaining headway and credence was that Lincoln at Hampton Roads had taken a sheet of paper, written at the top the one word "Union," and shoving it across the table toward Stephens, had said, "Let me have that one condition and you can write below it whatever peace terms you choose." This reported repudiation of the Emancipation Proclamation was to the radicals a hair-raising piece of news.

On February 10 the tension began to let down. The House had been dealing with a variety of bills when the clerk announced a message from the President. All other business was suspended. The clerk began reading. Documents, letters, dispatches, poured forth in a long stream. It seemed almost as though Lincoln had awaited this hour. The pass written for Blair to Richmond, the letter of Davis to Blair which Blair carried to Lincoln, the reply of Lincoln to Blair meant for Blair to carry to Richmond and show to Davis, the rise of the phrases "our one common country" and "the two countries," the documents passing between the Confederate commissioners showing up at Grant's army lines and what passed between them and Grant, the further transactions between Eckert and the commissioners, the Lincoln letter of instructions to Seward with its three "indispensable" points, the dispatch to Grant to keep the war going no matter what he heard about peace, Grant's reply that he would sure keep the war going, the Eckert telegram in cipher to Lincoln which for the moment wrecked all chance of a conference, the long telegram of Grant to Stanton with Lincoln's brief comment that "this despatch . . . changed my purpose," the meeting at Hampton Roads and the reading of the commissioners' instruction from Davis that they were there "for the purpose of securing peace to the two countries," the negotiations ending with no result. The foregoing, "containing as is believed all the information sought," was respectfully submitted.

Pressmen from their gallery noted "absolute silence" from first to last during the reading of this message. Looking over the hall at the hundreds seated or standing, one might say, wrote Noah Brooks, they "had been suddenly turned to stone." Soon House members began exchanging smiles and glances of meaning. The President had never for a moment lost footing, had gone into a winding labyrinth where anything could happen and had come out without a flaw. "When the reading was over," and the full name of "Abraham Lincoln" signed to the communication was read by the clerk with a certain grandiloquence, Brooks heard "an instant and irrepressible storm of applause, begun by members on the floor, and taken up by the people in the gallery."

Washburne moved that 20,000 extra copies of the message be printed. "The entire loyal people of this country" would approve the "wisdom and discretion in the President of the United States" shown in this matter. Thad Stevens spoke. "The President has thought it was best to make the effort . . . I believe even those who thought his mission was unwise will accord to him sagacity and patriotism, and applaud his action."

To the Senate the President sent no such marshaled array of documents as he gave the House. To that graver and more sedate body, empowered to ratify treaties and conduct foreign affairs, went a copy of a long note written by the Secretary of State to Minister Adams at London, reciting the Hampton Roads negotiations.

An old order was passing. Now in the Supreme Court chambers for the first time a Negro was admitted to practice before that high tribunal: John S. Rock, an attorney of ability and good name in the city of Boston. The race issue writhed and snarled again in debates over the proposed Bureau for the Relief of Freedmen and Refugees. The bill gave the President power to appoint commissioners to control the bureau, with authority to distribute "abandoned lands" among the Negroes, to pay out money and supplies.

Overshadowing all other discussions across February were those on bills for recognizing as "legitimate" the government set up in Louisiana a year earlier under the guidance of Lincoln and the military commander of the department, General Banks. The election of state officers ordered by Banks for February 22, 1864, covered an area of about one-third of the state. The voters were 11,411 white men, each having taken the oath required by the President, and they made a total of more than one-fifth of the entire vote of the State of Louisiana in 1860. They had elected three Congressmen and a governor, Michael Hahn. At a later election they had chosen delegates to a constitutional convention which met in New Orleans in April. This convention abolished slavery in Louisiana "forever" by a vote of 72 to 13. It gave the ballot to white males only, yet it empowered the legislature to give the ballot to Negro soldiers of service in the Union Army and to Negroes who could read and write, meeting the qualifications Lincoln had suggested in his letter to Governor Hahn.

The new state governments the President had guided were "shadows" and not "realities," according to the opposition. For himself he wished to regard them as "important," as "earnestly struggling," as admittedly "short of complete success."

Not to the public of this hour could Lincoln have given the painful details and sorry embarrassments he confessed in peremptory letters to Union generals who were wrecking his work. On November 14, 1864, he had begun a letter to General S. A. Hurlbut, successor to Banks in command at New Orleans: "Few things, since I have been here, have impressed me more painfully than what, for four or five months past, has appeared as bitter military opposition to the new State Government of Louisiana." He had hoped he was mistaken as to the facts, but having seen copies of letters exchanged between Generals Hurlbut and E. R. S. Canby, the hope was gone. That two of his generals should join with secessionists in trying to undo his work was "incomprehensible"—and if continued would not be over-looked.

Banks was "very sore" at Sumner over his opposition to the Louisiana plan, so Sumner wrote to Franz Lieber. Also it was near fantasy that Mrs. Lincoln at this time was writing notes to Sumner asking him to use his influence to prevent Banks' appointment to the Cabinet, which she feared might take place.

On December 18 the President had met Monty Blair and General Banks in a White House hall and called them into his office. "They immediately began to talk about Ashley's bill," wrote Hay. The bill included recognition of the new state government of Louisiana. "The President had been reading it carefully & said that he liked it with the exception of one or two things which he thought rather calculated to conceal a feature which might be objectionable to some. The first was that under the provisions of that bill negroes would be made jurors & voters under the temporary governments." Banks observed: "Yes, that is to be stricken out . . . It would simply throw the Government into the hands of the blacks, as the white people under that arrangement would refuse to vote." This was in substance the same view Banks the year before had written to Lincoln.

For weeks across January and February Ashley's bill was debated and taken back to committee for revisions and modifications. Five times it was redrafted, always fixing cast-iron requirements to be followed in letting the seceded states come back into the Union. On the final vote it failed by 80 to 65, with 37 members not voting.

In the Senate, reconstruction acts ran a different course. There Trumbull of Illinois reported from the Judiciary Committee a joint resolution declaring that the United States recognized the Louisiana government "inaugurated under and by the convention which assembled on the 6th day of April, A.D., 1864, at the city of New Orleans, as the legitimate government of the said State, entitled to the guarantees and all other rights of a State government, under the Constitution of the United States." Senators Sumner, Wade and Howard spoke amazement and scorn that their former associate in opposition to the President now acted in behalf of the President's most earnest wishes. Serene and without a flicker of resentment, Trumbull led a parliamentary fight that had his old allies sore and desperate.

In late February it was seen that most of the Democrats would vote against recognizing the new Louisiana state government. It was again the familiar Lincoln "military despotism," said Garrett Davis of Kentucky, a horse thief Government which had illegally run off with some of the best horseflesh in Kentucky, impressed for Union Army cavalry. The outspoken fear of other Democrats was that a military rule directed by a Republican administration in Washington would favor the Negroes. On the other hand the outspoken fear of the five Republican Senators who joined the Democratic opposition was that under the new state government of Louisiana, if it should be recognized, the whites would control and refuse the ballot to the Negroes. Therefore these five Republicans sought to put a rider on the bill which would insure the Negro the right to vote in Louisiana, this to be a precedent imperative on all other reorganized states. Of Lincoln's "ten-per-cent principle" Wade would say, "A more absurd, monarchical, and anti-American principle was never announced on God's earth."

Trumbull had offered the figures on the Louisiana case. He gave the first complete details, the statistics and computations, showing that in the Louisiana polls the so-called "Lincoln's ten per cent" was nearer 20 per cent or more.

Leading all others in speeches of condemnation, in amendments, in motions to delay voting, was Sumner. In the Senate gallery from day to day sat one listener, one spectator, who charmed Sumner, fascinated him. She was to him the one woman in the world. He had fallen in love with her, Alice Mason Hooper, a niece of Jeremiah Mason of Boston. "His devotion had been marked and somewhat opposite to his usual stately ways," wrote Anna Laurens Dawes. "Among all the fascinating women of Washington she stood pre-eminent. Beauty, grace, a slender and stately form, a high-bred manner, and aristocratic reserve were all hers, and withal a special fascination, coming perhaps from the uncertain moods of an extremely variable temper —a temper which would pay its debts in the small coin of teasing or in the grand style, as fitted the mood of the hour." The match, the engagement to marry, came, wrote Miss Dawes, through "fascination and hope on the one side, fascination and ambition on the other." He was 57, a lifelong bachelor, and she at 27 sat in the gallery watching him, she with "the habits at once of a belle and a spoiled child, looking forward eagerly to the new gayeties of a senator's wife, and contemplating a near future when she should be mistress of the White House."

For her now, besides his regular public, Sumner performed, not knowing that soon after their marriage, soon after moving into a house of their own, his pride and will would come into collision with hers, they would part, he to meditate suicide and never after refer to her except as "that person." Now in February '65 he enjoyed it that his betrothed was in the gallery watching him in a parliamentary fight that called to his blood.

On the Senate floor Sumner rose to heights of stubborn granite and grandeur; also he sprawled in puddles of the ridiculous and the asinine. To brother Henry wrote Charles Francis Adams, Jr., "Sumner has run more than ever to seed, and now out-Sumners himself." Sumner argued that before he would recognize the new government of Louisiana, the right of Negroes to citizenship must be therewith guaranteed. The difference of view between Sumner and the President in this was much the same as it had been with the 13th Amendment, when Ashley had urged the President to send for Sumner and the President had replied: "I can do nothing with Mr. Sumner in these matters. While Mr. Sumner is very cordial with me, he is making his history in an issue with me on this very point. He hopes to succeed in beating the President so as to change this Government from its original form and make it a strong centralized power." Oddly enough, according to this, it was states' rights rather than Negro suffrage on which Sumner and Lincoln parted ways—and parted cordially, for Sumner never struck at Lincoln's motives.

There was laughter when Henderson inquired what had become of Sumner's "state suicide" theory. Was Louisiana in or out of the Union? Sumner: "It is in and it is not."

Sumner pressed toward the close of the debate: "The pretended State government in Louisiana is utterly indefensible . . . a mere seven-months' abortion, begotten by the bayonet in criminal conjunction with the spirit of caste."

The Senate February 27 postponed the measure by a vote of 34 to 12 "to to-morrow." This "to-morrow" never came. The session closed March 4 without a vote. Trumbull spoke his belief that there would have been a clear majority for the resolution had it not been fought by Sumner. In the last days of the session Sumner piled his desk high with documents, books, papers, notes, gave the word he was going to filibuster. He would stand and speak and read till the session officially ended. Thus he would kill three bills —a tax, a tariff and an appropriation bill. The Senate gave in. Sumner had his way. Louisiana was out. Lincoln's foremost immediate project was lost, for the time. Another Congress, further events, would pass on Louisiana.

The tangled episode of Louisiana's political fate came to its climax and diminuendo. Heavy folios of narrative would be required to tell the entire story in all its chaotic and troubled lights. Passions—the same passions that had made the war—ran through all the breath of it. Yet Sumner in all his stubborn course of procedure had cast no aspersion on the President. And Lincoln in his turn had kept a perfect serenity toward Sumner. Each had stood by his sincere convictions as spoken to the other in early winter discussions.

About this time, according to an incident later related by Joseph G. Cannon of Danville, Illinois, several Northern Congressmen in Lincoln's office were calling for retaliation. They wanted hangings of "rebel" leaders. Representative James K. Moorhead was making a second and more vitriolic attack than his first when Lincoln leaned across his table, shot out an arm and pointed a long finger: "Mr. Moorhead, haven't you lived long enough to know that two men may honestly differ about a question and both be right?"

Out of Savannah February 1 Sherman had moved, his plan of campaign a secret. A dispatch had come to Stanton and Lincoln that his route was inland. Before starting Sherman had said this march would be ten times as difficult, ten times more important, than the one from Atlanta to the sea.

In two columns with outriding cavalry Sherman's 60,000 men moved over the soil of the state that had led off in secession. Continuous winter rains had swollen all streams. Country not under water was mud and quagmire. They marched day on day with rain about two days out of three. They crossed five large navigable rivers, swollen torrents. At times every private in the army served as a pioneer, split saplings and carried fence rails for corduroy roads, laid pontoons, cleared entanglements. They waded streams, no time to bridge. Some forces worked for hours waist-deep in icy flood-waters. One captured Confederate trooper, seeing these exploits, told the 104th Illinois, "If your army goes to hell, it will corduroy the road." General Joseph E. Johnston said later, "I made up my mind there had been no such army since the days of Julius Caesar."

Confederate forces of about 15,000, chiefly under General Wade Hampton, made no headway in stopping the Northern invaders, who seemed to have saved their fury for South Carolina. Troops of the 15th corps were heard to say, "Here is where treason began and, by God, here is where it shall end." Officially Sherman's orders, as in Georgia, were against wanton violence and destruction, but Sherman did not repeat them now. In his own later words: "My aim then was to whip the rebels, to humble their pride, to follow them to their inmost recesses, and make them fear and dread us." Over the South arose a tradition that Sherman had raved in wrath, "I'm going to bring every Southern woman to the washtub."

Undoubtedly his men went farther in robbery, violence and vicious capers than he cared to have them, but their toils and marches, their readiness for hardship and fighting, were such that Sherman could not bring himself to penalize them. For himself he slept in a tree one night of flood, another night on a hard board church pew, living mostly as plain as any private.

Foragers stripped the country of many farm buildings, farm animals, fences, much property, and food of all kinds. The railroads were torn up, and weather permitting, bridges burned, cotton bales set blazing, vacant dwellings and barns fired. Looters and bummers stole jewelry, watches and silverware, smashed pianos and shattered mirrors, though the extent and the manner of these outrages became an issue of veracity as between Northern and Southern witnesses.

It was heartbreak time in South Carolina. The final dooms were weaving, Mrs. Chesnut writing February 22: "Charleston and Wilmington have surrendered. I have no further use for a newspaper. I never want to see another one as long as I live . . . Shame, disgrace, beggary, all have come at once, and are hard to bear—the grand smash! Rain, rain, outside, and naught but drowning floods of tears inside." She couldn't bear it, and rushed downstairs and out through the rainstorm to the home of the Reverend Mr. Martin, who said, "Madam, Columbia is burned to the ground." Mrs. Chesnut bowed her head and sobbed aloud.

In bloody actions of February 5, 6 and 7 Grant had so struck at Lee that by no chance could Lee send any men toward Sherman. In Washington February 22 by order of the President there was a night illumination of the high domed building on the top of Capitol Hill—lights and singing bright windows in celebration of victories resulting in Columbia, Charleston, Wilmington, and a fresh wide area coming again under the U.S. flag.

CHAPTER 59

The Second Inaugural

O F LITTLE help toward Lincoln's second inaugural address in a few days was the widely circulated *Leslie's Weekly* which on its front page February 25, 1865, said Lincoln showed "pigheadedness in retaining McClellan" so long, and that his retention of "worthless" Cabinet members had earned him "the strongly expressed contempt of Congress." In fact, "There is no man of less consequence in these United States than Abraham Lincoln of Illinois. A schoolboy would deserve flogging for sending out documents of such prodigious moment as come from his pen in phrases so mean and unbecoming."

On March 4, 1865, hours before noon, Lincoln in a Senate wing room considered and signed bills. A parade on Pennsylvania Avenue from the White House to the Capitol moved in a light drizzle of rain and cold, gusty winds. A muddy paste coated the sidewalks lined with spectators. On one wagon platform printers from the Typographical Society, a labor union, ran a hand press and scattered programs of the day's events. A battalion of Negro troops in Union Army blue marched, and the Negro Grand Lodge of Odd Fellows.

Toward noon flocks of women streamed around the Capitol, "crinoline smashed, skirts bedaubed, velvet and laces streaked with mud." And the women, noted Brooks, kept unfailing good nature though "such another dirty crowd probably never was seen." In the galleries women in wide crinoline "filled the seats like a cloud," not a man finding a seat. "Diamonds flashed, feathers nodded (damply), bright faces gleamed, and the noise of feminine tongues was like a swarm of bees." Senator Foot of Vermont rapped his gavel for order but "a rippling storm of small talk in the galleries went on."

Invited notables trod to their reserved seats. Noah Brooks wrote of Mrs. Lincoln, attended by Senator Anthony, seated in the Diplomatic Gallery, and a buzz when the Justices of the Supreme Court entered in their black robes. A few stray governors came in, then the Diplomatic Corps, in gold lace, feathers and white pantaloons. One ambassador had to unbutton himself to get his feet on the floor. Members of the House moved in at noon, then the Cabinet.

In the middle of the front row sat Lincoln; as the clock struck twelve his eyes turned with those of others to the entrance of Andrew Johnson, Vice-President-elect, escorted by Senator Doolittle. Johnson after introduction rose with no papers, saying impromptu to the Senators, to the Supreme Court, that their power came from the mass of the people, and further, "You, Mr. Secretary Seward, Mr. Secretary Stanton, the Secretary of the Navy [he couldn't quite dig up the name of Welles], and the others who are your associates—you know that you have my respect and my confidence —derive not your greatness and your power alone from President Lincoln." He was in a mood. "Humble as I am, plebeian as I may be deemed, permit me in the presence of this brilliant assemblage to enunciate the truth that courts and cabinets, the President and his advisers, derive their power and their greatness from the people."

Part of this, of course, was Andrew Johnson's traditional stump speech. "I, though a plebeian boy, am authorized by the principles of the Government under which I live to feel proudly conscious that I am a man, and grave dignitaries are but men." He was overdoing the business of being a plebeian.

By now Hamlin had pulled at Johnson's coattails while the Senate clerk, John W. Forney, with whom Johnson had been drinking the evening before, whispered loud, hoping to catch Johnson's eye and flag him down.

Johnson swept on into thanking God that Tennessee had never been out of the Union, and declaring flatly, "No State can go out of this Union; and moreover, Congress cannot eject a State from the Union."

Far more sorry than funny was this performance—the sour note of the day. His face flushed, his voice hoarse, Johnson looked worn and sick. For weeks that winter he had been in bed with typhoid fever and general exhaustion from heavy labors amid terrific excitement. He had written to Lincoln inquiring whether by any precedents he could stay in Nashville and take his oath of office. Lincoln had wired: "It is our unanimous conclusion that it is unsafe for you not to be here on the fourth of March. Be sure to reach here by that time." In Hamlin's room in the Senate building he poured one tumbler of whisky and drank it down, and according to Hamlin, just before going into the overheated Senate chamber, drank another, saying, "I need all the strength for the occasion I can have."

As Johnson got well into his speech several Republican Senators bent their heads, unable to look at him. Sumner covered his face with his hands. Seward, wrote Noah Brooks, was "bland and serene as a summer day" and Stanton seemed "petrified." Speed "sat with eyes closed." Senators "turned and twisted" in their chairs. When Johnson had repeated inaudibly the oath of office, he turned, took the Bible in his hand, "and facing the audience, said, with a loud, theatrical voice and gesture, 'I kiss this Book in the face of my nation of the United States.'"

At Lincoln's side sat Senator Henderson of Missouri, who noticed Lincoln's head drooping in humiliation. As Senator Henderson offered his arm to Lincoln for taking their place in the march to the inaugural platform outside, Henderson heard Lincoln say to a marshal, "Do not let Johnson speak outside."

A day or two later Hugh McCulloch spoke to Lincoln about alarm in some quarters. What would happen to the country if Lincoln should be suddenly removed and Johnson replaced him? Lincoln after a moment's hesitation and with unusual seriousness: "I have known Andy for many years. He made a bad slip the other day, but you need not be scared. Andy ain't a drunkard."

The procession to the Capitol portico formed and moved. The drizzle of rain had stopped. "A tremendous shout, prolonged and loud, arose from the surging ocean of humanity," wrote Noah Brooks. The President with invited notables took the platform. Then the sergeant at arms of the Senate arose and with raised hands got the crowd still. And Abraham Lincoln, rising tall, gaunt and outstanding, stepped forward to read his inaugural address. Applause roared, again and again was repeated, and finally died far away on the outer fringe of the throng.

In a silence almost profound the audience now listened. Seldom had a President been so short-spoken about the issues of so grave an hour. He read his carefully and deliberately prepared address:

[Fellow Countrymen:] At this second appearing to take the oath of the presidential office, there is less occasion for an extended address than there was at the first. Then a statement, somewhat in detail, of a course to be pursued, seemed fitting and proper. Now, at the expiration of four years, during which public declarations have been constantly called forth on every point and phase of the great contest which still absorbs the attention, and engrosses the energies of the nation, little that is new could be presented. The progress of our arms, upon which all else chiefly depends, is as well known to the public as to myself; and it is, I trust, reasonably satisfactory and encouraging to all. With high hope for the future, no prediction in regard to it is ventured.

On the occasion corresponding to this four years ago, all thoughts were anxiously directed to an impending civil-war. All dreaded it—all sought to avert it. While the inaugeral address was being delivered from this place, devoted altogether to *saving* the Union without war, insurgent agents were in the city seeking to *destroy* it without war—seeking to dissol[v]e the Union, and divide effects, by negotiation. Both parties deprecated war; but one of them would *make* war rather than let the nation survive; and the other would *accept* war rather than let it perish. And the war came.

One eighth of the whole population were colored slaves, not distributed generally over the Union, but localized in the Southern part of it. These slaves constituted a peculiar and powerful interest. All knew that this interest was, somehow, the cause of the war. To strengthen, perpetuate, and extend this interest was the object for which the insurgents would rend the Union, even by war; while the government claimed no right to do more than to restrict the territorial enlargement of it. Neither party expected for the war, the magnitude, or the duration, which it has already attained. Neither anticipated that the *cause* of the conflict might cease with, or even before, the conflict itself should cease. Each looked for an easier triumph, and a result less fundamental and astounding. Both read the same Bible, and pray to the same God; and each invokes His aid against the other. It may seem strange that any men should dare to ask a just God's assistance in wringing their bread from the sweat of other men's faces; but let us judge not that we be not judged. The prayers of both could not be answered; that of neither has been answered fully. The Almighty has His own purposes. "Woe unto the world because of offences! for it must needs be that offences come; but woe to that man by whom the offence cometh!" If we shall suppose that American Slavery is one of those offences which, in the providence of God, must needs come, but which, having continued through His appointed time, He now wills to remove, and that He gives to both North and South, this terrible war, as the woe due to those by whom the offence came, shall we discern therein any departure from those divine attributes which the believers in a Living God always ascribe to Him? Fondly do we hope—fervently do we pray—that this mighty scourge of war may speedily pass away. Yet, if God wills that it continue, until all the wealth piled by the bond-man's two hundred and fifty years of unrequited toil shall be sunk, and until every drop of blood drawn with the lash shall be paid by another drawn with the sword, as was said three thousand years ago, so still it must be said "the judgments of the Lord, are true and righteous altogether"

With malice toward none; with charity for all; with firmness in the right, as God gives us to see the right, let us strive on to finish the work we are in; to bind up the nation's wounds; to care for him who shall have borne the battle, and for his widow, and his orphan—to do all which may achieve and cherish a just, and a lasting peace, among ourselves, and with all nations.

A subdued handclapping and occasional cheers punctuated the address. Reporters noticed at the final paragraph many moist eyes and here and there tears coursing down faces unashamed.

The clerk of the Supreme Court brought the Bible. Then Lincoln, laying his right hand on an open page of the Book, repeated the oath of office after Chief Justice Chase, bent forward, kissed the Book and arose to full height again.

Presenting the Book to Mrs. Lincoln afterward, the Chief Justice pointed to the pencil-marked verses kissed by the President, in the fifth chapter of Isaiah:

None shall be weary nor stumble among them; none shall slumber nor sleep; neither shall the girdle of their loins be loosed, nor the latchet of their shoes be broken:

Whose arrows are sharp, and all their bows bent, their horses' hoofs shall be counted like flint, their wheels like a whirlwind.

Like the Gettysburg Address, and more particularly the House Divided speech, the second inaugural took on varied meanings. To some it was a howl for vengeance, to others a benediction and a plea—with deep music.

"Everyone likes a compliment," wrote Lincoln to Thurlow Weed with thanks for good words, and giving his own estimate of his address. He expected it "to wear as well as—perhaps better than—any thing I have produced; but I believe it is not immediately popular. Men are not flattered by being shown that there has been a difference of purpose between the Almighty and them."

In the evening the White House was open for a reception. "The platform in front of the entrance, the walks and drives back of the Avenue, were packed with people," noted Lieutenant Ashmun of the guards. Occasionally a lady fainted or became terrified and would have to be taken out over the heads of the close-packed crowd. From 8 until 11 Lincoln spent in almost continuous handshaking. Newsmen wrote that he shook hands with more than 6,000 persons.

The crowds vanished and in the still midnight the White House looked to the guard Crook, "as if a regiment of rebel troops had been quartered there, with permission to forage." Mementoes were wanted. "A great piece of red brocade, a yard square almost, was cut from the window-hangings of the East Room. Flowers from the floral designs in the lace curtains were cut out. Some arrests were made, after the reception, of persons concerned in the disgraceful business." The President, noted Crook, was "distressed greatly." Usually he was so calm about things. Crook noted his saying, "Why should they do it? How can they?"

An American crowd, "a motley democratic crowd, such as could be seen in no royal country, and of which we are justly proud," ran the version of Adelaide W. Smith, an army nurse. She had met one Lieutenant Gosper, their friendship not ordinary. In a skirmish before Petersburg his right leg had been shot away and Miss Smith had been his nurse. She wrote, "We fell into the long procession of couples approaching the President." Swept along, Miss Smith and Lieutenant Gosper on his crutch finally saw Lincoln. To their surprise he stepped out before the two of them, took the hand of Lieutenant Gosper, and in a voice unforgettable, was saying, "God bless you, my boy!"

The two of them moved on, the lieutenant happy and saying to Ada Smith, "Oh! I'd lose another leg for a man like that!"

Mary Abigail Dodge, a trim little 109-pound woman, widely known for her sparkling magazine and newspaper writings, had on March 7, 1861, in a White House crowd put out her hand saying, "Mr. Lincoln, I am very sorry for you, but indeed I must shake hands with you," hearing him, "Ah! *your* hand doesn't hurt me." Now on March 4, 1865, in her little village of Hamilton, Massachusetts, she wrote him a letter he may have read more than once:

I only wish to thank you for being so good—and to say how sorry we all are that you must have four years more of this terrible toil. But remember what a triumph it is for the right, what a blessing to the country—and then your rest shall be glorious when it does come!

You can't tell anything about it in Washington where they make a noise on the slightest provocation— But if you had been in this little speck of a village this morning and heard the soft, sweet music of unseen bells rippling through the morning silence from every quarter of the far-off horizon, you would have better known what your name is to this nation.

May God help you in the future as he has helped you in the past and a people's love and gratitude will be but a small portion of your exceeding great reward.

CHAPTER 60

Endless Executive Routine

WHERE others had made little or no headway at calming Missouri, General Grenville M. Dodge as military commander was to try his hand. More than any other state Missouri was seeing civil war, neighbors arrayed against neighbors, with roving guerrillas and bushwhackers, barn-burners, midnight shootings, Lincoln writing to Dodge January 15 of "so much irregular violence in Northern Missouri as to be . . . almost depopulating it." He suggested that Dodge consider "an appeal to the people there to go to their homes, and let one another alone," possible withdrawal of troops where they seemed an irritation. In suggesting steps he believed practical, Lincoln voiced a faith in humanity not easy to apply in Missouri at that hour.

In the weeks following inauguration, according to one of Sumner's secretaries, "Mr. Lincoln bestowed more tokens of good-will on Sumner than on any other senator." It seemed that for any Senators or Congressmen whose co-operation Lincoln sought, he would go out of his way to grant them offices or favors. During four years and one month of presidential appointive powers, Lincoln, according to a later estimate, removed 1,457 out of a possible 1,639 officials. In many responsible wartime positions the strictest of loyalty was a requirement; all under doubt had to go. In the building of a loyalist Government Lincoln carried a heavy load.

The old and tried friend of true steel loyalty, Isaac N. Arnold, while giving all he had for Lincoln in Washington, had lost his seat in Congress, but was staying on in Washington to write a biography of Lincoln and a history of the overthrow of slavery. Lincoln offered him a choice of two good offices and Arnold was thinking it over.

Fessenden had resigned as Secretary of the Treasury and begun his third term as Senator from Maine. Leading bankers and many Western politicians favored Maine-born Hugh McCulloch, who in 1833 had settled in Fort Wayne, Indiana, and won his way to the top circles of banking. Lincoln asked McCulloch to call and, as they shook hands, "I have sent for you, Mr. McCulloch, to let you know that I want you to be Secretary of the Treasury." McCulloch accepted with "distrust" of his ability; the Senate unanimously confirmed his appointment.

To replace the resigned John P. Usher Lincoln sent the name of James Harlan, U.S. Senator from Iowa, to be Secretary of the Interior, which the Senate also confirmed. Harlan was a frontier educator who had been superintendent of public instruction in Iowa in 1847 and president of Iowa Wesleyan University in 1863. Welles wrote that the President told the Cabinet he had talked with Usher about the necessity for his resigning because two in the Cabinet from Indiana were one too many.

In some British political and journalistic circles a war scare was on. Lincoln and Seward had their conferences over how to convey assurances to Britain that the United States was not preparing for violence overseas.

The President heard Seward, Speed and Welles one day discuss the rights of courts or of Congress to go beyond public records and demand any papers whatsoever from any department of the Government. Seward pointed to the private, locked shelves of the President, saying, "They will demand those papers." "But those," said the President, according to Welles, "are private and confidential, a very different affair." "Call them what you please," said Seward, "you cannot retain them from Congress or the court if you concede the principle in this case [involving records of court-martial trials] . . . the Secretary of the Navy . . . must not furnish them copies nor must he testify." Without being convinced of Seward's points, the President was an attentive listener, and, wrote Welles, "I think his faith was somewhat shaken." The President said: "We will look into this matter fully and carefully. If the Secretary of State is right, we shall all of us be of his opinion, for this is a big thing, and this question must have been up and passed on before this day." He decided a legal opinion should come from the Attorney General with questions framed for him to answer. "The matter closed for the present," wrote Welles, "by the President instructing me not to give my evidence or copies till this question is decided."

Seward during this conference had been not merely annoyed but angry. "He denied," wrote Welles, "that the public papers of any Department were to be subjected to private examination, and most emphatically denounced any idea of furnishing copies on the claim or demand of any State court or any court in a private suit. If it was conceded in a single instance, it must be in all."

In a period of less than seven weeks Lincoln had guided the delicate legislative passage of the 13th Amendment; had conducted the elaborate finesse of the Hampton Roads conference; had gone through the broils of the failure to secure recognition for Louisiana; had kept in touch with Grant and Sherman, naval affairs, the draft sending fresh replacements to the armies; had attended to a regular grist of courts-martial, arbitrary arrests, habeas corpus, pardons; had chosen two new Cabinet members; had written his second inaugural and taken oath for a second term; had passed on hundreds of applications for office. And on Tuesday, March 14, for the first time he held a Cabinet meeting as he lay in bed, worn and haggard from emotional stress and overwork.

Seward brought up "a paper for excluding blockade-runners and persons in complicity with the Rebels from the country." The appointment of John P. Hale as Minister to Spain came up. Hale had been merciless and slashing in criticisms of the Navy Department. "Seward tried to gloss it over. Wanted Hale to call and see me," wrote Welles, "and make friends with Fox." Horizontal in bed the President, in a way, rested.

Eighteen days after reinauguration Brooks' news letter noted the President's health as "worn down by the constant pressure of office-seekers and legitimate business, so that for a few days he was obliged to deny himself to all comers." Since a new rule held to strictly, of closing the office doors at three in the afternoon, "receiving only those whom he prefers during the evening hours," the President was looking better.

Once after handling a grist of callers that included a Senator seeking to honor the Monroe Doctrine by a war with France, and a poor scrub woman who wished merely the privilege of daily earning wages by shining the Treasury Building floors, Lincoln said to Brooks, "When I get through with such a day's work there is only one word that can express my condition, and that is—*flabbiness*." Again to Brooks he referred to "the tired spot which can't be got at."

The patience of the American people the President thought something matchless and touching; he was never weary of commending it, noted Brooks, "I have seen him shed tears when speaking of the cheerful sacrifice of the light and strength of so many happy homes throughout the land."

For so long a time now in one crisis after another the President had seen the judgments of supposedly good minds, some rated among "the best minds," so utterly wrong, so completely mistaken, so ready with advice that would have brought wreck and ruin beyond retrieving, that he had a deeper and surer feeling about his own reason and vision in the face of chaos. This feeling in some moods bordered on arrogance. Or if not arrogance a cold self-assurance, a refusal to say Yes to the proposals of even the so-called best minds until he had tested those proposals in the fire and the ice of his own mind and heart in long deliberations.

During four years the President had spoken many confidences and eased his mind freely to Brooks; their friendship had deepened. At no time in delicate moments of tangled affairs had Brooks mistaken his place. So the quiet understanding was that probably the following summer he was to be appointed private secretary to the President, Nicolay and Hay taking places in the Paris legation. Brooks had the required gravity—and humor—with loyalty, affection and sympathy, even though he had no special admiration for Nicolay and Hay.

That the White House couple were an oddly mated pair seemed to be generally assumed. When in January Mrs. Lincoln dismissed a doorkeeper who had held the post since the Jackson administration, it was chronicled briefly in the newspapers. With more Union victories in sight and with her husband elected to four more years in the White House, there was less of malicious rumor published about her—though gossip still ran on, some of it not idle or ill-meant.

At the inaugural ball, March 6, the President with Speaker Colfax entered the long marble hall of the Patent Office. The leading lady of the grand march was Mrs. Lincoln, and her escort Senator Sumner. It meant at least they were on speaking terms, that the President and his parliamentary foe, divided on principles, had not parted as personal friends. Mrs. Lincoln had a warm personal regard for Sumner. She sent him little notes, flowers from the White House conservatory and seemed to admire him in about the degree she hated Seward.

Indications were that Mrs. Lincoln chiefly shaped the military status of young Robert. In the White House Mrs. Lincoln's sister, Emilie Todd Helm, in her diary in November '63 wrote: "She [Mrs. Lincoln] is frightened about Robert going into the army. She said today to Brother Lincoln (I was reading in another part of the room but could not help overhearing the conversation): 'Of course, Mr. Lincoln, I know that Robert's plea to go into the army is manly and noble and I want him to go, but oh! I am so frightened he may never come back to us!' " From the father came the plea, as Mrs. Helm heard it, "Many a poor mother, Mary, has had to make this sacrifice and has given up every son she had and lost them all."

Mrs. Helm recorded a call from General Sickles and Senator Harris at the White House: "Senator Harris turned to Mrs. Lincoln abruptly and said: 'Why isn't Robert in the army? He is old enough and strong enough to serve his country. He should have gone to the front some time ago.' Sister Mary's face turned white as death and I saw that she was making a desperate effort at self-control. She bit her lip, but answered quietly, 'Robert is making his preparations now to enter the Army, Senator Harris; he is not a shirker as you seem to imply for he has been anxious to go for a long time. If fault there be, it is mine, I have insisted that he should stay in college a little longer as I think an educated man can serve his country with more intelligent purpose than an ignoramus.' "

The mother had had her wish. Her boy had stayed on at Harvard and graduated. It was probably by agreement with Mrs. Lincoln, that Lincoln on January 19, 1865, wrote to Grant: "Please read and answer this letter as though I was not President, but only a friend. My son, now in his twenty second year, having graduated at Harvard, wishes to see something of the war before it ends. I do not wish to put him in the ranks, nor yet to give him a commission, to which those who have already served long, are better entitled, and better qualified to hold. Could he, without embarrassment to you, or detriment to the service, go into your Military family with some nominal rank, I, and not the public, furnishing his necessary means? If no, say so without the least hesitation, because I am as anxious, and as deeply interested, that you shall not be encumbered as you can be yourself."

Grant replied that he would be glad to have the son "in my military family in the manner you propose." What then followed in this delicate arrangement was reported by Grant's staff member Colonel Horace Porter: "The President replied that he would consent to this upon one condition: that his son should serve as a volunteer aide without pay or emoluments; but Grant dissuaded him from adhering to that determination, saying that it was due to the young man that he should be regularly commissioned, and put on an equal footing with other officers of the same grade. So it was finally settled that Robert should receive the rank of captain and assistant adjutant-general; on February 23 he was attached to the staff of the general-in-chief. The new acquisition to the company at headquarters soon became exceedingly popular. He had inherited many of the genial traits of his father, and entered heartily into all the social pastimes at headquarters. He was always ready to perform his share of hard work, and never expected to be treated differently from any other officer on account of his being the son of the Chief Executive of the nation."

Press reports of February gave the President's income tax payment for the year at $1,279.13. Around the query "How much is Mr. Lincoln worth in money?" there seemed to be little curiosity. His salary of $25,000 a year was the largest steady income he had ever had. It was paid each month in Treasury Department warrants, with the income tax deducted. These payments Lincoln had invested in more than $75,000 worth of U.S. securities, of which more than $50,000 were "registered bonds bearing 6 per cent interest, payable in coin."

In mid-March came Senator John B. Henderson of Missouri with two lists of men and boys held in military prisons in his state or nearby. All sorts of appeals had been coming to the Senator, and before leaving for home he wanted to clear up as many of these cases as he could. He laid before Lincoln first a list of those he considered fairly innocent. Lincoln looked it over. "Do you mean to tell me, Henderson, that you wish me to let loose all these people at once?" Henderson said Yes; the war was nearly over; the time had come to try generosity and kindness. "Do you really think so?" asked Lincoln. Henderson was sure he thought so; he was trying to slow down the guerrilla warfare of his torn and weary state. "I hope you are right," said Lincoln, "but I have no time to examine this evidence. If I sign this list as a whole, will you be responsible for the future good behavior of the men?" Henderson would. "Then I will take the risk and sign it," said Lincoln as he began writing the word "Pardoned" after each name of some man convicted by a military commission, finally writing a general order of release.

Henderson thanked the President and then pulled out his second list, names of men maybe not so very innocent but maybe safe to take a chance on. "I hope," said Lincoln, according to Henderson's account, "you are not going to make me let loose another lot." Yes, Henderson thought it good policy, safer and better than holding them in jails. "Yes," said Lincoln, "but you know I am charged with making too many mistakes on the side of mercy." Henderson was sure he was right and said the President ought to sign out the whole batch. "Well, I'll be durned if I don't," said the President, this being, noted Henderson, "the only time I ever heard Mr. Lincoln use a word which approached profanity." As he handed the list back, Lincoln said: "Now, Henderson, remember you are responsible to me for those men. If they do not behave, I shall have to put you in prison for their sins."

Solidarity was wanted. For the Jewish chiropodist Zacharie, Stanton must arrange a pass to Savannah and let Zacharie bring back his father and sisters, if he so wished. Blumenberg, a Baltimore Jew, Lincoln wrote Stanton in the same letter, should have a hearing. Blumenberg had "raised troops—fought, and been wounded. He should not be dismissed in a way that disgraces and ruins him without a hearing." At Bardstown, Kentucky, ran a telegraphed order, "Let no depredation be committed upon the property or possessions of the Sisters of Charity of Nazareth Academy." And two orders addressed "To whom it may concern" specified that Sisters of Mercy in charge of military hospitals in Chicago or Washington should be furnished such provisions as they desired to purchase, "and charge same to the War Department."

The man-hunter approach as often as possible was to be avoided. Some such point of view seemed more and more to animate Lincoln in the latest war flares and shadows. Against Stanton's express wishes, and knowing well that Stanton would be furious should he hear of it, Lincoln took his own whimsical course and released three secession leaders, one a brigadier general.

In the case of John Y. Beall, however, Lincoln decided the evidence proved Beall a spy, a pirate and a privateersman, leading a band which had captured vessels on the Great Lakes, seized cargoes and money, scuttled one steamer, and failed in a plan to release the Confederate prisoners on Johnson's Island. A mass of formidable influence came forward seeking from the President a commutation of death sentence to life imprisonment. Money was poured out and a vast personal influence enlisted. Over and again Lincoln and Major General John A. Dix, commanding the Department of the East, gave the same answers, Lincoln saying, "General Dix may dispose of the case as he pleases—I will not interfere!" General Dix saying, "All now rests with the President—as far as my action rests there is not a gleam of hope." And no word having come from Lincoln or Dix, Captain John Y. Beall of the Confederate Army on February 24, 1865, was hanged.

"I've had more questions of life and death to settle in four years than all the other men who ever sat in this chair put together," said Lincoln to Bromwell of Illinois, with Seward and others present. "No man knows the distress of my mind. The case of Beall on the Lakes—there had to be an example. They tried me every way. They wouldn't give up. But I had to stand firm. I even had to turn away his poor sister when she came and begged for his life, and let him be executed, and he was executed, and I can't get the distress out of my mind yet." Bromwell noticed Lincoln's eyes moisten, and turned and saw other eyes in the room the same.

On March 11 went forth the President's proclamation that any and all deserters, wherever they might be and no matter what had happened to carry their feet away from the army, on return to their regiments or companies "shall be pardoned."

On some matter of no moment Greeley had a brief interview in early March and had a feeling Lincoln was worn down to his last physical reserves. "His face was haggard with care and seamed with thought and trouble. It looked care-ploughed, tempest-tossed and weather-beaten." On March 21, however, the editor of the Baltimore *American and Commercial Advertiser* watched him an hour in the morning and an hour in the afternoon receiving many difficult visitors, and, "The President looked extremely well, seemed in excellent spirits, and bore none of those evidences of debility or failing health which the New York *Tribune* daily talks about." On one office envelope Charles A. Dana took notice of the word "Assassination" in Lincoln's handwriting. Of death threat letters Dana had taken to the President, Dana wrote, "He looked at them but made no special remark, and, in fact, seemed to attach very little importance to them. I left them with him."

Harriet Beecher Stowe one winter evening had asked if he did not feel a great relief over the prospect of the war soon coming to a close. And Lincoln had answered, she said, in a sad way: "No, Mrs. Stowe, I shall never live to see peace. This war is killing me."

CHAPTER 61

Lincoln Visits Grant's Army—Grant Breaks Lee's Line

DOWN Pennsylvania Avenue one day, wrote Noah Brooks, moved "a Confederate regimental band which had deserted in a body with its instruments, and was allowed to march through the streets of the national capital playing Union airs."

Congressman Ashley, just from Grant's headquarters, reported to Lincoln of Grant saying, "For every three men of ours dead, five of theirs; for every three of our cattle dead, five of theirs." And picking up some paper from a table and crushing it in his hand, "Tell the President I have got them like that!" Ashley said, "It made the cold chills run over me."

Sheridan had driven Early's army out of the Shenandoah Valley and reported in late March 780 barns burned, 420,000 bushels of wheat taken, also 700,000 rounds of ammunition, 2,557 horses, 7,152 head of beef cattle. So often now the wagons of Lee went out for food and came back empty. In comparison the Union army had nearly all needs in supplies running over.

After long bickering, with the Confederate Senate reversing itself and by a majority of one voting to arm the slaves for defense, President Davis signed the bill. At last the Negro slave was to be put in the Confederate Army to fight for his master. This was their one final hope for more soldiers.

As from Lee had come to Mrs. Chesnut an impressive saying: "This is the people's war; when they tire, I stop." She wrote as though she believed in this hour Lee had said it. When a certain order of passion, faith and endurance goes down, its final extinction is miraculously swift, Mrs. Chesnut mused. It was like the snuffing out of a candle: "One moment white, then gone forever."

To one White House caller Lincoln gave his picture of the major strategy of recent weeks. "Grant has the bear by the hind leg while Sherman takes off the hide." Pointing on a map, he said that Sherman when last heard of had his cavalry, vanguard and infantry columns here, there and there, "expecting to bring them all together *here*." Then after a pause: "Now when he does that, he'll—but that reminds *me* of the horsedealer in Kentucky who got baptized in the river. The ceremony once over he insisted on it a second time. The preacher hesitated but the horse-trader had his way. And when he came up from the second ducking he gasped, 'There now! Now I can tell the devil to go to hell!' "

Up across North Carolina marched Sherman to Fayetteville, then to Goldsboro, where he paused for rest. Behind them toward Savannah lay 425 miles of foraged and ravaged country. Since July '63 his men had come on their feet no less than 2,500 miles, fording ordinary streams and flooded rivers, through rains and hot sun. Many were ragged, their trousers half gone from tussling through underbrush. More than half had thrown away their worn-out shoes, some walking barefoot, others with feet wrapped in blanket pieces. They leaped and shouted as they slid into new issues of shoes, uniforms, overcoats, at Goldsboro. The troops were mainly from the West, the Midwest and the Northwest.

Lincoln was to leave Washington to see Grant and have a breakaway from many pressures at Washington. And he might go over with Grant what terms should end the war. Early in March he had written an order through Stanton indicating Grant was to have no conference with General Lee unless on purely military affairs: ". . . you are not to decide, discuss, or confer upon any political questions. Such questions the President holds in his own hands, and will submit them to no military conferences or conventions."

The President was to sail from Washington on the *Bat*, a fast, comfortable, well-armed dispatch boat. Then came later orders for Captain Barnes to report at the White House, where, noted the Captain, "Mr. Lincoln received me with great cordiality, but with a certain kind of embarrassment, and a look of sadness which rather embarrassed me. After a few casual remarks he said that Mrs. Lincoln had decided that she would accompany him to City Point—could the *Bat* accommodate her and her maidservant?"

Barnes was ushered into Mrs. Lincoln's presence, noting that "she received me very graciously, standing with arms folded." Her wishes: "I am going with the President to City Point, and I want you to arrange your ship to take me, my maid and my officer [or guard], as well as the President." Barnes was bothered. He went to Fox. They agreed the *Bat* couldn't be fixed over. Together they went to the White House. There "in very funny terms the President translated our difficulties." Fox promised another and better boat. On the unarmed and less safe though more spacious *River Queen*, with the *Bat* as convoy, the Lincoln family made the trip, Tad sleeping in a stateroom with the guard Crook.

Grant came aboard at City Point. Any hour he expected the enemy, because of their forces dwindling through desertion, to make a desperate attempt to crash the Union lines and force a path toward joining Johnston in North Carolina.

In a jolting coach over the military railroad from City Point toward the front Lincoln rode past scenery where in the first daylight hours that morning men had been mowed down by fort guns and men had fought hand to hand with bayonet and clubbed musket. Confederate troops under General John B. Gordon had taken Fort Stedman and pressed on with the aim of destroying a railroad and Union supply stores. The Union troops had rallied, had driven the enemy back and retaken Fort Stedman—and Lincoln's breakfast hour, as he wired Stanton, saw the fight "ending about where it began."

Lincoln saw close up the results of desperate combat on more than a small scale. Reports gave Union losses at 500 killed and wounded, 500 captured; Confederate losses 800 killed and wounded, 1,800 captured.

While the President journeyed to the front via railway, Mrs. Lincoln was joined by Mrs. Grant, who was living with her family on the ship *Mary Martin.* The two women rode in an ambulance over a muddy, rough corduroy road. They were to join the President and Meade's staff in reviewing Crawford's division. As the wagon rolled along, Adam Badeau, Grant's secretary, seated with his back to the horses and facing the ladies, did his best at conversation, mentioning that all the wives of officers at the army front had been ordered to the rear, a sure sign of big action soon to come. Not a lady had been allowed to stay at the front, continued Badeau, unaware of what he was getting into, not a lady except Mrs. Griffin, the wife of General Charles Griffin, she having a special permit from the President.

Swift as a cat leap, Mrs. Lincoln: "What do you mean by that, sir? Do you mean to say that she saw the President alone? Do you know that I never allow the President to see any woman alone?" Badeau saw the face of a woman boiling with rage. He tried smiling toward this face, to show there was no malice. Badeau's smile was timed wrong. "That's a very equivocal smile, sir," he now heard. "Let me out of this carriage at once. I will ask the President if he saw that woman alone."

Badeau and Mrs. Grant tried to smooth and quiet her but failed. Mrs. Lincoln ordered Badeau to have the driver stop, and Badeau hesitating, she thrust her arms past him and took hold of the driver. By now however Mrs. Grant was able to coax Mrs. Lincoln to be still and to wait. As they alighted at the reviewing ground General Meade walked up, paid his respects to Mrs. Lincoln, escorted her away, later returning her with diplomatic skill, Mrs. Lincoln informing Badeau, "General Meade is a gentleman, sir. He says it was not the President who gave Mrs. Griffin the permit, but the Secretary of War." Thus ran Badeau's account.

Badeau and Mrs. Grant agreed "the whole affair was so distressing and mortifying that neither of us must ever mention it again." No inkling of it seemed to reach Meade, who wrote to his wife of her own visit to his headquarters that week "it seems so like a dream I can hardly realize you have been here." The President had spoken of Mrs. Meade, "expressed regret that your visit should have been so abruptly terminated," while "Mrs. Lincoln spoke very handsomely of you and referred in feeling terms to our sad bereavement [the recent death of a child]."

On the soil where Union countercharges began Lincoln saw the dead in blue and gray and butternut lying huddled and silent, here and there the wounded gasping and groaning. He saw a collection of prisoners taken that morning, a ragged and dusty crew, and remarked "on their sad condition," noted Barnes. "They had fought desperately and were glad to be at rest. Mr. Lincoln was quiet and observant, making few comments." On the train a "worn and haggard" Lincoln saw the loading of the Union wounded. "He remarked that he had seen enough of the horrors of war, that he hoped this was the beginning of the end." Wrote the guard Crook of this day, "I saw him [Lincoln] ride over the battlefields at Petersburg, the man with the hole in his forehead and the man with both arms shot away lying, accusing, before his eyes."

Beyond the immediate scene Lincoln gazed on that day other fighting had gone on. The Union troops advanced along the whole of Lee's right, taking entrenched picket lines. The Union estimate put their own losses at 2,080 as against 4,800 to 5,000 Confederate. Lee next day was writing Davis, "I fear now it will be impossible to prevent a junction between Grant and Sherman."

Lincoln sat for a while at the headquarters campfire, according to Colonel Horace Porter, "and as the smoke curled about his head during certain shiftings of the wind he brushed it away from time to time by waving his right hand in front of his face." To Grant and staff men gathered around he spoke of "appalling difficulties" the administration had met, field losses, troubles in finance and foreign affairs, how they had been overcome by the unswerving patriotism of the people, the devotion of the loyal North, and the superb fighting qualities of the troops. He drifted into a more cheerful vein and got into his storytelling stride by way of the Trent Affair, reeling off an elaborate version of the barber and his worried customer: "He began by lathering face, nose, eyes and ears, stropped his razor on his boot, and then made a drive at the man's countenance as if he had practised mowing in a stubble-field. He cut a bold swath across the right cheek, carrying away the beard, a pimple, and two warts. The man in the chair ventured to remark: 'You appear to make everything level as you go.' 'Yes,' said the barber; 'and if this handle don't break, I guess I'll get away with most of what's there.' The man's cheeks were so hollow that the barber couldn't get down into the valleys with the razor, and the ingenious idea occurred to him to stick his finger in the man's mouth and press out the cheeks. Finally he cut clear through the cheek and into his own finger. He pulled the finger out of the man's mouth, snapped the blood off it, glared at him, and cried: 'There, you lantern-jawed cuss, you've made me cut my finger!' And so England will discover that she has got the South into a pretty bad scrape by trying to administer to her, and in the end she will find that she has only cut her own finger."

The laugh following this subsided, and Grant asked, "Mr. President, did you at any time doubt the final success of the cause?" And Lincoln, leaning forward in his camp chair, with an emphatic right-hand gesture: "Never for a moment."

Next day Barnes "found Mr. Lincoln quite recovered," lamenting the loss of life, confident the war was ending, pleased at news that Sheridan from the Shenandoah Valley had moved in a big swing around Lee's army to the north and arrived safe at Harrison's Landing to join Grant that day.

The President's eyes caught on three tiny kittens, wandering, mewing as if lost. He picked up one and asked it, "Where is your mother?" Someone answered, "The mother is dead." And as he petted the little one: "Then she can't grieve as many a poor mother is grieving for a son lost in battle." Gathering the two others in his hands, he put them on his lap, stroked their fur, and according to Admiral Porter, meditated, "Kitties, thank God you are cats, and can't understand this terrible strife that is going on."

The *River Queen* moved down the James River and from her deck Lincoln saw the bank lined with men shouting, laughing, swimming, watering their horses—Sheridan's men washing off the dust and grit of the Shenandoah

Valley. They spotted the President and sent him cheers. The *River Queen* passed through a naval flotilla. The crews cheered the Commander in Chief, saw his tall frame in a long-tailed black frock coat, a cravat of black silk carelessly tied, a black silk hat. Barnes noted, "As he passed each vessel he waved his high hat, as if saluting friends in his native town, and seemed as happy as a school boy."

Up the James steamed the *River Queen* to Aiken's Landing for a field review of part of the Army of the James. Sheridan came aboard. The President ended his long-held handshake. "General Sheridan, when this peculiar war began I thought a cavalryman should be at least six feet four high, but"—still gazing down on the short General—"I have changed my mind—five feet four will do in a pinch."

Ord on one side, Grant on the other, escorted the President over a rough corduroy road two miles to the reviewing ground. An ambulance followed bringing Mrs. Lincoln and Mrs. Grant in care of Colonel Horace Porter and Adam Badeau. Improved springs on the ambulance only served to toss the occupants higher, but Mrs. Lincoln in fear that they would miss the review asked Porter for more speed. The driver accommodated till the mud flew from the horses' heels, and the ladies' hats were jammed and heads bumped against the top of the wagon. "Mrs. Lincoln now insisted on getting out and walking," wrote Porter, "but as the mud was nearly hub-deep, Mrs. Grant and I persuaded her that we had better stick to the wagon as our only ark of refuge."

Meantime the President, with a squadron of 20 or more officers and orderlies, rode through woods and swamp. Standing at "parade rest" the division had waited for hours. The troops cheered the Commander in Chief. The review over, shellfire began on the enemy picket line in sight, heavy skirmishing lines moved forward, took the picket-line trenches, swelled the day's total of prisoners to 2,700, repulsed two fierce counterattacks, ending the day with Union losses of about 2,000 to 4,000 Confederate.

Colonel Theodore Lyman of Meade's staff at this review had his first look at Lincoln and wrote to his wife: "The President is, I think, the ugliest man I ever put my eyes on; there is also an expression of plebeian vulgarity in his face that is offensive (you recognize the recounter of coarse stories). On the other hand, he has the look of sense and wonderful shrewdness, while the heavy eyelids give him a mark of almost genius. He strikes me, too, as a very honest and kindly man; and, with all his vulgarity, I see no trace of low passions in his face. On the whole, he is such a mixture of all sorts, as only America brings forth. He is as much like a highly intellectual and benevolent Satyr as anything I can think of. I never wish to see him again, but, as humanity runs, I am well content to have him at the head of affairs."

Mrs. Lincoln and Mrs. Grant had arrived late for the review but in time for Mrs. Lincoln to see Mrs. Ord riding near the President in the reviewing column, though equally near her husband, who was the immediate commander of the troops under review. Seeing the ambulance drive in on the parade line, Mrs. Ord excused herself with, "There comes Mrs. Lincoln and Mrs. Grant—I think I had better join them." The accounts of Barnes, Porter and Badeau as to what then happened agreed that there were embarrassing moments and bitterly pathetic exhibitions, Badeau's later recollections being more complete in detail, though having slight discrepancies. It seemed, however, that as Mrs. Ord joined them, Mrs. Lincoln furiously exclaimed: "What does this woman mean by riding by the side of the President and ahead of me? Does she suppose that *he* wants *her* by the side of *him?*" She went into a frenzy that mingled extravagant rage and drab petulance. "All that Porter and I could do," wrote Badeau, "was to see that nothing worse than words occurred." They feared some wild scene of violence enacted before the troops so calmly standing at "present arms." One outburst flung itself at Mrs. Grant: "I suppose you think you'll get to the White House yourself, don't you?" Mrs. Grant kept cool, saying she was quite satisfied with her present position, that it was far greater than she had ever expected to attain. Mrs. Lincoln: "Oh! you had better take it if you can get it. 'Tis very nice." Then the slings of reproach were sent at Mrs. Ord, with Mrs. Grant quietly and at some risk defending her friend.

A nephew of Secretary Seward, a young major and a member of General Ord's staff, a joker, rode alongside and blurted out with a rich grin: "The President's horse is very gallant, Mrs. Lincoln. He insists on riding by the side of Mrs. Ord." This of course helped no one. Mrs. Lincoln cried, "What do you mean by that?" and young Major Seward shied away in a crazy gallop.

When the review had ended—and the troops were moving toward the enemy picket lines and death and wounds—Mrs. Lincoln in the presence of a group of officers, according to Badeau, hurled vile names at Mrs. Ord and again asked what Mrs. Ord meant by following the President. Enough of this sent Mrs. Ord into tears, into asking what in the world she had done. Mrs. Lincoln stormed till she spent her strength. A manner of silence ensued. Porter believed "Mrs. Lincoln had suffered so much from the fatigue and annoyances of her overland trip that she was not in a mood to derive much pleasure from the occasion." Badeau saw "everybody shocked and horrified." Barnes found Mrs. Grant silent and embarrassed. "It was a painful situation, from which the only escape was to retire. Mrs. Ord and myself with a few officers rode back to City Point."

On the return trip of the *River Queen*, "the President seemed to recover his spirits," according to Horace Porter, who thought perhaps the strength and fighting quality he witnessed that afternoon in the Army of the James "had served to cheer him up." Whatever his mood, whatever the trouble he might be disguising, he told Colonel Porter one of his favorite funny stories, repeating the same story later to Grant.

Of what happened that evening of March 26 when the *River Queen* returned to her moorings at City Point Badeau wrote: "That night the President and Mrs. Lincoln entertained General and Mrs. Grant and the General's staff at dinner on the steamer, and before us all Mrs. Lincoln berated General Ord to the President, and urged that he should be removed. He was unfit for his place, she said, to say nothing of his wife. General Grant sat next and defended his officer bravely."

Lincoln and Grant said good night. With the war and more on his hands the President was not at ease. Out in the dark night along a 40-mile front 100,000 men and more lived hugging the dirt of the earth, some in tents but more in huts and shelters. Soon they might go into the wildest, bloodiest battle of the whole war. Beyond lay the solemn matter of what kind of a peace should be signed. Yet along with these problems was a personal grief.

He sent off the ship an orderly who about 11 o'clock awakened Captain Barnes with a message that the President would like to see him. Barnes stepped into his clothes in a hurry, boarded the *River Queen*, and found Mr. and Mrs. Lincoln awaiting him in the upper saloon. A few essentials Captain Barnes would disclose: "Mr. Lincoln took little part in the conversation which ensued, which evidently followed some previous discussion with Mrs. Lincoln, who had objected very strenuously to the presence of other ladies at the review, and had thought that Mrs. Ord had been too prominent in it; that the troops were led to think she was the wife of the President, who had distinguished her with too much attention. Mr. Lincoln very gently suggested that he had hardly remarked her presence; but Mrs. Lincoln was not to be pacified, and appealed to me to support her views. Of course I could not umpire such a question, and could only state why Mrs. Ord and myself found ourselves in the reviewing column, and how immediately we withdrew from it upon the appearance of the ambulance with Mrs. Lincoln and Mrs. Grant. I extricated myself as well as I could, but with difficulty, and asked permission to retire, the President bidding me good-night sadly and gently."

Amid the scenes created by the disordered brain of a tragically afflicted woman, young Captain Barnes felt himself drawn to the one person he saw as writhing inwardly more than any other, writing, "I came to feel an affection for him that none other inspired." The melancholy of Lincoln he believed related in part to the torments Mrs. Lincoln was under. "I had the greatest sympathy for her and for Mr. Lincoln, who I am sure felt deep anxiety for her," Barnes noted. "His manner towards her was always that of the most affectionate solicitude, so marked, so gentle and unaffected that no one could see them together without being impressed by it." Though a common undertone phrase for her was "crazy woman," Barnes' more humanly decent description ran: "She was at no time well; the mental strain upon her was great, betrayed by extreme nervousness approaching hysteria, causing misapprehensions, extreme sensitiveness as to slights or want of politeness or consideration."

At intervals during this City Point visit, however, several credible observers without particular prejudice agreed in the main with Badeau's account that "Mrs. Lincoln repeatedly attacked her husband in the presence of officers because of Mrs. Griffin and Mrs. Ord." As for the head of the state, wrote Badeau, "He bore it as Christ might have done, with supreme calmness and dignity; he called her 'mother', pleaded with eyes and tones, endeavored to explain or palliate the offenses of others, till she turned on him like a tigress; and then he walked away," hiding his face that others might not see it. Toward Mrs. Grant, Mary Todd Lincoln showed no relenting, according to Badeau once rebuking the General's wife, "How dare you be seated until I invite you?"

Barnes reported as usual to the President, received "marked kindness," and in a small stateroom converted into an office heard Lincoln read dispatches from Stanton and from the front, while Tad ran in and out, sometimes "clinging to his father and caressed affectionately by him." Barnes inquired about Mrs. Lincoln, hoping she had recovered from the fatigue of the previous day. "Mr. Lincoln said she was not well at all, and expressed the fear that the excitement of the surroundings was too great for her or for any woman."

In the roomy log cabin of Grant, Lincoln spent the forenoon mainly in talk with Admiral David D. Porter, Grant a listener "in grim silence, or only answering direct questions from Mr. Lincoln" in monosyllables. In very good spirits that morning was Lincoln, thought Barnes. "Running his hands with an upward movement through his rumpled hair he would stretch himself out, and look at the listeners in turn as though for sympathy and appreciation." Grant, however, "seldom smiled." He was thinking about his armies. If Lee escaped the net now spread, the war might go another year or two— or longer.

Four years now since Fort Sumter at Charleston had crumbled. Now that captured fort was under repair, and Stanton, Admiral Dahlgren, William Lloyd Garrison, Henry Ward Beecher and Nicolay to represent the President, were preparing to go down and hold a flag-raising ceremony of speeches and prayers, with the Union banner again floating from that citadel where the war had begun.

A steamer put Sherman ashore at City Point late in the afternoon of March 27. Grant was there waiting. They walked to Grant's cabin. Sherman had talked nearly an hour when Grant interrupted. "I'm sorry but the President is aboard the *River Queen*." They took Admiral Porter and soon the three found Lincoln alone in the after cabin. Sherman and Lincoln after nearly four years again faced each other. The conversation ranged from laughter to solemnity.

Next morning, March 28, on the *River Queen* came a conference of the three pivotal Northern men of the war, with Admiral Porter present. Both Grant and Sherman supposed that one or the other of them would have to fight one more bloody battle, and that it would be the *last*. "Mr. Lincoln exclaimed, more than once," wrote Sherman, "that there had been blood enough shed, and asked us if another battle could not be avoided." The generals told Lincoln they could not control that event.

Sherman came now to a momentous point. He wrote of it later: "I inquired of the President if he was all ready for the end of the war. What was to be done with the rebel armies when defeated? And what should be done with the political leaders, such as Jeff. Davis, etc.? Should we allow them to escape, etc.? He said he was all ready; all he wanted of us was to defeat the opposing armies, and to get the men composing the Confederate armies back to their homes, at work on their farms and in their shops. As to Jeff. Davis, he was hardly at liberty to speak his mind fully, but intimated that he ought to clear out, 'escape the country,' only it would not do for him to say so openly."

Lincoln was this day talking with two men like himself terribly intimate with awful authority. They were hammering out a national fate. Before them hazards and intricacies lay too vast to put on paper. Lincoln hesitated at outlining for his generals any peace terms or reconstruction policies beyond the few simple conditions he had named at Hampton Roads.

In Europe at that hour could be heard the prediction that Sherman would take over the Washington Government and run it. Delane of the London

Times spoke fears of that event. For two years Lincoln and these two generals had been welding a strange partnership that worked. Amid malice, conspiracy, jealousies, amid crooked and crazy entanglements of human impulse and motive that made the war a dismal swamp-jungle affair, the three held together. Of each of them it had been graphically said that he was intensely American and could have been born and made nowhere but in the "U.S.A." They read each other now by signals, intentions and hopes.

Sherman was eager to hear any specific recommendations that might have occurred to the mind of the President. Of the answers Sherman later wrote: "Mr. Lincoln was full and frank in his conversation, assuring me that in his mind he was all ready for the civil reorganization of affairs at the South as soon as the war was over; and he distinctly authorized me to assure Governor Vance and the people of North Carolina that, as soon as the rebel armies laid down their arms, and resumed their civil pursuits, they would at once be guaranteed all their rights as citizens of a common country; and that to avoid anarchy the State governments then in existence, with their civil functionaries, would be recognized by him as the government *de facto* till Congress could provide others . . . His earnest desire seemed to be to end the war speedily, without more bloodshed or devastation, and to restore all the men of both sections to their homes . . . When at rest or listening, his legs and arms seemed to hang almost lifeless, and his face was care-worn and haggard; but, the moment he began to talk, his face lightened up, his tall form, as it were, unfolded, and he was the very impersonation of good-humor and fellowship."

The three Northern pivotal men were parting, Sherman to remember Lincoln in a most simple manner: "Sherman, do you know why I took a shine to Grant and you?" "I don't know, Mr. Lincoln, you have been extremely kind to me, far more than my deserts." "Well, you never found fault with me."

Lincoln and Sherman had done most of the talking, Grant not mentioning a matter he later brought before Lincoln. "I told him that I had been very anxious to have the Eastern armies vanquish their old enemy. If the Western armies should be even upon the field, operating against Richmond and Lee, the credit would be given to them for the capture, by politicians and noncombatants from the section of country which those troops hailed from. Western members [of Congress] might be throwing it up to the members of the East that they were not able to capture an army, or to accomplish much but had to wait until the Western armies had conquered all the territory south and west of them, and then come on to help them capture the only army they had been engaged with. Mr. Lincoln said he saw that now, but had never thought of it before, because his anxiety was so great that he did not care where the aid came from so the work was done."

Back at City Point Lincoln kept close to Grant, whose company he would lose in a day or two, when a big push was to begin and Grant would live at the fighting front with his troops in motion.

That sword of Robert E. Lee—how it had vanished and come back and held its ground beyond prophecies! With those valiant bayonets on which the Confederate Government had been carried for three years, could Lee again swing round and baffle pursuit, perhaps win to the mountains, fight guerrilla style till he could recruit a new army?

What did the night's darkness hold? Would Grant take Lee? If he did, then both the structure and the dream of a Confederate States of America were sunk with the fabrics of all shadows and dust. A republican Union of States cemented and welded with blood and iron would stand for a long time among World Power nations, committed to government of, by, and for the people. Only for the assurance of that reality had Lincoln cared to toil and groan these last four years of burdens and bitterness.

Beyond the screen and mist of the night lay what? Peach blooms and apricot blossoms had risen in the air the last few days in rare spots. April was near. What of this April?

At 8:30 the morning of March 29, 1865, Lincoln went ashore from the *River Queen* to Grant's shanty. They were putting the horses aboard the railroad train that was to take Grant and his staff to the Petersburg front.

Mrs. Grant stood by, her face pale and sorrowful. At the door Grant kissed her, over and again, joined Lincoln; the two walked down to the railroad platform. "Mr. Lincoln looked more serious than at any other time since he had visited headquarters," noted Horace Porter. "The lines in his face seemed deeper, and the rings under his eyes were of a darker hue. It was plain that the weight of responsibility was oppressing him." At the train the President gave a warm handshake to the General and to each member of the staff, and then stood near the rear end of the car while they went aboard. The train was ready to start. They all raised their hats in respect to the President. His hat went off to them and his voice was broken and he couldn't hide it as he called to them: "Good-by, gentlemen. God bless you all! Remember, your success is my success." The whistle sounded. The train moved. Grant was off to a campaign all hoped would be his last and the last of the war.

Lighting a cigar Grant went over plans with staff officers, once saying: "The President is one of the few who has not attempted to extract from me a knowledge of my movements, although he is the only one who has right to know them. He will be the most anxious man in the country to hear from us. I think we can send him some good news in a day or two."

Fair weather of several days on the evening of March 29 gave way to torrents from the sky. Fields became beds of quicksand. Troops waded in mud above their ankles. Horses sank to their bellies and had to be pulled out with halters. Wagon wheels sank to the hubs and in some cases above the axles to the wagon box. Roads became sheets of water. Marching on such terrain was only worse than trying to sleep in wet blankets on soaked ground. On March 30 men's tempers showed. Rawlins gloomed and Grant held that soon as the weather cleared up the roads the men would be gay again.

Having studied his map, as he relayed telegrams to Stanton, Lincoln commented: "Judging by the two points from which General Grant telegraphs, I infer that he moved his headquarters about one mile since he sent the first of the two dispatches." Also to Stanton, Lincoln wired the personal item that Mrs. Lincoln had started for Washington, and he would thank Stanton "to see that our coachman is at the Arsenal wharf at Eight (8) o'clock to-morrow morning, there wait until she arrives."

Sheridan went on dashing where the fire was most furious, waving his battle flag, praying, swearing, shaking his fist, yelling threats and blessings. With fixed bayonets and a final rousing cheer, the Union columns under General Ayres overran the enemy earthworks, swept everything before them, killed or captured in their immediate front every man whose legs had not saved him.

Lincoln while this battle raged did his best at picturing it from a dispatch sent by Grant. He wired Seward that "Sheridan, aided by Warren, had at 2. P.M. pushed the enemy back so as to retake the five forks, and bring his own Head Quarters up . . ." The next two days Lincoln sent to Stanton a series of Grant's dispatches, relayed as Grant wrote them, and these the Secretary of War gave to the press. Thus millions of readers in the North had what they took as authentic information about the crumbling of Lee's lines foreshadowing the fall of Richmond.

Anxious Northern readers, including a horde of speculators and gamblers, saw in the public prints that Sheridan with his cavalry and the 5th corps had captured three brigades of infantry, several thousand prisoners—that Grant had telegraphed at 4:30 P.M. April 2: "The whole captures since the army started out will not amount to less than 12,000 men, and probably fifty pieces of artillery . . . All seems well with us, and everything is quiet just now." And Lincoln had telegraphed Grant: "Allow me to tender to you, and all with you, the nations grateful thanks . . . At your kind suggestion, I think I will visit you to-morrow."

At a lesser price than predicted Lee's army was cut off from Richmond, and on the night of April 2 his troops, ordered out of Petersburg and other points on the line, were reconcentrating to march west. Lincoln boarded a railroad car at City Point and rode to Petersburg, where Grant and his staff were waiting, ready to go. Grant wrote of their meeting, "About the first thing that Mr. Lincoln said to me was: 'Do you know, general, that I have had a sort of sneaking idea for some days that you intended to do something like this.'" At City Point Lincoln wired Stanton at 5 P.M. this April 3: ". . . staid with Gen. Grant an hour & a half and returned here. It is certain now that Richmond is in our hands, and I think I will go there to-morrow."

As Lincoln visited the sick and wounded among avenues of hospital tents at City Point that week, Adelaide Smith, the nurse, heard the camp talk that when the President's party came to one set of tents young Dr. Jerome Walker of the Sanitary Commission pointing at them said, "Mr. President, you do not want to go in there." "Why not, my boy?" "They are sick rebel prisoners." "That is just where I do want to go," and he strode in and shook hands from cot to cot.

Shot-torn in both hips, lay Colonel Harry L. Benbow, who had commanded three regiments at Five Forks. And according to Colonel Benbow: "He halted beside my bed and held out his hand. I was lying on my back, my hands folded across my breast. Looking him in the face, 'Mr. President,' I said, 'do you know to whom you offer your hand?' 'I do not,' he replied. 'Well,' said I, 'you offer it to a Confederate colonel who has fought you as hard as he could for four years.' 'Well,' said he, 'I hope a Confederate colonel will not refuse me his hand.' 'No, sir,' I replied, 'I will not,' and I clasped his hand in both of mine."

Over 5,000 men of both sides were in City Point hospitals. Lincoln tried to visit every last man of them but couldn't find time to make the complete rounds. His right arm lame from handshaking, the head surgeon said it certainly must ache. Lincoln smiled, mentioned "strong muscles," stepped out the door of the surgeon's shanty, took an ax, sent chips of logs flying, then paused and slowly with his right arm raised the ax till he was holding it at full horizontal without a quiver. Before leaving he was offered what he might like by way of a drink. He took a glass of lemonade.

CHAPTER 62

Richmond Falls—Appomattox

ON THE Sabbath day of April 2, 1865, in the Davis family pew of St. Paul's Episcopal Church, seated erect and calm under the chancel, was Jefferson Davis. An adjutant, mud on his boots, a hard-riding man, came up the aisle in a swift military stride and handed a paper to Davis, who read the words Lee had long delayed: "I advise that all preparation be made for leaving Richmond tonight. I will advise you later, according to circumstances." Davis arose, walked to the War Department, telegraphed to Lee that a move from Richmond that night would "involve the loss of many valuables, both for the want of time to pack and of transportation." Lee in the field on receiving this message, according to one of his staff men, tore it into bits, saying, "I am sure I gave him sufficient notice," and replied calmly by telegraph to Davis that it was "absolutely necessary" to abandon the position that night.

By railroad at 11 that Sabbath night, Davis with his Cabinet and other officials left their capital city, their Executive Mansion, their arsenals and stores, arriving safely in Danville the next afternoon. Word spread in Richmond that Lee's army had taken its last man and gun out of Petersburg—and Richmond would fall next. On railroad trains, on wagons, carts, buggies, gigs, on horses piled with bundles and belongings, the Government and many citizens in flight had a moving day.

Burning and dynamiting of bridges, arsenals and warehouses went on through the night. Heavy smoke clouds rose from cotton warehouses. Just after daylight April 3 a crowd of thousands of men, women and children swarmed at the doors of a commissary depot. Many of them had not tasted a full, nourishing meal in months. Behind those depot doors they had heard —and heard correctly—were barrels of ham, bacon, whisky, flour, sugar, coffee. Why these had not gone to General Lee's half-starved army weeks before was for responsible officials to answer. Rampaging humans broke through those depot doors, so long guarded. Raging, laughing, snarling, the crowd surged in.

General Godfrey Weitzel received the surrender of Richmond that morning of April 3 at the city hall. By midafternoon his troops had stopped the rioting and main disorders.

In Washington, wrote David Homer Bates, "Lincoln's despatch from City Point gave us in the War Department the first news of the capture of Petersburg and Richmond." Shortly after that message, came the first one in four years wired from Richmond, General Weitzel saying: "We took Richmond at 8:15 this morning." The news spread fast. Press extras sent the excitement higher. Thousands crowded around the War Office; Stanton spoke gratitude to Almighty God for deliverance.

Record-breaking crowds lined the saloon bars. From the Capitol on to the White House and executive buildings, Pennsylvania Avenue took on bunting and banners. The sky was shaken by a salute of 800 guns. In the streets people hugged each other, men made up old quarrels, marched singing and prankish.

From City Point the *Malvern* with Lincoln aboard steamed toward Richmond. Dead horses floated by, broken ordnance, wrecked boats. Nearing Richmond, the *Malvern* went aground. Admiral Porter ordered a 12-oared barge to carry the President ashore. Lincoln, Tad and Crook sat amid the oarsmen. A gig holding Barnes and a few others acted as escort. Lincoln was reminded of a fellow who failed at getting high or low offices and finally "he asked me for an old pair of trousers. It is well to be humble."

At a place called Rockett's the little barge landed the President. The receiving crowd ashore was, according to Porter and Crook, entirely Negro. By the grapevine some had heard here was Lincoln. One old-timer of 60 sprang forward: "Bress de Lawd, dere is de great Messiah!" He fell on his knees and bowed at the President's feet, other Negroes doing the same. The President: "Don't kneel to me. You must kneel to God only and thank him for your freedom." From corners that had seemed deserted suddenly sprang black folk, some silent and awe-struck, others turning somersaults and yelling with joy. With some Lincoln shook hands.

Twelve armed sailors formed an escort. At his left the President had Porter and Captain Penrose, at his right Crook holding Tad by the hand. This procession began its march. Barnes saw a lone cavalryman at a street corner and sent him galloping to Weitzel's headquarters with the news of who was coming. Wrote Crook: "Every window was crowded with heads. But it was a silent crowd. There was something oppressive in those thousands of watchers without a sound, either of welcome or hatred. I think we would have welcomed a yell of defiance. I stole a look sideways at Mr. Lincoln. His face . . . had the calm . . . of a brave man . . . ready for whatever may come."

Nearly two miles along dusty streets on a warm April day this little presidential party marched to the center of Richmond. Not a soldier, citizen, horse or wagon had met them. The President had stopped a moment to gaze at Libby Prison, according to Porter, and on someone calling, "Pull it down," he replied, "No, leave it as a monument."

The cavalry escort arrived and led them to the Confederate Executive Mansion, a two-story house fronted with tall Colonial pillars, now the headquarters of General Weitzel and the temporary government. Dusty and sweating from his walk amid sights of burned buildings, wreckage on the streets and terror in the air, Lincoln sank into a chair at a long table, "pale and haggard, utterly worn out," noted Barnes, his first words, "I wonder if I could get a glass of water." It interested him to know this was the chair in which Jefferson Davis had sat and over this table had handled high documents.

With a cavalry escort and with Weitzel, Porter and others, Lincoln rode in a carriage over the city, seeing some of the 700 burned dwellings and stores, Libby Prison, Castle Thunder, thousands of homeless whites and Negroes. Into the disordered building where the now fugitive Confederate Congress had held its sessions, Lincoln was ushered. And if he was reminded of any anecdote no one made a record of it—though it was said his eyes often had a dreaminess.

Weitzel's aide Graves went along on this ride, and of it wrote that he heard General Weitzel ask one very important question: What should he, Weitzel, do in regard to this conquered people? "President Lincoln replied," wrote Graves, "that he did not wish to give any orders on that subject, but as he expressed it, 'If I were in your place, I'd let 'em up easy, let 'em up easy.' "

Porter and Crook heaved sighs of relief on getting the President aboard the *Malvern*, which had now been brought upriver. Any one of many kinds of fools could have taken a pot shot at Lincoln that day.

At noon April 6 Mrs. Lincoln arrived at City Point in a party of important persons, including Senator Sumner. And on this day Lincoln telegraphed Grant that Seward had been thrown from his carriage, seriously injured, and this with other matters would take him to Washington soon. At Richmond, he wished Grant to know, he had met Judge Campbell and put in Campbell's hands "an informal paper" repeating the Hampton Roads peace conditions, "and adding that if the war be now further persisted in by the rebels, confiscated property shall, at the least, bear the additional cost; and that confiscations shall be remitted to the people of any State which will now promptly, and in good faith, withdraw its troops and other support, from resistance to the government. Judge Campbell thought it not impossible that the rebel Legislature of Virginia would do the latter, if permitted; and accordingly, I addressed a private letter to Gen. Weitzel (with permission for Judge Campbell to see it)."

The matter was delicate—but Lincoln was taking a chance. He was meeting fully and squarely any leanings toward the Union, any changed attitude that might have developed among the Virginia legislative members. Having once officially seceded their state from the Union now they could officially return if they chose. They could construe for themselves the extent of dignity and authority accorded them by the President's telegram to Weitzel dated April 6 at City Point: "It has been intimated to me that the gentlemen who have acted as the legislature of Virginia, in support of the rebellion, may now desire to assemble at Richmond, and take measures to withdraw the Virginia troops, and other support from resistance to the General government. If they attempt it, give them permission and protection, until, if at all, they attempt some action hostile to the United States, in which case you will notify them and give them reasonable time to leave;

& at the end of which time, arrest any who may remain. Allow Judge Campbell to see this, but do not make it public."

Of this attempt at results by legal device Lincoln wrote Grant he did not think it probable anything would come, "but I have thought best to notify you, so that if you should see signs, you may understand them."

Grant wired Lincoln a message from Sheridan reporting captures of several thousand prisoners, including Custis Lee, the son of General Robert E. Lee, and Generals Ewell, Kershaw, Button, Corse and Debray, Sheridan closing his dispatch, "If the thing is pressed I think that Lee will surrender." Lincoln wired Grant: "Gen. Sheridan says 'If the thing is pressed I think that Lee will surrender.' Let the *thing* be pressed."

An estimate of Lincoln, partly as General Lee failed to see him, came from a later commentator, an intimate of the documented Lee, a four-volume biographer of Lee. This set forth Lincoln in the role of a spokesman, a sayer. "Lee's balancing of the ponderables on the military scales was accurate," ran this picture. "He could not realize, and few even in Washington could see, that an imponderable was tipping the beam. That imponderable was the influence of President Lincoln. The Richmond government had discounted his every moderate utterance and had capitalized his emancipation proclamation in order to stiffen Southern resistance. The Confederate people had mocked him, had despised him, and had hated him. Lee himself, though he had avoided unworthy personal animosities and doubtless had included Mr. Lincoln in his prayers for all his enemies, had made the most of the President's military blunders and fears . . . He was much more interested in the Federal field-commanders than in the commander-in-chief. After the late winter of 1863-64, had Lee known all the facts, he would have given as much care to the study of the mind of the Federal President as to the analysis of the strategical methods of his immediate adversaries. For that remarkable man, who had never wavered in his purpose to preserve the Union, had now mustered all his resources of patience and of determination. Those who had sought cunningly to lead him, slowly found that he was leading them. His unconquerable spirit, in some mysterious manner, was being infused into the North as spring approached."

Lincoln in Virginia relaxed a little, eased off the Washington burdens. It was the nearest approach to a vacation he had had since the war began. It wasn't much of a holiday to look at the ruins of Richmond, nor an interval of sport to shake hands in tent hospitals with men fever-smitten and bullet-mutilated. But Washington with its intrigue and smug satisfactions was worse. Grant and others thought they saw Lincoln's anxiety diminish in the City Point stay of 15 days.

On Saturday, April 8, the *River Queen* was leaving for Washington. A military band came on board, and after several pieces, Lincoln called for "Dixie," saying, "That tune is now Federal property." The musicians were surprised. Lincoln wanted it to be a good-will song of the reunited states.

On Sunday, April 9, steaming up the Potomac, Mrs. Lincoln, noted Sumner, spoke of Jefferson Davis: "Do not allow him to escape the law—he must be hanged!" The President replied calmly, "Judge not, that ye be not judged." And by Sumner's account, when pressed again by the remark that the sight of Libby Prison made it impossible to pardon the Confederate chief, Lincoln repeated twice over the words, "Judge not, that ye be not judged."

The roofs of Washington came into view. Sumner in a carriage with the President and Mrs. Lincoln, drove to the White House. Then straight to the home of Seward the President drove. Four days before on a sunny spring afternoon Seward in his customary daily drive, in company with his son and daughter, had watched his fast young horses prance and go, had enjoyed it. Suddenly the horses took fright and plunged into a wild runaway. Seward stood up, tried for a leap to the pavement, was thrown in the air, and when a crowd gathered he was unconscious. Taken home, physicians found the right shoulder badly dislocated, the jaw broken on both sides, his slow and partial return to consciousness coming with agonizing pain. His wife had journeyed from Auburn, New York, with heartache saw his face so bruised, swollen, discolored, his voice so changed and hoarse, that he seemed a man she had never before seen. At first he wandered in delirium, but on the third day was again in his right mind.

The gaslights in the house were turned low as Lincoln entered, the rooms quiet, everyone moving softly and speaking in whispers. On a bed in the center of his second-floor room lay the Secretary of State, swathed in bandages. Young Frederick Seward guided the President, who sat down on the side of the bed near the left arm of the sick and broken man. The wounded right arm was at times crazy with pain. The face looked out from a steel frame that held the jaw for healing. Lincoln spoke softly, solemnly, his greetings and sympathy. From the swollen tongue came with pain and effort the hoarse whisper, "You are back from Richmond?"

Lincoln leaned across the bed, rested on an elbow so as to bring his face nearer to the face of his friend, and told of many things he had seen and heard on the trip to City Point. Seward listened, his mind eager. "They were left together for a half hour or more," wrote the son Frederick. "Then the door opened softly, and Mr. Lincoln came out gently, intimating by a silent look and gesture that Seward had fallen into a feverish slumber and must not be disturbed."

In ten days of latter March and early April Lee had lost 19,000 men to Grant as prisoners. In a series of desperate fights the total of Lee's killed and wounded ran high—and of effective troops he had none to spare. The race westward on parallel lines was clocked with running battles. The one day's stop at Amelia Court House instead of expected food supplies for Lee's men saw nothing at all. The rank and file of the army must march on slim rations, mainly of parched corn. At Sayler's Creek enough of the Union army had overtaken Lee to force a combat that resulted in Lee's saying to one of his officers, "General, that half of our army is destroyed." The cannon of Lee were on short rations as well as the foot soldiers and cavalry horses. The artillerists knew that in a straight frontal battle they wouldn't have shells to last through.

Grant knew probably better than anyone that he could beat this army, smash pieces of it and send it recoiling in retreat. But he wouldn't swear he could capture it. To bag such an army of proved wit and flair—to take the whole of it and end the war—that was something else. Anything could happen.

While Lincoln journeyed toward Washington the night of April 8, Grant in the rear of the Army of the Potomac pressing Lee's rear guard, stopped at a farmhouse with a sick headache. He spent the night bathing his feet in hot water and mustard, putting mustard plasters on his wrists and the back of his neck, moving restlessly on a sitting-room sofa trying to snatch a little sleep. His mind had concentrated intensely on notes he had written to Lee and Lee's answers. Each of these great and adroit commanders was making deep guesses about what was going on in the mind of the other. Grant however believed he knew the mind and feeling of Lincoln beyond instructions. Their many talks at City Point made him sure of what he could offer Lee that would be as though from the President. He sent Lee another note to the effect that while he had "no authority to treat on the subject of peace," he would however state "that I am equally anxious for peace with yourself, and the whole North entertains the same feeling." Lee read the note as an invitation for him to meet Grant and discuss terms of surrender, this in line with Grant's hope "that all our difficulties may be settled without the loss of another life."

On Palm Sunday morning, April 9, 1865, across the path of Lee's army and blocking its way stood the cavalry of Phil Sheridan. At five o'clock that morning General Lee on high ground studied the landscape and what it held. Eight o'clock came. Also came word that Sheridan's cavalry had fallen slowly back and widened out. Behind the cavalry, and screened by woodland, waited heavy bodies of infantry in blue, the troops of Ord and Griffin, who had made an almost incredible march of 30 miles the night and day before, coming up at daybreak to support Sheridan and invite battle. To the left, to the rear, were other Union lines.

Lee's staff officers heard him say, "There is nothing left me to do but to go and see General Grant, and I would rather die a thousand deaths." "Oh, General," protested one, "what will history say of the surrender of the army in the field?" "Yes, I know they will say hard things of us! They will not understand how we were overwhelmed by numbers. But that is not the question, Colonel: The question is, is it right to surrender this army. If it is right, then I will take all the responsibility."

Lee sent a note asking Grant for an interview "with reference to the surrender of this army." Grant at once wrote Lee to name the place for their meeting. Grant riding toward the front said to Colonel Horace Porter, "The pain in my head seemed to leave me the moment I got Lee's letter."

At the McLean house on the edge of Appomattox village, 95 miles west of Richmond, the two great captains of men faced each other in a little room and Lee gave over his army to Grant—Lee tall and erect, Grant short and stoop-shouldered; Lee 58 years old with silver hair, near the evening of life, Grant 42 with black hair and unspent strength of youth yet in him; Lee in a clean and dazzling military outfit, Grant in a rough-worn and dusty blouse telling his high rank only by the three stars on the shoulders, apologizing to Lee that he had come direct from the field and hadn't had time to change his uniform.

Lee inside was writhing over the bitter ordeal, and Grant later admitted he was embarrassed—though both wore grave, inscrutable faces and no one could have read the mixed feelings masked by the two commanders. "I met

Lincoln reading Second Inaugural address at Capitol front March 4, 1865 [Meserve].

The Last Photographs of Lincoln

By Alexander Gardner, April 10, 1865, the day after Lee's surrender at Appomattox. Tad is shown with his father, upper left [Meserve].

you once before, General Lee," began Grant in even voice, "while we were serving in Mexico . . . I have always remembered your appearance, and I think I should have recognized you anywhere." "Yes, I know I met you on that occasion, and I have often thought of it and tried to recollect how you looked, but I have never been able to recall a single feature."

Talk about Mexico ran into memories of that war when they both wore blue. Grant just about forgot why they were there, it seemed. Lee brought him to the point. "I suppose, General Grant, that the object of our present meeting is fully understood. I asked to see you to ascertain upon what terms you would receive the surrender of my army."

Grant went on as between two good neighbors. "The terms I propose are those stated substantially in my letter of yesterday—that is, the officers and men surrendered to be paroled and disqualified from taking up arms again until properly exchanged, and all arms, ammunition and supplies to be delivered up as captured property." "Those," said Lee, "are about the conditions I expected would be proposed."

Grant, seated at a table, put it in writing, his staff aides and corps commanders standing by; Lee was seated with his aide Colonel Charles Marshall standing behind his chair. Grant rose, stepped over to Lee and handed him the paper scrawled in pencil. Lee took out spectacles, pulled a handkerchief and wiped the glasses, crossed his legs, read slowly and carefully the strangest and most consequential paper that had ever met his eyes. And with his first touch of warmth he said to Grant, "This will have a very happy effect on my army."

Grant asked for any further suggestions. Lee had one. In his army the cavalrymen and artillerists owned their horses; he wanted these men to have their mounts for spring plowing on their farms. Grant said: "I take it that most of the men in the ranks are small farmers, and as the country has been so raided by the two armies, it is doubtful whether they will be able to put in a crop to carry themselves and their families through the next winter without the aid of the horses they are now riding." So without changing the written terms he would instruct officers receiving paroles "to let all the men who claim to own a horse or mule take the animals home with them to work their little farms." Lee showed relief. "This will have the best possible effect upon the men. It will be very gratifying and will do much toward conciliating our people."

Lee shook hands with some of Grant's generals who offered theirs, bowed, then turned to Grant saying that a thousand Union prisoners had been living the last few days on parched corn only; they required attention, and of provisions "I have, indeed, nothing for my own men." This was discussed briefly and Grant directed that 25,000 rations be sent to Lee's men.

Lee wrote an acceptance of Grant's terms, signed it, and the documents of surrendering an army were completed. There remained only such formalities as roll call and stacking of arms. Union gunners made ready to fire a salute of grand national triumph, but Grant forbade any signs of rejoicing over a broken enemy he hoped hereafter would no longer be an enemy.

Lee rode among his men—who crowded around him crying, "We'll fight 'em yet"—and explained, with tears and in a choked voice, that they had fought the war together, he had done his best, and it was over. Many were dazed. Some wept. Others cursed and babbled. The army could die but never surrender, they had hoped. Yet they still worshiped Lee. They touched his hands, his uniform; they petted his horse Traveller, smoothing his flanks with their hands. One man, throwing down his musket, cried to the blue heaven: "Blow, Gabriel, blow! My God, let him blow, I am ready to die!"

McLean's House, where Lee surrendered

For Grant it was one more odd day. Three times now he had bagged a whole army, at Fort Donelson, at Vicksburg, at Appomattox. He had kept his pledge to Lincoln that he would do his best to avoid a final bloody battle.

Next day it rained. The paroles numbered 28,231. Grant and Lee sat their horses between lines for a farewell talk. Grant said that not a man in the South had so great an influence with soldiers and people as General Lee, that if Lee would now advise the surrender of the other armies his advice would be followed. Lee said he could not do this without first consulting Davis. And with no misunderstandings Grant and Lee said good-by.

One of the great Confederate combat leaders, General John B. Gordon, had sat his horse and spoken farewell to his men. Some he had seen weeping as they folded burnt and shot-pierced battle flags and laid them on the stacked arms of surrender. As he told his troops of his own grief he tried to give them hope to rebuild out of the poverty and ashes to which many would return. Gordon could never forget a Kentucky father who lost two sons, one dying for the North, the other for the South. Over the two graves of his soldier boys the father set up a joint monument inscribed "God knows which was right."

From Appomattox Grant telegraphed Stanton at 4:30 P.M. April 9: "General Lee surrendered the Army of Northern Virginia this afternoon on terms proposed by myself."

The war was over. It would have various dying flares in a sunset sky. The costs and sacrifices could never be forgotten. There would be hates and rankling memories. The war nevertheless had spent itself and had gone now into a realm of memory and hallucination, a national ordeal and fever over and past.

Newsmen wrote their stories, put on the wires the glad tidings, and then went out and got drunk, or as Noah Brooks said, "unbent themselves." Cannon boomed over Washington at dawn. Over muddy streets surged people singing and cheering. Government departments gave their clerks another holiday.

The area in front of the White House filled with an enormous crowd. Brass bands had their music interrupted by guns. Tad showed at the well-known window from which the President always spoke; the crowd roared as he waved a captured Confederate flag. Hats went in the air with volleys of yells as the President came out to look at a throng where hatless men were now throwing into the air other men's hats and wild emotion poured out in screams that rose and curved in rockets. As the heaving surface of hats, faces and arms quieted down, the President spoke brief congratulations on the occasion, said arrangements were made for a formal celebration. "I propose closing up this interview by the band performing a particular tune . . . I have always thought 'Dixie' one of the best tunes I have ever heard."

Over the North that day of April 10 everything done before in victory celebrations was done again—but longer, oftener and with complete and final enthusiasm. To the prowar celebrants were joined the antiwar people, peace men and women who had always said the war was a cruel and costly failure; they too were glad now. So many, even many of the loyal ones, had been heartsick about the way it dragged for four years beyond all first expectations. Great God, but Lincoln must be thankful today. Hurrah for the Union! Hurrah for Lincoln! Hurrah for Grant and Sherman, the grand right and left arms of Lincoln! Get out the flags. Hang out every rag in the house that looks like a flag. Hang out red, white and blue bunting. Make a show. Great Jehovah, but we're glad the war's over! Men on horseback rode up and down swinging cowbells and tooting horns. Men tied tin cans to sticks, to ropes, and stood on street corners rattling their noisemakers.

The night saw torches and transparencies, bonfires, songs and howling. Nobody could be too foolish this day. Men climbed lampposts, stood upright on bareback horses. Laughing men rode sober-faced mules, riding backward and brandishing the mule's tail at onlookers. For many there was nothing to do but get drunk. Shake hands once, shake hands again, put your arms around anybody, today we love everybody, the war is over, throw your hat on the windmill, throw your hat over the moon.

In Willard's an elderly gentleman having had a few drinks, but not too many for the day, leaped up on the bar and led the crowd in singing "Praise God from whom all blessings flow."

Motley wrote of 20,000 businessmen in New York City uncovering their heads and singing in unison the psalm of thanksgiving: "Praise God."

CHAPTER 63

"Not in Sorrow, but in Gladness of Heart"

APRIL 11 the President issued a proclamation closing Southern ports. Any ship or vessel from beyond the United States trying to enter these ports with articles subject to duties, "the same, together with its tackle, apparel, furniture and cargo, shall be forfeited to the United States."

Also of this date was a proclamation barring from all U.S. ports the war vessels of any foreign country whose ports refused equal privileges and immunities to U.S. war vessels. The home war fading, the Union could risk challenging other countries.

The President spent his best working hours this day on his speech for the evening. He was seizing the initiative to set in motion his own reconstruction program. Not until next December would Congress meet, not unless he called a special session. He intended to speak to the country so plainly that before Congress met, he could hope the majority of the people would be with him.

A loose, informal, nameless aggregate of political power was responsive to him, with common understandings; he was their voice for remolding Southern society and politics toward peaceful resumption of their place as states in the old Union. He knew his American people. Panic, want, fanaticism, race hatred, cries for retribution, lust for big money and fortunes, these were spread over the country. Lincoln had his choice of going with those who, to win a complete and abstract justice for the Negro, would not hesitate about making the South a vast graveyard of slaughtered whites, with Negro state governments established and upheld by Northern white bayonets. The caldron of war hate still boiled under the surface rejoicing of April 10 over Appomattox. The passions of Sumner, Wade and others had become a habit with them and their followers.

A "carefully written paper" rather than a speech the President held in waiting for the crowd. With bands of music and banners of freedom, with shouting and hoorah, an immense throng poured into the area in front of the White House. Many were the surging calls and cries for the President. "There was something terrible," thought Noah Brooks, "in the enthusiasm with which the beloved Chief Magistrate was received. Cheers upon cheers, wave after wave of applause, rolled up, the President patiently standing quiet until it was all over."

He began to read his speech holding a candle in his left hand and the manuscript in the right. "Speedily becoming embarrassed with the difficulty of managing the candle and the speech," wrote Brooks, "he made a comical motion with his left foot and elbow, which I construed to mean that I should hold his candle for him, which I did." Then, "We meet this evening, not in sorrow, but in gladness of heart . . . A call for a national thanksgiving is being prepared, and will be duly promulgated . . . To Gen. Grant, his skilful officers, and brave men, all belongs. The gallant Navy stood ready, but was not in reach to take active part."

This to the crowd was in somewhat the expected tone. Then the key changed. The crowd was "perhaps surprised," thought Brooks. The President read on, dropped to the floor each written page when read, and became aware that Tad was picking them up as they dropped. He could hear Tad, unseen to the crowd, calling for "another" and "another" of the fluttering sheets. He read on: "By these recent successes the re-inauguration of the national authority—reconstruction—which has had a large share of thought from the first, is pressed much more closely upon our attention. It is fraught with great difficulty. Unlike the case of a war between independent nations, there is no authorized organ for us to treat with. No one man has authority to give up the rebellion for any other man. We must simply begin with, and mould from, disorganized and discordant elements."

Those of the crowd who had come for hoorah wondered how much more of it there would be. It was a little heavy, it seemed. Others knew he was talking not to the thousands on the White House lawn but to the whole American and European world.

Three years he had been studying what to do about getting Louisiana properly back into the Union. "From about July 1862, I had corresponded with different persons, supposed to be interested, in seeking a reconstruction of a State government for Louisiana. When the Message of 1863, with the plan before mentioned, reached New-Orleans, Gen. Banks wrote me that he was confident the people, with his military co-operation, would reconstruct, substantially on that plan. I wrote him, and some of them to try it; they tried it, and the result is known. Such only has been my agency in getting up the Louisiana government. As to sustaining it, my promise is out, as before stated. But, as bad promises are better broken than kept, I shall treat this as a bad promise, and break it, whenever I shall be convinced that keeping it is adverse to the public interest. But I have not yet been so convinced."

Off to the discard he was throwing those labored legal arguments in Congress that the seceded states through the act of secession had "committed suicide" and thereby were no longer states. "Good for nothing at all," he held this question. "A merely pernicious abstraction." He would offer this reasoning: "We all agree that the seceded States, so called, are out of their proper practical relation with the Union; and that the sole object of the government, civil and military, in regard to those States is to again get them into that proper practical relation . . .

"The amount of constituency, so to speak, on which the new Louisiana government rests, would be more satisfactory to all, if it contained fifty, thirty, or even twenty thousand, instead of only about twelve thousand, as it does. It is also unsatisfactory to some that the elective franchise is not given to the colored man. I would myself prefer that it were now conferred on the very intelligent, and on those who serve our cause as soldiers. Still the question is not whether the Louisiana government, as it stands, is quite all that is desirable. The question is 'Will it be wiser to take it as it is, and help to improve it; or to reject, and disperse it?' 'Can Louisiana be brought into proper practical relation with the Union *sooner* by *sustaining,* or by *discarding* her new State Government?'

"Some twelve thousand voters in the heretofore slave-state of Louisiana have sworn allegiance to the Union, assumed to be the rightful political power of the State, held elections, organized a State government, adopted a free-state constitution, giving the benefit of public schools equally to black and white, and empowering the Legislature to confer the elective franchise upon the colored man. Their Legislature has already voted to ratify the constitutional amendment recently passed by Congress, abolishing slavery throughout the nation. These twelve thousand persons are thus fully committed to the Union, and to perpetuate freedom in the state—committed to the very things, and nearly all the things the nation wants—and they ask the nations recognition, and it's assistance to make good their committal. Now, if we reject, and spurn them, we do our utmost to disorganize and disperse them."

He gave his forecast, spoke as a sad prophet: "We in effect say to the white men 'You are worthless, or worse—we will neither help you, nor be helped by you.' To the blacks we say 'This cup of liberty which these, your old masters, hold to your lips, we will dash from you, and leave you to the chances of gathering the spilled and scattered contents in some vague and undefined when, where, and how.' If this course, discouraging and paralyzing both white and black, has any tendency to bring Louisiana into proper practical relations with the Union, I have, so far, been unable to perceive it."

He would turn from these dark visions. "If, on the contrary, we recognize, and sustain the new government of Louisiana the converse of all this is made true. We encourage the hearts, and nerve the arms of the twelve thousand to adhere to their work, and argue for it, and proselyte for it, and fight for it, and feed it, and grow it, and ripen it to a complete success. The colored man too, in seeing all united for him, is inspired with vigilance, and energy, and daring, to the same end. Grant that he desires the elective franchise, will he not attain it sooner by saving the already advanced steps toward it, than by running backward over them? Concede that the new government of Louisiana is only to what it should be as the egg is to the fowl, we shall sooner have the fowl by hatching the egg than by smashing it."

He came to his closing words. "Important principles may, and must, be inflexible. In the present *'situation'* as the phrase goes, it may be my duty to make some new announcement to the people of the South. I am considering, and shall not fail to act, when satisfied that action will be proper."

As he stood for a moment taking the plaudits of the crowd, he smiled to the candle-bearer Brooks. "That was a pretty fair speech, I think, but you threw some light on it."

There were applause and cheers, with no such uproar as had begun the evening. The speech had been too long, too closely reasoned, to please a big crowd. He would hear from the country about the speech. What he heard would help guide him further. His powers were vast. Before Congress met in December he might put through a series of decisions and actions that would channel and canal future policy for years, in accord with his outspoken designs of this evening.

The New York *Tribune* reported the speech "fell dead, wholly without effect on the audience," and furthermore, "it caused a great disappointment and left a painful impression." Other newspapers noted frequent applause and "silent attention" between the punctuations of applause.

On the calendars the day of April 11 was marked off. Midnight came. The lighted windows of the White House had darkened. The curves of light shining from the Capitol dome were gone. The moist air stayed on. Washington slept in the possession of a mist that crept everywhere, finespun, intangible, elusive.

CHAPTER 64

Negotiations—An Ominous Dream

STANTON and others were in a fury over what they feared had been open recognition of the seceded Virginia Legislature by the Federal Executive. Before the incident could come to a boiling point, Lincoln swept away all preparations with a telegram to Weitzel. From the operator Albert Chandler he borrowed a Gillott's small-barrel pen—No. 404—and, while standing, wrote:

I have just seen Judge Campbell's letter to you of the 7th. He assumes as appears to me that I have called the insurgent Legislature of Virginia together, as the rightful Legislature of the State, to settle all differences with the United States. I have done no such thing. I spoke of them not as a Legislature, but as "the gentlemen who have *acted* as the Legislature of Virginia in support of the rebellion" ... as Judge Campbell misconstrues this ... let my letter to you, and the paper to Judge Campbell both be withdrawn or, countermanded, and he be notified of it. Do not now allow them to assemble; but if any have come, allow them safe-return to their homes.

A careful diary entry of Welles indicated that the President strongly inclined to let the insurgent Virginia Legislature have wide powers, that he peremptorily stopped that legislature from convening because once more his Cabinet of select advisers was against him—and it was one of the cases where it was better to go along with them—and wait. The "so-called legislature," Welles told the President, "would be likely to propose terms which might seem reasonable, but which we could not accept."

Seward was among those who mainly favored the President's policy of good will, of being generous and taking chances on double-dealing. Through different processes of thought, "we frequently arrived at the same conclusion," Seward described their joint operations; on the large questions "no knife sharp enough to divide us."

Among those high in the Government persistently vocal for punishing the defeated Confederates was Vice-President Johnson. To Dana in Richmond he insisted "their sins had been enormous," and if they were let back into the Union without punishment the effect would be bad, raising dangers in the future.

To Grant it came that Vice-President Johnson in Washington, in Richmond, had an "ever-ready" remark: "Treason is a crime and must be made odious." To Southern men who went to Johnson for assurances that they might begin some sort of rebuilding, he offered vehement denunciations. To Grant this was a sorry performance, Grant believing that the Lincoln view had behind it "the great majority of the Northern people, and the soldiers unanimously," the Lincoln view favoring "a speedy reconstruction on terms that would be the least humiliating to the people who had rebelled against their government." Grant also believed with Lincoln that a majority of the Northern people were not in favor of votes for the Negro. "They supposed that it would naturally follow the freedom of the negro, but that there would be a time of probation, in which the ex-slaves could prepare themselves for the privileges of citizenship before the full right would be conferred."

Sherman's ideas about peace terms and reconstruction, it would be too easy to say, were identical with those of Grant. The Union general who more than any other favored a war strategy of punishment and destruction of the South decidedly favored a mild and kindly peace policy. Between Sherman and Joe Johnston was not merely respect but a curious affection. They always fought fair and clean, each having admiration for the style of the other. Not often does it happen in war, but a fellowship had grown up between the two commanders. Neither Sherman nor Johnston had ever owned slaves. Both disliked Jefferson Davis. Grant knew Sherman would drive no hard bargain.

In the balances of early April the three high commanders and a million soldiers were, to use Grant's word, "unanimous" for ending the war on practically any terms that would bring a restored Union with slavery gone.

To Carpenter, Dana, Brooks and others, came an anecdote used by Lincoln when he was asked what he would do with Jefferson Davis. Lamon had his version of Lincoln saying: "When I was a boy in Indiana, I went to a neighbor's house one morning and found a boy of my own size holding a coon by a string. I asked him what he had and what he was doing. He says, 'It's a coon. Dad cotched six last night, and killed all but this poor little cuss. Dad told me to hold him until he came back, and I'm afraid he's going to kill this one too; and oh, Abe, I do wish he would get away!' 'Well, why don't you let him loose?' 'That wouldn't be right; and if I let him go, Dad would give me hell. But if he would get away himself, it would be all right.' Now," said Mr. Lincoln, "if Jeff Davis and those other fellows will only get away, it will be all right. But if we should catch them, and I should let them go, 'Dad would give me hell.'" It was not unpleasant for Lincoln to look back and consider that in all his speeches and papers no one could find a phrase of hate or personal evil wish against the head of the Confederate Government.

The two men who most often warned Lincoln about his personal safety were Stanton and Lamon. To Lamon he had laughing retorts. The envelope on which he had written "Assassination," wherein he filed threat letters, numbered 80 items in latter March. He told Seward, "I know I am in danger; but I am not going to worry over threats like these."

Lamon took no ease about this matter because of a dream Lincoln told him. To Lamon he spoke more than once of his failure to produce again the double image of himself in a looking glass, which he saw in 1860 lying on a lounge in his home in Springfield. One face held glow of life and breath, the other shone ghostly pale white. "It had worried him not a little . . . the mystery had its meaning, which was clear enough to him . . . the lifelike image betokening a safe passage through his first term as President; the ghostly one, that death would overtake him before the close of the second."

Sternly practical and strictly logical man that Lincoln was, using relentless scrutiny of facts and spare derivations of absolutes from those facts, he nevertheless believed in dreams having validity for himself and for others. According to Lamon's study, Lincoln held that any dream had a meaning if you could be wise enough to find it. When a dream came Lincoln sought clues from it. Once when Mrs. Lincoln and Tad were away he telegraphed her to put away a pistol Tad was carrying. "I had an ugly dream about him."

To Lamon it was appropriate that Lincoln held the best dream interpreters were the common people. "This accounts in large measure for the profound respect he always had for the collective wisdom of the plain people,—'the children of Nature,' he called them." The very superstitions of the people had roots of reality in natural occurrences. "He esteemed himself one of their number, having passed the greater part of his life among them."

Of the dream that came to Lincoln this second week of April '65, Lamon wrote that it was "the most startling incident" that had ever come to the man, of "deadly import," "amazingly real." Lincoln kept it to himself for a few days; then one evening at the White House, with Mrs. Lincoln, Lamon and one or two others present, he began talking about dreams and led himself into telling the late one that haunted him. Of his written account of the evening, Lamon said, "I give it as nearly in his own words as I can, from notes which I made immediately after its recital."

Mrs. Lincoln remarked, "Why, you look dreadfully solemn; do *you* believe in dreams?" "I can't say that I do," returned Mr. Lincoln; "but I had one the other night which has haunted me ever since. After it occurred, the first time I opened the Bible, strange as it may appear, it was at the twenty-eighth chapter of Genesis, which relates the wonderful dream Jacob had. I turned to other passages, and seemed to encounter a dream or a vision wherever I looked. I kept on turning the leaves of the old book, and everywhere my eye fell upon passages recording matters strangely in keeping with my own thoughts,—supernatural visitations, dreams, visions, etc."

He now looked so serious and disturbed that Mrs. Lincoln exclaimed: "You frighten me! What is the matter?" "I am afraid," said Mr. Lincoln, seeing the effect his words had upon his wife, "that I have done wrong to mention the subject at all; but somehow the thing has got possession of me, and, like Banquo's ghost, it will not down."

This set on fire Mrs. Lincoln's curiosity. Though saying she didn't believe in dreams, she kept at him to tell what it was he had seen in his sleep that now had such a hold on him. He hesitated, waited a little, slowly began, his face in shadows of melancholy:

"About ten days ago I retired very late. I had been up waiting for important dispatches from the front. I could not have been long in bed when I fell into a slumber, for I was weary. I soon began to dream. There seemed to be a death-like stillness about me. Then I heard subdued sobs, as if a number of people were weeping. I thought I left my bed and wandered downstairs. There the silence was broken by the same pitiful sobbing, but the mourners were invisible. I went from room to room; no living person was in sight, but the same mournful sounds of distress met me as I passed along. It was light in all the rooms; every object was familiar to me; but where were all the people who were grieving as if their hearts would break? I was puzzled and alarmed. What could be the meaning of all this? Determined to find the cause of a state of things so mysterious and so shocking, I kept on until I arrived at the East Room, which I entered. There I met with a sickening surprise. Before me was a catafalque, on which rested a corpse wrapped in funeral vestments. Around it were stationed soldiers who were acting as guards; and there was a throng of people, some gazing mournfully upon the corpse, whose face was covered, others weeping pitifully. 'Who is dead in the White House?' I demanded of one of the soldiers. 'The President,' was his answer; 'he was killed by an assassin!' Then came a loud burst of grief from the crowd, which awoke me from my dream. I slept no more that night; and although it was only a dream, I have been strangely annoyed by it ever since."

"That is horrid!" said Mrs. Lincoln. "I wish you had not told it. I am glad I don't believe in dreams, or I should be in terror from this time forth." "Well," responded Mr. Lincoln, thoughtfully, "it is only a dream, Mary. Let us say no more about it, and try to forget it."

The dream had shaken its dreamer to the depths, noted Lamon. As he had given the secret of it to others he was "grave, gloomy, and at times visibly pale, but perfectly calm." To Lamon afterward, in a reference to it Lincoln quoted from *Hamlet*, "To sleep; perchance to dream! ay, *there's the rub!*"— stressing the last three words.

Once again and with playful touches, bringing his sense of humor into use as though he might laugh off the dream, he said to Lamon: "Hill, your apprehension of harm to me from some hidden enemy is downright foolishness. For a long time you have been trying to keep somebody—the Lord knows who—from killing me. Don't you see how it will turn out? In this dream it was not me, but some other fellow, that was killed. It seems that this ghostly assassin tried his hand on someone else. And this reminds me of an old farmer in Illinois whose family were made sick by eating greens. Some poisonous herb had got into the mess, and members of the family were in danger of dying. There was a half-witted boy in the family called Jake; and always afterward when they had greens the old man would say, 'Now, afore we risk these greens, *let's try 'em on Jake. If he stands 'em*, we're all right.' Just so with me. As long as this imaginary assassin continues to exercise himself on others I can stand it." He then became serious and said: "Well, let it go. I think the Lord in His own good time and way will work this out all right. God knows what is best."

This last he gave with a sigh, and in a way as if talking to himself with no friend Lamon standing by.

CHAPTER 65

The Calendar Says Good Friday

FROM mid-April '61 to mid-April '65 some 3,000,000 men North and South had seen war service—the young, the strong, the physically fit, carrying the heavy load and taking the agony. The fallen of them had seen Antietam, Murfreesboro, Fredericksburg, Chancellorsville, the Wilderness, Spotsylvania, Cold Harbor, each a shambles, a human slaughterhouse. In the burned and blackened Shenandoah Valley were enough embers of barns and men to satisfy any prophet of doom. From Malvern Hill and Gettysburg down to Chickamauga, Chattanooga, Island Number 10, Vicksburg, the Red River and beyond, the burying grounds deep and shallow held the consecrated dead.

They were a host proven in valor and sacrifice—swept to the Great Beyond. No man who actually and passionately loved the cause of either flag could evade moments when he reproached himself for being alive. Robert E. Lee had those moments, well attested. So did Abraham Lincoln. His Gettysburg speech and his letter to Mrs. Bixby had an undeniable undertone of this reproach.

Killed in action or dead from wounds and disease were some 620,000 Americans, 360,000 from the North, 260,000 from the South—planted in the tomb of the earth, spectral and shadowy. They were phantoms never absent from Lincoln's thoughts. Possibly from that vanished host, rather than from the visible and living, Lincoln took his main direction and moved as though the word "reconciliation" could have supreme beauty if he could put it to work.

In Greensboro, North Carolina, at a rather ordinary house, in an upstairs room having a bed, a few small chairs, a table with pen and ink, Jefferson Davis, with four remaining Cabinet members and two veteran generals, held a final meeting over the affairs of the Confederate States of America, its government, its armies and prospects. They agreed a letter should be written to Sherman asking for terms. Johnston asked Davis to write it—which he did. They parted.

The sunset of the Confederacy had shaded over into evening stars, into lasting memories of a Lost Cause. Some would find welfare and kindness in the old Union. Two sections of the country fought a duel and came out with honors enough for both—this was the philosophy of some who really loved two flags—and why was a mystery, their personal secret. Some who had starved and suffered and taken wounds in the rain and lived on the food of rats and lost everything except a name for valor and endurance—some of these could never repent or be sorry.

As Davis packed his kit for moving farther south he knew there were not a few in the North who wished to see him hang on a sour-apple tree. One report credited Lincoln with saying: "This talk about Mr. Davis tires me. I hope he will mount a fleet horse, reach the shores of the Gulf of Mexico, and ride so far into its waters that we shall never see him again."

Lincoln sat for a photograph by Alexander Gardner—and for the first time when facing a camera in the four years of his administration permitted a smile to wreath his face. Until this camera register in the second week of April '65, he had most often been grave and somber. Now he smiled. The hurricane was spent, the high storm winds gone down. Rough weather and choppy seas were ahead—but the worst was over and could not come again. He hoped for good will and mutual trust and let that hope shine on his face.

Slimmer than a single cobweb thread was the hope that the President would call an extra session of Congress and let the legislative end of the Government dictate the reconstruction. When Speaker Colfax saw Lincoln about it he heard the President say he should "put it off as long as possible."

Crusader opposition to the President saw a long hard fight ahead. They would have to break Lincoln's control of his party. They would have to pry loose from him several powerful Northern economic factors that had not suffered loss at his hands and expected favors to come. They had not yet been able to solve the political genius by which he had so repeatedly foiled those seeking to unhorse him. Phillips, Sumner, Wade, Stevens, were not sure what strategy would overcome the odds against them. But they were sure the fight must be made; the Executive must somehow be shorn of his power. On the calendar it was Holy Week and April 14th was Good Friday. Some were to say they had never before this week seen such a shine of beneficence, such a kindling glow, on Lincoln's face. He was down to lean flesh and bone, 30 pounds underweight, his cheeks haggard, yet the inside of him moved to a music of peace on earth and good will to men. He let it come out in the photograph Gardner made this Holy Week.

The schedule for this day as outlined beforehand was: office business till eight; breakfast and then interviews till the Cabinet meeting at 11; luncheon, more interviews, a late afternoon drive with Mrs. Lincoln; an informal meeting with old Illinois friends; during the day and evening one or more trips to the War Department; another interview, then to the theater with Mrs. Lincoln and a small party. Such was the prepared docket for this Good Friday.

The city of Washington outside the White House kept on being gay. Flags and bunting still flew across streets. Churchgoers in large numbers heard Good Friday sermons of the Prince of Peace having brought unutterable blessings to the country.

In Washington General Grant had arrived from the front, heard shouts of welcome, and in trying to walk from his hotel to the War Department had to call on the police to help make a path through the curious, cheering throngs. The Secretary of War had announced that after "consultation with the lieutenant-general," it was decided to stop all drafting and recruiting.

At breakfast with Robert the President heard his son tell of life at the front, and he probably did, as one story ran, take up a portrait of Robert E. Lee his son had brought him, and after placing it on the table scan it long, saying: "It is a good face. I am glad the war is over at last."

After breakfast came Speaker Colfax. Other callers included Congressman Cornelius Cole of California, a Grand Rapids, Michigan, lawyer, W. A.

Howard, and the "lame-duck" Senator John P. Hale of New Hampshire. The President emphasized restoration of good will between the two sections whose war had ended.

Senator John A. J. Creswell came, one of the Union men who kept Maryland from secession. Creswell said that an old friend had drifted South, got into the Confederate Army, fallen into Federal hands, and was now a prisoner. "I know the man acted like a fool, but he is my friend and a good fellow. Let him out, give him to me, and I will be responsible for him."

"Creswell," said Lincoln, "you make me think of a lot of young folks who once started out Maying. To reach their destination they had to cross a shallow stream, and did so by means of an old flat boat. When they came to return, they found to their dismay that the old scow had disappeared. They were in sore trouble, and thought over all manner of devices for getting over the water, but without avail. After a time one of the boys proposed that each fellow should pick up the girl he liked the best and wade over with her. The masterly proposition was carried out, until all that were left upon the island was a little short chap and a great, long, gothic-built elderly lady. Now, Creswell, you are trying to leave me in the same predicament. You fellows are all getting your own friends out of this scrape, and you will succeed in carrying off one after another until nobody but Jeff Davis and myself will be left on the island, and then I won't know what to do. How should I feel? How should I look lugging him over? I guess the way to avoid such an embarrassing situation is to let them all out at once."

Others came seeking pardons, releases, discharges, which Lincoln wrote with an easier hand than he could while the war was on. A fever of a bright new time coming possessed many this day. "Washington was a little delirious," wrote Crook. Everybody was celebrating. The kind of celebration depended on the kind of person. It was merely a question of whether the intoxication was mental or physical. A stream of callers came to congratulate the President.

Lincoln was disinclined to go to the theater party planned by Mrs. Lincoln. A third-rate drama, *Our American Cousin*, which the star Laura Keene had carried to popularity, was showing at Ford's Theatre. But Mrs. Lincoln had set her heart on it, and on his suggestion she invited General and Mrs. Grant. And General Grant accepted, the newspapers were announcing.

Grant however had changed his mind. Mrs. Grant, in all probability, had told the General that the more she thought about it, the more it seemed impossible that she could endure an evening with the unfortunate woman she had last seen in such outbursts of temper and rages of jealousy at City Point. The General himself, anyone who knew him would testify, could see no fun in such a social evening.

Grant sat that morning in his first session with a President and a Cabinet. Welles wrote in his diary the President's comment on re-establishing law and order and new state governments in the South. Changing Welles' report from the third person to the first, Lincoln said:

"I think it providential that this great rebellion is crushed just as Congress has adjourned and there are none of the disturbing elements of that body to hinder and embarrass us. If we are wise and discreet we shall reanimate the States and get their governments in successful operation, with order prevail-

ing and the Union reestablished before Congress comes together in December . . . I hope there will be no persecution, no bloody work after the
war is over. No one need expect me to take any part in hanging or killing
those men, even the worst of them. Frighten them out of the country, open
the gates, let down the bars, scare them off"—throwing up his hands as if
scaring sheep. "Enough lives have been sacrificed."

Early in this Good Friday session of the Cabinet curiosity was sharp about
army news. Stanton had not arrived. Grant said he was hourly expecting to
hear from Sherman. Wrote Welles: "The President remarked it would, he
had no doubt, come soon, and come favorable, for he had last night the usual
dream which he had preceding nearly every great and important event of the
War. Generally the news had been favorable which succeeded this dream,
and the dream itself was always the same. I inquired what this remarkable
dream could be. He said it related to your (my) element, the water; that he
seemed to be in some singular, indescribable vessel, and that he was moving
with great rapidity towards an indefinite shore; that he had this dream preceding Sumter, Bull Run, Antietam, Gettysburg, Stone River, Vicksburg,
Wilmington, etc. General Grant said Stone River was certainly no victory,
and he knew of no great results which followed from it. The President said
however that might be, his dream preceded that fight. 'I had,' the President
remarked, 'this strange dream again last night, and we shall, judging from
the past, have great news very soon. I think it must be from Sherman. My
thoughts are in that direction, as are most of yours.' "

Young Frederick Seward attended this Cabinet meeting as Acting Secretary
of State in place of his father, who still lay abed with a broken jaw. Young
Seward's account of the session added details that escaped Welles. Curiosity
was spoken about the "rebel" leaders. Would they escape? Would they be
caught and tried, and if so, what would be the penalties? "All those present
thought that, for the sake of general amity and good will, it was desirable to
have as few judicial proceedings as possible." "I suppose, Mr. President," said
Postmaster General Dennison, "you would not be sorry to have them escape
out of the country?" "Well," came a slow answer, "I should not be sorry to
have them out of the country; but I should be for following them up pretty
close, to make sure of their going."

As to various details of any new state government, Seward heard the President: "We can't undertake to run State governments in all these Southern
States. Their people must do that—though I reckon that at first some of them
may do it badly."

So the Cabinet session of Friday, April 14, came to an end with the expectation that on Tuesday, April 18, they would again meet and resume discussion of how to bind up the nation's wounds.

A new British Minister, Sir Frederick Bruce, had arrived in Washington
and was awaiting presentation to the President. Young Seward asked at what
time the next day would it be convenient? Lincoln paused a moment, then:
"Tomorrow at two o'clock?" Seward supposed it would be in the Blue Room.
"Yes, in the Blue Room," said Lincoln.

Chaplain Neill came to Lincoln's office with a Vermont colonel seeking a
brigadier general's commission Lincoln had signed. The President had not
returned from lunch. Neill was looking among papers on the President's desk.

Lincoln came in eating an apple. "I told him for what I was looking," wrote Neill of this, "and as I talked he placed his hand on the bell-pull, when I said, 'For whom are you going to ring?' Placing his hand upon my coat, he spoke but two words,—'Andrew Johnson.' Then I said, 'I will come in again.' As I was leaving the room the Vice-President had been ushered in, and the President advanced and took him by the hand." Seldom had Lincoln and Johnson met. Definitely Lincoln had on several occasions avoided a conference sought by Johnson. Before Johnson left Lincoln would have sounded and fathomed him on immediate issues.

A black woman faint from hunger and a five-mile walk arrived at the White House gate, where the guards queried, "Business with the President?" and heard her grimly: "Befo' Gawd, yes." "Let her pass—they'll stop her further on," she heard one guard say as she took a deep breath and went on. The main entrance guard stopped her: "No further, madam. Against orders." In a flash she darted under his arm and went straight to the guard at the farther door. "Fo' Gawd's sake, please lemme see Mistah Lincoln." "Madam, the President is busy. He can not see you."

Either a cry she gave or the little tumult of her coming had reached inside, because, as she afterward related: "All of a sudden de do' open, and Mistah Lincoln hissef stood lookin' at me. I knowed him, fo' dar wuz a whimsy smile on his blessed face, an' he wuz a sayin' deep and sof'-like, 'There is time for all who need me. Let the good woman come in.' "

He heard Nancy Bushrod tell of her life with her husband Tom, how they were slaves on the old Harwood plantation near Richmond till the Emancipation Proclamation brought them to Washington. Tom joined a regiment with the Army of the Potomac, leaving Nancy with twin boys and a baby girl. At first his pay kept coming every month. Then it stopped. The soldiers were behind in pay from the Government. She had tramped seeking work but Washington was overrun with Negro help. Could the President help her get Tom's pay?

He heard her through and, according to Nancy, told her: "You are entitled to your soldier-husband's pay. Come this time tomorrow and the papers will be signed and ready for you." And as Nancy told it, "I couldn't open my mouf to tell him how I'se gwine 'membah him fo'evah for dem words, an' I couldn't see him kase de tears wuz fallin'." He called her back. "My good woman, perhaps you'll see many a day when all the food in the house is a single loaf of bread. Even so, give every child a slice and send your children off to school." With that, the President bowed "lak I wuz a natchral bawn lady."

Assistant Secretary of War Dana had a report that Jacob Thompson, the Confederate commissioner in Canada who had fomented raids, explosions and various disorders in the Great Lakes region, was to arrive in Portland this night of April 14 to take a steamer for Liverpool. Stanton said promptly, "Arrest him!" and changed to: "No, wait; better go over and see the President." Dana found Lincoln with his coat off in a closet attached to the office, washing his hands. "Halloo, Dana!" said the President. "What is it now?" "Well, sir, here is the Provost Marshal of Portland, who reports that Jacob Thompson is to be in that town to-night, and inquires what orders we have to give." "What does Stanton say?" "Arrest him." "Well," continued Lincoln, drawling the words, "no, I rather think not. When you have an elephant by the hind leg, and he's trying to run away, it's best to let him run."

This answer Dana carried back to the War Department, which on Stanton's wish sent no reply to the Provost Marshal's anxious inquiry. If the Marshal on his own initiative should make the arrest, Stanton would have Thompson where he wanted him—without having ordered the arrest.

A long afternoon carriage drive made an interlude. Mrs. Lincoln told Crook and others later of her query whether some friends should be invited for this drive, Lincoln saying No, he wanted "just ourselves." As the carriage rolled along he talked about the next four years in Washington, how he hoped afterward perhaps for a trip abroad, then a return to Springfield, perhaps law practice and a prairie farm on the banks of the Sangamon. Mrs. Lincoln spoke too of a happiness moving him, a happiness so strange and unusual that she could not read it, and it troubled her. She quoted him as saying, "I never felt so happy in my life," and a fear crossed her as she replied, "Don't you remember feeling just so before our little boy died?"

Walking over to the War Department late this afternoon of April 14, Lincoln did one thing perhaps for the first time. Always others had brought up the matter of possible harm to come to him—and he had laughed them off or promised to take care. In this instance it was Lincoln who first mentioned it, according to Crook's account. They passed some drunken men, profane, violent, irresponsible. And Lincoln turned, saying, "Crook, do you know, I believe there are men who want to take my life?" And after a pause, half to himself, "And I have no doubt they will do it."

Lincoln's tone was so calm and sure that Crook found himself saying, "Why do you think so, Mr. President?" "Other men have been assassinated"—this still in the manner of half talking to himself. "I hope you are mistaken, Mr. President," offered Crook. And after a few paces in silence, Lincoln in a more ordinary tone: "I have perfect confidence in those who are around me—in every one of you men. I know no one could do it and escape alive. But if it is to be done, it is impossible to prevent it."

Of this visit to the telegraph office, Cipher-Operator Charles A. Tinker wrote, "Lincoln . . . came . . . while I was transmitting a cipher dispatch that was couched in very laconic terms. Lincoln read the dispatch, and after taking in the meaning of the terse phrases, he turned to me and with his accustomed smile said, 'Mr. Tinker, that reminds me of the old story of the Scotch lassie on her way to market with a basket of eggs for sale. She had just forded a small stream with her skirts well drawn up, when a wagoner on the opposite side of the stream called out, "Good morning, my lassie; how deep's the brook and what's the price of eggs?" She answered, "Knee deep and a sixpence." ' Mr. Lincoln, still with a smile, lifted his coat tails in imitation of the maiden and passed into Secretary Stanton's room adjoining."

After a short conference in Stanton's office Lincoln came out, Crook noticing that the "depression" or "intense seriousness" had passed. "He talked to me as usual." Of the theater party planned for the evening he said: "It has been advertised that we will be there, and I cannot disappoint the people. Otherwise I would not go. I do not want to go." This surprised Crook, who knew well the ease and enjoyment Lincoln usually found at the theater. So Crook meditated, "It seems unusual to hear him say he does not want to go tonight." At the White House door he stood facing his guard a moment and then, "Good-bye, Crook." This puzzled Crook somewhat. Until then it had always been "Good-night, Crook."

At the White House Congressman Samuel Shellabarger of Ohio pleasantly asked that one of his constituents be appointed to a staff position in the Army. Lincoln pleasantly said he was reminded of when he was a young man in Illinois and a woman in the neighborhood made shirts. "An Irishman went to her and ordered a white shirt for some special function. The woman made it, and laundered it and sent it to her customer. When he got it the Irishman found the shirt had been starched all the way around, instead of only in the bosom, and he returned it with the remark that he didn't want a shirt that was all collar. The trouble with you, Shellabarger, is that you want the army all staff and no army." Thus Shellabarger told it to his Buckeye friend J. Warren Keifer.

Dick Oglesby, the new Governor of Illinois, and Dick Yates, the new U.S. Senator from Illinois, had an evening hour at the White House with Lincoln. They were home folks. Oglesby was salty and Yates convivial. Lincoln read to them horseplay humor from the latest outpouring of Petroleum Vesuvius Nasby, said Oglesby, perhaps including a letter dated April 10 wherein the satirist took his fling as follows: "I survived the defeet uv Micklellan (who wuz, trooly, the nashen's hope and pride likewise), becoz I felt assoored that the rane uv the Goriller Linkin wood be a short wun; that in a few months, at furthest, Ginral Lee wood capcher Washington, depose the ape, and set up there a constooshnal guverment, based upon the great and immutable trooth that a white man is better than a nigger." The Confederates had "consentratid" and lost their capital. "Linkin rides into Richmond! A Illinois rale-splitter, a buffoon, a ape, a goriller, a smutty joker, set hisself down in President Davis's cheer, and rites dispatchis! . . . This ends the chapter. The Confederasy hez at last consentratid its last consentrate. It's ded. It's gathered up its feet, sed its last words, and deceest . . . Linkin will serve his term out—the tax on whisky won't be repeeled—our leaders will die off uv chagrin, and delirium tremens and inability to live so long out uv offis, and the sheep will be skattered. Fare-well, vane world." This extravaganza rested Lincoln. It had the flavor Oglesby liked. And Yates could take it.

After dinner Speaker Colfax called by appointment. He asked whether the President intended to call an extra session of Congress during the summer. The President assured him he had no such intention. This left Colfax free for a trip to the West Coast. Lincoln gave him a message to the mountain regions that their gold and silver mines must count in a coming peace prosperity. Colfax spoke of how uneasy all had been over his going to Richmond and taking risks amid the tumult there. "He replied," noted Colfax, "pleasantly and with a smile (I quote his exact words), 'Why, if anyone else had been President and gone to Richmond, I would have been alarmed too; but I was not scared about myself a bit.'"

Congressman George Ashmun of Massachusetts waited below, said a card brought in. A loyal party man, presiding chairman of the 1860 convention that had nominated Lincoln for President, he was entitled to a hearing. One published report assumed to give concretely the gist of their interview. Ashmun spoke for a client of his who had a cotton claim against the Government and he desired a "commission" appointed to examine and decide on the merits of the case. Lincoln was quoted as replying rather warmly: "I have done with 'commissions.' I believe they are contrivances to cheat the Government out of every pound of cotton they can lay their hands on." Ashmun's face flushed. He answered that he hoped the President meant no personal imputation. Lincoln saw that his sudden and sharp comment on such "commissions" had been taken as personal and he had wounded a good friend, instantly saying: "You did not understand me, Ashmun. I did not mean what you inferred. I take it all back." He would see Ashmun first of all callers on the docket next morning, and taking a card, wrote:

> April 14, 1865.
> Allow Mr. Ashmun
> & friend to come in
> at 9 A.M. tomor-
> row—
>   A. Lincoln

They joined Colfax, Mrs. Lincoln and Noah Brooks. The President was unusually cheerful, thought Brooks, "never more hopeful and buoyant concerning the condition of the country, full of fun and anecdotes," though he had no enthusiasm about the play for the evening, felt "inclined to give up the whole thing." The party stepped out on the White House portico, Lincoln going toward the carriage, saying, "Grant thinks we can reduce the cost of the army establishment at least a half million a day, which, with the reduction of expenditures of the navy, will soon bring down our national debt to something like decent proportions, and bring our national paper up to a par, or nearly so, with gold—at least so they think."

Good old Isaac N. Arnold of Chicago came along, mentioned his errand as Lincoln was stepping into the carriage, and was answered, "Excuse me now. I am going to the theater. Come and see me in the morning."

CHAPTER 66

Blood on the Moon

IN THE carriage into which the President and his wife stepped were Henry Reed Rathbone, assigned by Stanton to accompany the President, and his fiancée, Miss Clara Harris. He was 28 years old, of a well-to-do clan of Rathbones in Albany, New York, a major of volunteers since November '62, a trusted War Office attaché. His sweetheart was the daughter of Judge Ira Harris of Albany, since 1861 U.S. Senator from New York.

The guard with Lincoln this evening was John F. Parker, one of the four officers detailed from the Metropolitan Police Force of the city for White House duty in staying close to the President and keeping a sharp eye on anyone who might have designs on the life and person of the President. Of these four guards only one, it afterward appeared, had a questionable record—and he was John F. Parker. On this evening he was 35 years old lacking one month; born in Frederick County, Virginia, he had worked at the carpenter's trade in Washington, enlisted in the Army as a three-month man, in '61 joining the Metropolitan Police as a patrolman. At his home on 750 L Street he had a wife and three children.

In March and April of '63 Parker was on trial on various charges: of being found asleep on a streetcar when he should have been patrolling his beat; of conduct unbecoming an officer through five weeks of residence in a house of prostitution, where it was alleged he had been drunk, had been put to bed, had fired a revolver through a window; the board found he was "at a house of ill fame with no other excuse than that he was sent for by the Keeper (Miss Annie Wilson)," although there was "no evidence that there was any robbery there or disturbance of the peace or quiet of that neighborhood." The list of trials, the repeated similar charges against Parker, the board's findings in the evidence showed conclusively that he was of loose habits rather than a steady reliable man.

How Parker found his way into the White House to begin with was not clear in the records. On April 3, however, when he was drafted for army service, Mrs. Lincoln on Executive Mansion stationery had written to the District of Columbia Provost Marshal, James R. O'Beirne, a certificate "that John F. Parker . . . has been detailed for duty at the Executive Mansion by order of [signed] Mrs. Lincoln."

The carriage left the White House with its four occupants, coachman Francis Burns holding the reins, and alongside him the footman and valet Charles Forbes. At Ford's Theatre, Burns pulled up his horses. Forbes swung down to the sidewalk and opened the carriage door. The President and his wife stepped out, followed by Major Rathbone and Miss Harris. The guard Parker was at hand. The party walked into the theater at about nine o'clock. An usher led them to their box. The audience in their 1,000 seats saw or heard that the President had arrived. They applauded; many rose from their seats; some cheered. The President paused and nodded his acknowledgment of their welcome to him.

On the stage proceeds a play written 14 years before by the English dramatist Tom Taylor; on rehearsal he decided it was not for the British public and later had sent it to the New York producer Lester Wallack, who had told Laura Keene it would fit her. She had put it on, but after a fairly good run it has about reached its limit.

The play proceeds, not unpleasant, often stupid, sprinkled with silly puns, forced humor. The story centers around the Yankee lighting his cigar with an old will, burning the document to ashes and thereby throwing a fortune of $400,000 away from himself into the hands of an English cousin. The audience agrees it is not bad. The applause and laughter say the audience is having a good time.

From the upholstered rocking armchair in which Lincoln sits he can see only the persons in the box with him, the players on the stage and any persons off stage on the left. The box has two doors. The door forward is locked. The President's party has the roominess and convenience of double space, extra armchairs, side chairs, a small sofa. In the privacy achieved he is in sight only of his chosen companions, the actors he has come to see render a play, and the few people who may be off stage to the left.

This privacy however is not as complete as it seems. A few feet behind the President is the box door, the only entry to the box unless by a climb from the stage. In this door is a small hole, bored that afternoon to serve as a peep-hole—from the outside. Through this peephole it is the intention of the Out-sider who made it with a gimlet to stand and watch the President, then at a chosen moment to enter the box. This door opens from the box on a nar-row hallway that leads to another door opening on the balcony of the theater.

Through these two doors the Outsider must pass in order to enter the President's box. Close to the door connecting with the balcony two inches of plaster have been cut from the brick wall of the narrow hallway. The intention of the Outsider is that a bar placed in this cut-away wall niche and then braced against the panel of the door will hold that door against intruders, will serve to stop anyone from interference with the Outsider while making his observations of the President through the gimleted hole in the box door.

At either of these doors, the one to the box or the one from the balcony to the hallway, it is the assigned duty and expected responsibility of John F. Parker to stand or sit constantly, with unfailing vigil. A Ward Lamon or an Eckert on this duty would probably have noticed the gimleted hole, the newly made wall niche, and been doubly watchful.

"The guard . . . acting as my substitute," wrote the faithful Crook later, "took his position at the rear of the box, close to an entrance leading into the box . . . His orders were to stand there, fully armed, and to permit no unauthorized person to pass into the box. His orders were to stand there and protect the President at all hazards. From the spot where he was thus sta-tioned, this guard could not see the stage or the actors; but he could hear the words the actors spoke, and he became so interested in them that, in-credible as it may seem, he quietly deserted his post of duty, and walking down the dimly-lighted side aisle, deliberately took a seat."

The custom was for a chair to be placed in the narrow hallway for the guard to sit in. The doorkeeper Buckingham told Crook that such a chair was provided this evening for the accommodation of the guard. "Whether Parker occupied it at all, I do not know," wrote Crook. "Mr. Buckingham is of the impression that he did. If he did, he left it almost immediately, for he confessed to me the next day that he went to a seat, so that he could see the play." The door to the President's box is shut. It is not kept open so that the box occupants can see the guard on duty.

Either between acts or at some time when the play was not lively enough to suit him or because of an urge for a pony of whisky under his belt, John F. Parker leaves his seat in the balcony and goes down to the street and joins companions in a little whiff of liquor—this on the basis of a statement of the coachman Burns, who declared he stayed outside on the street with his car-riage and horses, except for one interlude when "the special police officer [meaning John F. Parker] and the footman of the President [Forbes] came up to him and asked him to take a drink with them; which he did." Thus circumstances favor the lurking and vigilant Outsider.

The play goes on. The evening and the drama are much like many other evenings when the acting is pleasant enough, the play mediocre, the audience having no thrills of great performance but enjoying itself.

Out in a main-floor seat is one Julia Adelaide Shephard, writing a letter to her father about this Good Friday evening at the theater. "Cousin Julia has just told me," she reports, "that the President is in yonder upper right hand private box so handsomely decked with silken flags festooned over a picture of George Washington. The young and lovely daughter of Senator Harris is the only one of his party we see as the flags hide the rest. But we know Father Abraham is there like a Father watching what interests his children. The American cousin has just been making love to a young lady who says she'll never marry but for love but when her mother and herself find out that he has lost his property they retreat in disgust at the left hand of the stage while the American cousin goes out at the right. We are waiting for the next scene."

And the next scene? The next scene is to crash and blare and flare as one of the wildest, one of the most inconceivable, fateful and chaotic that ever stunned and shocked a world that heard the story.

The moment of high fate is not seen by the theater audience. Only one man sees that moment. He is the Outsider, the one who waited and lurked and made his preparations. He comes through the outer door into the little hallway, fastens the strong though slender bar into the two-inch niche in the brick wall, and braces it against the door panel. He moves softly to the box door and through the little hole studies the box occupants and his Human Target seated in an upholstered rocking armchair. Softly he opens the door and steps toward his prey, in his right hand a one-shot brass derringer pistol, a little eight-ounce vest-pocket weapon winged for death, in his left hand a steel dagger. He is cool and precise and times his every move. He raises the derringer, lengthens his right arm, runs his eye along the barrel in a line with the head of his victim less than five feet away—and pulls the trigger.

A lead ball somewhat less than a half-inch in diameter crashes into the left side of the head of the Human Target, into the back of the head, in a line with and three inches from the left ear. "The course of the ball was obliquely forward toward the right eye, crossing the brain in an oblique manner and lodging a few inches behind that eye. In the track of the wound were found fragments of bone, which had been driven forward by the ball, which was embedded in the anterior lobe of the left hemisphere of the brain."

For Abraham Lincoln it is lights out, good night, farewell—and a long farewell to the good earth and its trees, its enjoyable companions, and the Union of States and the world Family of Man he has loved. He is not dead yet. He is to linger in dying. But the living man can never again speak, see, hear or awaken into conscious being.

Near the prompt-desk off stage stands W. J. Ferguson, an actor. He looks in the direction of the shot he hears, and sees "Mr. Lincoln lean back in his rocking chair, his head coming to rest against the wall which stood between him and the audience . . . well inside the curtains"—no struggle or move "save in the slight backward sway." Of this the audience knows nothing.

Major Rathbone leaps from his chair. Rushing at him with a knife is a strange human creature, terribly alive, a lithe wild animal, a tiger for speed, a wildcat of a man bareheaded, raven-haired—a smooth sinister face with

glaring eyeballs. He wears a dark sack suit. He stabs straight at the heart of
Rathbone, a fast and ugly lunge. Rathbone parries it with his upper right
arm, which gets a deep slash of the dagger. Rathbone is staggered, reels back.
The tigerish stranger mounts the box railing. Rathbone recovers, leaps again
for the stranger, who feels the hand of Rathbone holding him back, slashes
again at Rathbone, then leaps for the stage.

This is the moment the audience wonders whether something unusual is
happening—or is it part of the play? From the box railing the Strange Man's
leap for the stage is slightly interrupted. The draped Union flag of silk reaches
out and tangles itself in the spur of one riding boot, throwing him out of
control. He falls perhaps ten feet to the stage, landing on his left leg, breaking the shinbone a little above the instep.

Of what he has done the audience as yet knows nothing. They wonder
what this swift, raven-haired, wild-eyed Strange Man portends. They see him
rush across the stage, three feet to a stride, and vanish. Some have heard
Rathbone's cry "Stop that man!" Many have seen a man leap from a front
seat up on the stage and chase after the weird Stranger, crying "Stop that
man!" It is less than half a minute since the Strange Man mounted the box
railing, made the stage and strode off.

Off stage between Laura Keene and W. J. Ferguson he dashes at break-
neck speed, out of an entrance, 40 feet to a little door opening on an alley.
There stands a fast bay horse, a slow-witted chore boy nicknamed John Peanuts holding the reins. He kicks the boy, mounts the mare; hoofs on the
cobblestones are heard but a few moments. In all it is maybe 60 or 70 seconds since he loosed the one shot of his eight-ounce brass derringer.

Did the Strange Man now riding away on a fast bay horse pause a moment
on the stage and shout a dramatic line of speech? Some said he ran off as
though every second of time counted and his one purpose was escape. Others
said he faced the audience a moment, brandished a dagger still bloody from
slashing Rathbone, and shouted the state motto of Virginia, the slogan of
Brutus as he drove the assassin's knife into imperial Caesar: "*Sic semper
tyrannis*"—"Thus be it ever to tyrants."

The audience is up and out of its 1,000 seats, standing, moving. Panic is in
the air, fear over what may happen next. Many merely stand up from their
seats, fixed and motionless, waiting to hear what has happened. The question
is spoken quietly or is murmured anxiously—"What is it? What has happened?" The question is yelled with anguish—"For God's sake, what is it—
what has happened?"

A woman's scream pierces the air. Some say afterward it was Mrs. Lincoln.
The scream carries a shock and a creeping shiver to many hearing it. "He
has shot the President!" Men swarm up to the edge of the stage, over the
gas-jet footlights onto the stage. The aisles fill with people not sure where
to go.

Some 200 soldiers arrive to clear the theater. The wailing and the crazy
chaos let down in the emptying playhouse—and flare up again in the street
outside, where some man is accused of saying he is glad it happened, a sudden
little mob dragging him to a lamppost with a ready rope to hang him when

six policemen with clubs and drawn revolvers manage to get him away and jail him for safekeeping.

Mrs. Lincoln in the box sees her husband seated in the rocking chair, his head slumped forward. With little moaning cries she springs toward him and with her hands keeps him from tumbling to the floor. Major Rathbone has shouted for a surgeon, has run out of the box into the narrow hallway, and with one arm bleeding and burning with pain he fumbles to unfasten the bar between wall and door panel. An usher from the outside tries to help him. They get the bar loose. Back of the usher is a jam of people. He holds them back, allowing only one man to enter, a young-looking man with mustache and sideburns, 23-year-old Charles A. Leale, assistant surgeon, U.S. Volunteers.

Dr. Leale holds Mrs. Lincoln's outstretched hand while she cries "Oh, Doctor! Is he dead? Can he recover? Will you take charge of him? Do what you can for him. Oh, my dear husband! my dear husband!" He soothes her a little; he will do all that can possibly be done.

The man in the chair at first scrutiny seems to be dead, eyes closed, no certainty he is breathing. Dr. Leale with help from others lifts the man from the chair and moves him to a lying position on the floor. Dr. Leale lifts the eyelids and sees evidence of a brain injury. He rapidly passes the separated fingers of both hands through the blood-matted hair of the head, finding a wound and removing a clot of blood, which relieves pressure on the brain and brings shallow breathing and a weak pulse.

Dr. Leale bends over, puts a knee at each side of the body, and tries to start the breathing apparatus, attempts to stimulate respiration by putting his two fingers into the throat and pressing down and out on the base of the tongue to free the larynx of secretion. Dr. Charles Sabin Taft, an army surgeon lifted from the stage into the box, now arrives. Another physician, Dr. Albert F. A. King, arrives. Leale asks them each to manipulate an arm while he presses upward on the diaphragm and elsewhere to stimulate heart action. The body responds with an improvement in the pulse and the irregular breathing.

Dr. Leale is sure, however, that with the shock and prostration the body has undergone, more must now be done to keep life going. And as he told it later: "I leaned forcibly forward directly over his body, thorax to thorax, face to face, and several times drew in a long breath, then forcibly breathed directly into his mouth and nostrils, which expanded his lungs and improved his respirations. After waiting a moment I placed my ear over his thorax and found the action of the heart improving. I arose to the erect kneeling posture, then watched for a short time and saw that the President could continue independent breathing and that instant death would not occur. I then pronounced my diagnosis and prognosis: 'His wound is mortal; it is impossible for him to recover.'"

Brandy and water arrive. Dr. Leale slowly pours a small quantity into the President's mouth. It is swallowed and retained. While they are waiting for the President to gain strength, wrote Leale later, Laura Keene "appealed to me to allow her to hold the President's head. I granted this request, and she sat on the floor of the box and held his head in her lap. We decided that the

President could now be moved to a house where we might place him on a bed in safety."

Four soldiers from Thompson's Independent Battery C, Pennsylvania Light Artillery, lift the President by the trunk and legs, Dr. Taft carrying the right shoulder, Dr. King the left shoulder, Dr. Leale the head. They come to the door of the box. Dr. Leale sees the passageway packed with people. He calls out twice, "Guards, clear the passage!" A captain goes into action with troopers. They show muskets, bayonets, sabers. "Clear out!" rings the repeated order. "Clear out!" they cry to the curiosity seekers, and to some who hesitate and still insist on blocking passage. "Clear out, you sons of bitches!"

Then the solemn little group with their precious freight carried headfirst moves slowly through a space lined by protecting soldiers. At the stair head they shift so the feet are carried first. Two more soldiers join the original four in holding the President and moving him. As they go out of the door of the theater Dr. Leale is again asked if the President can be taken to the White House and answers, "No, the President would die on the way."

Overhead is night sky. Clouds of dark gray unfold and unroll and show a blazing white moon and fold and roll and cover it again. On Tenth Street between E Street and F humanity swirls and wonders and wants to know. "Is that the President they are carrying?" "Is it true that he was shot and will live?" "Oh, God, it can't be true!" "Where are they taking him?" "Who shot him?" "Was he stabbed or shot? I heard he was stabbed." "Was he shot bad or will he live?" "For God's sake, is there no chance for him?"

Packing Tenth Street straight across from the front door of Ford's Theatre is a crowd so massed that there is no hope of a path for those carrying the President unless something is done. The same captain who had managed clearance inside the theater comes to Leale: "Surgeon, give me your commands and I will see that they are obeyed." Leale asks the captain to clear a passage to the nearest house opposite. The captain draws a sword, commands the people to make an opening; they move back, and the procession begins its slow crossing. Several times they stop while Dr. Leale removes the newly gathered blood clots on the head wound. A barrier of men forms to keep back the crowds on each side of an open space leading to the house. Now comes the report that this house is closed. At the next house, Mr. Peterson's, No. 453 Tenth Street, Dr. Leale sees a man standing at the door with a lighted candle, beckoning them to come in. "This we did," ran Leale's account, "not having been interrupted in the slightest by the throngs in the street; but a number of the excited populace followed us into the house."

There they lay their stricken Friend of Man in the rented room of William Clark, a boarder in the house of William Peterson—on a plain wooden bed— at about 10:45 o'clock, somewhat less perhaps than a half-hour after the moment the trigger of the little eight-ounce derringer was pulled.

The President lies on his back in the center of the humble walnut bed. Now Dr. Leale holds the face upward to keep the head from rolling to either side. The long knee elevation troubles Leale. He orders the foot of the bed removed. Dr. Taft and Dr. King report it is a fixture. Leale requests it be broken. This it seems cannot be done with any satisfaction. Leale then has Lincoln moved so he lies diagonally across the bed and, propped with extra pillows, is gently slanted with a rest for head and shoulders, finally in a position of repose.

On white sheets lies the unconscious patient still in frock coat and long boots. Under the white sheets is a cornhusk mattress resting on rope lacings. The room fills with anxious people. Leale calls an officer, directs him to open a window, and to order all except the doctors and friends to leave.

After a short rest for the patient Leale decides to make a thorough physical examination to see if there are other wounds. He requests all except surgeons to leave the room. The captain reports all have left but Mrs. Lincoln, with whom he does not feel authorized to speak. Leale makes his wish known to Mrs. Lincoln and she leaves at once. They undress the patient, search the body from head to foot, finding no other wound. The lower extremities are cold; Leale sends a hospital steward for hot water and hot blankets. He sends for a large mustard plaster; this is applied over the solar plexus and to every inch of the entire anterior surface of the body.

The breath comes hard; pulse 44, feeble; the left pupil much contracted, the right widely dilated; both eyes totally insensible to light. The President is completely unconscious, an occasional sigh escaping with the labored breath.

In a nearby room Mrs. Lincoln has the company of Miss Harris, of several women who have arrived, and of the Reverend Dr. Gurley. Major Rathbone has fainted from loss of blood and is taken home. At intervals Mrs. Lincoln is notified she may visit her husband. Once she cries to him, "Live! you must live!" and again, "Bring Tad—he will speak to Tad—he loves him so."

Dr. Robert K. Stone, the Lincoln family physician, arrives, followed soon by Surgeon General Joseph K. Barnes and his assistant Dr. Charles H. Crane, who take charge. Dr. Leale reports to his chief what he has done. At 2 A.M. Dr. Barnes tries to locate the bullet and after a time further exploration for the bullet is considered of no avail.

The room is 15 feet long by 9 wide, entered from the hallway by a door having a large pane of glass covered with a curtain on the inside. A Brussels carpet is on the floor. The wallpaper is brown figured with white. Around are a few chairs, a plain bureau, a small wood stove, a washstand with pitcher and bowl. Here there is waiting for the end to come.

Outdoors a vagrant white moon, over which dark clouds had earlier rolled and unrolled their smokelike shadows, is now long hidden and lost behind a cold gray sky, an even monotone of a sky.

In the White House Robert Lincoln and John Hay sit gossiping pleasantly, Nicolay away at the Fort Sumter flag-raising. The doors burst open and several voices at once tell them the news. They run downstairs, take a carriage, cannot quite believe what they have heard. Slowly their carriage plows a path through the gathering thousands of people around Tenth Street. Dr. Stone gravely and tenderly tells Robert the worst: there is no hope. He chokes. The tears run down his face. After a time he recovers and does his best during hours of the night at comforting his mother.

At about the same hour and minute of the clock that the President is shot in Ford's Theatre a giant of a young man rides on a big one-eyed bay horse to the door of the Seward house on Lafayette Square, gets off his horse, rings the doorbell, says he is a messenger from the attending physician and has a package of medicine that must be personally delivered to the sickroom of the

Secretary of State. The servant at the door tries to stop the young man, who enters and goes up the stairs, suddenly to turn in a furious rush on Fred Seward, beating him on the head with the pistol, tearing the scalp, fracturing the skull and battering the pistol to pieces.

Young Seward grapples with the intruder, and in their scuffling the two of them come to the Secretary's room and fall together through the door. There Fred Seward fades out and for days knows nothing, in a stupor of unconsciousness. The Secretary's daughter and a soldier-nurse, Sergeant George T. Robinson, spring from their chairs. The murder-bent young giant knocks them right and left, gives Robinson a knife thrust, then rushes to the bed where the Secretary of State has lain nearly two weeks with a steel frame about the head and face. He stabs over and again at the throat of the sick man, delivers three ugly gashes in the cheek and neck. The steel frame foils a death gash. And the quick wit or odd luck of the victim still further foils him; the Secretary of State rolls off between the bed and the wall.

Now the stranger in the house hurls himself down the stairs, slashes an attendant on the way, is out of the front door unhurt, leaps into saddle and rides out Vermont Avenue toward an eastern suburb. Behind him he has left a quiet home transformed into a battlefield hospital, five persons bleeding from ghastly wounds, failing of death for any of them. Behind him too he has left a bloodstained knife, the battered pistol and his slouch felt hat.

This horror affair is the basis for the wildfire rumor that nearly all the Cabinet members have been assassinated. Senator Sumner finds a hack, is driven to Tenth Street above E, makes inquiries, is stopped by guards at the door of the Peterson house, says, "I *will* go in"—and his face and manner pass him. He quietly watches and waits, occasionally with moist eyes.

Two friends of Chase drop in to tell the Chief Justice the President has been shot. "My first impulse," Chase writes in his diary for April 14, "was to rise immediately and go to the President, but reflecting that I could not possibly be of any service, I resolved to wait for morning and further intelligence."

Secretary Welles is just falling asleep about 10:30 when his wife calls him. His messenger James Smith has arrived, excited, saying the President has been shot. In the Peterson house at the bedside of "the giant sufferer" Welles' outstanding impressions were: "He had been stripped of his clothes. His large arms, which were occasionally exposed, were of a size which one would scarce have expected from his spare appearance. His slow, full respiration lifted the clothes with each breath that he took. His features were calm and striking. I had never seen them appear to better advantage than for the first hour, perhaps, that I was there. After that, his right eye began to swell and that part of his face became discolored."

One by one the other Cabinet members arrive till all are in the Peterson house except Seward and McCulloch. Vice-President Andrew Johnson comes early for a brief visit.

At one in the morning, wrote the New York *Herald* man, "Senator Sumner was seated on the right of the President's couch, near the head, holding the right hand of the President in his own. He was sobbing like a woman, with his head bowed down almost on the pillow of the bed on which the President was lying."

Nerves are wearing away, faces haggard. Dr. Leale continues the one expedient of keeping the wound opening free from blood clot. The surgeons direct or perform every necessary act that comes to mind. They are supposed to be coldly practical, with no emotion to interfere with clear thinking, yet Surgeon Taft noted moments when "there was scarcely a dry eye in the room." To Dr. Leale it is vastly more than one more surgical case. From a distance he had loved the President. He had gone to Ford's Theatre chiefly to have a look at a public man he admired as a heroic character. So he is softly moved to a procedure he later described: "Knowledge that frequently just before departure recognition and reason return to those who have been unconscious caused me for several hours to hold his right hand firmly within my grasp to let him in his blindness know, if possible, that he was in touch with humanity and had a friend."

The one man dominant in the house is Edwin McMasters Stanton. He seems to have lived for this night, for the exercise of the faculties on which he prided himself. Over Washington wild rumors were running that a new uprising of the Confederacy was breaking, a city guerrilla warfare—that secretly armed secessionists were to swarm from their hiding places, take strategic points, and make a last desperate stand for the Confederate cause. "Stanton," wrote one of his friends, "instantly assumed charge of everything near and remote, civil and military." He ordered troops to keep clear the spaces around the house, to let no one enter the house except high Government officers and persons on special business. He sent for the District of Columbia Chief Justice David K. Cartter, who arrived soon and in an adjoining room began taking testimony, with a shorthand reporter present, of persons who might have evidence bearing on the high crime. To Charles A. Dana, Assistant Secretary of War, who could write shorthand, Stanton dictated telegrams to all parts of the country.

Stanton sent for several army officers to act as aides; directed General Thomas M. Vincent to take charge of affairs in the Peterson house; telegraphed to General Grant at Philadelphia that Lincoln had been shot and to return at once to Washington; telegraphed to Chief Kennedy of New York to send on his best detectives immediately; wrote and dispatched a note to Chief Justice Chase, saying the President could not live and to be ready to administer the oath of office to Vice-President Johnson; notified the Vice-President that the President was dying; and sent to the country and the people bulletin after bulletin concerning the tragedy and the President's condition. Thus, wrote a friend of Stanton, "he continued throughout the night, acting as president, secretary of war, secretary of state, commander-in-chief, comforter, and dictator."

As daylight began to slant through the windows, with its white clarity making the yellow gas jets and lamplights look garish and outdone, it became evident the President was sinking. Surgeon General Barnes, seated near the head of the bed, occasionally held his finger over the carotid artery to note its pulsation. Dr. Stone sat on the edge of the foot of the bed. Dr. Leale held the President's right hand, with an extended forefinger on the pulse.

At 5 A.M. the oozing from the wound ceased entirely and the breathing became stertorous and labored. On the haggard faces of the silent ones circled about, it was written more than once they thought the end had come.

From 11 at night until six in the morning Welles had "remained in the room . . . without sitting or leaving it." At six o'clock he went out of the house, tasted a deep breath of fresh air, looked up at a gloomy sky, and took a 15-minute walk. Every few rods were huddles and bunches of people, all anxious, all wanting to know what of the night, some of them having stood waiting all night and into the morning. One or more would step out from each of these groups and ask Welles, bearded and fatherly-looking, about the President. "Is there no hope?" He was impressed, reading "intense grief" on every face at his answer that the President could survive but a short time. "The colored people especially—and there were at this time more of them, perhaps, than of whites—were overwhelmed with grief."

A cold rain began falling. Out of a monotonous sky inexorably gray a cold rain began falling.

A little before seven Welles went into the room where a warm Friend of Man was going cold, moving into the final chill that all men at the last must know. "His wife soon after made her last visit to him. The death-struggle had begun. Robert, his son, stood with several others at the head of the bed. He bore himself well, but on two occasions gave way to overpowering grief and sobbed aloud, turning his head and leaning on the shoulder of Senator Sumner."

The last breath was drawn at 21 minutes and 55 seconds past 7 A.M. and the last heart beat flickered at 22 minutes and 10 seconds past the hour on Saturday, April 15, 1865. Dr. Barnes' finger was over the carotid artery, Dr. Leale's finger was on the right wrist pulse, and Dr. Taft's hand was over the cardium when the great heart made its final contraction.

The Pale Horse had come. To a deep river, to a far country, to a by-and-by whence no man returns, had gone the child of Nancy Hanks and Tom Lincoln, the wilderness boy who found far lights and tall rainbows to live by, whose name even before he died had become a legend inwoven with men's struggle for freedom the world over.

The voice of Phineas D. Gurley: "Let us pray." Kneeling at the bedside, his sonorous tones shook with submission to the Everlasting, to the Heavenly Father, with pleading that the dead man's country and family be comforted.

The widow was told. She came in and threw herself with uncontrollable moaning on the body. When later she went away the cry broke from her, "O my God, and I have given my husband to die!"

Over the drawn face muscles Dr. Leale moved a smoothing hand, took two coins from his pocket, placed them over the eyelids, and drew a white sheet over the face. Over the worn features had come, wrote John Hay, "a look of unspeakable peace." Stanton, it was said afterward, pronounced the words: "Now he belongs to the ages." By his wish this became legend.

The Cabinet, with Seward and McCulloch absent, met in the back parlor, arranged to notify the Vice-President and the Chief Justice of the Supreme Court, and to meet again at noon in the room of the Secretary of the Treasury and take action with the newly sworn-in President toward "preserving and promoting the public tranquillity."

The young surgeon, the good Dr. Leale, who all through the night had stood to his armpits in a vortex and a pit of desolation, had done all that could be done and was leaving the fated house where Mr. Peterson with a lighted candle had beckoned him in nine hours ago—it seemed nine years— nine hundred years.

"I left the house in deep meditation," ran his story. "In my lonely walk I was aroused from my reveries by the cold drizzling rain dropping on my bare head, my hat I had left in my seat in the theater. My clothing was stained with blood, I had not once been seated since I first sprang to the President's aid; I was cold, weary and sad." His eyes happened to fall on his wrists and the detachable cuffs. They had been laundered stiff and immaculately white. Now they were limp, wet, blood-soaked. He decided he would keep the cuffs as long as he lived. To him they were "stained with the martyr's blood."

Now there was a tincture of deep violet given to the Gettysburg phrases: "We cannot consecrate—we cannot hallow—this ground." Now there was a snow-white fabric crossed with sunset vermilion around the words written to the Boston widow woman: "The solemn pride that must be yours to have laid so costly a sacrifice upon the altar of freedom."

CHAPTER 67

Shock—The Assassin—A Stricken People

THE TOLLING of the bells began in Washington. Likewise in New York, Boston, Chicago, Springfield, Peoria, metropolitan centers and crossroads villages, the day had tolling bells hour on hour, flags at half-mast, the gay bunting, red, white and blue festoons brought down and crape or any fold of black put out and hung up for sign of sorrow.

Out on the Illinois prairie of Coles County they went to a farmhouse and told the news to an old woman who answered: "I knowed when he went away he'd never come back alive." This was Sally Bush Lincoln, prepared for her sorrow which came that day.

Edwin Booth, the world's foremost Shakespearian actor, lay abed in Boston the morning of April 15 when a servant came in and told him that his brother, John Wilkes Booth, had shot and killed the President. And as Edwin Booth related it to Joseph Jefferson, his mind "accepted the fact at once," for he thought to himself that his brother "was capable of just such a wild and foolish action." Edwin Booth added: "It was just as if I was struck on the forehead by a hammer." To General Grant's secretary, his old friend Adam Badeau, Edwin Booth on Sunday, April 16, wrote, "Abraham Lincoln was my President for, in pure admiration of his noble career and his Christian principles, I did what I never did before—I *voted* and *for* him!"

The man hunters and the fugitive John Wilkes Booth were second in national interest only to the death of Lincoln. Who was this Booth? Out of a mediocre fame he had now wrapped the letters of his name with a weird infamy. His own Southern heroes almost universally repudiated him as a madman, one who fought foul. And he was that—a lunatic—a diabolically cunning athlete, swordsman, dead shot, horseman, actor. Now his face and name were published with a War Department promise of $50,000 for his capture dead or alive.

John Wilkes Booth was one of ten children born to Mr. and Mrs. Junius Brutus Booth on a big wooded farm 25 miles from Baltimore. Junius Brutus Booth seemed to be a man filled with a compassion that often shook his controls and ran over into the pathetic, the ridiculous, even the comic. When he died in 1852 his feet had wandered before all shrines and altars and paid homage. He was brought up an Episcopalian; he made it a custom to keep some of the sacred days of the Koran; Catholic priests claimed him for one of their own because of his familiarity with their faith; and in synagogues he had been taken for a Jew when he joined fluently in their worship in their own tongue; Masons buried him in a Baptist vault. He was widely accepted as a figure in American cultural life, the supreme Shakespeare player.

He drank hard and often, and in moods and periods was definitely insane. In time Junius Brutus Booth came to sense the oncoming seizures of insanity and would make for home, where a rare and faithful wife nursed him through dark tortures. The daughter Asia wrote of these attacks being looked on in their home "with awe and reverence."

The son, John Wilkes Booth, had room to play, a 200-acre wooded farm, an oak-floored bedroom facing the east and the sunrise, on the walls deer antlers, swords, pistols, daggers, a bookcase holding Bulwer, Marryat, Byron, Shakespeare. Over the father's dark spells and grand whims, over Edwin's impenetrable melancholy, over the failings of others of the family, the mother and loyal Asia had no such brooding near to anguish as they gave the boy and youth Wilkes. They knew it was said "women spoiled him," that he did what he pleased and took what he wanted and kept his secrets. They saw vanity grow in him—vague, dark personal motives beyond reading and to be feared, projects and purposes vast with sick desire, dizzy with ego.

To the hanging of John Brown went J. Wilkes Booth as a lieutenant in the Richmond Grays. Though he hated John Brown's cause, he was fascinated and spellbound by the dramatic, lone-handed audacity of Old Ossawatomie.

His first stage successes came in Southern cities. As the Southern States moved into secession he moved North as a player. William Winter saw the young star's acting as "raw, crude and much given to boisterous declamation." He delighted in leaps and bounds while acting. The Baltimore *Sun* critic ticketed Wilkes Booth "the Gymnastic actor." There were fellow actors, such as E. L. Tilton, knocked into an orchestra pit while fencing with Wilkes Booth; some had been cut by his sword in mimic duels.

Over a piece of scenery more than five feet high, wrote W. J. Ferguson, he saw Wilkes Booth jump "with little effort." These unexpected feats were accepted as part of a "dashing buoyancy" natural to him. "I saw him, after a rehearsal," wrote Ferguson of Booth the swordsman, "take on two men at once with the foils and disarm them both within a few seconds." In a billiard-hall quarrel Ferguson saw Booth, swiftly and without anyone but Ferguson seeing him, throw a heavy book that hit a man in the back. The man turned, accused an innocent party, and started a free-for-all fight. The lights went out and Booth made his getaway, having had one more of his practical jokes.

In April '61, when Booth played with a stock company in Albany, the leading lady, Miss Henrietta Irving, rushed into his room at Stanwix Hall and with a dirk tried to stab him, landing only a light cut on his face. Then she retired to her own room and stabbed herself, though not seriously. A trifle short for heroic roles, noted Charles Wyndham, "he made up for the lack by his extraordinary presence and magnetism . . . He was the idol of women. They would rave of him, his voice, his hair, his eyes."

From '61 continuously as he traveled the North he spoke as openly as was convenient for the Confederate cause. In Albany the theater treasurer found him at breakfast one morning and explained that he would ruin his engagement there and put himself in personal danger if he went on talking secession. "Is not this a democratic city?" asked Booth. The reply: "Democratic? yes—but disunion, no!" After which Booth quieted in his talk, though sullen and sour about being gagged.

In '64 when he was filling fewer engagements because of a failing voice, Booth seemed to have a deepening sense of guilt over keeping himself in safety and comfort while the war raged and the Southern cause sank lower. His broodings took two directions. He would perform a deed saving the Southern cause while at the same time giving the world a breath-taking dramatic performance. In August '64 he won two recruits to "the enterprise," as they termed it. Samuel Arnold and Michael O'Laughlin, two former schoolmates of Booth at St. Timothy's Hall, after two years in the Confederate Army, considered themselves "engaged" with Booth as leader. The "enterprise," worked out in their talks, designed the "capture" or "abduction" of the President. Having gotten their prisoner out of Washington down to Richmond, they would exchange him for enough Confederate prisoners to win the war.

Most of the time until April 14, 1865, Booth lived in Washington, checking in and out of his National Hotel quarters, taking many trips on errands whose purpose he kept secret. He studied Lincoln's ways and habits, particularly as a theatergoer. At both Grover's Theatre and Ford's, Booth was at home, receiving his mail at Ford's. The entries and exits of these theaters knew him, every door, corner, hall, lobby, passageway, familiar to him. To the stock actors, stagehands, front-office employees, he was a distinguished figure whose nod they valued.

In November he rode a horse over Maryland and Virginia south of Washington, studied the roads, paths and hiding places by day or night. To Asia, in whom he had every trust, he gave an envelope later found to contain some bonds and oil stock certificates—and a letter. This gave the key to his scrambled brain, his vanity and self-importance, his desire to show the South that he was a Confederate hero even though they no longer loved him or cared about him. He referred in passing to his plan for making "a prisoner of this man, to whom she [the South] owes so much of her misery."

The letter indicated a "master mind," of a sort, holding sway over a little band of schemers and hopers meeting in a boardinghouse on H Street between Sixth and Seventh in Washington. They included a drugstore clerk, 20 years old, David E. Herold, out of work and seeking a job when Booth found him. Another was a hump-shouldered, scraggly-bearded fellow, dark, sly, fierce of looks though a coward in a pinch; he was of German descent, a carriage-maker at Port Tobacco, Virginia. Booth's promises of gold brought him in—George A. Atzerodt. Then there was a tall, broad-shouldered 20-year-old athlete joining ox and tiger in his frame, a veteran of Antietam and Chancellorsville, wounded at Gettysburg. In January '65 this youth after nearly four years of hard fighting at bloody salients had despaired of the Confederacy and deserted, happening in Baltimore when he was homeless, penniless, in rags, without money to buy food, to meet Booth, finding sympathy, praise, new clothes and money. This was the man known as Lewis Paine (Lewis Thornton Powell), whose entry into the Seward home had resulted in five persons stabbed and the Secretary of State narrowly missing a death wound. The keeper of the boardinghouse where the plotters met was the widow of a Confederate informer and dispatch-carrier, Mary E. Surratt.

Daily Mrs. Surratt saw her boarders acquainting themselves with weapons, holding vague whispered conversations, telling her nothing definite, intimating they would save the sinking Southern cause. The air had a touch of terror. Daily she crossed herself and more often hurried to church to pray. Mrs. Surratt's son John H., Jr., at first opposed and then gave way to Booth's eloquence. Just old enough to vote, six feet tall, slender but powerful, blond, with eyes sunken under a bulging forehead, he knew his footing more surely than the others. He quit his job as an Adams Express Company clerk to join Booth. With him came one Louis J. Weichmann, a wavering, suspicious and careful young man who had been Surratt's chum for two years at college when Surratt studied for the priesthood. Weichmann had been a schoolteacher in Washington, later getting a clerkship in the office of the commissary general of prisoners.

Of the two former Maryland schoolmates of Booth, Samuel Arnold was a farm hand who hated farm work, rather lazy, a student of books with an unmanageable vocabulary; Michael O'Laughlin was a Baltimore livery-stable worker, fairly good at handling horses and better yet at carrying liquor. The crew filled the seven bedrooms of Mrs. Surratt's boardinghouse. Some of them subsisted on money furnished by Booth, and all except Weichmann were led and lighted by Booth's stratagems and wildfire eloquence over the glory awaiting them all for their service to the Confederacy.

On at least one day Booth prowled the White House grounds with Paine. And if later statements of Paine to Major Thomas T. Eckert were correct, Booth directly suggested to the powerful young panther from Florida that he should go into the White House, send in his card, enter Lincoln's office like any one of many petitioners—and then and there shoot the President. Booth seemed to have taunted Paine with lacking nerve in this. Yet on Booth's suggestion Paine lurked among bushes in front of the White House conservatory. After a light rain had come a freeze with a crust of ice crackling under footsteps. Lincoln walked by in company with Eckert, and Paine heard Lincoln say, "Major, spread out, spread out, or we shall break through the ice." Paine in the bushes heard Lincoln telling Eckert of Illinois days once when neighbors returning from mill with their meal bags were crossing the frozen Sangamon River and as the ice cracked when they were part way over someone called the warning, "Spread out, spread out, or we shall break through the ice."

April 8 Washington is ablaze with flags and the North howling joy over the surrender of Lee's army. Paine, Atzerodt and Herold are left to Booth, awaiting his wish and whim. The evening of April 11 Booth is with Paine on the White House lawn near the window where the President speaks. He is shaken with rage at the President's saying the elective franchise, the ballot, should be given to the colored man, "the very intelligent, and . . . those who serve our cause as soldiers." He urges Paine to shoot the speaker, Paine protesting the risk is too great. The two walk away, Booth muttering, "That is the last speech he will ever make."

Events had swept away all doubts for Booth as to his course. He would be the whirlwind dark angel of retribution and justice—this was the fond wish. Never for a moment in the piled and ramified materials of evidence was there an indication that he examined his own heart and studied himself on the question of what was driving him on and whether he was first of all an actor. Until this week, believed his sister Asia, who perhaps understood him through a deeper love than he had ever had to search himself with, he was sane. "If Wilkes Booth was mad," she wrote, "his mind lost its balance between the fall of Richmond, and the terrific end."

In an inside coat pocket he carried the photographs of four actresses, beautiful women as the pictures rendered their faces, Fay Brown, Effie Germon, Alice Gray, Helen Western—and a fifth woman, half-smiling, later identified merely as "a Washington society woman." Whether any of them had intimacy of word and mind with him so as to know the seething concentrated purpose that swept aside all other passions—the later record revealed nothing.

John Deery, who kept a bar in front of Grover's Theatre, during this April week saw Booth often. Said Deery, "He sometimes drank at my bar as much as a quart of brandy in the space of less than two hours of an evening." Later Deery was to judge of this, "Booth was crazy, but he didn't show it." His theory was that any natural and inherited insanity dominating Booth this week was heightened and accentuated by liquor.

On April 12 Booth writes to a woman in New York who signs herself "Etta." She answers April 13, "Yes, Dear, I can heartily sympathize with you, for I too, have had the blues ever since the fall of Richmond, and like you, feel like doing something desperate." He has enlisted her in some phase of his projects and she lets him know: "I have not yet had a favorable opportunity to do what *you* wished, and I so solemnly promised, and what, in my own heart, I feel ought to be done. I *remember* what happiness is in store for us if we succeed in our present undertakings." She informs him that "the means you gave me when we parted" is gone. She quotes, "Money makes the mare go" and assures him, "I do as you desired and keep as secluded as a nun, which is not agreeable to me as you have found."

On April 14 Booth writes to his mother a letter dated "2 A.M." of that day. "Dearest Mother:" he begins. "I know you hardly expect a letter from me. Excuse brevity; am in haste. With best love to you all I am your affectionate son ever. John." That was all. To his mother, to his brother Edwin, to such friends as John T. Ford and John Deery, no inklings of a deed and a motive for which he is willing to pay with his life. The word "assassin," several commentators were to note, took root from the word "hashish" or "hasheesh," an East Indian drug that inflates the self-importance of the one eating it.

Between 11 and 12 o'clock of Good Friday morning, April 14, Booth comes to Ford's Theatre for his mail, hears that a messenger from the White House has engaged a box for the President that evening. He goes into action, hires a bay mare for himself to be ready at four o'clock in the afternoon. He calls on Mrs. Surratt just as she with Weichmann is leaving for Surrattsville, handing her a package holding a field glass to be delivered at a tavern there. To the empty Ford's Theatre he goes, seeing the two boxes thrown into one, the rocking chair brought for the President's corner of the box. He inspects locks, bores a hole through the box door, digs a niche in the plastered brick wall.

At seven in the evening Booth leaves his room at the National Hotel. In passing he asks the hotel clerk if he is going to Ford's Theatre this evening. The clerk hadn't thought about it. "There will be some fine acting there tonight," says Booth; he hurries to the Herndon House and sees Paine. They arrange their timing: at the same hour and minute of the clock that night Paine is to kill the Secretary of State and Booth is to kill the President. Atzerodt, run the further plans, is to kill Vice-President Johnson. Herold is to guide Paine to the Seward home and then hurry to the support of Atzerodt. On the street Booth talks with Atzerodt, who has heard of the fighting nerve of Andy Johnson and now tells Booth he enlisted for abduction but not killing. Atzerodt begs and whimpers. Booth storms at him and curses him.

Atzerodt, armed with a revolver he knows he can never use, drifts away, never to see Booth again. Early in the morning on foot headed toward his boyhood home 22 miles west of Washington, in Georgetown pawning his revolver for $10, was a muddled wanderer, one of the only three men in the world who could have told the police beforehand to the hour of Booth's intentions that night.

At a stable near Ford's and close to ten o'clock Booth, Paine and Herold get on their horses and part, Booth to go to Ford's, Herold to guide Paine to the Seward house. At the back door of Ford's Booth calls for the theater carpenter Spangler to hold his horse, enters and goes down under the stage, out of a private door into an alley and therefrom to the street in front of the theater. Spangler meantime calls the door boy John Peanuts to hold Booth's horse. Peanuts says he has to tend his door, Spangler saying if anything goes wrong to lay the blame on him. Out front on the street Booth sees the President's carriage at the curb, a crowd of curiosity seekers on the sidewalk, some of them waiting to have a look at the presidential party when it leaves the theater. The play is more than half over and a stir of voices and laughter drifts out from the windows to the lighted and cheerful street.

Booth walks past the doorkeeper Buckingham and with a pleasant smile and "You'll not want a ticket from *me?*" asks the time, and is pointed to the clock in the lobby. He requests a chew of tobacco from Buckingham, who draws a plug from which Booth takes a bite, as customary a proceeding as gentlemen of a previous generation exchanging snuff. On the street an actor who is to sing a new patriotic song asks the time and the theater costumer steps into the lobby and, looking at a large clock on the wall, calls out, "Ten minutes past ten." Booth opens a door from the lobby into the parquet, takes note of the presidential box, whether there are any visitors. He has seen *Our American Cousin* played and has calculated to fine points the strategic moment for his deed. Soon only one actor will be out front on the stage, only a woman and a boy in the wings. A laugh from the audience usually follows the exit of two ladies, a loud enough laugh perhaps to smother any unusual noises in a box.

Booth goes up the stairs leading to the dress circle, picks his way among chairs behind an outer row of seats, reaches the door of the passageway leading to the presidential box. He leans against the wall, takes a cool survey of the house. On the stage is only one actor. Booth knows him well, Harry Hawk, playing the character of Asa Trenchard, a supposedly salty American character. Mrs. Mountchessington has just left Asa alone with a rebuke that he was not "used to the manners of good society." Asa meditates alone over this: "Well, I guess I know enough to turn you inside out, old gal—you sockdologizing old mantrap."

Booth opens the door into the narrow hallway leading to the box, steps in, closes the door, fixes the bar in the mortised niche and against the door panel. On soft tiger feet he moves toward the box door, puts an eye to the hole bored through the door, sees his victim is precisely where he wishes and as he had planned. Softly he swings the door back and with his brass derringer pistol in the right hand and a long dagger in the other, he steps into the box.

Up till that instant any one of a million ordinary conceivable circumstances of fate could have intervened and made the next moment impossible. Yet not one of those potential circumstances arrived. What happened that next moment became world history—not because of him who did what was done, but because of the name, life and works of the victim of the deed.

"Think no more of him as your brother," wrote Edwin Booth to Asia; "he is dead to us now, as soon he must be to all the world, but imagine the boy you loved to be in that better part of his spirit, in another world." And referring to a weeping nameless betrothed one, Edwin added, "I have had a heart-broken letter from the poor little girl to whom he had promised so much happiness."

And the one man whose sworn duty it was to have intercepted the assassin—John F. Parker? There were charges brought against him by Superintendent A. C. Richards of the Metropolitan Police Force, "that Said Parker was detailed to attend and protect the President Mr. Lincoln, that while the President was at Ford's Theatre on the night of the 14th of April last, Said Parker allowed a man to enter the President's private Box and Shoot the President." But there was no trial on these charges, and it was not till three years later that Parker was to be dishonorably dismissed from the police force for sleeping on his beat.

Neither Stanton nor La Fayette C. Baker nor any member of Congress nor any newspaper metropolitan or rural, nor any accustomed guardian of public welfare, took any but momentary interest in the one guard sworn to a sacred duty who distinguished himself as a marvelous cipher, a more curious

derelict than any during the war shot by a firing squad for desertion, cowardice in the face of the enemy, or sleeping at the post of duty. The watch-
guards of public welfare all had other fish to fry, and it was to be many
years before the dereliction of John F. Parker, a nonentity and as such a
curiously odd number, was to be duly assessed.

How did Parker take the news of Lincoln's assassination? It woke some
lethargy in his bones. Probably all night long he wandered half-dazed over
the streets of Washington, stopping in saloons, gathering the news, wondering, bothering his head about what explanations he could make. At six
in the morning, according to the police blotter, he brought to headquarters
a woman of the streets he had arrested, her name Lizzie Williams. Parker
had decided he would make it a matter of record that he was on the job
as a police officer, that early in the morning he was on the job. So he
brings in a forlorn, bedraggled streetwalker—against whom he proved no
case, and Lizzie Williams was promptly discharged. This was his offering:
instead of intercepting the killer of the President shortly after 10 P.M. he
brings in to headquarters a battered and worn prostitute at 6 A.M. in a cold
gray rain and the sky a noncommittal monotone.

The guard Crook awoke in his home the morning after Good Friday to
hear the news, and his first thought was, "If I had been on duty at the
theater, I would be dead now." His next thought was to wonder whether his
fellow guard Parker was dead. Years later he was to wonder why the negli-
gence of the guard on duty had "never been divulged," writing: "So far as I
know, it was not even investigated by the police department. Yet, had he
[Parker] done his duty, President Lincoln would not have been murdered
by Booth." Crook reasoned that a single guard at the box entrance could have
made a struggle and an outcry that would have resulted in the disarming of
Booth. "It makes me feel rather bitter," wrote Crook, "when I remember
that the President had said, just a few hours before, that he knew he could
trust all his guards."

In company with Senator Ben Wade went Congressman Henry Laurens
Dawes to greet in the Kirkwood House the newly sworn-in President Andrew Johnson. And Wade's greeting, as Congressman Dawes told it to his
daughter Anna, ran: "Mr. Johnson, I thank God that you are here. Lincoln
had too much of the milk of human kindness to deal with these damned
rebels. Now they will be dealt with according to their deserts." This feeling
ran through a caucus of the Republican party radicals meeting that day to
consider, as Congressman George Julian phrased it, "a line of policy less
conciliatory than that of Mr. Lincoln."

Of the new President little was known, and from the Judge Advocate's
office, at headquarters of the Department of the South, Hilton Head, South
Carolina, John C. Gray, Jr., wrote to John C. Ropes: "He may turn out
more of a man than we hope. Henry Ward Beecher told an officer on the
dock [at Charleston] a few hours after the news was announced of Lincoln's
death, that Johnson's little finger was stronger than Lincoln's loins, and
though I have heard nothing so bad myself, I can see that a good many think
that Mr. Lincoln would have been too lenient with the rebels."

The single event of an assassination swept away a thousand foundations carefully laid and protected by the living Lincoln. A long series of delicate roots of human relationships the living Lincoln had nursed and guarded were torn up in a night.

One question was held pertinent: What from year to year during the war did Wilkes Booth meet that might generate a motive and play on it and shape it with finality? He saw and heard hundreds of men of the educated and privileged classes indulging in an almost unrestricted freedom of speech. Did they tell him anything else of import than that this one man had by his own whim and determination carried the war on through four devastating, howling, bitter years of agony? On the head of this one man Lincoln had been heaped a thousand infamies any one of which could easily inflame the mind of a vain and cunning fool. What was one more killing of a man in a land already strewn with corpses and cripples and famished skeletons in prisons?

The New York *Herald* on Easter Sunday, April 16, editorialized on the press as no factor of enlightenment, no sobering influence at all. It said directly that newspaper editors shared in the guilt of leading an assassin toward his bloody work. "It is as clear as day that the real origin of this dreadful act is to be found in the fiendish and malignant spirit developed and fostered by the rebel press North and South. That press has, in the most devilish manner, urged men to the commission of this very deed."

Party spirit and its mouthpieces, the press, the politicians and orators, came in for blame from *Harper's Weekly*. Directly and indirectly, openly and cunningly, the passions of men were set on fire by "the assertion that Mr. Lincoln was responsible for the war, that he had opened all the yawning graves and tumbled the victims in . . . Is it surprising that somebody should have believed all this, that somebody should have said, if there is a tyranny it can not be very criminal to slay the tyrant?"

Mrs. Chesnut saw a tide rolling toward her people, writing in her diary: "Lincoln, old Abe Lincoln, has been killed . . . Why? By whom? It is simply maddening . . . I know this foul murder will bring upon us worse miseries."

Sherman on his way to a conference with the Confederate General Joseph E. Johnston had a decoded telegram handed him from Stanton: "President Lincoln was murdered about 10 o'clock last night." Sherman pledged the operator to say nothing to anyone of the telegram. When Sherman and Johnston sat alone in a small farmhouse, Sherman handed over the telegram. Johnston read. On his forehead slowly came sweat "in large drops," as Sherman watched him, Sherman remembering so clearly and for so long a time afterward how one of the greatest of Confederate captains said that "Mr. Lincoln was the best friend they had" and the assassination was "the greatest possible calamity to the South." In the surrender terms they were to sign, Sherman's motive, according to his keenest interpreter, probably ranged around a thought: "Lincoln is dead. I will make his kind of a peace." When later the dread news was given to Sherman's army, many were ready to burn the city of Raleigh to the ground. Logan made speeches against it, other officers intervened, and discipline prevailed.

Now Laura Keene and Harry Hawk and the cast of *Our American Cousin* were in jail, detained for inquiry. Now the gentle sister Asia Booth was taken from her Philadelphia home to a Washington prison. Now the brother Edwin announced he would play no more drama for the American public— not for years, if ever again. Now the pursuit of the fugitive Jefferson Davis was urged more furiously by Stanton. Now a colonel had come to Charles A. Dana's house early of a morning to say, "Mr. Lincoln is dead and Mr. Stanton directs you to arrest Jacob Thompson." Lincoln had said No to this but now Stanton and a host of officials had no hesitations about drastic policies of punishment.

The fugitive Jefferson Davis wrote later of his dominant feeling: "The news [of the assassination] was to me very sad, for I felt that Mr. Johnson was a malignant man, and without the power or generosity which I believed Mr. Lincoln possessed." *Harper's Weekly* reported: "Roger A. Pryor stated in Petersburg that he believed Mr. Lincoln indispensable to the restoration of peace, and regretted his death more than any military mishap of the South. General Lee at first refused to hear the details of the murder . . . He said that when he dispossessed himself of the command of the rebel forces he kept in mind President Lincoln's benignity, and surrendered as much to the latter's goodness as to Grant's artillery. The General said that he regretted Mr. Lincoln's death as much as any man in the North."

Yet Booth had not entirely miscalculated. A small extremist minority element North and South exulted over his deed. In front of the New York post office April 15 a man saluted someone, "Did you hear of Abe's last joke?" In a few minutes he was encircled by raging men beating his head and crying "Hang him!" "Kill him!" "Hang the bastard up!" Police rescuers took a volley of bricks and stones. A young Englishman, Peter Britton, having had a few drinks, chronicled the New York *Herald*, walked Vandewater Street snarling oaths at Lincoln, saying, "I came a good ways to see the --- -- - ----- buried." Rescued by police from an excited crowd and taken before Justice Dowling, Britton was sentenced to six months in prison at hard labor. Police Sergeant Walsh of the 6th precinct, at the corner of Chatham and Pearl Streets threw a knockout blow to the mouth of one George Wells on hearing from that mouth: "Old Abe, the son of a bitch, is dead, and he ought to have been killed long ago." Justice Dowling sent Wells to prison for six months.

New York, the major draft-riot city, saw more of this tumult than other places. From coast to coast, however, there was a Copperhead minority to whom Booth was a hero. At Swampscott, Massachusetts, dispatches recited that one George Stone "said in public it was the best news we had received for four years, and gave three cheers." Citizens and soldiers tarred and feathered Stone. In most of these cases the offender spoke his first personal reaction to the news, without stopping to think of his community's reaction. The Lincoln-haters at first had no notion of how crushed with grief, how exquisitely sensitive, were an overwhelming number of Lincoln loyalists.

In Chicago on Madison Street and on Canal Street men and boys sent rocks crashing through the big glass windows of several places where a Copperhead saloonkeeper had hung in the front window a large portrait of J. Wilkes Booth.

The North was in grief. Everywhere the eye might turn hung the signs of this grief. The sermons, editorials, talk in streets, houses, saloons, railroad cars and streetcars, the black bunting and the crape—these were attempts to say something that could not be said. Men tried to talk about it and the words failed and they came back to silence. To say nothing was best. Lincoln was dead. Was there anything more to say? A great Friend of Man had suddenly vanished. Nothing could be done about it. Silence, grief and quiet resolves, these only were left for those who admired and loved and felt themselves close to a living presence that was one of them.

Thousands on thousands would remember as long as they lived the exact place where they had been standing or seated or lying down when the news came to them, recalling precisely in details and particulars where they were and what they were doing when the dread news arrived.

Hundreds of thousands there were who had been the foundation and groundwork of what he had done. These people—the basic Lincoln loyalist legion—had no words; they had only grief—sorrow beyond words. "A stricken people came to their altars." Whatever was sensitively and humanly aware wore crape, seen or unseen.

Far out on the rolling prairie of the Iowa frontier, a farmer rode a fast horse and shouted from the saddle, first to this neighbor and then the next, "Lincoln is shot!" or "Lincoln is dead—shot in a theater!" That was all. The rider was gone. They had heard him. They stood in their foot tracks, amazed, dumbstruck, sadly waited for further news, some saying, "What will the country do now?"

On an early morning streetcar in Philadelphia a good Quaker unrolled a morning newspaper, stared at it, and broke out: "My God! what is this? Lincoln is assassinated!" In the gray dawn on this streetcar men cupped their faces in their hands and on the straw-covered floor fell hot tears. The driver of the streetcar came in to make sure of what he heard. Then the driver went out and took the bells off his horses. And he drove on with his car filled with mourners, some silent, some sobbing.

Newsboys at their stands cried no headlines, handed the damp sheets from the press to the buyers, one boy noticed as he brushed with his dirty hand the tears from his dirty cheeks. In thousands of stores the merchants told the clerks they would close for the day; in many schools the sobbing teacher could only tell the children, "Go home, there will be no school today." The father, the children, coming home unexpected, the mother asked what was wrong and heard "Mama, they've killed the President" or "Our President is dead." Then the family hunted up crape or black cloth for the front doorway.

In Charleston, South Carolina, one old black woman walked a street looking straight ahead, wringing her hands and crying: "O Lawd! O Lawd! Marse Sam's dead! O Lawd! Uncle Sam's dead!" In Boston a thousand or more men found themselves on the Common, marching in a silent procession, two by two, not a word spoken, just walking, just seeing each other's faces, marching an hour or so and then slowly scattering, having reached some form of consolation in being together, seeing each other in mute grief.

In a home at Huntington, Long Island, a mother and son, Walt Whitman, heard the news early in the morning, sat at breakfast and ate nothing, sat at other meals during the day and ate nothing, silently passed newspaper extras to each other during the day and said little, the son deciding that as long as he lived he would on April 14 have sprigs of lilac in his room and keep it as a holy day for the man he later characterized as "the grandest figure on the crowded canvas of the drama of the nineteenth century."

Many of those who mourned knew there were times when with nothing to say, he said nothing, slept not at all, and wept at those times in a way that made weeping appropriate, decent, majestic.

Now Father Abraham was gone. Old Abe—there would be no more stories about him, alive there in the White House in Washington. They had saved the newspapers or they had clipped from the paper such pieces as the Gettysburg speech and the letter to Mrs. Bixby and the second in-augural. Now the newspapers had black borders, night's crape darkness, on the front-page columns. Now there was a memory to keep. That was left—the life he had lived—the meanings and the lights of that life. This could not be taken away.

Farmers in southern Illinois said the brown thrush no longer sang, that in the year to come the brown thrush never once sang. One Illinois boy going to town, holding his father's hand, having heard the church and town-hall bells all day, having seen only dark sorrow on all faces, looked up at the sky and found it strange the night stars were all out. Lincoln was dead—and yet as always the stars moved alive over the night dome.

Like a vast sunset of flame and changing gold ending a day and punctu-ating a period of time their faraway friend at Washington had vanished into the overhead planets and the same constellations of mist that had taken that long roll call of soldiers no longer answering "Here" to the company sergeant calling the names.

In a million and more American households they sought words that might help and assuage. "The land mourneth, every family apart," ran one Easter Sunday text. Also "The steps of a good man are ordered by the Lord: and He delighteth in his way." Over doorways, in store windows, on arches spanning streets, ran the legend "And the Lord blessed Abraham in all things."

On one arch of crape and white over Broadway in New York ran the sen-tence "The great person, the great man, is the miracle of history."

CHAPTER 68

A Tree Is Best Measured when It's Down

IN GREAT stone cathedrals of the cities, in modest frame churches of small towns, in little cabin churches at country crossroads, in hospital chapels and in at least one state prison, on Navy ships and in outdoor Army camp services, there were Easter Sunday sermons memorializing the dead President.

A large minority of Protestant ministers made reference to the death in a playhouse, the Reverend Justin Dewey Fulton in Tremont Temple, Boston, saying: "He was shot in a theatre. We are sorry for that. If ever any man had an excuse to attend a theatre, he had. The cares of office were heavy upon him. His brain reeled. His frame grew weak. In conversing with a friend, he said, 'Some think I do wrong to go to the opera and the theatre; but it rests me. I love to be alone, and yet to be with the people. A hearty laugh relieves me; and I seem better able after it to bear my cross.' This was his excuse. Upon it we will not pronounce a judgment. This we will say: we are all sorry our best loved died there. But take the truth with its shadow."

The Reverend Dr. Phineas D. Gurley in the New York Avenue Presbyterian Church in Washington, facing the Lincoln pew, would reveal a deep abhorrence: "Our lamented President fell in the theatre. Had he been murdered in his bed, or in his office, or on the street, or on the steps of the Capitol, the tidings of his death would not have struck the Christian heart of the country quite so painfully; for the feeling of that heart is that the theatre is one of the last places to which a good man should go."

Parts of the loathing undoubtedly Lincoln had heard from the pulpit, Dr. Gurley saying: "I have always regarded the theatre as in the main a school of vice and corruption—the illumined and decorated gateway through which thousands are constantly passing into the embrace of gaiety and folly, intemperance and lewdness, infamy and ruin. I have always hated and avoided it, and taught my children to avoid it."

One Reverend Dr. Duffield of Detroit, however, rivaled Dr. Gurley: "Would that Mr. Lincoln had fallen elsewhere than at the very gates of Hell—in the theater to which, through persuasion, he reluctantly went." The Reverend L. M. Glover in Jacksonville, Illinois, would rather it had occurred "in the street, in the council chamber, in the national museum or even the sanctuary of God."

That Lincoln, without being an affiliated churchman, had by a natural reverence, without affectation, won his way to many hearts of the clergy was evident in pulpit tributes paid him. In Boston the Reverend Samuel K. Lothrop mourned: "Brethren, but one theme can command your attention today . . . I feel almost incompetent to direct your thoughts this morning, as I have scarcely been able for the last twenty-four hours to collect and guide my own. Language is impotent." Over and again were the parallels drawn of Lincoln and Christ in blood of atonement dying for mankind, of Lincoln having his Judas no less than Christ. "The last and costliest offering which God demanded has been taken," said the Reverend C. B. Crane of the South Baptist Church of Hartford, Connecticut. "Jesus Christ died for the world, Abraham Lincoln died for his country."

Octavius Brooks Frothingham, pastor of the Third Congregational Unitarian Society in New York City, saw Lincoln as far spent. The people were sorrowing now not because of the crime but because they had lost a friend they loved simply as a man. "His belongings were nothing; dignities would not stick to him. His personal qualities protruded from his official skin, as the angular lines of his figure did from his court dress—as the bones of his great hands did from his kid gloves. The costumer, official or other, could make nothing of him. He was a character—not a doll. The decorators tried their hands on him in vain.

"The country does not go wild over him; it silently weeps for him; it does not celebrate him as a demigod—it mourns for him as a friend. He let the people work through him; and in his own esteem held a high place enough when he acted as an organ and an instrument. Such humility almost passes understanding—it runs into self-forgetfulness; it borders even on saintliness. He hoped little, expected nothing. A man of low temperament and sad nature, he worked and waited, waited and worked, bearing all things, enduring all things, but neither believing all things nor all things happening; bearing and enduring oh how much! even from his friends. What a history was written on that care-worn and furrowed face—of suffering accepted, sorrow entertained, emotions buried, and duty done!"

In scores of sermons was sounded the note of doom for the Southern leaders, for those who incarnated what the Reverend E. B. Webb of Boston termed "the same hell-born spirit that dastardly takes the life of our beloved President." Too long had "a driveling, morbid, perverted sense of justice" been permitted under the shadow of the Capitol at Washington. "It makes me shudder." Thus Mr. Webb in his Easter Sunday sermon stood in horror at the animating spirit of Lincoln in the Louisiana speech of April 11 and the final counsels with the Cabinet on April 14.

Many sermons and editorials likened Lincoln to Moses on Mount Pisgah, each taken away after the hard desert journey—and the Promised Land in sight. The Reverend J. M. Manning of Boston when he considered that Mr. Lincoln "disliked the sight of blood," that Mr. Lincoln "was melted by tears," that Mr. Lincoln was "made soft as woman by the tones of pleading wretchedness," said he would not attempt to scan the counsels of the Most High, though he must confess: "Perhaps it is better for us that we should be orphans today, than that he whom we loved to call 'Father' should have been spared. His paternal heart, had it still throbbed in life, might have proved too tender for the stern work we are yet to do." The Reverend W. S. Studley of Boston cried for multiple hangings of Southern traitors, and declared from the pulpit: "In dealing with traitors, Andrew Johnson's little finger will be thicker than Abraham Lincoln's loins. If the *old* president chastised them with whips, the *new* president will chastise them with scorpions."

In scores of sermons before large congregations of the well-to-do and influential, radicals pressed the need for trials and hangings of Southern leaders. In the Protestant churches of Boston such clergymen were in a large majority of the pulpits. In other cities and communities, however, the clergy in the main humbly held themselves to spiritual ministration and kept out of politics. The Reverend Edward Everett Hale in his Unitarian Church in Boston intimated that in the passions of the hour, including his own, it behooved good men to think twice and speak slow: "I dare not trust myself to speak a word regarding this simple, godly, good, great man . . . To speak of him I must seek some other hour." Mr. Hale saw the Republic as eternal, ready to live through successive assassinations, ending his sermon, "Fear not, little flock; it is your Father's good pleasure to give you the kingdom."

In like tone with the living Lincoln were many of the sermons in Roman Catholic churches and in Hebrew synagogues. "We pray," said Archbishop McCloskey in St. Patrick's Cathedral, New York, "that the sentiments of mercy and clemency and conciliation that so filled the heart of the beloved

President whom we have just lost will still actuate and guide the breast of him who, in this critical and trying hour, is called to fill his place."

Henry Ward Beecher threw himself with a flowing vitality into the occasion. Nothing now of that remark of his in Charleston a few days earlier that Johnson's little finger was stronger than Lincoln's loins. Beecher's Easter Sunday congregation in Plymouth Church, Brooklyn, filled all pews and added chairs in the aisles. Hundreds outside had failed to get in, scores had climbed up on the window sills to stand and listen. Beecher pointed to the murderer as one suckled and nursed in the slave system and its cruel and boisterous passions. Never would men forget that the slavery institution with its "mischiefs and monsters" had martyred one American President. "Never! while time lasts, while heaven lasts, while hell rocks and groans." The most often reprinted passage from sermons of this Easter Sunday was Beecher's closing. He pictured a coffined martyr moving in triumphal march, with cities and states as pallbearers, bells and cannon beating the hours. He intoned a dead march:

"Pass on, thou that has overcome! Your sorrows, oh people, are his peace! Your bells, and bands, and muffled drums, sound triumph in his ear. Wail and weep here; God made it echo joy and triumph there. Pass on!

"Four years ago, oh Illinois, we took from your midst an untried man, and from among the people. We return him to you a mighty conqueror. Not thine anymore, but the nation's; not ours, but the world's.

"Give him place, oh, ye prairies! In the midst of this great continent his dust shall rest, a sacred treasure to myriads who shall pilgrim to that shrine to kindle anew their zeal and patriotism.

"Ye winds that move over the mighty places of the West, chant his requiem! Ye people, behold a martyr whose blood, as so many articulate words, pleads for fidelity, for law, for liberty!"

Miss Anna Dickinson in her Academy of Music speech in Philadelphia cried for punishment of the Southern leaders. "Their crimes have rendered them unworthy of the respect of honest men." Where few or none in the North had gone beyond naming Jefferson Davis as suitable for the gallows, Miss Dickinson included General Robert E. Lee. She spoke of Lincoln's assassin and added, "Of the two, Lee is a viler murderer." In the tumult Wendell Phillips was saying nothing. He too could have moved the pools of public emotion. The event was involved. He would have one brief comment. Granted that Lincoln was a great oak. "We watered him," said Wendell Phillips, the agitator.

In black-border crape typography, in editorial comment, letters, poetical effusions, the newspapers went along with the public grief. The weekly periodicals, the monthly magazines, these too wore crape in the national mood. An issue of the New York *Herald* with its remarkable extended biographical sketch and its thorough news coverage in Washington sold out 15 minutes after its arrival. The price for an obtainable copy in Washington next day was $10. Under the heading "The Great Crime—Abraham Lincoln's Place in History" the *Herald* on April 17 published a shrewd and lavish portrayal. He was a *new* figure. All other nations of the human family would study him "as the type man of a new dynasty of nation-rulers," holding that "the best and strongest rule for every intelligent people is a government to be created by the popular will, and choosing for itself the representative in-strument who is to carry out its purposes." Gravely the *Herald*, naturally conservative though responsive to both property rights and human move-ments, noted: "The triumph of the democratic principle over the aristocratic in our recent contest is an assurance that time has revolved this old earth on which we live into a new and perhaps happier—perhaps sadder—era."

Lincoln was baffling, found the *Herald*. The more one gazed on him, the less easy it became to reckon what would be the end of his teachings. He was democracy beyond Cromwell or Napoleon, so completely modern that his like was not to be found in the past, "a character so externally uncouth, so pathetically simple, so unfathomably penetrating, so irresolute and yet so irresistible, so bizarre, grotesque, droll, wise and perfectly beneficent . . . It will take a new school of historians to do justice to this eccentric addition to the world's gallery of heroes; for while other men as interesting and original may have held equal power previously in other countries, it is only in the present age of steam, telegraphs and prying newspaper reporters that a sub-ject so eminent, both by genius and position, could have been placed under the eternal microscope of critical examination."

George William Curtis in *Harper's Weekly* was sure that those who knew Lincoln personally now felt "that the deep, furrowed sadness of his face seemed to forecast his fate." The nation had lost him, but it was something that he had lived to see daybreak. "He saw farther and deeper than others because he saw that in the troubled time upon which he was cast little could be wholly seen . . . he acquired a curious ascendency in the public confi-dence; so that if good men differed from his opinion they were inclined to doubt their own."

An old proverb known to woodsmen was fitting: "A tree is best measured when it's down." Often came the statement that over the world the whole civilized Family of Man shared in regrets or grief for the loss of a hero who belonged to humanity everywhere. The story of the living and actual Lin-coln had come to an end. Now began the vast epic tale of the authentic Lincoln tradition mingled with legend, myth, folklore. Believers and atheists, those of fixed doctrine or the freethinkers—both were to argue he was theirs. Letters and pamphlets were to picture him as Freemason or Spiritualist, as Protestant or Catholic or Jew or having Negro blood in his veins. The tee-totalers were to claim properly he was theirs because he never drank alcoholic liquors; the saloon crowd amid the sawdust and the spittoons were to say his stories alone put him in their class. Some had one sweeping claim: "He was humanity."

Lost in the huge and swelling choral acclaim were the few who agreed with the imperialist and Tory organ of London, the *Standard*, saying on April 21: "He was not a hero while he lived, and therefore his cruel murder does not make him a martyr." Of more import than the continued muddling and arrogance of the *Times* was the simple confession of the *Pall Mall Gazette:* "He was our best friend. He never lent himself to the purposes of that foolish and wicked minority which tried to set enmity between America and Eng-land. He never said or wrote an unfriendly word about us." Among the people of England, the masses whose sentiment kept the government from recognizing the Southern Confederacy, the mourning was genuine.

A letter to Mrs. Lincoln signed by Victoria Regina was deeply personal, woman to woman, the Queen saying: "No one can better appreciate than I can, who am myself *utterly broken-hearted* by the loss of my own beloved husband, who was the *light* of my life, my stay—*my all*—what your suffering must be; and I earnestly pray that you may be supported by Him to whom alone the sorely stricken can look for comfort." The House of Lords joined in an official address of sympathy to the American people.

In the French Senate and Chamber of Deputies imperialists and republicans joined in formal expressions of grief. A massive gold medal, bought with two-cent subscriptions from masses of people, was brought to the American Minister by a committee of liberals. It was for Mrs. Lincoln, with their message, "Tell her the heart of France is in that little box." In Germany many *Bunds* and *Vereins*, workingmen's clubs, co-operative societies, labor journals, spoke their loss. In Austria one parliamentary deputy noted a human memory taking on "supernatural proportions," Lincoln becoming "a myth, a type of the ideal democracy."

In Sweden flags were ordered at half-mast on the ships in harbor at Göteborg and there were expressions as in the *Nya Daglig Allehanda* of Stockholm: "It is a beautiful death, and Lincoln forever will be surrounded by the rays of impeccable glory. The time for impartial judgment will not come for many years." And in the harbor of Stockholm flags hung at half-mast on all ships. Excitement and sorrow rooted partly in Swedish sentiment over the victory of the *Monitor*, designed by John Ericsson and carrying guns invented by Admiral John Adolph Dahlgren. One observer wrote: "Our men clenched their fists in vain fury and our blue-eyed women shed many tears in memory of the remarkable man." In the harbors of Norwegian cities also flags were at half-mast. Thousands in that country had blood relations in Wisconsin and Minnesota regiments. Young Henrik Ibsen in a flowing turbulent poem, "The Murder of Abraham Lincoln," challenged Europe's right to mourn over the passing of the foremost son of democracy in the Western world.

In the Orient, China, Japan and Siam framed resolutions of condolence. To the four corners of the earth began the spread of the Lincoln story and legend. What he seemed to mean was reached for, Russia's Leo Tolstoy saying Lincoln had become a world folk legend through "peculiar moral powers and greatness of character . . . He was what Beethoven was in music, Dante in poetry, Raphael in painting and Christ in the philosophy of life. If he had failed to become President, he would be no doubt just as great, but only God could appreciate it." Of all great national heroes and statesmen of history Tolstoy was to say to the journalist James Creelman, "Lincoln is the only real giant." He named heroes but they were lesser than Lincoln "in depth of feeling and in certain moral power." Mystic shadows and a bright aura gathered around Lincoln's memory for the famous Russian. "Lincoln was . . . a Christ in miniature, a saint of humanity whose name will live thousands of years in the legends of future generations. We are still too near his greatness, and so can hardly appreciate his divine power; but after a few centuries more our posterity will find him considerably bigger than we do."

Lincoln, in Emerson's analysis, grew according to need. In the whirlwind of the war he was "no holiday magistrate, no fair-weather sailor . . . He is the true history of the American people in his time. Step by step he walked before them; slow with their slowness, quickening his march by theirs, the true representative of this continent; an entirely public man; father of his country."

The suave diplomat John Bigelow believed that in ordinary peacetime conditions Lincoln would have been a very ordinary President. In a wild crisis calling for a man deep in moral issues, the nation found Lincoln "even as the son of Kish found a crown while searching for his father's asses." His greatness was peculiar. "He was so modest by nature that he was perfectly content to walk behind any man who wished to walk before him . . . St. Paul hardly endured more indignities and buffetings without complaint."

Lincoln had stood as the national Fate, amid violence that was the shortest cut to a common Union of destiny for the states. Thus the Brazilian Minister Joaquin Nabuco who said, "I construe to myself that War as one of those illusions of life, in which men seem to move of their own free will, while they are really playing a tragedy composed by a Providence intent on saving their nation." Lincoln, as the leading player in the drama, "saw distinctly that the South was not a nationality, and that it could not think of being one, except during the hallucination of the crisis." In the velocities of modern change, the year 2000 would be governed by currents of political thought impossible to read. "But, whether the spirit of authority, or that of freedom, increases, Lincoln's legend will ever appear more luminous in the amalgamation of centuries, because he supremely incarnated both those spirits."

Walt Whitman would have blossoms and green branches piled on the coffin—armfuls of roses fresh as the morning—in loaded arms sprigs of lilac just off the bushes—brought and poured on the coffin. He would study sea-blown cities and moving harbor ships, the changing lights of the Ohio River shores and the flashing bosom of the wide Missouri, far-spreading prairies covered with grass and corn—he would in his psalm bring these to the coffin. He would consider the miracle of light so gentle and soft-born from the most excellent sun so calm and haughty—evening and the welcome of night and the stars—these too he would carry along in a threnody of praise to death —lovely and soothing death—the sure-enwinding arms of cool-enfolding death. He had listened to a hermit thrush singing in solemn shadowy cedars and still ghostly pines—under the evening star a carol of death with praise of its serene arrival and its husky whispering to "the huge and thoughtful night." This too he would bring to the coffin as his offertory and benediction, his chant of sane and sacred death. He gave it the title "When Lilacs Last in the Dooryard Bloom'd," in a closing line inscribing it "for the sweetest, wisest soul of all my days and lands—and this for his dear sake."

In thousands of commentaries Lincoln incarnated two results—Emancipation and Union. Two causes directed by Lincoln had won the war. Gone was the property status of the Negro, gone the doctrine of secession and states' rights. Black men could now move from where they were miserable to where they were equally miserable—now it was lawful for them to move. Now too for the Negro no longer was it a crime for him to be found reading a book nor was it any longer a crime to teach a Negro to read.

Now, too, as Lincoln had pledged, a whole mesh of trammels and clamps on Western migration were to be cut loose. The many homesteaders held back by political bickering could get going. And the Union Pacific railway could begin laying its rails; the jealousies suffocating it were out. With almost explosive force the industrial, financial and transportation systems of the North could be let loose, free to go. The war had done that. Now also, as a result flowing from the war, the United States was to take its place among nations counted World Powers. And as a World Power the expectation was it would be a voice of the teachings of Washington, Jefferson, Jackson—and Lincoln—speaking for republican government, for democracy.

Out of the smoke and stench, out of the music and violet dreams of the war, Lincoln stood perhaps taller than any other of the many great heroes. This was in the mind of many. None threw a longer shadow than he. And to him the great hero was The People. He could not say too often that he was merely their instrument.

CHAPTER 69

Vast Pageant, Then Great Quiet

IN THE East Room of the White House lay the body of a man, embalmed and prepared for a journey. On a platform under a canopy of folds and loops of black silk and crape rested the coffin. Tassels, shamrock leaves, silver stars and silver cords could be seen on facings and edges. A shield with a silver plate had the inscription:

Abraham Lincoln
Sixteenth President of the United States
Born Feb. 12, 1809
Died April 15, 1865

It was Tuesday, April 18, and outside surged the largest mass of people that had ever thronged the White House lawn, the estimate 25,000. In two columns they filed through the East Room, moving along the two sides of the coffin, many pale and limping soldiers out of the convalescent wards of the hospitals, many women and children sobbing and weeping aloud as they passed, pausing only the slightest moment for a look.

On Wednesday, April 19, arrived 60 clergymen, the Cabinet members, the Supreme Court Justices, important officials, foreign Ministers, General Grant with white sash across his breast, the new President Andrew Johnson—600 dignitaries in all. Mrs. Lincoln was still too distracted to be present, but Robert Lincoln came.

Bishop Matthew Simpson of the Methodist Episcopal church offered prayer that smitten hearts might endure, might not be called upon for further sacrifices. A bitter cup from the hand of a chastening Divine Father had been given the mourning nation, said the Reverend Dr. Phineas D. Gurley in the funeral address. "His way is in the sea, and His path in the great waters; and His footsteps are not known . . . We bow, we weep, we worship . . . We will wait for His interpretation . . . He may purify us more in the furnace of trial, but He will not consume us."

The closing invocation was spoken by a Baptist clergyman, chaplain of the U.S. Senate, the Reverend Dr. E. H. Gray. The final ceremonial words spoken in the White House over the mute form of the author of the second inaugural and the Louisiana reconstruction speech of April 11 were: "O God, let treason, that has deluged our land with blood, and devastated our country, and bereaved our homes, and filled them with widows and orphans, and has at length culminated in the assassination of the nation's chosen ruler—God of justice, and avenger of the nation's wrong, let the work of treason cease, and let the guilty author of this horrible crime be arrested and brought to justice."

The services were over. The pallbearers took the silver handles. The bong of big bells on cathedrals struck and the little bells of lesser steeples chimed in, as across the spring sunshine came the tolling of all the church bells of Washington and Georgetown, and Alexandria across the river. Counting the minutes with their salutes came the hoarse boom of fort guns encircling the national capital and several batteries sent into the city.

Out of the great front door of the Executive Mansion for the last time went the mortal shape of Abraham Lincoln, 16th President of the United States. On the one-mile route to the Capitol, pavements and curbs were packed with onlookers, who also filled every roof, window, doorway, balcony and stairway. Sixty thousand spectators watched a parade of 40,000 mourners. From his sickbed, sore with his dagger wounds, Secretary Seward gazed from the window with mingled grief and thanks.

In the rotunda of the Capitol, under the great white dome that had come to its finished construction while the war raged, 12 sergeants of the Veteran Reserve Corps carried the coffin to a huge catafalque.

In silence during night watches the body of Lincoln lay with eyes never opening to see far above him the arches of the great dome that for him symbolized the Union. In the night watches while the guard mount changed, whispering, quiet on soft feet, into midnight and past into daybreak, midway between House and Senate chambers, midway between those seats and aisles of heartbreak and passion, he lay a horizontal clay tabernacle.

In the morning at ten o'clock the doors opened in special consideration for wounded soldiers from the hospitals, weak and battered men, some with empty sleeves, others on crutches, to file by. Afterward came the public, at times 3,000 to the hour, before midnight 25,000 persons.

Friday morning, April 21, saw the coffin placed aboard a special burial car at the Washington depot. Railroad-yard engine bells tolled and a far-stretching crowd stood with uncovered heads as the train of seven cars moved out of Washington for Baltimore.

This was the start of a funeral journey that was to take the lifeless body on a 1,700-mile route which included practically the same points and stops that the living form had made four years and two months before on the way to the first inauguration. Aboard the coaches were five men who had made that earlier journey: Colonel Ward Hill Lamon, Justice David Davis, General David Hunter, John G. Nicolay and John Hay. A committee of Senate and House members included Washburne, Yates and Arnold of Illinois, Harlan of Iowa and Julian of Indiana. Mrs. Lincoln, Robert and Tad were to undergo an ordeal; with them was their kinsman Ninian W. Edwards. The Illinois delegation aboard included Lincoln's first law partner John T. Stuart and such Sucker State familiars as Lyman Trumbull, William Bross, Jesse K. Dubois, Shelby M. Cullom and General John A. McClernand. Among state governors aboard were Oglesby of Illinois, Morton of Indiana, Brough of Ohio, Stone of Iowa.

Baltimore wore mourning everywhere and paid reverence; the human outpouring was unmistakable. More than surface changes had come to Maryland in the four furnace years. As the funeral train moved slowly over Pennsylvania soil, at lonely country crossroads were people and faces, horsemen, farmers with their wives and children, standing where they had stood for hours before, waiting, performing the last little possible act of ceremony and attention and love—with solemn faces and uncovered heads standing and gazing as the funeral car passed. In villages and small towns stood waiting crowds, sometimes with a little silver cornet band, often with flowers in hope the train might stop and they could leave camellias, roses, lilies-of-the-valley, wreaths of color and perfume. At York in a short stop six ladies came aboard and laid a three-foot wreath of red and white roses on the coffin.

Through heavy rains at Harrisburg came 30,000 in the night and morning to see the coffin in circles of white flowering almond. At noon on Saturday, April 22, in Philadelphia a half-million people were on hand for the funeral train. In Independence Hall stood the coffin. Outside the line of mourners ran three miles. "A young lady had her arm broken," said the New York *Herald*, "and a young child, involved in the crush, is said to have been killed. Many females fainted with exhaustion, and had to be carried off by their friends." Besides doors, through two windows in a double column a third of a million people entered and passed by the casket. A venerable Negro woman, her face indented and majestic as a relief map of the continent of Asia, laid evergreens on the coffin and with hot tears filling the dents and furrows, cried, "Oh, Abraham Lincoln, are you dead? Are you dead?" She could not be sure.

At Newark, New Jersey, on the morning of April 24 the train moved slowly amid acres of people, a square mile of them. At Jersey City was a like scene. The Empire State formally received the body from Governor Parker of New Jersey. A hearse moved through street crowds. The ferryboat *Jersey City* moved across the Hudson River, neared the wharf at Desbrosses Street. The Seventh Regiment National Guard formed a hollow square into which moved the funeral cortege. The procession marched to the City Hall through streets packed to capacity.

Never before, so everyone agreed, had New York put on such garb and completely changed its look so that it seemed another city. On the marble and brownstone fronts, in the ramshackle tenements of "those who live from hand to mouth," came out crape or black folds or drapery or black muslin, rosettes, sable emblems, what the news reporters termed "the habiliments of mourning."

From near noon Monday, April 24, to noon the next day the remains of Abraham Lincoln, horizontal amid white satin, lay in the City Hall. A vast outpouring of people hour by hour passed by to see this effigy and remembrance of his face and form. They came for many and varied reasons. Hundreds who had helped wreck, burn and loot this city, killing scores of policemen and Negroes in the draft and race riots of year before last, came now with curiosity, secret triumph, hate and contempt, a story traveling Manhattan that one entered a saloon hangout of their breed, saying, "I went down to the City Hall to see with my own eyes and be sure he was dead." An overwhelming many came as an act of faith and attestation; they had come to love him and follow him. The few women who sought to kiss his face were hurriedly moved on by the guards. Each might have had some sufficient reason; most of the boys at Malvern Hill and Gettysburg had mothers.

At noon on Tuesday, April 25, a procession moved from the City Hall to Ninth Avenue and the Hudson River Railroad depot. Nearly every race, nationality, religion, political faith, was represented among those who marched, near 100,000. The troops in Union Army blue alone numbered 20,000. The panoramic show took hours. It was massive, bizarre, spectacular, dazzling—yet somber. A hundred thousand strangers had come to New York to see it. The sidewalk, street, curb and window spectators ran perhaps to a million. At the procession's end came a delegation of 2,000 Negroes, some wearing the Union Army service blue. There had been mutterings from a draft- and race-riot element that they would "never let the damned niggers march." This would have interested the man in the hearse, could he have heard it. It was customary and expected. A telegram to General Dix spoke plain that the Secretary of War desired "no discrimination respecting color." And it was so ordered. At the Union Square exercises following the parade the Roman Catholic Archbishop McCloskey pronounced the benediction, Rabbi Isaacs of the Jewish Synagogue read from their scriptures, the Reverend Stephen H. Tyng of St. George's Church offered a prayer, the Reverend J. P. Thompson intoned Lincoln's second inaugural. Evening had come.

An epidemic of verse seized thousands. They sent their rhymed lines to the New York *Herald*, which publicly notified them that if it were all printed there would be no space for news, wherefore none at all would be printed. The Chicago *Tribune* editorially notified them it "suffered" from this "severe attack of poetry," that three days brought 160 pieces beginning either "Toll, toll, ye mourning bells" or "Mourn, mourn, ye tolling bells."

Up the Hudson River east bank the night of April 25 chugged the train of seven cars. On every mile of the route to Albany those on the train could see bonfires and torches, could hear bells and cannon and guns, could see forms of people and white sorry faces. Past midnight of April 25 into the morning hours of April 26 the columns of mourners passed the coffin in Albany.

On this morning of April 26, hunted like a wild beast and cornered like a rat, his broken shinbone betraying him, J. Wilkes Booth met his end. Near Bowling Green, Virginia, in a burning barn set afire from the outside, a bullet drove through his neck bone "perforating both sides of the collar," and he was dragged away from reaching flames and laid under a tree. Water was given him. He revived, to murmur from parched lips, "Tell my mother—

I died—for my country." He was carried to a house veranda, there muttering, "I thought I did for the best." He lingered for a time. A doctor came. Wilkes Booth asked that his hands might be raised so that he could look at them. So it was told. And as he looked on his hands, he mumbled hoarsely, "Useless! useless!" And those were his last words.

Across the Empire State that day and night it was mural monotone of mourning, the Erie Canal zone in sober grief with evergreens, flowers, sable emblems. The endless multitudinous effect became colossal. Thirty-six young ladies, gowned in white with black shoulder scarfs and the flag of their country, approached the dazzling when seen for the first time. But when seen and noted the 20th, 30th, 40th time, they took on a ritualist solemnity smoldering and portentous. Involved was the basis of the stubborn passion that had carried on four years of the bloodiest war known to mankind.

At Buffalo Millard Fillmore, one of the three living ex-Presidents of the United States, attended the funeral, which also was witnessed by the youth Grover Cleveland.

Reports had been published that the face in the coffin was shrunken and decayed to such an extent that perhaps good taste should forbid further exposure of it to public gaze. The embalmer on the train had several times by his craft wrought improvement. However this might be, there came from Toledo an old friend and a valued comforter of Lincoln, David R. Locke, who wrote under the pen name of Petroleum V. Nasby. He wrote now: "I saw him, or what was mortal of him in his coffin. The face had an expression of absolute content, of relief, at throwing off a burden such as few men have been called upon to bear—a burden which few men could have borne. I had seen the same expression on his living face only a few times, when, after a great calamity, he had come to a great victory. It was the look of a worn man suddenly relieved. Wilkes Booth did Abraham Lincoln the greatest service man could possibly do for him—he gave him peace."

At Cleveland the committee on arrangements had a pagoda put up in the city park, with open sides through which two columns could pass the coffin. Over the coffin Bishop Charles Pettit McIlvaine read from the Episcopal burial service. At ten o'clock when the park gates were shut it was said that more than 1,000,000 pilgrims from northern Ohio had paid their homage. A lashing wind drove torrents of rain as the night procession moved escorting the hearse through crowded streets to the depot.

From Cleveland to Crestline the rain kept on in torrents. Nevertheless at all towns and crossroads were the mourners, with uncovered heads, with torches and flags crossed with black. Five miles out from Columbus stood an old woman alone as the slow train came by, tears coursing down her furrowed cheeks. In her right hand she held out a black mourning scarf. With her left hand she stretched imploringly toward the rain-and-storm-bedraggled funeral car, reaching and waving toward it her handful of wild flowers, her bouquet and token.

In the rotunda of Ohio's capitol, on a mound of green moss dotted with white flowers, rested the coffin on April 28, while 8,000 persons passed by each hour from 9:30 in the morning till four in the afternoon. In the changing red-gold of a rolling prairie sunset, to the slow exultation of brasses rendering "Old Hundred" and the muffled booming of minute guns, the coffin was carried out of the rotunda and taken to the funeral train. It was now two weeks since the evening hour that Abraham Lincoln cheery and alive had left the White House in Washington to attend a performance in Ford's Theatre, and from his carriage had taken a final casual glance at the Executive Mansion where he had lived four years and 41 days.

The slow night run from Columbus to Indianapolis saw from the car windows a countryside of people thronging to the route of the coffin. At Pleasant Valley were bonfires. Nearly every town had its arch of evergreens, flags and black drapings. At Urbana ten young women strewed roses on the coffin, one of them breaking down in uncontrollable tears. At Piqua were 10,000 at midnight; at Richmond, Indiana, 10,000 again at three o'clock in the morning.

Tolling bells and falling rain at Indianapolis saw the coffin borne into the State House for a Sabbath to be remembered. On the slow night run to Chicago it was as in Ohio, thousands in Lafayette standing mute and daybreak not yet, thousands more at Michigan City. Now over flat lands ran the slow train, between it and the blue levels of Lake Michigan the long slopes of pine-crept dunes.

The day was Monday, May 1, but in effect the Chicago obsequies had begun the day before when Speaker Colfax delivered in Bryant Hall a formal funeral oration. To his portrait of Lincoln as the most forgiving of men Colfax joined allegations of Confederate atrocities: they had at Bull Run buried Union soldiers face downward and carved their bones into trinkets; they had wickedly and systematically starved Union prisoners to death. Colfax was for his own purposes still fomenting war hate and metaphorically waving a bloody shirt of incitation.

In the changed tone of the Chicago *Times* could be read the fact that among those who would gaze into the Lincoln coffin with a sincere grief this day would be at least a remnant of Copperheads. "There are not on this day mourners more sincere than the democracy of the Northern States. Widely as they have differed with Mr. Lincoln . . . they saw in the indications of the last few days of his life that he might command their support."

By railway train, by wagon or buggy and on horseback, something like 100,000 people had come into Chicago from all points of the Northwest. The vocal attempts at solemn grief often failed and were overdone. But there was a silent grief—broken only by choked snufflings, by low wailings, by almost inaudible moans—a loss afraid of words. There was a curious dumb sorrow, perhaps deeper than any other.

Slowly at Twelfth Street and Michigan Avenue the funeral train came to a stop. A procession of 50,000 people, witnessed by double as many, escorted the hearse to the courthouse. Not hitherto, however, had any Confederate soldiers marched—though here was a regiment of Confederate prisoners of war who had taken the oath of allegiance and aligned themselves for Union service. In the line of march and looking on, sharing something common, were native-born Yankees and Mayflower descendants, Sons and Daughters of the Revolution, Jews, Negroes, Catholics, Germans, Irishmen, Dutchmen, Swedes, Norwegians, Danes—the so-called "big bugs" and the so-called "ragtag and bobtail" for once in a common front.

A drizzle of rain fell, the streets slushy with a slippery mud. Occasionally planks or supporting two-by-fours of the wooden sidewalks crashed with spectators. Women fainted and two-horse ambulances came. Barkeepers were busy. So were pickpockets. The police-station cells were filled. Considering the extent of the swarming human crush, however, the day was orderly, even sedate.

All night long Monday, and through the early morning hours and all the day hours of Tuesday, the columns moved in and out of the courthouse. An estimated 125,000 people had taken their last glance at the Man from Illinois. A thousand men with blazing torches escorted the coffin to the funeral car for the slow night run to Springfield on the Alton Railroad.

At Joliet were midnight torches, evergreen arches, 12,000 people. Every town and village, many a crossroads and lonely farm, spoke its mournful salutation. Here and there an arch or a depot doorway had the short flash "Come Home."

Then at last home to Springfield. In the state capitol where he had spoken his prophet warnings of the House Divided, stood the casket. Now passed those who had known him long, part of the 75,000 who came. They were awed, subdued, shaken, stony, strange. They came from Salem, Petersburg, Clary's Grove, Alton, Charleston, Mattoon, the old Eighth Circuit towns and villages. There were clients for whom he had won or lost, lawyers who had tried cases with him and against, neighbors who had seen him milk a cow and curry his horse, friends who had heard his stories around a hot stove and listened to his surmises on politics and religion. All day long and through the night the unbroken line moved, the home town having its farewell.

On May 4 of this year 1865 anno Domini a procession moved with its hearse from the state capitol to Oak Ridge Cemetery. There on green banks and hillsides flowing away from a burial vault the crowded thousands of listeners and watchers heard prayers and hymns, heard the second inaugural read aloud. Bishop Matthew Simpson in a moving oration spoke as an in-

The burial vault at Springfield

terpreter and foreteller: "There are moments which involve in themselves eternities. There are instants which seem to contain germs which shall develop and bloom forever. Such a moment came in the tide of time to our land when a question must be settled, affecting all the powers of the earth. The contest was for human freedom. Not for this republic merely, not for the Union simply, but to decide whether the people, as a people, in their entire majesty, were destined to be the Governments or whether they were to be subject to tyrants or aristocrats, or to class rule of any kind. This is the great question for which we have been fighting, and its decision is at hand, and the result of this contest will affect the ages to come. If successful, republics will spread in spite of monarchs all over this earth." Came then from the people, noted the *Illinois State Journal*, exclamations of "Amen! thank God!"

Evergreen carpeted the stone floor of the vault. On the coffin set in a receptacle of black walnut they arranged flowers carefully and precisely, they poured flowers as symbols, they lavished heaps of fresh flowers as though there could never be enough to tell either their hearts or his.

And the night came with great quiet.

And there was rest.

The prairie years, the war years, were over.

SOURCES AND ACKNOWLEDGMENTS

The chief center of the research on the life of Lincoln before he became President was the Abraham Lincoln Association with its office in Springfield, Illinois, with funds subscribed by a national membership and with outside grants. From 1933 through 1941 the Association published four volumes, each giving "the day-by-day activities of Abraham Lincoln," where he was and what he was doing, so far as known by documents. Harry Pratt's two volumes, *Lincoln Day By Day 1809-1839* and *1840-1846*, are followed by Benjamin P. Thomas' for *1847-1853* and by Paul Angle's for *1854-1861*—the four books making a massive, formidable work that will be of use as long as there are sober and anxious students of Lincoln. Approaching the colossal is the nine-volume edition sponsored by the Association, published in 1953, *The Collected Works of Abraham Lincoln*. Heavy, exacting and thorough were the five-year labors of Roy P. Basler, editor, and Marion Dolores Pratt and Lloyd A. Dunlap, assistant editors. Their texts of letters, speeches, documents, are from originals or photostats of originals, except in a few instances which they report and discuss. This carefully documented assemblage of Lincoln utterance is possibly the best historical account by any one man on how and why the titanic war of 1861-1865 arose and was carried through. This utterance record of more than a million words holds the keys or clues to the subtle, wide-ranging personality of Lincoln more than any other work to be read and studied. A large one-volume compilation with an able biographical introduction is *The Life and Writings of Abraham Lincoln* (1940) by Philip Van Doren Stern. The most useful, well-annotated single volume in this field is *Abraham Lincoln: His Speeches and Writings* (1946) by Roy P. Basler.

From the Abraham Lincoln Association group and its associates came monographs revealing forgeries of four Lincoln letters printed earlier in books of reputation; they published evidence that the marble-enshrined log cabin at Hodgenville, Kentucky, is not the real and actual birth-cabin of Lincoln but rests on a tissue of traditions; they re-examined the legend of Ann Rutledge and Lincoln, made a strong case that the "romance" rested on conjecture and assumption while the often related grief and borderline insanity of Lincoln at her death were improbable. The Association reproduced in facsimile in 1938 a campaign biography, *Life of Abraham Lincoln* by W. D. Howells, with 14 corrections made by Lincoln's pencil in the summer of 1860; the value of such a book is in the corrections written in it and also in the bulk of statements that Lincoln let stand as fact.

Benjamin P. Thomas' book, *Lincoln's New Salem* (1934), brought to bear his long familiarity with that frontier community; it is the classic on Lincoln's "Alma Mater." Paul M. Angle's *Here I Have Lived: A History of Lincoln's*

Springfield 1821-1865 (1935) is a master report on Lincoln's home town. William E. Baringer's three volumes, *Lincoln's Vandalia* (1949), *Lincoln's Rise to Power* (1935), *A House Dividing* (1945), represent fresh research, especially on Lincoln in the Illinois Legislature and the intricacies of politics leading to Lincoln's nomination for President in 1860. A research not made thitherto appears in Donald W. Riddle's *Lincoln Runs for Congress* (1948). Harry Pratt's *Concerning Mr. Lincoln: In Which Abraham Lincoln Is Pictured as He Appeared to Letter Writers of His Time* (1944) gives swift and fleeting personal glimpses of Lincoln. Pratt's larger work, *Personal Finances of Abraham Lincoln* (1943), covers more ground than any previous studies of Lincoln's earnings and spendings and his sense about money. From the Abraham Lincoln Association, disbanded in 1953, for nearly 30 years there poured forth bulletins, books, a quarterly magazine, threshing out major and minor phases of the Lincoln story. Logan Hay, who died in 1942, is cherished as the founder and an ever-dynamic force in the Association.

All of the aforementioned books and publications came to print since I was writing *Abraham Lincoln: The Prairie Years*. Also in this period have come the important volumes of James G. Randall, *Lincoln the President: From Springfield to Gettysburg*, two volumes (1945) and *Lincoln the President: Midstream* (1952), this latter one of the most profound and charming studies of Lincoln. His *Lincoln and the South* (1945) and *Lincoln the Liberal Statesman* (1947) hold his keenly searching popular lectures and essays. And it happened that "Jim" Randall, greatly beloved, constantly an inspirational force in the field of Lincoln study, was himself taken away midstream of his great work. His widow, Ruth Painter Randall, published *Mary Lincoln: Biography of a Marriage* (1953), the most elaborately and scrupulously documented narrative of the girl who became wife and widow of Lincoln. There came from David Donald a skilled and brilliant book, *Lincoln's Herndon* (1948), the first book-length biography of Lincoln's law partner for 16 years. *Diplomat in Carpet Slippers* (1945) was Jay Monaghan's floodlight on Lincoln amid foreign affairs. *Lincoln and the Patronage* (1943) by Harry J. Carman and Reinhard H. Luthin has in extensive documented detail, in wide coverage, the appetites, connivings, whispers, howls of American politics and Lincoln at center. *Lincoln and the Press* (1951) by Robert S. Harper shows the uses of printer's ink in support, praise and defamation of an American President. *Lincoln and the War Governors* (1948) by William B. Hesseltine presents the state executives with whose co-operation or antagonism Lincoln had to deal. Margaret Leech's *Reveille in Washington: 1860-1865* (1941) is a pageant of scandal, drama, heroism, vividly written.

Lawyer Lincoln (1936) by Albert A. Woldman is an advance on former treatments of Lincoln in law practice, his *Lincoln and the Russians* (1952) presenting diplomats, letters, reports. *The First Lincoln Campaign* (1944) by Reinhard H. Luthin is an original and distinctive contribution stressing the economic factors and political personalities that clashed or interwove to make Lincoln the most "available" candidate for President in 1860. Again original and distinctive, probing deep among motives, is David M. Potter's *Lincoln and His Party in the Secession Crisis* (1942). T. Harry Williams is enlightening and worth scrutiny in *Lincoln and the Radicals* (1941) and *Lincoln and His Generals* (1952). The suave, breezy, eloquent, scrupulous Kentuckian,

William H. Townsend, has given us *Lincoln and Liquor* (1934) and *Lincoln in His Wife's Home Town* (1929), besides monographs of value. The objective viewpoints of a distinguished physician are in Dr. William A. Evans' *Mrs. Abraham Lincoln: A Study of Her Personality* (1932). A professor of mathematics, a veteran of two wars, Kenneth P. Williams was fully authorized to write his massive two-volume documented study, *Lincoln Finds a General* (1950). Independent and well written is Bruce Catton's *Mr. Lincoln's Army* (1951). Fletcher Pratt's *Stanton* (1953) is a military history of the war with Stanton as a central figure. John E. Washington in *They Knew Lincoln* (1942) sketches "Billy the Barber" and other Negroes in the personal life of Lincoln. George S. Bryan's *The Great American Myth* (1940) is a re-examination of facts and inventions regarding the murder of Lincoln. *The Mad Booths of Maryland* (1940) by Stanley Kimmel renders in wealth of detail the family and environment from which came Lincoln's assassin. The meditations of an idealist in poetry and philosophy are in T. V. Smith's *Abraham Lincoln and the Spiritual Life* (1951). The new biographies, Francis Brown's *Raymond of the Times* and Helen Nicolay's *Lincoln's Secretary* (1949) have their close-ups of Lincoln, as also does the five-million word *Diary of George Templeton Strong* (1952) edited by Allan Nevins. Basic as document and highly readable is *Lincoln and the Civil War in Diaries and Letters of John Hay* (1939) by Tyler Dennett. The controversial *Herndon's Lincoln: the True Story of a Great Life* (1889) in three volumes by William H. Herndon and Jesse W. Weik became available in a one-volume edition in 1930 with an introduction and notes by Paul M. Angle which make it the one Herndon edition most worth reading. Albert J. Beveridge died in 1927 before midstream of his two volumes published in 1928, *Abraham Lincoln: 1809-1858*. Emanuel Hertz died in 1940 shortly after publication of *The Hidden Lincoln* and *Lincoln Talks*. Oliver R. Barrett died seven months after my book, *Lincoln Collector*, was published in praise of his zeal and intelligence, its pages holding now some of the unity of his notable collection later auctioned. William E. Barton died in 1930, a year after the publication of *The Lineage of Lincoln*, a book two-fifths documents chiefly related to Lincoln kinfolk. The 1860-1861 New York *Herald* newsletters of Henry Villard, with deletions, are in *Lincoln on the Eve of '61* (1941). In *The American Iliad*, Otto Eisenschiml and Ralph Newman give a narrative of the Civil War by selected eyewitnesses and contemporaries. Eisenschiml's *In the Shadow of Lincoln's Death* (1940) relentlessly asks grim unanswerable questions. In *Legends that Libel Lincoln* (1946), Montgomery S. Lewis throws corrective light on three major libels. *Lincoln's War Cabinet* (1946) is a competent study by Burton J. Hendrick. George Fort Milton's *Abraham Lincoln and the Fifth Column* (1942) covers wide ground as to "Copperheads" and treasonable activities in the North. An elusive sweetheart flits through the pages of *Lincoln's Other Mary* (1946), the facts by R. Gerald McMurtry, the fiction by Olive Carruthers.

Benjamin P. Thomas, a trained historian, a resident of Springfield familiar with all the streets and roads most often traveled by Lincoln, personally acquainted with descendants of characters who figured in Lincoln's life, in 1952 published his one-volume *Abraham Lincoln*. As a narrative and close-up portrait of Lincoln it makes use of all early source materials and also the later accumulations which he often saw in manuscript before their publication; he was one of the most active workers, and at one time secretary, of the Abraham Lincoln Association. Thomas is out of Midwest soil and long broodings over Lincoln. Closing his book, he soberly affirms Lincoln: "Only with the slow march of time would it be given to most of his countrymen to understand the supreme meaning of his life . . . Because to him the American people were the leaders of an awakening of plain people the world over." When he was writing his one-volume Lincoln I told him, "If or when I get written and published a one-volume Lincoln, I hope and believe the two books will stand on the Lincoln shelf as good companions supplementing each other."

None of the foregoing books had been published at the time I was writing *Abraham Lincoln: The Prairie Years*. Most of them have seen publication since I wrote *Abraham Lincoln: The War Years*. All of them, however, have been used in the preparation of this one volume, for corrections or added lights. I have also used the files of *The Journal* of the Illinois State Historical Society, the Lincoln Memorial University's *Lincoln Herald*, the periodicals *Lincoln Lore* and *The Lincoln Kinsman* written by Louis A. Warren. To the stream of Lincoln source materials was added in 1941 the Herndon-Weik papers made available by Library of Congress purchase, and in 1947 the Robert T. Lincoln collection, a bequest to the Library. From the latter collection in 1948 came from David Mearns two volumes, *The Lincoln Papers*, with selections covering 1809 to July 4, 1861. A reader of these can step back into a generation of vanished Americans and see them in speaking likenesses, a variety of fine persons and odd fools.

In the preface to *The Prairie Years* I mentioned the Daniel Fish bibliography in 1906 listing 1,080 books and pamphlets about Lincoln and that of J. B. Oakleaf in 1925 listing 1,600 items. In 1945, however, came Jay Monaghan's listing of 3,958 items. By now, in 1954, there are more than 4,000 books and pamphlets dealing principally with Abraham Lincoln, his ancestry, wife and kin, even excluding such sources as the indispensable Welles and Browning diaries which deal with Lincoln incidentally. In 13 pages of a foreword to *The War Years* are enumerated and evaluated the array of source materials used in the writing of those four volumes.

The Blue and the Gray: the Story of the Civil War as Told by Participants, two volumes (1950), by Henry Steele Commager is a procession of witnesses and documents, Douglas Southall Freeman joining with others to attest its author as extraordinarily well equipped to present "a history of the Civil War in the words of those who fought it." The background of national events, the storms and the quiet between storms through which the American people moved from the 1847 Congress in which Lincoln had a seat to the 1861 inauguration of Lincoln, are presented as a moving panorama in Allan Nevins' *The Ordeal of the Union*, two volumes (1947), and *The Emergence of Lincoln*, two volumes (1950). These books embody vivid writing and vast research in original sources; they are important if not imperatively requisite for those who seek to know more concretely the wild onrushes of violent events along with quietly inexorable streams of invention, migration, territorial expansion, of those 14 years; they were shaping the national scene where Lincoln was fated to play the somber and leading role.

James O'Donnell Bennett's *Private Joe Fifer* (1936) quotes that Civil War soldier and governor of Illinois as having from Milton Hay the saying of

Lincoln, "You can fool some of the people all of the time and all of the people some of the time but you can't fool all of the people all of the time," Fifer adding, "In 1894, after my term as governor, I made a speech in Piatt County, this state, in which I repeated what Milt Hay had told me. The speech was printed in the St. Louis *Globe-Democrat*, the Chicago *Inter-Ocean* and other papers and thus the saying was first given publicity. None of the Lincoln biographers had ever discovered it."

In 1946 came *A Shelf of Lincoln Books* by Paul M. Angle, "a critical, selective bibliography of Lincolniana." He lists and evaluates 81 basic items, reporting their now generally accepted merits and deficiencies. Ralph Newman of the Abraham Lincoln Bookshop in Chicago lists 100 titles of the books he regards as most indispensable to the Lincoln student. In 1947 came Benjamin P. Thomas' *Portrait for Posterity*, a stormy, intensely human story of the procession of Lincoln biographers, their toils, hopes and miseries, their disputes, quarrels and quandaries. Thomas quotes from hundreds of letters they wrote. The book interweaves plots and characters into one of the strangest stories in American literary history. Thomas concludes: "The realist's ruthless searching gives the necessary facts. Yet the realist is ill-advised to scorn the idealist's sensitivity to those soul-qualities of Lincoln which documentary facts alone may not disclose."

INDEX

343, 363-5, 403, 413-5, 431, 435-6, 438,
480, 488, 524, 527, 529, 543-4, 551, 567,
572, 596, 602, 634, 641, 650, 654, 656, 662,
667-8, 695, 701-2, 714, 716
Wells, George, 726
Welton, Louis A., 587-8
Wentworth, John, 123, 145, 160, 168
West Virginia, 339-40
Wheeler, Joseph, 621
Whig party, 43, 48-9, 61, 64, 67-8, 80, 85,
88, 92, 97, 100, 103-4, 110, 118-9, 122-3
White, Andrew D., 563
White, Horace, 519
White House Landing, Va., 295-6
White, Hugh L., 48-9
White, Martha Todd, 244, 597
Whitehead, Gerrard, 597
Whiteside, Samuel, 30
Whitman, Walt, 400, 539, 578-9, 727, 734
Whitney, Henry C., 115, 121-3, 125, 127-
30, 151, 172, 181, 185, 194-5, 218, 225,
256, 260, 404, 480, 603
Whittier, John G., 100
Widney, John W., 578
Wiggins, Samuel, 66
Wilderness, The, Va., 508-10
Wilkes, Charles, 267-9
Wilkinson, Morton S., 332, 602
Williams, Archibald, 51
Williams, Jesse L., 405
Willis, N. P., 469
Wills, David, 439, 446
Wilmington, N. C., 636, 647, 661
Wilmot, David, 94, 97, 100

Wilmot Proviso, 97, 99-100, 103
Wilson, Frederick A., 487
Wilson, Henry, 243, 253, 348, 386, 537, 655
Wilson, Henry Clay, 487
Wilson, James F., 577
Wilson, James G., 481
Wilson, Robert L., 55
Wilson's Creek, Mo., 261-2
Winchester, Va., 550, 560
Wing, Henry E., 508, 579
Winter, William, 718
Winthrop, Robert C., 94, 553
Wintrup, John, 393
Wisconsin, 68, 119, 154, 173, 207, 492
Wood, Benjamin, 201, 420, 645
Wood, Bradford R., 405
Wood, Fernando, 201, 297, 406, 420, 488,
532, 552, 645
Wool, John E., 249, 294-5
Wooldridge, David, 50
Worden, John, 227, 291-2, 294
Work, Henry C., 475
Worthington, Thomas, 405
Wright, David M., 584-5
Wright, Erastus, 22
Wright, Horatio G., 529
Wyndham, Charles, 719

Yancey, William L., 169, 191, 238, 454
Yates, Richard, 187, 194, 438, 473, 511, 567,
705, 737
Young, Richard M., 51

Zacharie, Isachar, 391, 670